Oxford Handbook of Positive Psychology

OXFORD LIBRARY OF PSYCHOLOGY

Editor-in-Chief PETER E. NATHAN

Oxford Handbook of Positive Psychology

Edited by

C. R. Snyder

Shane J. Lopez

UNIVERSITY PRESS

2009

OXFORD
UNIVERSITY PRESS

Oxford University Press, Inc., publishes works that further Oxford University's objective
of excellence in research, scholarship, and education.

Oxford   New York
Auckland   Cape Town   Dar es Salaam   Hong Kong   Karachi
Kuala Lumpur   Madrid   Melbourne   Mexico City   Nairobi
New Delhi   Shanghai   Taipei   Toronto

With offices in
Argentina   Austria   Brazil   Chile   Czech Republic   France   Greece
Guatemala   Hungary   Italy   Japan   Poland   Portugal   Singapore
South Korea   Switzerland   Thailand   Turkey   Ukraine   Vietnam

Copyright © 2009 by Oxford University Press, Inc.

Published by Oxford University Press, Inc.
198 Madison Avenue, New York, New York 10016

www.oup.com

Oxford is a registered trademark of Oxford University Press

Library of Congress Cataloging-in-Publication Data
Oxford handbook of positive psychology / Edited by C. R. Snyder, Shane J. Lopez.
    p.   cm. — (Oxford library of psychology)
Includes bibliographical references and index.
ISBN 978-0-19-518724-3
1. Positive psychology.
I. Snyder, C. R.   II. Lopez, Shane J.
BF204.6.O95 2009
150.19′8—dc22

2008043836

9   8   7   6   5   4   3

Printed in the United States of America
on acid-free paper

CONTENTS

OXFORD LIBRARY OF PSYCHOLOGY

The *Oxford Library of Psychology,* a landmark series of handbooks, is published by Oxford University Press, one of the world's oldest and most highly respected publishers, with a tradition of publishing significant books in psychology. The ambitious goal of the *Oxford Library of Psychology* is nothing less than to span a vibrant, wide-ranging field and, in so doing, to fill a clear market need.

Encompassing a comprehensive set of handbooks, organized hierarchically, the *Library* incorporates volumes at different levels, each designed to meet a distinct need. At one level are a set of handbooks designed broadly to survey the major subfields of psychology; at another are numerous handbooks that cover important current focal research and scholarly areas of psychology in depth and detail. Planned as a reflection of the dynamism of psychology, the *Library* will grow and expand as psychology itself develops, thereby highlighting significant new research that will impact on the field. Adding to its accessibility and ease of use, the *Library* will be published in print and, later on, electronically.

The *Library* surveys psychology's principal subfields with a set of handbooks that capture the current status and future prospects of those major subdisciplines. This initial set includes handbooks of social and personality psychology, clinical psychology, counseling psychology, school psychology, educational psychology, industrial and organizational psychology, cognitive psychology, cognitive neuroscience, methods and measurements, history, neuropsychology, personality assessment, developmental psychology, and more. Each handbook undertakes to review one of psychology's major subdisciplines with breadth, comprehensiveness, and exemplary scholarship. In addition to these broadly conceived volumes, the *Library* also includes a large number of handbooks designed to explore in depth more specialized areas of scholarship and research, such as stress, health and coping, anxiety and related disorders, cognitive development, or child and adolescent assessment. In contrast to the broad coverage of the subfield handbooks, each of these latter volumes focuses on an especially productive, more highly focused line of scholarship and research. Whether at the broadest or most specific level, however, all of the *Library* handbooks offer synthetic coverage that reviews and evaluates the relevant past and present research and anticipates research in the future. Each handbook in the *Library* includes introductory and concluding chapters written by its editor to provide a roadmap to the handbook's table of contents and to offer informed anticipations of significant future developments in that field.

An undertaking of this scope calls for handbook editors and chapter authors who are established scholars in the areas about which they write. Many of the nation's and world's most productive and best-respected psychologists have agreed to edit *Library* handbooks or write authoritative chapters in their areas of expertise.

For whom has the *Oxford Library of Psychology* been written? Because of its breadth, depth, and accessibility, the *Library* serves a diverse audience, including graduate students in psychology and their faculty mentors, scholars, researchers, and practitioners in psychology and related fields. Each will find in the *Library* the information they seek on the subfield or focal area of psychology in which they work or are interested.

Befitting its commitment to accessibility, each handbook includes a comprehensive index, as well as extensive references to help guide research. And because the *Library* was designed from its inception as an online as well as a print resource, its structure and contents will be readily and rationally searchable online. Further, once the *Library* is released online, the handbooks will be regularly and thoroughly updated.

In summary, the *Oxford Library of Psychology* will grow organically to provide a thoroughly informed perspective on the field of psychology, one that reflects both psychology's dynamism and its increasing interdisciplinarity. Once published electronically, the *Library* is also destined to become a uniquely valuable interactive tool, with extended search and browsing capabilities. As you begin to consult this handbook, we sincerely hope you will share our enthusiasm for the more than 500-year tradition of Oxford University Press for excellence, innovation, and quality, as exemplified by the *Oxford Library of Psychology*.

Peter E. Nathan
Editor-in-Chief
Oxford Library of Psychology

C. R. Snyder

C. R. Snyder was a professor of Psychology and the M. Erik Wright Distinguished Professor of Clinical Psychology in the Department of Psychology at the University of Kansas, Lawrence. Dr. Snyder passed away on January 17, 2006.

Shane J. Lopez

Shane J. Lopez, PhD, is research director for the Clifton Strengths Institute and Gallup Senior Scientist in Residence. A college professor for 10 years, Shane leads the research on the links between strengths development, hope, academic success, and overall well-being. He collaborates with scholars around the world on these issues, and he specializes in hope and strengths enhancement for students from preschool through college graduation, advocating a whole-school strengths model that also builds the strengths expertise of educators and parents. Shane has provided strengths mentoring to thousands of college students, including academic, career, and life planning. He has helped develop assessments including the Children's Domain-Specific Hope Scale and the Strengths Self-Efficacy Measure. He co-wrote the statistical reports for the Clifton StrengthsFinder and the Clifton Youth StrengthsExplorer. Shane is also a licensed psychologist and director of the Gallup Well-Being Forum. His other publications with C. R. Snyder include *Positive Psychological Assessment* (APA) and *Positive Psychology: The Scientific and Practical Explorations of Human Strengths* (Sage).

CONTRIBUTORS

GLENN AFFLECK
Department of Community Medicine and
Health Care
University School of Medicine
Farmington, CT

NADIA AHMAD
Department of Psychology
University of Kansas
Lawrence, KS

JENNIFER L. AUSTENFELD
Department of Psychology
University of Kansas
Lawrence, KS

JAMES R. AVERILL
Department of Psychology
University of Massachusetts
Amherst, MA

PAUL B. BALTES
Max Planck Institute for Human Development
Berlin, Germany

C. DANIEL BATSON
Department of Psychology
University of Kansas
Lawrence, KS

JADE A. BENDER
Clinical Child Psychology Program
The University of Kansas
Lawrence, KS

JEREMY A. BLUMENTHAL
College of Law
Syracuse University
Syracuse, NY

JULIA K. BOEHM
Department of Psychology
University of California
Riverside, CA

ILONA BONIWELL
School of Psychology
University of East London
London, UK

JENNIFER D. BURT
Department of Educational Psychology
University of Nebraska
Lincoln, NE

DAVID CARUSO
Yale College Dean's Office
Yale University
New Haven, CT

CHARLES S. CARVER
Department of Psychology
University of Miami
Miami, FL

ERIC J. CASSELL
Weill Medical College
Cornell University
Ithaca, NY

JENNIFER S. CHEAVENS
Department of Psychology
The Ohio State University
Columbus, OH

JULIETTE CHRISTIE
Department of Psychology
The University of Georgia
Athens, GA

MICHAEL A. COHN
Osher Center for Integrative Medicine
University of California, San Francisco
San Francisco, CA

MIHALY CSIKSZENTMIHALYI
School of Behavioral and Organizational Sciences
Claremont Graduate University
Claremont, CA

J. J. CUTULI
Institute of Child Development
University of Minnesota
Minneapolis, MN

CHRISTOPHER G. DAVIS
Department of Psychology
Carleton University
Ottawa, Ontario, Canada

SALLY S. DICKERSON
Department of Psychology & Social Behavior
University of California
Irvine, CA

ED DIENER
Department of Psychology
University of Illinois at Urbana-Champaign
Champaign, IL

RICHARD A. DIENSTBIER
Department of Psychology
University of Nebraska
Lincoln, NE

DANA S. DUNN
Department of Psychology
Moravian College
Bethlehem, PA

LISA M. EDWARDS
Department of Counseling & Educational
Psychology
Marquette University
Milwaukee, WI

TIMOTHY R. ELLIOTT
Department of Educational Psychology
Texas A&M University
College Station, TX

BARBARA L. FREDRICKSON
Department of Psychology
University of North Carolina
Chapel Hill, NC

ARACELI FRIAS
Department of Psychology
Eastern Washington University
Cheney, WA

DANIEL FULFORD
Department of Psychology
University of Miami
Miami, FL

SHELLY L. GABLE
Department of Psychology
University of California
Santa Barbara, CA

MATTHEW W. GALLAGHER
Department of Psychology
University of Kansas
Lawrence, KS

RICH GILMAN
Department of Pediatrics
University of Cincinnati
Cincinnati, OH

MICHAEL C. GOTTLIEB
Private Practice
Dallas, TX

RUSSELL HALL
Department of Educational and Counseling
Psychology
University of Kentucky
Lexington, KY

MITCHELL M. HANDELSMAN
Department of Psychology
University of Colorado
Denver, CO

SUSAN HARRINGTON
School of Psychology
University of Leicester
Leicester, UK

JOHN H. HARVEY
Department of Psychology
University of Iowa
Iowa City, IA

CLYDE HENDRICK
Department of Psychology
Texas Tech University
Lubbock, TX

SUSAN S. HENDRICK
Department of Psychology
Texas Tech University
Lubbock, TX

P. PAUL HEPPNER
Department of Educational, School, and
Counseling Psychology
University of Missouri
Columbia, MO

JANETTE E. HERBERS
Institute of Child Development
University of Minnesota
Minneapolis, MN

RODERICK HETZEL
Staff Psychologist
Baylor University
Waco, TX

JOHN P. HEWITT
Department of Sociology
University of Massachusetts
Amherst, MA

RAYMOND L. HIGGINS
Department of Psychology
University of Kansas
Lawrence, KS

PETER H. HUANG
James Beasley Law School
Temple University
Philadelphia, PA

E. SCOTT HUEBNER
Department of Psychology
University of South Carolina
Columbia, SC

EILEEN HULME
Noel Academy for Strengths-Based
Leadership and Education
Azusa Pacific University
Azusa, CA

ALICE M. ISEN
Johnson Graduate School of
Management
Department of Psychology
Cornell University
Ithaca, NY

REBECCA J. JOHNSON
Department of Pediatrics
University of Missouri—Kansas City
Children's Mercy Hospitals and Clinics
Kansas City, MO

STEPHEN JOSEPH
School of Sociology & Social Policy
University of Nottingham
Nottingham, UK

TODD B. KASHDAN
Department of Psychology
George Mason University
Fairfax, VA

COREY L. M. KEYES
Department of Sociology
Emory University
Atlanta, GA

KERI J. BROWN KIRSCHMAN
Department of Psychology
University of Dayton
Dayton, OH

SAMUEL KNAPP
Pennsylvania Psychological
Association
Harrisburg, PA

UTE KUNZMANN
Department of Psychology
University of Leipzig
Leipzig, Germany

ELLEN LANGER
Department of Psychology
Harvard University
Cambridge, MA

SUZANNE C. LECHNER
Department of Psychiatry
University of Miami
Miami, FL

DONG-GWI LEE
Department of Psychology
Yonsei University
Seoul, South Korea

RICHARD M. LERNER
Institute for Applied Research in Youth
Development
Tufts University
Medford, MA

P. ALEX LINLEY
Centre for Applied Positive Psychology
Coventry, UK

DAVID A. LISHNER
Department of Psychology
University of Wisconsin Oshkosh
Oshkosh, WI

TODD D. LITTLE
Department of Psychology
University of Kansas
Lawrence, KS

FREDERICK G. LOPEZ
Department of Educational
Psychology
University of Houston
Houston, TX

SHANE J. LOPEZ
Clifton Strengths Institute
Omaha, NE

RICHARD E. LUCAS
Department of Psychology
Michigan State University
East Lansing, MI

FRED LUTHANS
Department of Management
University of Nebraska
Lincoln, NE

SONJA LYUBOMIRSKY
Department of Psychology
University of California
Riverside, CA

JAMES E. MADDUX
Department of Psychology
George Mason University
Fairfax, VA

ANNETTE MAHONEY
Department of Psychology
Bowling Green State University
Bowling Green, OH

NATALYA C. MAISEL
Department of Psychology
University of California
Los Angeles, CA

JOHN MALTBY
School of Psychology
University of Leicester
Leicester, UK

ANN S. MASTEN
Institute of Child Development
University of Minnesota
Minneapolis, MN

JOHN D. MAYER
Department of Psychology
University of New Hampshire
Durham, NH

MICHAEL E. MCCULLOUGH
Department of Psychology
University of Miami
Miami, FL

ROLLIN MCCRATY
Institute of HeartMath
Boulder Creek, CA

CHRISTOPHER J. MILLER
Department of Psychology
University of Miami
Miami, FL

PEGGY J. MYCEK
Department of Psychology & Social
Behavior
University of California
Irvine, CA

JEANNE NAKAMURA
School of Behavioral and Organizational
Sciences
Claremont Graduate University
Claremont, CA

KRISTIN NARAGON
Department of Psychology
University of Iowa
Iowa City, IA

KATE G. NIEDERHOFFER
The Dachis Corporation
Austin, TX

SUSAN NOLEN-HOEKSEMA
Department of Psychology
Yale University
New Haven, CT

REBECCA J. NORTH
Department of Psychology
University of Texas
Austin, TX

SHIGEHIRO OISHI
Department of Psychology
University of Virginia
Charlottesville, VA

ANTHONY D. ONG
Department of Human Development
Cornell University
Ithaca, NY

KENNETH I. PARGAMENT
Department of Psychology
Bowling Green State University
Bowling Green, OH

NANSOOK PARK
Department of Psychology
University of Rhode Island
Kingston, RI

BRIAN G. PAUWELS
Department of Psychology
Doane College
Crete, NE

JENNIFER TERAMOTO PEDROTTI
Department of Psychology and Child
Development
California Polytechnic State
University
San Luis Obispo, CA

JAMES W. PENNEBAKER
Department of Psychology
University of Texas
Austin, TX

CHRISTOPHER PETERSON
Department of Psychology
University of Michigan
Ann Arbor, MI

CYNTHIA L. S. PURY
Department of Psychology
Clemson University
Clemson, SC

KEVIN L. RAND
Department of Psychology
Indiana University—Purdue University
Indianapolis
Indianapolis, IN

AMY L. RESCHLY
Department of Educational Psychology &
Instructional Technology
University of Georgia
Athens, GA

MARIE-GABRIELLE J. REED
Hennepin County Medical Center
Minneapolis, MN

ROBERT A. REES
Institute of HeartMath
Boulder Creek, CA

MICHAEL C. ROBERTS
Clinical Child Psychology Program
The University of Kansas
Lawrence, KS

LINDSEY M. ROOT
Department of Psychology
University of Miami
Miami, FL

PETER SALOVEY
Department of Psychology
Yale University
New Haven, CT

SUSANNE SCHEIBE
Department of Psychology
Stanford University
Stanford, CA

MICHAEL F. SCHEIER
Department of Psychology
Carnegie Mellon University
Pittsburgh, PA

LAURIE A. SCHREINER
Department of Doctoral Higher
Education
Azusa Pacific University
Azusa, CA

JULIE SERGEANT
School of Social Welfare
University of Kansas
Lawrence, KS

SHAUNA L. SHAPIRO
Department of Counseling Psychology
Santa Clara University
Santa Clara, CA

SUSAN M. SHERIDAN
Department of Educational Psychology
University of Nebraska
Lincoln, NE

PAUL J. SILVIA
Department of Psychology
University of North Carolina
Greensboro, NC

DEAN KEITH SIMONTON
Department of Psychology
University of California
Davis, CA

C. R. SNYDER
Department of Psychology
University of Kansas
Lawrence, KS

ANNETTE L. STANTON
Department of Psychology
University of California
Los Angeles, CA

TRACY A. STEEN
Charles O'Brien Center for Addiction Treatment
University of Pennsylvania
Philadelphia, PA

MICHAEL F. STEGER
Department of Psychology
Colorado State University
Fort Collins, CO

SARAH J. SULLIVAN
Department of Psychology
University of California
Los Angeles, CA

WILLIAM B. SWANN, JR.
Department of Psychology
University of Texas
Austin, TX

BENJAMIN A. TABAK
Department of Psychology
University of Miami
Miami, FL

JUNE PRICE TANGNEY
Department of Psychology
George Mason University
Fairfax, VA

HOWARD TENNEN
Department of Community Medicine
and Health Care
University School of Medicine
Farmington, CT

SUZANNE C. THOMPSON
Department of Psychology
Pomona College
Pomona, CA

GITENDRA USWATTE
Department of Psychology
University of Alabama
Birmingham, AL

MICHAEL VAN GELDER
Department of Psychology
Eastern Washington University
Cheney, WA

VIVIAN L. VIGNOLES
Department of Psychology
University of Sussex
Brighton, UK

PHILIP C. WATKINS
Department of Psychology
Eastern Washington University
Cheney, WA

DAVID WATSON
Department of Psychology
University of Iowa
Iowa City, IA

MICHAEL L. WEHMEYER
Department of Special Education
University of Kansas
Lawrence, KS

GAIL M. WILLIAMSON
Department of Psychology
University of Georgia
Athens, GA

CHARLOTTE VAN OYEN WITVLIET
Department of Psychology
Hope College
Holland, MI

ALEX M. WOOD
School of Psychological Sciences
University of Manchester
Manchester, UK

BEATRICE A. WRIGHT
University of Kansas
Lawrence, KS

SEUNG HEE YOO
Department of Psychology
Yale University
New Haven, CT

CAROLYN M. YOUSSEF
College of Business
Bellevue University
Bellevue, NE

ALEX J. ZAUTRA
Department of Psychology
Arizona State University
Tempe, AZ

LISA M. PYTLIK ZILLIG
Department of Psychology
University of Nebraska
Lincoln, NE

PEGGY M. ZOCCOLA
Department of Psychology and
Social Behavior
University of California
Irvine, CA

TABLE OF CONTENTS

In less than a decade, positive psychology has caught the attention not only of the academic community but also of the general public. I just did a Google search for "positive psychology" and found 551,000+ hits. That is obviously impressive, although keeping all of us positive psychologists humble is that my searches for the "Olsen twins" and "Britney Spears" produced 4,770,000+ and 90,700,000+ hits, respectively.

It is still good that the larger world is interested in positive psychology, and probably even better that this interest does not entail morbid curiosity or the wish to witness a train wreck.

Regardless, the downside of the popularity positive psychology enjoys is the temptation for those of us associated with this new field to run ahead of what we know in pursuit of further popularity. So let us slow down and examine what positive psychology actually is and what we actually know.

Positive psychology is the "scientific" study of what makes life most worth living. It is a call for psychological science and practice to be as concerned with strength as with weakness; as interested in building the best things in life as in repairing the worst; and as concerned with making the lives of normal people fulfilling as with healing pathology.

Nowhere does this definition say or imply that psychology should ignore or dismiss the very real problems that people experience. Nowhere does it say or imply that the rest of psychology needs to be discarded or replaced. The value of positive psychology is to complement and extend the problem-focused psychology that has been dominant for many decades.

Several truisms underpin positive psychology. First, what is good in life is as genuine as what is bad—not derivative, secondary, epiphenomenal, illusory, or otherwise suspect. Second, what is good in life is not simply the absence of what is problematic. We all know the difference between not being depressed and bounding out of bed in the morning with enthusiasm for the day ahead. And third, the good life requires its own explanation, not simply a theory of disorder stood sideways or flipped on its head.

Positive psychology is psychology—psychology is science—and science requires checking theories against evidence. Accordingly, positive psychology is not to be confused with untested self-help, footless affirmation, or secular religion, no matter how good these may make us feel. Positive psychology is neither a recycled version of the power of positive thinking nor a sequel to *The Secret.*

Positive psychology will rise or fall on the science on which it is based. So far, the science is impressive. A great deal has been learned in recent years about the psychological good life, none of which was mentioned in any of the psychology courses I took a few decades ago.

The first edition of the *Handbook of Positive Psychology* both reflected the popularity of positive psychology and contributed to it, especially its scientific basis. Masterfully compiled and edited by my friends and colleagues, Rick Snyder and Shane Lopez, this handbook summarized what was known circa 2002 about positive psychology—theory, research, and application—and more importantly, it charted the future course of the field. Chapters were written by the leaders in positive psychology, and no one mailed in a contribution. Well, we all e-mailed them to Rick or to Shane, but you get the point. The *Handbook of Positive Psychology* earned a well-deserved place not just on bookshelves but on desks as well.

This edition of the *Oxford Handbook of Positive Psychology* promises to be even more useful to all interested in positive psychology. It updates and expands what is known. Again, it points to the future. And again, it was masterfully compiled and edited by Rick Snyder and Shane Lopez.

The future of positive psychology is bright, but there is one somber note I must sound. With the untimely passing of Rick Snyder, the field has lost one of its giants and one of its genuinely good guys. Rick was a well-known theorist and researcher, but he also labored mightily behind the scenes for the good of positive psychology. Rick, we will miss you. You may not be in Kansas anymore, but you are in our hearts and our minds. In that, we can take some solace.

The epitaph on the tombstone of baseball pioneer Jackie Robinson reads: "A life is not important except in the impact it has on other lives." If this is true, and I believe with my entire being that it is, then Rick Snyder led an important life and—indeed—continues to do so. On behalf of all of those touched by Rick Snyder, including those who will read this book, I express gratitude.

Christopher Peterson
University of Michigan
September 2008

MEMORIAM: REMEMBERING C.R. SNYDER: A HUMBLE LEGACY OF HOPE

C. R. Snyder was a professor of Psychology and the M. Erik Wright Distinguished Professor of Clinical Psychology in the Department of Psychology at the University of Kansas, Lawrence. Dr. Snyder passed away on January 17, 2006. The event was held on the beautiful campus of the University of Kansas, Rick's professional home for 34 years. In fact, the hall where we gathered stood only a few thousand feet from both Rick's academic home, Fraser Hall, and his beloved family home, a beautiful white colonial where he and his wife, Becky, welcomed friends, students, and colleagues. Stories about Rick's professional, personal, and downright hilarious exploits flowed between family, friends, students, and colleagues. We were a crowd sharing funny memories, giggling through sobs, and honoring Rick for his public and private contributions to psychology, society, and our lives. In this remembrance of my dear mentor and friend, I attempt to explain how one uncommonly good man tirelessly worked to help many others become the uncommonly good people he foresaw that they could be.

Rick Snyder had an uncanny talent for emotionally connecting with people through short, sincere interactions that could easily have become nothing more than small talk. Friends say he developed this skill out of necessity because, as the son of a salesman, his family moved nearly every year during his childhood and adolescence. In his adulthood, Rick's gift for emotional connections brought him warm relationships through which he seemed to happily do more giving than taking. His years of loving generosity for his family, colleagues, and students often left a transformative legacy. Indeed, Rick had a knack for giving what we needed, when we needed it. In my case, Rick took me under his wing the summer before my job at KU officially started. He treated me as an equal, and he never let me allow self-doubts to get in the way of my success as a professor. He often saw possibilities before I did, and he shared opportunities that both excited and daunted me. This was Rick's way, and it's a story I've heard repeatedly from his many mentees and colleagues.

Visiting with his other mentees at the memorial service made me realize that dozens of people had benefited similarly from what Rick called the "lifetime guarantee" on his mentoring. And as recent graduate Jennifer Cheavens reminded us, although we may have thought this guarantee would be fulfilled through personal visits, over the phone, and through e-mail notes, Rick's passing did not nullify the warranty. It simply means that Rick's positive influence will extend in ways we had not had to consider. We carry within us his teachings, to guide us in our efforts to live up to the example he set for us, to help us actually *be* the people he said he saw inside each of us. Indeed, his teachings make his guarantee good across *our* lifetimes.

The memorial service was moving and appropriately understated, as Rick was no fan of pomp or piety. Perhaps this is why he continually tried to teach the importance of having fun and the quiet dignity of maintaining our humility. Rick loved to say, "If you can't laugh at yourself, you have missed the biggest joke of all." He practiced what he preached; he laughed at his own gaffs just about daily. Through his own, quirky behavior, Rick made it safe to say, "I don't know" and "I messed up," and of course, he never let me take myself too seriously. Most importantly, he made me laugh, all the time. Whether Rick was dive-bombing me during a research meeting with one of the model planes in his office or he was breaking campus rules and a few laws by driving my wife's scooter across hallowed ground and squealing "Wheeee!" as he did it, that lovely man cracked me up.

During the memorial, colleagues remembered Rick as both King Midas and a working stiff. Both descriptions are apt. One of my favorite memories captures both facets of Rick. In 2000, along with several other leading contemporaries in positive psychology, Rick appeared on a two-hour *Good Morning America* special dedicated to sharing the social science on the good life. Rick chose to conduct a live experiment to demonstrate hope theory in action. So, on national network television, Rick had three of the cast members—the host, the medical expert, and the weather guy—participate in the cold pressor task, dunking their right fists to the bottom of a tank of freezing water for as long as they could stand it. After a short time, the weather guy removed his hand and shook some life back into it. A battle of wills ensued between the host and the medical expert and, as the segment was ending so the show could go to commercial, the medical expert had enough. The host, seemingly oblivious to the pain, vowed to keep his hand in the freezing water through the break. Upon returning from the commercial, the host asked Rick what the cold pressor task had to do with hope. Rick calmly detailed for the audience the basics of hope theory and the connection between hope and pain tolerance. He then revealed that the cast members had taken the hope scale prior to the show and that the ranking of their scores had accurately predicted how long each would be able to withstand the numbing pain of the cold water before calling it quits. To a casual observer, his results might have been viewed as "lucky" and to Rick's friends, this might have been construed as more evidence of his Midas touch. But I believe the success of his live, national demonstration was attributable to the "working stiff" mentality that Rick had for his research. His passion for his work led him to spend thousands of hours in his Hope Lab, and his hard work resulted in a deep understanding of how hope manifested in daily life. This allowed the award-winning teacher in Rick to take a risk to show an audience of millions one of the many ways hope manifests itself in their lives.

Unfortunately, Rick had an intimate knowledge of the relationship between hope and pain tolerance beyond what he learned through his scholarly work. Unbeknownst to many colleagues and students, Rick suffered from chronic, nearly debilitating chest and abdominal pain for the last 15 years of his life. The origin of the pain was never determined, and risky surgeries and aggressive treatments did little to curb his burning, daily hurt. Nevertheless, Rick coped. And coped. And coped. Even when diagnosed with transitional cell cancer in late

December 2005 (which was seemingly unrelated to his chronic illness), he coped as best he could, with Becky by his side the whole time.

Rick Snyder's scholarship demystified the concepts of excuse making, forgiveness, and hope for the world. The work he left behind shows us how to disconnect from past negative experiences through excuse making, how to free ourselves for future possibilities through forgiveness, and how to connect to positive future opportunities through hope. Along the way, Rick used his time to teach scores of us how to love and be loved, how to laugh at ourselves, how to work with passion, and how to cope. He taught me and many others how to be better people. I believe I speak for many when I say that, although I miss him terribly and every day I still wish I could talk to him, Rick's legacy in my life will be hope for our journey. His wise and loving lessons will carry me through challenges and adventures that I don't even know are coming, to the very last day of my own life. *This* is the hopeful legacy of a great teacher and a truly good man.

Shane J. Lopez
Omaha, Nebraska

PREFACE

Shane J. Lopez

Before C. R. "Rick" Snyder, hope was elusive to scholars and students of human behavior and the "fix it" philosophy dominated clinical psychology. As a result of his scholarship, collaborative spirit, and vision, an interdisciplinary group of researchers responded to his call for a *Handbook of Positive Psychology* with strong research on the best in people. Following his passing in 2006, contributors and Oxford University Press rallied to produce this volume, in honor of Rick.

This second edition of the *Oxford Handbook of Positive Psychology* was produced to help you look seriously at the positive in people and the world. To this end, I asked the contributors to provide a clear-eyed analysis of their specialty area and to distill it in such a way that the reader can find intellectual value and relevance in the ideas. The 120-plus contributors to the project did a masterful job. After reading each of these 65 chapters, several times, I have renewed excitement about popular positive psychology topics and I have deeper knowledge of topics that aren't part of the public conversation about optimal human functioning.

The volume is separated into 11 parts beginning with the "Major developments in positive psychology" which highlights inventions and discusses that reveal the potency of human strengths and positive emotions and highlights the new role of positive psychology practice. In "Positive psychology perspectives on human behavior," the chapters highlight the need for shifting our sole focus from weakness to an understanding of human behavior that includes a deep knowledge of strengths. "Positive psychology across the life span," the third part, expands what was previously known about positive human development.

The next five parts of the book summarize the research on positive psychology constructs and processes, ranging from subjective well-being to the biologically based toughness. A new section of the volume, "Positive institutions," discusses the role of good environments on positive behavior.

"Specific coping approaches" and "Toward better lives" highlight the pathways and strategies that can turn a good life into a great one. We purposefully end the volume with a discussion of happiness and meaning, two of the most desirable outcomes associated with positive psychology work.

My gratitude goes to Lori Handelman of Oxford University Press for her support of this project, and of me; Matthew Gallagher, the final recipient of Rick's mentoring guarantee and managing editor for this project; Christy Khan for her talent and willingness to serve; and Alli and Parrish Lopez for making me laugh everyday. My thanks also go to you, the reader, for keeping Rick's mission alive.

PART 1

Major Developments in Positive Psychology

A Case for Positive Psychology

Shane J. Lopez *and* Matthew W. Gallagher

Abstract

Pick up a magazine or a scholarly psychology journal and, chances are, you will read about the good work of a positive psychologist. Through the use of sound methods, positive psychologists answer hard questions about the best in people. This book serves as repository of answers to those tough questions. In this chapter, we argue that the work of positive psychology scholars is good for psychology, as a discipline, and for society. We also discuss what needs to be done to shore up the science and practice of positive psychology.

Keywords: positive psychology, social science, strengths

Positive psychology, the term, was first used in 1954 by Abraham Maslow in a book chapter where he noted that the "science of psychology has been far more successful on the negative than on the positive side. It has revealed to us much about man's shortcomings, his illness, his sins, but little about his potentialities, his virtues, his achievable aspirations, or his full psychological height. It is as if psychology has voluntarily restricted itself to only half its rightful jurisdiction, the darker, meaner half" (p. 354). More than 40 years later, Martin Seligman reintroduced the term and proclaimed that psychology was "half-baked" and more attention needed to be paid to the good in people and in the world. Quickly, research meetings sprang up in the United States in locales such as Philadelphia, Washington, DC, Lincoln, Lawrence, and Columbia and in far away retreats, including Grand Cayman and Akumal. The promise of this new brand of positive psychology was clear. By using the same techniques and tools that help us explain weakness and prevent or treat illness, we could enhance our understanding of strengths and promote well-being.

Some scholars of human behavior saw great potential in answering hard questions about the positive in people. Many of these scholars have contributed to this volume and it is this group of scholars and their

collective works that make the best case for positive psychology. Nevertheless, handing someone the *Handbook of Positive Psychology* is not always the best way to inform them of the added value of the work addressing strengths, positive emotions, and strong institutions. Here, we try to make a more succinct case for positive psychology's value to the discipline and to society. We also discuss the need to enhance science and the science-practice integration over the next decade of positive psychology work.

Making the Case for Positive Psychology

On occasion, we are asked to make a case for positive psychology. For example, most of the professors who have created positive psychology courses for their departments were challenged with the question "Why do we need a positive psychology course?" Other questions we have faced include, "Is there enough research to fill a handbook/textbook?", "Isn't this too esoteric for the general public?", and "Isn't this intellectual field just a playground for a select few?" We will answer each of these questions, as we did in actual discussions with deans, colleagues, publishers and editors, and friends in our attempt to demonstrate that positive psychology has a place in psychology and in the efforts of people to lead better lives.

Rounding Out Psychology

Maslow and Seligman's call for more serious attention to the positive side of life has been echoed by many, including visionaries in psychiatry such as Karl Menninger, and business gurus, notably Peter Drucker. Taking these calls one at a time and in historical sequence, Maslow (1954) argued for a augmentation of what was known about psychology to tell a complete story about human nature and to help people realize their full potential . . . not just to aid them in their work toward the absence of ills. Menninger (Menninger, Mayman, & Pruyser, 1963) reinvented psychiatry by demonstrating that mental illness was treatable, mental health was achievable, and both states could be studied. With a message for managers who wanted to boost their bottom line, Drucker (1993) simply stated that executives should build on strengths not weaknesses. In 1998, Seligman picked up the mantle of those who came before him, Maslow, Menninger, Drucker, and many others such as Marie Jahoda, Beatrice Wright, Albert Bandura, and Don Clifton, and paired scientific zeal with good timing to make positive psychology come alive and round out psychology.

We occasionally cite these historical events when trying to explain why we need positive psychology courses on campuses, but often it is more effective to note that wherever there is fear, there is hope. And, since abnormal psychology courses, which are required for most psychology majors, are about fear, related negative emotions, and illness, a positive psychology course serves to round out a student's knowledge base with the study of hope, positive emotions, and health. We can also detail how some of the best thinkers and researchers in psychiatry, sociology, economics, and business are contributing to this body of knowledge; so it exposes our students to research from other disciplines. That helps with the sell. What undermines the case that positive psychology rounds out psychology is the hyperfocus on what some critics refer to as happyology. Indeed, the lion's share of public storytelling about positive psychology work focuses on happiness and the shortcuts to it. While this coverage has made positive psychology courses and research more popular, this soft-hitting media possibly has made launching courses and getting grants more difficult.

Unifying Psychology

Psychology is carved up into specialties and divisions and filled with factions. Occasionally, one issue is intriguing enough to attract attention across the discipline, but the norm is that this issue is a divisive one. For example, the repressed memory debate grabbed the attention of developmentalists, memory researchers, forensic psychologists, and counseling, clinical, and school psychologists in the mid- to late 1990s. The debate over the veracity of repressed memories was standard fare in journals across the discipline and was the topic of cross-cutting panels at conferences. The debate brought us together—and then it divided us into camps arguing about what is real.

Positive psychology research, especially the operationalization of meaningful, yet fuzzy constructs such as hope, courage, and wisdom, has historically unified psychologists. Each of these constructs and many others were often defined and researched by collectives, with members from developmental psychology, social psychology, personality psychology, and clinical and counseling psychology. Researchers rallied around questions, shared new methods and approaches perfected in their specialty and in their own labs, and put old agendas aside for the sake of engaging in serious inquiry about topics that matter to all people. Positive psychology has provided reasons for talented scholars with overlapping interests to come together to ask and answer hard questions; all told, even when accounting for psychologists that have made cases against positive psychology, it has had unifying effect on the field.

Giving Psychology Away

Influential psychologists such as George Miller, George Albee, Raymond Fowler, and others have encouraged us to "give psychology away" over the decades. For the most part, we have been fairly successful at giving psychology away in the schools; high school courses have become commonplace and psychology majors outnumber most others on college campuses. We have also made a dent in educating the general public about mental illness and its prevention and treatment.

"Giving positive psychology away" seems to be an easy task. People not suffering from a mental disorder, more than 80% of the population on a given day, are trying to make sense of the world and use available information to make a good life. Positive psychology science and practice is accessible and this "new" information meets the daily needs of "normal" people.

Mass media grounded in principles of strengths development helps with the mission of giving positive psychology away. For example, Bandura spreads self-efficacy through carefully crafted soap operas (see population.org) that air on radio and/or television around the world. Companies such as Pepperidge Farm, maker of the Goldfish snack cracker, share optimism via an interactive website (see fishfulthinking.com) and packaging with mothers of children who love their product while viewers of "Paz the Penguin" of DiscoveryKids learn how to be hopeful, resilient learners. More than a million people are touched by one of these purveyors of positive psychology everyday.

Attracting More Talent to Psychology

Psychology, like any other science, explains the natural world through observation and experiment. Our findings are the products of those observations and experiments that are conducted by talented men and women across the world. The vibrancy of our science is dependent upon the commitment of these talented people to a lifelong pursuit of demystifying psychological phenomena. Positive psychology appears to attract those talented people.

Summer institutes, dissertation prizes, The Templeton Prize, and the Clifton Strengths Prize have encouraged the development of new scholars and have rewarded those who have made significant early career and lifelong contributions. None of these incentives explain the knocks on the office door or emails from bright, hardworking college students or retreads from the world of work who want to immerse themselves in the study of the positive. Knowing more about the good in people has a gravitational pull of some sort that is hard for some to resist. With the large numbers of people attracted to working on positive psychology research and programming, we are sure to connect with highly talented individuals who can make significant contributions.

Strengthening the Case for Positive Psychology

The case for positive psychology is easy to make, but it is also easy to undermine given the nature of the media attention received and varying quality of the research and practice that falls under the positive psychology umbrella. Here we contend that good science makes its own best case and we attempt to guide interested researchers toward sound, sophisticated methods that could tell a more complex story about positive human development. We also recommend testing theories and constructs in unison to determine, for example, the overlap or incremental value of optimism and hope when predicting changes in well-being over time. Finally, we encourage scientists and practitioners to work together toward solutions regarding how best to promote mental health.

Understanding of the Positive Psychology of Change

As the chapters in this revised edition make clear, the dramatic increase in positive psychology research has led to an improved understanding of the nature of positive mental health, the benefits of traits such as curiosity and hope, and the methods by which the findings of positive psychology can be used to improve the lives of individuals. Given that much of our science has real world applications that affect the lives of children and adults, we must continue to conduct rigorous science. Here we provide three recommendations that we believe could help advance the scientific basis of positive psychology: examining change, examining theories in unison, and integrating science and practice.

One of the underlying questions behind a portion of positive psychology research is whether it is possible to improve individual levels of well-being. This issue has significant relevance for individuals, public policy, and the health-care system. Given the weighty implications of this work, we must move beyond cross-sectional research designs and move toward models that account for dynamic change processes within individuals. Cross-sectional research can provide a wealth of information about how positive traits and various indices of mental health are associated with one another, but cross-sectional studies can never provide true tests of the causal models that are often put forth in our theories. Although it can be difficult and expensive to conduct longitudinal studies that can accurately demystify change, the methods and data analysis necessary to model change are becoming increasingly more accessible. The recent positive psychology research volume by Ong and Van Dulmen (2006) provides concrete examples of how longitudinal data analyzed using hierarchical linear modeling or growth curve modeling can be applied specifically to positive psychology research in order to provide a more sophisticated understanding of the latent trajectories of well-being. Of course, researchers should not use these advanced statistical analyses when they are not necessary or appropriate, but for positive psychology to continue to develop as a science, we believe that researchers will increasingly need to design studies that permit the appropriate modeling of individual trajectories and change.

Determining Overlap or Incremental Value of Theories and Constructs

As is clear from the number of new chapters in this edition of the handbook, the past few years have seen a remarkable growth in the development of new theories and measures of positive psychological constructs. In some ways this is great news, but there are also reasons to be cautious about this proliferation of constructs. In many instances, there is too little attention given to examining the incremental validity of these new constructs. It is important to demonstrate that multiple positive traits (e.g., hope and optimism) are associated with positive outcomes, but it is just as important, if not more so, to demonstrate the unique effects of these traits on positive outcomes and to demonstrate the contexts in which one trait might be more valuable than another. By examining our theories and constructs in unison, we can develop a more nuanced science of positive psychology that could articulate when, how, and why various constructs relate to one another.

Moving toward a Science-Practice Integration

We believe that as positive psychology continues to expand, it will be critical that the scientists and practitioners of positive psychology remain closely linked. Within the field of clinical psychology, there is an increasing disconnect between the theoretical orientations and methods endorsed by clinical researchers and practitioners. We believe this disconnect is unfortunate and hinders the work of both scientists and practitioners. Fortunately, because positive psychology training programs are just now being developed, as a field we have the opportunity to prevent the artificial and unfortunate separation between scientists and practitioners. By emphasizing research methods training and scholarly consumerism within positive psychology training programs, we could create a discipline in which practitioners are always either implementing empirically supported protocols, or helping to generate the empirical basis for new programs. In this way, we could ensure that positive psychology interventions remain firmly in the realm of science rather than pseudoscience, and can therefore more effectively apply the lessons learned from our research.

Beyond Making a Case for Positive Psychology

The fact that we were compelled to make the case for positive psychology in the lead chapter suggests that this subfield needs more intellectual backbone and more rigor, or that we have professional esteem issues. Well, this incarnation of positive psychology is only 10 years old, so strength and esteem are concerns, but we believe that the following 64 chapters can move us beyond the need for making a case for inclusion of positive psychology in mainstream psychology departments and toward discussions about how to meet the basic needs of children and adults and society at large.

Questions

1. What are some future applications of positive psychology that might meet societal needs?

2. What are the primary critiques of positive psychology and what evidence supports/refutes those critiques?

3. How could more talented graduate students and scholars be attracted to studying strengths, positive emotions, and strong institutions?

References

Drucker, P. F. (1993). *The effective executive.* New York: Harper Collins.

Maslow, A. H. (1954). *Motivation and personality.* New York: Brandeis University.

Menninger, K., Mayman, M., & Pruyser, P. W. (1963). *The vital balance.* New York: Viking Press.

Ong, A. D., & Van Dulmen, M. H. M. (2006). *Oxford handbook of methods in positive psychology.* New York: Oxford University Press.

Positive Psychology: Past, Present, and Future

Ed Diener

Abstract

This chapter briefly reviews the history of positive psychology, and the endeavor by scientists to answer the classic question posed by philosophers: What is the good life? One piece of evidence for the growth of positive psychology is the proliferation of measures to assess concepts such as happiness, well-being, and virtue. The chapter briefly reviews the importance of C. R. Snyder to the field of positive psychology. Several critiques of positive psychology are discussed. One valid critique is that there is too much emphasis within positive psychology on the individual, and too little focus on positive societies, institutions, and situations. We can profit from considering the various critiques because they will help us to improve the field. Positive psychology has important strengths, such as the number of young scholars and practitioners who are entering the field. The *Handbook of Positive Psychology* is an outstanding resource for all those who are working in this discipline, and also for others outside of the area, to gain broad knowledge of the important developments that are occurring in our understanding of positive human functioning.

Keywords: C. R. Snyder, history, positive psychology, quality of life, well-being

The Past, Present, and Future of Positive Psychology

It is an honor to introduce the second edition of the definitive reference work on positive psychology, the *Handbook of Positive Psychology*. It is a double honor to be able to write the introduction for this handbook because it was initiated by C. Richard "Rick" Snyder, in concert with Shane Lopez, and is now dedicated to Professor Snyder and his memory. Rick Snyder was a leader in the field of positive psychology, and I was thrilled when he and Professor Lopez asked me to write the introduction to this volume. We were all shocked and saddened by Dr. Snyder's untimely death during the preparation of the handbook. The chapters in this book are truly outstanding, and stand as convincing proof of Professor Snyder's legacy. I am grateful to be part of this excellent handbook, and I am certain that Rick Snyder would have been very proud of this volume.

The History of Positive Psychology

In one sense, positive psychology is thousands of years old, dating back to the thoughts of ancient philosophers and religious leaders who discussed character virtues, happiness, and the good society. More recently, in the last 100 years there have been behavioral scientists who have conducted scholarship and research on positive topics. For many decades, for instance, social psychologists have studied altruism, counselors have explored personality strengths, and sociologists have studied happiness. Pioneers such as Don Clifton (who studied human strengths), George Vaillant (who studies effective coping), Shelley Taylor (who studies health), Jane Piliavin (who studies helping and volunteerism), and Mihalyi Csikszentmihalyi (who studies flow and creativity) have worked in the field of positive psychology for decades, as have humanistic psychologists. However, what was missing was an integrated network to bring these scholars together in a common mission.

In another sense, positive psychology is less than a decade old. Around 1999, Martin E. P. Seligman began meeting with a group of scholars to form the positive psychology network. Seligman's audacious plan was to bring together the researchers and practitioners who were working on human strengths and positive attributes rather than focusing exclusively on human problems. This plan was amazingly effective, as a new field has emerged around the world in a matter of a few years. Prior to Seligman's efforts, those conducting scholarship on human strengths were usually working in relative isolation and sometimes in relative obscurity. Seligman's positive psychology initiative brought related scientists and practitioners together, and also helped to bring their work to the attention of others. Of course, the field grew rapidly in part due to Seligman's charisma and organizational skills, but it also grew for additional reasons. One of Seligman's important contributions was that although he recognized that positive applications are sorely needed, he always emphasized a scientific grounding for the field. Another aspect of the field is that it is open and democratic; anyone can "join."

Journalists often ask me why positive psychology has emerged now, after so many years, when psychology was focused primarily on human problems. One reason is that although our society still has problems, industrialized societies in many ways are better off than ever before (Easterbrook, 2003). Longevity is at an all-time high, human hunger is declining, people are more educated than ever before, and democratic governance is on the rise. Although certainly there are still threats and problems, such as global warming and terrorism (and the media often emphasizes these threats), most of our lives are blessed with ample resources, relative security, health, and unprecedented freedom. It makes sense, then, that we return to the philosophers' questions of what makes a good life and a good person. If affluence alone does not create a good life, what does? Concern for how to live a good life is natural once people's basic needs are met and threats are relatively contained. Unlike ancient societies, however, we have gained an enormous respect for the power of science in understanding, and therefore, we do not seek to understand human strengths only through rational thought but also through systematic scientific research. Positive psychology is a product of the importance now placed on science and the realization that we have the opportunity as never before in human history to create quality lives for ourselves.

Positive psychology strikes a resonant chord in society because many people are asking about their own quality of life and what will make a good life for them. Individuals have more freedom to pursue different life courses, and have knowledge of more alternatives. Thus, people are looking for information relevant to how to create a good life for themselves and for those they love. In individualistic societies—and the whole world is becoming more individualistic—people are taught to "follow your bliss." However, the best way to do this is not always self-evident, and people are looking for guidance on how to build a rewarding life, and how to build better societies. Although individualism allows people freedom, once material needs are met there is little guidance as to what should come next. Furthermore, individualism can create its own societal problems when individuals are not given sufficient grounding in positive psychology because they can make individual choices that are harmful to the group or nation. When individualism is pursued without concern for the well-being of the broader society, the outcomes can be destructive. Positive psychology emphasizes not only the actualization of the individual, but development within the framework of his or her contributions to other people and the world. Thus, our discipline is poised to answer questions that are pivotal to building healthier societies.

One other reason that positive psychology has grown is that many measures of strengths and positive phenomena have been developed—scales of optimism, virtues, life satisfaction, hope, creativity, meaning, and flow, to name just a few. Despite the obvious benefits of the self-report measures of strengths and well-being, there is a danger in relying solely on the self-report instruments. Positive psychologists also must use other methods of assessment, such as experience sampling, physiological, laboratory experimental, and behavior observation measures. In addition, we must be careful to include experimental designs and longitudinal studies in our studies of human strengths. We should avoid the error made in some fields of relying virtually exclusively on cross-sectional studies using only correlations of self-report measures.

On another front, positive psychology has become very popular with the media and with practitioners such as life coaches. There are dangers in this but also great opportunities. The danger is that we will rush to judgment on important issues and offer oversimplified answers. However, the opportunities are enormous in that positive psychologists can actually influence individuals and nations in substantive ways. The popular media can get our messages out to the public, and thus help us build a better world.

In any discussion about historical events, such as the emergence of the positive psychology movement in the late 1990s, a discussion of the large cultural trends is needed. I would be remiss, however, if I did not mention the second necessary influence on such events, and that is the important leaders involved. Our field owes a large debt to Martin E. P. Seligman and C. R. Snyder for their founding roles in positive psychology. I have enormous respect for both of them for their contributions to the field.

Rick Snyder was a distinguished professor of psychology, working at the University of Kansas from 1972 to 2006. He was a prolific researcher on positive topics, publishing 23 books and over 250 articles in his career. Rick was also an inspiring teacher, having received an unprecedented 27 teaching awards. Dr. Snyder's positive psychology scholarship was focused on *hope*, which he conceptualized more broadly than optimism, to include goal setting, pathway thinking, and agentic cognitions. Perhaps most noteworthy, Rick exemplified positive psychology in his own life, perpetually engaged, caring, and hopeful.

The Critics and the Future

Critics of positive psychology have emerged, and we would do well to evaluate their skepticism and learn from them when we can, rather than simply argue with them. One critique is that our field focuses too exclusively on the individual person, rather than considering the impact of neighborhoods, social groups, organizations, and governments in shaping positive behavior. Although there is research work in institutions, such as business organizations, it is true that most of the work in positive psychology has focused on the individual and factors within people. The psychology of positive institutions and of positive situations has received relatively less scholarly attention within the field, although we know that these areas are quite important. Thus, this is an important area that should be strengthened in positive psychology. It is encouraging that this handbook devotes substantial attention to positive institutions, and this presents an opportunity for contained growth of the field.

Another critique is that positive psychology is a cult, with "membership" open to insiders, but with boundaries that mark it off from the rest of the behavioral sciences. If this perception is widespread, it needs to be countered. Positive psychology must always have deep and frequent connections with the rest of the sciences and scholarly disciplines, and should never be a club of insiders; a broad interest from all scientists and practitioners should be encouraged. A related point is that positive psychology is not what the leaders of the field believe or define it to be; it is broader than that and should not be confined to the theories of a small set of scholars. For instance, the positive psychology of happiness is not what I say about subjective well-being; other positive psychologists can and should disagree with me at times and develop independent lines of scholarship. Indeed, positive psychology should be a large, democratic field in which debates and many viewpoints flourish.

Although there are notable leaders, such as Clifton, Seligman, Snyder, Csikszentmihalyi, and Emmons, the field must never be a cult in which one must believe what these individuals do. Positive psychology can avoid exclusivity by fostering connections with other fields and viewpoints, and must be welcoming to newcomers of various intellectual persuasions. The breadth of the field is exhibited in this book with the diversity of its authors. When one peruses the chapters in this volume, it is clear that positive psychology has strong ties to genetics and evolution, to neurobiology, to experimental and social psychology, and to other scientific areas. These ties should continue to grow as the field matures, and bridges to other areas of science will prevent the type of isolation that leads to stagnation of scholarly fields. It is also heartening to note that positive psychology is beginning to influence allied fields, such as anthropology, economics, philosophy, and developmental psychology.

A third critique of positive psychology is that the applications are outstripping the science. There is such a great demand for interventions that people have rushed to implement them, occasionally before the fundamental science is in place. To some extent this is inevitable because practitioners must act; they cannot wait for every issue to be resolved in a definitive way. Often they need to act with the best knowledge that is available. Nonetheless, we need researchers who continually point out the limits to our knowledge, and who continue to build a stronger scientific foundation. As is evident in this volume, positive psychologists who are working in applied areas are attempting to ground their work in scientific findings, and interventions are increasingly being tested empirically. The solid scientific foundations of our field are clearly evident in the chapters of this handbook.

A fourth critique of the field is that positive psychologists ignore past scholarship, as well as scholars who are not in the "fold," in doing their science. This is, of course, a mistake that we should always avoid. Psychologists, such as Marie Jahoda and Norman Bradburn, studied human happiness many decades ago, for example. Although we may not agree with everything that humanistic psychologists wrote, they had valuable insights and focused on "what is right" about individuals. Counseling psychologists have for many decades emphasized studying people's interests and strengths, and not simply focusing on what is wrong with them. Also, social welfare training and practice is deeply grounded in a strengths perspective. Thus, positive psychology has deep roots in past scholarship and practice, but should now bring together these diverse strands in an attempt to build an integrated discipline of the positive. There were intellectual giants in our past, and we do see farther because we stand on their shoulders. It is encouraging that one can see in the chapters in this volume that the scholarship of the past is integrated into the present directions of positive psychology.

A final critique of positive psychology, enunciated by the late eminent psychologist Richard Lazarus (2003), is that positive psychology is a Pollyanna view that ignores the negative in life. In fact, positive psychologists do not ignore what is negative in the human condition. However, they maintain that often one form of solution to problems, and in some cases the most effective one, is to build the positive rather than directly work on the problem. Another belief of positive psychologists is that we have for too long focused almost exclusively on the negative and on problems, and that positive aspects of humans are at least equally important, if not more so. Once again, the chapters of this volume demonstrate that we do not shy away from problems and challenges; we do not advance a sugar-coated view of life. Instead, positive psychologists do tackle problems while focusing on the positive in their approach to problems.

Whether the critiques of positive psychology are completely accurate or not, we can profit from them. The merits of the critiques may be of less importance than the open and active discourse they represent. What is important is that we examine our field in reference to the critiques, and use them to improve positive psychology. We should not be defensive about our field, but think about criticisms in order to learn from them. Some might think that answering criticisms is a strange way for a positive psychologist to introduce this volume. But the point is that we do not ignore the negative, and can even learn from it.

Furthermore, we can include the critics in our intellectual discussions in order to ensure continued growth in the field. For me, the outstanding work presented in this *Handbook of Positive Psychology* represents the best response to the critics.

Future Directions

Scholarship on positive psychology includes many different topics, including interest and flow, coping and resilience, virtue and character, intelligence and skills, creativity, and subjective well-being. Each of these phenomena can be analyzed at various levels, including the biological, cognitive, interpersonal, institutional, and societal. Some of these scholarly areas are in their infancy, whereas others are relatively well-developed. This volume includes reviews of both types of areas. The chapters in this volume review where we have made progress, but they are also valuable in showing where much work is still needed. The challenge, as the handbook makes clear, is that there are so many important topics waiting for deeper study.

One of the strengths that impresses me with the field of positive psychology is the number of young scholars who are entering the field as researchers and practitioners. Furthermore, the area is very popular with undergraduate students. Martin Seligman has emphasized from the beginning the critical importance of attracting young people to the field. For students, scholars, and the media alike, this handbook is a wonderful resource.

In what I have said thus far, I have emphasized the science and scholarship of positive psychology. However, the field is blossoming with applications and interventions, and this will continue to grow in the future. For example, executive life coaching will move beyond common sense and good judgment and will be built on scientific research. Clinical and counseling psychologists will continue to add positive interventions to their treatment regimens as the value of these is established with scientific studies. Developmental and educational psychologists will increasingly educate the public about how positive development can be assured. The national accounts of well-being, proposed by Martin Seligman and myself, are likely to be adopted in some nations, and will provide feedback to leaders on who is flourishing, and where societal interventions are needed. Assessments in which strengths and psychological problems are both measured, such as checkups for children, may come into existence. Whatever the directions, I am positive that there will be an explosion of applications of positive psychology, built on the excellent scholarship such as that presented in this handbook.

The goal of scientists, scholars, and practitioners in the field of positive psychology is to improve the quality of human life. We owe the authors of this volume a debt for the contributions they make here in this regard. Enjoy and savor this wonderful handbook.

Questions

1. What is the appropriate balance between science and practice in positive psychology?

2. How can positive psychology move in the direction of putting more focus on positive societies, organizations, and situations?

3. In what ways is happiness beneficial to effective functioning, and through what processes?

References

Easterbrook, G. (2003). *The progress paradox: How life gets better while people feel worse.* New York: Random House.

Lazarus, R. (2003). The Lazarus Manifesto for positive psychology and psychology in general. *Psychological Inquiry, 14,* 173–189.

Positive Emotions

Michael A. Cohn *and* Barbara L. Fredrickson

Abstract

Positive emotions include pleasant or desirable situational responses, ranging from interest and contentment to love and joy, but are distinct from pleasurable sensation and undifferentiated positive affect. These emotions are markers of people's overall well-being or happiness, but they also enhance future growth and success. This has been demonstrated in work, school, relationships, mental and physical health, and longevity. The *broaden-and-build theory of positive emotions* suggests that all positive emotions lead to broadened repertoires of thoughts and actions and that broadening helps build resources that contribute to future success. Unlike negative emotions, which are adapted to provide a rapid response to a focal threat, positive emotions occur in safe or controllable situations and lead more diffusely to seeking new resources or consolidating gains. These resources outlast the temporary emotional state and contribute to later success and survival.

This chapter discusses the nature of positive emotions both as evolutionary adaptations to build resources and as appraisals of a situation as desirable or rich in resources. We discuss the methodological challenges of evoking positive emotions for study both in the lab and in the field and issues in observing both short-term ("broaden") and long-term ("build") effects. We then review the evidence that positive emotions broaden perception, attention, motivation, reasoning, and social cognition and ways in which these may be linked to positive emotions' effects on important life outcomes. We also discuss and contextualize evidence that positive emotions may be detrimental at very high levels or in certain situations. We close by discussing ways in which positive emotions theory can be harnessed by both basic and applied positive psychology research.

Keywords: broadening, evolution, happiness, growth, resources

Positive emotions have long been studied as markers of people's overall well-being or happiness (Diener & Seligman, 2004; Kahneman, Kreuger, & Schkade, 2004), but looking at positive emotions as outcomes is just the beginning. In hundreds of well-controlled studies, positive emotions and experiences have also been shown to predict or contribute to valuable life outcomes (Lyubomirsky, King, & Diener, 2005), including greater satisfaction and success at work (Losada & Heaphy, 2004), improved immune function (Cohen, Doyle, & Turner, 2003), and even longer life (Danner, Snowdon, & Friesen, 2001; Levy, Slade, & Kunkel, 2002; Moskowitz, 2003; Ostir, Markides, & Black, 2000). We will use the "broaden-and-build theory" of positive emotions (Fredrickson, 1998, 2001) as a framework for reviewing the research on long-term effects and short-term mechanisms of positive emotions. We attempt to answer a central question: How is it that our fleeting experiences of joy, interest, or love—which can be so easily squelched or dismissed—produce lasting gains in strengths and well-being? At the end of the chapter we will address a larger question of particular interest to positive psychology: What is the role of positive emotion in a full and well-lived life?

Defining Positive Emotions

The theories of emotions that dominated psychology for most of its history proved fruitful for studying negative emotions but were often a poor fit for positive emotions (Fredrickson, 1998). In the past 10 years, positive emotions have come into their own. The renaissance in positive emotions research stems from two sources: a growing interest in the psychology of the "good life" (Fredrickson, 1998; Keyes & Haidt, 2002; Ryff & Singer, 1998) and several research programs that have sought to build an empirical, bottom-up model of positive emotions.

Although working definitions of emotions vary somewhat across researchers, consensus is emerging that emotions are best conceptualized as multicomponent response tendencies. Emotions involve not just subjective feelings but also attention and cognition, facial expressions, cardiovascular and hormonal changes, and more, unfolding over a relatively short time span (Cosmides & Tooby, 2000; Lazarus, 1991). Positive emotions subjectively resemble positive sensations (e.g., satiety, comfort) as well as undifferentiated positive moods. However, only positive emotions involve an appraisal of the situation (Oatley & Jenkins, 1996; Smith & Ellsworth, 1985) or the specific motivational effects we will discuss in this chapter.

Theorists differ as to how the differences between emotions are best modeled (e.g., Cosmides & Tooby, 2000; Russell, Weiss, & Mendelsohn, 1989; Smith & Ellsworth, 1985). However, there is general agreement that valence on a bipolar continuum from highly unpleasant to highly pleasant is a primary characteristic of every emotion (reviewed in Smith & Ellsworth, 1985). Indeed, this pleasantness rating may be one of the earliest determinations we make when processing sensory input from our environment (Chen & Bargh, 1999). An appraisal of pleasantness can arise when a stimulus fulfills a biological need (e.g., Cabanac, 1971), when it contributes to a personally relevant goal, or when it remedies a noxious or goal-inconsistent state.

Past research has suggested that positive emotions are less distinct and more likely to co-occur with one another than negative emotions (Barrett, Gross, Christensen, & Benvenuto, 2001; Fredrickson & Branigan, 2001; Smith & Ellsworth, 1985). This was in part because positive emotions differ on dimensions such as relatedness, moral judgment, and spiritual experience, which did not appear in the foundational appraisals research on negative emotions (Tong, 2006). The specific positive emotions individuals feel also vary due to personality differences (Shiota, Keltner, & John, 2006), cultural differences (Tsai, Knutson, & Fung, 2006), and variations in the ability to make fine distinctions among emotions (Tugade, Fredrickson, & Barrett, 2004).

Positive Emotions Versus Negative Emotions

Historically, emotions research has focused on negative emotions. The most general reason is that psychology as a whole has focused on understanding and ameliorating psychological problems (Seligman & Csikszentmihalyi, 2000). Although positive emotions can contribute to problems (e.g., mania, drug addiction), negative emotions are more prominent causes and effects of pathology and thus captured the majority of research attention. Studies of positive functioning and strengths have only recently begun to catch up, raising interest in the contributions of positive emotions. We argue later that even the study of pathology has been hindered by overlooking positive emotions, which play a critical role in recovering from adversity and developing compensatory strengths.

General theories of emotion are typically built with the more attention-grabbing negative emotions (e.g., fear and anger) as prototypes. A key idea in many theories is a link between each emotion and a "specific action tendency" (Frijda, 1986; Frijda, Kuipers, & Schure, 1989; Lazarus, 1991; Levenson, 1994; Oatley & Jenkins, 1996; Tooby & Cosmides, 1990). Fear, for example, produces motivation and physiological preparedness to escape, anger to attack, disgust to expel, and so on. These action tendencies are thought to have evolved because they helped our ancestors get out of life-or-death situations.

Positive emotions were often squeezed into these theories as an afterthought. Joy, for instance, was linked with aimless activation, interest with attending, and contentment with inactivity (Frijda, 1986). These tendencies seem far too general to be called specific, nor do they present the same obvious adaptive value as negative emotion tendencies (Ekman, 1992; Fredrickson, 1998; Lazarus, 1991). Our attempts to give positive emotions equal weight in shaping theories of emotion led us to develop the *broaden-and-build theory.*

The Broaden-and-Build Theory of Positive Emotions

Fredrickson's broaden-and-build theory of positive emotions holds that positive emotions "broaden" people's momentary thought–action repertoires and lead to actions that "build" enduring personal resources (Fredrickson, 1998, 2001).

The specific action tendencies of traditional models are appropriate descriptions of the function of negative emotions: In a life-threatening situation, a narrowed thought–action repertoire promotes quick and decisive action that carries direct and immediate benefit.[1]

Positive emotions, in contrast, seldom occur in response to life-threatening situations. Thus, there is less need for them to evoke specific, focused response tendencies. Instead, positive emotions lead to *broadened* and *more flexible* response tendencies, widening the array of thoughts and actions that come to mind (Fredrickson, 1998). Joy, for instance, creates the urge to play, whether physically, socially, or intellectually. Interest creates the urge to explore, take in new information and experiences, and expand the self in the process. Love—which we view as an amalgam of several positive emotions— creates urges to play with, learn about, and savor our loved ones. Broadened thought–action repertoires did not evolve because of their short-term survival benefits, the theory posits, but because of their long-term effects. Broadening "builds" personal resources.

Take play as an example. In many species, juveniles play with behaviors—like running into a flexible sapling or branch and catapulting oneself in an unexpected direction—that adults use exclusively for predator avoidance (Dolhinow, 1987). Social play also builds enduring resources. Laughter appears to signal openness to new, friendly interactions (broadening), which can lead to lasting social bonds and attachments (building; Gervais & Wilson, 2005). Shared amusement and smiles have many of the same effects (Keltner & Bonanno, 1997; Lee, 1983; Simons, McCluskey-Fawcett, & Papini, 1986). Childhood play also builds enduring intellectual resources by increasing levels of creativity (Sherrod & Singer, 1989) and fueling brain development (Panksepp, 1998). Similarly, the exploration prompted by the positive emotion of interest creates knowledge and intellectual complexity, and the savoring prompted by contentment produces self-insight and alters world views. So, each of these phenomenologically distinct positive emotions shares the downstream effect of augmenting personal resources, ranging from physical and social

resources to intellectual and psychological resources (see Fredrickson, 1998, 2001; Fredrickson & Branigan, 2001, for more detailed reviews).

The personal resources accrued during states of positive emotions are durable, outlasting the transient emotional states that led to their acquisition. These resources can be drawn on whenever they are needed, even if the individual does not feel positive at that moment (e.g., learning about a landscape out of curiosity, then using this knowledge while fleeing in terror). Figure 3.1 represents these three sequential effects of positive emotions: broadened mind-sets, built resources, and enhanced success in the future.

Short-Term and Long-Term Effects of Positive Emotions

Our empirical investigation of the broaden-and-build theory has rested on two hypotheses: the "broaden hypothesis," which targets the ways people change while experiencing a positive emotion, and the "build hypothesis," which targets the lasting changes that follow repeated positive emotional experiences over time.

The Broaden Hypothesis: Positive Emotions Broaden Perception, Thoughts, and Actions
VISUAL ATTENTION

The most cognitively basic form of the broaden effect we have examined appears in global–local visual processing tasks. Participants are asked to make a choice about a figure that can be categorized based either on its global, overall shape or on its local details (see Figure 2a). Positive emotions, with their broadened focus, produce a preference for the global level, whereas negative emotions often produce a preference for the details. This pattern holds both for emotionally relevant traits like optimism and anxiety (Basso, Schefft, Ris, & Dember, 1996) and for emotional states induced through a variety of means (Brandt, Derryberry, & Reed, 1992, cited in Derryberry & Tucker, 1994; Fredrickson & Branigan, 2005; Johnson & Fredrickson, 2005). Wadlinger & Isaacowitz (2006) tracked participants' eye movement and found that induced positive emotion broadens visual search patterns, leading to increased attention to peripheral stimuli.

COGNITION AND BEHAVIOR

Emotions affect both the focus and the process of cognition, and many long-standing findings on the effects of positive affect on cognition and behavior are consistent with the broaden hypothesis. Isen and

[1] A life-saving response need not involve action per se. Evolutionary research suggests that sadness may have evolved to *prevent* action at times when opportunities were too poor to merit expending any energy (Keller & Nesse, 2005).

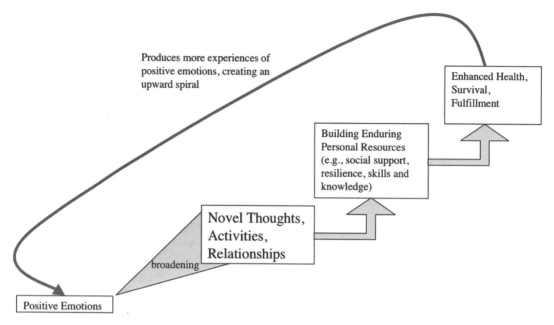

Fig. 3.1 The broaden-and-build theory of positive emotions.

colleagues tested the effects of positive states on a wide range of cognitive outcomes, ranging from creativity puzzles to simulations of complex, life-or-death work situations (Estrada, Isen, & Young, 1997). Her work demonstrates that positive emotions produce patterns of thought that are notably unusual (Isen, Johnson, Mertz, & Robinson, 1985), flexible and inclusive (Isen & Daubman, 1984), creative (Isen, Daubman, & Nowicki, 1987), and receptive to new information (Estrada et al., 1997). Rowe, Hirsch, & Anderson (2007) replicated Isen's findings of improved performance on the verbal-associative Remote Associates Test (Figure 3.2b) and found that this improvement was correlated with *decreased* performance on a visual task that required participants to narrow their range of attention.

In the domain of more personally relevant behavior, we (Fredrickson & Branigan, 2005) induced positive, negative, or no emotions in volunteer participants and then asked them to step away from the specifics of the induction and list all the things they felt like doing. Participants induced to feel positive emotions listed *more* and *more varied* potential actions relative to the neutral group; participants induced to feel negative emotions listed fewer potential actions than the neutral group. Similar research has shown that positive emotions produce more creative (Isen et al., 1987) and varied (Kahn & Isen, 1993) actions.

Another perspective on positive affect and cognition comes from the mood-as-information theorists. They have confirmed the beneficial effects of positive affect but also found a reduction in attention to detail and negative feedback, sometimes leading to an overreliance on heuristics or stereotypes (reviewed in the volume by Martin & Clore, 2001). However, other work suggests that people in positive emotional states are *more* likely to incorporate challenging evidence (Trope & Pomerantz, 1998) and carefully consider difficult problems (reviewed in Abele, 1992; Aspinwall, 1998).

The general term "broadened thought" could apply to either vague, heuristic thinking or thorough, nondefensive exploration, and little has been done to reconcile these opposing interpretations. What work there is suggests that *flexibility* and *openness* are important attributes of positive emotions' cognitive effects (Bless et al., 1996; Dreisbach & Goschke, 2004), and these effects can enhance or hinder performance depending on the task and the context.

SOCIAL COGNITION

Broadened social attention takes the form of enhanced attention to others and reduced distinctions between self and other or between different groups. Participants experiencing positive emotions report more overlap between their concept of themselves and their concept of their best friend (Waugh

Fig. 3.2 Three forms of broadened attention. (a) The participant is instructed to find the letter "T" as quickly as possible. It is present in both figures, but finding the first is facilitated by a broadened visual focus, while finding the second is facilitated by a narrowed (detail-oriented) focus (Fredrickson & Branigan, 2005; Johnson, 2005). (b) In this item from the Remote Associates Test, the participant is asked to find a word that ties the three stimulus words together. Participants are more likely to find the answer ("jack") when experiencing a positive emotion (Isen, Daubman, & Nowicki, 1987). (c) Caucasian individuals are typically poor at distinguishing a previously learned Black face from a new one and good at determining where a morphed series crosses from "more White" to "more Black." When experiencing positive emotions they recognize Black faces as well as they recognize White ones (Johnson & Fredrickson, 2005) and perform worse at dichotomous race categorization (Johnson, 2005).

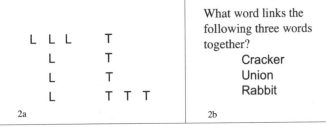

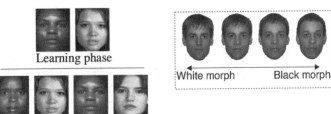

Learning phase

Identification Phase

White morph   Black morph

& Fredrickson, 2006; Waugh, Hejmadi, Otake, & Fredrickson, 2006) and become more imaginative and attentive regarding things they could do for friends (Otake, Waugh, & Fredrickson, in preparation). When a close relationship does not yet exist, induced positive emotions can increase trust (Dunn & Schweitzer, 2005) and may underlie the creation of a wide variety of bonds and interdependence opportunities (Cohn & Fredrickson, 2006; Gable, Reis, Impett, & Asher, 2004).

Positive emotions also broaden social group concepts and break down an essentialized sense of "us versus them" (Dovidio, Gaertner, Isen, Rust, & Guerra, 1995). We have discovered the same result in a racial context: When we induce positive emotions in participants, people become less racially biased in their face perception and simultaneously *worse* at perceiving physical differences between races (Figure 2c) (Johnson, 2005; Johnson & Fredrickson, 2005).

The studies we have discussed demonstrate variety in the broaden effect, but more importantly, the outcomes they involve can make a substantive difference in what people learn, who they befriend, and how they understand their lives. In other words, these "broadened" mind-sets can lead people to "build" enduring resources.

The Build Hypothesis

Although positive emotions are temporary and transient, they encourage a broadened range of actions, which over time builds enduring personal resources.

In nonhuman mammals, juvenile play is associated with developing behaviors later used in predator avoidance and aggressive fighting (Boulton & Smith, 1992; Caro, 1988) and improves learning skills on complex motor tasks (Einon, Morgan, & Kibbler, 1978). A review of the human literature by Lyubomirsky et al. (2005) found that positive emotions lead to outcomes ranging from satisfaction at work and in relationships to physical health and effective problem solving.

In a direct test of the build hypothesis, we randomly assigned working adults to experience enhanced daily positive emotions. Participants in the experimental group were trained in loving-kindness meditation, a practice similar to mindfulness meditation (Davidson et al., 2003; Kabat-Zinn, 2005) but which focuses on deliberately generating the positive emotions of compassion and love.

After 3 weeks of practice, meditators began reporting higher daily levels of various positive emotions compared to those in the waitlist control

Fig. 3.3 Results from a positive emotions intervention study. The intervention increased daily positive emotions, which led to building physical resources (top box), psychological resources (middle box), and social resources (bottom box). Resource building, in turn, led to increased life satisfaction.

group. After 8 weeks, meditators showed increases in a number of personal resources, including physical wellness, agency for achieving important goals, ability to savor positive experiences, and quality of close relationships. Mediation analyses suggested that these changes in resources were attributable to the increases in daily positive emotion and that these improved resources led those in the mediation group to judge their lives as more satisfying and fulfilling (see Figure 3; Fredrickson, Cohn, Coffey, Pek, & Finkel, 2008).

POSITIVE EMOTIONS AND STRESS

Prolonged negative situations like bereavement or joblessness evoke negative emotions but often cannot be solved by the kind of immediate, narrowly defined action that negative emotions encourage. Consistent with this view, studies have shown that grieving individuals who experienced some level of positive emotions alongside their negative ones showed greater psychological well-being a year or more later and that this occurs partly because positive emotions were associated with the ability to take a longer view and develop plans and goals for the future (Moskowitz, Folkman, & Acree, 2003; Stein, Folkman, Trabasso, & Richards, 1997). We found similar benefits of positive emotion in a longitudinal assessment of college students' emotions and mental health before and after the September 11 terrorist attacks (Fredrickson, Tugade, Waugh, & Larkin, 2003). Resilient participants were not devoid of negative emotions—they felt fear and grief much like their less resilient peers—but finding occasional opportunities to feel positive emotions seems to have alleviated some of the negative effects of a prolonged narrowed mind-set. Psychological resilience is also associated with the ability to distinguish many finely differentiated positive emotions (Tugade, Fredrickson, & Barrett, 2004); perhaps this is because a broad emotional lexicon makes it possible to find positive moments without denying the seriousness of a negative situation.

These results contradict common-sense criticisms that positive emotions are unhelpful or inappropriate for people in negative circumstances: Even adults dealing with suicidal thoughts (Joiner, Pettit, Perez, & Burns, 2001) or disclosure of childhood sexual abuse (Bonanno et al., 2002) showed better coping when some degree of positivity accompanied their painful feelings. In a longitudinal study of college students coping with ordinary life problems (Fredrickson & Joiner, 2002), we found that state positive emotions correlated with the use of creative and broad-minded coping strategies and that use of these strategies, in turn, predicted increased positive emotions 5 weeks later (above and beyond initial level of positive emotion). Research on pessimism and depression recognizes a self-reinforcing downward spiral; we are now finding evidence that positive emotions contribute to an upward spiral of increasing resources, life successes, and overall fulfillment.

POSITIVE EMOTIONS AND HEALTH

People who experience high levels of positive emotions tend to experience less pain and disability related to chronic health conditions (Gil et al., 1997), fight off illness and disease more successfully (Cohen & Pressman, 2006; Ong & Allaire, 2005), and even live longer (Danner et al., 2001; Levy et al., 2002; Moskowitz, 2003; Ostir et al., 2000). We believe that these findings may be explained by the ability of positive emotions to lift people out of stressed, narrowed states.

It is already established that the physiological changes that accompany negative emotions are beneficial for decisive, short-term action but detrimental to long-term health (Sapolsky, 1999), and that there are benefits to properly regulating the stress response (McEwen & Seeman, 1999). We have explored whether positive emotions help with regulation, neutralizing the body's biochemical stress response once a threat is past.

We exposed participants to an anxiety-provoking experience, ended the experience, and then showed them an emotional film clip, all while measuring their biological stress responses. Participants in the two positive emotion conditions (mild joy and contentment) recovered more quickly than those viewing a neutral clip, who recovered more quickly than those viewing a sad clip (Fredrickson, Mancuso, Branigan, & Tugade, 2000, study 1; see also Fredrickson & Levenson, 1998). When there was no stressor, none of the films had any biological effect (Fredrickson et al., 2000, study 2). In other words, the positive films are not notable for what they *do* to the cardiovascular system, but rather for what they can *undo* within this system. We have also discovered that people who are generally resilient against negative events recover more quickly and that they do so by self-generating positive emotions during the recovery process (Tugade & Fredrickson, 2004).

We take these laboratory experiments as a microcosm for the influence of emotions on coping and of coping on health. Imagine that some individuals typically seek positive emotions to help them quickly bounce back from life's stressors, while others spend more time remaining physiologically activated and prepared to react, even after the threat is gone. Over time, the latter group will accumulate more physiological wear and tear and be more vulnerable to a wide range of stress-related illness (Kiecolt-Glaser, McGuire, Robles, & Glaser, 2002; McEwen & Seeman, 1999). Whether the undo effect of positive emotions factors into long-term health in this way is a challenging and deeply important question for future research.

Measuring Positive Emotions
Self-Report Measures

There are few self-report emotion measures that do justice to the diversity of positive emotions. Often specificity is not critical, and many studies generate valid results with a single-item question about emotional valence, possibly combined with arousal level (Russell et al., 1989). The popular Positive and Negative Affect Schedule (PANAS) measure (Watson, Wiese, Vaidya, & Tellegen, 1999) is designed for theoretical reasons to differentiate high-arousal emotions only and underrepresents low-arousal positive emotions. The Multiple Affect Adjective Check List (MAACL; Larsen & Sinnett, 1991) has a full positive affect subscale, but with 132 items, it is often not feasible to use as part of experimental research.

The modified Differential Emotions Scale (mDES; Fredrickson et al., 2003) asks participants to assess how intensely they are experiencing 20 discrete emotions. We developed the mDES to include both low- and high-arousal examples of both positive and negative emotions (e.g., contentment, excitement, sadness, and anxiety). Thus, it is useful both for finely categorizing a person's emotion experience and for measuring his or her overall level of positive and negative emotion. The mDES also includes emotion-like states without an inherent valence, such as surprise, and emotions that are considered less prototypical and so may be reported participants independently, such as interest and compassion. By varying the response options, the mDES can measure either intensity or frequency of either present or recalled emotions. The mDES uses terms that most participants are familiar with and takes only 1–2 min to complete, so it balances the goals of quick assessment and emotional breadth.[2]

Facial Measures

Self-report measures share a number of flaws. They are vulnerable to desirable responding; they distract participants from the task or experience at hand; and they cannot measure emotions that are too subtle to reach conscious awareness but that still affect cognition (e.g., Winkelman & Berridge, 2004). They are also poor at demonstrating the course of an emotion over time. For these purposes, psychophysiological measures may be better. In *facial electromyography* (facial EMG), electrical sensors placed on the face detect changes in muscle tension. Positive emotions cause activity in the *zygomasticus major* and the *obicularis oculi*, the two muscles used in a spontaneous (nonposed) smile. This occurs even if the participant is not aware of any change and an observer would not be able to detect a smile. Another option is Ekman and Friesen's (1978) Facial Action Coding System (FACS), a procedure for describing the movement of all facial muscle groups, including those that display emotion. Facial EMG is more sensitive to small changes, whereas FACS can discriminate a wider range of emotions. Both are useful as covert measures of emotional change over time.

Future Directions
Physiological and Neurological Connections

We are eager to see empirical findings on positive emotions embedded in a broader physiological

[2] The most current version of the mDES is available at http://www.positiveemotions.org

context. A review by Ashby, Isen, and Turken (1999) suggests that the broaden effect may be associated with release of mesolimbic dopamine, which enhances cognitive flexibility, set switching, and proactive curiosity. Notably, this is the same neurological system Berridge and Robinson (2003) associated with the motivational component of positive affect. It is also the mesolimbic dopamine system that is inhibited by older antipsychotic drugs, which lead to notable cognitive narrowing and rigidity (Berger et al., 1989). There is no doubt that the neurological substrate of the broaden effect will turn out to be more complex than a single neurotransmitter or neuronal system, but Ashby et al.'s (1999) observations help pave the way for future investigation.

Scattered results linking physiology and positive emotional effects are emerging in other areas. Haidt (2005) has early but suggestive evidence linking elevation and other moral emotions to changes in vagal tone. Results from neuroimaging studies demonstrate heightened left-hemispheric activation both while experiencing positive emotions and tonically in individuals with higher trait positive emotionality (Davidson, 2004). Our work on the undo effect (Fredrickson & Levenson, 1998; Fredrickson et al., 2000) demonstrates that positive emotions can reduce the duration of cardiovascular response evoked by a stressor. As we learn more about how positive emotions are situated in the brain and body, we will be able to make better predictions about emotions and health and take advantage of more research from medical and animal research.

Interventions

Interventions based on the resource-building effects of positive emotions require us to have emotion inductions that are reliable and continue to work over time. Emmons and McCullough (2003) have designed an intervention based on counting blessings; Sheldon and Lyubomirsky (2006) have combined counting blessings with visualizing one's best possible self, and Seligman, Steen, and Park (2005) had participants count blessings, express gratitude, and practice using their signature strengths. Our research on loving-kindness meditation produced the strongest evidence to date that induced positive emotions lead to gains in resources, but its intervention is cumbersome and resource intensive. Positive emotions research needs a variety of inductions that can work with different populations, different lifestyles, and different levels of resources and

participant commitment. We encourage future research on popular or folk methods for changing one's emotional state to see if we can empirically verify and harness their effects. Related areas of psychology can also help: practitioners of cognitive-behavioral therapy have a stable of techniques for generating positive emotions as a bulwark against depression (Beck, 1995), and these may be adaptable for nondepressed individuals as well.

Properties of Specific Emotions

So far, the empirical evidence suggests that the broaden effect is common to many positive emotions and may describe their most general shared effect on cognition and attention. However, different positive emotions should also have distinct thought–action repertoires, subjective components, and physiological effects. For example, Tiedens and Linton (2001) compared the cognitive effects of contentment and pleasant surprise along a certainty–uncertainty continuum, and Gonzaga, Turner, Keltner, Campos, and Altemus (2006) studied cognitive, behavioral, and biological distinctions between romantic love, friendship, and sexual desire. Tong (2006) found that distinguishing different positive emotions may require attention to dimensions of experience that researchers have not previously thought of as inherent to emotion, such as social connection and spiritual experience.

Models

The broaden-and-build theory provides a description of the short-term effects of positive emotions and a plausible mechanism for long-term growth, but at a very general level. There is much more to learn about how the broaden effect works and what it does in specific situations. How does a broad mind-set affect perceived familiarity with and interest in a new relationship partner? In a learning situation, is it likely to increase interest in the topic at hand or increase the tendency to switch between topics? In what situations does it lead to heuristic use versus careful processing?

Conclusion: Positive Emotions and Positive Psychology

Positive psychology's domain includes both the hedonic definition of happiness—good moods and pleasurable experiences—and the eudaemonic definition—personal growth, meaningful occupation, and connection with others. These have sometimes been portrayed as conflicting, and positive psychology has sometimes had to emphasize the eudaemonic to counter media portrayals of the field as Pollyannaish or emotionally manic. We see the emerging view of positive emotions as undoing this dichotomy. Evolution shaped the enjoyable emotions of friendship because investing energy in another person does not always promote survival immediately, but it reliably does over time. We evolved the ability to feel interest to move us through the idle stage of learning about a new topic (e.g., an animal's migratory patterns, the nuances of a landscape) to the point where we develop potentially life-saving knowledge. Positive emotions contribute to both the pleasurable life and the good life.

Many positive emotions are related to immediate pleasure, and there is no question that positive emotions are also part of arrogance, addiction, and complacency. However, in most cases we see positive emotions as part of humanity's toolbox for growth: Positive emotions allow us to sample the rewards of the future in the present.

We encourage positive psychologists to consider the resource-building value of positive emotions in their work. When studying people who are successful in their own lives, we should remember to seek positive emotional mediators for their successful behaviors. When designing interventions, we should remember that positive emotions encourage participants to stick with a program (Csikszentmihalyi, 2003) and also help move them from entrenched habits to new and adaptive ways of acting (Fredrickson & Losada, 2005).

Our critics do sound a useful warning: A full scientific understanding of positive emotions should include the pitfalls and boundary conditions of their benefits. For example, although more securely attached infants show faster cognitive development, insecure attachment may be an appropriate response to threatening or unreliable family circumstances. Positive emotions help undo the lingering cardiovascular effects of stressors, but people in particularly dangerous circumstances may have good reason to remain ready to act, even when a threat appears to be gone. Additionally, there is some suggestion that extremely high levels of positive emotions, untempered by sufficient negative emotions, can degrade performance (Diener, 2004; Fredrickson & Losada, 2005). We would like to develop a nuanced understanding of when positive emotions can help resolve a negative situation (as in Fredrickson et al., 2003; Moskowitz et al., 2003; Stein et al., 1997) and when they might be dangerous, excessive, or unacceptably costly.

Despite these caveats, we believe there is good reason to celebrate and encourage positive emotions. Research on critical ratios of positivity to negativity (Fredrickson & Losada, 2005; Gottman, 1994) suggests that most individuals and groups are on the low end. There are important questions about when and how to experience positive emotions and which emotions are appropriate in different situations, but few of us are fortunate enough to have the problem of simply experiencing too much joy, interest, contentment, or love. If we were to make a recommendation based on the current state of the research, it is that people should cultivate positive emotions as a regular feature of their lives without giving up their ability to react to good and bad events as they come. Negative emotions help us respond to threats, avoid risks, and appropriately mark losses, while positive emotions help us take advantage of everything life has to offer.

Future Questions About Positive Emotions

1. Is broadening one thing or many? Is there a single underlying biological, neurological, or psychological state that increases the breadth of perception, motivation, attention, and social cognition, or are these all separate but conceptually related adaptations? If they are separate, why does broadening in one domain appear to be associated with broadening in others? If they are unified, then what features of distinct positive emotions or distinct situations determine the type of broadened thoughts and actions that will result?

2. When is a broadened thought–action repertoire beneficial? Some evidence suggests that positive emotions can interfere with intense attention and detail-oriented thinking, but many real-world situations clearly benefit from both close attention to details and openness to new ideas or unexpected information. It will be especially critical to understand how the broaden effect plays out in a variety of task, work, and study contexts.

3. If positive emotions are widely beneficial, why don't we experience more of them? A variety of research indicates that most people would benefit from modest increases in their daily levels of positive emotions. Are there benefits, in either the evolutionary or the modern context, to a conservative approach to positive emotions? Or are there potentially remediable features of the modern world that cause many people to experience more worry and distress and less interest, joy, and contentment than would be optimal?

References

Abele, A. (1992). Positive versus negative mood influences on problem solving. *Polish Psychological Bulletin, 23*, 187–202.

Ashby, F. G., Isen, A. M., & Turken, U. (1999). A neuropsychological theory of positive affect and its influence on cognition. *Psychological Review, 106*, 529–550.

Aspinwall, L. (1998). Rethinking the role of positive affect in self-regulation. *Motivation and Emotion, 22*(1), 1–32.

Barrett, L. F., Gross, J., Christensen, T. C., & Benvenuto, M. (2001). Knowing what you're feeling and knowing what to do about it: Mapping the relation between emotion differentiation and emotion regulation. *Cognition and Emotion, 15*, 713–724.

Basso, M. R., Schefft, B. K., Ris, M. D., & Dember, W. N. (1996). Mood and global-local visual processing. *Journal of the International Neuropsychological Society, 2*, 249–255.

Beck, J. S. (1995). *Cognitive therapy: Basics and beyond.* New York: Guilford.

Berger, H. J. C., van Hoof, J. J. M., van Spaendonck, K. P. M., Horstink, M. W. I., van den Bercken, J. H. L., Jaspers, R., et al. (1989). Haolperidol and cognitive shifting. *Neuropsychologia, 27*, 629–639.

Berridge, K. C., & Robinson, T. E. (2003). Parsing reward. *Trends in Neurosciences, 26*, 507–513.

Bless, H., Clore, G., Schwarz, N., Golisano, V., Rabe, C., & Wölk, M. (1996). Mood and the use of scripts: Does a happy mood really lead to mindlessness? *Journal of Personality and Social Psychology, 71*(4), 665–679.

Bonanno, G. A., Keltner, D., Noll, J. G., Putnam, F. W., Trickett, P. K., LeJune, J., et al. (2002). When the face reveals what words do not: Facial expressions of emotion, smiling, and the willingness to disclose childhood sexual abuse. *Journal of Personality and Social Psychology, 83*, 94–110.

Boulton, M. J., & Smith, P. K. (1992). The social nature of play fighting and play chasing: Mechanisms and strategies underlying cooperation and compromise. In J. H. Barkow, L. Cosmides, & J. Tooby (Eds.), *The adapted mind: Evolutionary psychology and the generation of culture* (pp. 429–444). New York: Oxford University Press.

Cabanac, M. (1971). Physiological role of pleasure. *Science, 173*, 1103–1107.

Caro, T. M. (1988). Adaptive significance of play: Are we getting closer? *Tree, 3*, 50–54.

Chen, M., & Bargh, J. (1999). Consequences of automatic evaluation: Immediate behavioral dispositions to approach or avoid the stimulus. *Personality and Social Psychology Bulletin, 25*(2), 215–224.

Cohen, S., Doyle, W. J., & Turner, R. B. (2003). Emotional style and susceptibility to the common cold. *Psychosomatic Medicine, 65*, 652–657.

Cohen, S., & Pressman, S. D. (2006). Positive affect and health. *Current Directions in Psychological Science, 15*, 122–125.

Cohn, M. A., & Fredrickson, B. L. (2006). Beyond the moment, beyond the self: Shared ground between selective investment theory and the broaden-and-build theory of positive emotions. *Psychological Inquiry, 17*, 39–44.

Cosmides, L., & Tooby, J. (2000). Evolutionary psychology and the emotions. In M. Lewis & J. M. Haviland-Jones (Eds.), *Handbook of Emotions* (2nd ed., pp. 91–115). New York: Guilford.

Csikszentmihalyi, M. (2003). *Good business: Leadership, flow, and the making of meaning.* New York: Penguin.

Danner, D. D., Snowdon, D. A., & Friesen, W. V. (2001). Positive emotions in early life and longevity: Findings from the nun study. *Journal of Personality and Social Psychology, 80*, 804–813.

Davidson, R. J. (2004). What does the prefrontal cortex "do" in affect: Perspectives on frontal EEG asymmetry research. *Biological Psychiatry, 67*, 219–233.

Davidson, R. J., Kabat-Zinn, J., Schumacher, J., Rosenkrantz, M., Muller, D., Santorelli, S. F., et al. (2003). Alterations in brain and immune function produced by mindfulness meditation. *Psychosomatic Medicine, 65*, 564–570.

Derryberry, D., & Tucker, D. M. (1994). Motivating the focus of attention. In P. M. Neidenthal & S. Kitayama (Eds.), *The heart's eye: Emotional influences in perception and attention* (pp. 167–196). San Diego, CA: Academic Press.

Diener, E. (February 2004). *Very happy people and success in domains of life.* Talk presented at the meeting of the Society for Personality and Social Psychology, New Orleans, LA.

Diener, E., & Seligman, M. E. P. (2004). Beyond money: Toward an economy of well-being. *Psychological Science in the Public Interest, 5*, 1–31.

Dolhinow, P. J. (1987). At play in the fields. In H. Topoff (Ed.), *The natural history reader in animal behavior* (pp. 229–237). New York: Columbia University Press.

Dovidio, J., Gaertner, S., Isen, A., Rust, M., & Guerra, P. (1995). Positive affect and the reduction of intergroup bias. In C. Sedikides, J. Schopler, & C. A. Insko (Eds.), *Intergroup cognition and intergroup behavior* (pp. 337–366). Mahway, NJ: Erlbaum.

Dreisbach, G., & Goschke, T. (2004). How positive affect modulates cognitive control: Reduced perseveration at the cost of increased distractibility. *Journal of Experimental Psychology: Memory and Cognition, 30*, 343–353.

Dunn, J., & Schweitzer, M. (2005). Feeling and believing: The influence of emotion on trust. *Journal of Personality and Social Psychology, 88*(6), 736–748.

Einon, D. F., Morgan, M. J., & Kibbler, C. C. (1978). Brief periods of socialization and later behavior in the rat. *Developmental Psychobiology, 11*, 213–225.

Ekman, P. (1992). An argument for basic emotions. *Cognition and Emotion, 6*, 169–200.

Ekman, P., & Friesen, W. V. (1978). *Facial action coding system: A technique for the measurement of facial movement.* Palo Alto, CA: Consulting Psychologists Press.

Emmons, R. A., & McCullough, M. E. (2003). Counting blessings vs. burdens: An experimental investigation of gratitude and subjective well-being in daily life. *Journal of Personality and Social Psychology, 84*, 377–389.

Estrada, C. A., Isen, A. M., & Young, M. J. (1997). Positive affect facilitates integration of information and decreases anchoring in reasoning among physicians. *Organizational Behavior and Human Decision Processes, 72*, 117–135.

Fredrickson, B. L. (1998). What good are positive emotions? *Review of General Psychology, 2*, 300–319.

Fredrickson, B. L. (2001). The role of positive emotions in positive psychology: The broaden-and-build theory of positive emotions. *American Psychologist, 56*, 218–226.

Fredrickson, B. L., & Branigan, C. (2001). Positive emotions. In T. J. Mayne & G. A. Bonnano (Eds.), *Emotion: Current issues and future directions.* New York: Guilford.

Fredrickson, B. L., & Branigan, C. (2005). Positive emotions broaden thought—action repertoires: Evidence for the broaden-and-build model. *Cognition and Emotion, 19*, 313–332.

Fredrickson, B. L., Cohn, M. A., Coffey, K., Pek, J., & Finkel, S. M. (2008). Open hearts build lives: Positive emotions, induced through meditation, build consequential personal resources. *Journal of Personality and Social Psychology, 95*, 1045–1062.

Fredrickson, B. L., & Joiner, T. (2002). Positive emotions trigger upward spirals toward emotional well-being. *Psychological Science, 13*, 172–175.

Fredrickson, B. L., & Levenson, R. W. (1998). Positive emotions speed recovery from the cardiovascular sequelae of negative emotions. *Cognition and Emotion, 12*, 191–220.

Fredrickson, B. L., & Losada, M. F. (2005). Positive affect and the complex dynamics of human flourishing. *American Psychologist, 60*, 678–686.

Fredrickson, B. L., Mancuso, R. A., Branigan, C., & Tugade, M. (2000). The undoing effect of positive emotions. *Motivation and Emotion, 24*, 237–258.

Fredrickson, B. L., Tugade, M. M., Waugh, C. E., & Larkin, G. (2003). What good are positive emotions in crises? A prospective study of resilience and emotions following the terrorist attacks on the United States on September 11th, 2001. *Journal of Personality and Social Psychology, 84*, 365–376.

Frijda, N. H. (1986). *The emotions.* Cambridge: Cambridge University Press.

Frijda, N. H., Kuipers, P., & Schure, E. (1989). Relations among emotion, appraisal, and emotional action readiness. *Journal of Personality and Social Psychology, 57*, 212–228.

Gable, S. L., Reis, H. T., Impett, E. A., & Asher, E. R. (2004). What do you do when things go right? The intrapersonal and interpersonal benefits of sharing positive events. *Journal of Personality and Social Psychology, 87*, 228–245.

Gervais, M., & Wilson, D. S. (2005). The evolution and functions of laughter and humor: A synthetic approach. *Quarterly Review of Biology, 80*, 395–451.

Gil, K. M., Edens, J. L., Wilson, J. J., Raezer, L. B., Kinney, T. R., Schultz, W. H., et al. (1997). Coping strategies and laboratory pain in children with sickle cell disease. *Annals of Behavioral Medicine, 19*, 22–29.

Gonzaga, G. C., Turner, R. A., Keltner, D., Campos, B., & Altemus, M. (2006). Romantic love and sexual desire in close relationships. *Emotion, 6*, 163–179.

Gottman, J. M. (1994). *What predicts divorce? The relationship between marital processes and marital outcomes.* Hillsdale, NJ: Erlbaum.

Haidt, J. (2005). *The happiness hypothesis: Finding the modern truth in ancient wisdom.* New York: Basic Books.

Isen, A. M., & Daubman, K. A. (1984). The influence of affect on categorization. *Journal of Personality and Social Psychology, 47*, 1206–1217.

Isen, A. M., Daubman, K. A., & Nowicki, G. P. (1987). Positive affect facilitates creative problem solving. *Journal of Personality and Social Psychology, 52*, 1122–1131.

Isen, A. M., Johnson, M. M. S., Mertz, E., & Robinson, G. F. (1985). The influence of positive affect on the unusualness of word associations. *Journal of Personality and Social Psychology, 48*, 1413–1426.

Johnson, K. J. (2005). *We all look the same to me: Positive emotions eliminate the own-race bias in face recognition.* Unpublished doctoral dissertation, University of Michigan, Ann Arbor, MI.

Johnson, K. J., & Fredrickson, B. L. (2005). "We all look the same to me": Positive emotions eliminate the own-race bias in face recognition. *Psychological Science, 16*, 875–881.

Joiner, T. E., Pettit, J. W., Perez, M., & Burns, A. B. (2001). Can positive emotion influence problem-solving among suicidal adults? *Professional Psychology: Research and Practice, 32*, 507–512.

Kabat-Zinn, J. (2005). *Full catastrophe living: Using the wisdom of your body and mind to face stress, pain, and illness* (15th Anniversary ed.). New York: Bantam.

Kahn, B. E., & Isen, A. M. (1993). The influence of positive affect on variety seeking among safe, enjoyable products. *Journal of Consumer Research, 20*, 257–270.

Kahneman, D., Kreuger, A. B., & Schkade, D. A. (2004). A survey method for characterizing daily life experience: The day reconstruction method. *Science, 306*, 1776–1780.

Keller, M. C., & Nesse, R. M. (2005). Is low mood an adaptation? Evidence for subtypes with symptoms that match precipitants. *Journal of Affective Disorders, 86*, 27–35.

Keltner, D., & Bonanno, G. A. (1997). A study of laughter and dissociation: Distinct correlates of laughter and smiling during bereavement. *Journal of Personality and Social Psychology, 73*, 687–702.

Keyes, C. L. M., & Haidt, J. (Eds.). (2002). *Flourishing: Positive psychology and the life well lived.* Washington, DC: APA Press.

Kiecolt-Glaser, J. K., McGuire, L., Robles, T. F., & Glaser, R. (2002). Emotions, morbidity, and mortality. *Annual Review of Psychology, 53*, 83–107.

Larsen, R. J., & Sinnett, L. (1991). Meta-analysis of manipulation validity. *Personality and Social Psychology Bulletin, 17*, 323–334.

Lazarus, R. S. (1991). *Emotion and adaptation.* New York: Oxford University Press.

Lee, P. C. (1983). Play as a means for developing relationships. In R. A. Hinde (Ed.), *Primate Social Relationships* (pp. 82–89). Oxford: Blackwell.

Levenson, R. W. (1994). Human emotions: A functional view. In P. Ekman & R. J. Davidson (Eds.), *The nature of emotion: Fundamental questions* (pp. 123–126). New York: Oxford University Press.

Levy, B. R., Slade, M. D., & Kunkel, S. R. (2002). Longevity increased by positive self-perceptions of aging. *Journal of Personality and Social Psychology, 83*, 261–270.

Losada, M., & Heaphy, E. (2004). The role of positivity and connectivity in the performance of business teams: A non-linear dynamics model. *American Behavioral Scientist, 47*(6), 740–765.

Lyubomirsky, S. L., King, L., & Diener, E. (2005). The benefits of frequent positive affect: Does happiness lead to success? *Psychological Bulletin, 131*, 803–855.

McEwen, B. S., & Seeman, T. (1999). Protective and damaging effects of mediators of stress: Concepts of allostasis and allostatic load. *Annals of the New York Academy of Sciences, 896*, 30–47.

Martin, L. L., & Clore, G. (Eds.). (2001). *Theories of mood and cognition: A user's guidebook.* Mahwah, NJ: Lawrence Erlbaum.

Moskowitz, J. T. (2003). Positive affect predicts lower risk of AIDS mortality. *Psychosomatic Medicine, 65*, 620–626.

Moskowitz, J. T., Folkman, S., & Acree, M. (2003). Do positive psychological states shed light on recovery from bereavement? Findings from a 3-year longitudinal study. *Death Studies, 27*, 471–500.

Oatley, K., & Jenkins, J. M. (1996). *Understanding emotions.* Cambridge, MA: Blackwell.

Ong, A. D., & Allaire, J. C. (2005). Cardiovascular intraindividual variability in later life: The influence of social connectedness and positive emotions. *Psychology and Aging, 20*, 476–485.

Ostir, G. V., Markides, K. S., & Black, S. A. (2000). Emotional well-being predicts subsequent functional independence and survival. *Journal of the American Geriatrics Society, 48*, 473–478.

Otake, K., Waugh, C. E., & Fredrickson, B. L. *Positive emotions unlock other-focused thinking.* Manuscript in preparation.

Panksepp, J. (1998). Attention deficit hyperactivity disorders, psychostimulants, and intolerance of childhood playfulness: A tragedy in the making? *Current Directions in Psychological Science, 7,* 91–98.

Rowe, G., Hirsch, J., & Anderson, A. K. (2007). Positive affect increases the "breadth" of attentional selection. *Proceedings of the National Academy of Sciences, 104,* 383–388.

Russell, J. A., Weiss, A., & Mendelsohn, G. A. (1989). Affect grid: A single-item scale of pleasure and arousal. *Journal of Personality and Social Psychology, 57,* 493–502.

Ryff, C. D., & Singer, B. (1998). The contours of positive human health. *Psychological Inquiry, 9,* 1–28.

Sapolsky, R. M. (1999). The physiology and pathophysiology of unhappiness. In D. Kahneman, E. Diener, & N. Schwarz (Eds.), *Well-being: The foundations of hedonic psychology* (pp. 453–469). New York: Russell Sage Foundation.

Seligman, M. E. P., & Csikszentmihalyi, M. (2000). Positive psychology: An introduction. *American Psychologist, 55,* 5–14.

Seligman, M. E. P., Steen, T. A., & Park, N. (2005). Positive psychology progress: Empirical validation of interventions. *American Psychologist, 60,* 410–421.

Sheldon, K. M., & Lyubomirsky, S. (2006). How to increase and sustain positive emotion: The effects of expressing gratitude and visualizing best possible selves. *Journal of Positive Psychology, 1,* 73–82.

Sherrod, L. R., & Singer, J. L. (1989). The development of make-believe play. In J. Goldstein (Ed.), *Sports, games and play* (pp. 1–38). Hillsdale, NJ: Lawrence Erlbaum.

Shiota, M. N., Keltner, D. & John, O. P. (2006). Positive emotion dispositions differentially associated with Big Five personality and attachment style. *The Journal of Positive Psychology, 1,* 61–71.

Simons, C. J. R., McCluskey-Fawcett, K. A., & Papini, D. R. (1986). Theoretical and functional perspective on the development of humor during infancy, childhood, and adolescence. In L. Nahemow, K. A. McCluskey-Fawcett, & P. E. McGhee (Eds.), *Humor and aging* (pp. 53–77). San Diego, CA: Academic Press.

Smith, C. A., & Ellsworth, P. C. (1985). Patterns of cognitive appraisal in emotion. *Journal of Personality and Social Psychology, 48,* 813–838.

Stein, N. L., Folkman, S., Trabasso, T., & Richards, T. A. (1997). Appraisal and goal processes as predictors of psychological well-being in bereaved caregivers. *Journal of Personality and Social Psychology, 72,* 872–884.

Tiedens, L. Z., & Linton, S. (2001). Judgment under emotional certainty and uncertainty: The effects of specific emotions on information processing. *Journal of Personality and Social Psychology, 81,* 973–988.

Tong, E. M. W. (2006). *The cognitive phenomenology of positive emotions.* Unpublished doctoral dissertation, University of Michigan.

Tooby, J., & Cosmides, L. (1990). The past explains the present: Emotional adaptations and the structure of ancestral environments. *Ethology and Sociobiology, 11,* 375–424.

Trope, Y., & Pomerantz, E. (1998) Resolving conflicts among self-evaluative motives: Positive experiences as a resource for overcoming defensiveness. *Motivation and Emotion, 22*(1), 53–72.

Tsai, J. L., Knutson, B., & Fung, H. H. (2006). Cultural variation in affect valuation. *Journal of Personality and Social Psychology, 90,* 288–307.

Tugade, M., & Fredrickson, B. L. (2004). Resilient individuals use positive emotions to bounce back from negative emotional experiences. *Journal of Personality and Social Psychology, 86,* 320–333.

Tugade, M. M., Fredrickson, B. L., & Barrett, L. F. (2004). Psychological resilience and positive emotional granularity: Examining the benefits of positive emotions on coping and health. *Journal of Personality, 72,* 1161–1190.

Wadlinger, H. A., & Isaacowitz, D. M. (2006). Positive affect broadens visual attention to positive stimuli. *Motivation and Emotion, 30,* 89–101.

Watson, D., Wiese, D., Vaidya, J., & Tellegen, A. (1999). The two general activation systems of affect: Structural findings, evolutionary considerations, and psychobiological evidence. *Journal of Personality and Social Psychology, 76,* 820–838.

Waugh, C. E., & Fredrickson, B. L. (2006). Nice to know you: Positive emotions, self–other overlap, and complex understanding in the formation of a new relationship. *Journal of Positive Psychology, 1,* 93–106.

Waugh, C. E., Hejmadi, A., Otake, K., & Fredrickson, B. L. (2006). *Positive emotions and self–other overlap in American and Indian students.*Unpublished raw data.

Winkelman, P., & Berridge, K. C. (2004). Unconscious emotions. *Current Directions in Psychological Science, 13,* 120–123.

CHAPTER
4

Classifying and Measuring Strengths of Character

Christopher Peterson *and* Nansook Park

Abstract

What is the good of a person? Answers to this question lie at the heart of traditional moral philosophy as well as contemporary positive psychology. For the past few years, we have been involved in a project describing important strengths of character and ways to measure them. Our research program is sometimes identified as the Values in Action (VIA) project. The VIA classification includes two dozen strengths of character on which our research has focused. Various VIA measures comprise a family of assessment devices that measure individual differences in the strengths in the classification. The present contribution describes the process by which the VIA classification was created, the ways character strengths are measured, and empirical findings: distribution and demographics; correlates and consequences; origins and development; deliberate cultivation; interventions; and structure and trade-offs. Work is ongoing to refine our measures and to use empirical findings to generate theory. Especially important lines of future research include the relationship of character strengths to hard outcome measures, cultural differences and similarities, development, interventions, and the processes by which strengths of character give rise to actual behavior. Our project supports the premise of positive psychology that attention to good character sheds light on what makes life worth living.

Keywords: assessment, character, life satisfaction, virtue, VIA classification

What is the good of a person? Answers to this question lie at the heart of traditional moral philosophy as well as contemporary positive psychology (Peterson, 2006). In their introduction to positive psychology, Seligman and Csikszentmihalyi (2000) described the study of positive traits as a central pillar of this new field, and Park and Peterson (2003) proposed that positive traits link together the other pillars of positive psychology: positive experiences and positive institutions. Positive traits enable positive experiences, which have important consequences in the contexts of the family, the workplace, and the community.

Centuries ago, the Athenian philosophers—Socrates, Plato, and especially Aristotle—framed morality in terms of good character and in particular virtues, traits of character that make someone good (Rachels, 1999). Asian philosophers like Confucius also enumerated virtues that made a person morally

praiseworthy and more importantly contributed to the good society (Smart, 1999).

In the Western world, this framing of morality in terms of virtues changed with the growing influence of Christianity, which saw God as the giver of laws by which one should live. Righteous conduct no longer stemmed from inner virtues but rather from obedience to the commandments of God. Whereas the early Greeks regarded reason as chief among the virtues, Christian thinkers like St. Augustine distrusted reason. One must subordinate oneself to God, whether it seemed "reasonable" to do so or not (consider the dilemma of Job).

The guiding question of moral philosophy therefore changed from inquiries about the characteristics of a good person to "What are the right things to do?" As Christianity waned in importance, what has been called Divine Law gave way to a secular equivalent dubbed Moral Law. Human reason was reintroduced to the philosophy of morality, but the focus remained on specifying the rules of right conduct.

In more recent decades, philosophy returned to the ethics of virtue, starting with Anscombe's (1958) influential criticism that moral philosophy was incomplete because it rested on the notion of a law without a lawgiver. Virtue ethics is the contemporary approach within philosophy to strengths of character, and as psychologists, we find virtues a more agreeable topic than laws. Virtues pertain to people and the lives that they actually lead (Yearley, 1990). Said another way, scientific psychology is not in a position to prescribe the moral life but is well equipped to describe the what, how, and why of good character.

For the past few years, we have been involved in a project describing important strengths of character and ways to measure them. Our research program is sometimes identified as the Values in Action (VIA) project, after the nonprofit organization—the VIA Institute—that sponsored the initial work (see http://www.viastrengths.org). The VIA classification includes two dozen strengths of character on which our research has focused (Peterson & Seligman, 2004). Various VIA measures comprise a family of assessment devices that measure individual differences in the strengths in the classification. The most general use of the term VIA is to describe a vocabulary for psychologically informed discourse on the qualities of a person worthy of moral praise.

History of the VIA Project

Positive psychology's foray into character began in 1999 when a core group of scholars[1] assembled to create a tentative list of human strengths. Christopher Peterson and Martin Seligman continued this work, elaborating the initial list, presenting it at various conferences, and refining it after discussions with conference participants. Between conferences, Peterson and Seligman devised a framework for defining and conceptualizing strengths. Also critical were surveys of literatures that addressed good character, from psychiatry, youth development, philosophy, and of course psychology (e.g., Peterson, 2003).

Helpful as well were what can be called virtue catalogs—list of character strengths from historical luminaries like Charlemagne and Benjamin

Franklin, contemporary figures like William Bennett and John Templeton, and imaginary sources like the Klingon Empire. Also consulted were virtue-relevant messages in Hallmark greeting cards, bumper stickers, *Saturday Evening Post* covers by Norman Rockwell, personal ads, popular song lyrics, graffiti, tarot cards, the profiles of Pokémon characters, and the residence halls of Hogwarts.

Another component of the project was the development of ways to assess character strengths. Peterson began to devise character measures for adults, and Nansook Park took the lead in devising measures for children and youth and for directing cross-cultural investigations. For this part of the project, we reviewed popular children's books to understand developmentally appropriate expressions of various character strengths. A monograph describing the classification was published in 2004 (Peterson & Seligman, 2004), and the present contribution provides a summary and update.

When our work began, the initial question was how to approach good character. Is character but one thing, either present or absent? Is character culturally bound or socially constructed, making generalization futile? Can character, however it is defined, be explained by a single theory drawn from psychology, education, philosophy, or theology?

Here is how we answered these basic questions. We approached good character as a family of characteristics, each of which existed in degrees, and we decided not to wed our approach to a given theory. An impetus for the project was the need to know more about good character, and no consensual theory had emerged within psychology or elsewhere. We took to calling our project an aspirational classification, meaning that it attempted to specify mutually exclusive and exhaustive categories of moral traits without claiming finality or a deep theory (Bailey, 1994).

We relied on virtue ethics to help us think through the meaning of good character. Here is a representative definition of a virtue (Yearley, 1990, p. 13):

> a disposition to act, desire, and feel that involves the exercise of judgment and leads to a recognizable human excellence or instance of human flourishing. Moreover, virtuous activity involves choosing virtue for itself and in light of some justifiable life plan.

This definition of a virtue sounds very much the meaning of a trait as used in personality psychology today. We like the definition by Baumrind (1998) that character is personality evaluated. Character strengths are the subset of personality traits on

---

[1] This group included Donald Clifton, Mihaly Csikszentmihalyi, Ed Diener, Kathleen Hall Jamieson, Robert Nozick, Daniel Robinson, Martin Seligman, and George Vaillant.

which we place moral value. Introversion and extraversion, for example, are traits with no moral weight. Kindness and teamwork in contrast are morally valued, which is why they are considered character strengths.

The VIA Classification

Candidate strengths accumulated, and ways to reduce and systematize the list were needed. Useful in this regard was a literature review by Katherine Dahlsgaard, who read the texts of the world's influential religious and philosophical traditions (e.g., the books of *Exodus* and *Proverbs* in the case of Judaism, the *Analects* in the case of Confucianism, and so on), exhaustively listed the virtues discussed in each, and then identified a core set of virtues acknowledged as important in all (Dahlsgaard, Peterson, & Seligman, 2005):

- wisdom and knowledge—cognitive strengths entailing the acquisition and use of knowledge
- courage—emotional strengths involving the exercise of will to accomplish goals in the face of opposition, external or internal
- humanity—interpersonal strengths that involve "tending and befriending" others
- justice—civic strengths underlying healthy community life
- temperance—strengths protecting against excess
- transcendence—strengths that forge connections to the larger universe and provide meaning

This list is limited to literate traditions, but it is notable that fieldwork by Biswas-Diener (2006) verified that these sorts of virtues were also acknowledged and cultivated among the nonliterate Maasai and Inughuit. So, Dahlsgaard's core virtues provided an overall scheme for classifying more specific character strengths.

The second step in simplifying the list was specifying criteria for saying that a candidate strength belonged in the classification:

- ubiquity—is widely recognized and celebrated across cultures
- fulfilling—contributes to individual fulfillment, satisfaction, and happiness broadly construed
- morally valued—is valued in its own right and not as a means to an end
- does not diminish others—elevates others who witness it, producing admiration, not jealousy
- nonfelicitous opposite—has obvious antonyms that are "negative"

- traitlike—is an individual difference with demonstrable generality and stability
- measurable—has been successfully measured by researchers as an individual difference
- distinctiveness—is not redundant (conceptually or empirically) with other character strengths
- paragons—is strikingly embodied in some individuals
- prodigies—is precociously shown by some children or youth
- selective absence—is missing altogether in some individuals
- institutions—is the deliberate target of societal practices and rituals that try to cultivate it

These criteria were abstracted from the best examples of character strengths that had been gathered and then used to winnow the list. Not all of the VIA character strengths meet all 12 criteria, but in each case the majority of the criteria are satisfied (Park & Peterson, 2006b). The VIA classification includes 24 positive traits organized in terms of the six core virtues (Table 4.1).

Caveats are in order. First, the hierarchical organization—strengths under virtues—is a conceptual scheme and not a hypothesis to be tested with data. Indeed, our empirical investigations of the structuring of character strengths yield a coherent picture but not exactly the one implied in Table 4.1.

Second, there exist culture-bound strengths—positive traits valued in some places but not others—such as ambition, achievement, and autonomy in the contemporary United States. Their absence from the VIA classification means that they failed the ubiquity criterion. Depending on the interests and purposes of a researcher or practitioner, attention to these culture-bound strengths may be important.

Third, we now believe that some of the 24 strengths are cut from a different moral cloth than the others. Strengths like humor and zest are not morally valued in their own right but become morally valued when coupled with other strengths in the classification. So, a humorous person is simply funny, but a humorous person who is kind is very special and morally praiseworthy. We call these value-added strengths and intend to study them further.

Fourth, we expect change in the classification. Some existing strengths may be dropped, and others may be combined. Still other strengths may be added, and among those suggested to us are compassion, patience, and tranquility. Our criteria provide the guidelines for changing the VIA classification.

Table 4.1 VIA classification of strengths

1. Wisdom and Knowledge

- creativity: thinking of novel and productive ways to do things
- curiosity: taking an interest in all of the ongoing experience
- open-mindedness: thinking things through and examining them from all sides
- love of learning: mastering new skills, topics, and bodies of knowledge
- perspective: being able to provide wise counsel to others

2. Courage

- authenticity: speaking the truth and presenting oneself in a genuine way
- bravery: *not* shrinking from threat, challenge, difficulty, or pain
- perseverance: finishing what one starts
- zest: approaching life with excitement and energy

3. Humanity

- kindness: doing favors and good deeds for others
- love: valuing close relations with others
- social intelligence: being aware of the motives and feelings of self and others

4. Justice

- fairness: treating all people the same according to notions of fairness and justice
- leadership: organizing group activities and seeing that they happen
- teamwork: working well as member of a group or team

5. Temperance

- forgiveness: forgiving those who have done wrong
- modesty: letting one's accomplishments speak for themselves
- prudence: being careful about one's choices; *not* saying or doing things that might later be regretted
- self-regulation: regulating what one feels and does

6. Transcendence

- appreciation of beauty and excellence: noticing and appreciating beauty, excellence, and/or skilled performance in all domains of life
- gratitude: being aware of and thankful for the good things that happen
- hope: expecting the best and working to achieve it
- humor: liking to laugh and joke; bringing smiles to other people
- religiousness: having coherent beliefs about the higher purpose and meaning of life

As mentioned, the VIA classification was presented in a monograph describing what was known and what was not known about each of the included strengths: paradigm cases, consensual definition, historical background, measurement, correlations and consequences of having or lacking the strength, development, enabling and disabling conditions, gender and cultural differences, and interventions thought to build the strength (Peterson & Seligman, 2004). The monograph was intended as a framework for conducting future research and creating new interventions.

Measures

We have been busy during the past few years with measuring the 24 VIA strengths (Park & Peterson, 2006b; Peterson, Park, & Seligman, 2005). To date, we have devised and evaluated (a) focus groups to flesh out the everyday meanings of character strengths among different groups; (b) self-report questionnaires suitable for adults and young people; (c) structured interviews to identify what we call signature strengths; (d) informant reports of how target individuals rise to the occasion (or not) with appropriate strengths of character (e.g., hope when encountering setbacks); (e) a content analysis procedure for assessing character strengths from unstructured descriptions of self and others; (f) strategies for scoring positive traits from archived material like obituaries; and (g) case studies of nominated paragons of specific strengths. We also note our ongoing attempts to devise interventions to change character strengths. To the degree that our interventions successfully target specific character strengths as we measure them, we have additional evidence that they are discrete individual differences.

Space does not permit a detailed description of what we have learned about the reliability and validity of these different methods. Suffice it to say that we have successfully established the internal consistency of our questionnaire measures and their test–retest stability over several months. We have investigated their validity with the known-groups procedure and more generally by mapping out their correlates (Park & Peterson, 2006c). Although we anticipate that these different methods will converge in the strengths they identify for given individuals, we note that each assessment strategy should also provide unique information about good character. Available data suggest convergence but not redundancy.

To develop and validate measures for adults, we did not rely on college student samples. Although young adults have strengths of character, we were persuaded by previous thinkers from Aristotle (2000) to Erik Erikson (1963) that good character is most apt to be found among those who are mature, who have done more than rehearse work and love.

In addition to traditional methods of collecting data, we also used the Internet to reach a wide range of adults. We placed our tentative questionnaires online (see http://www.authentichappiness.org). Critical to the appeal of this method, we believe, is that upon completion of the measures, respondents are given instant feedback about their top five strengths. In addition to expediting our research, this strategy has taught us something about character: Being able to put a name to what one does well is intriguing to people and even empowering. So far, more than 500,000 people from all 50 U.S. states and some 200 different nations have completed our questionnaires.

These Internet respondents may not be a representative sample of the United States or world population, but we stress the diversity of our respondents across virtually all demographic contrasts (other than computer literacy). Recently, researchers have shown that Internet studies typically enroll more diverse samples than conventional studies using psychology subject pool samples at colleges or universities and that they are as valid as traditional research methods (Gosling, Vazire, Srivastava, & John, 2004).

Our measures of the VIA strengths allow a systematic study of character in multidimensional terms. Past research on good character has focused on one component of character at a time, leaving unanswered questions about the underlying structure of character within an individual. Some individuals may be creative and authentic but are neither brave nor kind, or vice versa (Park, 2004). Furthermore, measuring a full range of positive traits may reduce concerns about socially desirable responding by allowing most research participants to say something good about themselves. Although we are open to the possibility that some people may altogether lack the strengths in our classification, the data show that virtually everyone has some notable strengths of character. We have taken to calling these signature strengths, and they are akin to what Allport (1961) once identified as personal traits. Signature strengths are positive traits that a person owns, celebrates, and frequently exercises. In interviews with adults, we find that everyone can readily identify a handful of strengths as very much their own, typically between three and seven (as Allport proposed). Our hypothesis is that the exercise of signature strengths is particularly fulfilling.

Empirical Findings

Measures make empirical research possible, and here is some of what we have learned to date.

Distribution and Demographics

Our Internet procedure makes it possible to compare people around the world. For example, we compared scores from 111,676 adult respondents from 54 nations and all 50 U.S. states and found striking convergence in the relative prevalence of the 24 different VIA strengths (Park, Peterson, & Seligman, 2006). In almost all nations, from Azerbaijan to Zimbabwe, the most commonly endorsed strengths were kindness, fairness, authenticity, gratitude, and open-mindedness, and the lesser strengths included prudence, modesty, and self-regulation. Except for religiousness, comparisons within the U.S. sample showed no differences as a function of state or geographical region. We speculate that our results revealed something about universal human nature and/or the character requirements minimally needed for a viable society.

We also looked at demographic correlates of the VIA strengths within the U.S. sample. There are some modest and sensible differences. Females score higher than males for the interpersonal strengths of gratitude, kindness, and love. Older adults score higher than younger adults on strengths of temperance. Respondents with more education love learning more than those with less education. Those who are married are more forgiving than those who were unmarried. African Americans and Asian Americans are more religious than European Americans.

In contrast to adults, the most common strengths among youth were gratitude, humor, and love, and the lesser strengths included prudence, forgiveness, religiousness, and self-regulation (Park & Peterson, 2006c). Hope, teamwork, and zest were relatively more common among youth than adults, whereas appreciation of beauty, authenticity, leadership, and open-mindedness were relatively more common among adults than youth.

What about the strengths of very young children? We coded open-ended parental descriptions of young children and found a sensible pattern (Park & Peterson, 2006a). The modal child, as seen by his or her parents, is one who is loving, kind, creative, humorous, and curious. These results also confirm theoretical speculation that some strengths of character—authenticity, gratitude, modesty, forgiveness, and open-mindedness—are not common among young children.

Correlates and Consequences

Evidence concerning the correlates of the VIA strengths is accumulating. So, among adults, several strengths in particular show a robust relation with life satisfaction, happiness, and psychological well-being measured in different ways: love, gratitude, hope, curiosity, and zest (Park, Peterson, & Seligman, 2004). Among youth, the robust predictors of life satisfaction are love, gratitude, hope, and zest (Park & Peterson, 2006c). And among very young children, those described by their parents as showing love, zest, and hope are also described as happy (Park & Peterson, 2006a).

In addition to life satisfaction, the following outcomes are related to character strengths in the VIA classification:

- Academic achievement among school children is predicted by temperance strengths and by perseverance.
- Military performance among West Point cadets is predicted by the strength of love.

- Teaching effectiveness is predicted by teacher zest, humor, and social intelligence.
- The tendency to regard one's work as a calling (as opposed to a way to pay the bills) is predicted by zest.

In our current studies, we are using longitudinal designs and focusing on "hard" outcome measures like workplace productivity and health (Peterson & Park, 2006).

Origins and Development

We know less about the origins of character strengths than their consequences, but our preliminary studies find modest convergence between the character strengths of parents and those of their children (Park & Peterson, 2006c). Helping to make sense of these patterns is a twin study showing that many of the VIA strengths have moderate levels of heritability, as do other personality traits (Steger, Hicks, Kashdan, Krueger, & Bouchard, 2007). More interesting was the finding that several of the traits (e.g., love of learning, open-mindedness) showed some influence of shared family environment and that still others (e.g., humor, teamwork) showed some influence of nonshared family environment. Further research of a fine-grained nature is of course needed to map out the processes by which character strengths are forged.

In several retrospective studies, we have looked at the apparent effects of profound life events on character strengths, again finding sensible patterns. Physical illness and psychological disorder have a short-term and across-the-board negative effect on the level of character strengths, although for some people, certain character strengths actually are higher following such events (Peterson, Park, & Seligman, 2006). So, serious physical illness (from which one has recovered) is linked to increases in bravery, kindness, and humor, and severe psychological disorder (that has resolved) is linked to increases in appreciation of beauty and love of learning. Increases in these strengths were related to higher life satisfaction.

These findings do not mean that people need trauma, illness, or disorder to increase their character strengths. In fact, our data showed that in general, people with these unfortunate life histories reported lower life satisfaction than people who did not. However, these results suggest that in the wake of negative life events, certain character strengths may work as a buffer and help to maintain or even increase well-being despite challenges.

Along these lines, trauma is also associated with increased levels of certain character strengths. In a study of American adults responding to our online measure before and after the events of 9/11, we found that the strengths of religiousness, hope, and love were elevated for 6 months, a temporal pattern not shown among European respondents (Peterson & Seligman, 2003). These strengths, the so-called theological virtues of St. Paul, are core Western virtues and may reflect the operation of processes specified in terror management theory, which proposes that the possibility of death leads people to reaffirm central cultural beliefs and values (Pyszczynski, Solomon, & Greenberg, 2002).

Our results have a larger significance for positive psychology. When the field was first articulated by Seligman and Csikszentmihalyi (2000), it was carefully distanced from business-as-usual psychology and its concern with problems. But as critics of positive psychology have observed, it is not always possible to segregate the positive in life from the negative (Lazarus, 2003), and our data suggest that crisis may be the crucible of good character. In any event, these sorts of findings would not have been discovered without the premise of positive psychology that attention to strength is worthwhile even following challenge.

Deliberate Cultivation

Some researchers have looked as well at how character strengths included in the VIA classification can be cultivated. This work is in its infancy, and to date, only a handful of strengths have been seriously considered, like hope (optimism), gratitude, kindness, social intelligence, leadership, creativity, and fairness (Park & Peterson, 2008). The problem with these endeavors, as seen from the vantage of the VIA project, is that they focus on one strength of character at a time. Unanswered is whether other strengths, not on focus and not measured, are changed as well.

In the meantime, we offer the following observations about the cultivation of good character among the young. We follow Aristotle (2000) in believing that good character is shown only in habitual action. Psychologists know a great deal about habits and the steps that establish them. First is to establish the baseline of the habit in question. The VIA measures we have created are a good place to start, but these are typically summaries based on global self-report.

We suggest that individuals also be encouraged to keep track of strength opportunities and how they rose to the occasion. If the target strength is bravery, the strength opportunity is any situation in which fear is experienced yet some action still needs to be taken despite the fear: for example, standing up for an unpopular opinion. Did one do what is needed or not?

Goals are not enough. One also needs to have plans for reaching these goals. Our literature reviews suggest that these plans are optimal when they combine didactic instruction with hands-on experience and extensive practice. Think about it, talk about it, and do it—over and over again. Goals should be difficult and specific but at the same time allow successes along the way in order to sustain motivation (Locke, Shaw, Saari, & Latham, 1981).

Structure and Trade-offs

Our classification of character strengths under core virtues is a conceptual scheme and not an empirical claim. The question remains of how the VIA strengths related to one another. One answer comes from an exploratory factor analysis of data from an adult sample, in which we first standardized subscale scores within individual respondents, thereby removing response sets like extremity (Peterson, 2006). Oblique factor analysis (which allows factors to be correlated) revealed a clear two-factor solution, shown in Figure 1 along with our interpretation of the two factors: heart versus mind and self versus other. This is a circumplex model, meaning that strengths close together comfortably co-occur, whereas those more distant are less compatible.

Can someone have all of the character strengths, or are trade-offs among them inevitable as people conduct their everyday lives? Figure 1 implies that trade-offs do occur and that people make them in characteristic ways. All things being equal, some of us will tend to be kind, whereas others of us will tend to be honest. The structure of these trade-offs might reveal something about how the real world allows good character to present itself.

Note in Figure 4.1 how the character strengths associated with happiness and life satisfaction tend to reside north of the equator (in the heart quadrants), whereas those associated with achievement are located south (in the head quadrants). Perhaps the very small associations found between life satisfaction and education, income, and status—despite all the apparent benefits that these bring—reflect the operation of these trade-offs. Our additional analyses suggest that respondents with a high school degree tend to score higher than those with college degrees on many of the "focus on others" strengths, and those with a college degree tend to score higher than those with a high

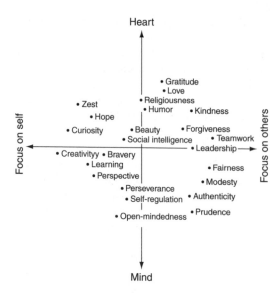

Fig. 4.1 The structure of character.

school degree of many of the "focus on self" strengths (cf. Snibbe & Markus, 2005).

We have also looked at the issue of balance among character strengths by calculating the standard deviation of scores within individuals. People whose character strengths had lower standard deviations—that is, whose scores are less discrepant with one another and arguably more balanced—reported higher life satisfaction, especially if they were older adults. Perhaps, the integration of one's strengths with maturity reflects wisdom (Erikson, 1963).

The Future

We will continue to refine our measures and to use empirical findings to generate theory. As noted, our attention is turning to hard outcome measures, to cultural differences and similarities, to development, to interventions, and to the processes by which strengths of character give rise to actual behavior. Our project supports the premise of positive psychology that attention to good character sheds light on what makes life worth living. As Aristotle (2000) proposed long ago, happiness is the purpose of life, and living in accordance with one's virtues is how to achieve happiness.

Questions

1. Do strengths of character encourage physical health, achievement, and social engagement; if so, how?

2. How can strengths of character be taught?

3. Are there cultural differences and similarities in strengths of character?

References and Recommended Readings*

Allport, G. W. (1961). *Pattern and growth in personality.* New York: Holt, Rinehart, & Winston.

Anscombe, G. E. M. (1958). Modern moral philosophy. *Philosophy, 33,* 1–19.

Aristotle (2000). *The Nicomachean ethics* (R. Crisp, Trans.). Cambridge: Cambridge University Press.

Bailey, K. D. (1994). *Typologies and taxonomies: An introduction to classification techniques.* Thousand Oaks, CA: Sage.

Baumrind, D. (1998). Reflections on character and competence. In A. Colby, J. James, & D. Hart (Eds.), *Competence and character through life* (pp. 1–28). Chicago: The University of Chicago Press.

Biswas-Diener, R. (2006). From the equator to the north pole: A study of character strengths. *Journal of Happiness Studies, 7,* 293–310.

Dahlsgaard, K., Peterson, C., & Seligman, M. E. P. (2005). Shared virtue: The convergence of valued human strengths across culture and history. *Review of General Psychology, 9,* 209–213.

Erikson, E. (1963). *Childhood and society* (2nd ed.). New York: Norton.

Gosling, S. D., Vazire, S., Srivastava, S., & John, O. P. (2004). Should we trust Web-based studies? A comparative analysis of six preconceptions about Internet questionnaires. *American Psychologist, 59,* 93–104.

Lazarus, R. S. (2003). Does the positive psychology movement have legs? *Psychological Inquiry, 14,* 93–109.

Locke, E. A., Shaw, K. N., Saari, L. M., & Latham, G. (1981). Goal setting and task performance: 1969–1980. *Psychological Bulletin, 90,* 124–152.

Park, N. (2004). Character strengths and positive youth development. *Annals of the American Academy of Political and Social Science, 591,* 40–54.

Park, N., & Peterson, C. (2003). Virtues and organizations. In K. S. Cameron, J. E. Dutton, & R. E. Quinn (Eds.), *Positive organizational scholarship: Foundations of a new discipline* (pp. 33–47). San Francisco: Berrett-Koehler.

Park, N., & Peterson, C. (2006a). Character strengths and happiness among young children: Content analysis of parental descriptions. *Journal of Happiness Studies, 7,* 323–341.

*Park, N., & Peterson, C. (2006b). Methodological issues in positive psychology and the assessment of character strengths. In A. D. Ong & M. van Dulmen (Eds.), *Handbook of methods in positive psychology* (pp. 292–305). New York: Oxford University Press.

Park, N., & Peterson, C. (2006c). Moral competence and character strengths among adolescents: The development and validation of the values in action inventory of strengths for youth. *Journal of Adolescence, 29,* 891–905.

Park, N., & Peterson, C. (2008). The cultivation of character strengths. In M. Ferrari & G. Potworowski (Eds.), *Teaching for wisdom* (pp. 57–75). Mahwah, NJ: Erlbaum.

Park, N., Peterson, C., & Seligman, M. E. P. (2004). Strengths of character and well-being. *Journal of Social and Clinical Psychology, 23,* 603–619.

Park, N., Peterson, C., & Seligman, M. E. P. (2006). Character strengths in fifty-four nations and the fifty U.S. states. *Journal of Positive Psychology, 1,* 118–129.

Peterson, C. (2003). Classification of positive traits in youth. In R. M. Lerner, F. Jacobs, & D. Wertlieb (Eds.), *Promoting positive child, adolescent, and family development: A handbook of program and policy innovations* (Vol. 4, pp. 227–255). Thousand Oaks, CA: Sage.

Peterson, C. (2006). *A primer in positive psychology.* New York: Oxford University Press.

Peterson, C., & Park, N. (2006). Character strengths in organizations. *Journal of Organizational Behavior, 27,* 1–6.

Peterson, C., Park, N., & Seligman, M. E. P. (2005). Assessment of character strengths. In G. P. Koocher, J. C. Norcross, & S. S. Hill, III (Eds.), *Psychologists' desk reference* (2nd ed., pp. 93–98). New York: Oxford University Press.

Peterson, C., Park, N., & Seligman, M. E. P. (2006). Greater strengths of character and recovery from illness. *Journal of Positive Psychology, 1,* 17–26.

Peterson, C., & Seligman, M. E. P. (2003). Character strengths before and after September 11. *Psychological Science, 14,* 381–384.

*Peterson, C., & Seligman, M. E. P. (2004). *Character strengths and virtues: A handbook and classification.* New York: Oxford University Press/Washington, DC: American Psychological Association.

Pyszczynski, T., Solomon, S., & Greenberg, J. (2002). *In the wake of 9/11: The psychology of terror.* Washington, DC: American Psychological Association.

Rachels, J. (1999). *The elements of moral philosophy* (3rd ed.). New York: McGraw-Hill.

Seligman, M. E. P., & Csikszentmihalyi, M. (2000). Positive psychology: An introduction. *American Psychologist, 55,* 5–14.

Smart, N. (1999). *World philosophies.* New York: Routledge.

Snibbe, A. C., & Markus, H. R. (2005). You can't always get what you want: Educational attainment, agency, and choice. *Journal of Personality and Social Psychology, 88,* 703–720.

Steger, M. F., Hicks, B., Kashdan, T. B., Krueger, R. F., & Bouchard, T. J., Jr. (2007). Genetic and environmental influences on the positive traits of the values in action classification, and biometric covariance with normal personality. *Journal of Research in Personality, 41,* 524–539.

Yearley, L. H. (1990). *Mencius and Aquinas: Theories of virtue and conceptions of courage.* Albany, NY: State University of New York Press.

Positive Psychology Applications

P. Alex Linley, Stephen Joseph, John Maltby, Susan Harrington, *and* Alex M. Wood

Abstract

Applied positive psychology is concerned with facilitating good lives and enabling people to be at their best. It is as much an approach as a particular domain of inquiry. As shown throughout this chapter, positive psychology has applications that span almost every area of applied psychology and beyond. In clinical psychology, counseling and psychotherapy, applied positive psychology builds on the traditions of humanistic psychology and Carl Rogers' client-centered therapy. It challenges the dominant assumptions of the medical model and promotes a dimensional, rather than dichotomous, understanding of mental health and mental illness. Beyond the alleviation of psychopathology, applied positive psychology has also seen the development of specific happiness-increase interventions, including counting one's blessings, using signature strengths, and paying a gratitude visit. In education, applied positive psychology has been used to promote flow in the classroom, as well as harnessing children's strengths to aid their learning and development. Forensic applications of positive psychology are represented by the good lives model of offender management, which focuses on the adaptive satisfaction of human needs. In Industrial Organizational (I/O) psychology, positive psychology applications are represented throughout work on transformational leadership, employee engagement, positive organizational scholarship, positive organizational behavior, appreciative inquiry, and strengths-based organization. In society, more broadly, applied positive psychology is shown to influence the development of life coaching and the practice of executive coaching, while population approaches are being explored in relation to epidemiology and the promotion of social well-being. Having reviewed these diverse areas, the chapter then goes on to consider the theoretical basis for applied positive psychology; the questions of *who* should apply positive psychology, as well as *where* and *how*; and whether positive psychology applications could be universally relevant. The chapter concludes by considering what the future of applied positive psychology may hold and suggesting that the discipline has the potential to impact positively on people throughout the world.

Keywords: applications, future, positive psychology, theory

The practice of positive psychology is about facilitating good lives, or about enabling people to be at their best. The breadth of the definition is indicative of just how broadly we see the field of positive psychology applications. Positive psychology is not a "thing" as such, but much more an approach, a way of doing things, and it is this that inspires its applied breadth (see Linley, Joseph, Harrington, & Wood, 2006). Previously, we have defined applied positive psychology as "the application of positive psychology research to the facilitation of optimal human functioning," and we went on to note that this work would be carried on "at the level of the individual, the group, the organization, the community, or the society . . . across the full range of human functioning, from disorder and distress to health and fulfilment" (Linley & Joseph, 2004a, p. 4). As the work reviewed in this chapter shows, these broad applications of positive psychology are now beginning to happen.

Given the breadth of positive psychology applications, but constrained by the space limitations of this chapter, our coverage of each area is of necessity brief. However, in the sections that follow we set out to provide an overview of some of the work that has been done so far in applying positive psychological approaches to the major domains of psychological practice. These include clinical, health, educational, occupational, and forensic psychology, and also counseling and psychotherapy. In addition, we review two areas that positive psychology applications are influencing greatly: happiness interventions and life coaching. Finally, we conclude by identifying some of the key questions and opportunities for the applications of positive psychology, in relation to fundamental assumptions, theory development, areas of application, and universality of findings and applications.

Before we begin though, it may be helpful to consider just what the outcome variables of relevance to positive psychology applications may be. There has perhaps been too much emphasis to date on happiness as the outcome variable of interest to positive psychology. While happiness is indeed important—and also much neglected in traditional psychology research and practice—it is also important to recognize that it is not the *only* outcome variable, or even, necessarily, the most important one. When we define positive psychology applications as being about facilitating good lives, or about enabling people to be at their best, we are referring to a vast constellation of positive states, traits, experiences, groups, communities, organizations, societies, and environments that people may deem desirable. In the sections that follow, we will consider the major domains of positive psychology applications.

Clinical, Counseling and Health Psychology, Counseling and Psychotherapy

The emergence of positive psychology has served to highlight that there are a number of approaches within humanistic and existential psychology that already offer a wealth of ideas and approaches, that are concerned with movement toward more optimal functioning and well-being. Further, positive psychology also has served to generate new techniques that promise to be useful in a range of clinical, therapeutic, and health-care settings.

Person-Centered Approach and Positive Therapy

The most obvious example of how humanistic psychology can inform positive psychology applications is that of client-centered therapy (CCT), an approach originally developed by Carl Rogers

(1951) in the 1950s. We have written in detail elsewhere about how CCT offers a positive psychological way of working (see Joseph & Linley, 2004, 2005, 2006a). In brief, CCT is a positive psychological approach because it is based on the person-centered meta-theoretical position that people are intrinsically motivated toward optimal functioning.

CCT proposes that it is the client who is his or her own best expert and that it is in the relationship between therapist and client that movement toward optimal functioning is able to develop, an idea that resonates closely with other recent developments in psychotherapy research (e.g., Hubble & Miller, 2004; Wampold, 2001), and the extensive evidence base on the role of the relationship in therapeutic outcomes (see Bozarth & Motomasa, 2005; Martin, Garske, & Davis, 2000). Understanding the importance of relationship factors promises to provide the foundation stone for much applied work in clinical and health psychology, not only in the therapeutic relationship itself but also in the development of intervention work focused on the facilitation of extra therapeutic social support from family, friends, and the community (see Taylor & Sherman, 2004).

The main implication of positive psychology for clinical and health psychology is its influence on how clinical and health psychologists may begin to think differently about the fundamental assumptions underpinning their work, and to move toward the adoption of other conceptions than the illness ideology and the medical model, which are currently the dominant paradigms in the field.

Positive Psychology versus the Medical Model

Positive psychology promotes nonmedical model–based ways of understanding human experience (see Joseph & Linley, 2006b). It is through these new ways of thinking that positive psychology has the potential to be of most interest to clinical, counseling, and health psychologists, and counselors and psychotherapists. Indeed, we are careful to note that much of what is now considered under the rubric of positive psychology has historical roots in counseling psychology (Lopez et al., 2006) and humanistic psychology (Taylor, 2001), among others (Linley & Joseph, 2004a), and we should be mindful of the lessons that can be learned from these approaches.

In their critical analysis of the philosophical origins of clinical psychology and their subsequent development of what they describe as an agenda for "positive clinical psychology," Maddux, Snyder, and Lopez (2004) argued that clinical psychology is defined by its illness ideology. Maddux et al. reject these implicit medical model assumptions and instead developed the assumptions of what they describe as a positive clinical psychology (see also chap. 7): *Assumption No. 1*: Positive clinical psychology is concerned with everyday problems in living, not just extreme maladaptive functioning. *Assumption No. 2*: Psychopathology, clinical problems, and clinical populations, differ "only in degree," rather than in kind, from normal problems in living, falling somewhere on a "continuum" of human functioning. This is a "dimensional model" rather than a categorical model. *Assumption No. 3*: Psychological disorders are *not* analogous to biological or medical diseases. Rather, they are reflective of problems in the person's interactions with his or her environment, and not only and simply of problems within the person himself or herself. *Assumption No. 4*: The role of the positive clinical psychologist is to identify human strengths and promote mental health as assets that buffer against weakness and mental illness.

Maddux et al. (2004; see also chap. 7) call for positive psychology to develop a new vision. We concur that it is through the reconceptualization of the fundamental assumptions underlying practice that positive psychology may have its greatest impact on clinical and health psychology. Our view is that the person-centered assumption of an intrinsic tendency toward growth and development, or actualizing tendency, is most consistent with the positive psychology evidence (Joseph & Linley, 2006a; Linley & Joseph, 2004b; Patterson & Joseph, 2007).

New Developments in Practice

Recent efforts have generated new techniques and ways of working with particular client groups based on empirical positive psychology evidence. We summarize these approaches below.

WELL-BEING THERAPY

Well-being therapy was developed by Fava and colleagues (e.g., Fava, Rafanelli, Cazzaro, Conti, & Grandi, 1998; Ruini & Fava, 2004). It is based on Ryff's (1989) six domains of psychological well-being, namely environmental mastery, personal growth, purpose in life, autonomy, self-acceptance, and positive relations with others. Well-being therapy is described as a short-term psychotherapeutic strategy that extends over eight sessions, with each session ranging from 30 to 50 min. It emphasizes self-observation, including the use of a structured diary, and the interaction between the

client and the therapist (Ruini & Fava, 2004, p. 374). To date, well-being therapy has been used very effectively with people suffering from affective disorders (Fava, Rafanelli, Cazzaro, et al., 1998), recurrent depression (Fava, Rafanelli, Grandi, Conti, & Belluardo, 1998), and generalized anxiety disorder (Fava et al., 2005).

MINDFULNESS-BASED COGNITIVE THERAPY

Mindfulness has long been recognized as a means for improving self-awareness, thereby allowing one to make more informed and deliberate choices. Recent empirical work from the positive psychology tradition has shown how mindfulness is associated with a host of well-being indicators (Brown & Ryan, 2003). Mindfulness-based approaches also provide possible means of fostering self-determination and self-awareness, and thereby allow the satisfaction of basic psychological needs for autonomy, competence, and relatedness (Brown & Ryan, 2004), which are believed to underpin much of human well-being (Ryan & Deci, 2000). There is growing evidence to support the effectiveness of this approach (see, e.g., Ma & Teasdale, 2004) and for its use with a variety of clinical as well as nonclinical conditions (Grossman, Niemann, Schmidt, & Walach, 2004).

QUALITY OF LIFE THERAPY

Quality of Life Therapy, developed by Frisch (2006), provides a collection of cognitive therapy techniques that therapists can use to help clients move toward greater happiness. It employs what is called the CASIO model as a blueprint for interventions. The CASIO model consists of four components that provide the framework for thinking about particular areas of life, and a fifth component for thinking about other areas of life: **C**ircumstances or Characteristics of an area of life; **A**ttitude about, perception, and interpretation of an area; **S**tandards of fulfilment or achievement; **I**mportance a person places on an area for overall happiness; and **O**ther areas of life. Thus, using this blueprint, clients are encouraged to change their circumstances, think differently, set themselves new standards, change their priorities about what's important in life, and think about other areas of life. To date, there are not outcomes studies available in relation to this approach, and this should be a focus of future research.

POSITIVE PSYCHOTHERAPY

Applying the principles and major tenets of positive psychology to psychotherapy led Seligman, Rashid, and Parks (2006) to develop positive psychotherapy.

This therapeutic approach rests on the central premise that building positive emotions, strengths, and meaning are efficacious in the treatment of psychopathology. Its fundamental assumptions are similar to those of positive therapy (Joseph & Linley, 2006a) in that it holds that people have an inherent tendency for growth and fulfilment; that positive emotions and strengths are authentic and real, rather than epiphenomena of psychological disorders; and that focusing on strengths and meaning is a means for ameliorating psychopathology. Preliminary work has indicated that positive psychotherapy is at least as efficacious for major depression as traditional pharmacological treatments (Seligman et al., 2006).

CLINICAL APPROACHES TO POSTTRAUMATIC GROWTH

In our own work, we have been concerned with the concept of posttraumatic growth, or how people change and grow positively following trauma. In thinking about how clinicians may work with people following trauma in such a way that promotes and facilitates the person's capacity for growth and positive change, Tedeschi and Calhoun (2004; Calhoun & Tedeschi, 1999) are explicit in noting that therapy that seeks to facilitate posttraumatic growth is always client-led, moving at the client's pace and in the client's direction. These therapeutic positions are very much concordant with how we would understand positive therapy. Elsewhere in our work (Joseph & Linley, 2005), we have elaborated on a person-centred organismic valuing theory of how people adapt positively following stressful and traumatic events, and this provides a solid foundation from which to develop a more specified positive psychological therapy for the facilitation of growth following trauma.

Extending Positive Psychology to Other Clinical Populations

Other work has extended positive psychology applications to work with people diagnosed with schizophrenia, and behavioral disorders (Ahmed & Boisvert, 2006), as well as to work with people across the mental health spectrum (Joseph & Worsley, 2005). There has also been impetus toward happiness interventions with nonclinical populations, as we describe in the next section.

Specific Happiness Interventions

Until recently, it was believed that people's overall levels of happiness were essentially unchangeable. Happiness seems to have some genetic basis (Lykken, 1999), and people quickly return to their baseline state of happiness following improved life circumstances (the "hedonic treadmill" effect; Brickman & Campbell, 1971), both of which led many scientists to conclude that happiness change initiatives were doomed. More recently Diener, Lucas, and Scollon (2006) have argued that these traditional assumptions about the hedonic treadmill need to be revised, and Lyubomirsky and colleagues (Lyubomirsky, Sheldon, & Schkade, 2005, chap. 63; Sheldon & Lyubomirsky, 2004) have suggested that 50% of happiness is genetic, 10% is due to life circumstances, and 40% is determined by the actions we choose to perform. Successful happiness interventions have focused on this changeable 40%, and while research is still in its infancy, there is a clear suggestion that happiness can be sustainably changed. Importantly, for happiness change initiatives to be successful, Sheldon and Lyubomirsky (2004) specify that interventions must have person-activity fit; people must be prepared to put in the necessary effort; and people must habitually use different happiness intervention activities in order to avoid hedonic adaptation effects.

In the earliest scientific studies of happiness interventions, Fordyce (1977, 1983) reported seven studies (with times ranging from 2 weeks to 18 months) where participants were randomly assigned to either a happiness intervention, or a placebo condition. He found that 14 activities increased happiness, such as spending more time socializing, strengthening your closest relationships, and becoming more active. Notably, the successful interventions seemed to focus on intentional activities, as Lyubomirsky et al. (2005) would suggest. Fordyce's early work was also extended by Lichter, Haye, and Kammann (1980), who developed a cognitive retraining approach to happiness, and found significant increases in happiness, relative to a control group, in two experiments.

More recently, Seligman, Steen, Park, and Peterson (2005) evaluated the effectiveness of five interventions, relative to a placebo condition. Increased happiness and decreased depression over a 6-month period were found in two conditions, where participants either (a) took a survey to discover their five signature strengths, and used these strengths in a new and different way for a week, or (b) wrote down three things that went well each day for 1 week. In a third condition, participants were given 1 week to write and then deliver a letter of gratitude in person to someone who had been especially kind to them but had never been properly thanked. This intervention had the largest effect on happiness and depression of any condition, but the effect only lasted up to 1 month. The successful exercises were self-reinforcing, in that the people who experienced long-term benefits were those who had chosen to continue the exercises from the intervention beyond the 1-week experimental period.

Two of the successful interventions reported by Seligman et al. (2005) involved gratitude—either toward other people, or life in general. Other research (Emmons & McCullough, 2003) also has shown that interventions that promote a focus on the good things in life increase positive affect and satisfaction with life. It is possible that interventions to increase gratitude may help avoid habituation following improved life circumstances (cf. Watkins, 2004; chap. 41). Further, given that gratitude seems to be a broadly prosocial affect (McCullough, Kilpatrick, Emmons, & Larson, 2001), further investigation is needed into whether gratitude interventions increase perceived or actual social resources, and whether these increased resources mediate the effect of gratitude interventions on happiness and well-being.

The effects of happiness interventions, and the advances that have been made already in our understanding of the possibility of sustainably increasing happiness, as well as some of the mechanisms for doing so, hold tremendous promise. Given that Seligman et al.'s (2005) results were fully mediated by self-sustained activities beyond the 1-week experimental period, and the perennial problems of treatment adherence in pharmacological treatments, it may be that positive psychology-driven happiness interventions have much to offer in relation to the treatment of more serious affective disorders.

Education and the Teaching of Positive Psychology

The role of positive psychology in education is becoming well recognized in the school literature (see Huebner et al., this volume), driven in part by the publication of positive psychology special issues of *School Psychology Quarterly* (2003) and *Psychology in the Schools* (2004). The role of positive psychology in education is primarily focused on encouraging and rewarding the multitude of talents and strengths a child has, by presenting opportunities for displays of these talents and strength each day, rather than for penalizing them for their deficits (Clonan, Chafouleas, McDougal, & Riley-Tillman, 2004; Huebner & Gilman, 2003).

Theory and research in the positive psychology of education extends to all aspects of the educational experience and curriculum. For example, Clonan et al. (2004) outline a vision of the positive psychology school, concentrating on areas of prevention (to reduce stress), consultation (across the curriculum and different service providers), and competency development (in academic skills and positive peer experience and interaction). However, the challenge for positive psychology is to establish what the key components of positive psychology "look like" within a school, how the teaching and natural environment can be used to capitalize on positive psychological principles, and how a school can maintain and plan for sustained change (Clonan et al., 2004).

The focus of positive psychology applied to education has also been extended to consideration of the role of effective upward social comparisons in learning, growth, and development (Cohn, 2004); teaching students to make wise judgments (Reznitskaya & Sternberg, 2004); and the effective teaching of positive psychology as a subject in its own right (Baylis, 2004; Fineburg, 2004). Furthermore, driven in part by the positive psychology movement, attention is now turning to what we might do to make schools happy places (Layard, 2005; Martin, 2005; Noddings, 2003).

APPLYING STRENGTHS IN SCHOOL AND COLLEGE

Within education, there have been specific attempts to apply and celebrate strengths in the classroom, with college students, 10–14-year-old students, and younger children (Liesveld & Miller, 2005). The Gallup Organization has developed and delivered the StrengthsQuest educational program (Clifton & Anderson, 2002) across a variety of higher education colleges and universities. The program is now being extended to 10–14-year-old students (Anderson, 2005), and preliminary reports from teachers using the program have been positive (e.g., Austin, 2006; Henderson, 2005). Within the United Kingdom, a project has been run across a group of primary schools (ages 5–11 years) under the title of Celebrating Strengths (Fox Eades, 2008). This project has linked strengths to specific festivals and events throughout the school calendar and has included activities such as the strengths-based classroom (recognizing the strengths of all class members), victory logs (record books noting students' achievements), and celebrations of "what went well."

Forensic Psychology and Offender Rehabilitation

Positive psychology and forensic psychology may seem like strange bedfellows, but over the past two decades increasing empirical evidence has begun to suggest that criminal recidivism can be reduced by rehabilitating offenders as opposed to punishment alone (Andrews & Bonta, 1998). Typically, such rehabilitation utilizes the "risk-need" approach, which focuses on reducing the likelihood of recidivism by assessing and treating the associated dynamic risk factors, the primary aim being to protect the community from further harm. More recently, Ward (2002; Ward & Mann, 2004) has developed an "enhancement" model called the "good lives model" (GLM), which focuses on human well-being and locates rehabilitation in a more constructive, strengths-based, capabilities approach. Rehabilitation seeks to improve the capabilities of the offender, thus improving their quality of life and reducing their likelihood of committing further crimes against the community.

The GLM of rehabilitation focuses on the core ideas of human identity and agency, psychological well-being, and the potential to live an alternative life to a criminal lifestyle (Ward & Gannon, 2006). It is based on the fundamental assumption that human beings are intrinsically active and goal-seeking, constantly constructing meaning and a sense of purpose in their lives. Individuals strive to achieve valued aspects of human life, primary human goods that include activities, experiences, and states of mind that are intrinsically beneficial and enhance individual flourishing and well-being, and hence are sought for their own sake rather than as a means to an end. Within this model, consideration is still given to risk factors for offending, but these risk factors are viewed as obstacles to achieving these valued outcomes, rather than as the focus in their own right.

The aim of the GLM of rehabilitation is to provide the offender with a concrete understanding of how they may live a realistic good life that is beneficial and fulfilling. Rehabilitation seeks to enhance the external conditions (e.g., social support) and internal conditions (e.g., skills, values, capabilities) that will enable the person to secure the primary human goods they have identified as personally meaningful in socially acceptable, noncriminal ways, resulting in both an increased sense of personal identity and agency, and reduced recidivism. This approach has been used effectively on a trial basis within the British prison population (Ward & Mann, 2004), and appears to have the potential for a major rethinking of how we approach the rehabilitation and reintegration of offenders into society.

Industrial/Organizational Psychology and the World of Work

Positive psychology applied to the world of work is an emerging discipline, but one which has

tremendous potential to effect people's working lives for the better (see Linley, Harrington, & Page, in press). For example, the pioneering work of The Gallup Organization has shown that playing to people's strengths (Hodges & Clifton, 2004) and creating an engaged workforce (Harter, Schmidt, & Keyes, 2003) have major bottom-line business benefits. Other examples of research from a positive psychology perspective that pertains to the world of work include those of transformational leadership, employee engagement, positive organizational scholarship and positive organizational behavior, and appreciative inquiry (AI). We address each of these in turn, but refer interested readers to Linley et al. (in press) for a fuller coverage of positive psychology applied to work.

TRANSFORMATIONAL LEADERSHIP

Transformational leadership is characterized by four core behaviors: "idealized influence," "inspirational motivation," "intellectual stimulation," and "individualized consideration" (see Bass, 1998). Taken together, these behaviors result in leaders whose actions are determined by what they believe is right, rather than by the easy or expedient option. They inspire their employees to reach for stretch goals, encourage them to think autonomously and challenge the established ways of doing things. Finally, they demonstrate individualized concern for each employee's development and well-being.

Sivanathan, Arnold, Turner, and Barling (2004) argue that transformational leadership leads to an increase in employee well-being through four mediating psychological processes: increasing "self-efficacy," that is, an individual's belief in their own ability, which is positively related to increases in motivation and job performance; increasing "trust in management," that is, belief in their leader, which helps to mitigate the feelings of uncertainty and threat that modern organizations create; "meaningful work," that is, belief that they are making a valuable contribution; and increasing "organizational identity," that is, employees' sense of social identity and belonging with the organization. These latter two areas also have been identified as key elements of a culture that engenders employee engagement (Stairs, 2005).

EMPLOYEE ENGAGEMENT

Employee engagement is defined as the degree of commitment to a particular job, and comprises of rational commitment (driven by goals such as financial reward or professional development) and emotional commitment (driven by a deeper belief in the value of the job). This concept of employee commitment is similar to the relational and transactional components of the psychological contract (Rousseau, 1995). Stairs (2005) argues that the application of positive psychology can create higher levels of emotional commitment, individual performance, and positive discretionary behaviors, resulting in enhanced organizational productivity and profitability. Empirically, employee engagement has been shown to be consistently linked with better organizational outcomes, including employee retention, fewer sick days, enhanced customer satisfaction, and increased financial turnover and profit (Harter, Schmidt, & Hayes, 2002; Harter et al., 2003).

POSITIVE ORGANIZATIONAL SCHOLARSHIP AND POSITIVE ORGANIZATIONAL BEHAVIOR

Two further examples of creating positive cultures that focus on employees' strengths and positive behaviors are positive organizational scholarship (POS; Cameron, Dutton, & Quinn, 2003) and positive organizational behavior (POB; Luthans, 2002, this volume). POS focuses on identifying and developing positive organizational characteristics that lead to exceptional individual and organizational performance. POS investigates positive deviance, that is, the ways in which organizations and their members may flourish and prosper by developing strengths such as resilience, restoration, and vitality.

POB seeks to improve employee performance and organizational competitive advantage by focusing on state-like strengths and psychological capacities that are positive, measurable, developable, and performance-related. Luthans, Avey, Avolio, Norman, and Combs (2006) identified four key components of POB: "self-efficacy" (having the confidence to take on and succeed at challenging tasks); "optimism" (positivity regarding future success); "hope" (flexible perseverance toward succeeding at future goals); and "resiliency" (ability to successfully bounce back from problems and adversity). Luthans et al. (2006) have applied the principles of positive psychology to create a positive capital intervention (PCI) that develops these four strengths in organizational members. They report preliminary results that demonstrate small but significant increases in the psychological capital of managers and argue that sustained increases in psychological capital will result in increased employee performance and organizational profitability.

APPRECIATIVE INQUIRY

AI is a narrative-based process of positive organizational change that works through a process called the AI 4-D cycle. The AI 4-D cycle involves "discovery" (identifying the best of what is); "dream" (creating a results-oriented vision and higher purpose); "design" (articulating an organizational design that is capable of drawing on the organization at its best); and "destiny" (strengthening the positive, affirmative capability of the organization to build hope and sustain momentum for ongoing positive change). This process has been elaborated to create a model of positive organizational change that increases inquiry into the appreciable world and relatedness to others through the "elevation of inquiry" (asking more questions about the positive); the "fusion of strengths" (connecting the strengths of organizational members to a shared vision); and the "activation of energy" that follows from this (Cooperrider & Sekerka, 2003). AI has received considerable attention and achieved many successes in the world of organization development. It operates from many of the same core assumptions as positive psychology, although integration between AI and positive psychology has been slow to manifest, but is now beginning.

Life Coaching

An area of application where positive psychology has found a ready and welcoming home is coaching. We believe that there are four primary reasons for this (see Linley & Harrington, 2005). First, both positive psychology and coaching psychology are explicitly concerned with the enhancement of performance and well-being. Second, both have implicitly challenged practitioners to question the fundamental assumptions that they hold about human nature (Linley & Joseph, 2004b). Third, positive psychology has infused an interest in the psychology of human strengths, an area that provides significant potential for coaches in harnessing a client's potential in the service of their goals and desired outcomes (Linley & Harrington, 2006). Fourth, there have been many calls for an evidence base to underpin coaching (Grant, 2006), and positive psychology is well placed to provide some of the evidence that supports coaching interventions.

There is a dearth of coaching research, whether positive psychology based or otherwise. This is likely because coaching is only now moving from first to second generation (Kauffman & Scoular, 2004). First-generation coaches established the profession and brought it to the attention of the business world, being led by coaching gurus who inspired and enthused others from their own wealth of talents and experience. The shift now to second-generation coaching is reflected in the need for coaching to be based on explicit psychological principles and grounded in a solid evidence base, something that is only just beginning. Specifically in relation to positive psychology and coaching, one early study has demonstrated that cognitive-behavioral solution-focused life coaching can be an effective means of enhancing goal striving, well-being, and hope (Green, Oades, & Grant, 2006). However, as much as there are very strong theoretical integrations between positive psychology and coaching, empirical validations and assessments of coaching processes and outcomes from a positive psychology perspective are sorely needed. Further, there is very little work that examines positive psychology in relation to executive coaching (but see Burke & Linley, 2007).

Population Approaches and Public Policy

Population approaches to improving mental health have been proposed by Huppert (2004) and Keyes (chap. 9). The work of Rose (1992) demonstrated that the prevalence of many common diseases in a given population or subpopulation is directly related to population mean of the underlying risk factors; therefore, by changing the mean of the risk factors, we should be able to change the prevalence. This hypothesis has also been supported for psychiatric disorders, including psychological distress as measured by the GHQ-30 (Anderson, Huppert, & Rose, 1993; Goldberg, 1978) and the common psychological disorders of depression and anxiety (Melzer, Tom, Brugha, Fryers, & Meltzer, 2002). As such, Huppert argued, population approaches could be effectively employed to facilitate population health and well-being through using population-level interventions.

Similar work is being carried out by Population Communications International (http://www.population.org), which works with local partners to deliver culturally sensitive radio and television soap operas that address the societal factors that limit people's ability to make choices that lead to better health, enhance their educational prospects, and encourage sustainable development. They achieve this through using characters in the soap operas to model the behaviors that promote family health, stable communities, and a sustainable environment. Much of this work is informed by Bandura's decades of research on social modeling and self-efficacy (e.g., Bandura, 1997).

A population-based approach also has been used by the Positive Parenting Program (Triple P) in Australia. The Positive Parenting Program is a family intervention program that is designed to prevent behavioral, emotional, and developmental problems in children up to the age of 16. It aims to achieve this through promoting and developing the knowledge, skills, and confidence of parents (Sanders, 2003; Sanders, Markie-Dadds, & Turner, 2002).

Sanders, Montgomery, and Brechman-Toussaint (2000) reported on the effectiveness of a 12-episode television series, *Families*, that was aimed at improving disruptive child behavior and family relationships. Each episode of *Families* lasted for approximately 20–30 min, and included a feature story about family issues, together with a segment of 5–7 min that presented parents with guidelines and instructions for using a range of parenting strategies to address common child behavioral problems, to prevent problems from occurring, and to help teach children in learning new skills and master difficult tasks. These segments also presented the viewer with a modeled demonstration of the suggested strategies. The initial report, based on 56 parents of children aged 2–8 years, showed that the prevalence of disruptive behavior dropped from 43% to 14%, with the effects being maintained at a 6-month follow-up.

Other population-based approaches to the practice of positive psychology are largely centered on the achievement of happiness as a public policy aim. Veenhoven (2004) has demonstrated why the greatest happiness principle ("the greatest happiness for the greatest number") is a legitimate policy aim, and Diener (Diener, 2000; Diener & Seligman, 2004) and Kahneman (Kahneman, Krueger, Schkade, Schwarz, & Stone, 2004) have argued for national indicators of subjective well-being. The focus on happiness as a public policy concern underpins the Gallup World Poll; is the pursuit of Gross National Happiness (GNH) in the Himalayan Kingdom of Bhutan; has been the subject of a Prime Minister's Strategy Unit report in the United Kingdom (Donovan & Halpern, 2001); and is the subject of policy debates between the two major British political parties (e.g., David Cameron, Leader of the Conservative Party's, focus on "general well-being"; Smith, 2006).

Within the United Kingdom, the New Economics Foundation, the Centre for Confidence and Well-Being, and the Centre for Applied Positive Psychology are all engaged with promoting the principles and practice of positive psychology. The New Economics Foundation (NEF; http://www.neweconomics.org)

describes itself as an "independent 'think-and-do' tank [that] believes in economics as if people and the planet mattered." A large part of their work focuses on the role of well-being in a flourishing society, and their research and actions are directed toward this end (see Marks & Shah, 2004; Marks, Shah, & Westall, 2004). The Centre for Confidence and Well-Being was founded to tackle the Scots crisis of confidence through promoting activities and events that can bring about attitudinal change in Scotland and a shift toward more positive self-belief (see Craig, 2005; also http://www.centreforconfidence.co.uk). The Centre for Applied Positive Psychology (CAPP) was founded to take academic research in positive psychology and apply it in real-world settings, across the areas of work, education, and health. Its mission is *Strengthening the World* (see http://www.cappeu.org and Linley, 2008). These three centers are notable because they all operate independently of university affiliations and hence represent an important step toward the "real-world" dissemination and applications of positive psychology, something that we believe is imperative if the positive psychology approach is to achieve its own potential.

Major Questions and Future Directions

This chapter has briefly scoped some of the major domains of positive psychology applications and reviewed some of the key findings and lessons from them; but it also raises a number of major questions that will inform the future directions, and efficacy or otherwise, of positive psychology applications. We address what we see as the four most pressing of these questions.

What Are the Fundamental Assumptions That Underpin Positive Psychology Applications?

As we indicated at the beginning of the chapter, positive psychology causes us to reexamine our fundamental assumptions about human nature and hence about how we might work best with people. We have been explicit in our work (e.g., Joseph & Linley, 2004; Linley & Joseph, 2004b) that the fundamental assumption we find most compelling in relation to the research evidence from positive psychology, and the implications this has for the ways in which we engage with people, is the view that human beings possess an inherent, constructive developmental tendency toward growth and fulfilment, or actualizing tendency, to use Rogers' term. However, this is not strictly an empirical question—or at least a question that lends itself to easy empirical scrutiny. As such we must ultimately make an assumption that fits best with our personal convictions and our reading of the research evidence. This is what we have done in subscribing to this approach, and we invite others to examine their own fundamental assumptions in relation to positive psychology applications, with a view to establishing if there are competing assumptions that may better fit both the subjective and objective data we have before us. If positive psychology can agree—even broadly—on its core fundamental assumptions, this will provide a concrete foundation from which we can build.

What Is the Theoretical Basis for Positive Psychology Applications?

Intrinsically related to this question of fundamental assumptions is the issue of the deep theoretical basis that underpins positive psychology and its applications. At the moment, to our knowledge, quite simply, there isn't one. Positive psychology does not have an integrating theory that ties together the wide range of findings from research and practice, and this inevitably limits its advances. However, we have proposed elsewhere (Joseph & Linley, 2006a) that the meta-theory of the person-centered approach, first articulated by Carl Rogers, provides a core basis for positive psychology theory development. It also challenges the illness ideology and medical model that is implicit within much of psychological thinking (Joseph & Linley, 2006b; Maddux et al., 2004), and provides an integrative theoretical framework that maps many existing positive psychological constructs (Patterson & Joseph, 2007; Sheldon, 2004). Developing a deep theory that integrates what is known about optimal human functioning with what is known about psychopathology and distress will generate considerable advances in positive psychology applications.

Who Should Apply Positive Psychology, and Where?

Is positive psychology the province only of positive psychologists? Or even only of psychologists? We argue, comprehensively, that it is not. Positive psychology is not restricted, and should not be restricted, to just psychology. It is a much broader approach to the questions of what it means to be human and to live well, and these questions cut across a host of disciplines, including, for example, sociology, anthropology, philosophy, ethics, economics, and public policy. To restrict positive psychology to just psychologists would be to sell short or even sell out the world-changing potential of the approach. In contrast, and as we have argued else-where (Linley, 2006; Linley et al., 2006), the goal of positive psychologists should be to spread the positive psychology message as far and as wide as we are able. This may be best achieved through integration and bridge building with other disciplines, but also through the conduct of well-designed and well-controlled scientific research that demonstrates the compelling benefits that a positive psychological approach delivers. This means also that positive psychology applications should not be, and are not being, contained only within academic psychology departments, or only in the hands of formal applied psychology practitioners. Rather, the most progressive advances in positive psychology applications will come through partnership and collaboration with areas where we can have the greatest difference and touch the greatest number of lives—at work, in education, and through health, as well as through politics, public policy, and population approaches.

Are Positive Psychology Applications Universal?

A question that may justly be leveled at all of the interventions and applications we have reviewed above is the extent to which the approaches and findings hold across different cultures and populations. In short, the state of knowledge is that we simply do not know. Although, there is evidence for the consistency of strengths rankings across different nations (Park, Peterson, & Seligman, 2006), and evidence to suggest that subjective well-being is universally valued (Diener & Suh, 2000), if systematically overestimated in Western cultures (Diener, Napa Scollon, Oishi, Dzokoto, & Suh, 2000), these are hardly bases from which to conclude that the positive psychology applications would be as relevant and effective in Bangalore as they are in Boston. We are reminded of Lopez et al.'s (2002) story of the Mexican fisherman, and sadly recognize that in the intervening years, cross-cultural studies of positive psychology—and especially positive psychology applications—have not moved on as much as we might like. That said, we would also do well to remember—as Constantine and Sue (2006) remind us—that studying multicultural aspects of positive psychology does not require us to travel many thousands of miles: Many of us now live in multicultural societies that provide ample testing grounds—as well as ample need—for positive psychology applications. This, surely, would constitute a major advance in moving positive psychology out from its traditional White, Anglo-American heritage.

What Does the Future Hold for Positive Psychology Applications?

Arguments initially leveled against the positive psychology movement were its perceived emphasis on the "positive" at the exclusion of the "negative" (Held, 2004), and its failure to fully acknowledge and build on its historical antecedents. An important first step for positive psychology applications then is the integration of positive and negative and the application of positive psychology approaches to traditional areas of focus for "business-as-usual" psychology. The application of positive psychology to the treatment of depression (Seligman et al., 2006), to recovery from traumatic events (Joseph & Linley, 2005), and to new understandings of clinical psychology (Duckworth, Steen, & Seligman, 2005; chap. 7) are welcome examples of this integration, which serve to mitigate this criticism and usher in a new, more integrative approach to the understanding and improvement of the human condition. Similarly, there have now been more explicit efforts to link positive psychology to past efforts through special issues of journals including the *Journal of Humanistic Psychology* and *The Counseling Psychologist*, and further efforts in this regard are to be encouraged, especially interdisciplinary approaches that seek to introduce a positive psychological perspective to such domains as economics, politics, and social policy.

The success or failure of these activities will determine the future of positive psychology applications in relation to the most pressing question that is faced—namely, will positive psychology applications become marginalized through the narrow pursuit of happiness, or will they blossom through their broader integration into personal, organizational, and social initiatives designed to enhance human flourishing in the home through education, at work, and throughout life? The breadth of positive psychology applications reviewed here suggests that positive psychology already has moved beyond the narrow pursuit of happiness, and as such, we may indeed be witnessing the beginning of a new world order that strives to create flourishing human lives through enabling people to be at their best whether in love, at work, or through play.

In Conclusion

In this chapter, we have reviewed the breadth of positive psychology applications, and yet still cannot claim to be anywhere near comprehensive. However, we hope that this chapter stands as a testament to the hundreds of people who are developing and delivering positive psychology applications, and to the many thousands of people who could likely lead better lives as a result. The future of positive psychology applications lies in the hands of us all, both as researchers and practitioners, and as human beings, and in working with positive psychology we have a rare opportunity to leave our world with a better legacy—carpe diem.

Questions for the Future

1. What is the smallest thing that applied positive psychology could do to make the biggest difference?

2. How can we best "give applied positive psychology away" to people?

3. What would be an applied positive psychology perspective on the major social challenges facing us today?

References

Ahmed, M., & Boisvert, C. M. (2006). Using positive psychology with special mental health populations. *American Psychologist, 61*, 333–335.

Anderson, E. C. (2005). Strengths-based educating: A concrete way to bring out the best in students—and yourself. *Educational Horizons, 83*, 180–189.

Anderson, J., Huppert, F. A., & Rose, G. (1993). Normality, deviance, and minor psychiatric morbidity in the community. *Psychological Medicine, 23*, 475–485.

Andrews, D. A., & Bonta, J. (1998). *The psychology of criminal conduct* (2nd ed.). Cincinnati, OH: Anderson Publishing.

Austin, D. B. (2006). Building on a foundation of strengths. *Educational Horizons, 84*, 176–182.

Bandura, A. (1997). *Self-efficacy: The exercise of control.* New York: W H Freeman.

Bass, B. M. (1998). *Transformational leadership: Industrial, military and educational impact.* Mahwah, NJ: Erlbaum.

Baylis, N. (2004). Teaching positive psychology. In P. A. Linley & S. Joseph (Eds.), *Positive psychology in practice* (pp. 210–217). Hoboken, NJ: Wiley.

Bozarth, J. D., & Motomasa, N. (2005). Searching for the core: The interface of client-centered principles with other therapies. In S. Joseph & R. Worsley (Eds.), *Person-centred psychopathology: A positive psychology of mental health* (pp. 293–309). Ross-on-Wye, England: PCCS Books.

Brickman, P., & Campbell, D. T. (1971). Hedonic relativism and planning the good society. In M. H. Appley (Ed.), *Adaptation-level theory: A symposium* (pp. 287–302). New York: Academic Press.

Brown, K. W., & Ryan, R. M. (2003). The benefits of being present: Mindfulness and its role in psychological well-being. *Journal of Personality and Social Psychology, 84*, 822–848.

Brown, K. W., & Ryan, R. M. (2004). Fostering healthy self-regulation from within and without: A self-determination theory perspective. In P. A. Linley & S. Joseph (Eds.), *Positive psychology in practice* (pp. 105–124). Hoboken, NJ: Wiley.

Burke, D., & Linley, P. A. (2007). Enhancing goal self-concordance through coaching. *International Coaching Psychology Review, 2*(1), 62–69.

Calhoun, L. G., & Tedeschi, R. G. (1999). *Facilitating posttraumatic growth: A clinician's guide.* Mahwah, NJ: Lawrence Erlbaum.

Cameron, K. S., Dutton, J. E., & Quinn, R. E. (Eds.). (2003). *Positive organizational scholarship: Foundations of a new discipline.* San Francisco, CA: Berrett-Koehler.

Clifton, D. O., & Anderson, E. C. (2002). *StrengthsQuest: Discover and develop your strengths in academic, career, and beyond.* Washington, DC: The Gallup Organization.

Clonan, S. M., Chafouleas, S. M., McDougal, J. L., & Riley-Tillman, T. C. (2004). Positive psychology goes to school: Are we there yet? *Psychology in the Schools, 41*, 101–110.

Cohn, M. A. (2004). Rescuing our heroes: Positive perspectives on upward comparisons in relationships, education, and work. In P. A. Linley & S. Joseph (Eds.), *Positive psychology in practice* (pp. 218–237). Hoboken, NJ: Wiley.

Constantine, M. G., & Sue, D. W. (2006). Factors contributing to optimal human functioning in people of color in the United States. *The Counseling Psychologist, 34*, 228–244.

Cooperrider, D. L., & Sekerka, L. E. (2003). Toward a theory of positive organizational change. In K. S. Cameron, J. E. Dutton, & R. E. Quinn (Eds.), *Positive organizational scholarship: Foundations of a new discipline* (pp. 225–240). San Francisco, CA: Berrett-Koehler.

Craig, C. (2005). Scotland's tipping point. In K. MacAskill (Ed.), *Agenda for a new Scotland: Visions of Scotland.* Edinburgh, UK: Luath Press.

Diener, E. (2000). Subjective well-being: The science of happiness and a proposal for a national index. *American Psychologist, 55*, 34–43.

Diener, E., Lucas, R. E., & Scollon, C. N. (2006). Beyond the hedonic treadmill: Revising the adaptation theory of well-being. *American Psychologist, 61*, 305–314.

Diener, E., Napa Scollon, C. K., Oishi, S., Dzokoto, V., & Suh, E. M. (2000). Positivity and the construction of life satisfaction judgments: Global happiness is not the sum of its parts. *Journal of Happiness Studies, 1*, 159–176.

Diener, E., & Seligman, M. E. P. (2004). Beyond money: Toward an economy of well-being. *Psychological Science in the Public Interest, 5*, 1–31.

Diener, E., & Suh, E. M. (2000). Measuring subjective well-being to compare the quality of life of cultures. In E. Diener & E. M. Suh (Eds.), *Culture and subjective well-being* (pp. 3–12). Cambridge, MA: MIT Press.

Donovan, N., & Halpern, D. (2001). *Life satisfaction: The state of knowledge and implications for government.* London: Downing Street Strategy Unit. Retrieved from http://www.strategy.gov.uk/2001/futures/attachments/ls/paper.pdf

Duckworth, A. L., Steen, T. A., & Seligman, M. E. P. (2005). Positive psychology in clinical practice. *Annual Review of Clinical Psychology, 1*, 629–651.

Emmons, R. A., & McCullough, M. E. (2003). Counting blessings versus burdens: An experimental investigation of gratitude and subjective well-being in daily life. *Journal of Personality and Positive Psychology, 84*, 377–389.

Fava, G. A., Rafanelli, C., Cazzaro, M., Conti, S., & Grandi, S. (1998). Well-being therapy: A novel psychotherapeutic approach for residual symptoms of affective disorders. *Psychological Medicine, 28*, 475–480.

Fava, G. A., Rafanelli, C., Grandi, S., Conti, S., & Belluardo, P. (1998). Prevention of recurrent depression with cognitive-behavioral therapy. *Archives of General Psychiatry, 55*, 816–820.

Fava, G. A., Ruini, C., Rafanelli, C., Finos, L., Salmaso, L., Mangelli, L., et al. (2005). Well-being therapy of generalized anxiety disorder. *Psychotherapy and Psychosomatics, 74*, 26–30.

Fineburg, A. C. (2004). Introducing positive psychology to the introductory psychology student. In P. A. Linley & S. Joseph (Eds.), *Positive psychology in practice* (pp. 197–209). Hoboken, NJ: Wiley.

Fordyce, M. W. (1977). Development of a program to increase personal happiness. *Journal of Counseling Psychology, 24,* 511–521.

Fordyce, M. W. (1983). A program to increase happiness: Further studies. *Journal of Counseling Psychology, 30,* 483–498.

Fox Eades, J. (2008). *Celebrating strengths: Building strengths-based schools.* Coventry, UK: CAPP Press.

Frisch, M. B. (2006). *Quality of life therapy: Applying a life satisfaction approach to positive psychology and cognitive therapy.* Hoboken, NJ: Wiley.

Goldberg, D. P. (1978). *Manual of the General Health Questionnaire.* London: NFER-Nelson.

Grant, A. M. (2006). A personal perspective on professional coaching and the development of coaching psychology. *International Coaching Psychology Review, 1,* 12–22.

Green, L. S., Oades, L. G., & Grant, A. M. (2006). Cognitive-behavioral, solution-focused life coaching: Enhancing goal striving, well-being, and hope. *Journal of Positive Psychology, 1,* 142–149.

Grossman, P., Niemann, L., Schmidt, S., & Walach, H. (2004). Mindfulness-based stress reduction and health benefits. *Journal of Psychosomatic Medicine, 57,* 35–43.

Harter, J. K., Schmidt, F. L., & Hayes, T. L. (2002). Business-unit-level relationship between employee satisfaction, employee engagement, and business outcomes: A meta-analysis. *Journal of Applied Psychology, 87,* 268–279.

Harter, J. K., Schmidt, F. L., & Keyes, C. L. M. (2003). Well-being in the workplace and its relationship to business outcomes: A review of the Gallup studies. In C. L. M. Keyes & J. Haidt (Eds.), *Flourishing: Positive psychology and the life well-lived* (pp. 205–224). Washington, DC: American Psychological Association.

Held, B. S. (2004). The negative side of positive psychology. *Journal of Humanistic Psychology, 44,* 9–46.

Henderson, G. (2005). The power of teaching students using strengths. *Educational Horizons, 83,* 202–204.

Hodges, T. D., & Clifton, D. O. (2004). Strengths-based development in practice. In P. A. Linley & S. Joseph (Eds.), *Positive psychology in practice* (pp. 256–268). Hoboken, NJ: Wiley.

Hubble, M. A., & Miller, S. D. (2004). The client: Psychotherapy's missing link for promoting a positive psychology. In P. A. Linley & S. Joseph (Eds.), *Positive psychology in practice* (pp. 335–353). Hoboken, NJ: Wiley.

Huebner, E. S., & Gilman, R. (2003). Toward a focus on positive psychology in school psychology. *School Psychology Quarterly, 18,* 99–102.

Huppert, F. A. (2004). A population approach to positive psychology: The potential for population interventions to promote well-being and prevent disorder. In P. A. Linley & S. Joseph (Eds.), *Positive psychology in practice* (pp. 693–709). Hoboken, NJ: Wiley.

Joseph, S., & Linley, P. A. (2004). Positive therapy: A positive psychological theory of therapeutic practice. In P. A. Linley & S. Joseph (Eds.), *Positive psychology in practice* (pp. 354–368). Hoboken, NJ: Wiley.

Joseph, S., & Linley, P. A. (2005). Positive adjustment to threatening events: An organismic valuing theory of growth through adversity. *Review of General Psychology, 9,* 262–280.

Joseph, S., & Linley, P. A. (2006a). *Positive therapy: A meta-theory for positive psychological practice.* London: Taylor & Francis.

Joseph, S., & Linley, P. A. (2006b). Positive psychology versus the medical model? *American Psychologist, 61,* 332–333.

Joseph, S., & Worsley, R. (Eds.) (2005). *Person-centred psychopathology: A positive psychology of mental health.* Ross-on-Wye, UK: PCCS Books.

Kahneman, D., Krueger, A. B., Schkade, D. A., Schwarz, N., & Stone, A. A. (2004). Toward national well-being accounts. *American Economic Review, 94,* 429–434.

Kauffman, C., & Scoular, A. (2004). Toward a positive psychology of executive coaching. In P. A. Linley & S. Joseph (Eds.), *Positive psychology in practice* (pp. 287–302). Hoboken, NJ: Wiley.

Layard, R. (2005). *Happiness: Lessons from a new science.* London: Allen Lane.

Lichter, S., Haye, K., & Kammann, R. (1980). Increasing happiness through cognitive retraining. *New Zealand Psychologist, 9,* 57–64.

Liesveld, R., & Miller, J. A. (2005). *Teach with your strengths: How great teachers inspire their students.* New York: Gallup Press.

Linley, A. (2008). *Average to A+: Realising strengths in yourself and others.* Coventry, UK: CAPP Press.

Linley, P. A. (2006). Counseling psychology's positive psychological agenda: A model for integration and inspiration. *The Counseling Psychologist, 34,* 313–322.

Linley, P. A., & Harrington, S. (2005). Positive psychology and coaching psychology: Perspectives on integration. *The Coaching Psychologist, 1*(1), 13–14.

Linley, P. A., & Harrington, S. (2006). Strengths coaching: A potential-guided approach to coaching psychology. *International Coaching Psychology Review, 1,* 37–46.

Linley, P. A., Harrington, S., & Page, N. (Eds.). (in press). *Oxford handbook of positive psychology and work.* New York: Oxford University Press.

Linley, P. A., & Joseph, S. (2004a). Applied positive psychology: A new perspective for professional practice. In P. A. Linley & S. Joseph (Eds.), *Positive psychology in practice* (pp. 3–12). Hoboken, NJ: Wiley.

Linley, P. A., & Joseph, S. (2004b). Toward a theoretical foundation for positive psychology in practice. In P. A. Linley & S. Joseph (Eds.), *Positive psychology in practice* (pp. 713–731). Hoboken, NJ: Wiley.

Linley, P. A., Joseph, S., Harrington, S., & Wood, A. M. (2006). Positive psychology: Past, present, and (possible) future. *The Journal of Positive Psychology, 1,* 3–16.

Lopez, S. J., Magyar-Moe, J. L., Petersen, S. E., Ryder, J. A., Krieshok, T. S., O'Byrne, K. K., et al. (2006). Counseling psychology's focus on positive aspects of human functioning. *The Counseling Psychologist, 34,* 205–227.

Lopez, S. J., Prosser, E. C., Edwards, L. M., Magyar-Moe, J. L., Neufeld, J. E., & Rasmussen, H. N. (2002). Putting positive psychology in a multicultural context. In C. R. Snyder & S. J. Lopez (Eds.), *Handbook of positive psychology* (pp. 700–714). New York: Oxford University Press.

Luthans, F. (2002). Positive organizational behavior: Developing and managing psychological strengths. *Academy of Management Executive, 16,* 57–72.

Luthans, F., Avey, J. B., Avolio, B. J., Norman, S. M., & Combs, G. M. (2006). Psychological capital development: Toward a micro-intervention. *Journal of Organizational Behaviour, 27,* 387–393.

Lykken, D. T. (1999). *Happiness: What studies on twins show us about nature, nurture, and the happiness set-point.* Racine, WI: Golden Books Publishing.

Lyubomirsky, S., Sheldon, K. M., & Schkade, D. (2005). Pursuing happiness: The architecture of sustainable change. *Review of General Psychology, 9,* 111–131.

Ma, S. H., & Teasdale, J. D. (2004). Mindfulness-based cognitive therapy for depression: Replication and exploration of differential relapse prevention effects. *Journal of Consulting and Clinical Psychology, 72,* 31–40.

McCullough, M. E., Kilpatrick, S., Emmons, R. A., & Larson, D. (2001). Is gratitude a moral affect? *Psychological Bulletin, 127,* 249–266.

Maddux, J. E., Snyder, C. R., & Lopez, S. J. (2004). Toward a positive clinical psychology: Deconstructing the illness ideology and constructing an ideology of human strengths and potential. In P. A. Linley & S. Joseph (Eds.), *Positive psychology in practice* (pp. 320–334). Hoboken, NJ: Wiley.

Marks, N., & Shah, H. (2004). *A well-being manifesto for a flourishing society.* London: New Economics Foundation.

Marks, N., Shah, H., & Westall, A. (2004). *The power and potential of well-being indicators: Measuring young people's well-being in Nottingham.* London: New Economics Foundation.

Martin, D. J., Garske, J. P., & Davis, M. K. (2000). Relation of the therapeutic alliance with outcome and other variables: A meta-analytic review. *Journal of Consulting and Clinical Psychology, 68,* 438–450.

Martin, P. (2005). *Making happy people: The nature of happiness and its origins in childhood.* London: Fourth Estate.

Melzer, D., Tom, B. D. M., Brugha, T. S., Fryers, T., & Meltzer, H. (2002). Common mental disorder symptom counts in populations: Are there distinct case groups above epidemiological cut-offs? *Psychological Medicine, 32,* 1195–1201.

Noddings, N. (2003). *Happiness and education.* New York: Cambridge University Press.

Park, N., Peterson, C., & Seligman, M. E. P. (2006). Character strengths in fifty-four nations and the fifty U.S. states. *Journal of Positive Psychology, 1,* 118–129.

Patterson, T., & Joseph, S. (2007). Person-centered personality theory: Support from self-determination theory and positive pschology. *Journal of Humanistic Psychology, 47,* 117–139.

Reznitskaya, A., & Sternberg, R. J. (2004). Teaching students to make wise judgments: The "Teaching for Wisdom" program. In P. A. Linley & S. Joseph (Eds.), *Positive psychology in practice* (pp. 181–196). Hoboken, NJ: Wiley.

Rogers, C. R. (1951). *Client-centred therapy: Its current practice, implications and theory.* Boston, MA: Houghton Mifflin.

Rose, G. (1992). *The strategy of preventive medicine.* Oxford: Oxford University Press.

Rousseau, D. M. (1995). *Psychological contracts in organizations: Understanding written and unwritten agreements.* London: Sage.

Ruini, C., & Fava, G. A. (2004). Clinical applications of well-being therapy. In P. A. Linley & S. Joseph (Eds.), *Positive psychology in practice* (pp. 371–387). Hoboken, NJ: Wiley.

Ryan, R. M., & Deci, E. L. (2000). Self-determination theory and the facilitation of intrinsic motivation, social development, and well-being. *American Psychologist, 55,* 68–78.

Ryff, C. D. (1989). Happiness is everything, or is it? Explorations on the meaning of psychological well-being. *Journal of Personality and Social Psychology, 57,* 1069–1081.

Sanders, M. R. (2003). Triple P—positive parenting program: A population approach to promoting competent parenting. *Australian e-Journal for the Advancement of Mental Health,* 2(3).

Sanders, M. R., Markie-Dadds, C., & Turner, K. M. T (2002). The role of the media and primary care in the dissemination of evidence-based parenting and family support interventions. *The Behavior Therapist,* 25, 156–166.

Sanders, M. R., Montgomery, D. T., & Brechman-Toussaint, M. L. (2000). The mass media and the prevention of child behaviour problems: The evaluation of a television series to promote positive outcomes for parents and their children. *Journal of Child Psychology and Psychiatry, 41,* 939–948.

Seligman, M. E. P., Rashid, T., & Parks, A. C. (2006). Positive psychotherapy. *American Psychologist, 61,* 774–788.

Seligman, M. E. P., Steen, T. A., Park, N., & Peterson, C. (2005). Positive psychology progress: Empirical validation of interventions. *American Psychologist, 60,* 410–421.

Sheldon, K. M. (2004). *Optimal human being: An integrated, cross-disciplinary approach.* Mahwah, NJ: Erlbaum.

Sheldon, K. M., & Lyubomirsky, S. (2004). Achieving sustainable new happiness: Prospects, practices, and prescriptions. In P. A. Linley & S. Joseph (Eds.), *Positive psychology in practice* (pp. 127–145). Hoboken, NJ: Wiley.

Sivanathan, N., Arnold, K. A., Turner, N., & Barling, J. (2004). Leading well: Transformational leadership and well-being. In P. A. Linley & S. Joseph (Eds.), *Positive psychology in practice* (pp. 241–255). Hoboken, NJ: Wiley.

Smith, D. (2006, June 4). Birth of a big Tory idea (News review). *The Sunday Times,* Section 4, p. 2.

Stairs, M. (2005). Work happy: Developing employee engagement to deliver competitive advantage. *Selection and Development Review, 21*(5), 7–11.

Taylor, E. (2001). Positive psychology and humanistic psychology: A reply to Seligman. *Journal of Humanistic Psychology, 41,* 13–29.

Taylor, S. E., & Sherman, D. K. (2004). Positive psychology and health psychology: A fruitful liaison. In P. A. Linley & S. Joseph (Eds.), *Positive psychology in practice* (pp. 305–319). Hoboken, NJ: Wiley.

Tedeschi, R. G., & Calhoun, L. G. (2004). A clinical approach to posttraumatic growth. In P. A. Linley & S. Joseph (Eds.), *Positive psychology in practice* (pp. 405–419). Hoboken, NJ: Wiley.

Veenhoven, R. (2004). Happiness as a public policy aim: The greatest happiness principle. In P. A. Linley & S. Joseph (Eds.), *Positive psychology in practice* (pp. 658–678). Hoboken, NJ: Wiley.

Wampold, B. E. (2001). *The great psychotherapy debate: Models, methods, and findings.* Mahwah, NJ: Lawrence Erlbaum.

Ward, T. (2002). Good lives and the rehabilitation of offenders: Promises and problems. *Aggression and Violent Behavior, 7,* 513–528.

Ward, T., & Gannon, T. A. (2006). Rehabilitation, etiology, and self-regulation: The comprehensive good lives model of treatment for sexual offenders. *Aggression and Violent Behavior, 11*(1), 77–94.

Ward, T., & Mann, R. (2004). Good lives and the rehabilitation of offenders: A positive approach to sex offender treatment. In P. A. Linley & S. Joseph (Eds.), *Positive psychology in practice* (pp. 598–616). Hoboken, NJ: Wiley.

Watkins, P. C. (2004). Gratitude and subjective well-being. In R. A. Emmons & M. E. McCullough (Eds.), *The psychology of gratitude* (pp. 167–192). New York: Oxford University Press.

Positive Psychology Within a Cultural Context

Jennifer Teramoto Pedrotti, Lisa M. Edwards, *and* Shane J. Lopez

Abstract

As our capacity for communication with nations across the globe increases through the advances of technology, our interactions with others with different worldviews also become more frequent. This exposure to diversity on so many levels requires a better understanding of the multiple contexts in which people from different cultural backgrounds live and the strengths they possess that help them experience well-being. In order to define the characteristics that may be viewed as strengths in different groups, we must make efforts to remember that cultural rules and norms often dictate what can be called a strength versus a weakness. It is imperative that we are able to recognize that strengths may look very different in different contexts and that these diverse manifestations may come from a variety of worldviews. More work must be done in order to develop a better understanding of the way that cultural context plays a role in the operationalization, manifestation, and measurement of strengths in diverse groups. The following chapter provides a history of the connections between culture and positive psychology and discusses current issues regarding the link between cultural context and various personal characteristics. Examples from culturally sensitive positive psychological theory and research are also given in order to illustrate how researchers are better exploring positive psychology within a cultural context.

Keywords: culture, strengths, positive psychology, context

> The good citizen is a "citizen of the world . . ." thinking about humanity as it is realized in the whole world is valuable for self-knowledge: we see ourselves and our customs more clearly when we see our own ways in relation to those of others. (Nussbaum, 1997, p. 59)

As nations become more and more diverse across the world, and as we interact more frequently through trade, collaboration, and advances of technology, it becomes necessary to include a discussion of cultural context in studying any human variant. Discussions of culture fit naturally within the field of psychology at large, and particularly well within the area of positive psychology and its concentration on strength as important to, and present within, the lives of all individuals. Positive psychologists have begun to recognize this importance over the last

few decades and have begun to attempt to build a community "where the word 'equality' can truly be applied to the abilities of all citizens to pursue their goals" (Lopez et al., 2000, p. 238). In discussing strengths and virtues, it becomes imperative to define these variables within the appropriate cultural context, however, and to view their diverse manifestations from a variety of viewpoints.

In this chapter, we examine a variety of frameworks that can be used to understand and foster healthy functioning. We will review a brief history of the way in which culture and positive psychology fit together, and cover current debates about the level of importance it plays today in the field. We also will describe exemplars of strengths-based theory and research that take cultural context into account.

Cross-Cultural Psychology and Multiculturalism: Definitional Clarity

Many authors have given definitions of the term "culture" but scholars often disagree in terms of which facets must be included in this definition (Kroeber & Kluckhohn, 1952; Triandis, 1996). In an attempt to bring some of these definitions together, Triandis defines culture as consisting of "*shared* elements that provide the standards for perceiving, believing, evaluating, communicating, and acting among those who share a language, a historic period and a geographic location" (p. 408). These elements are then passed down through the generations allowing for small adaptations as other factors shift and change, and may include "unexamined assumptions" (Triandis, 1996, p. 408) that are taken for granted as part of a cultural group's worldview.

It is also important in our treatment of this broad topic to distinguish between the concepts of "cross-cultural psychology" and "multiculturalism." While cross-cultural psychology can be defined as "comparisons across cultures or countries, as opposed to comparisons of groups within one society" (Mio, Barker-Hackett, & Tumambing, 2006, p. 294), multiculturalism refers more to the interaction among various cultures within one context: for example that which exists within the culturally diverse United States (Mio et al., 2006). At this point, it is important that studies investigating differences between members of different nations *and* studies examining strengths of those from different cultural groups within countries continue to be conducted. It is equally important that we not confuse the cross-cultural and multicultural aspects of research as investigation of different populations and issues occurs. For example, a study about Chinese individuals and their levels of happiness (as compared to the happiness of Koreans or Japanese) may not be relevant to the reported well-being of Chinese American individuals and to their attempts to lead flourishing lives within the United States. Though it is possible that Chinese heritage may influence the views of this group of Americans, we cannot assume that these two groups are the "same." As we make efforts in the larger field of psychology to give the appropriate attention to "the fourth force," as multiculturalism is often described (Pedersen, 1990), we must in turn recognize the importance of cultural context in discussing strengths and virtues in our teaching, research, and practice.

Culture-Free or Culturally Embedded? Perspectives on Strengths in a Cultural Context

In today's research within the field of positive psychology, two main views have emerged in terms of how to view strengths from a cultural perspective. Though both camps stipulate that all cultures have strengths, one camp proposes that some strengths exist universally across cultures, whereas the other believes that what is called a strength or a virtue is determined by cultural values and context (Snyder & Lopez, 2007).

Culture-Free Perspective

Culture-free proponents state that in research investigations across several cultural groups, universal attributes have been found that can be classified as strengths across each of these diverse cultures (Peterson & Seligman, 2004). The researchers from this viewpoint argue that the objectivity inherently present within the field of social science can "transcend particular cultures and politics and approach universality" (Seligman & Csikszentmihalyi, 2000, p. 5). To support their view, these researchers state that they have been able to identify 24 personal strengths and believe these to be present and viewed as beneficial in all cultures and societies (Snyder & Lopez, 2007). These 24 strengths are the basis of the Values in Action classification of strengths (VIA; Peterson & Seligman, 2004)—an assessment designed to determine personal strengths in individuals. One example is the concept of happiness; in the culture-free viewpoint it is accepted that all people want to be happy (Myers, 1992) and that in this way we are all similar despite our different cultural backgrounds. Finally, culture-free proponents also make the assumption that a researcher's own culture, and the values that accompany it, do not enter into his or her professional work. Instead, this camp of researchers believes that as scientists we should be able to move beyond these personal characteristics by using validated and reliable methods of research.

Culturally Embedded Perspective

Researchers in the other camp argue that strengths can only be viewed accurately from within a cultural context and disagree with the assertions that cultural values do not influence professional work (Constantine & Sue, 2006;

Snyder & Lopez, 2007). Though this group of researchers agrees that strengths can be found in all cultures and societies, they posit that strengths may manifest differently depending on cultural context. For example, a concept such as compassion may exist in both Eastern and Western cultures, but may be viewed differently or valued more strongly in one culture or another. A concept such as happiness may not be the goal of all individuals from all cultures (Ahuvia, 2001; Pedrotti, 2007; Snyder & Lopez, 2007) as others have previously thought. In addition, the behaviors associated with this strength in one culture may not be the same as behaviors associated with it in another culture (Sandage, Hill, & Vang, 2003). The American Psychological Association (2003) has encouraged researchers, practitioners, and academics to develop particular competencies in working with individuals from different backgrounds than their own, or in conducting research with these populations, and has in this way endorsed the culturally embedded view of psychology in general. This view can be applied directly to strengths within the culturally embedded positive psychology viewpoint.

Those operating from a multicultural framework state that human functioning cannot be considered in a vacuum; thus culture and context are a part of the everyday human experience. As such, many scholars have chosen to operate from a culturally embedded viewpoint as opposed to a culture-free stance (Pedrotti & Edwards, in press; Sue & Constantine, 2003). It seems clear that a decision regarding what types of characteristics and actions are deemed positive for a particular individual will be guided and influenced by the cultural environment and the salience of various cultural values in this individual's life (Christopher, 2005; Constantine & Sue, 2006; Leong & Wong, 2003; Pedrotti & Edwards, in press; Snyder & Lopez, 2007; Sue & Constantine, 2003).

Moving from Models of Inferiority to Models Recognizing Strengths in Diversity

Early psychological models of racial and ethnic differences examined distinctions from a deficiency perspective. Deviations from the characteristics of the dominant culture were viewed through an ethnocentric lens that interpreted any differences negatively and indicative of weakness or pathological functioning.

The "inferiority model" was an early paradigm, which was used to explain racial and ethnic differences that were based on a history of racist rationalization. This model (as described in a review by Kaplan & Sue, 1997) attributed variability in functioning to biological differences. The "natural inferiority" argument contended that if members of certain racial and ethnic groups were inherently incapable of advancing in society, then it was useless to attempt to adjust the existing environment to provide equal or favorable opportunities. Of course, the fundamental attribution errors inherent to this model were illuminated when biological explanations for racial and ethnic differences were not supported by human genetic research (see reviews of related research in Jackson, 1992; Zuckerman, 1990).

In the "deficit model" it was proposed that ethnic differences were the result of immutable environmental mechanisms, rather than biological factors (Allport, 1954). Prejudice was purported to be a key factor in creating stress that adversely affected minority group members' ability to excel (Sue, 1983). Higher rates of distress in racial and ethnic minorities were attributed to hostile environmental circumstances (Carter, 1994) that elicited inferior or self-destructive coping strategies. Although this model focused greater attention on the effects of prejudice and unequal social conditions, it still cast minority group members in the shadow of inferiority (Kaplan & Sue, 1997), and did not adequately address the complexity of individual differences.

The field of psychology moved away from deficiency or inferiority models to explanatory models recognizing the importance of culture. These models, known as "cultural pluralism" models, acknowledged that specific cultural experiences contribute to healthy functioning and engender unique strengths. Within these models it is proposed that racial or ethnic groups should remain distinct cultural entities, while simultaneously promoting larger common goals. For example, in the United States, a Latino/an American would be expected to retain his or her culture of origin, while still promoting traditional American values such as individualism. Cultural pluralism is not a reflection of the United States' outdated "melting pot" idea (i.e., ethnic groups combine with the dominant American culture to produce a universal American identity). Instead this model champions a "unity in diversity" position that, according to Kaplan and Sue (1997), succeeds more as an idealized description of cultural group relations than as an explanatory model for viewing and working with multicultural populations.

Pedersen (1996) proposed that, rather than characterizing cultural groups in rigid categories, there is a need to combine the many different "cultural identities" each person presents in distinct situations. The "cultural grid" is an open-ended model that matches social system variables (i.e., demographics, status, and affiliation) with patterns of cognitive variables (i.e., expectations and values). It was developed to help identify and describe the cultural aspects of a situation, assisting researchers and clinicians in the formation of hypotheses that include complex cultural perspectives, as well as intercultural differences and explanations. The result is an orientation that allows group variables to be combined with individual cognitive perspectives in a single framework for the purpose of anticipating an individual's "personal cultural" response to specific situations.

The emerging model in psychological perspectives that take culture into account establishes that each person has a unique culture, both independently and connected to the larger society (Chin, 1993). The "human diversity model" broadens the focus of research beyond merely racial, ethnic, and cultural issues to include varied groups and populations with unique differences, strengths, and histories. The umbrella of human diversity allows researchers to focus on patterns unique to specific groups or populations, and/or universal group processes. This expands conceptualization options unequivocally, allowing recognition of the importance of cultural variables upon functioning.

Chin (1993) made strides in the direction of understanding diversity by elucidating a "psychology of difference" to invoke changes in assumptive models to develop a more comprehensive framework, valuing differences and the context of culture. This requires that clinicians and researchers actively engage in (a) presenting a positive presentation of values, potentials, and lifestyle of the culturally different client; (b) shifting from a deficit hypothesis to a difference hypothesis; (c) recognizing that cultural differences exist; (d) examining frameworks that are biased against these differences; and (e) acknowledging that cultural behaviors are adaptive and have withstood the test of time. Thus, cultural behaviors should be examined for their inherent health-promoting values.

A full explanatory model that not only recognizes individual cultural strengths and weaknesses, but potentially sheds light on factors that would help maximize the strengths of all individuals, will require further expansion. It is our contention that such a model will flow out of a psychological science committed to studying what works (Lopez et al., 2002). Thus, we will cluster observations about

manifestations of psychological processes so that we can clarify what works for individuals and the broader community. This scientific review along with the recommendations offered will provide a framework for positive human diversity models.

Exemplar Research in Multiculturalism and Positive Psychology

In this section we highlight areas of research and studies that have increased our understanding of positive psychology in a cultural context, and which continue to inform our conceptualizations of optimal functioning among individuals of different backgrounds.

Specifically, we highlight exemplar investigations of strengths among racially and ethnically diverse individuals and countries, and we describe efforts to identify and elucidate culturally specific strengths.

A Multicultural Investigation of Optimism

Chang (1996a) investigated optimism and pessimism in Asian Americans and Caucasian Americans to emphasize the importance of testing whether constructs are equivalent across cultures. Chang examined the utility of optimism and pessimism in predicting problem-solving behaviors, depressive symptoms, general psychological symptoms, and physical symptoms. In general, the results of this study revealed that Asian Americans were significantly more pessimistic than Caucasian Americans (according to the Extended Life Orientation Test; Chang, Maydeu-Olivares, & D'Zurilla, 1997), but not significantly different in their level of optimism. These findings were corroborated when data from an independent sample were examined (Chang, 1996b). Chang notes that his findings might suggest that Asian Americans are generally more negative in their affectivity than Caucasian Americans; however, he found that there were no significant differences in reported depressive symptoms between the two groups. In fact, optimism was negatively correlated with both general psychological symptoms and physical symptoms for Asian Americans but not for Caucasian Americans. Also, problem solving was found to be negatively correlated with depressive symptoms for Asian Americans but unrelated for Caucasian Americans. Finally, it was revealed that while pessimism was negatively correlated with problem-solving behaviors for Caucasian Americans, it was positively correlated for Asian Americans.

Despite the utility of group difference multicultural research, Chang (1996a, 1996b) revealed the need to assess the equivalence of specific constructs across cultures rather than merely measure differences in levels of the construct. This need clearly can be understood if one were to suggest an intervention focused on reducing pessimism in the Asian American participants in Chang's study without knowing the psychological correlates of pessimism in Asian American samples. In this case, reducing pessimism levels for Asian Americans could conceivably lead to a decreased utilization of problem-solving behaviors. These constructs must be understood in a multicultural framework in order to interpret their magnitudes in terms of their utility for the cultural group. Only after they are placed in this framework, can the development of culturally appropriate interventions proceed in a responsible manner.

Cross-Cultural Investigations of Subjective Well-Being

In colloquial terms, subjective well-being (SWB) is known as "happiness," and it is only in the past 25 years that researchers have successfully studied this variable empirically (Diener, 2000). Diener, Suh, Lucas, & Smith (1999) have operationalized SWB as being comprised of both cognitive-judgmental and affective components. Life satisfaction, or a person's evaluation of the quality of his or her life (Diener, 1994), represents the cognitive-judgmental component of SWB. The affective components of SWB are positive (presence of) and negative (absence of) affect.

Researchers (Diener, Oishi, & Lucas, 2003; Diener & Suh, 2000; Suh & Oishi, 2004) have investigated factors associated with SWB at the individual and cultural levels, both within and across nations. At the individual level, SWB has been found to correlate with many factors, including good health, enough education, fit between personality and culture, personal growth, purpose in life, self-acceptance, sense of self-determination, having many acquaintances, and receiving social support from many close friends (Triandis, 2000).

A large body of research exists looking at differences in SWB across groups in nations (Deaton, 2008; Diener & Diener, 1995; Diener, Diener, & Diener, 1995; Howell & Howell, 2008; Suh, Diener, Oishi, & Triandis, 1998), providing clues to correlates of life satisfaction in diverse cultures. In a review of national differences in SWB, Diener and Suh (1999) reported that people living in individualistic cultures have higher levels of life satisfaction than those in collectivist cultures. While collectivist cultures give priority to the in-group and define the self in relational terms, individualist cultures, such as

the United States, encourage independence, attention to personal opinions and feelings, and autonomy. The distinctions between these cultural variables suggest that SWB may be more salient to individualists, and that attributes traditionally associated with well-being may not be as relevant for members of collectivist cultures (Suh, 2002).

Research looking at SWB across nations also has shown that individuals in wealthier nations report higher levels of life satisfaction (Deaton, 2008; Howell & Howell, 2008), though the processes by which national wealth and well-being are connected are unclear (Diener & Suh, 1999). Philosophically, material poverty should not preclude the attainment of well-being for individuals who are oppressed or disadvantaged and relegated to lower socioeconomic levels in society, and finding other approaches to happiness, including such avenues as spirituality, optimism, and flow, is essential for these individuals to reach their maximum potential (Csikszentmihalyi, 1999).

Diener (2000) noted that individuals from various societies might value happiness in different ways. Indeed, the importance placed on well-being by some cultural groups may provide clues to cross-national differences in levels of SWB, and may also reveal unique aspects of culture. For example, adults from the Pacific Rim of Asia placed less importance on SWB than respondents from Latin America, which is supported by findings that East Asians may be willing to sacrifice positive emotions in order to achieve important goals (Diener, Oishi, & Lucas, 2003). These nuances across cultures regarding the importance and predictors of SWB provide many potential areas for continued research.

Culture and the Construction of Self

Markus and Kitayama (1991) described a framework of how individuals perceive themselves in relation to their culture, and this framework has served as the basis for a number of studies about well-being. These authors suggest that one important difference among cultural groups has to do with the types of self-construals that individuals make, and that these self-construals can be "independent" or "interdependent." An independent self-construal is characteristic of Western cultures such as North America, which share a belief in independence of the self from others, and an emphasis on internal abilities, thoughts, and feelings. The independent self-construal reflects ideals of independence, self-actualization, and autonomy, and emphasizes socially disengaging behaviors such as asserting or protecting one's own rights (Kitayama, Markus, & Kurokawa, 2000, p. 95).

In contrast, an interdependent construal is understood in reference to the context or culture of which the self is related. The interdependent self-construal reflects a view on connectedness, meeting others' expectations, and facilitation of interpersonal harmony. This theory posits that those with interdependent self-construals will have an enhanced ability to blend in with the group and will likely engage in self-criticism more than self-enhancement (Heine & Lehaman, 1995; Kitayama et al., 2000). The interdependent self-construal has been associated with non-Western cultures, where socially engaging behavior, such as taking one's proper place in society, is emphasized (Kitayama et al., 2000, p. 95).

Self-construal theory has served as the basis for research about well-being, cognitions, and emotion among individuals from Western and non-Western backgrounds. As an example, Kitayama et al. (2000) studied Japanese and American college students and their reported emotional states in daily life. Consistent with theory, they found that "good feelings" were associated with interdependence of the self in Japan, but with independence of the self in the United States. These dimensions of self-construal have thus served as a useful framework for understanding different conceptions of the self in culture across groups.

Culturally Relevant Strengths

In addition to studying the applicability and relevance of certain positive constructs in the lives of culturally diverse individuals and groups, researchers also are beginning to explore strengths that emerge directly from a particular cultural background, such as ethnic identity, familism, bicultural competence, and religion/spirituality (Lopez et al., 2002; Sue & Constantine, 2003). The field has thus seen a shift from generalizing findings about strengths to all individuals, to investigating strengths within a culture or community that may be unique to that group. In many cases, this research has started with qualitative approaches that allow for the study of individual meanings within a social context (Morrow, Rakhsha, & Castaneda, 2001), but many of these areas incorporate both qualitative and quantitative methodology.

Specifically, researchers are investigating the role of cultural strengths as buffers against the negative effects of stress, and/or as variables that promote optimal functioning. For example, ethnic identity, or the meaning or importance of ethnicity to an individual at a given time (Phinney, 1992, 2003),

has been shown to buffer the negative effects of discrimination stressors in the lives of youth and adults of color (Lee, 2005; Romero & Roberts, 2003a; Yoo & Lee, 2005). Researchers are investigating how religion and spirituality may influence well-being in adults of diverse backgrounds (Blaine & Crocker, 1995; Sue & Constantine, 2003), and how familism plays a role in life satisfaction among Mexican American youth (Edwards & Lopez, 2006). Researchers are also beginning to understand how racial/ethnic minority youth and adults exhibit bicultural competence, or the ability to navigate cultural contexts (LaFromboise, Coleman, & Gerton, 1993; Romero & Roberts, 2003b).

It is not difficult to imagine numerous other culturally relevant strengths that can be studied by researchers. For example, Hays (2001, p. 106) provides a useful list of culturally related personal, interpersonal, and environmental strengths. Personal strengths include bilingual or multilingual skills, pride in one's culture, and wisdom. Interpersonal supports may be extended families, traditional celebrations and rituals, and cultural or group-specific networks. Finally, examples of environmental conditions that can serve as cultural strengths include cultural foods or a space for prayer or meditation. Research focused on some of these individual- and community-level resources will likely provide more culturally relevant conceptions of well-being (Sue & Constantine, 2003).

Considering Culture in Practice

Researchers, psychologists, and educators are beginning to integrate findings about culture and positive psychology and see how worldviews, cultural frameworks, and constructs come together in work with youth and adults. In this section we describe several strategies for conceptualization and assessment of strengths/weakness and optimal human functioning that emerge from recent theory and research about positive psychology in a cultural context. Simple strategies for identifying strengths of people and environments may prove useful for researchers, practitioners, managers, and educators who attempt to make individuals, organizations, and communities more positive.

It is important to understand the diverse strengths that people possess personally and in their environment. The four-front approach (Wright, 1991; Wright & Lopez, 2002) provides a useful framework for understanding strengths and deficiencies in an individual's life. As is evident by our field's history of overlooking strengths in people of diverse backgrounds, as well as ignoring the role of cultural context and environment (Lopez et al., 2006), there is a need to purposefully identify and acknowledge strengths and positive coping strategies of all individuals. With the four-front approach, clinicians gather information about (a) strengths and assets of the client, (b) deficiencies and undermining characteristics of the client, (c) resources and opportunities in the environment, and (d) deficiencies and destructive factors in the environment. This information can be gathered using multiple methods, including observation, discussion with the client, and standardized assessments, and clinicians are encouraged to integrate the material into the therapeutic process (Edwards, Holtz, & Green, 2007). This balanced approach allows for more holistic conceptualizations of client functioning and encourages both clinician and client to reflect on the context and its influence on the individual (Pedrotti, Edwards, & Lopez, 2008).

Understanding the multiple identities that each individual exemplifies is particularly important for appreciating their diversity. A useful framework for conceptualizing the diverse identities that individuals possess is the ADDRESSING model (Hays, 2001, 2007). Hays suggests that clients be described across the following dimensions: Age, Disability (acquired), Disability (developmental), Religion, Ethnicity, Sexual orientation, Socioeconomic status, Indigenous heritage, National origin, and Gender. Professionals who consider this variety of identities will likely have a broader, more complex understanding of an individual's background and potential strengths.

Future Directions for Studying Strengths and Well-Being in a Cultural Context

One area of investigation may be to look more closely at measures currently being used to determine personal strengths to determine if they have cultural equivalence for various groups. As discussed above, strengths may have different definitions in different cultures (conceptual equivalence), may not be measured as accurately by various instruments in different cultural groups (measurement equivalence), or may not be translated appropriately to ensure linguistic equivalence, or that the same meanings of terms and descriptions exists from group to group (Mio et al., 2006). For example, the VIA classification of strengths (VIA; Peterson & Seligman, 2004) is a widely used measure including 240 items on five-point Likert scales (Very Much Like Me to Very Much Unlike Me) and is designed to determine an individual's top five "signature strengths." It is unclear if the questions appropriately reflect strengths for all individuals. (Ongoing research by Nansook Park of University of Rhode Island and colleagues is examining cross-national and cross-cultural strengths data.) One item, for instance, states "As a leader, I treat everyone equally regardless of experience" and if answered toward the affirmative loads on the "Fairness" scale: denoted a positive quality (or "virtue") by this scale and defined as "Treating all people the same according to notions of fairness and justice; not letting personal feelings bias decisions about others" (Peterson & Seligman, 2004). This item may be interpreted very differently, however, by members from different cultural backgrounds. While an individualistic participant might value those who treat all equally, this equal treatment for all philosophy might not be a positive trait for members of cultures that have a more stratified social structure in which treating different social groups with the status they deserve is thought to be a positive action. Another item states, "I do not like to stand out in a crowd"; this item may be viewed very differently by Western individuals (with popular sayings such as "The squeaky wheel gets the grease") and Eastern individuals (with popular sayings such as "The nail that sticks out gets hammered down"). Thus, these examples must be considered in utilizing various scales to measure strengths and scales such as this and others must be tested to determine their level of equivalence between groups. Until then, such scales must be interpreted with much client feedback and with great caution so as not to pathologize various behaviors that may be culturally appropriate in some groups (Pedrotti & Edwards, in press).

Identifying these resources and seeing how they actually function to promote well-being can provide empirically based knowledge to be applied to prevention and intervention techniques. For example, findings about different ways in which youth and adults learn to be bicultural (LaFromboise et al., 1993) can inform efforts to improve well-being among immigrants in the United States. Mixed method studies that explore phenomena qualitatively and quantitatively may be particularly useful for gaining a more complex understanding of a particular topic while simultaneously testing theoretical models (Hanson, Creswell, Plano Clark, Petska, & Creswell, 2005). As such, studies that explore the cultural context and processes of biculturalism may shed light on how many racial/ethnic minorities promote well-being in everyday life.

As the practice of measuring strengths across domains and in various contexts (school, home, workplace, etc.) becomes more common, and the calls for national well-being indices begin to resonate, understanding how the best in people manifests within and across cultures becomes imperative. Culture counts; our research and practice must reflect that.

Questions

1. How can we continue to work toward developing positive interventions that take culture and context into account? What key points should be emphasized to ensure the success of culturally competent, strength-based interventions?

2. How might our empirical understanding of biculturalism and other cultural strengths increase? What methods can be employed to gather this information?

3. How can current strength-based measures be modified and revised to be more culturally inclusive of diverse groups?

References

Ahuvia, A. (2001). Well-being in cultures of choice: A cross-cultural perspective. *American Psychologist, 56,* 77–78.

Allport, G. W. (1954). *The nature of prejudice.* Reading, MA: Addison-Wesley.

American Psychological Association. (2002). Ethical principles of psychologists and code of conduct. *American Psychologist, 57,* 1060–1073.

Blaine, B., & Crocker, J. (1995). Religiousness, race, and psychological well-being: Exploring social psychological mediators. *Personality and Social Psychology Bulletin, 21,* 1031–1041.

Carter, J. H. (1994). Racism's impact on mental health. *Journal of the National Medical Association, 86,* 543–547.

Chang, E. C. (1996a). Cultural differences in optimism, pessimism, and coping: Predictors of subsequent adjustment in Asian American and Caucasian American college students. *Journal of Counseling Psychology, 43,* 113–123.

Chang, E. C. (1996b). Evidence for the cultural specificity of pessimism in Asians vs. Caucasians: A test of a general negativity hypothesis. *Personality and Individual Differences, 21,* 819–822.

Chang, E. C., Maydeu-Olivares, A., & D'Zurilla, T. J. (1997). Optimism and pessimism as partially independent constructs: Relationship to positive and negative affectivity and psychological well-being. *Personality and Individual Differences, 23,* 433–440.

Chin, J. L. (1993). Toward a psychology of difference: Psychotherapy for a culturally diverse population. In J. L. Chin, V. De La Cancela, & Y. M. Jenkins (Eds.), *Diversity in psychotherapy. The politics of race, ethnicity, and gender* (pp. 69–91). Westport, CN: Praeger.

Christopher, J. C. (2005). Situating positive psychology. *Naming and nurturing: The e-newsletter of the Positive Psychology Section of the American Psychological Association's Counseling Psychology Division, 17,* 2, 3–4.

Constantine, M., & Sue, D. W. (2006). Factors contributing to optimal human functioning of people of color in the United States. *The Counseling Psychologist, 34,* 228–244.

Csikszentmihalyi, M. (1999). If we are so rich, why aren't we happy? *American Psychologist, 54,* 821–827.

Deaton, A. (2008). Income, health, and well-being around the world: Evidence from the Gallup World Poll. *Journal of Economic Perspectives, 22,* 53–72.

Diener, E. (1994). Assessing subjective well-being: Progress and opportunities. *Social Indicators Research, 31,* 103–157.

Diener, E. (2000). Subjective well-being. *American Psychologist, 55,* 34–43.

Diener, E., & Diener, M. (1995). Cross-cultural correlates of life satisfaction and self-esteem. *Journal of Personality and Social Psychology, 68,* 653–663.

Diener, E., Diener, M., & Diener, C. (1995). Factors predicting the subjective well-being of nations. *Journal of Personality and Social Psychology, 69,* 851–864.

Diener, E., Oishi, S., & Lucas, R. (2003). Personality, culture, and subjective well-being: Emotional and cognitive evaluations of life. *Annual Review of Psychology, 54,* 403–425.

Diener, E., & Suh, E. M. (1999). National differences in subjective well-being. In D. Kahneman, E. Diener, & N. Schwarz (Eds.), *Well-being: The foundations of hedonic psychology.* New York: Russell Sage Foundation.

Diener, E., Suh, E. M., Lucas, R., & Smith, H. (1999). Subjective well-being: Three decades of progress. *Psychological Bulletin, 125,* 276–302.

Diener, E., & Suh, E. M. (2000). *Culture and subjective well-being.* Cambridge: The MIT Press.

Edwards, L. M., Holtz, C. A., & Green, M. B. (2007). Promoting strengths among culturally diverse youth in schools. *School Psychology Forum, 2,* 39–49.

Edwards, L. M., & Lopez, S. J. (2006). Perceived family support, acculturation, and life satisfaction in Mexican American youth: A mixed methods exploration. *Journal of Counseling Psychology, 53,* 279–287.

Jackson, F. L. C. (1992). Race and ethnicity as biological constructs. *Race and Ethnicity, 2,* 120–125.

Hanson, W. E., Creswell, J. W., Plano Clark, V. L., Petska, K. S., & Creswell, J. D. (2005). Mixed methods research designs in counseling psychology. *Journal of Counseling Psychology, 52,* 224–235.

Hays, P. A. (2001). *Addressing cultural complexities in practice.* Washington, DC: American Psychological Association.

Hays, P. A. (2007). *Addressing cultural complexities in practice: Assessment, diagnosis, and therapy* (2nd ed.). Washington, DC: American Psychological Association.

Heine, S. J., & Lehaman, D. R. (1995). Cultural variation in unrealistic optimism: Does the West feel more invulnerable than the East? *Journal of Personality and Social Psychology, 68,* 595–607.

Howell, R. T., & Howell, C. J. (2008). The relation of economic status to subjective well-being in developing countries: A meta-analysis. *Psychological Bulletin, 134,* 536–560.

Kaplan, J. S., & Sue, S. (1997). Ethnic psychology in the United States. In D. F. Halpern & A. E. Voiskounsky (Eds.), *States of mind. American and post-Soviet perspectives on contemporary issues in psychotherapy* (pp. 349–369). New York: Oxford University Press.

Kitayama, S., Markus, H. R., & Kurokawa, M. (2000). Culture, emotion, and well-being: Good feelings in Japan and the United States. *Cognition and Emotion, 14,* 93–124.

Kroeber, A. L., & Kluckhohn, C. (1952). *Culture: Critical review of concepts and definitions.* Cambridge, MA: Peabody Museum.

LaFromboise, T., Coleman, H., & Gerton, J. (1993). Psychological impact of biculturalism: Evidence and theory. *Psychological Bulletin, 114,* 395–412.

Lee, R. M. (2005). Resilience against discrimination: Ethnic identity and other-group orientation as protective factors for Korean Americans. *Journal of Counseling Psychology, 52,* 36–44.

Leong, F. T. L., & Wong, P. T. P. (2003). Optimal human functioning from cross-cultural perspectives: Cultural competence as an organizing framework. In W. B. Walsh (Ed.), *Counseling psychology and optimal human functioning* (pp. 123–150). Mahwah, NJ: Lawrence Erlbaum.

Lopez, S. J., Edwards, L. M., Pedrotti, J. T., Prosser, E. C., Walton, S. L., Spalitto, S. V., et al. (2006). Beyond the DSM: Assumptions, alternatives, and alterations. *Journal of Counseling and Development, 84,* 259–267.

Lopez, S. J., Gariglietti, K. P., McDermott, D., Sherwin, E. D., Floyd, R. K., Rand, K., et al. (2000). Hope for the evolution of diversity: On leveling the field of dreams. In C. R. Snyder (Ed.), *The handbook of hope* (pp. 220–240). San Diego, CA: Academic Press.

Lopez, S. J., Prosser, E. C., Edwards, L. M., Magyar-Moe, J., Neufeld, J., & Rasmussen, H. (2002). Putting positive psychology in a multicultural context. In C. R. Snyder & S. J. Lopez (Eds.), *The handbook of positive psychology* (pp. 700–714). New York: Oxford Press.

Markus, H. R., & Kitayama, S. (1991). Culture and the self: Implications for cognition, emotion, and motivation. *Psychological Review, 98,* 224–253.

Mio, J. S., Barker-Hackett, L., & Tumambing, J. D. (2006). *Multicultural psychology: Understanding our diverse communities.* Boston, MA: McGraw-Hill.

Morrow, S. L., Rakhsha, G., & Castaneda, C. L. (2001). Qualitative research methods for multicultural counseling. In J. G. Ponterotto, J. M. Casas, L. A. Suzuki, & C. M. Alexander (Eds.), *Handbook of multicultural counseling* (pp. 575–603). Thousand Oaks, CA: Sage.

Myers, D. G. (1992). *The pursuit of happiness.* New York: Avon Books.

Nussbaum, M. C. (1997). *Cultivating humanity.* Cambridge, MA: Harvard University Press.

Pedersen, P. B. (1990). The multicultural perspective as a fourth force in counseling. *Journal of Mental Health Counseling, 12,* 93–95.

Pedersen, P. B. (1996). Intercultural counseling: U. S. perspectives. In D. W. Sue, A. E. Ivey, & P. B. Pedersen, (Eds.), *A theory of multicultural counseling and therapy.* Pacific Grove, CA: Brooks/Cole Publishing Co.

Pedrotti, J. T. (2007). Eastern perspectives on positive psychology. In C. R. Snyder & S. J. Lopez (Eds.), *Positive psychology: The scientific and practical explorations of human strengths* (pp. 37–50). Thousand Oaks, CA: Sage.

Pedrotti, J. T., & Edwards, L. M. (in press). The intersection of positive psychology and multiculturalism in counseling. In J. Ponterotto, M. Casas, L. Suzuki, & C. Alexander (Eds.), *Handbook of multicultural counseling* (3rd ed.). Thousand Oaks, CA: Sage.

Pedrotti, J. T., Edwards, L. M., & Lopez, S. J. (2008). Working with multiracial clients in therapy: Bridging theory, research and practice. *Professional Psychology: Research and Practice, 39,* 192–201.

Peterson, C., & Seligman, M. E. P. (2004). *Character strengths and virtues: A handbook and classification.* Washington, DC: American Psychological Association.

Phinney, J. S. (1992). The multigroup ethnic identity measure: A new scale for use with diverse groups. *Journal of Adolescent Research, 7,* 156–176.

Phinney, J. S. (2003). Ethnic identity and acculturation. In K. M. Chun, P. Organista, & G. Marin (Eds.), *Acculturation: Advances in theory, measurement, and applied research* (pp. 63–81). Washington, DC: American Psychological Association.

Romero, A. J., & Roberts, R. E. (2003a). The impact of multiple dimensions of ethnic identity on discrimination and adolescent's self-esteem. *Journal of Applied Social Psychology, 33,* 2288–2305.

Romero, A. J., & Roberts, R. E. (2003b). Stress within a bicultural context for adolescents of Mexican descent. *Cultural Diversity and Ethnic Minority Psychology, 9*(2), 171–184.

Sandage, S., Hill, P. C., & Vang, H. C. (2003). Toward a multicultural positive psychology: Indigenous forgiveness and Hmong culture. *The Counseling Psychologist, 31,* 564–592.

Seligman, M. E. P., & Csikszentmihalyi, M. (2000). Positive psychology: An introduction. *American Psychologist, 55,* 5–14.

Snyder, C. R., & Lopez, S. J. (2007) *Positive psychology: The scientific and practical explorations of human strengths.* Thousand Oaks, CA: Sage.

Sue, D. W., & Constantine, M. G. (2003). Optimal human functioning in people of color in the United States. In B. W. Walsh (Ed.), *Counseling Psychology and optimal human functioning* (pp. 151–169). New Jersey: Lawrence Erlbaum.

Sue, S. (1983). Ethnic minority issues in psychology: A reexamination. *American Psychologist, 38,* 583–592.

Suh, E. (2002). Culture, identity consistency, and subjective well-being. *Journal of Personality and Social Psychology, 83,* 1378–1391.

Suh, E., Diener, E., Oishi, S., & Triandis, H. C. (1998). The shifting basis of life satisfaction judgments across cultures: Emotions versus norms. *Journal of Personality and Social Psychology, 74,* 482–493.

Suh, E., & Oishi, S. (2004). Culture and subjective well-being: Introduction to the special issue. *Journal of Happiness Studies, 5,* 219–222.

Triandis, H. C. (1996). The psychological measurement of cultural syndromes. *American Psychologist, 51,* 407–415.

Triandis, H. C. (2000). Cultural syndromes and subjective well-being. In E. Diener & E. M. Suh (Eds.), *Culture and subjective well-being* (pp. 13–36). Cambridge, MA: The MIT Press.

Wright, B. A. (1991). Labeling: The need for greater person–environment individuation. In C. R. Snyder & D. R. Forsyth (Eds.), *The handbook of social and clinical psychology* (pp. 469–487). New York: Pergamon.

Wright, B. A., & Lopez, S. J. (2002). Widening the diagnostic focus: A case for including human strengths and environmental resources. In C. R. Snyder & S. J. Lopez (Eds.), *Handbook of positive psychology* (pp. 26–44). New York: Oxford University Press.

Yoo, H. C., & Lee, R. M. (2005). Ethnic identity and approach-type coping as moderators of the racial discrimination/well-being relation in Asian Americans. *Journal of Counseling Psychology, 52,* 497–506.

Zuckerman, M. (1990). Some dubious premises in research and theory on racial differences: Scientific, social, and ethical issues. *American Psychologist, 45,* 1297–1303.

PART 2

Positive Psychology Perspectives on Human Behavior

Stopping the "Madness": Positive Psychology and Deconstructing the Illness Ideology and the DSM

James E. Maddux

Abstract

This chapter describes the traditional view of clinical psychology as a discipline and profession that is steeped in an "illness ideology." This illness ideology has roots in clinical psychology's early connections with psychiatry and medicine and limits clinical psychology to the study of what is worst and weakest about people rather than what is best and bravest about people. The historical, cultural, and professional causes of this ideology are discussed, with an emphasis on the social construction and deconstruction of the *Diagnostic and Statistical Manual of Mental Disorders* as the manifestation of the illness ideology that has the greatest detrimental influence on clinical psychology. The chapter also proposes that the illness ideology be replaced with a positive psychology ideology that emphasizes well-being, satisfaction, happiness, interpersonal skills, perseverance, talent, wisdom, personal responsibility, and what makes life worth living.

Keywords: diagnostic categories, *Diagnostic and Statistical Manual of Mental Disorders*, dimensional models of psychopathology, illness ideology, social construction of mental disorder

The ancient roots of the term "clinical psychology" continue to influence our thinking about the discipline long after these roots have been forgotten. "Clinic" derives from the Greek *klinike* or "medical practice at the sickbed," and "psychology" derives from the Greek *psyche*, meaning "soul" or "mind" (*Webster's New Collegiate Dictionary*, 1980). Although few clinical psychologists today literally practice at the bedsides of their patients, too many of its practitioners ("clinicians") and most of the public still view clinical psychology as a kind of "medical practice" for people with "sick souls" or "sick minds." Positive psychology provides a long overdue opportunity for changing clinical psychology's view of itself and the way it is viewed by the public.

How Clinical Psychology Became "Pathological"

The short history of clinical psychology suggests that change will not come easily. With the founding of the first "psychological clinic" in 1896 at the University of Pennsylvania, Lightner Witmer started the field of clinical psychology (Reisman, 1991).

Witmer and other early clinical psychologists worked primarily with children who had learning or school problems—not with "patients" with "mental disorders" (Reisman, 1991; Routh, 2000). Thus, they were influenced more by psychometric theory and its emphasis on careful measurement than by psychoanalytic theory and its emphasis on psychopathology. Following Freud's 1909 visit to Clark University, however, psychoanalysis and its derivatives soon came to dominate both psychiatry and clinical psychology (Korchin, 1976).

Other developments encouraged clinical psychologists to devote their attention to psychopathology and to view people through the lens of the disease model. First, although clinical psychologists' academic training took place in universities, their practitioner training primarily occurred in psychiatric hospitals and clinics (Morrow, 1946, cited in Routh, 2000) where they worked mostly as psychodiagnosticians under the direction of psychiatrists. Second, after World War II (1946), the Veterans Administration joined the American Psychological Association in developing training centers and standards for clinical psychologists. Because these early training centers were in VA hospitals, the training of clinical psychologists continued to occur primarily in psychiatric settings. Third, the National Institute of Mental Health was founded in 1947 and "thousands of psychologists found out that they could make a living treating mental illness" (Seligman & Csikszentmihalyi, 2000, p. 6).

By the 1950s, the practice of clinical psychology was characterized by four basic assumptions about its scope and about the nature of psychological adjustment and maladjustment (Barone, Maddux, & Snyder, 1997). First, clinical psychology is concerned with psychopathology—deviant, abnormal, and maladaptive conditions. Second, psychopathologies differ in kind, not just in degree, from everyday problems in living. Third, psychopathologies are analogous to biological or medical diseases and reside somewhere "inside" the individual. Fourth, the clinician's task is to identify (diagnose) the disorder (disease) inside the person (patient) and to prescribe an intervention (treatment) that will eliminate (cure) the internal disorder (disease).

Clinical Psychology Today: The Illness Ideology and the DSM

Once clinical psychology became "pathologized," there was no turning back. Albee (2000) suggests that "the uncritical acceptance of the medical model, the organic explanation of mental disorders, with psychiatric hegemony, medical concepts, and language" (p. 247) was the "fatal flaw" of the standards for clinical psychology training that were established at the 1950 Boulder Conference. He further suggests that this fatal flaw "has distorted and damaged the development of clinical psychology ever since" (p. 247). Indeed, things have changed little since 1950. The four basic assumptions described previously continue to serve as implicit guides to clinical psychologists' activities. In addition, the language of clinical psychology remains the language of medicine and pathology—the language of the *illness ideology*. Terms such as *symptom, disorder, pathology, illness, diagnosis, treatment, doctor, patient, clinic, clinical,* and *clinician* emphasize abnormality over normality, maladjustment over adjustment, and sickness over health. They promote the dichotomy between normal and abnormal behaviors, clinical and nonclinical problems, and clinical and nonclinical populations. They situate the locus of human adjustment and maladjustment inside the person rather than in the person's interactions with the environment or in sociocultural values and institutions. Finally, they portray people who seek help as passive victims of intrapsychic and biological forces beyond their direct control and who therefore should be the passive recipients of an expert's care.

This pathology- and medically oriented clinical psychology has outlived its usefulness. Decades ago, the field of medicine began to shift its emphasis from the treatment of illness to the prevention of illness and later from the prevention of illness to the enhancement of health. Health psychologists acknowledged this shift almost three decades ago (e.g., Stone, Cohen, & Adler, 1979) and have been influential ever since in facilitating it. Clinical psychology needs to make a similar shift or it will soon find itself struggling to establish a clear identity and a clear purpose among the mental health professions and disciplines.

Making this shift and building a "positive clinical psychology" will require abandoning the language of the illness ideology and adopting a language from positive psychology that offers a new way of thinking about human behavior. In this new language, ineffective patterns of behaviors, cognitions, and emotions are problems in living, not disorders or diseases. These problems in living are located not inside individuals but in the interactions between the individual and other people, including the culture at large. People seeking assistance in enhancing the quality of their lives are clients or students, not patients. Professionals who specialize in facilitating psychological health are teachers, counselors, consultants, coaches, or even social activists, not clinicians or doctors. Strategies and techniques for enhancing the quality of lives are educational, relational, social, and political interventions, not medical treatments. Finally, the facilities to which people will go for assistance with problems in living are centers, schools, or resorts, not clinics or hospitals. Such assistance might even take place in community centers, public and private schools, churches, and people's homes rather than in specialized facilities.

The major barrier to abandoning the language of the illness ideology and adopting the language of positive psychology is that the illness ideology is enshrined in the most powerful book in psychiatry and clinical psychology—the, *Diagnostic and Statistical Manual of Mental Disorders*—(DSM). First published in the early 1950s (American Psychiatric Association (APA), 1952) and now in either its fourth or sixth edition (APA, 2000) (depending on whether or not one counts the revisions of the third and fourth editions as "editions"), the DSM provides the organizational structure for almost every textbook and course on abnormal psychology and psychopathology for undergraduate and graduate students, as well as almost every professional book on the assessment and treatment of psychological problems. So revered is the DSM that in many clinical programs (including mine until recently) students are required to memorize parts of it line by line, as if it were a book of mathematical formulas or a sacred text.

Although most of the previously noted assumptions of the illness ideology are explicitly disavowed in the DSM-IV's introduction (APA, 1994), practically every word thereafter is *inconsistent* with this disavowal. As long as clinical psychology worships at this icon of the illness ideology, change toward a more positive clinical psychology will be impossible. What is needed, therefore, is a kind of iconoclasm, and the icon in need of shattering is the DSM. The goal is not the DSM's destruction but its *deconstruction*—an examination of the social forces that serve as its power base and of the implicit intellectual assumptions that provide it with a pseudo-scientific legitimacy. This deconstruction will be the first stage of a reconstruction of our view of human behavior and problems in living.

The Social Deconstruction of the DSM

As with all icons, powerful sociocultural, political, professional, and economic forces built the illness ideology and the DSM and continue to sustain them. Thus, to begin this iconoclasm, we must realize that our conceptions of psychological normality and abnormality, along with our specific diagnostic labels and categories, are not facts about people but *social constructions*—abstract concepts that were developed collaboratively over time through the implicit and explicit collaborations of theorists, researchers, professionals, consumers, and the culture in which all are embedded and that represent a shared view of the world. For this reason, we cannot say that "mental disorder" and the numerous diagnostic categories of the DSM were "discovered" in the same manner that an archeologist discovers a buried artifact or a medical researcher discovers a virus. Instead, they were "invented." This is not to say that they are "myths" (Szasz, 1974) or that the distress of people who are labeled as mentally disordered is not real. Instead, it is to say that these disorders do not "exist" and "have properties" in the same manner that artifacts and viruses do. For these reasons, a taxonomy of mental disorders such

as the DSM "does not simply describe and classify characteristics of groups of individuals, but ... actively 'constructs' a version of both normal and abnormal" (Parker, Georgaca, Harper, McLaughlin, & Stowell-Smith, 1995, p. 93).

The illness ideology's conception of *mental disorder* and the various specific DSM categories of mental disorders are not mappings of psychological facts about people. Instead, they are social artifacts that serve the same sociocultural goals as our constructions of race, gender, social class, and sexual orientation—that of maintaining and expanding the power of certain individuals and institutions and maintaining social order, as defined by those in power (Beall, 1993; Parker et al., 1995; Rosenblum & Travis, 1996). As are these other social constructions, our concepts of psychological normality and abnormality are tied ultimately to social values—in particular, the values of society's most powerful individuals, groups, and institutions—and the contextual rules for behavior derived from these values (Parker et al., 1995; Rosenblum & Travis, 1996). Thus, the ongoing debate over the definition of *mental disorder* and who gets to define it and the continual revisions of the DSM comprise not a search for truth but a struggle for the personal, political, and economic power that derives from the authority to determine what and whom society views as normal and abnormal.

Medical philosopher Lawrie Resnek (1987) has demonstrated that even our definition of physical disease "is a normative or evaluative concept" (p. 211) because to call a condition a disease "is to judge that the person with that condition is less able to lead a good or worthwhile life" (p. 211). If this is true of physical disease, it is certainly also true of psychological "disease." Because they are social constructions that serve sociocultural goals and values, our notions of psychological normality–abnormality and health–illness are linked to our assumptions about how people should live their lives and about what makes life worth living. This truth is illustrated clearly in the APA's 1952 decision to include homosexuality in the first edition of the DSM and its 1973 decision to revoke its disease status (Kutchins & Kirk, 1997; Shorter, 1997; Wilson, 1993). This issue was also in the forefront of the controversies over posttraumatic stress disorder, paraphilic rapism, and masochistic personality disorder (Kutchins & Kirk, 1997), as well as caffeine dependence, sexual compulsivity, low-intensity orgasm, sibling rivalry, self-defeating personality, jet lag, pathological spending, and impaired sleep-related painful erections, all of which were proposed for inclusion in DSM-IV (Widiger & Trull, 1991). Therefore, Widiger and Sankis (2000) somewhat missed the mark when they stated that "social and political concerns might be hindering a recognition of a more realistic and accurate estimate of the *true rate* of psychopathology" (p. 379, emphasis added). A "true rate" of psychopathology does not exist apart from the social and political concerns involved in the construction of the definition of psychopathology in general and specific psychopathologies in particular.

With each revision, the DSM has had more and more to say about how people should live their lives and about what makes life worth living. The number of pages increased from 86 in 1952 to almost 900 in 1994, and the number of mental disorders increased from 106 to 297. As the boundaries of "mental disorder" have expanded with each DSM revision, life has become increasingly pathologized, and the sheer numbers of people with diagnosable mental disorders has continued to grow. The framers of the DSM have been gradually pathologizing almost every conceivable human problem in living.

Consider some of the "mental disorders" found in the DSM-IV. Premenstrual emotional change is Premenstrual Dysphoric Disorder. Cigarette smokers have Nicotine Dependence. If you drink large quantities of coffee, you may develop Caffeine Intoxication or Caffeine-Induced Sleep Disorder. Being drunk is Alcohol Intoxication. If you have "a preoccupation with a defect in appearance" that causes "significant distress or impairment in . . . functioning" (p. 466), you have a Body Dysmorphic Disorder. A child whose academic achievement is "substantially below that expected for age, schooling, and level of intelligence" (p. 46) has a Learning Disorder. Toddlers who throw tantrums have Oppositional Defiant Disorder. Even Sibling Relational Problems, the bane of parents everywhere, have found a place in *DSM-IV,* although not yet as an official mental disorder.

Human sexual behavior comes in such variety that determining what is "normal" and "adaptive" is a daunting task. Nonetheless, sexual behavior has been ripe for pathologization in the DSM-IV. Not wanting sex often enough is Hypoactive Sexual Desire Disorder. Not wanting sex at all is Sexual Aversion Disorder. Having sex but not having orgasms or having them too late or too soon is considered an Orgasmic Disorder. Failure (for men) to maintain "an adequate erection . . . that causes marked distress or interpersonal difficulty" (p. 504) is a Male Erectile Disorder. Failure (for women) to attain or maintain

"an adequate lubrication or swelling response of sexual excitement" (p. 502) accompanied by distress is Female Sexual Arousal Disorder. Excessive masturbation used to be considered a sign of a mental disorder (Gilman, 1988). Perhaps in DSM-V not masturbating at all, if accompanied by "marked distress or interpersonal difficulty," will become a mental disorder (Autoerotic Aversion Disorder).

Over the past several years, we have witnessed numerous media reports of epidemics of internet addiction and road rage. Discussions of these new "disorders" have turned up at scientific meetings and are likely to find a home in the DSM-V if the media and mental health professions continue to collaborate in their construction, and if treating them and writing books about them becomes lucrative.

The trend is clear. First, we see a pattern of behaving, thinking, feeling, or desiring that deviates from some fictional social norm or ideal; or we identify a common complaint that, as expected, is displayed with greater frequency or severity by some people than others; or we decide that a certain behavior is undesirable, inconvenient, or disruptive. We then give the pattern a medical-sounding name, preferably of Greek or Latin origin, and capitalize it.

Eventually, the new term may be reduced to an acronym, such as OCD (Obsessive-Compulsive Disorder), ADHD (Attention-Deficit/Hyperactive Disorder), and BDD (Body Dysmorphic Disorder). The new disorder then becomes viewed as a disease-like entity. As news about "it" spreads, people begin thinking they have "it"; medical and mental health professionals begin diagnosing and treating "it"; and clinicians and clients begin demanding that health insurance policies cover the "treatment" of "it." Alan Ross (1980) referred to this process as the *reification* of the disorder. In light of the awe with which mental health professionals view their diagnostic terms and the power that such terms exert over both professional and client, a better term for this process may be the *reification* of the disorder.

We are fast approaching the point at which everything that human beings think, feel, do, and desire that is not perfectly logical, adaptive, or efficient will be labeled a mental disorder. It is time to stop the "madness."

The Intellectual Deconstruction of the DSM: An Examination of Faulty Assumptions

In addition to its sociocultural foundation, the DSM has an intellectual foundation. This foundation consists of a number of assumptions about human behavior and how to understand it that do not hold up very well to logical scrutiny.

Faulty Assumption I: Categories Are Facts about the World

The basic assumption of the DSM is that a system of socially constructed categories is a set of facts about the world. At issue here is not the Reliability of classifications in general or of the DSM in particular—that is, the degree to which we can define categories in a way that leads to consensus in the assignment of things to categories. Instead, the issue is the validity of such categories. The validity of a classification system refers not to the extent to which it provides an accurate "map" of reality but, instead, to the extent to which it serves the goals of those who developed it. For this reason, all systems of classification are arbitrary. This is not to say that all classifications are capricious or thoughtless, but that, they are constructed to serve the goals of those who develop them. Philosopher Alan Watts (1951) once asked whether it is better to classify rabbits according to the characteristics of their fur or according to the characteristics of their meat. He answered by saying that it depends on whether you are a furrier or a butcher. How you choose to classify rabbits depends on what you want to *do* with them. Neither classification system is more valid or "true" than the other. We can say the same of all classification systems. They are not "valid" (true) or "invalid" (false); they are only more or less useful. Thus, we can evaluate the validity of a system of representing reality only by evaluating its utility, and its utility can be evaluated only in reference to a set of chosen goals, which in turn are based on values. Therefore, instead of asking "How true is this system of classification?" we have to ask, "What do we value? What goals do we want to accomplish? How well does this system help us accomplish them?" Thus, we cannot talk about "diagnostic validity *and* utility" (Nathan & Langenbucher, 1999, p. 88, emphasis added) as if they are different constructs. They are one and the same.

Too often we mistakenly believe that "making sense out of life is impossible unless the flow of events can somehow be fitted into a framework of rigid forms" (Watts, 1951, pp. 3–44). Unfortunately, once we construct our categories, we see them as representing "things," and we confuse them with the real world. We come to believe that, as Gregory Kimble (1995) said, "If there is a word for it, there must be a corresponding item of reality. If there are two words, there must be two realities and they must be different" (p. 70). What we fail to realize is that, as Alan Watts (1966) said, "However much we divide, count, sort, or classify [the world] into particular things and events, this is no more than a way of thinking about the world. It is never *actually* divided" (p. 54). Also, as a result of confusing our categories with the real world, we also too often confuse classifying with understanding, and labeling with explaining (Ross, 1980; Watts, 1951). We forget that agreeing on the names of things does not mean that we understand and can explain the things named.

Faulty Assumption II: We Can Distinguish between Normal and Abnormal

The second faulty assumption of the DSM is that we can establish clear criteria for distinguishing between normal and abnormal thinking, feeling, and behaving and between healthy and unhealthy psychological functioning. Although it is stated in the DSM-IV that "there is no assumption that each category of mental disorder is a completely discrete entity with absolute boundaries dividing it from other mental disorders or from no mental disorder" (APA, 1994, p. xxii), the subsequent 800 pages that are devoted to descriptions of categories undermine the credibility of this claim.

This *discontinuity* assumption is mistaken in three ways. First, it runs counter to an assumption made by virtually every major personality theorist—that adaptive and maladaptive psychological phenomena differ not in kind but in degree and that continuity exists between normal and abnormal and between adaptive and maladaptive functioning. Even the psychoanalytic approaches, the most pathologizing of all theories, assume that psychopathology is characterized not by the presence of underlying unconscious conflicts and defense mechanisms, but by the degree to which such conflicts and defenses interfere with functioning in everyday life (Brenner, 1973).

Second, it runs counter to yet another basic assumption made by most contemporary theorists and researchers in personality, social, and clinical psychology—that the processes by which maladaptive behavior is acquired and maintained are the same as those that explain the acquisition and maintenance of adaptive behavior. No one has yet demonstrated that the psychological processes that explain the problems of people who present themselves to mental health professionals ("clinical populations") and those who do not ("nonclinical populations") differ from each other. There are no reasons to assume that behaviors judged to be "normal" and behaviors that violate social norms and are judged to be "pathological" are governed by different processes (Leary & Maddux, 1987).

Third, and most importantly, the discontinuity assumption runs counter to the growing body of empirical evidence that normality and abnormality, as well as effective and ineffective psychological functioning, lie along a continuum, and that so-called psychological disorders are simply extreme variants of normal psychological phenomena and ordinary problems in living (Krueger, Watson, & Barlow, 2005, chap. 9; Widiger & Samuel, 2005). This *dimensional approach* is concerned not with classifying people or disorders but with identifying and measuring individual differences in psychological phenomena such as emotion, mood, intelligence, and personal styles (e.g., Lubinski, 2000). Great differences among individuals on the dimensions of interest are expected, such as the differences we find on formal tests of intelligence. As with intelligence, any divisions made between normality and abnormality are socially constructed for convenience or efficiency but are not to be viewed as indicative of true discontinuity among "types" of phenomena or "types" of people. Also, statistical deviation is not viewed as necessarily pathological, although extreme variants on either end of a dimension (e.g., introversion–extraversion, neuroticism, intelligence) may be maladaptive if they signify inflexibility in functioning.

Faulty Assumption III: Categories Facilitate Clinical Judgment

Proponents of diagnostic categories often argue that such categories facilitate understanding patients or clients and are an aid to clinical judgment and decision making. In many ways, however, diagnostic categories can cloud professional judgments by helping set into motion a "vicious cycle" in which error and bias are encouraged and maintained despite the professional's good intentions.

This cycle begins with four beliefs that the professional brings to the initial encounter with a client. The first is that there is a dichotomy between normal and abnormal psychological functioning. The second is that distinct syndromes called *mental disorders* actually exist and have real properties. The third is that the people who come to "clinics" must have a "clinical problem" and that problem must fit one of these syndromes. The fourth is that he or she is an accurate observer

of others, an unbiased and objective gatherer and processor of information about others, and an objective decision maker.

These beliefs lead to a biased and error-prone style of interacting with, thinking about, and gathering information about the client. Especially pernicious is a bias toward confirmatory hypothesis testing in which the professional seeks information supportive of the assumption that the client has a clinically significant dysfunction or mental disorder. The use of this strategy increases the probability of error and bias in perception and judgment. Furthermore, the vagueness of the criteria for normality and abnormality (or health and pathology) and for specific mental disorders provides ample opportunity for the commission of the errors and biases in perception and judgment that have been demonstrated by research on decision making under uncertainty (Dawes, 1998). Finally, because the DSM describes only categories of disordered or unhealthy functioning, it offers little encouragement to search for evidence of healthy functioning. Thus, a fundamental negative bias is likely to develop in which the professional pays close attention to evidence of pathology and ignores evidence of health (chap. 8).

These errors and biases lead the professional to gather information about and form impressions of the client that, although not highly accurate, are consistent with the professional's hypotheses. Accordingly, the professional gains a false sense of confidence in her social perception and judgment abilities. In turn, she comes to believe that she knows pathology when she sees it and that people indeed do fit the categories described by the DSM. Because clients readily agree with the professional's assessments and pronouncements (Snyder, Shenkel, & Lowery, 1977), the professional's confidence is bolstered by this "evidence" that she is correct.

Because of this false feedback and subsequent false sense of accuracy and confidence, over time the professional becomes increasingly confident and yet increasingly error-prone, as suggested by research showing a positive correlation between professional experience and error and bias in perceiving and thinking about clients (e.g., Garb, 1998). Thus, the professional plunges confidently into the next clinical encounter even more likely to repeat the error-prone process.

Faulty Assumption IV: Categories Facilitate Intervention

The ultimate goal of a system for organizing and understanding human behavior and its "disorders" is the development of methods for relieving suffering and enhancing well-being. Therefore, to determine the validity of a system for classifying "mental disorders," we need to ask not "How true is it?" but "How well does it facilitate the design of effective ways to help people live more satisfying lives?"

Because effective interventions must be guided by theories and concepts, designing effective interventions requires a conceptualization of human functioning that is firmly grounded in a theory of how patterns of behavior, thought, and emotion develop and how they are maintained despite their maladaptiveness. By design, however, the DSM is purely descriptive and atheoretical. Because it is atheoretical, it does not deal with the etiology of the disorders it describes and therefore cannot provide theory-based conceptualizations of the development and maintenance of adjustment problems that might lead to intervention strategies. Because a system of descriptive categories includes only lists of generic problematic behaviors ("symptoms"), it may suggest somewhat vaguely *what* needs to be changed, but it cannot provide guidelines for *how* to facilitate change.

Beyond the Illness Ideology and the DSM

The deconstruction of the illness ideology and the DSM leaves us with the question, "But what will replace them?" Positive psychology offers a replacement for the illness ideology. Positive psychology emphasizes well-being, satisfaction, happiness, interpersonal skills, perseverance, talent, wisdom, and personal responsibility. It is concerned with understanding what makes life worth living, with helping people become more self-organized and self-directed, and with recognizing that "people and experiences are embedded in a social context" (Seligman & Csikszentmihalyi, 2000, p. 8). Unlike the illness ideology, which is grounded in certain social values that implicitly and explicitly tell people how to live their lives, positive psychology "would inform individuals' choices along the course of their lives, but would take no stand on the desirability of life courses" (Seligman & Csikszentmihalyi, 2000, p. 12).

What will replace the DSM is difficult to predict. An attractive alternative is the recent Values in Action (VIA) classification of strengths (Peterson & Seligman, 2004, chap. 4). The goal of the VIA classification is to identify and define *character strengths*. A character strength is defined as "a disposition to act, desire, and feel that involves the exercise of judgment and leads to a recognizable human excellence or instance of human flourishing"

(Yearly, 1990, p. 13). Among the many character strengths that have received attention from researchers over the past several years are curiosity (chap. 34), forgiveness (chap. 40), creativity (chap. 24), hope (chap. 30), social and emotional intelligence (chap. 22), and personal control (chaps. 25 and 31). As research on these and other positive human attributes makes its way into the curriculum of clinical psychology graduate programs, a greater consideration of people's assets and strengths will eventually find its way into the practice of clinical psychology (see chap. 5).

Three other alternative approaches to the DSM have been on the scene for some time. The dimensional approach noted previously is concerned with describing and measuring continua of individual differences rather than constructing categories. It assumes that people will display considerable statistical deviation in behavioral, cognitive, and emotional phenomena and does not assume that such deviation is, per se, maladaptive or pathological.

Interpersonal approaches begin with the assumption that "maladjusted behavior resides in a person's recurrent transactions with others . . . [and] results from . . . an individual's failure to attend to and correct the self-defeating, interpersonally unsuccessful aspects of his or her interpersonal acts" (Kiesler, 1991, pp. 443–444). These approaches focus not on the behavior of individuals but on the behavior of individuals interacting in a system with others (Benjamin, 1996; Kiesler, 1991).

Case formulation approaches posit that the most useful way to understand psychological and behavioral problems is not to assign people and their problems to categories but to formulate hypotheses "about the causes, precipitants, and maintaining influences of a person's psychological, interpersonal, and behavioral problems" (Eells, 1997, p. 1). Because case formulations are guided by theory, they are the antithesis of DSM's atheoretical, descriptive approach. Case formulation has been given the most attention by behavioral and cognitive theorists, but it also has advocates from psychoanalytic, time-limited psychodynamic, interpersonal, and experiential perspectives (Eells, 1997). Despite their diversity, case formulation approaches share an avoidance of diagnostic categories and labels; a concern with understanding not what the person *is* or what the person *has* but with what the person does, thinks, and feels; and an emphasis on developing theory-guided interventions tailored to the individual's specific needs and goals.

Despite their differences, these three approaches share a rejection of the illness ideology's emphasis on pathology, its assumption that pathology resides inside of people, and its rigid system of categorization and classification. Also, because they set the stage for an examination of both adaptive and maladaptive functioning, they share a basic compatibility with the principles and goals of positive psychology.

Conclusion

The illness ideology has outlived its usefulness. The positive psychology movement offers a rare opportunity for a reorientation and reconstruction of our views of clinical psychology through a reconstruction of our views of psychological health and human adaptation and adjustment. We need a clinical psychology that is grounded not in the illness ideology but in a positive psychology ideology that rejects (a) the categorization and pathologization of humans and human experience, (b) the assumption that so-called mental disorders exist in individuals rather than in the relationships between the individual and other individuals and the culture at large, and (c) the notion that understanding what is worst and weakest about us is more important than understanding what is best and bravest.

This change in ideology must begin with a change in the language we use to talk about human behavior and the problems that human beings experience in navigating the courses of their lives—a change from the language of the illness ideology to the language of positive psychology. Because the language of the illness ideology is enshrined in the DSM, this reconstruction must begin with a deconstruction of this icon of the illness ideology.

The illness ideology and the DSM were constructed to serve and continue to serve the social, political, and economic goals of those who shared in their construction. They are sustained not only by the individuals and institutions whose goals they serve, but also by an implicit set of logically flawed and empirically unsupported assumptions about how best to understand human behavior—both the adaptive and the maladaptive. We need to make clinical psychologists more aware of both the socially constructed nature of the assumptions about psychological disorders that guide their professional activities and the logical and empirical weaknesses of these assumptions. We need to question the often unquestioned sociocultural forces and philosophical assumptions that provide the foundation for the illness ideology, the DSM, and our "distorted and damaged" clinical psychology. Finally, we need to encourage our students, the public, and our policy makers to do the same.

Future Questions

1. Will mental health professionals ever agree on a definition of "mental disorder," "psychopathology," and related terms?

2. Will dimensional views of psychological normality and abnormality eventually replace the current categorical system?

3. What are the most important ways in which positive psychology can have an impact on theory, research, and professional practice in clinical psychology?

References

Albee, G. W. (2000). The Boulder model's fatal flaw. *American Psychologist, 55,* 247–248.

American Psychiatric Association. (1952). *Diagnostic and statistical manual of mental disorders.* Washington, DC: American Psychiatric Association.

American Psychiatric Association. (1994). *Diagnostic and statistical manual of mental disorders* (4th ed.). Washington, DC: American Psychiatric Association.

American Psychiatric Association. (2000). *Diagnostic and statistical manual of mental disorders* (4th ed., Text rev.). Washington, DC: American Psychiatric Association.

Barone, D. F., Maddux, J. E., & Snyder, C. R. (1997). *Social cognitive psychology: History and current domains.* New York: Plenum.

Beall, A. E. (1993). A social constructionist view of gender. In A. E. Beall & R. J. Sternberg (Eds.), *The psychology of gender* (pp. 127–147). New York: Guilford.

Benjamin, L. S. (1996). *Interpersonal diagnosis and treatment of personality disorders* (2nd ed.). New York: Guilford.

Brenner, C. (1973). *An elementary textbook of psychoanalysis.* New York: Anchor Books.

Dawes, R. M. (1998). Behavioral decision-making and judgment. In D. T. Gilbert, S. T. Fiske, & G. Lindzey (Eds.), *Handbook of social psychology* (Vol. 1, pp. 497–548). New York: McGraw-Hill.

Eells, T. D. (1997). Psychotherapy case formulation: History and current status. In T. D. Eells (Ed.), *Handbook of psychotherapy case formulation* (pp. 1–25). New York: Guilford.

Garb, H. N. (1998). *Studying the clinician: Judgment research and psychological assessment.* Washington, DC: American Psychological Association.

Gilman, S. L. (1988). *Disease and representation.* Ithaca, NY: Cornell University Press.

Kiesler, D. J. (1991). Interpersonal methods of assessment and diagnosis. In C. R. Snyder & D. R. Forsyth (Eds.), *Handbook of social and clinical psychology* (pp. 438–468). New York: Pergamon.

Kimble, G. (1995). Psychology stumbling down the road to hell. *The General Psychologist, 31,* 66–71.

Korchin, S. J. (1976). *Modern clinical psychology.* New York: Basic Books.

Krueger, R. F., Watson, D., & Barlow, D. H. (2005). Introduction to the special section: Toward a dimensionally based taxonomy of psychopathology. *Journal of Abnormal Psychology, 114*, 491–493.

Kutchins, H., & Kirk, S. A. (1997). *Making us crazy: DSM: The psychiatric bible and the creation of mental disorders.* New York: Free Press.

Leary, M. R., & Maddux, J. E. (1987). Toward a viable interface between social and clinical/counseling psychology. *American Psychologist, 42*, 904–911.

Lubinski, D. (2000). Scientific and social significance of assessing individual differences: "Sinking shafts at a few critical points." *Annual Review of Psychology, 51*, 405–444.

Morrow, W. R. (1946). The development of psychological internship training. *Journal of Consulting Psychology, 10*, 165–183.

Nathan, P. E., & Langenbucher, J. W. (1999). Psychopathology: Description and classification. *Annual Review of Psychology, 50*, 79–107.

Parker, I., Georgaca, E., Harper, D., McLaughlin, T., & Stowell-Smith, M. (1995). *Deconstructing psychopathology.* London: Sage.

Peterson, C., & Seligman, M. E. P. (2004). *Character strengths and virtues: A classification and handbook.* New York: Oxford University Press/Washington, DC: American Psychological Association.

Reisman, J. M. (1991). *A history of clinical psychology.* New York: Hemisphere.

Resnek, L. (1987). *The nature of disease.* New York: Routledge & Kegan Paul.

Rosenblum, K. E., & Travis, T. C. (Eds.). (1996). *The meaning of difference: American constructions of race, sex and gender, social class, and sexual orientation.* New York: McGraw-Hill.

Ross, A. O. (1980). *Psychological disorders of children: A behavioral approach to theory, research, and therapy* (2nd ed.). New York: McGraw-Hill.

Routh, D. K. (2000). Clinical psychology training: A history of ideas and practices prior to 1946. *American Psychologist, 55*, 236–240.

Seligman, M. E. P., & Csikszentmihalyi, M. (2000). Positive psychology: An introduction. *American Psychologist, 55*, 5–14.

Shorter, E. (1997). *A history of psychiatry.* New York: Wiley.

Snyder, C. R., Shenkel, R. J., & Lowery, C. (1977). Acceptance of personality interpretations: The "Barnum effect" and beyond. *Journal of Consulting and Clinical Psychology, 45*, 104–114.

Stone, G. C., Cohen, F., & Adler, N. E. (Eds.). (1979). *Health psychology: A handbook.* San Francisco: Jossey-Bass.

Szasz, T. J. (1974). *The myth of mental illness.* New York: Harper & Row.

Watts, A. (1951). *The wisdom of insecurity.* New York: Vintage Books.

Watts, A. (1966). *The book: On the taboo against knowing who you are.* New York: Vintage Books.

Webster's New Collegiate Dictionary. (1980). Springfield, MA: G. & C. Merriam Company.

Widiger, T. A., & Samuel, D. B. (2005). Diagnostic categories or dimensions? A question for the diagnostic and statistical manual of mental disorders—fifth edition. *Journal of Abnormal Psychology, 114*, 494–504.

Widiger, T. A., & Sankis, L. M. (2000). Adult psychopathology: Issues and controversies. *Annual Review of Psychology, 51*, 377–404.

Widiger, T. A., & Trull, T. J. (1991). Diagnosis and clinical assessment. *Annual Review of Psychology, 42*, 109–134.

Wilson, M. (1993). DSM-III and the transformation of American psychiatry: A history. *American Journal of Psychiatry, 150*, 399–410.

Yearly, L. H. (1990). *Mencias and Aquinus: Theories of virtue and conceptions of courage.* Albany, NY: State University of New York Press.

Widening the Diagnostic Focus: A Case for Including Human Strengths and Environmental Resources

Beatrice A. Wright *and* Shane J. Lopez

Abstract

In positive psychology, we must challenge a common error of professional psychology, today: making diagnostic, treatment, and policy decisions primarily on deficiencies of the person instead of giving serious consideration to "deficits" and "strengths" of both person and environment. This mission may seem disheartening in that it requires greater rather than less cognitive complexity. Yet this multifaceted focus is crucial if two system concepts—whole person and behavior as a function of person in interaction with environment—are to be taken seriously (Lewin, 1935). Practice and research that fall short of attending to this person–environment interaction does a disservice to remedial possibilities and personal integrity. We have divided this chapter into two parts. In the first part, we present enlightening concepts together with supporting research. In the second part, we apply the insights gained to professional practice and research and make specific recommendations regarding each of the issues raised.

Keywords: balanced assessment, deindividuation, diagnosis, labeling, strengths

Enlightening Concepts
Labeling, Distinctiveness, and Deindividuation

The problem of labeling will always be a problem. This assertion embraces two quite different meanings of the word "problem." In the first instance, the problem refers to perplexing questions proposed for investigation and academic discussion. In the second instance, the reference is to problems that add to disadvantagement caused by negative labeling.

Labeling literature and the body of related research are vast. They range over work on impression formation (interpersonal perception), prejudice (attitudes), discrimination (behavior), deviancy (social edicts), ethnocentrism (in-group vs. out-group), semantics and semiotics (meaning of speech and symbols), labels (identity, diagnosis), and stereotypes (beliefs). Even research on categorizing objects (object perception) is relevant.

To label is to give a name to things grouped together according to a shared characteristic(s). Because labels stand for something, they are abstractions. They organize and simplify the world and seemingly make it more understandable. For labeling purposes, differences among members of the labeled group are secondary, if not unimportant, so long as they do not violate the rules of inclusion. Thus, the label "American" or the label "fruit" encompasses an enormous diversity within each of these categories.

Grouping and labeling also require differentiating an out-group. "American" and "fruit" are communicable labels because there are other people and edibles that are excluded from these classifications. It can be expected, therefore, that labeling groups leads to a muting of perceived within-group differences and a highlighting of perceived between-group differences. Such muting and highlighting of differences have received considerable support in a variety of laboratory studies. Two experiments are described here: one involves objects and the other, people. They were selected to underscore the fact that the process of grouping (labeling, categorizing) involves basic dynamic properties regardless of whether the grouping is of people or objects.

In the first experiment by Tajfel and Wilkes (1963), research participants were shown a series of eight lines whose lengths differed from each other by a constant ratio. In one condition, the letter *A* appeared above each of the four shorter lines, and the letter *B* appeared above each of the four longer lines. In other conditions, the four *A*s and the four *B*s either were attached to the lines indiscriminately or did not appear. The participants estimated the length of the lines in random order, and they reported that lines belonging to the two systematically labeled classes A and B were farther apart in length than in the unclassified or haphazardly classified conditions. Moreover, with the repeated experience of estimating the lines in successive trials, participants increased the judged similarity of stimuli belonging to the same systematically labeled class, as compared with the other two conditions. In short, the participants overestimated differences in adjacent lines across categories A and B and underestimated differences in length within the categories.

The second experiment by Doise, Deschamps, and Meyer (1978) concerns social perception. The research participants were asked to describe photographs of children using a list of trait adjectives. There were two conditions. In one condition, the participants were presented with six photographs at one time, grouped according to sex (three boys, three girls), and described each photograph. In the second condition, the research participants were initially presented with only three same-sex photographs (boys or girls) to describe. Following that, they were shown the three photographs of the other sex to describe. Thus, these participants did not know in advance that they would rate photographs of both sexes, whereas the participants in the first condition realized this from the beginning. The researchers reported that those participants who had the two sexes in mind at the outset tended to perceive smaller intrasex differences and larger intersex differences than those participants who did not anticipate rating the photographs of the other sex.

Based on these two experiments, we can conclude that the perception of within-group differences was diminished, whereas between-group differences were exaggerated. Another way to put this is that group members are perceived as more similar to each other and more dissimilar to out-group members than when they remain as unclassified objects or individuals.

A different type of evidence for within-group deindividuation (attenuation of differences) emerges when "the stream of behavior" of group members is divided into meaningful units. Wilder (1984) took advantage of the idea that behavior, rather than being perceived as a continuous stream, is "chunked" in order to impart meaning (Barker, 1963; Barker & Wright, 1955). He reasoned that behavior would be divided into larger chunks when the person is viewed as a member of a group rather than as an individual. In the experiment, research participants were asked to divide the videotaped behaviors of one of four people into meaningful action units. In the group condition, the four people were identified as a group, whereas in the nongroup condition they were described as having come together by chance. The results showed that research participants chunked the behavior of group members into fewer meaningful units than when the people were seen as aggregates of individuals. Our inference is that the behavior of an individual who is perceived as a member of a group is less informative.

Deindividuation has yet other consequences. Experimenters have shown that the beliefs as well as the behavior of people perceived as members of a group tend to be seen as more similar than in the case of people viewed as individuals (Wilder, 1978). Also, more information that is consistent than inconsistent with the group label will tend to be remembered. In one study, for example, more "librarian-like" behavior was recalled about the person when she was presented as a librarian instead of a waitress (Cohen, 1981). For further research on the implications of the categorization process, the reviews by Tajfel (1978) and Wilder (1986) are recommended.

What needs to be emphasized is that human perception is coerced by the mere act of grouping things together. Within-group attenuation and between-group accentuation of differences are a product of categorization and may well be a general law that operates in the case of classification of both objects and people. Moreover, inasmuch as labeling identifies group membership, the mere act of labeling leads to both deindividuation of group members and accentuation of differences with outgroups. Such influence poses an enormous challenge to psychology, whether with respect to clinical practice or research. Fundamental questions surface: Does deindividuation have negative consequences? When, what are they, and for whom? What are the costs of emphasizing distinctiveness between groups? If differences are accentuated, what happens to the similarities between groups? And where is the environment in all this? The challenge to psychology will be explored further and partial solutions formulated in the second part of this chapter.

Labeling and the Fundamental Negative Bias

The discussion thus far has dealt with the effects of perceiving something as a member of a group (category, class of things) regardless of whether the affixed label is neutral or evokes a value-laden train of thought. But labels that identify group memberships of people (or of objects, for that matter) are usually not neutral but instead signal positive or negative evaluations. These value differentials, as compared with "neutral" categories, have been shown to enhance still further the perceived similarities within categories and the perceived differences between categories (Tajfel, 1978, p. 62). Accordingly, the problem of within-group deindividuation is compounded.

Basic Proposition

The fundamental negative bias involves basic propositions regarding the concepts of saliency, value, and context (Wright, 1988): If something stands out sufficiently (saliency); and if, for whatever reason, it is regarded as negative (value); and if its context is vague or sparse (context), then the negative value of the object of observation will be a major factor in guiding perception, thinking, and feeling to fit its negative character. This proposition has a parallel in the positive side of bias; namely, where something is perceived as salient, positive, and in a sparse context, then positivity will be a major factor in guiding subsequent cognitive-affective events. Because the fundamental negative bias contributes so insidiously to prejudice and disadvantagement, the focus is on this bias in the following discussion.

That the affective value of something, in the absence of counteracting contextual factors, can become a potent force in influencing what a person thinks and feels about it can be understood in terms of the concept of similarity as a unit-forming factor (Heider, 1958; Wertheimer, 1923). Similarity between entities, be they external objects or intrapsychic events, is a powerful factor in perceiving them as a unit, that is, as belonging together. An especially salient type of similarity among entities is their affective quality. Things that are positive are alike in engendering a force toward them; negative things, a force away from them. Combining positive and negative qualities subjects the person to forces in opposing directions.

Experiments on Context

EXTERNAL CONTEXT

"Context" refers to the set of conditions within which something is perceived and that influences that thing's meaning. The context can refer to conditions external to the perceiver or to intrapsychic predispositions of various sorts. A few experiments bearing on the significance of external context with regard to the fundamental negative bias are presented in the following.

In an important yet simple experiment, reactions to the label "blindness" as compared with "blind people," and "physical handicap" as compared with "physically handicapped people" were examined (Whiteman & Lukoff, 1965). That the condition itself was evaluated far more negatively than were people with the condition is not surprising. Still, the question remains as to how to account for the difference. The explanation can be found in the fundamental negative bias. Blindness, the salient condition, generally is valued negatively. When no context existed to alter its meaning, its negativity guided the reaction accordingly. When, however, the positive concept "person" was added, a context was provided that moderated the dominant position of the negative condition. It was the context that in effect changed the concept to be rated. And that is just the point. Contexts bring about diverse structures of meaning. Also noteworthy here is the classic work of Asch (1952), where he clearly demonstrated the importance of context in perception of people.

The context can be positive or negative. In the previous example, the concept of "person" provided a positive context and therefore constrained the negative spread. Researchers also have shown that, as the positive character of the context becomes even more salient, attitudes become more favorable. This was demonstrated, for example, in an experiment in which attitudes toward a person who was labeled with a particular problem (e.g., former mental patient, amputee) became more positive when that person was described as functioning adequately than when the negatively labeled person stood alone (Jaffe, 1966).

If a positive context can constrain negative evaluation, we might surmise that a negative context could increase the negativity of the object of observation, augmenting the fundamental negative bias in controlling attitudes. Thus, in one experiment, attitudes toward a person described as physically disabled and as having undesirable personality traits tended to be more negative than those toward a comparably described, able-bodied person (Leek, 1966). Such intensified reactions have also been demonstrated with respect to race (Dienstbier, 1970) and people with mental disorders (Gergen & Jones, 1963).

Besides affecting the "processing" of information presented about a person, the fundamental negative bias also influences information "sought" about a person. This was demonstrated in a study specifically designed to explore implications of the fundamental negative bias (Pierce, 1987). The research participants, simulating the role of a counselor, were asked what they would like to know about a client. The client, Joan, was identified either as just having been released from a psychiatric ward (salient negative) or as just having graduated from college (salient positive). In both cases, she was described further as seeking help because she was "feeling somewhat anxious and uncertain about her future, including her job and other issues in her life." The research participants selected 24 items of information they would like to know about Joan the client, from a list of 68 items, half of which referred to something positive (e.g., "Is Joan intelligent?") and half to something negative (e.g., "Is Joan cruel?"). Significantly, more negative items were selected in the case of the former psychiatric patient than the college graduate, apparently reflecting the belief that the negative information would be more relevant. Although there may be some basis in fact for this belief, the differential preference for negatives in the two cases poses a particular challenge for those who believe in the importance of calling special attention to positive personal traits. Bear in mind that the only revealed difference between the clients was identification as former psychiatric patient versus college graduate. Parenthetically, the subjects also rated Joan, as they believed the helping agency would, less positively in the former case.

The meaning of "external context" should be clarified. External context is not limited to a network of externally presented personal attributes but includes the external situation as well. The fact that the meaning of observations can be altered by the situation in which person perception takes place is well known. In the previous study (Pierce, 1987), two simulated situations were compared. One was that of a counseling center that "seeks out the strengths and assets of people"; the other was a psychological clinic that "deals with the emotional and behavioral problems of people." When the client was identified as attending a psychological clinic, whether as a former mental patient or as a college student, the research participants checked significantly more negative-information items that would be sought by the agency, and the client was evaluated less positively than when she was identified as attending a counseling center. In this experiment, the orienting function of the helping agency (the external situational context) played an important role in determining the affective course that cognition would take.

INTRAPSYCHIC CONTEXT

In addition to conditions externally imposed, factors internal to the person can also provide the main context for influencing perception. A variety of personal dispositions, such as personality traits and values, are potentially important in this regard. With respect to the fundamental negative bias, it is known that people who are more ethnocentric are more likely to view minority group members negatively than people who are less ethnocentric (English, 1971a, 1971b). This personality trait could provide the kind of internal context that maximizes the saliency of any negative attribute presented by the external stimulus conditions of an out-group; it could even have the power to lead the perceiver to ignore positive attributes. The same line of reasoning holds for values. It seems plausible that a strong value placed on human dignity, for example, would have the potential to exert a significant influence in organizing perception in a way that forestalls the fundamental negative bias.

Motivation should be mentioned as still another potentially important internal factor that can affect the potency of the fundamental negative bias. For example, the evaluator might benefit in some way by devaluating another, as when there is a need to feel superior. Such a motive could easily reinforce the fundamental negative bias, even to the extent of discrediting what would ordinarily be regarded as positive aspects of the other person. The converse is also true. Thus, humanistic and religious concerns could be a motivating force that creates a positive context of beliefs and principles in which to view people. These are a few examples of personal dispositions that conceivably support or compete with the power of the fundamental negative bias.

INSIDER VERSUS OUTSIDER PERSPECTIVES

The contrasting viewpoints of the "insider" and "outsider" corral a different set of context conditions in terms of which judgments are made (Dembo, 1964, 1970). The insider (also referred to as the "actor") is the person experiencing his or her own behavior, feelings, or problems. The outsider is the person observing or evaluating someone else. Both clinicians and researchers are outsiders with respect to the views and feelings of the clients and participants they are studying. Several types of investigations involving insider–outsider perspectives are described subsequently.

Research on the "mine—thine problem" is especially revealing because the research participant is placed in the position of both insider and outside observer as he or she engages in the assigned task (Wright, 1983). A simple way to conduct the experiment is to ask participants to list the initials of five people they know well in one column and beside each initial indicate that person's worst handicap (limitation, shortcoming, disability, or problem). Then, next to each of the five handicaps they are asked to write what they regard as their own worst handicap. They are then asked to circle the one from each pair they would choose for themselves if they had a choice. Next, they are asked to write two numbers on a slip of paper to indicate the number of times their own and the others' worst handicaps were chosen, the sum of the two normally being five. These slips are then collected so that the number frequencies can be displayed and discussed.

The results are dramatic and consistent. The number of times one's own handicap or problem is reclaimed clearly exceeds the frequency of choosing the others'. Among the five choices, it is common for subjects to select their own handicap five, four, or three times—rarely less frequently.

The difference between what is taken into account by the insider and outsider becomes appreciated in a personally direct way in the group's attempt to explain the results. Explanations include the following: they are used to their own handicap (familiarity); they have learned how to deal with it (coping); it is a part of the self and one's history (self-identity). Keep in mind that the subject is an insider when considering his or her own handicap and an outsider when regarding the other person's. Consequently, the other person's handicap more or less stands alone as a labeled negative condition and is therefore perceptually more insulated from context factors that could check the spread of its negative affect.

Other investigators have shown that patients (the insiders) tend to have a more positive outlook than do others viewing their situation (Hamera & Shontz, 1978; Mason & Muhlenkamp, 1976). Still other researchers have shown that mental hospital patients, mothers on welfare, and clients at a rehabilitation center (i.e., the insiders) tend to rate themselves as above average in how fortunate they are, whereas people viewing their situation from the outside judge them to be below average (Wright & Howe, 1969). This phenomenon, known as the "fortune phenomenon," was first noted by Dembo, Leviton, and Wright (1956/1975).

Based on our knowledge of research bearing on the perspectives of insiders and outsiders, not only does the meaning of the experience or label appear to differ, but so, too, are insiders generally more inclined than outsiders to take into account positives in their troubling situations. It seems clear that the context in which the judgments are made differs greatly in the two cases. Insiders place the significance of the problem in a life context so that the span of realities connected with it is wide. Only some aspects are negative; others are clearly positive (e.g., coping, identity), and it is this broad context that restrains the spread of negative effects. On the other hand, to outsiders the other person's problem more or less tends to stand alone, especially when it is represented by a label. In this case, the context is sparse or simplified, and the negativity of the problem dominates the train of thought.

RELATIVE POTENCY OF POSITIVES VERSUS NEGATIVES

The problem of context raises the question of the relative potency of positive and negative attributes. There is strong and accumulating evidence that under many conditions people tend to weigh negative aspects more heavily than positive aspects (Kanouse & Hanson, 1971). The following experiment is illustrative (Feldman, 1966). Research participants rated each of 25 statements containing a different adjective to describe the person, given the context "He is a (e.g., wise) man." A 9-point rating scale was used, ranging from good to bad. The participants also rated the statement when it included both a positive and a negative adjective (e.g., wise and corrupt). The potency of each adjective was determined by comparing the ratings of the statement when the adjective was used alone and when it appeared as a pair. The results were clear. The most powerful trait adjectives were negative. That is, overall ratings of people described by both a positive and a negative label were more negative than would be predicted by simply averaging the scale values assigned to each used singly.

From the study previously described on the fundamental negative bias (Pierce, 1987), we can also glean evidence concerning the potency value of negatives. Recall that in that study, subjects sought information about a client from the perspective of a counseling center that focused on strengths and assets, or a psychological clinic that focused on emotional and behavior problems. At the end of the experiment, the subjects were asked to write an essay expressing their views as to whether the kind of information sought about the client would have been different had the client gone to the alternate agency for help (the psychological clinic in the case of the client at the counseling center, and vice versa). Whereas none of the subjects spontaneously indicated that the problem-oriented psychological clinic would have been less adequate than the counseling center to meet the client's needs, some subjects questioned whether a strength-focused agency could help the client resolve her problems even though she might feel better about herself for a short while.

Several explanations of the greater potency (weight) given to negatives than positives have been proposed. First, negative information may become more salient because it arouses vigilance. Also, negative experiences do not "let go" of the person; the person ruminates about them, thereby increasing their presence and potency. Moreover, the norms of society are positive. Any negative deviation stands out and is given added weight because of its normative violation. Another explanation for the disproportionate weight given to negative attributes is that they are more likely to reduce or cancel the value of positive attributes than vice versa. Finally, Kogan and Wallach (1967) have suggested that the special saliency of negatives may have a physiological basis insofar as evidence exists for the relative independence of reward and punishment systems in the brain. These separate systems may have evolved in the Darwinian sense, producing approach and avoidance tendencies of unequal strength.

The greater potency of negatives, however, should not be taken to mean that negatives facilitate a broader, more flexible, or more integrated organization of cognitive material. On the contrary, it appears that positive affect is superior in this regard. For example, in a variety of studies it has been shown that both positive affect and positive material cue a wider range of associations than negative material (Isen, 1987). This point is especially relevant when considering action to change matters for the better, as in the case of treatment settings. A further point needs to be emphasized, namely, that the added potency of negatives places a heavy demand on context factors in holding the fundamental negative bias in check.

LABELING AND NEGLECT OF ENVIRONMENTAL CONSIDERATIONS

Thus far, we have dealt with the general effects of grouping people and objects by some labeling device and the effects when the label connotes something negative. As we have seen, within-group deindividuation and between-group accentuation of

differences tend to occur. Additionally, when a label is both negative and salient within a sparse context, it tends to invite more negative associations than when the context is expanded to include positive aspects. The insider versus outsider perspective is important in this regard. Furthermore, the negative preoccupation is exacerbated by the added weight ordinarily given to negatives. The point was stressed that the negative preoccupation can be checked by embedding the label in a cognitive-affective context (external/intrapsychic) that alters the significance of the label. We now turn our attention to the obscurity of the environment in the labeling process.

PERSON AND ENVIRONMENT AS FIGURE AND GROUND

We begin by noting that people frequently are labeled (grouped) solely by personal attributes: race, gender, age, intellectual level, physical condition, emotional status, and so forth. These attributes describe the person, not the environment. Even in cases where the label alludes to a particular environment, the label is generally interpreted as providing information about the person. Thus, such labels as mental hospital patients, rehabilitation clients, librarians, prisoners, and third graders essentially define the kind of person one is referring to, not the kind of environment. The label directs attention to patients, not hospitals; prisoners, not prisons; librarians, not libraries. At best, the environment remains as a vague background against which the person is featured.

The prominence of the person as figure and the vagueness of the environment are further supported by the nature of environments and people. People are active, moving in space, commanding attention by their behavior. Environments are less visible when perceiving persons and therefore less apprehendable. The environment provides the medium that allows the person to act, just as sound waves are the medium that allows the person to hear (Heider, 1926). In both cases, the sound heard and the person behaving are more easily apprehended than the mediating conditions. Unless the environment stands out because it is the object of study (in ecology, for example), or because of some commanding event, as when an earthquake strikes (physical environment) or a child is sexually abused (social environment), the environment overwhelmingly remains hidden in our thinking about and evaluating a person.

An additional factor contributing to the saliency of the person and the eclipse of the environment is that the person and his or her behavior are tied together by proximity; that is, the person is present whenever the behavior occurs. Proximity, like similarity, has long been recognized as a unit-forming factor. Thus, closeness in time and space between person and behavior creates a strong force toward accounting for the person's behavior in terms of properties of the person to the neglect of the environment. Even the expression "the person's behavior" uses the possessive case to tie the behavior to the person and not to the environment. Moreover, as the person moves from place to place, the constancy is the person, not the environment.

CAUSAL ATTRIBUTION

Major consequences for seeking and understanding the causes of behavior follow from the figure–ground relationship between person and environment. Despite the fact that most people would agree that both physical and social environments affect behavior, the role of the environment is easily neglected because of its obscurity. The aforementioned study of information sought about a client bears on this point (Pierce, 1987). When the research participants were asked to indicate which of the initial pool of about 100 information items were irrelevant to the problems presented, a much larger percentage of environmental than person-attribute items were so judged (77% vs. 17%), with this occurring in spite of the fact that the contents of these items were not trivial. They touched on crime, pollution, standard of living, and education—environmental areas that clearly could be considered significant.

Additional factors affecting the relative saliency of person and environment in causal attribution are discussed subsequently. In order, they are insider versus outsider perspectives, covariation, just world phenomenon, focal task, and values and motivation.

INSIDER VERSUS OUTSIDER PERSPECTIVES

The difference in the two perspectives was introduced in connection with the fundamental negative bias, where it was shown that the insider is relatively more inclined than the outsider to take into account positives in a troubling situation. Now let us examine how the two perspectives influence the saliency of person versus environment and therefore causal attribution.

The overall conclusion, based on several lines of investigation, is that the insider is more apt than the outsider to attribute his or her own behavior to properties of the environment, whereas the outside

observer more frequently sees the other person's traits as the source of the behavior (Goldberg, 1978). This general result is nicely shown in an experiment in which the research participants were asked to describe five people, including themselves, by selecting from each of 20 pairs of trait opposites (e.g., energetic vs. relaxed) the trait that most nearly applied to the person, or by checking the alternative option, "depends on the situation" (Nisbett, Caputo, Legant, & Maracek, 1973). The participants more frequently checked "depends on the situation" when describing themselves (the insider) than when they were in the position of observers describing someone else (e.g., best friend, peer acquaintance).

In a second study, it was demonstrated that the weight given to person and environment depends on the focus of attention of the insider and outsider (Storms, 1973). In this experiment, the focus of the insider's attention was shifted to approximate the visual focus of an observer. There were two parts to this experiment. The first part was a live situation in which two participants conversed with each other. This session was videotaped, with separate cameras focused on each of the conversants. In the second part, each member of the dyad watched the videotape that had been focused on himself or herself, thereby assuming the visual vantage point of an outsider observer.

In both live and video situations, the participants indicated the degree to which they felt their own behavior (how friendly, talkative, nervous, and domineering they were) was affected (a) by their own personality and (b) by the nature of the situation (e.g., other person's behavior). In the live situation, the subjects as insiders attributed their behavior significantly more frequently to the environment than in the videotape situation, where their visual attention approximated that of an observer. It should also be pointed out that in this experiment, as well as the preceding one in which five persons were rated, the research participants attributed their own behavior to personal traits more frequently than to the situation whether they were in the position of insiders or outside observers. This is because behavior still remains "attached to the person" even when the person is the insider, although in this position the person is more sensitive to the environment than when in the position of an outsider.

In a third study, the insider and outsider roles were simulated (Snyder, Shenkel, & Schmidt, 1976). Research participants assumed the role of counselor (outsider) or client (insider) as they listened to a taped therapy interview ostensibly of a client who either was seen for the first time or was chronic (in counseling five different times). In the interview, the client asserted that her situation caused her problems. Once again, the problems of the client were seen as significantly more personality-based when the ratings were made from the point of view of the counselor than of the client, a difference that held in the case of both the first-time and the chronic client.

COVARIATION

The perception of "what varies with what" is a powerful factor in the determination of causes (Kelley, 1973). That is, where behavior is seen to vary with the person, explanation is sought in terms of personal attributes. Where behavior is seen to vary with the situation, characteristics of the situation are held accountable. It is now proposed that because of the saliency of the person in understanding a person's behavior, the attributes of the person initially become the arena for the explanatory search (Wright, 1983). Only when this probe proves unrewarding is the search expanded to include the environment.

As an illustration, consider the difference in attribution outcome when the behavior under scrutiny is atypical or typical. In his classic work, Heider (1958) pointed out, "If we know that only one person succeeded or only one person failed out of a large number in a certain endeavor, then we shall ascribe success or failure to this person—to his great ability or to his lack of ability. On the other hand, if we know that practically everyone who tries, succeeds, we shall attribute the success to the task" (p. 89). We then say that the task was easy or, in the case of general failure, that the task was hard.

The inferential process in the two cases can be described as follows. The judgment that a particular behavior is typical or deviant requires comparing the behavior of people at the start, simply because behavior is "tied to" people. At this stage, the environment does not enter. If an adequate explanation of the behavior can be found in person characteristics, person attribution takes place. In the interest of parsimony, the explanatory process then stops because there is no felt need to seek further explanation by examining the environment. It is only when cogent personal characteristics do not readily surface that the need to explain shifts attention to the environment, thus ushering in an additional stage in the inferential process.

It is further proposed that in the case of "atypical behavior," personal characteristics more readily emerge than in the case of "typical behavior." It is relatively easy to account for a child's inattentiveness, for example, in terms of presumed hyperactivity, mental retardation, or some other characteristic of the child when most children are able to attend to the task. With such closure in the attribution search, there is no need to pursue the matter further by inquiring about possible contributing situational factors, such as class size or home difficulties. There is even no felt need to ask whether the child is inattentive in other situations, such as on the playground. In short, the atypical behavior is seen to covary with the person, not with the situation. Snyder (1977) has shown that a person-based attribution of behavior correlates significantly and positively with the perceived degree of the person's maladjustment.

In the case of typical behavior, however, the course of events often takes a different turn. Consider the case where almost all members of a classroom are inattentive. It is not ordinarily concluded that the class is hyperactive or mentally retarded or delinquent. An observer would tend to reserve such judgment for special classes of labeled children. Instead, the teacher's skill in keeping order might be questioned or the overcrowded classroom noted. These probes enlarge the causal network to include the situation. Thus, when the search for personal traits is not adequate to the task of accounting for common behavior, the perceiver moves to the next possible explanatory source—namely, the situation.

Apparently, once attention is directed to the situation, other situations are drawn into the comparative process. If an observer holds overcrowding accountable for the inattentiveness, it is because the inattentiveness is felt to contrast with behavior in less crowded classes. Similarly, behavior typical at a tennis match is ascribed to the nature of the situation, only because the behavior is understood to change with the situation. The side-to-side head turning occurs when the ball is volleyed from court to court, not during interludes; or it occurs at tennis matches, not at concerts. However, if a few individuals were observed to be engaged in "non-tennis"-oriented activity, the behavior would likely be attributed to boredom or some other personal attribute.

The covariation process described previously is particularly threatening to atypical groups, however they are labeled (e.g., mentally ill, disabled). This is because once they and their behavior are identified as atypical—nonnormative, deviant—the covariation process captures many seemingly plausible personal traits in its causal net, thereby aborting the causal search. The result is that environmental considerations are effectively screened out.

THE JUST WORLD PHENOMENON

A third factor in causal attribution involves consideration of both reality and what ought to be. Theory and research support the idea that human beings are inclined to feel that suffering and punishment, like joys and rewards, should be deserved (Asch, 1952; Heider, 1958). This sentiment is aptly referred to as the "just world phenomenon" (Lerner, 1970). Belief in a just world can be maintained by "blaming the victim." This has been shown in a series of laboratory experiments summarized by Lerner (1970). Blaming is manifested when the suffering is viewed as a consequence or punishment of some form of sin, wrongdoing, or irresponsibility. Because of the need to bring "ought" and "reality" into balance, the poor tend to be blamed for their poverty, and the person who is raped is blamed for the rape.

A scale has been developed to measure individual differences concerning belief in a just world (Rubin & Peplau, 1975). Results indicate that believers are more likely than nonbelievers to admire fortunate people and derogate victims, thus maintaining the notion that people in fact get what they deserve.

To be sure, "ought and reality" can be aligned by altering reality to fit what ought to be. Such is the goal of reformers and activists whose efforts are directed at environmental change (e.g., legal, political, social, economic). Yet, as we have seen, because it is the suffering of a person (or people) that is being explained, the focus quite naturally becomes the person, not the environment. It takes a broader view to be able to scan other situations and to recognize the possible covariation between suffering and situations.

Although the just world phenomenon applies equally to advantaged and disadvantaged groups, it adds to the problems of those who are already burdened. Whenever the suffering is justified by perceiving the person as its main cause, possible environmental circumstances are overlooked.

TASK FOCUS

The explanatory search in understanding behavior is also guided by the task undertaken by the investigator. Where the task is to form an impression of the person, to understand the person's behavior, to characterize the person in terms of descriptions, labels, or diagnoses, the task itself directs the perceiver's attention to the person. Where the task is to describe the environment in which people function, however, the focus of attention shifts to families, homes and schools, neighborhoods and parks, places of work and worship, and so forth. A vocabulary then emerges to describe and label the characteristics of situations that influence behavior (Stokols & Altman, 1987). Ecological psychology is one representative of this focus (Barker, 1963; Schoggen, 1989). Its vocabulary includes such phrases as "behavior settings" and "penetration" which refer to the power of different functional positions in the setting. Another representative of systematic environmental attention is behavior modification approaches that focus on the connection between environmental contingencies and the reinforcement and extinction of behavior. Terms used are "schedules of reinforcement," "chaining," and "conditioned reinforcers." There are also studies in which the focus is upon socioeconomic-behavioral correlates of broad environmental categories such as urban and rural.

The focus of helping agencies varies. Some concentrate on changing the person's situation, as is the case of social service and employment agencies. Others focus on changing the person; schools and treatment centers are examples. People are referred to one or another agency according to whether the problem is seen to be intrinsic to the person or to the environment.

Thus, the perceived source of difficulties critically affects referral decisions. This was clearly shown in an experiment in which participants, serving as counselors in a simulated referral agency, assigned clients to one or another agency after learning of the problem (Batson, 1975). When the client's situation was held primarily accountable for the problem, referrals were more likely to be directed to social service agencies than to institutions oriented toward changing the person, whereas the reverse was true when the problem was judged to reside in the client.

Where the primary mission of a treatment center is to change the person, assessment procedures will be directed toward describing and labeling person attributes. The danger is that the environment scarcely enters the equation in understanding behavior.

OTHER FACTORS IN NEGLECT OF ENVIRONMENTAL CONSIDERATIONS

Just as intrapsychic factors were mentioned as supporting or diminishing the power of the fundamental negative bias, so do these factors need to be recognized in the mix of factors that influence the figure–ground relationship between person and environment. The ideology of rugged individualism, for example, focuses on the person as the responsible agent. On the other hand, values and ideology can direct attention to the environment, as in the case of reformers and activists who argue for integration or segregation. Also, ego-defensive forces may create a need to blame the person or the environment. By blaming the poor, for example, one may feel personally competent or unobliged to contribute to remediation. By blaming the environment, one may see a way to assuage personal guilt by shifting responsibility from the self to others. Snyder (1990) has drawn attention to the need to preserve a sense of control, this being a principal motivation on the part of both the society and the individual in holding people responsible for their actions.

Additionally, the environment may be perceived as fixed, as too difficult to change. Effort may therefore be expended on changing the person. A case in point is the misperception that job tasks and the work environment are immutable. Instead of trying to modify them, the potential worker may be denied employment, directed elsewhere, or trained for a different occupation. The net effect is that the person, not the environment, needs to change. The concept of "reasonable accommodations," however, shifts the focus to the environment. Increasingly, modifying the work environment, physically or through rule change, is becoming evident.

Further clarification of basic conceptual and methodological issues is sorely needed to resolve the problem of environmental neglect. Without that, corrective measures will remain limited, a basic reason being that the forces toward perceiving people and their attributes are overpowering. Conyne and Clack (1981), who referred to the environment as an "untapped force for change," constructed an environmental classification matrix that offers diverse conceptualizations of environmental factors. In a text that resulted from a 1989 national conference that focused on organism–environment interaction, Wachs and Plomin (1991) clear the path to a better understanding of the environment by addressing conceptual and methodological roadblocks frequently encountered in behavioral research. Fortunately, the volume edited by Friedman and Wachs (1999) presents a comprehensive review of insights and proposals concerned with conceptualizing and measuring organism–environment integration that should help stimulate ways of overcoming environmental neglect. Bear in mind

that the forces toward perceiving people and not environments in causal attribution are so strong that it will take a counteracting commitment to overcome them.

Implications for Professional Practice and Research

The wide array of factors discussed thus far alert us to psychological decoys that easily lead the professional astray in practice and research. Recommendations based on this understanding are offered as safeguards in each case.

Clinical Settings

Clinical settings are established to help solve problems—physical, mental, or emotional. And that is part of the problem. Being problem oriented, the clinician easily concentrates on pathology, dysfunction, and troubles, to the neglect of discovering those important assets in the person and resources in the environment that must be drawn upon in the best problem-solving efforts (Wright & Fletcher, 1982).

Consider the following example. A counselor, seeking consultation concerning the rehabilitation of a delinquent youth, presented the case of 14-year-old John to the first author of this chapter. The following 10 symptoms were listed: assault, temper tantrums, stealing (car theft), fire setting, self-destructive behavior (jumped out of a moving car), threats of harm to others, insatiable demand for attention, vandalism, wide mood swings, and underachievement in school. On the basis of these symptoms, the diagnosis on Axis I of the *Diagnostic and Statistical Manual of Mental Disorders* (DSM-III-R; American Psychiatric Association, 1987) was conduct disorder, undersocialized, aggressive, and with the possibility of a dysthymic disorder; on Axis II, passive aggressive personality. No physical disorders were listed on Axis III. The psychosocial stressors, rated as extreme on Axis IV, noted the death of his mother when John was a baby and successive placement with various relatives and homes. On Axis V, John's highest level of adaptive functioning was rated as poor.

Following perusal of this dismal picture, Wright asked the counselor whether John had anything going for him. The counselor then mentioned that John kept his own room in order, took care of his personal hygiene, liked to do things for others (although on his own terms), liked school, and had an IQ of 140. Notice how quickly the impression of John changes once positives in the situation are brought out to share the stage with the problems.

Before that, the fundamental negative bias reigned supreme. Whereas the fact of John's delinquency had led to the detection of all sorts of negatives about his conduct and situation, the positives remained unconsidered. Is this case atypical? Only in its extreme neglect of strengths, we venture to say. Even a casual review of psychological reports of cases at mental health facilities will reveal how common it is for troublesome aspects to overshadow those that hold promise.

Notice also that the positives in John's case had been neglected with respect to both personal characteristics and significant environments. Environmental stresses are briefly noted on Axis IV, the axis that requires such specification. But the counselor did not indicate any environmental supports that could be provided by John's relatives, school, or community. Were such environmental resources nonexistent, or did they remain hidden and unexplored?

There are at least two reasons that contribute to the elusiveness of environmental resources in the assessment procedures of person-centered treatment settings. Because it is the person who is to be treated, attention is focused on the person. The consequence is that assessment procedures are inclined toward the person, not the environment. Adequate attention to resources in the environment is also made more difficult by the fundamental negative bias. Just as the negative train of thought gives short shrift to assets of the person, so it also does to resources in the environment. The affective shift required makes it more "natural" to disregard positives in the environment when trying to understand problems.

Hardly anyone would argue that the environment should be ignored, and yet we know how easily the environment fades into oblivion. Some may take the position that no one profession can do the entire job of assessment, pointing out that it is the psychologist's responsibility to examine people, whereas social workers are specifically trained to examine circumstances in the home, school, and other community settings. However, the conclusion that psychologists are therefore absolved from seriously considering environmental factors is not warranted.

The covariation principle discussed earlier provides a readily available self-monitoring check to assist in bringing environmental issues to the foreground. The general question "Does this behavior or problem occur in all situations?" forces one to review the many types of situations in the person's life.

THE FOUR-FRONT APPROACH TO ASSESSMENT

Once the power of the fundamental negative bias and the forces that keep the environment at bay are recognized, it becomes clear that the assessment and diagnostic processes need to be engaged on four fronts. Professionals must give serious attention to (a) deficiencies and undermining characteristics of the person, (b) strengths and assets of the person, (c) lacks and destructive factors in the environment, and (d) resources and opportunities in the environment.

Highlighting positives as well as negatives in both the person and the environment serves vital purposes. It provides a framework to counteract deindividuation. It affects the significance of the negatives and enlarges remediation possibilities. It also encourages the "discovery" of assets and resources that can be developed in serving human potential.

A brief example of the efficacy of using assets to remediate deficits involves the case of a middle-aged man whose visual-spatial skills were impaired by a stroke (Chelune, 1983). The neuropsychologist was able to demonstrate the potential utility of using the client's intact verbal skills as a means of compensating for his considerable difficulty with copying a cross. When the man was instructed to "talk himself through" such tasks, he was able to do them without difficulty. If only the impaired side of his functioning had been attended to, remediation possibilities would have been limited.

In accord with the approach on four fronts, an attempt was made to correct common oversights that appeared in the behavior checklists on children's intake forms at mental health centers (Fletcher, 1979). These checklists essentially pointed out child problems but rarely, if at all, included items pertaining to child assets or the environment. A checklist was therefore constructed consisting of four separate parts: (a) Child Problems (39 items; e.g., temper outbursts, mean to others); (b) Child Assets (39 items; e.g., affectionate, finishes tasks); (c) Environmental Problems (21 items; e.g., family fights, lack of recreational opportunities); and (d) Environmental Resources (21 items; e.g., grandparent(s), school). Notice that the problems and assets on the child side were made equal in number, as were the problems and resources on the environmental side, but that the child items far exceeded the environmental items. This disparity, which occurred in spite of a serious attempt to correct it, reflects the greater availability of person categories in our lexicon than environmental categories.

Information bearing on the four fronts can be obtained through the many types of assessment procedures available. It is essential that psychological tests are selected that are designed to uncover personal strengths and assets just as tests are selected that are sensitive to deficits and pathology. Systematic identification of environmental restraints and resources can be achieved via questionnaires, observation, and collateral sources of information. Recent advancements in the development of environment models and assessment tools (see Friedman & Wachs, 1999) make measurement of the objective, subjective, and temporal components of the environment possible.

The task of integrating data from four fronts is a challenging one. It is challenging because the four domains represent a dynamic whole in which the client's functioning needs to be grasped. Not only do the strengths and limitations of the client influence each other, but also the client's behavior and environment are mutually interdependent. Assessment is a cyclical process of building tentative understanding of issues involving the client within this complex network of factors.

Throughout the assessment process, the psychologist is urged to remain on guard lest positives in the person and situation remain overlooked because of the intrusion of the fundamental negative bias and environmental neglect. In this regard, recommendations have been made on how to interview for client strengths and minimize bias in clinical work (Spengler, Strohmer, Dixon, & Shivy, 1995).

To ensure that positives are not submerged by negatives, it was proposed (Wright, 1991) that assets and deficits approximate an equal amount of space in psychological reports and equal time at case conferences. This "equal space and time" guideline serves as a concrete reminder of the importance of seriously attending to both aspects. Observing this rule of equity is quite challenging. Adding a strengths section to a verbal or written report may be the first step toward being able to interweave information about pathology and strengths in psychological assessment.

Finally, it is imperative when presenting psychological data that the clinician demonstrate respect for the client's struggle with problems in daily living or more severe dysfunction. Focusing on how the repertoire of client strengths and environmental resources can enable the client in that struggle is the best way to ensure fundamental support and regard for the client.

THE DIAGNOSTIC AND STATISTICAL MANUAL OF MENTAL DISORDERS

The *Diagnostic and Statistical Manual of Mental Disorders* has been widely accepted in the United States as the diagnostic tool of mental health clinicians

and researchers. The last revision, DSM-IV (American Psychiatric Association, 1994), describes over 400 categories of mental disorder grouped according to 16 major classes. The disorders are typically described in terms of diagnostic features, prevalence, course, cultural considerations, and so forth. Five axes are provided for recording information to help the clinician plan treatment and predict outcome (Axis I, Clinical Disorders and Other Conditions That May Be a Focus of Attention; Axis II, Personality Disorders and Mental Retardation; Axis III, General Medical Conditions; Axis IV, Psychosocial and Environmental Problems; and Axis V, Global Assessment of Functioning).

An enormous amount of research and care have gone into the DSMs. Because DSM is such an important document, it is fitting that we examine some of the ideas that have determined its nature. The recommendations offered center around the problems of deindividuation, the fundamental negative bias, and environmental neglect.

DEINDIVIDUATION

The evidence is clear. Affixing a label (diagnosis in the present instance) leads to a muting of differences within the labeled group. DSM-IV developers remind the clinician that "individuals sharing a diagnosis are likely to be heterogeneous even in regard to the defining features of the diagnosis." They emphasize the need to "capture additional information that goes far beyond diagnosis" in order to accent the unique characteristics of individuals that may influence how they manage their lives (American Psychiatric Association, 1994, p. xxii).

But within-group deindividuation is so insidious that all too readily it reaches the ultimate point of dehumanization in which the person is then made equivalent to the disorder. The devaluative implication of such terminological equivalence was first recognized by Wright (1960). The DSM developers also caution, "A common misconception is that a classification of mental disorders classifies people, when actually what are being classified are disorders that people have" (American Psychiatric Association, 1994, p. xxii), and clinicians should avoid labeling people as schizophrenics or alcoholics and instead should use the more accurate but admittedly more cumbersome "an individual with Schizophrenia" or "an individual with Alcohol Dependence" (American Psychiatric Association, 1994, p. xxii). It is our belief, however, that the two caveats concerning homogenization of individuality and dehumanization, wise as they are, cannot stem the tide of deindividuation so long as a few diagnostic labels dominate perception. What is needed is greater individuation in terms of the four-front approach.

THE FUNDAMENTAL NEGATIVE BIAS

So long as the main diagnostic categories are disorders, relatively little effort will be expended on personal assets and environmental resources. The DSM working group made an attempt to offset this danger by including the Global Assessment of Functioning Scale (Axis V). It is provided to assist this assessment, yet it actually serves as a global assessment of dysfunction, namely, the extent to which individuals are languishing or suffering. That is, only a small range of scores on the 100-point scale (approximately 75–100) describes functioning that is adequate, good, or superior. The remainder of the scale is coordinated to functioning, ranging from slightly impaired to harming self or others. Lopez, Prosser, LaRue, Ulven, and Vehige (2000) proposed that the Global Assessment Scale be restructured by having anchors of 1, 50, and 100 reflective of severely impaired functioning, good health, and thriving, respectively. It should also be noted that a "scant few pages" are devoted to Axis V, in contrast to the "hundreds of pages" devoted to diagnosing mental disorders. Small wonder that the aforementioned report of the delinquent youth was so negatively one-sided, and small wonder that attention to deficits and pathology so commonly overwhelms the reporting of strengths and assets in mental health agencies.

The rejoinder may be that it is the job of mental health agencies to diagnose and deal with problems, and that problems refer to dysfunction, not to well-functioning areas. But the rejoinder to this point of view is that inasmuch as the person functions as a whole system in which healthy and dysfunctional characteristics affect each other, both aspects must be given serious attention in diagnosis and treatment plans. Surely it makes a difference to both diagnosis and treatment if a client is aware of his or her difficulties, is willing to accept help, is responsible, is kind, and gets along with others. Systematic research can help to clarify which personal assets need to be singled out, how they cluster, and how to present them—on profiles, checklists, rating scales, for example.

NEGLECT OF ENVIRONMENTAL CONSIDERATIONS

Axis IV, DSM-IV, bears the title "Psychosocial and Environmental Problems." It was devised in recognition of the fact that the environment is not inconsequential in understanding and diagnosing mental disorder. Still, Axis IV must be considered barely a first step in meeting the challenge of addressing environmental influences on human behavior. First to be observed is that this axis refers to psychosocial and environmental "problems, not resources." The neglect of the positive is so profound that DSM-IV developers caution users against listing "so-called positive stressors, such as a job promotion" on this axis unless they "constitute or lead to a problem" (American Psychiatric Association, 1994, p. 29). Again, positive attributes or characteristics of the person or situation are relegated to the background. Axis IV is helpful insofar as its guidelines draw attention to the environment—problems regarding family, occupation, living circumstances, and so forth. Even so, very little space and attention are devoted to this axis, and no axis directs attention to environmental supports.

RECOMMENDATIONS FOR THE DSM AND ITS ALTERNATIVES

The themes of this chapter, with its focus on the problems of deindividuation, the fundamental negative bias, and environmental neglect, strongly suggest that the four-front approach become the model for future DSM revisions. How else can positives as well as negatives in both the person and the environment be made sufficiently salient to allow an integrated assessment of the whole person-in-environment? Is it too impractical to envision a diagnostic manual consisting of four volumes, one addressing each front? Can anything short of that do justice to the goal of optimizing diagnostic and remediation efforts on behalf of the client? An added benefit would be the likely impetus given to conceptually clarifying significant aspects of the person-in-environment.

There are other recommendations regarding the current diagnostic system. We have already argued for the inclusion of environmental resources on Axis IV and for modifications to Axis V of the current five-axis system. Also, Lopez et al. (2000) present the outline for what could constitute an Axis VI designed to guide the clinician in identifying client strengths, resources, and virtues.

Finally, the Developmental Diagnostic Classification System (Ivey & Ivey, 1998) constitutes a reengineering of the diagnostic classification framework that is grounded in a developmental focus and the assumption that all behavior is adaptive. This new system focus emphasizes detection of what is working in the client's life and capitalizes on human strengths.

Revisions of the DSM have been based on research garnered from extensive reviews of the literature and on consultation with experts from different disciplines. The developers state, "More than any other nomenclature of mental disorders, DSM-IV is grounded in empirical evidence" (American Psychiatric Association, 1994, p. xvi). They also point out that "to formulate an adequate treatment plan, the clinician will invariably require considerable information about the person being evaluated beyond that required to make a DSM-IV diagnosis" (American Psychiatric Association, 1994, p. xxv). What is not recognized is that the additional information required must also be buttressed by research that details personal strengths as well as difficulties. These are the domains of the four-front approach. Greater conceptual clarification of the nature of this interdependent network requires continuing investigation.

Whether or not the DSM is used, the recommendations proposed here can be applied in clinical practice. These recommendations refer to the four-front approach, approximating equal time and space to assets as to deficits in psychological reports and at case conferences, and to uncovering the environment by covarying problematic behavior with situations in the person's life.

The main themes argued in this chapter also raise issues bearing on the conduct and interpretation of research. A few examples are discussed in the following.

Research Practices
COMPARING CONDITIONS AND GROUPS IN RESEARCH

The difference in perspectives of the outsider and insider, as well as the power of the fundamental negative bias, alert us to certain pitfalls that need to be avoided in interpreting research. Consider an experiment that compared reactions of able-bodied persons to confederate interviewers with and without a simulated disability. (Because there is no need to indict a particular researcher, this study is not identified here.) All things were kept equal in the two conditions except for the independent variable. Although the main finding was that the interviewer with the disability was consistently rated more favorably on a variety of personality characteristics (e.g., more likable, better attitude), the results were interpreted as supporting research indicating the operation of a sympathy effect to avoid the appearance of rejection or prejudice.

A number of points need to be emphasized. First, the investigator was seduced into attending to the disability variable as the salient factor in the experiment because "all other things were kept equal." Second, these controls kept the investigator, as observer, from attending to the context of the interview as "experienced by the research participants." Instead, the negative value attributed to the disability stood alone in determining the negative flow of thoughts and feelings, leaving the investigator to become trapped by the fundamental negative bias, even to the extent of treating findings favoring the interviewer with the disability as if they were negative.

For the research participants, however, the situation appeared very different. They knew nothing about the behavior of the interviewer being held constant in two experimental conditions in which only the interviewer's physical appearance varied. All they were aware of was an interviewer whose status and behavior were positive. Thus, instead of the context being obliterated, the context was decidedly positive. Under these circumstances, response intensification occurred, a finding that fits with other research. The research participants may have appreciated the interviewer's apparent success in meeting the challenges of his or her disability and therefore perceived the interviewer as having special qualities as a cause or consequence of such success. The conclusion is compelling that two vastly different situations were evaluated, one as perceived by the research participants and a very different one by the experimenter.

Researchers must become sensitized to possible differences in perspective between themselves and subjects, especially in terms of the saliency and context of variables under study. They also must become aware of the power of the fundamental negative bias to influence their own thinking when the independent variable carries a negative connotation or label (disability in this experiment).

The preceding discussion relates to research in which participants are assigned to different conditions, not to research in which the behavior of distinct groups of people is compared. In the latter case, special precautions need to be taken lest the label identifying the groups controls the investigator's thinking. In countless studies, there are comparisons of males and females, Blacks and Whites, people with and without disabilities, heterosexuals and homosexuals, and so forth. All too often, between-group differences are attributed solely to the group characteristic made visible by the label (e.g., gender, race). Other factors such as the generally large overlap in behavior between groups, within-group differences, and differences in the groups' life circumstances are frequently ignored or discounted. The consequent between-group distinctiveness, within-group deindividuation, and environmental neglect have serious societal implications that need to be thought through by researchers. At the very least, the "something else perhaps" notion, proposed by the philosopher Herbert Feigl (1953), bears reemphasizing to avoid "nothing but" interpretations based on a salient, labeled variable. Feigl also reminded us that the investigator must be pressed to discover "what's what" by systematic research.

THE PROBLEM OF STATISTICAL SIGNIFICANCE

The fact that the null hypothesis cannot be proven statistically (Fisher, 1955) adds to the complexity of the issues raised here. Similarities between groups, typically regarded as null findings, are therefore discounted. The consequence for understanding different groups is serious, and in the case of groups that are already disadvantaged, ignoring similarities adds to the disadvantagedness.

A variety of statistical procedures to help eliminate the bias against accepting the null hypothesis (i.e., similarities between groups) have been proposed. Traditionally, researchers use the 0.01 or 0.05 alpha level of significance to refer to the small probability that the obtained difference between groups could be due to chance. One proposal is that the high end of the probability range could be used to suggest the likelihood of similarity (rather than exact equivalence) between groups (Wright, 1988, p. 16). While it is true that the null hypothesis cannot logically be proven and can "at most be confirmed or strengthened" (Fisher, 1955), it should be noted that large p values do in fact "confirm or strengthen" the hypothesis that group differences are small or nonexistent. In that case, one could conclude that the obtained difference is unreliable as a difference but reliable as a similarity. The similarity, then, would have to be judged to determine whether it is of psychological importance, just as a statistically significant difference has to be so judged. Of course, relevant research criteria, such as reliability and validity of measures used, would have to be evaluated.

The point is that investigators, by giving weight to similarities as well as to differences between groups, achieve better understanding of the data and help to stem the automatic slide toward between-group accentuation of differences. A further fact that should not be overlooked is that perceived similarities promote positive intergroup relations. Additional arguments, evidence, and procedures to counteract prejudice against accepting the null hypothesis can be found in Greenwald (1975).

THE PROBLEM OF ATTITUDE TESTS OF STEREOTYPES

When measuring attitudes toward a particular group, the intent is to get at stereotypes, attitudes that are tied to the label designating the group. If the label connotes something negative to the respondent, as is often the case, for example, with regard to mental disorder, disability, poverty, and homosexuality, then the label is likely to give rise to a negative mind-set in answering the items, especially because the label, as an abstraction, is separated from particular people and circumstances.

Contributing to this mind-set is a preponderance of negatively focused items that frequently, although not always, characterize attitude tests about groups stigmatized in some way. This negative loading may be a manifestation of the fundamental negative bias inasmuch as the test constructor may be led by the group's stigmatized status to formulate items that imply devaluation. It may also be considered a way to minimize the influence of "social desirability," that is, a subject's inclination to respond favorably to items expressing what is proper.

In any case, the negative loading can have several unacceptable consequences. First, we should be concerned lest a preponderance of negatively worded items orients thinking toward the negative side of possibilities, thereby strengthening a negative-response bias. Also, rejecting a negative statement is not the same, affectively and cognitively, as affirming a positive statement. Rejecting the idea, for example, that a particular group is often conniving or lazy does not imply the opposite belief, that the group is often honest or eager to work. Both types of statements are needed to guard against a negative bias and to offer respondents the opportunity to express attitudes that reflect genuinely positive, as well as negative, feelings and beliefs.

In addition, an overload of negatively worded items could provide a misleading educational experience, leading the respondent to begin to believe disparaging statements that had not been entertained before. The possibility of this happening is increased by evidence showing that people tend to give more weight to negative aspects of something than to positive aspects. To counteract the excessive weight that might be given to negative items, the most obvious suggestion is to include at least the same number, and preferably a greater number, of positively worded items.

Another concern relates to the nature of stereotyping itself. Although it is understandable that attitude tests avoid differentiations among group members captured by the label, the possible deleterious effects of an ostensible scientific instrument that homogenizes people in this way are of concern. Deindividuation flies in the face of decades of research showing that a label or diagnosis tells us very little about what a person is like inasmuch as individuals are unique in their combination of interests, values, abilities, circumstances, and so forth. Because of the nature of stereotypes, however, the tests themselves have to ignore this uniqueness. To minimize stereotyping effects of such tests, it is recommended that research participants be cautioned against this possibility during debriefing.

Another urgently needed recommendation is that researchers spend at least as much effort searching for and uncovering positive attitudes as they do negative ones. To agree with this, recommendation depends on believing that positive attitudes toward disadvantaged groups not only exist but also are as important as negative attitudes, for two reasons. First, attitudes are typically ambivalent, and when evaluated within this more complex matrix, the perception of the group is likely to change. A telling example discussed earlier is the attitude change that took place toward the delinquent youth as soon as positive traits were brought to the fore. Second, positive attitudes are also important because it is these attitudes that have to be drawn on, built upon, and spread in the effort to overcome disparaging beliefs and feelings of one group toward another.

Positive Psychology: Just Another Label?

The label of "positive psychology" represents those efforts of professionals to help people optimize human functioning by acknowledging strengths as well as deficiencies, and environmental "resources" in addition to stressors. Label us hopeful optimists (please) because we believe that this enlarged focus is essential in clarifying what works in people's lives. Many issues were raised in this chapter. We hope that readers will be encouraged to consider the conceptual reasoning, evidence, and recommendations in both their ongoing scholarly work and their clinical practice.

Note

This chapter updates Wright, B. A. (1991). Labeling: The need for greater person–environment individuation. In C. R. Snyder & D. R. Forsyth (Eds.), *The handbook of social and clinical psychology: A health perspective.* New York: Pergamon.

Questions for Future Study

1. Would the use of a four-front approach to clinical assessment limit the effects of deindividuation or the fundamental negative bias in clinical practice?

2. How could the use of four-front approach to clinical assessment reshape how clinicians plan and implement interventions for their clients?

3. How could strengths-based assessments be incorporated into future iterations of the *Diagnositic and Statistical Manual of Mental Disorders*?

References

American Psychiatric Association. (1987). *Diagnostic and statistical manual of mental disorders* (3rd ed., Rev.). Washington, DC: Author.

American Psychiatric Association. (1994). *Diagnostic and statistical manual of mental disorders* (4th ed.). Washington, DC: Author.

Asch, S. E. (1952). Forming impressions of personality. *Journal of Abnormal and Social Psychology, 41,* 258–290.

Barker, R. G. (Ed.). (1963). *The stream of behavior.* New York: Appleton-Century-Crofts.

Barker, R. G., & Wright, H. F. (1955). *Midwest and its children.* New York: Harper and Row.

Batson, C. D. (1975). Attribution as a mediator of bias in helping. *Journal of Personality and Social Psychology, 32,* 455–466.

Chelune, G. J. (1983, August). *Neuropsychological assessment: Beyond deficit testing.* Paper presented at the 91st annual convention of the American Psychological Association, Anaheim, CA.

Cohen, C. E. (1981). Person categories and social perception: Testing some boundaries of the processing effects of prior knowledge. *Journal of Personality and Social Psychology, 40,* 441–452.

Conyne, R. K., & Clack, R. J. (1981). *Environmental assessment and design: A new tool for the applied behavioral scientist.* New York: Praeger.

Dembo, T. (1964). Sensitivity of one person to another. *Rehabilitation Literature, 25,* 231–235.

Dembo, T. (1970). The utilization of psychological knowledge in rehabilitation. *Welfare Review, 8,* 1–7.

Dembo, T., Leviton, G. L., & Wright, B. A. (1956/1975). Adjustment to misfortune: A problem of social-psychological rehabilitation. *Artificial Limbs, 3*(2), 4–62. (Reprinted in *Rehabilitation Psychology, 2,* 1–100.)

Dienstbier, R. A. (1970). Positive and negative prejudice with race and social desirability. *Journal of Personality, 38,* 198–215.

Doise, W., Deschamps, J. C., & Meyer, G. (1978). The accentuation of intracategory similarities. In H. Tajfel (Ed.), *Differentiation between social groups: Studies in the social psychology of intergroup relations* (pp. 159–168). (European Monographs in Social Psychology 14.) London: Academic Press.

English, R. W. (1971a). Assessment, modification and stability of attitudes toward blindness. *Psychological Aspects of Disability, 18*(2), 79–85.

English, R. W. (1971b). Correlates of stigma toward physically disabled persons. *Rehabilitation Research and Practice Review, 2,* 1–17.

Feigl, H. (1953). The scientific outlook: Naturalism and humanism. In H. Feigl & M. Brodbeck (Eds.), *Readings in the philosophy of science* (pp. 8–18). New York: Appleton-Century-Crofts.

Feldman, S. (1966). Motivational aspects of attitudinal elements and their place in cognitive interaction. In S. Feldman (Ed.),

Cognitive consistency: Motivational antecedents and behavioral consequences (pp. 75–108). New York: Academic Press.

Fisher, R. (1955). Statistical method and scientific induction. *Journal of the Royal Statistical Society, 17*, 69–78.

Fletcher, B. L. (1979). *Creating a child intake form for use in a mental health center*. Unpublished manuscript, University of Kansas, Lawrence.

Friedman, S. L., & Wachs, T. D. (Eds.). (1999). *Measuring environment across the lifespan*. Washington, DC: American Psychological Association.

Gergen, K. L., & Jones, E. E. (1963). Mental illness, predictability and affective consequences as stimulus factors in person perception. *Journal of Abnormal and Social Psychology, 67*, 95–104.

Goldberg, L. R. (1978). Differential attribution to trait-descriptive terms to oneself as compared to well-liked, neutral, and disliked others: A psychometric analysis. *Journal of Personality and Social Psychology, 36*, 1012–1028.

Greenwald, A. G. (1975). Consequences of prejudice against the null hypothesis. *Psychological Bulletin, 82*, 1–20.

Hamera, E. K., & Shontz, F. C. (1978). Perceived positive and negative effects of life-threatening illness. *Journal of Psychosomatic Research, 22*, 419–424.

Heider, F. (1926). Ding und medium. *Symposion, 1*, 109–157.

Heider, F. (1958). *The psychology of interpersonal relations*. New York: Wiley.

Isen, A. M. (1987). Positive affect, cognitive processes, and social behavior. In L. Berkowitz (Ed.), *Advances in experimental social psychology* (Vol. 20, pp. 203–254). Orlando, FL: Academic Press.

Ivey, A. E., & Ivey, M. B. (1998). Reframing DSM-IV: Positive strategies from developmental counseling and therapy. *Journal of Counseling and Development, 76*, 334–350.

Jaffe, J. (1966). Attitudes of adolescents toward the mentally retarded. *American Journal of Mental Deficiency, 70*, 907–912.

Kanouse, D. E., & Hanson, L. R., Jr. (1971). Negativity in evaluations. In E. E. Jones et al. (Eds.), *Attribution: Perceiving the causes of behavior* (pp. 47–62). Morristown, NJ: General Learning Press.

Kelley, H. H. (1973). Process of causal attribution. *American Psychologist, 28*, 107–128.

Kogan, N., & Wallach, M. A. (1967). Risk taking as a function of the situation, the person, and the group. In G. Mandler, P. N. Kogan, & M. A. Wallach (Eds.), *New directions in psychology III* (pp. 111–278). New York: Holt, Rinehart, and Winston.

Leek, D. F. (1966). *Formation of impressions of persons with a disability*. Unpublished master's thesis, University of Kansas, Lawrence.

Lerner, M. J. (1970). The desire of justice and reactions to victims. In J. Macaulay & L. Berkowitz (Eds.), *Altruism and helping behavior* (pp. 205–229). New York: Academic Press.

Lewin, K. (1935). *A dynamic theory of personality*. New York: McGraw-Hill.

Lopez, S. J., Prosser, E. C., LaRue, S., Ulven, J. C., & Vehige, S. (2000). *Practicing positive psychology*. Unpublished manuscript.

Mason, L., & Muhlenkamp, A. (1976). Patients' self-reported affective states following loss and caregivers' expectations of patients' affective states. *Rehabilitation Psychology, 23*, 72–76.

Nisbett, R. E., Caputo, C., Legant, P., & Maracek, J. (1973). Behavior as seen by the actor and as seen by the observer. *Journal of Personality and Social Psychology, 27*, 154–164.

Pierce, D. L. (1987). *Negative bias and situation: Perception of helping agency on information seeking and evaluation of clients*. Unpublished master's thesis, University of Kansas, Lawrence.

Rubin, Z., & Peplau, L. A. (1975). Who believes in a just world? *Journal of Social Issues, 31*, 65–89.

Schoggen, P. (1989). *Behavior settings: A revision of Barker's ecological psychology*. Stanford, CA: Stanford University Press.

Snyder, C. R. (1977). "A patient by any other name" revisited: Maladjustment or attributional locus of problem? *Journal of Consulting and Clinical Psychology, 45*, 101–103.

Snyder, C. R. (1990). Self-handicapping processes and sequelae: On the taking of a psychological dive. In R. L. Higgins, C. R. Snyder, & S. Berglas, *Self-handicapping: The paradox that isn't* (pp. 107–150). New York: Plenum.

Snyder, C. R., Shenkel, R. J., & Schmidt, A. (1976). Effects of role perspective and client psychiatric history on locus of problem. *Journal of Consulting and Clinical Psychology, 44*, 467–472.

Spengler, P. M., Strohmer, D. C., Dixon, D. N., & Shivy, V. A. (1995). A scientist-practitioner model of psychological assessment: Implications for training, practice and research. *The Counseling Psychologist, 23*, 506–534.

Stokols, D., & Altman, I. (Eds.). (1987). *Handbook of environmental psychology* (Vols. 1–2). New York: Wiley.

Storms, M. D. (1973). Videotape and the attribution process: Reversing actors' and observers' points of view. *Journal of Personality and Social Psychology, 27*, 165–175.

Tajfel, H. (Ed.). (1978). *Differentiation between social groups: Studies in the social psychology of intergroup relations* (European Monographs in Social Psychology 14). London: Academic Press.

Tajfel, H., & Wilkes, A. (1963). Classification and quantitative judgment. *British Journal of Psychology, 54*, 101–114.

Wachs, T. D., & Plomin, R. (1991). *Conceptualization and measurement of organism–environment interaction*. Washington, DC: American Psychological Association.

Wertheimer, M. (1923). Untersuehungen zur Lehre von der gestalt (Examination of the lessons of gestalt): II. *Psychologishe Forschung, 4*, 301–350.

Whiteman, M., & Lukoff, I. F. (1965). Attitudes toward blindness and other physical handicaps. *Journal of Social Psychology, 65*, 135–145.

Wilder, D. A. (1978). Perceiving persons as a group: Effects on attributions of causality and beliefs. *Social Psychology, 1*, 13–23.

Wilder, D. A. (1984). *Effects of perceiving persons as a group on the information conveyed by their behavior*. Unpublished manuscript, Rutgers University, New Brunswick, NJ.

Wilder, D. A. (1986). Social categorization: Implications for creation and reduction of intergroup bias. In L. Berkowitz (Ed.), *Advances in experimental social psychology* (Vol. 19, pp. 291–355). Orlando, FL: Academic Press.

Wright, B. A. (1960). *Physical disability: A psychological approach*. New York: Harper and Row.

Wright, B. A. (1983). *Physical disability: A psychosocial approach* (2nd ed.). New York: Harper and Row.

Wright, B. A. (1988). Attitudes and the fundamental negative bias. In H. E. Yuker (Ed.), *Attitudes toward persons with disabilities* (pp. 3–21). New York: Springer.

Wright, B. A. (1991). Labeling: The need for greater person–environment individuation. In C. R. Snyder & D. R. Forsyth (Eds.), *The handbook of social and clinical psychology* (pp. 469–487). New York: Pergamon.

Wright, B. A., & Fletcher, B. L. (1982). Uncovering hidden resources: A challenge in assessment. *Professional Psychology, 13*, 229–235.

Wright, B. A., & Howe, M. (1969). *The fortune phenomenon as manifested in stigmatized and non-stigmatized groups*. Unpublished manuscript, University of Kansas, Lawrence.

Toward a Science of Mental Health

Corey L. M. Keyes

Abstract

This chapter summarizes the research on the dual-continua model of mental health and mental illness. Studies supported this model and therefore the view that the presence of mental health is more than the absence of mental illness. Mental health is conceived of as a constellation of dimensions of subjective well-being, specifically hedonic and eudaemonic measures of subjective well-being. Specifically, the mental health continuum ranges from languishing, moderate, to flourishing mental health. These classifications are important for distinguishing and predicting level of functioning for individuals with and without a current mental disorder. Among individuals free of a mental disorder, flourishing individuals report the fewest missed days of work, the fewest half-day or greater work cutbacks, the healthiest psychosocial functioning, high resilience, and high intimacy), the lowest risk of cardiovascular disease, the lowest number of chronic physical diseases at all ages, the fewest health limitations of activities of daily living, and lower health-care utilization. Even among adults with a mental disorder during the past 12 months, those who are flourishing functioned better than those with moderate mental health, who in turn functioned better than those who were languishing. The findings strongly support the adoption of a more positive paradigm to treatment, prevention, and promotion of population mental health.

Keywords: flourishing, happiness, mental health, psychological well-being, subjective well-being

There have been at least three conceptions of health throughout human history worldwide—pathos, salus, and hale. The pathogenic approach is the first, most historically dominant vision, derived from the Greek word *pathos*, meaning suffering or an emotion-evoking sympathy. The pathogenic approach views health as the absence of disability, disease, and premature death. The second approach is the salutogenic approach, which can be found in early Greek and Roman writings and was popularized by Antonovsky (1979) and humanistic scholars. Derived from the Latin word *salus*, meaning health, the salutogenic approach views health as the presence of positive states of human capacities and functioning in thinking, feeling, and behavior (Strümpfer, 1995). The third approach is the complete state model, which derives from the ancient word for health as being *hale*, meaning whole. This approach is exemplified in the World Health Organization's (1948) definition of overall health as a complete state, consisting of the presence of positive state of human capacities and functioning as well as the absence of disease or infirmity.

By subsuming the pathogenic and salutogenic paradigms, the whole states approach is the only paradigm that can achieve true population health in the 21st century. The model of health as a complete state will be illustrated through a review of the author's research on mental health as a complete state. Borrowing from the World Health Organization's (1948) definition of health, here I define mental health as not merely the absence of psychopathology, but the presence of sufficient levels of emotional, psychological, and social well-being (Keyes, 2002, 2005a, 2005b).

Mental Health as "Something Positive"

Until recently, mental health as something more than the absence of psychopathology remained undefined, unmeasured, and therefore unrecognized at the level of governments and nongovernmental organizations. In 1999, the Surgeon General, then Dr. David Satcher, conceived of mental health as "... a state of successful performance of mental function, resulting in productive activities, fulfilling relationships with people, and the ability to adapt to change and to cope with adversity" (U.S. Public Health Service, 1999, p. 4). In 2004, the World Health Organization published an historic first report on mental health promotion, conceptualizing mental health as not merely the absence of mental illness, but the presence of "... a state of well-being in which the individual realizes his or her own abilities, can cope with the normal stresses of life, can work productively and fruitfully, and is able to make a contribution to his or her community" (World Health Organization, 2004, p. 12).

These definitions affirmed the existing behavioral and social scientific vision of mental health as not merely the absence of mental illness, but the presence of something positive. Social and psychological scientists have been studying "something positive" in the domain of subjective well-being—individuals' evaluations and judgment of their own lives—for about 50 years (e.g., Gurin, Veroff, & Feld, 1960; Jahoda, 1958; see also Keyes, 2006). This research has yielded 13 specific dimensions of subjective well-being in the U.S. adult population. When factor-analyzed, studies show that the manifold scales measuring subjective well-being represent the latent structure of hedonic well-being (i.e., positive emotions toward one's life) and eudaemonic well-being (i.e., psychological well-being and social well-being) in adults (Keyes, Shmotkin, & Ryff, 2002; McGregor & Little, 1998; Ryan & Deci, 2001) and in a nationally representative sample of adolescents between the ages of 12 and 18 (Keyes, 2005c).

Subjective well-being research yielded clusters of mental health symptoms that mirror the cluster of symptoms used in the text revision of the fourth edition of the *Diagnostic and Statistical Manual of Mental Disorders* (DSM-IV-TR; American Psychiatric Association, 2000) to diagnose a major depressive episode (MDE). In the same way that depression requires symptoms of *an*-hedonia, mental health consists of symptoms of hedonia such as emotional vitality and positive feelings toward one's life. In the same way that major depression consists of symptoms of *mal*-functioning, mental health consists of symptoms of positive functioning. Table 9.1 presents clusters of symptoms of mental health. The diagnosis of states of mental health was modeled after the DSM-III-R approach to diagnosing MDE (Keyes, 2002). Each

measure of subjective well-being is considered a symptom because it represents an outward sign of an unobservable state. Latent, or directly unobservable, conditions must be inferred from symptoms. Moreover, mental health, like mental illness, is identifiable only as collections of signs and symptoms that, as a syndrome, reflect an underlying state of health or its absence.

To be diagnosed as "flourishing" in life, individuals must exhibit high levels on at least one measure of hedonic well-being and high levels on at least six measures of positive functioning. Individuals who exhibit low levels on at least one measure of hedonic well-being and low levels on at least six measures of positive functioning are diagnosed as "languishing" in life. Languishing in the absence of mental health is synonymous with saying that it is a state of being mentally *un*-healthy. To be languishing is to be in a state of being stuck, stagnant, or empty, and devoid of positive functioning in life. Adults who are "moderately mentally healthy" do not fit the criteria for either flourishing or languishing in life. A continuous assessment sums all measures of mental health that are coded into 10-point ranges after the Global Assessment of Functioning (GAF) approach in the DSM-III-R. For reasons reviewed by Kessler (2002) in the domain of psychopathology, I have used— and would recommend that others use—both the categorical and continuous assessment for mental health, because each approach provides valuable information and to see whether results and conclusions vary by each approach (see chap. 8).

Findings reviewed next are from several published papers that analyzed data from the MacArthur Foundation's 1995 Midlife in the United States (MIDUS) Survey. This survey was a random-digit-dialing sample of noninstitutionalized English-speaking adults between the ages of 25 and 74 living in the 48 contiguous states. The MIDUS survey used DSM-III-R (American Psychiatric Association, 1987) criteria to diagnose four mental disorders (i.e., MDE, panic, generalized anxiety, and alcohol dependence), which were operationalized by the Composite International Diagnostic Interview-Short Form (CIDI-SF) scales (Kessler, Andrews, Mroczek, Ustun, & Wittchen, 1998).

The Dual-Continua Model

Confirmatory factor analysis was used to test the theory that the MIDUS measures of mental health and mental illness belong to two latent continua. Three scales served as indicators of mental health: the summed scale of emotional well-being

Table 9.1 Categorical Diagnosis of Mental Health (i.e., Flourishing)

Diagnostic Criteria	Symptom Description
Hedonia: requires high level on at least one symptom scale (Symptoms 1 or 2)	1. Regularly cheerful, in good spirits, happy, calm and peaceful, satisfied, and full of life (*positive affect past 30 days*)
	2. Feels happy or satisfied with life overall or domains of life (*avowed happiness or avowed life satisfaction*)[a]
Positive functioning: requires high level on six or more symptom scales (Symptoms 3–13)	3. Holds positive attitudes toward oneself and past life and concedes and accepts varied aspects of self (*self-acceptance*)
	4. Has positive attitude toward others while acknowledging and accepting people's differences and complexity (*social acceptance*)
	5. Shows insight into own potential, sense of development, and open to new and challenging experiences (*personal growth*)
	6. Believes that people, social groups, and society have potential and can evolve or grow positively (*social actualization*)
	7. Holds goals and beliefs that affirm sense of direction in life and feels that life has a purpose and meaning (*purpose in life*)
	8. Feels that one's life is useful to society and the output of his or her own activities are valued by or valuable to others (*social contribution*)
	9. Exhibits capability to manage complex environment, and can choose or manage and mold environments to suit needs (*environmental mastery*)
	10. Interested in society or social life: feels society and culture are intelligible, somewhat logical, predictable, and meaningful (*social coherence*)
	11. Exhibits self-direction that is often guided by his or her own socially accepted and conventional internal standards and resists unsavory social pressures (*autonomy*)
	12. Has warm, satisfying, trusting personal relationships and is capable of empathy and intimacy (*positive relations with others*)
	13. Has a sense of belonging to a community and derives comfort and support from community (*social integration*)

[a] Life domains may include employment and marriage or close interpersonal relationship (e.g., parenting).

(i.e., single item of satisfaction + scale of positive affect), the summed scale of psychological well-being (i.e., six scales summed together), and the summed scale of social well-being (i.e., the fives scales summed together). Four summary measures served as indicators of mental illness, with each being operationalized as the number of symptoms of the following mental disorders: generalized anxiety, panic disorder, MDE, and alcohol dependence. Two competing theories—the single-factor and the two-factor model—were tested. The single-factor model hypothesizes that the measures of mental health and mental illness reflect a single—a latent—factor, support for which would indicate that the absence of mental illness implies the presence of mental health. The two-factor model hypothesizes that the measures of mental illness represent the latent factor of mental health that is distinct from, but correlated with, the latent factor of mental illness that is represented by the measures of mental illness. The data strongly supported the

two-factor model, which was a nearly perfect fitting model to the MIDUS data (Keyes, 2005a).

The latent factor of mental illness correlated -0.53 with the latent factor of mental health. As predicted, there is a modest association between mental health and mental illness; level of mental health tends to increase as level of mental illness decreases. The modest correlation suggests that the latent constructs of mental health and mental illness are distinctive. This distinctiveness raises the empirical question of the risk of an episode of mental illness as level of mental health decrease. Languishing adults report the highest prevalence of any of the four mental disorders as well as the highest prevalence of reporting two or more mental disorders during the past year. In contrast, flourishing individuals report the lowest prevalence of any of the four 12-month mental disorders or their comorbidity. Compared with languishing or flourishing, moderately mentally healthy adults were at intermediate risk of any of the mental disorders or two or more mental disorders during the past year. Thus, the 12-month risk of MDE, for example, is over 5 times greater for languishing than flourishing adults.

Support for the two-factor model provides the strongest scientific evidence to date in support of the complete health approach to mental health. That is, the evidence indicates that the absence of mental illness does not imply the presence of mental health, and the absence of mental health does not imply the presence of mental illness. Thus, neither the pathogenic (i.e., focus on the negative) nor salutogenic (i.e., focus on the positive) approaches alone accurately describe the mental health of a population. Rather, mental health is a complete state that is best studied through the combined assessments of mental health with mental illness. Complete mental health is a state in which individuals are free of mental illness and they are flourishing. Of course, flourishing may sometimes occur with an episode of mental illness, and moderate mental health and languishing can both occur with and without a mental illness.[1]

Mental Health as Flourishing Is Salutary

Research has supported the hypothesis that anything less than complete mental health results in increased impairment and disability (Keyes, 2002, 2004, 2005a, 2005b). For example, adults diagnosed as completely mentally healthy functioned superior to all others in terms of reporting the fewest workdays missed, fewest workdays cut back by one-half, the lowest rate of cardiovascular disease (CVD), the lowest level of health limitations of activities of daily living, the fewest chronic physical diseases and conditions, the lowest health-care utilization, and the highest levels of psychosocial functioning. In terms of psychosocial functioning, this meant that completely mentally healthy adults report the lowest level of perceived helplessness (e.g., low perceived control in life), the highest level of functional goals (e.g., knowing what they want from life), the highest level of self-reported resilience (e.g., that they try to learn from adversities), and the highest level of intimacy (e.g., that they have very close relationships with family and friends). In terms of all of these measures, completely mentally healthy adults functioned better than

adults with moderate mental health, who in turn functioned better than adults who were languishing.

Just over 20% of adults in the MIDUS study had an episode of at least one of the four mental disorders. Adults with a mental illness who had either moderate level of mental health or were flourishing reported fewer workdays missed, fewer workdays' cutback, and fewer health limitations of daily living than languishing adults. Thus, languishing individuals who also had one or more mental disorders functioned worse than all others on every criterion. Adults with a mental illness who also had either moderate mental health or flourishing function no worse than adults who were languishing and did not have a mental disorder. Thus, mental illness that is combined with languishing is more dysfunctional than the situation when a mental illness occurs in the context of moderate mental health or flourishing. Put differently, level of mental health within the population that has had an episode of mental illness distinguishes level of functioning.

The complete mental health diagnostic states have been shown to be independent risk factors for CVD (Keyes, 2004). In this paper, I focus on the combination of the categorical diagnosis of mental health with MDE, because the latter has been shown to be a risk factor for heart and arterial diseases. The unadjusted prevalence of any CVD was 8% among completely mentally healthy adults, compared with 12% of adults with moderate mental health, 12% of adults who were languishing, and 13% of adults with "pure" depression (i.e., had MDE but also fit the criteria for moderate mental health or flourishing). Among adults who were languishing and had an episode of major depression, the prevalence of any CVD was 19%. In multivariate analyses, completely mentally healthy adults had the lowest risk of a CVD. In fact, adults who fit the criteria for anything less than complete mental health had levels of relative risk for CVD that were comparable to the relative risk associated with diabetes, smoking cigarettes, and lack of physical exercise.

A recent paper (Keyes, 2005b) investigated the association of the complete mental health diagnoses with chronic physical conditions associated with age. The MIDUS survey included self-reported assessments of 27 chronic physical health conditions adapted from the Medical Outcomes Study. The complete mental health diagnosis was associated with 85% of the chronic physical conditions measured in the MIDUS survey (the Keyes 2005b paper focused only on MDE as the form of mental illness). The prevalence of chronic physical conditions was highest among adults

---

[1] In papers published to date (Keyes, 2002, 2004, 2005a, 2005b), individuals with a mental illness who were moderately mentally healthy or flourishing were collapsed into one group, because few flourishing individuals report an episode of mental illness and pooling these groups did not affect the results.

who are languishing and had an episode of major depression, and lowest among completely mentally healthy adults. The prevalence of chronic physical conditions was slightly higher among moderately mentally healthy adults than completely mentally healthy adults, whereas languishing adults reported even more chronic conditions than adults with moderate mental health.

Overall, adults with major depression and languishing had an average of 4.5 chronic conditions. Adults with depression but also had moderate mental health or flourishing had an average of 3.1 chronic conditions, which was the same as adults who were languishing but without any mental illness. Moderately mentally healthy adults without any mental illness had an average of 2.1 chronic conditions, compared with adults with complete mental health who had an average of 1.5 chronic conditions. Multivariate regression analyses confirmed that, when compared against completely mental healthy adults, chronic physical conditions increased as the level of mental health decreased. It is noteworthy that mental health status was a significant predictor of chronic physical conditions even after adjustment for the usual sociodemographic variables as well as body mass index, diabetes status, smoking status, and level of physical exercise.

Multivariate analyses also revealed statistically significant interactions of age with two of the complete mental health diagnostic states. While chronic physical conditions increased with age, there were two interaction effects: languishing by age and languishing with an episode of major depression by age. Young languishing adults have an average of one more chronic condition than young flourishing adults; midlife languishing adults report an average of about 1.7 more conditions than flourishing midlife adults; and languishing older adults have an average of 2.6 more chronic conditions than flourishing older adults. Similarly, young languishing adults with MDE report an average of 2.6 more chronic conditions than flourishing young adults; midlife languishing adults with MDE have an average of 3.5 more conditions than flourishing midlife adults; and languishing older adults who also had MDE have an average of 4.2 more chronic conditions than flourishing older adults. In short, languishing with, and languishing without, a mental illness is associated with increased chronic physical disease with age.

Results from this study suggest two important findings. First, adults who were completely mentally healthy had the lowest number of chronic physical conditions at all ages. Second, the youngest adults who were languishing had the same number of chronic physical conditions as older flourishing adults. Younger languishing adults who also had MDE had 1.5 more chronic conditions than older flourishing adults. In other words, the absence of mental health—whether it is languishing or languishing combined with a mental illness—appears to compound the risk of chronic physical disease with age.

In turn, Keyes and Grzywacz (2005) have found health-care utilization to be lowest among adults who are flourishing. Rates of overnight hospitalizations over the past year, outpatient medical visits over the past year, and number of prescription drugs were lowest among adults who were flourishing and physically healthy, followed by adults who were either flourishing but had physical illness conditions or adults who were not flourishing but were physically healthy. In short, complete mental health—that is, flourishing and the absence of mental illness—should be central to any national debate about health-care coverage and costs. Rather than focusing all discussions around health-care delivery and insurance, our nation must increase and protect the number of individuals who are healthy, driving down the need for health care.

Prevalence: Too Little Flourishing

The evidence just reviewed suggests that flourishing, a central component of complete mental health, is a desirable condition that any community, corporation, or government would want to protect or promote in its citizens. How much of the adult population is mentally healthy?

Figure 9.1 presents the point prevalence estimates previously reported in Keyes (2005a) with one exception. Figure 9.1 reports the prevalence of the relatively rare but important group of adults who, despite flourishing, reported at least one or more mental disorders. Only 17% of adults who were free of a mental illness during the past year fit the criteria for flourishing in life. Most of the adult population, that is, 51%, did not have an episode of mental illness but were only moderately mentally healthy. Worse yet, 10% of adults are mentally *un*-healthy, as they are languishing and did not fit the criteria for any of the four mental disorders—and languishing adults averaged 1 symptom of mental illness, suggesting that languishers may not be a subsyndromal form of mental illness. In addition, 23% of adults fit the criteria for one or more of the four mental disorders measured in the MIDUS survey. Of that 23%, 7% had a mental illness and fit the criteria for languishing, meaning individuals had an episode of mental illness along with the absence of mental health

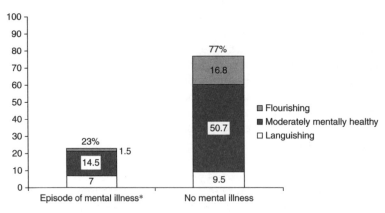

Fig. 9.1 Complete mental health: Prevalence of 12-month DSM-III-R mental disorders by mental health in the MIDUS study of U.S. adult population, ages 25–74 in 1995.

*Major depressive episode, panic disorder, generalized anxiety disorder, or alcohol dependence.

(i.e., languishing). Of the 23% with a mental illness, 14.5% had moderate mental health and 1.5% were flourishing.

The goal of any approach to a population's mental health should be (a) the reduction of mental illness and (b) the promotion of rates of complete mental health. Whereas it would be ideal if 60%, for example, of the population were flourishing and free of mental illness, barely 2 in every 10 adults are truly mentally healthy. Too many adults experience an episode of mental illness in a year, and too few adults are flourishing. Such findings suggest a need for national investments in the promotion of mental health as flourishing. The size of the adult population with moderate mental health, and its proximity to being completely mentally healthy, indicates a cost-effective leverage point for increasing national mental health. Evidence reviewed earlier suggests that reducing the size of the moderate mental health group by increasing its mental health could substantially reduce direct (e.g., health-care usage) and indirect (e.g., workdays missed) costs.

Conclusions

Measures of mental illness and measure of mental health form two distinct continua in the U.S. population. Measures of disability, chronic physical illness, psychosocial functioning, and health-care utilization reveal that anything less than flourishing is associated with increased impairment and burden to self and society. Only a small proportion of individuals free of a common mental disorder are mentally healthy, that is, "flourishing." Thus, the absence of mental illness is not the presence of mental health; flourishing individuals function markedly better than all others, but

only a fifth of the U.S. adult population is flourishing (Keyes, 2002, 2003, 2004, 2005a, 2005b).

The paradigm of mental health research and services in the United States must change in this century from pathogenic to the complete states approach. This paradigm seeks to understand the causes of mental illness and the causes of mental health (i.e., flourishing) to create and implement effective treatments, prevention, and promotion efforts in the population. To achieve a mentally healthier nation, we must simultaneously reduce the number of cases of mental illness and increase the number of individuals who are flourishing. Toward that end, Congress and policy makers should lobby to amend the "Healthy People" objectives to increase the rates of flourishing rather than only decrease the rates of specific disease conditions. In turn, branches within the National Institutes of Health should be expanded to include "salutogenic" laboratories for basic and applied science. Centers for Disease Control and Prevention can focus its state-wide surveillance of health conditions to include not only mental illness and distress but also the presence and absence of mental health. Counseling and clinical psychology programs would also need to increase faculty and training in "salutogenic" approaches to therapy.

Three Questions for Future Research

1. Does positive mental health cause mental illness? That is, do improvements in positive mental health decrease, while declines in positive mental health increase, the risk of mental illness?

2. What variables predict changes in positive mental health? That is, what is the epidemiology of flourishing?

3. Do patients with mental illness under treatment respond better to different forms of therapy depending on their level of positive mental health? That is, does a patient's positive mental health play a role in treatment response and risk of relapse after completion of therapy?

References

American Psychiatric Association. (1987). *Diagnostic and statistical manual of mental disorders* (3rd ed., Rev.). Washington, DC: Author.

American Psychiatric Association. (2000). *Diagnostic and statistical manual of mental disorders* (4th ed., Text rev.). Washington, DC: Author.

Antonovsky, A. (1979). *Health, stress, and coping*. San Francisco, CA: Jossey-Bass.

Gurin, G., Veroff, J., & Feld, S. (1960). *Americans view their mental health*. New York: Basic Books.

Jahoda, M. (1958). *Current concepts of positive mental health*. New York: Basic Books.

Kessler, R. C. (2002). The categorical versus dimensional assessment controversy in the sociology of mental illness. *Journal of Health and Social Behavior, 43*, 171–188.

Kessler, R. C., Andrews, G., Mroczek, D., Ustun, B., & Wittchen, H.-U. (1998). The world health organization composite international diagnostic interview short form (CIDI-SF). *International Journal of Methods in Psychiatric Research, 7*, 171–185.

Keyes, C. L. M. (2002). The mental health continuum: From languishing to flourishing in life. *Journal of Health and Social Behavior, 43*, 207–222.

Keyes, C. L. M. (2003). Complete mental health: An agenda for the 21st century. In C. L. M. Keyes & J. Haidt (Eds.), *Flourishing: Positive psychology and the life well-lived* (pp. 293–312). Washington, DC: American Psychological Association Press.

Keyes, C. L. M. (2004). The nexus of cardiovascular disease and depression revisited: The complete mental health perspective and the moderating role of age and gender. *Aging and Mental Health, 8*, 266–274.

Keyes, C. L. M. (2005a). Mental illness and/or mental health? Investigating axioms of the complete state model of health. *Journal of Consulting and Clinical Psychology, 73*, 539–548.

Keyes, C. L. M. (2005b). Chronic physical disease and aging: Is mental health a potential protective factor? *Ageing International, 30*, 88–104.

Keyes, C. L. M. (2005c). The subjective well-being of America's youth: Toward a comprehensive assessment. *Adolescent and Family Health, 4*, 3–11.

Keyes, C. L. M. (2006). Subjective well-being in mental health and human development research worldwide: An introduction. *Social Indicators Research, 77*, 1–10.

Keyes, C. L. M., & Grzywacz, J. G. (2005). Health as a complete state: The added value in work performance and healthcare costs. *Journal of Occupational and Environmental Medicine, 47*, 523–532.

Keyes, C. L. M., Shmotkin, D., & Ryff, C. D. (2002). Optimizing well-being: The empirical encounter of two traditions. *Journal of Personality and Social Psychology, 82*, 1007–1022.

McGregor, I., & Little, B. R. (1998). Personal projects, happiness, and meaning: On doing well and being yourself. *Journal of Personality and Social Psychology, 74*, 494–512.

Ryan, R. M., & Deci, E. L. (2001). On happiness and human potentials: A review of research on hedonic and eudaimonic well-being. *Annual Review of Psychology, 52*, 141–166.

Strümpfer, D. J. W. (1995). The origins of health and strength: From "salutogenesis" to "fortigenesis." *South African Journal of Psychology, 25*, 81–89.

U.S. Public Health Service. (1999). *Mental health: A report of the Surgeon General*. Rockville, MD: Author.

World Health Organization. (1948). World Health Organization constitution. In *Basic Documents*. Geneva: Author.

World Health Organization. (2004). *Promoting mental health: Concepts, emerging evidence, practice* (Summary report). Geneva: Author.

Modeling Positive Human Health: From Covariance Structures to Dynamic Systems

Anthony D. Ong *and* Alex J. Zautra

Abstract

In this chapter, we illustrate how recent advances in longitudinal methodology can be applied to diverse issues of interest to positive psychologists. The aim of the chapter is to describe how contemporary theories of well-being may be empirically evaluated using a variety of research designs and analytic techniques that can fully capture the complexity and dynamics of positive human health. Throughout, we identify unresolved methodological challenges associated with the measurement and analysis between- and of within-person phenomena and elaborate on the implications of these challenges for process research in positive psychology.

Keywords: dynamic systems, growth curves, longitudinal

> The life, the fortune and the happiness of every one of us depend on our knowing something about the rules of a game infinitely more difficult than chess. The chessboard is the universe, the pieces are the phenomena of the universe. The player on the other side is hidden from us. We know that his play is always fair, just and patient. But we also know, to our cost, that he never overlooks a mistake, or makes the smallest allowance for ignorance. To the man who plays well, the highest stakes are paid, with the sort of flowering generosity with which the strong show delight in strength. And he who plays ill is check-mated—without haste and without remorse. What I mean by education is learning the rules of this mighty game.
>
> —*Thomas H. Huxley* (1948), *A Liberal Education*

The rules for doing research that can net the highest stakes in understanding are, to a considerable extent, the rules of design and measurement. Many forms of data analysis can lead to the same conclusion when a study is well designed, but even the most intricate and powerful data analysis methods cannot extract a dependable basis for understanding when a study is poorly designed.

Design is critical. At the core of good design is good measurement. If the variables of an otherwise adequate design are not measured well, if they are not reliable and reliably independent, the results from analysis, however intricate and powerful these may be, can be of little value and may be quite misleading. It is therefore important to know the design properties of measurements, for these properties indicate what the results from analyses can and cannot reveal.

In this chapter, we illustrate how recent advances in longitudinal methodology can be applied to diverse issues of interest to positive psychologists. Although we do not intend to provide an in-depth review, we do strive to critically evaluate and address conceptual and methodological issues surrounding the need for (a) reliable and theory-driven measures of positive health and well-being, (b) study designs that link information at different levels of analysis, and (c) innovative methodological approaches that are sensitive to complex dynamic relationships. Progress on these issues requires a greater understanding of process. The aim of this chapter is to help build such understanding by describing how contemporary theories of well-being (i.e., subjective well-being and psychological well-being) may be empirically evaluated using a variety of research designs (e.g., longitudinal panel designs, intensive bursts designs) and analytic techniques (e.g., growth curve analysis and dynamic systems analysis) that can fully capture the complexity and dynamics of positive human health. We conclude with a brief discussion of methodological issues that might profitably be considered in future research.

Elaborating the "Positive" in Positive Psychology

Any theory that purports to be scientific should account for the extant evidence—ideally all of the evidence. It should also give indications of where new evidence should be sought that can test the theory and lead to modifications. A clear and detailed theoretical model thus is a necessary foundation for all empirical research. In an everyday sense of things, positive psychology is a theory of human strengths and potentials to which there are individual differences within the human species. Among the strengths and potentials that characterize humans in contrast to other species are some that allow for description of one individual as different from another. In all languages of the world there are words used to describe positive aspects of human functioning in which people differ. These positive aspects of human health have been referred to with the term "well-being." Positive psychology is thus a theory of human well-being.

There is a problem in describing theory in this way, however. Well-being is a singular word. But the accumulated evidence indicates that there is more than one kind of quality that is said to be characteristic of human well-being. These qualities appear to be positively correlated, but no unifying principle (such as the principle that unites different forms of energy—kinetic, heat, chemical, etc.) has been established that unites different forms of well-being. Thus, the problem is that use of the singular word "well-being" fosters belief that different positive human experiences are all forms of one thing, well-being, when the empirical evidence points to many more. It is possible that there is one organizing principle pervading all human well-being. It is reasonable that there should be. It would be valuable to have a measure of it. But the evidence adduced thus far does not indicate that principle. Studies that can lead to such discovery therefore need to be based on good understanding of empirical measurement evidence.

Measuring Dimensions of Positive Health and Well-Being

The theories of subjective well-being (SWB; Diener, 1984) and psychological well-being (PWB; Ryff, 1989) were developed in response to simple structure evidence of covariation among measures of human well-being. The theories are largely descriptive—and account of what are the dimensions that characterize the human capacity for generating and coping with complexities. But the theories are also a description of variables with which measures of human well-being correlate, and an account of how and why such relationships come about. The theories are thus also explanatory. Although both theories aim to describe how people evaluate their lives, each gives emphasis to different aspects of this evaluation.

SWB defines evaluations in terms of three elements: reports of positive and negative affect and judgments of overall life satisfaction (Diener, 1994). A key assertion of this model is that positive emotion defines a dimension of well-being that cannot be accounted for through the assessment of subjective distress, depressed affects, or other negative emotions (Watson, Clark, & Tellegen, 1988). Overall life satisfaction then is thought to depend on the promotion of positive states, the diminution of negative affects, and the cognitive structures that support judgments that weigh the positive in life more heavily than the negative.

In contrast, PWB parses well-being into six elements: judgments of self-acceptance, personal growth, purpose in life, positive relations with others, environmental mastery, and autonomy (Ryff & Keyes, 1995, chap. 9). The authors of this approach distinguish their model as one that focuses on stable, "stick-to-the-ribs," qualities of the person in comparison to models of happiness that rely on subjective reports of positive states that are more transitory. Indeed, measures of the positive differ dramatically in the proportion of variance in their scores that constitute a stable trait (see Kenny & Zautra, 2001) versus a state, which varies within a person over time. Seen in this light, the two approaches, SWB and PWB, may be thought of as more complementary, tackling different temporal aspects of the assessment of well-being.

Considerable progress has been made in identifying and measuring the separate elements of SWB and PWB. Reliable measures of these elements have been developed—the Positive and Negative Affect Schedule (PANAS; Watson et al., 1988), the Satisfaction With Life Scale (SWLS; Diener, Emmons, Larsen, & Griffin, 1985), and the PWB scales (Ryff, 1989). Different forms of evidence have been put forth to indicate the validity of these elements. Evidence of discriminant validity of SWB elements has been supported with multi-trait, multi-method analyses (Lucas, Diener, & Suh, 1996). Evidence of convergent validity of PWB elements has been indicated with common factor analyses (Ryff & Keyes, 1995). And evidence for the convergent and discriminant validity of all nine SWB and PWB elements has been supported with confirmatory factor analyses (Keyes, Shmotkin, & Ryff, 2002). Thus it has become clear that the phenomenon referred to as "well-being" is a mosaic of many component parts. This mosaic, such as it is, can be partitioned into a parsimonious set of dimensions, representing measurements that imperfectly account for individual differences among a large number of these components.

The Need for Idiographic Evidence

Although the foundational evidence has provided a basis for understanding the phenomenon of well-being, other basic information is needed to establish the nature of the phenomenon. That is, individuals are believed to exhibit coherent patterns of experience that cannot be fully described or explained merely by locating individuals within a fixed system of trait dimensions (Allport, 1966). Although nomothetic (between-person) analyses have yielded converging evidence for the construct validity of measures of SWB and PWB, very little attention has been given to investigating idiographic (within-person) relations among these elements (Ong, Horn, & Walsh, 2006).

Perhaps, nowhere more than in positive psychology is the importance of repeated measurement

and analysis so essential (Ong & van Dulmen, 2006). Studies that include only one occasion of measurement provide a good example of ambiguities that arise when an assumption of stability is made. These ambiguities have been described in detail by Nesselroade (1991a). When participants are measured on only one occasion, the "interindividual" variability in the measurements can reflect three different sources: (a) stable differences among people (traits), (b) "intraindividual" variability (states), and (c) temporal measurement error. These three possible sources of variation are inextricably confounded when data are obtained on only one occasion, and it is impossible to separate them (Nesselroade, 1991b).

Because phenomena also may vary reliably and lawfully within individuals, conclusions based on nomothetic research are premature without idiographic information (Nesselroade, 1991b). With few exceptions (e.g., Wessman & Ricks, 1966; Zevon & Tellegen, 1982), however, construct validation of SWB and PWB measures has been based largely on nomothetic rather than idiographic research. Little is known about whether the separate elements of SWB and PWB can be reliably and independently observed within individuals studied across time. To our knowledge, no study has provided evidence indicating that the reliability and independence of measurements that have been indicated in between-person analyses of both SWB and PWB (i.e., Keyes et al., 2002) also obtain for within-person observations of these phenomena. Evidence of this possibility is needed if SWB and PWB theories are to move beyond being simple descriptive empirical generalization of research findings to provide some indications of how positive health and well-being is organized within individuals, how such experience develops across the life span, or how individual differences in well-being come about.

The Need for Evidence of Measurement Invariance

Implicit in the comparison of groups and individuals is the assumption of equivalence of measurement. This assumption, however, is rarely tested directly in research in positive psychology. Yet the interpretation of either "interindividual" or "intraindividual" results, based on nonequivalent measurements, is riddled with ambiguity (Horn & McArdle, 1992). Evidence of measurement invariance is fundamentally important for evaluating both nomothetic and idiographic evidence. For in each case, before any construct validation results can be sensibly interpreted, there must be assurances that the scales measure the same attributes in the same way in different groups and circumstances. If scales do not measure the same factors (a) in the same way in different groupings of people or (b) in the same people measured in different places and times, there is no logical basis for interpreting the results of analyses of differences between means or variances or correlations (Meredith & Horn, 2001).

Do people interpret the items of SWB and PWB scales in comparable ways? A consistent finding in the literature is that women score slightly lower than men on measures of SWB (Lucas & Gohm, 2000), but significantly higher than men on PWB measures of Positive Relations with Others and Personal Growth (Ryff & Keyes, 1995). Although these observed differences may reflect valid psychological differences between men and women, it is also possible that the item content of certain SWB and PWB measures may differentially capture aspects of well-being that women are more likely to endorse, whereas the item content of other measures may summarize aspects of well-being that men are more likely to endorse (Ong et al., 2006). Establishing that an instrument is factorially invariant, therefore, provides evidence not only that respondents from different groups can be legitimately compared on the same scale, but also that observed group mean differences in raw scores reflect valid and meaningful group differences at the level of the latent variable assumed to underlie those scores. Evidence of measurement invariance across time, thus, is a necessary prerequisite for understanding all other evidence pertaining to the temporal validity of such constructs (Horn & McArdle, 1992; Meredith & Horn, 2001).

In essence, these concerns are all related to the larger issue of establishing the validity of measures of processes that are going on inside the person's head. Behavioral scientists rarely have been comfortable with the assumption that avowals of happiness and other states of well- and ill-being bear a one-to-one correspondence with actual states of well-being of the organism, and are even less comfortable with the assumption that the degree of accuracy of these accounts of subjective states is equivalent across people differing in personality, intelligence, and social situation. Recent advances in brain imaging have taken this question to a new level, pairing self-reports of emotive states with neural activation in regions of the brain known to be associated with those states. The evidence accumulated thus far suggests that there is considerable correspondence between self-reports of emotion and activation of

brain regions, but also that people can differ substantially in the degree of excitation in response to stimuli that provoke an emotional state (Craig, 2005).

Designing Studies of Change

Because the process of change represents a main, central issue for the study of positive psychology, needed are research designs that can capture ongoing processes of growth and adaptation. In this section, we highlight the utility of longitudinal panel and intensive bursts designs. Arguments are presented that bear on the value of these designs as underutilized approaches that appear particularly appropriate to the investigation of intraindividual change and variability in SWB and PWB. Throughout, we argue that the strength of the process approach is an essential shift away from cross-sectional, single-variable explanations toward person-centered accounts of positive health.

Longitudinal Panel Designs

Many of the most interesting research questions addressed in positive psychology relate to how individuals change over time and what factors influence the development of adaptive change. Longitudinal panel designs are particularly well suited for evaluating models of "long-term" change or development. In the typical longitudinal panel design, (a) data are collected at two or more points in time, (b) the same sample of people is interviewed at distinct points in time, and (c) data from the respondents are compared across these time points to monitor patterns of change. Although longitudinal panel designs vary with respect to the composition of the sample, the number of follow-up assessments, and the intervals between assessments, such designs share two defining characteristics. First, the same research participants, who constitute the "panel," are measured for two or more points in time (the measurement periods or "waves"). Second, at least one variable is measured for two or more waves. This is the "longitudinal" aspect of the data, which allows the measurement of qualitative or quantitative change within individuals from one wave to the next. In contrast to the longitudinal panel design, "cross-sectional" designs involve the assessment of research participants at only one measurement point (for a review, see Raudenbush, 2000).

Intensive Bursts Designs

There are times when the investigator is interested in closely observing change while it is occurring. In comparison with longitudinal panel designs, intensive bursts designs allow researchers to observe processes of "short-term" change within a rapidly changing window of time. The use of electronic diaries (e.g., palm pilots) allows for the study of the determinants and consequences of changes in well-being within people's everyday lives. The short time intervals between events and self-reports improve accuracy and reduce bias. In addition to these improvements in measurement precision, repeated assessments of the same person over time solves a serious problem in inference that plagues research in this area. Variables that predict differences between people on an outcome like happiness may have no effect or even the opposite effect on the same outcome when measured as a change within the person observed over time (Tennen & Affleck, 1996). Only careful studies that evaluate changes over time in both the independent and dependent variable can safely make such assertions. Finally, electronic diaries have methodological advantages that are connected to the use of intensive bursts designs. First, electronic diaries allow individuals to report their behavior and experiences over the range of situational circumstances experienced in everyday life. Second, they allow for statistical modeling of behavior over time. Third and most important, such procedures can test, rather than assume, the validity of the nomothetic approach.

Methodologies That Are Sensitive to Dynamic Relationships

In addition to designing studies of change, one critical aspect of testing theories of change is fitting models of change to empirical data. In this section, we describe analytic possibilities that are available for longitudinal panel designs and for intensive bursts designs. We focus our comments on two general data analysis strategies, namely those associated with growth curve modeling and dynamic systems analysis, respectively. For a more thorough discussion of other statistical approaches for modeling change, the interested reader is referred to Collins and Horn (1991), Collins and Sayer (2000), Kenny and Zautra (2001), McArdle and Hamagami (2001), and Raudenbush (2001).

Growth Curve Modeling

One of the major goals of positive psychology is to determine factors that influence normal and optimal development. These factors may be fixed at a particular level (e.g., gender, ethnicity) or variable (e.g., physical health, emotions). Traditional statistical methods such as repeated measures analysis of variance cannot take into account the time-varying nature of covariates. The most commonly used approach to modeling change in continuous variables that allow for time-varying covariates is "growth curve models." Growth curve models, such as hierarchical linear models (Raudenbush, 2000), fit growth trajectories for individuals and relate characteristics of these individual growth trajectories (e.g., slope) to covariates. Because these models typically involve relatively few occasions of measurements, longitudinal panel designs are generally the temporal design of choice when fitting growth curve models. The individual growth trajectory can be expressed as

$$Y_{ti} = \beta_{0i} + \beta_{1i}x_{ti} + e_{ti}$$

for a linear model of growth. Y_{ti} represents individual i's outcome score at time t, where $t = 1, \ldots, T$; x_{ti} represents the measure of time for individual i; and β_{0i} and β_{1i} represent the intercept and slope, respectively, of linear growth for individual i. This is often referred to as the level 1 equation. The intercept and slope parameters are random effects; in other words, they may vary across individuals, as reflected in the need for the i subscript denoting individual. This leads directly to the level 2 equations:

$$\beta_{0i} = \gamma_{00} + u_{0i}$$

$$\beta_{1i} = \gamma_{10} + u_{1i}$$

Growth curve modeling is an appropriate technique for studying individual change because repeated measures can be considered as nested within individuals and can be represented as a two-level hierarchical model. At the within-person level, each individual's development is modeled as a unique growth trajectory. At between-person level, the growth parameters of these trajectories become the outcome variables, which are then modeled as a function of person-level characteristics. Consider a growth trajectory of SWB for individual A with intercept β_{0A} and slope β_{1A}. The level 2 equations state that individual A's intercept β_{0A} can be decomposed into two components: the grand mean of all the β_{0i}'s for all individuals, γ_{00}, and β_{0A}'s deviation from this grand mean, u_{0A}. Likewise, individual A's slope β_{1A} can be decomposed into two components: the grand mean of all the β_{1i}'s for all individuals, γ_{10}, and β_{1A}'s deviation from this grand mean, u_{1A}. Interindividual variability in intercepts is expressed in the variance of the u_{0i}'s, and interindividual variability in slope is expressed in the variance of the u_{1i}'s.

It is possible to include predictors in addition to time (or even instead of time) in the level 1 equation, and to include time-invariant predictors in the level 2 equation. For excellent overviews of growth curve and hierarchical linear models for longitudinal panel studies, the reader is referred to Raudenbush (2000), McArdle and Nesselroade (2003), and Maxwell and Tiberio (2007).

Dynamic Systems Analysis

A recent implementation of intensive bursts designs is dynamic systems analysis. Fundamentally, a dynamical systems approach offers a way to formalize concepts of self-regulation. The focus is on modeling or representing the relationships between the current state of a variable or an ensemble of variables and the subsequent state of such variables (Boker & Nesselroade, 2002). One key advantage of the dynamic systems approach over other approaches to modeling dynamic processes is the capacity to represent "shocks" or other inputs from outside the individual.

For example, consider a model of self-regulation that reflects a "pendulum with friction," which is hypothesized to best exemplify the intraindividual disregulation that may result from exposure to daily stress. This model is referred to as a "damped linear oscillator." The equation for the damped linear oscillator can be expressed as a linear regression formula in which the acceleration of the pendulum is the outcome variable and the position and velocity of the pendulum are the predictor variables (Boker, 2001). From a developmental perspective, "velocity" may refer to the linear change in the system (e.g., change in mood), and "acceleration" may pertain to the curvature (e.g., the speed with which the mood change occurs). Differential equation models express effects within a system in terms of their derivatives (i.e., the instantaneous rates of change of the variables), as well as in terms of the values of the variables themselves. For example, a differential equation model of emotion regulation following stress might relate daily affect to its slope, or first derivative (i.e., how rapidly an individual's mood was changing). A more complete model might include effects related to its curvature, or second derivative (i.e., how rapidly mood was accelerating and decelerating in its change). These three parameters—initial position (emotion/affect), velocity (change), and acceleration (speed of change)—represent a dynamical system in which the relationships between them define a central tendency of a family of trajectories that any one individual might have (Boker & Nesselroade, 2002).

The regression coefficients from this structural equation model, in turn, define order parameters (e.g., frequency and decay rate) of the system that best represents the interrelations between variability in affect and stress over time. The dynamic systems approach is both efficient and powerful, since it can identify intraindividual fluctuations in dynamics using relatively sparse data.

Summary and Conclusions

We have strived to demonstrate in this chapter that positive psychology is a theory with many facets. But to recognize that positive psychology has many facets is merely to start to understand it. Just what are the facets? How do they emerge in culture and in individuals? What are their functions? How do they change and evolve over time? We offer no definitive answers to these questions. Rather, we have attempted to provide a general orienting framework that can guide the thinking of researchers about positive psychological phenomena, sensitize them to the kinds of data that are needed to study these phenomena, and suggest fruitful lines of analyses and interpretation of their effects.

In particular, we have suggested that scientific understanding has moved away from the idea that human well-being can be well represented by a single dimension. Evidence accumulated over the course of this century has made it clear that the phenomenon of human well-being is multidimensional. Therein lies a problem in identifying particularly happy individuals; therein lies a problem of determining where to look for particularly happy individuals; therein lies a difficulty of examining a hypothesis stipulating that, on average, happy people will display more wisdom and character than unhappy people. Jahoda (1958) brought attention to this problem 50 years ago and it still does not have a ready solution. The use of eudaemonic indicators solves one problem but introduces another: In what sense is one better off with a higher "purpose in life," to take one example, if unhappiness accompanies it? A reliance on measures of physical health as outcomes has been a steadying influence, but it is important to identify the implicit model that underlies the use of health as an outcome for studies in positive psychology.

We also have suggested that one major limitation of current theorizing in positive psychology is inherent in the very properties of extant measurement tools. That is, most theories of well-being (SWB and PWB) are described in terms of Cartesian coordinates or factors. These factors may be rotated into an infinity of different positions, each equally adequate for describing the relationships among dimensions of well-being, but each calling for different concepts and different languages for describing human well-being. A metatheory of simple structure has guided the rotation that has been accepted as the basic structure of SWB and PWB theory. This metatheory requires that manifest dimensions of well-being relate to a finite number of factors. This is a reasonable requirement for studies designed to indicate it—and many studies have been so designed—but it is not an indication of how well-being *must* be organized to account for relationships that are observed within and across individuals.

Finally, we have underscored the importance of taking a process approach to understanding the complexity of positive human health and well-being. Extant theories of SWB and PWB provide few details about how well-being develops or about how positive psychological states interact and work together to produce optimal human functioning.

These theories thus do little to indicate the dynamics of human adaptation. The kind of system that ultimately will best describe such adaptation and its development, contend will be functional and will map on to the human brain. Over time, such a system might be more nearly of the form of a spiral of Archimedes, out of which evolves a repetitive building on what is known (induction), which leads to deductions that generate empirical studies and more induction, which leads to further deductions, which spawn further induction, and so on. In the long run, knowing that science is a never-ending search for better explanations and that no theory is ever complete we can be confident that SWB and PWB theories will be replaced by a better theory.

Future Questions

1. How is positive health and well-being organized across individuals?

2. How does positive health and well-being develop across the lifespan?

3. How do individual differences in positive health and well-being come about?

References

Allport, G. W. (1966). Traits revisited. *American Psychologist, 21,* 1–10.

Boker, S. M. (2001). Differential models and differential structural equation modeling of intraindividual variability. In L. M. Collins & A. G. Sayer (Eds.), *New methods for the analysis of change* (pp. 5–27). Washington, DC: American Psychological Association.

Boker, S. M., & Nesselroade, J. R. (2002). A method for modeling the intrinsic dynamics of intraindividual variability: Recovering the parameters of simulated oscillators in multi-wave panel data. *Multivariate Behavioral Research, 37,* 127–160.

Collins, L. M., & Horn, J. L. (Eds.). (1991). *Best methods for the analysis of change: Recent advances, unanswered questions, future directions.* Washington, DC: American Psychological Association.

Collins, L. M., & Sayer, A. G. (2000). Modeling growth and change processes: Design, measurement, and analysis for research in social psychology. In C. M. Judd & H. T. Reiss (Eds.), *Handbook of research methods in social and personality psychology* (pp. 478–495). New York: Cambridge University Press.

Craig, A. D. (2005). Forebrain emotional asymmetry: a neuroanatomical basis? *Trends in Cognitive Sciences, 9,* 566–571.

Diener, E. (1984). Subjective well-being. *Psychological Bulletin, 95,* 542–575.

Diener, E. (1994). Assessing subjective well-being: Progress and opportunities. *Social Indicators Research, 31,* 103–157.

Diener, E., Emmons, R. A., Larsen, R. J., & Griffin, S. (1985). The satisfaction with life scale. *Journal of Personality Assessment, 49,* 71–75.

Horn, J. L., & McArdle, J. J. (1992). A practical and theoretical guide to measurement invariance in aging research. *Experimental Aging Research, 18,* 117–144.

Huxley, T. H. (1948). *Selections from the essays of Thomas Henry Huxley.* New York: Crofts Classics.

Jahoda, M. (1958). *Current concepts in positive mental health.* New York: Basic Books.

Kenny, D. A., & Zautra, A. (2001). Trait-state models for longitudinal data. In L. M. Collins & A. G. Sayer (Eds.), *New methods for the analysis of change* (pp. 243–263). Washington, DC: American Psychological Association.

Keyes, C. L. M., Shmotkin, D., & Ryff, C. D. (2002). Optimizing well-being: The empirical encounter of two traditions. *Journal of Personality and Social Psychology, 82,* 1007–1022.

Lucas, R. E., Diener, E., & Suh, E. (1996). Discriminant validity of well-being measures. *Journal of Personality and Social Psychology, 71,* 616–628.

Lucas, R. E., & Gohm, C. L. (2000). Age and sex differences in subjective well-being across cultures. In E. M. Suh & E. Diener (Eds.), *Culture and subjective well being* (pp. 291–317). Cambridge: The MIT Press.

Maxwell, S., & Tiberio, S. (2007). Multilevel models of change: Fundamental concepts and relationships to mixed models and latent growth curve models. In A. D. Ong & M. H. V. Dulmen (Eds.), *Oxford handbook of methods in positive psychology* (pp. 439–452). New York: Oxford University Press.

McArdle, J. J., & Hamagami, F. (2001). Latent difference score structural models for linear dynamic analyses with incomplete longitudinal data. In L. M. Collins & A. G. Sayer (Eds.), *New methods for the analysis of change* (pp. 139–175). Washington, DC: American Psychological Association.

McArdle, J. J., & Nesselroade, J. R. (2003). Growth curve analysis in contemporary psychological research. In W. F. Velicer & J. A. Schinka (Eds.), *Handbook of psychology: Research methods in psychology* (pp. 447–480). New York: Wiley.

Meredith, W., & Horn, J. L. (2001). The role of factorial invariance in modeling growth and change. In L. M. Collins & A. G. Sayer (Eds.), *New methods for the analysis of change* (pp. 203–240). Washington, DC: American Psychological Association.

Nesselroade, J. R. (1991a). The warp and woof of the developmental fabric. In R. M. Downs, L. S. Liben, & D. S. Palermo (Eds.), *Visions of aesthetics, the environment & development: The legacy of Joachim F. Wohlwill* (pp. 214–242). Hillsdale, NJ: Erlbaum.

Nesselroade, J. R. (1991b). Interindividual differences in intraindividual change. In L. M. Collins & J. L. Horn (Eds.), *Best methods for the analysis of change: Recent advances, unanswered questions, future directions* (pp. 92–105). Washington, DC: American Psychological Association.

Ong, A. D., Horn, J. L., & Walsh, D. A. (2006). Stepping into the light: Modeling the dynamics of hedonic and eudaemonic well-being. In A. D. Ong & M. van Dulmen (Eds.), *Oxford handbook of methods in positive psychology* (pp. 12–25). New York: Oxford University Press.

Ong, A. D., & van Dulmen, M. (Eds.). (2006). *The Oxford handbook of methods in positive psychology.* New York: Oxford University Press.

Raudenbush, S. W. (2000). Comparing personal trajectories and drawing causal inferences from longitudinal data. *Annual Review of Psychology, 52,* 501–525.

Raudenbush, S. W. (2001). Toward a coherent framework for comparing trajectories of individual change. In A. G. Sayer & L. M. Collins (Eds.), *New methods for the analysis of change* (pp. 33–64). Washington, DC: American Psychological Association.

Ryff, C. D. (1989). Happiness is everything, or is it? Explorations on the meaning of psychological well-being. *Journal of Personality and Social Psychology, 57,* 1069–1081.

Ryff, C. D., & Keyes, C. L. M. (1995). The structure of psychological well-being revisited. *Journal of Personality and Social Psychology, 69,* 719–727.

Tennen, H., & Affleck, G. (1996). Daily processes in coping with chronic pain: Methods and analytic strategies. In N. S. Endler & M. Zeidner (Eds.), *Handbook of coping: Theory, research, applications* (pp. 151–177). Oxford: Wiley.

Watson, D., Clark, L. A., & Tellegen, A. (1988). Development and validation of brief measures of positive and negative affect: The PANAS scales. *Journal of Personality and Social Psychology, 54,* 1063–1070.

Wessman, A. E., & Ricks, D. F. (1966). *Mood and personality.* Oxford: Holt, Rinehart, and Winston.

Zevon, M. A., & Tellegen, A. (1982). The structure of mood change: An idiographic/nomothetic analysis. *Journal of Personality and Social Psychology, 43,* 111–122.

Positive Ethics: Themes and Variations

Mitchell M. Handelsman, Samuel Knapp, *and* Michael C. Gottlieb

Abstract

Psychology has a history of approaching ethics from a rule-based perspective. The APA Ethics Code was developed by focusing on problematic behaviors, and ethics training is often concerned with helping psychologists protect themselves from ethics complaints and lawsuits. Recently, many scholars have been focusing on positive approaches to ethics. Positive ethics shifts the emphasis from following rules and avoiding discipline to encouraging psychologists to aspire to their highest ethical ideals. Such a positive focus might help psychologists consider ethical issues in a broader context that could contribute to better decision making and better integration of professional rules with personal principles and values. Positive ethics might also contribute to a greater degree of openness so that psychologists feel freer to seek the assistance of others. We discuss several major trends in the literature under the themes of self-awareness, professional awareness, and global awareness. Self-awareness includes understanding our own values and motives. Being more reflective about our values may help us develop ethical sensitivity—the ability to recognize ethical dimensions in our work even when no dilemmas or conflicts exist. Self-awareness also includes taking care of ourselves in all areas of our lives, and developing virtues—character traits that allow us to fulfill both personal and professional moral motivations. Our second theme, professional awareness, includes ethical acculturation, which refers to integrating our personal and professional moralities throughout our professional development. We need to understand the moral traditions that underlie our ethical reasoning. We can also prevent many ethical problems and dilemmas by anticipating them, obtaining consultation, and engaging in continuing education. Our third theme—global awareness— includes multicultural sensitivity, political sensitivity, and civic virtue.

Keywords: ethical acculturation, ethics, positive ethics, self-care, virtue ethics

Psychology, as a profession, is young, and contemporary notions of professional ethics have developed relatively recently. Only after disclosure of the Nazi atrocities of World War II did professions focus on how to behave ethically. For example, documents such as the Nuremburg Code of 1947 and the 1964 Declaration of Helsinki (Levine, 1986) were written with the purpose of protecting research participants from abuse (Appelbaum, Lidz, & Meisel, 1987).

Also during the post–World War II period, as veterans returned to pursue their interrupted educational goals, professional psychology came into its own. The young professionals of that time were acutely aware of how people had been abused under the guise of research, and so wanted to establish higher standards for themselves and their nascent profession. Given this historical context, it is easy to understand why an emerging profession wanted to develop an ethics code. Because professionals are placed in powerful positions by society, because they have the opportunity to both help and harm others, and because of their fiduciary obligations to those in their care, their behavior should be regulated.

The American Psychological Association (APA) produced its first ethics code in 1953 (APA, 1953), creating this document by soliciting examples of critical incidents or problematic situations faced by researchers and practitioners (Kimmel, 1988; Pope & Vetter, 1992). By using real ethical dilemmas as examples, the authors hoped the code would achieve some level of ecological validity. This approach was well received, and it continued as the basis for many future revisions of the code.

It was not until 1992 that APA modified the overall organization of the code (APA, 1992). This version began with a section of aspirational principles that, with some modifications, was retained in the 2002 revision (APA, 2002). These principles are derived from overarching principles of biomedical ethics (Beauchamp & Childress, 2001) and set the foundation—if not the tone—for the standards that follow. The principles are promoting human welfare and avoiding harm; being faithful and responsible; maintaining one's integrity; promoting justice and fairness; and respecting the rights and dignity of others. The aspirational principles make a clear statement about the identity and values of psychologists, and they closely resemble the goals that motivate people to become psychologists.

Unfortunately, the influence of these aspirational principles has been small. The profession—whose code was developed by focusing on problematic behaviors and minimum standards—still turns in the direction of emphasizing the enforceable standards. For example, the APA (2002) code contains 626 words explaining five broad principles and 7,857 words specifying 89 standards. The outcome of this "remedial" (Knapp & VandeCreek, 2006, p. 4) emphasis is unfortunate. Rather than encouraging its trainees and members to do the right thing for others and society, the profession teaches them how to circle the wagons to protect themselves from ethics complaints and lawsuits. Bersoff (1994) described this aptly when he noted, "The current code, at best, builds an ethical floor but hardly urges us to reach for the ceiling" (p. 385).

As professional practice has become more complex, and society more litigious, psychologists have become alienated from the moral roots of the profession and find it difficult to discuss ethical issues in a way that actualizes their vision of what it means to be a professional. We believe it is time for a mid-course correction. In this chapter, we bring together several threads from the fields of positive psychology and professional ethics that form a basis for further study and application of ethical excellence.

Positive Ethics

The advent of the positive psychology initiative provided us with an opportunity to address our concerns. In 2002, we wrote, "Current notions of professional ethics focus too heavily on avoiding or punishing misconduct rather than promoting the highest ethical conduct. We contend that . . . the prevailing models of ethics are too rule-bound or defensive" (Handelsman, Knapp, & Gottlieb, 2002, p. 732). With this as a premise, we proposed that the profession refocus its efforts in the direction of what we termed "positive ethics." The goal of positive ethics was to shift the primary emphasis from avoiding discipline to a "more balanced and integrative approach that includes encouraging psychologists to aspire to their highest ethical potential" (p. 731).

Although we first used the term positive ethics (Handelsman et al., 2002), the concept of seeking guidance from overarching ethical theories and principles is not new. For example, Brown (1994) warned psychologists not to let ethics become "a concrete wall hemming us in, forbidding us from human connectedness" (p. 276). Kitchener (2000) urged psychologists "to turn to the foundational ethical principles and theories" (p. 20), and Bricklin (2001) noted that being ethical means more than just obeying the law. Fisher (1994) argued for a duty-based (rather than rule-based) perspective to resolve ethical dilemmas in research.

We proposed that an explicit and comprehensive emphasis on positive ethics might accomplish a number of things. First, a positive emphasis might help psychologists consider ethical issues in a broader context. That is, ethical decision making should include a greater awareness of personal and professional values as well as social influences. Providing an alternative to models of "ethical sickness" (Handelsman et al., 2002, p. 732) may help psychologists explore their own values and find personal bases for actions consistent with their professional obligations. By looking at obligations from this perspective, psychologists could strive for their professional best instead of settling for the professional minimum.

Second, we feared that too many students and colleagues failed to see the relationship between enforceable standards and overarching ethical values. A positive emphasis might expand awareness and help them better integrate the profession's rules with its aspirational principles.

Third, the profession has advanced to the point where many practitioners are specialized and work in highly technical and complex areas. Such an environment demands great thoughtfulness when ethical dilemmas arise. In an atmosphere of anxiety over professional liability, professionals might feel deterred from seeking the consultation of trusted colleagues precisely at a time when they need it the most. Positive ethics might contribute to a greater degree of openness so that colleagues feel freer to seek the assistance of others.

Recent scholarship has shifted the ethical discourse into more positive directions; in this chapter, we review several of these trends. We have organized our discussion into three basic themes, moving from the micro- to the macro-level: (a) self-awareness, (b) professional awareness, and (c) global awareness. These themes overlap and cannot be appreciated or applied in a linear manner; however, we believe this structure helps us organize and understand some disparate threads in the literature that can help psychologists strive for ethical excellence and develop a comprehensive professional identity.

Self-Awareness
Values and Motives

Like others, psychologists seek meaningful goals and authentic happiness. Although few psychologists have formally studied philosophical ethics, most have developed a personal set of values influenced by their upbringing, religious tradition, and/ or cultural background. For most psychologists, their career choice was an opportunity to actualize their values, such as reducing suffering and helping others live better lives.

Psychologists who strive for ethical excellence seem to place great value on their professional activities. They seem to have what Rest (1986) called moral motivation, or the ability to prioritize moral values relative to other values and act on those values. Recent research (e.g., Greitemeyer, Fischer, Kastenmueller, & Frey, 2006) has focused on moral courage—the ability to act on moral values in spite of the personal or professional consequences.

Outstanding psychologists also reflect on their personal motives and acknowledge the self-interest involved in their professional activities so they can modulate appropriate professional gratifications— for example, making money, feeling good about good decisions made by clients, professional recognition—and separate them from inappropriate motivations such as sexual exploitation. In this regard, Pope, Sonne, and Greene (2006) provided an extremely useful guide to initiating discussions of topics that have traditionally been taboo. At first glance, the topics that Pope et al. discuss appear to be quite negative (e.g., sexual feelings in therapy,

disgust, racial prejudice). However, the positive contribution the authors make highlights the need to recognize and discuss the entire range of feelings and motives that can influence ethical judgment and behavior.

Ethical Sensitivity

Being more self-reflective and mindful (Seif, 2006) of their values and motives may help psychologists be more sensitive to the ethical dimensions inherent in their work. Rest (1986) referred to this notion as moral sensitivity, and Tjeltveit (1999, 2006) discussed "ethical acuity" (1999, p. 272; i.e., the ability to recognize the ethical dimensions of situations).

In ethics training, case studies are seen as valuable tools (Pettifor, Estay, & Paquet, 2002). Unfortunately, many case examples only present conflicts between ethical principles; they may give the impression that ethical deliberation is needed only in dilemmatic situations. Although it is important to know how to respond when dilemmas arise, Tjeltveit and others (e.g., de las Fuentes, Willmuth, & Yarrow, 2005) have recognized the importance of ethical reflection and sensitivity even in situations where no dilemmas exist. Knapp and VandeCreek (2003) discussed psychologists' supererogatory obligations, suggesting that we consider the moral requirements that go beyond the minimum required by codes, rules, and statutes (see also Knapp, Gottlieb, & Handelsman, 2004).

Ethical sensitivity is a useful skill, but self-reflection is not perfect (Dunning, Heath, & Suls, 2004). Thus, even as psychologists develop their sensitivity and reasoning skills, the need for consultation does not diminish. We will have more to say about consultation later.

Self-Care

The link between individual well-being and higher goals was recognized by Immanuel Kant. Although Kant believed that the goal of life was to fulfill one's moral obligations, he stated that "to secure one's own happiness is a duty, at least indirectly; for discontent with one's condition, under a pressure of many anxieties and amidst unsatisfied wants, might easily become a great temptation to transgression of duty" (1785/1988, p. 23). In other words, the lack of happiness may inhibit people from fulfilling their duties.

Professional activities cannot provide all of life's satisfactions; the field of psychology also presents challenges that can foster discouragement and demoralization. For example, psychology students can be in for rude awakenings when they encounter patients who display extreme hostility or despair, students who lack motivation to learn, or research colleagues who use questionable methodology to promote their research.

One rationale for psychologists taking care of themselves comes from Standard 2.06 of the APA (2002) code, which prohibits psychologists from doing work when they know or should know that their personal problems may prevent them from acting competently. However, good self-care should go beyond just avoiding incompetence. Without neglecting other obligations, psychologists should strive for personal well-being and happiness (Norcross & James, 2005). Self-care includes paying attention to relationships and social support (Coster & Schwebel, 1997), balancing time and emotional investment, peer consultation, personal psychotherapy, and physical well-being.

Self-care entails recognition that a meaningful life is one that uses signature strengths in the fulfillment of important goals that transcend the self (Seligman, 2002). Consistent with positive psychology, self-care should focus on ways psychologists can fulfill their highest aspirations. For example, psychologists who practice good self-care may be more likely to experience flow (Csikszentmihalyi, 1990) and wisdom (Baltes, Gluck, & Kunzmann, 2002). Psychologists who pursue personal well-being should be better able to fulfill their professional obligations (Barnett, Johnston, & Hillard, 2006). For example, applying the work of Frederickson (2002), we would predict that psychologists who experience more positive emotions are better at professional decision making. Fredrickson concluded that "we should cultivate positive emotions in our own lives and in the lives of those around us not just because doing so makes us feel good in the moment but also because doing so will transform us to be better people" (p. 131).

Virtues

Rule-based or principle-based ethics invites us to ask the question, "What should (or shouldn't) I do?" Values clarification invites us to ask, "What do I believe?" Virtue ethics (Jordan & Meara, 1990; Meara, Schmidt, & Day, 1996) takes the next step and encourages us to ask, "Who should I be?" Fowers (2005) saw the Aristotelian ideal of the virtuous person—who "knows how to act well and does so gladly" (p. 73)—as a goal for psychologists. He concluded, "The science and practice of psychology are inherently ethical endeavors that we

can pursue best if we are clear about the goods we seek and cultivate the character strengths that support that pursuit" (2005, pp. x–xi).

A number of researchers are investigating virtues empirically. Peterson and Seligman (2004) identified six virtues that have appeared across time and cultures: courage, justice, humanity, temperance, transcendence, and wisdom. Walker and Hennig (2004) identified moral exemplars as being just, brave, and caring. Osswald, Greitemeyer, Fischer, and Frey (2006) found evidence that activating moral prototypes—making people aware of these qualities in themselves or others—influences ethical behavior. We believe this may be a more promising approach than fear-based risk management training strategies (Gleicher & Petty, 1992; Jepson & Chaiken, 1990).

One implication of appreciating and measuring virtue as an element of professional ethics is the suggestion that virtue, or character and fitness, should be used as a criterion for admission to graduate training programs (Johnson & Campbell, 2004; Pipes, Holstein, & Aguirre, 2005). Pipes et al. argued that training programs "must select individuals whose character includes qualities such as truthfulness, personal responsibility, and integrity" (2005, p. 332).

In regard to virtues as selection criteria, the theory is ahead of the application. Johnson and Campbell (2004) found that directors of clinical training programs were concerned about the character and fitness of their applicants, and rated virtues such as integrity, prudence, and caring as very important. They also noted, however, that current methods of assessing character—including letters of recommendation and interviews—are not very useful. A subsequent study (Johnson, Porter, Campbell, & Kupko, 2005) found that state licensing boards were inconsistent in their assessment of character and fitness of applicants for licensure. Perhaps the empirical work on virtues and moral prototypes will soon have practical applications in the screening of graduate applicants and the assessment of students' progress in training programs. It is to issues of professional training and development that we now turn our attention.

Professional Awareness
Ethical Acculturation

Ethical sensitivity is important in its own right, but it also forms a major component of professional identity development that we have called "ethical acculturation" (Handelsman, Gottlieb, & Knapp,

2005, p. 59). The ethical acculturation model, based on Berry's (2003) model of acculturation, is a more positive alternative to many traditional models of ethics training in which students become passive recipients of rules, principles, and guidelines.

The ethical acculturation model conceives of professional development—from the first day of graduate school until retirement—as an acculturation process in which the major task is the integration of preexisting ethical values, thoughts, and traditions, with the ethical traditions and values that characterize the culture of psychology. Integration involves synthesizing one's own moral sense into professional deliberations as well as recognizing when conflicts exist between them. The acculturation model invites trainers to get to know students' backgrounds, and to understand conflicts students may experience as acculturation stressors requiring choices rather than as intellectual or moral failures (Bashe, Anderson, Handelsman, & Klevansky, 2007; Gottlieb, Handelsman, & Knapp, 2008; Knapp & VandeCreek, 2006).

Pipes et al. (2005) also discussed the relationship between personal and professional ethics. They noted that the APA (2002) Ethical Standards are not applicable to personal behavior but that the boundary between personal and professional behavior is not always clear. Thus, it is important to be reflective about that boundary and attempt a "fusion" (p. 331) between personal and professional values. "In this sense, the emphasis is not on 'What am I free to do in my personal life that is unregulated by the Code?' but rather 'What are those enduring values that cut across my professional life and my personal life?'" (Pipes et al., 2005, p. 331).

Pipes et al. (2005) argued that virtue ethics is a good way to help psychologists think through the relationship between personal and professional behaviors. "Virtue ethics... suggests that the kind of person someone is (in some total sense) drives what the person does and how the person thinks in the professional as well as in the personal realm" (p. 330).

Ethical Reasoning and Decision Making

With the goal of fusion or integration, ethical reasoning and decision making—what Rest (1986) called moral judgment—takes on a broader role than simply helping psychologists choose actions that are just good enough to avoid sanctions. Actualizing ethical ideals involves using our own motives, values, supererogatory obligations (Knapp & VandeeCreek, 2003), and practical wisdom

(Fowers, 2005) to make decisions that are morally praiseworthy.

Moral Traditions

If full ethical acculturation and excellent decision making are to be achieved, psychologists need to appreciate the variety of moral traditions that underlie both their own sense of ethics and the ethical culture of psychology. Knapp and VandeCreek (2004) argued that an appreciation of the moral foundations of the ethics code will help reduce a sense of alienation that some psychologists may feel from the profession. If the ethics code were seen as reflecting a common set of values, psychologists might identify more with the professional culture and be more willing to comply with its provisions and more able to apply ethical standards in ambiguous situations.

Although few psychologists have formally studied philosophical ethics, most have developed a personal set of ethical values. For many psychologists, their career choice was an opportunity to help people, reduce suffering, and live out important ideals. These goals may be manifested in character strengths such as compassion, wisdom, courage, justice, temperance, or spirituality (Seligman, 2002). However, others may conceptualize the desired behaviors in terms of fulfillment of the principle of utility (Mill, 1861/1987), upholding ethical principles (Beauchamp & Childress, 2001), the ethics of care (Gilligan, Ward, & Taylor, 1988), or feminist ethics (Lerman & Porter, 1990). Despite differences in terminology, these and other ethical theories overlap significantly regarding the aspirational behaviors that they promote.

Part of developing ethical sensitivity, according to Tjeltveit (2006), is "identifying ethical sources" (p. 196), that is, the roots of our own ethical beliefs. Tjeltveit cited Taylor's (1989) notion of ethical retrieval, and wrote:

> Retrieval of one's ethical heritage, the implicit and perhaps unconscious source of automatic ethical assumptions, may be particularly important.... This retrieval permits us to develop intellectually firsthand nuanced ethical commitments, commitments that are at once consistent with who we have been that— because carefully examined—become fully ours in the present.
> (Tjeltveit, 2006, p. 196)

Two specific techniques to help trainees and practicing psychologists achieve retrieval are the ethics autobiography (Bashe et al., 2007) and the morality genogram, developed by Weinberg and described by de las Fuentes and colleagues (2005). Both techniques invite students to write about their backgrounds and value traditions that might help or hinder them as they become professionals.

Exploring moral traditions also means thinking carefully about such basics as the value of what we produce (Fowers, 2005; Tjeltveit, 1999). For example, Tjeltveit (2006) argued that psychologists' and clients' notions of the good life can vary greatly, due to cultural differences, personal experiences, stage in therapy, and other factors. "To work with diverse clientele and to refine and sharpen our own ethical perspectives, we need to learn about a diverse array of ethical perspectives and visions of the good life" (Tjeltveit, 2006, p. 199).

Prevention

One consequence of ethical acculturation and increased awareness of ethical traditions and decision-making strategies is that some problematic behavior may be prevented. Some situations may not become dilemmatic if psychologists are already acting at high ethical levels with regard to such issues as informed consent, conflicts of interest, and integrity.

Knapp (2003) outlined positive ways to maintain this level of functioning, including consultation and continuing education. In this regard, 14 states required continuing ethics education in 2002 when the first edition of this handbook was published. As of 2007, that number was 22. Peer consultation may be especially useful (Knapp, 2003) if discussions can be free and open; Pope et al. (2006) provide an excellent resource for accomplishing this goal. Even risk management approaches can be made more patient oriented with a focus on ethical ideals (Bennett et al., 2007).

Global Awareness
Multicultural Sensitivity

There is an unquestionable need for the culture of psychology to be more knowledgeable about and welcoming to diverse populations—both among its clientele and students. Efforts are being made to ensure the ability of professional psychologists to serve the health-care needs of diverse populations by improving and increasing training in cultural competence (APA, 2003; Constantine & Sue, 2005), and through greater involvement of diverse groups in professional psychology.

One common argument in support of such initiatives is that they serve the interests of psychologists. This argument notes that the population of the United States is becoming more diverse (by 2050 a majority of Americans will belong to a group which is now considered a minority) and, unless psychologists are competent to work with them, psychological services will become marginalized and less relevant to a majority of Americans. Similarly, the APA Presidential Task Force on Enhancing Diversity (2005) argued that "changing APA to be more welcoming benefits not only marginalized groups but APA itself" (p. 15). The self-interest argument, however, is a weak one. According to this standard, if an emphasis on multiculturalism were no longer financially beneficial, these initiatives would be discontinued.

We contend that multiculturalism, as other policy issues, should be evaluated from the standpoint of an overarching positive ethical framework (Arredondo & Toporek, 2004). For example, Fowers and Davidov (2006) presumed that taking a multicultural perspective would be a character trait of a person who strives for personal virtues, such as fairness, open-mindedness, and compassion. They also recognized that justifications for multicultural sensitivity could be derived from other ethical theories.

Political Sensitivity and Action

The personal qualities or virtues that motivate psychologists to strive for the best in their professional relationships also may motivate psychologists to strive for civic virtue. Civic virtue or civic engagement refers to the meaningful involvement in and contribution to the community as a whole (Doyle, 2004). For the average citizen, civic virtue means more than just abstaining from violating the law. It can include participation in nonprofit or charitable activities, voting, leadership, and acting in other ways that promote community well-being. For psychologists, civic virtue also can involve serving on committees of their local, state, or national psychological association, offering professional presentations, writing articles, mentoring younger colleagues, and sharing their expertise. Another level of civic virtue would be to serve society at large by serving on the boards of community organizations, working for reduced fees for worthwhile community agencies or on other projects, and using psychological knowledge to create programs that have more and more global effects (e.g., Bandura, 2006).

Civic engagement or virtue includes involvement in the political process, either regarding issues related to the profession (e.g., advocating for adequate public access to quality psychological services) or issues on the local, state, national, or global levels, such as civil liberties or human rights. In fact, Koocher (2006) has argued that psychology itself, through APA and other organizations, should reciprocate the benefits society has bestowed on it by becoming involved in political advocacy.

Conclusion

In spite of almost daily news reports about unethical practices in all professions, there is room for optimism about more positive approaches to ethics. For example, the ethical acculturation model has been cited in some textbooks in psychology (e.g., Knapp & VandeCreek, 2006; Sommers-Flanagan & Sommers-Flanagan, 2007), and has appeared in the literature of other professions, such as community college leadership (Anderson, Harbour, & Davies, 2007). In business, Campbell (2006) wrote about compliance education in terms that reflect a positive approach: "When we focus on compliance alone, we are setting the bar too low.... Something more holistic is increasingly required." He saw a need for business ethics to become "embedded in every action we take and ... no longer an inelegant appendage." Other writers in business have equated positive business ethics with an ultimate goal of service rather than profit (Handy, 2002; "A Proper Perspective on Profit," 2006).

As psychologists, we have the advantage of being able to study the conditions that may make positive ethics more attainable, and we urge our research colleagues to address these important issues. To the extent that positive psychology helps psychologists understand how to promote human well-being, every development in positive psychology is a development for positive ethics.

Questions for the Future

1. Can ethics training be made more effective by incorporating positive themes?

2. Under what conditions do psychologists invoke ethical themes (virtues, principles, etc.) when they make professional decisions?

3. Can a more explicit emphasis on ethical virtues or moral background increase our ability to select exceptional candidates for professional training?

References

American Psychological Association. (1953). *Ethical standards of psychologists.* Washington, DC: Author.

American Psychological Association. (1992). Ethical principles of psychologists and code of conduct. *American Psychologist, 47,* 1597–1611.

American Psychological Association. (2002). Ethical principles of psychologists and code of conduct. *American Psychologist, 57,* 1060–1073.

American Psychological Association. (2003). Guidelines on multicultural education, training, research, practice, and organizational change for psychologists. *American Psychologist, 58,* 377–402.

American Psychological Association, Task Force on Enhancing Diversity. (2005). *Final report.* Washington, DC: American Psychological Association.

Anderson, S. K., Harbour, C. P., & Davies, T. G. (2007). Professional ethical identity development and community college leadership. In D. Hellmich (Ed.), *Ethical leadership in the community college: Bridging theory and daily practice* (pp. 61–77). Bolton, MA: Anker.

Appelbaum, P. S., Lidz, C. W., & Meisel, A. (1987). *Informed consent: Legal theory and clinical practice.* New York: Oxford University Press.

Arredondo, P., & Toporek, R. (2004). Multicultural counseling competencies = ethical practice. *Journal of Mental Health Counseling, 26,* 44–55.

Baltes, P. B., Gluck, J., & Kunzmann, U. (2002). Wisdom: Its structure and function in regulating successful life span development. In C. R. Snyder & S. J. Lopez (Eds.), *Handbook of positive psychology* (pp. 327–347). New York: Oxford University Press.

Bandura, A. (2006, October). Global applications of social cognitive theory for human betterment. Presentation at the Fifth International Positive Psychology Summit, Washington, DC.

Barnett, J. E., Johnston, L. C., & Hillard, D. (2006). Psychotherapist wellness as an ethical imperative. In L. VandeCreek & J. B. Allen (Eds.), *Innovations in clinical practice: Focus on health and wellness* (pp. 257–271). Sarasota, FL: Professional Resources Press.

Bashe, A., Anderson, S. K., Handelsman, M. M., & Klevansky, R. (2007). An acculturation model for ethics training: The ethics autobiography and beyond. *Professional Psychology: Research and Practice, 38,* 60–67.

Beauchamp, T., & Childress, J. (2001). *Principles of biomedical ethics* (5th ed.). New York: Oxford University Press.

Bennett, B. E., Bricklin, P. M., Harris, E., Knapp, S., VandeCreek, L., & Younggren, J. (2007). *Patient focused risk management.* Rockville, MD: APAIT.

Berry, J. W. (2003). Conceptual approaches to acculturation. In K. M. Chun, P. B. Organista, & G. Marin (Eds.), *Acculturation: Advances in theory, measurement, and applied research* (pp. 17–37). Washington, DC: American Psychological Association.

Bersoff, D. (1994). Explicit ambiguity: The 1992 Ethics Code as oxymoron. *Professional Psychology: Research and Practice, 25,* 382–387.

Bricklin, P. (2001). Being ethical: More than obeying the law and avoiding harm. *Journal of Personality Assessment, 77,* 195–202.

Brown, L. (1994). Concrete boundaries and the problem of literal-mindedness: A response to Lazarus. *Ethics and Behavior, 4,* 275–282.

Campbell, C. (2006, June 15). Online education and services: A new education. *Legalweek.com.* Retrieved July 5, 2006 from http://www.legalweek.com/ViewItem.asp?id=29405

Constantine, M. G., & Sue, D. W. (Eds.). (2005). *Strategies for building multicultural competence in mental health and educational settings.* Hoboken, NJ: Wiley.

Coster, J. S., & Schwebel, M. (1997). Well-functioning in professional psychologists. *Professional Psychology: Research and Practice, 28,* 5–13.

Csikszentmihalyi, M. (1990). *Flow, the psychology of optimal experience.* New York: Harper Collins.

de las Fuentes, C., Willmuth, M. E., & Yarrow, C. (2005). Competency training in ethics education and practice. *Professional Psychology: Research and Practice, 36,* 362–366.

Doyle, R. (2004, June). Civic culture. *Scientific American, 290,* 34.

Dunning, D., Heath, C., & Suls, J. M. (2004). Flawed self-assessment: Implications for health, education, and the workplace. *Psychological Science in the Public Interest, 5,* 69–106.

Fisher, C. B. (1994). Reporting and referring research participants: Ethical challenges for investigators studying children and youth. *Ethics and Behavior, 4,* 87–95.

Fowers, B. J. (2005). *Virtue and psychology: Pursuing excellence in ordinary practices.* Washington, DC: American Psychological Association.

Fowers, B., & Davidov, M. (2006). The virtue of multiculturalism: Personal transformation, character and the openness to the other. *American Psychologist, 61,* 581–594.

Frederickson, B. (2002). Positive emotions. In C. R. Snyder & S. J. Lopez (Eds.), *Handbook of positive psychology* (pp. 120–134). New York: Oxford University Press.

Gilligan, C., Ward, J., & Taylor, J. (Eds.). (1988). *Mapping the moral domain.* Cambridge, MA: Harvard University Press.

Gleicher, F., & Petty, R. E. (1992). Expectations of reassurance influence the nature of fear-stimulated attitude change. *Journal of Experimental Social Psychology, 28,* 86–100.

Gottlieb, M. C., Handelsman, M. M., & Knapp, S. (2008). Some principles for ethics education: Implementing the acculturation model. *Training and Education in Professional Psychology, 2,* 123–128.

Greitemeyer, T., Fischer, P., Kastenmueller, A., & Frey, D. (2006). Civil courage and helping behaviour: Differences and similarities. *European Psychologist, 11,* 90–98.

Handelsman, M. M., Gottlieb, M. C., & Knapp, S. (2005). Training ethical psychologists: An acculturation model. *Professional Psychology: Research and Practice, 36,* 59–65.

Handelsman, M. M., Knapp, S., & Gottlieb, M. C. (2002). Positive ethics. In C. R. Snyder & S. J. Lopez (Eds.), *Handbook of positive psychology* (pp. 731–744). New York: Oxford University Press.

Handy, C. (2002). What's a business for? *Harvard Business Review, 80*(12), 49–55.

Jepson, C., & Chaiken, S. (1990). Chronic issue-specific fear inhibits systematic processing of persuasive communications. *Journal of Social Behavior and Personality, 5,* 61–84.

Johnson, B., & Campbell, C. (2004). Character and fitness requirements for professional psychologists: Training directors' perspectives. *Professional Psychology: Research and Practice, 35,* 405–411.

Johnson, B., Porter, K., Campbell, C., & Kupko, E. (2005). Character and fitness requirements for professional psychologists: An examination of state licensing application forms. *Professional Psychology: Research and Practice, 36,* 73–81.

Jordan, A., & Meara, N. (1990). Ethics and the professional practice of psychologists: The role of virtues and principles. *Professional Psychology: Theory and Practice, 21,* 106–114.

Kant, I. (1785/1988). *Fundamental principles of the metaphysics of morals.* Amherst, NY: Prometheus Books.

Kimmel, A. J. (1988). *Ethics and values in applied social research.* Newbury Park, CA: Sage.

Kitchener, K. S. (2000). *Foundations of ethical practice, research, and teaching in psychology.* Mahwah, NJ: Lawrence Erlbaum.

Knapp, S. (2003, August). Prevention of ethical problems: An overview of existing and proposed strategies. In A. Tjeltveit (Chair), *Positive strategies to prevent ethical problems in psychotherapy practice.* Symposium conducted at the meeting of the American Psychological Association, Toronto.

Knapp, S., Gottlieb, M., & Handelsman, M. (2004, Spring). Living up to your ethical ideals: Three reminders for psychotherapists. *Psychotherapy Bulletin, 39*(2), 14–18, 24.

Knapp, S., & VandeCreek, L. (2003, Fall). Do psychologists have supererogatory obligations? *Psychotherapy Bulletin, 38*(3), 29–31.

Knapp, S., & VandeCreek, L. (2004). A principle-based analysis of the 2002 American Psychological Association's Ethics Code. *Psychotherapy: Theory, Research, Practice and Training, 41,* 247–254.

Knapp, S. J., & VandeCreek, L. D. (2006). *Practical ethics for psychologists: A positive approach.* Washington, DC: American Psychological Association.

Koocher, G. P. (2006, February). Speaking against torture. *Monitor on Psychology, 37,* 5.

Lerman, H., & Porter, N. (Eds.). (1990). *Feminist ethics in psychotherapy.* New York: Springer.

Levine, R. (1986). *Ethics and regulations of clinical research* (2nd ed.). Baltimore: Urban and Schwarzenber.

Meara, N., Schmidt, L., & Day, J. (1996). Principles and virtues: A foundation for ethical decisions, policies, and character. *The Counseling Psychologist, 24,* 4–77.

Mill, J. S. (1861/1987). Utilitarianism. In A. Ryan (Ed.), *John Stuart Mill and Jeremy Bentham: Utilitarianism and other essays* (pp. 272–338). New York: Penguin.

Norcross, J. C., & James, D. G. (2005). Therapist self-care checklist. In G. P. Koocher, J. C. Norcross, & S. S. Hill, III (Eds.), *Psychologists' desk reference* (pp. 677–682). New York: Oxford University Press.

Osswald, S., Greitemeyer, T., Fischer, P., & Frey, D. (2006, October). Moral exemplarity and prosocial behavior: Do distinct moral prototypes differentially correspond to helping behavior, moral courage and heroism and do they predict the associated behavior? Poster presented at the Fifth International Positive Psychology Summit, Washington, DC.

Peterson, C., & Seligman, M. E. P. (2004). *Character strengths and virtues: A handbook and classification.* New York: Oxford University Press.

Pettifor, J. L., Estay, I., & Paquet, S. (2002). Preferred strategies for learning ethics in the practice of a discipline. *Canadian Psychology, 43,* 260–269.

Pipes, R. B., Holstein, J. E., & Aguirre, M. G. (2005). Examining the personal–professional distinction: Ethics codes and the difficulty of drawing a boundary. *American Psychologist, 60,* 325–334.

Pope, K. S., Sonne, J. L., & Greene, B. (2006). *What therapists don't talk about and why.* Washington, DC: American Psychological Association.

Pope, K. S., & Vetter, V. A. (1992). Ethical dilemmas encountered by members of the American Psychological Association: A national survey. *American Psychologist, 47,* 397–411.

A Proper Perspective on Profit. (2006, Spring). *The Graduate Review*. Retrieved July 5, 2006 from http://www.spu.edu/prospects/grad/enews/spring_2006/gradreview1.html

Rest, J. R. (1986). *Moral development: Advances in research and theory*. New York: Praeger.

Seif, B. (2006, May). Positive ethics: An inside job. *Pennsylvania Psychologist, 69*, 10–15.

Seligman, M. (2002). *Authentic happiness*. New York: Free Press.

Sommers-Flanagan, R., & Sommers-Flanagan, J. (2007). *Becoming an ethical helping professional: Cultural and philosophical foundations*. New York: Wiley.

Taylor, C. (1989). *Sources of self: The making of the modern identity*. Cambridge, MA: Harvard University Press.

Tjeltveit, A. C. (1999). *Ethics and values in psychotherapy*. London: Routledge.

Tjeltveit, A. C. (2006). To what ends? Psychotherapy goals and outcomes, the good life, and the principle of beneficence. *Psychotherapy: Theory, Research, Practice and Training, 43*, 186–200.

Walker, L. J., & Hennig, K. H. (2004). Differing conceptions of moral exemplarity: Just, brave and caring. *Journal of Personality and Social Psychology, 86*, 629–647.

PART 3

Positive Psychology Across the Lifespan

Resilience in Development

Ann S. Masten, J. J. Cutuli, Janette E. Herbers, *and* Marie-Gabrielle J. Reed

Abstract

Resilience in human development is defined in relation to positive adaptation in the context of significant adversity, emphasizing a developmental systems approach. A brief history and glossary on the central concepts of resilience research in developmental science are provided, and the fundamental models and strategies guiding the research are described. Major findings of the first four decades of research are summarized in terms of protective and promotive factors consistently associated with resilience in diverse situations and populations of young people. These factors—such as self-regulation skills, good parenting, community resources, and effective schools—suggest that resilience arises from ordinary protective processes, common but powerful, that protect human development under diverse conditions. The greatest threats posed to children may be adversities that damage or undermine these basic human protective systems. Implications of these findings for theory and practice are discussed, highlighting three strategies of fostering resilience, focused on reducing risk, building strengths or assets, and mobilizing adaptive systems that protect and restore positive human development. The concluding section outlines future directions of resilience research and its applications, including rapidly growing efforts to integrate research and prevention efforts across disciplines, from genetics to ecology, and across level of analysis, from molecules to media.

Keywords: adaptation, competence, protective factor, resilience, strengths

Introduction

Humans have been fascinated since ancient times with stories of people who overcome adversity to succeed in life, but the scientific study of resilience in children began in the 1960s and 1970s (Masten, 2007). Pioneering investigators (e.g., Norman Garmezy, Lois Murphy, Michael Rutter, & Emmy Werner) argued that understanding such phenomena held the potential to transform practice and policies to promote competence and prevent or ameliorate problems in the lives of children threatened by risk or adversity. These pioneers inspired four decades of research on resilience in development that has provided models, methods, and findings with profound implications for theory, research, and intervention.

The goal of this chapter is to highlight results of resilience research to date and their implications for the future. Following a brief history of resilience research, we describe key models and corresponding methods characteristic of research on resilience. We summarize major findings and conclusions from this body of work in terms of protective systems for development and resilience in children. These fundamental protections bear a noteworthy resemblance to many of the chapter titles of this volume. We conclude that resilience arises from basic adaptation systems that protect human development under diverse conditions and discuss the implications of resilience research for theory, intervention, policy, and future research.

History of the Study of Resilience in the Behavioral Sciences

The idea of individual resilience in the face of adversity has been around for a very long time, as evident in myths, fairy tales, art, and literature that portray heroes and heroines who surmount great obstacles (Campbell, 1970). Beginning in the nineteenth century, scientists in diverse fields, ranging from biology to psychoanalysis, focused their attention on human adaptation (Masten, Burt, & Coatsworth, 2006; Mayr, 1982). Early concepts of the ego, mastery motivation, competence, and self-efficacy in twentieth-century psychology particularly emphasized positive aspects of adaptation in development. Yet, at the same time, the burgeoning literature on mental health and problems in children and adolescents was dominated by research on risk and the treatment of symptoms. In her classic 1962 book, *The Widening World of Childhood*, Lois Murphy decried the negative focus of research on individual differences in children: "It is something of a paradox that a nation which has exulted in its rapid expansion and its scientific-technological achievements should have developed in its studies of childhood so vast a 'problem' literature" (p. 2).

Murphy's words were a harbinger of change. A decade later, the systematic study of resilience in psychology emerged from the study of children at risk for problems and psychopathology (Luthar, 2006; Masten, 2007; Masten & Obradović, 2007). By the 1960s, psychologists and psychiatrists interested in the etiology of psychopathology had begun longitudinal studies of children believed to be "at risk" for serious problems because of their biological heritage (e.g., a parent with schizophrenia), perinatal hazards (e.g., premature birth), or their environments (e.g., poverty). Some of these investigators were struck by the common observation of children, purportedly at high risk for problems, who were developing quite well, and they recognized the significance of these phenomena for intervention as well as for scientific theory (Anthony, 1974; Garmezy, 1971, 1974; Murphy & Moriarty, 1976; Rutter, 1979; Werner & Smith, 1982). These investigators inspired the first generation of research on resilience.

In the early publications on resilience and in the press about such phenomena, successful high-risk children were referred to variously as "invulnerable," "stress-resistant," or "resilient." Eventually "resilient" became the dominant descriptor for such individuals, and the domain of research was labeled the study of *resilience*.

Conceptual Models of Resilience
Defining Resilience

In research on children over the past four decades, resilience generally refers to *patterns of positive adaptation during or following significant adversity or risk*. Resilience is an inferential concept, in that two major judgments must be rendered to diagnose resilience. First, there is a judgment that individuals are at least "doing okay" with respect to a set of expectations for behavior. Second, there must be significant exposure to risk or adversity that has posed a serious threat to good outcomes. Thus, the study of resilience phenomena requires that investigators define (a) the criteria or method for identifying positive adaptation or development and (b) the past or current presence of conditions that threaten to disrupt positive adaptation or harm development. In studies of individual development, resilience describes a class of phenomena where individuals show positive adaptation and development despite exposure to experiences or conditions associated with negative outcomes.

The meaning of resilience and the methods of translating definitions into operation in research have been the subject of considerable debate and controversy over the years (Curtis & Cicchetti, 2003; Luthar, 2006; Luthar & Brown, 2007; Luthar, Cicchetti, & Becker, 2000; Masten, 1999; Yates, Egeland, & Sroufe, 2003). Nonetheless, findings from a diverse literature point with striking regularity to the same conclusions. Given the considerable degree of debate and confusion about defining resilience and related concepts, we provide a glossary of how these terms are used in this chapter in Table 12.1.

Defining and Assessing Positive Adaptation and Good Developmental Outcomes

Diverse criteria have been used for judging good adaptation in studies of resilience. These include positive behavior such as the presence of social and academic achievements, the presence of other behaviors desired by society for people of this age, happiness or life satisfaction, and the absence of undesirable behavior, including mental illness, emotional distress, criminal behavior, or risk-taking behaviors. In the developmental literature, many investigators define good outcomes on the basis of a history of success in meeting age-related standards of behavior widely known as *developmental tasks*.

Developmental tasks refer to expectations of a given society or culture in historical context for the behavior of children in different age periods and situations (Elder, 1998; Masten & Coatsworth, 1998; Masten et al., 2006). These are the social milestones for development, presumed to guide socialization practices. They may vary from one culture to another to some degree, but these broad tasks presumably depend on human capabilities and societal goals that are widely shared across cultures.

Table 12.1 Glossary of key terms

Resilience	Positive adaptation in the context of significant challenges, variously referring to the capacity for, processes of, or outcomes of successful life-course development during or following exposure to potentially life-altering experiences
Developmental tasks	Major expectations of a given society or culture in historical context for the behavior of children in different age periods and situations, representing criteria by which progress in individual development is judged
Risk	An elevated probability of an undesirable outcome
Risk factor	A measurable characteristic of a group of individuals or their situation that predicts negative outcome on a specific outcome criterion. Stressful life events (stressors) are one type of risk factor
Cumulative risk	The total effect of multiple risk factors combined or the piling up in time of multiple risk factors
Risk gradient	A visual depiction of risk or cumulative risk showing how a negative criterion of outcome rises as a function of rising risk level
Asset	A measurable characteristic of a group of individuals or their situation that predicts positive outcome with respect to a specific criterion. A predictor of positive outcomes across levels of risk, statistically reflecting a positive association between the characteristic and the outcome, or an elevated probability of a desirable outcome
Promotive factor	Used synonymously with "asset" in resilience science
Protective factor	A measurable characteristic of a group of individuals or their situation that predicts positive outcome in the context of risk or adversity. Purists reserve this term for predictors that work "only" under adversity (like an airbag in an automobile) or that have a larger positive effect on outcome when risk is high compared to when risk is low (to distinguish a protective factor from an asset that works the same way at all levels of risk)
Cumulative protection	The presence of multiple protective influences in an individual's life, either within or across time. A common goal of comprehensive prevention programs

For example, toddlers are expected to learn to walk and talk, and to obey simple instructions of parents. Older children are expected in most societies to learn at school, to get along with other children, and to follow the rules of classroom, home, and community. In the United States and many other economically developed countries, successful youth are expected to graduate from high school and gain the education and occupational skills needed for economic independence, to abide by the law, to have close friends and romantic relationships, and to begin to contribute to society. Resilient children and youth manage to meet developmental task expectations even though they have faced significant obstacles to success in life.

One of the most interesting debates in the resilience literature has focused on whether the criteria should include good *internal* adaptation (positive psychological well-being vs. emotional distress and problems) as well as good *external* adaptation. Both camps agree that external adaptation standards must be included when defining resilience. Some investigators, however, also include indicators of emotional health and well-being as additional defining criteria, whereas others study the internal dimensions of

behavior as concomitants or predictors of resilience. This debate reflects the dual nature of living systems. Human individuals are living organisms that must maintain coherence and organization as a unit and also function as part of larger systems, such as families and communities (Masten, 2007).

A second interesting issue is whether to define resilience in children as functioning in the normative, average range ("doing okay") or excelling. Stories of heroic survival or media accounts of resilient people tend to highlight outstanding achievements in the face of adversity. However, most investigators have set the bar at the level of the normal range, no doubt because their goal is to understand how individuals maintain or regain normative levels of functioning and avoid significant problems in spite of adversity—a goal shared by many parents and societies.

In studies of resilient children and youth, typical measures of good outcome assess the following domains: academic achievement (grades and test scores, staying in school, graduating from high school); conduct (rule-abiding behavior vs. antisocial behavior); peer acceptance and friendship; normative mental health (few symptoms of internalizing or externalizing behavior problems); and involvement in age-appropriate activities (extra-curricular activities, sports, community service). Most studies include multiple indicators of good functioning or outcome rather than a single domain of functioning.

Good outcomes are not enough to define resilience, however. Such children could be called competent, well-adjusted, or simply "normal." Resilient children must also have overcome some kind of threat to good adaptation, which means they must meet a second type of criterion.

Defining and Assessing Threats to Good Adaptation or Development

Many different kinds of threats and hazards to individual functioning and development have been considered in studies of resilience (Luthar, 2006; Masten, Best, & Garmezy, 1990). These include premature birth, divorce, maltreatment, exposure to domestic or neighborhood violence, parental illness or psychopathology, poverty, homelessness, and the massive (community level) traumas of war and natural disasters. Such threats are well-established *risk factors* for development because there is good evidence that such conditions/experiences elevate the probability of problems among children in the group of people who share this risk exposure.

Initially, in the study of resilience, many investigators focused on a single indicator to define risk. It was apparent quickly, however, that risk factors often co-occur and pile up over time. Furthermore, different risk factors often predict similar problems, partly because they tend to co-occur over time. Consequently, there was a shift to studying *cumulative risk* (Masten et al., 1990; Obradović, Shaffer, & Masten, in press).

Cumulative risk assessment has taken two major forms: risk indices and stressful life experience scores. Cumulative risk scores often sum the number of risk factors present in a child's life, typically including a number of socio-demographic status variables such as "single parent household" or "parent did not finish high school," whereas negative life experience scores typically sum the number of negative life events or experiences encountered during a period of time, sometimes weighting these experiences by intensity or severity (Obradović et al., in press). Thus, in studies of resilience, resilient children may be defined as those who are doing well despite the presence of many risk factors or numerous negative life experiences in their life histories.

Issues abound in the assessment of adversity and risk, and a full discussion of them is beyond the scope of this chapter. Examples of controversies include whether to count stressful experiences that depend on the behavior of the individual, whether to assign severity weights to events or simply add them up, whether to consider subjective perceptions or objective judgments about the stressfulness of experiences, and whether life event reports are reliable (Dohrenwend, 1998; Masten, 1999; Obradović et al., in press; Zimmerman, 1983).

Assessing Promotive and Protective Factors

Given that children clearly can develop competence even when risk is very high, investigators of resilience must also consider the question of "What makes a difference?" To do so requires one to examine the qualities of individuals and their environments (or their interactions) that might explain why some people fare better than others in the context of adversity. The concepts of promotive factors and protective factors, along with related processes, have been defined for research (see glossary in Table 12.1). Assets, resources, or promotive factors are closely related terms for general predictors of better outcomes that appear to forecast good adaptation in similar ways across levels of risk. The notions of human, social, and material capital have similar connotations: these are various resources that people may draw on as needed for adaptive success. *Protective factors*, in contrast, have a special role when risk or adversity is high. These characteristics or processes (such as good learning skills or parenting quality) may predict better outcomes for everyone, but they appear to be even more important under certain conditions of higher risk or adversity.

Models of Resilience

Two major approaches have characterized the research on resilience in development (Masten, 2001). *Variable-focused* approaches examine the statistical connections and patterns among measures of characteristics of individuals, environments, and experiences in an effort to ascertain what accounts for good outcomes when risk or adversity is high. This method effectively draws on the power of the whole sample or an entire risk group as well as the strengths of multivariate statistics to identify clues to resilience processes. Variable-focused approaches are well suited to searching for specific protective factors or influences for particular aspects of adaptation. *Person-focused* approaches identify resilient people and try

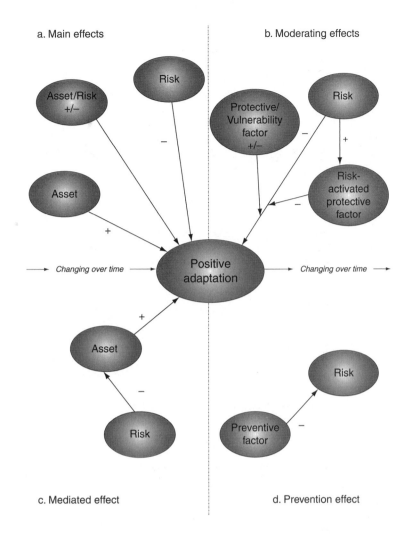

Fig. 12.1 Models of resilience illustrating additive, interactive, and indirect models of how risks, assets, and protective factors could influence a desired outcome of interest. (See discussion in the text.)

to understand how they differ from other people who are not faring as well in the face of adversity or those who have not been challenged by serious threats to development. This approach reflects the perspective that resilience is usually judged in terms of a whole person and also in terms of multiple dimensions of adaptive functioning simultaneously. In other words, resilience is configural because individuals typically are judged to be doing well in several important ways at once, rather than just one way. This approach is well suited to studying diverse lives through time.

VARIABLE-FOCUSED MODELS OF RESILIENCE

Several variable-focused models of resilience have been tested in the empirical literature, including additive models, interactive models, and indirect models, also known respectively as main effects, moderating, and mediating models.

In the simplest model, the additive effects of risk factors, asset/resource factors, and continuously distributed dimensions of asset/risk variables are examined in relation to a positive outcome of interest (see Figure 12.1a). In this model, the assets and risks contribute independently to how well a child is doing on the outcome of interest. Pure risk factors have negative effects on the outcome of interest when they occur, but do not necessarily have an effect if absent, such as the loss of a parent. Pure assets have positive influences if they are present, but do not have negative effects if they are absent (like a musical talent). However, many attributes are not "pure" risks or assets, but rather operate along a continuum of risk to asset with two poles, where one end is bad and the other end is good with respect to the outcome of interest (such as the level of intellectual skills or the quality of parenting with respect to academic achievement). While assets may be helpful across all levels of risk, the presence of

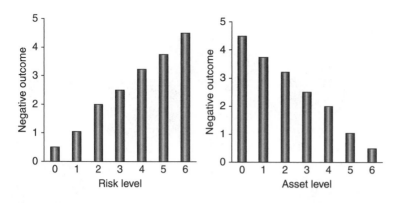

Fig. 12.2 A typical risk gradient showing negative outcome as a function of risk level (on the left) and its inverse, plotting negative outcome as a function of assets (on the right), a hypothetical "asset gradient."

these resources can theoretically counterbalance high levels of risk and produce a competent outcome. This possible role of assets is referred to as a "compensatory effect" (Garmezy, Masten, & Tellegen, 1984). Interventions that attempt to boost the presence of assets to counterbalance risk are based on an additive model.

Risk/asset gradients also reflect additive models of this kind. A typical cumulative risk gradient is shown on the left side of Figure 12.2, where the level of a negative outcome is plotted as a function of the number of risk factors. Risk factors in such models often include well-established risks, such as a single-parent household, a mother who did not finish high school, a large family size, or income below the poverty level (Obradović et al., in press). Other risk gradients are formed by showing the outcome in relation to level of disadvantage on a dimensional indicator of risk, such as socioeconomic status. Such risk indices predict a wide range of public health outcomes, including mortality rates, academic attainment, and physical and mental health, across many societies (Keating & Hertzman, 1999).

Additive models may also reflect assets, strengths, or resources present in an individual's life. In contrast to risk gradients, "asset gradients" can be used to predict positive outcomes, as illustrated on the right in Figure 12.2. Often, one can think of an asset gradient as the inverse of a risk gradient because many of the most common risk indicators also reflect asset status or one end of an asset–risk dimension. "Risks" are arbitrarily labeled by the negative end of a continuum that contains "assets" on the opposite pole, which means that a low risk score also means that there is a high asset score. A positive psychology perspective might emphasize that the children low on such risk gradients typically are those with more assets and advantages: with two better educated parents, good income, the benefits that go along

with higher socioeconomic status, etc. As mentioned above, there are also a class of pure assets that are not necessarily detrimental if absent (e.g., some kind of talent), and these assets may very well be present in children on the high end of a risk gradient. However, even in studies that measure pure risk factors (negative life events for example), the low-risk children are still more likely to have a greater accumulation of assets (pure or otherwise), because negative events are less likely to occur in advantaged families with effective parenting, more education, safer neighborhoods, good medical care, etc.

Interactive models are shown in Figure 12.1b. In these cases, there are moderating effects in which the relation of the risk factor to the outcome of interest depends on another variable. The moderating variable alters the observed relation of the risk/adversity variable to the outcome. In other words, the risk effects vary at different levels of the moderating variable. Such moderators have been called "vulnerability" and "protective" factors. Two kinds of interaction effects are illustrated. One kind of moderator is always functioning and operates to reduce or increase the impact of the impending threat on the life of a person. Individual differences in temperament or personality are among the most widely studied moderators of this kind. The second kind of moderator is "threat-activated"—it is triggered in response to impending threat. Airbags in automobiles function in this way, as does the human immune system. Emergency social services (e.g., crisis nursery, foster care) are designed on this model, to be triggered in response to a perceived threat (e.g., imminent harm to a child). A parent who is doing a good job may take special actions in the face of a serious new threat to a child's life or well-being. Similarly, a child's own coping efforts could operate this way if special efforts are made to reduce the impact of a particular threat to one's self.

Interventions that attempt to provide new emergency systems or to improve how systems respond to threats in order to ameliorate the impact of hazards on the lives of individuals are based on this kind of model.

Indirect models of resilience are illustrated in Figure 12.1c. Not all possibilities are included, but the depicted model illustrates the phenomenon of mediated effects, where a powerful influence on outcome is itself affected by risks and resources. Many of the threats that have the potential to harm child development may work indirectly by harming crucial assets or protective factors in children's lives, such as their parents. Mediation models can be viewed as efforts to understand how "distal" threats have effects more "proximal" to a child or as breaking down the process of risk into sequences with more steps. Interventions in which there is an attempt to improve the quality of key predictors of child outcome, such as parental effectiveness, are often based on such mediator models (Masten & Shaffer, 2006). These interventions, for example, may attempt to help children indirectly by supporting effective parenting during a crisis.

One other indirect model, illustrated in Figure 12.1d, is the invisible effect of total prevention, when an intervention or a powerful protective factor prevents the risk/threatening condition from occurring at all. One of the prevention successes of the twentieth century provides an example. The occurrence of the risk factor of premature birth was greatly reduced by improved prenatal care in many countries. Similarly, an alert parent may intervene to head off a negative event prior to its occurrence.

Figures 12.1a–d are a convenient way to illustrate various models of resilience, but it is important to keep in mind that these models vastly oversimplify the processes by which resilience unfolds in real lives through time. First, these models are static. In life, the systems and influences that act as risks and assets are continually interacting, changing, and often influencing each other. Thus, a child's behavior influences the quality of parenting he receives and the behavior of his teachers; subsequently the behavior of parents or teachers toward the child influences the child's behavior, and so on. In reality, there are few "one-way arrows" in life. Transactional models that capture the mutual influences over time resulting from the continual interaction of living systems, their environments, and their experiences are difficult to portray in two-dimensional pictures.

Second, the variable-focused models that focus on a single aspect of "outcome" or one dimension of

the criterion for good adaptation will not capture the overall pattern of resilience in a person's life, which is multifaceted and configural. Person-focused models attempt to get a handle on these holistic patterns.

PERSON-FOCUSED MODELS OF RESILIENCE

Three types of person-focused models have played a key role in resilience research. One kind of model derives from the single case study of individuals who have inspired larger-scale investigations or illustrate findings from larger studies in which they are embedded. Case studies are not in themselves conceptual models of resilience, but case studies do serve a heuristic purpose of inspiring models to explain natural phenomena. Individual cases illustrate potential pathways of resilience that can suggest both models and areas of interest for future empirical study. Case reports of resilience can be found throughout the resilience literature (see, e.g., the case of "Sara" reported by Masten & O'Connor, 1989).

A second person-focused model of resilience is based on identifying a resilient subgroup of very high-risk individuals who do well. This is a classic approach in the resilience field, exemplified by the most important longitudinal study of resilience to date, the Kauai longitudinal study initiated in 1955 (Werner & Smith, 1982, 1992, 2001). In this study of a large birth cohort, a high-risk group of children was identified according to multiple risk indicators that were present before the age of 2. Then the outcomes of these children, how well they were doing on multiple developmental and mental health markers at around 10 and 18 years old, were examined to identify a subgroup of resilient children. Resilient children could then be compared to their peers in the high-risk group who did not fare well. Results indicated many differences beginning at an early age that favored the resilient group, including better quality of care in infancy, higher self-worth and intellectual functioning in childhood, and more support from "kith and kin" (Werner & Smith, 1992).

This approach often results in evidence of striking differences in the assets and protective factors characterizing the lives of resilient versus maladaptive children from risky backgrounds. However, there are some limitations as well. Often, results indicate that the resilient group was exposed to less adversity (they come from a lower risk level on a risk gradient), and, even when risk levels are comparable, it is not clear whether the correlates of resilience are general assets that promote good outcomes at all

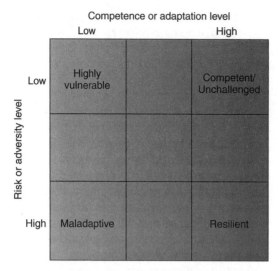

Competence or adaptation level

	Low	High
Low	Highly vulnerable	Competent/ Unchallenged
High	Maladaptive	Resilient

Risk or adversity level

Fig. 12.3 A full diagnostic model of resilience that identifies groups by two sets of criteria for (a) adversity level and (b) good outcome or competence on one or more criteria. Comparisons of "corner" groups hold particular interest: the resilient, who are high on both adversity and good outcomes; the maladaptive, who are high on adversity but who have negative outcomes; the competent-unchallenged, who are low on adversity with good outcomes; and the vulnerable, who do not do well even though adversity is low.

levels of risk, or they represent protective factors that have special effects at high risk levels. This question cannot be answered using this approach because low-risk groups are not included in the analyses. This led to a third approach, which includes low-risk children, with the goal of comparing the resilient group to lower-risk (adaptive and maladaptive) peers as well as high-risk, maladaptive peers.

Full diagnostic models of resilience classify children on the two major aspects of individual lives: good outcomes and adversity/risk. Figure 12.3 illustrates this model. In the Project Competence study of resilience (Masten et al., 1999), this strategy was used to complement variable-focused analyses. Youth from a normative urban sample were classified as high, middle/mixed, or low on competence based on the pattern of success for three major developmental tasks for their age group: academic achievement, rule-abiding conduct versus antisocial behavior, and social competence with peers. Youth classified as high in competence had achieved at least average success on all three developmental tasks. They were also classified on lifetime adversity exposure, based on life histories of negative experiences out of their control (such as death of a parent or close friend, marital conflict, violence of an alcoholic parent, accidents or health crises of family members). Lifetime adversity was

rated as high (severe to catastrophic exposure), average, or low (below average levels of exposure for the cohort). The goal was to compare the four corner groups (see Figure 12.3). As found in other studies, however, there was a nearly "empty cell" for low adversity exposure and low competence (very few children with low adversity exposure were doing poorly). Thus, resilient youth were compared to two other groups, their maladaptive peers, who shared a history of severe to catastrophic adversity but differed markedly in outcome, and their competent peers, who were similar in outcome but differed markedly because they had low adversity backgrounds. Results indicated that resilient youth have much in common with competent youth who have not faced adversity, in that they share many of the same assets, both personal ones like good intellectual skills and family assets like effective parenting. Both groups differed dramatically in resources from their maladaptive peers, who faced great adversity with much less human and social capital. Results of this study suggest that there are fundamental processes that not only lead to normative competence, but also protect development in the context of adversity.

PATHWAY MODELS

Both the classic and the full diagnostic models of resilience implicitly span considerable amounts of time. This is because the risks and achievements by which resilience is judged are not momentary phenomena, but rather characterize experiences and functioning that unfold over time. Currently, there is growing interest in more systematic pathway models of resilience that address patterns of behavior over time in more explicit ways. This interest reflects a general trend in developmental theory toward more complex dynamic systems models that account for major patterns in the life course (Yates et al., 2003).

Figure 12.4 illustrates three resilient pathways that could arise from a host of cumulative influences. Life course is plotted over time with respect to how an individual is doing on a global index of good versus maladaptive development. All individuals in this diagram have experienced significant adversity. Path A reflects a child growing up in a high-risk environment who nonetheless steadily functions well in life. Path B reflects a child who is doing well, is diverted by a major blow (perhaps a traumatic experience), and recovers. Path C reflects a late-bloomer or "catch-up" pattern, in which a high-risk child who is not doing well is provided with life-altering chances or opportunities that

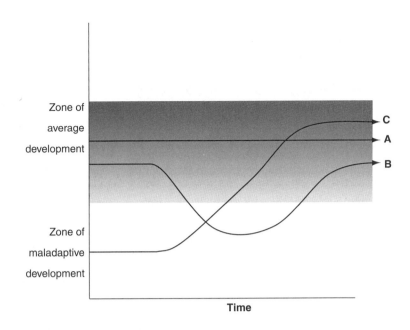

Fig. 12.4 Resilience pathways over the life course. Path A illustrates the developmental course of a high-risk child who consistently does well in life. Path B shows the course of a child who initially does well and then is diverted by a major blow and later recovers to good functioning. Path C illustrates the late-bloomer pattern where a child burdened by disadvantage begins to do well after major improvements in rearing conditions.

permit her to reestablish a more developmentally normative level of functioning. One example of this involves orphanage-reared Romanian children who were adopted by families in Western countries. Most of these children went from profound deprivation in the orphanage to normative or enriched rearing environments in their adoptive homes. Children who were adopted internationally before they were 6 months old were quite likely to follow path C and "catch up" to noninstitutionalized domestic adoptees in weight, height, and cognitive functioning by the time they were 4 years old (Rutter & English and Romanian Adoptees (ERA) Study Team, 1998). Furthermore, they were less likely to have impairments across seven different domains of functioning when they were 6 and 11 years old, suggesting that their adoptive families provided them with the necessary environments to allow the children to rebound from experiencing early adversity (Kreppner et al., 2007). There are also reports of maladaptive high-risk youth who seek or respond to turning points or "second-chance opportunities" in life, such as military service, positive romantic relationships, or religious conversions, and turn their lives in new directions (Laub, Nagin, & Sampson, 1998; Roisman, Masten, Coatsworth, & Tellegen, 2004; Rutter, 1990; Werner & Smith, 1992).

TRANSACTIONAL MODELS ACROSS LEVELS OF ANALYSIS

Developmental pathways are difficult to study, as lives unfold from myriad transactions among systems and in idiosyncratic ways. Researchers interested in pathway models of resilience and development have a formidable agenda in front of them as they begin to address the goal of providing a more comprehensive account of how these transactions produce development. As a result, there is growing interest in the integration of research across disciplines and levels of analysis to study processes of resilience (Cicchetti & Curtis, 2007; Lester, Masten, & McEwen, 2006; Masten, 2007).

To date, the majority of research on resilience has focused on the linkages among psychosocial risks and protective influences as they relate to behavioral outcomes in development. An example would be the study of children living in poverty (psychosocial risk) with good parental support (psychosocial protection), who perform at or above national norms on measures of academic achievement (behavioral outcome). However, developmental theories about resilience are much more dynamic than the research to date, and assume that many levels across multiple systems are involved in many processes that lead to resilience (Cicchetti & Curtis, 2007; Curtis & Cicchetti, 2003; Masten & Obradović, 2007; Yates et al., 2003).

In dynamic systems models of resilience, risks, assets, and protective factors may be represented at multiple levels of analysis, in genes, cells, neurological or physiological structure or functioning, psychological variables (e.g., personality, intelligence), families and peer groups, school and neighborhood factors, and broader contextual influences like culture, ethnicity, local/state/federal social policies, etc. One current challenge lies in elucidating how assets, risks, and protective factors transact across these levels to produce positive or negative outcomes. As research progresses on the processes that produce resilience, investigators are expanding their models to incorporate knowledge and methodologies across levels and traditionally distinct fields, such as neuroscience, genomics, education, economics, sociology, anthropology, and public health (Cicchetti & Blender, 2004; Curtis & Cicchetti, 2003; Lester et al., 2006; Luthar, 2006; Luthar & Brown, 2007; Masten, 2007). The goal is to produce more detailed models of risk and resilience that include mediators and moderators operating across systems, considered at multiple levels over time. For example, a moderation model could involve findings linking social support (psychosocial protection) with lower rates of depression (behavioral outcome) among children who experienced both maltreatment (psychosocial risk) and genetic risk for depression (Kaufman et al., 2004; see also Cicchetti & Blender, 2004).

A mediational model could involve positive early caregiving being linked to lasting differences in hypothalamic-pituitary-adrenal axis functioning (which acts to constrain some aspects of physiological arousal during periods of acute stress), which in turn is linked to lower levels of psychopathology and greater levels of adaptive functioning (Gunnar, Fisher, & The Early Experience, Stress, and Prevention Network, 2006). These models incorporate findings across scientific fields and multiple levels of analysis to better explain the processes by which risks, assets, and protective factors result in resilient outcomes.

A Summary of Findings on Resilience in Development

Findings from a wide-ranging and diverse literature on resilience in children and youth converge with compelling regularity on a set of individual, relationship, and environmental attributes associated with good adjustment and development under a variety of life-course threatening conditions

Table 12.2 Protective factors for psychosocial resilience in children and youth

In the child
Problem-solving skills
Self-regulation skills for self-control of attention, arousal, and impulses
Easy temperament in infancy; adaptable personality later in development
Positive self-perceptions or self-efficacy
Faith and a sense of meaning in life
A positive outlook on life
Talents valued by self and society
General appealingness or attractiveness to others

In the family and close relationships
Positive attachment relationships
Close relationships to competent, prosocial, and supportive adults
Authoritative parenting (high on warmth, structure/monitoring, and expectations)
Positive family climate with low discord between parents
Organized home environment
Postsecondary education of parents
Parents with qualities listed as protective factors within the child (above)
Parents involved in child's education
Socioeconomic advantages
Connections to prosocial and rule-abiding peers
Romantic relationships with prosocial and well-adjusted partners

In the community and relationships with organizations
Effective schools
Ties to prosocial organizations (such as schools, clubs, or scouting)
Neighborhoods with high "collective efficacy"
High levels of public safety
Good emergency social services (such as 911 or crisis nursery services)
Good public health and health-care availability

across cultural contexts (Luthar, 2006; Masten, 2001, 2007). A list of the most commonly reported potential protective factors against developmental hazards found in studies of psychosocial resilience is presented in Table 12.2. These protective factors measure differential attributes of the child, the family, other relationships, and the major contexts in which children and youth develop, such as school and neighborhood. The most salient individual characteristics include cognitive skills and personality differences related to effective problem solving, self-regulation, and adaptability to stress. Many of the characteristics that consistently have been found to predict good adaptation in the context of risk are the subject of chapters in this volume, including self-efficacy, self-worth, problem solving, positive relationships, faith or spirituality, and humor.

The most widely reported family attributes are related to the quality of parenting available to the child and socioeconomic advantages. Parents who provide love and support, as well as structure and high expectations, generally appear to protect child development across a wide variety of situations and cultures. Relationship bonds to other competent and involved adults and (as young people grow older) to prosocial peers or romantic partners are also widely reported correlates and predictors of resilience. Additionally, in the larger arenas in which children grow up, there are protective factors in multiple contexts which provide structure, safety, opportunities to learn and to develop talents, adult role models, support for cultural and religious traditions, and many other resources. Given that many of the attributes of child or environment on this list also have been implicated as predictors of good development in low-risk children, it is important to consider their meaning in development.

Masten (2001) has argued that there are fundamental human adaptation systems that serve to keep behavioral development on course and facilitate recovery from adversity when more normative conditions are restored. These protective systems presumably have emerged from processes of biological and cultural evolution that have shaped human capacity for adaptation. Some of these systems have been the subject of extensive theoretical and empirical study in psychology, whereas others have been left to other disciplines or neglected. Systems that have received some attention in psychology would include the following: attachment relationships and parenting; pleasure-in-mastery motivational systems; self-regulatory systems for emotion, arousal, and behavior; families; as well as formal education systems, culture belief systems, and religion or spirituality. In the case of some systems, such as cultural beliefs and organizations, other disciplines, such as anthropology and sociology, may have contributed more than psychology.

Within resilience research, the processes underlying specific protective factors have not been the subject of extensive study to date, though there have been numerous calls for such research (Luthar, 2006; Masten et al., 1990; Rutter, 1990). The most powerful tests of theories about resilience processes can be achieved through experiments designed to promote resilience by manipulating a specific promotive or protective process. This is accomplished when a well-designed intervention or prevention trial (with random assignment to groups) influences a process of interest and shows that the change in this process is related to predicted changes in the children. However, it is also the case where experiments that were not explicitly designed to test a resilience model provide corroborating evidence of resilience theory. Many of the successful experiments to prevent problems in children appear to work by promoting or mobilizing the same assets and protective systems implicated by resilience research (Luthar, 2006; Masten, 2007; Masten et al., 2006).

Fostering Resilience: Implications for Policy and Practice

The findings on resilience suggest that the greatest threats to children are those adversities that undermine basic human protective systems. It follows that efforts to promote competence and resilience in at-risk children should focus on strategies that prevent damage to, restore, or compensate for threats to these basic systems. For example, prenatal care, nutritional programs, early childhood education, adequate medical care, and good schools all promote or protect brain development, attention, thinking, and learning, thereby promoting the healthy development of systems that appear to play a powerful role in the lives of children who successfully negotiate challenges to development.

Also crucial are programs and policies that support effective parenting and the availability of competent adults in the lives of children. The best-documented asset of resilient children is a strong bond to a competent and caring adult, which need not be a parent. Ensuring that children have such an adult in their lives must be the first order of business.

Resilience models and findings suggest that programs will be most effective when they tap into powerful adaptation systems. One example is provided by the mastery motivational system. When development is proceeding normally, humans are motivated to learn about the environment and derive pleasure from mastering new skills. Children need opportunities to experience success at all ages. This means that families, schools, and communities have a responsibility to provide such opportunities and to ensure that the talents of each child are developed. One of the great differences in the lives of children growing up in the middle class versus poverty is in the richness of opportunities for achievement that feed the mastery motivation system. Feelings of self-confidence and self-efficacy grow from mastery experiences. Children who feel effective persist in the face of failure and achieve greater success because of their efforts (Bandura, 1997).

Much has been written about programs that work for children at risk. Based on the resilience literature, we would expect that successful programs for children at risk would safeguard and foster basic but powerful protective systems for human development.

Strategies for Fostering Resilience

The models and lessons arising from research on resilience suggest three major kinds of strategies for prevention and intervention programs. Conceptually, the work on resilience suggests that we need to move positive goals to the forefront. *Promoting healthy development and competence is as important, if not more important, than preventing problems, and will serve the same end.* As a society, we will do well to nurture human capital, investing in the competence of our children. This means understanding how the capacity for academic achievement, rule-abiding behavior, and good citizenship develops. It is important to identify risks and prevent them whenever possible, but it is also important to identify assets and protective systems, and support these to the best of our knowledge. Three basic strategies for intervention are suggested by resilience research, as illustrated in Table 12.3.

Risk-focused strategies are designed to reduce the exposure of children to hazardous experiences. Examples of risk-focused strategies include prenatal care to prevent premature births, school reforms to reduce the stressfulness of school transitions for young adolescents, and community efforts to prevent homelessness through housing policies. Here the intent is to remove or reduce threat exposure.

Table 12.3 Examples of strategies for promoting resilience in children and youth

Risk-focused strategies: Preventing/reducing risk and stressors
Prevent or reduce the likelihood of low birth weight or prematurity through prenatal care
Screen for and treat depression in mothers of newborns
Prevent homeless episodes through housing policy or emergency assistance
Reduce neighborhood crime or violence through community policing
Clean up asbestos, lead, land mines where children live or play
Avoid multiple foster care placements

Asset-focused strategies: Improving number or quality of resources or social capital
Provide food, water, shelter, medical, or dental care
Provide a tutor, nurse, or guardian *ad litem*
Organize activity clubs for children or build a recreation center
Educate parents about child development and effective parenting
Restore community services after a disaster
Train care providers, corrections staff, or police in child development
Educate teachers about child development and effective teaching

Process-focused strategies: Mobilizing the power of human adaptation systems
Foster secure attachment relationships between infants and parents through parental-sensitivity training or home-visiting programs for new parents and their infants
Nurture healthy brain development through high-quality nutrition and early childhood programs
Nurture mentoring relationships for children through a program to match children with potential mentors
Support healthy family formation and function through education and policies
Build self-efficacy through graduated success models of teaching
Encourage friendships of children with prosocial peers in healthy activities, such as extracurricular activities
Support cultural traditions that provide children with adaptive rituals and opportunities for bonds with prosocial adults, such as religious education or classes for children where elders teach ethnic traditions of dance, meditation, etc.

Asset-focused strategies are designed to increase the amount of, access to, or quality of resources children need for positive development. Examples of resources that are assumed to have direct effects on children include tutors or recreation centers with programs for children. Other assets are assumed to operate indirectly to the benefit of children, through strengthening the social or financial capital in a child's life. Examples include the establishment of literacy or job programs for parents, and programs to provide teachers with more training or resources, so that they can be more effective in the classroom (e.g., Benson, Galbraith, & Espeland, 1995).

Process-focused strategies are designed to mobilize the fundamental protective systems for human development. In this case, efforts go beyond simply removing risk or adding assets but instead attempt to influence *processes* that will change a child's life. Examples include programs designed to improve the quality of attachment relationships or efforts to build self-efficacy through a sequence of graduated mastery experiences that enable children to experience success and motivate them to succeed in life.

Comprehensive intervention efforts to change the life chances of children at risk include all three of these strategies. Examples include Head Start (Zigler & Styfco, 2001), the Abecedarian Project (Campbell, Ramey, Pungello, Sparling, & Miller-Johnson, 2002), the Chicago Child-Parent Centers (Reynolds et al., 2007), the Fast Track prevention trial for conduct problems (Conduct Problems Prevention Research Group, 2002), and the Seattle Social Development Project (Hawkins, Guo, Hill, Battin-Pearson, & Abbott, 2001). In effect, these programs aim to prevent or reduce problems in development by promoting good adaptation. Each has a different model and emphasis, yet they all utilize multiple strategies to reduce risk and increase protection in children's lives. Findings from successful interventions corroborate the findings from the resilience literature, implicating highly similar protections and processes.

Conclusions and Future Directions for Resilience Research

Of all the knowledge gained from research on developmental resilience, one conclusion stands out: resilience in children arises from *ordinary processes*. Evidence indicates that the children who "make it" have basic human protective systems operating in their favor. Resilience does not come from rare and special qualities, but from the operations of ordinary

human systems in the biology and psychology of children, from their relationships in the family and community, and from schools, religions, cultures, and other aspects of societies (Masten, 2001).

Positive psychology, the focus of this handbook, represents a return to the study of how these systems and their interactions give rise to good adaptation and development, as well as resilience. The interest in positive adaptation evident in the early history of psychology is enjoying a renaissance that was rekindled in part by the study of resilient children in the 1960s, 1970s, and 1980s.

The study of resilience in development has produced a shift in the frameworks for understanding and helping children at risk or already in trouble. This change is evident in new conceptualization of the goals of prevention and intervention that now address competence as well as problems. It is also apparent in assessments that include strengths in addition to risks and problems. Theories about the etiology of behavior problems and mental illness must now explain why some people who experience hazards and risks associated with psychopathology nevertheless develop into competent and healthy individuals. Policy makers concerned about the large numbers of children at risk for problems, now ask "what works?" to prevent such problems and to promote favorable youth development; they also ask how this knowledge can be effectively harnessed to enhance the human capital of society.

Fortified by the groundwork of a first generation of research, investigators of resilience now must address some tough questions about how naturally occurring resilience operates and whether these processes can be initiated or facilitated by design in policies or practice (Luthar & Brown, 2007). The corresponding biological processes of resilience, from genes to neurological development and functioning for example, are still just beginning to be considered (Cicchetti & Curtis, 2007; Curtis & Cicchetti, 2003; Lester et al., 2006; Luthar, 2006). The study of healthy physical development also must be integrated with the study of healthy psychological development in children growing up under favorable and unfavorable conditions. It also has become evident that the classification systems for psychopathology need an overhaul to address the role of positive adaptation more effectively in defining, assessing, and treating disorder (see Masten & Curtis, 2000; Masten et al., 2006). As studies of resilience go forward, explanations must include additional influences on development and their interface, which requires going beyond the traditional boundaries of psychological science. This research promises a more thorough appreciation of how it is that certain children beat the odds and succeed in life. Armed with this understanding, policy makers and preventive interventionists can make informed decisions to bring about the best possible outcomes in all children.

It is not possible to prevent all of the hazards that jeopardize the lives and well-being of children and youth. Therefore, we must learn how to preserve, protect, and recover good adaptation and development that has been or will be threatened by adversity and risk exposure. This is the ongoing goal of resilience studies in developmental science.

Questions about the Future

1. With advances in methods for studying genes and gene action, as well as brain development and brain function, the study of resilience processes across levels of analysis is becoming feasible. Given that relationships are at the top of the list of important protective systems for human resilience, how might future studies integrate assessments at the genetic, neural, and relational levels to study the processes by which relationships work?

2. How can disciplines work together to prepare populations for resilience in the face of major disasters of nature or human design, such as terrorist attacks, flu pandemic, or hurricanes, that threaten protective systems of human life across many levels, from the individual immune systems to families, communities, and the ecosystem?

3. As globalization occurs, how will the unique protective influences of specific cultures be preserved and what kind of new protective systems will emerge?

Acknowledgments

Resilience concepts described in this chapter were developed in the context of the Project Competence studies of competence and resilience at the University of Minnesota, with the collaboration of Norman Garmezy and Auke Tellegen, and grant support from the William T. Grant Foundation, the National Institute of Mental Health, the National Science Foundation, the National Institute of Child Health and Human Development, the University of Minnesota Center for Urban and Regional Affairs, and McKnight Professorships to the first author. Preparation of this chapter was also facilitated by a grant to the first author from the National Science Foundation (BCS-0745643) and a Predoctoral Training Fellowship to J. J. Cutuli from the Center for Neurobehavioral Development at the University of Minnesota.

References and Recommended Readings*

Anthony, E. J. (1974). The syndrome of the psychologically invulnerable child. In E. J. Anthony & C. Koupernik (Eds.), *The child in his family: Children at psychiatric risk* (pp. 529–545). New York: Wiley.

Bandura, A. (1997). *Self-efficacy: The exercise of control.* New York: W. H. Freeman.

Benson, P. L., Galbraith, J., & Espeland, P. (1995). *What kids need to succeed.* Minneapolis, MN: Free Spirit.

Campbell, J. (1970). *The hero with a thousand faces.* New York: World.

Campbell, F A., Ramey, C. T., Pungello, E., Sparling, J., & Miller-Johnson, M. (2002). Early childhood education: Young adult outcomes from the Abecedarian Project. *Applied Developmental Science, 6*(1), 42–57.

Cicchetti, D., & Blender, J. A. (2004). A multiple-levels-of-analysis approach to the study of developmental processes in maltreated children. *Proceedings of the National Academy of Sciences, 101,* 17325–17326.

Cicchetti, D., & Curtis, W. J. (Eds.) (2007). Special issue: A multilevel approach to resilience. *Development and Psychopathology, 19*(3).

Conduct Problems Prevention Research Group. (2002). Predictor variables associated with positive Fast Track outcomes at the end of third grade. *Journal of Abnormal Child Psychology, 30*(1), 37–52.

Curtis, W. J., & Cicchetti, D. (2003). Moving research on resilience into the 21st century: Theoretical and methodological considerations in examining the biological contributors to resilience. *Development and Psychopathology, 15,* 773–810.

Dohrenwend, B. P. (Ed.). (1998). *Adversity, stress, and psychopathology.* New York: Oxford University Press.

Elder, G. H. (1998). The life course as developmental theory. *Child Development, 69,* 1–12.

Garmezy, N. (1971). Vulnerability research and the issue of primary prevention. *American Journal of Orthopsychiatry, 41,* 101–116.

Garmezy, N. (1974). The study of competence in children at risk for severe psychopathology. In E. J. Anthony & C. Koupernik (Eds.), *The child in his family: Vol. 3. Children at psychiatric risk* (pp. 77–97). New York: Wiley.

Garmezy, N., Masten, A. S., & Tellegen, A. (1984). The study of stress and competence in children: A building block for developmental psychopathology. *Child Development, 55,* 97–111.

Gunnar, M. R., Fisher, P. A., & The Early Experience, Stress, and Prevention Network. (2006). Bringing basic research on early experience and stress neurobiology to bear on preventive interventions for neglected and maltreated children. *Development and Psychopathology, 18,* 651–677.

Hawkins, J. D., Guo, J., Hill, K. G., Battin-Pearson, S., & Abbott, R. D. (2001). Long-term effects of the Seattle Social Development Intervention on school-bonding trajectories. *Applied Developmental Science, 5,* 225–236.

Kaufman, J., Yang, B. Z., Douglas-Palumberi, H., Houshyar, S., Lipschitz, D., Krystal, J. H., et al. (2004). Social supports and serotonin transporter gene moderate depression in maltreated children. *Proceedings of the National Academy of Sciences, 101,* 17316–17321.

Keating, D., & Hertzman, C. (Eds.). (1999). *Developmental health and the wealth of nations: Social, biological and educational dynamics.* New York: Guilford.

Kreppner, J. M., Rutter, M., Beckett, C., Castle, J., Colvert, E., Grothues, C., et al. (2007). Normality and impairment following profound early institutional deprivation: A longitudinal examination through childhood. *Developmental Psychology, 43*(4), 931–946.

Laub, J. H., Nagin, D. S., & Sampson, R. J. (1998). Trajectories of change in criminal offending: Good marriages and the desistance process. *American Sociological Review, 63*, 225–238.

*Lester, B. M., Masten, A. S., & McEwen, B. S. (Eds.). (2006). *Resilience in Children* (Vol. 1094). New York: Academy of Sciences.

*Luthar, S. S. (2006). Resilience in development: A synthesis of research across five decades. In D. Cicchetti & D. J. Cohen (Eds.), *Developmental psychopathology: Vol. 3. Risk, disorder, and adaptation* (2nd ed., pp. 739–795). Hoboken, NJ: Wiley.

Luthar, S. S., & Brown, P. J. (2007). Maximizing resilience through diverse levels of inquiry: Prevailing paradigms, possibilities, and priorities for the future. *Development and Psychopathology, 19*, 931–955.

Luthar, S. S., Cicchetti, D., & Becker, B. (2000). The construct of resilience: A critical evaluation and guidelines for future work. *Child Development, 71*, 543–562.

Masten, A. S. (1999). Resilience comes of age: Reflections on the past and outlook for the next generation of research. In M. D. Glantz & J. Johnson (Eds.), *Resilience and development: Positive life adaptations* (pp. 281–296). New York: Plenum.

Masten, A. S. (2001). Ordinary magic: Resilience processes in development. *American Psychologist, 56*, 227–238.

*Masten, A. S. (2007). Resilience in developing systems: Progress and promise as the fourth wave rises. *Development and Psychopathology, 19*, 921–930.

Masten, A. S., Best, K. M., & Garmezy, N. (1990). Resilience and development: Contributions from the study of children who overcome adversity. *Development and Psychopathology, 2*, 425–444.

Masten, A. S., Burt, K., & Coatsworth, J. D. (2006). Competence and psychopathology in development. In D. Cicchetti & D. J. Cohen (Eds.), *Developmental psychopathology: Vol. 3. Risk, disorder, and adaptation* (2nd ed., pp. 687–738). Hoboken, NJ: Wiley.

Masten, A. S., & Coatsworth, J. D. (1998). The development of competence in favorable and unfavorable environments: Lessons from successful children. *American Psychologist, 53*, 205–220.

Masten, A. S., & Curtis, W. J. (2000). Integrating competence and psychopathology: Pathways toward a comprehensive science of adaptation in development. *Development and Psychopathology, 12*, 529–550.

Masten, A. S., Hubbard, J. J., Gest, S. D., Tellegen, A., Garmezy, N., & Ramirez, M. (1999). Competence in the context of adversity: Pathways to resilience and maladaptation from childhood to late adolescence. *Development and Psychopathology, 11*, 143–169.

*Masten, A. S., & Obradović, J. (2007). Disaster preparation and recovery: Lessons from research on resilience in human development. *Ecology and Society, 13*(1), 9. http://www.ecologyandsociety.org/vol 13/iss1/art9/

Masten, A. S., & O'Connor, M. J. (1989). Vulnerability, stress, and resilience in the early development of a high-risk child. *Journal of the American Academy of Child and Adolescent Psychiatry, 28*, 274–278.

Masten, A. S., & Shaffer, A. (2006). How families matter in child development: Reflections from research on risk and resilience. In A. Clarke-Stewart & J. Dunn (Eds.), *Families count: Effects on child and adolescent development* (pp. 5–25). Cambridge: Cambridge University Press.

Mayr, E. (1982). *The growth of biological thought: Diversity, evolution, and inheritance.* Cambridge, MA: Belknap Press of Harvard University Press.

Murphy, L. B. (1962). *The widening world of childhood: Paths toward mastery.* New York: Basic Books.

Murphy, L. B., & Moriarty, A. E. (1976). *Vulnerability, coping, and growth: From infancy to adolescence.* New Haven, CT: Yale University Press.

Obradović, J., Shaffer, A., & Masten, A. S. (in press). Risk in developmental psychopathology: Progress and future directions. In L. C. Mayes & M. Lewis (Eds.), *The environment of human development: A handbook of theory and measurement.* New York: Cambridge University Press.

Reynolds, A. J., Temple, J. A., Ou, S.-R., Robertson, D. L., Mersky, J. P., Topitzes, J. W., et al. (2007). Effects of a school-based, early childhood intervention on adult health and well-being. *Archives of Pediatrics and Adolescent Medicine, 161*, 730–739.

Roisman, G. I., Masten, A. S., Coatsworth, J. D., & Tellegen, A. (2004). Salient and emerging developmental tasks in the transition to adulthood. *Child Development, 75*(1), 123–133.

Rutter, M. (1979). Protective factors in children's responses to stress and disadvantage. In M. W. Kent & J. E. Rolf (Eds.), *Primary prevention of psychopathology: Vol. 3. Social competence in children* (pp. 49–74). Hanover, NH: University Press of New England.

Rutter, M. (1990). Psychosocial resilience and protective mechanisms. In J. Rolf, A. S. Masten, D. Cicchetti, K. H. Nuechterlein, & S. Weintraub (Eds.), *Risk and protective factors in the development of psychopathology* (pp. 181–214). New York: Cambridge University Press.

Rutter, M., & English and Romanian Adoptees (ERA) Study Team. (1998). Developmental catch-up and deficit, following adoption after severe global early privation. *Journal of Child Psychology and Psychiatry, 39*, 465–476.

Werner, E. E., & Smith, R. S. (1982). *Vulnerable but invincible: A study of resilient children.* New York: McGraw-Hill.

Werner, E. E., & Smith, R. S. (1992). *Overcoming the odds: High risk children from birth to adulthood.* Ithaca, NY: Cornell University Press.

Werner, E. E., & Smith, R. S. (2001). *Journeys from childhood to mid-life: Risk, resilience, and recovery.* Ithaca, NY: Cornell University Press.

Yates, T. M., Egeland, B., & Sroufe, L. A. (2003). Rethinking resilience: A developmental process perspective. In S. S. Luthar (Ed.), *Resilience and vulnerability: Adaptation in the context of childhood adversities* (pp. 234–256). New York: Cambridge University Press.

Zigler, E., & Styfco, S. J. (2001). Extended childhood intervention prepares children for school and beyond. *Journal of the American Medical Association, 285*(18), 1378–2380.

Zimmerman, M. (1983). Methodological issues in the assessment of life events: A review of issues and research. *Clinical Psychology Review, 3*, 339–370.

Positive Psychology for Children and Adolescents: Development, Prevention, and Promotion

Keri J. Brown Kirschman, Rebecca J. Johnson, Jade A. Bender, *and* Michael C. Roberts

Abstract

The goal of this chapter is to inform the reader of the unique facets of childhood as they relate to the research and application of positive psychology, provide reference to exemplary work in this area, and identify research needs for the future. Researchers have noted the need, particularly when working with children and adolescents, to examine strengths and positive aspects of development rather than focusing solely on psychopathology and other possible negative outcomes. Positive psychology offers such an approach. This chapter reviews current research in hope, optimism, benefit finding, and quality of life in children and adolescents, highlighting measurement issues and notable interventions for each of these concepts. Developmental considerations, prevention and promotion, and settings for the delivery of positive psychology to children and adolescents are discussed. Despite the development in positive psychology measurement and intervention for children, much more research is needed in this area. Future exploration of the interrelatedness among hope, optimism, growth finding, and other positive psychology variables is needed. There are many youth programs and interventions that have a positive psychology orientation; however, methodologically sound, systematic research planned a priori is needed. Thus, interventions and evaluations of programs to promote hope or optimism in children and adolescents are prime areas for future work.

Keywords: benefit finding, children, hope, optimism, quality of life

A whole stack of memories never equal one little hope.
—*Charles M. Schulz*

Historically, the study of the psychology of childhood has paralleled that of adults, with the focus primarily on psychopathology, maladjustment, and problem behaviors. This pathology model has been applied to children with significant emotional and behavioral disorders that may pose major problems for parents, teachers, and peers and result in their pathology receiving the greatest attention. More recently, however, the focus increasingly has become one of perceiving the competencies of the child and his or her family and enhancing growth in psychological domains. Positive psychology embodies these efforts.

Whereby the basic tenets of positive psychology (described elsewhere in this Handbook) do not differ when referring to the special population of children and adolescents, to blindly apply these concepts without considering the unique aspects of childhood would be naive at best, and likely counterproductive. Adult-oriented theories and intervention techniques "have never sufficed in other areas of mental health intervention... [because] work with children requires a developmental perspective which recognizes the process of continual change over time in the psychology of children" (Roberts & Peterson, 1984, p. 3). In our view, well-formulated positive psychology literature takes a developmental perspective. The goal of this chapter is to inform the reader of these unique facets of childhood as they relate to the research and application of positive psychology, provide reference to exemplary work in this area, and identify research needs for the future.

Concepts such as coping and resiliency suggest that children and adolescents are capable of positive responses even in negative environmental situations or life events such as abuse, trauma, or chronic illness. Siegel (1992) called for increased attention to the variety of areas in which such positive responses can be seen, including individual differences in children's behavioral, emotional, and physiological responsiveness to their environment. Siegel indicated that each child may respond quite differently to an environmental stressor and that "individual-differences factors can influence both a child's response to stress and his or her use of coping strategies" (p. 4). An important aspect of coping is that the same mechanisms of responding to stress are involved in life events that are not as major as divorce or disease, but are the daily hassles of human existence. In much of the earlier literature and still to some extent today, coping or resilience concepts are thought of only as responses to a stressor, usually a major one, not as a positive behavioral style of adjusting, adapting, accommodating, and assimilating to an ever-changing environment in a child's life. In a positive psychology orientation, however, a comprehensive and inclusive conceptualization of coping views these adaptations as normal developmental events with much common origin and function. Additionally, there is an increasing recognition that growth and enhancement to achieve physical and psychological well-being occur through these adaptations.

Beyond specific psychological concepts, such as coping, others have noted the need, particularly working with adolescents, to examine the strengths and positive assets of developmental stages rather than focusing on the multitude of stressors and potential negative outcomes (Johnson, Roberts, & Worell, 1999). Johnson and Roberts (1999) recognized that "looking at strengths rather than deficits, opportunities rather than risks, assets rather than liabilities is slowly becoming an increasing presence in the psychotherapy, education, and parenting literature" (p. 5). For instance, Dryfoos (1998) reviewed the programs aimed at assisting adolescents and concluded that successful ones emphasized optimism and hope and were growth enhancing for the adolescents and their families. Further, an approach that examines strengths and emphasizes a positive-psychology orientation may be preferred by adolescents (Ginsburg et al., 2002).

Frequently, the focus has been on taking children with problems and doing something to change them. Positive psychology has something to offer this process, for example, developing social skills in a child with behavior problems, or capitalizing on a child's existing strengths. A larger application of positive psychology, however, would be to view it in terms of prevention and promotion. More recent conceptualizations have focused attention on normal development for most children, but also on considering how pathology might be avoided through early intervention and enhanced environments for "all" children. Thus, the application of concepts of positive psychology has moved to arenas where children without identified needs can be targeted, for example, in schools, pediatrician's offices, and in faith-based organizations.

In this chapter, we will describe the four conceptualizations of hope, optimism, benefit finding, and quality of life as related to positive psychology for children and adolescents. This examination of the literature provides a general overview, highlighting measurement and future research directions and is illustrative of the potential utility of positive psychology in the study of child development.

Hope
Definition and Concept

Snyder and his colleagues have defined hope as a cognitive set involving an individual's beliefs in his or her capability to produce workable routes to goals (waypower or pathways) and beliefs in his or her own ability to initiate and sustain movement toward those goals (willpower or agency; Snyder, 1994; Snyder et al., 1991; Snyder, Hoza, et al., 1997; see chap. 30). They have suggested that hope is an important construct in understanding how individuals, including children, deal with stressors in their lives, avoid becoming mired down in problem behaviors, and use past experiences to develop strategies for working toward goals in an adaptive, effective manner.

Snyder and his colleagues proposed that most children have the intellectual capacity to use hopeful, goal-directed thinking. Boys and girls have similar levels of hope and tend to be biased somewhat positively in their perceptions of the future, although it has been argued that this is typical and adaptive (Snyder, Hoza, et al., 1997). This bias may be appropriate to help children develop and sustain thoughts of positive outcomes even if they are realistically untenable, and it appears that high-hope children do this as they successfully deal with stressful events in childhood. The research thus far indicates that, for most children, hope is relatively high, and that even children with comparatively low hope rarely indicate that they have no hope (Snyder, McDermott, Cook, & Rapoff, 1997). Measures of children's self-reported hope correlate positively with self-reported competency, and children with higher levels of hope report feeling more positively about themselves and less depressed than children with lower levels of hope (Snyder, 1994).

Measurement

A measure of children's hope, the Children's Hope Scale (CHS), was developed by Snyder, Hoza, et al. (1997). The measure has two subscales comprised of three items each that correspond to the conceptual model: agency (willpower) and pathways (waypower). Several versions of the CHS have been designed for different age groups and for different purposes. These versions include the Young Children's Hope Scale (YCHS) Story Form (for ages 5–8 years), Self-Report Form (for ages 5–9 years), and Observer Rating Form (for teachers, parents, and other adults); and for older children, the Children's Hope Scale (CHS) Self-Report Form (for ages 9–16 years) and an Observer Rating Form. Adolescents aged 16 and over can complete the Trait Hope Scale or the State Hope Scale, which have been designed for adults and also come with observer rating forms.

Data collected during the development of the CHS indicate that the CHS demonstrates high test–retest reliability for intervals up to 1 month (Snyder, Hoza, et al., 1997). Subsequent research indicates that the CHS has adequate internal consistency and criterion-related validity, and support has been found for the correlated, two-factor conceptual model underlying the CHS (Valle, Huebner, & Suldo, 2004). Research with the CHS has shown that the two subscales correlate 0.50–0.70. Snyder, McDermott, et al. (1997) labeled three different patterns of scores that tend to describe children's hope based on the combination of their agency and pathways subscores: small hope (low agency and low pathways), half hope (one low and one high), and high or large hope (high agency and high pathways). The authors suggest that interventions may be tailored to address either low agency or low pathways, or both, but research has not yet addressed this possibility.

Research Examining Hope in Children

Increasingly more research has explored hope in children. A small number of studies suggest that children's hope moderately predicts school-related achievement. Worrell and Hale (2001) found that adolescents at risk for dropping out of high school were less likely to do so if they had high hope, compared to those with low hope. Gilman, Dooley, and Florell (2006) found that adolescents in both high and average hope groups reported less school and psychological distress, higher personal adjustment and global satisfaction, greater participation in extracurricular activities, and higher self-reported GPA than adolescents in the low hope group.

Hope has also been explored in children considered to be "at-risk." Hinton-Nelson, Roberts, and Snyder (1996) gathered information from junior high students attending a school in close proximity to a high crime area to explore the relations among exposure to violence, hope, and perceived vulnerability to victimization. The authors hypothesized that children who had been exposed to violence would have lower levels of hope, but this was not the case: children in this sample reported levels of hope similar to that of other groups. Participants who had witnessed violence, but had less personal or direct experience with violence, reported the highest levels of hope, and participants with higher hope were less likely to believe they would die a violent death. In contrast, participants with direct exposure to violence tended to predict violent deaths for themselves. The authors concluded that, while these young people acknowledged the violence around them, they were able to sustain high hope as long as they did not experience violence directly.

In a similar study investigating hope and its correlates in children considered to be "at risk," Hagen, Myers, and Mackintosh (2005) administered self-report measures of hope, perceived social support, and internalizing and externalizing behavior to children (ages 6–12 years) of incarcerated women. Hope was positively correlated to perceived social support and negatively correlated to internalizing and externalizing problems. Hope continued to predict fewer internalizing and externalizing problems even after controlling for social support and level of stress. Wilson, Syme, Boyce, Battistich, and Selvin (2005) examined the relations among hope, neighborhood conditions, and substance use. Their results indicated that substance use was related to higher perceived neighborhood disorder and to a lower sense of hope.

Hope has been suggested as a useful concept to examine in pediatric populations, because children who are chronically ill or injured are often required to cope with or adjust to difficult conditions. In one study, Lewis and Kliewer (1996) examined the relations among hope, coping strategies, and adjustment in a group of children with sickle-cell disease (SCD). Results revealed that hope was negatively related to anxiety, but that coping strategies moderated this relationship. Specifically, children with SCD who had high levels of hope and who reported using primarily active coping strategies (distraction, seeking social support) reported less anxiety. The authors concluded that knowing both a child's level of hope and the types of coping behaviors he or she is using are important for understanding variations in psychological adjustment to chronic illness.

In another study, Barnum, Snyder, Rapoff, Mani, and Thompson (1998) hypothesized that high-hope thinking may be protective, allowing children to function effectively in spite of obstacles and challenges in their lives. They examined predictors of adjustment (social support, family environment, burn characteristics, demographics, hope) in two adolescent groups: burn survivors and matched controls. They found few differences between the two groups. For both groups, higher hope scores predicted lower externalizing behavior scores, and social support and hope both significantly contributed to the prediction of global self-worth. Barnum et al. (1998) suggested that adolescents who report higher levels of hope may think in ways that generate positive solutions, and may feel more capable of enacting a variety of behaviors to solve problems, thereby reducing the need to act out in problematic ways. An increase in the ability to problem-solve and generate positive solutions may translate into actions that facilitate disease management. In one study, high levels of hope were predictive of children's adherence to their asthma treatment regimen (Berg, Rapoff, Snyder, & Belmont, 2007).

In another study examining a pediatric population, Connelly (2005) explored the relations among family functioning, quality of life, and hope in children with juvenile rheumatoid arthritis and their parents. Child-reported hope was not related to a measure of quality of life, but was modestly, negatively correlated with parent-reported family functioning, indicating that children's hope was lower when parental dissatisfaction with family functioning was high.

Intervention

Given that hope appears to be related to school achievement, adjustment, and adaptive behavior, among other factors, research has begun to look at ways to intervene to promote and improve children's hope (Snyder, Feldman, Shorey, & Rand, 2002). McDermott et al. (1996; described in McDermott & Hastings, 2000) discussed a program in which school-aged children were read stories of high-hope children and participated in discussions aimed at how participants might incorporate hope into their own lives. The intervention resulted in modest, positive changes on measures of hope. More recently, a hope intervention using multimodal educational strategies for middle school–aged children has shown promise (Pedrotti, Lopez, & Krieshok, 2008). Students participated in five weekly sessions in small groups of 8–12. Program components included identifying hopeful and unhopeful language, the pairing of youth into "hope buddies" to communicate future goals with their peers, and students writing their own personal hope stories. Hope scores, as measured by the CHS, were significantly higher for those students who participated in the program when compared with nonparticipants and remained elevated 6 months post intervention.

Other studies have examined whether psychosocial interventions that were not designed to target hope specifically might nevertheless influence children's hope. McNeal et al. (2006) examined children's and adolescents' hope upon admission to a residential facility utilizing the teaching family treatment model, and then again 6 months later. The Child Behavior Checklist (CBCL) was also administered at admission as a general measure of emotional and behavioral problems. The authors found that children with higher CBCL scores at admission reported less hopeful agency thinking, but their hope increased at a faster rate than children with lower CBCL scores. In addition, waypower hopeful thinking increased significantly over the first 6 months of treatment for the group overall. In another study that examined hope in children enrolled in an intervention program, Brown and Roberts (2001) assessed hope in at-risk children participating in a 6-week performing arts summer day camp. Children in the camp participated in intense dance training, psychosocial groups, and wrote hope-themed essays. Results indicated that hope scores increased significantly over the 6 weeks, and remained elevated and stable at 4-month follow-up. These two studies cannot pinpoint which elements of each comprehensive intervention influenced hope, but do suggest that hope can be influenced through positive intervention.

Thus far, few studies have investigated interventions targeting hope. Future research should examine the effectiveness of hope-themed interventions and curriculum, pinpoint which individuals or groups might benefit from such intervention, and determine how observed changes in hopeful thinking impact adjustment and behavior.

Optimism

Definition and Concept

Optimism has been conceptualized as both an explanatory style and a pattern of positive expectations (dispositional optimism) for the future (see Carver & Scheier, 2001; Gillham, Shatte, Reivich, & Seligman, 2001). We will be focusing on optimism as an explanatory style in youth, and the interested reader is referred to chap. 28 for more on dispositional optimism. When it is defined in terms of explanatory style, optimism refers to how an individual thinks about the causality of an event. That is, an optimist is defined as a person who sees defeat as temporary, confined to a particular case, and not his or her direct fault (Seligman, 1991). A pessimist, on the other hand, believes bad events will last a long time and undermine everything he or she does, and that these events were his or her fault. Thus, the way that a person explains positive or negative events to him or herself determines whether he or she is optimistic or pessimistic. This explanatory style is evident in how an individual thinks about the causes of events. A pessimist dwells on the most catastrophic causes for the event, whereas an optimist can see that there are other possible, less catastrophic causes for the same event. For example, two children receive poor grades on a test. The pessimistic child might say to himself, "I'm stupid and can't get anything right," whereas the optimistic child might say to herself "I need to study a little harder next time." In summary, Seligman stated that the way in which a person explains events has three dimensions: permanent versus temporary, universal versus specific, and internal versus external. This explanatory style can be acquired by children and adults and has been labeled "learned optimism."

Considerable research has been conducted on the benefits of learned optimism and the costs of pessimism. Optimists tend to do better in school and college than pessimists. The physical and mental health of optimists tends to be better, and optimists may even live longer than pessimists (Seligman, 1991). Optimists also tend to cope with adverse situations in more adaptive ways (Scheier &

Carver, 1993). Adolescents who are optimistic tend to be less angry (Puskar, Sereika, Lamb, Tusaie-Mumford, & McGuinness, 1999) and abuse substances less often (Carvajal, Claire, Nash, & Evans, 1998). Conversely, pessimists tend to give up more easily, get depressed more often, have poorer health, be more passive (Seligman, 1991), have more failure in work and school, and have more social problems (Peterson, 2000). Despite the appearance that optimism and pessimism may be at two ends of a continuum, with optimism as the better end, this conception has come into question and some researchers have taken a turn toward looking at the potential disadvantages of intense optimism and the advantages of pessimism in certain circumstances (Norem & Chang, 2001).

Seligman, Reivich, Jaycox, and Gillham (1995) described four sources for the origins of optimism. The first possible source is genetics. A second source is the child's environment, in which parental modeling of explanatory styles seems to be a strong influence on children's levels of optimism. A third source for optimism is also an environmental influence, in the form of criticism that a child receives from parents, teachers, coaches, or other adults. For instance, if an adult criticizes a rather permanent ability of a child (e.g., "You just can't learn this"), the child is more likely to develop a pessimistic explanatory style. A fourth way in which optimism develops is through life experiences that promote either mastery or helplessness. Life events such as divorce, death in the family, or abuse can affect how a child describes causes to him- or herself. Events such as these tend to be permanent, and many times the child is unable to stop or reverse the event.

In light of all the benefits of being optimistic and the costs of being pessimistic, is it best for a child to be optimistic all the time? Seligman et al. (1995) noted that there are limits to optimism. Children must see themselves in a realistic light in order for them to successfully challenge their automatic negative thoughts. Teaching children to be realistic helps them perceive the beginnings of negative self-attribution (e.g., "I flunked the test because I am stupid") and challenges them to see where they might be able to overcome a fault (e.g., "I flunked the test because I didn't study enough. Next time I'll study harder").

Measurement

One assessment tool for measuring optimism in children is the Children's Attributional Style Questionnaire (CASQ; Seligman et al., 1995).

This instrument is a 48-item forced-choice questionnaire that assesses explanatory style for both positive and negative hypothetical events. The questions measure whether the child's attributions about positive or negative events are stable or unstable, global or specific, and internal or external. The revised version, the CASQ-R (Thompson, Kaslow, Weiss, & Nolen-Hoeksema, 1998), has been truncated to 24 items. The validity of the CASQ-R is comparable to that of the original CASQ; however, the reliability may be weaker.

Interventions

The Penn Resiliency Program is a 12-session intervention that helps young adolescents identify and make changes to their explanatory style (Reivich, Gillham, Chaplin, & Seligman, 2005). Cognitive-behavioral therapy is used to increase resilience by building skills, such as the ability to identify multiple, accurate causes of a problem and balance optimistic thoughts with the reality of a situation. Adolescents are taught to identify negative beliefs, to evaluate those beliefs by examining evidence for and against them, and to generate more realistic alternatives. The goal of the program is to take adolescents who are at either extreme of the explanatory style, pessimism or optimism, and build flexibility in problem solving. The results of the intervention are encouraging. Researchers found that the children who were in the intervention condition demonstrated improved explanatory styles and reported lower rates of depressive symptoms in the years following the intervention. Children who completed the program in preadolescence were able to deal with the challenges they faced in adolescence more effectively and had less depression than children in the control group. Thus, this study demonstrates the importance of teaching children the skills of learned optimism before they reach puberty, but late enough in childhood for them to understand the concepts.

The study of optimism in children is fairly new, and many aspects have yet to be researched. Results thus far seem to indicate that optimism can be taught, and learned optimism can be helpful in alleviating and even preventing some of the problems of childhood and adolescence. Optimism may be a very valuable tool that children can use to negotiate the challenges and adversity they are sure to face.

Quality of Life
Definition and Concept

Quality of life (QOL) is a multidimensional concept and includes physical, mental, spiritual, and social aspects that contribute to one's sense of well-being (Institute for the Future, 2000). Although definitions for QOL have lacked consistency, elements most noted in the literature include the importance of "subjective" reports of one's well-being and considerations of social, emotional, and cognitive development when measuring QOL during childhood and adolescence. For example, social aspects of QOL may be perceived as more important by adolescents as compared with younger children or adults. Thus, collecting only objective measures of QOL (e.g., presence of a disability) is incomplete. An individual's perceptions of his or her unique situation must be assessed as well. Further, cultural influences on children and adolescent's perception of QOL must be considered; however, research in this area is in its infancy (Olson, Lara, & Frintner, 2004).

Concern about the well-being of children and adolescents has fueled the interest in measurement of QOL for a number of purposes. Broadly, there has been interest in examining the QOL of various subgroups of American youth via population monitoring (Centers for Disease Control and Prevention, 2000; Topolski, Edwards, & Patrick, 2004). For example, QOL has been used to aid in the identification of health disparities among school children (Varni, Burwinkle, & Seid, 2006). Socioeconomic, physical, or mental health conditions that might impact QOL have been examined. QOL has been reportedly lower for children who are obese (Schwimmer, Burwinkle, & Varni, 2003), have attention-deficit/hyperactive disorder (ADHD; Klassen, Miller, & Fine, 2004), and are from urban elementary schools (Mansour et al., 2003). In addition to identifying subgroups of children and adolescents who may have lower QOL, assessing QOL more globally may lead to identification of levels of QOL that may serve to enhance general well-being and serve as protective factors during times of stress. Topolski and colleagues (2001) found that adolescents who reported higher levels of QOL were engaged in fewer risk behaviors (e.g., drug abuse). Additionally, Upton, Maddocks, Eiser, Barnes, and Williams (2005) report the utility of a QOL instrument to assess the success of foster child placements for children in public care.

Health-related quality of life (HRQOL) for children and adolescents with acute and chronic health problems has received considerable attention in recent years (Drotar, 1998; Koot & Wallander, 2001). HRQOL is more specific than overall QOL and acknowledges that disease processes and treatment may have a deleterious impact on a child or adolescent's overall well-being. The notion of HRQOL originated with the World Health Organization's (1948) definition "Health is a state of complete physical, mental, and social well-being, and not merely the absence of disease or infirmity" (p. 1). A child with pediatric headaches, for example, may be functioning well as determined by physiological markers, but may have significant impairment in HRQOL if the illness has caused significant absences from school resulting in feelings of social inadequacy. The converse is true as well, whereby a child with a health impairment may report high levels of HRQOL despite the medical stressor. This higher perceived QOL may serve as an adaptive framework that enhances the child's ability to cope with the day-to-day aspects of their medical regimen, the chronicity of the medical illness, and promote the child's overall well-being.

HRQOL facilitates clinical decisions by providing a medium for children and adolescents with a pediatric or psychiatric illness to report the impact of the disease course and treatment regimen on their overall QOL (Drotar, 2004). These data, in turn, can be used to inform treatment decisions. Eiser (2004) advocated for HRQOL assessments in addition to standard survival statistics in clinical trials. HRQOL can be coupled with adherence measures to better develop a treatment plan that a child and family can adhere to, thus minimizing the impact on a child's perceived quality of their life. Pediatric patients and families who score lower on HRQOL measures can be targeted for psychosocial interventions. Additionally, individuals interested in the delegation of limited health resources have also recognized the utility of measuring the HRQOL (Kaplan, 2001). Measuring QOL in the medical setting may assist health professionals in demonstrating to third-party payers the effectiveness of particular interventions.

Measurement

The measurement of QOL in children and adolescents is replete with challenges (Drotar, 2004). Early measures of QOL primarily focused on subjective proxy-reports, including parents, nurse, teachers, and physician reports of the child's QOL; however, low concordance between respondents has been found (Guyatt, Juniper, Griffith, Feeny, & Ferrie, 1997; Theunissen et al., 1998). Although age-appropriate modifications are necessary, self-report QOL information can be reliably obtained from children as young as 6–7 years of age (Feeny, Juniper, Ferrie, Griffith, & Guyatt, 1998; Riley, 2004). Development of alternative methods of gathering accurate information from younger children regarding their perceived well-being is needed (Rebok et al., 2001).

In recent years, the measurement of pediatric HRQOL has gained considerable momentum with reliable and valid measures of QOL present for clinical and research endeavors (Drotar, 2004; Drotar, Schwartz, Palermo, & Burant, 2006). The following section will describe primarily HRQOL measures and recent advances in applying these measures to evaluate QOL in children and adolescents without chronic illnesses.

In the measurement of HRQOL, general and disease-specific pediatric QOL measures are available. General measures of QOL can be used with children with low-incidence childhood diseases and for cross-condition comparisons (Drotar et al., 1998). Generic HRQOL measures generally include assessment of physical (e.g., participation in sports, activity limitations), psychological (e.g., positive emotions, cognitive functioning), and social (e.g., making friends) domains (Rajmil et al., 2004). The Child Health Questionnaire (CHQ; Landgraf, Abetz, & Ware, 1996) is a noncategorical measure of HRQOL in children and adolescents 5–18 years of age that assesses physical, emotional, and social aspects of QOL. Children and adolescents of at least 10 years of age complete an 87-item self-report of QOL. Parent report forms are available in a 50-item version, as well as a shorter 28-item format. The longer parent format has demonstrated construct validity for measuring constructs of physical and psychosocial health in children and adolescents with and without chronic illnesses (Drotar, Schwartz, Palermo, & Burant, 2006).

Disease-specific measures of QOL have been developed for specific pediatric illnesses and may be more sensitive in determining the differential effects of treatments within one illness domain. Often, physical symptoms associated with the course and treatment of the illness, as well as health status, psychological and adaptive functioning, and family functioning are assessed when the disease-specific measures are used. Consequently, different QOL measures have been developed for use with various childhood conditions including cystic fibrosis (Modi & Quittner, 2003), diabetes (Diabetes Control and Complications Trial (DCCT) Research Group, 1988), epilepsy (Ronen, Streiner, Rosenbaum, & Canadian Pediatric

Epilepsy Network, 2003), asthma (Mishoe et al., 1998; Townsend et al., 1991), and being born with limb deficiencies (Pruitt, Seid, Varni, & Setoguchi, 1999). In the case of children's asthma, a multidisciplinary team assesses QOL in the domains of symptomatology, activity limitations, and emotional functioning (Townsend et al., 1991). The QOL measure of diabetes assesses disease impact as well as school life and relationships with peers (Ingersoll & Marrero, 1991).

When evaluating HRQOL, it may be best to use both a general and a disease-specific module for the most comprehensive assessment of QOL (Powers, Patton, Hommel, & Hershey, 2003). One assessment module that considers QOL in specific pediatric populations via disease modules, and yet also includes a complementary inventory to be used with populations free of disease (i.e., the Generic Core Scales), is the Pediatric Quality of Life Inventory (PedsQL™ 4.0; Varni, Seid, & Kurtin, 2001). Disease-specific modules are available for asthma, arthritis, cancer, cardiac disease, and diabetes. The PedsQL™ 4.0 Generic Core Scales have 23 items that assess physical, emotional, social, and school functioning in the past month (Varni, Seid, Knight, Uzark, & Szer, 2002). Self-report forms are available for children and adolescents aged 5–18; parallel parent report forms are available for youth aged 2–18. The Generic Core Scales can be used to assess QOL in healthy school and community populations (Varni, Burwinkle, & Seid, 2006). For example, the Generic Core Scales have been found to predict health-care access for children enrolled in a statewide health insurance program in California (Varni, Burwinkle, Seid, & Skarr, 2003).

Interventions

The measurement of QOL can add clinical relevance to the results of outcome studies following medical or psychological interventions (Eiser, 2004). Drotar (2004) noted the importance of defining and identifying clinically significant levels of change in QOL to help guide treatment decisions. In addition, measuring QOL can better identify individuals with pediatric conditions who find the treatment to interfere with important aspects of their lives and therefore are less likely to adhere to the prescribed medical regimen (Drotar et al., 1998). Information collected through the use of QOL measures may lead to additional support or intervention for the child. For example, Boggs and Durning (1998) used the Pediatric Oncology Quality of Life Scale as a screening measure to determine which

children would be most likely to benefit from psychological services. Research on additional clinical applications of QOL measures has been noted as an important area for future research (Drotar, 2004).

Benefit Finding and Growth
Definition and Concept

Benefit finding, sense making, posttraumatic growth (PTG), and stress-related growth are among the most common terms used to refer to the positive cognitions that individuals assign to a traumatic event and the positive outcomes associated with those cognitions. While some researchers (e.g., Davis, Nolen-Hoeksema, & Larson, 1998) recommend differentiating between these terms, most research does not discriminate. Thus, as a class, these terms represent the idea that individuals who have experienced a traumatic event, such as a chronic illness, death of a loved one, or natural disaster, often perceive and undergo growth. Examples of such growth include reprioritizing one's life goals, feeling closer to loved ones, and undergoing positive personality changes, such as increased empathy and patience. Generally speaking, theories (e.g., Janoff-Bulman, 1999; Taylor, 1983) suggest that such positive growth occurs because one's personal beliefs about the world are shattered by the experience of a traumatic event. In order to rebuild one's world view, cognitive adaptations that emphasize the value and significance of the event are used to make sense of what happened. One aspect that remains unclear, however, is whether benefit finding describes actual growth, perceived growth, or both (Park & Helgeson, 2006). The perception of growth may be just as important as veridical growth; however, it is important that researchers move toward discriminating between the two to help clarify between process and outcome. In addition to better defining growth, Ickovics and colleagues (2006) report that it is necessary to conceptualize models that integrate the developmental process and growth. In other words, future theories of benefit finding and growth should strive to illustrate the impact of growth on development and vice versa.

Research on the impacts of benefit finding in adults has proliferated in the past 5 years (see Helgeson, Reynolds, & Tomich, 2006). According to a meta-analytic review of benefit finding in adults, the relationship between benefit finding and well-being remains unclear. More specifically, findings indicate that while benefit finding is related to greater positive well-being and less depression, it is also related to more intrusive thoughts about the traumatic event. Despite a plethora of research on benefit finding in adults, there are only a handful of studies that address benefit finding in children, adolescents, and their families. The first studies to examine benefit finding regarding an event that impacted the child or adolescent looked at the effect of the traumatic event on mothers (see Affleck, Tennen, & Gershman, 1985; Rini et al., 2004). More recently, three studies have directly addressed benefit finding in children and adolescents. Two studies have suggested that most children and their parents report benefits following the cancer experience; however, the reported relationships between benefit finding and posttraumatic stress are incongruous (Barakat, Alderfer, & Kazak, 2006; Phipps, Long, & Ogden, 2007). Thus, future research needs to determine if the positive outcomes associated with benefit finding in adults hold true for children and adolescents. The third study published to date that focused on adolescents fostered more insight into relationship between benefit finding and well-being. Ickovics and colleagues (2006) found different growth profiles depending on the type of event (i.e., teenage pregnancy, death of a loved one), and an interaction between growth and time. In essence, the researchers reported that adolescents with higher PTG at baseline started off with lower levels of distress and continually declined; whereas, adolescents with lower PTG started off with higher distress and the distress took longer to decline. Thus, despite decreases in distress, those with lower PTG scores remained more distressed at long-term follow-up then those with higher PTG scores. Due to the conflicting findings presented by research on adults and children, the question of whether benefit finding is adaptive remains. Several researchers (i.e., Affleck & Tennen, 1996; Park & Helgeson, 2006) postulated that as long as the severity of the traumatic event is acknowledged, benefit finding is not maladaptive.

Measurement

Two methods have been used to assess benefit finding. First, single item, open-ended questions, such as "What, if any, positive consequences have ensued from this experience?" have been used (Affleck & Tennen, 1996). One support for the continued use of these types of questions lies in the idea that it may not be the number of benefits perceived so much as the perception of at least one positive outcome that is related to well-being. Second, measures that list several types of benefits and ask the child to report whether those

benefits describe them have been created. For instance, the Benefit Finding Scale for Children (Phipps et al., 2007) is a downward extension of a scale used by Tomich and Helgeson (2004). The 10-item self-report scale begins with the question stem, "Having had my illness," and asks the child to respond using a 5-point Likert scale. Ickovics and colleagues (2006) also developed a downward extension of the Posttraumatic Growth Inventory (PTGI: Tedeschi & Calhoun, 1996). In order to make the scale more adolescent friendly, they modified the wording, simplified the Likert scale, and deleted the religiosity subscale. Finally, Barakat and colleagues (2006) used the perceptions of change in self subscale on the Impact of Traumatic Stressors Interview Schedule (ITSIS: Kazak et al., 2001) to interview adolescent cancer survivors and their parents about any changes that resulted from the cancer experience; however, this subscale has not been independently evaluated for use as a measure of PTG.

Considering the finding that the type of measure used can significantly impact the outcomes of a study (e.g., Helgeson et al., 2006), a combination of open-ended questions and lists of benefits may be the best method until further research can better direct measurement practices. Other future measurement considerations include differentiating between actual and perceived growth, including objective reports (e.g., parents, teachers), developing measures that assess both positive and negative growth, and creating measures that are nonspecific to the type of traumatic event.

Intervention

Despite the apparent clinical implications of benefit finding, interventions developed specifically to increase benefit finding are absent. The question of whether or not benefit finding is a spontaneous process could be posed; however, cognitive-behavioral therapy and writing interventions have been associated with growth in a few adult studies (e.g., Antoni et al., 2001; Weinrib, Rothrock, Johnsen, & Lutgendorf, 2006). Despite a lack of interventions, several recommendations for components of interventions have been posited. For instance, Kessler, Galea, Jones, and Parker (2006) suggested encouraging the mass media to promote positive cognitions following major disasters, and Ickovics and colleagues (2006) suggested implementing interventions in schools, churches, health clinics, and community centers that focus on child and adolescent issues. Parents should also be considered as a point of intervention.

As the limited child and adolescent research suggests, researchers and clinicians are just now on the cusp of understanding and defining the concept of benefit finding. Thus, the area is wide open and waiting for research to examine the consequences, methods of measurement, and interventions of benefit finding.

Related Concepts of Positive Psychology

There are several concepts related to the positive psychology of children in addition to the aforementioned (e.g., competence-based primary prevention, assets-based community development). Many of these approaches to bettering the lives of children highlight a positive psychology orientation, whether directly acknowledged or not. Two concepts that have received considerable attention are family-centered positive psychology (FCPP) and positive youth development.

FCPP aims to enhance functioning of the family unit, not just the functioning of the individual child or adolescent. FCPP holds the following tenets: interventions should build on preexisting family strengths, families should contribute to identifying needs, a focus on both process and outcome data, and an emphasis on strengthening social networks for the family (Sheridan, Warnes, Cowan, Schemm, & Clarke, 2004 chap. 52). Evaluating and promoting strengths in families has been found to have desirable outcomes for children and adolescents. For example, positive interactions with family have been found to promote psychological well-being for adolescents who were overweight or at risk for being overweight (Fulkerson, Strauss, Neumark-Sztainer, Story, & Boutelle, 2007). However, further research to establish the utility of FCPP is needed (Sheridan et al., 2004).

Like FCPP, positive youth development focuses on the strengths of children and involves the communities in which they live. The Commission on Positive Youth Development (2005) notes that "The positive youth development approach aims at understanding, educating, and engaging children in productive activities rather than at correcting, curing, or treating them for maladaptive tendencies or so-called disabilities" (p. 501). Youth development programs focus on broad-based skill development instead of targeting a specific problem-behavior (e.g., teen pregnancy). As such, interventions attempt to recognize the strengths of youth, even the most troubled youth, and build on those strengths. In a review of 15 youth development programs, Roth, Brooks-Gunn, Murray, and Foster (1998) found that programs that were effective tended to involve caring adults, involve youth in all phases of the intervention from inception to implementation, instill hope, result in end products such as performances (e.g., plays), and focus on community development. Empirical investigations for many of the programs labeled "youth development" are lacking, however, and increased rigor in the methodology of future studies has been suggested (Larson, 2000).

Important Considerations for Positive Psychology as it Relates to Children
Developmental Perspective

Good positive psychology theory and research in the area of childhood and adolescents must maintain a developmental perspective, one that considers all life stages prior to adulthood, rather than considering childhood only as the period preceding adulthood. In using a developmental approach, Maddux, Roberts, Sledden, and Wright (1986) noted that researchers should consider a future orientation in which any effort at intervention is considered important because of its potential to improve future health status (i.e., in adulthood), *as well as* considering the impact of interventions on the child's current functioning. Regarding the latter, Maddux and colleagues (1986) suggested that "each period of life receive attention to the particular problems evident in that period" (p. 25). Thus, there should be a focus on the health status of children while they *are* children, rather than recognizing children's importance only because the children will become adults in the future.

The uniqueness of child and adolescent development needs to be recognized in all theories, measures, and applications of positive psychology concepts. A certain level of cognitive maturity is necessary for the measurement and implementation of interventions designed to increase specific positive psychological phenomenon, for example, finding growth or meaning in traumatic experiences (Milam, Ritt-Olson, & Unger, 2004). In terms of measurement, it is no longer acceptable to adapt instruments designed for use with adults in a downward extension to use with children or adolescents. Instead, instruments must assess those competencies and indices of well-being that are central to childhood and adolescence.

Several questions that consider a developmental perspective remain unanswered and are deserved of research attention. Are there sensitive periods for positive psychology-oriented interventions, and if so at what age ranges is it most effective to intervene?

For example, the development of character strengths of "love" may be best intervened at the time of infant attachment, whereas aspects of open-mindedness may not be fruitful until a later childhood or adolescence (Park & Peterson, 2006). When do particular character strengths develop and what experiences in childhood and adolescence might erode strengths? For example, character strengths of hope, teamwork, and zest were reportedly higher for adolescents as compared to adults (Park, Peterson, & Seligman, 2005). How might these be maintained to be beneficial into young adulthood?

Prevention and Promotion

Developmental considerations will improve positive psychology's efforts at preventing development of childhood problems and increasing the promotion of mental and physical health. In fact, childhood may be the optimal time to promote healthy attitudes, behavior, adjustment, and prevention of problems (Roberts & Peterson, 1984). As noted by Seligman, Steen, Park, and Peterson (2005), clinicians should be "as concerned about how to keep certain strengths from eroding on the journey to adulthood as we are with how to build others from scratch" (p. 412). Prevention and promotion efforts in childhood attempt to improve the quality of life for the child "during childhood" and for that child's "later" adulthood. As noted by Peterson and Roberts (1986), prevention efforts often take a developmental perspective and focus on competency enhancement that "is likely to be most effective when applied during the time of greatest competency acquisition, which is during childhood for many skills such as language, social abilities, or self-efficacy beliefs" (p. 623). Such enhancement of positive psychology thinking, such as encouraging hope, would similarly be most effective at these early stages of human development.

Settings for Service Delivery

Clinicians and researchers are increasingly focused on enhancing and facilitating children's development, whatever the setting or circumstances. In medical settings, pediatric psychologists have been charged with promoting healthy lifestyles, and preventing the development of health-risk behaviors in children who are currently healthy (Roberts, Brown, Boles, Mashunkashey, & Mayes, 2003; Wilson & Evans, 2003). For example, in medical settings, enhancing the psychosocial growth of children involves making changes in the hospital architecture that welcome and support children and families, staff training to recognize and facilitate children's needs and development at all times, and medical procedures that allow children appropriate input and control regarding what is done to them (Johnson, Jeppson, & Redburn, 1992). In addition, much focus has been on bolstering social supports for chronically ill children and their families, with promising results of increased psychological adjustment (Fuemmeler, Mullins, & Carpentier, 2006). This finding has been extended to providing social support for parents; Brown and colleagues (2007) reported that perceived social support for mothers with breast cancer was related to decreased reports of psychopathology in their children. Similarly, schools can be envisioned as settings where children can experience empowerment and enhanced development rather than places where the focus is on stresses and challenges (Donnelly, 1997; Schorr, 1997). Teachers may serve as mentors in positive psychology. A model of teacher utilization of positive psychology in their classrooms has been developed (Akin-Little, Little, & Delligatti, 2004), but the long-term effects of using a positive psychology orientation have not yet been studied. Other programs have focused on enhancing children's problem-solving abilities.

Like schools, other community settings may serve as meaningful arenas for helping children learn the "good life." Pediatricians and other primary care physicians may be in a position to provide "doses" of positive psychology; however, the current practice, feasibility, and efficacy of this has not been examined (Hershberger, 2005). Religious centers encourage faith and spirituality, two aspects of positive psychology that have not been given significant attention in relation to children. As noted by health researchers, "Spiritual factors promote good health, . . . and contribute to the state of wellness that characterize health" (Institute for the Future, 2000, p. 190). Additional consideration of faith and religion in the lives of children and adolescents is needed.

Researchers have recognized the importance of employing multiple contexts and cross-discipline efforts for encouraging well-being in children, and have begun to explore the practicalities of this approach (Masten, 2001; Power, 2003; Power, DuPaul, Shapiro, & Kazak, 2003). Conjoined efforts among psychologists, teachers, parents, health-care providers, and spiritual and other community leaders in the promotion of hope, optimism, quality of life, and other aspects of positive psychology would likely be beneficial to children and adolescents as they go about the day-to-day stressors of being children.

Future Research Directions

While research efforts for positive psychology topics such as hope and optimism have increased since the first edition of this Handbook, the relative dearth of these studies in writing this chapter suggests continued effort is needed in a number of areas. Hope, optimism, quality of life, and growth finding have been explored more fully in the literature; however, the interrelatedness among such positive psychology concepts is in need of examination. In an exemplary study using structural equation modeling, Shogren, Lopez, Wehmeyer, Little, and Pressgrove (2006) assessed the comparability and relationships between hope, self-determination, optimism, and locus of control and found these constructs to be significantly related in a sample of adolescents with and without cognitive disabilities. Further, levels of hope and optimism predicted life satisfaction in both groups of adolescents. Further scholarship evaluating the relationship among these variables is needed. Snyder and Lopez (2002) stated, "greater attention needs to be paid to the overlap of constructs so as to ascertain shared operative processes and the shared variance in optimal functioning" (p. 756).

Studies of the positive psychology topics of hope and optimism, as examples, have typically employed cross-sectional designs. Longitudinal models would elucidate the sequence of development and what influences change over time. Additionally, these studies will likely lead to a better understanding of the stability of hope, optimism, and related concepts during childhood and adolescence.

Interventions and evaluations of programs to promote hope or optimism are also prime areas for further work. Interventions may enhance the positive frames for all children, or for those with special stresses. In the latter case, applications may be necessary with children who have a chronic illness or with those experiencing psychological problems or disruptive life events, such as divorce, death, or relocation. There are many youth programs and interventions that have a positive psychology orientation; however, methodologically sound, systematic research planned a priori is needed. All too often, community programs designed for children and adolescents are implemented without adequate funding for a strong evaluation component of the rigor necessary to provide meaningful analyses of components that may be central to the successful promotion of well-being in children and adolescents.

Most importantly, because positive psychology seems inherently linked to preventive efforts to improve children's lives, the concepts of positive psychology need to be integrated into prevention theory and programming. Behavioral measures of positive psychology concepts, such as hope, need to be developed and integrated into the theories. These behaviors can then be used as affirmative outcome measures in prevention and intervention programs. Research establishing utility of positive psychology in the prevention of problems for children and adolescents is needed. Further, efforts to demonstrate cost-effectiveness of these programs are needed to increase potential of future funding for prevention efforts.

In the next decade, we hope to see evidence-based practices based on principles of positive psychology emerge for children and adolescents, steeped in a developmental perspective, and considering the multiple contexts in which children learn and play. Positive psychology has been theorized to have much to offer for children who have been identified as having various challenges or in "at-risk" populations, as well as for all children in order to live life more fully, and beyond being simply "free from psychopathology." The full contribution of the field of positive psychology will be demonstrated through a better understanding of more effective interventions that also address prevention, treatment of problems, and the promotion of well-being. The field of positive psychology as it relates to children and adolescents is replete with opportunities for research.

Key Questions

1. What is the interrelatedness of children's hope, optimism, quality of life, and other positive psychology concepts?

2. What is the utility of positive psychology in promoting health for specific groups of children and adolescents (e.g., children with chronic illness, adolescents from disadvantaged backgrounds)?

3. What is the stability of hope, optimism and related constructs during childhood, adolescence, and into adulthood?

Acknowledgment

The authors thank Janette Reinke for her contributions in an earlier version of this chapter.

References

Affleck, G., & Tennen, H. (1996). Construing benefits from adversity: Adaptational significance and dispositional underpinnings. *Journal of Personality, 64*, 899–922.

Affleck, G., Tennen, H., & Gershman, K. (1985). Cognitive adaptations to high risk infants: The search for mastery,

POSITIVE PSYCHOLOGY FOR CHILDREN AND ADOLESCENTS

meaning, and protection from future harm. *American Journal of Mental Deficiency, 89*, 653–656.

Akin-Little, K. A., Little, S. G., & Delligatti, N. (2004). A preventative model of school consultation: Incorporating perspectives from positive psychology. *Psychology in the Schools, 41*, 155–162.

Antoni, M., Lehman, J., Kilbourn, K., Boyers, A., Culver, J., Alferi, S., et al. (2001). Cognitive-behavioral stress management intervention decreases the prevalence of depression and enhances benefit finding among women under treatment for early-stage breast cancer. *Health Psychology, 20*, 20–32.

Barakat, L., Alderfer, M., & Kazak, A. (2006). Posttraumatic growth in adolescent survivors of cancer and their mothers and fathers. *Journal of Pediatric Psychology, 31*, 413–419.

Barnum, D. D., Snyder, C. R., Rapoff, M. A., Mani, M. M., & Thompson, R. (1998). Hope and social support in the psychological adjustment of children who have survived burn injuries and their matched controls. *Children's Health Care, 27*, 15–30.

Berg, C. J., Rapoff, M. A., Snyder, C. R., & Belmont, J. M. (2007). The relationship of children's hope to pediatric asthma treatment adherence. *Journal of Positive Psychology, 2*, 176–184.

Boggs, S. R., & Durning, P. (1998). The pediatric oncology quality of life scale: Development and validation of a disease-specific quality of life measure. In D. Drotar (Ed.), *Measuring health-related quality of life in children and adolescents* (pp. 187–202). Mahwah, NJ: Lawrence Erlbaum.

Brown, K. J., & Roberts, M. C. (2001, August). *Outcome evaluations of a dance camp for inner-city youth.* Paper presented at the 109th Annual Convention of the American Psychological Association, San Francisco.

Brown, R. T., Fuemmeler, B., Anderson, D., Jamieson, S., Simonian, S., Kneuper Hall, R. et al. (2007). Adjustment of children and their mothers with breast cancer. *Journal of Pediatric Psychology, 32*, 297–308.

Carvajal, S. C., Clair, S. D., Nash, S. G., & Evans, R. I. (1998). Relating optimism, hope, and self-esteem to social influences in deterring substance use in adolescence. *Journal of Social and Clinical Psychology, 17*, 443–465.

Carver, C. S., & Scheier, M. F. (2001). Optimism, pessimism, and self-regulation. In E. Chang (Ed.), *Optimism and pessimism: Implications for theory, research, and practice* (pp. 31–51). Washington, DC: American Psychological Association.

Centers for Disease Control and Prevention. (2000). *Measuring healthy days: Population assessment of health-related quality of life.* Atlanta, GA: Author.

Commission on Positive Youth Development. (2005). Positive perspective on youth development. In D. L. Evans, E. B. Foa, R. E. Gur, H. Hendin, C. P. O'Brien, M. E. P. Seligman, & B. T. Walsh (Eds.), *Treating and preventing adolescent mental health disorders: What we know and what we don't know* (pp. 497–530). New York: Oxford University Press.

Connelly, T. W. (2005). Family functioning and hope in children with juvenile rheumatoid arthritis. *The American Journal of Maternal/Child Nursing, 30*, 245–250.

Davis, C., Nolen-Hoeksema, S., & Larson, J. (1998). Making sense of loss and benefiting from the experience: Two construals of the meaning. *Journal of Personality and Social Psychology, 75*, 561–574.

Diabetes Control, & Complications Trial (DCCT) Research Group. (1988). Reliability and validity of a diabetes quality of life measures for the DCCT. *Diabetes Care, 11*, 725–732.

Donnelly, M. (1997). Changing schools for changing families. *Family Futures, 1*, 12–17.

Drotar, D. (1998). (Ed.), *Measuring health-related quality of life in children and adolescents.* Mahwah, NJ: Lawrence Erlbaum.

Drotar, D. (2004). Measuring child health: Scientific questions, challenges, and recommendations. *Ambulatory Pediatrics, 4*, 353–357.

Drotar, D., Levi, R., Palermo, T. M., Riekert, K. A., & Robinson, J. R., & Walders, N. (1998). Clinical applications of health-related quality of life assessment for children and adolescents. In D. Drotar (Ed.), *Measuring health-related quality of life in children and adolescents* (pp. 329–339). Mahwah, NJ: Lawrence Erlbaum.

Drotar, D., Schwartz, L., Palermo, T., & Burant, C. (2006). Factor structure of the child health questionnaire-parent form in pediatric populations. *Journal of Pediatric Psychology, 31*, 127–138.

Dryfoos, J. G. (1998). *Safe passages: Making it through adolescence in a risky society.* Oxford: Oxford University Press.

Eiser, C. (2004). Use of quality of life measures in clinical trials. *Ambulatory Pediatrics, 4* (Suppl. 4), 395–399.

Feeny, D., Juniper, E., Ferrie, P. J., Griffith, L. E., & Guyatt, G. H. (1998). Why not just ask the kids? Health-related quality of life in children with asthma. In D. Drotar (Ed.), *Measuring health-related quality of life in children and adolescents* (pp. 171–185). Mahwah, NJ: Lawrence Erlbaum.

Fuemmeler, B. F., Mullins, L. L., & Carpentier, M. (2006). Peer friendship issues and emotional well-being. In R. T. Brown (Ed.), *Pediatric hematology/oncology: A biopsychosocial approach* (pp. 100–108). New York: Oxford University Press.

Fulkerson, J. A., Strauss, J., Neumark-Sztainer, D., Story, M., & Boutelle, K. (2007). Correlates of psychosocial well-being among overweight adolescents: The role of family. *Journal of Consulting and Clinical Psychology, 75*, 181–186.

Gillham, J. E., Shatte, A. J., Reivich, K. J., & Seligman, M. E. P. (2001). Optimism, pessimism, and explanatory style. In E. Chang (Ed.), *Optimism and pessimism: Implications for theory, research, and practice* (pp. 3153–3175). Washington, DC: American Psychological Association.

Gilman, R., Dooley, J., & Florell, D. (2006). Relative levels of hope and their relationship with academic and psychological indicators among adolescents. *Journal of Social and Clinical Psychology, 25*, 166–178.

Ginsburg, K. R., Alexander, P. M., Hunt, J., Sullivan, M., Zhao, H., & Cnaan, A. (2002). Enhancing their likelihood for a positive future: The perspective of inner-city youth. *Pediatrics, 109*, 1136–1143.

Guyatt, G. H., Juniper, E. F., Griffith, L. E., Feeny, D. H., & Ferrie, P. J. (1997). Children and adult perceptions of childhood asthma. *Pediatrics, 99*, 165–168.

Hagen, K. A., Myers, B. J., & Mackintosh, V. H. (2005). Hope, social support, and behavioral problems in at-risk children. *American Journal of Orthopsychiatry, 75*, 211–219.

Helgeson, V., Reynolds, K., & Tomich, P. (2006). A meta-analytic review of benefit finding and growth. *Journal of Consulting and Clinical Psychology, 74*, 797–816.

Hershberger, P. J. (2005). Prescribing happiness: Positive psychology and family medicine. *Family Medicine, 37*, 630–634.

Hinton-Nelson, M. D., Roberts, M. C., & Snyder, C. R. (1996). Early adolescents exposed to violence: Hope and vulnerability to victimization. *American Journal of Orthopsychiatry, 66*, 346–353.

Ickovics, J., Meade, C., Kershaw, T., Milan, S., Lewis, J., & Ethier, K. (2006). Urban teens: Trauma, posttraumatic growth, and emotional distress among female adolescents. *Journal of Consulting and Clinical Psychology, 74*, 841–850.

Ingersoll, G. M., & Marrero, D. G. (1991). A modified quality of life measure for youths: Psychometric properties. *The Diabetes Educator, 17*, 114–118.

Institute for the Future. (2000). *Health & health care 2010: The forecast, the challenge.* San Francisco: Jossey-Bass.

Janoff-Bulman, R. (1999). Rebuilding shattered assumptions after traumatic life events. In C. R. Snyder (Ed.), *Coping: The psychology of what works* (pp. 305–323). New York: Oxford University Press.

Johnson, B. H., Jeppson, E. S., & Redburn, L. (1992). *Caring for children and families: Guidelines for hospitals.* Bethesda, MD: Association for the Care of Children's Health.

Johnson, N. G., & Roberts, M. C. (1999). Passage on the wild river of adolescence: Arriving safely. In N. G. Johnson, M. C. Roberts, & J. Worell (Eds.), *Beyond appearances: A new look at adolescent girls* (pp. 3–18). Washington, DC: American Psychological Association.

Johnson, N. G., Roberts, M. C., & Worell, J. (Eds.). (1999). *Beyond appearances: A new look at adolescent girls.* Washington, DC: American Psychological Association.

Kaplan, R. M. (2001). Quality of life in children: A health care policy perspective. In H. M. Koot & J. L. Wallander (Eds.), *Quality of life in children and adolescent illness concepts, methods, and findings* (pp. 89–120). Hove, UK: Brunner-Routledge.

Kazak, A., Barakat, L., Alderfer, M., Rourke, M., Meeske, K., Gallagher, P., et al. (2001). Posttraumatic stress in survivors of childhood cancer and mothers: Development and validation of the Impact of Traumatic Stressors Interview Schedule (ITSIS). *Journal of Clinical Psychology in Medical Settings, 8*, 307–323.

Kessler, R., Galea, S., Jones, R., & Parker, H. (2006). Mental illness and suicidality after hurricane Katrina. *Bulletin of the World Health Organization, 84*, 930–939.

Klassen, A. F., Miller, A., & Fine, S. (2004). Health-related quality of life in children and adolescents who have a diagnosis of attention-deficit/hyperactivity disorder. *Pediatrics, 114*, 541–547.

Koot, H. M., & Wallander, J. L. (2001). *Quality of life in child and adolescent illness: Concepts, methods, and findings.* Hove, UK: Brunner-Routledge.

Landgraf, J. M., Abetz, L., & Ware, J. (1996). *The Child Health Questionnaire (CHQ): A user's manual.* Boston: The Health Institute, New England Medical Center.

Larson, R. W. (2000). Toward a psychology of positive youth development. *American Psychologist, 55*, 170–183.

Lewis, H. A., & Kliewer, W. (1996). Hope, coping, and adjustment among children with sickle cell disease: Tests of mediator and moderator models. *Journal of Pediatric Psychology, 21*, 25–41.

Maddux, J. E., Roberts, M. C., Sledden, E. A., & Wright, L. (1986). Developmental issues in child health psychology. *American Psychologist, 41*, 25–34.

Mansour, M. E., Kotagal, U., Rose, B., Ho, M., Brewer, D., Roy-Chaudhury, A., et al. (2003). Health-related quality of life in urban elementary schoolchildren. *Pediatrics, 111*, 1372–1381.

McDermott, D., & Hastings, S. (2000). Children: Raising future hopes. In C. R. Snyder (Ed.), *Handbook of hope: Theory, measures, and applications* (pp. 185–199). San Diego, CA: Academic Press.

McDermott, D., Hastings, S., Gariglietti, K. P., Gingerich, K., Callahan, B., & Diamond, K. (1996, April). *Fostering hope in the classroom.* Paper presented at the meeting of the Kansas Counseling Association, Salina.

McNeal, R., Handwerk, M. L., Field, C. E., Roberts, M. C., Soper, S., Huefner, J. C., et al. (2006). Hope as an outcome variable among youths in a residential care setting. *American Journal of Orthopsychiatry, 76*, 304–311.

Masten, A. S. (2001). Ordinary magic: Resilience processes in development. *American Psychologist, 56*, 227–238.

Milam, J. E., Ritt-Olson, A. & Unger, J. (2004). Posttraumatic growth among adolescents. *Journal of Adolescent Research, 19*, 192–204.

Mishoe, S. C., Baker, R. R., Poole, S., Harrell, L. M., Arant, C. B., & Rupp, N. T. (1998). Development of an instrument to assess stress levels and quality of life in children with asthma. *Journal of Asthma, 35*, 553–563.

Modi, A. C., & Quittner, A. L. (2003). Validation of a disease-specific measure of health-related quality of life for children with cystic fibrosis. *Journal of Pediatric Psychology, 28*, 535–546.

Norem, J., & Chang, E. (2001). A very full glass: Adding complexity to our thinking about the implications and application of optimism and pessimism in research. In E. C. Chang (Ed.), *Optimism and pessimism: Implications for theory, research, and practice* (pp. 347–367). Washington, DC: American Psychological Association.

Olson, L. M., Lara, M., & Frintner, M. P. (2004). Measuring health status and quality of life in U.S. children: Relationship to race, ethnicity, and income status. *Ambulatory Pediatrics, 4*(4), 377–386.

Park, C., & Helgeson, V. (2006). Introduction to the special section: Growth following highly stressful life events—current status and future directions. *Journal of Consulting and Clinical Psychology, 74*, 791–796.

Park, N., & Peterson, C. (2006). Character strengths and happiness among young children: Content analysis of parental descriptions. *Journal of Happiness Studies, 7*, 323–341.

Park, N., Peterson, C., & Seligman, M. E. P. (2005). Strengths of character and well-being among youth. Unpublished manuscript, University of Rhode Island.

Pedrotti, J. T., Lopez, S. J., & Krieshok, T. (2008). Making hope happen: A program for fostering strengths in adolescents. Manuscript submitted for publication.

Peterson, C. (2000). The future of optimism. *American Psychologist, 55*, 44–55.

Peterson, L., & Roberts, M. C. (1986). Community intervention and prevention. In H. C. Quay & J. S. Werry (Eds.), *Psychopathological disorders of childhood* (3rd ed., pp. 620–660). New York: Wiley.

Phipps, S., Long, A. M., & Ogden, J. (2007). Benefit finding scale for children: Preliminary findings from a childhood cancer population. *Journal of Pediatric Psychology, 32*, 1264–1271.

Power, T. J. (2003). Promoting children's mental health: Reform through interdisciplinary and community partnerships. *The School Psychology Review, 32*, 3–16.

Power, T. J., DuPaul, G. J., Shapiro, E. S., & Kazak, A. E. (2003). *Promoting children's health: Integrating school, family, and community.* New York: Guilford Press.

Powers, S. W., Patton, S. R., Hommel, K. A., & Hershey, A. D. (2003). Quality of life in childhood migraines: Clinical impact and comparison to other chronic illnesses. *Pediatrics, 112*, e1–5.

Pruitt, S. D., Seid, M., Varni, J. W., & Setoguchi, Y. (1999). Toddlers with limb deficiency: Conceptual basis and initial application of a functional status outcome measure. *Archives of Physical Medicine and Rehabilitation, 80*, 819–824.

Puskar, K. R., Sereika, S. M., Lamb, J., Tusaie-Mumford, K., & McGuinness, T. (1999). Optimism and its relationship to depression, coping, anger, and life events in rural adolescents. *Issues in Mental Health Nursing, 20*, 115–130.

Rajmil, L., Herdman, M., Fernandez de Sanmamed, M. J., Detmar, S., Bruil, J., Ravens-Sieberer, U., et al. (2004). Generic health-related quality of life instruments in children and adolescents: A qualitative analysis of content. *Journal of Adolescent Health, 34*(1), 37–45.

Rebok, G., Riley, A., Forrest, C., Starfield, B., Green, B., Robertson, J., et al. (2001). Elementary school-aged children's reports on their health: A cognitive interviewing study. *Quality of Life Research, 10*, 59–70.

Reivich, K., Gillham, J., Chaplin, T., & Seligman, M. E. P. (2005). From helplessness to optimism: The role of resilience in treating and preventing depression in youth. In S. Goldstein & R. Brooks (Eds.), *Handbook of resilience in children* (pp. 223–237). New York: Kluwer Academic.

Riley, A. W. (2004). Evidence that school-age children can self-report on their health. *Ambulatory Pediatrics, 4*, 371–376.

Rini, C., Manne, S., DuHamel, K., Austin, J., Ostroff, J., Boulad, F., et al. (2004). Mothers' perceptions of benefit following pediatric stem cell transplantation: A longitudinal investigation of the roles of optimism, medical risk, and sociodemographic resources. *Annals of Behavioral Medicine, 28*, 132–141.

Roberts, M. C., Brown, K. J., Boles, R. E., Mashunkashey, J. O., & Mayes, S. (2003). Prevention of disease and injury in pediatric psychology. In M. C. Roberts (Ed.), *Handbook of pediatric psychology* (3rd ed., pp. 84–98). New York: Guilford Press.

Roberts, M. C., & Peterson, L. (1984). Prevention models: Theoretical and practical implications. In M. C. Roberts & L. Peterson (Eds.), *Prevention of problems in childhood: Psychological research and applications* (pp. 1–39). New York: Wiley-Interscience.

Ronen, G. M., Streiner, D. L., Rosenbaum, P., & Canadian Pediatric Epilepsy Network. (2003). Health-related quality of life in children with epilepsy: Development and validation of self-report and parent proxy measures. *Epilepsia, 44*, 598–612.

Roth, J., Brooks-Gunn, J., Murray, L., & Foster, W. (1998). Promoting healthy adolescents: Synthesis of youth development program evaluations. *Journal of Research on Adolescence, 8*, 423–459.

Scheier, M. F., & Carver, C. S. (1993). On the power of positive thinking: The benefits of being optimistic. *Current Directions in Psychological Science, 2*, 26–30.

Schorr, L. B. (1997). *Common purpose: Strengthening families and neighborhoods to rebuild America.* New York: Anchor Books/Doubleday.

Schwimmer, J. B., Burwinkle, T. M., & Varni, J. W. (2003). Health-related quality of life of severely obese children and adolescents. *JAMA, 289*, 1813–1819.

Seligman, M. E. P. (1991). *Learned optimism.* New York: Alfred A. Knopf.

Seligman, M. E. P., Reivich, K., Jaycox, L., & Gillham, J. (1995). *The optimistic child.* Boston: Houghton-Mifflin.

Seligman, M. E. P., Steen, T., Park, N., & Peterson, C. (2005). Positive psychology progress: Empirical validation of interventions. *American Psychologist, 60*(5), 410–421.

Sheridan, S. M., Warnes, E. D., Cowan, R. J., Schemm, A. V., & Clarke, B. L. (2004). Family-centered positive psychology: Focusing on strengths to build student success. *Psychology in the Schools, 41*, 7–17.

Shogren, K. A., Lopez, S. J., Wehmeyer, M. L., Little, T. D., & Pressgrove, C. L. (2006). The role of positive psychology constructs in predicting life satisfaction in adolescents with and without cognitive disabilities: An exploratory study. *The Journal of Positive Psychology, 1*(1), 37–52.

Siegel, L. J. (1992). Overview. In A. M. La Greca, L. J. Siegel, J. L. Wallander, & C. E. Walker (Eds.), *Stress and coping in child health* (pp. 3–6). New York: Guilford.

Snyder, C. R. (1994). *The psychology of hope: You can get there from here.* New York: The Free Press.

Snyder, C. R., Feldman, D. B., Shorey, H. S., & Rand, K. L. (2002). Hopeful choices: A school counselor's guide to hope theory. *Professional School Counseling, 5*, 298–307.

Snyder, C. R., Harris, C., Anderson, J. R., Holleran, S. A., Irving, L. M., Sigmon, S. T., et al. (1991). The will and the ways: The development and validation of an individual-differences measure of hope. *Journal of Personality and Social Psychology, 60*, 570–585.

Snyder, C. R., Hoza, B., Pelham, W. E., Rapoff, M., Ware, L., Danovsky, M., et al. (1997). Development and validation of the Children's Hope Scale. *Journal of Pediatric Psychology, 22*, 399–421.

Snyder, C. R., & Lopez, S. J. (2002). The future of positive psychology: A declaration of independence. In C. R. Snyder & S. J. Lopez (Eds.), *Handbook of positive psychology* (pp. 751–768). New York: Oxford University Press.

Snyder, C. R., McDermott, D., Cook, W., & Rapoff, M. A. (1997). *Hope for the journey: Helping children through good times and bad.* Boulder, CO: Westview Press.

Taylor, S. (1983). Adjustment to threatening events: A theory of cognitive adaptation. *American Psychologist, 38*, 1161–1173.

Tedeschi, R. G., & Calhoun, L. G. (1996). The posttraumatic growth inventory: Measuring the positive legacy of trauma. *Journal of Traumatic Stress, 9*, 455–472.

Theunissen, N. C. M., Vogels, T. G. C., Koopman, H. M., Verrips, G. H. W., Zwinderman, K. A. H., Verloove-Vanhorick, S. P., et al. (1998). The proxy problem: Child report versus parent report in health-related quality of life research. *Quality of Life Research, 7*, 387–397.

Thompson, M., Kaslow, N., Weiss, B., & Nolen-Hoeksema, S. (1998). Children's Attributional Style Questionnaire-Revised: Psychometric examination. *Psychological Assessment, 10*, 166–170.

Tomich, P. L., & Helgeson, V. S. (2004). Is finding something good in the bad always good? Benefit finding among women with breast cancer. *Health Psychology, 23*, 16–23.

Topolski, T. D., Edwards, T. C., & Patrick, D. L. (2004). Toward youth self-report of health and quality of life in population monitoring. *Ambulatory Pediatrics, 4*, 387–394.

Topolski, T. D., Patrick, D. L., Edwards, T. C., Huebner, C. E., Connell, F. A., & Mount, K. K. (2001). Quality of life and health-risk behaviors among adolescents. *Journal of Adolescent Health, 29*, 426–435.

Townsend, M., Feeny, D., Guyatt, G., Furlong, W., Seip, A., & Dolovich, J. (1991). An evaluation of the burden of illness for pediatric asthmatic patients and their parents. *Annals of Allergy, 67*, 403–408.

Upton, P., Maddocks, A., Eiser, C., Barnes, P. M., & Williams, J. (2005). Development of a measure of the health-related quality of life of children in public care. *Child: Care, Health and Development, 31*, 409–415.

Valle, M. F., Huebner, E. S., & Suldo, S. M. (2004). Further evaluation of the Children's Hope Scale. *Journal of Psychoeducational Assessment, 22*, 320–337.

Varni, J. W., Burwinkle, T. M., & Seid, M. (2006). The PedsQL™ 4.0 as a school population health measure: Feasibility, reliability, and validity. *Quality of Life Research, 15*, 203–215.

Varni, J. W., Burwinkle, T. M., Seid, M., & Skarr, D. (2003). The PedsQL™ 4.0 as a pediatric population health measure: Feasibility, reliability, and validity. *Ambulatory Pediatrics, 3*, 329–341.

Varni, J. W., Seid, M., Knight, T. S., Uzark, K., & Szer, I. S. (2002). The PedsQL™ 4.0 Generic Core Scales: Sensitivity, responsiveness, and impact on clinical decision-making. *Journal of Behavioral Medicine, 25*, 175–193.

Varni, J. W., Seid, M., & Kurtin, P. S. (2001). PedsQL™ 4.0: Reliability and validity of the Pediatric Quality of Life Inventory version 4.0 Generic Core Scales in healthy and patient populations. *Medical Care, 39*, 800–812.

Weinrib, A., Rothrock, N., Johnsen, E., & Lutgendorf, S. (2006). The assessment and validity of stress-related growth in a community-based sample. *Journal of Consulting and Clinical Psychology, 74*, 851–858.

Wilson, D. K., & Evans, A. E. (2003). Health promotion in children and adolescents: An integration of psychosocial and environmental approaches. In M. C. Roberts (Ed.), *Handbook of pediatric psychology* (3rd ed., pp. 69–83). New York: Guilford.

Wilson, N., Syme, L. S., Boyce, T. W., Battistich, V. A., & Selvin, S. (2005). Adolescent alcohol, tobacco, and marijuana use: The influence of neighborhood disorder and hope. *American Journal of Health Promotion, 20*, 11–19.

World Health Organization. (1948). *Constitution of the World Health Organization basic document.* Geneva, Switzerland: World Health Organization.

Worrell, F. C., & Hale, R. L. (2001). The relationship of hope in the future and perceived school climate to school completion. *School Psychology Quarterly, 16*, 370–388.

The Positive Youth Development Perspective: Theoretical and Empirical Bases of a Strengths-Based Approach to Adolescent Development

Richard M. Lerner

Abstract

This chapter presents the conceptual foundations of the positive youth development (PYD) perspective by reviewing the history of theories about adolescent development and by specifying the key theoretical ideas defining the PYD perspective. By drawing in the main from the findings derived from the first longitudinal study of adolescents designed to test ideas associated with the PYD perspective—the 4-H Study of Positive Youth Development—illustrations are provided of the burgeoning empirical work assessing among diverse adolescents the usefulness of this strengths-based approach to youth. Finally, there is a discussion of the implications of PYD theory and research for future scholarship and applications aimed at improving the life chances of diverse adolescents.

Keywords: compensation model, developmental systems theory, ecological assets, intentional self-regulation optimization, positive youth development, risk and problem behaviors, selection

All adolescents have strengths, and their families, schools, faith institutions, and communities have resources that, when aligned with these strengths, can promote more positive development among young people (Lerner, 2004, 2005, 2007). The purpose of this chapter is to present the theoretical and empirical foundations of this strengths-based conception of youth, termed the "positive youth development" (PYD) perspective. This orientation to young people has arisen because of interest among developmental scientists in using developmental systems, or dynamic models of human behavior and development for understanding the plasticity of human development and, as well, the importance of relations between individuals and their real-world ecological settings as the bases of variation in the course of human development (Lerner, 2002, 2006).

This chapter presents the historical and conceptual foundations of the PYD perspective by reviewing briefly past theories of adolescent development and by specifying the key theoretical ideas defining the PYD perspective. In turn, I will illustrate the burgeoning empirical work being done to assess, among diverse adolescents, the usefulness of this strengths-based approach to youth development by drawing in the main from the findings derived from the first longitudinal study of adolescents designed to test ideas associated with the PYD perspective—the 4-H Study of Positive Youth Development (e.g., Gestsdóttir & Lerner, 2007; Jelicic, Bobek, Phelps, Lerner, & Lerner, 2007; Lerner et al., 2005; Phelps et al., 2007; Zarrett et al., in press; Zimmerman, Phelps, & Lerner, 2007, 2008).

As will be discussed later in the chapter, the 4-H study was designed to test the idea that when the strengths of youth are aligned across adolescence with family, school, and community resources (and, in particular, resources provided by community-based, out-of-school time youth development programs, such as 4-H, Boys & Girls Clubs, Big Brothers/Big Sisters, YMCA, and scouting), positive youth development (operationalized by the five Cs of competence, confidence, character, connection, and caring) and, as well, youth community "contributions" (the "sixth C" of PYD) will occur (Lerner, 2004, 2007; Lerner et al., 2005). Finally, I will consider briefly the implications of PYD theory and research for future scholarship and for applications of developmental science aimed at improving the life chances of diverse adolescents.

A Brief History of Theory about Adolescent Development

Adolescence spans the second decade of life (Lerner & Steinberg, in press), and has been described as a phase of life beginning in biology, with the advent of pubertal changes, and ending in society, with the historically, culturally, and socially constructed transition to young adulthood and the enactment of role choices forged during adolescence (Petersen, 1988). Given the multiple levels of organization within the ecology of human development that are involved in structuring the nature of developmental processes during this period, adolescence may be defined as the life-span period in which most of a person's biological, cognitive, psychological, and social characteristics are changing in an interrelated manner from what is considered childlike to what is considered adultlike. When most of a person's characteristics are in this state of change, the person is an adolescent.

Since the founding of the scientific study of adolescent development (Hall, 1904), the predominant conceptual frame for the study of this age period has been one of "storm and stress," or of an ontogenetic time of normative developmental disturbance (Freud, 1969). Typically, these deficit models of the characteristics of adolescence were predicated on biologically reductionist models of genetic or maturational determination (e.g., Erikson, 1968), and resulted in descriptions of youth as "broken" or in danger of becoming broken (Benson, Scales, Hamilton, & Sesma, 2006), as both dangerous and endangered (Anthony, 1969), or as "problems to be managed" (Roth & Brooks-Gunn, 2003). In fact, if positive development was discussed in the adolescent development literature—at least prior to the 1990s—it was implicitly or explicitly regarded as the absence of negative or undesirable behaviors (Benson et al., 2006). A youth who was seen as manifesting behavior indicative of positive development was depicted as someone who was *not* taking drugs or using alcohol, *not* engaging in unsafe sex, and *not* participating in crime or violence.

In short, for about the first 85 years of the scientific study of adolescent development, the field was framed almost exclusively by a deficit perspective about this period. Why? To address this question, we may divide the history of the field into three phases, beginning with the foundational contributions of G. Stanley Hall (1904).

The Beginning of the Scientific Study of Adolescence: The First Phase

Granville (G.) Stanley Hall (1844–1924) was the founder of the scientific study of adolescent development. In 1904, Hall published the first text on adolescence, a two-volume work entitled *Adolescence: Its psychology and its relations to physiology, anthropology, sociology, sex, crime, religion, and education*. Hall launched the study of adolescence with a theory that saw the period as one marked by "storm and stress." Hall believed that "ontogeny recapitulates phylogeny": The changes that occur in a person's life mirror the changes that occurred in the evolution of the human species. Human evolution, he believed, involved changes that moved us from being beast-like to being civilized. Adolescence corresponds to the period in evolution when humans changed from being beasts to being civilized. Therefore, adolescence is a time of overcoming one's beast-like impulses.

Few scientists believed the specifics of Hall's theory of recapitulation. However, his prominence in American psychology did influence the "general" conception that scientists—and society—had of adolescence, as a time of upheaval and stress. Other scholars studying adolescent development adopted, in their theories, Hall's idea that adolescence was a necessarily stressful period. For example, Anna Freud (1969) viewed adolescence as a universal period of developmental disturbance that involved upheavals in drive states, in family and peer relationships, in ego defenses, and in attitudes and values. Similarly, Erik Erikson (1968) spoke of adolescents as enmeshed in an identity crisis. In short, scientists defined young people as "at-risk" for behaving in uncivilized or problematic ways and therefore as being dangerous to themselves and to others. For much of the twentieth century most writing and research about adolescence was based on this deficit conception of young people.

The Second Phase of the Scientific Study of Adolescence

As early as the 1960s, research began to appear that showed that Hall's idea, that adolescence is a period of universal storm and stress, was not in fact universally true (e.g., Bandura, 1964; Douvan &

Adelson, 1966; Offer, 1969). Most young people do not have a stormy second decade of life, the period that most scientists denote as the adolescent period. In fact, although adolescents spend increasingly more time with peers than with parents, most adolescents still value their relations with parents enormously. Most adolescents have core values (e.g., about the importance of education in one's life, about social justice, and even about spirituality) that are consistent with those of their parents. In addition, most adolescents select friends who share these core values. Finally, there are numerous pathways (trajectories) across the adolescent years, and only some (a minority) of them reflect changes reflective of storm and stress.

Scholarship about adolescence during this second phase of the development of the field was not marked by the use of major or grand theories (e.g., psychoanalysis, learning theory, or cognitive developmental theory) framing empirical work (Lerner & Steinberg, in press). Rather, there was a burgeoning of research loosely tied to more molecular theories about the development of a particular facet of either (a) individual development, for example, ego identity development (e.g., Marcia, 1980); or (b) social development or youth–context relations, for instance, involving the effects of historical context on adolescent development (e.g., Elder, 1974; Nesselroade & Baltes, 1974) or parent–adolescent relations (e.g., Steinberg, Mounts, Lamborn, & Dornbusch, 1991). There were at least two contributions of great value that were associated with this research.

First, the level of empirical work regarding the development of individuals across the second decade of life elicited increasing interest in and enthusiasm about the study of adolescents and in enhancing their lives. For instance, the Carnegie Council on Adolescent Development was launched in the mid-1980s as a means to integrate research with application to address the problems of adolescence (Hamburg & Takanishi, 1996).

The research during this second phase thus both popularized and legitimated the field as an important area of scholarship within developmental science and, as well, helped the field to mature. Indicators of such maturity were the appearance of the first *Handbook of Adolescent Psychology* (Adelson, 1980); the organization of a scholarly society, the Society for the Study of Adolescence (SRA); and the launching of a major research journal sponsored by SRA, the *Journal of Research on Adolescence* (Lerner, 1991).

Second, the substance of the research being conducted during this period provided an empirical foundation for the synergistic generation, within the third stage of development of the field of adolescence, of the PYD perspective and of the use of research about adolescence as a key sample case for the elaboration of developmental systems theories of human development (Lerner & Steinberg, in press). In essence, the study of adolescent development was in large part a product and a producer of theoretical developments within the broader study of human development across the life span; the synergy between the study of adolescence and the elaboration of a developmental systems frame for the study of the life span would make, by the end of the 1990s, developmental systems theories the predominant theoretical lens for the conduct of developmental science (Lerner, 2006).

In short, the second decade of life emerged as a key sample case of the use of such theories for both basic research theory and for applications for promoting positive human development (Lerner & Steinberg, in press). It is useful to summarize some of the key research findings arising within the second phase of the development of the field of adolescence that provided the basis of the two above-noted contributions.

DIVERSITY IN THE FEATURES OF ADOLESCENT DEVELOPMENT

Not all young people undergo the transitions of adolescence in the same way, with the same speed, or with comparable outcomes. Individual differences are a key part of adolescent development, and are caused by differences in the timing of connections among biological, psychological, and societal factors—with none of these influences (e.g., biology) acting either alone or as the "prime mover" of change (Lerner, 2004). In other words, a major source of diversity in developmental trajectories are the systematic relations that adolescents have with key people and institutions in their social context, that is, their family, peer group, school, workplace, neighborhood, community, society, culture, and niche in history (Lerner, 2002). These person–context relations result in multiple pathways through adolescence (e.g., Offer, 1969).

MULTIPLE LEVELS OF CONTEXT ARE INFLUENTIAL DURING ADOLESCENCE

Adolescence is a period of extremely rapid transitions in physical characteristics. Indeed, except for infancy, no other period of the life cycle involves such rapid changes. While hormonal changes are part of the development of early adolescence

(Susman & Dorn, in press), they are not primarily responsible for the psychological or social developments during this period. Instead, the quality and timing of hormonal or other biological changes influence, and are influenced by, psychological, social, cultural, and historical factors (e.g., Stattin & Magnusson, 1990). For example, the physiological changes of early pubertal maturation have been linked to delinquency in adolescent girls, but only among girls who attend mixed-sex schools (Caspi, Lynam, Moffitt, & Silva, 1993) or among those who socialize with older friends instead of same-age friends (Stattin & Magnusson, 1990). Early maturation among girls in single-sex schools or in same-age peer groups was not linked with higher delinquency.

Indeed, global and pervasive effects of puberty on development do not seem to exist (Susman & Dorn, in press). When biological effects are found, they interact with contextual and experiential factors (e.g., the transition to junior high school) to influence academic achievement (Simmons & Blyth, 1987). In short, relations among hormonal and neural changes, personality and cognitive development, and the social contexts of youth illustrate the multiple levels of human life that are integrated throughout adolescent development.

ADOLESCENCE AS AN ONTOGENETIC LABORATORY

Given the structure and substance of the range of interrelated developments during adolescence, in the 1970s and 1980s many scholars of life-span development began to regard the adolescent period as an ideal "natural ontogenetic laboratory" for studying key theoretical and methodological issues in developmental science (Lerner & Foch, 1987; Steinberg & Morris, 2001). Examples come from research that studied the relations between individual-level changes (e.g., in personality, intelligence, or social relationships) and historical changes of both normative and non-normative character (e.g., Elder, 1974; Nesselroade & Baltes, 1974). There are several reasons for the special salience of the study of adolescent development to understanding the broader course of life-span development.

First, although the prenatal and infant period exceeds adolescence as an ontogenetic stage of rapid physical and physiological growth, the years from approximately 10 to 20 not only include the considerable physical and physiological changes associated with puberty but, as well, mark a time when the interdependency of biology and context in human development is readily apparent (Susman & Dorn, in press). Second, as compared to infancy, the

cognizing, goal setting, and relatively autonomous adolescent can, through reciprocal relations with his or her ecology, serve as an active influence on his or her own development, and the study of adolescence can inform these sorts of processes more generally (Lerner, 2002). Third, the multiple individual and contextual transitions into, throughout, and out of this period, involving the major institutions of society (family, peers, schools, and the workplace), engage scholars interested in broader as well as individual levels of organization and, as well, provide a rich opportunity for understanding the nature of multilevel systemic change.

Finally, developmental scientists were also drawn to the study of adolescents because of the historically unprecedented sets of challenges to the healthy development of adolescents that arose during the latter decades of the twentieth century (Lerner, 1995) and, as well, because interest in age groups other than adolescents nevertheless frequently involved this age group. For example, interest in infants often entailed the study of teenage mothers and interest in middle and old age frequently entailed the study of the "middle generation squeeze," wherein the adult children of aged parents cared for their own parents while simultaneously raising their own adolescent children.

In sum, during the second phase of the development of the field of adolescence, there was increasing documentation of the diversity of adolescent development and of the nature of the interrelations of individual and context that were involved in shaping the specific directions of change found across this period of life. These findings provided evidence for plasticity of development (i.e., for systematic variation in the course of ontogenetic change); substantial plasticity in the direction of intraindividual change could be inferred to exist as a consequence of the range of interindividual differences in intraindividual change found to be present across the second decade of life.

However, despite these findings the predominant lens for conceptualizing the nature of adolescence continued to be one that implicitly or explicitly used a deficit model of youth. Indeed, even at this writing, literally hundreds of millions of federal tax dollars continue to be spent each year to reduce or prevent the problems "caused" by the alleged deficits of adolescents. These problems include alcohol use and abuse; unsafe sex and teenage pregnancy; school failure and dropout; crime and delinquency; and depression and self-harming behaviors.

Of course, one cannot deny the existence of problems during the adolescent years, or the importance of efforts to prevent problems. Nevertheless, the advent of a developmental systems perspective (Lerner, 2002, 2004; Lerner & Steinberg, in press) about adolescence led, over the course of the still ongoing third phase of development of the field of adolescence, to the idea that the best way to prevent problem behaviors was to focus on adolescent strengths, not deficits, and to promote positive changes across the second decade of life.

The Third Phase of the Scientific Study of Adolescence

The third phase in the development of the field of adolescence has been marked by at least three foci: a focus on developmental systems ideas as a frame for research and application (Lerner, 2002); an interest in application that involves interactions among, and occasionally collaborations involving, researchers and practitioners in the field of youth development; and an interest in the ideas associated with the PYD perspective, both for advancing theory and research within the scholarly community and for enhancing policies and programs for youth within the practitioner community. In many ways, the interest in PYD integrates the other two foci of concern within the third phase of the field's development.

Accordingly, it is important to understand the origins, foundations, and features of the PYD perspective. In addition, it is equally important to understand the empirical standing of this approach to adolescence. The remainder of this chapter will discuss these issues.

The Positive Youth Development Perspective

In the late 1990s and early 2000s, psychological science paid increasing attention to the concept of "positive psychology" (e.g., Seligman, 1998, 2002). Current PYD scholarship is now informed by this important work (e.g., Damon, 2004; Lerner, 2004, 2007). However, the emergence of the PYD perspective during the third phase of the study of adolescence was linked more to biology and comparative psychology than to the study of human psychology.

Origins of the PYD Perspective

The roots of the PYD perspective are found in the work of comparative psychologists (e.g., Gottlieb, Wahlsten, & Lickliter, 2006; Schneirla, 1957) and biologists (e.g., Novikoff, 1945a, 1945b; von Bertalanffy, 1933) who had been studying the plasticity of developmental processes that arose from the "fusion" (Tobach & Greenberg, 1984) of biological

and contextual levels of organization. The use of these ideas about the import of levels of integration in shaping ontogenetic change began to impact the human developmental sciences in the 1970s (Cairns, 2006; Gottlieb et al., 2006; Lerner, 2002, 2006; Overton, 2006). Examples are the theoretical papers by Overton (1973) and Lerner (1978) on how the nature–nurture controversy may be resolved by taking an integrative, relational perspective about genetic and contextual influences on human development.

Accordingly, to understand the direction of scholarship within the third phase of the study of adolescent development, it is important to understand the scholarship that was conducted about adolescence as both a product and a producer of the broader scholarly approach to the study of the entire human life span that had been ongoing for a much longer period, for about 40 years (Baltes, Lindenberger, & Staudinger, 2006). I believe that it is difficult to overestimate the importance of the synergy between the growing influence of developmental systems theories within developmental science and the elaboration of a strengths-based approach to the study of adolescent development within the third phase of the development of the field of adolescence.

Interest in developmental systems theories and in a strengths-based view of adolescence was evidenced by a growing emphasis on "relations" among levels of organizations, and not on the "main effects" of any level itself, as constituting the fundamental units of analysis in developmental science (e.g., see Brandtstädter, 2006; Bronfenbrenner & Morris, 2006; Magnusson & Stattin, 2006; Rathunde & Csikszentmihalyi, 2006). Indeed, as reflected by the range of chapters in the most recent (sixth) edition of the *Handbook of Child Psychology* (Damon & Lerner, 2006), developmental science now includes a range of diverse instantiations of developmental systems theories. Nevertheless, the commonalities across such models (Damon & Lerner, 2008; Lerner, 2006) operationalize the fundamental features of the approach to theories. The defining features of developmental systems theories are summarized in Table 14.1.

Defining Features of Developmental Systems Theories

As described in the table, the possibility of adaptive developmental relations between individuals and their contexts and the potential plasticity of human development that is a defining feature of ontogenetic

Table 14.1 Defining features of developmental systems theories

A relational meta-model

Predicated on a postmodern philosophical perspective that transcends Cartesian dualism, developmental systems theories are framed by a relational meta-model for human development. There is, then, a rejection of all splits between components of the ecology of human development, e.g., between nature- and nurture-based variables, between continuity and discontinuity, or between stability and instability. Systemic syntheses or integrations replace dichotomizations or other reductionist partitions of the developmental system.

The integration of levels of organization

Relational thinking and the rejection of Cartesian splits are associated with the idea that all levels of organization within the ecology of human development are integrated, or fused. These levels range from the biological and physiological through the cultural and historical.

Developmental regulation across ontogeny involves mutually influential individual $\longleftrightarrow$ context relations

As a consequence of the integration of levels, the regulation of development occurs through mutually influential connections among all levels of the developmental system, ranging from genes and cell physiology through individual mental and behavioral functioning to society, culture, the designed and natural ecology, and, ultimately, history. These mutually influential relations may be represented generically as Level 1 $\longleftrightarrow$ Level 2 (e.g., Family $\longleftrightarrow$ Community) and, in the case of ontogeny, may be represented as individual $\longleftrightarrow$ context.

Integrated actions, individual $\longleftrightarrow$ context relations, are the basic unit of analysis within human development

The character of developmental regulation means that the integration of actions—of the individual on the context and of the multiple levels of the context on the individual (individual $\longleftrightarrow$ context)—constitute the fundamental unit of analysis in the study of the basic process of human development.

Temporality and plasticity in human development

As a consequence of the fusion of the historical level of analysis—and therefore temporality—within of the levels of organization comprising the ecology of human development, the developmental system is characterized by the potential for systematic change, by plasticity. Observed trajectories of intraindividual change may vary across time and place as a consequence of such plasticity.

Plasticity is relative

Developmental regulation may both facilitate and constrain opportunities for change. Thus, change in individual $\longleftrightarrow$ context relations is not limitless, and the magnitude of plasticity (the probability of change in a developmental trajectory occurring in relation to variation in contextual conditions) may vary across the life span and history. Nevertheless, the potential for plasticity at both individual and contextual levels constitutes a fundamental strength of all humans' development.

Intraindividual change, interindividual differences in intraindividual change, and the fundamental substantive significance of diversity

The combinations of variables across the integrated levels of organization within the developmental system that provide the basis of the developmental process will vary at least in part across individuals and groups. This diversity is systematic and lawfully produced by idiographic, group differential, and generic (nomothetic) phenomena. The range of interindividual differences in intraindividual change observed at any point in time is evidence of the plasticity of the developmental system, and makes the study of diversity of fundamental substantive significance for the description, explanation, and optimization of human development.

Optimism, the application of developmental science, and the promotion of positive human development

The potential for and instantiations of plasticity legitimate an optimistic and proactive search for characteristics of individuals and of their ecologies that, together, can be arrayed to promote positive human development across life. Through the application of developmental science in planned attempts (i.e., interventions) to enhance (e.g., through social policies or community-based programs) the character of humans' developmental trajectories, the promotion of positive human development may be achieved by aligning the strengths (operationalized as the potentials for positive change) of individuals and contexts.

Multidisciplinarity and the need for change-sensitive methodologies

The integrated levels of organization comprising the developmental system require collaborative analyses by scholars from multiple disciplines. Multidisciplinary knowledge and, ideally, interdisciplinary knowledge is sought. The temporal embeddedness and resulting plasticity of the developmental system requires that research designs, methods of observation and measurement, and procedures for data analysis be change-sensitive and able to integrate trajectories of change at multiple levels of analysis.

change within the dynamic, developmental system (Gottlieb et al., 2006; Thelen & Smith, 2006) stand as distinctive features of the developmental systems approach to human development and, as well, provide a rationale for making a set of methodological choices that differ in design, measurement, sampling, and data analytic techniques from selections made by researchers using split or reductionist approaches to developmental science. Moreover, the emphasis on how the individual acts on the context to contribute to the plastic relations with the context that regulate adaptive development (Brandtstädter, 2006) fosters an interest in person-centered (as compared to variable-centered) approaches to the study of human development (Magnusson & Stattin, 2006; Overton, 2006; Rathunde & Csikszentmihalyi, 2006).

Furthermore, given that the array of individual and contextual variables involved in these relations constitutes a virtually open set (e.g., there are over 70 trillion potential human genotypes and each of them may be coupled across life with an even larger number of life-course trajectories of social experiences; Hirsch, 2004), the diversity of development becomes a prime, substantive focus for developmental science (Lerner, 2004; Spencer, 2006). The diverse person, conceptualized from a strengths-based perspective (in that the potential plasticity of ontogenetic change constitutes a fundamental strength of all humans; Spencer, 2006), and approached with the expectation that positive changes can be promoted across all instances of this diversity as a consequence of health-supportive alignments between people and settings (Benson et al., 2006), becomes the necessary subject of developmental science inquiry.

It is in the linkage between the ideas of plasticity and diversity that a basis exists for the extension of developmental systems thinking to the field of adolescence and for the field of adolescence to serve as a "testing ground" for ideas associated with developmental systems theory. This synergy has had at least one key outcome, that is, the forging of a new, strengths-based vision of and vocabulary for the nature of adolescent development. In short, the plasticity–diversity linkage within developmental systems theory and method provided the basis for the formulation of the PYD perspective.

Components of the PYD Perspective

Beginning in the early 1990s, and burgeoning in the first half decade of the twenty-first century, a new vision and vocabulary for discussing young people has emerged. These innovations were framed by the developmental systems theories that were engaging the interest of developmental scientists. The focus on plasticity within such theories led in turn to an interest in assessing the potential for change at diverse points across ontogeny, those spanning from infancy through the 10th and 11th decades of life (Baltes et al., 2006). Moreover, these innovations were propelled by the increasingly more collaborative contributions of researchers focused on the second decade of life (e.g., Benson et al., 2006; Damon, 2004; Lerner, 2004), practitioners in the field of youth development (e.g., Floyd & McKenna, 2003; Pittman, Irby, & Ferber, 2001), and policy makers concerned with improving the life chances of diverse youth and their families (e.g., Cummings, 2003; Gore, 2003).

These interests converged in the formulation of a set of ideas that enabled youth to be viewed as resources to be developed, and not as problems to be managed (Roth & Brooks-Gunn, 2003). These ideas may be discussed in regard to two key hypotheses. Each hypothesis is associated with two subsidiary hypotheses. The first hypothesis pertains to the operationalization of PYD. The second is concerned with the relations between individuals and contexts that, within developmental systems models (see Table 14.1), provide the basis of human development.

HYPOTHESIS 1. PYD IS COMPRISED OF FIVE CS

Based on both the experiences of practitioners and on reviews of the adolescent development literature (Eccles & Gootman, 2002; Lerner, 2004; Roth & Brooks-Gunn, 2003), "five Cs"—competence, confidence, connection, character, and caring—were hypothesized as a way of conceptualizing PYD (and of integrating all the separate indicators of it, such as academic achievement or self esteem). These five Cs were linked to the positive outcomes of youth development programs reported by Roth and Brooks-Gunn (2003). In addition, these "Cs" are prominent terms used by practitioners, adolescents involved in youth development programs, and the parents of these adolescents in describing the characteristics of a "thriving youth" (King et al., 2005).

Hypothesis 1A. Contribution Is the "6th C"

A hypothesis subsidiary to the postulation of the "five Cs" as a means to operationalize PYD is that, when a young person manifests the Cs across time (when the youth is thriving), he or she will be on a life trajectory toward an "idealized adulthood" (Csikszentmihalyi & Rathunde, 1998; Rathunde &

Csikszentmihalyi, 2006). Theoretically, an ideal adult life is marked by integrated and mutually reinforcing contributions to self (e.g., maintaining one's health and one's ability so as to remain an active agent in one's own development) and to family, community, and the institutions of civil society (Lerner, 2004; Sherrod, Flanagan, & Youniss, 2002). An adult engaging in such integrated contributions is a person manifesting adaptive developmental regulations (Brandtstädter, 2006).

Hypothesis 1B. PYD and Risk/Problem Behaviors Are Inversely Related

A second subsidiary hypothesis to the one postulating the five Cs is that there should be an inverse relation within and across development between indicators of PYD and behaviors indicative of risk behaviors or internalizing and externalizing problems. Here, the idea—forwarded in particular by Pittman and her colleagues (e.g., Pittman et al., 2001) in regard to applications of developmental science to policies and programs—is that the best means to prevent problems associated with adolescent behavior and development (e.g., depression, aggression, drug use and abuse, or unsafe sexual behavior) is to promote positive development.

HYPOTHESIS 2. YOUTH–CONTEXT ALIGNMENT PROMOTES PYD

Based on the idea that the potential for systematic intraindividual change across life (i.e., for plasticity) represents a fundamental strength of human development, the hypothesis was generated that, if the strengths of youth are aligned with resources for healthy growth present in the key contexts of adolescent development—the home, the school, and the community—then enhancements in positive functioning at any one point in time (i.e., well-being; Lerner, 2004) may occur; in turn, the systematic promotion of positive development that may occur across time (i.e., thriving; e.g., Lerner, 2004; Lerner et al., 2005) can be achieved.

Hypothesis 2A. Contextual Alignment Involves Marshaling Development Assets

A key subsidiary hypothesis to the notion of aligning individual strengths and contextual resources for healthy development is that there exist, across the key settings of youth development (i.e., families, schools, and communities), at least some supports for the promotion of PYD. Termed "developmental assets" (Benson et al., 2006), these resources constitute the social and ecological "nutrients" for the growth of healthy youth.

Hypothesis 2B. Community-Based Programs Constitute Key Developmental Assets

There is broad agreement among researchers and practitioners in the youth development field that the concept of developmental assets is important for understanding what needs to be marshaled in homes, classrooms, and community-based programs to foster PYD (Benson et al., 2006; Lerner, 2007). In fact, a key impetus for the interest in the PYD perspective among both researchers and youth program practitioners, and thus a basis for the collaborations that exist among members of these two communities, is the interest that exists in ascertaining the nature of the resources for positive development that are present in youth programs, for example, in the literally hundreds of thousands of the after-school programs delivered either by large, national organizations, such as 4-H, Boys & Girls Clubs, scouting, Big Brothers/Big Sisters, YMCA, or Girls, Inc., or by local organizations.

The focus on youth programs is important not only for practitioners in the field of youth development, however. In addition, the interest on exploring youth development programs as a source of developmental assets for youth derives from theoretical interest in the role of the macro-level systems effects of the ecology of human development on the course of healthy change in adolescence (Bronfenbrenner & Morris, 2006); interest derives as well from policy makers and advocates, who believe that at this point in the history of the United States community-level efforts are needed to promote positive development among youth (e.g., Cummings, 2003; Gore, 2003; Pittman et al., 2001).

Conclusions about the PYD Perspective

Replacing the deficit view of adolescence, the PYD perspective sees "all" adolescents as having strengths (by virtue of at least their potential for change). The perspective suggests that increases in well-being and thriving are possible for all youth through aligning the strengths of young people with the developmental assets present in their social and physical ecology.

Although still at a preliminary stage of progress, there is growing empirical evidence that, with some important qualifications, the general concepts and main and subsidiary hypotheses of the PYD perspective find empirical support (Lerner, Phelps, Bowers, & Forman, in press). Using findings derived from the 4-H Study of Positive Youth Development (e.g., Lerner et al., 2005; Phelps et al., 2007) as a sample case, I will briefly review this evidence.

The 4-H Study of Positive Youth Development

The 4-H Study of Positive Youth Development is a longitudinal investigation supported by a grant from the National 4-H Council. The study began in 2002–2003 by studying a national cohort of about 1,700 fifth grade youth (from 13 states across all regions of the United States) and their parents. At the time of this writing, the study is in its seventh wave of data collection (2008–2009), studying 11th graders, and involving about 5,000 youth from 34 states and about 2,500 of their parents. The 4-H study was designed to test a model about the role of ecological developmental assets and individual actions in the promotion of PYD, as conceptualized by the "five Cs" of PYD and of the "sixth C" of contribution, and in the diminution of problem and risk behaviors. These latter behaviors were operationalized by measures of internalizing problems such as depression, risk behaviors such as smoking, drinking, and drug use, and externalizing problems such as school bullying. Full details of the methodology of the 4-H study have been presented in several publications (e.g., Gestsdóttir & Lerner, 2007; Jelicic et al., 2007; Lerner et al., 2005; Phelps et al., 2007; Theokas & Lerner, 2006).

The increase in sample size that exists across the waves of the study occurs because the 4-H study uses a form of longitudinal sequential design (Baltes, Reese, & Nesselroade, 1977). Fifth graders, gathered during the 2002–2003 school year (Wave 1 of the study), were the initial cohort within this design and this cohort was the only one studied in Wave 1. However, to maintain at least initial levels of power for within-time analyses and to assess the effects of retesting, all subsequent waves of the study involve the addition of a "retest control" cohort of youth of the current grade level of the initial cohort; this new cohort is then followed longitudinally. Accordingly, in Wave 2 of the study (sixth grade for the initial cohort), a retest control group of sixth graders who were new to the study were gathered; these youth became members of a second longitudinal cohort. Similarly each subsequent wave of the study introduces a new cohort which is then followed longitudinally throughout the rest of the study.

The 4-H study data set may be used to illustrate the empirical evidence bearing on the main and subsidiary hypotheses of the PYD perspective. Given that prior to the 4-H study, there were no data indicating the reality of the five Cs, and thus no measure that could be used to test the purported positive outcomes of the individual–context

alignments of concern in the second hypothesis associated with the PYD perspective, we began the 4-H study by seeking to test ideas derived from the first hypothesis.

Exploring Hypothesis 1: The Five Cs, Contribution, and the Relation between PYD and Risk/Problem Behaviors

Using the fifth grade data from the first wave of assessment within the 4-H study, Lerner et al. (2005) provided initial evidence for the five Cs and PYD constructs. Lerner et al. (2005) reported that the results of an initial structural equation modeling (SEM) analysis used to test the "five Cs" model proved to be adequate. Lerner et al. (2005) found evidence that the five Cs exist as latent constructs accounting for variance in several desirable "surface traits" (e.g., in regard to "competence," measures of academic, social, and vocational abilities), and of their convergence on a second-order construct of PYD. Moreover, consistent with the predictions associated with Hypotheses 1A and 1B, discussed earlier, additional evidence was presented that PYD correlated positively with the purported "sixth C" of youth contribution (Lerner, 2004) and negatively with indices of risk and problem behaviors (Lerner et al., 2005).

Jelicic et al. (2007), using data from the first two waves of the 4-H study (i.e., fifth and sixth grades), extended the findings of Lerner et al. (2005). Jelicic et al. reported that Grade 5 PYD covaried positively with Grade 6 scores for youth contribution and negatively with scores for risk and problem behaviors.

Accordingly, the findings of Lerner et al. (2005) and Jelicic et al. (2007) provide evidence that for 4-H study participants overall, there is evidence for the existence of the five Cs of PYD, for the existence of the "sixth C" of contribution, and for positive relations among these Cs and, in turn, for inverse relations between the Cs and risk/problem behaviors. However, other findings from the 4-H study data set suggest that the developmental relations among the Cs and risk/problem behavior are more nuanced.

Using data from Grades 5, 6, and 7, Phelps et al. (2007) assessed the patterns of change over time associated with PYD and of risks/problem behaviors. Results indicated that five PYD trajectories represented changes across grades and three trajectories were associated with indicators of both internalizing and externalizing problems. Although Hypothesis 1B involves the expectation that most youth across the early adolescent period would show change over time marked by the coupling of increases in PYD and decreases in risk/problem behaviors, only about one-sixth of all youth in the sample manifested this particular pattern of change. Other youth remained stable over time, showed increases in PYD and risk, or declined in PYD.

A study by Zimmerman et al. (2008) both replicated and extended the findings of the Phelps et al. (2007) study. Using data from Grades 5, 6, 7, and 8, Zimmerman et al. assessed the patterns of change associated with indicators of PYD, contribution, and risk/problem behavior. Results indicated that five PYD trajectories represent change across grades, four trajectories were associated with indicators of youth contribution, four trajectories were associated also with indicators of depressive symptoms, and three trajectories were associated with indicators of risk/problem behaviors. Youth had diverse combinations of these trajectories of positive and problematic behaviors.

The multiplicity of patterns of conjoint trajectories for PYD and risks/problem behaviors means that the PYD model needs to be revised in at least two ways. First, theoretical revision and subsequent empirical research needs to accommodate to the fact that even youth at the highest levels of PYD development over the course of early adolescence (Grades 5 through 8) can show, as well, increases in risk and problem behaviors. Second, earlier ideas about the possibility of foregoing prevention efforts when PYD was promoted (e.g., Pittman et al., 2001) need to be revised in light to the findings of Phelps et al. (2007) and Zimmerman et al. (2008). Both prevention and promotion efforts need to be pursued, given that trajectories of PYD and of risk/problem behaviors are intertwined in diverse ways across the early adolescent years.

In short, 4-H study findings suggest that the first set of hypotheses about the PYD perspective need to be revised to ask, "What trajectories of growth in PYD and contribution covary with what trajectories of change in risk/problem behaviors, for what youth, living in what settings?" We also have to ask, "What individual and contextual processes are involved in these diverse developmental patterns?" This latter question pertains to the second set of PYD hypotheses. Findings from the 4-H study pertinent to this set of hypotheses also require revisions in the PYD perspective.

Exploring Hypothesis 2: Youth–Context Alignment, Developmental Assets, and the Role of Out-of-School-Time Youth Development Programs

To assess whether youth–context alignment promoted PYD, Theokas and Lerner (2006) and Brown (2008) measured four types of ecological assets

identifiable in the homes, schools, and communities of 4-H study participants (Grade 5 through Grade 7). These assets involve, first, individuals in the lives of youth—parents, teachers, and community mentors, for instance. The second domain of ecological assets is the physical and institutional resources present in the social environment (these assets index opportunities for learning, recreation, and engagement with individuals and the physical world). The third domain of assets is collective, activity which includes mutual engagement between community members, parents, youth, school personnel, and institutions of society. The fourth domain is accessibility, which involves the ability of youth to partake of human resources and resource opportunities.

Theokas and Lerner (2006) used fifth-grade data to assess, in each of three settings (the home, the school, and the community), the relations between these four domains of actual developmental assets and indices of PYD and risk/problem behaviors. Four communities within the larger 4-H study data set were studied, viz. Worcester (Massachusetts), Puma (Arizona; which includes Tucson), Missoula (Montana), and Dade County (Florida, which includes Miami). In all communities, scores for the ecological assets were significantly related to both positive and problematic outcomes in expected directions. For instance, ecological assets increased the positive prediction of PYD (accounting for an additional 18% of the variance), above demographic predictors (e.g., sex, race, SES); in turn, these assets were negatively related to internalizing problems, that is, an additional 14% of the variance (beyond demographic predictors) was accounted for by the ecological assets.

Theokas and Lerner (2006) also found that some assets were particularly important in specific contexts. For example, collective activity in the family was the only ecological asset that predicted decreased risk behaviors. Family assets accounted for larger portions of the variance for all outcomes with the exception of "contribution," for which school assets accounted for more variance. Moreover, in the family context, collective activity (e.g., eating dinner together) was the chief predictor of PYD. In the school, accessibility (e.g., small school size and low teacher:student ratios) was most important; in the community, the presence of a mentor was the most important asset.

Using the same four communities studied by Theokas and Lerner (2006), Brown (2008) extended the fifth grade findings developmentally. Brown studied participants across Grades 5–7. She determined whether neighborhood assets moderated the effect of adolescent involvement in out-of-school activities on positive and negative developmental outcomes. The results revealed a complex interplay between individual-level factors, activity involvement, and neighborhood assets. Activity involvement differentially affected youth outcomes depending upon the ecological context in which they were embedded.

For example, activity involvement had the greatest influence on youth living in neighborhoods with limited physical resources. In addition, boys and girls were affected differently by both the amount of time spent in activities and the types of neighborhood supports available. Youth living in lower-assets neighborhoods benefited more than their counterparts living in high-assets neighborhoods from participation in activities when looking at outcomes of dysfunction. Once again, then, data from the 4-H study suggest that a more nuanced understanding of person–context relations is needed to fully capture the range of relations between youth and contexts that are involved in PYD.

Moreover, assessing the role of ecological assets in the youth–context alignments expected to be linked to PYD is only part of the task in exploring the second hypothesis. In the context of the developmental systems model of mutually influential person–context relations framing the PYD perspective (Lerner, 2004, 2005), it is necessary to identify and appraise the importance of strengths of youth that, when aligned with ecological assets, are associated with PYD. What may comprise such strengths?

Gestsdóttir and Lerner (2008) hypothesized that processes of intentional self-regulation may constitute such strengths. They noted that adolescence is a period of marked change in the person's cognitive, physical, emotional, and social development (in the individual's relations with the people and institutions of the social world), and that these changes place adaptational demands on adolescents. Adaptation involves relations between the actions of adolescents upon the context and the action of the context on them, a bidirectional process that has been labeled developmental regulation. The attributes and means through which the adolescent contributes to such regulation may be termed self-regulation. Accordingly, Gestsdóttir and Lerner proposed that the development of intentional self-regulation in adolescence would be linked to the PYD and, as well, to lower levels of risk/problem behaviors.

To explore this idea, Gestsdóttir and Lerner used the model of Selection, Optimization, and Compensation (SOC), developed by Baltes, Baltes, and Freund (e.g., Baltes & Baltes, 1990; Baltes et al., 2006; Freund & Baltes, 2002), to conceptualize and index intentional self-regulation in adolescence. Accordingly, Gestsdóttir and Lerner (2007) found that fifth and sixth graders' scores on SOC, both within and across time, were related to indicators of positive and negative development in predicted directions. In turn, Zimmerman et al. (2007), studying participants from Grades 5 through 7, found that statistically significant but substantively minor changes in SOC scores existed across the three grades. As such, Zimmerman et al. (2007) also found that Grade 5 SOC scores were significant predictors of subsequent development. Grade 5 SOC scores positively predicted Grade 7 scores on the five Cs of PYD and negatively predicted Grade 7 depression, delinquency, and risk behaviors. Moreover, in the previously discussed study by Zimmerman et al. (2008), SOC scores were found to predict which youth were in the highest trajectories of PYD and "contribution" from Grades 5 to 8 and, as well, in the lowest trajectories of risk/problem behaviors across these grades.

In short, while current research associated with the 4-H study is integrating the assessment of SOC and of ecological assets in the appraisal of PYD, findings to date indicate that both internal strengths and ecological assets covary in theoretically expected ways with PYD, contribution, and risk/problem behaviors. However, as with the revisions of the first set of hypotheses that were linked to findings from the 4-H study, the findings that are pertinent to these second hypotheses suggest that we need to ask how variation in individual strengths, when linked to different assets in various settings, results in particular patterns of relations among PYD, contribution, and risk/problem behaviors. This more nuanced question will necessarily be complicated further when the remaining issue to be addressed in regard to the second hypothesis—the links between PYD and community-based out-of-school-time (OST) activities, and in particular youth development (YD) programs, such as 4-H and Boys & Girls Clubs, etc.—is considered. Data from the 4-H Study also illustrate that there is evidence that OST programs and, specifically, YD programs, are associated with PYD. However, as before, the nature of this relationship is more complicated than framed in the initial formulation of this hypothesis.

Using information presented by Eccles and Gootman (2002) about the diversity of community-based activities available in the lives of youth, Balsano, Phelps, Theokas, Lerner, and Lerner (in press) assessed the OST activities of youth in regard to a set of structured after-school activities and programs that were categorized into four groupings: (1) youth development (YD) programs (e.g., 4-H, YMCA/YWCA, Boys & Girls Clubs, Scouts, Big Brothers/Big Sisters); (2) sports; (3) arts (e.g., music, drama, dance); and (4) other after-school clubs. Youth also participate in unstructured activities including playing with friends and homework completion and, as well, have after-school jobs. However, both to explore facets of Hypothesis 2 and because, compared with unstructured after-school activities, structured activities are associated more often with indicators of positive development (e.g., Mahoney, Vandell, Simpkins, & Zarrett, in press), Balsano et al. focused on structured activities.

Across Grades 5 and 6, youth OST activity involvement was characterized by a changing and diverse array of activities in which youth participated, and there were some gender differences in patterns of youth participation and in links between participation and scores for PYD. For example, boys were more likely to participate in some sports and girls were more likely to participate in some instances of the arts. In addition, girls scored higher in PYD than boys, and PYD scores were significantly associated with breadth of OST activity participation for girls but not for boys.

Zarrett et al. (in press) explored further the association between patterns of OST activities and PYD. Using data from Grades 5 through 7, Zarrett et al. assessed the relations among sports participation (the most frequent instance of OST activities; Balsano et al., in press) and other OST activities, including YD programs, and positive and problematic youth development. Any benefits of sports participation were found to depend in part on specific combinations of multiple activities in which youth participated along with sports. In particular, participation in a combination of sports and YD programs was related to PYD and youth contribution, even after controlling for the total time youth spent in OST activities and their sports participation duration.

The findings of Zarrett et al. (in press), when combined with other reports from the 4-H study, underscore a key theme in the 4-H study data that have been presented to illustrate the empirical status of the PYD perspective: there is considerable support for this strengths-based approach to the study of adolescent development; at the same time, however, the complexity, nuances, and qualifications of developmental trends pertinent to the sets of hypotheses framing the field suggest that both theoretical refinement and considerable additional longitudinal research will be needed to more fully understand how the links between the developing strengths of youth and the resources available in their homes, schools, and communities can best be combined to assure thriving across the second decade of life.

In short, the two PYD hypotheses need to be recast to ask what individual strengths, of what youth, at what points in their adolescence, when combined with what ecological assets, in what settings (family, school, and community) are associated with what combination of PYD, contribution, and risk/problem behavior trajectories? The formulation of this revised, multicomponent, developmental, and relational question leads to some concluding comments.

Conclusions

The stereotype that there is a single pathway through the adolescent years—for instance, one characterized by inevitable "storm and stress" (Hall, 1904)—cannot stand in the face of current knowledge about diversity in adolescence; evidence for strengths in youth; findings regarding the presence and bases of trajectories of positive development; and results of initial longitudinal assessments that document the number of different pathways of PYD across at least the early adolescent years. Accordingly, in future research and applications pertinent to adolescence, scholars and practitioners must extend their conception of this period to focus on changing relations between the individual characteristics of a youth and his or her complex and distinct ecology.

Contemporary developmental science—predicated on a relational metatheory and focused on the use of developmental systems theories to frame research on dynamic relations between diverse individuals and contexts—constitutes an approach that may integrate the scholarship pertinent to these diverse levels of organization and, by so doing, may facilitate understanding of the means to capitalize on the strengths of young people and their contexts in the service of promoting positive human development. As has been demonstrated by reviewing the ongoing work of the 4-H Study of Positive Youth Development, developmental systems approaches have the promise of providing important insights about the diverse ways in which adolescents, in dynamic exchanges with their ecologies, can develop along positive pathways.

As Bronfenbrenner (2005) eloquently puts it, it is these relations that make human beings human. As such, the PYD perspective suggests that, if we are to conduct good science about adolescent development, we must study youth and contexts in integrative, developmental manners. Such work can inform policies and programs uniquely, helping to characterize the multiple ways that the strengths of diverse youth can be transformed into positive developmental pathways. I believe that we can better serve America's and the world's youth, families, and communities through this approach to science. Continued scholarly and societal investment in such work can enhance the likelihood that strong, active, and contributing youth will be emblematic of the future of civil society.

Three Future Questions about the Field

1. What is the impact of the strengths-based, PYD perspective on research and applications derived from deficit conceptions of adolescence?

2. How do the key hypotheses associated with the PYD perspective need to be revised in light of current findings from the 4-H Study of Positive Youth Development?

3. What are the chief challenges in transforming theory and research about PYD into policy and program initiatives aimed at enhancing the lives of diverse adolescents?

Acknowledgments

A prior version of this chapter was prepared for the Workshop on the Science of Adolescent Health and Development, National Research Council /Institute of Medicine of the National Academy of Sciences. The preparation of this chapter was supported in part by grants from the National 4-H Council and the John Templeton Foundation. I am grateful to my colleagues and students participating in the 4-H Study of Positive Youth Development for their collaboration in the research reviewed in this chapter.

References

Adelson, J. (Ed.). (1980). *Handbook of adolescent psychology.* New York: Alan Guttmacher Institute.

Anthony, E. J. (1969). The reactions of adults to adolescents and their behavior. In G. Caplan & S. Lebovici (Eds.), *Adolescence: Psychosocial perspectives* (pp. 54–78). New York: Basic Books.

Balsano, A., Phelps, E., Theokas, C., Lerner, J. V., & Lerner, R. M. (in press). Patterns of early adolescents' participation in youth developing programs having positive youth development. *Journal of Research on Adolescence.*

Baltes, P. B., & Baltes, M. M. (1990). Psychological perspectives on successful aging: The model of selective optimization with compensation. In P. B. Baltes & M. M. Baltes (Eds.), *Successful aging: Perspectives from the behavioral sciences* (pp. 1–34). New York: Cambridge University Press.

Baltes, P. B., Lindenberger, U., & Staudinger, U. M. (2006). Lifespan theory in developmental psychology. In R. M. Lerner (Ed.), *Handbook of child psychology: Vol. 1. Theoretical models of human development* (6th ed., pp. 569–664). Hoboken, NJ: Wiley.

Baltes, P. B., Reese, H. W., & Nesselroade, J. R. (1977). *Life-span developmental psychology: Introduction to research methods.* Monterey, CA: Brooks/Cole.

Bandura, A. (1964). The stormy decade: Fact or fiction? *Psychology in the School, 1,* 224–231.

Benson, P. L., Scales, P. C., Hamilton, S. F., & Sesma, A., Jr. (2006). Positive youth development: Theory, research, and applications. In R. M. Lerner (Ed.), *Handbook of child psychology: Vol. 1. Theoretical models of human development* (6th ed., pp. 894–941). Hoboken, NJ: Wiley.

Brandtstädter, J. (2006). Action perspectives on human development. In R. M. Lerner (Ed.), *Handbook of child psychology: Vol. 1. Theoretical models of human development* (6th ed., pp. 516–568). Hoboken, NJ: Wiley.

Bronfenbrenner, U. (2005). *Making human beings human: Bioecological perspectives on human development.* Thousand Oaks, CA: Sage.

Bronfenbrenner, U., & Morris, P. A. (2006). The bioecological model of human development. In R. M. Lerner (Ed.), *Handbook of child psychology: Vol. 1. Theoretical models of human development* (6th ed., pp. 793–828). Hoboken, NJ: Wiley.

Brown, J. S. (2008). The role of ecological context and activity involvement in youth developmental outcomes: Differential impacts of asset poor and asset rich neighborhoods. Unpublished dissertation. Ithaca, NY: Cornell University.

Cairns, R. B. (2006). The making of developmental psychology. In R. M. Lerner (Ed.), *Handbook of child psychology: Vol. 1. Theoretical models of human development* (6th ed., pp. 89–165). Hoboken, NJ: Wiley.

Caspi, A., Lynam, D., Moffitt, T. E., & Silva, P. A. (1993). Unraveling girls' delinquency: Biological, dispositional, and contextual contributions to adolescent misbehavior. *Developmental Psychology, 29,* 19–30.

Csikszentmihalyi, M., & Rathunde, K. (1998). The development of the person: An experiential perspective on the ontogenesis of psychological complexity. In R. M. Lerner (Ed.), *Handbook of child psychology: Vol. 1. Theoretical models of human development* (5th ed., pp. 635–684). New York: Wiley.

Cummings, E. (2003). Foreword. In D. Wertlieb, F. Jacobs, & R. M. Lerner (Eds.), *Handbook of applied developmental science: Promoting positive child, adolescent, and family development through research, policies, and programs: Vol. 3. Promoting positive youth and family development: Community systems, citizenship, and civil society* (pp. ix–xi). Thousand Oaks, CA: Sage.

Damon, W. (2004). What is positive youth development? *Annals of the American Academy of Political and Social Science, 591,* 13–24.

Damon, W., & Lerner, R. M. (Eds.). (2006). *Handbook of child psychology* (6th ed.). Hoboken, NJ: Wiley.

Damon, W., & Lerner, R. M. (2008). *Child and adolescent development: An advanced course.* Hoboken, NJ: Wiley.

Douvan, J. D., & Adelson, J. (1966). *The adolescent experience.* New York: Wiley.

Eccles, J. S., & Gootman, J. A. (Eds.). (2002). *Community programs to promote youth development/committee on community-level programs for youth.* Washington, DC: National Academy Press.

Elder, G. H., Jr. (1974). *Children of the Great Depression: Social change in life experiences.* Chicago: University of Chicago Press.

Erikson, E. H. (1968). *Identity, youth, and crisis*. New York: Norton.

Floyd, D. T., & McKenna, L. (2003). National youth serving organizations in the United States: Contributions to civil society. In R. M. Lerner, F. Jacobs, & D. Wertlieb (Eds.), *Handbook of applied developmental science: Promoting positive child, adolescent, and family development through research, policies, and programs: Vol. 3. Promoting positive youth and family development: Community systems, citizenship, and civil society* (pp. 11–26). Thousand Oaks, CA: Sage.

Freud, A. (1969). Adolescence as a developmental disturbance. In G. Caplan & S. Lebovici (Eds.), *Adolescence* (pp. 5–10). New York: Basic Books.

Freund, A. M., & Baltes, P. B. (2002). Life-management strategies of selection, optimization, and compensation: Measurement by self-report and construct validity. *Journal of Personality and Social Psychology, 82,* 642–662.

Gestsdóttir, S., & Lerner, R. M. (2007). Intentional self-regulation and positive youth development in early adolescence: Findings from the 4-H Study of Positive Youth Development. *Developmental Psychology, 43*(2), 508–521.

Gestsdóttir, G., & Lerner, R. M. (2008). Positive development in adolescence: The development and role of intentional self regulation. *Human Development, 51,* 202–224.

Gore, A. (2003). Foreword. In R. M. Lerner & P. L. Benson (Eds.), *Developmental assets and asset-building communities: Implications for research, policy, and practice* (pp. xi–xii). Norwell, MA: Kluwer.

Gottlieb, G., Wahlsten, D., & Lickliter, R. (2006). The significance of biology for human development: A developmental psychobiological systems view. In R. M. Lerner (Ed.), *Handbook of child psychology: Vol. 1. Theoretical models of human development* (6th ed., pp. 210–257). Hoboken, NJ: Wiley.

Hall, G. S. (1904). *Adolescence: Its psychology and its relations to psychology, anthropology, sociology, sex, crime, religion, and education.* New York: Appleton.

Hamburg, D. A., & Takanishi, R. (1996). Great transitions: Preparing American youth for the 21st century—the role of research. *Journal of Research on Adolescence, 6,* 379–396.

Hirsch, J. (2004). Uniqueness, diversity, similarity, repeatability, and heritability. In C. Garcia Coll, E. Bearer, & R. M. Lerner (Eds.), *Nature and nurture: The complex interplay of genetic and environmental influences on human behavior and development* (pp. 127–138). Mahwah, NJ: Lawrence Erlbaum.

Jelicic, H., Bobek, D., Phelps, E. D., Lerner, J. V., & Lerner, R. M. (2007). Using positive youth development to predict contribution and risk behaviors in early adolescence: Findings from the first two waves of the 4-H Study of Positive Youth Development. *International Journal of Behavioral Development, 31*(3), 263–273.

King, P. E., Dowling, E. M., Mueller, R. A., White, K., Schultz, W., Osborn, P., et al. (2005). Thriving in adolescence: The voices of youth-serving practitioners, parents, and early and late adolescents. *Journal of Early Adolescence, 25*(1), 94–112.

Lerner, R. M. (1978). Nature, nurture, and dynamic interactionism. *Human Development, 21,* 1–20.

Lerner, R. M. (1991). Editorial: Continuities and changes in the scientific study of adolescence. *Journal of Research on Adolescence, 1,* 1–5.

Lerner, R. M. (1995). *America's youth in crisis: Challenges and options for programs and policies.* Thousand Oaks, CA: Sage.

Lerner, R. M. (2002). *Concepts and theories of human development* (3rd ed.). Mahwah, NJ: Lawrence Erlbaum.

Lerner, R. M. (2004). *Liberty: Thriving and civic engagement among American youth.* Thousand Oaks, CA: Sage.

Lerner, R. M. (2005, September). *Promoting positive youth development: Theoretical and empirical bases.* White paper prepared for the Workshop on the Science of Adolescent Health and Development, National Research Council/Institute of Medicine. Washington, DC: National Academies of Science.

Lerner, R. M. (2006). Developmental science, developmental systems, and contemporary theories. In R. M. Lerner (Ed.), *Handbook of child psychology: Vol. 1. Theoretical models of human development* (6th ed., pp. 1–17). Hoboken, NJ: Wiley.

Lerner, R. M. (2007). *The good teen: Rescuing adolescents from the myths of the storm and stress years.* New York: The Crown Publishing Group.

Lerner, R. M., & Foch, T. T. (Eds.). (1987). *Biological–psychosocial interactions in early adolescence.* Hillsdale, NJ: Erlbaum.

Lerner, R. M., Lerner, J. V., Almerigi, J., Theokas, C., Phelps, E., Gestsdóttir, S., et al. (2005). Positive youth development, participation in community youth development programs, and community contributions of fifth grade adolescents: Findings from the first wave of the 4-H Study of Positive Youth Development. *Journal of Early Adolescence, 25*(1), 17–71.

Lerner, J. V., Phelps, E., Forman, Y. E., & Bowers, E. (in press). Positive youth development. In. R. M. Lerner & L. Steinberg (Eds.), *Handbook of adolescent psychology* (3rd ed.). Hoboken, NJ: Wiley.

Lerner, R. M., & Steinberg, L. (Eds.). (In press). *Handbook of adolescent psychology* (3rd ed.). Hoboken, NJ: Wiley.

Magnusson, D., & Stattin, H. (2006). The person in the environment: Towards a general model for scientific inquiry. In R. M. Lerner (Ed.), *Handbook of child psychology: Vol. 1. Theoretical model of human development* (6th ed., pp. 400–464). New York: Wiley.

Mahoney, J., Vandell, D., Simpkins, S., & Zarrett, N. (in press). Adolescent out-of-school activities. In R. M. Lerner & L. Steinberg (Eds.), *Handbook of adolescent psychology* (3rd ed). Hoboken, NJ: Wiley.

Marcia, J. E. (1980). Identity in adolescence. In J. Adelson (Ed.), *Handbook of adolescent psychology* (pp. 159–187). New York: Wiley.

Nesselroade, J. R., & Baltes, P. B. (1974). Adolescent personality development and historical change: 1970–1972. *Monographs from the Society for Research in Child Development, 9*(154), 1–80.

Novikoff, A. B. (1945a). The concept of integrative levels and biology. *Science, 101,* 209–215.

Novikoff, A. B. (1945b). Continuity and discontinuity in evolution. *Science, 101,* 405–406.

Offer, D. (1969). *The psychological world of the teen-ager.* New York: Basic Books.

Overton, W. F. (1973). On the assumptive base of the nature–nurture controversy: Additive versus interactive conceptions. *Human Development, 16,* 74–89.

Overton, W. F. (2006). Developmental psychology: Philosophy, concepts, methodology. In R. M. Lerner (Ed.), *Handbook of child psychology: Vol. 1. Theoretical models of human development* (6th ed., pp. 18–88). Hoboken, NJ: Wiley.

Petersen, A. C. (1988). Adolescent development. *Annual Review of Psychology, 39,* 583–607.

Phelps, E., Balsano, A., Fay, K., Peltz, J., Zimmerman, S., Lerner, R. M., et al. (2007). Nuances in early adolescent development trajectories of positive and of problematic/risk behaviors: Findings from the 4-H Study of Positive Youth Development. *Child and Adolescent Clinics of North America, 16*(2), 473–496.

Pittman, K., Irby, M., & Ferber, T. (2001). Unfinished business: Further reflections on a decade of promoting youth development. In P. L. Benson & K. J. Pittman (Eds.), *Trends in youth development: Visions, realities and challenges* (pp. 4–50). Norwell, MA: Kluwer.

Rathunde, K., & Csikszentmihalyi, M. (2006). The developing person: An experiential perspective. In R. M. Lerner (Ed.), *Handbook of child psychology: Vol. 1. Theoretical models of human development* (6th ed., pp. 465–515). Hoboken, NJ: Wiley.

Roth, J. L., & Brooks-Gunn, J. (2003). What exactly is a youth development program? Answers from research and practice. *Applied Developmental Science, 7*, 94–111.

Schneirla, T. C. (1957). The concept of development in comparative psychology. In D. B. Harris (Ed.), *The concept of development* (pp. 78–108). Minneapolis, MN: University of Minnesota.

Seligman, M. E. P. (1998). Building human strength: Psychology's forgotten mission. *APA Monitor, 29*(1), 2.

Seligman, M. E. P. (2002). Positive psychology, positive prevention, and positive therapy. In C. R. Snyder & S. Lopez (Eds.), *Handbook of positive psychology*. New York: Oxford University Press.

Sherrod, L.R., Flanagan, C., & Youniss, J. (2002). Dimensions of citizenship and opportunities for youth development: The what, why, when, where, and who of citizenship development. *Applied Developmental Science, 6*(4), 264–272.

Simmons, R. G., & Blyth, D. A. (1987). *Moving into adolescence: The impact of pubertal change and school context.* Hawthorne, NJ: Aldine.

Spencer, M. B. (2006). Phenomenological variant of ecological systems theory (PVEST): A human development synthesis applicable to diverse individuals and groups. In R. M. Lerner (Ed.), *Handbook of child psychology: Vol. 1. Theoretical models of human development* (6th ed., pp. 829–893). Hoboken, NJ: Wiley.

Stattin, H., & Magnusson, D. (1990). *Pubertal maturation in female development.* Hillsdale, NJ: Erlbaum.

Steinberg, L., & Morris, A. S. (2001). Adolescent development. *Annual Review of Psychology, 52*, 83–110.

Steinberg, L., Mounts, N. S., Lamborn, S. D., & Dornbusch, S. M. (1991). Authoritative parenting and adolescent adjustment across varied ecological niches. *Journal of Research on Adolescence, 1*, 19–36.

Susman, E. J., & Dorn, L. D. (in press). Puberty: Its role in development. In R. M. Lerner & L. Steinberg (Eds.), *Handbook of adolescent psychology* (3rd ed.). Hoboken, NJ: Wiley.

Thelen, E. & Smith, L. B. (2006). Dynamic systems theories. In R. M. Lerner (Ed.), *Handbook of child psychology: Vol. 1. Theoretical models of human development* (6th ed., pp. 258–312). Hoboken, NJ: Wiley.

Theokas, C., & Lerner, R. M. (2006). Observed ecological assets in families, schools, and neighborhoods: Conceptualization, measurement and relations with positive and negative developmental outcomes. *Applied Developmental Science, 10*(2), 61–74.

Tobach, E., & Greenberg, G. (1984). The significance of T. C. Schneirla's contribution to the concept of levels of integration. In G. Greenberg & E. Tobach (Eds.), *Behavioral evolution and integrative levels* (pp. 1–7). Hillsdale, NJ: Erlbaum.

Von Bertalanffy, L. (1933). *Modern theories of development.* London: Oxford University Press.

Zarrett, N., Fay, K., Carrano, J., Li, Y., Phelps, E., & Lerner, R. M. (in press). More than child's play: Variable- and pattern-centered approaches for examining effects of sports participation on youth development. *Developmental Psychology.*

Zimmerman, S., Phelps, E., & Lerner, R. M. (2007). Intentional self-regulation in early adolescence: Assessing the structure of selection, optimization, and compensations processes. *European Journal of Developmental Science, 1*(3), 272–299.

Zimmerman, S., Phelps, E., & Lerner, R. M. (2008). Positive and negative developmental trajectories in U.S. adolescents: Where the PYD perspective meets the deficit model. *Research in Human Development, 5*(3), 153–165.

Aging Well in the 21st Century: Challenges and Opportunities

Gail M. Williamson *and* Juliette Christie

Abstract

Contrary to popular belief, the majority of adults over the age of 65 are physically and psychologically healthy. They are not cognitively deficient, socially isolated, or lonely, nor do they drain society's resources. They are aging well, and to the extent that they are able to engage in valued activities, they will continue to do so. A key component of adapting to growing older is the ability to maintain the sense of personal control that can be threatened by normal aging processes. The Activity Restriction Model of Depressed Affect proposes that to age successfully is to maintain physical and cognitive functioning via engagement in personally meaningful activities. Indeed, activity restriction—or the inability to continue normal activities that often follows stessful life events such as debilitating illness—is a major factor in poorer mental health outcomes. Potential contributors to activity restriction and depression are identified. Interventions to reduce activity restriction in older adults should focus on promoting manageable activities, taking into consideration individual differences in functional, psychological, and social resources.

Keywords: activity restriction, depression, older adults, physical functioning, successful aging

Getting old is something most people dread. But, as one of our grandfathers often said, "Being old is better than the only available alternative." If we are fortunate, we will age. If we are truly fortunate, we will age well, remaining vital and actively engaged with life. It is this challenge that has fostered the movement toward promoting "successful aging." Indeed, aging well is quite possible, and with the aid of current research in gerontological science, critical issues can now be targeted to help our aging population live well in the years to come.

History of Aging and Outlook for the Future

Historically, attitudes about aging have been fraught with mythical thinking, a short-sightedness we are just beginning to overcome. Traditionally, old people have been viewed as sick, cognitively inept, isolated, a financial drain on society, and depressed by their circumstances. These attitudes and the projected increase in elderly people within the next few years have seduced scholars,

commentators, and policy makers into the doomsday philosophy that our society is about to be overwhelmed by people who are disabled, requiring constant care, and not making worthwhile contributions. With fewer children per capita than previous generations, a major concern is that when the Baby Boomers age into disability, there will be fewer adult children available to provide care, creating a demand for formal (e.g., nursing home) care that may severely (if not, impossibly) tax societal resources.

Of course, as with any substantial demographic shift, there are concerns to be addressed. With these challenges, however, come opportunities, and the central purpose of this chapter is to summarize evidence indicating that there are offsetting parallel, positive arguments to these catastrophic predictions. Many solutions revolve around actions that should be and, in some cases, already are being taken at the governmental and societal levels. Fortunately, aging individuals and their immediate social networks can solve many problems without resorting to public assistance. The solution lies in changes in behavior that will enable older adults to continue to engage in valued normal activities with each advancing year. First, however, we need to take a realistic look at today's elders and what future generations can expect as they age.

Are Old People Sick People?

An important truth is that most adults over age 65 are remarkably healthy. Rates of disability, even among the very old (i.e., those over age 95), as well as the percentage (and absolute numbers) of nursing home residents have been steadily declining since 1982. Along with increasingly widespread public knowledge and acceptance of the behavioral aspects of chronic illness, advances in medical technology forecast an even rosier old age for Baby Boomers and subsequent generations. In addition, older adults are quite skilled in making gradual lifestyle changes to accommodate diminishing physical abilities. Also, nature is remarkably forgiving. In other words, it is never too late to begin a healthful lifestyle.

Are Old People Cognitively Deficient?

Cognitive abilities naturally slow down with increasing age. However, the "use it or lose it" adage about sexual functioning also applies to learning and memory abilities. Short of organic disorders (e.g., Alzheimer's disease), older adults in cognitively challenging environments show minimal, if any, declines in thinking and learning abilities. Like any other age group, when elderly people are less mentally challenged, their cognitive performance declines. Older adults typically encounter mental challenges less frequently than the college students to whom they usually are compared, but they can learn new things—and learn them quite well. Moreover, whether people believe they can learn and remember is crucial. The lesson here is that aging adults bear some responsibility for making sure that they engage in cognitively challenging activities.

Using current and emerging technologies will improve cognitive capacities of seniors, and those who make the effort to gain technological expertise will benefit most from these advances. The first step may involve no more than learning to use an automated teller machine (ATM), but that effort can promote subsequent skills. "Neurobic exercises" both preserve and improve brain and memory functions. Routine activities that require little cognitive effort can exacerbate cognitive decline. Accordingly,

researchers recommend actively seeking new and enjoyable experiences—simply because they are different.

Are Old People Isolated and Lonely?

Recent evidence suggests that the stereotypical view that older individuals deplete the energies of an ever-diminishing support system is insubstantial. To the contrary, social networks remain remarkably stable in size throughout the life span, with the number of close relationships among noninstitutionalized older adults equaling those of younger people. Network losses do occur over the life span through death, relocation, and retirement, but even among very old people, new social relationships are formed to replace lost ones.

In addition to possessing the capability to deal with changes in support networks, the aging Baby Boomers will be afforded technological advantages. With their computer competencies, they will likely use e-mail to maintain contact with family members and friends. We already have evidence that they are more likely than their younger counterparts to access internet information and support from a wide spectrum of people who share their needs and concerns.

Do Old People Drain Society's Resources?

The benefits elders receive have been scrutinized as potentially wasted and taking away from "more needy" groups and the overall economic well-being. Evidence does not support such broad-sweeping interpretations. First, older adults vary as widely as their younger counterparts in health, financial security, and willingness to accept public support. Second, senior citizen benefits depend on social status and past work experience, favoring high income earners with a continuous work history, that is, white middle class men. The stereotype of these "advantaged" oldsters has been used to justify reforms aimed at decreasing benefits for all elders. Without Social Security, however, the percentage of people over age 65 who live in governmentally defined poverty would increase from 12% to 50%. Thus, cuts in Social Security would hit hardest those who need them most.

Older adults do not drain societal resources. Future elders are more educated than their predecessors and, with their higher earnings, will continue to save after retirement rather than "spend down" their assets. Even those who do not continue to work for pay make substantial contributions. "Paid" work tends to be overvalued in our society, but unpaid (e.g., in the home, volunteer efforts) and underpaid (e.g., working in fast-food restaurants and bagging groceries) activities contribute a great deal to the social enterprise. When given the opportunity, large numbers of seniors eagerly do volunteer work and take on low-paying part-time jobs. But, the most telling, and least appreciated, example of the financial contributions of older adults is the economic value of the care they provide to disabled family members, estimated in 1999 to be between $45 and $200 billion annually. Put simply, older adults contribute a great deal to society—whether or not they collect a paycheck.

Should they choose to continue to work for pay, Baby Boomers and subsequent generations will be more advantaged than any previous generation. Attitudes about older workers are changing, as are the attitudes of older workers themselves. Because of post–Baby Boom declines in birth rates, as the Baby Boomers age, the number of employable adults will decrease relative to the number of new jobs. Following the law of supply and demand, older workers will be more valued and sought after. Moreover, younger retirees and Baby Boomers are looking at retirement as both a lifestyle transition and a new opportunity. Nearly 70% of Boomers expect to continue working after retirement, and those who do not feel ready to retire will not be compelled to do so.

The traditional retirement age of 65 has lost much of its significance. In terms of health and life expectancy, age 70 today is roughly the equivalent of age 65 in the 1930s when Social Security was established. Indeed, changing health status and attitudes have led to age 65 no longer being considered "old." Although most individuals who have at least adequate financial resources will retire at the usual time or earlier, they will be able to choose to continue working either because they want to or feel the need to supplement their retirement benefits.

The point to be made here revolves around personal choice. We have known for a long time that people who feel in control and who can make choices about the important aspects of their lives are both physically healthier and less depressed than those who perceive that they lack personal control.

Are Old People Depressed?

Evidence substantiating the presumed incidence of higher levels of depression among older adults is less than overwhelming, largely because of variations in the group under consideration and how "depression" is defined. In certain segments of the population, clinically relevant depressive syndromes, including major and minor depression, may affect 13–15% of older adults. And, while empirical findings do indicate higher rates of "depression" among disabled older adults, the same is true in younger adults with disabilities. The truth is that, overall, clinical depression is not more, and probably is less, prevalent in older than younger adults. Indeed, there is evidence that elders cope more effectively with stressful life events than do younger adults. Over the life course, through life experiences and successfully coping with various stressors, the typical adult builds adaptive attitudes that generalize to coping with new stressors. A key component is personal control. Regardless of age, people are motivated to exercise control over the important aspects of their lives. Solving the problems that go along with getting older (e.g., death of a spouse) simply may not be possible. Consequently, those who adapt well will shift their focus from actively trying to change the situation to managing stress-related emotional reactions by, for example, accepting the situation and continuing to function as normally as possible. By doing so, they will maintain a sense of control.

The Activity Restriction Model of Depressed Affect

Exemplifying the impact of loss of control, activity restriction has been operationalized as the inability to continue normal, valued activities (e.g., self-care, care of others, doing household chores, going shopping, visiting friends) that often follows stressful life events such as debilitating illness. According to the Activity Restriction Model of Depressed Affect, major life stressors lead to poorer mental health outcomes *because* they disrupt normal, valued activities. In other words, activity restriction mediates the association between stress and mental health.

Individual Differences in Activity Restriction

Stressful life circumstances are not the only contributors to activity restriction. Individuals differ in important ways. Age is one of these factors. Older adults tolerate similar levels of pain better than do younger adults, a phenomenon most commonly attributed to the increased exposure to pain and disabling conditions that older people experience. Indeed, experience, rather than chronological age matters more in terms of predicting those who will restrict their activities in the wake of stressful events.

In other words, old age need not foster either activity restriction or depression.

Another potentially important contributor to coping with stress is financial resources. Inadequate income interferes with normal activities. Moreover, if financial resources are merely perceived as being less than adequate, activities are more restricted. Thus, when life becomes stressful, a first line of defense may be to cut back on normal activities that involve spending money, for example, shopping, recreation, and hobbies.

Aside from demographic factors, aspects of the individual's personality also contribute to activity restriction. Some people cope in maladaptive ways across all situations throughout their lives. In contrast, there are those who routinely face the situation, rationally evaluate possible solutions, seek help and information as appropriate, and, if all else fails, accept that the problem has occurred, deal with their emotional reactions, and make every effort to resume life as usual.

Another important individual difference is social support. People with stronger social support resources cope better with all types of stressful life events, and routine activities are facilitated by social support. Comparable benefits are seen in people who merely perceive that social support is available if it is needed, and the benefits of perceiving that one has supportive others remain after controlling for demographics (e.g., age, financial resources), illness severity, and personality variables. Social support, however, appears to be a function of personality variables that, in turn, influence activity restriction. Those with more socially desirable characteristics (e.g., dispositional optimism) also have more supportive social ties and, therefore, may be less subject to activity restriction.

Summary of Current Research Findings

The forecast for our aging population is that, more than ever before, older adults will be physically, cognitively, psychologically, and socially healthy. Still, significant numbers of elders will be disabled, socially isolated, and depressed. From accumulating evidence, it is now clear that people consistently become depressed in the wake of stressful life events largely because those events disrupt their ability to go about life as usual, and that illness severity, younger age (or lack of experience), inadequate income, less social support, and personality variables contribute to this effect.

In their acclaimed book, *Successful Aging*, Rowe and Kahn (1998) proposed that there are three components of successful aging: (a) avoiding disease;

(b) engagement with life; and (c) maintaining high cognitive and physical function. They further proposed that each of these factors is "to some extent independent of the others" (p. 38). We do not disagree with this categorization. However, we argue that these factors are less inclusive and independent than Rowe and Kahn suggest. Not only do numerous other factors (e.g., personality, financial resources) influence how well one ages, but also Rowe and Kahn's three components can be subsumed by the construct of maintaining a lifestyle that involves normal, valued, and beneficial activities.

Our first counterargument is that avoiding disease is largely a function of routine activities. Temperance in detrimental behavior (e.g., smoking) is related to better physical health, less disability, and greater longevity. Second, engaging with life is virtually synonymous with continuing valued personal activities. People who feel engaged with life are those who engage in personally meaningful activities. In the Activity Restriction Model, it is postulated that continuing to be involved in personally relevant activities (whether intellectual, physical, or social) is what matters most. Finally, Rowe and Kahn (1998) advocate maintaining high cognitive and physical functioning as the third key to aging successfully. When confronted with seemingly overwhelming life events, the telling factor may well be the extent to which at least a semblance of normal activities can continue.

Interventions to Increase Activity and Decrease Depression

In the Activity Restriction Model, coping with stress is posited to be a complex, multifaceted process that is influenced by numerous factors. With age, physical and psychological stressors often become less controllable. Successful interventions may require helping elders shift from problem-focused to emotion-focused coping mechanisms. By acknowledging that depressed affect is a function of restricted normal activities, we can design interventions to reduce both activity restriction and depression. Efforts to increase activity should focus on identifying manageable activities and available resources. Programs can be implemented to engage aging adults in pastimes that not only meet their specific interests and needs but also fit their functional capacities.

Beyond evaluating demographic characteristics such as age and financial resources, a second line of intervention involves assessing stable traits that predispose people to restrict their normal activities.

Early interventions could then target those most at risk for poor adaptation. For instance, people low in optimism do not cope effectively or adjust well to stress. They also have less supportive social ties, increasing their vulnerability to activity restriction. High levels of neuroticism are related to a maladaptive coping style that may include foregoing pleasurable activities. When faced with disrupting life events, individuals who are less agentically oriented and do not have a strong sense of mastery will have more difficulty finding ways to continue their rewarding activities. In addition, those who are low in the dispositional predilection to hope for positive outcomes are less likely to conceptualize ways to continue (or replace) valued activities or to persist in their efforts to do so, particularly when pathways to achieving these goals are blocked. Once individuals who may be predisposed to restrict activities have been identified, a particularly fruitful line of intervention may be an adaptation of Hope Therapy.

Social support, like personality and experience, interacts with health-related variables to affect normal activities. With more supportive social support networks, activity restriction is less likely. Thus, identifying community-residing older adults with deficits in social support is another important avenue for intervention. Specifically, the particular aspects of social support that are either absent or most distressing need to be identified such that treatment can be targeted accordingly. Deficits in social support can range from instrumental (e.g., grocery shopping) to emotional (e.g., coping with life changes). Available resources often are underutilized because family and friends are not aware of the elder's needs. Thus, a prime point of intervention is to identify resources and facilitate social network cooperation.

Directions for Future Research

The Activity Restriction Model of Depressed Affect, like other models of stress and coping, implies that the causal path is unidirectional—that is, stress causes activity restriction that, in turn, causes negative affect. Without doubt, this model can be turned on its head such that, as clinicians have long known, being depressed causes people to forego many of their previously enjoyed activities. In fact, one of the better behavioral treatments for depression is to motivate patients to become more socially and physically active. Controlled experimental studies are needed to clarify previous results by demonstrating that strategies designed to increase activity

level will, in fact, improve well-being. In addition, identifying differences between people who will tolerate discomfort in order to continue engaging in meaningful activities and those who will not voluntarily make such efforts under similar levels of discomfort will bring us closer to successful intervention programs.

Concluding Comments

Contrary to common belief, growing old in the twenty-first century is not likely to be an unpleasant experience for most people, nor are older adults likely to overwhelm societal resources with their needs. Clearly, physical, mental, social, and financial well-being are intertwined, and aging successfully depends, to a large extent, on effectively coping with age-related life events.

As specified in the Activity Restriction Model of Depressed Affect, people experience decrements in mental health in direct proportion to how stress interferes with their normal activities. Therefore, those who age well are those who feel in control of at least some of the important aspects of their lives and maintain the normal activities they value most. The association between stress and adjustment is multifaceted and complex; however, if people are motivated and facilitated to continue at least some of their valued activities, they should be physically and psychologically healthier. Indeed, maintaining normal activities may be the key to aging successfully.

Questions for the Future

1. Given current and projected economic trends, is successful aging still a reality?

2. What public policy changes are needed to ensure the continued development and successful maintenance of continuing care retirement communities (CCRCs) that facilitate living well and "in place"?

3. How might state and local governments improve public transportation services to enable older adults to maintain their lifestyles?

Acknowledgments

Manuscript preparation was supported by the National Institute on Aging (AG15321, G. M. Williamson, principal investigator) and further facilitated by a fellowship from the Institute for Behavioral Research at The University of Georgia.

Reference

Rowe, J. W., & Kahn, R. L. (1998). *Successful aging.* New York: Pantheon Books.

New Territories of Positive Life-Span Development: Wisdom and Life Longings

Susanne Scheibe, Ute Kunzmann, *and* Paul B. Baltes

Abstract

In search for concepts that help understand how individuals strive for growth and perfection within the boundaries and constraints of human lives, we describe theory and research on the concepts of wisdom, or expert knowledge about human nature and the life course, and *Sehnsucht* (life longings), the recurring and strong desire for ideal (utopian), alternative states and expressions of life. Both represent relatively new concepts on the agenda of lifespan research, originating from an interest in identifying major topics of public and humanist discourse about the potentials and constraints of life-span development and finding ways to measure them with the methods of normative psychological science. Despite their complexity and multiple meanings, progress has been made in the theory-driven operationalization of wisdom and life longings, allowing new insights into their ontogenesis and role for positive development. Emerging research shows that wisdom and life longings do not directly promote a hedonic life orientation or happiness: neither the insight that life is incomplete (wisdom) nor the experience of this incompleteness (life longings) is compatible with feelings of unequivocal joy and pleasure. Yet, there is emerging evidence that they contribute to other aspects of positive development, emphasizing personal growth, meaning, and the aligning of one's own and other's well-being. We suggest that future research should focus on the links of wisdom and life longings with multiple developmental outcomes and the possible interplay of both concepts in promoting positive development.

Keywords: functionality, life longings, ontogenesis, *Sehnsucht*, wisdom

Philosophers, theologians, and psychologists have long considered and discussed the criteria for a good or perfect life and the different ways in which humans strive for optimality and perfection (cf. Baltes, 2004; Baltes, Glück, & Kunzmann, 2002). Given that the concept of development is inherently linked to notions of growth (Harris, 1957; Lerner, 2002) and improvement-oriented intervention (Tetens, 1777), within the field of psychology, developmental psychologists have been key players in this endeavor. The search for improvement and optimality, however, occurs in the context of developmental constraints, including limited resources, restricted opportunities, and blocked pathways. This is especially true for later phases of adulthood when people face a reduced remaining lifetime to pursue their goals, declines in physical and cognitive functioning, as well as losses of social partners and roles (e.g., Baltes & Mayer, 1999; Schaie, 2005).

Two concepts, which have been the focus of our research, reflect the dynamic interplay between two motivational principles: striving for perfection and growth and compensating for constraints, losses, and the chronic incompleteness of life. These are "wisdom," or expert knowledge about human nature and the life course (Baltes & Kunzmann, 2003; Baltes & Smith, 1990; Baltes & Staudinger, 2000; Kunzmann & Baltes, 2005); and *Sehnsucht* ("life longings"), the recurring and strong desire for ideal (utopian), alternative states and expressions of life (Baltes, 2008; Scheibe, Freund, & Baltes, 2007).

Both concepts have been major topics of public and humanist discourse about life and life-span development. However, they have rarely been addressed in the context of psychological research—arguably because of their multiple meanings and complexity and the challenges that are involved when studying them empirically. As we will review in this chapter, a small but growing field of research has suggested that the few existing psychological definitions and operationalizations of wisdom and life longings do meet the standards of normative psychological science. Even more important, we shall argue that studying concepts such as wisdom and life longings makes a meaningful, if not necessary, contribution not only to the field of aging but also to a positive psychology approach (see also Baltes & Kunzmann, in press; Baltes & Smith, 1990, 2008; Kunzmann & Baltes, 2005; Scheibe, Kunzmann, & Baltes, 2007).

Positive Psychology and the Study of Wisdom and Life Longings

Wisdom and life longings fit well into the general notion of positive psychology, the science of what makes life worth living (Seligman & Csikszentmihalyi, 2000). The positive psychology initiative aims to counteract a presumably one-sided focus of twentieth-century psychology on negative experiences and the dysfunctional. Although proponents of positive psychology may have overstated the focus on negativity in past psychological research, it certainly is worthwhile to strengthen research that explicitly addresses positive subjective experiences, desirable individual traits, civic virtues, as well as the positive aspects and gains that adult development and aging may bring about (see also Baltes, 2004; Baltes et al., 2002).

Within the positive psychology framework, our goal has been to provide a balanced view emphasizing both positive and negative aspects of human experience. This balanced view is consistent with a central proposition of life-span developmental psychology, namely that gains and losses, the positive and the negative, are always intertwined; every phase of life and every developmental change simultaneously involves benefits and costs (Baltes, 1987, 1997; Baltes, Lindenberger, & Staudinger, 2006; Brandtstädter, 1984, 1998). Even in the best scenario possible, life does not consist of unlimited opportunities and exclusively positive experiences; it always involves constraints, challenges, threats, losses, and difficult, sometimes even traumatic, life events. If one considers life as a whole, these negative experiences are often the rule rather than the exception. Therefore, one important aspect of a positive psychology is to acknowledge that negative realities do exist and that studying the ways in which people learn to accept them as important parts of life or manage to deal with them constructively is critical to gaining a better understanding of human nature and life-span development (see also Aspinwall & Staudinger, 2003).

In this spirit, wisdom and life longings are not unequivocally positive phenomena in the sense that they directly and inevitably optimize a person's level of well-being in a hedonistic sense. Striving for wisdom or indulging in life longings even appears to have costs in terms of hedonistic pleasures. However, there is reason to believe that wisdom and life longings are both linked to another central facet of the good life—personal growth, integrity, and a concern for the well-being of others (e.g., Baltes, 2004; Baltes & Kunzmann, 2004; Baltes & Staudinger, 2000; Kunzmann & Baltes, 2003a, 2003b, 2005; Scheibe, Kunzmann, et al., 2007; for the distinction between the two aspects of a good life, growth and happiness, see, for example, Kunzmann, Stange, & Jordan, 2005; Labouvie-Vief & Medler, 2002; McGregor & Little, 1998).

As we discuss in the following, wisdom and life longings both deal with life's potentials *and* constraints. Persons high on wisdom-related knowledge are presumably motivated to understand the complex and sometimes paradoxical nature of life, view events and experiences from multiple perspectives, and simultaneously consider the gains and losses inherent in any developmental change (Kunzmann & Baltes, 2003b). Similarly, life longings involve at the same time ideal conceptions of self and development (personal utopias of life) and a sense of incompleteness and imperfection, leading to ambivalent, bittersweet emotions. Persons with moderate- to high-level expressions of life longings may be highly critical of themselves and their lives, may have high ideals and seek to attain them, and at the same time, may realize that perfection is an ideal rather than a goal that can be reached. Given these insights and experiences, it is unlikely that wiser persons and persons with strong life longings have an abundance of pleasant feelings. However, wisdom and life longings may contribute to a good life and a positive development by facilitating personal growth and a balancing of various, sometimes conflicting and negative, personal experiences, goals, and values.

Wisdom: Knowledge about Life's Potentials and Constraints

At the core of the concept of wisdom is the notion of a perfect, perhaps utopian,[1] integration of knowledge and character, mind, and virtue (e.g., Baltes & Kunzmann, 2003; Baltes & Staudinger, 2000). Although the psychology of wisdom is a relatively new field, several promising theoretical and operational definitions of wisdom have been developed in recent years (for reviews see Baltes & Smith, 2008; Baltes & Staudinger, 2000; Kramer, 2000; Kunzmann & Baltes, 2005; Staudinger, 2008; Sternberg, 1990, 1998). In these models, wisdom is thought to be different from other human strengths in that it facilitates an integrative and holistic approach toward life's challenges and problems—an approach that embraces past, present, and future dimensions of phenomena, values different points of views, considers contextual variations, and acknowledges the uncertainties inherent in any sense making of the past, present, and future.

A second important feature of wisdom is that it involves an awareness that individual and collective well-being are tied together so that one cannot exist without the other. In this sense, wisdom has been said to refer to time-tested knowledge that guides our behavior in ways that optimize productivity on the level of individuals, groups, and even society (e.g., Kramer, 2000; Sternberg, 1998).

Finally, wisdom has been linked to the ancient idea of a good life which has been thought to involve a preference for personal growth and self-actualization (e.g., Kekes, 1995). Therefore, the acquisition of wisdom during ontogenesis may often be incompatible with a hedonic life orientation and a predominantly pleasurable, passive, and sheltered life. Given their interest in self-realization and the maximization of a common good, wiser people are likely to partake in behaviors that contribute, rather than consume, resources (Kunzmann & Baltes, 2003a, 2003b; Sternberg, 1998). Also, an interest in understanding the significance and deeper meaning of phenomena, including the blending of developmental gains and losses, most likely is linked to emotional complexity rather than pleasantness (Labouvie-Vief, 1990).

There are generally two ways of studying wisdom in psychological research (Baltes & Kunzmann, 2004). A first approach, which is grounded in social and personality psychology, is to focus on the nature of wise persons, that is, their intellectual, motivational, and emotional characteristics (e.g., Ardelt, 2004; Erikson, 1980; Wink & Helson, 1997). A second approach that we have pursued is to define wisdom as a body of highly developed knowledge on the basis of relevant psychological and cultural-historical wisdom work (Baltes & Smith, 1990; Baltes & Staudinger, 2000). This approach proceeds from the idea that a comprehensive definition of wisdom requires going beyond the individual and her characteristics, simply because wisdom is an ideal rather than a state of being.

The Berlin Wisdom Model

Proceeding from and integrating work on the aging mind and personality, life-span developmental theory, and cultural-historical work on wisdom, in the Berlin paradigm, wisdom has been defined as highly valued and outstanding expert knowledge about dealing with fundamental, that is existential, problems related to the meaning and conduct of life (Baltes, 2004; Baltes & Kunzmann, 2003; Baltes & Smith, 1990; Baltes & Staudinger, 2000; Dittmann-Kohli & Baltes, 1990; Dixon & Baltes, 1986). These problems are typically complex and poorly defined, and have multiple, yet unknown, solutions. Deciding on a particular career path, accepting the death of a loved one, dealing with personal mortality, or solving long-lasting conflicts among family members exemplify the type of problem that calls for wisdom-related expertise. In contrast, more circumscribed everyday problems can be effectively handled by using more limited abilities. To solve a math problem, for example, wisdom-related expertise usually is neither necessary nor particularly helpful.

Five criteria were developed to describe this body of knowledge in more detail. Expert knowledge about the meaning and conduct of life is thought to approach wisdom if it meets "all" five criteria, namely (a) rich "factual knowledge" about human nature and the life course; (b) rich "procedural knowledge" about ways of dealing with life problems; (c) "life-span contextualism," that is, an awareness and understanding of the many contexts of life, and of how they relate to each other and change over the life span; (d) "value relativism and tolerance," that is, an acknowledgment of individual, social, and cultural differences in values and life priorities; and (e) "knowledge about handling uncertainty," including the limits of one's own knowledge.

---

[1] By utopian, we mean idealized or perfect, that is, something that goes beyond usual levels of functioning and that cannot be fully reached.

Assessment of Wisdom-Related Knowledge

The Berlin wisdom paradigm is based on a modified version of the method of "thinking aloud" (Ericsson & Simon, 1984). Specifically, after a warm-up phase, participants are instructed to say out loud everything that crosses their minds when they think about a given hypothetical life problem. One might be: "Imagine that someone gets a call from a good friend who says that he or she cannot go on anymore and wants to commit suicide." Another problem reads: "A 15-year-old girl wants to get married right away. What could one consider and do?" Trained raters evaluate responses to those problems by using the five criteria that were specified as defining wisdom-related knowledge. The assessment of wisdom-related knowledge on the basis of these criteria exhibits satisfactory reliability and validity. For example, middle-aged and older public figures from Berlin nominated as life-experienced and wise by a panel of journalists—independently of the Berlin definition of wisdom—were among the top performers in laboratory wisdom tasks and outperformed similar-aged adults who were not nominated (Baltes, Staudinger, Maercker, & Smith, 1995).

THE BERLIN WISDOM PARADIGM: SELECTED FINDINGS

The Berlin research program on wisdom has addressed a broad range of questions concerning the development of wisdom, including individual and social factors that facilitate or hinder its acquisition and refinement during ontogenesis. Other research has focused on the activation of wisdom-related knowledge in a given situation. This laboratory work has provided evidence that wisdom-related knowledge can be activated by relatively simple short-term interventions. Finally, there is research dealing with the links between wisdom-related knowledge and psychological adaptation or what has been called the good life (for reviews see Baltes & Staudinger, 2000; Kunzmann & Baltes, 2005; Kunzmann & Stange, 2006; Staudinger, 1999a). We will briefly review some of the major findings in the following sections.

The Development of Wisdom during Ontogenesis

Although laypeople and scientists have considered wisdom a human strength that is closely and positively linked to old age (Baltes & Smith, 1990; Heckhausen, Dixon, & Baltes, 1989), it is not a normative developmental achievement in adulthood and old age. Consistent with the idea that wisdom is a goal that few people—if any—will fully achieve, high levels of wisdom-related knowledge are rare. Many adults are on the way to wisdom, but very few people approach high wisdom scores as measured by the Berlin wisdom tasks. Therefore, many wise individuals may be relatively old, but most older people most likely are not wise.

But what is the empirical evidence? Pasupathi, Staudinger, and Baltes (2001) reported that wisdom-related knowledge considerably increased during adolescence and young adulthood (i.e., between age 14 and 20). As to be expected, studying older adults did not evince marked further changes for the average case. Specifically, in four studies with a total sample size of 533 individuals ranging in age from 20 to 89 years, the relationship between wisdom-related knowledge and chronological age was virtually zero and nonsignificant (Baltes & Smith, 1990; Staudinger, 1999b). Within the limitations of cross-sectional data, this evidence suggests that, on a group level of analysis, wisdom-related knowledge remains stable over the adult years into the sixties and seventies (for reviews see Baltes & Kunzmann, in press; Kunzmann & Baltes, 2005; Staudinger, 1999b).

For wisdom-related knowledge and judgment to develop during the second half of life, factors other than age are critical. Correlational evidence from adult samples suggests that it takes a complex coalition of expertise-enhancing factors from different domains, ranging from persons' personality and social-cognitive style (e.g., social intelligence, openness to experience) to their immediate social context (e.g., presence of role models) to societal and cultural conditions (e.g., exposure to societal transitions). For example, those who are open to new experiences, who have a higher level of what has been called psychological mindedness (i.e., interest in and responsiveness to the inner needs, motives, and experiences of others; Gough, 1964), who think about the how and why of an event rather than simply whether it is good or bad, or who are oriented both toward personal growth and the well-being of others display higher levels of wisdom knowledge (Kunzmann & Baltes, 2003b; Staudinger, Lopez, & Baltes, 1997; Staudinger, Maciel, Smith, & Baltes, 1998). Higher levels of creativity and lower levels of conservative cognitive styles (i.e., adhering to existing rules, minimizing change, and avoiding ambiguous situations) and oligarchic cognitive styles (i.e., experience of tension when pursuing multiple goals; Sternberg, 1997) are also predictive of wisdom as measured with the Berlin paradigm. Finally, there is evidence that adults who specialize in professions that provide extensive training and practice in difficult and uncertain life matters (e.g., clinical psychology) show higher wisdom-related performance than professionals from fields in which training and job tasks were not specifically dedicated to dealing with fundamental life problems (Staudinger, Smith, & Baltes, 1992).

Together, these findings suggest an explanation for the lack of age differences in wisdom-related knowledge. Specifically, some of the identified wisdom-facilitative factors have been shown to decline with age (e.g., openness to experience; McCrae et al., 2000), other factors seem to increase with age (e.g., generativity and values revolving around the well-being of others; Kunzmann et al., 2005), and yet others show no relationship to age at all (e.g., cognitive styles *sensu* Sternberg, 1997). The age-associated system of changes appears to be too complex to permit a simple linear increase in wisdom-related knowledge with advancing age (see also Baltes & Kunzmann, in press). Nevertheless, it may well be that certain subgroups of individuals will experience age-related gains and that wisdom-related knowledge can be activated and enhanced by explicit interventions.

The Activation of Wisdom-Related Knowledge

Many adults presumably are interested in learning more about the ways of improving their levels of wisdom-related knowledge. The psychological wisdom literature has suggested three strategies (Baltes & Kunzmann, in press; Glück & Baltes, 2006; Stange & Kunzmann, 2008). One strategy involves organizing one's life around the factors that have been shown to predict individual differences in wisdom during adulthood and old age. For example, one may attempt to develop wisdom by finding role models and mentors, pursuing certain professions, or developing certain motivational orientations and values. In the long run, this strategy may help the individual attain sustainable improvement in wisdom.

A second way of improving one's wisdom-related knowledge is to attend structured courses explicitly designed to teach skills and thinking styles that can be considered preconditions or components of wisdom. Sternberg and his colleagues have implemented such a wisdom training in an educational setting (Sternberg, 2001). Their curriculum, which currently is being evaluated, addresses diverse topics ranging from an introduction to scientific definitions of wisdom to discussions of specific wisdom components (e.g., value tolerance and approaching a common good) to encouraging students to use particular wise individuals as role models.

A third strategy of enhancing wisdom-related knowledge refers to short-term interventions that help people access and express their existing wisdom-related knowledge more effectively (Baltes & Kunzmann, in press; Glück & Baltes, 2006; Stange & Kunzmann, 2008). Three such interventions have been successfully tested within the Berlin wisdom paradigm. Staudinger and Baltes (1996) tested a first intervention that was based on the idea that wisdom is a social phenomenon. The study suggests that individuals will increase the quality of their activated wisdom-related knowledge if they engage in actual or imagined consultations with others before dealing with a complex and serious life problem. A second intervention study suggests that people's wisdom-related knowledge can be improved by activating knowledge about variations among cultures. Specifically, imagining to travel around the world and reflecting on the differences and similarities among different locations, people, and cultures before dealing with a wisdom problem can improve the quality of people's wisdom-related knowledge (Böhmig-Krumhaar, Staudinger, & Baltes, 2002). Finally, there is evidence that at least some individuals can improve their wisdom-related performance by consciously trying to be wise. A simple instruction "to try to give a wise response to a wisdom task" was enough to improve wisdom-related performance when dealing with a life problem—at least for people with an above-average profile of wisdom resources such as high intelligence, openness to experience, and good social relations (Glück & Baltes, 2006). Taken together, this evidence suggests that wisdom-related knowledge is not fixed, rather it is dynamic and can be improved by relatively simple social and cognitive strategies.

The Relation between Wisdom and Indicators of Successful Development

The question of whether wisdom includes the application of knowledge in everyday life has provoked considerable division within both the humanities and the social sciences. On the one hand, wisdom has been seen as being quite remote from manifest behavior. Particularly, in Eastern philosophical traditions, truly wise persons are thought to avoid immediate action and to sometimes demonstrate their competence by refraining from any action at all (Assmann, 1994).

On the other hand, several modern philosophers influenced by the tradition of early Greek philosophy have proposed that wisdom is closely linked to our everyday behaviors. In this tradition, wisdom has been thought to be a resource that facilitates a good life on both an individual and a societal level (e.g., Kekes, 1995).

On the basis of philosophical work in the early Greek tradition and our own theoretical work in this area, we have predicted that the values and behaviors of people with high levels of wisdom-related knowledge will indicate a striving for a good life. One aspect of a good life in the early Greek tradition refers to the balancing of personal and common interests (see also Sternberg, 1998). A second aspect refers to the preference for personal growth and self-actualization—even if this preference opposes happiness in a hedonistic and materialistic sense (Baltes et al., 2002; Kunzmann & Baltes, 2003a).

To begin to investigate the idea that there is a link between wisdom-related knowledge and psychological indicators of a good life, Kunzmann and Baltes (2003a) conducted a questionnaire study with an age-heterogeneous sample of young, middle-aged, and older adults. As expected, adults with higher levels of wisdom-related knowledge reported less preference for self-oriented values revolving around a pleasurable and comfortable life. Instead, they reported preferring self-oriented values such as personal growth and insight, as well as a preference for other-oriented values related to environmental protection, societal engagement, and the well-being of friends. People with high levels of wisdom-related knowledge also showed less preference for conflict management strategies that reflect either a one-sided concern with one's own interests (i.e., dominance), a one-sided concern with others' interests (i.e., submission), or no concern at all (i.e., avoidance). As predicted, they preferred a cooperative approach reflecting a joint concern for one's own and the opponent's interests (i.e., cooperation). Finally, people with high levels of wisdom-related knowledge reported that they experience self-centered pleasant feelings less frequently (e.g., happiness, amusement) but process-oriented and environment-centered positive emotions more frequently (e.g., interest, inspiration).

These findings are promising in that they clearly oppose the view that wisdom-related knowledge is an abstract body of theoretical knowledge that is relevant only for philosophical discourse about hypothetical problems. Rather, wisdom-related knowledge makes a difference for people's affective experiences, values, and behavioral choices in everyday life. More generally speaking, wisdom-related knowledge seems to go hand in hand with a joint concern for developing one's own and others' potential.

Experiencing Personally Life's Potentials and Constraints: Adding Life Longings (*Sehnsucht*) to the Agenda of Positive Life-Span Research

In comparison to wisdom which involves generalized knowledge about human nature and the life course, *Sehnsucht* (life longings) can be regarded as personalized, experiential knowledge and awareness of the fundamental conditions of life, including the incompleteness and imperfection of life. *Sehnsucht* denotes the recurring, strong feeling that life is incomplete or imperfect, coupled with a desire for ideal (utopian), alternative states and experiences of life. For example, a person may be unhappy about certain aspects of her marriage and dream about a fulfilling partnership with somebody she once was in love with. This two-sided focus elicits ambivalent, bittersweet emotions. The concept of *Sehnsucht* is very prominent in everyday culture, the arts, and the humanities, particularly in the German and European cultural context (Clair, 2005; Vosskamp, 2004).

A Psychological Conceptualization of Life Longings: Six Characteristics

Taking everyday language and the humanities as a point of departure, we derived a psychological conceptualization of *Sehnsucht* within the framework of life-span psychology (Baltes, 2008; Scheibe, Freund et al., 2007). *Sehnsucht's* dictionary definition is "a high degree of intense and often painful desire for something, particularly if there is no hope to attain the desired or when its attainment is uncertain, still far away" (Grimm & Grimm, 1854–1871/1984). Similar to Zeitgeist, *Sehnsucht* is difficult to translate into English. We suggested the term "life longings" as a translation to emphasize the holistic character of *Sehnsucht*, as well as its extension across multiple domains and times of life (Scheibe, Freund et al., 2007).

Considering the dictionary definition of *Sehnsucht*, general principles of life-span psychology (Baltes, 1987), and previous (mostly conceptual) psychological work on the topic (Belk, Ger, & Askegaard, 2003; Holm, 1999; Palaian, 1993; Ravicz, 1998), we derived six core characteristics. In studies with German and U.S. samples of adults aged 18–91 years, these six characteristics proved to be a useful description of the experiential "gestalt" or structure of life longings (Baltes, 2008; Scheibe, Blanchard-Fields, Wiest, & Freund, 2009; Scheibe, Freund et al., 2007). First is the observation that a central aspect of the experience of life longings is a "feeling of incompleteness and a sense of imperfection" of one's life. Something is missing that appears essential for a meaningful life and if attained, promises to make life more complete (Boesch, 1998; Holm, 1999). Second is the observation that life longings are directed at an idealized alternative to the imperfect present, that is, "personal utopias" of desired alternative expressions of life. Utopian ideals may represent individuals' memories or expectations of highly positive developmental states and conceptions of the ideal life course or self; they can be approximated but they cannot be fully attained (Boesch, 1998).

Third, life longings extend beyond the present into the past and future; they have a "tritime focus." They can be directed at memories of past peak experiences (e.g., moments of intense joy, positive feelings associated with a past life phase or place) that one desires to reexperience in the present and future, and at peak experiences envisioned for the future. The fourth characteristic is "emotional ambivalence" (Belk et al., 2003; Boesch, 1998; Palaian, 1993). This attribute is consistent with the notion that development is multifunctional and always involves both gains and losses (Baltes, 1987; Brandtstädter, 1984; Labouvie-Vief, 1981). The emotional quality of life longings is postulated to be inherently ambivalent or "bittersweet," combining pleasant feelings elicited by utopian fantasies with unpleasant feelings of disappointment and frustration as these fantasies are out of reach.

Fifth is the notion that life longings elicit "reflective and evaluative processes" dealing with the consideration of one's actual developmental state, self-critical reflection on the past, present, and (expected) future, as well as an exploratory search for optimal ways of living. Finally, we assume with Boesch (1991, 1998) that life longings are rich in "symbolic meaning." Life longings are more than a specific, concrete behavior or experience. Instead, specific objects or targets of life longings should be linked to more encompassing mental and emotional representations for which they stand. A specific longing (e.g., for an embrace by a loved one) is considered a life longing only if the desired state is linked with a broader configuration of thoughts and feelings that are relevant for multiple domains or times of life.

Assessment of Life Longings

Based on the framework of the six life-longing characteristics, our research group developed a self-report procedure to assess life longings in adults (Scheibe, Freund et al., 2007). This procedure combines idiographic and nomothetic techniques. In the idiographic part, participants are asked to generate a list of life longings, that is, dreams about, strong desires, or wishes for persons, objects, experiences, events, or conditions of life or the world that are intense, enduring or recurring, and very unlikely or not easily attainable at present. This is preceded by a warm-up task, in which they are asked to reflect on different life phases (childhood, youth, adulthood, old age) or life domains (relationships with other persons, health and personal situation, self-view). Reported life longings deal primarily with social relationships, such as a fulfilling partnership, true friendship, or the lasting well-being of family members (Kotter-Grühn, Wiest, Zurek, & Scheibe, in press). Other frequently mentioned topics concern the self-image or state of mind (e.g., inner peace), health (e.g., recovering from serious illness, being active until old age), leisure (e.g., traveling the world), and work-related issues (e.g., becoming head of a company).

In the nomothetic part, participants rate their two or three most important life longings on scales covering the six characteristics of life longings (personal utopia, sense of incompleteness, tritime focus, ambivalent emotions, life reflection and evaluation, and symbolic richness) and other important characteristics (e.g., frequency and intensity, functional significance, and controllability of life longings). The scales evince acceptable internal consistencies in both German and U.S. samples and substantial retest stabilities across 5 weeks (Kotter-Gruehn, Scheibe, Blanchard-Fields, & Baltes, 2009; Scheibe, Blanchard-Fields et al., 2009; Scheibe, Freund et al., 2007) and can be used to link life longings to other person characteristics, such as emotional well-being.

Selected Findings from a New Project on Life Longings

Given the novelty of the psychological concept of life longings, one goal of our research has been to investigate commonalities and differences with well-articulated related concepts like goals, regrets, or the ideal self. A second research question addressed the ontogenesis of life longings, that is, when in the life course do life longings emerge and what is their course in adulthood and old age? Third, we started to explore the possible functions of life longings for development and their relation to indicators of positive development or the good life.

Divergent Validity: Comparing Life Longings with Related Concepts

The most notable concept related to life longings is the concept of personal goals. Like life longings, goals are directed at positive outcomes and give directionality to life. Importantly, however, goals operate primarily at the behavioral level: people strive at attaining their goals by formulating specific implementation intentions and by engaging in goal-relevant behaviors. Life longings, in contrast, are utopian and unattainable in principle; they work mainly at the level of imagination and fantasy (Boesch, 1998; Scheibe, Freund et al., 2007). Consistent with this view, a study comparing personal life longings and goals found that goals were reported to be more concrete and controllable (i.e., one knows the steps necessary for their achievement) than life longings, and to have a stronger influence on the structuring of everyday life (Mayser, Scheibe, & Riediger, 2008). Life longings, in contrast, were rated to be more emotionally bittersweet (painful and pleasurable at the same time), utopian, and long-term oriented than goals. Both goal and life-longing characteristics were related to individuals' life satisfaction; yet, in line with the stronger role of goals in structuring everyday life, the association between goals and life satisfaction was stronger than that between life longings and life satisfaction.

Recent research investigating one specific aspect of incompleteness, the wish to have a child in middle-aged childless women, shows that goals and life longings emerge under different conditions (Kotter-Gruehn et al., 2009). When the wish for children was intense and at the same time perceived as attainable (as might be the case for relatively young heterosexual women with a partner), women tended to describe this wish as a goal. However, when the wish for children was intense and long-lasting (as might be the case in older women past the developmental deadline of childbearing), women tended to describe this wish more as a life longing.

Divergent validity of life longings in comparison to goals can also be found at the level of subjective conceptions and in comparison to further concepts like regret and the ideal self. Scheibe, Freund, and Blanchard-Fields (2009) investigated persons' beliefs about the typical states and traits associated with the activation of life longings, goals, regret, and the ideal self. Consistent with the characteristic of emotional ambivalence and the two-edged focus on positive ideals and incompleteness, participants regarded both positive and negative states as typical for the experience of life longings, and they linked the frequent experience of life longings with both positive (e.g., agreeableness, openness) and negative personality traits (e.g., neuroticism, low environmental mastery). Goals and the ideal self were rated higher on positive than negative states and linked with a well-adjusted personality profile. Regret, in contrast, was rated higher on negative than positive states and linked with a maladaptive personality profile. Together, these findings support the divergent validity of the construct of life longings, demonstrating its uniqueness in relation to other, already existing concepts.

Age and the Expression of Life Longings

Like wisdom, we expect the frequency and relevance of life longings to increase from childhood to young adulthood and to remain largely stable across adulthood and old age (Scheibe, Freund et al., 2009). This assumption is based on our theory that assigns to life longings complex cognitive, affective, and motivational components that likely only become fully expressed in late adolescence or early adulthood. For example, symbolic richness, tritime focus, and reflection and evaluation require autobiographical reasoning and memory, abilities that only become fully available in middle to late adolescence (Bluck & Habermas, 2001; Staudinger, 2001).

Accordingly, the basic structure of life longings presumably has been established when entering adulthood. Paralleling the ontogenesis of wisdom (Baltes & Kunzmann, 2003; Baltes & Staudinger, 2000), subsequent adult changes are expected to be determined more by factors other than chronological age, such as personality, cognitive style, motivational orientations, and life experiences. Confirming this view, in our sample ranging in age from 19 to 81, five of the six core characteristics of life longings (personal utopia, ontogenetic tritime focus, ambivalent emotions, life reflection and evaluation, and symbolic richness) were invariant across adult age groups (Scheibe, Freund et al., 2009). Only the aspect of incompleteness was lower in older participants, suggesting that with age, people are able to approximate their ideal and actual views of themselves (Ryff, 1991). Stability across age groups also was found in terms of the covariance structure of the six characteristics.

Interesting adult age differences emerged with regard to a sense of control over life longings. Compared to younger adults, older adults reported feeling more able to regulate their experience of life longings, but less able to translate their life longings into goals and goal-related action. These findings conform with the emerging picture of stable or even improved emotional functioning and emotional control in later periods of adulthood (Isaacowitz, Charles, & Carstensen, 2000), yet a reduced capacity to shape the external environment according to own desires and preferences (Brandtstädter & Renner, 1990; Lachman & Weaver, 1998).

Whereas the structure and intensity of life longings appears to be invariant across adulthood, specific contents of life longings differ. We submit that life longings are directed at those age-related themes and tasks that are relevant as individuals wrestle with incompleteness and imperfection in achieving their goals, and as they review, manage, and plan their lives as a whole. Thus, current and past (unattained) developmental tasks and themes should be in the foreground. Scheibe, Freund et al. (2007; see also Scheibe, Blanchard-Fields et al., 2009) asked adult participants to rate the extent to which their three life longings were related to each of the 13 thematic categories. Ratings were consistent with a focus of life longings on current developmental tasks. For example, work/education was rated higher in young and middle-aged adults and lower in older adults. Work-related life longings may reflect developmental tasks of occupational development in young adults and work–family balance in middle-aged adults. Results also were consistent with a focus of life longings on past, perhaps unresolved developmental tasks. For example, partnership was most often targeted by life longings of middle-aged adults and less so in those of younger and older participants. Establishing a partnership is considered a primary task of young adulthood. However, a fulfilling partnership may be more like a concrete, action-relevant goal in this life period, whereas middle-aged adults may realize the unattainability of this wish, recognizing its symbolic and utopian nature.

The Relation between Life Longings and Successful Development

Do life longings have any functional significance for the planning, evaluation, and management of life development and thus contribute to successful development? As discussed previously, life longings are likely more strongly related to indicators of personal growth than to pleasant feelings and hedonism. Why should life longings promote personal growth?

In recent studies, we found that life longings have two important developmental functions (Scheibe, Blanchard-Fields et al., 2009; Scheibe, Freund et al., 2007). Participants with high-level expressions of life longings reported that their life longings (a) provide a general orientation and directionality to development and (b) helped them to regulate losses and incompleteness. With regard to directionality, reflecting on aspects of life that are incomplete on the one hand, and events and experiences that would make life more complete on the other, may guide persons to select and pursue those goals that are most suited to promote a sense of well-being and meaning. In this sense, life longings may function as a vision or overarching goal from which more concrete goals are derived.

Certainly, not every life longing is turned into a goal and pursued actively. The sense of directionality is dependent on the assessment that the targets of life longings are at least partly attainable. Yet, experiences of life longings are assumed to often occur together with experiences of loss or blocked goals, and the insight that not all desirable goals can be realized. Unattainable goals may be transformed into life longings; that is, people can withdraw active efforts at pursuing these goals without relinquishing them completely. At the level of fantasy and imagination, people can nurture something that they have to do without in objective reality. In this sense, life longings may serve as a mechanism of managing conditions of loss, failure, and unattainability. This function of life longings was more strongly endorsed by older adults. Certainly, later stages of life bring more and more threats to the realization of personal goals, as aging is associated with accumulating losses (Baltes & Smith, 2003) and a shortening in remaining lifetime (Lang & Carstensen, 2002). Therefore, using life longings as a strategy to manage loss and unattainability may become increasingly important with advancing age.

Yet, the function of managing nonrealizability is also relevant in younger ages, particularly when persons are confronted with constraints or blocked goals in important, self-defining life domains. We investigated the assumed transformation process from goals to life longings for an important life goal that is shared by many people but cannot be attained by everyone: the goal to have children (Kotter-Gruehn et al., 2009). Middle-aged childless women were assigned to hypothetical stages of the transformation process from goal to life longing. Women who were classified as having passed the transformation process (i.e., they reported a weak goal, but strong life longing to have children) were older and their child wish was less attainable, both subjectively and objectively, than women classified to be before the transition (reporting a strong goal, but weak life longing to have children) or in transition (reporting a strong goal and a strong life longing to have children). These women no longer reported deriving much directionality from their life longing to have children, yet they strongly felt that their life longing helped them to deal with their lack by nurturing fantasies of having a child.

Going one step further, we also investigated the relation of life longings with subjective well-being. It is unlikely that life longings directly translate into high levels of happiness. Having very frequent and intense life longings likely is associated with a high degree of incompleteness of life and the perception that important aspirations were not and never will be reached. This should be particularly true for persons who have low control over their life longings. Indeed, we found that life longings have costs in the hedonic aspect of subjective well-being. Specifically, we found that persons with high-level expressions of life longings reported lower happiness and psychological well-being, more desire for change, and higher negative affectivity (Kotter-Gruehn et al., 2009; Scheibe, Blanchard-Fields et al., 2009; Scheibe, Freund et al., 2007). These negative associations were moderated by the degree to which persons reported a sense of control over the onset, course, and end of life longing–related thoughts and emotions. When a high degree of control was reported, negative correlations reached the range of zero or even positive associations. Among childless women, transforming the blocked goal to have a child into a life longing seemed to be beneficial for well-being when women had high control over the experience of this life longing and when other self-regulation strategies (goal disengagement and reengagement) failed. Such findings reinforce the important role that a sense of control plays in the conduct and evaluation of life (Baltes & Baltes, 1986; Lachman, 2006).

So far, little attention has been paid to the relationship between life longings and personal growth. Here, positive associations can be expected. Life longings entail the imaginary anticipation of highly positive psychological states that surpass the status quo and elicit processes of self-critical reflection about oneself, others, and life in general—hence, they may promote self-insight, creativity, and wisdom. Such links have been suggested in previous theoretical writings on life longings (Boesch, 1998; Hogrebe, 1994; Vogt, 1993). Future research should explore the links between life longings and topics like self-concept complexity, self-insight, creativity, wisdom, and generativity.

Conclusions and Future Directions

In this chapter, we have emphasized that personal development across the life span involves a striving for growth and perfection that occurs within a reality of constraints, losses, and incompleteness (Baltes, 1997; Baltes et al., 2006; Scheibe, Kunzmann, et al., 2007). Reflecting this notion, our goal within a positive psychology has been to understand how gains and losses, the positive and the negative, are interrelated. Adversity and negative life events eventually may facilitate personal growth and presumably positive life events may have negative consequences after all (Aspinwall & Staudinger, 2003). Wisdom and life longings are two concepts that are ideally suited to address these complexities. Both concepts deal with positivity in its most radical form, that is, psychological utopia. At the same time, however, they reflect an awareness that life inherently is incomplete and imperfect. Therefore, wisdom and life longings do not directly promote a hedonic life orientation or sense of happiness. Neither the insight that life is incomplete (wisdom-related knowledge) nor the experience of this incompleteness (life longings) seems to be compatible with feelings of joy, enthusiasm, and happiness. Nevertheless, we argue that they contribute to a meaningful and satisfying life. In this chapter, we first reported supporting evidence for these predictions. Specifically, our findings suggest a positive correlation between wisdom-related knowledge and developmental outcomes reflecting an interest in self-actualization and helping others grow. There is also evidence suggesting that life longings have important developmental functions, including the provision of directionality in life and the management of loss and unattainable personal goals and projects.

One avenue for future research is to study the links between wisdom-related knowledge and life longings on the one hand and multiple developmental outcomes on the other hand more systematically and from a process-oriented perspective. For example, in what ways do the experience of life longings and the availability of wisdom-related knowledge help people deal with concrete life situations characterized by uncertainty and incompleteness so that they will grow themselves and help others grow?

Future research should further examine the possible interplay of life longings and wisdom in promoting positive development. Wisdom-related knowledge about the potentials and constraints of life may help adults develop mature and adaptive forms of life longings. For example, knowledge about the contexts, limits, and uncertainties of life may help to put one's own ongoing subjective experiences in perspective and may make it easier to accept that one cannot have everything in life, that one always has to make choices, thus facilitating more positive feelings toward one's life longings. Vice versa, personally experiencing the potentials and constraints of life may promote the acquisition of more abstract and general wisdom-related knowledge. In other words, dreaming about ideals and highest potentials on the one hand and experiencing the impossibility of their (complete) fulfillment and the limits of life on the other may help persons to acquire knowledge about the potentials, contexts, limits, and uncertainties of life. This type of knowledge does not remain purely theoretical but is connected with emotionally meaningful personal experiences. In fact, several wisdom researchers have argued that wisdom can be acquired only through learning from one's own experiences, not "vicariously" through reading books or through others' instructions (Sternberg, 1998). Given this reciprocal relationship, it is likely that experiencing personally the potentials and constraints of life (life longings) and knowing about the potentials and constraints of life (wisdom) may conjointly foster positive development, particularly personal growth.

Studying concepts such as wisdom and life longings forces us to acknowledge that human nature and life-span development inherently are complex and involve positive and negative aspects that interact in multiple and time-lagged ways. From our point of view, disentangling and understanding this complexity should be at the heart of the field of positive psychology. Approaching this fascinating endeavor from different perspectives and scientific disciplines will eventually lead to a more comprehensive understanding of human life and life-span development.

Questions for the Future

1. How do individuals apply their wisdom-related knowledge to real-life problems requiring complex and consequential decisions?

2. Under which conditions is the experience of incompleteness of life (life longings) beneficial for individuals' development?

3. Can wisdom and life longings, the knowledge and the personal experience of the potentials and constraints of life, conjointly foster positive development, particularly personal growth?

References

Ardelt, M. (2004). Wisdom as expert knowledge system: A critical review of a contemporary operationalization of an ancient concept. *Human Development, 47,* 257–285.

Aspinwall, L. G., & Staudinger, U. M. (2003). A psychology of human strengths: Some central issues of an emerging field. In L. G. Aspinwall & U. M. Staudinger (Eds.), *A psychology of human strengths: Fundamental questions and future directions for a positive psychology* (pp. 9–22). Washington, DC: American Psychological Association.

Assmann, A. (1994). Wholesome knowledge: Concepts of wisdom in a historical and cross-cultural perspective. In D. L. Featherman, R. M. Lerner, & M. Perlmutter (Eds.), *Life-span development and behavior* (Vol. 12, pp. 187–224). Hillsdale, NJ: Erlbaum.

Baltes, M. M., & Baltes, P. B. (1986). *The psychology of control and aging.* Hillsdale, NJ: Lawrence Erlbaum.

Baltes, P. B. (1987). Theoretical propositions of life-span developmental psychology: On the dynamics between growth and decline. *Developmental Psychology, 23,* 611–626.

Baltes, P. B. (1997). On the incomplete architecture of human ontogeny: Selection, optimization, and compensation as foundation of developmental theory. *American Psychologist, 52,* 366–380.

Baltes, P. B. (2004). Wisdom: The orchestration of mind and virtue. Unpublished book. Retrievable at http://www.mpib-berlin.mpg.de/en/institut/dok/full/baltes/orchestr/Wisdom_compl.pdf

Baltes, P. B. (2008). Entwurf einer Lebensspannen-Psychologie der Sehnsucht: Utopie eines vollkommenen und perfekten Lebens [A lifespan psychological approach to the study of Sehnsucht (life longings): Utopia of a perfect and complete life]. *Psychologische Rundschau, 59,* 77–86.

Baltes, P. B., Glück, J., & Kunzmann, U. (2002). Wisdom: Its structure and function in regulating successful life span development. In C. Snyder & S. J. Lopez (Eds.), *Handbook of positive psychology* (pp. 327–347). New York: Oxford University Press.

Baltes, P. B., & Kunzmann, U. (2003). Wisdom: The peak of human excellence in the orchestration of mind and virtue. *The Psychologist, 16,* 131–133.

Baltes, P. B., & Kunzmann, U. (2004). The two faces of wisdom: Wisdom as a general theory of knowledge and judgment about excellence in mind and virtue vs. wisdom as everyday realization in people and products. *Human Development, 47*(5), 290–299.

Baltes, P. B., & Kunzmann, U. (in press). Wisdom and aging: The road toward excellence in mind and character. In D. Park & N. Schwarz (Eds.), *Cognitive aging: A primer*. Philadelphia, PA: Psychology Press.

Baltes, P. B., Lindenberger, U., & Staudinger, U. M. (2006). Life span theory in developmental psychology. In R. M. Lerner (Ed.), *Handbook of child psychology: Vol. 1. Theoretical models of human development* (6th ed., pp. 569–664). Hoboken, NJ: Wiley.

Baltes, P. B., & Mayer, K. U. (1999). *The Berlin aging study: Aging from 70 to 100*. New York: Cambridge University Press.

Baltes, P. B., & Smith, J. (1990). The psychology of wisdom and its ontogenesis. In R. J. Sternberg (Ed.), *Wisdom: Its nature, origins, and development* (pp. 87–120). New York: Cambridge University Press.

Baltes, P. B., & Smith, J. (2003). New frontiers in the future of aging: From successful aging of the young old to the dilemmas of the fourth age. *Gerontology, 49*, 123–135.

Baltes, P. B., & Smith, J. (2008). The fascination of wisdom: Its nature, ontogeny, and function. *Perspectives on Psychological Science, 3*, 56–64.

Baltes, P. B., & Staudinger, U. M. (2000). Wisdom: A metaheuristic (pragmatic) to orchestrate mind and virtue toward excellence. *American Psychologist, 55*, 122–136.

Baltes, P. B., Staudinger, U. M., Maercker, A., & Smith, J. (1995). People nominated as wise: A comparative study of wisdom-related knowledge. *Psychology and Aging, 10*(2), 155–166.

Belk, R. W., Ger, G., & Askegaard, S. (2003). The fire of desire: A multisited inquiry into consumer passion. *Journal of Consumer Research, 30*, 326–351.

Bluck, S., & Habermas, T. (2001). Extending the study of autobiographical memory: Thinking back about life across the life span. *Review of General Psychology, 5*, 135–147.

Boesch, E. E. (1991). *Symbolic action theory and cultural psychology*. New York: Springer.

Boesch, E. E. (1998). *Sehnsucht: Von der Suche nach Glück und Sinn [Longing: About the search for happiness and meaning]*. Bern, Switzerland: Huber.

Böhmig-Krumhaar, S. A., Staudinger, U. M., & Baltes, P. B. (2002). In search of more tolerance: Testing the facilitative effect of a knowledge-activating mnemonic strategy on value relativism. *Zeitschrift für Entwicklungspsychologie und Pädagogische Psychologie, 34*, 30–43.

Brandtstädter, J. (1984). Personal and social control over development: Some implications of an action perspective in life-span developmental psychology. In P. B. Baltes & O. G. Brim Jr. (Eds.), *Life-span development and behavior* (Vol. 6, pp. 1–32). New York: Academic Press.

Brandtstädter, J. (1998). Action perspectives on human development. In R. M. Lerner (Ed.), *Handbook of child psychology: Vol. 1. Theoretical models of human development* (5th ed., pp. 807–863). New York: Wiley.

Brandtstädter, J., & Renner, G. (1990). Tenacious goal pursuit and flexible goal adjustment: Explication and age-related analysis of assimilative and accommodative strategies of coping. *Psychology and Aging, 5*, 58–67.

Clair, J. (Ed.). (2005). *Melancholie: Genie und Wahnsinn in der Kunst [Melancholy: Genius and madness in the arts]*. Ostfildern-Ruit: Hatje Cantz.

Dittmann-Kohli, F., & Baltes, P. B. (1990). Toward a neofunctionalist conception of adult intellectual development: Wisdom as a prototypical case of intellectual growth. In C. Alexander & E. Langer (Eds.), *Higher stages of human development: Perspectives on adult growth* (pp. 54–78). New York: Oxford University Press.

Dixon, R. A., & Baltes, P. B. (1986). Toward life-span research on the functions and pragmatics of intelligence. In R. J. Sternberg & R. K. Wagner (Eds.), *Practical intelligence: Nature and origins of competence in the everyday world* (pp. 203–235). Cambridge: Cambridge University Press.

Ericsson, K. A., & Simon, H. A. (1984). *Protocol analysis: Verbal reports as data*. Cambridge, MA: MIT Press.

Erikson, E. H. (1980). *Identity and the life cycle*. New York: Norton.

Glück, J., & Baltes, P. B. (2006). Using the concept of wisdom to enhance the expression of wisdom knowledge: Not the philosopher's dream but differential effects of developmental preparedness. *Psychology and Aging, 21*, 679–690.

Gough, H. G. (1964). *The California Psychological Inventory*. Palo Alto, CA: Consulting Psychologists.

Grimm, J., & Grimm, W. (1854–1871/1984). *Deutsches Wörterbuch Bd. 1–33. [German dictionary Vols. 1–33]*. Munich, Germany: Deutscher Taschenbuchverlag. (Reprinted from German Dictionary by J. Grimm & W. Grimm, 1854–1871, Leipzig: Hirzel).

Harris, D. B. (Ed.). (1957). *The concept of development*. Minneapolis, MN: University of Minnesota Press.

Heckhausen, J., Dixon, R. A., & Baltes, P. B. (1989). Gains and losses in development throughout adulthood as perceived by different age groups. *Developmental Psychology, 25*, 109–121.

Hogrebe, W. (1994). *Sehnsucht und Erkenntnis: Antrittsvorlesung an der Friedrich-Schiller-Universität Jena am 11.11.1993 [Longing and gaining insight: First lecture at the Friedrich Schiller University Jena on 11 November 1993]*. Erlangen and Jena, Germany: Palm & Enke.

Holm, O. (1999). Analyses of longing: Origins, levels, and dimensions. *Journal of Psychology, 133*, 612–630.

Isaacowitz, D. M., Charles, S. T., & Carstensen, L. L. (2000). Emotion and cognition. In F. I. M. Craik & T. A. Salthouse (Eds.), *The handbook of aging and cognition* (2nd ed., pp. 593–631). Mahwah, NJ: Lawrence Erlbaum.

Kekes, J. (1995). *Moral wisdom and good lives*. Ithaca, NY: Cornell University Press.

Kotter-Gruehn, D., Scheibe, S., Blanchard-Fields, F., & Baltes, P. B. (2009). Developmental emergence and functionality of *Sehnsucht* (life longings): The sample case of involuntary childlessness in middle-aged women. Manuscript submitted for publication.

Kotter-Grühn, D., Wiest, M., Zurek, P. P., & Scheibe, S. (in press). What is it we are longing for? Psychological and demographic factors influencing the contents of Sehnsucht (life longings). *Journal of Research in Personality*.

Kramer, D. A. (2000). Wisdom as a classical source of human strength: Conceptualization and empirical inquiry. *Journal of Social and Clinical Psychology, 19*, 83–101.

Kunzmann, U., & Baltes, P. B. (2003a). Beyond the traditional scope of intelligence: Wisdom in action. In R. J. Sternberg, J. Lautrey, & T. I. Lubart (Eds.), *Models of intelligence: International perspectives* (pp. 329–343). Washington, DC: American Psychological Association.

Kunzmann, U., & Baltes, P. B. (2003b). Wisdom-related knowledge: Affective, motivational, and interpersonal correlates. *Personality and Social Psychology Bulletin, 29*, 1104–1119.

Kunzmann, U., & Baltes, P. B. (2005). The psychology of wisdom: Theoretical and empirical challenges. In R. J. Sternberg & J. Jordan (Eds.), *A handbook of wisdom: Psychological perspectives* (pp. 110–135). New York: Cambridge University Press.

Kunzmann, U., & Stange, A. (2006). Wisdom as a classical human strength: Psychological conceptualizations and empirical inquiry. In A. D. Ong & M. Van Dulmen (Eds.), *Varieties of positive experience: Structure, variability, and change* (pp. 306–322). New York: Oxford University Press.

Kunzmann, U., Stange, A., & Jordan, J. (2005). Positive affectivity and lifestyle in adulthood: Do you do what you feel? *Personality and Social Psychology Bulletin, 31,* 574–588.

Labouvie-Vief, G. (1981). Proactive and reactive aspects of constructivism: Growth and aging in life-span perspective. In R. M. Lerner & N. A. Busch-Rossnagel (Eds.), *Individuals as producers of their development: A life-span perspective* (pp. 197–230). New York: Academic Press.

Labouvie-Vief, G. (1990). Wisdom as integrated thought: Historical and developmental perspectives. In R. J. Sternberg (Ed.), *Wisdom: Its nature, origins, and development* (pp. 52–83). New York: Cambridge University Press.

Labouvie-Vief, G., & Medler, M. (2002). Affect optimization and affect complexity: Modes and styles of regulation in adulthood. *Psychology and Aging, 17,* 571–588.

Lachman, M. E. (2006). Perceived control over aging-related declines: Adaptive beliefs and behaviors. *Current Directions in Psychological Science, 15,* 282–286.

Lachman, M. E., & Weaver, S. L. (1998). Sociodemographic variations in the sense of control by domain: Findings from the MacArthur studies of midlife. *Psychology and Aging, 13,* 553–562.

Lang, F. R., & Carstensen, L. L. (2002). Time counts: Future time perspective, goals, and social relationships. *Psychology and Aging, 17,* 125–139.

Lerner, R. M. (2002). *Concepts and theories of human development.* Mahwah, NJ: Erlbaum.

Mayser, S., Scheibe, S., & Riediger, M. (2008). (Un)reachable? An empirical differentiation of goals and life-longings. *European Psychologist, 13,* 126–140.

McCrae, R. R., Costa, P. T., Jr., Ostendorf, F., Angleitner, A., Hrebickova, M., Avia, M. D., et al. (2000). Nature over nurture: Temperament, personality, and life span development. *Journal of Personality and Social Psychology, 78,* 173–186.

McGregor, I., & Little, B. R. (1998). Personal projects, happiness, and meaning: On doing well and being yourself. *Journal of Personality and Social Psychology, 74,* 494–512.

Palaian, S. K. (1993). The experience of longing: A phenomenological investigation (emotion, desires) (Doctoral dissertation, The Union Institute, 1993). *Dissertation Abstracts International, 54,* 1678B.

Pasupathi, M., Staudinger, U. M., & Baltes, P. B. (2001). Seeds of wisdom: Adolescents' knowledge and judgment about difficult life problems. *Developmental Psychology, 37,* 351–361.

Ravicz, L. (1998). The experience of longing (desire, yearning) (Doctoral dissertation, University of Tennessee, Knoxville, 1998). *Dissertation Abstracts International, 60,* 2958B.

Ryff, C. D. (1991). Possible selves in adulthood and old age: A tale of shifting horizons. *Psychology and Aging, 6,* 286–295.

Schaie, K. (2005). *Developmental influences on adult intelligence: The Seattle longitudinal study.* New York: Oxford University Press.

Scheibe, S., Blanchard-Fields, F., Wiest, M., & Freund, A. (2009). Longing for optimal (utopian) states of life in Germany and the United States: A cross-cultural study on *Sehnsucht* (life longings). Manuscript submitted for publication.

Scheibe, S., Freund, A. M., & Baltes, P. B. (2007). Toward a developmental psychology of *Sehnsucht* (life longings): The optimal (utopian) life. *Developmental Psychology, 43,* 778–795.

Scheibe, S., Freund, A. M., & Blanchard-Fields, F. (2009). What is new about *Sehnsucht*? Differentiating Sehnsucht (life longings) from goals, the ideal self, and regret in laypersons'

conceptions and personal experience. Manuscript submitted for publication.

Scheibe, S., Kunzmann, U., & Baltes, P. B. (2007). Wisdom, life longings, and optimal development. In J. A. Blackburn & C. N. Dulmus (Eds.), *Handbook of Gerontology: Evidence-based approaches to theory, practice, and policy* (pp. 117–142). Hoboken, NJ: Wiley.

Seligman, M. E. P., & Csikszentmihalyi, M. (2000). Positive psychology: An introduction. *American Psychologist, 55,* 5–14.

Stange, A., & Kunzmann, U. (2008). Fostering wisdom: A psychological perspective. In M. Ferrari & G. Potworowski (Eds.), *Fostering wisdom* (pp. 171–185). New York, NY: Springer.

Staudinger, U. M. (1999a). Social cognition and a psychological approach to an art of life. In F. Blanchard-Fields & B. T. Hess (Eds.), *Social cognition and aging* (pp. 343–375). New York: Academic Press.

Staudinger, U. M. (1999b). Older and wiser? Integrating results on the relationship between age and wisdom-related performance. *International Journal of Behavioral Development, 23,* 641–664.

Staudinger, U. M. (2001). Life reflection: A social-cognitive analysis of life review. *Review of General Psychology, 5,* 91–99.

Staudinger, U. M. (2008). A psychology of wisdom: History and recent developments. *Research in Human Development, 5,* 107–120.

Staudinger, U. M., & Baltes, P. B. (1996). Interactive minds: A facilitative setting for wisdom-related performance? *Journal of Personality and Social Psychology, 71,* 746–762.

Staudinger, U. M., Lopez, D. F., & Baltes, P. B. (1997). The psychometric location of wisdom-related performance: Intelligence, personality, and more? *Personality and Social Psychology Bulletin, 23,* 1200–1214.

Staudinger, U. M., Maciel, A., Smith, J., & Baltes, P. B. (1998). What predicts wisdom-related performance? A first look at personality, intelligence, and facilitative experiential contexts. *European Journal of Personality, 12*(1), 1–17.

Staudinger, U. M., Smith, J., & Baltes, P. B. (1992). Wisdom-related knowledge in a life review task: Age differences and the role of professional specialization. *Psychology and Aging, 7,* 271–281.

Sternberg, R. J. (Ed.). (1990). *Wisdom: Its nature, origins, and development.* New York: Cambridge University Press.

Sternberg, R. J. (1997). *Thinking styles.* New York: Cambridge University Press.

Sternberg, R. J. (1998). A balance theory of wisdom. *Review of General Psychology, 2,* 347–365.

Sternberg, R. J. (2001). Why schools should teach for wisdom: The balance theory of wisdom in educational settings. *Educational Psychologist, 36,* 227–245.

Tetens, J. N. (1777). *Philosophische Versuche über die menschliche Natur und ihre Entwicklung [Philosophical essays on human nature and its development].* Leipzig, Germany: Weidmanns Erben und Reich.

Vogt, M. C. (1993). Der anthropologische Zusammenhang zwischen Sehnsucht und Sucht [The anthropological relationship between longing and addiction]. Unpublished doctoral dissertation, University of Zurich, Zurich, Switzerland.

Vosskamp, W. (2004). *Ein anderes Selbst: Bild und Bildung im deutschen Roman des 18. und 19. Jahrhunderts [The other self].* Göttingen, Germany: Wallstein.

Wink, P., & Helson, R. (1997). Practical and transcendent wisdom: Their nature and some longitudinal findings. *Journal of Adult Development, 4,* 1–15.

PART 4

Emotional Approaches

Subjective Well-Being: The Science of Happiness and Life Satisfaction

Ed Diener, Shigehiro Oishi, *and* Richard E. Lucas

Abstract

This chapter reviews the scientific research on subjective well-being. Subjective well-being consists of a person's cognitive and affective evaluations of his or her life. First, the authors will provide a brief historical review of research on subjective well-being. Second, they will summarize the main measurement issues (e.g., the validity of self-reports, memory bias). Third, they will present the major theoretical approaches to this area of research (e.g., need and goal satisfaction theories, process or activity theories, genetic and personality predisposition theories). Finally, the authors will review current findings (e.g., hedonic adaptation, the effect of intervention, cultural variation) and suggest future directions for the study of subjective well-being.

Keywords: happiness, life satisfaction, positive psychology, subjective well-being

Scientists who study subjective well-being assume that an essential ingredient of a good life is that the person herself likes her life. Subjective well-being is defined as a person's cognitive and affective evaluations of his or her life as a whole. These evaluations include emotional reactions to events as well as cognitive judgments of satisfaction and fulfillment. Thus, subjective well-being is a broad concept that includes experiencing high levels of pleasant emotions and moods, low levels of negative emotions and moods, and high life satisfaction.

History of Subjective Well-Being Research

Throughout history, philosophers and religious leaders have suggested that diverse characteristics such as love, wisdom, and nonattachment are the cardinal elements of a fulfilled existence (see McMahon, 2006, for review). Utilitarians such as Jeremy Bentham, however, argued that the presence of pleasure and the absence of pain are the defining characteristics of a good life (1789/1948). Thus, the utilitarians were the intellectual forerunners of

subjective well-being researchers, focusing on the emotional, mental, and physical pleasures and pain that individuals experience. Although there are other desirable personal characteristics beyond whether a person is happy (Ryan & Deci, 2001; Ryff & Singer, 1998), the individual with abundant joy has one key ingredient of a good life.

Early in the twentieth century, empirical studies of subjective well-being began to take shape. As early as 1925, Flugel studied moods by having people record their emotional events and then summing their emotional reactions across moments. Flugel's work was the forerunner of modern experience sampling approaches to measuring subjective well-being online as people go about their everyday lives. After World War II, survey researchers began polling people about their happiness and life satisfaction using simple global survey questionnaires. The pollsters studied large numbers of people who were often selected to produce representative samples of nations. George Gallup, Gerald Gurin and his colleagues, and Hadley Cantril pioneered the use of large-scale surveys as an assessment technique.

They asked people questions such as, "How happy are you?" with simple response options varying from "very happy" to "not very happy."

Although early subjective well-being studies were characterized by very short scales, many important discoveries were made. In 1969, for example, Norman Bradburn showed that pleasant and unpleasant affects are somewhat independent and have different correlates—they are not simply opposites of one another. Thus, the two affects must be studied separately to gain a complete picture of individuals' well-being. This finding had important implications for the field of subjective well-being: it showed that clinical psychology's attempts to eliminate negative states would not necessarily foster positive states. The elimination of pain may not result in a corresponding increase in pleasure; ridding the world of sadness and anxiety will not necessarily make it a happy place.

Wilson reviewed the relatively small amount of research on "avowed happiness" in 1967, and Diener (1984) provided a review of the much larger database on subjective well-being that had accumulated by the mid-1980s. By that time, the field was becoming a science (Diener, 1984). Since Diener's review was published, a number of books have appeared on the topic of subjective well-being (e.g., Argyle, 2001; Myers, 1992; Strack, Argyle, & Schwarz, 1991), and Diener, Suh, Lucas, and Smith authored a new *Psychological Bulletin* review of the literature in 1999. In 2005, Lyubomirsky, King, and Diener published another *Psychological Bulletin* reviewing the consequences of happiness. Two handbooks related to subjective well-being (Eid & Larsen, 2008; Kahneman, Diener, & Schwarz, 1999), a book (Diener & Suh, 2000), and an *Annual Review of Psychology* article dedicated to cross-cultural differences (Diener, Oishi, & Lucas, 2003) also provide more thorough reviews of this area. The scientific discipline of subjective well-being has grown rapidly since the mid-1980s. One major reason for this is that researchers succeeded in developing scientific methods for studying subjective well-being.

Measurement of Subjective Well-Being

Early survey instruments usually posed a single question about people's happiness or life satisfaction. As the field matured, more multi-item scales appeared, with greater reliability and validity than the single-item instruments. Lucas, Diener, and Suh (1996) demonstrated that multi-item life satisfaction, pleasant affect, and unpleasant affect scales formed factors that were separable from each other, as well as from other constructs such as self-esteem. A number of happiness, affect, and life satisfaction measures are now available, and we present the five-item Satisfaction With Life Scale (Diener, Emmons, Larsen, & Griffin, 1985; Pavot & Diener, 1993) in the appendix.

A major concern of researchers in the field is whether self-report instruments are valid. After all, people might report that they are happy but not truly experience high subjective well-being. Sandvik, Diener, and Seidlitz (1993) found that self-report measures converge with other types of assessment including expert ratings based on interviews with respondents, experience sampling measures in which feelings are reported at random moments in everyday life, participant's memory for positive versus negative events in their lives, the reports of family and friends, and smiling. However, global judgments of life satisfaction do not faithfully correspond to the average mood or level of satisfaction experienced across many different moments or domains because these judgments are likely to be influenced by a person's current mood, his or her beliefs about happiness, and the ease of retrieving positive and negative information (Kahneman, Krueger, Schkade, Schwarz, & Stone, 2004, for suggestions regarding solutions to these problems; Robinson & Clore, 2002; Schwarz & Strack, 1999, for review). Thus, additional assessment devices based on memory, informant reports, and experience sampling are likely to supplement the information obtained from global measures (Schimmack, 2003; Scollon, Kim-Prieto, & Diener, 2003). In some cases the alternative measures may yield different answers about who is happiest (e.g., Diener & Suh, 1999, Table 22.1; Oishi, 2002; Riis, Loewenstein, & Baron, 2005).

Although global reports are more vulnerable to judgmental biases than online reports, global reports of well-being are still valuable because (a) they offer insight into the fascinating psychological processes by which people construct global judgments about their lives, and (b) they often predict future decisions (Wirtz, Kruger, Scollon, & Diener, 2003) and important life outcomes, such as relationship stability (Oishi & Sullivan, 2006), better than momentary reports of well-being. In global reports we also discover how a person summarizes his or her life as a whole, and this synopsis captures each person's values and individuality. Indeed, there are systematic individual and cultural differences in the type of information individuals use when making life satisfaction judgments. For instance, achievement-oriented individuals judge their life satisfaction based largely on their success in achievement domains (Oishi, Diener, Suh, & Lucas, 1999), whereas sensation seekers judge their life satisfaction based on how much excitement they have in life (Oishi, Schimmack, & Colcombe, 2003). Furthermore, chronically happy people tend to report being very satisfied with a global domain such as education, even when they are only mildly satisfied with the corresponding, specific domains such as textbooks and lectures. Interestingly, this positivity bias (i.e., tendency to evaluate global domains more positively than the corresponding specific domains) is particularly strong among Puerto Ricans and Columbians and particularly weak among Japanese, Koreans, and Chinese (Diener, Scollon, Oishi, Dzokoto, & Suh, 2000). Thus, global reports of life satisfaction are not the arithmetic average of various life domains or moments, but they reflect an individual's satisfaction with personally important domains of life and their interpretation of overall life. In a sense then, these are two varieties of happiness and satisfaction—evaluations of specific aspects of life and online at-the-moment feelings of well-being versus larger, global judgments about one's happiness and satisfaction (Kim-Prieto, Diener, Tamir, Scollon, & Diener, 2005).

Theoretical Approach to Subjective Well-Being

Many theories of happiness have been proposed since Aristotle's insights. These theories can be categorized into three groups: (a) need and goal satisfaction theories; (b) process or activity theories; and (c) genetic and personality predisposition theories. The first constellation of theories centers on the idea that the reduction of tensions (e.g., the elimination of pain and the satisfaction of biological and psychological needs) leads to happiness. Freud's (1933) pleasure principle and Maslow's (1970) hierarchical needs model represent this approach. In support of this view, Sheldon, Elliot, Kim, and Kasser (2001) found that the degree to which individuals' needs were met was positively associated with the degree of their life satisfaction.

Whereas need satisfaction theorists assume that the satisfaction of basic needs will result in happiness, activity theorists maintain that engagement in an activity itself provides happiness. Most notably, Csikszentmihalyi (1975) suggested that people are happiest when they are engaged in interesting activities that match their level of skill. He called the state of mind that results from this matching of challenges and skill "flow," and he argued that people who often experience flow tend to be very happy. Goal researchers (e.g., Brunstein, 1993; Emmons, 1986) agree that having important goals and making progress toward goals are reliable indicators of well-being, and therefore goal theories can combine the elements of need satisfaction and pleasurable activity in explaining subjective well-being.

Both needs theorists and activity theorists argue that subjective well-being will change as individuals approach their goals or engage in interesting activities. By contrast, trait theorists argue that there is an element of stability in people's levels of well-being that cannot be explained by the stability of the conditions of people's lives, and that subjective well-being is strongly influenced by stable personality dispositions. For instance, Diener, Sandvik, Seidlitz, and Diener (1993) found that stability in subjective well-being was comparable among people whose income went up, went down, or stayed the same over 10 years. Similarly, Costa, McCrae, and Zonderman (1987) reported that the life satisfaction of people who experienced major life changes was as stable as the life satisfaction of people who lived in stable circumstances (see Schimmack & Oishi, 2005, for a meta-analysis on stability). These results have led some theorists to suggest that although life events can influence subjective well-being, people eventually adapt to these changes and return to biologically determined "set-points" or "adaptation-levels" (e.g., Headey & Wearing, 1992).

One reason for the stability of subjective well-being is that there is a substantial genetic component to it; to some degree people are born prone to being happy or unhappy. For example, Tellegen et al. (1988) examined monozygotic twins who were reared apart and compared them to dizygotic twins who were also reared apart, as well as to monozygotic and dizygotic twins who were raised together. After comparing the similarities of the various types of twins, Tellegen et al. estimated that 40% of the variability in positive emotionality and 55% of the variability in negative emotionality could be predicted by genetic variation (see also Stubbe, Posthuma, Boomsma, & De Geus, 2005). These estimates allow for environmental influences (as shown by Scollon & Diener, 2006), but genes do appear to influence characteristic emotional responses to life circumstances.

When one examines personality influences in more detail, the traits that are most consistently linked to subjective well-being are extraversion and neuroticism (Diener & Lucas, 1999). In particular, one specific facet of extraversion, cheerfulness, and one specific facet of neuroticism, depression, explain individual differences in life satisfaction more than global traits of extraversion and neuroticism as a whole (Schimmack, Oishi, Furr, & Funder, 2004).

Differences in subjective well-being also result from stable individual differences in how people think about the world. Differences in the accessibility of pleasant versus unpleasant information, as well as the accuracy and efficiency with which people process pleasant versus unpleasant information influence subjective well-being (Robinson & Kirkeby, 2005; Robinson, Vargas, Tamir, & Solberg, 2004). Happy people attend to and recall the pleasant aspects of life more than others (Tamir & Robinson, 2007). Also, happy people tend to use broad, abstract criteria in judging their own lives, whereas unhappy people tend to use concrete criteria (Updegraff & Suh, 2007). Similarly, certain cognitive dispositions such as hope (Snyder et al., 1991) and optimism (e.g., Scheier & Carver, 1993) appear to influence subjective well-being. It is not just who we are that matters to happiness, but how we think about our lives.

Current Subjective Well-Being Findings
Demographic Correlates of Subjective Well-Being

Income is consistently related to subjective well-being in both within-nation (e.g., Diener et al., 1993) and between-nation analyses (e.g., Diener et al., 1993). However, at both the individual and national level, income changes over time seem to have little net effect on subjective well-being (Diener & Suh, 1998; Diener et al., 1993; see however Veenhoven & Hagerty, 2006). Goals and expectations must be taken into account to understand the relation between income and subjective well-being; the benefits of a rising income are offset if one's material desires increase even faster than wealth (Solberg, Diener, Wirtz, Lucas, & Oishi, 2002).

Age is also related to subjective well-being, but the effects are small and depend on the component of subjective well-being being measured (see Mroczek, 2001, for review). For example, in an international sample of 40 nations, Diener and Suh (1998) found that although pleasant affect declined across age cohorts, life satisfaction and unpleasant affect showed little change. Marital status is also correlated with subjective well-being, but the effects

of marriage can differ for men and women. Furthermore, in a large-scale longitudinal study Lucas, Clark, Georgellis, and Diener (2003) found that marriage did not lead to lasting changes in happiness. Moreover, there was a selection bias (personality effect) such that those who would eventually marry were happier than those who would not even long before the marriage occurred. Thus, the underlying mechanisms linking various demographic variables and subjective well-being need to be clarified in the future.

Hedonic Adaptation

Since Brickman, Coates, and Janoff-Bulman's (1978) famous study that compared lottery winners to patients with spinal cord injuries, many have come to believe that human beings can and do adapt to many life events, and that life events do not have a significant long-term effect on one's well-being. Recently, however, this interpretation has been challenged (see Lucas, 2007a; Veenhoven, 1991, for reviews). Large-scale longitudinal projects revealed that people do not adapt to drastic changes in life circumstances such as becoming disabled (Lucas, 2007b), divorced (Lucas et al., 2003), or unemployed (Lucas, Clark, Georgellis, & Diener, 2004). Namely, many unfortunate individuals who experience these radical changes in life circumstances do not return to their pre-incidence level of happiness, and, therefore, the concept of a "setpoint" should not be deemed fixed (Diener, Lucas, & Scollon, 2006). Thus, despite the strong association between temperament and subjective well-being, life events and circumstances do matter to one's subjective well-being.

Besides the large longitudinal studies mentioned previously, Wilson, Gilbert, and their colleagues (Wilson, Centerbar, Kermer, & Gilbert, 2005) have begun exploring the underlying mechanisms of hedonic adaptations, using an experimental method. For instance, these researchers have shown that providing an explanation for a positive event sped up hedonic adaptation to the event. In other words, when a positive event occurred, an individual would feel happy for a longer period of time if he or she did not find out why this event happened. The effort to alter hedonic adaptation has just begun. Clearly, the scientific investigation into how to prevent hedonic adaptation to a positive event is an exciting research agenda and will likely make an important contribution to subjective well-being research and positive psychology in the future.

The Effect of Interventions

Fordyce (1977, 1983) created an intervention program based on the idea that people's subjective well-being can be increased if they learn to imitate the traits of happy people, such as being organized, keeping busy, spending more time socializing, developing a positive outlook, and working on a healthy personality. Fordyce found that the program produced increases in happiness compared to a placebo control, as well as compared to participants in conditions receiving only partial information. Most impressive, he found lasting effects of the intervention in follow-up evaluations 9–28 months after the study.

Recently, a number of additional effective interventions on happiness have been reported, ranging from kindness interventions (Otake, Shimai, Tanaka-Matsumi, Otsui, & Fredrickson, 2006) and gratitude interventions (Emmons & McCullough, 2003) to variants of the writing intervention (King, 2001; Lyubomirsky, Sousa, & Dickerhoof, 2006). Recent intervention studies are clearly promising. However, more diverse dependent variables and measuring instruments would be desirable, as well as explorations of which interventions are most beneficial, and why (see Seligman, Steen, Park, & Peterson, 2005, for an excellent starting point in this direction).

Objective Consequences of Subjective Well-Being

Lyubomirsky, King, and Diener (2005) recently summarized over 200 articles that studied the outcomes of happiness, and they found that by and large, happiness assessed at one point was associated with positive outcomes later. For instance, cheerful people were making more money decades later than less cheerful people. Moreover, happy people were more likely to be in a stable romantic relationship than less happy people a decade later. In a meta-analysis, Pressman and Cohen (2005) also showed many benefits of positive affect on health (e.g., fewer symptoms, less pain, better pulmonary function).

The relationship between level of happiness and important life outcomes is, however, not always linear. For instance, the highest levels of educational achievement and income were obtained by moderately happy people, not by the happiest people (Oishi, Diener, & Lucas, 2007). Thus, the optimal level of happiness is not the highest possible level, but the moderate level of happiness, at least in terms of educational and vocational achievement. Interestingly, however, the happiest people did best when it came to romantic relationships.

Culture and Subjective Well-Being

In recent years, cultural differences in subjective well-being have been explored, with the realization that there are profound differences in what makes people happy (see Diener et al., 2003; Suh & Koo, 2008, for review). For example, self-esteem and consistency in self-perception are less strongly associated with life satisfaction in collectivistic cultures than in individualistic cultures (Diener & Diener, 1995; Suh, 2002). In contrast, relationship harmony and social support are more strongly associated with life satisfaction in collectivistic cultures than in individualistic cultures (Kwan, Bond, & Singelis, 1997). Similarly, interpersonally engaging emotions are more strongly associated with happiness in Japan than in the United States, whereas interpersonally disengaging emotions (e.g., pride) are more strongly associated with happiness in the United States than in Japan (Kitayama, Mesquita, & Karasawa, 2006). Also, interpersonal contexts (e.g., being alone vs. being with friends) have a stronger impact on the affective experiences of Japanese and Indians than on those of Americans (Oishi, Diener, Scollon, & Biswas-Diener, 2004). Several theorists have recently proposed various mediators for cultural differences in the mean levels of happiness, such as wealth, justice, and trust (Tov & Diener, 2008), lay beliefs about happiness (e.g., there is a limited amount of happiness one can feel in life; Suh & Koo, 2008), and specificity of judgment criteria (e.g., "getting an A" vs. "doing well"; Oishi & Sullivan, 2005; Updegraff & Suh, 2007).

Future Research

It is still unclear to what extent individual and cultural differences found in global reports are accurate reflections of differences in online experiences or are manifestations of processes related to the global way people see themselves (Oishi, 2002; Scollon, Diener, Oishi, & Biswas-Diener, 2004, for an initial effort). Thus, it is first important to increase our understanding of what each type of well-being measure reflects and to develop reliable and valid non-self-report measures (e.g., biological and cognitive measures) of well-being in the future (c.f. Ryff et al., 2006). Second, more attention should be paid to developmental processes. In particular, gene–environment interaction needs to be spelled out in the future to advance our understanding of "when" and "to whom" a particular life event has a lasting impact (e.g., Caspi et al., 2003). Third, a longitudinal approach should be taken in an investigation of society and culture. Specifically, the way in which changes in macro systems (e.g., political, economic, and cultural) have an impact on people's well-being should be examined more carefully to create the happy societies Bentham and others envisioned.

In conclusion, the science of subjective well-being is now thriving. Although the happy person is more likely to be from a wealthy nation and to have enough resources to pursue his or her particular goals, characteristics such as a positive outlook, meaningful goals, close social relationships, and a temperament characterized by low worry are very important to high subjective well-being. We look forward to the day when effective interventions based on scientific findings will provide a readily available way to increase happiness.

Three Questions about the Future of Subjective Well-Being Research

1. When is happiness helpful to effective functioning and when it is not? And in what circumstances and cultures is happiness helpful?

2. Will there be development of the measure of subjective well-being that is superior to existing self-reports both in terms of psychometric properties and time efficiency?

3. To what extent will molecular genetics of subjective well-being be discovered and conceptually linked to individual- (e.g., personality), interpersonal- (e.g., marriage), and societal- (e.g., culture, political system) level phenomena?

References and Recommended Readings*

*Works that provide a good overview of the field for those new to the area.

*Argyle, M. (2001). *The psychology of happiness*. New York: Taylor & Francis.

Bentham, J. (1789/1948). *Introduction to the principles and morals of legislation*. London: University of London Athlone Press.

Bradburn, N. M. (1969). *The structure of psychological well-being*. Chicago: Aldine.

Brickman, P., Coates, D., & Janoff-Bulman, R. (1978). Lottery winners and accident victims: Is happiness relative? *Journal of Personality and Social Psychology, 36*, 917–927.

Brunstein, J. (1993). Personal goals and subjective well-being: A longitudinal study. *Journal of Personality and Social Psychology, 65*, 1061–1070.

Caspi, A., Sugden, K., Moffitt, T. E., Taylor, A., Craig, I. W., Harrington, H., et al. (2003). Influence of life stress on depression: Moderation by a polymorphism in the 5-HTT gene. *Science, 201*, 386–389.

Costa, P. T., Jr., McCrae, R. R., & Zonderman, A. (1987). Environmental and dispositional influences on well-being: Longitudinal follow-up of an American national sample. *British Journal of Psychology, 78*, 299–306.

Csikszentmihalyi, M. (1975). *Beyond boredom and anxiety*. San Francisco: Jossey-Bass.

*Diener, E. (1984). Subjective well-being. *Psychological Bulletin, 93*, 542–575.

Diener, E., & Diener, M. (1995). Cross-cultural correlates of life satisfaction and self-esteem. *Journal of Personality and Social Psychology, 68*, 653–663.

Diener, E., Emmons, R. A., Larsen, R. J., & Griffin, S. (1985). The satisfaction with life scale. *Journal of Personality Assessment, 49*, 71–75.

Diener, E., & Lucas, R. E. (1999). Personality and subjective well-being. In D. Kahneman, E. Diener, & N. Schwarz (Eds.), *Well-being: The foundations of hedonic psychology* (pp. 213–229). New York: Russell Sage Foundation.

Diener, E., Lucas, R. E., & Scollon, C. N. (2006). Beyond the hedonic treadmill: Revising the adaptation theory of well-being. *American Psychologist, 61*, 305–314.

Diener, E., Oishi, S., & Lucas, R. E. (2003). Culture, personality, and well-being. *Annual Review of Psychology, 54*, 403–425.

Diener, E., Sandvik, E., Seidlitz, L., & Diener, M. (1993). The relationship between income and subjective well-being: Relative or absolute? *Social Indicators Research, 28*, 195–223.

Diener, E., Scollon, C. N., Oishi, S., Dzokoto, V., & Suh, E. M. (2000). Positivity and the construction of life satisfaction judgments: Global happiness is not the sum of its parts. *Journal of Happiness Studies, 1*, 159–176.

Diener, E., & Suh, E. M. (1998). Subjective well-being and age: An international analysis. In K. W. Schaie & M. P. Lawton (Eds.), *Annual Review of Gerontology and Geriatrics* (Vol. 17, pp. 304–324). New York: Springer.

Diener, E., & Suh, E. M. (1999). National differences in subjective well-being. In D. Kahneman, E. Diener, & N. Schwarz (Eds.), *Well-being: The foundations of hedonic psychology* (pp. 434–450). New York: Russell Sage Foundation.

*Diener, E., & Suh, E. M. (Eds.). (2000). *Subjective well-being across cultures*. Cambridge, MA: The MIT Press.

*Diener, E., Suh, E., Lucas, R., & Smith, H. (1999). Subjective well-being: Three decades of progress. *Psychological Bulletin, 125*, 276–302.

Eid, M., & Larsen, R. J. (2008). *The science of subjective well-being*. New York: Guilford.

Emmons, R. A. (1986). Personal strivings: An approach to personality and subjective well-being. *Journal of Personality and Social Psychology, 51*, 1058–1068.

Emmons, R. A., & McCullough, M. E. (2003). Counting blessing versus burdens: An experimental investigation of gratitude and subjective well-being in daily life. *Journal of Personality and Social Psychology, 84*, 377–389.

Flugel, J. C. (1925). A quantitative study of feeling and emotion in everyday life. *British Journal of Psychology, 9*, 318–355.

Fordyce, M. W. (1977). Development of a program to increase personal happiness. *Journal of Counseling Psychology, 24*, 511–520.

Fordyce, M. W. (1983). A program to increase happiness: Further studies. *Journal of Counseling Psychology, 30*, 483–498.

Freud, S. (1933/1976). New introductory lectures on psychoanalysis. In J. Strachey (Ed. & Trans.), *The complete psychological works* (Vol. 16). New York: Norton.

Headey, B., & Wearing, A. (1992). *Understanding happiness: A theory of subjective well-being*. Melbourne: Longman Cheshire.

*Kahneman, D., Diener, E., & Schwarz, N. (Eds.). (1999). *Well-being: The foundations of hedonic psychology*. New York: Russell Sage Foundation.

Kahneman, D., Krueger, A. B., Schkade, D. A., Schwarz, N., & Stone, A. A. (2004). A survey method for characterizing daily life experience: The day reconstruction method. *Science, 306,* 1776–1780.

Kim-Prieto, C., Diener, E., Tamir, M., Scollon, C., & Diener, M. (2005). Integrating the diverse definitions of happiness: A time-sequential framework of subjective well-being. *Journal of Happiness Studies, 6,* 261–300.

King, L. A. (2001). The health benefits of writing about life goals. *Personality and Social Psychology Bulletin, 27,* 798–807.

Kitayama, S., Mesquita, B., & Karasawa, M. (2006). Cultural affordances and emotional experience: Socially engaging and disengaging emotions in Japan and the United States. *Journal of Personality and Social Psychology, 91,* 890–903.

Kwan, V. S. Y., Bond, M. H., & Singelis, T. M. (1997). Pancultural explanations for life satisfaction: Adding relationship harmony to self-esteem. *Journal of Personality and Social Psychology, 73,* 1038–1051.

Lucas, R. E. (2007a). Adaptation and the set-point model of subjective well-being: Does happiness change after major life events? *Current Directions in Psychological Science, 16,* 75–79.

Lucas, R. E. (2007b). Long-term disability is associated with lasting changes in subjective well-being: Evidence from two nationally representative longitudinal studies. *Journal of Personality and Social Psychology, 92,* 717–730.

Lucas, R. E., Clark, A. E., Georgellis, Y., & Diener, E. (2003). Reexamining adaptation and the set point model of happiness: Reactions to changes in marital status. *Journal of Personality and Social Psychology, 84,* 527–539.

Lucas, R. E., Clark, A. E., Georgellis, Y., & Diener, E. (2004). Unemployment alters the set point for life satisfaction. *Psychological Science, 15,* 8–13.

Lucas, R. E., Diener, E., & Suh, E. (1996). Discriminant validity of well-being measures. *Journal of Personality and Social Psychology, 71,* 616–628.

Lyubomirsky, S., King, L., & Diener, E. (2005). The benefits of frequent positive affect: Does happiness lead to success? *Psychological Bulletin, 131,* 803–855.

Lyubomirsky, S., Sousa, L., & Dickerhoof, R. (2006). The costs and benefits of writing, talking, and thinking about life's triumphs and defeats. *Journal of Personality and Social Psychology, 90,* 692–708.

McMahon, D. M. (2006). *Happiness: A history.* New York: Atlantic Monthly Press.

Maslow, A. H. (1970). *Motivation and personality.* New York: Harper & Row.

Mroczek, D. K. (2001). Age and emotion in adulthood. *Current Directions in Psychological Science, 10,* 87–90.

*Myers, D. G. (1992). *The pursuit of happiness: Who is happy and why.* New York: William Morrow.

Oishi, S. (2002). Experiencing and remembering of well-being: A cross-cultural analysis. *Personality and Social Psychology Bulletin, 28,* 1398–1406.

Oishi, S., Diener, E., & Lucas, R. E. (2007). The optimal level of well-being: Can we be too happy? *Perspectives on Psychological Science, 2,* 346–360.

Oishi, S., Diener, E., Scollon, C. N., & Biswas-Diener, R. (2004). Cross-situational consistency of affective experiences across cultures. *Journal of Personality and Social Psychology, 86,* 460–472.

Oishi, S., Diener, E., Suh, E., & Lucas, R. E. (1999). Value as a moderator in subjective well-being. *Journal of Personality, 67,* 157–184.

Oishi, S., Schimmack, U., & Colcombe, S. (2003). The contextual and systematic nature of life satisfaction judgments. *Journal of Experimental Social Psychology, 39,* 232–247.

Oishi, S., & Sullivan, H. (2005). The mediating role of parental expectations in culture and well-being. *Journal of Personality, 73,* 1267–1294.

Oishi, S., & Sullivan, H. W. (2006). The predictive value of daily vs. retrospective well-being judgments in relationship stability. *Journal of Experimental Social Psychology, 42,* 460–470.

Otake, K., Shimai, S., Tanaka-Matsumi, J., Otsui, K., & Fredrickson, B. L. (2006). Happy people become happier through kindness: A counting kindnesses intervention. *Journal of Happiness Studies, 7,* 361–375.

Pavot, W., & Diener, E. (1993). Review of the satisfaction with life scale. *Psychological Assessment, 5,* 164–172.

Pressman, S. D., & Cohen, S. (2005). Does positive affect influence health? *Psychological Bulletin, 131,* 925–971.

Riis, J., Loewenstein, G., & Baron, J. (2005). Ignorance of hedonic adaptation to hemodialysis: A study using ecological momentary assessment. *Journal of Experimental Psychology: General, 134,* 3–9.

Robinson, M. D., & Clore, G. L. (2002). Belief and feeling: Evidence for an accessibility model of emotional self-report. *Psychological Bulletin, 128,* 934–960.

Robinson, M. D., & Kirkeby, B. S. (2005). Happiness as a belief system: Individual differences and priming in emotion judgments. *Personality and Social Psychology Bulletin, 31,* 1134–1144.

Robinson, M. D., Vargas, P. T., Tamir, M., & Solberg, E. C. (2004). Using and being used by categories: The case of negative evaluations and daily well-being. *Psychological Science, 15,* 521–526.

Ryan, R. M., & Deci, E. L. (2001). On happiness and human potentials: A review of research on hedonic and eudaimonic well-being. *Annual Review of Psychology, 52,* 141–166.

Ryff, C. D., Dienberg Love, G., Urry, H. L., Muller, D., Rosenkranz, M. A., Friedman, E. M., et al. (2006). Psychological well-being and ill-being: Do they have distinct or mirrored biological correlates? *Psychotherapy and Psychosomatics, 75,* 85–95.

Ryff, C. D., & Singer, B. (1998). The contours of positive human health. *Psychological Inquiry, 9,* 1–28.

Sandvik, E., Diener, E., & Seidlitz, L. (1993). Subjective well-being: The convergence and stability of self-report and non-self-report measures. *Journal of Personality, 61,* 317–342.

Scheier, M. F., & Carver, C. S. (1993). On the power of positive thinking: The benefits of being optimistic. *Current Directions in Psychological Science, 2,* 26–30.

Schimmack, U. (2003). Affect measurement in experience sampling research. *Journal of Happiness Studies, 4,* 79–106.

Schimmack, U., & Oishi, S. (2005). The influence of chronically accessible and temporarily accessible information on life satisfaction judgments. *Journal of Personality and Social Psychology, 89,* 395–406.

Schimmack, U., Oishi, S., Furr, F. M., & Funder, D. C. (2004). Personality and life satisfaction: A facet level analysis. *Personality and Social Psychology Bulletin, 30,* 1062–1075.

Schwarz, N., & Strack, F. (1999). Reports of subjective well-being: Judgmental processes and their methodological implications. In D. Kahneman, E. Diener, & N. Schwarz (Eds.), *Well-being: The foundations of hedonic psychology* (pp. 61–84). New York: Russell Sage Foundation.

Scollon, C. N., & Diener, E. (2006). Love, work, and changes in extraversion and neuroticism over time. *Journal of Personality and Social Psychology, 91*, 1152–1165.

Scollon, C. N., Diener, E., Oishi, S., & Biswas-Diener, R. (2004). Emotions across cultures and methods. *Journal of Cross-cultural Psychology, 35*, 304–326.

Scollon, C. N., Kim-Prieto, C., & Diener, E. (2003). Experience sampling: Promises and pitfalls, strengths and weaknesses. *Journal of Happiness Studies, 4*, 5–34.

Seligman, M. E. P., Steen, T. A., Park, N., & Peterson, C. (2005). Positive psychology progress: Empirical validation of interventions. *American Psychologist, 60*, 410–421.

Sheldon, K. M., Elliot, A. J., Kim, Y., & Kasser, T. (2001). What is satisfying about satisfying events? Testing 10 candidate psychological needs. *Journal of Personality and Social Psychology, 80*, 325–339.

Snyder, C. R., Harris, C., Anderson, J. R., Holleran, S. A., Irving, L. M., Sigmon, S. T., et al. (1991). The will and the ways: Development and validation of an individual differences measure of hope. *Journal of Personality and Social Psychology, 60*, 570–585.

Solberg, E. C., Diener, E., Wirtz, D., Lucas, R. E., & Oishi, S. (2002). Wanting, having, and satisfaction: Examining the role of desire discrepancies in satisfaction with income. *Journal of Personality and Social Psychology, 83*, 725–734.

*Strack, F., Argyle, M., & Schwarz, N. (Eds.). (1991). *Subjective well-being: An interdisciplinary perspective*. Oxford: Pergamon.

Stubbe, J. H., Posthuma, D., Boomsma, D. I., & De Geus, E. J. C. (2005). Heritability of life satisfaction in adults: A twin-family study. *Psychological Medicine, 35*, 1581–1588.

Suh, E. M. (2002). Culture, identity, consistency, and subjective well-being. *Journal of Personality and Social Psychology, 83*, 1378–1391.

Suh, E. M., & Koo, J. (2008). Comparing SWB across cultures and nations: The "what" and "why" questions. In M. Eid & R. J. Larsen (Eds.), *The science of subjective well-being* (pp. 414–427). New York: Guilford.

Tamir, M., & Robinson, M. D. (2007). The happy spotlight: Positive mood and selective attention to rewarding information. *Personality and Social Psychology Bulletin, 33*, 1124–1136.

Tellegen, A., Lykken, D. T., Bouchard, T. J., Wilcox, K. J., Segal, N. L., & Rich, S. (1988). Personality similarity in twins reared apart and together. *Journal of Personality and Social Psychology, 54*, 1031–1039.

Tov, W., & Diener, E. (2008). The well-being of nations: Linking together trust, cooperation, and democracy. In B. A. Sullivan, M. Snyder, & J. L. Sullivan (Eds.), *Cooperation: The political psychology of effective human interaction* (pp. 323–342). Maden, MA: Blackwell Publishing.

Updegraff, J. A., & Suh, E. M. (2007). Happiness is a warm abstract thought: Self-construal abstractness and subjective well-being. *Journal of Positive Psychology, 2*, 18–28.

Veenhoven, R. (1991). Is happiness relative? *Social Indicators Research, 24*, 1–34.

Veenhoven, R., & Hagerty, M. (2006). Rising happiness in nations 1946–2004. *Social Indicators Research, 79*, 421–436.

Wilson, W. (1967). Correlates of avowed happiness. *Psychological Bulletin, 67*, 294–306.

Wilson, T. D., Centerbar, D., Kermer, D., & Gilbert, D. T. (2005). The pleasures of uncertainty: Prolonging positive moods in ways people do not anticipate. *Journal of Personality and Social Psychology, 88*, 5–21.

Wirtz, D., Kruger, J., Scollon, C. N., & Diener, E. (2003). What to do on spring break? The role of predicted, online, and remembered experience in future choice. *Psychological Science, 14*, 520–524.

Appendix: Satisfaction With Life Scale (Diener, Emmons, Larsen, & Griffin, 1985)

Below are five statements that you may agree or disagree with. Using the 1–7 scale indicate your agreement with each item by placing the appropriate number on the line preceding that item. Please be open and honest in your responding.

7—Strongly agree
6—Agree
5—Slightly agree
4—Neither agree nor disagree
3—Slightly disagree
2—Disagree
1—Strongly disagree

_____ In most ways my life is close to my ideal
_____ The conditions of my life are excellent
_____ I am satisfied with my life
_____ So far I have gotten the important things I want in life
_____ If I could live my life over, I would change almost nothing

Scoring and interpretation of the scale

Add up your answers to the five items and use the following normative information to help in "interpretation":

5—9	Extremely dissatisfied with your life
10—14	Very dissatisfied with your life
15—19	Slightly dissatisfied with your life
20	About neutral
21—25	Somewhat satisfied with your life
26—30	Very satisfied with your life
31—35	Extremely satisfied with your life

Most Americans score in the 21–25 range. A score above 25 indicates that you are more satisfied than most people.

Flow Theory and Research

Jeanne Nakamura *and* Mihaly Csikszentmihalyi

Abstract

This chapter describes flow, the experience of complete absorption in the present moment, and the experiential approach to positive psychology that it represents. We summarize the model of optimal experience and development that is associated with the concept of flow, and describe several ways of measuring flow, giving particular attention to the experience sampling method. We review some of the recent research concerning the outcomes and dynamics of flow, its conditions at school and work, and interventions that have been employed to foster flow. Finally, we identify some of the promising directions for flow research moving into the future.

Keywords: flow, human development, motivation, optimal functioning, subjective experience

What constitutes a good life? Few questions are of more fundamental importance to a positive psychology. Flow research has yielded one answer, focusing on full involvement in the present moment. From the perspective of flow, "a good life is characterized by complete absorption in what one does." In this chapter, we describe the flow model of optimal experience and development, explain how flow has been measured, discuss recent work in this area, and identify directions for future research.

Optimal Experience and Its Role in Development

Studying the creative process in the 1960s (Getzels & Csikszentmihalyi, 1976), Csikszentmihalyi observed that when work on a painting was going well, the artist persisted single-mindedly, disregarding hunger, fatigue, and discomfort—yet lost interest in the product once it was completed. Flow research and theory had their origin in a desire to understand this phenomenon of intrinsically motivated, or "autotelic," activity—activity rewarding in and of itself (*auto* = self, *telos* = goal), regardless of extrinsic rewards that might result from the activity.

Significant research had been conducted previously on intrinsic motivation (Deci & Ryan, 1985). Nevertheless, no systematic empirical research had been undertaken to clarify the "subjective phenomenology" of intrinsically motivated activity. Csikszentmihalyi (1975/2000) investigated the nature and conditions of enjoyment by interviewing chess players, rock climbers, dancers, and others who emphasized enjoyment as the main reason for pursuing an activity. The conditions for entering flow include:

• perceived challenges, or opportunities for action, that stretch but do not overmatch existing skills;
• clear proximal goals and immediate feedback about the progress being made.

Under these conditions, experience seamlessly unfolds from moment to moment and one enters a subjective state with the following characteristics:

• intense and focused concentration on the present moment;
• merging of action and awareness;
• loss of reflective self-consciousness (i.e., loss of awareness of oneself as a social actor);

- a sense that one can control one's actions; that is, a sense that one can in principle deal with the situation because one knows how to respond to whatever happens next;
- distortion of temporal experience (typically, a sense that time has passed faster than normal);
- experience of the activity as intrinsically rewarding, such that often the end goal is just an excuse for the process.

The reported phenomenology was remarkably similar across different leisure and work settings.

When in flow, the individual operates at full capacity (cf. de Charms, 1968; Deci, 1975; White, 1959). The state is one of dynamic equilibrium. Entering flow depends on establishing a balance between perceived action capacities and action opportunities (cf. optimal arousal, Berlyne, 1960; Hunt, 1965). The balance is fragile. If challenges exceed skills, one first becomes vigilant and then anxious; if skills exceed challenges, one first relaxes and eventually becomes bored. A visual representation of this landscape shows the quality of experience as a function of the ratio between perceived challenges and skills (Figure 18.1). Shifts in subjective state provide feedback about the changing relationship to the environment. Anxiety or boredom presses a person to adjust his or her level of skill and/or challenge, in order to escape the aversive state and reenter flow.

The original account of the flow state has proven robust. The experience is reported in similar terms across lines of class, gender, and age, as well as across cultures (Asakawa, 2004; Delle Fave & Massimini, 2004) and different kinds of activity.

Flow research was pursued throughout the 1980s and 1990s in the laboratories of Csikszentmihalyi in Chicago and colleagues in Italy (Csikszentmihalyi & Csikszentmihalyi, 1988; Inghilleri, 1999; Massimini & Carli, 1988; Massimini & Delle Fave, 2000). It yielded several refinements of the model of experiential states and dynamics in which the flow concept is embedded.

The flow concept has been employed by researchers studying optimal experience (e.g., leisure, play, sports, art, intrinsic motivation), and by practitioners addressing contexts where fostering positive experience is especially important (in particular, formal schooling at all levels). In addition, the concept has had growing impact outside academia, in such spheres as popular culture, professional sports, and business.

Initially, work on flow was assimilated by psychology primarily within the humanistic tradition of Maslow and Rogers (McAdams, 1990), or as part of the empirical literature on intrinsic motivation and interest (e.g., Deci & Ryan, 1985; Renninger, Hidi, & Krapp, 1992). In recent years, a model of the individual as a self-regulating organism interacting with the environment has become increasingly central in psychology (e.g., Brandstadter, 2006; Magnusson & Stattin, 2006). This is highly compatible with the model of psychological functioning and development associated with the flow concept (Inghilleri, 1999; Rathunde & Csikszentmihalyi, 2006).

Because the flow experience is shaped by both person and environment, it involves "emergent motivation" in an open system (Csikszentmihalyi, 1985): What happens at any moment is responsive to what happened immediately before, rather than being dictated by a preexisting intentional structure located within person (e.g., a trait) or environment (e.g., a role or script). Motivation is emergent in the sense that "proximal goals" arise out of the interaction. The next section introduces the companion notion of emergent long-term goals, such as new interests.

Sports, games, and other "flow activities" provide goal and feedback structures that make flow more likely. But one can find flow in almost any activity, even working a cash register, ironing clothes, or driving a car. It is subjective challenges and skills, not objective ones, which influence the quality of a person's experience. Similarly a person who is involved in a flow activity may not enter flow if

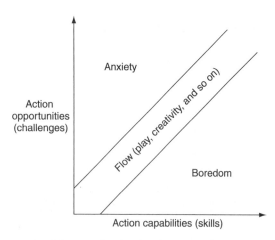

Fig. 18.1 The original model of the flow state. Flow is experienced when perceived opportunities for action are in balance with the actor's perceived skills. Adapted from Csikszentmihalyi (1975/2000).

distractions or excessive challenges disrupt the experience.

Flow, Complexity, and Development

When attention is completely absorbed in the challenges at hand, the individual achieves an ordered state of consciousness (see Nakamura & Csikszentmihalyi, 2002a, for fuller discussion of the relations between flow and attentional processes). Thoughts, feelings, wishes, and action are in harmony. Subjective experience is both differentiated and integrated, the defining qualities of a complex phenomenon.

The notion of complexity applies in a second sense, as well. The flow state is intrinsically rewarding and leads the individual to seek to replicate flow experiences; this introduces a selective mechanism into psychological functioning that fosters growth (Massimini & Delle Fave, 2000). As people master challenges in an activity, they develop greater levels of skill and the activity ceases to be as involving as before. To continue experiencing flow, they must engage progressively more complex challenges. The optimal level of challenge stretches existing skills (cf. Vygotsky, 1978), resulting in more complex capacities for action. This factor distinguishes the flow model from theories that define optimal challenge in terms of either a homeostatic equilibrium point to be returned to or a maximum level of challenge to be reached (Moneta & Csikszentmihalyi, 1996). A flow activity provides a system of graded challenges, able to accommodate a person's continued and deepening enjoyment as skills grow.

The tendency of the self toward complexity is a source of new goals and interests as well as new capacities for action in relation to existing interests (Csikszentmihalyi & Nakamura, 1999). Descending a staircase is an almost unnoticed means to an end for the person on foot, but might be a beckoning opportunity for flow to a person on a skateboard. In this second sense, emergent motivation means we can come to experience a new or previously unengaging activity as intrinsically motivating if we once find flow in it.

The Autotelic Personality

As noted previously, flow theory and research have focused on phenomenology rather than personality. The goal has been to understand the dynamics of momentary experience and the conditions under which it is optimal. The capacity to experience flow appears to be nearly universal. Nevertheless, people vary widely in the frequency of reported flow. People also differ in the quality of their experience, and in their desire to be doing what they are doing, when their capacities and their opportunities for action are simultaneously high. This suggests that the latter balance represents an important but not a sufficient condition for flow.

From the beginning, Csikszentmihalyi (1975/2000) recognized the possibility of an "autotelic personality," a person who tends to enjoy life or "generally does things for their own sake, rather than in order to achieve some later external goal" (Csikszentmihalyi, 1997, p. 117). This kind of personality is distinguished by "meta-skills," which enable the individual to enter the flow and stay in it. These meta-skills include a general curiosity and interest in life, persistence, and low self-centeredness, which result in the ability to be motivated by intrinsic rewards.

By adding a temporal perspective to the concept of autotelic personality, Csikszentmihalyi and Nakamura (in press) argued that optimal life-span development involves the formation of "psychological capital" (PK). PK refers to an even broader set of meta-skills or learned habits that allow a person not only to enjoy whatever he or she does at the moment, but at the same time increase the likelihood of enjoying future experiences. Thus a person who experienced flow only when involved in extreme sports, or when playing chess, might not build PK because these sources of enjoyment are likely to dry up later in life. Nor would a person develop PK by spending years in drudgery, hoping to enjoy life later.

Measuring Flow and Autotelic Personality

Researchers have developed several means of measuring intra-individual (e.g., cross-context) and inter-individual differences in flow experiences. In addition, some effort has been made to measure autotelic personality, the disposition to experience flow.

Measuring Flow

Subjective experience has been viewed as falling outside the sphere of scientific inquiry throughout many of the years since the decline of introspectionist psychology. This has recently been changing, however (Richardson, 1999), leading to increased interest in the methods used in flow research. Several self-report tools are being used, including interviews, paper-and-pencil measures, and the experience sampling method. Other methods have been added to the tool kit in recent years.

INTERVIEW

The flow concept emerged from qualitative accounts of how it feels when an activity is going well (Csikszentmihalyi, 1975/2000). The semistructured interview provides a holistic, emic account of the flow experience in real-life contexts. It was a critical tool in first delineating dimensions and dynamics of the flow experience. It continues to be the approach of choice in exploratory research (e.g., Reed, Schallert, & Deithloff, 2002) and studies directed toward rich, integrated description (Jackson, 1995; Neumann, 2006; Perry, 1999).

QUESTIONNAIRE

Paper-and-pencil measures have been used widely when the goal is not to identify but instead to measure dimensions of the flow experience, and/or differences in its occurrence across contexts or individuals. The Flow Questionnaire presents respondents with several passages describing the flow state and asks whether they have had the experience, how often, and in what activities (Csikszentmihalyi & Csikszentmihalyi, 1988).

The 10-item Flow Scale (Mayers, 1978) elicits an estimate of the frequency with which the respondent experiences dimensions of flow in specified activities (e.g., "I get involved," "I get direct clues as to how well I am doing"). Delle Fave and Massimini (1988) employed the Flow Questionnaire and Flow Scale in tandem to identify flow activities and then compare the person's rating of the flow dimensions for his or her primary flow activity with those for a standardized set of everyday activities. In contrast to these global estimates of the frequency of flow in specified activities, a scale assessing the flow state in the respondent's "current" pursuit was developed for use in German and translated into several additional languages (Rheinberg, Vollmeyer, & Engeser, 2003).

Extensive psychometric work by Jackson and colleagues (Jackson & Eklund, 2002, 2004; Jackson & Marsh, 1996) produced two parallel 36-item scales to measure (a) the frequency of flow in a given activity (Dispositional Flow Scale, DFS-2) and (b) the degree to which flow dimensions characterize a just-completed experience or event (Flow State Scale, FSS-2). While designed to measure flow within physical activities, the scales have been used successfully to study other pursuits such as music, theatre, and computing; two short flow scales for general use have recently been developed (Jackson,

Martin, & Eklund, 2008). Finally, researchers continue to develop questionnaire measures of flow in particular activities, such as work (Bakker, 2008).

EXPERIENCE SAMPLING METHOD

Interview and global-rating approaches rely on retrospective reconstruction of past experience, and respondents must average across many discrete experiences to compose a picture of the typical subjective experience when things are going well, and then estimate the frequency or intensity of this experience. The study of flow progressed in large part because researchers in the 1970s developed a tool uniquely suited to the study of situated experiential states, including optimal experience. Descriptions of the Experience Sampling Method (ESM) can be found elsewhere (Csikszentmihalyi & Larson, 1987; Hektner, Schmidt, & Csikszentmihalyi, 2006). Briefly, participants carry paging devices that signal them, at preprogrammed times, to complete a questionnaire describing the moment at which they were paged. The method takes multiple random samples from the stream of actual everyday experience.

ESM studies of flow have focused on the sampled moments when (a) the "conditions for flow" exist, based on the balance of challenges (or opportunities for action) and skills (abilities to deal with the situation); and/or (b) the "flow state" is reported. The latter usually is measured by aggregating reported levels of concentration, enjoyment, and intrinsic motivation. These three dimensions provide a reasonable proxy for what is in reality a much more complex state of consciousness. Fuller discussion of the study of flow with the ESM can be found elsewhere (Csikszentmihalyi & Rathunde, 1993; Hektner, Schmidt, & Csikszentmihalyi, 2006; Nakamura & Csikszentmihalyi, 2002a; Schmidt, Shernoff, & Csikszentmihalyi, 2006). In an adaptation of naturalistic experience sampling, Abuhamdeh studied competition within an Internet chess club; players' ratings provided an objective measure of challenge and skill levels, which was compared with their enjoyment of the game (Abuhamdeh & Csikszentmihalyi, 2008).

OBJECTIVE MEASUREMENT

The ESM yields a corpus of moments in flow, particularly when large numbers of experience samples are collected, but necessarily interrupts the flow experience. Custodero (1998) triangulated interview and observational data to construct a behavioral measure of flow during young children's musical performance. While her primary motivation was to devise a measure of flow for a population with limited capacity to report inner states, her work represents one of the few efforts to identify behavioral markers of flow. The technique is painstaking and time-intensive, however. With colleagues including Fredrik Ullen, one of our current goals is to identify physiological markers of flow that would permit tracking of the dynamics of flow without disrupting it (Blom & Ullen, 2008). ESM research suggests that enjoyment and involvement are associated with significantly lower salivary cortisol levels than expected for time of day (Adam, 2005), implying lower stress levels and lower blood pressure.

LABORATORY MANIPULATION

With this same aim of studying the dynamics of flow, several researchers have tracked or controlled theoretically key experiential conditions, usually the levels of challenge and skill in an activity such as an online game or learning situation, and elicited self-reports of flow (e.g., Pearce, Ainley, & Howard, 2005; Rheinberg & Vollmeyer, 2003). Moller has developed a computer game procedure that promises to give researchers a standardized laboratory manipulation for controlled study of the dynamics of flow (Moller, Csikszentmihalyi, Nakamura, & Deci, 2007; see also Keller & Bless, 2008).

Measuring the Autotelic Personality

As interest in the autotelic personality has grown, researchers have sought a way to measure it with the naturalistic data generated by the ESM. "Time spent in the high-challenge, high-skill situations conducive to flow" has been the most widely used measure of the general propensity toward flow (Adlai-Gail, 1994; Asakawa, 2004; Hektner, 1996). However, time in flow also reflects the range of action opportunities that happen to be available in the individual's environment during the sampling period. Other researchers therefore have operationalized the disposition as "intrinsic motivation in high-challenge, high-skill situations," reflected in low mean scores on the item "I wish to be doing something else" when subjective challenges and skills are both above average (e.g., Csikszentmihalyi & LeFevre, 1989). We anticipate that measures of psychological capital will encompass what has been known as autotelic personality, such as the possession of "meta-skills" for the regulation of experience (Csikszentmihalyi & Nakamura, 1989, in press; Csikszentmihalyi, Rathunde, & Whalen, 1993).

Recent Directions in Flow Research
Consequences of Flow

According to this model, experiencing flow encourages a person to persist in and return to an activity because of the experiential rewards it promises, and thereby fosters the growth of skills over time. Several studies linked flow to commitment and achievement during high school (Carli, Delle Fave, & Massimini, 1988; Mayers, 1978; Nakamura, 1988). A longitudinal ESM study of talented high school students showed a relationship between quality of experience and persistence. Students still committed to their talent area at age 17 were compared to peers who had disengaged. Four years earlier, those currently still committed had experienced more flow and less anxiety than their peers when engaged in school-related activities; they also were more likely to have identified their talent area as a source of flow (Csikszentmihalyi et al., 1993). In a longitudinal study of students talented in mathematics (Heine, 1996), those who experienced flow in the first part of a course performed better in the second half, controlling for initial abilities and GPA; in studies of two university courses, flow predicted semester-end performance (Engeser, Rheinberg, Vollmeyer, & Bischoff, 2005). Because the self grows through flow experiences, we also might expect time spent in flow to predict self-esteem. Correlational studies with ESM data support this expectation (Adlai-Gail, 1994; Wells, 1988).

In the work domain, several studies connected flow to such positive outcomes as work satisfaction (Bryce & Haworth, 2002). Researchers linked teachers' experience of flow to students' cognitive engagement (Basom & Frase, 2004) and to students' experience of flow (Bakker, 2005).

Longitudinal research suggests that in addition to enhancing positive outcomes, mastering challenges in daily life may protect against negative outcomes (Schmidt, 1999). For adolescents who had experienced high adversity at home and/or school, the availability of challenging activities, involvement in these activities, and sense of success when engaged in them were all associated with lower delinquency 2 years later.

The Nature and Dynamics of Flow

The positive correlates and outcomes of flow undoubtedly account for some of the interest paid to it in recent years. However, this interest, in a sense, misses the point. From the perspective of the individual, the flow state is a self-justifying experience; it is, by definition, an end in itself.

A distinct strand of research can be traced forward from the original study of flow activities. In this work, interviews have yielded domain-specific descriptions of deep flow in diverse activities: elite and nonelite sport (Jackson & Csikszentmihalyi, 1999; Kimiecik & Harris, 1996), social activism (Colby & Damon, 1992), aesthetic experience (Csikszentmihalyi & Robinson, 1990), literary writing (Perry, 1999), and scholarly and creative work more generally (Csikszentmihalyi, 1996; Neumann, 2006). These studies confirm how universal the flow state is across different activities. Research also is yielding nuanced pictures of flow within particular contexts. The dynamics of flow are being studied in domains including sports and games, computer and Web usage, education, and work.

FLOW AT SCHOOL

A growing body of research addresses different educational contexts. Studies of school types, pedagogies, and instructional practices are illustrative. In an ESM study of middle schools, Montessori students experienced more flow, and were more motivated in school, than students attending matched traditional institutions (Rathunde & Csikszentmihalyi, 2005). Regarding classroom activities, active pedagogies such as cooperative learning provided more flow than passive pedagogies such as listening to lectures, both for high school (Shernoff, Csikszentmihalyi, Shneider, & Shernoff, 2003) and college (Peterson & Miller, 2004) students. In a study of instructional-discourse strategies, Turner et al. (1998) identified elementary school math classrooms where students reported challenges and skills that were in balance and above average for the sample; the teachers tended to "scaffold" instruction, negotiating understanding, giving autonomy, and encouraging intrinsic motivation, rather than being highly directive and evaluative and using extrinsic controls. Turner and Meyer (2004) observe that supportive instructional practices are critical if students are to embrace academic challenges rather than finding them threatening, even when the challenges are carefully modulated.

FLOW AT WORK

In addition to the research on learning, several studies have addressed the work experience of teachers. A recent British study suggested that primary and secondary teachers experience flow with high frequency, and that their levels of flow may exceed those of workers in several other professions (Morgan, 2005). Research on teachers also has examined antecedents of flow. Among facilitators identified are self-efficacy (Basom & Frase, 2004) and job resources (Bakker, 2005); some of the latter (e.g., performance feedback) directly provide proximal conditions for entering flow while others (e.g., social support, coaching by supervisors) are thought to function like skills to help workers meet the challenges of their work. Bakker's work suggests that underprovision of resources, like inadequate levels of skill, can lead to anxiety, and overprovision of resources, like excess of skill, can lead to boredom. A longitudinal study (Salanova, Bakker, & Llorens, 2006) offered evidence of a "positive upward spiral": Both personal resources (i.e., self-efficacy beliefs) and organizational resources (e.g., social support) positively affected work-related flow and, in addition, work-related flow positively affected the resources that workers mobilize.

Also in the work context, an intriguing line of research concerns the "paradox of work" first reported by Csikszentmihalyi and Lefevre (1989) in a U.S. sample. ESM studies of Swiss (Schallberger & Pfister, 2001) and German (Rheinberg, Manig, Reinhold, Engeser, & Vollmeyer, 2007) workers have confirmed that flow is higher at work and yet happiness or satisfaction is higher at leisure. Csikszentmihalyi and Lefevre suggested that cultural biases undermine the perception of work as enjoyable despite the positive quality of experience. Schallberger and Pfister's fine-grained analysis of emotional states in the two contexts suggests a second interpretation, that work does indeed provide the positive activation associated with flow and long-term growth, but leisure provides a reduction of negative activation (e.g., stress) that is associated with short-term well-being.

TEMPORAL DYNAMICS

There is growing research interest in the temporal dynamics of flow, across different time frames. The flow model distinguishes between proximal conditions and elements of the flow state, but it does not specify the temporal sequencing of these elements. Several researchers have addressed how these dimensions relate to one another. For example, modeling of ESM data shows that attentional involvement (concentrating and feeling involved) partially mediates the relationship between optimal challenge and the experience of enjoyment (Abuhamdeh, 2008). The full set of conditions and dimensions has been organized in several models of the phenomenology of flow that start with antecedent conditions and end in outcomes (e.g., Quinn, 2005). Other researchers have examined the process of entering flow (Jackson, 1995; Massimini, Csikszentmihalyi, & Delle Fave, 1988; Perry, 1999; Reed et al., 2002); the fluctuation of flow or involvement over the course of one experience, for example, studying for an exam (Reed, Hagen, Wicker, & Schallert, 1996); and the fluctuation of flow over the course of a series of events, such as rehearsals leading up to a musical performance (Kraus, 2003).

THE EXPERIENTIAL LANDSCAPE

As new ESM studies have been conducted, the general features of the experiential landscape defined by the interaction of challenges and skills have been clarified. Massimini and colleagues recognized that flow is fostered when challenges and skills are in balance and, in addition, both are above average levels for the individual. The Milan group also differentiated the challenge/skill terrain into eight experiential "channels" (Figure 18.2). A simplified version divides the same space into four quadrants defined by whether challenges and skills are above the personal mean (high) or below it (low). The high-challenge, low-skill ("anxiety") quadrant is characterized, as expected, by high stakes but low enjoyment and low motivation. Only in the high-challenge, high-skill ("flow") quadrant are these variables plus concentration and self-esteem simultaneously above the personal mean. In contrast, all the variables are below average in the low-challenge,

low-skill ("apathy") quadrant. Concentration, self-esteem, and importance to future goals peak in the "flow" quadrant whereas enjoyment and wish to be doing the activity are actually somewhat higher in the low-challenge, high-skill quadrant (cf. Moneta, 2004). The quality of experience under the latter conditions is partially positive even though stakes are not high and attention is unfocused. The current mapping of the experiential landscape labels this quadrant "relaxation" to capture the mixed nature of the subjective state, which is less aversive than originally thought. A large-scale ESM study of adolescents found schoolwork is prevalent in the "anxiety" quadrant; structured leisure, schoolwork, and work in the "flow" quadrant; socializing and eating in the "relaxation" quadrant; and passive leisure and chores in the "apathy" quadrant (Csikszentmihalyi & Schneider, 2000).

We speculate that two kinds of experiences might be intrinsically rewarding: one that involves conservation of energy (relaxation), the other involving the use of skills to seize ever greater opportunities (flow). It is consistent with current understandings of evolution to suppose that both these strategies for coping with the environment, one conservative and the other expansive, were selected over time as important components of the human behavioral repertoire, even though they motivate different—in some sense, opposite—behaviors. By contrast, the two distinctly aversive situations, which organisms are presumably programmed to avoid, are those in which one feels overwhelmed by environmental

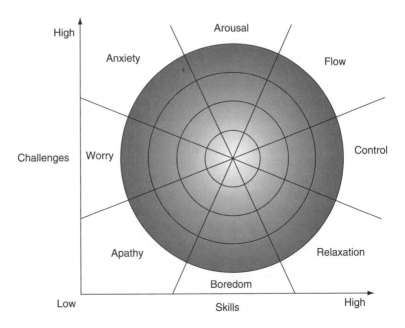

Fig. 18.2 One representation of the current model of the flow state. Flow is experienced when perceived challenges and skills are above the actor's average levels; when they are below, apathy is experienced. Intensity of experience increases with distance from the actor's average levels of challenge and skill. Adapted from Csikszentmihalyi (1997).

demands (anxiety), or left with nothing to do (apathy).

Finally, a growing body of research is examining how dispositions, such as motivational orientation, affect the experiencing of flow. Naturalistic research shows that high trait intrinsic motivation is associated with subjectively faster passage of time, less attention to the time, and more losing track of the time (Conti, 2001), and with a stronger (quadratic) relationship between level of challenge and degree of task enjoyment (Abuhamdeh, 2008; cf. Moneta, 2004). In other studies, success-motivated individuals reported more flow than failure-motivated individuals during a laboratory task (Puca & Schmalt, 1999) and need for achievement moderated the relationship between having a high-challenge, high-skill job, and task enjoyment (Eisenberger, Jones, Stinglhamber, Shanock, & Randall, 2005).

Interventions and Programs to Foster Flow

Flow researchers have discussed how their findings might be applied (Csikszentmihalyi, 1990, 1996, 2003; Csikszentmihalyi & Robinson, 1990; Jackson & Csikszentmihalyi, 1999; Perry, 1999). The relevance of the flow concept is increasingly noted in occupational therapy (Emerson, 1998; Rebeiro & Polgar, 1998) and social policy affecting the disabled (Delle Fave & Massimini, 2005).

Flow principles have been translated into practice in various contexts. Two types of intervention can be distinguished: (a) those seeking to shape activity structures and environments so that they foster flow or obstruct it less; and (b) those attempting to assist individuals in finding flow. The former include interventions to make work a greater source of flow. The Swedish state-owned transportation company, Green Cargo, had been losing money since its founding in 1889. When Stefan Falk joined the executive ranks in 2003, he instituted new techniques based on flow principles. Line managers were trained to identify workers' distinctive strengths; they then met regularly with each worker to set clear goals, find the appropriate level of challenges, and provide timely feedback. In 2004, the firm was profitable for the first time in 115 years and the flow-based program was credited as an important factor in the transformation (Marsh, 2005). In other domains, several museums, including Los Angeles' Getty Museum, incorporated flow principles during the design of exhibits and buildings. Flow principles informed product design at Nissan USA, with the goal of making use of the product more enjoyable.

Educational settings present an important arena for applying an understanding of flow. The Key School in Indianapolis (Whalen, 1999), a K-12 public school, opened in 1987; it seeks to (a) create a learning environment that fosters flow experiences and (b) help students form interests and develop the capacity and propensity to experience flow. In the Flow Activities Center, students have regular opportunities to choose and engage in pursuits related to their own interests. In Denmark, educators are integrating flow principles into the curriculum and pedagogy of schools from kindergarten onward (Knoop & Lyhne, 2006; Kristensen & Andersen, 2004) and schools are assessing student flow experience and other aspects of positive functioning.

The most direct efforts to assist individuals in finding flow lie in the sphere of psychotherapy. The Milan group built on their extensive program of basic research to develop therapeutic interventions aimed at transforming the structure of daily life toward more positive experience. Psychiatric interventions informed by flow theory have been successful in diverse cultural settings, including Nicaragua and northern Somalia (Inghilleri, 1999). In Italy, the ESM, guided by flow theory, has provided a tool for identifying patterns in everyday experience and ways in which these might be transformed (Delle Fave & Massimini, 1992, 2005; Inghilleri, 1999; Massimini, Csikszentmihalyi, & Carli, 1987).

Many therapies focus on conflict, under the assumption that once this is worked through, well-being will automatically follow. The therapeutic approach described here reverses figure and ground. Use of flow principles allows therapy to be reoriented toward building on interests and strengths, taking advantage of the growth of skill and confidence (cf. Wells, 1988) that attends flow experience, and enabling the individual to reduce dysphoric experience as a by-product of this growth.

A common theme of educational and therapeutic applications of flow principles bears underlining. Their goal is not to foster the state of flow directly, but rather to help individuals identify activities that they enjoy and learn how to invest their attention in the work of these activities.

Directions for Future Research

Many current areas of flow theory, research, and application are likely to extend fruitfully into the future. New research directions identified in the work of Nakamura and Csikszentmihalyi (2002a) also remain promising. Others are just emerging. For example, theory (Dietrich, 2004) and experimentation (Ullen, personal communication, 2006) on the neuropsychology of flow are beginning.

Current societal changes give new urgency to some questions about flow. For example, fundamental questions concern the nature of the attentional processes that foster flow and the way optimal attentional practices are formed (Hamilton, 1983). The ever-increasing pace of life and the proliferating claims on attention due to new technologies—the challenges of so-called multi-tasking, the pervasiveness of "attention robbers" (Metzinger, personal communication, 2004)—highlight the importance of attention regulation and its impact on quality of experience. Understanding the dynamics (Asakawa, 2004) and development (Rathunde, 1997) of the autotelic personality thus gains importance. In Asakawa's (2004) ESM study of Japanese college students, autotelics reported more balanced levels of challenge and skill than did non-autotelics. In addition, they more often reported that challenges exceeded skills than that skills exceeded challenges, whereas the reverse characterized non-autotelics. A related issue is the question of how children and adolescents learn what goals deserve attention. Extended to take into account life-span development, this becomes the study of how psychological capital is formed, allowing the pursuit of meaningful goals that provide flow throughout a person's life.

Other societal changes give new access to standing questions about flow. For example, despite its implication in development and in the positive quality of life, flow's amoral character has always been clear. Past research has shown that fire-setting and other activities damaging to self or others can afford flow, and has suggested that flow activities can become addictive. In recent years, researchers have begun to ask whether experiencing flow can lead to addictive playing of computer games. Cyber-behavior, a domain widely analyzed from a flow perspective, has the advantage of being fairly easily studied. It thus stands to yield more insight than an activity like fire-setting into the evolution, persistence, and consequences, of problem flow. The overarching goals are to compare the dynamics of seeking flow in one activity rather than another, and understand the long-term effects of these choices.

Another fertile direction is the situating of flow within the broader landscape of positive functioning. For example, some positive psychologists (e.g., Ryan & Deci, 2001; Waterman, 1993) posit two models of well-being and conceptualize flow as an aspect of "eudaemonia," or self-realization, viewing this as the counterpoint to "hedonia," or pleasure. Nakamura described the growth of flow experiences into sources of vital engagement through the accumulation of life-historical, interpersonal, and other connections that endow absorbing activities with meaning (Nakamura & Csikszentmihalyi, 2002b). Seligman's (2002) tripartite model of happiness treats flow as the main manifestation of "engaged" lives. Guided by Seligman's model, Peterson, Park, and Seligman (2005) measured adults' orientations toward achieving happiness through pleasure, meaning, or engagement (flow).

Conclusion

Research on flow contributes knowledge to several topics that are of central importance to positive psychology. In the first place, it illuminates the phenomenology of optimal experience, answering the question: What is it like to live fully, to be completely involved in the moment? Second, it leads to questions about the long-term consequences of optimal experience: Does the sum of flow over time add up to a good and happy life? Or only under certain conditions, that is, if the person develops the meta-skills to manage attention and enjoy meaningful challenges? Furthermore, this line of research tries to unravel the conditions that act as obstacles or facilitators to optimal experience, focusing especially on the most prominent institutions such as the family, schools, and the workplace. Although it seems clear that flow serves as a buffer against adversity and prevents pathology, its major contribution to the quality of life consists in endowing momentary experience with value.

Questions

1. What are the long-term effects of different flow activities on the quality of individual lives?

2. How can flow be increased in the major areas of life, for example, education, work, relationships, free time?

3. How does the experience of flow relate to other aspects of positive functioning?

References

Abuhamdeh, S. (2008). What makes an intrinsically motivated activity intrinsically motivating? The role of challenge. Unpublished doctoral dissertation, University of Chicago.

Abuhamdeh, S., & Csikszentmihalyi, M. (2008). The effects of intrinsic and extrinsic motivational orientation in the competitive context. Manuscript under review.

Adam, E. (2005). Momentary emotion and cortisol levels in the everyday lives of working parents. In B. Schneider & L. Waite (Eds.), *Being together, working apart* (pp. 105–133). Cambridge: Cambridge University Press.

Adlai-Gail, W. (1994). Exploring the autotelic personality. Unpublished doctoral dissertation, University of Chicago.

Asakawa, K. (2004). Flow experience and autotelic personality in Japanese college students: How do they experience challenges in daily life? *Journal of Happiness Studies, 5*(2), 123–154.

Bakker, A. B. (2005). Flow among music teachers and their students: The crossover of peak experiences. *Journal of Vocational Behavior, 66*(1), 26–44.

Bakker, A. B. (2008). The work-related flow inventory: Construction and initial validation of the WOLF. *Journal of Vocational Behavior, 72*, 400–414.

Basom, M. R., & Frase, L. (2004). Creating optimal work environments: Exploring teacher flow experiences. *Mentoring and Tutoring, 12*(2), 241–258.

Berlyne, D. (1960). *Conflict, arousal, and curiosity*. New York: McGraw-Hill.

Blom, O., & Ullen, F. (2008). *The psychophysiology of flow during music performance*. Talk presented at the Fourth European Conference on Positive Psychology, Opatija, Croatia.

Brandstadter, J. (2006). Action perspectives on human development. In R. M. Lerner (Ed.), *Handbook of child psychology* (Vol. 1, pp. 516–568). New York: Wiley.

Bryce, J., & Haworth, J. (2002). Wellbeing and flow in sample of male and female office workers. *Leisure Studies, 23*, 249–263.

Carli, M., Delle Fave, A., & Massimini, F. (1988). The quality of experience in the flow channels: Comparison of Italian and U.S. students. In M. Csikszentmihalyi & I. Csikszentmihalyi (Eds.), *Optimal experience* (pp. 288–306). Cambridge: Cambridge University Press.

Colby, A., & Damon, W. (1992). *Some do care*. New York: Free Press.

Conti, R. (2001). Time flies: Investigating the connection between intrinsic motivation and the experience of time. *Journal of Personality, 69*(1), 1–26.

Csikszentmihalyi, M. (1985). Emergent motivation and the evolution of the self. *Advances in Motivation and Achievement, 4*, 93–119.

Csikszentmihalyi, M. (1990). *Flow*. New York: Harper & Row.

Csikszentmihalyi, M. (1996). *Creativity*. New York: HarperCollins.

Csikszentmihalyi, M. (1997). *Finding flow*. New York: Basic.

Csikszentmihalyi, M. (1975/2000). *Beyond boredom and anxiety*. San Francisco: Jossey-Bass.

Csikszentmihalyi, M. (2003). *Good business*. New York: Viking.

Csikszentmihalyi, M., & Csikszentmihalyi, I. (Eds.). (1988). *Optimal experience*. Cambridge: Cambridge University Press.

Csikszentmihalyi, M., & Larson, R. (1987). Validity and reliability of the experience sampling method. *Journal of Nervous and Mental Disease, 175*, 526–536.

Csikszentmihalyi, M., & LeFevre, J. (1989). Optimal experience in work and leisure. *Journal of Personality and Social Psychology, 56*(5), 815–822.

Csikszentmihalyi, M., & Nakamura, J. (1989). The dynamics of intrinsic motivation: A study of adolescents. In R. Ames & C. Ames (Eds.), *Research on motivation in education* (pp. 45–71). New York: Academic Press.

Csikszentmihalyi, M., & Nakamura, J. (1999). Emerging goals and the self-regulation of behavior. *Advances in social cognition, 12*, 107–118.

Csikszentmihalyi, M., & Nakamura, J. (in press). Psychological capital. In S. Lopez (Ed.), *Encyclopedia of positive psychology*. Oxford, UK: Blackwell.

Csikszentmihalyi, M., & Rathunde, K. (1993). The measurement of flow in everyday life. *Nebraska Symposium on Motivation, 40*, 57–97.

Csikszentmihalyi, M., Rathunde, K., & Whalen, S. (1993). *Talented teenagers*. Cambridge: Cambridge University Press.

Csikszentmihalyi, M., & Robinson, R. (1990). *The art of seeing*. Malibu, CA: J. Paul Getty Museum and the Getty Center for Education in the Arts.

Csikszentmihalyi, M., & Schneider, B. (2000). *Becoming adult: How teenagers prepare for the world of work*. New York: Basic.

Custodero, L. (1998). Observing flow in young people's music learning. *General Music Today, 12*(1), 21–27.

de Charms, R. (1968). *Personal causation*. New York: Academic Press.

Deci, E. (1975). *Intrinsic motivation*. New York: Plenum.

Deci, E., & Ryan, R. (1985). *Intrinsic motivation and self-determination in human behavior*. New York: Plenum.

Delle Fave, A., & Massimini, F. (1988). Modernization and the changing contexts of flow in work and leisure. In M. Csikszentmihalyi & I. Csikszentmihalyi (Eds.), *Optimal experience* (pp. 193–213). Cambridge: Cambridge University Press.

Delle Fave, A., & Massimini, F. (1992). The ESM and the measurement of clinical change: A case of anxiety disorder. In M. deVries (Ed.), *The experience of psychopathology* (pp. 280–289). Cambridge: Cambridge University Press.

Delle Fave, A., & Massimini, F. (2004). The cross-cultural investigation of optimal experience. *Ricerche di Psicologia, 27*, 79–102.

Delle Fave, A., & Massimini, F. (2005). The relevance of subjective well-being to social policies: Optimal experience and tailored intervention. In F. Huppert et al. (Eds.), *The science of well-being* (pp. 379–402). Oxford: Oxford University Press.

Dietrich, A. (2004). Neurocognitive mechanisms underlying the experience of flow. *Consciousness and Cognition, 13*(4), 746–761.

Eisenberger, R., Jones, J. R., Stinglhamber, F., Shanock, L., & Randall, A. T. (2005). Flow experiences at work: For high need achievers alone? *Journal of Organizational Behavior, 26*, 755–775.

Emerson, H. (1998). Flow and occupation: A review of the literature. *Canadian Journal of Occupational Therapy, 65*, 37–43.

Engeser, S., Rheinberg, F., Vollmeyer, R., & Bischoff, J. (2005). Motivation, Flow-Erleben und Lernleistung in universitären Lernsettings. *Zeitschrift für Pädagogische Psychologie, 19*(3), 159–172.

Getzels, J. W., & Csikszentmihalyi, M. (1976). *The creative vision*. New York: Wiley.

Hamilton, J. A. (1983). Development of interest and enjoyment in adolescence. *Journal of Youth and Adolescence, 12*, 355–372.

Heine, C. (1996). Flow and achievement in mathematics. Unpublished doctoral dissertation, University of Chicago.

Hektner, J. (1996). Exploring optimal personality development: A longitudinal study of adolescents. Unpublished doctoral dissertation, University of Chicago.

Hektner, J. M., Schmidt, J. A., & Csikszentmihalyi, M. (2006). *Experience sampling method*. Thousand Oaks, CA: Sage.

Hunt, J. (1965). Intrinsic motivation and its role in development. *Nebraska Symposium on Motivation, 12*, 189–282.

Inghilleri, P. (1999). *From subjective experience to cultural change.* Cambridge: Cambridge University Press.

Jackson, S. A. (1995). Factors influencing the occurrence of flow state in elite athletes. *Journal of Applied Sport Psychology, 7*, 138–166.

Jackson, S. A., & Csikszentmihalyi, M. (1999). *Flow in sports.* Champaign, IL: Human Kinetics.

Jackson, S. A., & Eklund, R. C. (2002). Assessing flow in physical activity: The Flow State Scale-2 (FSS-2) and Dispositional Flow Scale-2 (DFS-2). *Journal of Sport and Exercise Psychology, 24*, 133–150.

Jackson, S. A., & Eklund, R. C. (2004). *The flow scales manual.* Morgantown, WV: Fitness Information Technology.

Jackson, S. A., & Marsh, H. W. (1996). Development and validation of a scale to measure optimal experience: The flow state scale. *Journal of Sport and Exercise Psychology, 18*, 17–35.

Jackson, S. A., Martin, A. J., & Eklund, R. C. (2008). Long and short measures of flow: Examining construct validity of the FSS-2, DFS-2, and new brief counterparts. *Journal of Sport and Exercise Psychology, 30*, 561–587.

Keller, J., & Bless, H. (2008). Flow and regulatory compatibility: An experimental approach to the flow model of intrinsic motivation. *Personality and Social Psychology Bulletin, 34*, 196–209.

Kimiecik, J. C., & Harris, A. T. (1996). What is enjoyment? A conceptual/definitional analysis with implications for sport and exercise psychology. *Journal of Sport and Exercise Psychology, 18*, 247–263.

Knoop, H. H., & Lyhne, J. (Eds.). (2006). *Et Nyt Laeringslandskab.* Copenhagen: Dansk Psykologisk Forlag.

Kraus, B. N. (2003). Musicians in flow: Optimal experience in the wind ensemble rehearsal. Unpublished doctoral dissertation, Arizona State University.

Kristensen, R., & Andersen, F. O. (2004). *Flow, Opmaerksomhed og Relationer.* Frederikshavn: Danilo.

McAdams, D. P. (1990). *The person.* San Diego: Harcourt Brace Jovanovich.

Magnusson, D., & Stattin, H. (2006). The person in context. In R. M. Lerner (Ed.), *Handbook of child psychology* (Vol. 1, pp. 400–464). New York: Wiley.

Marsh, A. (2005, August). The art of work. *Fast Company*, pp. 77–79.

Massimini, F., & Carli, M. (1988). The systematic assessment of flow in daily experience. In M. Csikszentmihalyi & I. Csikszentmihalyi (Eds.), *Optimal experience* (pp. 266–287). Cambridge: Cambridge University Press.

Massimini, F., Csikszentmihalyi, M., & Carli, M. (1987). The monitoring of optimal experience: A tool for psychiatric rehabilitation. *Journal of Nervous and Mental Disease, 175*(9), 545–549.

Massimini, F., Csikszentmihalyi, M., & Delle Fave, A. (1988). Flow and biocultural evolution. In M. Csikszentmihalyi & I. Csikszentmihalyi (Eds.), *Optimal experience* (pp. 60–81). Cambridge: Cambridge University Press.

Massimini, F., & Delle Fave, A. (2000). Individual development in a bio-cultural perspective. *American Psychologist, 55*, 24–33.

Mayers, P. (1978). Flow in adolescence and its relation to school experience. Unpublished doctoral dissertation, University of Chicago.

Moller, A., Csikszentmihalyi, M., Nakamura, J., & Deci, E. (2007). *Developing an experimental induction of flow.* Poster presented at the Annual Meeting of the Society for Personality and Social Psychology, Nashville.

Moneta, G. (2004). The flow model of intrinsic motivation in Chinese: Cultural and personal moderators. *Journal of Happiness Studies, 5*, 181–217.

Moneta, G., & Csikszentmihalyi, M. (1996). The effect of perceived challenges and skills on the quality of subjective experience. *Journal of Personality, 64*(2), 275–310.

Morgan, S. J. (2005). *JobLab: A study into the experience of teaching.* Crawley: CrossLight.

Nakamura, J. (1988). Optimal experience and the uses of talent. In M. Csikszentmihalyi & I. Csikszentmihalyi (Eds.), *Optimal experience* (pp. 319–326). Cambridge: Cambridge University Press.

Nakamura, J., & Csikszentmihalyi, M. (2002a). The concept of flow. In C. R. Snyder & S. J. Lopez (Eds.), *Handbook of positive psychology* (pp. 89–105). New York: Oxford University Press.

Nakamura, J., & Csikszentmihalyi, M. (2002b). The construction of meaning through vital engagement. In C. Keyes & J. Haidt (Eds.), *Flourishing* (pp. 83–104). Washington, DC: APA Books.

Neumann, A. (2006). Professing passion: Emotion in the scholarship of professors at research universities. *American Educational Research Journal, 43*(3), 381–424.

Pearce, J. M., Ainley, M., & Howard, S. (2005). The ebb and flow of online learning. *Computers in Human Behavior, 21*(5), 745–771.

Perry, S. K. (1999). *Writing in flow.* Cincinnati, OH: Writer's Digest Books.

Peterson, S. E., & Miller, J. A. (2004). Comparing the quality of students' experiences during cooperative learning and large-group instruction. *Journal of Educational Research, 97*(3), 123–133.

Peterson, C., Park, N., & Seligman, M. (2005). Orientations to happiness and life satisfaction: The full life versus the empty life. *Journal of Happiness Studies, 6*(1), 25–41.

Puca, R. M., & Schmalt, H.-D. (1999). Task enjoyment: A mediator between achievement motives and performance. *Motivation and Emotion, 23*(1), 15–29.

Quinn, R. W. (2005). Flow in knowledge work: High performance experience in the design of national security technology. *Administrative Science Quarterly, 50*, 610–641.

Rathunde, K. (1997). Parent–adolescent interaction and optimal experience. *Journal of Youth and Adolescence, 26*, 669–689.

Rathunde, K., & Csikszentmihalyi, M. (2005). Middle-school students' motivation and quality of experience: A comparison of Montessori and traditional school environments. *American Journal of Education, 111*, 341–371.

Rathunde, K., & Csikszentmihalyi, M. (2006). The development of the person: An experiential perspective. In W. Damon & R. M. Lerner (Eds.), *Handbook of child psychology* (Vol. 1, pp. 465–515). Hoboken, NJ: Wiley.

Rebeiro, K. L., & Polgar, J. M. (1998). Enabling occupational performance: Optimal experiences in therapy. *Canadian Journal of Occupational Therapy, 66*, 14–22.

Reed, J. H., Hagen, A. S., Wicker, F. W., & Schallert, D. L. (1996). Involvement as a temporal dynamic: Affective factors in studying for exams. *Journal of Educational Psychology, 88*(1), 101–109.

Reed, J. H., Schallert, D. L., & Deithloff, L. F. (2002). Investigating the interface between self-regulation and involvement processes. *Educational Psychologist, 37*(1), 53–57.

Renninger, K. A., Hidi, S., & Krapp, A. (1992). *The role of interest in learning and development.* Hillsdale, NJ: Erlbaum.

Rheinberg, F., Manig, Y., Reinhold, K., Engeser, S., & Vollmeyer, R. (2007). Flow bei der arbeit, doch Gluck in der Freizeit: Zielausrichtung, Flow und Glucksgefuhle [Flow during work but happiness during leisure time: Goals, flow, and happiness]. *Zeitschrift für Arbeits- und Organisationspsychologie, 51,* 105–115.

Rheinberg, F., & Vollmeyer, R. (2003). Flow-Erleben in einem Computerspiel unter experimentell variierten Bedingungen. *Zeitschrift für Psychologie, 211*(4), 161–170.

Rheinberg, F., Vollmeyer, R., & Engeser, S. (2003). Die Erfassung des Flow-Erlebens. In J. Stiensmeier-Pelster & F. Rheinberg (Eds.), *Diagnostikvon Motivation und Selstkonzept* (pp. 261–279). Göttingen: Hogrefe.

Richardson, A. (1999). Subjective experience: Its conceptual status, method of investigation, and psychological significance. *Journal of Personality, 133*(5), 469–485.

Ryan, R., & Deci, E. (2001). On happiness and human potentials: A review of research on hedonic and eudaimonic well-being. *Annual Review of Psychology, 52,* 141–166.

Salanova, M., Bakker, A. B., & Llorens, S. (2006). Flow at work: Evidence for an upward spiral of personal and organizational resources. *Journal of Happiness Studies, 7*(1), 1–22.

Schallberger, U., & Pfister, R. (2001). Flow-Erleben in Arbeit und Freizeit: Ein Untersuchung zum Paradox der Arbeit mit der Experience Sampling Method. *Zeitschrift für Arbeits- und Organisationspsychologie, 45*(4), 176–187.

Schmidt, J. (1999). Overcoming challenges. Unpublished doctoral dissertation, University of Chicago.

Schmidt, J. A., Shernoff, D. J., & Csikszentmihalyi, M. (2006). Individual and situational factors related to the experience of flow in adolescence: A multilevel approach. In A. D. Ong & M. H. M. van Dulmen (Eds.), *Oxford handbook of methods in positive psychology* (pp. 542–558). New York: Oxford University Press.

Seligman, M. E. P. (2002). *Authentic happiness.* New York: Free Press.

Shernoff, D. J., Csikszentmihalyi, M., Shneider, B., & Shernoff, E. S. (2003). Student engagement in high school classrooms from the perspective of flow theory. *School Psychology Quarterly, 18*(2), 158–176.

Turner, J. C., & Meyer, D. K. (2004). A classroom perspective on the principle of moderate challenge in mathematics. *Journal of Educational Research, 97*(6), 311–318.

Turner, J. C., Meyer, D. K., Cox, K. E., Logan, C., DiCintio, M., & Thomas, C. T. (1998). Creating contexts for involvement in mathematics. *Journal of Educational Psychology, 90*(4), 730–745.

Vygotsky, L. (1978). *Mind in society.* Cambridge, MA: Harvard University Press.

Waterman, A. S. (1993). Two conceptions of happiness: Contrasts of personal expressiveness (eudaimonia) and hedonic enjoyment. *Journal of Personality and Social Psychology, 64*(4), 678–691.

Wells, A. (1988). Self-esteem and optimal experience. In M. Csikszentmihalyi & I. Csikszentmihalyi (Eds.), *Optimal experience* (pp. 327–341). Cambridge: Cambridge University Press.

Whalen, S. (1999). Challenging play and the cultivation of talent: Lessons from the Key School's flow activities room. In N. Colangelo & S. Assouline (Eds.), *Talent development III* (pp. 409–411). Scottsdale, AZ: Gifted Psychology Press.

White, R. (1959). Motivation reconsidered: The concept of competence. *Psychological Review, 66,* 297–333.

Positive Affectivity: The Disposition to Experience Positive Emotional States

David Watson *and* Kristin Naragon

Abstract

Positive affectivity is a trait that reflects stable individual differences in positive emotional experience; high levels of the trait are marked by frequent feelings of cheerfulness, enthusiasm, and energy. Positive affectivity is relatively independent from negative affectivity, as these traits developed in response to different evolutionary pressures. Similar to personality traits, trait affect is structured hierarchically. Although there is not a clear consensus regarding the lower-order components of positive affectivity, we emphasize a model that includes components of Joviality, Self-Assurance, and Attentiveness. Different measures of positive affectivity are reviewed, as well as relations to overlapping constructs such as extraversion, happiness, and subjective well-being.

In terms of its biological bases, positive affectivity is moderately heritable and is linked to left prefrontal brain activation, likely mediated by the dopaminergic system. There are few demographic or environmental factors that are systematically related to levels of positive affectivity; for instance, the trait does not differ according to age or gender. However, frequency of social activity and identification as religious/spiritual are both positively correlated with positive affectivity.

Positive affect is relevant to a number of important domains. For example, low levels of positive affectivity are characteristic of numerous psychological disorders (particularly depression). Current marital and job satisfaction can be predicted based on previous measurement of positive affectivity. Positive affectivity is also related to better physical health, such as increased resistance to infectious illnesses. Finally, although mean levels of positive affectivity do not appear to differ greatly across cultures, there is evidence that culture may influence cross-situational stability and perceptions of trait affect. We conclude by showing that although temperament is an important factor in determining levels of positive affectivity, individuals are still free to take action to increase their happiness in lasting ways.

Keywords: extraversion, happiness, mood, subjective well-being, trait affect

In this chapter, we examine the broad disposition of positive affectivity, a trait that reflects stable individual differences in positive emotional experience. Individuals high on this dimension experience frequent and intense episodes of pleasant, pleasurable mood; generally speaking, they are cheerful, enthusiastic, energetic, confident, and alert. By contrast, those who are low in positive affectivity report substantially reduced levels of happiness, excitement, vigor, and confidence. Positive affectivity is a moderately stable trait over time and individuals demonstrate consistent mood levels across different situations, such as social interactions, being alone, and working (Costa & McCrae, 1992; Watson, 2000). Reflecting the general neglect of many positive psychology topics, positive affectivity was overlooked until the 1980s. Based on the past two decades of accrued research, however, a clear scholarly overview of the construct can be given.

Differentiating Positive and Negative Affectivity

Over the past few decades, researchers have established that two largely independent factors—

positive affect and negative affect—comprise the basic dimensions of emotional experience. These two broad dimensions have been identified in both intra- and interindividual analyses, and they emerge consistently across diverse descriptor sets, time frames, response formats, languages, and cultures (Watson, 1988; Watson & Clark, 1997b). Both of these dimensions can be assessed either as a short-term state or as a long-term trait (in which case they typically are referred to as "positive affectivity" and "negative affectivity," respectively).

These two affect dimensions represent the subjective components of more general biobehavioral systems that evolved to address very different evolutionary tasks (Tomarken & Keener, 1998; Watson, Wiese, Vaidya, & Tellegen, 1999). Specifically, negative affect is a component of the withdrawal-oriented Behavioral Inhibition System. The essential purpose of this system is to keep the organism out of trouble by inhibiting behavior that might lead to pain, punishment, or some other undesirable outcome. In sharp contrast to negative affect, positive affect is a component of the approach-oriented Behavioral Facilitation System, which directs organisms toward situations and experiences that potentially may yield pleasure and reward. This system is adaptive in that it ensures the procuring of resources (e.g., food and water, warmth and shelter, the cooperation of others, sexual partners) that are essential to the survival of both the individual and the species.

Given that they reflect very different evolutionary pressures, it is not surprising that negative and positive affects naturally are highly distinctive dimensions that are associated with fundamentally different classes of variables. For instance, as we detail subsequently, they correlate quite differently with general traits of personality. In light of these differential correlates, it is essential that these dimensions be assessed and analyzed separately.

The Hierarchical Structure of Positive Affectivity

Self-rated affect is hierarchically structured and must be viewed at two fundamentally different levels: a higher-order level that consists of the general negative and positive affect dimensions, and a lower-order level that represents specific types of affect (Watson & Clark, 1992a, 1992b, 1997b). In other words, both of these broad dimensions can be deconstructed into several correlated yet ultimately distinct affects, much like general intelligence can be subdivided into specific abilities. In this hierarchical model, the upper level reflects the overall "valence" of the

affects (i.e., whether they represent pleasant or unpleasant mood states) whereas the lower level reflects the specific "content" of mood descriptors (i.e., the distinctive qualities of each specific type of affect).

Little agreement exists regarding the specific types of positive affect, and this is reflected in substantial discrepancies in content among measures of positive mood. For instance, the Differential Emotions Scale (DES; Izard, Libero, Putnam, & Haynes, 1993), Multiple Affect Adjective Check List-Revised (MAACL-R; Zuckerman & Lubin, 1985), and Profile of Mood States (POMS; McNair, Lorr, & Dropplemann, 1971) each model positive affect differently. We will emphasize a structural model—based on extensive factor analyses—that distinguishes among three moderately to strongly related subcomponents of positive affect. Scales assessing each of these facets are included in the Expanded Form of the Positive and Negative Affect Schedule (PANAS-X; Watson & Clark, 1999): Joviality (eight items; e.g., "cheerful," "happy," "lively," "enthusiastic"), self-assurance (six items; e.g., "confident," "strong," "daring"), and attentiveness (four items; e.g., "alert," "concentrating," "determined"). The respondent rates each affect descriptor on a 5-point intensity scale, and the directions can be adapted to measure affectivity over different time periods (e.g., right now, during the past week, in general).

Table 19.1 reports correlations among these specific positive affects—along with the general negative affect scale of the PANAS-X—in a combined sample of more than 3,000 undergraduates (1,375 from Southern Methodist University, 1,761 from the University of Iowa; Watson & Clark, 2002). The respondents rated the extent to which they generally experienced each mood term. Two aspects of these data are noteworthy. First, the joviality, self-assurance and attentiveness scales are strongly interrelated, with correlations ranging from .48 to .57; from this, we can infer that these scales all reflect a common higher-order factor. Second, the positive mood scales all are weakly related to general negative affect, with correlations ranging from only −.14 (self-assurance) to −.21 (joviality). Based on these data, we again can observe (a) the distinctiveness of positive and negative emotional experience and (b) the importance of assessing them separately.

Measures of Positive Affectivity
Positive Affectivity Scales

The relevant assessment literature has never been subjected to a thorough review, and convergent and discriminant validity data are lacking for many

Table 19.1 Correlations among general negative affectivity and specific types of positive affectivity

Scale	Joviality	Self-assurance	Attentiveness
Joviality	—		
Self-assurance	.57	—	
Attentiveness	.53	.48	—
General negative affect	−.21	−.14	−.17

Note: $N = 3,136$. All correlations are significant at $p < .01$, two-tailed.

measures. Consequently, the conclusions drawn from these data must be tentative.

For the sake of convenience, measures of positive affectivity can be divided into two basic types. First, many widely used affect inventories have a "general" form (in which respondents rate their typical, average feelings) that can be used to measure this trait. For instance, the DES, the MAACL-R, and the PANAS-X all have trait versions that allow one to assess various aspects of the dimension. Unfortunately, researchers have failed to examine the convergence among these different trait instruments.

Second, many personality inventories contain scales relevant to the construct; examples include the Activity and Positive Emotions facet scales of the Revised NEO Personality Inventory (NEO PI-R; Costa & McCrae, 1992), the Well-Being scale of the Multidimensional Personality Questionnaire (MPQ; Tellegen, in press), and the Positive Temperament scale of the General Temperament Survey (GTS; Clark & Watson, 1990). Watson and colleagues have collected data establishing moderate to strong links among several of these measures. For instance, in a sample of 328 college students, the GTS Positive Temperament scale correlated .62 and .48 with the NEO PI-R Activity and Positive Emotions scales, respectively (Watson & Clark, 1994). Relatedly, Clark (1993) reported a correlation of .73 between the GTS Positive Temperament and MPQ Well-Being scales in a sample of 251 college students. In addition, the trait PANAS-X scales have demonstrated moderate to strong correlations with these personality measures: the GTS Positive Temperament scale correlated .55 with general positive affect, .57 with joviality, .43 with self-assurance, and .36 with attentiveness (Watson & Clark, 1993).

Based on these data, one can conclude that these scales reflect the same basic domain of personality; however, the correlations are not high enough to suggest that these measures are completely interchangeable. Because of this, it is somewhat hazardous to collapse results obtained using different instruments. At this stage of the literature, unfortunately, it is necessary to do so.

Measures of Related Constructs

Wherever possible, we rely on data from pure, established measures of positive affectivity in the following sections. Because of gaps in the existing literature, however, it will also be necessary to draw on evidence based on closely related constructs. For instance, measures of happiness and subjective well-being tend to be strongly correlated with positive affectivity scales. However, they also have a secondary component of low negative affectivity (in other words, happy people tend to report both high positive affectivity and low negative affectivity), so these indices do not represent pure measures of positive affectivity (Myers & Diener, 1995; Watson & Clark, 1997b). Similarly, global self-esteem scales tend to be complex mixtures of high positive affectivity and low negative affectivity (Watson, Suls, & Haig, 2002).

Positive affectivity scales also are strongly and systematically related to general traits of personality, particularly extraversion (Lucas, Diener, Grob, Suh, & Shao, 2000; Watson & Clark, 1992b, 1997a; Watson et al., 1999). It will be helpful, in this regard, to examine positive affectivity in relation to the complete five-factor (or "Big Five") model of personality. Extensive structural analyses of personality descriptors consistently have revealed five broad higher-order trait factors: extraversion, agreeableness, conscientiousness, neuroticism, and openness to experience (Costa & McCrae, 1992; Watson & Clark, 1992b).

We computed correlations between trait affectivity and the Big Five in the combined undergraduate sample that was described previously. All respondents completed trait forms of the general negative affect scale and the various positive affectivity scales of the PANAS-X. In addition, they were administered one of several different Big Five

Table 19.2 Correlations between positive and negative affectivity and measures of the Big Five personality traits

Affect scale	E	A	C	N	O
Negative affectivity					
General negative affect	−.26	−.33	−.23	**.58**	−.14
Positive affectivity					
General positive affect	**.49**	.22	.39	−.35	.23
Joviality	**.60**	.31	.22	−.36	.15
Self-assurance	**.47**	−.05	.16	−**.41**	.21
Attentiveness	.28	.23	**.53**	−.26	.19

Note: $N = 3,136$. All correlations are significant at $p < .01$, two-tailed. Correlations of |.40| and greater are shown in boldface. E = extraversion; A = agreeableness; C = conscientiousness; N = neuroticism; O = openness.

instruments; we standardized the scores in each individual sample to eliminate differences in metric across these Big Five measures, which allowed us to combine them in an overall analysis (see Table 19.2; Watson & Clark, 2002). Replicating previous findings in this area (Watson & Clark, 1992b), negative affectivity is very strongly related to neuroticism (overall $r = .58$) and more modestly correlated with the other traits. By contrast, the general positive affect scale is most strongly linked ($r = .49$) with extraversion. Consistent with earlier research (Watson & Clark, 1992b), however, we also observe considerable specificity at the lower-order level. That is, extraversion is strongly correlated with joviality ($r = .60$), moderately correlated with self-assurance ($r = .47$), and only modestly related to Attentiveness ($r = .28$). Indeed, attentiveness scores are much more highly related to conscientiousness ($r = .53$) than to extraversion. Extraversion obviously is highly relevant to any discussion of positive affectivity; accordingly, we will make use of extraversion-based results in subsequent sections.

Summary of Research Findings
Causes and Correlates of Positive Affectivity
GENETIC EVIDENCE

What causes mean-level differences in positive affectivity? First, this trait clearly is strongly heritable. Most of the available data are based on measures of extraversion. Heritability estimates for extraversion derived from twin studies generally fall in the .40–.60 range, with a median value of approximately .50 (Clark & Watson, 1999). Adoption studies yield somewhat lower heritability estimates, but this largely may be due to their failure to assess nonadditive genetic variance. Finally, based on results from both twin and adoption studies, it appears that the common rearing environment

(i.e., the effects of living together in the same household) exerts little influence on this trait (Clark & Watson, 1999).

Although the literature involving pure measures of positive affectivity is much smaller, it has yielded very similar results. Researchers using the MPQ Well-Being scale have reported heritability estimates in the .40–.50 range (Finkel & McGue, 1997; Tellegen et al., 1988). Similarly, Jang, McCrae, Angleitner, Riemann, and Livesley (1998) obtained heritabilities of .38 for both the NEO PI-R Positive Emotions and Activity scales, whereas Eid, Riemann, Angleitner, and Borkenau (2003) reported heritabilities of .36 and .45 for Positive Affect and Energy, respectively. Moreover, consistent with the data for extraversion, these studies indicate that the common rearing environment essentially has no effect on the development of positive affectivity.

NEUROBIOLOGICAL BASIS OF POSITIVE AFFECTIVITY

How do these innate genotypic differences manifest themselves as phenotypic differences in positive emotionality? Davidson, Tomarken, and their colleagues have demonstrated that happy individuals tend to show relatively greater resting activity in the left prefrontal cortex than in the right prefrontal area; conversely, dysphoric individuals display relatively greater right anterior activity. Unfortunately, it has proven difficult to isolate the specific effects of left versus right prefrontal activity in these studies. However, it appears that positive affectivity primarily reflects the level of resting activity in the left prefrontal area, whereas negative affectivity is more strongly associated with right frontal activation (Davidson, Jackson, & Kalin, 2000; Tomarken & Keener, 1998).

This left prefrontal activity, in turn, can be linked to the mesolimbic dopaminergic system, which has been strongly implicated in the operation of the Behavioral Facilitation System and in the subjective experience of positive mood (Depue & Collins, 1999; Wacker, Chavanon, & Stemmler, 2006). Taken together, these data suggest that the dopaminergic system plays a key role in both left frontal activation and phenotypic differences in positive affectivity. Depue, Luciana, Arbisi, Collins, and Leon (1994) examined this idea by administering biological agents known to stimulate dopaminergic activity, and then measuring the strength of the system's response. Consistent with their expectation, Depue and colleagues found that various measures of dopaminergic activity were strongly correlated with individual differences in positive affectivity, but were unrelated to negative affectivity.

DEMOGRAPHIC AND ENVIRONMENTAL CORRELATES

An enormous literature has examined how numerous demographic variables—age, gender, marital status, ethnicity, income and socioeconomic status, and so on—are related to individual differences in happiness, life satisfaction, and trait affectivity (for reviews, see Argyle, 1987; Myers & Diener, 1995; Watson, 2000). From these studies, it is clear that objective demographic factors are relatively weak predictors of happiness and positive affectivity. For instance, positive affectivity scores are not systematically related to age (Clark & Watson, 1999; Watson & Walker, 1996). Along these same lines, variables such as annual income, level of educational attainment, and socioeconomic status are, at best, weakly related to happiness and well-being (Myers & Diener, 1995; Watson, 2000). Similarly, men and women report virtually identical levels of happiness and positive affectivity (Watson, 2000; Watson & Clark, 1999). Thus, an individual's capacity for positive affectivity is not seriously limited by objective conditions such as gender, age, wealth, and status.

Two variables consistently have emerged as significant predictors of positive affectivity. First, positive affectivity—but not negative affectivity—is moderately correlated with various indicators of social behavior, including number of close friends, frequency of contact with friends and relatives, making new acquaintances, involvement in social organizations, and overall level of social activity (Myers & Diener, 1995; Watson, 2000; Watson & Clark, 1997a). Thus, those who are high in positive affectivity tend to be extraverts who are socially active. The underlying causality appears to be bidirectional, with social activity and positive affectivity mutually influencing each other (Watson, 2000; Watson & Clark, 1997a).

On the one hand, it is well established that social interaction typically produces a transient elevation in positive mood (Watson, 2000); on the other hand, it also is true that feelings of cheerfulness, liveliness, and enthusiasm are associated with an enhanced desire for affiliation and an increased preference for interpersonal contact (Lucas et al., 2000).

Second, people who describe themselves as "spiritual" or "religious" report higher levels of happiness than those who do not; this effect has been observed both in the United States and in Europe (Myers & Diener, 1995; Watson, 2000). We have found that religion and spirituality are positively related to positive affectivity, but are unrelated to negative affectivity (Clark & Watson, 1999; Watson & Clark, 1993). Why are spiritual and religious people happier? Two basic explanations have been offered (Myers & Diener, 1995; Watson, 2000). First, religion may provide people with a profound sense of meaning and purpose in their lives, thereby supplying them with plausible answers to the basic existential questions of life. Second, religious activity simply may represent a particular variety of social behavior. In other words, membership in a religious denomination allows people to congregate together, espouse shared views, and form supportive relationships. Consistent with this explanation, people who are religious rate themselves as being less lonely than those who are not (Argyle, 1987).

Broader Significance of the Trait
LINKS TO PSYCHOPATHOLOGY

Low levels of positive affectivity are associated with a number of clinical syndromes, including social phobia, agoraphobia, posttraumatic stress disorder, schizophrenia, eating disorder, and the substance disorders (Mineka, Watson, & Clark, 1998; Watson, 2000). However, low positive affectivity plays a particularly salient role in the mood disorders (Clark, Watson, & Mineka, 1994; Mineka et al., 1998; Watson, 2000; Watson, Gamez, & Simms, 2005). It is strongly linked to the melancholic subtype of major depression, which is characterized by either a "loss of pleasure in all, or almost all, activities" or a "lack of reactivity to usually pleasurable stimuli" (American Psychiatric Association, 2000, p. 420). It also is noteworthy that positive affectivity scores have predicted the subsequent development of depression in prospective data. These findings raise the intriguing possibility that lack of positive affectivity may be an important vulnerability factor for mood disorder (Clark et al., 1994).

This link with positive affectivity also may help to explain the cyclic course of the mood disorders. This cyclicity is most apparent in the bipolar disorders, in which the individual fluctuates between well-defined episodes of mania (or hypomania) and depression. Similarly, major depression tends to occur in episodes that may spontaneously remit over time (American Psychiatric Association, 2000). Moreover, melancholic depression frequently shows a marked diurnal pattern in which the symptoms are worst in the morning and then lessen in strength over the course of the day. Finally, the mood disorders can show a marked seasonal pattern, as is exhibited in seasonal affective disorder, which is characterized by the onset of a prolonged depressive episode during the late fall or early winter. It surely is not coincidental that these circadian and seasonal trends parallel those observed with positive mood (Watson, 2000).

JOB AND MARITAL SATISFACTION

Individuals who are high in positive affectivity feel good about themselves and their world. Consequently, they report greater satisfaction with important aspects of their lives, as well as more success across multiple domains such as work and relationships (Lyubomirsky, King, & Diener, 2005). For instance, positive affectivity is a significant predictor of job satisfaction (Connolly & Viswesvaran, 2000; Watson & Slack, 1993). Watson and Slack (1993) used a prospective design in which employees initially completed a measure of positive affectivity (a short-form of the MPQ Well-Being scale) and then rated their job satisfaction more than 2 years later (M interval = 27 months). Positive affectivity remained a significant, moderate predictor of various aspects of job satisfaction (with correlations ranging from .27 to .44), even when the measures were separated by a considerable time interval. Staw, Bell, and Clausen (1986) report even more striking evidence along these same lines. They found that a 17-item Affective Disposition scale (which represents a combination of high positive affectivity and low negative affectivity)—assessed when the participants were adolescents—was a significant predictor of job satisfaction nearly 50 years later, even after controlling for objective differences in work conditions. Furthermore, positive affectivity is also strongly related to personal accomplishment (an individual's sense of adequacy and effectiveness on the job) and organizational commitment (see Thoresen, Kaplan, Barsky, Warren, & de Chermont, 2003, for a meta-analysis).

On the basis of these data, we can conclude that trait affectivity plays an important etiological role in overall job satisfaction.

Positive affectivity is also significantly correlated with marital and relationship satisfaction. Watson, Hubbard, and Wiese (2000) examined this issue in two different samples, one consisting of 74 married couples, and the other comprised of 136 dating couples. Positive emotionality had correlations with satisfaction that ranged from .24 to .48 across these two samples. These data are cross-sectional, so that it is unclear whether scores on this dimension can predict relationship satisfaction prospectively. It also should be noted that marital satisfaction and job satisfaction are themselves linked, and there is some evidence that mood (particularly positive affect) may mediate this relationship (Heller & Watson, 2005).

PHYSICAL HEALTH

Although much of the research linking positive affect to physical health has focused on state mood, there is also a body of research examining trait affectivity. It should be noted that many of the studies do not use pure measures of positive affect, but rather related constructs such as life satisfaction and happiness. With regard to objective health measures, numerous studies have shown that positive affectivity prospectively predicts increased longevity in the community dwelling elderly population (Danner, Snowdon, & Friesen, 2001; Ostir, Markides, Black, & Goodwin, 2000; Parker, Thorslund, & Nordstrom, 1992). However, this association has not been consistently found in other populations. Positive affectivity has also been linked to resistance to developing infectious illnesses. For example, Cohen, Doyle, Turner, Alper, and Skoner (2003) aggregated daily mood scores to create measures of trait positive and negative affectivity. They then exposed participants to viruses known to cause the common cold. Those with high positive affectivity were less likely to develop a cold subsequent to exposure, even after controlling for factors such as negative affectivity and baseline immunity.

Positive affectivity is also associated with better physical health in studies using subjective report. For instance, among both diseased and healthy populations, those who are higher in positive affectivity report fewer symptoms and less pain (De Gucht, Fischler, & Heiser, 2004; Kvaal & Patodia, 2000).

How can we explain the link between positive affectivity and improved health? One possibility is that positive affectivity changes how people "perceive" their health and bodies, rather than changing their physical state directly. This is supported by the finding that given similar objective markers of disease, those high in positive affectivity report fewer and less severe symptoms (Cohen et al., 2003). Positive affectivity also may influence health through its association with healthy behaviors, such as better sleep habits (Fosse, Stickgold, & Hobson, 2002), increased exercise (Watson, 2000), and improved coping skills (Salovey, Rothman, Detweiler, & Steward, 2000). Finally, there is some evidence that positive affectivity may directly affect nervous system activation and hormones that impact disease processes (Cohen et al., 2003; Polk, Cohen, Doyle, Skoner, & Kirschbaum, 2005). To gain a clearer understanding of how positive affectivity relates to health, we need more studies that use pure measures of positive affectivity and that control for the influence of negative affectivity (Pressman & Cohen, 2005).

CULTURAL INFLUENCES

What role does culture play in our experience of positive affectivity? In terms of mean level differences across cultures, studies have yielded inconsistent results. There is some evidence that individualist, rich, and democratic cultures may have higher levels of subjective well-being than collectivistic, poor, and totalitarian cultures (Diener & Suh, 2000). Based on the responses of more than 6,000 college students, Lucas et al. (2000) reported that the structure of extraversion and positive affect was identical across 39 different countries. In a study of Caucasian American, Hispanic American, Japanese, and Indian college students, Oishi, Diener, Scollon, and Biswas-Diener (2004) found equal temporal stability in affective experiences across cultures when mood was measured at random moments over 7 days. Other evidence suggests that temperament has a larger effect on the "actual" affective experiences of individuals (thus explaining the commonalities in affectivity across cultures), while cultural factors play a larger role in the individual's conception of their "ideal" (or most valued) affective experiences (Tsai, Knutson, & Fung, 2006). Overall, there are more similarities than differences in the positive affective experiences of individuals from different cultures.

One cultural variable that may impact positive affectivity and extraversion is the degree of individualism (independent self-conceptualization) versus collectivism (interdependent self-conceptualization) in the culture. For instance, in the large-scale study described previously, Lucas et al. (2000) found that individualism versus collectivism moderated the strength of the association between extraversion and positive affect, with weaker correlations emerging in collectivist countries. Individualism versus collectivism may also impact the within-person cross-situational consistency of affective experience. Oishi et al. (2004) measured mood while participants were in various situations, such as being alone versus with someone else. The situation had a greater impact on the individual's level of positive affect in more collectivist cultures than in individualist cultures, with affective experience remaining more stable regardless of the situation in the latter. Thus, individual differences in positive affectivity may be more consistent and salient in individualistic cultures.

Raising Positive Affectivity

As we have shown, positive affectivity levels are not highly constrained by objective life conditions. Indeed, Diener and Diener (1996) demonstrated that most people—including the poor and the physically handicapped—describe themselves as experiencing at least moderate levels of positive affectivity. Nevertheless, the fact remains that many of us are not as happy as we would like to be. Surely, few of us would object to feeling more cheerful and energetic than we currently are. This raises a crucial issue: Is true, long-term change really possible? Various lines of evidence suggest that major life events typically exert a significant influence on well-being only in the short term, and that people eventually adapt to them and gradually move back to their preexisting baseline or "set-point" (Diener, Lucas, & Scollon, 2006; Myers & Diener, 1995; Watson, 2000). Furthermore, as was discussed earlier, positive affectivity levels clearly are strongly influenced by hereditary factors that influence the functioning of the central nervous system. These data suggest that some people simply may be destined to be more cheerful and enthusiastic than others, regardless of major life events or any systematic attempts at change.

One may easily exaggerate, however, the constraints imposed by genetic and biological factors. Indeed, recent research by Lyubomirsky and others has indicated that, while changes in circumstance may have little permanent impact on positive affectivity, intentional activity changes can lead to lasting higher levels of happiness (e.g., Diener et al., 2006; Sheldon & Lyubomirksy, 2006). Behavior geneticists repeatedly have attacked the overly simplistic view that evidence of heritability necessarily implies that change is impossible. As Weinberg (1989) put it, "There is a myth that if a behavior or characteristic is genetic, it cannot be changed. Genes do not fix behavior. Rather, they establish a range of possible reactions to the range of possible experiences that environments can provide" (p. 101). In other words, inherited genotypes simply establish the maximum and minimum phenotypic values that are possible for a given individual; environmental factors then are free to determine exactly where the person falls within this range. Furthermore, unless a person already has reached his or her maximum phenotypic value (a condition that should occur rarely, if at all), it should be possible to increase positive affectivity significantly, regardless of the phenotypic value. Consequently, the genetic and biological data should not induce a fatalistic resignation; we still are free to increase our positive affectivity and to move closer toward our potential maximum.

Future Questions

1. We currently lack consensus regarding the lower-order components of positive affectivity. What are the specific facets that define this higher-order dimension?

2. We now have good evidence that levels of negative affectivity have increased over the past few decades, such that the average person today is reporting higher levels of negative emotionality than in the past. However, we lack parallel data regarding positive affectivity: Are we witnessing any systematic changes in overall levels of this trait over time?

3. How does positive affectivity interact with negative affectivity in influencing both physical and psychological health? For example, can high levels of positive emotionality serve as a protective factor to reduce the risk of illness or mental disorder in individuals who also are high in negative emotionality?

References

American Psychiatric Association. (2000). *Diagnostic and statistical manual of mental disorders* (4th ed., Text rev.). Washington, DC: Author.

Argyle, M. (1987). *The psychology of happiness*. New York: Methuen.

Clark, L. A. (1993). *Schedule for Nonadaptive and Adaptive Personality (SNAP): Manual for administration, scoring, and interpretation*. Minneapolis, MN: University of Minnesota Press.

Clark, L. A., & Watson, D. (1990). The General Temperament Survey. Unpublished manuscript, University of Iowa, Iowa City, IA.

Clark, L. A., & Watson, D. (1999). Temperament: A new paradigm for trait psychology. In L. A. Pervin & O. P. John (Eds.), *Handbook of personality* (2nd ed., pp. 399–423). New York: Guilford.

Clark, L. A., Watson, D., & Mineka, S. (1994). Temperament, personality, and the mood and anxiety disorders. *Journal of Abnormal Psychology, 103*, 103–116.

Cohen, S., Doyle, W. J., Turner, R. B., Alper, C. M., & Skoner, D. P. (2003). Emotional style and susceptibility to the common cold. *Psychosomatic Medicine, 65*, 652–657.

Connolly, J. J., & Viswesvaran, C. (2000). The role of affectivity in job satisfaction: A meta-analysis. *Personality and Individual Differences, 29*, 265–281.

Costa, P. T., Jr., & McCrae, R. R. (1992). *Revised NEO Personality Inventory (NEO-PI-R) and NEO Five-Factor Inventory (NEO-FFI) professional manual*. Odessa, FL: Psychological Assessment Resources.

Danner, D. D., Snowdon, D. A., & Friesen, W. V. (2001). Positive emotions in early life and longevity: Findings from the nun study. *Journal of Personality and Social Psychology, 80*, 804–813.

Davidson, R. J., Jackson, D. C., & Kalin, N. H. (2000). Emotion, plasticity, context, and regulation: Perspectives from affective neuroscience. *Psychological Bulletin, 126*, 890–909.

De Gucht, V., Fischler, B., & Heiser, W. (2004). Neuroticism, alexithymia, negative affect, and positive affect as determinants of medically unexplained symptoms. *Personality and Individual Differences, 36*, 1655–1667.

Depue, R. A., & Collins, P. F. (1999). Neurobiology of the structure of personality: Dopamine, facilitation of incentive motivation, and extraversion. *Behavioral and Brain Sciences, 22*, 491–569.

Depue, R. A., Luciana, M., Arbisi, P., Collins, P., & Leon, A. (1994). Dopamine and the structure of personality: Relation of agonist-induced dopamine activity to positive emotionality. *Journal of Personality and Social Psychology, 67*, 485–498.

Diener, E., & Diener, C. (1996). Most people are happy. *Psychological Science, 7*, 181–185.

Diener, E., Lucas, R. E., & Scollon, C. N. (2006). Beyond the hedonic treadmill: Revising the adaptation theory of well-being. *American Psychologist, 61*, 305–314.

Diener, E., & Suh, E. M. (Eds.). (2000). *Culture and subjective well-being*. Cambridge: The MIT Press.

Eid, M., Riemann, R., Angleitner, A., & Borkenau, P. (2003). Sociability and positive emotionality: Genetic and environmental contributions to the covariation between different facets of extraversion. *Journal of Personality, 71*, 319–346.

Finkel, D., & McGue, M. (1997). Sex differences and nonadditivity in heritability of the Multidimensional Personality Questionnaire scales. *Journal of Personality and Social Psychology, 72*, 929–938.

Fosse, R., Stickgold, R., & Hobson, J. A. (2002). Emotional experience during rapid-eye-movement sleep in narcolepsy. *Sleep, 25*, 724–732.

Heller, D., & Watson, D. (2005). The dynamic spillover of satisfaction between work and marriage: The role of time and mood. *Journal of Applied Psychology, 90*, 1273–1279.

Izard, C. E., Libero, D. Z., Putnam, P., & Haynes, O. M. (1993). Stability of emotion experiences and their relations to traits of personality. *Journal of Personality and Social Psychology, 64*, 847–860.

Jang, K. L., McCrae, R. R., Angleitner, A., Riemann, R., & Livesley, W. J. (1998). Heritability of facet-level traits in a cross-cultural twin sample: Support for a hierarchical model of personality. *Journal of Personality and Social Psychology, 74*, 1556–1565.

Kvaal, S. A., & Patodia, S. (2000). Relations among positive affect, negative affect, and somatic symptoms in a medically ill patient sample. *Psychological Reports, 87*, 227–233.

Lucas, R. E., Diener, E., Grob, A., Suh, E. M., & Shao, L. (2000). Cross-cultural evidence for the fundamental features of extraversion. *Journal of Personality and Social Psychology, 79*, 452–468.

Lyubomirsky, S., King, L., & Diener, E. (2005). The benefits of frequent positive affect: Does happiness lead to success? *Psychological Bulletin, 131*, 803–855.

McNair, D. M., Lorr, M., & Droppleman, L. F. (1971). *Manual: Profile of mood states*. San Diego, CA: Educational and Industrial Testing Service.

Mineka, S., Watson, D., & Clark, L. A. (1998). Comorbidity of anxiety and unipolar mood disorders. *Annual Review of Psychology, 49*, 377–412.

Myers, D. G., & Diener, E. (1995). Who is happy? *Psychological Science, 6*, 10–19.

Oishi, S., Diener, E., Scollon, C. N., & Biswas-Diener, R. (2004). Cross-situational consistency of affective experiences across cultures. *Journal of Personality and Social Psychology, 86*, 460–472.

Ostir, G. V., Markides, K. S., Black, S. A., & Goodwin, J. S. (2000). Emotional well-being predicts subsequent functional independence and survival. *Journal of the American Geriatrics Society, 48*, 473–478.

Parker, M., G., Thorslund, M., & Nordstrom, M. L. (1992). Predictors of mortality for the oldest old. A 4-year follow-up of community-based elderly in Sweden. *Archives of Gerontology and Geriatrics, 14*, 227–237.

Polk, D. E., Cohen, S., Doyle, W. J., Skoner, D. P., & Kirschbaum, C. (2005). State and trait affect as predictors of salivary cortisol in healthy adults. *Psychoneuroendocrinology, 30*, 261–272.

Pressman, S. D., & Cohen, S. (2005). Does positive affect influence health? *Psychological Bulletin, 131*, 925–971.

Salovey, P., Rothman, A. J., Detweiler, J. B., & Steward, W. T. (2000). Emotional states and physical health. *American Psychologist, 55*, 110–121.

Sheldon, K. M., & Lyubomirsky, S. (2006). Achieving sustainable gains in happiness: Change your actions, not your circumstances. *Journal of Happiness Studies, 7*, 55–86.

Staw, B., Bell, N. E., & Clausen, J. A. (1986). The dispositional approach to job attitudes: A lifetime longitudinal test. *Administrative Science Quarterly, 31*, 56–77.

Tellegen, A. (in press). *Multidimensional Personality Questionnaire*. Minneapolis, MN: University of Minnesota Press.

Tellegen, A., Lykken, D. T., Bouchard, T. J., Jr., Wilcox, K. J., Segal, N. L., & Rich, S. (1988). Personality similarity in twins reared apart and together. *Journal of Personality and Social Psychology, 54*, 1031–1039.

Thoresen, C. J., Kaplan, S. A., Barsky, A. P., Warren, C. R., & de Chermont, K. (2003). The affective underpinnings of job perceptions and attitudes: A meta-analytic review and integration. *Psychological Bulletin, 129*, 914–945.

Tomarken, A. J., & Keener, A. D. (1998). Frontal brain asymmetry and depression: A self-regulatory perspective. *Cognition and Emotion, 12*, 387–420.

Tsai, J. L., Knutson, B., & Fung, H. H. (2006). Cultural variation in affect valuation. *Journal of Personality and Social Psychology, 90*, 288–307.

Wacker, J., Chavanon, M.-L., & Stemmler, G. (2006). Investigating the dopaminergic basis of extraversion in humans: A multilevel approach. *Journal of Personality and Social Psychology, 91*, 171–187.

Watson, D. (1988). The vicissitudes of mood measurement: Effects of varying descriptors, time frames, and response formats on measures of Positive and Negative Affect. *Journal of Personality and Social Psychology, 55*, 128–141.

Watson, D. (2000). *Mood and temperament*. New York: Guilford.

Watson, D., & Clark, L. A. (1992a). Affects separable and inseparable: On the hierarchical arrangement of the negative affects. *Journal of Personality and Social Psychology, 62*, 489–505.

Watson, D., & Clark, L. A. (1992b). On traits and temperament: General and specific factors of emotional experience and their relation to the Five-Factor Model. *Journal of Personality, 60*, 441–476.

Watson, D., & Clark, L. A. (1993). Behavioral disinhibition versus constraint: A dispositional perspective. In D. M. Wegner & J. W. Pennebaker (Eds.), *Handbook of mental control* (pp. 506–527). New York: Prentice-Hall.

Watson, D., & Clark, L. A. (1994). [Associations between the SNAP and NEO-PI-R trait scales]. Unpublished raw data.

Watson, D., & Clark, L. A. (1997a). Extraversion and its positive emotional core. In R. Hogan, J. Johnson, & S. Briggs (Eds.), *Handbook of personality psychology* (pp. 767–793). San Diego, CA: Academic Press.

Watson, D., & Clark, L. A. (1997b). Measurement and mismeasurement of mood: Recurrent and emergent issues. *Journal of Personality Assessment, 68*, 267–296.

Watson, D., & Clark, L. A. (1999). *The PANAS-X: Manual for the Positive and Negative Affect Schedule—Expanded form*. Retrieved from University of Iowa, Department of Psychology Web site: http://www.psychology.uiowa.edu/Faculty/Watson/Watson.html

Watson, D., & Clark, L. A. (2002). [Associations between the PANAS-X scales and the Big Five personality traits]. Unpublished raw data.

Watson, D., Gamez, W., & Simms, L. J. (2005). Basic dimensions of temperament and their relation to anxiety and depression: A symptom-based perspective. *Journal of Research in Personality, 39*, 46–66.

Watson, D., Hubbard, B., & Wiese, D. (2000). General traits of personality and affectivity as predictors of satisfaction in intimate relationships: Evidence from self- and partner-ratings. *Journal of Personality, 68*, 413–449.

Watson, D., & Slack, A. K. (1993). General factors of affective temperament and their relation to job satisfaction over time. *Organizational Behavior and Human Decision Processes, 54*, 181–202.

Watson, D., Suls, J., & Haig, J. (2002). Global self-esteem in relation to structural models of personality and affectivity. *Journal of Personality and Social Psychology, 83*, 185–197.

Watson, D., & Walker, L. M. (1996). The long-term stability and predictive validity of trait measures of affect. *Journal of Personality and Social Psychology, 70*, 567–577.

Watson, D., Wiese, D., Vaidya, J., & Tellegen, A. (1999). The two general activation systems of affect: Structural findings, evolutionary considerations, and psychobiological evidence. *Journal of Personality and Social Psychology, 76*, 820–838.

Weinberg, R. A. (1989). Intelligence and IQ: Landmark issues and great debates. *American Psychologist, 44*, 98–104.

Zuckerman, M., & Lubin, B. (1985). *Manual for the MAACL-R: The Multiple Affect Adjective Check List Revised*. San Diego, CA: Educational and Industrial Testing Service.

The Social Construction of Self-Esteem

John P. Hewitt

Abstract

Self-esteem is examined here as an object of cultural discourse and as a socially constructed emotion grounded in mood. Scientific and popular conceptions of self-esteem share an emphasis on the person's acceptance by self and others, the evaluation of performance, social comparison, and the efficacy of individual action as the important roots of self-esteem. The present analysis deconstructs these elements, treating them not as psychological universals but rather as deeply rooted in the competing themes of American culture. The discourse of self-esteem translates these themes into personal terms, enabling the person's understanding of where he or she stands in relation to such contradictory emphases as individuality versus community, striving for success versus self-acceptance, or the quest for happiness as a future state versus contentment with one's present lot. The socially constructed, discursive nature of self-esteem does not preclude an examination of its underlying psychological reality, which is here conceived as mood. Self-esteem provides a way of experiencing and interpreting mood, which functions to encourage and inhibit conduct in various situations depending upon the individual's ongoing experiences. Mood is a universal response to positive and negative experiences; self-esteem is a particular construction of mood fitted to a culture and its dominant and competing themes. The analysis considers how self-esteem binds the person to particular cultural emphases and examines the limitations of the contemporary self-esteem movement.

Keywords: affect, culture, emotion, mood, self

From the psychology of William James to the contemporary industry dedicated to its study and promotion, self-esteem has held a central place in the scholarly and popular understanding of the person in the United States. In this chapter I will examine self-esteem as an element of a culture that emphasizes the importance of the individual self even while making the self problematic; suggest reasons why the experience and discourse of self-esteem have been socially constructed; and show how this approach to self-esteem adds to our understanding of the individual in contemporary society.

The study of self-esteem has spawned an enormous research literature (see, for example, Baumeister, Campbell, Krueger, & Vohs, 2003; Gecas & Burke, 1995; Mecca, Smelser, & Vasconcellos, 1989; Owens, Stryker, & Goodman,

2001). Here, rather than summarize its complex findings, I ask what the concept of self-esteem means in cultural terms. I take the position that psychological findings about self-esteem are not universal or essential facts but discoveries about the psychology of socially, culturally, and historically situated human beings. My first task is therefore one of deconstruction.

Deconstructing the Discourse of Self-Esteem

The contemporary understanding of self-esteem is rooted in four ideas—acceptance, evaluation, comparison, and efficacy—that show strong and historically persistent resonance in American culture. To the modern mind, self-esteem seems anchored in unqualified acceptance of the child early in life, the receipt of positive evaluations from relevant others, favorable comparisons with others and with ideal versions of the self, and the capacity for efficacious action. Self-esteem is thought to be dependent upon the child's acceptance within the social fold. It is built early on a foundation of security, trust, and unconditional love. Later, whatever standards of evaluation are employed, positive evaluations will enhance self-esteem and negative evaluations will damage it. Likewise, self-esteem is enhanced when the person is able to make favorable comparisons with other people or with an ideal self, and it is enhanced when the person acts effectively in his or her physical or social environment (Damon, 1995; Gecas & Schwalbe, 1983; Owens, 1995; Rosenberg, 1979; Swann, 1996; Wills, 1981).

These elements, thought by social scientists and lay persons alike to underlie self-esteem, are deeply embedded in contemporary American culture. This culture emphasizes the individual's responsibility to create a social world or to carve out a place in an existing one where he or she can be warmly embraced. It is the individual who must cultivate and make friends, establish occupational or professional ties, or find a mate. Likewise, American culture makes available numerous situations in which the individual is exposed to evaluation, imagines the evaluations others are making, or engages in self-evaluation. Children are graded in school, rated on their athletic or musical prowess and accomplishments, and assigned to "popular" or "unpopular" peer groups. Adults are evaluated for their appearance and work performance. There are numerous occasions on which individuals reflect on how well or ill they fare in comparison with relevant others or with possible or desirable versions of themselves. Parents compare their children with those of others, assess their own accomplishments relative to their aspirations, and strive to keep up with the social standing of their friends and neighbors. And it is the individual who possesses the capacity and responsibility to act independently and effectively (Bellah, Madsen, Sullivan, Swidler, & Tipton, 1985; Hewitt, 1998).

American culture does not, however, present a single face with respect to acceptance, evaluation, comparison, and efficacy (Erikson, 1976; Hewitt, 1989, 1998). Although the social world often is portrayed as an interpersonal oyster for the individual to crack and enjoy, Americans also look wistfully for places where acceptance is guaranteed and "everybody knows your name." Schools do not apply evaluative criteria with equal rigor in all aspects of students' activities: Academic standards often are lax,

whereas only those with talent and a capacity for hard work make the varsity football team or the school orchestra. Children are told to work hard and achieve but also that they have the right to feel good about themselves no matter how they do, that they should compete only with themselves, and that failure at a task does not mean they are not worthy human beings (Hewitt, 1998). Finally, there is a countervailing communitarian impulse in American culture that mitigates its intense individualism. For some people under some conditions, self-worth is established by membership in a group and association with its members, social comparisons are between groups, and individuals take pride from group accomplishments.

This ambivalence about acceptance, evaluation, comparison, and efficacy is linked to other ambiguities and strains in American culture. Americans are urged by their Declaration of Independence to feel entitled to the "pursuit of happiness" and by long tradition to believe each person deserves a chance at success. But the meanings of happiness and success have never been clear, and this ambiguity is a key to the psychology of Americans. Happiness is defined both as a future state of enjoyment dependent upon successful individual effort and as satisfaction with one's current place in life. Everyone deserves a chance at success, but for some it is the brass ring of social and financial advancement, while for others it is the contented application of effort to a vocation even without hope of fame or fortune (Hewitt, 1989).

Americans also show considerable ambivalence about equality, specifically whether to emphasize equality of opportunity or equality of condition. The former emphasizes a level playing field: Everybody should have a fair start at the game and play under the same rules. But the belief that Americans are entitled to equality of condition also has adherents, and the scope of conditions that fall under "equal rights" has expanded. Happiness and success have to some degree become defined as rights rather than as prizes to be sought and won.

Differing versions of self-esteem mirror these contrasting meanings of success, happiness, and equality. One cluster of meanings emphasizes that self-esteem is not a right but a privilege, to be achieved by individual effort and development of appropriate attitudes and behavior. The other cluster emphasizes that self-esteem is an entitlement, that its acquisition should require no behavioral changes, and that the individual can bootstrap himself or herself to self-affirming feelings. Long-standing cultural disputes are thus encoded in new terms, and so also reproduced, as people debate the real nature of self-esteem and wonder on what basis they can feel "right" about themselves.

The language of self-esteem translates deeply rooted cultural issues into personal terms: Have I found a place where I belong and others like or respect me? Am I as happy or as successful as I could be? Am I entitled to think better of myself than I do? How can I feel better about me? What must I do to feel better? How can I justify the way I feel about myself? For those who are engaged in the "pursuit" of happiness and success and who feel themselves well on the way, "self-esteem" is a way of characterizing—and experiencing—their positive feelings about their lives. A view of self-esteem as something earned by virtue of effort and accomplishment validates their way of pursuing happiness and success. For those who feel themselves not far enough along on the path, talk of earning self-esteem is a motivational spur to further effort. It provides a way of imagining a future self and, in doing so, focusing present efforts on its attainment.

By contrast, those who espouse communitarian rather than individualist definitions of self, as well as those who have tried but failed in a future-oriented quest for success and happiness, also can find in the discourse of self-esteem the basis for comforting and reassuring self-perceptions. I am entitled to feel good about myself, one might say, because friends and family value me for virtues that transcend financial success. I am good and virtuous in their world. I am happy with who I am, for even though I have not gone far professionally or financially, I am content with my life and with those among whom I live.

The discourse of self-esteem thus provides a common language that Americans use to discuss felt difficulties with self-validation and in the same breath address cultural contradictions. This language bridges competing definitions of success and happiness, providing for both competitive striving and self-acceptance, contentment in the present, and excitement about the future. Moreover, it bridges individualism and collectivism, providing a central concept—self-esteem—on whose attainment all can agree even as they disagree on the proper means of attaining it. In creating the concept of self-esteem and laying the basis for a popular discourse about it, social scientists thus inadvertently contribute to what Michel Foucault called "technologies of the self," creating the very terms and instruments whereby the self is experienced (Martin, Gutman, & Hutton, 1998). Their professional work has in

turn fueled the efforts of legions of "conceptual entrepreneurs" who market the idea of self-esteem as well as techniques for its improvement.

The Reality of Self-Esteem

How can we most usefully conceive the nature and experience of self-esteem? The approach I recommend here defines self-esteem as a socially constructed emotion. Not merely psychological states, socially constructed emotions are situated experiences. They arise at predictable times and places under the influence of role requirements as well as status relationships, success or failure in the attainment of socially prescribed goals, and the actual or imagined evaluative judgments of others. Self-esteem is a reflexive emotion that has developed over time in social processes of invention, that individuals learn to experience and to talk about, that arises in predictable social circumstances, and that is subject to social control (Smith-Lovin, 1995). Anchoring self-esteem within the realm of emotions gives a more precise theoretical formulation than its more common definition as the evaluative dimension of self-regard and better captures the reality of the experience from the individual's standpoint. Defining the emotion of self-esteem as a social construction permits consideration of cultural variations in self-esteem but at the same time allows one to examine its underlying visceral, physiological, and neurological correlates.

Affect is a central element of the experience of self. Moreover, the range of affect that may be directed toward the self is for all practical purposes the same as the range of affect of which humans are capable. Fear, anger, hatred, love, pride, satisfaction, anxiety, loathing, shame, guilt, embarrassment, and the like all figure in the experience of self in varying degrees and circumstances. None of these forms of self-directed affect is by itself the core of self-esteem. Yet what social scientists and lay people alike understand as self-esteem is in one way or another tied to these emotional experiences. When social scientists seek to develop items to measure self-attitudes, we readily turn to pride, shame, hatred, satisfaction, and other words in the cultural vocabulary of emotions as ways of communicating to subjects the kinds of self-reports we want from them.

The key term for grasping the socially constructed emotion of self-esteem is "mood," a term that I employ in its conventional sense of a generalized aroused or subdued disposition. At one extreme lies euphoria—a pervasive good feeling that the individual might describe in a variety of culturally available terms: energized, happy, "psyched," self-confident, elated. At the other extreme lies dysphoria—a similarly pervasive feeling described in culturally opposite terms such as listless, sad, fearful, anxious, or depressed. In a state of mood closer to euphoria, the individual is aroused, organized, ready to act; in a state closer to dysphoria, the individual is more reserved, fearful, and reluctant to act. I posit that mood is a crucial animal experience; that it lies close to neurological, physiological, and visceral reality; that variations in mood are universal and can be explained in general terms; and that culture provides the words used to label mood.

Self-esteem is not the only word attached to the universal human experience of mood. People tending toward euphoria may report that they are "happy," "excited," or "self-confident," or that they "feel good" or are "in a good mood." They may respond to self-esteem measures in ways that lead a social scientist to attribute high self-esteem to them. They may strike a clinician as healthy or, if too euphoric, as manic. And if they have access to the discourse of self-esteem, as nearly everyone nowadays does, they may say that they have high self-esteem. Variations in mood are describable by a variety of culturally provided terms, none of which provides the basis for an analysis of the nature of mood, its level, or of fluctuations in it.

Labels for mood have social and cultural origins. The contemporary individual afflicted with a mood disorder, for example, has access to the social machinery of psychiatry and its array of diagnostic categories, therapies, and medicines. He or she will thus have the opportunity—and sometimes be under considerable social pressure—to accept a label of major depression and to take the steps recommended by psychologists, social workers, or psychiatrists. The seventeenth-century New England Puritan who had similar feelings of sadness, lack of self-worth, and morbid social sensitivity might well have been encouraged to look within. Believing in humankind's inherently sinful nature and uncertain of his or her own state of grace, such an individual would have found a different explanation for the same underlying feelings, and a program of self-scrutiny and repentance would have been recommended.

The interpretation of underlying affective states, perhaps especially ones so generalized as mood, thus depends upon the social processes that create and certify knowledge and assign its implementation to various experts. Interpretations also are shaped by the goals and values of particular cultures. Arguably the depressed Puritan found himself or herself

culturally, if not personally, more at ease, for a dark mood could at least be assigned religious meaning and thus be accommodated by others. Contemporary Americans are enjoined to be happy and self-confident, and thus find in depression and low self-esteem painful personal experiences that their social world does not readily tolerate.

Mood, which has been extensively studied by psychologists, poses a complex challenge to social and psychological theory. Mood is both an unperceived background of everyday action and an object of attention in its own right; it influences thoughts and actions, but it is also something people think about and act toward (Morris, 1989). It is influenced by events in the person's world but also by endogenous factors of which the individual has no knowledge. Hence, a "good" or "bad" mood may result from the reality or appearance of positive or negative events, but also independently of events as a result of malfunctioning neurotransmission.

Although the word "mood" sometimes (Isen, 1984) is used synonymously with "affect," Batson's (1990) distinction between "affect," "mood," and "emotion" is more helpful. "Affect" is the most general and primitive of the terms, and following Zajonc (1980), Batson argues that it serves to inform the organism about the more and less valued "states of affairs" it experiences. Changes toward more valued states of affairs produce positive affect, whereas changes toward less valued states produce negative affect. "Mood" is a more complex affective state, because it entails more or less well-formed "expectations" about the future experience of positive or negative affect. Mood is constituted by a change in expectation (together with the affective state evoked by the change), and thus refers to "the fine-tuning of one's perception of the general affective tone of what lies ahead" (Batson, 1990, p. 103). "Emotions" are present-oriented, focused on the person's relationship to a specific goal. Whereas the experience of a positive mood implies the expectation of more positive affect in the future, the emotion of joy arises in the present as goals are attained or attained more fully than imagined.

These ideas suggest that affect, mood, and emotion powerfully shape the development and maintenance of ties between the individual and the social order. Culture supplements psychologically intrinsic satisfactions with its own menu of approved goals and definitions of positive affect. The social order governs access to the cognitive and material means of pursuing a socially approved goal—knowing what to do and how to do it, and having the resources needed to realize a desired end. Hence, the sources of positive affect, of changes in the expectation of positive affect, and of the person's capacity to act so as to create positive events lie in culture and society. External events shape affect, mood, and emotion, resulting in a tendency for people to do what others require, encourage, or make possible. Following socially approved courses of action to approved goals produces positive affect, inclines individuals to anticipate more such affect in the future, and rewards them with positive emotions in each succeeding present.

This strong social determinism is in three ways defective. First, it does not take sufficient account of the need to interpret mood or of the potential for interpretive variability. Morris (1989) suggests that mood is figure as well as ground. As Batson (1990) defines it, mood is a more or less well-defined set of "expectations" about the future. And as a sociologist might put it, mood begins with an affective state but becomes mood only as the individual invokes a culturally supplied vocabulary and formulates those expectations in specific terms. Affective states demand interpretation, and it is in the process of interpretation that moods and emotions are created.

Interpretations vary, for there is no firm link between an affective state and the individual's perception of its origins or of the steps that might produce a more desired state. People make errors in attribution. Culture provides alternative goals and alternative vocabularies for experiencing mood and emotion. Hence, it is not necessarily obvious to the individual what actions will produce a more desirable affective result, and the link between social demands and individual lines of conduct is therefore sometimes problematic.

Second, the link between mood and events is complex. Events do produce positive and negative affect and so shape the expectation of future affective states. Thus, affective arousal influences mood, which in turn influences the person's approach to (or avoidance of) objects in the future. However, two psychological phenomena warn against excessive social determinism. The "positivity offset" helps explain people's willingness sometimes to depart from established, socially patterned forms of conduct. Even without positive affective arousal there is a bias toward approaching an object even at great distance from it. How else, as Cacioppo and Gardner (1999, p.191) point out, could we expect the organism "to approach novel objects, stimuli, or contexts." Likewise, organisms react more strongly to negative stimuli than to positive ones. Presumably this negativity bias evolved to protect the organism against the untoward consequences of its own exploratory actions. Moreover, endogenous factors may govern mood on schedules independent of external events. Depression may arise spontaneously and for no reason apparent either to the observer or to the depressed person. We refer to depression as a "mood disorder" precisely because it subverts an orderly link between events and mood.

Third, mood shapes the person's perception of the social world and his or her experiences in it. The significance of events and of those who produce them is not given solely in the events themselves, for affect strongly influences what we see and how we make sense of it. Affect shapes attention and perception (Zajonc, 1998), memory (Phelps & Anderson, 1997), and altruism (Batson, 1990). Indeed, Isen (1984) argues that "affective states—even mild and even positive affective states—can influence thoughts, cognitive processing, and social behavior in some remarkable ways" (pp. 179–180). Thus, illustratively, people in a positive affective state seem to remember positive events better than negative ones (Isen, 1984). Positive moods increase helping behavior; more precisely, events that enhance mood make it more likely that those whose moods are enhanced will help others who were not responsible for the enhanced mood (Batson, 1990). And mood influences the way we think about other persons through a mood-congruent judgment effect. Improvements in mood are accompanied by more positive views of other people (Mayer & Hanson, 1995).

From the standpoint of a psychologically informed social theory, positive mood is most usefully seen as encouraging the perception of the social world in relatively benign and nonthreatening terms. It fosters the perception of a self at ease with its others, one capable of taking actions they will find acceptable or at least understandable. It furthers the perception of a self that is accepted by friends and available for role-based interaction with strangers. By contrast, negative mood encourages the perception of a hostile social world and a self at risk in it. The dysphoric self is not a self at ease but an anxious self—anxious about what to do, about how others will respond, about the likelihood of taking successful action. It is a self located in a social world that may turn hostile at any moment, that may conceal its true attitudes, that may erect obstacles in the person's path. A euphoric person imagines a social world where it is easy to perceive opportunities, friendly and receptive others, and successful lines of conduct. A dysphoric person imagines a social world filled with obstacles, resistant or unfriendly others, and limited chances for success.

Mood, Self-Esteem, and Discourse

Self-esteem has been constructed in an American cultural context that enjoins the pursuit of happiness and success. Although subject to conflicting definitions, these are nonetheless culturally important goals. When culture sets goals, people respond in two ways that are key to the analysis. First, they respond affectively to their pursuit and attainment of these goals. Success and failure generate positive and negative "affect" and produce changes in "mood," that is, in expectations of future affect. Mood is in part a product of how successfully the person has formed attachments to the social world and of how well he or she has achieved its culturally enjoined goals. A sense of membership in the social world and of proper attainment of cultural ideals engenders elevated mood; failure in these respects engenders depressed mood.

Second, people respond to mood by interpreting it. Individuals interpret their mood experiences by utilizing a language that is available to them as members of a social world and participants in its culture. They engage in discourse that explores cultural goals, their success or failure in attaining them, and the resulting affective experiences. To understand mood and its relationship to self-esteem, then, we must examine the linguistic opportunities that are available to individuals and the forces that constrain their selection.

Self-esteem is a recent linguistic opportunity for Americans. Although psychologists and sociologists have used the word for over 100 years, it gained popular currency only in the last third of the twentieth century. The construction of the language and emotion of self-esteem has come about in response to the American cultural polarities discussed previously. The polarities themselves are long-standing ones and they have been dealt with culturally in a variety of ways. It is the vocabulary of self-esteem that is relatively new.

The historically dominant pole of American culture emphasizes success as a result of individual achievement, happiness as a future state to be sought by individual effort, and equality of opportunity to seek success and happiness. The individual is a voluntary member of a social world and either succeeds or fails as an individual. Such cultural circumstances engender individual mood responses, for some will fail badly, others will succeed greatly, and most will fall somewhere in the middle. The interpretation of mood in this cultural moment, however, is unlikely to involve self-esteem. For even where the term and the experience of self-esteem exist, classic instrumental individualism (Bellah et al., 1985) has its own linguistic convention for interpreting the individual's experiences of success and failure, and its prominent terms are "pride" and "shame."

It is difficult to imagine enterprising nineteenth-century American farmers and mechanics feeling or speaking of their "self-esteem" as enhanced by their success in wresting a living from the earth or creating new machines and industries. Rather, we today think of them—as they thought of themselves—as "proud" of their accomplishments and "ashamed" when they fell short. Much the same was true of the industrialists of the late nineteenth century, and it remains true of individuals who subscribe to contemporary versions of instrumental individualism. They are proud when they succeed and ashamed when they fail. Pride is grounded in mood in much the same way as self-esteem is so anchored. But it is not the same emotion, for pride conveys images of self-respect and dignity, and the proud individual imagines an audience that applauds effort, hard work, achievement against the odds, and self-regard that is deserved because it has been earned.

Similarly, to fall short of one's own goals or the expectations of one's fellows engenders the emotion of shame. One who accepts an ethic of achievement is disappointed, downcast, depressed, and most of all ashamed when he or she fails. Like pride, shame interprets mood by emphasizing the individual's responsibility for a course of action and its outcome. The individual feels that he or she has failed and must therefore present a shameful face to the judging, evaluating world.

Self-esteem, in contrast, answers to the opposing pole of American culture, which emphasizes "expressive" individualism. Here, success and happiness are more likely to be viewed as entitlements, or at least to be subject to relaxed standards of evaluation. Thus, one is entitled to feel happy and successful regardless of one's station in life, or at the very least one can find validation of the right to feel contentment in lesser accomplishments. The social world, in this view, owes the individual both a respectable place and respect for occupying it. The watchword is equality of condition, not of opportunity.

It is this cultural configuration that fosters a language and emotion of self-esteem. Present from the beginning, this opposing moment of the culture recently has found its voice in the language of self-esteem, as well as more broadly in humanistic psychology, in both secular and religious "positive thinking," and in assorted other popular psychologies and therapies that have proliferated in American life. Self-esteem has not driven out other words, nor has it trumped pride/shame as a principle motivating social emotion. Instrumental individualism is unlikely to disappear anytime soon.

Self-esteem does, however, support a different relationship between the individual and the social order. Pride and shame presume a relationship in which culture and society set goals for individuals and provide means for attaining them, and in which individuals readily accept cultural guidance. People feel proud and speak of pride when they achieve cultural ideals to which they feel positively attached. Self-esteem, in contrast, presumes a relatively more problematic, often oppositional relationship between the individual and the social world, one in which the individual feels at risk (cf. Turner, 1976). It is no accident that the self-esteem movement perceives, albeit mistakenly (Baumeister et al., 2003), an epidemic of low self-esteem and mounts a campaign to remedy the situation. In its frame of reference, self-esteem is an entitlement always at risk in a hostile, denigrating, judgmental social world.

What is the gain in transforming our view of self-esteem from a universal psychological trait and motivating force to a socially constructed emotion grounded in mood? It lies mainly in a more precise understanding of the challenge to the self posed by the social and cultural world in which we live, and of the ways human beings cope. To grasp how individuals function in that world, we must understand the emotional economy it creates for them and examine how they respond to it.

The emotion of self-esteem, the study of self-esteem, and a social movement that proposes to promote individual well-being and solve social problems by fostering self-esteem have arisen in a culture that puts the individual self on a shaky center stage. The discourse of self-esteem attempts to respond by articulating a cultural vision of a satisfying personal life that runs explicitly counter to the dominant competitive, instrumental individualism. It proposes an alternative world in which the individual has a right to an assured place, evaluations are not the sole basis of positive self-feeling, social comparison is subdued, and all have the capacity for efficacious action and the right to positive self-regard. Where modern life often depresses and enervates, those who emphasize self-esteem argue, they wish to elevate and energize.

The discourse of self-esteem mounts a decidedly weak critique of American culture and a program of action unlikely to change it appreciably. Programs that seek to elevate individual self-esteem through positive thinking and other forms of psychological bootstrapping merely pose a weaker expressive individualism against a dominant instrumental individualism. Such programs thus reproduce an existing set of cultural definitions rather than challenging them. They convey the illusion of action to solve personal and social problems, but in doing so accept the terms of the debate as it has been constructed by the dominant individualism.

More crucially for the present analysis, the discourse of self-esteem is apt to confuse a sign of well-being with its essence. This is so in two senses. First, "reasonably" good self-esteem provides an indication that mood is working within optimal limits to motivate and caution human action. Self-esteem is a measure of the person's expectation of positive events and, accordingly, her or his willingness to approach objects and others. Second, and more broadly, good self-esteem is indicative of a positive and integral personal and social identity (cf. Hewitt, 1989)—that is, a sense that one is located securely in the social world, competent to meet its challenges, ready to participate in life with others, and able to balance social demands and personal desires (cf. Scheff, 1990).

Although self-esteem is a desirable state (or trait) because of what it signifies about personal well-being, it has become reasonably clear that the most effective way to achieve good self-esteem is not by implementing programs in schools and other locations to improve it (Baumeister et al., 2003). The fundamental mistake of the self-esteem movement is not to emphasize its importance but to imagine that self-esteem is itself the goal to be pursued. Conditions that promote optimal human functioning also promote self-esteem, and these fundamental conditions are the ones worth pursuing: acceptance within a social fold, a sense of security, cultural competence, and the capacity to reconcile personal goals and social expectations.

Questions

1. How will the emotional economy in which self-esteem has been socially constructed be transformed in the future and how will these changes shape the experience and discourse of self-esteem?

2. Will the increasingly sophisticated psychological and social psychological understanding of self-esteem, which emphasizes self-esteem as an outcome

of other experiences, shape the popular self-esteem movement, which emphasizes self-esteem as an important goal in itself?

3. Can the analysis of self-esteem as a socially constructed emotion grounded in mood form a basis for researches that examine, in situ, how the experience and discourse of self-esteem function in everyday life?

References and Recommended Readings*

Batson, C. D. (1990). Affect and altruism. In B. S. Moore & A. M. Isen (Eds.), *Affect and social behavior* (pp. 89–125). Cambridge: Cambridge University Press.

Baumeister, R. F., Campbell, J., Krueger, J., & Vohs, K. (2003). Does high self-esteem cause better performance, interpersonal success, happiness, or healthier lifestyles? *Psychological Science in the Public Interest, 4*, 1–44.

Bellah, R. N., Madsen, R., Sullivan, W. M., Swidler, A., & Tipton, S. (1985). *Habits of the heart: Individualism and commitment in American life.* Berkeley, CA: University of California Press.

Cacioppo, J. T., & Gardner, W. L. (1999). Emotion. In *Annual Review of Psychology* (Electronic ed.), 1999, Gale Group.

*Damon, W. (1995). *Greater expectations: Overcoming the culture of indulgence in America's homes and schools.* New York: Free Press.

Erikson, K. T. (1976). *Everything in its path.* New York: Simon and Schuster.

*Gecas, V., & Burke, P. (1995). Self and identity. In K. Cook, G. A Fine, & J. S. House (Eds.), *Sociological perspectives on social psychology* (pp. 41–67). Boston: Allyn and Bacon.

Gecas, V., & Schwalbe, M. (1983). Beyond the looking-glass self: Social structure and efficacy-based self-esteem. *Social Psychology Quarterly, 46*, 77–88.

*Hewitt, J. P. (1989). *Dilemmas of the American self.* Philadelphia: Temple University Press.

*Hewitt, J. P. (1998). *The myth of self-esteem: Finding happiness and solving problems in America.* New York: St. Martin's.

Isen, A. M. (1984). Toward understanding the role of affect in cognition. In R. S. Wyer, Jr., & T. K. Srull (Eds.), *Handbook of social cognition* (Vol. 3, pp. 179–236). Hillsdale, NJ: Erlbaum.

Martin, L. H., Gutman, H., & Hutton, P. H. (Eds.). (1988). *Technologies of the self: A seminar with Michel Foucault.* Amherst, MA: University of Massachusetts Press.

Mayer, J. D., & Hanson, E. (1995). Mood-congruent judgment over time. *Personality and Social Psychology Bulletin, 21*, 237–244.

*Mecca, A. M., Smelser, N. L., & Vasconcellos, J. (Eds.). (1989). *The social importance of self-esteem.* Berkeley, CA: University of California Press.

Morris, W. N. (1989). *Mood: The frame of mind.* New York: Springer-Verlag.

Owens, K. (1995). *Raising your child's inner self-esteem: The authoritative guide from infancy through the teen years.* New York: Plenum.

Owens, T. J., Stryker, S., & Goodman, N. (Eds.). (2001). *Extending self-esteem theory and research: Social and psychological currents.* Cambridge: Cambridge University Press.

Phelps, E. A., & Anderson, A. K. (1997). Emotional memory: What does the amygdala do? *Current Biology, 7*, 311–314.

*Rosenberg, M. (1979). *Conceiving the self.* New York: Basic Books.

Scheff, T. J. (1990). *Microsociology: Discourse, emotion, and social structure.* Chicago: University of Chicago Press.

Smith-Lovin, L. (1995). The sociology of affect and emotion. In K. Cook, G. A. Fine, & J. S. House (Eds.), *Sociological perspectives on social psychology* (pp. 118–148). Boston: Allyn and Bacon.

*Swann, W. (1996). *Self-traps: The elusive quest for higher self-esteem.* New York: Freeman.

Turner, R. H. (1976). The real self: From institution to impulse. *American Journal of Sociology, 81*, 989–1016.

Wills, T. A. (1981). Downward comparison principles in social psychology. *Psychological Bulletin, 90*, 245–271.

Zajonc, R. B. (1980). Feeling and thinking: Preferences need no inferences. *American Psychologist, 35*, 151–175.

Zajonc, R. B. (1998). Emotions. In D. T. Gilbert, S. T. Fiske, & L. Gardner (Eds.), *Handbook of social psychology* (pp. 591–634). New York: Oxford University Press.

Coping Through Emotional Approach: Emerging Evidence for the Utility of Processing and Expressing Emotions in Responding to Stressors

Annette L. Stanton, Sarah J. Sullivan, *and* Jennifer L. Austenfeld

Abstract

Emotional approach coping (EAC) is a construct encompassing the intentional use of emotional processing and emotional expression in efforts to manage adverse circumstances. The construct was developed in an attempt to reconcile a discrepancy between the empirical coping literature, in which an association between the use of emotion-focused coping and maladjustment often is reported, and literature in other areas describing the adaptive roles of emotional processing and expression. At least two significant limitations in the way emotion-focused coping has been operationalized help explain this discrepancy: widely disparate coping strategies, both approach-oriented and avoidance-oriented, are designated as emotion-focused coping in the literature, and some emotion-focused coping items in published measures are confounded with expressions of distress or self-deprecation.

To address these problems in measurement, the EAC scale was developed. The measure includes two correlated but distinct subscales: Emotional Processing (i.e., attempts to acknowledge, explore, and understand emotions) and Emotional Expression (i.e., verbal and/or nonverbal efforts to communicate or symbolize emotional experience). Recent research using this psychometrically sound measure has provided evidence that EAC enhances adjustment to stressors including infertility, sexual assault, and breast cancer. The findings are not uniform, however, and further study of moderators such as the interpersonal context, the nature of the stressor, cognitive appraisals of the stressor, and individual differences is needed, along with additional study of mechanisms for the effects of EAC. Although emotional processing and expression are core components of many clinical approaches, specific measurement of EAC thus far has been limited to only a few clinical intervention trials. An understanding of who benefits from EAC in which contexts and how these benefits accrue will require continued integration of findings from stress and coping research, emotion science, and clinical studies.

Keywords: coping, emotion, emotional approach, stress

When people encounter significant stressors, such as the diagnosis of a life-threatening disease or a major setback at work, they call upon numerous strategies to manage them. Is it better for one's health and well-being to process and express the attendant emotions fully, to suppress them, or to frame the experience cognitively such that it carries little emotional impact? Accumulating evidence suggests that attempts at suppression and avoidance of emotions often exact a psychological and physiological toll, whereas cognitive reappraisal of the stressor can carry adaptive affective, cognitive, and social consequences (for a review, see John & Gross, 2004). But what about processing and expressing emotions? Evidence for the merits of this approach appears decidedly more mixed. In this chapter, we discuss the contrasting literatures regarding the adaptiveness of actively processing and expressing emotions, describe the development of a construct to reflect coping through emotional approach, examine research addressing the conditions under which and how such coping confers benefits, and provide examples of clinical interventions that promote emotional processing and expression.

History of the Construct

Our interest in coping with adversity through actively processing and expressing emotions emerged from an attempt to reconcile several lines of theory and research on stress, coping, and emotion. A number of theories of emotion emphasize its adaptive, organizing elements. For example, Levenson (1994) argued that emotions "alter attention, shift certain behaviors upward in response hierarchies, and activate relevant associative networks in memory," as well as generate "a bodily milieu that is optimal for effective response" (p. 123). The adaptive consequences of attending to and expressing emotions have also emerged in research on expressive disclosure through writing (see Frattaroli, 2006; Smyth, 1998, for reviews) and on such clinical approaches as emotion-focused therapy (EFT; e.g., Greenberg & Watson, 2006).

In contrast, other theorists have characterized the experience of intense emotion as dysfunctional and as an impediment to rational processes (see Averill, 1990, for a review). Further, in the empirical literature on stress and coping, measures to assess one's attempts to manage emotions surrounding stressors (i.e., emotion-focused coping; Lazarus & Folkman, 1984) have demonstrated robust relations with maladaptive outcomes. In an illustrative review of the PsycInfo database from 1995 through 1998, we identified more than 100 studies in which the relation between emotion-focused coping and adjustment was examined in an adult or adolescent sample (Stanton, Parsa, & Austenfeld, 2002). Three measures containing emotion-focused coping content were used most frequently: the Ways of Coping Questionnaire (Lazarus & Folkman, 1984), the COPE (Carver, Scheier, & Weintraub, 1989), and the Coping Inventory for Stressful Situations (CISS; Endler & Parker, 1990, 1994). When we reviewed findings of studies including the two subscales most relevant to processing and expressing emotions (i.e., CISS Emotion-Oriented Coping scale and COPE Focus on and Venting of Emotion scale), a consistent association (albeit primarily cross-sectional) emerged between those scales and such indicators of maladjustment as depressive or anxious symptoms, neuroticism, and dissatisfaction with life.

Why might one question the validity of the conclusion that the relation of emotion-focused coping and distress is "perhaps the most consistent finding in the coping literature" (Coyne & Racioppo, 2000,

p. 657)? We contend that the manner in which emotion-focused coping has been operationalized in coping measures accounts in part for the association of emotion-focused coping with dysfunctional outcomes (Stanton, Danoff-Burg, Cameron, & Ellis, 1994; Stanton, Kirk, Cameron, & Danoff-Burg, 2000). First, emotion-focused coping is a broad construct, entailing behaviors oriented both toward approaching and avoiding the stressor and associated emotions. Accordingly, wide latitude is apparent in items designed to operationalize emotion-focused coping (e.g., "I let my feelings out," "I blame myself for becoming too emotional," "I say to myself 'this isn't real'"), some of which are inversely correlated (Scheier, Weintraub, & Carver, 1986). A related point is that researchers sometimes refer to "emotion-focused coping" rather than to a specific facet (e.g., avoidance) of that umbrella construct when they draw conclusions about its adaptiveness. Second, in several instruments, a number of emotion-focused coping items contain expressions of distress (e.g., "Become very tense") or self-deprecation (e.g., "Focus on my general inadequacies"). It is difficult to imagine that such items would not be associated with indicators of maladjustment.

The contention that coping measures are confounded with adjustment outcomes is supported by the finding that clinical psychologists rate a majority of published, emotion-oriented coping items as symptomatic of psychopathology (study 1, Stanton et al., 1994). In addition, coping items written specifically to exclude expressions of distress and self-deprecation evidence discriminant validity with measures of adjustment, whereas confounded items overlap significantly with measures of poor functioning (study 2, Stanton et al., 1994). These problems in the operationalization of emotion-focused coping led to our attempt to create psychometrically sound measures of coping through identifying, processing, and expressing emotions under stressful conditions.

Assessment of Coping through Emotional Approach

Although a number of self-report instruments are available relevant to emotion regulation (e.g., Berkeley Expressivity Questionnaire, Gross & John, 1995; Emotional Expressiveness Questionnaire and Ambivalence over Emotional Expressiveness Questionnaire, King & Emmons, 1990), they are not designed to evaluate emotional processing and expression as coping approaches. Hence, we developed and tested a set of emotional approach items free of content indicating distress or self-deprecation (Stanton, Kirk et al., 2000). Emotional processing (EP) and emotional expression (EE) emerged as two distinct factors of emotional approach coping (EAC) through exploratory (study 1) and confirmatory (study 3) factor analysis. The EP items reflect active attempts to acknowledge, explore, and understand emotions (e.g., "I acknowledge my emotions," "I take time to figure out what I'm really feeling"). The EE items represent active verbal and/or nonverbal efforts to communicate or symbolize emotional experience (e.g., "I feel free to express my emotions," "I take time to express my emotions").

The EAC scales have been tested using situational (i.e., specific stressor) and dispositional (i.e., "indicate what you generally do, feel, and think when you experience stressful situations") instruction sets. They demonstrate high internal consistency reliability and test–retest reliability at 4 weeks in both versions (see Austenfeld & Stanton, 2004, for a review of psychometric properties and descriptive statistics) and are uncorrelated with social desirability (Segerstrom, Stanton, Alden, & Shortridge, 2003; studies 1 and 3, Stanton, Kirk et al., 2000). Although distinct from other coping strategies, EP and EE evidence moderately positive correlations with approach-oriented strategies including problem-focused coping and seeking social support (Stanton, Danoff-Burg et al., 2000; Stanton, Kirk et al., 2000) and are uncorrelated with (Stanton, Danoff-Burg et al., 2000; Stanton, Kirk et al., 2000) or negatively correlated with (Smith, Lumley, & Longo, 2002) avoidant strategies such as mental disengagement.

The EP and EE subscales are moderately to highly intercorrelated, but their distinctiveness has also been demonstrated. For example, family members are better able to estimate each other's presumably more public coping through EE than their EP (study 2, Stanton, Kirk et al., 2000), and the EE scale correlates more highly with self-report measures of emotional expressiveness and family expressiveness than does the EP scale (studies 1 and 3, Stanton, Kirk et al., 2000). In addition, several studies described in the next section have demonstrated distinct relations of the EP and EE scales with measures of adjustment.

Use of EAC strategies varies significantly by gender in some samples (see Austenfeld & Stanton, 2004), with women tending to report more EP and/or EE than men, whereas other studies have not identified a gender difference (e.g., Smith et al., 2002). The relations of EAC with dispositional variables tend to vary by gender in young adults. In undergraduate women, EP is positively associated with adaptive traits such as hope and instrumentality and negatively correlated with maladaptive variables such as neuroticism and trait anxiety. In undergraduate men, EP is unrelated to the adaptive measures and correlated positively with ruminative and distracting reactions to depressive symptoms (studies 1 and 3, Stanton, Kirk et al., 2000). A closer examination of the relationship of EP to rumination and other forms of repetitive thought in undergraduates (study 1, Segerstrom et al., 2003) did not reveal significant gender differences, but did support a distinction between EP and measures of repetitive thought generally associated with negative outcomes including depressive rumination and pervasive worry.

Dispositional variables particularly relevant to EAC are the emotional ability and regulation constructs, such as emotional intelligence. Lumley, Gustavson, Partridge, and Labouvie-Vief (2005) provided an analysis of relationships among measures of emotional intelligence, alexithymia, and EAC. The authors found moderate, positive associations of EAC with a self-report measure of mood regulation skills, which represents a subset of emotional intelligence, but lower correlations ($r \approx .20$) with a performance-based measure of emotional intelligence. They reported moderate, negative correlations of EAC scales with a self-report measure of alexithymia, a construct reflecting difficulties with identifying and communicating emotions. In a study of 162 African American adults, Peters (2006) also found a moderate, negative association of EAC with alexithymia. Taken together, findings provide reasonable support for the convergent and discriminant validity of the EAC scales.

Recent Research on Coping through Emotional Approach
Cross-sectional Research

Research employing both the specific EAC scales developed by Stanton and colleagues, as well as related measures, indicates that coping through emotional approach offers psychological benefits under particular circumstances. For example, in a cross-sectional study with a medical population, Smith et al. (2002) found that EAC was associated uniquely with lower affective pain and depressive symptoms in men and women living with chronic myofascial pain, and that in men EE was associated with lower sensory pain and physical impairment. These relationships held after controlling for negative affect, education, and marital status. Peters

(2006), found that EAC was negatively related to trait anxiety and depression in African American adults, and a study of 248 young adults revealed that higher EE was associated with fewer anhedonic depressive symptoms (Kashdan, Zvolensky, & McLeish, 2008). Although several cross-sectional analyses demonstrate relationships of EAC with positive psychological adjustment, the links between EAC and salutary outcomes are not completely consistent. For example, a small, cross-sectional study of women with a maternal history of breast cancer observed no relationship between EAC and posttraumatic stress symptoms (Mosher, Danoff-Burg, & Brunker, 2005), but a significant relation of EP with greater posttraumatic growth (Mosher, Danoff-Burg, & Brunker, 2006).

Longitudinal Research

Cross-sectional designs cannot elucidate the degree to which EAC contributes to positive adjustment versus the degree to which psychological health promotes the use of EAC. Fortunately, there is a growing body of longitudinal research investigating the role of EAC in adjustment following stressful life events. There is evidence that EAC confers psychological benefit to individuals coping with an array of specific stressful experiences including infertility, sexual assault, and breast cancer. In couples coping with infertility, EAC predicts decreased depressive symptomatology in both members of heterosexual couples following an unsuccessful insemination attempt (Berghuis & Stanton, 2002). Furthermore, findings from this study suggest that EAC benefits partners as well as individuals: high EAC in male partners was protective against depressive symptomatology in female partners low in EAC. Terry and Hynes (1998) also observed a prospective positive relationship between EAC and psychological adjustment in a sample of women coping with infertility (although note that their EAC measure included items related to social support). These studies suggest that EAC can be beneficial when people confront stressors such as infertility that are perceived as relatively uncontrollable.

In a sample of sexual assault survivors, Frazier, Mortensen, and Steward (2005) demonstrated that increases in the EE component of EAC were associated with increases in feelings of control over the recovery process, and that such feelings of control were associated with decreasing distress following the assault (but note that EE did not mediate the relation between perceived control and distress). The researchers (Frazier, Tashiro, Berman, Steger, &

Long, 2004) also demonstrated that an increase in approach-oriented coping (a composite of EE and cognitive restructuring) was associated with increasing reports of positive life change over time and that coping partially mediated the relations of social support with positive change trajectories.

Coping through emotional approach has also been investigated in the context of breast cancer, where the most consistent evidence emerges for the benefits of EE. Stanton, Danoff-Burg, and colleagues (2000) explored the effects of EAC in a 3-month longitudinal study of women who recently had completed breast cancer treatment. After controlling for dependent variables at initial assessment, participant age, and coping strategies other than emotional approach, they found that, in comparison to women low in coping through EE at study entry, highly expressive women reported an increase in vigor and a decrease in distress at follow-up. For women who perceived their social environment as highly receptive, coping through EE also predicted improved quality of life. Manne, Ostroff, and colleagues (2004) found that coping through EE approximately 4 months following breast cancer diagnosis predicted an increase in posttraumatic growth over the next 18 months for women with breast cancer. This relationship was not found for the women's partners, but patients reported more growth when their partners reported high use of EE. However, Lechner, Carver, Antoni, Weaver, and Phillips (2006, study 2) did not find an association of emotionally expressive coping and finding benefit in the breast cancer experience at approximately 2 months after surgery or at 5-year follow-up.

There is some evidence that the benefits of coping through EE extend to the domain of physical health. Emotionally expressive breast cancer patients in Stanton, Danoff-Burg et al. (2000) had fewer medical appointments for cancer-related morbidities during the course of the study, as well as improved perceived physical health. One longitudinal epidemiological study revealed that a different measure of coping through EE during the first month following diagnosis of breast cancer predicted longer survival at 8-year follow-up for African American and European American women, particularly for women who also reported available emotional support (Reynolds et al., 2000).

EP appears to evidence a distinct pattern of relations with adaptive outcomes. In the Stanton, Danoff-Burg et al. (2000) longitudinal study of breast cancer patients, some evidence emerged for the association between EP and better adjustment in zero-order correlations, but processing predicted increased distress in regression analyses, when EE was controlled statistically. The researchers speculated that EP might facilitate diminished distress to the extent that it is channeled through EE and that the variance unique to processing might represent a ruminative component, particularly when processing continues for months after stressor onset (note that women entered the study approximately 6 months after diagnosis). Lechner et al. (2006, study 2) reported a concurrent association of cancer-related EP and finding benefit in the cancer experience at approximately 2 months after surgery, but early EP did not predict benefit finding at a 5-year follow-up. Manne, Ostroff et al. (2004) found that higher EP by partners (but not breast cancer patients) at approximately 4 months after diagnosis predicted maintenance of their own posttraumatic growth over time, whereas lower processing predicted declining posttraumatic growth. Certainly, the effects of EP and EE might be time-dependent, such that attempts to acknowledge and understand emotions are more likely to be adaptive when they occur relatively early in the stressor trajectory, facilitating efficient EE and goal pursuit (see also study 3, Stanton, Kirk et al., 2000). The temporal trajectory of EP and EE in relation to adjustment requires study.

Moderators of the Relations between EAC and Outcomes

Contrary to the findings on emotion-focused coping in the stress and coping literature, research using measures that assess the degree to which people actively process and express their emotions suggests that EAC strategies can contribute to psychological and physical health. Yet, consistent with Lazarus and Folkman's (1984) account of the varying utility of coping mechanisms across situations, the benefits of coping through emotional approach are likely to vary as a function of contextual and personal variables. First, the receptiveness of the interpersonal context in which an individual processes and expresses emotions may well influence the relief derived from EAC (Lepore, Silver, Wortman, & Wayment, 1996; Stanton, Danoff-Burg et al., 2000). Given that EAC is related to positive adjustment even when social support is statistically controlled (Stanton et al., 1994; Stanton, Danoff-Burg et al., 2000; Stanton, Kirk et al., 2000), however, even individuals in emotionally inhospitable environments may benefit from emotional approach strategies when given contextually appropriate outlets for emotions.

Second, both the nature of the stressor and the individual's appraisal of the stressor may moderate the likelihood that individuals will employ EAC as well as the advantage that it confers. For example, Park, Armeli, and Tennen (2004a) asked undergraduates to rate the controllability of the day's most stressful event as well as how they coped, and found that students used more EAC in response to stressors they appraised as relatively more uncontrollable. Such matching of coping strategy and stressor appraisal also might be important to consider in pairing interventions with the individuals who are most likely to benefit from them. In light of their finding that individuals who appraise their cancer experience as being at least moderately stressful report more posttraumatic growth than individuals who appraise it as only mildly stressful, Lechner and colleagues (2006) assert that it may be useful to target expressive disclosure interventions toward those individuals who appraise a given stressor as a significant challenge. Furthermore, the nature of individuals' appraisals of stressors is also likely to influence the specific emotions that arise. Given that the acceptability of specific emotions varies by culture and context, certain emotions may be more conducive to EAC when context is taken into account.

Some longitudinal work has indicated that the utility of EP and EE varies by gender. Stanton et al. (1994) investigated the influence of a preliminary measure of EAC on adjustment over time in a sample of young women and men. After controlling for initial levels of dependent variables, they found that EAC predicted increased life satisfaction and decreased depressive symptomatology over time in young women coping with a self-nominated stressor, whereas EAC predicted poorer adjustment over time in young men. Some gender-related effects also emerged in an experience-sampling design conducted over 14 days with lesbians and gay men (Beals, Peplau, & Gable, 2009), which targeted daily experiences of the opportunity to disclose sexual orientation. On days in which disclosure occurred, EP regarding sexual orientation was beneficial for women and detrimental for men with regard specifically to daily negative affect. However, greater EP regarding sexual orientation was associated with greater daily life satisfaction and positive affect for both sexes. Research in infertile couples also has demonstrated that EAC can be beneficial for both women and men (Berghuis & Stanton, 2002).

Finally, individual differences, such as skill in employing emotional approach techniques for specific emotions without alienating social support networks, also might modify the tendency to employ EAC as well as the impact of those strategies on adjustment. We would speculate that individuals high in perceived emotional intelligence are more likely to use active coping, including emotional approach, in part because they are more skilled in its appropriate use and have received reinforcement for its appropriate use in the past (Salovey, Stroud, Woolery, & Epel, 2002). Conversely, Zuckerman, Knee, Kieffer, and Gagne (2004) found that holding highly unrealistic control beliefs was associated with lower endorsement of EP and EE as coping strategies. The researchers argue that individuals who cling to unrealistic notions of control are unwilling to cope through processing emotions because such careful evaluation of situations might entail relinquishing illusions of control. Finally, personality attributes such as hope, anxiety sensitivity, and others also can moderate the strength and direction of effects of EAC on adjustment. For example, Stanton, Danoff-Burg et al. (2000) found that breast cancer patients' emotionally expressive coping was beneficial for women high in hope with regard to distress and medical appointments for cancer-related morbidities and was unrelated to outcomes for women low in hope. Kashdan et al. (2008) found that, in young adults with low anxiety sensitivity, high EE was related to lower agoraphobic cognitions, whereas in young adults with high anxiety sensitivity, high EE was related to higher cognitions. Moderated effects also emerged in a daily process study by Park, Armeli, and Tennen (2004b); for undergraduates high in social enhancement motives and low in sensation seeking who also had a family history of alcohol abuse, EAC was associated with greater alcohol use.

Mechanisms for the Effects of EAC

What intervening variables might explain the relationship between EAC and positive psychological adjustment? Stanton, Parsa, and Austenfeld (2002) proffered that "coping through emotional approach may serve as a successful vehicle for goal clarification and pursuit" (p. 153), citing its mediating role between the dispositional hope and outcomes (Stanton, Danoff-Burg et al., 2000). Thus, processing and expressing emotions may facilitate the direction of attention toward goals that are of most importance to an individual, the identification of barriers to achieving those goals, and the generation of new pathways to reaching them (Stanton et al., 2002). Such an interpretation is consistent with findings linking emotionally expressive coping with problem-focused coping (Stanton, Kirk et al., 2000).

The effects of EAC also might be due in part to the inherent exposure to the stressful event involved in actively processing and expressing emotions. Repeated exposure to emotions may impart positive adjustment through both physiological habituation as well as cognitive reappraisal of the stressor and related affirmation of positive personal qualities associated with confronting the stressful experience (e.g., Creswell et al., 2007; Low, Stanton, & Danoff-Burg, 2006; Pennebaker, Mayne, & Francis, 1997; study 4, Stanton, Kirk et al., 2000).

Finally, the use of EAC may help individuals appropriately select and maximally draw upon their social environments (e.g., Carstensen, 1998; Manne, Ostroff et al., 2004). In a small sample of patients diagnosed with (or at risk of) malignant melanoma and their partners, Lichtenthal, Cruess, Schuchter, and Ming (2003) found that patients' greater use of EAC was associated with higher correspondence between patients' received and partners' provided support, suggesting that patients high in EAC were better able to communicate their needs for support. In the same vein, Rini, Dunkel Schetter, Hobel, Glynn, and Sandman (2006) demonstrated an indirect relationship between EE and diminished anxiety in a study of pregnant women and their partners. Along with other variables such as secure attachment, greater coping through EE in pregnant women formed a latent construct reflecting interpersonal orientation. Interpersonal orientation was associated with stronger marital quality and greater effectiveness of social support, which in turn predicted reduction in anxiety over the course of pregnancy (also see Huizink, de Medina, Mulder, & Visser, 2002). Thus, the salutary outcomes of coping through emotional approach may arise through both intrapersonal and interpersonal pathways.

Summary and Directions

In sum, a growing body of literature suggests that coping through processing and expressing emotions is helpful for some individuals facing particular stressful encounters. Certainly, there is far to go in understanding the consequences of processing and expressing specific negative emotions (e.g., Lieberman & Goldstein, 2006; Trierweiler, Eid, & Lischetzke, 2002), as well as the influence of positive emotional experience in this process (e.g., Folkman & Moskowitz, 2004; Fredrickson, 2001).

Specification of the unique characteristics of adaptive EP in contrast to rumination also requires continued study (e.g., Kross, Ayduk, & Mischel, 2005). Increasingly specific understanding of for whom, under what circumstances, and how EAC is most effective will be invaluable in the next generation of clinical interventions.

Emotional Processing and Expression in Clinical Interventions

With the increasing integration of emotion science into approaches to psychotherapy, emotion regulation has emerged as a unifying construct (e.g., Moses & Barlow, 2006). Moreover, a disturbance in core affective processing is viewed as a shared characteristic of many psychological disorders (e.g., Barrett, Mesquita, Ochsner, & Gross, 2007). Effective EP and EE are acknowledged as central to positive change across several major psychotherapeutic traditions (see Whelton, 2004, for a review). Developed by Greenberg and colleagues (e.g., Greenberg & Watson, 2006), EFT views awareness, tolerance, and utilization of negative emotions, as well as enjoyment of positive emotions, as central to psychological adjustment. A meta-analysis of four randomized, controlled studies of EFT in married couples demonstrated reduction of marital distress (Johnson, Hunsley, Greenberg, & Schindler, 1999). In studies of the related process-experiential therapy as a treatment for depression, depth of EP predicts positive outcomes (Pos, Greenberg, Goldman, & Korman, 2003; Watson & Bedard, 2006). Therapies that encourage EP and EE have also been shown to produce favorable outcomes in medical populations (Giese-Davis et al., 2002; Spiegel, Bloom, Kraemer, & Gottheil, 1989). In a randomized, controlled trial, women with metastatic breast cancer who participated in group supportive-expressive therapy reported improvement in facets of emotion regulation, with less suppression of negative affect and more restraint of aggressive, impulsive, inconsiderate, and irresponsible behavior relative to controls (Giese-Davis et al., 2002). Acceptance and commitment therapy (e.g., Hayes, Luoma, Bond, Masuda, & Lillis, 2006) and dialectical behavior therapy (e.g., Lynch, Chapman, Rosenthal, Kuo, & Linehan, 2006) are two additional approaches in which attention to and regulation of emotion are key components.

Coping researchers have developed group treatments to compare the utility of problem-focused and emotion-focused strategies, in which the emotion-focused interventions typically include emotional approach strategies. A controlled comparison of problem-focused to emotion-focused counseling for bereavement (Schut, Stroebe, van den Bout, & de Keijser, 1997) revealed a significant gender difference, with problem-focused counseling more beneficial for women, and emotion-focused counseling more beneficial for men. The benefits of emotion-focused coping for men appeared only at longer-term follow-up, 7 months post intervention. In a controlled trial comparing problem-focused with emotion-focused group treatment for infertile women (McQueeney, Stanton, & Sigmon, 1997), both treatment groups evidenced decreased distress at treatment completion relative to controls, but the emotion-focused group also evidenced enhanced adjustment at 1-month follow-up. The problem-focused group was more likely to attain parenthood at 18-month follow-up than the other two groups, suggesting that problem-focused group members may have been more persistent in their efforts to become parents.

Another controlled comparison of problem-focused to emotion-focused group interventions examined these strategies in the context of worksite stress (Bond & Bunce, 2000). The emotion-focused intervention, based on Acceptance and Commitment Therapy (ACT; Hayes et al., 2006), facilitated emotional approach and acceptance, whereas the problem-focused intervention trained participants to identify and alleviate workplace stressors. Both treatments increased psychological adjustment and propensity to innovate at work, but via somewhat different mechanisms; ACT enhanced acceptance of negative emotions and thoughts, whereas the problem-focused treatment increased direct attempts to modify work stressors. This study demonstrates that although mechanisms may differ, both emotion- and problem-focused coping strategies are potentially helpful in the coping process. In the spirit of integration, one intervention that incorporates, rather than compares, both emotion-focused and problem-focused strategies is Folkman and colleagues' Coping Effectiveness Training (CET; 1991), in which participants learn to select particular coping strategies for specific facets of stressful situations. In HIV-positive men, CET improved perceived stress, burnout, and anxiety (but not depressive symptoms) relative to control conditions, and coping self-efficacy mediated intervention effects on the first two outcomes (Chesney, Chambers, Taylor, Johnson, & Folkman, 2003).

More recently, EAC has been specifically measured in controlled studies of interventions.

A cognitive-behavioral stress management (CBSM) group intervention for women with early-stage breast cancer (Antoni et al., 2001), which includes encouragement of EP and EE, reduced the prevalence of moderate depressive symptoms relative to a control group, and increased benefit finding and optimism, effects that were maintained at 3-month follow-up. EAC increased in CBSM relative to the control condition, and it was correlated with increased benefit finding during and after the intervention. Although EAC was not found to mediate the relation between CBSM and benefit finding in that trial, it did act as a mechanism for CBSM effects on several outcomes in a second trial with breast cancer patients (Antoni, Carver, & Lechner, 2009). A four-session creative arts intervention, which was intended to enhance EE, reduced negative affect in women with breast cancer, but did not increase the use of EE compared to controls (Puig, Lee, Goodwin, & Sherrard, 2006). Manne, Babb, Pinover, Horwitz, and Ebbert (2004) tested a psychoeducational group intervention for wives of men with prostate cancer and found no significant differences between the treatment and control groups on either posttreatment distress or EAC (although the treatment group evidenced a nonsignificant trend toward more EAC). The researchers noted, however, that distress declined over time in the control group, and the study had limited power to detect differences in distress.

At present, minimal evidence has emerged for EAC as a mechanism for psychosocial intervention effects. Perhaps active attempts to process and express emotions surrounding a stressor subside once they have been successful in resolving the associated emotions. Thus, EAC efforts might be expected to increase during psychosocial intervention, but actually might diminish after effective resolution. Alternatively, EAC may be most effective in subsets of these samples (e.g., participants high in emotional intelligence), and therefore the action of EAC may be more frequently observed through careful analyses of interaction with person variables.

Although not intended as a clinical intervention, experimental trials of expressive disclosure, in which participants are asked to write (or talk) about their deepest feelings and thoughts regarding a stressor (Pennebaker & Beall, 1986), are also relevant, both with regard to their demonstration of the benefits of processing and expressing emotions (see Frattaroli, 2006, for a review) and to emerging evidence that EAC can moderate these effects. Stanton, Kirk, and colleagues (2000, study 4) randomly assigned undergraduates who were coping with a parent's psychological or physical health problem to talk about either their emotions related to their parent's disorder or the facts of their parent's disorder over two sessions. A coping by condition interaction emerged such that participants who were high on coping through EE with regard to their parent's disorder (assessed prior to the experimental task) displayed lower physiological arousal and negative affect when assigned to talk about their emotions relative to participants in other conditions. Similarly, in an expressive disclosure trial with medical students writing about their clinical clerkships (Austenfeld, Paolo, & Stanton, 2006), participants high in EAC benefited more than did those low on EAC when they were assigned to the expressive disclosure condition relative to other conditions. Added to the evidence for moderated effects in longitudinal studies, these findings point to the need to consider the interplay of person characteristics and environmental contingencies when evaluating the utility of coping approaches.

Conclusions

In contrast to earlier conclusions in the stress and coping literature that emotion-focused coping is maladaptive, more recent research reveals that coping through active attempts to acknowledge, understand, and express emotions can carry salutary consequences. However, attributes of the interpersonal context, the stressful experience, and the individual are important moderators of the utility of coping through emotional approach. The integration of stress and coping research, emotion science, and controlled tests of related clinical interventions holds promise in illuminating the roles of coping through processing and expressing emotions in influencing health and well-being.

Questions for Future Research

1. How does the processing and expression of specific emotions, both negative and positive, influence stress-related adjustment?

2. Under what conditions does coping through emotional processing and expression facilitate or hinder adaptive functioning?

3. What are the biopsychosocial mechanisms through which EAC affects psychological and physical health?

References

Antoni, M. H., Carver, C. S., & Lechner, S. C. Enhancing positive adaptation: Example intervention during treatment for breast cancer. In C. L. Park, S. C. Lechner, M. H. Antoni, & A. L. Stanton (Eds.), *Medical illness and positive life change: Can crisis lead to personal transformation?* (pp. 197–214). Washington, DC: American Psychological Association.

Antoni, M. H., Lehman, J. M., Kilbourn, K. M., Boyers, A. E., Culver, J. L., Alferi, S. M., et al. (2001). Cognitive-behavioral stress management intervention decreases the prevalence of depression and enhances benefit finding among women under treatment for early-stage breast cancer. *Health Psychology, 20,* 20–32.

Austenfeld, J. L., Paolo, A. M., & Stanton, A. L. (2006). Effects of writing about emotions versus goals on psychological and physical health among third-year medical students. *Journal of Personality, 74,* 267–286.

Austenfeld, J. L., & Stanton, A. L. (2004). Coping through emotional approach: A new look at emotion, coping, and health-related outcomes. *Journal of Personality, 72,* 1335–1363.

Averill, J. R. (1990). Inner feelings, works of the flesh, the beast within, diseases of the mind, driving force, and putting on a show: Six metaphors of emotion and their theoretical extensions. In D. E. Leary (Ed.), *Metaphors in the history of psychology* (pp. 104–132). New York: Cambridge University Press.

Barrett, L. F., Mesquita, B., Ochsner, K. N., & Gross, J. J. (2007). The experience of emotion. *Annual Review of Psychology, 58,* 373–403.

Beals, K. P., Peplau, L. A., & Gable, S. L. (2009). Stigma management and well-being: The role of perceived social support, emotional processing, and suppression. Submitted manuscript.

Berghuis, J. P., & Stanton, A. L. (2002). Adjustment to a dyadic stressor: A longitudinal study of coping and depressive symptoms in infertile couples over an insemination attempt. *Journal of Consulting and Clinical Psychology, 70,* 433–438.

Bond, F.W., & Bunce, D. (2000). Mediators of change in emotion-focused and problem-focused worksite stress management interventions. *Journal of Occupational Health Psychology, 5,* 156–163.

Carstensen, L. L. (1998). A life-span approach to social motivation. In J. Heckhausen & C. S. Dweck (Eds.), *Motivation and self-regulation across the life span* (pp. 341–364). Cambridge: Cambridge University Press.

Carver, C. S., Scheier, M. F., & Weintraub, J. K. (1989). Assessing coping strategies: A theoretically based approach. *Journal of Personality and Social Psychology, 56,* 267–283.

Chesney, M. A., Chambers, D. B., Taylor, J. M., Johnson, L. M., & Folkman, S. (2003). Coping effectiveness training for men living with HIV: Results from a randomized clinical trial testing a group-based intervention. *Psychosomatic Medicine, 65,* 1038–1046.

Coyne, J. C., & Racioppo, M. W. (2000). Never the twain shall meet? Closing the gap between coping research and clinical intervention research. *American Psychologist, 55,* 655–664.

Creswell, J. D., Lam, S., Stanton, A. L., Taylor, S. E., Bower, J. E., & Sherman, D. K. (2007). Does self-affirmation, cognitive processing, or discovery of meaning explain cancer-related health benefits of expressive writing? *Personality and Social Psychology Bulletin, 33,* 238–250.

Endler, N. S., & Parker, J. D. A. (1990). *Coping Inventory for Stressful Situations (CISS): Manual.* Toronto, ON: Multi-Health Systems.

Endler, N. S., & Parker, J. D. A. (1994). Assessment of multi-dimensional coping: Task, emotion, and avoidance strategies. *Psychological Assessment, 6,* 50–60.

Folkman, S., Chesney, M., McKusick, L., Ironson, G., Johnson, D. S., & Coates, T. J. (1991). Translating coping theory into intervention. In J. Eckenrode (Ed.), *The social context of coping* (pp. 239–259). New York: Plenum.

Folkman, S., & Moskowitz, J. T. (2004). Coping: Pitfalls and promise. *Annual Review of Psychology, 55,* 745–774.

Frattaroli, J. (2006). Experimental disclosure and its moderators: A meta-analysis. *Psychological Bulletin, 132,* 823–865.

Frazier, P. A., Mortensen, H., & Steward, J. (2005). Coping strategies as mediators of the relations among perceived control and distress in sexual assault survivors. *Journal of Counseling Psychology, 52,* 267–278.

Frazier, P., Tashiro, T., Berman, M., Steger, M., & Long, J. (2004). Correlates of levels and patterns of positive life changes following sexual assault. *Journal of Consulting and Clinical Psychology, 72,* 19–30.

Fredrickson, B. L. (2001). The role of positive emotions in positive psychology: The broaden-and-build theory of positive emotions. *American Psychologist, 56,* 218–226.

Giese-Davis, J., Koopman, C., Butler, L. D., Classen, C., Cordova, M., Fobair, P., et al. (2002). Change in emotion-regulation strategy for women with metastatic breast cancer following supportive-expressive group therapy. *Journal of Consulting and Clinical Psychology, 70,* 916–925.

Greenberg, L. S., & Watson, J. C. (2006). *Emotion-focused therapy for depression.* Washington, DC: American Psychological Association.

Gross, J. J. & John, O. P. (1995). Facets of emotional expressivity: Three self-report factors and their correlates. *Personality and Individual Differences, 19,* 555–568.

Hayes, S. C., Luoma, J. B., Bond, F. W., Masuda, A., & Lillis, J. (2006). Acceptance and commitment therapy: Model, processes and outcomes. *Behaviour Research and Therapy, 44,* 1–25.

Huizink, A. C., de Medina, P. G. R., Mulder, E. J. H., & Visser, G. H. A. (2002). Coping in normal pregnancy. *Annals of Behavioral Medicine, 24,* 132–140.

John, O. P., & Gross, J. J. (2004). Healthy and unhealthy emotion regulation. *Journal of Personality, 62,* 1301–1333.

Johnson, S. M., Hunsley, J., Greenberg, L., & Schindler, D. (1999). Emotionally focused couples therapy: Status and challenges. *Clinical Psychology: Science and Practice, 6,* 67–79.

Kashdan, T. B., Zvolensky, M. J., & McLeish, A. C. (2008). Anxiety sensitivity and affect regulatory strategies: Individual and interactive risk factors for anxiety-related symptoms. *Journal of Anxiety Disorders, 22,* 429–440.

King, L. A., & Emmons, R. A. (1990). Conflict over emotional expression: Psychological and physical correlates. *Journal of Personality and Social Psychology, 58,* 864–877.

Kross, E., Ayduk, O., & Mischel, W. (2005). When asking "why" does not hurt: Distinguishing rumination from reflective processing of negative emotions. *Psychological Science, 16,* 709–715.

Lazarus, R. S., & Folkman, S. (1984). *Stress, appraisal, and coping.* New York: Springer.

Lechner, S. C., Carver, C. S., Antoni, M. H., Weaver, K. E., & Phillips, K. M. (2006). Curvilinear associations between benefit finding and psychosocial adjustment to breast cancer. *Journal of Consulting and Clinical Psychology, 74,* 828–840.

Lepore, S. J., Silver, R. C., Wortman, C. B., & Wayment, H. A. (1996). Social constraints, intrusive thoughts, and depressive symptoms among bereaved mothers. *Journal of Personality and Social Psychology, 70,* 271–282.

Levenson, R. W. (1994). Human emotion: A functional view. In P. Ekman & R. J. Davidson (Eds.), *The nature of emotion: Fundamental questions* (pp. 123–126). New York: Oxford University Press.

Lichtenthal, W. G., Cruess, D. G., Schuchter, L. M., & Ming, M. E. (2003). Psychosocial factors related to the correspondence of recipient and provider perceptions of social support among patients diagnosed with or at risk for malignant melanoma. *Journal of Health Psychology, 8*, 705–719.

Lieberman, M. A., & Goldstein, B. A. (2006). Not all negative emotions are equal: The role of emotional expression in online support groups for women with breast cancer. *Psycho-oncology, 15*, 160–168.

Low, C. A., Stanton, A. L., & Danoff-Burg, S. (2006). Expressive disclosure and benefit finding among breast cancer patients: Mechanisms for positive health effects. *Health Psychology, 25*, 181–189.

Lumley, M. A., Gustavson, B. J., Partridge, R. T., & Labouvie-Vief, G. (2005). Assessing alexithymia and related emotional ability constructs using multiple methods: Interrelationships among measures. *Emotion, 5*, 329–342.

Lynch, T. R., Chapman, A. L., Rosenthal, M. Z., Kuo, J. R., & Linehan, M. M. (2006). Mechanisms of change in dialectical behavior therapy: Theoretical and empirical observations. *Journal of Clinical Psychology, 62*, 459–480.

McQueeney, D. A., Stanton, A. L., & Sigmon, S. (1997). Efficacy of emotion-focused and problem-focused group therapies for women with fertility problems. *Journal of Behavioral Medicine, 20*, 313–331.

Manne, S., Babb, J., Pinover, W., Horwitz, E., & Ebbert, J. (2004). Psychoeducational group intervention for wives of men with prostate cancer. *Psycho-oncology, 13*, 37–46.

Manne, S., Ostroff, J., Winkel, G., Goldstein, L., Fox, K., & Grana, G. (2004). Posttraumatic growth after breast cancer: Patient, partner, and couple perspectives. *Psychosomatic Medicine, 66*, 442–454.

Moses, E. B., & Barlow, D. H. (2006). A new unified treatment approach for emotional disorders based on emotion science. *Current Directions in Psychological Science, 15*, 146–150.

Mosher, C. E., Danoff-Burg, S., & Brunker, B. (2005). Women's posttraumatic stress responses to maternal breast cancer. *Cancer Nursing, 28*, 399–405.

Mosher, C. E., Danoff-Burg, S., & Brunker, B. (2006). Posttraumatic growth and psychosocial adjustment of daughters of breast cancer survivors. *Oncology Nursing Forum, 33*, 543–551.

Park, C. L., Armeli, S., & Tennen, H. (2004a). Appraisal-coping goodness of fit: A daily Internet study. *Personality and Social Psychology Bulletin, 30*, 558–569.

Park, C. L., Armeli, S., & Tennen, H. (2004b). The daily stress and coping process and alcohol use among college students. *Journal of Studies on Alcohol, 65*, 126–135.

Pennebaker, J. W., & Beall, S. (1986). Confronting a traumatic event: Toward an understanding of inhibition and disease. *Journal of Abnormal Psychology, 95*, 274–281.

Pennebaker, J. W., Mayne, T. J., & Francis, M. E. (1997). Linguistic predictors of adaptive bereavement. *Journal of Personality and Social Psychology, 72*, 863–871.

Peters, R. M. (2006). The relationship of racism, chronic stress emotions, and blood pressure. *Journal of Nursing Scholarship, 38*, 234–240.

Pos, A. E., Greenberg, L. S., Goldman, R. N., & Korman, L. M. (2003). Emotional processing during experiential treatment of depression. *Journal of Consulting and Clinical Psychology, 71*, 1007–1016.

Puig, A., Lee, S. M., Goodwin, L., & Sherrard, P. A. D. (2006). The efficacy of creative arts therapies to enhance emotional expression, spirituality, and psychological well-being of newly diagnosed Stage I and Stage II breast cancer patients: A preliminary study. *The Arts in Psychotherapy, 33*, 218–228.

Reynolds, P., Hurley, S., Torres, M., Jackson, J., Boyd, P., Chen, V. W., et al. (2000). Use of coping strategies and breast cancer survival: Results from the Black/White Cancer Survival Study. *American Journal of Epidemiology, 152*, 940–949.

Rini, C., Dunkel Schetter, C., Hobel, C. J., Glynn, L. M., & Sandman, C. A. (2006). Effective social support: Antecedents and consequences of partner support during pregnancy. *Personal Relationships, 13*, 207–229.

Salovey, P., Stroud, L. R., Woolery, A., & Epel, E. S. (2002). Perceived emotional intelligence, stress reactivity, and symptom reports: Further explorations using the trait meta-mood scale. *Psychology and Health, 17*, 611–627.

Scheier, M. F., Weintraub, J. K., & Carver, C. S. (1986). Coping with stress: Divergent strategies of optimists and pessimists. *Journal of Personality and Social Psychology, 51*, 1257–1264.

Schut, H. A. W., Stroebe, M. S., van den Bout, J., & de Keijser, J. (1997). Intervention for the bereaved: Gender differences in the efficacy of two counselling programmes. *British Journal of Clinical Psychology, 36*, 63–72.

Segerstrom, S. C., Stanton, A. L., Alden, L. E., & Shortridge, B. E. (2003). A multidimensional structure for repetitive thought: What's on your mind, and how, and how much? *Journal of Personality and Social Psychology, 85*, 909–921.

Smith, J. A., Lumley, M. A., & Longo, D. J. (2002). Contrasting emotional approach coping with passive coping for chronic myofascial pain. *Annals of Behavioral Medicine, 24*, 326–335.

Smyth, J. M. (1998). Written emotional expression: Effect sizes, outcome types, and moderating variables. *Journal of Consulting and Clinical Psychology, 66*, 174–184.

Spiegel, D., Bloom, J. R., Kraemer, H. C., & Gottheil, E. (1989). Effect of psychosocial treatment on survival of patients with metastatic breast cancer. *Lancet, ii*, 888–891.

Stanton, A. L., Danoff-Burg, S., Cameron, C. L., Bishop, M. M., Collins, C. A., Kirk, S. B., et al. (2000). Emotionally expressive coping predicts psychological and physical adjustment to breast cancer. *Journal of Consulting and Clinical Psychology, 68*, 875–882.

Stanton, A. L., Danoff-Burg, S., Cameron, C. L., & Ellis, A. P. (1994). Coping through emotional approach: Problems of conceptualization and confounding. *Journal of Personality and Social Psychology, 66*, 350–362.

Stanton, A. L., Kirk, S. B., Cameron, C. L., & Danoff-Burg, S. (2000). Coping through emotional approach: Scale construction and validation. *Journal of Personality and Social Psychology, 74*, 1078–1092.

Stanton, A. L., Parsa, A., & Austenfeld, J. L. (2002). The adaptive potential of coping through emotional approach. In C. R. Snyder & S. J. Lopez (Eds.), *Handbook of positive psychology* (pp. 148–158). New York: Oxford University Press.

Terry, D. J., & Hynes, G. J. (1998). Adjustment to a low-control situation: Reexamining the role of coping responses. *Journal of Personality and Social Psychology, 74*, 1078–1092.

Trierweiler, L. I., Eid, M., & Lischetzke, T. (2002). The structure of emotional expressivity: Each emotion counts. *Journal of Personality and Social Psychology, 82*, 1023–1040.

Watson, J. C., & Bedard, D. L. (2006). Clients' emotional processing in psychotherapy: A comparison between cognitive-behavioral and process-experiential therapies. *Journal of Consulting and Clinical Psychology, 74*, 152–159.

Whelton, W. J. (2004). Emotional processes in psychotherapy: Evidence across therapeutic modalities. *Clinical Psychology and Psychotherapy, 11*, 58–71.

Zuckerman, M., Knee, C. R., Kieffer, S. C., & Gagne, M. (2004). What individuals believe they can and cannot do: Explorations of realistic and unrealistic control beliefs. *Journal of Personality Assessment, 82*, 215–232.

The Positive Psychology of Emotional Intelligence

Peter Salovey, John D. Mayer, David Caruso, *and* Seung Hee Yoo

Abstract

Emotional intelligence is contextualized historically and defined as a set of four interrelated abilities focused on the processing of emotional information. These four abilities involve (a) perceiving emotions, (b) using emotions to facilitate cognitive activities, (c) understanding emotions, and (d) managing emotions in oneself and other people. Emotional intelligence is best measured as a set of abilities using tasks rather than self-judgment scales. When emotional intelligence is measured in this way it shows discriminant validity with respect to "cognitive" intelligence, personality traits, and social desirability, which is generally not the case for self-judgment measures. The ability-based measure of emotional intelligence most often used in research is the Mayer–Salovey–Caruso Emotional Intelligence Test (MSCEIT), a reliable instrument that is associated with positive outcomes in social situations, families, educational settings, and the workplace. Promising interventions designed to improve emotional intelligence have been developed for school children and managers. The effectiveness of these interventions needs to be evaluated systematically.

Keywords: competencies, emotions, emotional intelligence, intelligence, MSCEI

> Out of the marriage of reason with affect there issues clarity with passion. Reason without affect would be impotent, affect without reason would be blind.
> —(*Tomkins*, 1962, p. 112)

During the second half of the 1990s, emotional intelligence and EQ (we much prefer the former term to the latter) were featured as the cover story in at least two national magazines (Gibbs, 1995; Goleman, 1995a), received extensive coverage in the international press (e.g., Alcalde, 1996; Miketta, Gottschling, Wagner-Roos, & Gibbs, 1995; Thomas, 1995), were named the most useful new words or phrases for 1995 by the American Dialect Society (1995, 1999; Brodie, 1996), and made appearances in syndicated comic strips. What is this construct, and why has it been so appealing?

Emotional intelligence (EI) represents the ability to perceive, appraise, and express emotion accurately and adaptively; the ability to understand emotion and emotional knowledge; the ability to access and/or generate feelings when they facilitate cognitive activities and adaptive action; and the ability to regulate emotions in oneself and others (Mayer & Salovey, 1997). In other words, EI refers to the ability to process emotion-laden information competently and to use it to guide cognitive activities like problem solving and to focus energy on required behaviors. The term suggested to some that there might be other ways of being intelligent than those emphasized by standard IQ tests, that one might be able to develop these abilities, and that an EI could be an important predictor of success in personal relationships, family functioning, and the workplace. The term is one that instills hope and suggests promise, at least as compared to traditional notions of crystallized intelligence. For these very reasons, EI belongs in positive psychology. The purpose of this chapter is to review the history of and current research on EI and to determine whether our positive assessments of it are appropriate or misplaced.

History of the Concept

Turning to the field of psychology, there are two references to EI prior to our work on this concept. First, Mowrer (1960, pp. 307–308) famously concluded that "the emotions . . . do not at all deserve being put into opposition with 'intelligence' . . . they are, it seems, themselves a high order of intelligence." Second, Payne (1983/1986) used the term in an unpublished dissertation. A framework for an EI, a formal definition, and suggestions about its measurement were first described in two articles that we published in 1990 (Mayer, DiPaolo, & Salovey, 1990; Salovey & Mayer, 1990).

The tension between exclusively cognitive views of what it means to be intelligent and broader ones that include a positive role for the emotions can be traced back many centuries. For example, the Stoic philosophers of ancient Greece focused on virtue and viewed emotion as too individualistic and self-absorbed to be a reliable guide for insight and wisdom. Later, the Romantic movement in late-eighteenth century and early-nineteenth century Europe stressed how emotion-rooted intuition and empathy could provide insights that were unavailable through logic alone.

The modern interest in EI stems, perhaps, from a similar dialectic in the field of human abilities research. Although narrow, analytically focused definitions of intelligence predominated much of this century, following Cronbach's (1960) often cited conclusion that a social intelligence was unlikely to be defined and had not been measured, cracks in the analytic intelligence edifice began to appear in the 1980s. For example, Sternberg (1985) challenged mental abilities researchers to pay more attention to creative and practical aspects of intelligence, and Gardner (1983/1993) even defined an intrapersonal intelligence that concerns access to one's feeling life, the capacity to represent feelings, and the ability to draw upon them as a means of understanding and guide for behavior. Shortly thereafter, in their controversial book *The bell curve*, Herrnstein and Murray (1994) revived debate about the genetic basis for traditionally defined intelligence and the degree to which intelligence is affected by environmental circumstances. Paradoxically, instead of crystallizing support for the genetic intelligence position, the effect of *The bell curve* was to energize many educators, investigators, and journalists to question whether the traditional view of intelligence was conceptualized too narrowly, and to embrace the notion that there might be other ways to be smart and succeed in the world.

It was in this context that we wrote our 1990 articles, introducing EI as the ability to understand feelings in the self and others, and to use these feelings as informational guides for thinking and action (Salovey & Mayer, 1990). At that time, we described three core components of EI—appraisal and expression, regulation, and utilization—based on our reading and organizing of the relevant literature rather than on empirical research. Since this original article, we have refined our conceptualization of EI so that it now includes four dimensions (Mayer & Salovey, 1997; Mayer, Salovey, & Caruso, 2004), which we will discuss later in this chapter.

Our work was reinforced by neuroscientists' interest in showing that emotional responses were integral to "rational" decision making (e.g., Damasio, 1994). Through our theorizing, we also helped to stimulate the writing of the best-selling book, *Emotional Intelligence*, in which Goleman (1995b) promised that EI rather than analytical intelligence predicts success in school, work, and home. Despite the lack of data to support some of Goleman's claims, interest in EI soared, with books appearing monthly in which the authors touted the value of EI in education (Schilling, 1996), child-rearing (Gottman & DeClaire, 1997; Shapiro, 1997), the workplace (Cooper & Sawaf, 1997; Goleman, 1998; Ryback, 1998; Simmons & Simmons, 1997; Weisinger, 1998), and personal growth (Epstein, 1998; Salerno, 1996; Segal, 1997; Steiner & Perry, 1997). Very little of this explosion of available resources on EI represented empirically oriented scholarship.

There also has been great interest in the development of measures to assess the competencies involved in EI. Not surprisingly, a plethora of supposed EI scales and batteries of varying psychometric properties appeared (e.g., Bar-On, 1997; Cooper & Sawaf, 1997; Schutte et al., 1998). In reality, these instruments tapped self-reported personality constructs, and they were disappointing in terms of their discriminant and construct validities (Brackett & Mayer, 2003; Davies, Stankov, & Roberts, 1998; Mayer, Salovey, & Caruso, 2008). As an alternative, we have been arguing for the value of conceptualizing EI as a set of abilities and to measure it as such (Mayer, Salovey, & Caruso, 2000a, 2000b; Mayer,

Salovey, Caruso, & Sitarenios, 2001; Mayer, Salovey, Caruso, & Sitarenios, 2003). We will describe this approach to measurement later in the chapter.

Current Model of Emotional Intelligence

What follows is a brief summary of our ability theory of EI, displayed in Table 22.1; more detailed presentations can be found elsewhere (e.g., Mayer, Caruso, & Salovey, 1999; Mayer & Salovey, 1997; Salovey, Bedell, Detweiler, & Mayer, 2000; Salovey & Grewal, 2005; Salovey, Woolery, & Mayer, 2001). Although there is sometimes empirical utility in considering EI as a unitary construct, most of our work suggests that it can be divided into four branches. The first of these branches, "perceiving emotions," involves

Table 22.1 The four-branch model of emotional intelligence

Perceiving emotions

Ability to identify emotion in one's physical and psychological states
Ability to identify emotion in other people
Ability to express emotions accurately and to express needs related to them
Ability to discriminate between accurate/honest and inaccurate/dishonest feelings

Using emotions (to facilitate cognition)

Ability to redirect and prioritize thinking on the basis of associated feelings
Ability to generate emotions to facilitate judgment and memory
Ability to capitalize on mood changes to appreciate multiple points of view
Ability to use emotional states to facilitate problem solving and creativity

Understanding emotions

Ability to understand relationships among various emotions
Ability to perceive the causes and consequences of emotions
Ability to understand complex feelings, emotional blends, and contradictory states
Ability to understand transitions among emotions

Managing emotions

Ability to be open to feelings, both pleasant and unpleasant
Ability to monitor and reflect on emotions
Ability to engage, prolong, or detach from an emotional state
Ability to manage emotions in oneself
Ability to manage emotions in others

Based on Mayer & Salovey, 1997.

recognizing and inputting verbal and nonverbal information from the emotion system. The second branch, "using emotions," refers to using emotions as part of cognitive processes such as creativity and problem solving. The third branch, "understanding emotions," involves cognitive processing of emotion, that is, insight and knowledge brought to bear about one's feelings or the feelings of others. Our fourth branch, "managing emotions," concerns the regulation of emotions in oneself and in other people.

The first branch of EI begins with the capacity to perceive feelings. EI is impossible without the competencies involved in this first branch (see also Saarni, 1990, 1999). If each time unpleasant feelings emerged, people turned their attentions away; they would learn very little about feelings. Emotional perception involves registering, attending to, and deciphering emotional messages as they are expressed in facial expressions, voice tone, or cultural artifacts. A person who sees the fleeting expression of fear in the face of another understands much more about that other's emotions and thoughts than someone who misses such a signal.

The second branch of EI concerns emotional facilitation of cognitive activities. Emotions are complex organizations of the various psychological subsystems—physiological, experiential, cognitive, and motivational. Emotions enter the cognitive system both as cognized feelings, as is the case when someone thinks, "I am a little sad now," and as altered cognitions, as when a sad person thinks, "I am no good." Using emotions—branch 2—focuses on how emotion affects the cognitive system and, as such, can be harnessed for more effective problem solving, reasoning, decision making, and creative endeavors. Of course, cognition can be disrupted by emotions, such as anxiety and fear, but emotions also can prioritize the cognitive system to attend to what is important (Easterbrook, 1959; Mandler, 1975; Simon, 1982), and even to focus on what it does best in a given mood (e.g., Palfai & Salovey, 1993; Schwarz, 1990).

Emotions also change cognitions, making them positive when a person is happy, and negative when the person is sad (e.g., Forgas, 1995; Mayer, Gaschke, Braverman, & Evans, 1992; Salovey & Birnbaum, 1989; Singer & Salovey, 1988). These changes force the cognitive system to view things from different perspectives, for example, alternating between skeptical and accepting. The advantages of such alterations to thought are fairly apparent. When one's point of view shifts between skeptical and accepting, the individual can appreciate multiple vantage points and, as a consequence, think about a problem more deeply and creatively (e.g., Mayer, 1986; Mayer & Hanson, 1995). It is just such an effect that may lead people with mood swings toward greater creativity (Goodwin & Jamison, 1990; see also chap. 24).

Branch 3 involves understanding emotion. Emotions form a rich and complexly interrelated symbol set. The most fundamental competency at this level concerns the ability to label emotions with words and to recognize the relationships among exemplars of the affective lexicon. The emotionally intelligent individual is able to recognize that the terms used to describe emotions are arranged into families and that groups of emotion terms form fuzzy sets (Ortony, Clore, & Collins, 1988). Perhaps more importantly, the relations among these terms are deduced—that annoyance and irritation can lead to rage if the provocative stimulus is not eliminated, or that envy often is experienced in contexts that also evoke jealousy (Salovey & Rodin, 1986, 1989). The person who is able to understand emotions—their meanings, how they blend together, how they progress over time—is truly blessed with the capacity to understand important aspects of human nature and interpersonal relationships.

Partly as a consequence of various popularizations, and partly as a consequence of societal pressures to regulate emotions, many people primarily identify EI with its fourth branch, managing emotions. They hope EI will be a way of getting rid of troublesome emotions or emotional leakages into human relations, and rather hope to control emotions (Salovey, Bedell, Detweiler, & Mayer, 1999). Although this is one possible outcome of the fourth branch, optimal levels of emotional regulation may be moderate ones; attempts to minimize or eliminate emotion completely may stifle EI. Similarly, the regulation of emotion in other people is less likely to involve the suppressing of others' emotions but rather the harnessing of them, as when a persuasive speaker is said to "move" his or her audience.

Individuals use a broad range of techniques to regulate their moods. Thayer, Newman, and McClain (1994) believe that physical exercise is the single most effective strategy for changing a bad mood, among those under one's own control. Other commonly reported mood regulation strategies include listening to music, social interaction, and cognitive self-management (e.g., giving oneself a "pep talk"). Pleasant distractions (errands, hobbies, fun activities, shopping, reading, and writing) also are effective. Less effective (and, at times, counterproductive) strategies include passive mood management (e.g., television viewing, caffeine, food, and sleep), direct tension reduction (e.g., drugs, alcohol, and sex), spending time alone, and avoiding the person or thing that caused a bad mood. In general, the most successful regulation methods involve expenditure of energy; active mood management techniques that combine relaxation, stress management, cognitive effort, and exercise may be the most effective strategies for changing bad moods (reviewed by Thayer, Newman, & McClain, 1994). Central to emotional self-regulation is the ability to reflect upon and manage one's emotions; emotional disclosure provides one means of doing so. Pennebaker (1989, 1993, 1997) has studied the effects of disclosure extensively and finds that the act of disclosing emotional experiences in writing improves individuals' subsequent physical and mental health (see chap. 59).

Measuring EI

We believe that the most valid approach for assessing EI is the use of task-based, ability measures. Although self-report inventories assessing various aspects of EI have proliferated in recent years (e.g., Bagby, Parker, & Taylor, 1993a, 1993b; Bar-On, 1997; Catanzaro & Mearns, 1990; EQ Japan, 1998; Giuliano & Swinkels, 1992; Salovey, Mayer, Goldman, Turvey, & Palfai, 1995; Schutte et al., 1998; Swinkels & Giuliano, 1995), these constructs are difficult to distinguish from already measured aspects of personality (Brackett & Mayer, 2003; Davies et al., 1998); moreover, the correlation between emotional competency self-belief scores and actual competencies is disappointing (Brackett, Rivers, Shiffman, Lerner, & Salovey, 2006; Mayer et al., 1999). Therefore since the beginning of our work on EI, we have suggested that tasks that tap into the various competencies that underlie EI are likely to have more validity than self-report measures (e.g., Brackett & Mayer, 2003; Brackett et al., 2006; Mayer et al., 1990, 2008).

Task-based measures of emotional abilities developed on the basis of other theoretical frameworks may be useful in the assessment of EI. For example, in the Levels of Emotional Awareness Scale (LEAS) respondents are asked to describe their feelings about various stimuli and then these protocols are coded according to differentiations in the feeling language used (Lane, Quinlan, Schwartz, Walker, & Zeitlin, 1990). Another possibility is Averill and Nunley's (1992; see also Averill, 1999) test of emotional creativity in which participants are asked to write about situations in which they experience three different emotions simultaneously. Various measures of nonverbal emotional sending and receiving ability have also been

THE POSITIVE PSYCHOLOGY OF EMOTIONAL INTELLIGENCE

explored over the years (e.g., Buck, 1976; Freedman, Prince, Riggio, & DiMatteo, 1980; Matsumoto et al., 2000; Nowicki & Duke, 1994; Rosenthal, Hall, DiMatteo, Rogers, & Archer, 1979).

The first comprehensive, theory-based battery for assessing EI as a set of abilities was the Multifactor Emotional Intelligence Scale (MEIS), which has been refined and published as the Mayer–Salovey–Caruso Emotional Intelligence Test (MSCEIT) (Mayer, Salovey, & Caruso, 2002). They are administered via a computer interface or pencil and paper (Mayer, Caruso, & Salovey, 1998, 1999; Mayer et al., 2003). Both the MEIS and the MSCEIT are comprised of different tasks that assess the four branches of EI, reflecting the model of EI presented earlier: (a) perceiving emotions; (b) using emotions to facilitate thought and other cognitive activities; (c) understanding emotion; and (d) managing emotion in self and others (Mayer & Salovey, 1997; Mayer et al., 2003, 2004). The MSCEIT Branch 1 (perceiving emotions) is assessed by emotional perception tasks in faces, landscapes, and designs. Branch 2 (using emotions) is assessed by "sensations" tasks, measuring the ability to describe emotions in comparison with other sensory stimuli, and "facilitation" tasks, measuring the ability to identify emotions that would best facilitate thinking to carry out different behavioral tasks. Branch 3 (understanding emotions) is assessed by "blends" task, measuring the ability to identify emotions that make up complex emotions, and "changes" task, measuring the ability to understand when intensity of an emotion changes to or how an emotion changes into a different one. Branch 4's (managing emotions) two tasks measure "emotion management in the self" (emotion management tasks) and in "social situations" (emotion relationship tasks). These tasks ask participants to read scenarios and then rate four reactions to them according to how effective they are as emotion management strategies focused on the self or on others.

An issue that comes up in task-based tests of EI concerns what constitutes the correct answer. There are two methods for determining the "correct" answer: scoring using consensus or expert criterion (Mayer et al., 2003, 2004; Salovey & Grewal, 2005). Consensus scoring is based on responses of over 5,000 individuals whereas expert scoring is based on answers provided by 21 emotion researchers. To the extent that the respondent's answers match the consensus or experts' norm (depending on which scoring method is used), they would be scored as correct. Both scoring methods are reliable and highly correlated with each other ($r = .91$; Mayer et al., 2003; Salovey & Grewal, 2005).

In investigations using the MEIS and MSCEIT, we found support for the theoretical model of EI described earlier (Mayer & Salovey, 1997; Mayer et al., 2003). The interrcorrelations of the tasks in the MEIS and MSCEIT were positive and moderate: .20–.50 range for the MEIS and .17–.59 for the MSCEIT tasks. The factorial structure of MEIS recommended two equally viable factorial models: (a) a three- to four-factor solution that separated out factors of emotional perception, understanding, management, and, at times, using emotions to facilitate cognitive activities; or (b) a hierarchical structure that first describes a general factor, g_{ei}. Similarly, the MSCEIT yielded one-, two-, and four-factor solutions. The internal consistency of the MEIS is reasonably high: using consensus scoring, most of the 12 subscales had Cronbach alphas in the .70–.94 range (although two of the tasks of Branch 3 had alphas of .49 and .51; Ciarrochi, Chan, & Caputi, 2000). The internal consistency of MSCEIT is higher, in .76–.91 range, across expert and consensus scoring (Mayer et al., 2003).

The MEIS and MSCEIT as a whole correlate positively with verbal intelligence (but only in the $r = .35 – .54$ range), self-reported empathy, and parental warmth, and negatively with social anxiety and depression (Mayer et al., 1999; Zeidner, Shani-Zinovich, Matthews, & Roberts, 2005). The MEIS is not correlated with nonverbal measures of intelligence such as the Raven Progressive Matrices (Ciarrochi, Chan, & Caputi, 2000). The MSCEIT is weakly correlated with personality and other self-report measures of EI, providing evidence that MSCEIT is not just another personality measure (Brackett et al., 2006; Day & Carroll, 2004; Lopes, Salovey, & Straus, 2003; Roberts, Zeidner, & Matthews, 2001). It is also not correlated with social desirability (Lopes et al., 2003). Finally, and consistent with the idea that EI is a set of abilities that are developed through learning and experience, scores on EI measures improve with age (Mayer et al., 1999).

Current Research Findings

Individuals higher in EI as measured by the MEIS or MSCEIT were found to have better relationships with parents, friends, and romantic partners. They reported being more satisfied with their social relationships and the social support received from parents (Ciarrochi et al., 2000; Lopes et al., 2003). They also reported having more friends, feeling less conflict and antagonism with their close friends, and having higher-quality social relationships (Brackett, Mayer, & Warner, 2004; Ciarrochi et al., 2000; Lopes et al., 2003, 2004; Mestre, Guil, Lopes, Salovey, & Gil-Olarte, 2006). Romantic couples consisting of two low-total EI individuals reported more conflict and negative interactions and lower satisfaction with the relationship than couples that had at least one partner with high EI (Brackett, Warner, & Bosco, 2005). In most of these studies, EI was associated with the criterion variables even after controlling for personality and intelligence.

In addition to self-report, recent studies have employed other methods such as diaries, and ratings by friends and observers to assess social relationships. They yielded similar results showing that EI is important in such relationships. Those who were high on the emotion management branch of the MSCEIT were rated by their friends as providing more emotional support to friends and having a more positive relationship with friends that is full of intimacy, affection, and admiration (Lopes et al., 2004; Lopes, Salovey, Côté, & Beers, 2005). In a laboratory interaction study, men with higher EI were rated by observers as being more socially competent and engaged (Brackett et al., 2006). There is also some evidence that the positive role of EI in relationships may be replicated cross-culturally. In a diary study, German students higher on understanding emotion felt safer in interactions with others and perceived that the interaction partner found the interaction interesting and enjoyable; those higher on managing emotion felt more wanted and important during the interaction. Those high on emotion management also felt being positively perceived by members of the opposite-sex interactions (Lopes et al., 2004). There is also some evidence that EI may play a role in the attachment style of adults (Kafetsios, 2004).

Investigators have also examined adolescents' tobacco use and EI (Trinidad & Johnson, 2002; Trinidad, Unger, Chou, Azen, & Johnson, 2004; Trinidad, Unger, Chou, & Johnson, 2004, 2005). Higher EI was associated with lower tobacco use and a better understanding of the negative social effects of smoking. Similarly, Brackett and colleagues (Brackett & Mayer, 2003; Brackett et al., 2004) found that high EI was associated with less deviant behavior by adolescents such as lower use of drugs and alcohol and lower involvement in fights, gambling, and stealing.

Research on EI and academic performance has produced mixed findings. MSCEIT scores share zero or low correlations with grades and other indicators of academic achievement of both average and gifted students, particularly after controlling for general intelligence (Barchard, 2003; Bastian, Burns, & Nettelbeck, 2005; Brackett & Mayer, 2003; O'Connor & Little, 2003; Woitaszewski & Aalsma, 2004). On the other hand, emotion understanding and managing MSCEIT scores for high school male students in Spain positively predicted teacher ratings of their academic achievement and good academic behavior after controlling for IQ and Big Five (Mestre et al., 2006). There is also evidence of MEIS scores predicting the ability to solve difficult cognitive problems after controlling for general intelligence (Lam & Kirby, 2002) and MSCEIT emotion perception scores being correlated with individual performance on a decision-making task (Day & Carroll, 2004).

With regard to subjective happiness, EI has been associated with higher life satisfaction (Ciarrochi et al., 2000; but see also Mayer, Caruso & Salovey, 1999) and psychological well-being (Brackett & Mayer, 2003). A study using military personnel, however, found EI unrelated to life satisfaction and emotion perception ability and weakly correlated with higher job satisfaction (Livingston & Day, 2005). EI has been associated with lower self-perceived stress in the past week, but only for those who can clearly identify their emotions and intensely feel emotions (Gohm, Corser, & Dalsky, 2005).

EI, as assessed with the MSCEIT, also appears to be important in workplace situations. In a study conducted with employees of a Fortune 500 insurance company, EI was associated with percent merit increase, company rank, even when controlling for variables that are related to these factors such as age and education. It was also associated with peer-rated sociability and peer- and supervisor-rated contribution to positive work environment (Lopes, Grewal, Kadis, Gall, & Salovey, 2006).

Interventions to Improve EI

EI interventions are being developed aimed at raising EI in a variety of contexts.

Interventions in Education

With the availability of materials suggesting how teachers can cultivate EI in school children, there has been an increasing interest in the last decade in developing school-based programs focused on these abilities (Mayer & Cobb, 2000; Salovey & Sluyter, 1997). For example, in guidebook for developing EI curricula for elementary school students, Schilling (1996) recommends units on self-awareness, managing feelings, decision making, managing stress, personal responsibility, self-concept, empathy, communication, group dynamics, and conflict resolution. As should be obvious, the EI rubric is being applied quite broadly to the development of a range of social-emotional skills. As a result, many of the school-based interventions designed to promote EI are better classified under the more general label, Social and Emotional Learning (SEL) programs (Cohen, 1999a; Elias et al., 1997).

There are over 300 curriculum-based programs in the United States purporting to teach SEL (Cohen, 1999b). These range from those based on very specific social problem–solving skills training (e.g., Elias & Tobias, 1996) to more general conflict resolution strategies (e.g., Lantieri & Patti, 1996), to very broad programs organized around themes like "character development" (Lickona, 1991). One of the oldest SEL programs that has a heavy dose of EI development within it is the Social Development curriculum in the New Haven (Connecticut) public schools (Shriver, Schwab-Stone, & DeFalco, 1999; Weissberg, Shriver, Bose, & DeFalco, 1997). The New Haven Social Development program is a kindergarten through Grade 12 curriculum that integrates the development of social and emotional skills in the context of various prevention programs (e.g., AIDS prevention, drug use prevention, teen pregnancy prevention; see also Durlak, 1995). The curriculum provides 25–50 hr of highly structured classroom instruction at each grade level. Included in the early years of this curriculum are units on self-monitoring, feelings awareness, perspective taking (empathy), understanding nonverbal communication, anger management, and many other topics, some of which are loosely consistent with our model of EI. Although this program has not been evaluated in a randomized, controlled trial, a substantial survey administered every 2 years to New Haven schoolchildren has revealed positive trends since implementation of the program. For example, one change has been reduced school violence and feelings of hopelessness (Shriver et al., 1999). Another well-known EI curriculum is called Self Science, which was developed and field-tested at the Nueva School in Hillsborough (California) in first through eighth grades (Stone-McCown, Jensen, Freedman, & Rideout, 1998). The Self Science program begins with three assumptions: there is no thinking without feeling and no feeling without thinking; the more conscious one is of what one is experiencing, the more learning is possible; and, self-knowledge is integral to learning. The Self Science approach directly focuses on emotions in about half of the lessons. The goals of the Self Science curriculum include talking about feelings and needs; listening, sharing, and comforting others; learning to grow from conflict and adversity; prioritizing and setting goals; including others; making conscious decisions; and giving time and resources to the larger community (Stone-McCown et al., 1998).

For the past couple of years, Emotional Literacy in the Middle School (ELMS; Maurer & Brackett, 2004) program has been implemented in many schools throughout the United States and the United Kingdom. This program, designed for students between 10 and 13 years of age, aims to help students become emotionally literate by broadening their vocabulary and understanding of emotion words. Students learn to recognize, label, understand, and express emotions as well as to write about socio-emotional aspects of life. They also engage in projects to learn the four EI skills. For example, students learn about perceiving and using emotions skills by interpreting and analyzing emotions evoked by a given piece of music or by creating collages or mobiles related to various facial displays of emotion. All of the projects are followed up with group discussions. The ELMS also allows students to learn about cross-cultural differences in EI skills that exist in a diverse classroom environment.

Finally, many EI interventions for school children take place within other more specific prevention programs. A good example is the Resolving Conflict Creatively Program (RCCP) that began in the New York City public schools (Lantieri & Patti, 1996). The program goals include increasing awareness of the different choices available to children for dealing with conflicts; developing skills for making these choices; encouraging children's respect for their own cultural background and the backgrounds of others; teaching children how to identify and stand against prejudice; and increasing children's awareness of their role in creating a more peaceful world. A follow-up program, Peace in the Family, trains parents in conflict resolution strategies. RCCP training programs emphasize identifying one's own feelings in conflict situations and taking the perspective of and empathizing with others' feelings. In an evaluation that included 5,000 children participating in the RCCP program in New York City, hostile attributions and teacher-reported aggressive behavior dropped as a function of the number of conflict resolution lessons that the children had received, and academic achievement was highest among those children who received the most lessons (Aber, Brown, & Henrich, 1999; Aber, Jones, Brown, Chaudry, & Samples, 1998).

Although increasing numbers of SEL programs are being evaluated formally (e.g., Elias, Gere, Schuyler, Branden-Muller, & Sayette, 1991; Greenberg, Kushe, Cook, & Quamma, 1995), many still have not been subjected to empirical scrutiny. There is essentially no published research yet on whether these programs are effective by enhancing the kinds of skills delineated in our model of EI.

Interventions in the Workplace

Possible interventions to increase EI can also be found in the workplace (e.g., Caruso, Mayer, & Salovey, 2002; Cherniss & Goleman, 1998; Goleman, 1998). These workplace programs, however, are at a much earlier stage of development than those designed for the classroom. Furthermore, many of these workplace "EI" programs are really old and familiar training sessions on human relations, achievement motivation, stress management, and conflict resolution.

One promising approach to workplace EI is the Weatherhead MBA program at Case Western Reserve University, where training in social and emotional competency is incorporated into the curriculum for future business leaders (Boyatzis, Cowen, & Kolb, 1995). Although not focused explicitly on emotions per se, these MBA students receive experiences designed to promote initiative, flexibility, achievement drive, empathy, self-confidence, persuasiveness, networking, self-control, and group management. Communication and emotion-related skills are also increasingly being incorporated into physician training (Kramer, Ber, & Moores, 1989).

Perhaps the workplace program that addresses itself to EI most explicitly is the Emotional Competency Training Program at American Express Financial Advisors. The goal of the program is to assist managers in becoming "emotional coaches" for their employees. The training focuses on the role of emotion in the workplace and gaining an awareness of how one's own emotional reactions and the emotions of others affect management practices. Although systematic evaluation of this program has yet to be published, a higher business growth rate (money under management) has been found for the financial advisors whose managers had taken the training program as compared to those who had not (reported in Cherniss, 1999).

Directions for Future Research

Despite the rapid growth of interest in EI, the measurement of EI using ability-based indices is still in an early stage. As is inevitable for a new concept, EI has received some criticism. In particular, using an array of available and, for the most part, poorly validated instruments as the basis for analysis, the construct validity of EI has been questioned (Davies et al., 1998). It simply is premature to draw any such conclusions until investigators in our laboratory and other laboratories have completed and validated the appropriate ability-based measures of EI.

The area of EI is in need of energetic investigators interested in helping to refine the ability-based assessment of EI, and, subsequently, studying the predictive validity of EI (over and above other constructs) in accounting for important outcomes in school, workplace, family, and social relationships. Given the present status of instrument development and validation, we would encourage investigators to focus their energies on the refinement of ability measures of EI. Although we are confident that the MSCEIT will be the measurement instrument of choice for assessing EI as an ability, research needs to be conducted to measure EI with even greater precision and with more easily administered and briefer tests. Further work also will be needed before we can confidently claim that one method of scoring—expert or consensus—is clearly more valid than the others. And it will be necessary to investigate whether tests of EI are culture-bound or not. The fact is that we are in the early phase of research on EI, both in terms of measuring it as an ability and in showing that such measures predict significant outcomes.

After refining the measurement of EI, we are hoping that many investigators will join us in exploring what this construct predicts, both as an overall ability and in terms of an individual's profile of strengths and weaknesses. The domains in which EI may play an important part are limited only by the imagination of the investigators studying these abilities, and we are hoping to see an explosion of research in the near future establishing when EI is important—perhaps more so than conventional intelligence—and, of course, when it is not.

Finally, and reflecting the theme of this Handbook—positive psychology—attention will need to be focused on how EI can be developed through the life span. We suspect that work on the teaching and learning of emotion-related abilities might prove to be a useful counterpoint to the nihilistic conclusions of books like *The bell curve* and may, instead, suggest all kinds of ways in which emotionally enriching experiences could be incorporated into one's life. We need to remind ourselves, however, that work on EI is still in its infancy, and that what the field and general public need is more investigators treating it with serious empirical attention.

Three Questions about the Future of Emotional Intelligence

1. What skills and abilities related to the processing of emotional information are missing from the four-branch model?

2. What methods of assessing emotional intelligence can incorporate the measurement of more fluid abilities in ecologically valid contexts?

3. What are the longer-term consequences of interventions designed to enhance emotional intelligence in educational settings and workplaces?

Acknowledgment

Preparation of this chapter was facilitated by a grant from the National Cancer Institute (R01-CA68427).

References

Aber, J. L., Brown, J. L., & Henrich, C. C. (1999). *Teaching conflict resolution: An effective school-based approach to violence prevention*. New York: National Center for Children in Poverty, The Joseph L. Mailman School of Public Health, Columbia University.

Aber, J. L., Jones, S. M., Brown, J. L., Chaudry, N., & Samples, F. (1998). Resolving conflict creatively: Evaluating the developmental effects of a school-based violence prevention program in neighborhood and classroom context. *Development and Psychopathology, 10*, 187–213.

Alcalde, J. (1996, December). Inteligencia emocional? *Muy Interesante*, 41–46.

American Dialect Society. (1995). American Dialect Society: e-mail from Allan Metcalf. http://www.americandialect.org/excite/collections/adsl/011272.shtml

American Dialect Society. (1999). American Dialect Society: Words of the Year. http://www.americandialect.org/woty

Averill, J. R. (1999). Individual differences in emotional creativity: Structure and correlates. *Journal of Personality, 67*, 331–371.

Averill, J. R., & Nunley, E. P. (1992). *Voyages of the heart: Living an emotionally creative life*. New York: Free Press.

Bagby, R. M., Parker, J. D. A., & Taylor, G. J. (1993a). The twenty-item Toronto Alexithymia Scale: I. Item selection and cross-validation of the factor structure. *Journal of Psychosomatic Research, 38*, 23–32.

Bagby, R. M., Parker, J. D. A., & Taylor, G. J. (1993b). The twenty-item Toronto Alexithymia Scale: II. Convergent, discriminant, and concurrent validity. *Journal of Psychosomatic Research, 38*, 33–40.

Barchard, K. A. (2003). Does emotional intelligence assist in the prediction of academic success? *Educational and Psychological Measurement, 63*, 840–858.

Bar-On, R. (1997). *BarOn Emotional Quotient Inventory: A measure of emotional intelligence*. Toronto, ON: Multi-Health Systems.

Bastian, V. A., Burns, N. R., & Nettelbeck, T. (2005). Emotional intelligence predicts life skills, but not as well as personality and cognitive abilities. *Personality and Individual Differences, 39*, 1135–1145.

Boyatzis, R. E., Cowen, S. S., & Kolb, D. A. (1995). *Innovation in professional education: Steps on a journey to learning*. San Francisco: Jossey-Bass.

Brackett, M. A., & Mayer, J. D. (2003). Convergent, discriminant, and incremental validity of competing measures of emotional intelligence. *Personality and Social Psychology Bulletin, 29*, 1–12.

Brackett, M. A., Mayer, J. D., & Warner, R. M. (2004). Emotional intelligence and its relations to everyday behaviour. *Personality and Individual Differences, 36*, 1387–1402.

Brackett, M. A., Rivers, S. E., Shiffman, S., Lerner, N., & Salovey, P. (2006). Relating emotional abilities to social functioning: A comparison of self-report and performance measures of emotional intelligence. *Journal of Personality and Social Psychology, 91*, 780–795.

Brackett, M. A., Warner, R. M., & Bosco, J. S. (2005). Emotional intelligence and relationship quality among couples. *Personal Relationships, 12*, 197–212.

Brodie, I. (1996, January 5). Neutron bomb fall-out changes slang. *The Times*, p. 26.

Buck, R. (1976). A test of nonverbal receiving ability: Preliminary studies. *Human Communication Research, 2*, 162–171.

Caruso, D. R., Mayer, J. D., & Salovey, P. (2002). Emotional intelligence and emotional leadership. In R. Riggio, S. Murphy, & F. Pirozzolo (Eds.), *Multiple intelligences and leadership* (pp. 55–74). Mahwah, NJ: Lawrence Erlbaum.

Catanzaro, S. J., & Mearns, J. (1990). Measuring generalized expectancies for negative mood regulation: Initial scale development and implications. *Journal of Personality Assessment, 54*, 546–563.

Cherniss, C. (1999). *Model program summaries*. A technical report issued by the Consortium for Research on Emotional Intelligence in Organizations. Available at http://www.eiconsortium.org

Cherniss, C., & Goleman, D. (1998). *Bringing emotional intelligence to the workplace*. A technical report issued by the Consortium for Research on Emotional Intelligence in Organizations. Available at http://www.eiconsortium.org

Ciarrochi, J. V., Chan, A. Y. C., & Caputi, P. (2000). A critical evaluation of the emotional intelligence construct. *Personality and Individual Differences, 3*, 539–561.

Cohen, J. (Ed.). (1999a). *Educating minds and hearts: Social emotional learning and the passage into adolescence*. New York: Teachers College Press.

Cohen, J. (1999b). Social and emotional learning past and present: A psychoeducational dialogue. In J. Cohen (Ed.), *Educating minds and hearts: Social emotional learning and the passage into adolescence* (pp. 2–23). New York: Teachers College Press.

Cooper, R. K., & Sawaf, A. (1997). *Executive EQ: Emotional intelligence in leadership and organizations*. New York: Grosset/Putnam.

Cronbach, L. J. (1960). *Essentials of psychological testing*. New York: Harper and Row.

Damasio, A. R. (1994). *Descartes' error: Emotion, reason, and the human brain*. New York: Putnam Books.

Davies, M., Stankov, L., & Roberts, R. D. (1998). Emotional Intelligence: In search of an elusive construct. *Journal of Personality and Social Psychology, 75*, 989–1015.

Day, A. L., & Carroll, S. A. (2004). Using an ability-based measure of emotional intelligence to predict individual performance, group performance, and group citizenship behaviours. *Personality and Individual Differences, 36*, 1443–1458.

Durlak, J. A. (1995). *School-based prevention programs for children and adolescents*. Thousand Oaks, CA: Sage Publications.

Easterbrook, J. A. (1959). The effects of emotion on cue utilization and the organization of behavior. *Psychological Review, 66*, 183–200.

Elias, M. J., Gere M. A., Schuyler, T. F., Branden-Muller, L. R., & Sayette, M. A. (1991). The promotion of social competence: Longitudinal study of a preventive school-based program. *American Journal of Orthopsychiatry, 61*, 409–417.

Elias, M. J., & Tobias, S. E. (1996). *Social problem solving interventions in the schools*. New York: Guilford.

Elias, M. J., Zins, J. E., Weissberg, R. P., Frey, K. S., Greenberg, M. T., Haynes, N. M., et al. (1997). *Promoting social and emotional learning: Guidelines for educators*. Alexandria, VA: Association for Supervision and Curriculum Development.

Epstein, S. (1998). *Constructive thinking: The key to emotional intelligence*. Westport, CT: Praeger.

EQ Japan. (1998). *Emotional Quotient Inventory*. Tokyo: Author.

Forgas, J. P. (1995). Mood and judgment: The affect infusion model (AIM). *Psychological Bulletin, 117*, 39–66.

Freedman, H. S., Prince, L. M., Riggio, R. E., & DiMatteo, M. R. (1980). Understanding and assessing nonverbal expressiveness: The Affective Communication Test. *Journal of Personality and Social Psychology, 39*, 333–351.

Gardner, H. (1983/1993). *Frames of mind: The theory of multiple intelligences* (10th Anniversary Ed.). New York: Basic Books.

Gibbs, N. (1995, October 2). The EQ factor. *Time*, pp. 60–68.

Giuliano, T., & Swinkels, A. (1992, August). *Development and validation of the Mood Awareness Scale*. Paper presented at the annual meeting of the American Psychological Association, Washington, DC.

Gohm, C. L., Corser, G. C., & Dalsky, D. J. (2005). Emotional intelligence under stress: Useful, unnecessary, or irrelevant? *Personality and Individual Differences, 39*, 1017–1028.

Goleman, D. (1995a, September 10). Why your emotional intelligence quotient can matter more than IQ. *USA Weekend*, pp. 4–8.

Goleman, D. (1995b). *Emotional intelligence*. New York: Bantam.

Goleman, D. (1998). *Working with emotional intelligence*. New York: Bantam.

Goodwin, F. K., & Jamison, K. R. (1990). *Manic-depressive illness*. New York: Oxford University Press.

Gottman, J., & DeClaire, J. (1997). *The heart of parenting: Raising an emotionally intelligent child*. New York: Simon and Schuster.

Greenberg, M. T., Kushe, C. A., Cook, E. T., & Quamma, J. P. (1995). Promoting emotional competence in school-aged children: The effects of the PATHS curriculum. *Development and Psychopathology, 7*, 117–136.

Herrnstein, R. J., & Murray, C. (1994). *The bell curve: Intelligence and class in American life*. New York: Free Press.

Kafetsios, K. (2004). Attachment and emotional intelligence abilities across the life course. *Personality and Individual Differences, 37*, 129–145.

Kramer, D., Ber, R., & Moores, M. (1989). Increasing empathy among medical students. *Medical Education, 23*, 168–173.

Lam, L. T., & Kirby, S. L. (2002). Is emotional intelligence an advantage? An exploration of the impact of emotional and general intelligence on individual performance. *Journal of Social Psychology, 142*, 133–143.

Lane, R. D., Quinlan, D. M., Schwartz, G. E., Walker, P., & Zeitlin, S. B. (1990). The levels of emotional awareness scale: A cognitive-developmental measure of emotion. *Journal of Personality Assessment, 55*, 124–134.

Lantieri, L., & Patti, J. (1996). *Waging peace in our schools*. Boston: Beacon Press.

Lickona, T. (1991). *Educating for character: How our schools can teach respect and responsibility*. New York: Bantam.

Livingstone, H., & Day, A. L. (2005). Comparing the construct and criterion-related validity of ability-based and mixed-model measures of emotional intelligence. *Educational and Psychological Measurement, 65*, 757–779.

Lopes, P. N., Brackett, M. A., Nezlek, J. B., Schutz, A., Sellin, I., & Salovey, P. (2004). Emotional intelligence and social interaction. *Personality and Social Psychology Bulletin, 30*, 1018–1034.

Lopes, P. N., Grewal, D., Kadis, J., Gall, M., & Salovey, P. (2006). Evidence that emotional intelligence is related to job performance and affect and attitudes at work. *Psicothema, 18*, 132–138.

Lopes, P. N., Salovey, P., Côté, S., & Beers, M. (2005). Emotion regulation abilities and the quality of social interaction. *Emotion, 5*, 113–118.

Lopes, P. N., Salovey, P., & Straus, R. (2003). Emotional intelligence, personality, and the perceived quality of social relationships. *Personality and Individual Differences, 35*, 641–658.

Mandler, G. (1975). *Mind and emotion*. New York: Wiley.

Matsumoto, D., LeRoux, J. A., Wilson-Cohn, C., Raroque, J., Kooken, K., Ekman, P., et al. (2000). A new test to measure emotion recognition ability: Matsumoto and Ekman's Japanese and Caucasian Brief Affect Recognition Test (JACBART). *Journal of Nonverbal Behavior, 24*, 179–209.

Maurer, M., & Brackett, M. A. (2004). *Emotional literacy in the middle school: A six-step program to promote social, emotional, and academic learning*. Portchester, NY: National Professional Resources.

Mayer, J. D. (1986). How mood influences cognition. In N. E. Sharkey (Ed.), *Advances in cognitive science* (pp. 290–314). Chichester, UK: Ellis Horwood.

Mayer, J. D., Caruso, D. R., & Salovey, P. (1998). *Multifactor Emotional Intelligence Test (MEIS)*. (Available from John D. Mayer, Department of Psychology, University of New Hampshire, Conant Hall, Durham, NH 03824.)

Mayer, J. D., Caruso, D. R., & Salovey, P. (1999). Emotional intelligence meets traditional standards for an intelligence. *Intelligence, 27*, 267–298.

Mayer, J. D., & Cobb, C. D. (2000). Educational policy on emotional intelligence: Does it make sense? *Educational Psychology Review, 12*, 163–183.

Mayer, J. D., DiPaolo, M. T., & Salovey, P. (1990). Perceiving affective content in ambiguous visual stimuli: A component of emotional intelligence. *Journal of Personality Assessment, 54*, 772–781.

Mayer, J. D., Gaschke, Y., Braverman, D. L., & Evans, T. (1992). Mood-congruent judgment is a general effect. *Journal of Personality and Social Psychology, 63*, 119–132.

Mayer, J. D., & Hanson, E. (1995). Mood-congruent judgment over time. *Personality and Social Psychology Bulletin, 21*, 237–244.

Mayer, J. D., & Salovey, P. (1997). What is emotional intelligence? In P. Salovey & D. Sluyter (Eds.), *Emotional development and emotional intelligence: Implications for educators* (pp. 3–31). New York: Basic Books.

Mayer, J. D., Salovey, P., & Caruso, D. (2000a). Models of emotional intelligence. In R. J. Sternberg (Ed.), *The handbook of intelligence* (2nd ed., pp. 396–420). New York: Cambridge University Press.

Mayer, J. D., Salovey, P., & Caruso, D. (2000b). Emotional intelligence as Zeitgeist, as personality, and as a mental ability. In R. Bar-On & J. D. A. Parker (Eds.), *The handbook of emotional intelligence* (pp. 92–117). San Francisco: Jossey-Bass.

Mayer, J. D., Salovey, P., & Caruso, D. (2002). *Mayer–Salovey–Caruso Emotional Intelligence Test (MSCEIT)*. Toronto, ON: Multi-Health Systems.

Mayer, J. D., Salovey, P., & Caruso, D. (2004). Emotional intelligence: Theory, findings, and implications. *Psychological Inquiry, 15,* 197–215.

Mayer, J. D., Salovey, P., & Caruso, D. R. (2008). Emotional intelligence: New ability or eclectic traits? *American Psychologist, 63,* 503–517.

Mayer, J. D., Salovey, P., Caruso, D. R., & Sitarenios, G. (2001). Emotional intelligence as a standard intelligence. *Emotion, 3,* 232–242.

Mayer, J. D., Salovey, P., Caruso, D. R., & Sitarenios, G. (2003). Measuring emotional intelligence with the MSCEIT v 2.0. *Emotion, 3,* 97–105.

Mestre, J. M., Guil, R., Lopes, P. N., Salovey, P., & Gil-Olarte, P. (2006). Emotional intelligence and social and academic adaptation to school. *Psicothema, 18,* 112–117.

Miketta, G., Gottschling, C., Wagner-Roos, L., & Gibbs, N. (1995, October 9). Die neue Erfolgsformel: EQ. *Focus,* pp. 194–202.

Mowrer, O. H. (1960). *Learning theory and behavior.* New York: Wiley.

Nowicki, S., Jr., & Duke, M. P. (1994). Individual differences in the nonverbal communication of affect: The diagnostic analysis of Nonverbal Accuracy Scale. *Journal of Nonverbal Behavior, 18,* 9–35.

O'Connor, R. M., Jr., & Little, I. S. (2003). Revisiting the predictive validity of emotional intelligence: Self-report versus ability-based measures. *Personality and Individual Differences, 35,* 1893–1902.

Ortony, A., Clore, G. L., & Collins, A. (1988). *The cognitive structure of emotions.* Cambridge: Cambridge University Press.

Palfai, T. P., & Salovey, P. (1993). The influence of depressed and elated mood on deductive and inductive reasoning. *Imagination, Cognition, and Personality, 13,* 57–71.

Payne, W. L. (1983/1986). A study of emotion: Developing emotional intelligence; self-integration; relating to fear, pain and desire. *Dissertation Abstracts International, 47,* 203A (University Microfilms no. AAC 8605928). (Doctoral Dissertation at the Union Graduate School, Cincinnati, OH. Original dissertation work submitted and accepted, May, 1983.)

Pennebaker, J. W. (1989). Confession, inhibition, and disease. In L. Berkowitz (Ed.), *Advances in experimental social psychology* (Vol. 22, pp. 211–244). New York: Academic Press.

Pennebaker, J. W. (1993). Putting stress into words: Health, linguistic, and therapeutic implications. *Behavior Research and Therapy, 31,* 539–548.

Pennebaker, J. W. (1997). Writing about emotional experiences as a therapeutic process. *Psychological Science, 9,* 162–166.

Roberts, R. D., Zeidner, M., & Matthews, G. (2001). Does emotional intelligence meet traditional standards for an intelligence? Some new data and conclusions. *Emotion, 1,* 196–231.

Rosenthal, R., Hall, J. A., DiMatteo, M. R., Rogers, P., & Archer, D. (1979). *Sensitivity to nonverbal communication: A profile approach to the measurement of individual differences.* Baltimore: Johns Hopkins University Press.

Ryback, D. (1998). *Putting emotional intelligence to work: Successful leadership is more than IQ.* Boston: Butterworth-Heinemann.

Saarni, C. (1990). Emotional competence: How emotions and relationships become integrated. In R. A. Thompson (Ed.), *Socioemotional development: Nebraska symposium on motivation* (Vol. 36, pp. 115–182). Lincoln, NE: University of Nebraska Press.

Saarni, C. (1999). *Developing emotional competence.* New York: Guilford.

Salerno, J. G. (1996). *Emotional quotient (EQ): Are you ready for it?* Oakbank, SA: Noble House of Australia.

Salovey, P., Bedell, B., Detweiler, J. B., & Mayer, J. D. (1999). Coping intelligently: Emotional intelligence and the coping process. In C. R. Snyder (Ed.), *Coping: The psychology of what works* (pp. 141–164). New York: Oxford University Press.

Salovey, P., Bedell, B. T., Detweiler, J. B., & Mayer, J. D. (2000). Current directions in emotional intelligence research. In M. Lewis & J. M. Haviland-Jones (Eds.), *Handbook of emotions* (2nd ed., pp. 504–520). New York: Guilford.

Salovey, P., & Birnbaum, D. (1989). The influence of mood on health-relevant cognitions. *Journal of Personality and Social Psychology, 57,* 539–551.

Salovey, P., & Grewal, D. (2005). The science of emotional intelligence. *Current Directions in Psychological Science, 14,* 281–285.

Salovey, P., & Mayer, J. D. (1990). Emotional intelligence. *Imagination, Cognition, and Personality, 9,* 185–211.

Salovey, P., Mayer, J. D., Goldman, S. L., Turvey, C., & Palfai, T. P. (1995). Emotional attention, clarity, and repair: Exploring emotional intelligence using the Trait Meta-Mood Scale. In J. W. Pennebaker (Ed.), *Emotion, disclosure, and health* (pp. 125–154). Washington, DC: American Psychological Association.

Salovey, P., & Rodin, J. (1986). Differentiation of social-comparison jealousy and romantic jealousy. *Journal of Personality and Social Psychology, 50,* 1100–1112.

Salovey, P., & Rodin, J. (1989). Envy and jealousy in close relationships. *Review of Personality and Social Psychology, 10,* 221–246.

Salovey, P., & Sluyter, D. (Eds.). (1997). *Emotional development and emotional intelligence: Implications for educators.* New York: Basic Books.

Salovey, P., Woolery, A., & Mayer, J. D. (2001). Emotional intelligence: Conceptualization and measurement. In G. Fletcher & M. Clark (Eds.), *The Blackwell handbook of social psychology* (pp. 279–307). London: Blackwell.

Schilling, D. (1996). *Fifty activities for teaching emotional intelligence: Level I. Elementary.* Torrance, CA: Innerchoice Publishing.

Schutte, N. S., Malouff, J. M., Hall, L. E., Haggerty, D. J., Copper, J. T., Golden, C. J., et al. (1998). Development and validation of a measure of emotional intelligence. *Personality and Individual Differences, 25,* 167–177.

Schwarz, N. (1990). Feelings as information: Informational and motivational functions of affective states. In E. T. Higgins & E. M. Sorrentino (Eds.), *Handbook of motivation and cognition* (Vol. 2, pp. 527–561). New York: Guilford.

Segal, J. (1997). *Raising your emotional intelligence: A practical guide.* New York: Holt.

Shapiro, L. E. (1997). *How to raise a child with a high EQ: A parents' guide to emotional intelligence.* New York: HarperCollins.

Shriver, T. P., Schwab-Stone, M., & DeFalco, K. (1999). Why SEL is the better way: The New Haven Social Development program. In J. Cohen (Ed.), *Educating minds and hearts: Social emotional learning and the passage into adolescence* (pp. 43–60). New York: Teachers College Press.

Simmons, S., & Simmons, J. C. (1997). *Measuring emotional intelligence.* Arlington, TX: Summit Publishing Group.

Simon, H. A. (1982). Comments. In M. S. Clark & S. T. Fiske (Eds.), *Affect and cognition* (pp. 333–342). Hillsdale, NJ: Erlbaum.

Singer, J. A., & Salovey, P. (1988). Mood and memory: Evaluating the network theory of affect. *Clinical Psychology Review, 8*, 211–251.

Steiner, C., & Perry, P. (1997). *Achieving emotional literacy: A personal program to increase your emotional intelligence.* New York: Avon.

Sternberg, R. J. (1985). *The triarchic mind: A new theory of human intelligence.* New York: Penguin.

Stone-McCown, K., Jensen, A. L., Freedman, J. M., & Rideout, M. C. (1998). *Self-science: The emotional intelligence curriculum* (2nd ed.). San Mateo, CA: Six Seconds.

Swinkels, A., & Giuliano, T. A. (1995). The measurement and conceptualization of mood awareness: Monitoring and labeling one's mood states. *Personality and Social Psychology Bulletin, 21*, 934–939.

Thayer, R. E., Newman, J. R., & McClain, T. M. (1994). Self-regulation of mood: Strategies for changing a bad mood, raising energy, and reducing tension. *Journal of Personality and Social Psychology, 67*, 910–925.

Thomas, B. (1995, December 13). A la recherche du QE perdu. *Le Canard Enchaîné*, p. 5.

Tomkins, S. S. (1962). *Affect, imagery, and consciousness: Vol. 1. The positive affects.* New York: Springer.

Trinidad, D. R., & Johnson, A. (2002). The association between emotional intelligence and early adolescent tobacco and alcohol use. *Personality and Individual Differences, 32*, 95–105.

Trinidad, D. R., Unger, J. B., Chou, C.-P., Azen, S. P., & Johnson, C. A. (2004). Emotional intelligence and smoking risk factors in adolescents: Interactions on smoking intentions. *Journal of Adolescent Health, 34*, 46–55.

Trinidad, D. R., Unger, J. B., Chou, C.-P., & Johnson, C. A. (2004). The protective association of emotional intelligence with psychosocial smoking risk factors for adolescents. *Personality and Individual Differences, 36*, 945–954.

Trinidad, D. R., Unger, J. B., Chou, C.-P., & Johnson, C. A. (2005). Emotional intelligence and acculturation to the United States: Interactions on the perceived social consequences of smoking in early adolescents. *Substance Use and Misuse, 40*, 1697–1706.

Weisinger, H. (1998). *Emotional intelligence at work: The untapped edge for success.* San Francisco: Jossey-Bass.

Weissberg, R. P., Shriver, T. P., Bose, S., & DeFalco, K. (1997). Creating a district wide social development project. *Educational Leadership, 54*, 37–39.

Woitaszewski, S. A., & Aalsma, M. C. (2004). The contribution of emotional intelligence to the social and academic success of gifted adolescents as measured by the Multifactor Emotional Intelligence Scale—Adolescent version. *Roeper Review, 27*, 25–30.

Zeidner, M., Shani-Zinovich, I., Matthews, G., & Roberts, R. D. (2005). Assessing emotional intelligence in gifted and non-gifted high school students: Outcomes depend on the measure. *Intelligence, 33*, 369–391.

Emotional Creativity: Toward "Spiritualizing the Passions"

James R. Averill

Abstract

Emotional states are typically viewed negatively: Our fears, angers, and sorrows seem to outweigh our joys and pleasures. Yet, it is hard to imagine life without ostensibly negative emotions. The solution, Nietzsche suggested, is to spiritualize the passions, the negative as well as the positive. And what might that entail? Whatever else, spiritualizing the passions requires creativity. In this chapter, we explore how standard criteria for creativity (novelty, effectiveness, and authenticity) apply to emotional as well as to intellectual and artistic responses. In a similar vein, we show how characteristics commonly associated with spiritual experiences (meaning, vitality, and connectedness) apply to emotionally creative responses. Finally, data are presented that relate individual differences in emotional creativity to a spiritualization of the passions, at the high end of the creativity continuum; and to its opposite, a despiritualization of the passions (neurosis), at the low end.

Keywords: alexithymia, creativity, emotion, neurosis spirituality

The relation between emotions and creativity is charged with ambivalence. In schools we encourage creativity, and in the arts and sciences, we praise its achievement. A person, it seems, cannot be too creative. By contrast, a person who is too prone to emotion risks being labeled as immature, uncouth, boorish, or worse. Even our language seems to disparage emotions: Most nonemotional words have a positive connotation; the opposite is true of emotional words, where the negative outnumber the positive by roughly 2 to 1 (Averill, 1980a).

The way creativity and emotions are evaluated in everyday affairs is reflected in our scientific theories. For example, creativity is regarded as a late evolutionary development, whereas the emotions are typically treated as holdovers from our infrahuman past; correspondingly, creativity is seated in the neocortex, whereas emotions are relegated to paleocortical and subcortical regions of the brain; and, from a cognitive perspective, creativity is classed among the "higher" thought processes, whereas emotions often are treated

as noncognitive—a psychological euphemism for "lower" thought processes.

Nevertheless, our everyday and scientific conceptions of emotion and creativity can be misleading. The primary purpose of this chapter is to illustrate how emotions are compatible with creativity—indeed, can themselves be creative products. A secondary purpose is reflected in the subtitle to the chapter, "spiritualizing the passions," which I adopt from Nietzsche (1889/2003). I will not speculate about Nietzsche's meaning of this phrase.[1] Suffice

[1] Nietzsche (1889/2003) recognized that the passions often "drag down their victim by the weight of their folly" ("Morality as Anti-nature," p. 1). The solution, he believed, is not to extirpate the passions, which would be inimical to life, but to spiritualize (*vergeistigen*) them. In one sense, this involves a "return to nature," but not in the sense envisioned by Rousseau, whose romanticism Nietzsche disparaged. Nietzsche's (1889/2003) vision was not "a going-back but a *going-up*—up into a high, free, even frightful nature and naturalness, such as plays with great tasks, is *permitted* to play with them" ("Expeditions of an Untimely Man," p. 48, italics in original).

it to say that, as used in this chapter, spiritualization has no necessary ontological implications—a belief, for example, in a nonmaterial mode of existence. Acts of creation—or re-creation, as in aesthetic experiences (Averill, Stanat, & More, 1998; Richards, 1998)—provide the reference point for spiritualizing the passions as here conceived.

In addition to presenting a model of emotion in which emotional creativity makes theoretical sense, I review briefly some empirical research on individual difference in emotional creativity, with special reference to alexithymia and mystic-like experiences—two conditions that represent low and high points along the continuum of emotional creativity. I also explore how neurotic syndromes can be interpreted as emotional creativity gone awry—a despiritualization of the passions, so to speak.

Historical Background in Brief

The idea of emotional creativity is a straightforward extension of a social-constructionist view of emotion (Averill, 1980b, 1984, 2004). It is not, however, limited to any one theoretical perspective, as the following examples illustrate. Otto Rank (1932), a student of the arts and onetime disciple of Freud, believed that many neurotic syndromes reflect creative impulses that are expressed in ways detrimental to the individual—a point that will be discussed in more detail subsequently. Starting from a different perspective, and ending up at the other end of the neurotic–healthy spectrum, Abraham Maslow (1971) defined "primary" creativity as the ability to be inspired, to become totally immersed in the matter at hand, and to experience those "peak" moments that are "a diluted, more secular, more frequent version of the mystical experience" (p. 62). I would only add that emotional creativity is not limited to a few extreme (peak or mystical) experiences but can encompass a wide variety of emotions experienced in everyday life.

In his *Varieties of Religious Experience*, William James (1902/1961) observed that "When a person has an inborn genius for certain emotions, his life differs strangely from that of ordinary people, for none of their usual deterrents check him" (p. 215). Again, I would add a caveat: Creativity in the emotional domain is not limited to a few persons of "inborn genius" any more than is creativity in the intellectual and artistic domains so limited (Richards, 2007).

In contemporary theory and research, a number of concepts bear a family resemblance to emotional creativity, for example, emotional intelligence (chap. 22), emotional competence (Saarni, 1999), intra- and interpersonal intelligences (Gardner, 1993), and constructive thinking (Epstein, 1998). There are important differences in the theoretical underpinnings to these concepts (for comparisons, see Averill, 2004, 2007). What these concepts have in common is an emphasis on the functional or adaptive aspects of emotional behavior.

Emotions as Syndromes

The model of emotion on which the present analysis is based has been presented in detail elsewhere (e.g., Averill, 2005; Averill & Nunley, 1992; Averill & Thomas-Knowles, 1991). Only a brief summary is provided here. By emotions, I mean those states of affairs recognized in ordinary language by such terms as "anger," "grief," and "love." These are syndromes, that is, coordinated sets of responses to situations appraised as beneficial or harmful to the person. The operative term here is "coordinated." Research attests that the way the elements that constitute an emotional syndrome are organized is not "hardwired" into the nervous system and hence invariant; on the contrary, they are only loosely related and vary from one situation and person to another. This is true not only of instrumental acts (hitting, running, etc.) and expressive reactions (smiling, frowning, etc.), but also of peripheral and central neural mechanisms that mediate emotions (Barrett, 2006). That being the case, the question arises: What provides meaning and coherence to an emotional syndrome on any given occasion?

The way a person appraises the situation is an important factor in determining the nature and course of an emotional episode. However, as Dewey (1895) pointed out long ago in a much neglected analysis, appraisals are part of the emotion, not external or antecedent to it (see, also, Solomon, 1993). Thus, we are still left with making sense of the entire syndrome—the appraisal as well as the coordinated responses.

In order to lend substance to an otherwise abstract analysis, it might be helpful at this point to introduce a concrete example. LaBarre (1947) described the following episode of grief manifested by a Kiowa woman at her brother's funeral: "She wept in a frenzy, tore her hair, scratched her cheeks, and even tried to jump into the grave ..." (p. 55). Within most modern, industrialized societies, this would appear to be a histrionic reaction, even for the loss of a dear brother. According to LaBarre, however, the deceased brother was not dear to the woman; yet, neither was her reaction histrionic.

"I happened to know," he writes, "that [the woman] had not seen her brother for some time, and there was no particular love lost between them: she was merely carrying on the way a decent woman should among the Kiowa. Away from the grave, she was immediately chatting vivaciously about some other topic. Weeping is used differently among the Kiowas" (p. 55).

Was the Kiowa woman merely playing the role of a grief-stricken sister? Not if we interpret her performance as feigned. There is no reason to believe the woman was insincere in her grief. From a social perspective, grief *is* a role that societies create in order to facilitate transition following bereavement, and that people may enact with greater or lesser involvement (Averill & Nunley, 1993). This is not to gainsay the importance of biology—grievous hurt at the loss of a loved one is part of what keeps us together as members of a social species. However, biology only sets the stage; it does not write the script. In the final analysis, emotional syndromes are lent coherence by culturally specific beliefs and rules.

When emotional beliefs and rules are internalized by individuals during socialization, and linked with deeply held values or current concerns, we may speak of emotional ("hot" cognitive) schemas. An emotional episode occurs when relevant schemas are activated by situational cues (facilitated, on occasion, by internal conditions, such as physiological arousal from extraneous sources). In oft-recurring situations, emotional schemas may exist preformed in the mind (or brain) of the individual. When the situation is unusual and the episode complex, however, emotional schemas may be constructed "on-line," as an episode develops. In constructing a schema on-line, a person has recourse to a large database of experience stored in memory, as well as the beliefs and rules about the proper course of the emotion. Depending on the circumstances and the person's goals, only a subset of this stored information may be accessed in a given episode. A good deal of improvisation is thus possible, even inevitable, as an episode progresses.

Emotions as Creative Products

Nothing in the above analysis precludes emotions from creative change. The criteria for judging an emotional response as creative are the same as those for judging an artistic or intellectual response creative, namely, "novelty," "effectiveness," and "authenticity."

The criterion of novelty implies something new or different. However, a novel response may simply be bizarre. To be considered creative, the response must also be effective—for example, aesthetically (as in art), practically (as in technology), or interpersonally (as in leadership). But adding effectiveness to novelty is still not sufficient. The creative response should also be an authentic expression of the person's own beliefs and values, and not a mere copy of another's expectations.

The criterion of authenticity has been particularly emphasized by Arnheim (1966, p. 298) for works of art; to make a complex issue short, authenticity is what distinguishes an original painting, say, from an imitation, no matter how novel or aesthetically pleasing the latter might be. Emotions, too, can be more or less authentic (Salmela, 2005). An emotion that does not reflect a person's own beliefs and values cannot be considered fully creative, no matter how novel or effective.

Individual Differences in Emotional Creativity

Not everyone is equally creative in the emotional domain any more than in the intellectual or artistic domains. Years of preparation typically are required before creativity is achieved within the arts and sciences (Hayes, 1981; Weisberg, 1986). There is no reason to believe the situation to be different in the domain of emotion. Some people think about and try to understand their emotions; and they are sensitive to the emotions of others. Such people, we may presume, are on average better prepared emotionally than are their more indifferent—but not necessarily less reactive—counterparts.

To explore individual differences in the ability to be emotionally creative, a 30-item Emotional Creativity Inventory (ECI) has been constructed (Averill, 1999a). Seven of the items refer to emotional preparedness. The remaining items address the three criteria for creativity discussed previously. Specifically, 14 items refer to the novelty of emotional experiences; 5 to effectiveness; and 4 to authenticity. Factor analysis indicates that the ECI can be broken down into three facets. The first facet comprises the "preparedness" items; the second facet, the "novelty" items; and the third facet, a combination of the "effectiveness and authenticity" items. Sample items from the three facets are presented in Table 23.1.

Scores on the ECI have been related to a variety of behavioral and personality variables, including peer ratings of emotional creativity (study 2,

Table 23.1. Sample items from the three facets of the Emotional Creativity Inventory

Preparation (2 of 7 items)
When I have strong emotional reactions, I search for reasons for my feelings.
I pay attention to other people's emotions so that I can better understand my own.

Novelty (4 of 14 items)
My emotional reactions are different and unique.
I have felt combinations of emotions that other people probably have never experienced.
I sometimes experience feelings and emotions that cannot be easily described in ordinary language.
I like to imagine situations that call for unusual, uncommon, or unconventional emotional reactions.

Effectiveness/Authenticity (3 of 9 items)
My emotions help me achieve my goals in life.
The way I experience and express my emotions helps me in my relationships with others.
My outward emotional reactions accurately reflect my inner feelings.

Table 23.2. Correlations of the Emotional Creativity Inventory with Alexithymia and Mysticism scales

	Emotional Creativity Inventory			
Scale	Preparedness	Novelty	Effectiveness/Authenticity	Total
Alexithymia (*n = 89*)				
F1: Difficulty identifying	−.01	.39***	−.45***	.02
F2: Difficulty describing	−.24*	.18	−.64***	−.25*
F3: Externally oriented	−.65***	−.46***	−.37***	−.61***
Mysticism (*n = 91*)				
F1: General	.26**	.46***	.09	.39***
F2: Religious	.40***	.40***	.25*	.46***

*$p < .05$, **$p < .01$, ***$p < .001$, two-tailed tests.

Averill, 1999a), the creative expression of emotions in words and pictures (Gutbezahl & Averill, 1996; Ivcevic, Brackett, & Mayer, 2007), and the productive use of solitude (Long, Seburn, Averill, & More, 2003). I will limit the present discussion to two variables of particular relevance to this chapter, namely alexithymia and mysticism. The relevant data are presented in Table 23.2.

Alexithymia and the Language of Emotion

Persons with alexithymia suffer from an impoverished fantasy life, a reduced ability to experience positive emotions, and poorly differentiated negative affect (Taylor, 1994). The Toronto Alexithymia Scale (TAS-20) is commonly used to measure the condition (Bagby, Parker, & Taylor, 1994). This scale consists of three factors: Factor 1 assesses a person's "difficulty identifying feelings" as distinct, say, from bodily sensations; Factor 2 reflects "difficulty describing feelings" or communicating feelings to others; and Factor 3 indicates a preference for "externally oriented thinking," that is, a focus on situational details as opposed to one's own thoughts and feelings. The top half of Table 23.2 presents the correlations between the three facets of the ECI (Preparedness, Novelty, and Effectiveness/Authenticity), as well as the Total score, and the three dimensions of the TAS-20, based on a sample of 89 university students (see study 5, Averill, 1999a, for details).

People who are emotionally creative as well as those with alexithymia have difficulty identifying and describing their emotional experiences, as indicated by the positive association between the Novelty subscale of the ECI and the F1 and F2 factors of the TAS-20 ($r = .39$ and .18, respectively). However, the source of the difficulty is different for the two conditions. For people with alexithymia, the difficulty stems from an impoverished inner life; for emotionally creative persons, it stems from the complexity and originality of their experiences. As one of the items in the ECI reads, "I would have to be a poet or novelist to describe the kinds of emotions I sometimes feel, they are so unique."

When describing events that "lack" emotional content, people with alexithymia can be quite fluent, even poetic. This sometimes makes it difficult to distinguish alexithymia from emotional creativity. Consider the following stanzas from the poem *No Platonique Love* by William Cartwright, a seventeenth-century Oxford don:

Tell me no more of minds embracing minds,
  And hearts exchang'd for hearts;
That Spirits Spirits meet, as Winds do Winds
  And mix their subt'lest parts;
That two unbodi'd Essences may kiss,
And then like Angels, twist and feel one bliss.

I was that silly thing that once was wrought
  To practice this thin Love;
I climb'd from Sex to Soul, from Soul to Thought;
  But thinking there to move,
Headlong I roll'd from Thought to Soul, and then
From Soul I lighted at the Sex agen.[2]

Perèz-Rincòn (1997) has used this poem to illustrate alexithymia, presumably on the basis of the poet's stated inability to appreciate love abstractly, in Thought, but only concretely, in Sex. Based on the poem alone, that is not a reasonable interpretation. From the little we know of Cartwright's life, however, he was not at a loss for words in describing his emotional experiences, as the following observation by a contemporary illustrates: "Those wild beasts (the Passions) being tuned and composed to tameness and order, by his sweet and harmonious language" (Lloyd, 1668, cited by Goffin, 1918, p. xvii). Cartwright's poem is like a reversible figure. When viewed from a different perspective, the image it presents changes from a picture of alexithymia to a picture of emotional creativity.

Love—even the thick, sexual love touted by Cartwright—does not just happen. It requires thought (preparation), and the quality of thought makes a difference in the novelty, effectiveness, and authenticity of subsequent behavior. Having "climb'd from Sex to Soul, from Soul to Thought" could Cartwright return to Sex again, unchanged? Only if he were suffering a complete disjunction between thought and feeling, a condition more akin to psychopathy than alexithymia. More likely, Sex was transformed by Cartwright's Thought into something more than mere copulation; and, conversely, his Thought was transformed by Sex into something more than abstract contemplation.

Poetry is not the only means by which novel emotions may be given effective and authentic expression, but words possess a special power in determining the realities as well as our ideas of emotion. Like a tree, language sends its roots deep into the soil from which it draws sustenance, and the soil may be transformed in the process. Yet even at their poetic best, words are often insufficient to express some of our most profound and creative emotional insights, including those that we might label mystical.

Spirituality: The Mysticism of Everyday Life

Full-blown mystical experiences are as rare as they are difficult to describe. In more mild degree, however, mystic-like experiences are surprisingly common (Greeley, 1974; Laski, 1968). The bottom half of Table 23.2 presents the correlations, based on a sample of 91 university students, between the ECI and a measure of self-reported mystical experiences (Hood, 1975). Hood's scale comprises two dimensions: Factor 1, "General Mysticism," emphasizes the unity of experience, the transcendence of space and time, the loss of ego boundaries, and a sense that all things are alive; and F2, "Religious Interpretation," emphasizes the holiness or sacredness of experience, as well as feelings of peace and joy. As Table 23.2 indicates, the ECI total score was associated with the General Mysticism subscale ($r = .39$) and with the Religious Interpretation subscale ($r = .46$). All three

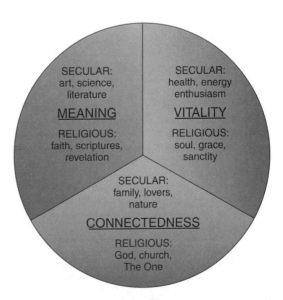

Fig. 23.1 Three characteristics of spiritual experiences, as viewed from secular and religious perspectives.

---

[2] From Goffin (1918), reprinted with the permission of Cambridge University Press.

facets of the ECI contributed to these relations, but particularly Preparedness and Novelty.[3]

To place these results in a broader context, let us return to Nietzsche's call for a "spiritualization of the passions." From a psychological perspective, there are two ways of looking at spirituality. The first is as an emotional state per se, represented in extreme form by mystical experiences.[4] The second is as an attribute of other emotional states, to the extent that they share features in common with mystical experiences. Emotional creativity, I suggest, is associated not only with the tendency toward mystical experiences, as the data in Table 23.2 suggest, but also with the tendency to imbue other, more mundane emotions with mystic-like qualities.

Three features are characteristic of mystical states and hence are relevant to spiritualizing the passions. These are a sense of vitality, connectedness, and meaningfulness (Averill, 1999b). Each of these features can be approached from either a secular or religious perspective, as illustrated in Figure 23.1.

VITALITY

In one of its most common usages, spirituality implies a sense of aliveness, as when a person is described as "high-spirited." Reified in animistic religions, spirits may dwell in any object—a volcano, say, or a tree—from whence they venture forth, creating mischief in human affairs, for good of ill.

However, we need not reify spiritual feelings into spiritual beings. From a secular perspective, the important point is that spirituality (in the sense of vitality) involves more than simply being alive—that could be said of an amoeba. Vitality also implies the ability to be creative.

CONNECTEDNESS

One of the most common features of spiritual experiences is a feeling of union or harmony with another. Sexual love and the love of a parent for a child are common metaphors as well as triggers for such feelings. However, the "other" with which one identifies need not be a person; it may be conceived broadly as humanity, nature, or even the ground of all being, as in the Hindu concept of Brahman.

MEANINGFULNESS

Spiritual experiences are rich in significance. However, like an encrypted message, the meaning of the experience may not be immediately apparent, which fact only adds to the sense of profundity. From a religious perspective, revelation and scripture typically are used to help decipher the meaning of spiritual experiences. From a secular perspective, science, art, and literature serve similar functions.

None of the above criteria is inconsistent with the way everyday emotions are—or at their best, can be—experienced. An event that does not touch on a person's concerns in a "meaningful" way will not elicit an emotional response, and the person who does not respond emotionally to such an event is lacking "vitality." The criterion of "connectedness" is more ambiguous when applied to everyday emotional experiences. Emotional outbursts are often disruptive of interpersonal relationships. That is one reason why, as noted in the introduction to this chapter, emotions frequently have been depicted as the animal in human nature, to be subdued by "higher" thought processes.

"Spiritualizing the passions" was Nietzsche's way of calling not for subduing the emotions, but for their elevation; not "a going-back but a *going-up*—up into a high, free, even frightful nature and naturalness" (see Footnote 1). Nietzsche's phrasing may seem unduly flamboyant. Therefore, let us consider a more familiar, even hackneyed expression: "Getting in touch with your true feelings." What in the course of events makes a feeling seem "true"? And do true feelings already exist in the mind/brain of the individual, simply waiting to be revealed ("touched")? Or are they newly created as an episode unfolds?

---

[3] Some of the items in Hood's original scale overlap in content with items from the Novelty subscale of ECI. A reanalysis suggested that these items could be eliminated without destroying the integrity or meaning of the F1 and F2 subscales. The data presented in Table 23.2 are for the emended subscales (see Averill, 1999a, Study 4, for details). The correlation between the "total" score on the ECI and the "total" score on the original mysticism scale was ($r = .46$, $p < .01$). In effect, elimination of overlapping items had little influence on the relation between the two scales.

[4] According to the model described previously, emotional states are determined, in part, by the cultural beliefs and rules (implicit theories) that help shape emotional syndromes and their cognitive representations (schemata). The model does not fit all emotions equally. In particular, states of acute depression, anxiety, and mysticism lie at its periphery. I will discuss depression further on (see Footnote 5). With regard to mysticism, Rothberg (1990) points to the lengthy and rigorous training that typically precedes the attainment of a full mystical experience; we should entertain the possibility, he suggests, that such training is occasionally successful in transcending all cultural categories, including those that help define the self as an independent entity. Katz (1992), on the other hand, argues that a careful reading of mystical reports reveals a subtle but uneliminable influence of cultural beliefs and rules. This dispute pertains to the most extreme forms of mystical experience, where a dismantling of cognitive schemas at least approaches completion. Such occurrences are rare, if ever, and for the uninitiated are more likely to produce direful anxiety than mystical bliss.

Such questions provided grist for a study by Morgan and Averill (1992). Participants were asked to describe an episode of "true feelings" and to contrast it with an episode of similar length and intensity, but one they would not classify in the same manner. Most participants had no difficulty recalling relevant incidents. Generalizing from their descriptions, emotions that are considered "true" typically occur during periods of challenge or transition, such as the establishment or breakup of a love relationship, taking a new job, or otherwise having one's core beliefs and values contested. More than other intense emotional experiences (e.g., fear of injury during an approaching automobile accident), "true" feelings are powerfully felt struggles to modify, restore, or enhance a sense of self. The initial stage of a true-feeling episode may be marked by confusion, depression, and anxiety. The true feelings emerge from this emotional fog as resolution is achieved.

In short, "spiritualizing the passions" requires that one's emotions be rendered "true," that is, integrated with the beliefs and values hat help constitute a person's sense of self, both as an individual and in relation to others. It is an emotionally creative process in service of the self.[5]

Applications

If self-realization and expansion involve a spiritualization of the passions, neuroses of many types—not just alexithymia—might be characterized as a form of despiritualization. Not only are neurotic syndromes deficient in the features described above for spiritualization (vitality, connectedness, and meaningfulness), they also are contrary to the three criteria for emotional creativity discussed previously (novelty, effectiveness, and authenticity). Neurotic behavior—for example, a hysterical conversion reaction—may be unique (abnormal) in that it violates conventional norms; however, it is hardly novel from the individual's perspective as it becomes oft-repeated, uncontrollable, and unyielding to change. Neurotic behavior also is ineffective, at least in the long term, and is not a true or authentic reflection of the individual's core beliefs and values (Averill & Nunley, 1992, chap. 13).

The above considerations suggest that some of the techniques used to foster creativity in other settings (see, for example, Nickerson, 1999) might be fruitfully incorporated into psychotherapy. These techniques fall into four broad categories: (a) preparedness—gaining knowledge and expertise within a domain; (b) motivation—cultivating a desire to innovate on what is known, and a willingness to take risks; (c) imagination—learning to envision new approaches and realities; and (d) self-monitoring—guiding and assessing one's own efforts for effectiveness. But more than new techniques, emotional creativity suggests a different way of looking at the emotions and their disorders. Most therapies still treat the emotions (at least so-called "basic" emotions) as primitive reactions that may be regulated, but not fundamentally altered. That belief can become a self-fulfilling prophecy.

The applications of emotional creativity are not limited to psychotherapy. To a certain extent, we are all emotional Luddites—we find it difficult to adjust to change. To illustrate, conduct the following thought experiment. What emotional adjustments would be necessary if you and others were to live to be 150–200 years old? Could you remain faithfully married to the same person for over 100 years, "until death do you part"? How long might you remain in a career before you were burnt out, or sought other challenges? Questions such as these could easily be multiplied. The point is simply that major accommodations would be required on the individual as well as social levels.

The above thought experiment is not mere fancy. Advances in genetic engineering and medicine eventually may double the human life span; much of the scientific knowledge is in place, and its feasibility has been demonstrated in lower (invertebrate) organisms. The extension to mammals and ultimately humans seems more a matter of when, not if. Referring to that eventuality, John Harris (2000), who holds the Sir David Alliance Chair of Bioethics at the University of Manchester, has advised that "we should start thinking now about how we can live decently and creatively with the prospect of such lives" (p. 59).

---

[5] Of all emotional states, episodes of endogenous depression might seem the least amenable to spiritualization in the sense described here. And that is generally the case. The depressed person feels empty, tends to withdraw from human contact, and experiences life as pointless. For want of a better explanation, in many cultures the condition is attributed to "soul loss" (Shweder, 1985). Even so, some people, especially those of unusual creative potential, can turn even depression into a vital and meaningful experience. Jamison (1993) provides many examples in her book on manic-depressive illness. The following observation by Herman Melville is representative: "The intensest light of reason and revelation combined, can not shed such blazonings upon the deeper truths in man, as will sometimes proceed from his own profoundest gloom. Utter darkness is then his light.... Wherefore is it, that not to know Gloom and Grief is not to know aught that an heroic man should learn" (quoted by Jamison, 1993, p. 216).

Increased life expectancy is a goal of modern medicine—if Ponce de León were alive today, he would better be a physician than an explorer searching for the fountain of youth. Needless to say, most of the challenges that we face as individuals, nations, and a global community are not so avidly sought as longevity. Political oppression, poverty, ethnic and religious strife, overpopulation, and degradation of the environment are but a few of the more obvious threats to human well-being. None of these will yield to technological fixes alone. Their solution also depends on a willingness to adapt emotionally. Emotional innovation, however, does not come easy. The reason is not that emotions are hardwired into our nervous system and hence impervious to change. If the arguments and data presented in this chapter have any validity, the difficulty lies elsewhere.

Concluding Observations

Emotions embody the values of society. This is true even of those emotions considered most basic, the list of which varies from one culture and historical epoch to another. In contemporary Western societies, if you strip all connotations of right and wrong, good and bad, from concepts such as love, anger, grief, and fear, you also strip them of much of their meaning and significance. It follows that if you change an emotion in fundamental ways you call into question the values embodied by the emotion. Not surprisingly, then, attempts at emotional innovation typically meet with skepticism, even condemnation. The resistance is not entirely without warrant: Many emotional innovations, like genetic mutations, may prove more harmful than beneficial; moreover, like biological evolution, social advances follow an uncertain path. Thus, there is no guarantee that emotional innovations will meet with success, or even what success might mean. But if the task is difficult, and the outcome uncertain, that is no reason for disheartenment. Positive psychology promises challenge more than comfort; emotional creativity is part of that challenge.

Questions

1. What foreseeable environmental and social changes will require corresponding changes in the emotional life of people?

2. How can creativity be nurtured in the emotional as well as in the intellectual and artistic domains?

3. What selective ("weeding out") mechanisms may be needed to control for possible unintended consequences (e.g., disruptive side effects) of emotional creativity?

References

Arnheim, R. (1966). *Toward a psychology of art*. Berkeley, CA: University of California Press.

Averill, J. R. (1980a). On the paucity of positive emotions. In K. R. Blankstein, P. Pliner, & J. Polivy (Eds.), *Assessment and modification of emotional behavior* (pp. 7–45). New York: Plenum.

Averill, J. R. (1980b). A constructivist view of emotion. In R. Plutchik & H. Kellerman (Eds.), *Emotion: Theory, research and experience: Vol. I. Theories of emotion* (pp. 305–339). New York: Academic Press.

Averill, J. R. (1984). The acquisition of emotions during adulthood. In C. Z. Malatesta & C. Izard (Eds.), *Affective processes in adult development* (pp. 23–43). Beverly Hills, CA: Sage.

Averill, J. R. (1999a). Individual differences in emotional creativity: Structure and correlates. *Journal of Personality, 67*, 331–371.

Averill, J. R. (1999b). Spirituality: From the mundane to the meaningful—and back. *Journal of Theoretical and Philosophical Psychology, 18*, 101–126.

Averill, J. R. (2004). A tale of two snarks: Emotional intelligence and emotional creativity compared. *Psychological Inquiry, 15*, 228–233.

Averill, J. R. (2005). Emotions as mediators and as products of creative activity. In J. Kaufman & J. Baer (Eds.), *Creativity across domains: Faces of the muse* (pp. 225–243). Mahwah, NJ: Erlbaum.

Averill, J. R. (2007). Together again: Emotion and intelligence reconciled. In G. Matthews, M. Zeidner, & R. D. Roberts, R. D. (Eds.), *Emotional intelligence: Knowns and unknowns* (pp. 49–71). New York: Oxford University Press.

Averill, J. R., & Nunley, E. P. (1992). *Voyages of the heart: Living an emotionally creative life*. New York: The Free Press.

Averill, J. R., & Nunley, E. P. (1993). Grief as an emotion and as a disease. In M. S. Stroebe, W. Stroebe, & R. O. Hansson (Eds.), *The handbook of bereavement* (pp. 77–90). New York: Cambridge University Press.

Averill, J. R., Stanat, P., & More, T. A. (1998). Aesthetics and the environment. *Review of General Psychology, 2*, 153–174.

Averill, J. R., & Thomas-Knowles, C. (1991). Emotional creativity. In K. T. Strongman (Ed.), *International review of studies on emotion* (Vol. 1, pp. 269–299). London: Wiley.

Bagby, R. M., Parker, J. D. A., & Taylor, G. J. (1994). The twenty-item Toronto Alexithymia Scale—I. Item selection and cross-validation of the factor structure. *Journal of Psychosomatic Research, 38*, 23–32.

Barrett, L. F. (2006). Solving the emotion paradox: Categorization and the experience of emotion. *Personality and Social Psychology Review, 10*, 20–46.

Dewey, J. (1895). The theory of emotion: II. The significance of emotions. *Psychological Review, 2*, 13–32.

Epstein, S. (1998). *Constructive thinking: The key to emotional intelligence*. Westport, CT: Praeger.

Gardner, H. (1993). *Frames of mind: The theory of multiple intelligences* (10th anniversary ed.). New York: Basic Books.

Goffin, R. C. (1918). *The life and poems of William Cartwright*. Cambridge: The University Press.

Greeley, A. M. (1974). *Ecstasy: A way of knowing*. Englewood Cliffs, NJ: Prentice-Hall.

Gutbezahl, J., & Averill, J. R. (1996). Individual differences in emotional creativity as manifested in words and pictures. *Creativity Research Journal, 9*, 327–337.

Harris, J. (2000, April 7). Intimations of immortality. *Science, 288*, 59.

Hayes, J. R. (1981). *The complete problem solver*. Philadelphia: Franklin Institute Press.

Hood, R. W., Jr. (1975). The construction and preliminary validation of a measure of reported mystical experience. *Journal for the Scientific Study of Religion, 14*, 29–41.

Ivcevic, Z., Brackett, M. A., & Mayer, J. D. (2007). Emotional intelligence and emotional creativity. *Journal of Personality, 75*, 199–235.

James, W. (1902/1961). *Varieties of religious experience*. New York: Collier Books.

Jamison, K. R. (1993). *Touched with fire*. New York: The Free Press.

Katz, S. T. (Ed.). (1992). *Mysticism and language*. New York: Oxford University Press.

LaBarre, W. (1947). The cultural basis of emotions and gestures. *Journal of Personality, 16*, 48–68.

Laski, M. (1968). *Ecstasy: A study of some secular and religious experiences*. New York: Greenwood Press.

Long, C. R., Seburn, M., Averill, J. R., & More, T. A. (2003). Solitude experiences: Varieties, settings, and individual differences. *Personality and Social Psychology Bulletin, 29*, 578–583.

Maslow, A. H. (1971). *The farther reaches of human nature*. New York: Viking Press.

Morgan, C., & Averill, J. R. (1992). True feelings, the self, and authenticity: A psychosocial perspective. In D. D. Franks & V. Gecas (Eds.), *Social perspectives on emotion* (Vol. 1, pp. 95–124). Greenwich, CT: JAI Press.

Nickerson, R. S. (1999). Enhancing creativity. In R. J. Sternberg (Ed.), *Handbook of creativity* (pp. 392–430). Cambridge: Cambridge University Press.

Nietzsche, F. (1889/2003). *Twilight of the idols* (Trans. R. J. Hollingdale). London: Penguin Classics.

Perèz-Rincòn, H. (1997). Alexithymia considered as a survival of an archaic structure of language: Importance of Bruno Snell's theories. *New Trends in Experimental and Clinical Psychiatry, 13*, 159–160.

Rank, O. (1932). *Art and artist* (Trans. L. Lewison). New York: Agathon Press.

Richards, R. (1998). The subtle attraction: Beauty as a force in awareness, creativity, and survival. In S. W. Russ (Ed.), *Affect, creative experience, and psychological adjustment* (pp. 191–213). Philadelphia: Brunner Mazel.

Richards, R. (Ed.). (2007). *Everyday creativity and new views of human nature*. Washington, DC: American Psychological Association.

Rothberg, D. (1990). Contemporary epistemology and the study of mysticism. In R. K. C. Forman (Ed.), *The problem of pure consciousness* (pp. 163–210). New York: Oxford University Press.

Saarni, C. (1999). *The development of emotional competence*. New York: Guilford.

Salmela, M. (2005). What is emotional authenticity? *Journal for the Theory of Social Behavior, 35*, 219–240.

Shweder, R. A. (1985). Menstrual pollution, soul loss, and the comparative study of emotions. In A. Kleinman & B. Good (Eds.), *Culture and depression: Studies in the anthropology and cross-cultural psychiatry of affect and disorder* (pp. 182–215). Berkeley, CA: University of California Press.

Solomon, R. C. (1993). *The passions*. Indianapolis, IN: Hackett Publishing Co.

Taylor, G. J. (1994). The alexithymia construct: Conceptualization, validation, and relationship with basic dimensions of personality. *New trends in experimental and clinical psychiatry, 10*, 61–74.

Weisberg, R. W. (1986). *Creativity: Genius and other myths*. New York: W. H. Freeman and Company.

PART 5

Cognitive Approaches

Creativity

Dean Keith Simonton

Abstract

Because creativity is often viewed as a highly positive human capacity both at the individual and societal levels, the chapter provides an overview of what psychologists have learned about this phenomenon. After beginning with the definition of creativity in terms of adaptive originality, the review turns to how measurement depends on whether creativity is to be treated as a process, a person, or a product. The next section of the review concentrates on the principal empirical results, with special focus on the two findings that would seem to be especially germane for positive psychology, namely (a) the impact of early trauma on creative development and (b) the relation between creativity and psychopathology. This section is followed by a discussion of the two key theoretical issues that pervade research on creativity: the nature–nurture question and the small-c versus big-C creativity question. Once these empirical and theoretical matters have been discussed, the article can progress to a treatment of some practical applications. These applications concern creativity-improving techniques that can be implemented during childhood, adolescence, or adulthood. The chapter closes with a brief discussion of the most fruitful directions for future research on creativity. Despite the tremendous accumulation of knowledge about the phenomenon, a lot of unanswered questions remain.

Keywords: creativity, environment, genetics, genius, intervention

Introduction

People are almost universal in their appreciation of creativity. This is true in home and at school, and whether at work or at play. Rarely is it perceived as a negative quality for a person to possess. Likewise, people vary considerably in the magnitude of creativity that they can or usually do display. While some students put together rather humdrum papers and projects, others fulfill the same course requirements with impressive imagination and wit. While some inventors may rest content with making minor improvements in already established technologies, others devise revolutionary inventions that dramatically transform our daily lives.

Creativity is so highly valued as a human resource that most modern societies have special means to encourage those of its citizens who exhibit creative behavior. At the most basic level, patent and copyright laws have been implemented so as to allow individuals to enjoy the fruits of their creative labors. At an even higher level of creative achievement, there are the honors and awards bestowed upon the most outstanding exemplars of creativity. Thus, the Nobel Prizes are awarded to the best creators in the sciences and literature, and each major literary tradition will have its own set of special prizes recognizing their best writers (Pulitzer, Cervantes, Goethe, etc.). Likewise, the Academy Awards and Golden Globe Awards are granted to those who create the most notable films.

The worth of creative behavior may even continue to be recognized long after the creator has died. If the accomplishment is truly exceptional, the creator may "go down in history" as a "creative genius." These are people who have left a "name behind," such as Aristotle, Descartes, Shakespeare, Michelangelo, and Beethoven in Western civilization, and Ibn Sina, Shankara, Zhu Xi, Firdawsi,

Murasaki Shikibu, Kalidasa, Du Fu, Wang Wei, Unkei, and Toyo Sesshu in Eastern civilizations. Indeed, these names are often taken as indicative of the creative vitality of any given civilization at a particular point in time. When a culture is overflowing with eminent creators, it is said to exhibit a "Golden Age," whereas when examples of creative genius become few and far between, the culture is said to have entered a "Dark Age." Hence, creativity often is viewed as a human capacity that has both individual and sociocultural utility and value.

Given the foregoing considerations, it is impossible to imagine the emergence of a bona fide positive psychology that does not include creativity among its topics. I subsequently will examine what psychologists know about this crucial phenomenon (see also Runco, 2004). I first discuss various measurement approaches, and then review some key empirical findings and central theoretical issues. After treating some of the practical applications, I close by suggesting the prospects for future work on the topic of creativity.

Measurement Approaches

Before a concept can be measured, it first must be defined. Fortunately, at least in the abstract, there is virtually universal agreement on what creativity is (Simonton, 2000b). In particular, creativity usually is said to entail the generation of ideas that fulfill the two following conditions.

1. Creativity must be "original." These days, no one can be called "creative" who decides to "reinvent the wheel," nor can one earn that ascription for writing the lines "To be, or not to be." Creative ideas are novel, surprising, unexpected. Originality is a necessary but not sufficient criterion for creativity, which brings us to the second condition.

2. Creativity must be "adaptive." Someone who decides to make a blimp out of solid concrete can no doubt claim considerable originality, but whether this strange idea "can fly" is quite a different matter. Similarly, someone may propose a highly unusual advertising slogan like "The worst wurst in the West," but whether that phrase will convince potential consumers to buy more of that brand of sausage is highly unlikely.

Given the general definition of creativity as "adaptive originality," how can it be best measured? This turns out to be difficult. Creativity researchers have not agreed on the optimal instrument for assessing individual differences on this trait (Simonton, 2003b). The reason for this lack of consensus is that creativity can manifest itself in three distinct ways (Simonton, 2003d). First, creativity may be viewed as some kind of mental "process" that yields adaptive and original ideas. Second, it can be seen as a type of "person" who exhibits creativity. Third, creativity can be analyzed in terms of the concrete "products" that result from the workings of the creative process or person. Each of these three manifestations suggests rather distinct measures, as will become apparent next.

The Creative Process

If the emphasis is on the thought processes that yield creative ideas, then the best assessment approach should be to tap individual differences in access to these processes. This was the approach adopted by Guilford (1967). He began by proposing a profound distinction between two kinds of thinking. "Convergent" thought involves the convergence on a single correct response, such as is characteristic of most aptitude tests, like those that assess intelligence. "Divergent" thought, in contrast, entails the capacity to generate many alternative responses, including ideas of considerable variety and originality. Guilford and others have devised a large number of tests purported to measure the capacity for divergent thinking (Simonton, 2003b). Typical is the Alternate Uses Test, in which the subject must come up with many different ways of using a common object, such as a paper clip or brick.

Another test that views the creative process in a manner similar to divergent thinking is the Remote Associates Test, or RAT, of Mednick (1962). This test was based on the premise that creativity involves the ability to make rather remote associations between separate ideas. Highly creative individuals were said to have a flat hierarchy of associations in comparison to the steep hierarchy of associations of those with low creativity. A flat associative hierarchy means that for any given stimulus, the creative person has numerous associations available, all with roughly equal probabilities of retrieval. Because such an individual can generate many associative variations, the odds are increased that he or she will find that one association that will make the necessary remote connection. The RAT can therefore be said to operate according to an implicit variation-selection model of the creative process.

Although these tests have been validated against other criteria of creative performance (e.g., Carson, Peterson, & Higgins, 2005), it has become clear that generalized tests do not always have as much predictive validity as measures more specifically tailored to a particular domain of creativity (Simonton, 2003b).

The Creative Person

To the extent that the content of the creative process is domain specific, it would seem necessary to construct as many creativity instruments as there are creative domains. Fortunately, an alternative psychometric tactic exists that is based on the assumption that the creative individual is distinctively different in various personal characteristics. Especially pertinent is the evidence that creative people display personality profiles that depart from the average person (Feist, 1998). Creative personalities tend to possess those characteristics that would most favor the production of both numerous and diverse ideas. In particular, creative individuals tend to be independent, nonconformist, unconventional, even bohemian; they also tend to have wide interests, greater openness to new experiences, and a more conspicuous behavioral and cognitive flexibility and boldness (Simonton, 2008a). The only major complication in this general picture is that the personality profiles of artistic creators tend to differ noticeably from those of scientific creators (Feist, 1998). In a nutshell, the creative scientists tend to fall somewhere between the creative artists and noncreative personalities in terms of their typical traits.

The Creative Product

Because process- and person-based creativity measures are relatively easy to design and administer, the bulk of the literature on creativity has tended to use them. Yet one might argue that the ultimate criterion of whether someone can be considered creative is whether or not that individual has successfully generated a product that meets both the requirements of creative behavior—originality and adaptiveness. This product-based assessment is more direct and objective, but it also has more than one operational definition. One approach is to simply ask individuals to identify what they would consider samples of their creative activities, such as poems, paintings, and projects (Carson, Peterson, & Higgins, 2005; Richards, Kinney, Lunde, Benet, & Merzel, 1988a). Another approach is to have research participants generate creative products under controlled laboratory conditions, and then have these evaluated by independent judges (e.g., Amabile, 1996; Smith, Ward, & Finke, 1995; Sternberg & Lubart, 1995). These two operational definitions have the advantage that they are best designed to assess individual differences in more everyday forms of the phenomenon.

Yet it is obvious that at higher levels of creative activity, the investigator can go beyond a participant's self-report or a judge's subjective evaluation. Inventors hold patents, scientists publish journal articles, dramatists write plays, directors create movies, and so forth. Hence, cross-sectional variation in creativity can be assessed in terms of individual differences in the output of such professionally or culturally acknowledged works (e.g., Simonton, 1991a, 1991b, 1997). Investigators may count total output (quantity), select output (quality), or output influence (impact). For example, researchers of scientific creativity may tabulate the total number of publications, just those publications that are actually cited in the literature, or the total number of citations those publications have received (Feist, 1993; Simonton, 2004b). Happily, researchers have demonstrated quite conclusively that these three alternative measures correlate very highly among each other (e.g., Simonton, 1992).

If creative persons have generated a substantial body of highly influential products, it is inevitable that they should attain eminence for their accomplishments (Simonton, 1991c). In fact, the single most powerful predictor of eminence in any creative domain is the number of works an individual has contributed (Simonton, 1991a, 1991b, 1997). Accordingly, sometimes cross-sectional variation in creativity will be assessed using some variety of eminence indicator (e.g., Feist, 1993; Simonton, 1992). These may include expert ratings, the receipt of major honors, or having entries in biographical dictionaries and encyclopedias (e.g., Simonton, 1998).

Empirical Findings

Judging from the previous section, there seems to be an embarrassment of riches when it comes to the assessment of creativity. This superfluity, however, is only superficial. One of the most critical findings in the empirical research is that these alternative measures tend to display fairly respectable intercorrelations (Carson, Peterson, & Higgins, 2005; Eysenck, 1995). In other words, creative products tend to emerge from creative persons who use the creative process in generating their output. The correlations are by no means perfect, but they do suggest that each instrument is gauging the same fundamental reality. Consequently, the various measures often yield the same general conclusions about the nature of human creativity. In any case, because extensive reviews are readily available elsewhere (Simonton, 2008a), the best choice here is to discuss just two sets of empirical findings that have special relevance for a positive psychology of creativity. These concern early trauma and psychological disorder.

Early Trauma

According to the empirical literature, child prodigies and intellectually gifted children tend to have enjoyed rather happy childhoods (Feldman & Goldsmith, 1986; Terman, 1925). That is, their parents provided them with financially comfortable homes and ample intellectual and aesthetic stimulation; their parents had stable marriages, and the children were both physically healthy and educationally successful. Yet when researchers turn to highly creative individuals, a rather contrasting picture emerges (Goertzel, Goertzel, & Goertzel, 1978; Ludwig, 1995; Roe, 1953; Sulloway, 1996). The family may have experienced severe economic ups and downs, and the parents' marriage may have fallen far short of the ideal; the child may have been sickly or have endured some physical or cognitive disability. More remarkably, early development of the future creator may have been plagued with one or more traumatic experiences, such as the loss of one or both parents in childhood or adolescence (Eisenstadt, 1978; Roe, 1953; Sulloway, 1996). Yet what makes these findings all the more intriguing is that the same developmental events also are associated with negative life outcomes, such as juvenile delinquency or suicidal depression (Eisenstadt, 1978).

This peculiar paradox suggests that under the right conditions, exposure to traumatic or difficult experiences early in life can make a positive contribution to the development of creative potential. Perhaps those who have the capacity to "rise to the challenge" will benefit, and creativity itself may be an adaptive response to such circumstances (Eisenstadt, 1978). Events that might have yielded a societal misfit instead produce an individual who can respond constructively with an adulthood of creative achievement rather than disappointment or alienation.

Psychological Disorder

One of the oldest debates in the study of creativity is the "mad-genius controversy" (Simonton, 2005). On the one hand are those who believe that outstanding creativity is positively associated with psychopathology, a belief that goes back as far as Aristotle. There are others, such as humanistic psychologists, who see creativity as a symptom of mental health, not illness. Based on the empirical research on this issue suggests, it appears that there is some truth in both viewpoints (Eysenck, 1995; Simonton, 2005).

On the one hand, the rates of apparent psychological disorder in samples of highly creative individuals do seem to be somewhat higher than in the general population (Eysenck, 1995; Richards, Kinney, Lunde, Benet, & Merzel, 1988b). The incidence rates are especially elevated for those who pursue artistic forms of creative expression (Jamison, 1993; Ludwig, 1995; Simonton, 2004b). Furthermore, there is a positive relation between the amount of psychopathological symptoms and the level of creative achievement attained (Barron, 1969; Eysenck, 1995; Ludwig, 1995). Of special interest are the findings that creativity and psychopathology are positively associated with reduced latent inhibition, that is, with the reduced capacity to filter out extraneous information (Carson, Peterson, & Higgins, 2003; Eysenck, 1995). Finally, and perhaps most provocatively, family lines with a disproportionate numbers of individuals with psychological disorders also are more likely to have highly creative individuals (Juda, 1949; Karlson, 1970; Richards et al., 1988b). As such, pathological and creative pedigrees tend to overlap to a degree that far exceeds chance expectation.

On the other hand, the empirical research also suggests that creativity and psychopathology are by no means equivalent (Simonton, 2005). For one thing, creative individuals often have character traits, such as high ego-strength, which are not found in clinical populations (Barron, 1969; Eysenck, 1995). However bizarre their thoughts or behaviors may be, creators remain in self command—even exploiting their eccentricities for creative ends. In addition, their symptomatology usually falls well below pathological levels. Though their profiles do not lie in the normal range, they also do not reach truly pathological levels—they are at the borderline between the normal and the abnormal. In addition, creative individuals usually have higher levels of intelligence that enable them to convert their unusual thoughts into original but still adaptive ideas (Carson, Peterson, & Higgins, 2003; Simonton, 2005).

When one places these psychopathology findings alongside those for traumatic experiences, a significant lesson emerges: Events and traits that might severely disable or retard personal development can sometimes be converted into forces for positive growth. Or, if that is too strong an inference, one can safely infer the following optimistic alternative: Such events and conditions need not prevent the development of exceptional creativity. Indeed, people can be phenomenally robust, as they transform "liabilities" into assets.

Theoretical Issues

Despite the abundance of empirical findings, creativity researchers continue to wrestle with profound theoretical questions, two of which involve nature versus nurture and small-c versus big-C creativity.

The Nature–Nurture Issue

Is creativity born or made, or some combination of the two? Research suggests that creativity reflects a complex interaction of genetic and environmental factors (Eysenck, 1995; Simonton, 2008b). For example, genes may contribute to creativity according to a multiplicative (emergenic) rather than a simple additive model (Simonton, 1999b). As a further complication, it very well may be that various environmental influences interact with genetic factors with equally complex functional relationships (Eysenck, 1995). To some extent, creative development requires a specific congruence between genetic inheritance and environmental stimulation. This intricate genetic–environmental determination helps to explain why creativity may display a highly skewed cross-sectional distribution in the general population (Simonton, 1999a). When optimal creative development requires a precise configuration of many different factors, it makes it more difficult for people to emerge who have the total package.

Small-c versus Big-C Creativity

Small-c enhances everyday life and work with superior problem-solving skills, whereas big-C creativity makes lasting contributions to culture and history. In the first case, we are speaking of the creative person, whereas in the latter case we are talking about the creative genius. The enigma is whether these two grades of creative behavior are qualitatively or quantitatively distinct. If everyday creativity is qualitatively different from genius-level creativity, then the personal attributes underlying the first may be different from those responsible for the second (e.g., any tendency toward psychopathology). If the two are only quantitatively different, however, then the factors that predict levels of small-c creativity would also predict levels of big-C creativity. The evidence to date supports the notion that these two grades represent regions on a continuous scale of creative activity (Eysenck, 1995; Simonton, 2004b).

Practical Applications

If creativity truly is a highly desirable human characteristic, then it certainly would be valuable to know how to facilitate it. Consequently, it should come as no surprise that a considerable amount of research has focused on how people can become more creative. These creativity-enhancement methods have been aimed at childhood and adolescence, as well as adulthood. I review these next.

Early Development

Children are naturally creative. Creativity appears in their fantasy play, for example. Were it not for the stultifying influences of home and school, it often is thought that this conspicuous creativity would persist into adulthood. Thus, the pressure to "behave," "grow up," and "mature" stifles creative capacities. As such, children get the message that their creative endeavors are "childish" in the eyes of adults. This view of creative development is consistent with creative adults' tendencies to exhibit childlike traits such as openness to experience, playfulness, and rich imagination (Feist, 1998). This view also suggests that if the goal is to enhance creativity, the place to begin would be the home and the place to continue such creativity lessons would be the school. In the former case, parents should encourage their children's creative activities, even if this means that the parents must relinquish considerable control over how their children spend their time (e.g., perhaps little attention to school homework). In the latter case, more attention would have to be given to the development of educational systems that nurture rather than inhibit creative classroom expressions and behaviors. There are many recommendations about implementing such changes (e.g., Colangelo & Davis, 2002), with the presumable benefit being a society replete with highly creative adults.

Yet the foregoing view is overly optimistic. In the first place, it may not be accurate to assume that, without the external constraints imposed at home and school, childhood creativity would automatically transform into adulthood creativity. For instance, a similar developmental pattern is observed in the higher mammals (such as carnivores and primates)—where playful youth invariably converts into serious maturity. Hence, the longitudinal shift may reflect endogenous rather than exogenous factors. In addition, it should be emphasized that many of the personal attributes contributing to adult creativity have respectable heritability coefficients, thereby signifying that environmental influences may play a minor role (Simonton, 1999b). Closely related to this point is the existence of substantial individual differences in the characteristics that contribute to adulthood creativity. It may well be that only a relatively small proportion of the population enjoys the distinctive intellectual and dispositional profile that would enable them to manifest significant levels of creativity as adults. By adopting this perspective, the primary goal would be to identify those children with the most creative potential and then place them in special programs for the gifted and talented (see, e.g., Lubinski, Webb, Morelock, & Benbow, 2001). Although this implication might seem elitist, it may be more practical than trying to make every child into little creative geniuses (Winner, 1996). Needless to say, such an intervention would run counter to the basic egalitarianism that supposedly guides educational policy in many school systems.

The practical advantage of more select programs becomes especially apparent when we take into consideration the tremendous amount of investment required to convert the promise of youth to the accomplishments of maturity. Researchers have shown that it takes years of intense study and practice for someone to acquire the capacity to make creative contributions (Ericsson, 1996; Simonton, 2000a). Moreover, this special training very often must depend on the attentive guidance of mentors, teachers, and coaches (Bloom, 1985; Simonton, 1992). Thus, successful creative development typically necessitates an exceptional commitment of parental and school resources.

Adult Encouragement

Adults vary greatly in their creative potentials. Some may have very little capacity for generating new ideas, others may have enough to adapt well to everyday problems at home and work, whereas still others will attain levels worthy of the designation "creative genius." These individual differences do not operate in isolation, however, from various situational factors that enhance or inhibit the realization of creative potential. In this latter regard, many psychologists have investigated some of these situational influences. For example, a person's creativity is affected by extrinsic reward, evaluative supervision, and time pressure (Amabile, 1996). Such factors often operate in very complex ways to raise or lower creativity. For instance, rewards can harm creativity under

some circumstances, but enhance it under different conditions (Eisenberger & Cameron, 1996).

In the foregoing studies, the researchers focused on how various situations affect individual creativity. Yet in many applied settings—such as the research, development, or marketing teams in industry—creativity occurs as a group phenomenon (Paulus & Nijstad, 2003). The question then becomes how to nurture the creative performance of the entire group, not just the individual group members. Indeed, the assumption is that group creativity often can achieve what cannot be accomplished by the various persons working separately. This assumption is the basis of various "brainstorming" techniques. Researchers conclude that this approach to group creativity only works well under a specified set of complex circumstances (Paulus & Nijstad, 2003). Hence, creativity consultants in industrial and organizational settings must do their utmost ensure that these particular conditions are met.

Creativity can take place in a variety of groups, including those that encompass whole domains, traditions, cultures, and civilizations. For instance, as noted earlier, particular creative activities in the arts or sciences may exhibit periods of florescence ("Golden Ages") alternating with periods of decadence or stagnation ("Dark Ages"). Hence, some researchers have concentrated on the political, economic, cultural, and social conditions that most favor the emergence and maintenance of eras in which creativity blossoms across many creative endeavors (Simonton, 2003a). On the one hand, certain circumstances, such as military conflict and political anarchy, depress creative activity in most domains (Simonton, 1990). On the other hand, different conditions such as the infusion of cultural diversity—through immigration, political fragmentation, or nationalistic revolt—can revive creativity (Simonton, 2004a). Thus, to the degree that these events are under the control of a nation's leaders, countries can adopt policies that discourage or encourage creativity among its citizens.

Future Directions

Although psychologists have produced an impressive body of research on creativity, research still has an enormous potential for growth on three fronts. First, many research questions remain that deserve far more attention. For example, there is a relative dearth of research on how creativity develops and manifests itself in various underrepresented populations, such as women and ethnic minorities (Ochse, 1991). More work also is needed on the genetic basis of individual differences in creativity, using the latest theoretical and methodological advances in behavior genetics (Simonton, 1999b). Lastly, the field would benefit from ambitious longitudinal studies that focus specifically on creative development from childhood through adulthood (cf. Subotnik & Arnold, 1994). Indeed, it would be most advantageous to extend the span of such longitudinal analysis so as to determine the nature of creativity in the final years of life (Lindauer, 2003).

Second, the psychological study of creativity would be greatly strengthened by a comprehensive and precise theoretical framework. It is not that the field lacks theoretical perspectives. On the contrary, there presently are many promising theories. Perhaps, however, there are too many available theories. The proponents of psychoanalytic, Gestalt, behaviorist, and humanistic schools have offered their explanations for creativity, but no one theory has emerged as the consensual one in the field. Recently I have proposed combinatorial models of the creative process, person, and product that hold considerable promise (Simonton, 2003d, 2004b). Although originally designed to explain scientific creativity, the models are easily extended to other forms of creativity, such as that occurring in the arts (Simonton, 2004c). Besides explaining a wide range of phenomena, these combinatorial models have the additional advantage that they can be derived from Darwinian theories of the creative process (Simonton, 1999a). As a result, it has the potential of integrating creativity with other topics covered in evolutionary psychology (Simonton, 2003c). Until some comprehensive framework is widely adopted, creativity research will lack theoretical coordination.

Third and last, practical new methods are needed for enhancing both personal and societal creativity. That is, to become full participants in the positive psychology initiative, researchers ultimately must produce real improvements in both everyday and genius-grade manifestations of creativity. In part, this desideratum will be achieved automatically as our empirical and theoretical knowledge expands. Practical applications also may emerge, however, from advances outside of psychological research. Especially interesting possibilities on this latter point relate to the advent of the personal computer and the Internet linking virtually all of the computers in the world. Tremendous advances already have been made in writing computer programs to successfully simulate the creative process (Dartnall, 2002), and the communication networks between computers have provided the basis for "electronic brainstorming" (e.g., Roy, Gauvin, & Limayem, 1996). These innovations eventually may reach the point where linking each individual's brain with other thinking entities will magnify creativity both individually and collectively. These entities would be distributed throughout the world, and would consist of both neurological and electronic units— both other human brains and sophisticated computer programs. The result could be a collective creative genius capable of producing a global Golden Age unlike any this earth has so far witnessed.

Thus, if psychological researchers can increase our understanding and use of creativity continues along the lines suggested in this chapter, not only will psychology become more positive, but the world should become more positive as well.

Three Questions about Topic's Future

1. Is it possible to devise a theory of creativity that encompasses all aspects of the phenomenon? Or is the phenomenon so complex that we must resign ourselves to a large number of mini-theories or restricted models? Can one theory really treat the process, person, and product forms of creativity operating at both everyday and genius levels?

2. What kinds of methodological advances are necessary to enhance our understanding of creativity in all its manifestations? For example, can we anticipate major new contributions from brain imaging, behavior genetics, or multilevel modeling? Is the field ripe for a new burst of creativity in the scientific study of creativity?

3. Can new interventions be devised to enhance both the development and manifestation of creativity? Can these techniques apply universally or must they be especially tailored to target distinct groups with respect to age, gender, ethnicity, and the like?

References

Amabile, T. M. (1996). *Creativity in context*. Boulder, CO: Westview.

Barron, F. X. (1969). *Creative person and creative process*. New York: Holt, Rinehart & Winston.

Bloom, B. S. (Ed.). (1985). *Developing talent in young people*. New York: Ballantine Books.

Carson, S., Peterson, J. B., & Higgins, D. M. (2003). Decreased latent inhibition is associated with increased creative achievement in high-functioning individuals. *Journal of Personality and Social Psychology, 85*, 499–506.

Carson, S., Peterson, J. B., & Higgins, D. M. (2005). Reliability, validity, and factor structure of the Creative Achievement Questionnaire. *Creativity Research Journal, 17*, 37–50.

Colangelo, N., & Davis, G. A. (Eds.). (2002). *Handbook of gifted education* (3rd ed.). Boston: Allyn & Bacon.

Dartnall, T. (Ed.). (2002). *Creativity, cognition, and knowledge: An interaction.* Westport, CT: Praeger.

Eisenberger, R., & Cameron, J. (1996). Detrimental effects of reward: Reality or myth? *American Psychologist, 51,* 1153–1166.

Eisenstadt, J. M. (1978). Parental loss and genius. *American Psychologist, 33,* 211–223.

Ericsson, K. A. (Ed.). (1996). *The road to expert performance: Empirical evidence from the arts and sciences, sports, and games.* Mahwah, NJ: Erlbaum.

Eysenck, H. J. (1995). *Genius: The natural history of creativity.* Cambridge: Cambridge University Press.

Feist, G. J. (1993). A structural model of scientific eminence. *Psychological Science, 4,* 366–371.

Feist, G. J. (1998). A meta-analysis of personality in scientific and artistic creativity. *Personality and Social Psychology Review, 2,* 290–309.

Feldman, D. H., & Goldsmith, L. T. (1986). *Nature's gambit: Child prodigies and the development of human potential.* New York: Basic Books.

Goertzel, M. G., Goertzel, V., & Goertzel, T. G. (1978). *300 eminent personalities: A psychosocial analysis of the famous.* San Francisco: Jossey-Bass.

Guilford, J. P. (1967). *The nature of human intelligence.* New York: McGraw-Hill.

Jamison, K. R. (1993). *Touched with fire: Manic-depressive illness and the artistic temperament.* New York: Free Press.

Juda, A. (1949). The relationship between highest mental capacity and psychic abnormalities. *American Journal of Psychiatry, 106,* 296–307.

Karlson, J. I. (1970). Genetic association of giftedness and creativity with schizophrenia. *Hereditas, 66,* 177–182.

Lindauer, M. S. (2003). *Aging, creativity, and art: A positive perspective on late-life development.* New York: Kluwer Academic/Plenum.

Lubinski, D., Webb, R. M., Morelock, M. J., & Benbow, C. P. (2001). Top 1 in 10,000: A 10-year follow-up of the profoundly gifted. *Journal of Applied Psychology, 86,* 718–729.

Ludwig, A. M. (1995). *The price of greatness: Resolving the creativity and madness controversy.* New York: Guilford.

Mednick, S. A. (1962). The associative basis of the creative process. *Psychological Review, 69,* 220–232.

Ochse, R. (1991). Why there were relatively few eminent women creators. *Journal of Creative Behavior, 25,* 334–343.

Paulus, P. B., & Nijstad, B. A. (Eds.). (2003). *Group creativity: Innovation through collaboration.* New York: Oxford University Press.

Richards, R., Kinney, D. K., Lunde, I., Benet, M., & Merzel, A. P. C. (1988a). Assessing everyday creativity: Characteristics of the Lifetime Creativity Scales and validation with three large samples. *Journal of Personality and Social Psychology, 54,* 476–485.

Richards, R., Kinney, D. K., Lunde, I., Benet, M., & Merzel, A. P. C. (1988b). Creativity in manic-depressives, cyclothymes, their normal relatives, and control subjects. *Journal of Abnormal Psychology, 97,* 281–288.

Roe, A. (1953). *The making of a scientist.* New York: Dodd, Mead.

Roy, M. C., Gauvin, S., & Limayem, M. (1996). Electronic group brainstorming: The role of feedback on productivity. *Small Group Research, 27,* 215–247.

Runco, M. (2004). Creativity. *Annual Review of Psychology, 55,* 657–687.

Simonton, D. K. (1990). Political pathology and societal creativity. *Creativity Research Journal, 3,* 85–99.

Simonton, D. K. (1991a). Career landmarks in science: Individual differences and interdisciplinary contrasts. *Developmental Psychology, 27,* 119–130.

Simonton, D. K. (1991b). Emergence and realization of genius: The lives and works of 120 classical composers. *Journal of Personality and Social Psychology, 61,* 829–840.

Simonton, D. K. (1991c). Latent-variable models of posthumous reputation: A quest for Galton's G. *Journal of Personality and Social Psychology, 60,* 607–619.

Simonton, D. K. (1992). Leaders of American psychology, 1879–1967: Career development, creative output, and professional achievement. *Journal of Personality and Social Psychology, 62,* 5–17.

Simonton, D. K. (1997). Creative productivity: A predictive and explanatory model of career trajectories and landmarks. *Psychological Review, 104,* 66–89.

Simonton, D. K. (1998). Achieved eminence in minority and majority cultures: Convergence versus divergence in the assessments of 294 African Americans. *Journal of Personality and Social Psychology, 74,* 804–817.

Simonton, D. K. (1999a). *Origins of genius: Darwinian perspectives on creativity.* New York: Oxford University Press.

Simonton, D. K. (1999b). Talent and its development: An emergenic and epigenetic model. *Psychological Review, 106,* 435–457.

Simonton, D. K. (2000a). Creative development as acquired expertise: Theoretical issues and an empirical test. *Developmental Review, 20,* 283–318.

Simonton, D. K. (2000b). Creativity: Cognitive, developmental, personal, and social aspects. *American Psychologist, 55,* 151–158.

Simonton, D. K. (2003a). Creative cultures, nations, and civilizations: Strategies and results. In P. B. Paulus & B. A. Nijstad (Eds.), *Group creativity: Innovation through collaboration* (pp. 304–328). New York: Oxford University Press.

Simonton, D. K. (2003b). Creativity assessment. In R. Fernández-Ballesteros (Ed.), *Encyclopedia of psychological assessment* (Vol. 1, pp. 276–280). London: Sage.

Simonton, D. K. (2003c). Human creativity: Two Darwinian analyses. In S. M. Reader & K. N. Laland (Eds.), *Animal innovation* (pp. 309–325). New York: Oxford University Press.

Simonton, D. K. (2003d). Scientific creativity as constrained stochastic behavior: The integration of product, process, and person perspectives. *Psychological Bulletin, 129,* 475–494.

Simonton, D. K. (2004a). Creative clusters, political fragmentation, and cultural heterogeneity: An investigative journey though civilizations East and West. In P. Bernholz & R. Vaubel (Eds.), *Political competition, innovation and growth in the history of Asian civilizations* (pp. 39–56). Cheltenham, UK: Edward Elgar.

Simonton, D. K. (2004b). *Creativity in science: Chance, logic, genius, and Zeitgeist.* Cambridge: Cambridge University Press.

Simonton, D. K. (2004c). Creativity as a constrained stochastic process. In R. J. Sternberg, E. L. Grigorenko, & J. L. Singer (Eds.), *Creativity: From potential to realization* (pp. 83–101). Washington, DC: American Psychological Association.

Simonton, D. K. (2005). Are genius and madness related? Contemporary answers to an ancient question. *Psychiatric Times, 22*(7), 21–23.

Simonton, D. K. (2008a). Genius and creativity. In O. P. John, R. W. Robins, & L. A. Pervin (Eds.), *Handbook of personality: Theory and research* (3rd ed., pp. 679–698). New York: Guilford.

Simonton, D. K. (2008b). Scientific talent, training, and performance: Intellect, personality, and genetic endowment. *Review of General Psychology, 12*, 28–46.

Smith, S. M., Ward, T. B., & Finke, R. A. (Eds.). (1995). *The creative cognition approach*. Cambridge, MA: The MIT Press.

Sternberg, R. J., & Lubart, T. I. (1995). *Defying the crowd: Cultivating creativity in a culture of conformity*. New York: Free Press.

Subotnik, R. F., & Arnold, K. D. (Eds.). (1994). *Beyond Terman: Contemporary longitudinal studies of giftedness and talent*. Norwood, NJ: Ablex.

Sulloway, F. J. (1996). *Born to rebel: Birth order, family dynamics, and creative lives*. New York: Pantheon.

Terman, L. M. (1925). *Mental and physical traits of a thousand gifted children*. Stanford, CA: Stanford University Press.

Winner, E. (1996). *Gifted children: Myths and realities*. New York: Basic Books.

The Role of Personal Control in Adaptive Functioning

Suzanne C. Thompson

Abstract

A sense of personal control is an important resource that helps people maintain emotional stability and successfully negotiate their way through life. People foster their perceived control by focusing on reachable goals, creating new avenues for control, and accepting difficult-to-change circumstances. In general, perceived control need not be realistic in order to have beneficial effects, although in the area of health promotion, overestimating one's control can reduce the motivation to engage in protection. Research on ethnic differences in the benefits of a sense of personal control suggests that those from more collectivistic cultures or subcultures may be less benefited by a sense of personal control, relying instead on a socially derived sense of control. Successful interventions to enhance personal control include programs that bolster coping skills, give options and decisions to participants, and provide training that encourages attributions to controllable factors. Future research should further explore ethnic differences in the effects of personal control, the consequences of unrealistic control perceptions, and interventions to enhance the sense of control.

Keywords: acceptance, control motivation, ethnic differences, interventions, perceived control

The focus of positive psychology is on adaptive functioning, including the human capacity to maintain emotional well-being despite setback, major trauma, and the ups and downs of ordinary life. Perceived control is particularly relevant to this positive focus on the ability to find a meaningful life even in difficult circumstances. What is amazing about personal control is not just the adaptive function it serves, but the incredible capacity many people have for keeping a sense of control in circumstances that appear to offer limited options. In this chapter, I first will cover the background of the perceived control concept in psychology and the mechanisms by which control has positive effects. Then, control measurement and the adaptiveness of personal control beliefs when they seem to contradict reality are addressed. Finally, individual differences in a sense of control, interventions to enhance control, and future directions are covered.

Overview of Perceived Control Research and Theory

Perceived control—the judgment that one has the means to obtain desired outcomes and to avoid undesirable ones—has a long history as a central idea in psychological theory and research. In major theoretical approaches, scholars have attempted to explicate various aspects of perceived control, including why it is important (Miller, 1979; White, 1959), the variety of deficits associated with a lack of control (Seligman, 1975), and the role of control in coping with stressful life circumstances (Taylor, 1983).

Perhaps the most fundamental conceptualization of perceived control is Geary's (1998) evolutionary framework in which the desire for control serves as the basic motivation that guides all other motives, emotions, cognitions, and social behaviors. Wanting to have control has been adaptive because humans with this desire are more likely to obtain resources that are critical for survival and reproduction. Other theorists who do not specifically espouse an evolutionary framework also have claimed that a control drive is the central motivation guiding human behavior and development (Heckhausen & Schulz, 1995; White, 1959).

In keeping with the view that the control motive is basic to the human condition, researchers have demonstrated its many benefits. Perceptions of control are associated with better coping with stressful life circumstances (Glass, McKnight, & Valdimarsdottir, 1993; Litt, 1988; Thompson, Sobolew-Shubin, Galbraith, Schwankovsky, & Cruzen, 1993). Those with more perceived control are less anxious and depressed in the face of chronic illnesses (Griffin & Rabkin, 1998; Thompson, Nanni, & Levine, 1994) and less traumatized by victimization (Regehr, Cadell, & Jensen, 1999). In addition, those with a stronger sense of perceived control are more likely to take needed action to improve or protect their physical health (Peterson & Stunkard, 1989; Rodin, 1986).

Perceived control also provides benefits in the workplace (Parkes, 1989), as well as educational settings (Dicintio & Gee, 1999; Eccles et al., 1991). For example, children with a mastery orientation seek challenge in their tasks and persist even in the face of obstacles (Dweck, 1999). In almost every life arena, one's sense of personal control has positive implications for emotional well-being, for the likelihood that action is taken, for physical health, and for general adaptive functioning.

Why Is a Sense of Control Beneficial?

The question of why a sense of control is important to psychological well-being does not have one simple answer. A number of advantages to perceived control have been identified and, depending on the situation, one or more of these benefits may be critical.

According to the evolutionary perspective on perceived control, humans have been shaped through evolution to prefer a sense of control. Throughout human history, people who experienced positive emotions and a sense of well-being when they had control were more likely to work to have control and to manipulate the environment in ways that increased the chances that they and their offspring would survive. Those with a drive for control were more likely to survive and pass on their genes, resulting in an innate desire for control.

Perceptions of control also are advantageous because they may prompt individuals to take action

and avoid stressful situations. More specifically, a sense of control activates problem solving and attention to solutions. Another reason why personal control is beneficial is that a sense of control allows one to prepare for an upcoming stressor and ensure that the situation will not become intolerable (Miller, 1979). Thus the potentially negative event is not as stressful when it is accompanied by a belief in personal control.

Finally, a sense of uncontrollability has been associated with increased physiological reactivity to stress and depressed immune functioning (Brosschot et al., 1998; Dantzer, 1989). Thus, persons with a sense of control may protect themselves against the potentially health-compromising physiological effects of stress.

What People Do to Get a Sense of Control

Thompson and Wierson (2000) suggest that people use at least three strategies to maintain control even in difficult circumstances: changing to goals that are reachable in the current situation, creating new avenues for control, and accepting current circumstances.

First, making progress toward goals is an important source of perceived control and general well-being (see Snyder, 1996). When progress on an important goal is not possible, people who are flexible in identifying attainable alternate goals will be able to maintain a sense of control by finding satisfying, attainable alternatives. On this point, Brandstadter and Rothermund (1994) found that older adults maintain a strong sense of general control by deemphasizing the importance of goals that have become difficult to achieve and focusing instead on more reachable goals. Although it would not be adaptive to relinquish goals too readily, flexibility in the face of unreachable goals helps sustain perceptions of control.

Second, identifying and cultivating the areas of personal control that are still available is an effective way to maintain overall levels of control. For example, chronically ill individuals can influence the course of their illness by obtaining extensive medical information, getting good medical care, following the course of treatment, reducing stress in their lives, and investigating alternate types of treatment. Because predictability enhances a sense of control (Thompson, 1981), just getting information on the causes and course of one's disease and treatment options can increase perceived control.

Third, there is the strategy of acceptance which is based on Rothbaum, Weisz, and Snyder's (1982) distinction between primary and secondary control. Primary control is the same as perceived control as it is defined in this chapter: the perception that one can get desired outcomes. Secondary control involves accepting one's life circumstances as they are, instead of working to change them. Acceptance can be achieved in a variety of ways, including finding benefits and meaning in the loss and in one's life situation. Even in an overall negative experience, many individuals are able to find some benefits or advantages in their situation (see chap. 60). For example, stroke patients report that their stroke helped them appreciate life and their spouse and that they have grown from the experience (Thompson, 1991). Secondary control is associated with better adjustment to difficult circumstances such as Parkinson's disease (McQuillen, Licht, & Licht, 2003). Acceptance increases a sense of control because it helps people feel less like helpless victims and reduces the discrepancy between desired and achieved outcomes.

Measuring Perceptions of Control

Many ways to measure perceived control are available, reflecting the complexity of the construct. Perceived control can refer to general perceptions such as overall control in one's life or to specific areas such as control in the academic arena. Generally, it is best to select measures that are geared to the context being addressed. For example, school-related perceived control (e.g., as measured with the Intellectual Achievement Responsibility Questionnaire; Crandall, Katkovsky, & Crandall, 1965) is likely to be a better predictor of academic achievement than is general control. However, if the research question is focused on overall levels of control (e.g., a study addressing decline in overall control associated with aging) or if comparisons are to be made across different domains, then a widely used general measure of control, the Pearlin and Schooler Mastery Scale (Pearlin & Schooler, 1978), is available.

Another distinction among control measures refers to the assessment of overall control versus the components of control judgments. Perceived control can be decomposed into two parts: (a) "locus of control," which is the perception that most people's outcomes are influenced by personal action (internal) versus outside forces or other people (external); and (b) "self-efficacy," which refers to the belief that one personally has the ability to enact the actions that are necessary to get desired outcomes. Perceived control is the combination of an internal locus (i.e., outcomes depend on personal action) and self-efficacy (i.e., I have the skills to take effective action).

A further important distinction concerns the time frame of the perceived control judgment. Frazier and her colleagues (Frazier, 2003; Frazier, Berman, & Steward, 2001) have found that present and future control have positive effects on psychological adjustment, but past control is either unrelated to adjustment or associated with worse outcomes.

Realism and Illusion in the Effects of Personal Control

Having a sense of control is typical of those who handle stress well, so the construct fits well with the positive psychology focus of this book. However, the possibility that having a strong sense of control has a downside as well as being a mark of good functioning needs to be addressed. Is perceived control useful only if it is an accurate reflection of one's capabilities?

Several lines of research address this question. One involves laboratory studies of illusory control in which the actual level of control over a task is manipulated and participants are asked to estimate their control after completing the task (Alloy & Abramson, 1979). Those who overestimate their control tend to be better copers and more persistent on tasks (Alloy & Clements, 1992).

Correlational studies of coping with traumatic life events such as chronic illness also shed light on the adaptiveness of illusory control. Presumably, people with more serious loss or trauma have less real control, yet perceived control is just as beneficial for those who are facing more severely restrictive or adverse circumstances as it is for those in better circumstances (Helgeson, 1992; Reed, Taylor, & Kemeny, 1993; Thompson et al., 1993), indicating that control does not have to be realistic to be beneficial. Thus, despite the reasonableness of the assumption that control needs to be realistic to be adaptive, the empirical results for coping with failure on laboratory tasks and with negative live events suggest otherwise.

That is not the whole story, however. Health behavior deficits associated with illusory control were examined by Thompson, Kent, Thomas, and Vrungos (1999) and they found that college students and gay men in the community who used more general illusory control in their thinking about HIV susceptibility also were more likely to use ineffective ways to protect against exposure to

HIV. Furthermore, college research participants who received an intervention to undermine their illusions of control over protection from HIV and other sexually transmitted diseases reported more effective protection (e.g., condom use) in the 3-month period following the study than did those whose illusions were left intact (Thompson, Kyle, Vrungos, & Swan, 2002). These studies suggest that overestimations of control may be maladaptive in the context of health-related behaviors.

How might we explain the varying results regarding illusory control that have emerged from the coping and the health behavior studies? Many people may combine the best of both worlds by regularly overestimating their control, but at critical junctures, being more honest with themselves and making accurate assessments of their control (Taylor & Armor, 1996). These ideas explain why people who are coping with difficult life circumstances derive benefits from perceptions of control even if these judgments are overestimations of their actual control.

A different situation exists in the area of health-protective behaviors. Some people may be motivated to overestimate their control over health behaviors so as to avoid having to make difficult changes, that is, use condoms 100% of the time. Illusory beliefs in the effectiveness of easier measures to avoid HIV such as partner screening or serial monogamy maintain a sense of protection without having to enact the more difficult strategies of consistent condom use or abstinence (Thompson et al., 1999). Thus, when the driving motive for overestimating control is to avoid an effective, but difficult behavior, then illusory control can be maladaptive.

Individual Differences

Depressive thinking is one individual difference that can affect judgments of control. Research on illusions of control in laboratory settings where the actual contingencies are manipulated has revealed that nondepressed individuals have higher estimates of their control than their depressed counterparts (Alloy & Abramson, 1982; Martin, Abramson, & Alloy, 1984). It is the nondepressed as compared to the depressed individuals who are more likely to overestimate their control.

The relationship between demographic factors and perceived control has also been examined. Judgments of control tend to stay stable throughout the adult years, with declines coming only in the later years (Mirowsky, 1995; Nelson, 1993) or not at all (Lachman, 1991; Peng & Lachman, 1993).

Perceived control is adaptive throughout the range of ages that have been studied (Andersson, 1992; Brandstadter & Rothermund, 1994). In fact, Rodin (1986) has suggested that a sense of control may have greater benefits for older than younger individuals.

Other studies have examined the effects of ethnicity and culture on control perceptions. Researchers have found that people in a variety of countries realize benefits from perceived control. The perceived control of both Russian adults (Bobak, Pikhart, Hertzman, Rose, & Marmot, 1998) and adolescents from Eastern European countries (Grob, Little, Wanner, Wearing, & Euronet, 1996) is associated with better psychological well-being.

A somewhat different story emerges from Asian and African American populations. For instance, several studies found that both Asian Americans and Asians in Asia have lower levels of perceived control than do non-Asians in the United States (Liu & Yussen, 2005; Sastry & Ross, 1998). In addition, several studies find a relatively weak relationship between perceived control and psychological outcomes among Asian and African Americans. Wong, Heiby, Kameoka, and Dubanoski (1999) surveyed both Asian American and White elder adults and found more perceived control was associated with less depression only for the White elders. In the previously mentioned Sastry and Ross (1998) study, there were weaker relationships between perceived control and psychological distress for Asian Americans and Asians than for non-Asians. Thompson, Collins, Newcomb, and Hunt (1996) found a similar result for African American and White U.S. samples: More perceived control was strongly associated with better adjustment for White inmates, but no relationship emerged for the African Americans. It may be that people in less individualist cultures derive less benefit from individual-level perceptions of control.

One possibility that has been explored recently is that those from collectivist cultures find group-based control more useful than individual-level perceived control. In support of this, several studies have found that control exercised through social relationships is higher in collectivist cultures (Ashman, Shiomura, & Levy, 2006) and is associated with better psychological outcomes (Schaubroeck, Lam, & Xie, 2000; Spector, Sanchez, Siu, Salgado, & Ma, 2004).

Interventions to Increase Control

An important research focus has been to enhance the control perceptions of those who are in low-control circumstances. Comprehensive interventions that involve teaching stress reduction and coping skills are one approach. The idea is that successful experience in reducing stress and handling problems will increase a sense of control. Along these lines, Cunningham, Lockwood, and Cunningham (1991) gave cancer patients a psychoeducational program with seven weekly 2-hr sessions that produced higher perceptions of self-efficacy. Similarly, Telch and Telch (1986) found that group coping skills instruction improved self-efficacy for cancer patients. Slivinske and Fitch (1987) tested a comprehensive control-enhancing intervention for elderly individuals that focused on enhanced responsibility, stress management, physical fitness, and spirituality. The group that received the intervention had a significant increase in perceived control and overall functioning. Parker et al. (1988) provided rheumatoid arthritis patients with cognitive behavioral therapy and training in coping problem solving, distraction, and self-management, which had the effect of less catastrophizing and stronger perceptions of control over pain. A cognitive behavioral treatment program for pain patients had the positive effect of reducing feelings of helplessness (Katz, Ritvo, Irvine, & Jackson, 1996), and a similar program for people with arthritis decreased pain, fatigue, and anxiety (Barlow, Turner, & Wright, 1998). These studies have found positive effects, but given the comprehensive nature of the interventions, we cannot deduce that it was the enhancement of control per se that produced the positive effects.

A second approach has been to use interventions that are more closely focused on specifically enhancing control. In several studies, people have been encouraged to participate more in their treatment or treatment decisions. For example, Johnston, Gilbert, Partridge, and Collins (1992) randomly assigned rehabilitation patients to a group who received a routine appointment letter with the message that their efforts would pay off, or to a control group who did not get this message. The group receiving the message had higher levels of perceived control and were more satisfied with information they received. In a study of patients with ulcer disease, participants were taught to read their own medical records and encouraged to ask questions of their medical care providers (Greenfield, Kaplan, & Ware, 1985). Other patients did not receive this intervention. Over time, those who received the instruction preferred a more active role in medical care and were more effective in obtaining information from their physicians.

A number of control interventions have been conducted in educational settings and work settings. For example, Bergin, Hudson, Chryst, and Resetar (1992) increased the perceived control of educationally disadvantaged young children, thereby improving their scores on standardized tests. In an impressive program of research on the importance of perceived control in education, Perry and his associates (Perry, 2003) have tested theory-based interventions for college students such as attribution retraining to increase causal attributions to controllable and modifiable explanations of academic performance. These interventions can reduce dropout rates and improve academic performance by enhancing students' sense of control (Perry, 2003; Perry & Penner, 1990).

Although many researchers have found positive effects associated with interventions to increase perceptions of control, some studies have found mixed results. Reich and Zautra (1991) used a comprehensive control enhancement intervention with at-risk older adults (bereaved or disabled). The intervention involved cognitive and behavioral techniques to increase perceived control with random assignment to one of three levels of an intervention: control-enhanced, placebo-contact, or a no-contact group. The control enhancement increased mental health for individuals with a high internal locus of control, but the placebo-contact group worked best for those with a low internal locus. Those who were low in internality were actually better off if they were encouraged to be dependent. Craig, Hancock, Chang, and Dickson (1998) found that a cognitive-behavioral therapy intervention for patients with spinal cord injuries increased feelings of control only for participants who initially had low feelings of control. Another study found that a control-enhancing intervention for managers of a trucking company increased job satisfaction, but only for those managers who had supportive supervisors (Logan & Ganster, 2005).

Overall, attempts to increase perceived control have shown some promise, especially if they increase general coping and stress reduction skills. Interventions in which patients are given more control may need to be matched to their desired level of control, and may be most effective for those who already are attuned to ways that they control outcomes and for those who are in an environment that is conducive to exercising control.

Future Directions

The concept of perceived control has generated a great deal of research and we now can reach some conclusions regarding its benefits and the circumstances under which it is adaptive. In general, perceptions of control help people maintain emotional well-being and deal effectively with life problems. Still, much remains to be discovered. Some suggestions for further research are discussed here.

Ethnic group differences in the adaptiveness of personal control is one area that needs further explication. Based on the studies discussed previously in this chapter, it seems that those from collectivist cultures do not derive as much benefit from a sense of personal control as do those from cultures with more individualistic orientations. Researchers need to establish the reliability of this effect, and determine what underlies it. More studies of perceived control that include members of various minority groups also are essential. It may be the case that minority group members and those from collectivist cultures possess a sense of control that does not rely on individual empowerment, but rather rests on using group influence. Standard measures of personal control may not adequately detect these group-oriented perceptions of control.

The question of the adaptiveness of overly optimistic estimates of one's control also needs further exploration. One issue is whether people are psychologically shaken by an incident that clearly indicates that they do not have as much control as they had imagined. Based on results to date, there does not appear to be a downside to overestimating one's control when in low control circumstances such as having a serious and debilitating chronic illness. In only a few studies, however, have researchers used the longitudinal designs that would be necessary to assess reactions before and after a disconfirmation of control. A second research issue regarding overestimations of control involves testing the effects of motives on overestimations of control. It may be that when people make overly optimistic judgments of their control to avoid undertaking a more difficult, but effective, course of action, their illusory control may have negative effects. When motives to avoid action prevail, illusory control may discourage rather than encourage effective action. More research, however, is needed on this topic before this view can be validated.

Finally, researchers need to explore more ways to increase perceived control in everyday life. Although a variety of interventions for those who are chronically ill or receiving medical care have been tested, there has been little research on interventions to increase personal control in ordinary life

circumstances. Many people are adept at finding a strong sense of personal control on their own, but for those who are not, control-enhancing programs could make the benefits of personal control more widely available. A central focus of positive psychology is to make beneficial ways of thinking and feeling available to the maximum number of people. Establishing environments where more people feel empowered to make positive changes in their lives is an important step in that direction.

Questions about the Future of Perceived Control Research

1. More research on ethnic differences in the adaptiveness of control needs to be done. Do individuals from more collectivist cultures get a sense of control from group membership as opposed to individual resources?

2. What are the effects of overestimating one's control? Some research finds problems with overly optimistic assessments of personal control and other research does not. Under what circumstances is it not adaptive to overestimate one's control?

3. What are the practical, effective ways to enhance personal control in a variety of settings such as schools, worksites, nursing homes, and hospitals?

References

Alloy, L. B., & Abramson, L. Y. (1979). Judgment of contingency in depressed and nondepressed students: Sadder but wiser? *Journal of Experimental Psychology: General, 108*, 441–483.

Alloy, L. B., & Abramson, L. Y. (1982). Learned helplessness, depression, and the illusion of control. *Journal of Personality and Social Psychology, 42*, 1114–1126.

Alloy, L. B., & Clements, C. M. (1992). Illusion of control: Invulnerability to negative affect and depressive symptoms after laboratory and natural stressors. *Journal of Abnormal Psychology, 101*, 234–245.

Andersson, L. (1992). Loneliness and perceived responsibility and control in elderly community residents. *Social Behavior and Personality, 7*, 431–443.

Ashman, O., Shiomura, K., & Levy, B. R. (2006). Influence of culture and age on control beliefs: The missing link of interdependence. *International Journal of Aging and Human Development, 62*, 143–157.

Barlow, J. H., Turner, A. P., & Wright, C. C. (1998). Sharing, caring, and learning to take control: Self-management training for people with arthritis. *Psychology, Health, and Medicine, 3*, 387–393.

Bergin, D. A., Hudson, L. M., Chryst, C. F., & Resetar, M. (1992). An afterschool intervention program for educationally disadvantaged young children. *The Urban Review, 24*, 203–217.

Bobak, M., Pikhart, H., Hertzman, C., Rose, R., & Marmot, M. (1998). Socioeconomic factors, perceived control, and self-reported health in Russia: A cross-sectional survey. *Social Science and Medicine, 47*, 269–279.

Brandstadter, J., & Rothermund, K. (1994). Self-percepts of control in middle and later adulthood: Buffering losses by rescaling goals. *Psychology and Aging, 9*, 265–273.

Brosschot, J. F., Godaert, G. L. R., Benschop, R. J., Olff, M., Ballieux, R. E., & Heijnen, C. J. (1998). Experimental stress and immunological reactivity: A closer look at perceived controllability. *Psychosomatic Medicine, 60*, 359–361.

Craig, A., Hancock, K., Chang, E., & Dickson, H. (1998). The effectiveness of group psychological intervention in enhancing perceptions of control following spinal cord injury. *Australian and New Zealand Journal of Psychiatry, 32*, 112–118.

Crandall, V. C., Katkovsky, W., & Crandall, V. J. (1965). Children's beliefs in their own control of reinforcements in intellectual-academic achievement situations. *Child Development, 36*, 91–109.

Cunningham, A. J., Lockwood, G. A., & Cunningham, J. A. (1991). A relationship between perceived self-efficacy and quality of life in cancer patients. *Patient Education and Counseling, 17*, 71–78.

Dantzer, R. (1989). Neuroendocrine correlates of control and coping. In A. Steptoe & A. Appels (Eds.), *Stress, personal control and health* (pp. 277–294). New York: Wiley.

Dicintio, M. J., & Gee, S. (1999). Control is the key: Unlocking the motivation of at-risk students. *Psychology in the Schools, 36*, 231–237.

Dweck, C. S. (1999). *Self-theories: Their role in motivation, personality, and development.* Philadelphia: Psychology Press.

Eccles, J. S., Buchanan, C. M., Flanagan, C., Fuligni, A., Midgley, C., & Yee, C. (1991). Control versus autonomy during early adolescence. *Journal of Social Issues, 47*(4), 53–68.

Frazier, P. A. (2003). Perceived control and distress following sexual assault: A longitudinal test of a new model. *Journal of Personality and Social Psychology, 84*, 1257–1269.

Frazier, P. A., Berman, M., & Steward, J. (2001). Perceived control and posttraumatic stress: A temporal model. *Applied and Preventive Psychology, 10*, 207–223.

Geary, D. C. (1998). *Male, female: The evolution of human sex differences.* Washington, DC: American Psychological Association.

Glass, D. C., McKnight, J. D., & Valdimarsdottir, H. (1993). Depression, burnout, and perceptions of control in hospital nurses. *Journal of Consulting and Clinical Psychology, 61*, 147–155.

Greenfield, S., Kaplan, S., & Ware, J. E. (1985). Expanding patient involvement in care. *Annals of Internal Medicine, 102*, 520–528.

Griffin, K. W., & Rabkin, J. G. (1998). Perceived control over illness, realistic acceptance, and psychological adjustment in people with AIDS. *Journal of Social and Clinical Psychology, 17*, 407–424.

Grob, A., Little, T. D., Wanner, B., Wearing, W., & Euronet. (1996). Adolescents' well-being and perceived control across 14 sociocultural contexts. *Journal of Personality and Social Psychology, 71*, 785–795.

Heckhausen, J., & Schulz, R. (1995). A life-span theory of control. *Psychological Review, 102*, 284–304.

Helgeson, V. S. (1992). Moderators of the relation between perceived control and adjustment to chronic illness. *Journal of Personality and Social Psychology, 63*, 656–666.

Johnston, M., Gilbert, P., Partridge, C., & Collins, J. (1992). Changing perceived control in patients with physical disabilities: An intervention study with patients receiving rehabilitation. *British Journal of Clinical Psychology, 31*, 89–94.

Katz, J., Ritvo, P., Irvine, M. J., & Jackson, M. (1996). Coping with chronic pain. In M. Zeidner & N. S. Endler (Eds.), *Handbook of coping: Theory, research, and applications* (pp. 252–278). New York: Wiley.

Lachman, M. E. (1991). Perceived control over memory aging: Developmental and intervention perspectives. *Journal of Social Issues, 47*(4), 159–175.

Litt, M. D. (1988). Self-efficacy and perceived control: Cognitive mediators of pain tolerance. *Journal of Personality and Social Psychology, 4*, 149–160.

Liu, Y., & Yussen, S. R. (2005). A comparison of perceived control beliefs between Chinese and American students. *International Journal of Behavioral Development, 29*, 14–23.

Logan, M. S., & Ganster, D. C. (2005). An experimental evaluation of a control intervention to alleviate job-related stress. *Journal of Management, 31*, 90–107.

Martin, D. J., Abramson, L. Y., & Alloy, L. B. (1984). Illusion of control for self and others in depressed and nondepressed college students. *Journal of Personality and Social Psychology, 46*, 125–136.

McQuillen, A. D., Licht, H., & Licht, B. G. (2003). Contributions of disease severity and perceptions of primary and secondary control to the prediction of psychosocial adjustment to Parkinson's disease. *Health Psychology, 22*, 504–512.

Miller, S. M. (1979). Controllability and human stress: Method, evidence, and theory. *Behavior Research and Theory, 17*, 287–306.

Mirowsky, J. (1995). Age and the sense of control. *Social Psychology Quarterly, 58*, 31–43.

Nelson, E. A. (1993). Control beliefs of adults in three domains: A new assessment of perceived control. *Psychological Reports, 72*, 155–165.

Parker, J. C., Frank, R. G., Beck, N. C., Smarr, K. L., Buescher, K. L., Phillips, L. R., et al. (1988). Pain management in rheumatoid arthritis patients: A cognitive-behavioral approach. *Arthritis and Rheumatism, 31*, 593–601.

Parkes, K. R. (1989). Personal control in an occupational context. In A. Steptoe & A. Appels (Eds.), *Stress, personal control, and health* (pp. 21–47). Oxford, UK: Wiley.

Pearlin, L., & Schooler, C. (1978). The structure of coping. *Journal of Health and Social Behavior, 19*, 2–21.

Peng, Y., & Lachman, M. E. (1993). *Primary and secondary control: Age and cultural differences.* Paper presented at the 101st Annual Convention of the American Psychological Association, Toronto, ON.

Perry, R. P. (2003). Perceived (academic) control and causal thinking in achievement settings. *Canadian Psychology, 44*, 312–331.

Perry, R. P., & Penner, K. S. (1990). Enhancing academic achievement in college students through attributional retraining and instruction. *Journal of Educational Psychology, 82*, 262–271.

Peterson, C., & Stunkard, A. J. (1989). Personal control and health promotion. *Social Science and Medicine, 28*, 819–828.

Reed, G. M., Taylor, S. E., & Kemeny, M. E. (1993). Perceived control and psychological adjustment in gay men with AIDS. *Journal of Applied Social Psychology, 23*, 791–824.

Regehr, C., Cadell, S., & Jensen, K. (1999). Perceptions of control and long-term recovery from rape. *American Journal of Orthopsychiatry, 69*, 110–115.

Reich, J. W., & Zautra, A. J. (1991). Experimental and measurement approaches to internal control in at-risk older adults. *Journal of Social Issues, 47*(4), 143–158.

Rodin, J. (1986). Aging and health: Effects of the sense of control. *Science, 233*, 1271–1276.

Rothbaum, F., Weisz, J. R., & Snyder, S. S. (1982). Changing the world and changing the self: A two-process model of perceived control. *Journal of Personality and Social Psychology, 42*, 5–27.

Sastry, J., & Ross, C. E. (1998). Asian ethnicity and the sense of personal control. *Social Psychology Quarterly, 61*, 101–120.

Schaubroeck, J., Lam, S. S., & Xie, J. L. (2000). Collective efficacy versus self-efficacy in coping responses to stressors and control: A cross-cultural study. *Journal of Applied Psychology, 85*, 512–525.

Seligman, M. E. P. (1975). *Helplessness: On depression, development, and death.* San Francisco: Freeman.

Slivinske, L. R., & Fitch, V. L. (1987). The effect of control enhancing interventions on the well-being of elderly individuals living in retirement communities. *The Gerontologist, 27*, 176–181.

Snyder, C. R. (1996). To hope, to lose, and to hope again. *Journal of Personal and Interpersonal Loss, 1*, 1–16.

Spector, P. E., Sanchez, J. I., Siu, O. L., Salgado, J., & Ma, J. (2004). Eastern versus Western control beliefs at work: An investigation of secondary control, socioinstrumental control, and work locus of control in China and the US. *Applied Psychology: An International Review, 53*, 38–60.

Taylor, S. E. (1983). Adjustment to threatening events: A theory of cognitive adaptation. *American Psychologist, 38*, 1161–1173.

Taylor, S. E., & Armor, D. A. (1996). Positive illusions and coping with adversity. *Journal of Personality, 64*, 873–898.

Telch, C. F., & Telch, M. J. (1986). Group coping skills instruction and supportive group therapy for cancer patients: A comparison of strategies. *Journal of Consulting and Clinical Psychology, 54*, 802–808.

Thompson, S. C. (1981). Will it hurt less if I can control it? A complex answer to a simple question. *Psychological Bulletin, 90*, 89–101.

Thompson, S. C. (1991). The search for meaning following a stroke. *Basic and Applied Social Psychology, 12*, 81–96.

Thompson, S. C., Collins, M. A., Newcomb, M. D., & Hunt, W. (1996). On fighting versus accepting stressful circumstances: Primary and secondary control among HIV-positive men in prison. *Journal of Personality and Social Psychology, 70*, 1307–1317.

Thompson, S. C., Kent, D. K., Thomas, C., & Vrungos, S. (1999). Real and illusory control over exposure to HIV in college students and gay men. *Journal of Applied Social Psychology, 29*, 1128–1150.

Thompson, S. C., Kyle, D., Vrungos, S., & Swan, J. (2002). Increasing condom use by undermining perceived invulnerability to HIV. *AIDS Education and Prevention, 14*, 505–514.

Thompson, S. C., Nanni, C., & Levine, A. (1994). Primary versus secondary and disease versus consequence-related control in HIV-positive men. *Journal of Personality and Social Psychology, 67*, 540–547.

Thompson, S. C., Sobolew-Shubin, A., Galbraith, M. E., Schwankovsky, L., & Cruzen, D. (1993). Maintaining perceptions of control: Finding perceived control in low-control circumstances. *Journal of Personality and Social Psychology, 64*, 293–304.

Thompson, S. C., & Wierson, M. (2000). Enhancing perceived control in psychotherapy. In C. R. Snyder & R. E. Ingram (Eds.), *Handbook of psychological change* (pp. 177–197). New York: Wiley.

White, R. W. (1959). Motivation reconsidered: The concept of competence. *Psychological Review, 66*, 297–333.

Wong, S. S., Heiby, E. M., Kameoka, V. A., & Dubanoski, J. P. (1999). Perceived control, self-reinforcement, and depression among Asian American and Caucasian American elders. *Journal of Applied Gerontology, 18*, 46–62.

Mindfulness Versus Positive Evaluation

Ellen Langer

Abstract

Mindfulness is a flexible state of mind that is characterized by openness to novelty, sensitivity to context, and engagement with the present moment. In this chapter, mindfulness is proposed to be a critical factor in determining individual performance and shaping our learning experiences. In particular, mindfulness appears to be crucial in helping us deal with the inevitable uncertainties in our lives and environments. The role that mindfulness plays in shaping evaluations, both positive and negative, is also discussed. Finally, it is suggested that the mindful individual is likely to choose to be positive and will experience both the advantages of positivity and the advantages of perceived control for well-being.

Keywords: engagement, evaluation, mindfulness, uncertainty

Life is a battle. On this point optimists and pessimists agree. Evil is insolent and strong; beauty enchanting but rare; goodness very apt to be weak; folly very apt to be defiant; wickedness to carry the day; imbeciles to be in very great places, people of sense in small, and mankind generally, unhappy.... In this there is mingled pain and delight, but over the mysterious mixture there hovers a visible rule, that bids us learn to will and seek to understand.

—*Henry James*

Introducing Mindfulness

What is considered evil, beautiful, good, folly, and wickedness are products of our mind. It is surely easier to be happy living in a world full of beauty and goodness. Just as surely, it is easier to be happy if we think these things of ourselves. This chapter will consider the ways our mindless use of evaluation, be it positive or negative, leads to our unhappiness; the direct effects of mindfulness on happiness; and why teaching mindfulness may reap more benefits than trying to teach people to be positive. Most will agree that pessimism is virtually synonymous with unhappiness. What might be

worth considering is how positive evaluations may lead to the same result.

Before proceeding, however, it is important to take at least a brief look at what mindfulness is and is not: It is a flexible state of mind—an openness to novelty, a process of actively drawing novel distinctions. When we are mindful, we become sensitive to context and perspective; we are situated in the present. When we are mindless, we are trapped in rigid mind-sets, oblivious to context or perspective. When we are mindless, our behavior is governed by rule and routine. In contrast, when we are mindful, our behavior may be guided rather than governed by rules and routines. Mindfulness is not vigilance or attention when what is meant by those concepts is a stable focus on an object or idea. When mindful, we are actively varying the stimulus field. It is not controlled processing (e.g., 31×267), in that mindfulness requires or generates novelty. Mindlessness is not habit, although habit is mindless. Mindlessness need not arise as a function of repeated experience. As demonstrated subsequently, mindlessness may come about on a single exposure to information.

For those of us who learned to drive many years ago, we were taught that if we needed to stop the car on a slippery surface, the safest way was to slowly, gently pump the brake. Today most new cars have antilock brakes. To stop on a slippery surface, now the safest thing to do is to step on the brake firmly and hold it down. Most of us caught on ice will still gently pump the brakes. What was once safe is now dangerous. The context has changed, but our behavior remains the same.

Much of the time we are mindless. Of course we are unaware when we are in that state of mind because we are "not there" to notice. To notice, we would have had to have been mindful. Yet over 25 years of research reveals that mindlessness may be very costly to us. In these studies we have found that an increase in mindfulness results in greater competence, health and longevity, positive affect, creativity, and charisma and reduced burnout, to name a few of the findings (see Langer, 1989, 1997).

Mindlessness comes about in two ways: either through repetition or on a single exposure to information. The first case is the more familiar. Most of us have had the experience, for example, of driving and then realizing, only because of the distance we have come, that we made part of the trip on "automatic pilot," as we sometimes call mindless behavior. Another example of mindlessness through repetition is when we learn something by practicing it so that it becomes like "second nature" to us. We try to learn the new skill so well that we do not have to think about it. The problem is that if we have been successful, it will not occur to us to think about it even when it would be to our advantage to do so.

Whether we become mindless over time or on initial exposure to information, we unwittingly lock ourselves into a single understanding of that information. For example, I learned that horses do not eat meat. I was at an equestrian event, and someone asked me to watch his horse while he went to get the horse a hot dog. I shared my fact with him. I learned the information in a context-free, absolute way and never thought to question when it might or

might not be true. This is the way we learn most things. It is why we are frequently in error but rarely in doubt. He brought back the hot dog. The horse ate it.

When information is given by an authority, appears irrelevant, or is presented in absolute language, it typically does not occur to us to question it. We accept it and become trapped in the mind-set, oblivious to how it could be otherwise. Authorities are sometimes wrong or overstate their case, and what is irrelevant today may be relevant tomorrow. When do we want to close the future? Moreover, virtually all the information we are given is presented to us in absolute language. As such, we tend to mindlessly accept it. Too often we mindlessly learn what we should love, hate, fear, respect, and so forth. Our learned emotional responses to people, things, ideas, and even ourselves control our well-being. Yet many of these responses are taken at face value. It seems easier that way than to question the underlying values and premises on which our evaluations are built.

Mindfulness, Uncertainty, and Automatic Behavior

Most aspects of our culture currently lead us to try to reduce uncertainty: We learn so that we will know what things are. In this endeavor we confuse the stability of our mind-sets with the stability of the underlying phenomena. We hold things still purportedly to feel in control, yet because they are always changing, we give up the very control we seek. Instead of looking for invariance, perhaps we should consider exploiting the power of uncertainty so that we can learn what things can become rather than what they are. If we made a universal attribution for our uncertainty, rather than a personal attribution for incompetence, much of the stress and incompetence we experience would diminish. Mindfulness, characterized by novel distinction-drawing, leads us in this direction. It makes clear that things change and loosens the grip of our evaluative mind-sets so that these changes need not be feared.

A large body of experimental studies, including our own, make a cogent case for the automaticity of most human behavior (see Bargh & Chartrand, 1999). The costs of the unconsidered nature of most social behavior are either overlooked or weighed against presumed benefits. The argument given for these benefits can be broken up into a normative part and a descriptive part. Neither is unproblematic. The normative part of the argument is a classic "resource constraint" proposition. Because cognitive work is costly, as the argument goes, cognitive commitments to the values and perspectives that we will bring to bear on a particular predicament are efficient. It is cognitive behavior that is well adapted to the circumstances of having to react to an environment that requires quick, decisive action. But for cognitive commitments, we would be "stuck," just like the ass in the medieval tale of Burridan, whose obsessive dithering between two stacks of hay leads him to starve to death. The alternative, a mindful engagement with the situation, is erroneously believed to lead to "analysis paralysis," which stifles decisive, purposive action.

This argument only works, however, if we accept that the environment is static and our understanding of it complete, or that we have discovered the "one best way" to deal with all possible eventualities. Both of these assumptions, however, are unrealistic. In our world, a world that is constantly changing in unpredictable ways, letting our beliefs die in our stead (Popper, 1973) is the hallmark of the successful individual. To be mindless is to close the future. At what point do we want to do this? Twentieth-century writing in epistemology teaches that scientific theories and models are regularly replaced by successors (Popper, 1959) whose premises are radically different from those of the incumbent theories. The succession of "paradigms" of scientific knowledge does not follow a path of "linear progress" toward more truthlike theories over time (Kuhn, 1981; Miller, 1994). Theories—or the models of the world or cognitive schemata that people use in order to choose between different courses of action—regularly change in fundamental ways, and the hallmark of rationality is not being able to salvage a theory from apparent refutation by the addition of fortifying hypotheses, but rather the ability to specify the conditions under which a theory will be abandoned (Lakatos, 1970).

Certainly, it is no less important for the individual to question her theories than it is for science. When information is processed mindlessly, the potential for reconsideration is abandoned. This typically happens by default and not design, so that even if it were to the individual's advantage to question her theories, it will not occur to her to do so. Bargh and his colleagues focus on the fact that the environment often requires "prompt" action (Bargh & Chartrand, 1999). What they fail to consider is that "adaptive," and therefore changing, actions also are required. Now, the emphasis is no longer on cognitive precommitments that aid actionability but rather on the ability to act while remaining open to the possibility that the theory on which the action is predicated may shortly be supplanted by a different theory. But if we are open to a potentially new theory, how can we take action? At this point, some are tempted to say analysis can paralyze us. Analysis paralysis, however, only follows if we assume that there is some level of analysis at which we may be able to identify a best theory. In this case we would keep searching for the "right" decision. Otherwise, there is no reason to be paralyzed by the process of reframing and reinterpreting the environment in terms of new models, because we know that all models are ultimately mistaken or can be significantly improved upon. We can take action in the face of uncertainty. Even a seemingly unassailable theory like Newton's formulation of classical mechanics was abandoned by modern physicists in favor of the relativistic picture of space and time, in spite of the fact that Newton's theory may very well be salvaged from refutation by the addition of "fortifying" hypotheses (Lakatos, 1970).

The ability to refine one's theory—or to alter it dramatically in the face of new circumstances—seems to be critically dependent upon our ability to withhold judgment about the "best one." We never abandon a "theory" because it has been refuted but rather because we have a better theory that has been more severely tested and has withstood those tests more competently (Lakatos, 1970).

Studies of learning behavior suggest that keeping multiple perspectives of the same phenomenon "alive" at any given time is critical to the process of learning from "experience." As an example of this, Thomas Kuhn (1981) noted in his analysis of Piaget's studies of the ways in which children learn about the concept of "speed," being able to simultaneously hold the mental models of "speed as blurriness of moving object" and the mental model of "speed as minimum time of object to destination" is critical to the children's ability to make correct inferences about the rates of motion of moving objects. At the least, it is clear that learning is not likely to take place if we are closed to new information.

Our studies (e.g., Bodner, Waterfield, & Langer, 2000; Chanowitz & Langer, 1981; Langer, Hatem, Joss, & Howell, 1989; Langer & Piper, 1987) showing that conditionalized presentation of information ("x could be seen as y") to students leads to better "performance" of the students on subsequent tests than does the unconditionalized presentation of information ("x is nothing but y," or "x is y") lend support to the notion that successful adaptive behavior depends on the "loosening" of the grip that our cognitive commitments have on our minds.

The argument for automatic behavior also relies on the questionable belief that automatic behavior is faster and somehow "easier" for people to engage. This deserves several comments. We might consider how often speed is really of the essence. To answer this, we may want to consider what the difference in speed is between mindless and mindful responses. We may produce the same response either mindfully or mindlessly. When we choose to do this, the difference in speed is likely to be trivial. On this point, my original work failed to make clear that while mindlessness closes us off to change, we also cannot be in a constant state of mindfully drawing distinctions about everything at once. To argue that mindlessness is rarely if ever beneficial means that we do not want to close ourselves off to possibility. Instead, we want to be either specifically mindful with respect to some particular content or "potentially" mindful. We may not want to notice the myriad ways each corn flake is different from the other, for example, but we do not want to be so automatic in what we do notice that we fail to see the metal nut that slipped into the bowl, either. A mindful breakfast, then, can take the same time as a mindless breakfast.

Furthermore, the need for exceptional speed, where milliseconds might matter, as in swerving the car to avoid hitting a child, may be avoided altogether by mindful behavior. When mindful, we often avert the danger not yet arisen.

In fact, mindfulness can increase, rather than decrease, one's performance. Consider states of "flow" (Csikszentmihalyi, 1990), which are characterized by a decrease in the effort required to process information and by an "enjoyment" of the experience of performance, "without" a loss of engagement or of the sense of being-in-the-present. It is difficult to argue that people who were found most likely to experience states of flow—such as surgeons and musicians—are also most likely to be automatic in their processing of the stimuli with which they interact. Similarly, our studies on the prevention of mindlessness (see Langer, 1989, 1997) show that when people learned mindfully, they were more likely to enjoy the learning experience than were people presented with an unconditional version of the same information.

The error in the proposition that automaticity is "easier" to engage in than is a conscious awareness and engagement with the present is a faulty comparison, whereby "automatic" processing is contrasted with "controlled processing" of information (which by definition is effortful). Mindfulness is orthogonal to controlled processing (see Langer, 1992). For the former, one is actively engaged in drawing novel distinctions (e.g., when does $1 + 1 = 1$?—when adding one wad of gum to one wad of gum); for the latter, one relies on distinctions previously drawn (e.g., as when we multiply 237×36). Thus, mindfulness may seem effortful when it is confused with controlled processing. Similarly, it may seem effortful when it is confused with stressful thinking. Events appear stressful when we are certain that a particular occurrence will necessarily lead to an outcome that is negative for us. It is hard to think about negative things happening to us. It is the mindless presumption that it will be negative that is hard, not mindfulness. Perhaps the ease of mindfulness becomes apparent when we consider that when we are fully engaged in our work, just as when we are at play, we seek novelty rather than certainty. Indeed, humor itself relies on mindfulness (which is why a joke already heard and remembered, without being newly considered, is rarely funny). Mindfulness is not a cold cognitive process. We may be mindful when we simply notice our peaceful reactions to the world around us.

Most of us have the mind-set that practice makes perfect. We often take as a given that we should learn "the" basics of complex skills so well that we do not have to think about them again, so that we can go on to master the finer points of the task. In an earlier work (Langer, 1997), I raised the question "Who decided what 'the' basics are?" To the extent that the learner differs from whoever that decision maker was, it may be advantageous to question *the* basics so that we can take advantage of our idiosyncratic strengths. Such questioning is ruled out when we are mindless. For example, it seems odd that a very small hand should hold a tennis racket the very same way a very large hand should and that in either case, the way should remain unchanged despite the weight of the racket. Does it make sense to freeze our understanding of a task at the point when we know the least about it? It is unlikely that experts do this; instead, they question basics. Our data (e.g., Langer & Imber, 1979) suggest that mindless practice leads to imperfect performance.

The costs of mindlessness go beyond performance decrements (see Langer, 1989, 1997). Even if our world (personal, interpersonal, and impersonal) were governed by certainty, it would be to our advantage to "be there" to experience it. In an uncertain world, mindlessness sets us up potentially to incur costs every time things change.

Uncertainty keeps us situated in the present. The perception of uncertainty leads to mindfulness, and mindfulness, in turn, leads to greater uncertainty. As such, mindfulness leads to engagement with the task at hand. Being situated in the present and involved in what we are doing are two ways mindfulness enables us to be content. Moreover, by drawing novel distinctions, we become sensitive to perspective, and in so doing, we come to see that evaluation is a function of our view rather than an inherent part of the stimulus. Our mindlessness regarding evaluation is perhaps the greatest cause of our unhappiness.

Mindlessness and Evaluation

We take for granted that evaluations exist independently of us. Each day we think and feel and act as if people, objects, and events were good or bad in themselves. For example, potholes, tax collectors, and divorce are bad, whereas caviar, philanthropists, and holidays are good. But we are essentially mindless to the fact that we have accepted value judgments that we have attached onto various events and objects and states of the world. We find something pleasing or displeasing because we choose to see it in a particular way. Such judgments are in our control, yet we too often are oblivious to this fact.

Things "out there" are not self-evidently good or bad. Sometimes we say this (e.g., "One man's passion is another man's poison"), yet our everyday experience signals otherwise. Potholes make cars slow down; a tax collector can be someone's beloved husband; divorce can be the best outcome for the child living in unspoken tension. When we are not locked into fixed evaluations, we have far more control than we think over our well-being. We have control over the experience of the present. The prevalence of value judgments in our lives reveals nothing about the world, but much about our minds. We judge and evaluate in order to do the "good" thing, to have the "right" thing, or do the "right" thing. The resulting feelings we identify with happiness. We are rarely immediately conscious of the purpose of our evaluations. Evaluation is something we use to make ourselves happy. As we shall see, however, the use of the evaluative mind-set is self-defeating, for it brings us unhappiness instead.

Many of our thoughts are concerned with whether what we or others are doing or thinking is good or bad. Evaluation is central to the way we make sense of our world, yet in most cases, evaluation is mindless. We say that there are two sides to the proverbial coin. Although we acknowledge that everything has advantages and disadvantages, we tend to treat things as good or bad in the balance. A more mindful approach would entail understanding not only that there are advantages and disadvantages to anything we may consider but that each disadvantage is "simultaneously" an advantage from a different perspective (and vice versa). With this type of mindful approach, virtually every unpleasant aspect of our lives could change.

"All behavior makes sense from the actor's perspective, or else the actor would not do it." This realization makes "all negative evaluations" of people suspect, and all action based on these predictions about people of questionable worth. If we are trying to predict what others will do in the future, and we believe the past is the best predictor, then it would behoove us to know better what the action meant to the actor.

A frog is put into a pot of water. The pot is slowly heated. The frog keeps adjusting and finally dies. Another frog is put into a pot of water. The heat is turned on very high. The frog notices the change and jumps out of the pot. When things "drastically" change for us, we notice a difference. Up until that time, we accommodate our experience into the extant frame we are using, and we seem to do this even when it is to our disadvantage. It does not occur to us to consider that the situation, our behavior, or the behavior of other people may be understood differently from the way we originally framed it. If we did, we could take advantage of cues that are less extreme to avoid the "heat."

Often negative evaluations lead us to give up. "Tomorrow will be better." "It's always darkest before the dawn." Implicit in these messages is the idea that we should give up the moment and accept that there are bad things.

Evaluation, positive or negative, is a state of mind. That does not mean that consequences are not real. It means that the number of consequences one could enumerate for any action are dependent on the individual's interest in noting them, and the evaluation of each of these consequences is dependent on the view taken of them. Events do not come with evaluations; we impose them on our experiences, and in so doing create our experience of the event. For pleasure, in winter Finns dip themselves in ice-cold water, and some Americans swim in the cold ocean; many watch horror movies and ride roller coasters for the purpose of becoming afraid.

Consider the following three different perspectives: (a) bad things are intolerable; (b) bad things happen, but if we just hold on, they will pass; and (c) bad things are context dependent—shift the context, and the evaluation changes. It is the third perspective that brings us most of what we currently value. Western culture currently teaches us only the second perspective. Even the saying "Every cloud has a silver lining" does not quite lead us to the third view. The implication here is that the bad thing will result in something good. Again we are expected to give up the moment and wait for it to pass, but now what will result is not just the passing of the bad but the arrival of something good. An optimist is said to be the one who, when surrounded by manure, knows there must be a pony in there somewhere. Again this is not what the third view is about. In this view there is an awareness that the very thing that is evaluated as negative is also positive. It is not that there may be five negative things and five positive—which surely is better than just seeing the negative—but that the ten things are both negative and positive, depending on the context we impose on them.

The previously noted cultural expressions are encouragement to "hope." Typically the encouragement to hope implicitly regards the present as necessarily bad. It is fine to want tomorrow to be good and to expect that it will be. When this is what we mean by encouraging hope, there is no problem. All too often, however, words of hope are expressed when people are feeling bad and they indirectly are led to accept that set of feelings. It is not fine to passively give up today. Such giving up follows from the view that is implicitly reinforced by the previous statements that events themselves are good or bad, rather than that our views make them good or bad.

Although the culture encourages us to be able to "delay gratification," waiting is mindless in that it suggests that there is no way to enjoy what is being done at the moment. Mindless hoping and learning to wait work against this concern. In one experiment aimed at testing these ideas, research participants were given cartoons to evaluate where the same task was defined as either work or play. When it was framed as work, it was found to be unpleasant, leading participants' minds to wander as they tried to just get through it. Although it was the same task, their response to it was very different as a function of the way they viewed it (Snow & Langer, 1997).

The downside of evaluation to intrapersonal processes is prodigious. We try to get through the "bad" times; we hesitate to decide because the "negative" consequences may be overwhelming. We try to feel better by comparing ourselves with those "worse off." We suffer guilt and regret because of the negative consequences we experience or have perpetrated on others. We lie because we see the negative aspects to our behavior and try to hide them from others. Each of these processes—social comparing, experiencing regret and guilt, and lying—implies that events are good or bad and that we must learn to accept them as they are and learn to deal with them, rather than to question our evaluation of them in the first place.

The implicit message given by the culture is that there is one yardstick by which to measure not just outcomes but ourselves and others. We look for new explanations only when all seems to fail. And, as with the frog, it may be too little, too late. For evaluation to be meaningful, we need to use a common metric. The problem enters when we are oblivious to the fact that many other potential yardsticks can be used, with very different results. The prevailing view in the coping literature is to allow a period of grieving so that the person can thereafter reengage in life-goal pursuits. Indeed, the very worst thing that one can do to persons who have just undergone a tragedy or loss is to have them see the situation differently (see Snyder, 1996). After loss, people may need to go through a period of grief and depression, and then after a period of time, goal-directed hopeful thought can be useful (see Feldman & Snyder, 2000). People who have undergone traumas want to be heard and have others listen to their "pains" rather than trying to "see" those pains differently. In this latter regard, friends or helpers will lose credibility as listeners if they become too prescriptive (Tennen & Affleck, 1999).

This view is not incompatible with the position being argued here. If the event is already negatively evaluated, it should be treated respectfully. Nevertheless, many "tragedies" initially could have been understood as opportunities at best, or inconveniences at worst.

The Multiple Meanings of Behavior

When the stories we tell ourselves are compelling and so much information seems to fit our interpretation, it is hard to understand why the other person just doesn't get it. And so we become evaluative. Presently, for many of us to feel right, someone else must be wrong. This dichotomous reasoning is the cause and consequence of an implicit acceptance of a single perspective. Behavior makes sense from the actor's perspective, or else it would not have occurred. I am right, and so are you. The task of successful interpersonal relating, then, may be to search for the information to make this point clear to us or simply accept that the behavior in question must have made sense.

Psychologists (e.g., Jones & Nisbett, 1972) have long described differences that result from the differences in perspective depending on whether one is responsible for some action, the actor, or whether one is an observer of that action. The findings suggest that as observers, we are more likely to attribute other people's behavior to dispositions and our own to situations. Situational attributions help keep us in the present. Dispositional attributions hold things still, presumably to enable us to predict the future. Because of our tendencies to confirm our hypotheses (Langer & Abelson, 1974), they instead may become self-fulfilling prophecies, creating a world less pleasant than it otherwise would be. Negative dispositional attributions keep us at a distance from people and thus reduce the chance to see that the attribution was wrong.

Past researchers have pointed out that behavior engulfs the field of our observation. Thus, as observers we see most clearly the action taken, while the situational constraints effecting those actions are less visible. As actors those situational constraints are felt more keenly. As actors we often know why we had to do whatever we did. We also know that in other circumstances we have behaved differently. Observers usually do not have this information.

While the research on attribution theory has certainly yielded important findings, there is another factor that needs to be highlighted that has not yet been examined, one that may account for even more of the interpersonal misunderstanding and concomitant unhappiness that people experience. Not only do people see different information depending on their vantage points and motivation, but, as implied earlier, people often see the "same" information differently. All of the behavior is accounted for but with a different label that carries with it a very different evaluative tone. Consider, for example, serious versus grim, flexible versus unpredictable, spontaneous versus impulsive, private versus secretive, and so on. "All" behavior is vulnerable to labels connoting these different evaluative tones. If our behavior is mindlessly engaged so we are essentially oblivious to why we did whatever we did; however, even as actors we become vulnerable to negative dispositions.

We often think we know other people, and because of this assumption we don't ask, and because we don't ask, we don't learn that the "same" event may look very different to someone else.

Often we don't know how other people feel unless we ask; we don't ask because we think we know. We think we know because we know how we would feel in the same situation. That is, we overestimate how similar other people are to ourselves. Lee Ross and colleagues have called this the "false consensus effect" (Ross, Greene, & House, 1977). We presume that our behavior makes sense and that all well-adjusted people would do the same thing. If someone does something different, he or she must then be "that kind of a person." For example, people in various experiments were asked to predict the opinions and attitudes of others about topics as varied as defense spending, soup, and what constituted appropriate behavior in various situations. Time and again, people overestimated the proportion of other people who feel or would behave as they do. Again, if I assume that all of us feel the same and I find out that you feel differently, it is your strange behavior that calls for explanation.

It may not be so much that we overestimate how similar others are to ourselves. The mistake we may make is that when we look at ourselves as observers, we see ourselves the same way we see others (Storms, 1973). However, when we take action, we may do so as mindful actors and not observers. Often we see the "same" behavior from different vantage points, but we label it quite differently—different with respect, primarily, to its evaluative tone. "We" may be interested in getting along with others, for example, but he may be seen as conforming.

One major problem with our tendency toward false consensus occurs when we turn it on ourselves. When we look back at our own behavior, now from the observer's vantage point, we may see ourselves as having behaved like "one of them." Because, as Kierkegaard noted, we live our lives going forward but understand them looking back, it is important to consider what we do as observers of other people. When we look back, we, too, are the objects of our inquiries and may treat ourselves the way others might. Those who are less evaluative of others will be less evaluative of themselves. This is the hidden cost of making downward social comparisons. We may feel temporarily good at seeing ourselves as superior to someone else, but when we turn things around, we become "him," the observed.

Consider a person's decision: X is an unpleasant feeling for me. If I do Y, the unpleasantness goes away. It would, then, seem sensible to do Y. Let us briefly consider drinking in this light. Going forward in time, we may feel depressed and empty. We learn that drinking eases the pain. If we do not acknowledge that the behavior initially made sense and only attend to the negative consequences of "excessive" drinking, after the emptiness passes, we do ourselves and others an injustice. The negative feelings that result from the awareness of these consequences probably lead to more drinking, and the cycle continues (Snyder, Higgins, & Stucky, 1983).

From the observers' perspective, for example, "too much" drinking clearly creates unwanted problems for the drinker. The drinker does not say to him- or herself, "I have had enough, but I think I'll drink more." He drinks as much as is deemed necessary to accomplish whatever his goal may be. The behavior is not irrational. It is undertaken to achieve a state of mind, and it most often accomplishes this. On the other hand, when we become observers of our actions, we may become more aware of the negative consequences of those actions. Looking back as observers of ourselves, we may see that we have caused harm to our livers or hurt our loved ones. Typically, we did not drink to bring about these ends. "Going forward" in time, the behavior was not driven by weakness. For most of us, it is easier to learn something new when we are feeling strong. At those times we feel up to the challenges that face us. It would seem, then, that learning how to manage stress or to understand alternative ways of dealing with emptiness, for example, if those are what prompted the drinking, would be easier if we felt good about ourselves. The point here is that we should feel better about ourselves if we see that in its own context, that is, from a going-forward mode, our behavior made sense. With that understanding, less costly alternatives for achieving our goal may be sought. In her doctoral research, Sharon Popp (personal communication, November 15, 1999) found that construction workers drank "excessively." Upon questioning, Popp found that when they were drinking, they opened up with each other and put their macho concerns aside. From these drinking interactions they discovered who they felt they could trust. Trust in their line of work is important. Should they drink or not? In more mundane circumstances, simply asking the question, "How may this behavior be sensible?" will quickly reveal reasonable understandings of our own behavior and that of other people. When we see behavior in a right and wrong frame, it is a question we do not think to ask.

Couples often come to feel that they see the same world, thus obviating the necessity for attention to actor–observer differences. Divorce statistics suggest otherwise.

Husband and wife are in two different rooms. Thinking it reasonable, she yells, " 'What are these?' She expects him to get up and go see what she is talking about, and usually she is not disappointed.

But one friend once struck back at his wife.... When his wife returned home one day, and shouted to him in his study, 'Did they come?,' the husband, not knowing what she was talking about, nevertheless said, 'Yes!' The wife shouted to him again. 'Where did you put them?' He shouted back, 'With the others' " (Fairle, 1978, p. 43).

Usually, couples do not get to see that they are seeing the same thing differently. "If we have the same frame of reference, we will respond in the same way."

The power of most great literature and movies is that we come to see the sense of the actor's behavior when the actions are in some way deplorable to us. The tension between the two may be the power of the work. Consider *Lolita*. If we could just have disgust for Humbert, there would be no problem. After all, grown men are not supposed to become sexually aroused and active with adolescent girls. Nabokov's skill reveals itself in drawing us inside this character so that we cannot so easily dismiss him. Behavior makes sense from the actor's perspective. Oedipus did not just kill his father. That would not have been interesting. We come to see how we could have made the same awful mistake. We tend to enjoy literature and film when we can identify with the characters. Simply being observers barely justifies the price we have paid for the popcorn. But great pieces, perhaps, let us identify with the protagonist and take us places we thought we would never go.

If we have the same experience, we will respond similarly. When we respond differently, we would be wise to conclude that the experience was different. This suggests that individual differences may be more differences in experience than differences in individuals. You and I have our hand on a hot radiator. I have to remove my hand more quickly than you. Are you braver or more able to endure pain? No. If you felt what I felt, you would remove your hand when I removed mine.

I see 10 horses running toward us. I am pleased they are coming to say hello. There are six of us, and everyone else runs for protection. They say I'm in denial. I compare myself to others and wonder what is wrong with me. I see 10 horses running toward us. I am pleased they are coming to say hello. There are six of us, and all but one are equally pleased the horses are approaching. One of us runs away for protection. That person is seen as cowardly. In both cases, the odd person makes an excuse for the difference in behavior. The rest do not get to learn that another perspective exists.

Interestingly, our culture provides us with norms that help us to misunderstand. If we or someone else commits an "error," we become contrite or indignant. Our response depends on whether, for example, we tell ourselves that "patience is a virtue" or "the early bird catches the worm." We may think we should have been satisfied with some outcome and not greedy if we think, "A bird in the hand is worth two in the bush" unless we think, "Nothing ventured nothing gained." We should not have been cowardly, "an eye for an eye," unless we think we should have "turned the other cheek." Even our most mundane behavior is hard to pin down: "Clothes make the man" versus "You can't judge a book by its cover." We can always make sense out of our behavior, or we can take ourselves to task, and the culture provides some of our evidence for whichever we choose. The problem is that much of the time most of us do not realize that there is a choice to be made.

Often, unaware of our motives, we tend to feel even more culpable or blaming when we call to mind any of these or similar refrains that suggest we should have known better. Just as each individual behavior has an individual perspective on it that lends reason to the action taken, so, too, does the opposite behavior.

Several seemingly mundane behaviors, both those taken as "bad" and some taken to be "good," look different when examined through this nonevaluative lens. Consider regret, making excuses, blame, and forgiveness in this new light.

Regrets

Regret happens under two conditions: when we are unhappy, and when we obscure the difference between our perspective at time one, when we took some action, and time two, when we evaluate the action we took. Regret is a prediction of our emotions: If we had chosen differently then, we would feel better now. If we feel fine now, the need for the prediction would not arise. When it does arise, it depends on the lack of awareness of the reasonableness of the action given the circumstances we faced at the time.

Much of the regret people experience concerns actions not taken. Perhaps the best way to feel bad is to see oneself as not having done anything when something could have been done. This is the most difficult case to deal with because any action taken can be used as at least some justification for not having taken some alternative action. "I couldn't get the phone because I was in the other room going through the mail, so I missed out on finding out about the trip in time to go" versus "I wasn't doing anything, and I missed the call and didn't find out in time to go." Are we ever really doing nothing?

To test whether future regrets could be prevented and "cured," we (Langer, Marcatonis, & Golub, 2000) conducted the following investigations. First, research participants showed up for a study on gambling in which they could win more than $100 and risk none of their own money. After the person showed up he or she was asked to wait until it was his or her turn, which would be indicated by a light above the waiting room door. Upon seeing the flashing light, the participant was to go to another floor in the building for the experiment. Participants were then randomly assigned to one of four conditions. We arranged it so that everyone missed an opportunity. Only those participants who were aware of spending their time well were expected to not feel regret.

Group 1: Participants in this group were simply told, "We do not need you to do anything at this time, so just wait until it is your turn."

Group 2: This was the same as Group 1, except that a Civil War documentary was playing on a VCR in the room.

Group 3: These subjects were invited to watch taped episodes of *Seinfeld* while they waited.

Group 4: These participants were asked to wait until it was their turn, but it was suggested that they spend the time thinking and feeling.

It was expected that Groups 1 and 2 would suffer the most regret; after all, to their minds, we reasoned, they were doing nothing and missed out on an opportunity. Although the mindful group, Group 4, was expected to feel the least regret, Group 3, based on popular ratings of the TV show, was expected to enjoy themselves and thus not regret the opportunity missed as much as the first two groups.

After waiting 20 min, the experimenter returned and informed the participants that they had missed their turn, and that two people who showed up won $200 and everyone else won at least $50. The experimenter checked the light above the door to show participants that it did indeed work.

Individuals in the Mindful condition (who were told to "be aware of what you are thinking and feeling" while they waited) (a) had a more positive experience as subjects; (b) found the experience of being a subject more beneficial; and (c) expressed less regret about the way they spent their time compared with individuals in the Civil War (CW) condition (who were allowed to watch a Civil War documentary) or those in the "Nothing" condition. Individuals in the Mindful condition were also more willing to participate in future investigations than were those in the CW or Nothing conditions.

It may be unreasonable, given the world we currently live in, to be happy or mindful all the time. If we were, as this research suggests, we might never have to experience regret. This work suggests that if the regretted action cannot be undone, any engaging activity may remove the negative feelings. Rethinking why the regretted action or inaction occurred, however, has the clear advantage of preventing its return. But the best alternative, it would seem, is to start out with the assumption that their behavior made sense to them at the time given the circumstances as they saw them, or else they would have behaved differently. This research tells us that when we are aware of why we are doing what we are doing, there is little room for self-recrimination.

Counterfactual thinking is the generation of alternatives that run contrary to the facts of what happened (Roese, 1997). Typically, the individual thinks that had he done otherwise, the outcome would have been better. Whereas upward comparisons, as in the social comparison literature, may initially result in feeling bad because of a realization of some positive alternative that might have been, over the long haul they may provide useful information and motivation for engaging in different behavior in the future: "If only I had taken her advice, this whole mess would have been avoided." Downward comparisons, in which we breathe a sigh of relief that we did not behave otherwise and thus avoided some negative outcome, result in positive feelings by contrast to what might have been: "Thank goodness I remembered to call, or else I, too, would have been fired."

It is true that if one imagines what else one might have done, there may be some experience of relief and the consideration of new information that may be of later use. Nevertheless, I would argue that there is a hidden downside to this kind of thinking. Surely if we proceed mindlessly, experience negative outcomes, and think about how we could have behaved differently, it is far better than believing we had no choice. But it is too easy for people to jump from "could have been" to "should have been" and then there arises the problem of how could we have been so stupid or incompetent not to have done it that way in the first place.

Counterfactual thinking occurs after the behavior has been engaged. Mindful thinking occurs before the activity has been engaged. This way people know

why they did what they decided to do and why they did not do otherwise. The consideration of alternatives may still lead to information that may be useful in the future but without the self-recriminations.

Moreover, every time we say to ourselves that we "should have," we implicitly reinforce the illusion of certainty and the single-minded evaluation of consequences. For example, "If only I had gone on Thursday instead, all would have been right with the world." Many mishaps could have occurred on Thursday that probably went into the reasoning to go on Wednesday. We no more know all the consequences that could have arisen now than we could have known then. The difference is that if we thought about it then, we would be aware that we could not have foreseen everything. The consequences we did consider may have looked different to us at the time before the decision was made. Now, after the fact, we experience regret by freezing the evaluation of these consequences. Before: "I told him about your appointment because he was getting angry at you, and I thought that would upset you." After: "I'm sorry I violated your privacy by telling him about your appointment." If we are mindful of alternative courses of action and alternative views of the potential consequences, then we are more likely to see the uncertainty inherent in the situation. If we proceed mindlessly, we often take the current view as the only reasonable view. Our self-respect suffers because we then feel we should have known.

Counterfactual thinking is more likely to occur after the experience of negative outcomes than positive outcomes (e.g., Klauer & Migulla, 1996; Sanna & Turley, 1996). Anger, depression, boredom, or essentially any unhappiness can trigger thoughts of how we might have done things differently in the past. If we proceed more mindfully, our perspective is forward-looking, not backward-looking.

Counterfactual thinking or regret is also more likely to occur the closer the person is to the sought-after goal. This tendency is so great that we even do it in situations that we take to be largely chance-determined. For instance, if we choose a lottery number that misses by one number, we experience more regret than if we miss by many numbers. The reason for this is that the closer we are to the goal, the easier it is to see how we might have behaved differently. Missing a train by 5 min seems worse to most of us than missing it by half an hour. The more mutable the situation, the more regret we feel. But all the while, we ignore that our actions made some sense to us and that is why we so engaged in them, whether the distance to some other goal was great or small.

The more normative the "appropriate" behavior is taken to be, the more regret we experience for our behavior (Kahneman & Miller, 1986). But, again, this analysis is after the fact. It is important to realize that many norms can be brought to bear on any situation before the fact. If after the fact we learn that "everyone" went to the party, we will feel more regret than if going to the party was not as typical. Before the fact we may consider many different parties and conclude that there is no norm for attendance; people are as likely to go as to not go. Before the fact, there are many sources of reasonable information to consider in making our decisions, with many possible consequences. After the fact, there are fewer paths that make sense because consequences are now apparent. Regret denies the utility of our past experience to our present situation.

Excuses

Ask 10 people if making excuses is good or bad. Next, ask them why. Virtually all will answer that making excuses is bad, and most will offer a view that amounts to saying that the excuse maker is not owning up to what she did. What does it mean to take responsibility for our actions? For which action should we be responsible?

Consider, again, that behavior always makes sense from the actor's perspective. If it did not, the actor would have done differently. People do not get up in the morning and say, "Today I'm going to be clumsy, inconsiderate, and hurtful." What were they intending when we experienced them that way? If we are not mindful of our intentions going forward, we become vulnerable to other people's characterization of our behavior looking back. The same behavior looks different from different perspectives. A negative view of our behavior necessitates an excuse.

What is the difference between an excuse and a reason? If I give an explanation that makes sense to us both, the explanation is taken as a reason for my action. When it is not accepted, a reason becomes an excuse. When it is not accepted, the actor's perspective is denied. The attribution of excuse making allows the person to whom the excuse is made to feel superior, at least for the moment. The cost is loss of genuine interaction and understanding.

If our behavior made sense going forward in time and we were mindless to our intentions, we may offer a reason that is unacceptable to the blamer, and it will be taken as an excuse. If we respect ourselves enough to know that what we did must have made sense to us even if we cannot remember why we did it, we will reject the accusation. The

alternative is that the behavior was the person's fault, engaged because he is bad. If he is not bad, then why did he do it? When people live in a world of absolute right and wrong without regard to perspective, any explanation different from their own is taken to be an excuse.

Our culture has confused reasons and excuses, with the result that the blamer has a ready reason not to listen. What does this mean when you think I am making excuses? Does it mean that I had no reason for what I did? I find myself saying, in such situations, "I know I care about you. Are you trying to persuade me that I don't?" "I know I'm a nice person. Are you trying to make me think I am not?"

The word "excuse" conveys an accusation on the part of the person to whom an explanation is given. It implies distrust regarding the speaker's motives and intentions. Our culture has become so tolerant of excuses that the difference between a reason and an excuse is not likely to be easily noticed. By obscuring the difference between the two, we unwittingly act as though our actions have no reasons, or that the only acceptable reason is one in which someone must look bad. As a result, self-respect suffers as others are given the final word over our intentions. If I paid attention to my actions before engaging in them, I would know why I did what I did after the action was completed. The cost of my mindlessness is that now I am more likely to accept your understanding of my behavior. What might have been a reason becomes an excuse.

If behavior makes sense from the actor's perspective, then we as actors become less vulnerable to other people's attributions of excuse making. Moreover, the very idea of an "excuse" reinforces the view that consequences are inherently negative.

Blame and Forgiveness

"To err is human, to forgive divine." Or is it? Again, ask 10 people whether forgiveness is good or bad. All will probably tell you that it is good. Forgiveness is something to which we should aspire. The more wronged we have been, the more divine it is to be able to forgive. Now ask 10 people if blame is good or bad. All will probably tell you that blame is bad. And yet to forgive, we have to blame. If we do not blame in the first place, there is nothing to forgive.

But there is a step before blame and forgiveness that needs our consideration. Before we blame, we have to experience the outcome as negative. If your behavior resulted in something positive for me, blame would hardly make sense. Those who see more negativity in the world are then those more likely to blame.

The same behavior makes many different senses. If we do not appreciate that we may look at a situation and see different things or see the same things differently, then we will remain stuck in an evaluative mind-set. If we remain in this mind-set, then we will experience negative outcomes that could have been experienced as positive. If we experience negative outcomes, then we will be tempted to find someone to blame. If we blame, at least we can try to forgive. To be *forgiving* is "better" than to be *unforgiving*. Understanding that the action made sense to the actor obviates the necessity for forgiveness.

Discrimination Is Not Evaluation

We can be discriminating without being evaluative. Noticing new things is the essence of mindfulness. Unquestioningly accepting a single-minded evaluation of what is noticed is mindless. Our culture is replete with examples of mindless evaluation. Sadly, it is hard to conjure up examples of a more mindful stance. We take an evaluative component as an essential part of our beliefs. Without knowing if something is good or bad, after all, how would we know whether to approach or avoid ideas, people, places, and things? Yet accepting evaluation, rather than mindful discrimination, as essential, we set ourselves up for the experience of feeling inadequate. By mindlessly attaching this evaluative component to our beliefs, we become victims of our mind-sets. We experience this reactivity only when things go wrong. These are the times we try to change; yet these are the times we are least equipped to do so.

With the awareness that we are responsible for our evaluations, we are more likely to use them in a conditional way. As such, we can stay responsive to our circumstances rather than become reactive to them as absolute evaluations lead us to be.

"When no news is bad news." If we give up evaluation, we give up the compliment but we are no longer vulnerable to the insult.

If someone compliments us, what is our reaction? If we are very pleased, it would suggest a certain amount of uncertainty about our level of skill. It also suggests a degree of vulnerability we would experience if we did not succeed. Imagine that somebody whose opinion you respected told you that you were great at spelling three-letter words. Chances are if you are over 10 years old, you would not be moved by this compliment. You know you can do it, so the feedback is essentially unimportant to you. Imagine

the same respected person told you that the way that you pronounce vowels is extraordinary. Again, you would be unlikely to be very moved. This time you are not taken in by the compliment because the issue probably does not matter much to you. In both cases, when you were not testing yourself, the compliment was unimportant. Here, then, is a way to protect ourselves from negative remarks: "If we don't take the compliment, we are not vulnerable to the insult."

The behaviorist literature tells us that there is positive and negative reinforcement. And there is positive and negative punishment. Positive reinforcement is the presentation of a positive stimulus—for example, a compliment. Negative reinforcement is the cessation of an aversive stimulus—for example, if someone is always insulting you, and now you do something and no insult follows, that behavior will be negatively reinforced. Reinforcement increases the response leading to it; whether it is positive or negative reinforcement, reinforcement feels good. Conversely, punishment is meant to stop the behavior leading to it. Positive punishment is the presentation of an aversive stimulus—for example, an insult. The interesting but less well known case is negative punishment: "the cessation of a positive stimulus"—time out from compliments. Because compliments feel so good, we are not inclined to look beyond them. Because compliments may help control us, there is little motivation for others to see their costs to us. Compliments, like insults, generally concern what we do and not who we are. As such, they help keep us in an evaluative frame of mind. Evaluating the self takes one out of the experience; self becomes object rather than actor. Ironically, with less experience, there is less of a self to evaluate.

If we give up evaluation, we give up downward social comparing.

> If you never assume importance
> You never lose it.
> (Lao Tse, *The Way of Life*)

The most frequent evaluation people make is to compare themselves with other people. When we want information about how to do a task better, we compare ourselves with others who are slightly better at the task. When we want to bolster our self-images, we compare ourselves with those who are less able then we are, that is, we make downward social comparisons.

A good deal of the work in psychology that deals with the "self" takes as a given that evaluation will occur and then proceeds to examine what information will be used and how it is used in making that evaluation. When evaluation does take place, it is carried out in the manner suggested by these researchers. The literature does not question whether or not there can be another way of being that is nonevaluative.

Leon Festinger (1954) went so far as to say that people have a drive to evaluate their opinions and abilities. When objective means for this comparison are not available, people make comparisons with others. People choose similar others for these comparisons. To feel good about themselves, people often make downward social comparisons. Regarding abilities, we make upward comparisons. I am more likely to compare my tennis skills with those of someone better than with those of someone I know cannot play as well. As Festinger was quick to note, of course in these upward comparisons I am not likely to compare myself with those far better than I am. I try, according to Festinger, to close the gap and become as similar to others as I can. There is also a tendency to reduce discrepancies regarding opinions. Both of these tendencies, regarding ability and opinion, implicitly reinforce the idea that there is a single view (a right and wrong), and that it is in our best interest to be like everyone else.

Is there any evidence that we can be completely nonevaluative? I do not know of any. Nevertheless, our own research suggests that this is the direction in which we might want to move. Johnny Welch, Judith White, and I (Langer, White, & Welch, 2000) conducted an investigation to look at the effect of being evaluative on negative emotions such as guilt, regret, stress, and the tendency to blame, keep secrets, and lie. First, we gave a questionnaire to people that simply asked them how often they compared themselves with other people, regardless of whether they saw themselves as better or worse. We then asked them to indicate how often they experienced the feelings or behaviors just noted (guilt, etc.). We divided the participants into two groups—those who answered that they frequently compared themselves with others and those who made these comparisons less often—and then looked at how often the two groups experienced the listed emotions and behaviors. The findings results were clear. Those who were less evaluative experienced less guilt, regret, and so on. Moreover, in response to the question, "In general, how well do you like yourself?" the less evaluative group was found to like themselves more.

The next step in our research was an experiment in which we (Yariv & Langer, 2000) either encouraged or discouraged people to make evaluations and found that, as in the questionnaire study, those who were more evaluative also suffered more.

We may stay evaluative because positive evaluation helps us feel good in the short run. As soon as we agree to accept a positive evaluation as reason to feel good about ourselves, however, we open the door for the damaging consequences of perceived failure. Surely, depression, suicide, and just feeling bad all result in whole or part from an evaluative stance.

If one tries and does not succeed, one could feel like a failure. Alternatively, one could conclude that the chosen way was not effective (Langer, 1989; Langer & Dweck, 1973).

James Joyce's famous book *The Dubliners* was rejected by 22 publishers. Gertrude Stein submitted poems to editors for about 20 years before one was accepted. Fred Astaire and the Beatles were also initially turned down. The list goes on (Bandura, 1997).

We have much control over the valence of our experience. Research participants actively drew 0, 3, or 6 novel distinctions while being engaged in disliked activities (listening to rap or classical music; watching football). We found that the more distinctions drawn, the more the activity was liked (Langer, 1997). That evaluations are malleable may also be seen in the classic research on the "mere exposure effect": The more often you see something, the more you like it. We had hypothesized that this effect would obtain primarily if, on repetition, participants drew novel distinctions—that is, if they were mindful. In this research, exposure was held constant, but participants drew several or few distinctions. The mere exposure effect seems to rely on mindful distinction drawing and not on exposure alone (Fox, Langer, & Kulessa, 2000). In either case, however, we have control over the valence of our experience.

Consider how we look for change when we observe our children and thus constantly draw novel distinctions. Our affection for our children only grows. We look for stability when we observe our spouses or partners. Sadly, too often our affection diminishes for our spouses or partners. Positive affect, thus, seems to depend on our willingness to mindfully engage another person.

The Myth of Inaction

Let us return to the question of analysis paralysis. Would giving up evaluation lead to inaction? After all, if you cannot believe your action will be successful or that you will want the final outcome you have worked for, why engage in it at all? The short answer is, "Why not?"

Consider what many experience as a midlife crisis. At some point in life, many people come to realize that nothing has any intrinsic meaning. There are three possible responses to this. Those who do not successfully emerge from this belief stay depressed and cynical at the meaninglessness of it all. Some ignore this belief and proceed as if they never had it, although all the while it lurks in the background. Finally, there are those who accept that everything can be equally meaningless or meaningful. This last group is the most likely to stay situated in a self-constructed meaningful present.

Similarly, a person can take action falsely believing that the action will result in a singularly desirable end state and repeatedly suffer surprise and disappointment. Instead, the same person can come to see that the action may not lead to the outcome, and the outcome may not be desirable anyway, and thus decide not to take any action. But a third option also presents itself. The person may be freed to take action because feared negative consequences are just as unpredictable as desired positive consequences, and even if they do occur, they also have another side. It is more satisfying to do something than to do nothing. Action is the way we get to experience ourselves. And so we act not to bring about an outcome but to bring about ourselves. In fact, when asked if they would hesitate to act if assured that the outcome to their prediction would be positive, people overwhelmingly say no. The fear of inaction has hidden in it the evaluative belief that making the "wrong" decision may be costly. Recent research we have conducted (Bodner et al., 2000; Langer & Lee, 2000), in fact, shows that people who are taught to reframe positive as negative, and vice versa, make their decisions more, not less, quickly. Giving up our evaluative tendencies does not seem to lead to inaction.

This is not to say that "inaction" is necessarily bad. Typically, or we see inaction as the absence of a particular action. That is, we do not make the phone call, buy the item, or attend the event. We need not see ourselves as inactive, but rather actively pursuing another course. If we realized this, we might be less afraid of giving up the illusion of evaluative stability.

In our attempts to understand behavior, psychologists may have unwittingly contributed to the unhappiness we are now directly attempting to change. As researchers we have been in the perspective of observer, more often than not, oblivious ourselves to how the same behavior may have different meaning when understood from the actor's perspective in addition to our own.

Mindfulness versus Positive Evaluation

Many years ago, we conducted an experimental investigation aimed at teaching people to be positive (Langer, Janis, & Wolfer, 1975). We looked at what the effects would be on preoperative stress of having a positive view of one's situation. We found that patients became less stressed, took fewer pain relievers and sedatives, and were able to leave the hospital sooner than comparison groups. Surely a single-mindedly positive view is likely to be more beneficial to health and well-being than a mindlessly negative view. But there are problems endemic to teaching people to view things positively. First, in the way we normally use language, if things can be positive, other things would then seem to be inherently negative. Second, because evaluation is taken to be an inherent part of outcomes, changing one evaluation from negative to positive may suggest more that the person was originally mistaken than that all outcomes may be viewed in a positive way. As such, positivity training may be less likely to generalize to new situations. Third, it would seem to follow that to be positive would be to accept positive statements by others (i.e., compliments), but to do so sets us up for negative punishment. Fourth, if being positive means we should be grateful that we are not as badly off as others might be (i.e., make downward social comparisons), then such gratitude comes at a very high cost. Fifth, and most important, if we teach people to be positive, we may unintentionally teach them to keep evaluation tied to events, ideas, and people, and thus we promote mindlessness.

When mindful, we may find solutions to problems that made us feel incompetent. We may avert the danger not yet arisen. By becoming less judgmental, we are likely to come to value other people and ourselves. All told, it would seem that being mindful would lead us to be optimistic, obviating the necessity for learning how to be positive.

Conclusions

While well-being is more likely to be related to positive than negative evaluations, positive evaluation makes negative evaluations appear to be independent of us. "Positive" experiences like hoping and forgiving, regret over past actions, and delaying gratification for a future goal all implicitly suggest that there is still potential negativity that one may have to confront. Positive evaluations, then, may implicitly rob us of control. Similarly, downward social comparisons may work in the short run to alleviate negative affect, but they set the stage for upward comparisons in the future. By contrast, mindfulness keeps us engaged and situated in the present. The mindful individual comes to recognize that each outcome is potentially simultaneously positive and negative (as is each aspect of each outcome), and that choices can be made with respect to our affective experience. Thus, the mindful individual is likely to choose to be positive and will experience both the advantages of positivity and the advantages of perceived control for well-being.

Questions for Future Research:

1. To what extent are individual differences in mindfulness shaped by culture?

2. What behaviors and psychological processes mediate the effects of mindfulness?

3. How can we design interventions to promote mindfulness and thereby improve well-being?

References

Bandura, A. (1997). *Self-efficacy: The exercise of control.* New York: Freeman.

Bargh, J., & Chartrand, T. (1999). The unbearable automaticity of being. *American Psychologist, 54,* 462–479.

Bodner, T., Waterfield, R., & Langer, E. (2000). Mindfulness in finance. Cambridge, MA: Harvard University (Manuscript in preparation).

Chanowitz, B., & Langer, E. (1981). Premature cognitive commitment. *Journal of Personality and Social Psychology, 41,* 1051–1063.

Csikszentmihalyi, M. (1990). *Flow: The psychology of optimal experience.* New York: Harper and Row.

Fairle, H. (October, 1978). My favorite sociologist. *The New Republic, 7,* 43.

Feldman, D. B., & Snyder, C. R. (2000). Hope, goals, and meaning in life: Shedding new light on an old problem. University of Kansas, Lawrence (Unpublished manuscript).

Festinger, L. (1954). A theory of social comparison processes. *Human Relations, 7,* 117–140.

Fox, B., Langer, E., & Kulessa, G. (2000). Mere exposure versus mindful exposure. Harvard University (Unpublished manuscript).

Jones, E., & Nisbett, R. (1972). The actor and the observer: Divergent perceptions of the causes of behavior. In E. E. Jones, D. E. Kanouse, H. H. Kelley, R. E. Nisbett, S. Valins, & B. Weiner (Eds.), *Attribution: Perceiving the causes of behavior* (pp. 79–94). Morristown, NJ: General Learning Press.

Kahneman, D., & Miller, D. T. (1986). Norm theory: Comparing reality to its alternatives. *Psychological Review, 93,* 136–153.

Klauer, K. C., & Migulla, K. J. (1996). Spontaneous counterfactual processing. *Zeitschrift für Sozialpsychologie, 26,* 34–42.

Kuhn, T. (1981). A function for thought experiments. In I. Hacking (Ed.), *Scientific revolutions* (pp. 6–27). New York: Oxford University Press.

Lakatos, I. (1970). Falsification and the methodology of scientific research programmes. In I. Lakatos & A. Musgrave (Eds.), *Criticism and the growth of knowledge* (pp. 91–196). New York: Cambridge University Press.

Langer, E. (1989). *Mindfulness.* Reading, MA: Addison-Wesley.

Langer, E. (1992). Interpersonal mindlessness and language. *Communication Monographs, 59,* 324–327.

Langer, E. (1997). *The power of mindful learning.* Reading, MA: Addison-Wesley.

Langer, E., & Abelson, R. (1974). A patient by any other name . . .: Clinician group differences in labeling bias. *Journal of Consulting and Clinical Psychology, 42,* 4–9.

Langer, E., & Dweck, C. (1973). *Personal politics.* Englewood Cliffs, NJ: Prentice-Hall.

Langer, E., Hatem, M., Joss, J., & Howell, M. (1989). Conditional teaching and mindful learning: The role of uncertainty in education. *Creativity Research Journal, 2,* 139–150.

Langer, E., & Imber, L. (1979). When practice makes imperfect. *Journal of Personality and Social Psychology, 37,* 2014–2025.

Langer, E., Janis, I., & Wolfer, J. (1975). Reduction of psychological stress in surgical patients. *Journal of Experimental Social Psychology, 11,* 155–165.

Langer, E., & Lee, Y. (2000). The myth of analysis paralysis. Cambridge, MA: Harvard University, unpublished data.

Langer, E., Marcatonis, E., & Golub, S. (2000). No regrets: The ameliorative effect of mindfulness. Cambridge, MA: Harvard University.

Langer, E., & Piper, A. (1987). The prevention of mindlessness. *Journal of Personality and Social Psychology, 53,* 280–287.

Langer, E., White, J., & Welch, J. (2000). Negative effects of social comparison. Cambridge, MA: Harvard University (Unpublished manuscript).

Lao, T. (1962). *The way of life* (Trans. W. Bynner). New York: Capricorn Books.

Miller, D. (1994). *Critical rationalism.* Chicago: Open Court.

Popper, K. R. (1959). *The logic of scientific discovery.* London: Hutchinson.

Popper, K. R. (1973). *Objective knowledge.* London: Routledge.

Roese, N. J. (1997). Counterfactual thinking. *Psychological Bulletin, 121,* 133–148.

Ross, L., Greene, D., & House, P. (1977). The false consensus effort: An egocentric bias in social perception and attribution process. *Journal of Personality and Social Psychology, 13,* 279–301.

Sanna, L. J., & Turley, K. J. (1996). Antecedents to spontaneous counterfactual thinking: Effects of expectancy violation and outcome valence. *Personality and Social Psychology Bulletin, 22,* 906–919.

Snow, S., & Langer, E. (1997). [The power of mindful learning]. Reading, MA: Addison-Wesley (Unpublished data, Reported in E. Langer).

Snyder, C. R. (1996). To hope, to lose, and hope again. *Journal of Personal and Interpersonal Loss, 1,* 3–16.

Snyder, C. R., Higgins, R. L., & Stucky, R. (1983). *Excuses: Masquerades in search of grace.* New York: Wiley-Interscience.

Storms, M. (1973). Videotape and the attribution process: Reversing actors' and observers' points of view. *Journal of Personality and Social Psychology, 27,* 165–175.

Tennen, H., & Affleck, G. (1999). Finding benefits in adversity. In C. R. Snyder (Ed.), *Coping: The psychology of what works* (pp. 278–304). New York: Oxford University Press.

Yariv, L., & Langer, E. (2000). Negative effects of social comparison. Cambridge, MA: Harvard University (Unpublished manuscript).

Perspectives on Time

Ilona Boniwell

Abstract

Time perspective is a preferential direction of an individual's thoughts toward the past, present, or future, which exerts a dynamic influence on their experience, motivation, thinking, and several aspects of behavior. This chapter discusses the theoretical and conceptual bases of this construct, as well as existing approaches to measuring time perspective, such as the Zimbardo Time Perspective Inventory. Major research findings with regard to time perspective are considered, including its influence on educational achievement, risk taking, and negative reminiscence. Further attention is paid to the patterns of relationships between various time perspective types and several aspects of well-being, highlighting the limitations associated with allowing any one time perspective to dominate. The idea of a balanced time perspective is suggested as an alternative to any particular temporal bias. In an optimally balanced time perspective, the past, present, and future components engage flexibly, in response to individuals' values and preferences, whilst taking into account a situation's context and demands at the same time.

Keywords: balanced time perspective, psychological time, psychology of time, time perspective

Philosophers, scientists, sociologists, and anthropologists have all studied time processes in a multitude of ways. One of the central philosophical debates of whether time is subjectively or objectively based has informed very different approaches to conceptualizing and studying time, and they have been subsequently utilized by social scientists. This chapter will first outline this debate before moving to consider the construct of time perspective (TP), one of the key areas of research within the subjective paradigm. The chapter will then introduce the reader to the theoretical foundations of TP, discuss the major approaches to its measurement, review relevant research findings and comment on possible future directions in research and practice.

The origins of this debate can be traced back to the early Greek philosophers Heraclitus and Zeno, arguing about the reality of change, and therefore time. Yet it is St. Augustine and Newton who are usually credited as the major proponents of the dichotomous perspective on the nature of time.

Augustine believed that time is nothing in reality, but exists only in the mind's comprehension of reality. "What then is time? If no one asks me, I know; if I want to explain it to a questioner, I do not know. But at any rate this much I dare affirm I know: that if nothing passed there would be no past time; if nothing were approaching, there would be no future time; if nothing were, there would be no present time.... It's in you, o my mind, that I measure time" (cited in Elliot, 1997, p. 14). Newton, on the other hand, argued that time is an infinitely large container for all events, and that the container exists with or without the events, maintaining thus that time has an objective quality.

The debate, which, throughout the centuries, attracted a number of noble advocates (see Boniwell, 2006), is reflected in the current representations of time that are also largely dualist. To summarize the existing positions, on the one hand, time is approached as an objective phenomenon that is sometimes called "geographical" or "clock" time.

This position regards time as linear and continuous, homogeneous, infinitely divisible, objective, and universal. Such a view is dominant in Western societies where time can be scheduled, measured, coordinated, and is externally created and reinforced by society. The objective perspective on time, however, can be seen as twofold in itself as it relies on two distinct meanings of objectivity. The first meaning concerns ontological objectivity, which is a claim that time has an independent existence from an observer. The second meaning of objectivity refers to the shared collective representation of time, which through the process of internalization leads to objectifying time and identifying it with the clock.

On the other hand, time is approached as an internal subjective phenomenon (Gorman & Wessman, 1977). This facet of time has been variously named by different theorists as "psychological time" (Golovakina & Kronick, 1989, p. 2), "time as it is processed by the human mind" or "subjective experience of time" (Levin & Zakay, 1989, p. 2), "the inner time of the mind" (Melges, 1982, p. 10), or "lived time" (Gorman & Wessman, 1977, p. 227). Psychological or lived time events, occurring simultaneously as marked by the calendar, can be experienced by individuals in very different ways: one event may seem vivid and still current, whereas another one is perceived as having occurred "ages ago." Thus, subjective time is influenced by pace, life stages, changes in life, contents and sequence of thoughts, feelings, and the activities of individuals (Hendricks & Peters, 1986). In subjective time, events may be discontinuous and their flow uneven. The same duration of events as measured by the clock may be experienced very differently when participants "lose" themselves in the process. Furthermore in one's mind time can flow backward as well as forward. This time has a unique significance and meaning for each individual.

Until relatively recently, temporal matters have not received much attention from the social sciences, but this pattern is now changing. Time has played a number of roles within research in that it can be approached as an independent and dependent variable of interest and as a key methodological factor (McGrath, 1988). Consistent with the dualist perspective on the nature of time, there appear to be two distinct approaches to studying time. The psychological study of objective time centers on time use or time budget research, concerned with the allocation of time to activities over a 24-hr period. Within a subjective paradigm, studies have focused on time estimation and subjective duration of experience, time personality, time congruity, time urgency, time intensity, polychronicity and monochronicity, subjective time use, and TP. However, one of the major dependent variables in experimental and cognitive psychology—reaction time (RT)—blends the objective recording of clock time with subjective responding. Research on time management also combines features of both approaches, relying largely on attitude surveys while tying time management behaviors to clock-related outcomes.

One of the key areas of research within subjective approaches to studying time concerns TP, or an individual's cognitive way of relating to the concepts of the past, present, and future, which affects decision making and subsequent actions. This construct may be of particular interest to positive psychologists because of its documented relationships with the measures of well-being and well-functioning (see, for example, Boniwell, 2005). The remainder of the chapter will consider this construct in more detail.

Time Perspective: Theoretical and Conceptual Bases of the Construct

Time perspective (TP) has been defined as a preferential direction of an individual's thoughts toward the past, present, or future, which exerts a dynamic influence on their experience, motivation, thinking, and several aspects of behaviour (De Volder, 1979). Lennings (1996) highlights both cognitive and affective aspects of the construct in his definition of TP as "a cognitive operation that implies both an emotional reaction to imagined time zones (such as future, present or past) and a preference for locating action in some temporal zone" (p. 72). In lay terms, TP is not unlike different colored spectacles through which one can look at the world. Wearing present-colored spectacles enables an individual to fully engage with the present moment, unaware of past determinants or future consequences. Putting on the spectacles of the past colors the present and the future in the shades of things gone. When looking at the world through future lenses, every action taken today is evaluated from the position of tomorrow.

Lewin (1948) was one of the first researchers to stress the importance of TP in the study of human behaviour. For him, the life space of an individual expanded across the temporal zones of past, present, and future, and influenced not only emotions and actions but also moral choices. More recent time researchers—notably Nuttin (1985), Cottle (1976), Wessman and Gorman (1977), Lennings (1996, 1998), and Zimbardo and Boyd (1999)—have supported the Lewinian belief that future and past events have a fundamental impact on present behavior to the extent that they are present in the person's everyday cognitive reasoning.

One literature review identifies up to 211 different ways of approaching the concept of TP (McGrath & Kelly, 1986). In an attempt to organize disperse findings originating from inconsistencies in defining and operationalizing TP, Kazakina (1999) writes of six major dimensions contributing to the construct, namely temporal orientation, extension, density, emotional valence, temporal continuity, and balance. "Temporal orientation" is defined as a preference for either the past, present, or future TP. "Temporal extension" is the length of time over which one projects cognitions and feelings into the past or future, with the longer future extension being associated with a range of favorable outcomes (such as delayed gratification, academic achievement, high IQ, and responsibility) in children and adults. A proportional allocation of significant events, experiences, or mental representations across time zones is known as "temporal density," while "emotional valence" refers to the affective attitudes that individuals associate with a certain temporal region. "Temporal continuity" is understood as the ability of a person to perceive their past, present, and future as meaningfully connected and integrated. Finally, "temporal balance" is enabled by the equality of thoughts and feelings attached to the past, present, and future and is theoretically associated with a balanced personality and the well-functioning of an individual (Rappaport, Enrich, & Wilson, 1985). Despite a wealth of research available, relatively few studies have considered TP in its complexity and across all three temporal zones, with the majority focusing on the future as an object of investigation (Kazakina, 1999).

The formation of TP is believed to be heavily influenced by the processes of socializing, modeling, education, cultural, and other environmental factors (Seginer, 2003; Zimbardo & Boyd, 1999). Heckel and Rajagopal (1975) compared the future TP among Indian and American college students and discovered striking differences in their extension of the future perspective, with American students having a longer future TP than their Indian counterparts. Levine and Barlett (1984) have found substantial cross-cultural differences in the future TP among both adults and students in Australia, Brazil, India, and the United States. Levine and Wolff (1985) developed a novel way of measuring TP of cultures in their studies of pace of time. Looking at three basic indicators of time—the accuracy of a country's bank clocks, the speed at which pedestrians walked, and the average time it took a postal clerk to sell a stamp—they compared six different countries. Japan appeared the leader in temporal pace, followed by the United States, England, Italy, Taiwan, and Indonesia.

Overall, Protestant nations tend to be more future oriented than Catholic nations, due to the enduring legacy of the Protestant work ethic, encouraging the pursuit of personal responsibility and the development of future tasks. In turn, the Gross National Product indices are higher among Protestant than among Catholic nations. Cultures with more individualistic focus tend to be more goal focused and future oriented than those emphasizing collectivism. Within countries, however, people living in southern areas tend to be more present oriented than those in northern regions (Boniwell & Zimbardo, 2004).

Empirical data point to systematic changes in TP, both across a life span and across a variety of situations (Gorman & Wessman, 1977; Melges, 1982, 1990; Nuttin, 1985; Shmotkin, 1991). Zimbardo and Boyd (1999) demonstrate that TP may be affected by situational forces (such as inflation), being on vacation, or under hypnosis. There is some evidence that an individual's TP varies in pathological conditions and abnormal states (Edlund, 1987; Friedman, 1990; Melges, 1982). For example Beiser (1987) has shown that during periods of acute stress refugees focus more on the present rather than the past or future, irrespective of their habitual temporal orientation. Nevertheless, despite being affected by upbringing and environmental forces, TP can become a relatively stable personality trait when a particular temporal bias comes to dominate one's outlook and behavior.

Measuring Time Perspective

Existing instruments devised to measure TP reflect the multiplicity of the approaches to the construct. A large number of the scales focus on one or two temporal regions, most often the future and/or present. Among these are a Future Anxiety Scale (Zaleski, 1996), the Consideration of Future Consequences Scale (Strathman, Gleicher, Boninger, & Edwards, 1994), and the Sensation-Seeking Scale that accentuates present-oriented perspective (Zuckerman, 1994). Bond and Feather

(1988) developed a well-known instrument called the Time Structure Questionnaire, which taps into subjective dimension of time. Present orientation is one of the five factors underlying their time structure construct. However, a multiple-dimension approach to measuring TP is strongly favored in the literature (Jones, 1994; Kazakina, 1999; Tismer, 1987). Early attempts to capture the complexity of TP in a single instrument range from the Circles Test (Cottle, 1976) to the Time Lines (Rappaport, Enrich, & Wilson, 1985) that were designed to elicit a spatial analog for the lengths of time subjects had lived relative to the length of life considered as still left. Other notable measures include the Time Reference Inventory (Roos & Albers, 1965), the Time Attitude Scale (Nuttin, 1985), the Time Competence Scale (Shostrom, 1964), and the Stanford Time Perspective Inventory (Zimbardo, 1990).

Few of the measures have enjoyed a widespread acceptance because of either their questionable psychometric properties or a limited focus on a single temporal zone. Having addressed many of the shortcomings of the previous attempts, a single, integrated TP scale has been developed, which combines the dimension of emotional valence with measuring temporal orientation across the past, present, and future. The Zimbardo Time Perspective Inventory (ZTPI; Zimbardo & Boyd, 1999) exhibits high test–retest reliability, as well as good convergent and discriminant validity. A consistent five-factor structure revealed through exploratory principal component factor analysis and further supported by confirmatory factor analysis explains 36% of variance. Five factors underlying the ZTPI—past-negative, past-positive, present-hedonistic, present-fatalistic and future factors—were derived from series of exploratory studies and have been continuously empirically refined. ZPTI appears to be the most frequently used scale in recent TP studies.

Considering a characteristic profile of an individual biased in the direction of each TP allows us to substantiate ZTPI factors. The person who is future oriented is concerned with working for future goals and rewards, often at the expense of present enjoyment, delaying gratification, and avoiding time-wasting temptations. The present situation is therefore contemplated in terms of future consequences. More specifically, people with future TP are more likely to floss their teeth, eat healthy foods, and get medical checkups regularly. Items on the future TP scale include, among others, "Meeting tomorrow's deadline and doing other necessary work come before tonight's play," and "When I want to achieve something, I set

goals and consider specific means for reaching those goals."

The ZTPI distinguishes between two very different ways of being focused on the present. The present-hedonistic person lives in and for the moment, is often a pleasure seeker, enjoys high-intensity activities, thrills, and new sensations, and is open to adventures. He or she would score highly on items such as "I take risks to put excitement in my life." Children are primarily present-hedonistically oriented. The downside of this orientation is the lack of regard for future consequences. The present-fatalistic TP, on the other hand, is characterized by helplessness, hopelessness, and a belief that spiritual, governmental, or other outside forces control one's life. This TP orientation is expressed by statements including "It doesn't make sense to worry about the future, since there is nothing that I can do about it anyway" and "Fate determines much in my life."

The past TP is associated with focus on family, tradition, history, and continuity of self over time. This too can be either positive or negative. The past-positive TP reflects a warm, pleasurable, though often sentimental view of one's past, with an emphasis on maintaining relationships with family and friends. The past-positive scale contains items such as "Happy memories of good times spring readily to mind" and "I enjoy stories about how things used to be in the 'good old times'." The past-negative TP is characterized by items such as "Painful past experiences keep being replayed in my mind." It reflects a generally negative, pessimistic, and aversive attitude toward the past, which may be based on actual traumatic life events or a negative reconstruction of past occurrences.

Major Research Findings

The TP construct has been found to be related to many attitudes and values, and predictive for a wide range of behaviors (Keough, Zimbardo, & Boyd, 1999; Zimbardo & Boyd, 1999; Zimbardo, Keough, & Boyd, 1997). Although many findings are significant, only those of particular interest to positive psychology are reviewed here.

In comparison to the other time orientations, an extensive amount of research has been carried out on the future TP. It is commonly argued that the future TP is what differentiates humans from animals, who are always in the present and lack the capacity for abstraction and conscious intentionality required for conceptualization of the future (Snyder, Rand, & Ritschel, 2006). There is much support to suggest that the future TP is associated with several positive outcomes, such as high motivation, sense of responsibility, ability to organize and plan actions, and self-efficacy (Lennings & Gow, 1997; Seijts, 1998). This orientation appears predominant in students and other learners across the boundaries of culture, gender, and socioeconomic status. De Volder and Lens (1982) found evidence that an extended future TP is an influential factor in academic performance improvement. Mello and Worrell (2006) report a significant positive association of educational achievement with future positive attitudes in a large sample of academically talented adolescents. Negatively correlated with depression and hopelessness (Breier-Williford & Bramlett, 1995), the future TP even predicts the extent to which unemployed people use their time constructively to seek jobs, rather than watching TV and engaging in other avoidant coping strategies (present oriented; Epel, Bandura, & Zimbardo, 1999).

Risk taking is a characteristic behavior of those high on either present-hedonistic and -fatalistic TP scores, which correlate positively to dangerous driving, frequent smoking, consumption of alcohol and drugs, and sexual promiscuity (Rothspan & Read, 1996; Keough, Zimbardo, & Boyd, 1999). In particular, the present-fatalistic attitude is depicted in a desire to live shorter lives and has been shown to be significantly positively associated with aggression, anxiety, and depression, and negatively with educational success (Mello & Worrell, 2006; Zimbardo & Boyd, 1999).

Ruminating on the past may be commonly paralleled with stagnation, yet it was found to be related to very different outcomes, depending on its valence. For example, Lyubomirsky and Nolen-Hoeksema (1995) have demonstrated that negative rumination is associated with predominantly past-negative orientation and also correlates with depression, anxiety, unhappiness, low self-esteem, and aggression. On the other hand, Bryant, Smart, and King (2005) have established that the frequency of naturally occurring positive reminiscing, a characteristic of the past-positive TP, predicted a perceived ability to enjoy life.

Relationship between Time Perspective and Subjective Well-Being

If TP is such a powerful influence on our behavior, its relationship with well-being cannot be overlooked. Given positive associations between the future TP and important life outcomes, a large number of theorists and researchers have claimed

that a focus on the future is fundamental to well-being and positive functioning (Kahana & Kahana, 1983; Kazakina, 1999; Wessman & Ricks, 1966; Wills, Sandy, & Yaeger, 2001; Zaleski, Cycon, & Kurc, 2001). On the other hand, Boniwell and Zimbardo (2004) have warned of the drawbacks of an excessive future orientation which are workaholism, minimizing the need for social connections, not taking time for occasional self-indulgence, nor being grounded in a sense of community and cultural traditions. Recent studies within positive psychology have found no relationship between the future TP as measured by ZTPI and various aspects of well-being (Boniwell et al. (under review); Foret, Steger, & Frazier, 2004; Tov, 2004), casting doubt on the supremacy of future orientation among the temporal zones.

There are conceptual grounds though to suggest that a time orientation with a focus on the present is a necessary prerequisite for well-being (Boyd-Wilson, Walkey, & McClure, 2002). The experience of well-being can only take place in the here and now, which give present orientation a special status. Yet emerging empirical evidence indicates only a modest positive association between the present hedonistic TP and life satisfaction and between the former and recreation satisfaction. Furthermore, the present-hedonistic TP appears to correlate positively with both positive and negative affect, possibly reflecting the tension between "work and play" attitudes (Boniwell et al. (under review); Tov, 2004).

It is, in fact, the past temporal orientation that shows the most robust associations with well-being measures. In a sample of older adults, Kazakina (1999) has established a positive relationship between the past-positive orientation and life satisfaction. These findings were supported by Boniwell et al. (under review), Foret et al. (2004), and Tov (2004) using student respondents. A similar pattern has emerged with regard to positive affect, meaning in life, and self-actualization. It may be that the positive past holds the keys to happiness. Consistent with this premise, Bryant et al. (2005) found that a 10-min daily reminiscing for a week resulted in the increase of happiness feelings, especially for those who used cognitive imagery as compared to memorabilia.

Balanced Time Perspective

Focusing predominantly on the future may bring academic success, or reminiscing may increase one's happiness, yet if a TP starts to dominate to the extent that it excludes or minimizes the others, it becomes dysfunctional. There are costs and sacrifices (often expressed through loss of human ties) associated with emphasizing an achievement-oriented future TP. Enjoying the moment and unreasonable risk taking seem to go hand in hand. Even positive past orientation has drawbacks that may include being excessively conservative, being cautious, avoiding change and openness to new experiences and cultures, sustaining the status quo, or trying to apply old solutions to the new problems.

A balanced TP has been proposed as a more positive alternative to living life as a slave to any particular temporal bias (Boniwell & Zimbardo, 2004). "In an optimally balanced time perspective, the past, present and future components blend and flexibly engage, depending on a situation's demands and our needs and values" (Zimbardo, 2002, p. 62). Essential to a balanced TP is the ability to switch between different TPs and being able to fully engage with the situation in hand, without lingering in an inappropriate temporal zone. There are early indications that people with the balanced TP are likely to be happier than the rest. A recent study by Boniwell et al. (under review) has operationalized balanced TP as scoring in the top 50% on all three positive TPs, and in the bottom 50% on the past-negative and present-fatalistic orientations. Good size relationships were observed between the balanced TP and several measures of well-being, many of which were higher than the relationships found for individual TP types.

Future Directions in Research and Practice

Although ZTPI appears reliable, valid, and easy to use, it offers a lot of scope for future development. Only 36% of the variance is explained by the five factors, calling for modification or expansion of the factor structure. Further studies utilizing confirmatory factor analysis are needed to assess the existing factor structure and psychometric properties of the subscales, similar to the studies carried out by Lennings (2000a, 2000b), who examined the precursor to ZTPI—the Stanford Time Perspective Inventory (Zimbardo, 1990). One of the most likely trajectories for expansion of the factor structure is the application of an affective dimension to the future ZTPI factor. It is theoretically possible to distinguish between the future-positive and future-anxious perspectives, characterized by different regulatory mechanisms underlying working for future rewards (e.g., integrated vs. introjected regulation; Ryan & Deci, 2000). It is plausible that

the lack of a relationship between the future TP and well-being can be explained by the lack of valence in the future ZTPI factor. Indeed, while Foret et al. (2004) found no association between the future TP and well-being, they report a positive relationship between the future-positive TP (which they defined as hope) and measures of meaning of life and life satisfaction. Furthermore, it is possible that other TP factors can be identified, for example, an atemporal factor, concerned with abstract thinking not bound by a temporal zone.

Further research is urgently required to enrich our understanding of the balanced TP. An intensive case study can shed more light on what it means to have a balanced TP and how it can be developed. The pattern of associations between a balanced TP and the Big Five, other personality variables, and different behaviors needs to be established. Furthermore, the relationships between TP and other constructs within a subjective paradigm of time (e.g., time personality, time urgency, polychronicity, and subjective time use) also deserve investigation.

Implicitly and explicitly, time is an important factor in one-to-one talking practices (such as psychotherapy and coaching). Some examples are potential differences in the subjective sense of time of the client and the therapist, as well as temporal processes at the points of encounter and ending. In terms of practical applications, Boniwell (2005) suggests several ways in which the construct of TP can be consciously and usefully applied in the consulting room. These include raising awareness of unproductive responses associated with habitual temporal orientations; devising strategies to develop underused temporal zones; finding the links and connections between past and present events and future aspirations in order to develop continuity; questioning the dominance of the future TP in Western societies; and evaluating an impact that this social belief has on individual lives.

The last point holds particular relevance for educational policy, which is predominantly future centered. Although undoubtedly useful in preparing children and young people for the world of work, it is also instrumental in the perpetuation of bias. It can be suggested on the basis of empirical evidence that in order to maximize both educational achievement and well-being, a greater emphasis needs to be placed on the development of a balanced TP. Giving equal importance, if not time, to valuing individual and community history, encouragement of social relationships, and intense experiential involvement in play and learning activities, alongside working for future rewards, may in the long run result in a more balanced and flexible society.

Questions

1. How can the Zimbardo Time Perspective Inventory be refined to include valence in the future time perspective factor?

2. What are the major mechanisms underlying the development of a balanced time perspective?

3. In what ways can the construct of time perspective be usefully addressed in applied settings?

References

Beiser, M. (1987). Changing time perspective and mental health among Southeast Asian refugees. *Culture, Health, and Psychiatry, 11*, 437–464.

Bond, M., & Feather, N. (1988). Some correlates of structure and purpose in the use of time. *Journal of Personality and Social Psychology, 55*, 321–329.

Boniwell, I. (2005). Beyond time management: How the latest research on time perspective and perceived time use can assist clients with time-related concerns. *International Journal of Evidence Based Coaching and Mentoring, 3*(2), 61–74.

Boniwell, I. (2006). Satisfaction with time use and its relationship with subjective well-being. Unpublished doctoral dissertation, The Open University.

Boniwell, I., Osin, E., Linely, P. A., & Ivanchenko, G. V. (under review). A question of balance: Time perspective and well-being in British and Russian samples. *Journal of Positive Psychology.*

Boniwell, I., & Zimbardo, P. G. (2004). Balancing time perspective in pursuit of optimal functioning. In P. A. Linley & S. Joseph (Eds.), *Positive Psychology in Practice* (pp. 165–178). Hoboken, NJ: Wiley.

Boyd-Wilson, B. M., Walkey, F. H., & McClure, J. (2002). Present and correct: We kid ourselves less when we live in the moment. *Personality and Individual Differences, 33*, 691–702.

Breier-Williford, S., & Bramlett, R. D. (1995). Time perspective of substance abuse patients: Comparison of the scales in Stratford Time Perspective Inventory, Beck Depression Inventory and Beck Hopelessness Scale. *Psychological Reports, 77*, 899–905.

Bryant, F. B., Smart, C. M., & King, S. P. (2005). Using the past to enhance the present: Boosting happiness through positive reminiscence. *Journal of Happiness Studies, 6*, 227–260.

Cottle, T. J. (1976). *Perceiving time.* New York: Wiley.

De Volder, M. (1979). Time orientation: A review. *Psychologica Belgica, 19*, 61–79.

De Volder, M., & Lens, W. (1982). Academic achievement and future time perspective as a cognitive motivational concept. *Journal of Personality and Social Psychology, 42*, 566–571.

Edlund, M. (1987). *Psychological time and mental illness.* New York: Gardner Press.

Elliot, M. K. (1997). Time, work, and meaning. Unpublished doctoral dissertation, Pacifica Graduate Institute.

Epel, E., Bandura, A., & Zimbardo, P. G. (1999). Escaping homelessness: The influences of self-efficacy and time perspective on coping with homelessness. *Journal of Applied Social Psychology, 29*, 575–596.

Foret, M. M., Steger, M. F., & Frazier, P. (2004). *Time perspective and well-being.* Poster presented at the 3rd International Positive Psychology Summit, Washington, DC.

Friedman, W. (1990). *About time.* Cambridge, MA: The MIT Press.

Golovakina, E. I., & Kronick, A. A. (1989). *Psihologichesloje vryemya lichnostyi (Psychological time of personality).* Kiev, Ukraine: Naukova Dumka.

Gorman, B. S., & Wessman, A. E. (1977). Images, values, and concepts of time in psychological research. In B. S. Gorman & A. E. Wessman (Eds.), *The personal experience of time* (pp. 217–263). New York: Plenum.

Heckel, R., & Rajagopal, J. (1975). Future time perspective in Indian and American college students. *Journal of Social Psychology, 95*, 131–132.

Hendricks, J., & Peters, C. B. (1986). The times of our lives: An integrative framework. *American Behavioral Scientist, 29*, 662–678.

Jones, J. M. (1994). An exploration of personality in human behaviour. In R. C. Schank & E. Langer (Eds.), *Beliefs, reasoning and decision making* (pp. 389–411). Hillsdale, NJ: Lawrence Erlbaum.

Kahana, E., & Kahana, B. (1983). Environmental continuity, futurity and adaptation of the aged. In G. D. Rowles & R. J. Ohta (Eds.), *Aging and milieu* (pp. 205–228). New York: Haworth Press.

Kazakina, E. (1999). Time perspective of older adults: Relationships to attachment style, psychological well-being and psychological distress. Unpublished doctoral dissertation, Columbia University.

Keough, K. A., Zimbardo, P. G., & Boyd, J. N. (1999). Who's smoking, drinking and using drugs? Time perspective as a predictor of substance use. *Basic and Applied Social Psychology, 21*, 149–164.

Lennings, C. J. (1996). Self-efficacy and temporal orientation as predictors of treatment outcome in severely dependent alcoholics. *Alcoholism Treatment Quarterly, 14*, 71–79.

Lennings, C. J. (1998). Profiles of time perspective and personality: Developmental considerations. *Journal of Psychology, 132*, 629–642.

Lennings, C. J. (2000a). The Stanford Time Perspective Inventory: An analysis of temporal orientation for research in health psychology. *Journal of Applied Health Behaviour, 2*, 40–45.

Lennings, C. J. (2000b). Optimism, satisfaction and time perspective in the elderly. *International Journal of Aging and Human Development, 51*(3), 168–181.

Lennings, C. J., & Gow, K. (1997). Time perspective, self-efficacy and academic achievement in nursing students. *Journal of Applied Social Behaviour, 4*, 37–51.

Levin, I., & Zakay, D. (Eds.). (1989). *Time and human cognition: A life-span perspective.* Amsterdam: North-Holland.

Levine, R. V., & Barlett, K. (1984). Pace of life, punctuality and coronary heart disease in six countries. *Journal of Cross-cultural Psychology, 28*, 129–137.

Levine, R., & Wolff, E. (1985). Social time: The heartbeat of culture. *Psychology Today, 19*(3), 29–35.

Lewin, K. (1948). *Resolving social problems.* New York: Harper.

Lyubomirsky, S., & Nolen-Hoeksema, S. (1995). Effects of self-focused rumination on negative thinking and interpersonal problem solving. *Journal of Personality and Social Psychology, 69*, 176–190.

McGrath, J. E. (1988). Time and social psychology. In J. E. McGrath (Ed.), *The social psychology of time: New perspectives* (pp. 134–148). Thousand Oaks, CA: Sage.

McGrath, J., & Kelly, J. (1986). *Time and human interaction: Towards a social psychology of time.* New York: Guildford.

Melges, F. T. (1982). *Time and the inner future.* New York: Wiley.

Melges, F. T. (1990). Identity and temporal perspective. In R. A. Block (Ed.), *Cognitive models of psychological time* (pp. 255–266). Hillsdale, NJ: Erlbaum.

Mello, Z. R., & Worrell, F. C. (2006). The relationship of time perspective to age, gender and academic achievement among academically talented adolescents. *Journal for the Education of the Gifted, 29,* 271–289.

Nuttin, J. (1985). *Future time perspective and motivation.* Hillsdale, NJ: Lawrence Erlbaum.

Rappaport, H., Enrich, K., & Wilson, A. (1985). Relation between ego identity and temporal perspective. *Journal of Personality and Social Psychology, 48,* 1609–1620.

Roos, P., & Albers, R. (1965). Performance of alcoholics and normals on a measure of temporal orientation. *Journal of Clinical Psychology, 21*(1), 34–36.

Rothspan, S., & Read, S. J. (1996). Present versus future time perspective and HIV risk among heterosexual college students. *Health Psychology, 15,* 131–134.

Ryan, R. M., & Deci, E. L. (2000). Self-determination theory and the facilitation of intrinsic motivation, and well-being. *American Psychologist, 55,* 68–78.

Seginer, R. (2003). Adolescent future orientation in culture and family settings. In W. Friedlmeier, P. Chakkarath, & B. Schwarz (Eds.), *Culture and human development: The importance of cross-cultural research to the social sciences.* Lisse, The Netherlands: Swets & Zietlinger.

Seijts, G. H. (1998). The importance of future time perspective in theories of work motivation. *Journal of Psychology, 132,* 154–169.

Shmotkin, D. (1991). The role of time orientation in life satisfaction across the life span. *Journal of Gerontology, 46,* 243–250.

Shostrom, E. L. (1964). An inventory for the measure of self-actualization. *Educational and Psychological Measurement, 24,* 207–218.

Snyder, C. R., Rand, K. L., & Ritschel, L. A. (2006). Hope over time. In L. J. Sanna & E. C. Chang (Eds.), *Judgments over time: The interplay of thoughts, feelings, and behaviors* (pp. 100–119). New York: Oxford University Press.

Strathman, A., Gleicher, F., Boninger, D., & Edwards, C. (1994). The consideration of future consequences: Weighting immediate and distant outcomes of behavior. *Journal of Personality and Social Psychology, 66,* 742–752.

Tismer, K. G. (1987). Psychological aspects of temporal dominance during adolescence. *Psychological Reports, 61,* 647–654.

Tov, W. (2004). *Time perspective and subjective well-being.* Poster presented at the 3rd International Positive Psychology Summit, Washington, DC.

Wessman, A. E., & Gorman, B. S. (1977). The emergence of human experience and concepts of time. In B. S. Gorman & A. E. Wessman (Eds.), *The personal experience of time* (pp. 4–55). New York: Plenum.

Wessman, A. E., & Ricks, D. F. (1966). *Mood and personality.* New York: Holt, Rinehart & Winston.

Wills, T. A., Sandy, J. M., & Yaeger, A. M. (2001). Time perspective and early-onset substance use: A model based on stress-coping theory. *Psychology of Addictive Behaviors, 15,* 118–125.

Zaleski, Z. (1996). Future anxiety: Concept measurement and preliminary research. *Personality and Individual Differences, 21,* 165–174.

Zaleski, Z., Cycon, A., & Kurc, A. (2001). Future time perspective and subjective well-being in adolescent samples. In P. Schmuck & K. M. Sheldon (Eds.), *Life goals and well-being: Towards a positive psychology of human striving* (pp. 58–67). Göttingen, Germany: Hogrefe & Huber.

Zimbardo, P. G. (1990). *Stanford Time Perspective Inventory manual.* Stanford, CA: Stanford University, Department of Psychology.

Zimbardo, P. G. (2002). Just think about it: Time to take our time. *Psychology Today, 35,* 62.

Zimbardo, P. G., & Boyd, J. N. (1999). Putting time in perspective: A valid, reliable individual-differences metric. *Journal of Personality and Social Psychology, 77,* 1271–1288.

Zimbardo, P. G., Keough, K. A., & Boyd, J. N. (1997). Present time perspective as a predictor of risky driving. *Personality and Individual Differences, 23,* 1007–1023.

Zuckerman, M. (1994). *Behavioral expressions and biological bases of sensation seeking.* New York: Cambridge University Press.

Optimism

Charles S. Carver, Michael F. Scheier, Christopher J. Miller, *and* Daniel Fulford

Abstract

Optimism is expecting good things to occur in one's life. Such positive expectations are associated with higher subjective well-being, even under conditions of stress or adversity. In contrast, pessimists respond to adversity with more intense negative feelings. There are also differences in the manner in which optimists and pessimists try to cope with adversity. Optimists tend to put the best face on the adversity, but they acknowledge its existence and its importance, and they try to do as much as possible to resolve whatever problems can be resolved. Pessimists are more likely to distance themselves from the problem and put off doing anything about it as long as possible. They are also more likely to give up trying, if things remain difficult. Some kinds of problem solution is proactive, engaged in before the problem arises. Optimists also tend to engage in such proactive efforts, including taking actions to minimize various kinds of health risks. Perhaps, as a consequence of these preventive steps, optimists also tend to have better health than pessimists. They seem to heal faster from wounds, and there is some evidence that when they are seriously ill they experience slower disease progression. It has been suggested that optimists sometimes are no better off than pessimists, and sometimes are worse off: that their confidence can get them into situations where it is difficult to cope effectively. Evidence of such negative effects of optimism does exist, but it is relatively sparse.

Keywords: confidence, coping, health, optimism, subjective well-being

Optimists are people who expect good things to happen; pessimists are people who expect bad things to happen. Folk wisdom has long held that this difference among people is important in many aspects of living. In this case, folk wisdom appears to be right. Optimists and pessimists differ in ways that have a big impact on their lives. They differ in how they approach problems, and they differ in the manner—and the success—with which they cope with adversity.

Scientific definitions of optimism and pessimism focus on expectations for the future, linking these ideas to a long line of expectancy-value models of motivation. Expectancy-value theories assume that behavior reflects the pursuit of goals: desired states or actions. People try to fit their behaviors to what they see as desirable. The more important is a goal to the person, the greater is its "value" (for more discussion

see Austin & Vancouver, 1996; Carver & Scheier, 1998). The second element is "expectancy"—confidence that the goal can be attained. If people doubt the goal can be reached, efforts toward it may sag even before the action starts. People confident about an eventual outcome will persevere even in the face of great adversity.

Optimism and pessimism are broad versions of confidence or doubt, pertaining to most situations in life rather than just one or two. Thus, optimists should tend to be confident and persistent in the face of challenge (even if progress is difficult or slow). Pessimists should be doubtful and hesitant in these same situations. Such differences in how people confront adversity have implications for ways people cope with stress (Scheier & Carver, 1992).

There are two ways to think about expectancies and how to measure them. One is to measure them directly, asking people whether they think their outcomes will be good or bad (Scheier & Carver, 1992). That is the approach taken here. It adds no more complexity to what we've said so far. Generalized expectancies—expectancies pertaining to the person's entire life space—are what we mean by "optimism" and "pessimism." It is measured by the Life Orientation Test-Revised, or LOT-R (Scheier, Carver, & Bridges, 1994—see Appendix). The LOT-R gives a continuous distribution of scores. Although we often refer to optimists and pessimists as though they were distinct groups, this is a verbal convenience. People actually range from very optimistic to very pessimistic, with most falling somewhere in between.

Another approach relies on the idea that people's expectancies for the future stem from their interpretations of the past (Peterson & Seligman, 1984, chap. 29). If past failures are interpreted as reflecting stable causes, expectancies will be pessimistic because the cause (relatively permanent) is likely to remain in force. If past failures are seen as reflecting unstable causes, the outlook for the future may be brighter because the cause may no longer be there. Some define optimism and pessimism in this way (Peterson & Seligman, 1984). This view differs from ours in important ways, but both share the theme that expectations for the future affect people's actions and experiences.

In this chapter, we describe some ways individual differences in optimism, measured as expectations for one's future, relate to variations in other important aspects of life. These aspects are grouped here in three sets: subjective well-being, coping responses, and physical well-being.

Optimism and Subjective Well-Being

One influence of optimism and pessimism is on how people feel when facing problems. When people face difficulty, the emotions they experience range from excitement and eagerness to anger, anxiety, and depression. The balance among feelings relates to variations in optimism. Optimists expect good outcomes, even when things are hard. This should yield a relatively positive mix of feelings. Pessimists expect bad outcomes. This should yield more negative feelings—anxiety, anger, sadness, or despair (Carver & Scheier, 1998; Scheier & Carver, 1992).

Relations between optimism and distress have been examined in people facing diverse difficulties. These include students entering college (Aspinwall & Taylor, 1992; Brissette, Scheier, & Carver, 2002); survivors of missile attacks (Zeidner & Hammer,

1992); people caring for cancer patients (Given et al., 1993) or Alzheimer's patients (Hooker, Monahan, Shifren, & Hutchinson, 1992; Shifren & Hooker, 1995); and people dealing with childbirth (Carver & Gaines, 1987), coronary artery bypass surgery (Fitzgerald, Tennen, Affleck, & Pransky, 1993; Scheier et al., 1989), aging (Giltay, Zitman, & Kromhout, 2006), failed attempts at in vitro fertilization (Litt, Tennen, Affleck, & Klock, 1992), bone marrow transplantation (Curbow, Somerfield, Baker, Wingard, & Legro, 1993), cancer (Carver et al., 1993; Friedman et al., 1992), and the progression of AIDS (Taylor et al., 1992).

These studies vary in complexity and thus what they can show. Researchers sometimes examine responses to an adverse event, but at only one time point. Such studies show that pessimists experience more distress afterward than optimists. What they can *not* show is whether pessimists had more distress even beforehand. Other studies assess people at multiple times. This gives a better picture of how distress shifts over circumstances. It also allows researchers to control for initial levels of distress. We focus here on this sort of study.

A very early study of optimism and emotional well-being (Carver & Gaines, 1987) examined the development of depressed feelings after childbirth. Women completed the LOT and a depression scale in the last third of their pregnancy. They completed the depression measure again 3 weeks after delivery. Optimism related to lower depression symptoms at initial assessment, and optimism predicted lower depression postpartum, controlling for the initial levels. Thus, optimism conferred resistance to postpartum depressive symptoms.

Several studies have examined people dealing with coronary artery bypass. One assessed people 1 month before surgery and 8 months afterward (Fitzgerald et al., 1993). Optimists had less presurgical distress, and (controlling for presurgical life satisfaction) optimists had more postsurgical life satisfaction. Analysis suggested that optimism about life funneled into a specific optimism about the surgery, and from there to satisfaction with life. A similar study by Scheier and colleagues (1989) found that optimists retained higher quality of life even up to 5 years after the surgery.

Optimism has also been studied in the context of other health crises. An example is treatment for breast cancer (Carver et al., 1993). Patients were interviewed at diagnosis, the day before surgery, a few days after surgery, and 3, 6, and 12 months later. Optimism (at initial assessment) predicted less distress over time, controlling for effects of medical variables and earlier distress. Thus, optimism predicted not just lower initial distress but also resilience against distress during the following year. A study of head and neck cancer patients yielded similar results (Allison, Guichard, & Gilain, 2000). Patients were assessed before treatment and 3 months afterward. Optimists reported higher quality of life before treatment and also posttreatment controlling for initial ratings.

Another medical context in which optimism has been studied is in vitro fertilization, a procedure that lets people overcome fertility problems. This study focused on people whose attempts at vitro fertilization were unsuccessful (Litt et al., 1992). Eight weeks beforehand, the researchers measured optimism, expectancies for fertilization success, distress, and the impact of infertility on participants' lives. Two weeks after notification of a negative pregnancy test, distress was measured again. None of the initial variables predicted follow-up distress (controlling for time-1 distress) except for pessimism.

Not only does optimism have a positive effect on the psychological well-being of people dealing with medical conditions, but it also influences well-being among caregivers. One project studied a group of cancer patients and their caregivers (Given et al., 1993). Caregivers' optimism predicted less depression and less impact of caregiving on their physical health. Similar results were found in research on caregiver spouses of Alzheimer's patients (Hooker et al., 1992; Shifren & Hooker, 1995): Optimism related to lower depression and greater well-being.

Other studies have looked at events that are difficult, but less extreme. For example, the start of college is a stressful time, and studies have examined students adjusting to their first semester of college (Aspinwall & Taylor, 1992; Brissette et al., 2002). Optimism and other variables were assessed when the students first arrived on campus. Measures of well-being were obtained at the end of the semester. Higher initial optimism predicted less distress at the end of the semester and greater development of friendship networks.

Optimism, Pessimism, and Coping

If optimists experience less distress than pessimists when dealing with difficulties, is it just because optimists are cheerful? Apparently not, because the differences often remain even when statistical controls are included for prior distress. There must be other explanations. In this section, we consider one of them: the coping strategies optimists and pessimists use. In many ways, this is just a more detailed depiction of the broad behavioral tendencies discussed at the outset. That is, people who are confident about the future continue trying, even when it's hard. People who are doubtful try to escape the adversity by wishful thinking, employ temporary distractions that don't help solve the problem, and sometimes even stop trying.

Such differences in coping have emerged in several studies. Early projects found that optimistic students reported both situational coping responses and general coping styles that differed from those of pessimists (Scheier, Carver, & Bridges, 2001). Optimism related to problem-focused coping, especially in controllable situations. Optimism also related to positive reframing and a tendency to accept the situation's reality. Optimism related to less denial and less of an attempt to distance oneself from the problem. Thus, optimists appear generally to be approach copers, and pessimists appear to be avoidant copers.

Other projects have studied coping strategies in specific contexts. Several studies described earlier also looked at coping. In their study of coronary artery bypass surgery, Scheier et al. (1989) assessed attentional-cognitive strategies as ways of dealing with the experience. Before surgery, optimists more than pessimists reported making plans for their future and setting goals for recovery. Optimists also focused less on negative aspects of the experience—distress and symptoms. Once surgery was past, optimists were more likely than pessimists to report seeking out information about what the physician would require of them in the months ahead. Optimists also were less likely to say they were suppressing thoughts about their symptoms. There was also evidence that the positive impact of optimism on quality of life 6 months later occurred through the indirect effect of these differences in coping.

The study of failed in vitro fertilization described earlier (Litt et al., 1992) also examined coping. Pessimism related to escape as a coping response. Escape, in turn, led to more distress after the fertilization failure. Optimists were also more likely than pessimists to report feeling they had benefited from the experience, for example, by becoming closer to their spouse.

Information on coping also comes from the study of AIDS patients described earlier (Taylor et al., 1992). Optimism predicted positive attitudes and tendencies to plan for recovery, seek information, and reframe bad situations more positively.

Optimists used less fatalism, self-blame, and escapism, and they didn't focus on negative aspects of the situation or try to suppress thoughts about their symptoms. Optimists also appeared to accept unchangeable situations rather than trying to escape them.

Relations between optimism and coping have also been the focus of studies of cancer patients. Stanton and Snider (1993) found that pessimistic women used more cognitive avoidance in coping with an upcoming biopsy than optimists. The avoidance appeared to mediate the relation of pessimism to prebiopsy distress. Cognitive avoidance prebiopsy also predicted postbiopsy distress among women with positive diagnoses.

Another study of cancer patients, mentioned earlier, examined how women coped with treatment for breast cancer during the first year (Carver et al., 1993). Both before and after surgery, optimism related to coping that involved accepting the reality of the situation, placing as positive a light on it as possible, and trying to relieve the situation with humor. Pessimism related to denial and giving-up tendencies at each time point. The coping responses related to optimism and pessimism also related to distress. Further analyses revealed that the effect of optimism on distress was largely indirect through coping, particularly postsurgery.

Another study also examined the role of coping in women treated for breast cancer (Schou, Ekeberg, & Ruland, 2005). Two coping strategies mediated the relationship between optimism and pessimism and quality of life 1 year after diagnosis. The greater fighting spirit of optimists (assessed before diagnosis) predicted better quality of life at the 1-year follow-up. Hopelessness/helplessness (reported by pessimists) predicted poorer quality of life.

In sum, it appears that optimists differ from pessimists both in stable coping tendencies and in the coping responses generated when confronting stressful situations (for detailed review see Solberg Nes & Segerstrom, 2006). In general, optimists use more problem-focused coping strategies than pessimists. When problem-focused coping is not a possibility, optimists turn to strategies such as acceptance, use of humor, and positive reframing. Pessimists tend to cope through overt denial and by mentally and behaviorally disengaging from the goals with which the stressor is interfering.

Particularly noteworthy is the contrast between acceptance and active denial. Denial (refusing to accept the reality of the situation) means trying to maintain a worldview that no longer is valid.

Acceptance implies restructuring one's experience to come to grips with the situation. This does not mean accepting and giving up. That reaction does not help. In fact, reacting to illness with resignation may actually hasten death (Greer, Morris, Pettingale, & Haybittle, 1990; Reed, Kemeny, Taylor, Wang, & Visscher, 1994). Acceptance of the diagnosis has very different consequences. By accepting that life is compromised (but not over), people develop adaptive parameters within which to live the time that's left. Acceptance may actually serve the purpose of keeping the person goal engaged, and indeed "life engaged" (Scheier & Carver, 2001).

Promoting Well-Being

Another coping difference concerns proactive coping, processes that promote good health and well-being rather than just reacting to adversity. Perhaps, optimists take active steps to ensure positive outcomes in their future. This would resemble problem-focused coping, except that no stressor yet exists.

There are many ways in which this might occur. One of them is seeking knowledge. One study investigated heart attack–related knowledge in a group of middle-aged adults. One might think that adults who are optimistic about their health might not make much effort to learn about risks related to heart attacks. Those high in dispositional optimism, however, actually knew more about the risk factors than those who were less optimistic (Radcliffe & Klein, 2002).

Proactive efforts in health promotion have also been examined among patients in a cardiac rehabilitation program (Shepperd, Maroto, & Pbert, 1996). Optimism related to success in lowering levels of saturated fat, body fat, and an index of overall coronary risk. Optimism also related to increases in exercise. Another study of the lifestyles of coronary artery bypass patients 5 years after surgery found optimists more likely than pessimists to be taking vitamins, eating low-fat foods, and to be enrolled in a cardiac rehabilitation program (Scheier & Carver, 1992).

Another proactive health-related behavior concerns HIV risk. By avoiding certain sexual practices (e.g., sex with unknown partners), people reduce risk of infection. One study of HIV-negative gay men found that optimists reported fewer anonymous sexual partners than pessimists (Taylor et al., 1992). This suggests that optimists were making efforts to reduce their risk, safeguarding their health.

Optimists appear to take action to minimize health risks. They do not simply stick their heads in the sand and ignore threats to well-being. They attend to risks, but do so selectively. They focus on risks that are applicable to them and relate to potentially serious health problems (Aspinwall & Brunhart, 1996). If the potential health problem is minor, or if it is unlikely to bear on them, their vigilance is not elevated. Optimists appear to scan their surroundings for threats to well-being but save their behavioral responses for threats that are truly meaningful.

Pessimism and Health-Defeating Behaviors

We characterized optimists throughout this discussion as persistent in trying to reach goals. Theory suggests that pessimists are less persistent and more likely to give up. There is, in fact, evidence of giving-up tendencies among pessimists, with bad consequences. For example, giving up may underlie various forms of substance abuse, such as excessive alcohol use, which is often seen as an escape from problems. This suggests that pessimists should be more vulnerable than optimists to such maladaptive behavior. Evidence supports this reasoning.

One study of women with a family history of alcoholism found that pessimists in that group were more likely than optimists to report drinking problems (Ohannessian, Hesselbrock, Tennen, & Affleck, 1993). In another study, people who had been treated for alcohol abuse were followed as they entered an aftercare program. Pessimists were more likely to drop out of that program and to return to drinking than optimists (Strack, Carver, & Blaney, 1987). Yet another study (Park, Moore, Turner, & Adler, 1997) found that optimistic pregnant women were less likely to engage in substance abuse during the course of their pregnancies.

A more recent study examined a different indicator of giving up: the disruption of normal social activities. Breast cancer patients reported illness-related disruption of social activities after treatment (Carver, Lehman, & Antoni, 2003). At each assessment, pessimism predicted more disruption, along with emotional distress and fatigue. When confronted with a health threat, pessimism led to a withdrawal from the very social activities that are important to a normal life.

Giving up can be reflected in many ways. Alcohol dulls awareness of failures and problems. People can ignore problems by distracting themselves with other activities. Sometimes, though, giving up is more complete. Sometimes people give up not just on specific goals, but on their lives, by suicide. Some are more vulnerable to suicide than others. It is commonly assumed that depression is the best indicator of suicide risk. But pessimism is actually a stronger predictor of this act, the ultimate disengagement from life (Beck, Steer, Kovacs, & Garrison, 1985).

In sum, a sizable body of evidence indicates that pessimism can lead people into self-defeating patterns. The result can be less persistence, more avoidance coping, health-damaging behavior, and potentially even an impulse to escape from life altogether. Without confidence about the future, there may be nothing to sustain life.

Optimism and Physical Well-Being

There is also some research linking optimism to physical well-being. In one such study, middle-aged women were tested for carotid intima thickness—an index of atherosclerosis in the carotid artery—at a baseline and a 3-year follow-up (Matthews, Raikkonen, Sutton-Tyrrell, & Kuller, 2004). Pessimism at the initial assessment predicted increases in intima thickness at follow-up. Optimists experienced almost no increase over the 3-year period.

In another project, Scheier and colleagues (1999) examined patterns of rehospitalization after coronary artery bypass surgery. The need for rehospitalization is very common in this population, but optimism significantly predicted lower likelihood of that occurring and a longer time before it occurred. Ironson and colleagues (2005) tested prospective links between optimism, coping, and disease progression among persons with HIV. Optimists displayed more proactive coping, less avoidant coping, and less disease progression.

Individual differences in healing and immunity have also been examined. In one study, men receiving a biopsy were followed throughout the healing process (Ebrecht et al., 2004). The sample was split into "slow healing" and "fast healing" groups. Slow healers had significantly lower optimism than the fast healers. In another study, older adults received an influenza vaccine, and optimism predicted a significantly better immune response 2 weeks later (Kohut, Cooper, Nickolaus, Russell, & Cunnick, 2002; for broader review of optimism and immunity, see Szondy, 2004). Other research has found, however, that optimism related to lower immune response under very high challenge (Segerstrom, 2006).

Research to date suggests that optimism and pessimism are psychological constructs that are relevant to biological outcomes, though the evidence on these outcomes is less consistent than for self-reports of health (Rasmussen, Scheier, & Greenhouse, 2009). One study even found that optimism predicts longer life—among 900 elderly Dutch persons, those reporting a high level of optimism at baseline were less likely to die over the next 10 years (Giltay, Geleijnse, Zitman, Hoekstra, & Schouten, 2004). Relations between optimism and physical well-being surely deserve further study.

Is Optimism Always Better than Pessimism?

Consistently throughout this chapter, we have portrayed optimists as better off than pessimists. They are less distressed when times are tough, they cope in ways that foster better outcomes, and they're better at taking the steps necessary to ensure that their futures continue to be bright. Although there are situations in which optimists are only slightly better off than pessimists and probably some where they have no advantage, there is remarkably little evidence that optimists are ever worse off than pessimists.

Several theorists have suggested that such situations do exist (e.g., Schwarzer, 1994; Tennen & Affleck, 1987), that optimism may be potentially damaging. The logic is this: Too much optimism might lead people to ignore a threat until it's too late, or might lead people to overestimate their ability to deal with it, resulting in poorer outcomes.

This appears to be generally not the case. However, occasional studies do suggest adverse effects of optimism. As noted earlier, there is some evidence that optimism predicts poorer immune response under relative high challenge (Segerstrom, 2006). One study also found that when an accumulation of life stress over a year's time becomes high, the buffering effect of optimism reverses (Chang & Sanna, 2003).

In another kind of project, Goodman, Chesney, and Tipton (1995) studied whether adolescent girls at risk for HIV infection sought information about HIV testing and agreed to have a test. Those higher in optimism were less likely to get the information and less likely to follow through with a test (see also Perkins, Leserman, Murphy, & Evans, 1993). However, several aspects of this study cast uncertainty on the findings. For one, this sample was unusually low in optimism. For another, no data were gathered on important variables such as whether the girls knew their partners' serostatus.

Possibly, the more optimistic girls had already established that their partners were HIV-negative. Nonetheless, this finding (along with the others noted) urges caution in drawing conclusions about universal benefits of optimism.

Does optimism foster a worldview that is fragile and easily shattered by trauma? Will optimists be less able to rebuild the shattered assumptions of their lives after experiencing a violent rape or having their home destroyed by fire or flood? Although such outcomes are possible, we know of no evidence that they occur. We instead expect optimists to accept their changed realities, reset their sights on the future, and continue to make the best of what they are facing. Pessimists may find their worldview confirmed by trauma or disaster, but we doubt they will take much satisfaction in that. Rather, they will continue to anticipate yet further adversity.

Cultural Issues

Much of what is known about optimism comes from studies of Westerners: mostly North Americans, predominantly of European descent. An important question is whether the knowledge from these studies generalizes to other groups. The information on that question is quite limited, but so far there have been both differences and similarities (Chang, 2002). One difference is that Asians seem to distinguish more sharply than European Americans between affirmation of an optimistic view and rejection of a pessimistic view. Overall mean differences in optimism have not stood out, but there have been some differences in patterns, the meaning of which is not entirely clear. In one study, an Asian American sample endorsed pessimism more than a European American sample; in another study, South Koreans endorsed pessimism less than European Americans (Chang, Sanna, & Yang, 2003). Thus far, the evidence suggests that optimism and pessimism relate to quality of life outcomes in the same general way across cultures (Chang, 2002). This area of inquiry will doubtlessly become more important over time.

Can Pessimists Become Optimists?

Given the many ways in which optimists' lives are better than those of pessimists, many ask if optimism can be acquired. Yes, change is possible, but there remain questions about how large a change can be expected and how permanent it will be. There also remain questions about whether an induced optimistic view acts in the same way—has the same beneficial effects—as a naturally occurring optimistic view.

The most straightforward way to turn a pessimist into an optimist is by techniques known collectively as cognitive-behavioral therapies. The logic behind these techniques is that people with problems make negative distortions in their minds. The negative thoughts cause negative affect and induce people to stop trying to reach their goals. Such distortions resemble what we would imagine as the interior monolog of the pessimist. The therapies aim to make the cognitions more positive, thereby reducing distress and fostering renewed effort.

It is important to recognize, though, that it can be unwise to substitute an unquestioning optimism for an existing doubt. Sometimes people are pessimistic because they have overly high aspirations. They demand perfection from themselves, hardly ever see it, and develop doubts about their adequacy. What they need is realistic goals, and practice setting alternative goals to replace what cannot be attained (Carver & Scheier, 2003; Wrosch, Scheier, Carver, & Schulz, 2003).

Concluding Comment

A growing literature confirms that people who dispositionally hold positive expectations for the future respond to difficulty or adversity in more adaptive ways than people who hold negative expectations. Expectancies influence how people approach these situations, and they influence the success with which people deal with them. Many questions remain unanswered. But we ourselves are optimistic about the future of work in this area, optimistic that research will continue to reveal the paths by which positive thinking can work to people's benefit.

Questions for the Future

1. How does optimism promote such health-related benefits as faster wound healing?
2. Is "acquired optimism" as beneficial as being born optimistic?
3. Does optimism have similar effects in cultures very different from American culture?

Acknowledgments

Preparation of this chapter was facilitated by support from the National Cancer Institute (CA64710, CA78995, and CA84944), the National Science Foundation (BCS0544617), and the National Heart, Lung, and Blood Institute (HL65111, HL65112, HL076852, and HL076858).

References

Allison, P. J., Guichard, C., & Gilain, L. (2000). A prospective investigation of dispositional optimism as a predictor of health-related quality of life in head and neck cancer patients. *Quality of Life Research, 9*, 951–960.

Aspinwall, L. G., & Brunhart, S. N. (1996). Distinguishing optimism from denial: Optimistic beliefs predict attention to health threats. *Personality and Social Psychology Bulletin, 22*, 993–1003.

Aspinwall, L. G., & Taylor, S. E. (1992). Modeling cognitive adaptation: A longitudinal investigation of the impact of individual differences and coping on college adjustment and performance. *Journal of Personality and Social Psychology, 61*, 755–765.

Austin, J. T., & Vancouver, J. B. (1996). Goal constructs in psychology: Structure, process, and content. *Psychological Bulletin, 120*, 338–375.

Beck, A. T., Steer, R. A., Kovacs, M., & Garrison, B. (1985). Hopelessness and eventual suicide: A 10-year prospective study of patients hospitalized with suicidal ideation. *American Journal of Psychiatry, 142*, 559–563.

Brissette, I., Scheier, M. F., & Carver, C. S. (2002). The role of optimism in social network development, coping, and psychological adjustment during a life transition. *Journal of Personality and Social Psychology, 82*, 102–111.

Carver, C. S., & Gaines, J. G. (1987). Optimism, pessimism, and postpartum depression. *Cognitive Therapy and Research, 11*, 449–462.

Carver, C. S., Lehman, J. M., & Antoni, M. H. (2003). Dispositional pessimism predicts illness-related disruption of social and recreational activities among breast cancer patients. *Journal of Personality and Social Psychology, 84*, 813–821.

Carver, C. S., Pozo, C., Harris, S. D., Noriega, V., Scheier, M. F., Robinson, D. S., et al. (1993). How coping mediates the effect of optimism on distress: A study of women with early stage breast cancer. *Journal of Personality and Social Psychology, 65*, 375–390.

Carver, C. S., & Scheier, M. F. (1998). *On the self-regulation of behavior*. New York: Cambridge University Press.

Carver, C. S., & Scheier, M. F. (2003). Three human strengths. In L. G. Aspinwall & U. M. Staudinger (Eds.), *A psychology of human strengths: Fundamental questions and future directions for a positive psychology* (pp. 87–102). Washington, DC: American Psychological Association.

Chang, E. C. (2002). Cultural influences on optimism and pessimism: Differences in Western and Eastern construals of the self. In E. C. Chang (Ed.), *Optimism and pessimism: Implications for theory, research, and practice* (pp. 257–280). Washington, DC: American Psychological Association.

Chang, E. C., & Sanna, L. J. (2003). Optimism, accumulated life stress, and psychological and physical adjustment: Is it always adaptive to expect the best? *Journal of Social and Clinical Psychology, 22*, 97–115.

Chang, E. C., Sanna, L. J., & Yang, K.-M. (2003). Optimism, pessimism, affectivity, and psychological adjustment in US and Korea: A test of a mediation model. *Personality and Individual Differences, 34*, 1195–1208.

Curbow, B., Somerfield, M. R., Baker, F., Wingard, J. R., & Legro, M. W. (1993). Personal changes, dispositional optimism, and psychological adjustment to bone marrow transplantation. *Journal of Behavioral Medicine, 16*, 423–443.

Ebrecht, M., Hextall, J., Kirtley, L.-G., Taylor, A. M., Dyson, M., & Weinman, J. (2004). Perceived stress and cortisol levels predict speed of wound healing in healthy male adults. *Psychoneuroendocrinology, 29*, 798–809.

Fitzgerald, T. E., Tennen, H., Affleck, G., & Pransky, G. S. (1993). The relative importance of dispositional optimism and control appraisals in quality of life after coronary artery bypass surgery. *Journal of Behavioral Medicine, 16*, 25–43.

Friedman, L. C., Nelson, D. V., Baer, P. E., Lane, M., Smith, F. E., & Dworkin, R. J. (1992). The relationship of dispositional optimism, daily life stress, and domestic environment to coping methods used by cancer patients. *Journal of Behavioral Medicine, 15*, 127–141.

Giltay, E. J., Geleijnse, J. M., Zitman, F. G., Hoekstra, T., & Schouten, E. G. (2004). Dispositional optimism and all-cause and cardiovascular mortality in a prospective cohort of elderly Dutch men and women. *Archives of General Psychiatry, 61*, 1126–1135.

Giltay, E. J., Zitman, F. G., & Kromhout, D. (2006). Dispositional optimism and the risk of depressive symptoms during 15 years of follow-up: The Zutphen Elderly Study. *Journal of Affective Disorders, 91*, 45–52.

Given, C. W., Stommel, M., Given, B., Osuch, J., Kurtz, M. E., & Kurtz, J. C. (1993). The influence of cancer patients' symptoms and functional states on patients' depression and family caregivers' reaction and depression. *Health Psychology, 12*, 277–285.

Goodman, E., Chesney, M. A., & Tipton, A. C. (1995). Relationship of optimism, knowledge, attitudes, and beliefs to use of HIV antibody test by at-risk female adolescents. *Psychosomatic Medicine, 57*, 541–546.

Greer, S., Morris, T., Pettingale, K. W., & Haybittle, J. L. (1990). Psychological response to breast cancer and 15-year outcome. *Lancet, i*, 49–50.

Hooker, K., Monahan, D., Shifren, K., & Hutchinson, C. (1992). Mental and physical health of spouse caregivers: The role of personality. *Psychology and Aging, 7*, 367–375.

Ironson, G., Balbin, E., Stuetzle, R., Fletcher, M. A., O'Cleirigh, C., Laurenceau, J.-P., et al. (2005). Dispositional optimism and the mechanisms by which it predicts slower disease progression in HIV: Proactive behavior, avoidant coping, and depression. *International Journal of Behavioral Medicine, 12*, 86–97.

Kohut, M. L., Cooper, M. M., Nickolaus, M. S., Russell, D. R., & Cunnick, J. E. (2002). Exercise and psychosocial factors modulate immunity to influenza vaccine in elderly individuals. *Journals of Gerontology: Series A. Biological Sciences and Medical Sciences, 57*, 557–562.

Litt, M. D., Tennen, H., Affleck, G., & Klock, S. (1992). Coping and cognitive factors in adaptation to in vitro fertilization failure. *Journal of Behavioral Medicine, 15*, 171–187.

Matthews, K. A., Raikkonen, K., Sutton-Tyrrell, K., & Kuller, L. H. (2004). Optimistic attitudes protect against progression of carotid atherosclerosis in healthy middle-aged women. *Psychosomatic Medicine, 66*, 640–644.

Ohannessian, C. M., Hesselbrock, V. M., Tennen, H., & Affleck, G. (1993). Hassles and uplifts and generalized outcome expectancies as moderators on the relation between a family history of alcoholism and drinking behaviors. *Journal of Studies on Alcohol, 55*, 754–763.

Park, C. L., Moore, P. J., Turner, R. A., & Adler, N. E. (1997). The roles of constructive thinking and optimism in psychological and behavioral adjustment during pregnancy. *Journal of Personality and Social Psychology, 73*, 584–592.

Perkins, D. O., Leserman, J., Murphy, C., & Evans, D. L. (1993). Psychosocial predictors of high-risk sexual behavior among HIV-negative gay men. *AIDS Education and Prevention, 5*, 141–152.

Peterson, C., & Seligman, M. E. P. (1984). Causal explanations as a risk factor for depression: Theory and evidence. *Psychological Review, 91*, 347–374.

Radcliffe, N. M., & Klein, W. M. P. (2002). Dispositional, unrealistic, and comparative optimism: Differential relations with the knowledge and processing of risk information and beliefs about personal risk. *Personality and Social Psychology Bulletin, 28*, 836–846.

Rasmussen, H. N., Scheier, M. F., & Greenhouse, J. B. (2009). Optimism and physical health: A meta-analytic review. Manuscript under review.

Reed, G. M., Kemeny, M. E., Taylor, S. E., Wang, H.-Y., & Visscher, B. R. (1994). "Realistic acceptance" as a predictor of decreased survival time in gay men with AIDS. *Health Psychology, 13*, 299–307.

Scheier, M. F., & Carver, C. S. (1992). Effects of optimism on psychological and physical well-being: Theoretical overview and empirical update. *Cognitive Therapy and Research, 16*, 201–228.

Scheier, M. F., & Carver, C. S. (2001). Adapting to cancer: The importance of hope and purpose. In A. Baum & B. L. Andersen (Eds.), *Psychosocial interventions for cancer* (pp. 15–36). Washington, DC: American Psychological Association.

Scheier, M. F., Carver, C. S., & Bridges, M. W. (1994). Distinguishing optimism from neuroticism (and trait anxiety, self-mastery, and self-esteem): A reevaluation of the Life Orientation Test. *Journal of Personality and Social Psychology, 67*, 1063–1078.

Scheier, M. F., Carver, C. S., & Bridges, M. W. (2001). Optimism, pessimism, and psychological well-being. In E. C. Chang (Ed.), *Optimism and pessimism: Implications for theory, research, and practice* (pp. 189–216). Washington, DC: American Psychological Association.

Scheier, M. F., Matthews, K. A., Owens, J. F., Magovern, G. J., Lefebvre, R. C., Abbott, R. A., et al. (1989). Dispositional optimism and recovery from coronary artery bypass surgery: The beneficial effects on physical and psychological well-being. *Journal of Personality and Social Psychology, 57*, 1024–1040.

Scheier, M. F., Matthews, K. A., Owens, J. F., Schulz, R., Bridges, M. W., Magovern, G. J., Sr., et al. (1999). Optimism and rehospitalization following coronary artery bypass graft surgery. *Archives of Internal Medicine, 159*, 829–835.

Schou, I., Ekeberg, O., & Ruland, C. M. (2005). The mediating role of appraisal and coping in the relationship between optimism–pessimism and quality of life. *Psycho-oncology, 14*, 718–727.

Schwarzer, R. (1994). Optimism, vulnerability, and self-beliefs as health-related cognitions: A systematic overview. *Psychology and Health, 9*, 161–180.

Segerstrom, S. C. (2006). How does optimism suppress immunity? Evaluation of three affective pathways. *Health Psychology, 25*, 653–657.

Shepperd, J. A., Maroto, J. J., & Pbert, L. A. (1996). Dispositional optimism as a predictor of health changes among cardiac patients. *Journal of Research in Personality, 30*, 517–534.

Shifren, K., & Hooker, K. (1995). Stability and change in optimism: A study among spouse caregivers. *Experimental Aging Research, 21*, 59–76.

Solberg Nes, L., & Segerstrom, S. C. (2006). Dispositional optimism and coping: A meta-analytic review. *Personality and Social Psychology Review, 10*, 235–251.

Stanton, A. L., & Snider, P. R. (1993). Coping with breast cancer diagnosis: A prospective study. *Health Psychology, 12*, 16–23.

Strack, S., Carver, C. S., & Blaney, P. H. (1987). Predicting successful completion of an aftercare program following treatment for alcoholism: The role of dispositional optimism. *Journal of Personality and Social Psychology, 53,* 579–584.

Szondy, M. (2004). Optimism and immune functions. *Mentalhigiene es Pszichoszomatika, 5,* 301–320.

Taylor, S. E., Kemeny, M. E., Aspinwall, L. G., Schneider, S. G., Rodriguez, R., & Herbert, M. (1992). Optimism, coping, psychological distress, and high-risk sexual behavior among men at risk for acquired immunodeficiency syndrome (AIDS). *Journal of Personality and Social Psychology, 63,* 460–473.

Tennen, H., & Affleck, G. (1987). The costs and benefits of optimistic explanations and dispositional optimism. *Journal of Personality, 55,* 377–393.

Wrosch, C., Scheier, M. F., Carver, C. S., & Schulz, R. (2003). The importance of goal disengagement in adaptive self-regulation: When giving up is beneficial. *Self and Identity, 2,* 1–20.

Zeidner, M., & Hammer, A. L. (1992). Coping with missile attack: Resources, strategies, and outcomes. *Journal of Personality, 60,* 709–746.

Appendix: Items of the Life Orientation Test-Revised (LOT-R), a measure of optimism versus pessimism

1. In uncertain times, I usually expect the best.
2. It's easy for me to relax. (Filler)
3. If something can go wrong for me, it will.[a]
4. I'm always optimistic about my future.
5. I enjoy my friends a lot. (Filler)
6. It's important for me to keep busy. (Filler)
7. I hardly ever expect things to go my way.[a]
8. I don't get upset too easily. (Filler)
9. I rarely count on good things happening to me.[a]
10. Overall, I expect more good things to happen to me than bad.

Note: Respondents indicate the extent of their agreement with each item using a 5-point scale ranging from "strongly disagree" (0) to "strongly agree" (4). After reverse-coding the negatively worded items (those identified with the superscript "a"), the six non-filler items are summed to produce an overall score. A hypothetical "neutral" response to all items would yield a score of 12; typically, however, the distribution is skewed somewhat toward the optimistic. Examples of average scores from two large samples (from Scheier et al., 1994) are 14.33 among college students and 15.16 among coronary bypass patients. Although there are no cutoff points that define people as optimists or as pessimists, it will be apparent that a score of 18 or higher is rather optimistic, whereas a score of 11 or 12 is not. Scores below 10 are rather pessimistic. From Scheier, M. F., Carver, C. S., & Bridges, M. W. (1994). Distinguishing optimism from neuroticism (and trait anxiety, self-mastery, and self-esteem): A reevaluation of the Life Orientation Test. *Journal of Personality and Social Psychology, 67,* 1063–1078. Reproduced with the permission of the authors and the American Psychological Association.

Optimistic Explanatory Style

Christopher Peterson *and* Tracy A. Steen

Abstract

So-called optimism has long given thoughtful people pause because of connotations of naiveté and denial, but optimism has become a more respectable stance, even among the sophisticated. Research has linked optimism to positive mood and good morale, to perseverance and effective problem solving, to achievement in a variety of domains, to popularity, to good health, and even to long life and freedom from trauma. In this chapter, we review what is known about one cognate of optimism—explanatory style, how people habitually explain the causes of events that occur to them. We trace the history of explanatory style research, which originated in studies of learned helplessness and depression as a way to make sense of the range of reactions in the wake of uncontrollable bad events. We focus on the neglected question of the origins of explanatory style, which seem to be multiple. We conclude by addressing issues that need to be considered by positive psychologists doing research on explanatory style. Research still focuses too much on negative outcomes, ignoring the premise of positive psychology that what makes life most worth living needs to be examined in its own right, not simply as the absence of problems.

Keywords: attributional reformulation, explanatory style, learned helplessness, optimism, pessimism

Optimism has a checkered reputation. Consider Dr. Pangloss, who blathered that this is the best of all possible worlds, or Pollyanna, who celebrated misfortunes befalling her and others. And how about contemporary politicians who spin embarrassing news into something wonderful? So-called optimism has long given thoughtful people pause because of connotations of naiveté and denial, but optimism has become a more respectable stance, even among the sophisticated. Research has linked optimism to positive mood and good morale, to perseverance and effective problem solving, to achievement in a variety of domains, to popularity, to good health, and even to long life and freedom from trauma (Peterson, 2000; Peterson & Bossio, 1991; Peterson & Park, 2007; Peterson & Steen, 2002; Seligman, 1990).

Our purpose in this chapter is to review what is known about one cognate of optimism—"explanatory style," how people habitually explain the causes of events that occur to them. We discuss studies on

explanatory style, focusing on the neglected question: "What are the origins of explanatory style?" We conclude by addressing issues that need to be considered by positive psychologists doing research on explanatory style (Peterson, 2000).

History: From Learned Helplessness to Explanatory Style

Learned helplessness was first described by psychologists studying animal learning (Peterson, Maier, & Seligman, 1993). Researchers immobilized a dog and exposed it to electric shocks that could be neither avoided nor escaped. Twenty-four hours later, the dog was placed in a situation in which shock could be terminated by a simple response. The dog did not make this response, however, and just sat, passively enduring the shock. This behavior was in marked contrast to dogs in a control group who reacted vigorously to the shock and learned readily how to turn it off.

The dog had learned to be helpless: When originally exposed to uncontrollable shock, it learned that nothing it did mattered. The shocks came and went independently of the dog's behaviors. Response-outcome independence was represented as an expectation of future helplessness then generalized to new situations to produce motivational, cognitive, and emotional deficits. The deficits that follow in the wake of uncontrollability have come to be known as the "learned helplessness phenomenon," and the associated cognitive explanation as the "learned helplessness model."

Human Helplessness

Psychologists interested in human problems were quick to see the parallels between learned helplessness as produced by uncontrollable events in the laboratory and maladaptive passivity as it exists in the real world. Thus, researchers began several lines of research on learned helplessness in people (Peterson et al., 1993).

In one line of work, helplessness in people was produced in the laboratory much as it was in animals, by exposing them to uncontrollable events and observing the effects. Unsolvable problems usually were substituted for uncontrollable electric shocks, but the critical aspects of the phenomenon remained: Following uncontrollability, people show a variety of deficits. In other studies, researchers documented further similarities between the animal phenomenon and what was produced in the human laboratory. Uncontrollable bad events made anxiety and depression more likely. Previous exposure to controllable events immunized people against learned helplessness. Similarly, forcible exposure to contingencies reversed helplessness deficits.

Several aspects of human helplessness differ from animal helplessness. First, uncontrollable bad events are more likely than uncontrollable good events to produce helplessness among human beings, probably because people are able to devise coherent (if not veridical) accounts for why good things happen to them. Thus, the intriguing phenomenon of "appetitive helplessness" among animals may have no reliable counterpart among people because they can readily create contingency interpretations.

More generally, people differ from animals in our sophistication of meaning making. As captured by the learned helplessness model, animals, of course, can learn that they do or do not have control over events. But people do much more, construing events in ways beyond their literal controllability. Rothbaum, Weisz, and Snyder (1982) suggested

that there are circumstances in which passivity, withdrawal, and submissiveness among people are not prima facie evidence of diminished personal control. Rather, these reactions may represent alternative forms of control achieved by aligning oneself with powerful external forces. For example, religion provides a worldview that can blunt the effects of not being able to control events.

A second asymmetry is "vicarious helplessness." Problem-solving difficulties can be produced in people if they simply see someone else confront uncontrollability (Brown & Inouye, 1978). Vicarious helplessness extends the potential ways in which helpless behavior can be produced in the natural world. The parameters of this phenomenon have not been investigated, and questions arise whether we can immunize people against vicarious helplessness or undo its effects via therapy.

A third difference is that small groups of people can be made helpless by exposure to uncontrollable events. So, when a group works at an unsolvable problem, it later shows group problem-solving deficits relative to another group with no previous exposure to uncontrollability (Simkin, Lederer, & Seligman, 1983). Group-level helplessness is not simply a function of individual helplessness produced among group members: When working alone, individual members of helpless groups show no deficits. Perhaps, these results can be generalized to larger groups, including complex organizations or even entire cultures. Again, the real-life implications of this phenomenon are intriguing, and future research seems indicated.

In another line of work, researchers proposed various failures of adaptation as analogous to learned helplessness and investigated the similarity between these failures and learned helplessness (Peterson et al., 1993). There are three criteria with which to judge the goodness of an application:

1. *Objective noncontingency.* The applied researcher must take into account the contingencies between a person's actions and the outcomes that he or she experiences. Learned helplessness is present only when there is no contingency between actions and outcomes. In other words, learned helplessness must be distinguished from extinction (where active responses once leading to reinforcement no longer do so) and from learned passivity (where active responses are contingently punished and/or passive responses are contingently reinforced).

2. *Cognitive mediation.* Learned helplessness also involves a characteristic way of perceiving,

explaining, and extrapolating contingencies. The helplessness model specifies cognitive processes that make helplessness more-versus-less likely following uncontrollable events (Peterson & Park, 2007). If measures of these processes are not sensibly related to ensuing passivity, then learned helplessness is not present.

3. *Cross-situational generality of passive behavior.* Finally, learned helplessness is shown by passivity in a situation "different" from the one in which uncontrollability was first encountered. Does the individual give up and fail to initiate actions that might allow him or her to control this situation? It is impossible to argue that learned helplessness is present without the demonstration of passivity in new situations. Other consequences may also accompany the behavioral deficits that define the learned helplessness phenomenon: cognitive retardation, low self-esteem, sadness, reduced aggression, immunosuppression, and physical illness.

In terms of these criteria, the best-fitting applications include depression; academic, athletic, and vocational failure; worker burnout; deleterious effects of crowding, unemployment, noise pollution, chronic pain, aging, mental retardation, and epilepsy; and passivity among ethnic minorities (Table 7-1, Peterson et al., 1993). Other popular applications are unproven or simply wrong, usually because the particular examples of passivity are better viewed as instrumental.

For example, victims of child abuse or domestic violence have been characterized as having "learned" to be helpless. A better argument is that they have learned to hold still. Such passivity is problematic when generalized, but the underlying process is not the one described by the learned helplessness model. The practical importance of distinguishing passivity due to learned helplessness from other types of passivity is that interventions to prevent or undo passive behavior need to be informed by the mechanisms at work.

As research ensued, it became clear that the original learned helplessness explanation was too simple, failing to account for the range of reactions that people display to uncontrollable events. Some people show the hypothesized deficits across time and situation, whereas others do not. Furthermore, failures of adaptation that the learned helplessness model presumably explains, such as depression, are often characterized by loss of self-esteem, about which the model is silent.

Attributional Reformulation and Explanatory Style

In an attempt to resolve these discrepancies, Abramson, Seligman, and Teasdale (1978) reformulated the helplessness model as applied to people by melding it with attribution theory. Abramson et al. explained the contrary findings by proposing that people ask themselves why uncontrollable (bad) events happen. The person's answer then sets parameters for subsequent helplessness. If the causal attribution is stable ("it's going to last forever"), then induced helplessness is long-lasting; if unstable, then it is transient. If the causal attribution is global ("it's going to undermine everything"), then subsequent helplessness is manifest across a variety of situations; if specific, helplessness is circumscribed. If the causal attribution is internal ("it's all my fault"), the person's self-esteem drops following uncontrollability; if external, self-esteem is left intact.

These hypotheses comprise the "attributional reformulation" of helplessness theory. This new theory left the original model in place, because uncontrollable events were still hypothesized to produce deficits when they gave rise to an expectation of response-outcome independence. The nature of these deficits was now said to be influenced by the causal attribution offered by the individual.

In some cases, the situation itself provides the explanation made by the person, and the extensive social psychology literature on causal attributions documents many influences on the process. In other cases, the person relies on his or her habitual way of making sense of events that occur, what is called one's "explanatory style" (Peterson & Seligman, 1984). People tend to offer similar explanations for disparate bad (or good) events. Explanatory style is therefore a distal, although important, influence on helplessness and the failures of adaptation that involve helplessness. An explanatory style characterized by internal, stable, and global explanations for bad events has been described as "pessimistic," and the opposite style—external, unstable, and specific explanations for bad events—has been described as "optimistic" (Buchanan & Seligman, 1995).

According to the attributional reformulation, explanatory style does not cause problems but rather is a dispositional risk factor. Given uncontrollable events and the lack of a clear situational demand on the proffered attribution for uncontrollability, explanatory style influences how the person responds. Helplessness will be long-lasting or transient, widespread or situational, damaging to self-esteem or not, in accordance with the individual's explanatory style.

In both the original and reformulated versions of the helplessness model, generalized expectations of response-outcome independence are the proximal cause of helplessness. Research in this tradition, however, has rarely looked at this mediating variable. Researchers instead measure explanatory style and correlate it with helplessness-related outcomes such as depression, illness, and failure. Invariably, those with an optimistic explanatory style fare better than those with a pessimistic explanatory style.

As explanatory style research has progressed and theory has been modified, the internality dimension has become of less interest (Abramson, Metalsky, & Alloy, 1989). It has more inconsistent correlates than stability or globality, it is less reliably assessed, and there are theoretical grounds for doubting its direct impact on expectations per se (Peterson, 1991). Internality may well conflate self-blame and self-efficacy, which explains why it fares poorly in empirical research.

Measures of Explanatory Style

Explanatory style typically is measured with a self-report questionnaire called the Attributional Style Questionnaire (ASQ; Peterson et al., 1982). In the ASQ, respondents are presented with hypothetical events involving themselves, and then asked to provide "the one major cause" of each event if it were to happen. Respondents then rate these provided causes along dimensions of internality, stability, and globality. Ratings are combined, keeping separate those for bad events and those for good events. Explanatory style based on bad events usually has more robust correlates than explanatory style based on good events, although correlations are typically in the opposite directions.

A second way of measuring explanatory style is with a content analysis procedure—the CAVE (an acronym for "content analysis of verbatim explanations")—that allows written or spoken material to be scored for naturally occurring causal explanations (Peterson, Schulman, Castellon, & Seligman, 1992). Researchers identify explanations for bad or good events, extract them, and have judges rate them along the scales of the ASQ. The CAVE makes possible longitudinal studies after-the-fact, so long as appropriate material can be located from early in the lives of individuals for whom long-term outcomes of interest are known.

Changing Explanatory Style

We know that cognitive therapy can change an individual's explanatory style from pessimistic to optimistic, reducing the extent of depressive symptoms (Seligman et al., 1988). We also know that cognitive-behavioral interventions that impart problem-solving skills can lead individuals to explain events more optimistically, preventing depression in the future (Gillham, Reivich, Jaycox, & Seligman, 1995).

For example, the Penn Resiliency Program (PRP) is a 12-session curriculum administered by school teachers and guidance counselors (Reivich, Gillham, Chaplin, & Seligman, 2005). The program contains two main components, one cognitive and the other based on social problem–solving techniques.

In the cognitive component, core cognitive techniques are translated, through the use of cartoons and skits, into a language that adolescents can understand and apply to their own lives. Group facilitators begin by teaching students about the link between thoughts and feelings. Then students learn how to evaluate the beliefs they have learned to recognize. Skits are used to help find differences between the beliefs of fictitious characters who are thriving and those who are not. By the end of these lessons, students have learned that pessimistic explanations of bad events are likely to result in undesirable outcomes.

In the social problem–solving component, students learn seven skills that help them better interact with this world: assertiveness, negotiation, relaxation, avoidance of procrastination, social skills, decision making, and problem solving. PRP has been successfully evaluated in school and managed care settings in both the United States and China (Gillham, Hamilton, Freres, & Patton, 2006). It has been extended to college students and to adults in the workplace. Current work concerns itself with the delivery of the PRP intervention through the Internet.

Origins of Explanatory Style

Explanatory style is therefore malleable, but what initially sets it in place? Researchers have not fully answered this question. We find isolated studies by various investigators documenting diverse influences on explanatory style. In few of these studies has more than one influence been investigated at a time. Hence, we cannot say what are the more important versus less important influences on explanatory style. Nor can we say how different influences interact.

Researchers have not studied explanatory style prior to age 8, when children are first able to respond to interview versions of the ASQ (Nolen-Hoeksema, 1986). We assume that explanatory style forms earlier, although we await appropriate assessment strategies to document this. This shortcoming aside, here is what is known about the natural history of explanatory style.

Genetics

Explanatory style is influenced by genetics. Schulman, Keith, and Seligman (1993) found that the explanatory styles of monozygotic twins were more highly correlated than the explanatory styles of dizygotic twins. This finding does *not* mean that there is an optimism gene. Genes may be indirectly responsible for the concordance of explanatory style among monozygotic twins. For example, genes influence attributes like intelligence and physical attractiveness, which in turn lead to more positive (and fewer negative) outcomes, which in turn may encourage an optimistic explanatory style.

Genetic influences aside, we presume that explanatory style is either acquired as a whole (e.g., when a child hears an explicit causal message from a parent or teacher) or abstracted from ongoing experience (e.g., when an individual ruminates on the meaning of failure or trauma and draws a causal conclusion). We can identify the former mode of acquisition as direct and the latter as indirect, although these may blur in actual instances.

Parents

Researchers have explored the relationship between the explanatory styles of parents and their offspring. Attributions by mothers and their children are usually the focus. The relevant data prove inconclusive, with some researchers finding convergence between the causal attributions of mothers and their children and others not (Peterson & Steen, 2002). Although few studies have looked at the explanatory styles of fathers and their children, Seligman and colleagues (1984) found that fathers' explanatory styles were *not* related to those of their children.

Perhaps the best way to make sense of these conflicting findings about explanatory styles of parents and their children is to take them at face value and conclude that explanatory style is transmitted to children by some parents but not by others. Researchers therefore must do something more than calculate simple correlations across generations. They need to investigate moderators of these occasional links. How much time do parents and children spend together? About what do they talk? Do causal explanations figure in this discourse?

Attention to mechanisms is especially important when we look at optimistic explanatory style. Why are some children able to endorse an optimistic outlook despite external influences that would seem to undercut optimism? Why do some children transcend whatever genetic influences there might be on explanatory style?

We assume that the explanatory style of children can be affected by their parents through simple modeling. Children are most likely to imitate those whom they perceive as powerful and competent, and most parents—although not all—fit this description. Children are attuned to the ways in which their parents interpret the world, and they therefore may be inclined to interpret their environments in a similar manner. If, for example, children repeatedly hear their parents give internal, stable, and global explanations for negative events, they are likely to adopt these pessimistic interpretations for themselves.

Another type of parental influence involves their interpretation of their children's behaviors. Criticism implying pessimistic causes has a cumulative effect on how children view themselves (Seligman, 1990). If a child says that she cannot find her house key, the parent may admonish the child as being careless, thus providing an internal, stable, and global explanation of the child's behavior. Alternatively, a parent may say that the child needs to work on becoming more organized, thus providing an internal, unstable, and specific attribution. One response enforces a pessimistic view of a relatively minor event, whereas the other response allows a more optimistic view.

Related to this point, Vanden Belt and Peterson (1991) found that how parents explain events involving their children has implications for their children's achievement and adjustment in the classroom. In their study, children whose parents had a pessimistic explanatory style vis-à-vis events involving their children tended to work below their potential in the classroom—perhaps because they had internalized their parents' outlook.

Another type of parental influence is indirect but probably quite important: whether a safe and coherent world is provided for the young child. Children from happy and supportive homes are more likely as adults to have an optimistic explanatory style (Franz, McClelland, Weinberger, & Peterson, 1994). This finding follows from the fact that parental encouragement and support diminishes fear of failure and enables children to take risks necessary to find and pursue their interests and talents. Success and confidence are generated, which in turn generate expectations of further success. Thus, optimism is fostered and nurtured through a series of confidence-building experiences. Along these lines, Marks (1998) cautioned that children who are congenitally deaf and blind are at particular risk for developing a pessimistic explanatory style if their condition elicits too much coddling or results in too many experiences of failure. Parents and caregivers face the challenging task of providing appropriate challenges that allow these children to exercise control over the environment.

What happens to children whose parents do not consistently encourage safe exploration of the world? Perez-Bouchard, Johnson, and Ahrens (1993) found that children (ages 8–14) of substance abusers were more likely to have a pessimistic explanatory style than children of parents without a history of substance abuse. One possible explanation of the link between parents' substance abuse and children's pessimism is that substance-abusing parents are less likely to be available to provide their children with the support and encouragement that facilitate successes. Furthermore, children of substance abusers may be forced to take on adult responsibilities beyond their developmental abilities, thus setting themselves up for failure rather than the success that fosters optimism. If children experience repeated failures, they learn that nothing they do makes a difference.

Teachers

As teachers administer feedback about children's performance, their comments may affect children's attributions about their successes and failures in the classroom. Heyman, Dweck, and Cain (1992) had kindergarteners role-play scenarios in which one of their projects was criticized by a teacher. Thirty-nine percent of the students displayed a helpless response to the teacher's criticism—exhibiting negative affect, changing their original positive opinions of the project to more negative ones, and expressing disinclinations toward future involvement in that type of project. In addition, those children were more likely to make negative judgments about themselves that were internal, stable, and global.

Mueller and Dweck (1998) demonstrated that even praise can be detrimental to children if focused on a trait perceived as fixed. In their study, children who were praised for intelligence displayed more characteristics of helplessness in response to difficulty or failure than did children praised for effort. Whether providing positive or negative feedback, a teacher's habitual explanations for children's performances can have a critical impact on their developing explanatory style.

Media

Do the media influence explanatory style? Levine (1977) reported that CBS and NBC newscasts modeled helplessness 71% of the time, thereby offering ample opportunity for the vicarious acquisition of helplessness. Gerbner and Gross (1976) also examined television shows and found that televised violence—whether fictional or actual—resulted in intensified feelings of risk and insecurity, promoting compliance with established authority. Explanatory style was not an explicit focus, but it seems plausible that a causal message was tucked into these phenomena (Wise & Rosqvist, 2006). Even when television produces positive feelings, helplessness may result when viewers learn to expect outcomes unrelated to behaviors (Hearn, 1991).

Although people of all ages watch television, young people may be especially susceptible to its influence. According to recent estimates, children in the United States watch more than 4 hr of television per day (American Academy of Pediatrics, 2006). Of particular concern is children's exposure to televised scenes of violence. From an explanatory style perspective, the issue is not televised violence per se but how its causes are portrayed.

Although to some extent television mirrors the world, its depictions of violence can be gratuitous. This is true not only of fictional portrayals but of news reports as well. When violence erupts anywhere in the world, television cameras arrive to record every facet of misery with numbing repetitiveness. Pictures of victims are displayed constantly; reporters review the sequence of events endlessly; and various professionals analyze the causes/effects as if they are paid by the word. Coverage is hourly, daily, lasting for weeks in some instances. In short, the medium ruminates on violence, tacitly encouraging the viewer to do the same, and rumination may take a toll, strengthening and cementing into place a pessimistic explanatory style.

Television's proclivity for ruminating in its news coverage compounds a tendency to magnify stories of violence in a way that slants factual presentation. It is not in the interest of networks to place temporal or specific parameters on a story. Instead, they benefit from interpreting a story from a pessimistic vantage, specifying the stability and globality of its impact and enlarging the story's import. Consider Joe Theisman's broken leg, the Rodney King beating, and the Abu Ghraib prison scandal—shown not only repeatedly but also in ways that make the world seem a terrible place. Unfortunately, the distortions in permanence and pervasiveness that serve the interest of the networks do not serve the best interests of young viewers who may adopt the implied style to which they are exposed. The positive psychology implication is that television can be more of a force for the good, not by changing its content but by altering the causal messages conveyed in stories and shows.

Trauma

Trauma also influences the explanatory style of children. Bunce, Larsen, and Peterson (1995) found that college students who reported experiencing a significant trauma (e.g., death of a parent, rape, or incest) at some point in their childhood or adolescence currently had a more pessimistic explanatory style than those students who had never experienced trauma. Even more specifically, Gold (1986) found that women who had been sexually victimized during their childhood and adolescence were more likely to have a pessimistic explanatory style than were women who had not been sexually victimized. Furthermore, even the divorce of parents, common in our modern society, puts children at greater risk for developing a pessimistic explanatory style (Seligman, 1990).

Because isolated traumas have been shown to influence the development of a pessimistic explanatory style, it is not surprising to find evidence that chronic abuse has a similar effect. Cerezo and Frias (1994) found that children (ages 8–13 years) whose parents had physically and emotionally abused them for at least 2 years had a more pessimistic explanatory style than did other children. Because of the often arbitrary nature and seemingly random occurrence of the punishments, the abused children learned that there was no way to prevent them. They learned to be helpless. A study of the explanatory styles of prison inmates provides additional evidence that chronic uncontrollable events influence explanatory style (Schill & Marcus, 1998). Inmates incarcerated 5 or more years had a more pessimistic explanatory style than did inmates incarcerated less than 1 year.

Conclusions

A great deal is known about the consequences of an optimistic versus pessimistic style of explaining the causes of events. Less is known about the origins of explanatory style, however, and thus we have summarized the pertinent research. Unaddressed by any study is a normative question: Is the typical person an optimist, a pessimist, or expectationally neutral (Peterson, 2006)? Said another way, does something unusual in the course of development need to occur in order to impart to someone an optimistic explanatory style? Is optimism simply the developmental default, deep-wired into human beings by evolution? Or is pessimism the default? Or perhaps the child is a blank slate, equally able to become an optimist or a pessimist, depending on the idiosyncratic influences to which he or she is exposed.

Certainly, many researchers have been drawn to the study of factors that make people pessimistic, although it is not clear if they are assuming that optimism needs no special explanation or instead that pessimism is a more pressing concern. Regardless, positive psychologists need to be concerned with how optimism *and* pessimism develop. To foreshadow a point we emphasize in the final section, we can assume neither that optimism is the simple opposite of pessimism nor that the determinants of optimism can be gleaned from the study of the determinants of pessimism.

Directions for Future Research: Explanatory Style as a Positive Psychology Concern

More needs to be done. In most explanatory style research, the focus has remained on outcomes of interest to the helplessness model: depression, illness, and failure. These are important, but the typical way of measuring these outcomes assigns zero points that correspond to *not* being depressed, *not* being ill, and *not* failing. This limitation can be glossed over by researchers describing what the data actually show. For example, if we find that pessimistic individuals are depressed and physically ill, we may glibly convey this result by saying that optimistic people are happy and healthy, even if our outcomes measures did not allow people to manifest happiness or health.

There is more to perseverance than the absence of helplessness, more to happiness than the absence of depression, and more to health than the absence of illness (Peterson, 2006). A sports cliché cautions that playing not to lose differs from playing to win. But somehow these obvious points can be ignored when optimism researchers interpret their findings. So long as outcome measures reflect only degrees of pathology, no conclusions can be drawn about well-being. This is an important lesson for positive psychologists of all stripes. It is not enough to study positive "predictors" like optimism; one must also study positive "outcomes" or—even better—outcomes that range from negative to positive. Only with this strategy will we have a complete positive psychology.

Some studies in the explanatory style tradition have included outcome measures that tap the full range of functioning. Usually, these have been studies of performance, in academic, athletic, and vocational domains. Here, the expected positive correlation between optimistic explanatory style and good performance is found. Unreported in such studies, though, is whether the correlation is a literal straight line rather than one that merely meanders upward. The distinction is important because it allows researchers to distinguish between the costs of pessimism versus the benefits of optimism.

As explanatory style researchers heed this call to study positive as well as negative outcomes, explanatory style based on good events might become more relevant than it has seemed in past research looking at negative outcomes. Abramson et al. (1989) suggested that the way people explain the causes of good events is related to how they savor their effects. Perhaps, good moods are created and sustained by savoring, and positive psychologists have directed our attention to the diverse benefits of positive emotions (Peterson & Park, 2007). Perhaps, thriving is under the sway of a "good" explanatory style just as helplessness is influenced by a "bad" explanatory style.

A valid criticism of explanatory style research to date is that it has looked much more at correlations between explanatory style and distant outcomes than at the mechanisms that lead from explanatory style to these outcomes. This imbalance is ironic given that learned helplessness research with animals has in recent years taken an ever closer look at the mechanisms—psychological and biological—that produce the helplessness phenomenon. Explanatory style researchers in contrast have rapidly moved from one outcome measure to another to still another. This restlessness has doubtlessly kept alive interest in explanatory style, but it has precluded a full understanding of learned helplessness.

Questions

1. What are the processes (mechanisms) by which explanatory style influences distant outcomes?

2. How can an optimistic explanatory style best be encouraged among children and adults?

3. Does "learned" optimism have the same consequences as naturally developed optimism?

References and Recommended Reading*

Abramson, L. Y., Metalsky, G. I., & Alloy, L. B. (1989). Hopelessness depression: A theory-based subtype of depression. *Psychological Review, 96,* 358–372.

*Abramson, L. Y., Seligman, M. E. P., & Teasdale, J. D. (1978). Learned helplessness in humans: Critique and reformulation. *Journal of Abnormal Psychology, 87,* 49–74.

American Academy of Pediatrics. (2006). *Television and the family*. Retrieved August 15, 2006, from http://www.aap.prg/family/tv1/htm

Brown, I., & Inouye, D. K. (1978). Learned helplessness through modeling: The role of perceived similarity in competence. *Journal of Personality and Social Psychology, 36,* 900–908.

*Buchanan, G. M., & Seligman, M. E. P. (Eds.). (1995). *Explanatory style*. Hillsdale, NJ: Erlbaum.

Bunce, S. C., Larsen, R. J., & Peterson, C. (1995). Life after trauma: Personality and daily life experiences of traumatized people. *Journal of Personality, 63,* 165–188.

Cerezo, M. A., & Frias, D. (1994). Emotional and cognitive adjustment in abused children. *Child Abuse and Neglect, 18,* 923–932.

Franz, C. E., McClelland, D. C., Weinberger, J., & Peterson, C. (1994). Parenting antecedents of adult adjustment: A longitudinal study. In C. Perris, W. A. Arrindell, & M. Eisemann (Eds.), *Parenting and psychopathology* (pp. 127–144). San Diego, CA: Academic Press.

Gerbner, G., & Gross, L. (1976). Living with television: The violence profile. *Journal of Communication, 26,* 173–199.

Gillham, J. E., Hamilton, J., Freres, D. R., & Patton, K. (2006). Preventing depression among early adolescents in the primary care setting: A randomized controlled study of the Penn Resiliency Program. *Journal of Abnormal Child Psychology, 34,* 203–219.

Gillham, J. E., Reivich, K. J., Jaycox, L. H., & Seligman, M. E. P. (1995). Prevention of depressive symptoms in schoolchildren: Two-year follow-up. *Psychological Science, 6,* 343–351.

Gold, E. R. (1986). Long-term effects of sexual victimization in childhood: An attributional approach. *Journal of Consulting and Clinical Psychology, 54,* 471–475.

Hearn, G. (1991). Entertainment manna: Does television viewing lead to appetitive helplessness? *Psychological Reports, 68,* 1179–1184.

Heyman, G. D., Dweck, C. S., & Cain, K. M. (1992). Young children's vulnerability to self-blame and helplessness: Relationship to beliefs about goodness. *Child Development, 63,* 401–415.

Levine, G. F. (1977). "Learned helplessness" and the evening news. *Journal of Communication, 27,* 100–105.

Marks, S. B. (1998). Understanding and preventing learned helplessness in children who are congenitally deaf-blind. *Journal of Visual Impairment and Blindness, 92,* 200–211.

Mueller, C. M., & Dweck, C. S. (1998). Praise for intelligence can undermine children's motivation and performance. *Journal of Personality and Social Psychology, 75,* 32–52.

Nolen-Hoeksema, S. (1986). Developmental studies of explanatory style, and learned helplessness in children. Unpublished doctoral dissertation, University of Pennsylvania.

Perez-Bouchard, L., Johnson, J. L., & Ahrens, A. H. (1993). Attributional style in children of substance abusers. *American Journal of Drug and Alcohol Abuse, 19*, 475–489.

*Peterson, C. (1991). Meaning and measurement of explanatory style. *Psychological Inquiry, 2*, 1–10.

*Peterson, C. (2000). The future of optimism. *American Psychologist, 55*, 44–55.

Peterson, C. (2006). *A primer in positive psychology.* New York: Oxford University Press.

Peterson, C., & Bossio, L. M. (1991). *Health and optimism.* New York: Free Press.

*Peterson, C., Maier, S. F., & Seligman, M. E. P. (1993). *Learned helplessness: A theory for the age of personal control.* New York: Oxford University Press.

Peterson, C., & Park, N. (2007). Explanatory style and emotion regulation. In J. J. Gross (Ed.), *Handbook of emotion regulation* (pp. 159–179). New York: Guilford.

Peterson, C., Schulman, P., Castellon, C., & Seligman, M. E. P. (1992). CAVE: Content analysis of verbatim explanations. In C. P. Smith (Ed.), *Motivation and personality: Handbook of thematic content analysis* (pp. 383–392). New York: Cambridge University Press.

*Peterson, C., & Seligman, M. E. P. (1984). Causal explanations as a risk factor for depression: Theory and evidence. *Psychological Review, 91*, 347–374.

Peterson, C., Semmel, A., von Baeyer, C., Abramson, L. Y., Metalsky, G. I., & Seligman, M. E. P. (1982). The Attributional Style Questionnaire. *Cognitive Therapy and Research, 6*, 287–299.

Peterson, C., & Steen, T. A. (2002). Optimistic explanatory style. In C. R. Snyder & S. J. Lopez (Eds.), *Handbook of positive psychology* (pp. 244–256). New York: Oxford University Press.

Reivich, K. J., Gillham, J. E., Chaplin, T. M., & Seligman, M. E. P. (2005). From helplessness to optimism: The role of resilience in treating and preventing depression in youth. In S. Goldstein & R. B. Brooks (Eds.), *Handbook of resilience in children* (pp. 223–237). New York: Kluwer.

Rothbaum, F., Weisz, J. R., & Snyder, S. S. (1982). Changing the world versus changing the self: A two-process theory of perceived control. *Journal of Personality and Social Psychology, 42*, 5–37.

Schill, R. A., & Marcus, D. K. (1998). Incarceration and learned helplessness. *International Journal of Offender Therapy and Comparative Criminology, 42*, 224–232.

Schulman, P., Keith, D., & Seligman, M. E. P. (1993). Is optimism heritable? A study of twins. *Behaviour Research and Therapy, 31*, 569–574.

*Seligman, M. E. P. (1990). *Learned optimism.* New York: Knopf.

Seligman, M. E. P., Castellon, C., Cacciola, J., Schulman, P., Luborsky, L., Ollove, M., et al. (1988). Explanatory style change during cognitive therapy for unipolar depression. *Journal of Abnormal Psychology, 97*, 13–18.

Seligman, M. E. P., Peterson, C., Kaslow, N. J., Tanenbaum, R. L., Alloy, L. B., & Abramson, L. Y. (1984). Attributional style and depressive symptoms among children. *Journal of Abnormal Psychology, 93*, 235–238.

Simkin, D. K., Lederer, J. P., & Seligman, M. E. P. (1983). Learned helplessness in groups. *Behaviour Research and Therapy, 21*, 613–622.

Vanden Belt, A., & Peterson, C. (1991). Parental explanatory style and its relationship to the classroom performance of disabled and nondisabled children. *Cognitive Therapy and Research, 15*, 331–341.

Wise, D., & Rosqvist, J. (2006). Explanatory style and well-being. In J. C. Thomas, D. L. Segal, & M. Hersen (Eds.), *Comprehensive handbook of personality and psychopathology, Vol. 1: Personality and everyday functioning* (pp. 285–305). Hoboken, NJ: Wiley.

Hope Theory

Kevin L. Rand *and* Jennifer S. Cheavens

Abstract

Hope is defined as the perceived ability to produce pathways to achieve desired goals and to motivate oneself to use those pathways. The historical origins of hope theory are reviewed. Definitions and explanations are given for the core concepts of Snyder's (1994c) cognitive model of hope, including goals, pathways, and agency. Goals are abstract mental targets that guide human behaviors. Pathways thought entails the perceived ability to generate multiple routes to desired goals. Agency thought entails the perceived ability to initiate and sustain movement along a pathway. Emotions are conceptualized as sequelae of goal-directed thoughts and actions and function as feedback regarding perceived success or failure of a goal pursuit. A temporal model of the goal pursuit process is presented, and the roles of hope cognitions at each phase of the sequence are explained. Several scales constructed based on hope theory and used in research are described. Research on hope is reviewed. Higher hope corresponds with superior academic and athletic performance, greater physical and psychological well-being, and enhanced interpersonal relationships. Future directions for research and application of hope theory are suggested, including distinguishing hope from other personality constructs, examining potential group differences in hope, exploring possible maladaptive aspects of hope, and using hope theory to understand and ameliorate current global crises.

Keywords: cognition, goals, hope, motivation, well-being

Snyder introduced his cognitive theory of hope nearly 20 years ago (Snyder, 1989). Since then, his original hypotheses have been studied by clinical psychologists (e.g., Chang, 1998; Cheavens, Feldman, Gum, Michael, & Snyder, 2006), social psychologists (e.g., Bryant & Cvengros, 2004; Carvajal, Clair, Nash, & Evans, 1998), allied health professionals (e.g., Barnum, Snyder, Rapoff, Mani, & Thompson, 1998), and other social scientists. Our goals for this chapter are to (a) provide a brief overview of hope theory; (b) present the scales commonly used to measure hope; (c) discuss the extant research and practical implications of hope theory; and (d) outline the future directions for research on hope. First, we will tell the story of how Snyder developed hope theory.

Origins of Hope Theory

Hope theory had its genesis in excuse making. In the late 1970s and early 1980s, Snyder and his colleagues were investigating the process of how people distance themselves from mistakes and failures (i.e., excuses; see Mehlman & Snyder, 1985). While engaged in this research on how people explain the things they "don't" want, Snyder began to develop hope theory as an attempt to better understand how people move closer to things they "do" want (viz. goals). In this sense, Snyder (1989) conceptualized hope as the "other side" of the excuse-making process.

The concept of hope has been around for millennia. In Greek mythology, hope was all that remained in Pandora's infamous jar after she unwittingly unleashed all of the evils into the world. Since then, hope has been both heralded and maligned. Take these historical examples: "Everything that is done in the world is done by hope" (Martin Luther) and "He that lives on hope will die fasting" (Benjamin Franklin quoted in Bartlett, 1968, p. 422).

By the twentieth century, scholars began to write about what seemed to be a universal human desire to seek goals as related to hope (Frank, 1975; Frankl, 1992; Melges & Bowlby, 1969; Menninger, 1959). The common theme in this literature is that hope involves the perception that one's goals can be achieved. In 1987, Snyder spent a sabbatical talking to people about hope and their goals. What he discovered was that when people discussed their goals, they mentioned two components: the routes to reach their goals and the motivation to use those routes. Snyder (1994a, 1994c) labeled these components "pathways" and "agency," and a new theory of hope was born. Using Snyder's definition (2002), hopeful thinking consists of the belief that one can find pathways to desired goals and the belief that one can muster the motivation to use those pathways.

An Overview of Hope Theory
Goals

A fundamental tenet of hope theory is that much of human behavior is goal directed. Goals are the mental targets that guide human action sequences. As such, goal thoughts are the foundation on which hope theory is built (Snyder, 1994a, 1994c, 1998). Goals can be verbal or visual representations. In other words, they can be manifested as self-statements (e.g., "I want to lose weight") or as mental images (e.g., picturing that new coat you saw in a store window). Goals vary in temporal frame (i.e., short term or long term). In addition, they can vary in terms of specificity, value, and importance. Initially, Snyder (1994a, 2002) argued that goals needed to be of sufficient value to occupy conscious thought. More recent research suggests, however, that much of human behavior can be guided by the pursuit of nonconscious goals (see Chartrand & Cheng, 2002). Additionally, Snyder (2002) has postulated that there are two basic types of goals: "approach goals" (e.g., getting into medical school) and "avoidance goals" (e.g., not getting the flu). Research suggests that people believe hope flourishes when the probability of goal attainment is intermediate (Averill, Catlin, & Chon, 1990).

Pathways

According to hope theory (and many other schools of thought), at some point in human evolution we developed the ability to conceptualize time in terms of past, present, and future (Snyder, 2002). As a result, humans can organize their behaviors in order to bring about desired future conditions (i.e., goals). Pathways thinking entails the perceived ability to generate routes connecting the present to this imagined future (i.e., connecting point A to point B). Thus, an individual perceives that he or she can generate at least one workable route to the desired goal. The production of multiple pathways is important when encountering barriers to goal pursuits, and research has demonstrated that high-hope people actually are effective at generating alternative pathways to goals (Irving, Snyder, & Crowson, 1998; Snyder, Harris, et al., 1991).

Agency

Agency is the motivational component in hope theory, and it is the perceived ability to use pathways to reach desired goals. Agency thinking involves self-referential thoughts about the ability to initiate and sustain movement along a pathway. Agency thoughts comprise affirming self-statements, such as "I can do this" (Snyder, Lapointe, Crowson, & Early, 1998). Agency thinking is important in all goal pursuits, but it becomes crucial in instances when people become blocked, because it helps people apply the necessary motivation to move along an alternate pathway (Snyder, 1994c).

There is some conceptual overlap between agency and Bandura's (1982, 1997) construct of self-efficacy. Specifically, Bandura defines efficacy expectancy as the situation-specific evaluation that an individual *can* carry out a particular course of action for a specific goal pursuit. In contrast, agency is a trait-like perception that an individual *will* carry out goal-directed actions for a wide range of goals (Snyder, 2002). Hence, agency differs from self-efficacy in that agency is more global than self-efficacy. In addition, agency reflects the intention to act rather than simply perceiving the ability to do so. Although research has shown that agency and self-efficacy are related, agency predicts unique variance in well-being above and beyond self-efficacy (Magaletta & Oliver, 1999).

Agency and Pathways Together

An important principle of Snyder's (1994a) theory is that hopeful thinking requires *both* the perceived ability to generate routes to a goal *and* the perceived ability/determination to use those routes. Hence, hope is "a positive motivational state that is based on an interactively derived sense of successful (1) agency (goal-directed energy) and (2) pathways (planning to meet goals)" (Snyder, Irving, & Anderson, 1991, p. 287). It is theorized that the relationship between pathways and agency thinking is transactional (both additive and iterative) such that in the midst of the goal pursuit, pathways thinking augments agency thinking, which, in turn, increases pathways thinking (see Snyder, Harris et al., 1991).

Hope and Emotions

Within hope theory, cognitive, as opposed to emotional, processes are emphasized. Emotions are hypothesized to be the "sequelae" of goal-directed thoughts and activities (Snyder, Rand, & Sigmon, 2002). Specifically, positive emotions stem from perceived progress (i.e., unimpeded movement or effectively overcoming obstacles) toward or attainment of a desired goal. In contrast, negative emotions result from perceived stagnation or setback in a goal pursuit.

Several correlational and experimental studies have shown that insurmountable goal blockages generate negative emotions in research participants, whereas successful goal pursuits or the overcoming of obstacles generate positive emotions (Snyder et al., 1996). Other investigators also have found evidence that people who encounter difficulties while pursuing important life goals experience decreased well-being (Diener, 1984; Emmons, 1986; Little, 1983; Omodei & Wearing, 1990; Palys & Little, 1983; Ruehlman & Wolchik, 1988). In addition, experimental manipulations have shown that thoughts about one's motivational state and the likelihood of particular outcomes give rise to emotions and not vice versa (Roseman & Evdokas, 2004).

Full Hope Model

Now that we have outlined the basic components in hope theory, we will discuss the temporal sequence of goal-directed thought. This sequence is outlined in Figure 30.1. Moving from left to right, there are three phases that influence the goal-directed thoughts of a goal pursuit: (a) an individual's learning history; (b) the preevent phase; and (c) the event sequence phase. An individual's learning history is important because the bases of agency and pathways thinking are formed during childhood (Snyder, 1994a, 1994c, 2002). Theoretically, pathways thinking develops when infants begin to make associations between co-occurring events (Schulman, 1991). Around the age of 1 year, a child begins to realize that she or he is a separate entity from other people (e.g., caregivers), engendering the insight that she or he can be a causal agent in chain-of-events sequences (Snyder, Rand, & Sigmon, 2002). This is the beginning of agency thinking.

The iterative processes of pathways and agency thinking are accompanied by emotional sets or moods that are based on the individual's accumulated experience with previous goal pursuits (Snyder, 2002). For example, a personal history replete with goal accomplishments and the successful overcoming of obstacles would give rise to an emotional set characterized by positive and active feelings (e.g., interest and curiosity) in the face of goal pursuits. Future goal pursuits are anticipated with the emotions that were evoked from past goal pursuits. Hence, high-hope individuals have emotion sets that routinely contain feelings of confidence and joy (Snyder, Cheavens, & Michael, 1999; Snyder, Harris et al., 1991; Snyder, Sympson, Michael, & Cheavens, 2000); whereas, low-hope individuals have emotion sets that are characterized by passive and negative feelings.

Now, we turn to the preevent phase of a particular goal pursuit. During the preevent analysis of a potential goal, an individual assesses the "outcome value" of the goal in question. If the goal is sufficiently important to warrant continued attention, then the individual moves into the event sequence phase. As an individual begins to pursue a goal, agency and pathways thinking repeatedly interact with the appraised outcome value (as indicated by the bidirectional arrows in Figure 30.1), allowing the individual to continuously monitor the outcome value of the goal pursuit in the context of the pathways available and the agency required to enact the available pathways. If the imagined outcome value of a goal pursuit is appraised as not being important enough to merit continued effort, then the goal pursuit can be stopped. This continuous outcome value check is important because sometimes the value of a goal cannot accurately be appraised until the goal pursuit has been initiated (Snyder, 2002).

As the individual enters the event sequence phase of the goal pursuit, goal-specific pathways and agency thoughts alternate and summate (as indicated by the bidirectional arrows in Figure 30.1). The iteration of pathways and agency throughout the event sequence influences the subsequent success of any given goal pursuit in a feed-forward manner (Snyder, Rand, & Sigmon, 2002). Once a particular goal pursuit is completed, the individual's appraisal of the process (i.e., success or failure) and the resultant emotions (i.e., positive or negative) cycle back to influence subsequent perceptions of pathways and agency capabilities for goals in that particular domain and in general. Repeated failures can result in the loss of hope, at least within a particular life domain (e.g., academics; Snyder, 2002).

At any given point in a goal pursuit, a person may encounter a stressor. Within hope theory, a stressor/

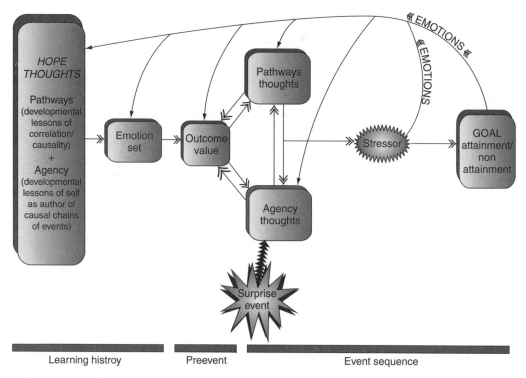

Fig. 30.1 Schematic of feed-forward and feedback functions involving agency and pathways goal-directed thoughts and emotions in hope theory.

obstacle is defined as any impediment that could jeopardize a goal pursuit (Snyder, 2002). The stressor generates emotions that feed back to influence pathways and agency thoughts related to the ongoing goal pursuit. The resultant emotions are a function of how the stressor is appraised. Although we posit that stressors elicit some initial negative emotions in everyone, high-hope individuals are more apt to experience concomitant positive emotions because they are more likely to see stressors as challenges to be overcome (Anderson, 1988; Snyder, Harris, et al., 1991).

Finally, another source of emotional influence in a goal pursuit is a surprise event (see Figure 30.1; Snyder, 2002). A surprise event is one that occurs outside the context of an ongoing goal pursuit and can be positive (e.g., receiving a call from a long-lost friend) or negative (e.g., finding out the friend lost his home in a hurricane). The emotions generated by the event affect the individual's agency thinking, generally by increasing or decreasing overall motivation. This agency is attached to a particular goal and pathways that are appropriate to the situation (e.g., helping the friend find a new place to live). The important thing to point out here is that occasionally emotions can be generated outside the context of a particular goal pursuit, but that these emotions are quickly incorporated into the ongoing goal-pursuit

thought process and influence the goal pursuit outcome (Snyder, 2002).

In summary, the hope model consists of both feed-forward (i.e., thoughts) and feedback mechanisms (i.e., thoughts and emotions) that influence a person's success in any given goal pursuit. This sequence is influenced both by dispositional characteristics of the individual (e.g., her or his learning history) and characteristics of the specific situation.

Individual Differences Scales
Trait Hope Scale

The adult Trait Hope Scale (Snyder, Harris et al., 1991) comprises four agency statements (e.g., "I energetically pursue my goals"), four pathways statements (e.g., "I can think of many ways to get out of a jam"), and four distracter items. Respondents are asked to rate the extent to which each statement applies to him or her based on an 8-point Likert scale (1 = definitely false through 8 = definitely true). The instrument has internal and temporal reliability, with two separate but related factors (i.e., pathways and agency) driven by an overarching hope factor (Babyak, Snyder, & Yoshinobu, 1993). The measure has received extensive convergent and discriminant validational support (see Cheavens, Gum, &

Snyder, 2000; Snyder, Harris et al., 1991). The Trait Hope Scale is shown in the Appendix.

State Hope Scale

The State Hope Scale (Snyder et al., 1996) consists of three pathways and three agency items in which respondents describe themselves in terms of how they are "right now." Studies have shown the State Hope Scale to have sound internal reliability and factor structure, in addition to convergent and discriminant validity (see Feldman & Snyder, 2000; Snyder et al., 1996).

Children's Hope Scale

The Children's Hope Scale (Snyder, Hoza et al., 1997) is designed to assess trait hope in children aged 8–16 years. It consists of three pathways and three agency items. It has been found to demonstrate internal and temporal reliability. Studies have supported its two-factor structure and its convergent and discriminant validities (see Moon & Snyder, 2000; Snyder, Hoza et al., 1997).

Hope and Life Outcomes

The impact of hope on different life outcomes has been theoretically discussed and empirically examined from several perspectives. In the following section, we briefly review the theoretical implications and research findings regarding hope's influence on the following life domains: (a) performance (i.e., academic and athletic); (b) well-being (i.e., physical health and psychological adjustment); and (c) interpersonal relationships.

Hope and Performance

Meeting the necessary academic milestones for movement toward long-term goals (e.g., graduation or later employment) is an almost ubiquitous goal among students. As such, higher levels of trait hope should, and do, correspond with greater academic achievement. For example, higher hope scores correlate with higher scores on subsequent achievement tests in elementary-school children (Snyder, Hoza et al., 1997), higher overall high school grade point averages (Snyder, Harris et al., 1991), and higher semester and overall grade point averages for college students (Chang, 1998; Curry, Maniar, Sondag, & Sandstedt, 1999; Curry, Snyder, Cook, Ruby, & Rehm, 1997; Snyder, Harris et al., 1991). In a longitudinal study of college students, higher levels of hope measured at the beginning of the students' first semester in college predicted higher cumulative grade point averages, higher graduation rates, and

lower dropout rates up to 6 years later, even after statistically controlling for intelligence, previous academic performance, self-esteem, and college-entrance exam scores (Snyder, Shorey et al., 2002; Snyder, Wiklund, & Cheavens, 1999).

Based on these links between hopefulness and academic success, hope-based interventions for at-risk students are currently being developed and tested. For example, projects at the Universities of Kansas and Wyoming consist of college classes designed to improve students' levels of hope and improve their academic performance (Curry et al., 1999; Snyder, Shorey, Rand, & Ritschel, 2005). In addition, Lopez and colleagues (Lopez, Bouwkamp, Edwards, & Teramoto Pedrotti, 2000) have had early success in promoting hope in junior high school students.

Another important area of performance is athletics. Based on hope theory, it is hypothesized that athletes with higher hope should be able to generate the best routes to accomplish their athletic goals and have more motivation to use these routes, resulting in increased success. Supporting this hypothesis, research has shown that Division I track athletes with higher versus lower levels of hope performed significantly better at their events, even when controlling for coaches' ratings of their natural athletic ability (Curry et al., 1997). In a study of female track athletes, Curry and colleagues found that combined State and Trait Hope Scale scores accounted for 56% of the variance related to actual athletic performance.

Hope and Well-Being

PHYSICAL HEALTH

As being physically healthy is an important goal for most, it follows that hopeful thinking should impact one's physical health. Snyder and colleagues (Snyder, Feldman, Taylor, Schroeder, & Adams, 2000) articulated the theoretical implications of hope in two domains of health-related goal pursuits: (a) avoiding future health problems (i.e., primary prevention); and (b) coping with extant health problems (i.e., secondary prevention).

Snyder and colleagues (Snyder, Feldman et al., 2000) speculated that higher levels of hope would correspond with being better able to attend to and use information about physical illnesses in order to facilitate prevention efforts. Related to this hypothesis, high-hope women performed better than low-hope women on a cancer facts test, even when controlling for previous academic performance and prior contact with others with cancer (Irving et al., 1998). Additionally, the high-hope women reported having stronger intentions to engage in cancer prevention activities than low-hope women. In another study, high-hope participants reported engaging in more physical exercise (an activity that is a major prophylactic against illness and disease) than low-hope participants (Harney, 1990). In a study of gay men, those with higher hope were less likely to engage in high-risk sexual behaviors than those with lower hope (Floyd & McDermott, 1998).

In addition to preventative behaviors, hope is likely to be inversely related to deliberate efforts to harm (e.g., suicide, self-injury, or violence toward others) as these efforts are incompatible with physical health goals. Related to this point, one recent study found that among hospital patients, those who recently engaged in parasuicidal behaviors reported having lower hope than matched control patients (Vincent, Boddana, & MacLeod, 2004). Moreover, the parasuicidal patients generated life goals that were less specific than their control counterparts and reported that they perceived these goals as more difficult, less likely to be achieved, and less within their control than the control patients.

Regardless of one's efforts at preventing illness or harm, people eventually succumb to some form of malady. Once a physical illness occurs, hope should emerge as an important factor in coping with and recovering from the illness (i.e., secondary prevention; see Snyder, 2002). Research has shown higher levels of hope to be associated with benefits in coping with burn injuries (Barnum et al., 1998), spinal cord injuries (Elliott, Witty, Herrick, & Hoffman, 1991), arthritis (Laird, 1992), fibromyalgia (Affleck & Tennen, 1996; Tennen & Affleck, 1999), and blindness (Jackson, Taylor, Palmatier, Elliott, & Elliott, 1998). This may be related, in part, to the ability of high-hope individuals to cope with pain associated with the disease process. An experiment using the cold-pressor task demonstrated that individuals with higher levels of trait hope were able to tolerate pain longer than individuals with lower levels of hope (Snyder, Berg et al., 2005). Another possible mechanism is that higher-hope individuals may have increased attention to useful illness-related information, which allows them to engage in more adaptive coping behaviors related to the illness. Consistent with this hypothesis, one study showed that higher levels of hope were associated with more frequent use of a Web site containing information on coping with a rare health condition as well as shorter self-reported duration of symptoms related to this condition (Vernberg, Snyder, & Schuh, 2005). In addition, another study showed that higher levels of hope corresponded with greater treatment adherence in children with asthma (Berg, Rapoff, Snyder, & Belmont, 2007).

PSYCHOLOGICAL ADJUSTMENT

As is the case with physical health, mental health can be understood from two basic domains: (a) maintaining psychological adjustment/preventing psychopathology (i.e., primary prevention); and (b) coping with and recovering from psychopathology (i.e., secondary prevention). In terms of primary prevention, hope may engender psychological well-being partly through the influence of successful goal pursuits on affectivity. Because emotions are posited to be the sequelae of goal pursuits, and hope facilitates goal pursuits, then higher levels of hope should correspond with more optimal patterns of affectivity. Consistent with this hypothesis, Snyder and colleagues (Snyder, Harris et al., 1991; Snyder, Hoza et al., 1997) have found that hope correlates positively with positive affect and inversely with negative affect. Similarly, in a 28-day daily diary study, higher hope was found to correlate positively with positive thoughts and negatively with negative thoughts (Snyder et al., 1996). In addition, high-hope college students reported feeling more inspired, energized, confident, and challenged by their goals than their low-hope peers (Snyder, Harris et al., 1991). In other studies, college students with higher levels of hope reported experiencing elevated feelings of self-worth and lower levels of depression (Snyder, Hoza et al., 1997; Snyder et al., 1996). The influence of hope on psychological well-being is not limited to the young. In a sample of older adults (mean age = 76 years), higher levels of hope were associated with greater life satisfaction and better perceived well-being, independent of objective measures of physical health and functional ability (Wrobleski & Snyder, 2005). One possible mechanism of hope's influence on psychological well-being is through meaning. Viktor Frankl (1966) argued that creating or finding meaning in life was the remedy for the angst associated with the "existential vacuum." Research has shown that trait hope correlates strongly ($rs = .70-.76$) with several measures of meaning in life (Feldman & Snyder, 1999).

Another mechanism by which hope is purported to influence psychological adjustment is through its influence on how people appraise and cope with stressors or goal obstacles. Higher-hope people are more likely than lower-hope people to find benefits in coping with their ongoing stressors (Affleck & Tennen, 1996; Tennen & Affleck, 1999). Additionally, high-hope people perceive that their hope will protect them against future stressors (Snyder, 2000), and this perception yields a higher general sense of confidence (Snyder, Feldman et al., 2000), resulting in a more general positive outlook on the future. Higher hope appears to moderate the relationship between unforeseen stressors and successful coping (see Snyder & Pulvers, 2001). For example, in a sample of high-risk children whose mothers were in prison, higher hope related to lower rates of behavioral problems, even after controlling for stress and social support (Hagen, Myers, & Mackintosh, 2005). In spite of lacking maternal access, having positive views of the future and confidence in their abilities to cope conferred protective benefits to these children.

When confronted with a stressor, higher- as compared to lower-hope people generate more strategies (pathways) for effectively coping with the stressor and express a greater likelihood of using these strategies (agency; Snyder, 1994c, 2000; Snyder, Harris et al., 1991). In contrast, compared to high-hope individuals, those with low hope are more likely to use avoidance as a coping strategy. Avoidance has been linked to distress and decreased psychological adjustment over time (Suls & Fletcher, 1985). Even when goal blockages are immutable, hopeful thinking confers benefits. High-hope people should have the cognitive flexibility to find alternative goals when their initial goals are truly blocked (Snyder, Rand, & Sigmon, 2002). In contrast, individuals with low hope tend to ruminate unproductively about being stuck (Michael, 2000; Snyder, 1999; see also Michael & Snyder, 2005) and cope through avoidance. By repeatedly using avoidance coping strategies, people with low hope do not learn from their past experiences (Snyder, Feldman et al., 2000). As such, they become stuck in a cycle of goal blockage, escape, and failure.

In spite of the most hopeful efforts to remain psychologically well, many will experience some form of clinically significant psychological distress. When this occurs, hope theory offers insight into the process of recovery. For years, Jerome Frank (1968, 1973, 1975) promulgated the view that hope was a common process across myriad psychotherapy techniques. Snyder and colleagues continued this line of thought by using hope theory as a framework for understanding how people improve in various forms of psychotherapy (Snyder, Ilardi, Cheavens, et al., 2000; Snyder, Ilardi, Michael, & Cheavens, 2000; Snyder, Michael, & Cheavens, 1999; Snyder & Taylor, 2000). Initially, most psychotherapy interventions provide the client with a "boost" of mental

energy (often referred to as a placebo effect). Irving and colleagues (2004) have argued that this represents an increase in agency thinking, fostered by the client's newly found belief that she or he can get better. Subsequently, each particular psychotherapy technique provides the client with the strategies for improving and maintaining her or his psychological well-being (i.e., insight in psychoanalysis, behavioral activation in behavior therapy, cognitive restructuring in cognitive therapy, etc.). These strategies are tantamount to pathways to the client's goal of regaining and maintaining psychological adjustment (Cheavens, Feldman, Woodward, & Snyder, 2006). Consistent with this hypothesis, one study found that agency scores were linked to improvement during the early stages of therapy and pathways scores were linked to improvement during the latter stages of therapy (Irving et al., 2004).

Hope theory has also been used to develop novel, promising individual (Lopez, Floyd, Ulven, & Snyder, 2000; see also Worthington et al., 1997) and group interventions (Cheavens et al., 2006; Klausner et al., 1998; Klausner, Snyder, & Cheavens, 2000). In addition, a pretreatment therapy preparation program based on hope theory has been successfully implemented (Irving et al., 2004). Furthermore, several self-help style texts have been written using hope theory to aid parents and teachers in helping children (McDermott & Hastings, 2000; McDermott & Snyder, 2000; Snyder, McDermott, Cook, & Rapoff, 1997) and for the benefit of adults (McDermott & Snyder, 1999).

INTERPERSONAL RELATIONSHIPS

Hopeful thinking is posited to begin in early childhood based on interactions between the child and her or his caregiver, peers, and teachers (Snyder, Cheavens, & Sympson, 1997), and there is empirical evidence that hopeful thinking is a consequence of secure and supportive relationships between child and adult caregiver (Shorey, Snyder, Yang, & Lewin, 2003). Connecting with other people is a fundamental human goal because goal pursuits almost always occur within the context of social commerce. One measure of the degree to which people are interested in connecting with others is the extent to which they are concerned about others' perceptions of them. Hence, the tendency to present oneself to others in a positive light can be thought of as adaptive and prosocial (Taylor, 1989). Higher levels of hope have been shown to have a slight, positive association with social desirability and positive self-presentation (Snyder, Harris et al., 1991;

Snyder, Hoza et al., 1997), suggesting that high-hope people have a healthy concern about the impressions they make on others.

Hopeful thinking is also important in helping to form human connections. People with high hope are likely to have close connections with other people, because they are interested not only in their own goals, but also in the goals of others in their lives (Snyder, 1994b, 1994c; Snyder, Cheavens, & Sympson, 1997). In addition, high-hope people have an enhanced ability to take the perspective of others (Rieger, 1993) and enjoy interacting with others (Snyder, Hoza et al., 1997). Indeed, research has shown that higher levels of hope are related to more perceived social support (Barnum et al., 1998), more social competence (Snyder, Hoza et al., 1997), and less loneliness (Sympson, 1999).

Future Directions

Although copious empirical and theoretical work has been conducted on Snyder's (1994a, 1994c, 2002) theory of hope, there still are many new areas to be explored. We will briefly discuss a few areas of research and practice that promise to offer intriguing insights into the roles that hope plays in the lives of people.

A common criticism of hope theory is that it is conceptually similar to other psychological constructs (e.g., optimism; see Aspinwall & Leaf, 2002). Snyder and colleagues (Snyder, 2002; Snyder, Rand, & Sigmon, 2002) have offered detailed explanations of the conceptual distinctions between hope and constructs, such as optimism, self-efficacy, and self-esteem. Still, an important area of future research is to explore the empirical support for these distinctions. Psychology as a field has long been criticized for its theoretical fragmentation. It will be crucial to empirically examine hope in conjunction with other constructs in order to better understand the nomological network and different sequelae of each phenomenon.

Another area that merits further study is group differences in hopeful thinking. For example, research consistently has shown no significant gender differences in hope; however, there is yet no theoretical explanation as to why. This finding is especially perplexing given the routine finding of gender differences on indices of adjustment (e.g., depressive symptoms; Nolen-Hoeksema, Larson, & Grayson, 1999). Given the connection between hopeful thinking and well-being that we previously have outlined, it seems peculiar to find gender differences in adjustment, but not hope. Also, more work is needed in understanding how different ethnic groups manifest hope

(Lopez, Gariglietti et al., 2000). For example, although some research has shown that the factor structure of hope is stable across various ethnic groups (Kato & Snyder, 2005; Roesch & Vaughn, 2006), there is evidence to suggest there may be differing relationships between hopeful thinking and the use of coping strategies across different ethnic groups (Danoff-Burg, Prelow, & Swenson, 2004). To the extent that we can understand how hope differentially impacts the well-being of different groups of people, the more likely we will be able to optimize human functioning for everyone.

Related to this point, an ongoing question is whether hope can be maladaptive for certain groups or in certain circumstances (i.e., false hope; see Snyder & Rand, 2000; Snyder, Rand, King, Feldman, & Taylor, 2002). Snyder and colleagues have offered theoretical reasons to doubt the existence of false hope; however, there still is a need to test these ideas empirically. Future research may uncover important information about the limits of hope in ameliorating the human condition.

Finally, the continued growth and expansion of hope theory into the realm of human interaction offers a tremendous opportunity for dealing with some of our greatest challenges in the modern world. Although hope theory is conceptualized at the individual level, the social implications are tremendous. Hopeful thought may be an antidote to fear and frustration, which we believe to be at the heart of many ongoing ills in the world (e.g., terrorism, warfare, and the erosion of civil liberties). To the extent that we can better understand people's fears and frustrations (and the destructive actions they take in response to these feelings) as functions of thwarted goals, the more likely we are as a global community to come up with tenable, long-term solutions. Perhaps this is the underlying lesson in the myth of Pandora.

Questions about the Future of Hope

1. What are the distinctions among hope and similar personality concepts, such as optimism and self-efficacy?

2. Are there circumstances where hope is maladaptive?

3. Can hope theory be used to understand and ameliorate current global crises (e.g., terrorism, war, and degradation of the environment)?

References

Affleck, G., & Tennen, H. (1996). Construing benefits from adversity: Adaptational significance and dispositional underpinnings. *Journal of Personality, 64*, 899–922.

Anderson, J. R. (1988). The role of hope in appraisal, goal-setting, expectancy, and coping. Unpublished doctoral dissertation, Department of Psychology, University of Kansas, Lawrence, KS.

Aspinwall, L. G., & Leaf, S. L. (2002). In search of the unique aspects of hope: Pinning our hopes on positive emotions, future-oriented thinking, hard times, and other people. *Psychological Inquiry, 13*, 276–288.

Averill, J. R., Catlin, G., & Chon, K. K. (1990). *Rules of hope*. New York: Springer-Verlag.

Babyak, M. A., Snyder, C. R., & Yoshinobu, L. (1993). Psychometric properties of the Hope Scale: A confirmatory factor analysis. *Journal of Research in Personality, 27*, 154–169.

Bandura, A. (1982). Self-efficacy mechanism in human agency. *American Psychologist, 37*, 122–147.

Bandura, A. (1997). *Self-efficacy: The exercise of control*. New York: Freeman.

Barnum, D. D., Snyder, C. R., Rapoff, M. A., Mani, M. M., & Thompson, R. (1998). Hope and social support in the psychological adjustment of pediatric burn survivors and matched controls. *Children's Health Care, 27*, 15–30.

Bartlett, J. (1968). *Familiar quotations*. Boston: Little, Brown, & Co.

Berg, C. J., Rapoff, M. A., Snyder, C. R., & Belmont, J. M. (2007). The relationship of children's hope to pediatric asthma treatment adherence. *Journal of Positive Psychology, 2*, 176–184.

Bryant, F. B., & Cvengros, J. A. (2004). Distinguishing hope and optimism: Two sides of a coin, or two separate coins? *Journal of Social and Clinical Psychology, 23*, 273–302.

Carvajal, S. C., Clair, S. D., Nash, S. G., & Evans, R. I. (1998). Relating optimism, hope, and self-esteem to social influences in deterring substance use in adolescents. *Journal of Social and Clinical Psychology, 17*, 443–465.

Chang, E. C. (1998). Hope, problem-solving ability, and coping in a college student population: Some implications for theory and practice. *Journal of Clinical Psychology, 54*, 953–962.

Chartrand, T. L., & Cheng, C. M. (2002). The role of nonconscious goal pursuit in hope. *Psychological Inquiry, 13*, 290–294.

Cheavens, J. S., Feldman, D., Gum, A., Michael, S. T., & Snyder, C. R. (2006). Hope therapy in a community sample: A pilot investigation. *Social Indicators Research, 77*, 61–78.

Cheavens, J. S., Feldman, D. B., Woodward, J. T., & Snyder, C. R. (2006). Hope in cognitive psychotherapies: On working with client strengths. *Journal of Cognitive Psychotherapy: An International Quarterly, 20*, 135–145.

Cheavens, J., Gum, A., & Snyder, C. R. (2000). The Hope Scale. In J. Maltby, C. A. Lewis, & A. Hill (Eds.), *A handbook of psychological tests* (Vol. 1, pp. 248–258). Lampeter, UK: Edwin Mellen.

Curry, L. A., Maniar, S. D., Sondag, K. A., & Sandstedt, S. (1999). An optimal performance academic course for university students and student-athletes. Unpublished manuscript, University of Montana, Missoula, MT.

Curry, L. A., Snyder, C. R., Cook, D. L., Ruby, B. C., & Rehm, M. (1997). The role of hope in student-athlete academic and sport achievement. *Journal of Personality and Social Psychology, 73*, 1257–1267.

Danoff-Burg, S., Prelow, H. M., & Swenson, R. R. (2004). Hope and life satisfaction in black college students coping with race-related stress. *Journal of Black Psychology, 30*, 208–228.

Diener, E. (1984). Subjective well-being. *Psychological Bulletin, 95*, 542–575.

Elliott, T. R., Witty, T. E., Herrick, S., & Hoffman, J. T. (1991). Negotiating reality after physical loss: Hope, depression, and disability. *Journal of Personality and Social Psychology, 61*, 608–613.

Emmons, R. A. (1986). Personal strivings: An approach to personality and subjective well-being. *Journal of Personality and Social Psychology, 51*, 1058–1068.

Feldman, D. B., & Snyder, C. R. (1999). Natural companions: Hope and meaning. Unpublished manuscript, University of Kansas, Lawrence, KS.

Feldman, D. B., & Snyder, C. R. (2000). The State Hope Scale. In J. Maltby, C. A. Lewis, & A. Hill (Eds.), *A handbook of psychological tests* (Vol. 1, pp. 240–245). Lampeter, UK: Edwin Mellen.

Floyd, R. K., & McDermott, D. (1998, August). *Hope and sexual risk-taking in gay men*. Paper presented at the American Psychological Association, San Francisco.

Frank, J. D. (1968). The role of hope in psychotherapy. *International Journal of Psychiatry, 5*, 383–395.

Frank, J. D. (1973). *Persuasion and healing* (Rev. ed.). Baltimore: Johns Hopkins University Press.

Frank, J. D. (1975). The faith that heals. *The Johns Hopkins Medical Journal, 137*, 127–131.

Frankl, V. (1966). What is meant by meaning? *Journal of Existentialism, 7*, 21–28.

Frankl, V. (1992). *Man's search for meaning: An introduction to logotherapy* (I. Lasch, Trans.). Boston: Beacon.

Hagen, K. A., Myers, B. J., & Mackintosh, V. H. (2005). Hope, social support, and behavioral problems in at-risk children. *American Journal of Orthopsychiatry, 75*, 211–219.

Harney, P. (1990). The Hope Scale: Exploration of construct validity and its influence on health. Unpublished master's thesis, Department of Psychology, University of Kansas, Lawrence, KS.

Irving, L. M., Snyder, C. R., Cheavens, J., Gravel, L., Hanke, J., Hilberg, P., et al. (2004). The relationships between hope and outcomes at pretreatment, beginning, and later phases of psychotherapy. *Journal of Psychotherapy Integration, 14*, 419–443.

Irving, L. M., Snyder, C. R., & Crowson, J. J., Jr. (1998). Hope and the negotiation of cancer facts by college women. *Journal of Personality, 66*, 195–214.

Jackson, W. T., Taylor, R. E., Palmatier, A. D., Elliott, T. R., & Elliott, J. L. (1998). Negotiating the reality of visual impairment. Hope, coping, and functional ability. *Journal of Clinical Psychology in Medical Settings, 5*, 173–185.

Kato, T., & Snyder, C. R. (2005). The relationship between hope and subjective well-being: Reliability and validity of the dispositional hope scale, Japanese version. *Japanese Journal of Psychology, 76*, 227–234.

Klausner, E. J., Clarkin, J. F., Spielman, L., Pupo, C., Abrams, R., & Alexopoulas, G. S. (1998). Late-life depression and functional disability: The role of goal-focused group psychotherapy. *International Journal of Geriatric Psychiatry, 13*, 707–716.

Klausner, E. J., Snyder, C. R., & Cheavens, J. (2000). Teaching hope to a population of older, depressed adults. In G. Williamson (Ed.), *Advances in aging theory and research* (pp. 295–310). New York: Plenum.

Laird, S. (1992). A preliminary investigation into prayer as a coping technique for adult patients with arthritis. Unpublished doctoral dissertation, Department of Psychology, University of Kansas, Lawrence, KS.

Little, B. R. (1983). Personal projects: A rationale and method for investigation. *Environment and Behavior, 15*, 273–309.

Lopez, S. J., Bouwkamp, J., Edwards, L. M., & Teramoto Pedrotti, J. (2000, October). *Making hope happen via brief interventions.* Paper presented at the 2nd Positive Psychology Summit, Washington, DC.

Lopez, S. J., Floyd, R. K., Ulven, J. C., & Snyder, C. R. (2000). Hope therapy: Helping clients build the house of hope. In C. R. Snyder (Ed.), *Handbook of hope: Theory, measures, and applications* (pp. 123–150). San Diego, CA: Academic Press.

Lopez, S. J., Gariglietti, K. P., McDermott, D., Sherwin, E. D., Floyd, R. K., Rand, K., et al. (2000). Hope for the evolution of diversity: On leveling the "Field of dreams." In C. R. Snyder (Ed.), *The handbook of hope* (pp. 223–242). New York: Academic Press.

McDermott, D., & Hastings, S. (2000). Children: Raising future hopes. In C. R. Snyder (Ed.), *Handbook of hope: Theory, measures, and applications* (pp. 185–199). San Diego, CA: Academic Press.

McDermott, D., & Snyder, C. R. (1999). *Making hope happen.* Oakland, CA: New Harbinger.

McDermott, D., & Snyder, C. R. (2000). *The great big book of hope: Help your children achieve their dreams.* Oakland, CA: New Harbinger.

Magaletta, P. R., & Oliver, J. M. (1999). The hope construct, will and ways: Their relationship with self-efficacy, optimism, and general well-being. *Journal of Clinical Psychology, 55*, 539–551.

Mehlman, R. C., & Snyder, C. R. (1985). Excuse theory: A test of the self-protective role of attributions. *Journal of Personality and Social Psychology, 49*, 994–1001.

Melges, R., & Bowlby, J. (1969). Types of hopelessness in psychopathological processes. *Archives of General Psychiatry, 20*, 690–699.

Menninger, K. (1959). The academic lecture on hope. *The American Journal of Psychiatry, 116*, 481–491.

Michael, S. T. (2000). Hope conquers fear: Overcoming anxiety and panic attacks. In C. R. Snyder (Ed.), *Handbook of hope: Theory, measures, and applications* (pp. 355–378). San Diego, CA: Academic.

Michael, S. T., & Snyder, C. R. (2005). Getting unstuck: The roles of hope, finding meaning, and rumination in adjustment to bereavement among college students. *Death Studies, 29*, 435–458.

Moon, C., & Snyder, C. R. (2000). The Children's Hope Scale. In J. Maltby, C. A. Lewis, & A. Hill (Eds.), *A handbook of psychological tests* (Vol. 1, pp. 160–166). Lampeter, UK: Edwin Mellen.

Nolen-Hoeksema, S., Larson, J., & Grayson, C. (1999). Explaining gender differences in depressive symptoms. *Journal of Personality and Social Psychology, 77*, 1061–1072.

Omodei, M. M., & Wearing, A. J., (1990). Need satisfaction and involvement in personal projects: Toward an integrative model of subjective well-being. *Journal of Personality and Social Psychology, 59*, 762–769.

Palys, T. S., & Little, B. R. (1983). Perceived life satisfaction and organization of personal projects systems. *Journal of Personality and Social Psychology, 44*, 1221–1230.

Rieger, E. (1993). Correlates of adult hope, including high- and low-hope adults' recollection of parents. Psychology honors thesis, Department of Psychology, University of Kansas, Lawrence, KS.

Roesch, S. C., & Vaughn, A. A. (2006). Evidence for the factorial validity of the dispositional hope scale: Cross-ethnic and cross-gender measurement equivalence. *European Journal of Psychological Assessment, 22*, 78–84.

Roseman, I. J., & Evdokas, A. (2004). Appraisals cause experienced emotions: Experimental evidence. *Cognition and Emotion, 18*, 1–28.

Ruehlman, L. S., & Wolchik, S. A. (1988). Personal goals and interpersonal support and hindrance as factors in psychological distress and well-being. *Journal of Personality and Social Psychology, 55*, 293–301.

Schulman, M. (1991). *The passionate mind.* New York: Free Press.

Shorey, H. S., Snyder, C. R. Yang, X., & Lewin, M. R. (2003). The role of hope as a mediator in recollected parenting, adult attachment, and mental health. *Journal of Social and Clinical Psychology, 22*, 685–715.

Snyder, C. R. (1989). Reality negotiation: From excuses to hope and beyond. *Journal of Clinical and Social Psychology, 8*, 130–157.

Snyder, C. R. (1994a). Hope and optimism. In V. S. Ramachandren (Ed.), *Encyclopedia of human behavior* (Vol. 2, pp. 535–542). San Diego, CA: Academic Press.

Snyder, C. R. (1994b, August). *Hope for the many vs. hope for the few.* Paper presented at the annual meeting of the American Psychological Association, Los Angeles.

Snyder, C. R. (1994c). *The psychology of hope: You can get there from here.* New York: Free Press.

Snyder, C. R. (1998). Hope. In H. S. Friedman (Ed.), *Encyclopedia of mental health* (pp. 421–431). San Diego, CA: Academic Press.

Snyder, C. R. (1999). Hope, goal blocking thoughts, and test-related anxieties. *Psychological Reports, 84*, 206–208.

Snyder, C. R. (2000). Hypothesis: There is hope. In C. R. Snyder (Ed.), *Handbook of hope: Theory, measures, and applications* (pp. 3–21). San Diego, CA: Academic Press.

Snyder, C. R. (2002). Hope theory: Rainbows in the mind. *Psychological Inquiry, 13*, 249–275.

Snyder, C. R., Berg, C., Woodward, J. T., Gum, A., Rand, K. L., Wrobleski, K. K., et al. (2005). Hope against the cold: Individual differences in trait hope and acute pain tolerance on the cold pressor task. *Journal of Personality, 73*, 287–312.

Snyder, C. R., Cheavens, J., & Michael, S. T. (1999). Hoping. In C. R. Snyder (Ed.), *Coping: The psychology of what works* (pp. 205–231). New York: Oxford University Press.

Snyder, C. R., Cheavens, J., & Sympson, S. C. (1997). Hope: An individual motive for social commerce. *Group Dynamics: Theory, Research, and Practice, 1*, 107–118.

Snyder, C. R., Feldman, D. B., Taylor, J. D., Schroeder, L. L., & Adams, V., III. (2000). The roles of hopeful thinking in preventing problems and enhancing strengths. *Applied and Preventative Psychology, 15*, 262–295.

Snyder, C. R., Harris, C., Anderson, J. R., Holleran, S. A., Irving, L. M., Sigmon, S. T., et al. (1991). The will and the ways: Development and validation of an individual-differences measure of hope. *Journal of Personality and Social Psychology, 60*, 570–585.

Snyder, C. R., Hoza, B., Pelham, W. E., Rapoff, M., Ware, L., Danovsky, M., et al. (1997). The development and validation of the Children's Hope Scale. *Journal of Pediatric Psychology, 22*, 399–421.

Snyder, C. R., Ilardi, S. S., Cheavens, J., Michael, S. T., Yamhure, L., & Sympson, S. (2000). The role of hope in cognitive behavior therapies. *Cognitive Therapy and Research, 24*, 747–762.

Snyder, C. R., Ilardi, S. S., Michael, S. T., & Cheavens, J. (2000). Hope theory: Updating a common process for psychological change. In C. R. Snyder & R. E. Ingram (Eds.), *Handbook of psychological change: Psychotherapy processes and practices for the 21st century* (pp. 128–153). New York: Wiley.

Snyder, C. R., Irving, L., & Anderson, J. R. (1991). Hope and health: Measuring the will and the ways. In C. R. Snyder & D. R. Forsyth (Eds.), *Handbook of social and clinical psychology: The health perspective* (pp. 285–305). Elmsford, NY: Pergamon.

Snyder, C. R., Lapointe, A. B., Crowson, J. J., Jr., & Early, S. (1998). Preferences of high- and low-hope people for self-referential input. *Cognition and Emotion, 12*, 807–823.

Snyder, C. R., McDermott, D., Cook, W., & Rapoff, M. (1997). *Hope for the journey: Helping children through the good times and the bad.* Boulder, CO: Westview.

Snyder, C. R., Michael, S. T., & Cheavens, J. (1999). Hope as a psychotherapeutic foundation for nonspecific factors, placebos, and expectancies. In M. A. Huble, B. Duncan, & S. Miller (Eds.), *Heart and soul of change* (pp. 179–200). Washington, DC: American Psychological Association.

Snyder, C. R., & Pulvers, K. (2001). Dr. Seuss, the coping machine, and "Oh, the places you will go." In C. R. Snyder (Ed.), *Coping and copers: Adaptive processes and people* (pp. 3–29). New York: Oxford University Press.

Snyder, C. R., & Rand, K. L. (2000, August). *Are "false" hopes really false?* Paper presented at the American Psychological Association, Washington, DC.

Snyder, C. R., Rand, K. L., King, E., Feldman, D., & Taylor, J. (2002). "False" hope. *Journal of Clinical Psychology, 58*, 1003–1022.

Snyder, C. R., Rand, K. L., & Sigmon, D. R. (2002). Hope theory: A member of the positive psychology family. In C. R. Snyder & S. J. Lopez (Eds.), *Handbook of positive psychology* (pp. 231–243). New York: Oxford University Press.

Snyder, C. R., Shorey, H. S., Cheavens, J., Pulvers, K. M., Adams, V. H., III, & Wiklund, C. (2002). Hope and academic success in college. *Journal of Educational Psychology, 94*, 820–826.

Snyder, C. R., Shorey, H. S., Rand, K. L., & Ritschel, L. A. (2005). A brief intervention to elevate hope in academically at-risk college students. Unpublished manuscript. University of Kansas, Lawrence, KS.

Snyder, C. R., Sympson, S. C., Michael, S. T., & Cheavens, J. (2000). The optimism and hope constructs: Variants on a positive expectancy theme. In E. C. Chang (Ed.), *Optimism and pessimism* (pp. 103–124). Washington, DC: American Psychological Association.

Snyder, C. R., Sympson, S. C., Ybasco, F. C., Borders, T. F., Babyak, M. A., & Higgins, R. L. (1996). Development and validation of the State Hope Scale. *Journal of Personality and Social Psychology, 70*, 321–335.

Snyder, C. R., & Taylor, J. D. (2000). Hope as a common factor across psychotherapy approaches: A lesson from the dodo's verdict. In C. R. Snyder (Ed.), *Handbook of hope: Theory, measures, and applications* (pp. 89–108). San Diego, CA: Academic Press.

Snyder, C. R., Wiklund, C., & Cheavens, J. (1999, August). *Hope and success in college.* Paper presented at the annual meeting of the American Psychological Association, Boston.

Suls, J., & Fletcher, B. (1985). The relative efficacy of avoidant and nonavoidant coping strategies: A meta-analysis. *Health Psychology, 4*, 249–288.

Sympson, S. C. (1999). Validation of the Domain Specific Hope Scale. Unpublished doctoral dissertation, University of Kansas, Lawrence, KS.

Taylor, S. E. (1989). *Positive illusions: Creative self-deception and the healthy mind.* New York: Basic Books.

Tennen, H., & Affleck, G. (1999). Finding benefits in adversity. In C. R. Snyder (Ed.), *Coping: The psychology of what works* (pp. 279–304). New York: Oxford University Press.

Vernberg, D., Snyder, C. R., & Schuh, M. (2005). Preliminary validation of a hope scale for a rare health condition using Web-based methodology. *Cognition and Emotion, 19*, 601–610.

Vincent, P. J., Boddana, P., & MacLeod, A. K. (2004). Positive life goals and parasuicide. *Clinical Psychology and Psychotherapy, 11*, 90–99.

Worthington, E. L., Jr., Hight, T. L., Ripley, J. S., Perrone, K. M., Kurusu, T. A., & Jones, D. R. (1997). Strategic hope-focused relationship-enrichment counseling with individuals. *Journal of Counseling Psychology, 44*, 381–389.

Wrobleski, K. K., & Snyder, C. R. (2005). Hopeful thinking in older adults: Back to the future. *Experimental Aging Research, 31*, 217–233.

Appendix: Adult Hope Scale
Goals Checklist

Directions: Read each item carefully. Using the scale shown below, please select the number that best describes YOU and put that number in the blank provided.

1 = Definitely False
2 = Mostly False
3 = Somewhat False
4 = Slightly False
5 = Slightly True
6 = Somewhat True
7 = Mostly True
8 = Definitely True

_____ 1. I can think of many ways to get out of a jam.

_____ 2. I energetically pursue my goals.

_____ 3. I feel tired most of the time.

_____ 4. There are lots of ways around any problem.

_____ 5. I am easily downed in an argument.

_____ 6. I can think of many ways in life to get the things that are most important to me.

_____ 7. I worry about my health.

_____ 8. Even when others get discouraged, I know I can find a way to solve the problem.

_____ 9. My past experiences have prepared me well for my future.

_____ 10. I've been pretty successful in life.

_____ 11. I usually find myself worrying about something.

_____ 12. I meet the goals I set for myself.

Self-Efficacy: The Power of Believing You Can

James E. Maddux

Abstract

The basic premise of self-efficacy theory is that "people's beliefs in their capabilities to produce desired effects by their own actions" (Bandura, 1997, p. vii) are the most important determinants of the behaviors people choose to engage in and how much they persevere in their efforts in the face of obstacles and challenges. Self-efficacy theory also maintains that these efficacy beliefs play a crucial role in psychological adjustment, psychological problems, physical health, as well as professionally guided and self-guided behavioral change strategies. This chapter provides an overview of self-efficacy theory and research by addressing three basic questions: (a) What is self-efficacy? (b) Where do self-efficacy beliefs come from? (c) Why is self-efficacy important? The chapter also discusses "collective efficacy"—group members' beliefs in their ability to collectively accomplish shared goals.

Keywords: collective efficacy, outcome expectancies, self-efficacy, self-regulation, social cognitive theory

> The very little engine looked up and saw the tears in the dolls' eyes. And she thought of the good little boys and girls on the other side of the mountain who would not have any toys or good food unless she helped. Then she said, "I think I can. I think I can. I think I can."
> —*The little engine that could* (Piper, 1930/1989)

Some of the most powerful truths also are the simplest—so simple that a child can understand them. The concept of "self-efficacy" deals with one of these truths—one so simple it can be captured in a children's book of 37 pages (with illustrations), yet so powerful that fully describing its implications has filled thousands of pages in scientific journals and books over the past three decades. This truth is that believing that you can accomplish what you want to accomplish is one of the most important ingredients—perhaps *the* most important ingredient—in the recipe for success. Any child who has read *The little engine that could* knows this is so. For 30 years,

hundreds of researchers have been trying to tell us *why* this is so.

The basic premise of self-efficacy theory is that "people's beliefs in their capabilities to produce desired effects by their own actions" (Bandura, 1997, p. vii) are the most important determinants of the behaviors people choose to engage in and how much they persevere in their efforts in the face of obstacles and challenges. Self-efficacy theory also maintains that these efficacy beliefs play a crucial role in psychological adjustment, psychological problems, physical health, as well as professionally guided and self-guided behavioral change strategies.

Since the publication of Albert Bandura's 1977 *Psychological Review* article titled "Self-Efficacy: Toward a Unifying Theory of Behavior Change," the term "self-efficacy" has become ubiquitous in psychology and related fields. Hundreds of articles on every imaginable aspect of self-efficacy have appeared in journals devoted to psychology, sociology, kinesiology, public health, medicine, nursing, and other fields. In this chapter, I attempt to summarize what we have learned from over three decades of research on self-efficacy. I will address three basic questions: What is self-efficacy? Where does it come from? Why is it important?

What Is Self-Efficacy?
A Very Brief History

Although the term "self-efficacy" is of recent origin, interest in beliefs about personal control has a long history in philosophy and psychology. Spinoza, David Hume, John Locke, William James, and (more recently) Gilbert Ryle have all struggled with understanding the role of "volition" and "the will" in human behavior (Russell, 1945; Vessey, 1967). The theories of effectance motivation (White, 1959), achievement motivation (McClelland, Atkinson, Clark, & Lowell, 1953), social learning (Rotter, 1966), and helplessness (Abramson, Seligman, & Teasdale, 1978) are just a few of the many theories that have sought to explore relationships between perceptions of personal competence and human behavior and psychological well-being (see also Skinner, 1995; Molden & Dweck, 2006). Bandura's 1977 article, however, formalized the notion of perceived competence as "self-efficacy," defined it clearly, and embedded it in a theory of how it develops and influences human behavior.

Defining Self-Efficacy

One of the best ways to get a clear sense of how self-efficacy is defined and measured is to distinguish it from related concepts. Self-efficacy is not perceived skill; it is what I believe I can do with my skills under certain conditions. It is not concerned with my beliefs about my ability to perform specific and trivial motor acts, but with my beliefs about my ability to coordinate and orchestrate skills and abilities in changing and challenging situations.

Self-efficacy beliefs are not simply predictions about behavior. Self-efficacy is concerned not with that I believe I *will* do but with what I believe I *can* do.

Self-efficacy beliefs are not casual attributions. Casual attributions are explanations for events, including my own behavior and its consequences.

Self-efficacy beliefs are my beliefs about what I am capable of doing.

Self-efficacy beliefs are not intentions to behave or intentions to attain a particular goal. An intention is what I say I will probably do; and research has shown that intentions are influenced by a number of factors, including, but not limited to, self-efficacy beliefs (Maddux, 1999a).

Self-efficacy is not self-esteem. Self-esteem is what I believe about myself, and how I feel about what I believe about myself. Efficacy beliefs in a given domain will contribute to my self-esteem only in direct proportion to the importance I place on that domain.

Self-efficacy is not a motive, drive, or need for control. I can have a strong need for control in a particular domain and still hold weak beliefs about my efficacy for that domain.

Self-efficacy beliefs are not outcome expectancies (Bandura, 1997) or behavior–outcome expectancies (Maddux, 1999a). A behavior–outcome expectancy is my belief that a specific behavior may lead to a specific outcome in a specific situation. A self-efficacy belief is the belief that I can perform the behavior or behaviors that produce the outcome.

Self-efficacy is not a personality trait. It is a set of beliefs about the ability to coordinate skills and abilities to attain desired goals in particular domains and circumstances. Measures of "general" self-efficacy have been developed (e.g., Chen, Gully, & Eden, 2001; Sherer et al., 1982; Tipton & Worthington, 1984) and are used frequently in research, but they have not been as useful as more specific self-efficacy measures in predicting what people will do under more specific circumstances (Bandura, 1997; Maddux, 1995).

Where Do Self-Efficacy Beliefs Come From?

Understanding how self-efficacy beliefs develop requires understanding a broader theoretical background. Self-efficacy is best understood in the context of social cognitive theory—an approach to understanding human cognition, action, motivation, and emotion that assumes that we are active shapers of rather than simply passive reactors to our environments (Bandura, 2001, 2006; Barone, Maddux, & Snyder, 1997; Molden & Dweck, 2006). Social cognitive theory's four basic premises, shortened and simplified, are

1. We have powerful cognitive capabilities that allow for the creation of internal models of experience, the development of innovative courses of action, the hypothetical testing of

such courses of action through the prediction of outcomes, and the communication of complex ideas and experiences to others. We also can engage in self-observation and can analyze and evaluate our own behavior, thoughts, and emotions. These self-reflective activities set the stage for self-regulation.

2. Environmental events, inner personal factors (cognition, emotion, and biological events), and behaviors are interactive influences. We respond cognitively, effectively, and behaviorally to environmental events. Also, through cognition we exercise control over our own behavior, which then influences not only the environment but also our cognitive, affective, and biological states.

3. "Self" and "personality" are socially embedded. They are perceptions (accurate or not) of our own and others' patterns of social cognition, emotion, and action as they occur in patterns of situations. Thus, self and personality are not simply what we bring to our interactions with others; they are created in these interactions, and they change through these interactions.

4. We are capable of self-regulation. We choose goals and regulate our behavior in the pursuit of these goals. At the heart of self-regulation is our ability to anticipate or develop expectancies—to use past knowledge and experience to form beliefs about future events and states and beliefs about our abilities and behavior.

These assumptions suggest that the early development of self-efficacy beliefs is influenced primarily by two interacting factors. First, it is influenced by the development of the capacity for symbolic thought, particularly the capacity for understanding cause–effect relationships and the capacity for self-observation and self-reflection. The development of a sense of personal agency begins in infancy and moves from the perception of the causal relationship between events, to an understanding that actions produce results, to the recognition that they can be the origin of actions that effect their environments. As children's understanding of language increases, so do their capacity for symbolic thought and, therefore, their capacity for self-awareness and a sense of personal agency (Bandura, 1997).

Second, the development of efficacy beliefs is influenced by the responsiveness of environments to the infant's or child's attempts at manipulation and control. Environments that are responsive to the child's actions facilitate the development of efficacy beliefs, whereas nonresponsive environments retard this development. The development of efficacy beliefs encourages exploration, which in turn enhances the infant's sense of agency. The child's social environment (especially parents) is usually the most important part of his or her environment. Thus, children usually develop a sense of efficacy from engaging in actions that influence the behavior of other people, which then generalizes to the nonsocial environment (Bandura, 1997). Parents can facilitate or hinder the development of this sense of agency not only by their responses to the infant's or child's actions, but also by encouraging and enabling the child to explore and master his or her environment.

Efficacy beliefs and a sense of agency continue to develop throughout the life span as we continually integrate information from five primary sources: performance experiences, vicarious experiences, imagined experiences, verbal persuasion, and physiological/emotional states.

Performance Experiences

Our own attempts to control our environments are the most powerful source of self-efficacy information (Bandura, 1997). Successful attempts at control that I attribute to my own efforts will strengthen self-efficacy for that behavior or domain. For example, if I get strong ratings of teaching effectiveness from my students, and if I attribute those ratings to my abilities as a teacher (vs. luck or easily pleased students), then my self-efficacy beliefs for teaching will probably be strengthened. Likewise, perceptions of failure that I attribute to lack of ability usually weaken self-efficacy beliefs.

Vicarious Experiences

Self-efficacy beliefs are influenced by our observations of the behavior of others and the consequences of those behaviors. We use this information to form expectancies about our own behavior and its consequences, depending on the extent to which we believe that we are similar to the person we are observing. Vicarious experiences generally have weaker effects on self-efficacy expectancy than do performance experiences (Bandura, 1997).

Imagined Experiences

We can influence self-efficacy beliefs by imagining ourselves or others behaving effectively or ineffectively in hypothetical situations. Such images may be derived from actual or vicarious experiences with situations similar to the one anticipated, or they may be induced by verbal persuasion, as when a psychotherapist guides a client through interventions, such as systematic desensitization and covert modeling (Williams, 1995). Simply imagining myself doing something well, however, is not likely to have as strong an influence on my self-efficacy as will an actual experience (Williams, 1995).

Verbal Persuasion

Efficacy beliefs are influenced by what others say to us about what they believe we can or cannot do. The potency of verbal persuasion as a source of self-efficacy expectancies will be influenced by such factors as the expertness, trustworthiness, and attractiveness of the source, as suggested by decades of research on verbal persuasion and attitude change (e.g., Eagly & Chaiken, 1993). Verbal persuasion is a less potent source of enduring change in self-efficacy expectancy than performance experiences and vicarious experiences.

Physiological and Emotional States

Physiological and emotional states influence self-efficacy when we learn to associate poor performance or perceived failure with aversive physiological arousal and success with pleasant feeling states. When I become aware of unpleasant physiological arousal, I am more likely to doubt my competence than if my physiological state were pleasant or neutral. Likewise, comfortable physiological sensations are likely to lead me to feel confident in my ability in the situation at hand. Physiological indicants of self-efficacy expectancy, however, extend beyond autonomic arousal. For example, in activities involving strength and stamina, such as exercise and athletic performances, perceived efficacy is influenced by such experiences as fatigue and pain (e.g., Bandura, 1997.)

Why Is Self-Efficacy Important?

Fully describing the many ways that self-efficacy beliefs are important would take hundreds of pages. I will focus on five areas: self-efficacy and psychological adjustment; self-efficacy and physical health; self-efficacy and self-regulation; self-efficacy and psychotherapy; and collective efficacy.

Self-Efficacy and Psychological Well-Being

Most philosophers and psychological theorists agree that a sense of control over our behavior, our environment, and our own thoughts and feelings is essential for happiness and a sense of psychological well-being. Feelings of loss of control are common among people who seek the help of psychotherapists and counselors.

Self-efficacy beliefs play a major role in a number of common psychological problems, Low self-efficacy expectancies are an important feature of depression (Bandura, 1997; Maddux & Meier, 1995). Depressed people usually believe they are less capable than other people of behaving effectively in many important areas of life. Dysfunctional anxiety and avoidant behavior are the direct result of low-self-efficacy beliefs for managing threatening situations (Bandura, 1997; Williams, 1995). Self-efficacy beliefs also play a powerful role in substance abuse problems and eating disorders (Bandura, 1997; DiClemente, Fairhurst, & Piotrowski, 1995). For each of these problems, enhancing self-efficacy for overcoming the problem and for implementing self-control strategies in specific challenging situations is essential to the success of therapeutic interventions (Bandura, 1997; Maddux, 1995).

Self-Efficacy and Physical Health

Most strategies for preventing health problems, enhancing health, and hastening recovery from illness and injury involve changing behavior. Research on self-efficacy has greatly enhanced our understanding of how and why people adopt healthy and unhealthy behaviors and of how to change behaviors that affect health (Bandura, 1997; Maddux, Brawley, & Boykin, 1995; O'Leary & Brown, 1995). Beliefs about self-efficacy influence health in two ways.

First, self-efficacy beliefs influence the adoption of healthy behaviors, the cessation of unhealthy behaviors, and the maintenance of behavioral changes in the face of challenge and difficulty. All of the major theories of health behavior, such as protection motivation theory (Maddux & Rogers, 1983; Rogers & Prentice-Dunn, 1997), the health belief model (Strecher, Champion, & Rosenstock, 1997), and the theory or reasoned action/planned behavior (Ajzen, 1988; Fishbein & Ajzen, 1975; Maddux & DuCharme, 1997), include self-efficacy as a key component (see also Maddux, 1993; Weinstein, 1993). In addition, researchers have shown that enhancing self-efficacy beliefs is crucial to successful change and maintenance of virtually every behavior crucial to health, including exercise, diet, stress management, safe sex, smoking cessation, overcoming alcohol abuse, compliance with treatment and prevention regimens, and disease detection behaviors such as breast self-examinations (Bandura, 1997; Maddux et al., 1995).

Second, self-efficacy beliefs influence a number of biological processes, which, in turn, influence health and disease (Bandura, 1997). Self-efficacy beliefs affect the body's physiological responses to stress, including the immune system (Bandura, 1997; O'Leary & Brown, 1995). Lack of perceived control over environmental demands can increase susceptibility to infections and hasten the progression of disease (Bandura, 1997). Self-efficacy beliefs also influence the activation of catecholamines, a family of neurotransmitters important to the management of stress and perceived threat, along with the endogenous painkillers referred to as endorphins (Bandura, 1997; O'Leary & Brown, 1995).

Self-Efficacy and Self-Regulation

Research on self-efficacy has added greatly to our understanding of how we guide our own behavior in the pursuit of desired goals. Self-regulation (simplified) depends on three interacting components (Barone et al., 1997): goals or standards of performance; self-evaluative reactions to performance; and self-efficacy beliefs.

Goals are essential to self-regulation because we attempt to regulate our actions, thoughts, and emotions to achieve desired outcomes. The ability to envision desired future events and states allows us to create incentives that motivate and guide our actions and standards against which to monitor our progress and evaluate both our progress and our abilities (chap. 30).

Self-evaluative reactions are important in self-regulation because our beliefs about the progress we are making (or not making) toward our goals are major determinants of our emotional reactions during goal-directed activity. These emotional reactions, in turn, can enhance or disrupt self-regulation.

Self-efficacy beliefs influence self-regulation in several ways. First, they influence the goals we set. The higher my self-efficacy in a specific achievement domain, the loftier will be the goals that I set for myself in that domain. Second, they influence our choices of goal-directed activities, expenditure of effort, persistence in the face of challenge and obstacles (Bandura, 1997), and reactions to perceived discrepancies between goals and current performance (Bandura, 1997). If I have strong efficacy beliefs, I will be relatively resistant to the disruptions in self-regulation that can result from difficulties and setbacks, and I will persevere. Perseverance usually produces desired results, and this success then increases my sense of efficacy (see also chap. 12).

Third, self-efficacy beliefs influence the efficiency and effectiveness of problem solving and decision making (see also chap. 32). When faced with complex decisions, people who have confidence in their ability to solve problems use their cognitive resources more effectively than do those people who doubt their cognitive skills (e.g., Bandura, 1997). Such efficacy usually leads to better solutions and greater achievement. In the face of difficulty, if I have high self-efficacy, I am likely to remain "task-diagnostic" and continue to search for solutions to problems. If my self-efficacy is low, however, I am more likely to become "self-diagnostic" and reflect on my inadequacies, which detracts from my efforts to assess and solve the problem (Bandura, 1997).

Self-Efficacy and Psychotherapy

I use the term "psychotherapy" to refer broadly to professionally guided interventions designed to enhance psychological well-being, while acknowledging that self-regulation plays an important role in all such interventions. Different interventions, or different components of an intervention, may be equally effective because they equally enhance self-efficacy for crucial behavioral and cognitive skills (Bandura, 1997; Maddux & Lewis, 1995).

Self-efficacy theory emphasizes the importance of arranging experiences designed to increase the person's sense of efficacy for specific behaviors in specific problematic and challenging situations. Self-efficacy theory suggests that formal interventions should not simply resolve specific problems, but should provide people with the skills and sense of efficacy for solving problems themselves. Some basic strategies for enhancing self-efficacy are based on the five sources of self-efficacy previously noted.

Performance experience. The phrase "seeing is believing" underscores the importance of providing people with tangible evidence of their success. When people actually can see themselves coping effectively with difficult situations, their sense of mastery is likely to be heightened. These experiences are likely to be most successful when both goals and strategies are specific. Goals that are concrete, specific, and proximal (short-range) provide greater incentive, motivation, and evidence of efficacy than goals that are abstract, vague, and set in the distant future (chap. 30). Specific goals allow people to identify the specific behaviors needed for successful achievement and to know when they have succeeded (chap. 30). For example, the most effective interventions for phobias and fears involve "guided mastery"—in vivo experience with the feared object or situation during therapy sessions, or between sessions as "homework" assignments (Williams, 1995). Recent technological advances now allow for the use of "virtual reality" experiences in the treatment of phobias and fears (e.g., Rothbaum et al., 2006). In cognitive treatments of depression, clients are provided structured guidance in arranging success experiences that will counteract low-self-efficacy expectancies (Maddux & Lewis, 1995).

Vicarious experience. Vicarious learning and imagination can be used to teach new skills and enhance self-efficacy for those skills. For example, modeling films and videotapes have been used successfully to encourage socially withdrawn children to interact with other children. The child viewing the film sees the model child, someone much like himself or herself, experience success and comes to believe that he or she too can do the same thing (Conger & Keane, 1981). In vivo modeling has been used successfully in the treatment of phobic individuals. This research has shown that changes in self-efficacy beliefs for approach behaviors mediate adaptive behavioral changes (Bandura, 1986; Williams 1995). Common everyday (nonprofessional) examples of the use of vicarious experiences to enhance self-efficacy include advertisements for weight loss and smoking cessation programs that feature testimonials from successful people. The clear message from these testimonials is that the listener or reader also can accomplish this difficult task. Formal and informal support groups—people sharing their personal experiences in overcoming a common adversity, such as addiction, obesity, or illness—also provide forums for the enhancement of self-efficacy.

Imagined experience. Live or filmed models may be difficult to obtain, but the imagination is an easily harnessed resource. Imagining ourselves engaging in feared behaviors or overcoming difficulties can be used to enhance self-efficacy. For example, cognitive therapy of anxiety and fear problems often involves modifying visual images of danger and anxiety, including images of coping effectively with the feared situation. Imaginal (covert) modeling has been used successfully in interventions to increase assertive behavior and self-efficacy for assertiveness (Kazdin, 1979). Systematic desensitization and implosion are traditional behavioral therapy techniques that rely on the ability to image coping effectively with a difficult situation (Emmelkamp, 1994). Because maladaptive distorted imagery is an important component of anxiety and depression, various techniques have been developed to help clients modify distortions and maladaptive assumptions contained in their visual images of danger and anxiety. A client can gain a sense of control over a feared situation by imagining a future self that can deal effectively with the situation.

Verbal persuasion. Most formal psychological interventions rely strongly on verbal persuasion to enhance a client's self-efficacy and encouraging small risks that may lead to small successes. In cognitive and cognitive-behavioral therapies (Holland, Stewart, & Strunk, 2006), the therapist engages the client in a discussion of the client's dysfunctional beliefs, attitudes, and expectancies and helps the client see the irrationality and self-defeating nature of such beliefs. The therapist encourages the client to adopt new, more adaptive beliefs and to act on these new beliefs and expectancies. As a result, the client experiences the successes that can lead to more enduring changes in self-efficacy beliefs and adaptive behavior. People also rely daily on verbal persuasion as a self-efficacy facilitator by seeking the support of other people when attempting to lose weight, quit smoking, maintain an exercise program, or summon up the courage to confront a difficult boss or loved one.

Physiological and emotional states. We usually feel more self-efficacious when we are calm than when we are aroused and distressed. Thus, strategies for controlling and reducing emotional arousal (specifically anxiety) while attempting new behaviors should enhance self-efficacy beliefs and increase the likelihood of successful implementation. Hypnosis, biofeedback, relaxation training, meditation, and medication are the most common strategies for reducing the physiological arousal typically associated with low self-efficacy and poor performance.

Collective Efficacy

This chapter has focused so far on the efficacy beliefs of individuals about themselves as individuals. Positive psychology and social cognitive theory both emphasize the social embeddedness of the individual. For this reason, I cannot leave the concept of efficacy locked inside the person. Accomplishing important goals in groups, organizations, and societies always has depended on the ability of individuals to identify the abilities of other individuals and to harness these abilities to accomplish common goals. Thus, in self-efficacy theory, it is recognized that no man or woman is an island and that there are limits to what individuals can accomplish alone. This idea is captured in the notion of "collective efficacy": "a group's shared belief in its conjoint capabilities to organize and execute the courses of action required for producing given levels of attainments" (Bandura, 1997, p. 477; also Zaccaro, Blair, Peterson, & Zazanis, 1995). Simply stated, collective efficacy is the extent to which we believe that we can work together effectively to accomplish our shared goals.

Despite a lack of consensus on its measurement (Bandura, 1997; Maddux, 1999b), collective efficacy has been found to be important to a number of collectives. The more efficacious spouses feel about their shared ability to accomplish important shared goals, the more satisfied they are with their marriages (Kaplan & Maddux, 2002). The same is true of college-age dating couples (Zapata & Maddux, 2006). The collective efficacy of an athletic team can be raised or lowered by false feedback about ability and can subsequently influence its success in competitions (Hodges & Carron, 1992). The individual and collective efficacy of teachers for effective instruction seems to affect the academic achievement of school children (Bandura, 1993, 1997). The effectiveness of self-managing work teams (Little & Madigan, 1994) and group "brainstorming" (Prussia & Kinicki, 1996) also seems to be related to a collective sense of efficacy. Researchers are also beginning to understand the origins of collective efficacy for social and political change (Fernandez-Ballesteros, Diez-Nicolas, Caprara, Barbaranelli, & Bandura, 2000). Of course, personal efficacy and collective efficacy go hand-in-hand because a "collection of inveterate self-doubters is not easily forged into a collectively efficacious force" (Bandura, 1997, p. 480).

Summary

In the past three decades, we have learned much about the role of self-efficacy beliefs and psychological adjustment and maladjustment, physical health, and self-guided and professionally guided behavior change. There is, of course, much more to be learned. In keeping with the agenda of positive psychology, I suggest two broad avenues of future research.

First, positive psychology emphasizes the development of positive human qualities and the facilitation of psychological health and happiness over the mere prevention of or remediation of negative human qualities and human misery. It also embraces the notion that individuals can be self-initiating agents for change in their own lives and the lives of others. The emphasis of social cognitive theory and self-efficacy theory on the development of "enablement"—providing people with skills for selecting and attaining the life goals they desire—over prevention and risk reduction is consonant with both of these emphases. Self-efficacy research concerned with enhancing our understanding of self-regulation will enhance our understanding of how to provide people with these enablement skills.

Second, positive psychology emphasizes the social embeddedness of the individual and acknowledges

that my individual success and happiness depends to a large degree on my ability to cooperate, collaborate, negotiate, and otherwise live in harmony with other people. In addition, the ability of businesses, organizations, communities, and governments (local, state, and national) to achieve their goals will increasingly depend on their ability to coordinate their efforts, particularly because these goals often conflict. For this reason, collective efficacy—including collective efficacy in organizations and schools, and efficacy for social and political change—provides numerous important questions for future research. In a world in which communication across the globe often is faster than communication across the street, and in which cooperation and collaboration in commerce and government is becoming increasingly common and increasingly crucial, understanding collective efficacy will become increasingly important.

The simple yet powerful truth that children learn from *The little engine that could* has been amply supported by over three decades of self-efficacy research—namely, that when equipped with an unshakable belief in one's ideas, goals, and capacity for achievement, there are few limits to what one can accomplish. As Bandura (1997) has stated, "People see the extraordinary feats of others but not the unwavering commitment and countless hours of perseverant effort that produced them" (p. 119). They then overestimate the role of "talent" in these accomplishments, while underestimating the role of self-regulation. The timeless message of research on self-efficacy is the simple, powerful truth that confidence, effort, and persistence are more potent than innate ability. In this sense, self-efficacy is concerned with human potential and possibilities, not limitations, thus making it a truly "positive" psychology.

Future Questions

1. It is clear that self-efficacy beliefs are important in the initiation of behavior changes, but additional research is needed on the role that self-efficacy beliefs play in the ongoing process of self-regulation. What is the complex interaction among self-efficacy beliefs and the other major components of self-regulation such as goals, intentions, plans, and so on?

2. Is there any utility in refining scales of "general self-efficacy" and continuing to use them in research?

3. What role do beliefs about collective efficacy play in organizational change and societal-level changes and movements (e.g., political movements)?

References

Abramson, L. Y., Seligman, M. E. P., & Teasdale, J. D. (1978). Learned helplessness in humans: Critique and reformulation. *Journal of Abnormal Psychology, 87*, 49–74.

Ajzen, I. (1988). *Attitudes, personality, and behavior.* Chicago: Dorsey Press.

Bandura, A. (1977). Self-efficacy: Toward a unifying theory of behavioral change. *Psychological Review, 84*, 191–215.

Bandura, A. (1986). *Social foundations of thought and action.* New York: Prentice-Hall.

Bandura, A. (1993). Perceived self-efficacy in cognitive development and functioning. *Educational Psychologist, 28*, 117–148.

Bandura, A. (1997). *Self-efficacy: The exercise of control.* New York: Freeman.

Bandura. A. (2001). Social cognitive theory: An agentic perspective. *Annual Review of Psychology, 52*, 1–26.

Bandura, A. (2006). Toward a psychology of human agency. *Perspectives on Psychological Science, 1*, 164–180.

Barone, D., Maddux, J. E., & Snyder, C. R. (1997). *Social cognitive psychology: History and current domains.* New York: Plenum.

Chen, G., Gully, S. M., & Eden, D. (2001). Validation of a new general self-efficacy scale. *Organizational Research Methods, 4*, 62–83.

Conger, J. C., & Keane, S. P. (1981). Social skills intervention in the treatment of isolated or withdrawn children. *Psychological Bulletin, 90*, 478–495.

DiClemente, C. C., Fairhurst, S. K., & Piotrowski, N. A. (1995). Self-efficacy and addictive behaviors. In J. E. Maddux (Ed.), *Self-efficacy, adaptation, and adjustment: Theory, research, and application* (pp. 109–142). New York: Plenum.

Eagly, A. H., & Chaiken, S. (1993). *The psychology of attitudes.* New York: Harcourt, Brace, Jovanovitch.

Emmelkamp, P. M. G. (1994). Behavior therapy with adults. In A. E. Bergin & S. L. Garfield (Eds.), *Handbook of psychotherapy and behavior change* (4th ed., pp. 379–427). New York: Wiley.

Fernandez-Ballesteros, R., Diez-Nicolas, J., Caprara, G. V. Barbaranelli, C., & Bandura, A. (2000). *Determinants and structural relation of personal efficacy to collective efficacy.* Unpublished manuscript, Stanford University.

Fishbein, M., & Ajzen, I. (1975). *Belief, attitude, intention, and behavior: An introduction to theory and research.* Reading, MA: Addison-Wesley.

Hodges, L., & Carron, A. V. (1992). Collective efficacy and group performance. *International Journal of Sport Psychology, 23*, 48–59.

Holland, S. D., Stewart, M. O., & Strunk, D. (2006). Enduring effects for cognitive behavior therapy in the treatment of depression and anxiety. *Annual Review of Psychology, 57*, 285–315.

Kaplan, M., & Maddux, J. E. (2002). Goals and marital satisfaction: Perceived support for personal goals and collective efficacy for collective goals. *Journal of Social and Clinical Psychology, 21*, 157–164.

Kazdin, A. E. (1979). Imagery elaboration and self-efficacy in the covert modeling treatment of unassertive behavior. *Journal of Consulting and Clinical Psychology, 47*, 725–733.

Little, B. L., & Madigan, R. M. (1994, August). *Motivation in work teams: A test of the construct of collective efficacy.* Paper presented at the annual meeting of the Academy of Management, Houston, TX.

McClelland, D. C., Atkinson, J. W., Clark, R. W., & Lowell, E. L. (1953). *The achievement motive.* New York: Appleton-Century-Croft.

Maddux, J. E. (1993). Social cognitive models of heath and exercise behavior: An introduction and review of conceptual issues. *Journal of Applied Sport Psychology, 5*, 116–140.

Maddux, J. E. (1995). Self-efficacy theory: An introduction. In J. E. Maddux (Ed.), *Self-efficacy, adaptation, and adjustment: Theory, research, and application* (pp. 3–36). New York: Plenum.

Maddux, J. E. (1999a). Expectancies and the social-cognitive perspective: Basic principles, processes, and variables. In I. Kirsch (Ed.), *How expectancies shape behavior* (pp. 17–40). Washington, DC: American Psychological Association.

Maddux, J. E. (1999b). The collective construction of collective efficacy. *Group Dynamics: Theory, Research, and Practice, 3*, 1–4.

Maddux, J. E., Brawley, L., & Boykin, A. (1995). Self-efficacy and healthy decision-making: Protection, promotion, and detection. In J. E. Maddux (Ed.), *Self-efficacy, adaptation, and adjustment: Theory, research, and application* (pp. 173–202). New York: Plenum.

Maddux, J. E., & DuCharme, K. A. (1997). Behavioral intentions in theories of health behavior. In D. Gochman (Ed.), *Handbook of health behavior research: I. Personal and social determinants* (pp. 133–152). New York: Plenum.

Maddux, J. E., & Lewis, J. (1995). Self-efficacy and adjustment: Basic principles and issues. In J. E. Maddux (Ed.), *Self-efficacy, adaptation, and adjustment: Theory, research, and application* (pp. 37–68). New York: Plenum.

Maddux, J. E., & Meier, L. J. (1995). Self-efficacy and depression. In J. E. Maddux (Ed.), *Self-efficacy, adaptation, and adjustment: Theory, research, and application* (pp. 143–169). New York: Plenum.

Maddux, J. E., & Rogers, R. W. (1983). Protection motivation and self-efficacy: A revised theory of fear appeals and attitude change. *Journal of Experimental Social Psychology, 19*, 469–479.

Molden, D. C., & Dweck, C. S. (2006). Finding "meaning" in psychology: A lay theories approach to self-regulation, social perception, and social development. *American Psychologist, 61*, 192–203.

O'Leary, A., & Brown, S. (1995). Self-efficacy and the physiological stress response. In J. E. Maddux (Ed.), *Self-efficacy, adaptation, and adjustment: Theory, research, and application* (pp. 227–248). New York: Plenum.

Piper, W. (1930/1989). *The little engine that could.* New York: Platt & Monk.

Prussia, G. E., & Kinicki, A. J. (1996). A motivational investigation of group effectiveness using social cognitive theory. *Journal of Applied Psychology, 81*, 187–198.

Rogers, R. W., & Prentice-Dunn, S. (1997). Protection motivation theory. In D. Gochman (Ed.), *Handbook of health behavior research: I. Personal and social determinants* (pp. 113–132). New York: Plenum.

Rothbaum, B. O., Anderson, P., Zimand, E., Hodges, L., Lang, D., & Wilson, J. (2006). Virtual reality exposure therapy and standard (in vivo) exposure therapy in the treatment for the fear of flying. *Behavior Therapy, 1*(37), 80–90.

Rotter, J. B. (1966). Generalized expectancies for internal versus external control of reinforcement. *Psychological Monographs, 80*(1, Whole No. 609).

Russell, B. (1945). *A history of Western philosophy.* New York: Simon & Schuster.

Sherer, M., Maddux, J. E., Mercandante, B., Prentice-Dunn, S., Jacobs, B., & Rogers, R. W. (1982). The self-efficacy scale: Construction and validation. *Psychological Reports, 51*, 633–671.

Skinner, E. A. (1995). *Perceived control, motivation, and coping.* Thousand Oaks, CA: Sage.

Strecher, V. J., Champion, V. L., & Rosenstock, I. M. (1997). The health belief model and health behavior. In D. Gochman

(Ed.), *Handbook of health behavior research: I. Personal and social determinants* (pp. 71–92). New York: Plenum.

Tipton, R. M., & Worthington, E. L. (1984). The measurement of generalized self-efficacy: A study of construct validity. *Journal of Personality Assessment, 48*, 545–548.

Vessey, G. N. A. (1967). Volition. In P. Edwards (Ed.), *Encyclopedia of philosophy* (Vol. 8, pp. 258–260). New York: Macmillan.

Weinstein, N. D. (1993). Testing four competing theories of health-protective behavior. *Health Psychology, 12*, 324–333.

White, R. W. (1959). Motivation reconsidered: The concept of competence. *Psychological Review, 66*, 297–333.

Williams, S. L. (1995). Self-efficacy, anxiety, and phobic disorders. In J. E. Maddux (Ed.), *Self-efficacy, adaptation, and adjustment: Theory, research, and application* (pp. 69–107). New York: Plenum.

Zaccaro, S., Blair, V., Peterson, C., & Zazanis, M. (1995). Collective efficacy. In J. E. Maddux (Ed.), *Self-efficacy, adaptation, and adjustment: Theory, research, and application* (pp. 305–330). New York: Plenum.

Zapta, S., & Maddux, J. E. (2006). Goals and relationship satisfaction among young dating couples: Perceived support for personal goals and collective efficacy for collective goals. Unpublished manuscript, George Mason University.

Problem-Solving Appraisal and Psychological Adjustment

P. Paul Heppner *and* Dong-gwi Lee

Abstract

How people typically respond to life's problems is of critical importance, particularly how they appraise their problem-solving skills and whether they generally approach or avoid the many problems of life. A critical strength or resource for coping with life's demands is a person's appraisal of his or her problem-solving skills and style. This chapter focuses on how problem-solving appraisal has been empirically demonstrated to be an important asset in living and an important component of positive psychology. Specifically, it begins with a brief history of applied problem-solving appraisal, followed by how it is measured. The Problem Solving Inventory (PSI) has been one of the most widely used self-report inventories in applied problem solving; the PSI has a strong empirical base, and it is strongly linked to a wide range of indices of psychological adjustment, physical health, a wide array of coping activities, and vocational adjustment. The chapter also provides a brief overview of problem-solving training interventions, and finally future research directions and conclusions. Because problem-solving appraisal is learned, this implies that it is amenable to change; this provides hope for millions of people to bring positive change to their lives through the integration of problem solving and positive psychology.

Keywords: positive life skills, problem-solving appraisal, problem solving inventory, problem-solving training, psychological adjustment

How people typically respond to life's problems is of critical importance, particularly how they appraise their problem-solving skills and whether they generally approach or avoid the many problems of life. Problems are solved by moving ahead. Some people bring many skills and strengths in solving the multitude of problems in life, whereas others have significant problem-solving deficits. The research evidence in this chapter will clearly indicate that how people appraise their problem solving affects not only how they cope with the problem but also their psychological adjustment.

Consider the case of two female college students, each of whom recently broke up with her boyfriend. After a year of dating, Tanya decided to end the romantic relationship. Although there were many qualities in Michael that Tanya liked, there also were nagging differences in some of their long-term goals, values, and approach to life that would not go

away. Although Tanya was feeling sad and "kind of down," after reflection she knew it was a good decision. She knew in her heart that the relationship would continue to pose difficulties as time passed, and she needed to end the relationship. Tanya also felt confident in her ability to meet and develop intimate relationships with other men. Even though Tanya was in a relationship that was not right for her, she was an effective problem solver and, most importantly, she appraised herself as an effective problem solver, both of which were important strengths that Tanya brought to coping with life's demands.

In contrast, Jennifer also recently broke up with her boyfriend. But a month later, Jennifer was quite depressed; when she tried to make up with her boyfriend, he refused. Jennifer felt she made a mistake and would never find a man like him again. She felt alone, anxious, and hopeless, had not studied much for the last three weeks, and was having a lot of difficulty sleeping. Jennifer lacked confidence in herself and felt herself slipping deeper into a dark hole; suicide had crossed her mind more than once in the last few weeks. Jennifer was not solving her problems very well, and she did not have a positive appraisal of her problem-solving ability.

These stories highlight how one's personal skills and resources affect responses to stressful life events. Positive psychology builds on people's strengths to enhance their well-being. A critical strength or resource for coping with life's demands is a person's appraisal of his or her problem-solving skills and style. This chapter focuses on how problem-solving appraisal has been empirically demonstrated to be an important asset in living and an important component of positive psychology. It begins with a brief history of applied problem-solving appraisal, how it is measured, a summary of the problem-solving appraisal literature, a brief overview of problem-solving training (PST) interventions, and finally future research directions and conclusions.

Brief History of the Applied Problem Solving

Because we are consistently confronted with attention-demanding problems, it is not surprising that psychologists have been exploring the problem-solving topic for years. Indeed, by the mid-1970s, the conceptions of problem solving included various learning (e.g., Skinner, 1974), Gestalt (e.g., Maier, 1970) and computer simulation approaches (e.g., Newell, Shaw, & Simon, 1963). In the bulk of this early research, the focus often has been on impersonal laboratory problems. In their landmark article, D'Zurilla and Goldfried (1971) reviewed applied problem-solving research to identify critical skills for helping individuals become more effective applied problem solvers. Subsequently, more attention was given to how people grapple with and solve personal, ambiguous, ill-defined problems (e.g., Janis & Mann, 1977), as well as implications for persons in the helping professions (e.g., Heppner, 1978).

In the early applied problem-solving literature, problem solving was conceptualized as a constellation of relatively discrete, cognitive abilities or thought processes. For example, the pioneering work in the late 1960s and 1970s of Shure, Spivack, and their colleagues investigated interpersonal cognitive problem-solving skills, such as problem sensitivity, means-ends thinking, alternative solution thinking, causal thinking, and consequential thinking (see Shure, 1982). In other early research, problem-solving skills were conceptualized within stage-sequential models, with an exemplar being the D'Zurilla and Goldfried (1971) five-stage model (general orientation, problem definition and formulation, generation of alternatives, decision making, and verification). This stage-sequential model led to the development of PST interventions (e.g., D'Zurilla, 1986; D'Zurilla & Nezu, 1982). Initially, the five stages were also used for conceptualizing psychotherapy activities (e.g., Heppner, 1978; Urban & Ford, 1971); later, with advances in our understanding of the complexities of information processing, more sophisticated information processing theories were developed within problem-solving frameworks (e.g., Anderson, 1983). Subsequently, scholars proposed more comprehensive analyses of the problem-solving activities in the psychotherapy process (Heppner & Krauskopf, 1987). In the 1990s, there was yet further refinement of applied problem-solving models and training (e.g., D'Zurilla & Nezu, 1999).

Model Advocated in This Chapter: Problem-Solving Appraisal

Persistent difficulties in the applied literature have involved the conceptualization and measurement of actual problem-solving skills, effectiveness, or competence (e.g., Gambrill, 2005; Heppner & Baker, 1997; Kendall & Fischler, 1984). Although this measurement remains problematic, in this chapter we will delve into a closely related construct—a person's appraisal of his or her problem-solving skills. Influenced by research on the importance of higher-order or meta-cognitive variables in various cognitive processes, Butler and Meichenbaum (1981) suggested that a crucial target is not just "the specific knowledge or processes that individuals may apply directly to the solution of problems, but with higher order variables that affect how (and whether) they will solve problems" (p. 219); subsequently, Bandura's (1986) work on self-efficacy provided empirical support for the existence of higher-order processes. Butler and Meichenbaum also emphasized the centrality of an individual's self-appraisal in his or her problem-solving ability. Similarly, other writers in the coping literature suggested that appraisal of one's ability is related to coping with stress (e.g., Antonovsky, 1979). Consistent with this view, Heppner and Petersen (1982) developed the Problem Solving Inventory (PSI) to assess problem-solving appraisal. In this chapter, we will concentrate on the role of problem-solving appraisal in the psychological adjustment process.

Measuring Problem-Solving Appraisal

Measures of applied problem solving include (a) the PSI (Heppner, 1988); (b) the Means-End Problem Solving Procedure (MEPS: Shure & Spivack, 1972); and (c) the Social Problem Solving Inventory (SPSI: D'Zurilla & Nezu, 1999). Only the PSI, however, is conceptualized as a global measure of problem-solving appraisal. As such, the PSI is distinct from indices of problem-solving orientation and skills (e.g., the SPSI). In this section, we will briefly describe the PSI and its applications for counseling.

Problem Solving Inventory

The PSI has been one of the most widely used self-report inventories in applied problem solving (Nezu, Nezu, & Perri, 1989). In the PSI, perceptions of one's problem-solving ability, style, behavior, and attitudes are assessed (Heppner, 1988; Heppner & Baker, 1997; Heppner & Wang, 2003). The PSI consists of 35 6-point Likert-type items (1 = "strongly agree" to 6 = "strongly disagree"), with a total score and three subscale scores (factors derived from a principal component analysis; Heppner & Petersen, 1982). The three subscales tap Problem-Solving Confidence (11 items), Approach-Avoidance Style (16 items), Personal Control (5 items), and 3 filler items. Problem-Solving Confidence is defined as an individual's self-assurance in a wide range of problem-solving activities, a belief and trust in one's problem-solving abilities (general problem-solving self-efficacy), and coping effectiveness. The Approach-Avoidance Style, as the label implies, refers to a general tendency to approach or avoid different problem-solving activities. Personal Control is defined as a belief in one's emotional and behavioral control (thereby reflecting emotional overreactivity and behavioral control; Heppner, 1988; Heppner & Baker, 1997). It should be noted that "higher scores on the PSI indicate a lack of problem-solving confidence, an avoidant problem-solving style, and an absence of personal control."

The PSI appears to be internally consistent and temporally stable; for example, the estimates of internal consistency and temporal stability (test–retest) over a two-week period for the total score and three factors are as follows: the total inventory, $\alpha = .90$, $r = .89$; Problem-Solving Confidence, $\alpha = .85$, $r = .85$; Approach-Avoidance Style, $\alpha = .84$, $r = .88$; and, Personal Control, $\alpha = .72$, $r = .83$ (Heppner & Petersen, 1982). In addition, researchers have provided a wide range of validity data

in support of the PSI's validity (see Heppner, 1988; Heppner & Baker, 1997). It is important to note that the three-factor structure of the PSI has been well replicated across various cultures, such as white college students (Heppner, Baumgardner, Larson, & Petty, 1988), Turkish college students (Sahin, Sahin, & Heppner, 1993), French Canadian adults (LaPorte, Sabourin, & Wright, 1988), and South African college students (Heppner, Pretorius, Wei, Lee, & Wang, 2002). The PSI is also easy to administer, typically requires 15 min for completion, and can be easily scored by hand or computer. The readability level is at the ninth grade (an adolescent version with fourth-grade reading level is also available).

With respect to counseling applications, the PSI can be used to quickly assess important information about the client's problem-solving style or appraisal that may facilitate or hinder his or her day-to-day functioning; moreover, the PSI can be used as a treatment outcome measure for PST interventions (aimed at client problems, such as depression, anxiety, dysfunctional thoughts, and career indecision; see Heppner, 1988; Heppner & Baker, 1997).

Summary of the Problem-Solving Appraisal Literature

Problem-solving appraisal using the PSI has been the focus of over 120 empirical investigations. In this section, we briefly summarize the topics of psychological adjustment, physical health, coping, and educational and vocational issues. We have been selective because of space limitations, but we do provide references for more detailed reviews.

Psychological Adjustment

Early in the evolution of this topic, researchers claimed that problem solving was linked to psychological adjustment (D'Zurilla & Goldried, 1971). In over 80 studies, researchers have examined the link between problem-solving appraisal and psychological health. We will briefly discuss the literature specifically related to (a) general psychological and social adjustment, (b) depression, (c) hopelessness and suicidal behavior, (d) alcohol use/abuse, (e) personality variables, and (f) childhood adjustment.

GENERAL PSYCHOLOGICAL AND SOCIAL ADJUSTMENT

Based on at least 24 studies (refer to Heppner, Witty, & Dixon, 2004) conducted with mostly college student populations, perceived effective (as compared with ineffective) problem solvers reported themselves to be "more" adjusted on (a) general measures, such as the Minnesota Multiphasic

Personality Inventory and Symptom Checklist-90 (e.g., Elliott, Herrick, & Witty, 1992); (b) specific measures of personality variables, such as positive self-concepts (e.g., Heppner, Reeder, & Larson, 1983) and locus of control (e.g., Cook & Heppner, 1997); (c) the frequency of personal problems (e.g., Heppner, Hibel, Neal, Weinstein, & Rabinowitz, 1982); (d) racial identity statuses in African American students (Neville, Heppner, & Wang, 1997); and (e) coping with grief experiences (Reid & Dixon, 2000). In addition, researchers have consistently found that positive problem-solving appraisal as tapped by the PSI is related to social skills as measured by self-report indices (see Heppner et al., 2004). For example, perceived effective (as compared to ineffective) problem solvers reported having (a) more social skills (e.g., Elliott, Godshall, Herrick, Witty, & Spruell, 1991); (b) less social uneasiness/distrust/distress (e.g., Larson, Allen, Imao, & Piersel, 1993); and (c) more social support (e.g., Wright & Heppner, 1991). Thus, there is a well-established association between positive problem-solving appraisal and better social and psychological adjustment.

DEPRESSION

There is extremely strong empirical support across a wide range of populations for a more positive problem-solving appraisal being assessed with less depression. For example, this relationship is statistically significant in at least 35 studies (refer to Heppner et al., 2004). In college student samples, these correlations typically range from .41 to .67 (e.g., Bonner & Rich, 1987). Additionally, similar statistically significant correlations have been found with persons who are in prison ($r = .52$, Bonner & Rich; 1990), patients with chronic low back pain ($r = .48$; Witty & Bernard, 1995), and adults with spinal-cord injuries ($r = .41$; Elliott, Herrick et al., 1992). Similar associations have also been found in other cultures such as South Africa (e.g., Pretorius & Diedricks, 1994), Turkey (Sahin et al., 1993), Canada (Marcotte, Alain, & Gosselin, 1999), and China (Cheng & Lam, 1997). Thus, the link between a more positive problem-solving appraisal and lower depression appears across populations and cultures.

Moreover, in at least nine studies investigators have indirectly or directly examined the moderating role of problem-solving appraisal in predicting depression (refer to Heppner et al., 2004). In nine studies where the moderating role of appraisal processes in regard to the stress and depression relationship is examined, the results of eight studies appear to support such moderation. Moreover, in the investigations, problem-solving appraisal, negative life events, and their interactions accounted for 40–60% of the variance in depression scores. In one study, Nezu and Ronan (1988) used a longitudinal design and controlled for premorbid levels of depression. Impressively, appraisal, negative life events, and their interactions accounted for 87% of the variance in depression scores. The moderating role of problem solving between life events and depression was also reported in a Chinese adolescent sample (Cheng & Lam, 1997). Taken together, it appears not only that perceived effective (as compared with ineffective) problem solvers report lower levels of depression, but also that perceived effective problem solvers under high levels of stress are particularly likely to exhibit lower depression. Thus, both positive problem-solving appraisal and its interaction with negative life events are important in predicting lower levels of depression.

HOPELESSNESS AND SUICIDAL BEHAVIOR

Schotte and Clum's (1982, 1987) diathesis-stress-hopelessness model of suicidal behavior suggests when people who have strong problem-solving abilities are exposed to naturally occurring conditions of high negative life stress, they are cognitively more able to develop effective alternative solutions for adaptive coping as compared with those deficient in problem solving. Subsequently, those with effective (as opposed to ineffective) problem solving skills, even under high stress, are less likely to experience hopelessness that puts the individual at risk for suicidal behavior. At least 12 studies have examined the relationship between problem-solving appraisal, hopelessness, and suicidal behavior to test Schotte and Clum's hypotheses and, in essence, provide strong support for the model (refer to Heppner et al., 2004). These investigations indicate that diminished problem-solving appraisal is a consistent and stable predictor of hopelessness and suicidal ideation. On the contrary, increases in perceived effective problem solving were associated with lower levels of hopelessness (e.g., Witty & Bernard, 1995) and suicidal ideation (e.g., Rudd, Rajab, & Dahn, 1994) across a variety of populations (e.g., college students, correctional inmates, psychiatric patients, and outpatient suicide ideators and attempters). Moreover, consistent with Schotte and Clum's theory, across all of the studies that measured both hopelessness and suicidal ideation, there was a stronger association between problem-solving appraisal and hopelessness ($r = .47–.62$) than between problem-solving appraisal and suicidal ideation ($r = .11-.43$). Although there was a main effect for problem-solving appraisal in predicting hopelessness and suicidal ideation across almost all these studies, in some studies, there also was an interaction with stress (e.g., Bonner & Rich, 1992). More specifically, as predicted by Schotte and Clum's model, perceived effective problem solvers under high levels of stress were likely to report low levels of hopelessness in three of six studies.

One investigation (Dixon, Heppner, & Rudd, 1994) directly tested and found strong support for the mediational role of hopelessness between problem solving and suicidal ideation. Consistent with the theory, Dixon et al. (1994) found that problem-solving appraisal was related to suicide ideation primarily through its impact on hopelessness, and accounted for 68% of the variance in suicidal ideation.

Although it is unclear why people with a perceived effective problem-solving style under high stress may be more able to ward off hopelessness and depression, one possible underlying mechanism may be the construct of hope, particularly agency and pathways (planning to meet goals; see Snyder, Michael, & Cheavens, 1999). Research has found that hope is a significant predictor of problem-focused appraisal (see Snyder et al., 1999). Future research might combine Snyder's hope theory with Schotte and Clum's theory to develop a more comprehensive model of problem solving, hopelessness, and suicidal behavior.

ALCOHOL USE/ABUSE

The proponents of cognitive-social learning approaches propose that individuals who abuse drugs and alcohol do so because they lack a sense of self-efficacy for coping with stressful situations. Thus, alcohol and drug consumption is their coping strategy for altering feelings of personal inadequacy. Support for this relationship between problem-solving appraisal and alcohol/drug usage emerges in at least six studies (refer to Heppner et al., 2004). For example, three studies (Godshall & Elliott, 1997; Heppner et al., 1982; Wright & Heppner, 1991) found a significant linear relationship between more positive problem-solving appraisal and less alcohol use/abuse. However, in two studies (Larson & Heppner, 1989; Williams & Kleinfelter, 1989), a more complex relationship between problem-solving appraisal and alcohol use/abuse emerged; there may be different drinking patterns associated with different components of problem-solving appraisal. Similarly,

one study (Slavkin, Heimberg, Winning, & McCaffrey, 1992) did not find a linear relationship between problem solving and alcohol abuse; but rather found an interesting interaction between the participants' alcohol abuse and parental drinking. In short, although there is some support for a significant linear relationship between a more positive problem-solving appraisal and less alcohol use/abuse, a more complex relationship may exist among these variables.

PERSONALITY VARIABLES

There is some evidence that problem-solving appraisal is associated with other personality variables. For example, in at least eight studies, researchers have also found a consistent association between a more positive problem-solving appraisal and lower anxiety (e.g., Larson, Piersel, Imao, & Allen, 1990). Moreover, a more positive problem-solving appraisal has been related to lower anger and higher curiosity. In these associations, stronger relationships appear with trait as opposed to state anxiety. Additionally, a more positive problem-solving appraisal has been related to a stronger sense of instrumentality in three studies (e.g., Heppner, Walther, & Good, 1995). Thus, it appears that problem-solving appraisal is associated more strongly with trait versus state variables, particularly anxiety and instrumentality.

CHILDHOOD ADJUSTMENT

There is some evidence for a link between mothers' problem-solving appraisal and children's behavior. For example, mothers' problem-solving appraisal scores were found to play a significant role, either in predicting preschool children's social and emotional development or in predicting role reversal behaviors (e.g., assuming parental roles), such as more direct coping behaviors in incest victims (e.g., Walker & Johnson, 1986). Another two studies found relationships between problem-solving appraisal and family environment and corporal punishment. For example, Shorkey, McRoy, and Armendariz (1985) reported that problem-solving appraisal by parents was associated with less reported use of parental punishment in child-rearing situations. If future research finds additional links among parental problem-solving appraisal, children's behavior, and parental punishment, PST with parents in remedial and preventive interventions may be a productive direction for future research.

Physical Health

Problem-solving appraisal has both theoretical and practical relevance to physical health. Positive problem-solving appraisal has been associated with positive health expectancies (e.g., Elliott & Marmarosh, 1994) and with fewer health complaints about premenstrual and menstrual pain, chronic pain, cardiovascular problems, and health problems in general (e.g., Elliott, 1992; see Heppner et al., 2004). These associations are stronger with clinical patients than with college students (Witty & Bernard, 1995). In addition, positive problem-solving appraisal has been found to be prospectively predictive of objective favorable behavioral health outcome complications, such as urinary track infections (e.g., Elliott, Pickelman, & Richeson, 1992).

In addition, four studies by Rath and colleagues (e.g., Rath, Hennessy, & Diller, 2003) consistently indicated that problem-solving appraisal was not only the most successful measure to differentiate brain injured adults from controls (even over standard neuropsychological measures of problem solving), but also the best predictor of community integration. Thus, Rath and associates concluded that the PSI is a very useful measure of evaluating functional problem-solving deficits in patients with traumatic brain injuries. In sum, positive problem-solving appraisal is associated with a range of physical health indices and is further evidence of a link between problem-solving appraisal and human adjustment.

Coping

Problem-solving appraisal has been conceptually linked with coping (Heppner & Krauskopf, 1987). In this section, we examine how problem-solving appraisal may be related to coping with stress across three different areas of research: hypothetical or laboratory problems, reported coping activities, and help seeking and use of helping resources.

HYPOTHETICAL OR LABORATORY PROBLEMS

One way that researchers have examined how people cope or solve problems is to present hypothetical or laboratory problems (e.g., water jar problems or anagram tasks; Wickelgren, 1974), and then study how participants grapple with those problems. The results here are mixed—the expected relationship between a more positive problem-solving appraisal and effective coping was found in three out of five studies (e.g., Nezu & Ronan, 1988). The complexity of the type of laboratory task might explain some of the discrepant results. In this regard, significant relationships were found in the three studies with more complex procedures and repeated trials. Therefore, future researchers might be well advised to use laboratory tasks that more

closely approximate real-life personal problems entailing uncertainty and sufficient complexity with repeated problem-solving trials (see Larson, Potenza, Wennstedt, & Sailors, 1995).

REPORTS OF COPING ACTIVITIES

Aligned with a cognitive transactional theory of coping (Lazarus & Folkman, 1984), some different researchers across at least 10 studies that utilized 13 separate samples that assessed various aspects of coping consistently found that a positive problem-solving appraisal was associated with reports of approaching and attempting to alter the cause of the stressful problem (e.g., MacNair & Elliott, 1992). Thus, a primary conclusion is that problem-solving appraisal is associated with the consistent report of actively focusing on the problem and attempting to resolve the cause of the problem (sometimes called problem-focused coping).

Why do people with a positive problem-solving appraisal tend to approach and engage in problem-focused coping? A possible explanation for the above pattern of results comes from a study by Baumgardner, Heppner, and Arkin (1986). Utilizing an experimental design in which they manipulated success or failure feedback to assess causal attributions, Baumgardner et al. found that the causal role of effort was a major distinguishing feature between the self-appraised effective and ineffective problem solvers; perceived effort was prominent for self-appraised effective problem solvers as a major cause of personal problems as well as their allegedly "failed" laboratory performance in solving a problem. Thus, it appears that effective problem solvers assume responsibility for personal problems; moreover, their increased effort attributions for "failured" coping attempts underscore that their effort relates to the approach, rather than the avoidance of personal problems.

HELP SEEKING AND RESOURCE UTILIZATION

The judicious use of one's environmental resources is important for coping with stressful events. Intuitively, effective problem solvers should be aware of their environment and efficiently use appropriate resources, whereas the opposite should be the case for ineffective problem solvers. In studies of college students, a more positive problem-solving appraisal has been found to be related to help-seeking variables—awareness, utilization of social support, and satisfaction with campus resources (e.g., Neal & Heppner, 1986).

In sum, there clearly is a relationship between a more positive problem-solving appraisal and beneficial coping activities. Although the research that has examined the link between problem-solving appraisal and hypothetical problem solving is equivocal, in other research, problem-solving appraisal consistently is associated with reports of approaching and attempting to resolve problems, as well as the awareness, utilization, and satisfaction with helping resources. Thus, problem-solving appraisal is clearly associated with an array of coping activities.

Vocational Issues

A person's career decision-making processes may be construed as a specific instance of problem solving (Holland & Holland, 1977). Indeed, problem-solving appraisal and career planning and decision making have been found to be related in at least 14 studies (e.g., Chartrand, Rose, Elliott, Marmarosh, & Caldwell, 1993; Flores, Ojeda, Huang, Gee, & Lee, 2006). Thus, how persons appraise their problem solving in general is related to how they approach a specific task, such as career decision making.

Problem-Solving Training Interventions

PST has involved teaching (a) specific component skills (e.g., problem definition and formulation); (b) a general problem-solving model; and (c) specific problem-solving skills in conjunction with other interventions (Heppner & Hillerbrand, 1991). In this section, we will briefly summarize the effectiveness of these three types of PST.

TEACHING SPECIFIC COMPONENT SKILLS

In this line of PST, research typically has focused on teaching cognitive skills within a specific problem-solving stage; typically the training is brief (e.g., 45 min) and an experimental, between-group design is often used (a treatment group vs. a no-treatment control group; see D'Zurilla & Nezu, 1982). Those persons in the specific problem-solving skills training group typically have outperformed those in the control group, although long-term stability of the training is less clear. For example, Nezu and D'Zurilla (1979) examined the effects of the decision-making skills training in three conditions: (a) specific training in decision making based on D'Zurilla and Goldfried's (1971) model; (b) teaching the general definition of decision making based on a utility approach; and (c) the control group with no instruction in decision making. Those in the first group were judged to be significantly more effective than persons in the other two groups.

TEACHING A GENERAL PROBLEM-SOLVING MODEL

In this approach, a general problem-solving model is used, such as the five-stage model of D'Zurilla and Goldfried (1971). The training usually includes didactics and practice in each of the stages over several training sessions, along with an applied integration step (Nezu, 1986). This approach is effective with many populations (e.g., psychiatric patients) and target goals (e.g., substance abuse and addictions, depression, stress and anxiety; D'Zurilla & Nezu, 1999). The persons in the group receiving the general PST typically have outperformed the individuals in control groups (see D'Zurilla & Nezu, 1982, 1999). For example, Platt, Husband, Hermalin, Cater, and Metzger (1993) reported that individuals with drug abuse problems who participated in a PST group for 10 weeks, relative to those in a control group, were significantly more likely to be employed at posttreatment and at a 6-month follow-up (see D'Zurilla & Nezu, 1982, 1999; Heppner & Hillerbrand, 1991).

TEACHING SPECIFIC SKILLS IN CONJUNCTION WITH OTHER INTERVENTIONS

PST has also been used as part of a treatment package including other interventions, such as anxiety management, communication skills, or study skills. This line of PST often consists of one or more problem-solving component skills. The PST has been effective in a wide range of populations (e.g., academic underachievers and psychiatric patients) and target goals (e.g., depression, phobias, marital and family problems, cigarette smoking, and weight problems). For example, in order to enhance stress management skills for women with low incomes supported by public assistance, Tableman, Marciniak, Johnson, and Rodgers (1982) examined the effectiveness of PST in conjunction with other interventions, such as stress reduction skills training, life planning, and goal-setting skills training. The participants in the combined training program manifested significant decreases in depression and anxiety.

In other research, problem-solving appraisal has been used as an outcome measure of PST. For example, in a PST group based on D'Zurilla and Nezu's (1982) general model, the participants reported a substantial increase in problem-solving appraisal as well as a concurrent decrease in depression at posttreatment and 6-month follow-up (Nezu, 1986). Likewise, Heppner et al. (1988) found that persons in an eight-week PST with a focus on self-management principles (e.g., self-analysis and self-reinforcement), as compared with those trained on specific problem-solving skills, showed posttreatment (and 1 year) improvements on the total PSI score and the Approach-Avoidance Style subscale.

Future Research Directions and Conclusions

Clearly, problem-solving appraisal has a significant role in positive psychology. How people appraise their problem-solving skills and style, as a psychological construct, is strongly linked to a wide range of indices of psychological adjustment. For example, a more positive (as opposed to negative) problem-solving appraisal has been associated with a positive self-concept, less depression and anxiety, and vocational adjustment. The PSI, as a measure of problem-solving appraisal, has a strong empirical base, and it portends to be of use to helping professionals.

Future research and theory development is needed to enhance our understanding of problem-solving appraisal and its role in coping and psychological adjustment. One promising direction may be to examine population issues, such as biological sex, ethnicity, socioeconomic status (SES), noncollege populations (e.g., adolescents, adults), people from countries other than the United States, as well as cultural issues to distinguish between universal ("etic") and culture-specific ("emic") problem-solving appraisals. Moreover, little is known about problem solving within different cultural contexts (e.g., African American culture, Asian culture), which holds great potential to be an exciting and fertile arena.

Another direction for future research is to examine the unique role of various components of problem-solving appraisal, as well as the combined effect of two or more of the PSI factors in creating more complex coping styles (e.g., reporting being confident but avoiding problems). Most of the previous research has utilized the total PSI score, but exciting new theoretical developments might occur through the examination of the various combinations of PSI factors. Similarly, we suggest that researchers pay more attention to the examination of more complex and comprehensive theoretical models of applied problem solving, with attention to moderating and mediating variables to identify more specific and complex relations (structural equation models) between problem-solving appraisal and psychological/ physical health. In addition, the relationship between problem-solving appraisal and problem-solving performance merits additional attention. It may be particularly promising to examine the link between problem-solving appraisal

and problem-solving effectiveness. Again, examining these complex issues may significantly facilitate a greater understanding of applied problem solving.

Problem-solving appraisal is learned, and most likely based on thousands of interactions with one's environment. Thus, it is of utmost importance to examine how one's problem-solving appraisal is developed from childhood onward. For example, it may be beneficial to examine to what extent parental modeling and training affect the early development of one's problem-solving appraisal. Likewise, to what extent does formal educational training play a later role in decreasing or enhancing a problem-solving appraisal in children and adolescents? Identifying the mechanisms that contribute to the development of individuals' problem-solving appraisal will enhance psychologists and other helping professionals to significantly promote the development not only of a positive problem-solving appraisal, but most likely problem-solving effectiveness as well.

In addition, it may be especially beneficial to examine how problem-solving appraisal may play a role in buffering people against effects of stressful life events. In this regard, researchers and practitioners are advised to explore a broad array of associations between problem-solving appraisal and adjustment-related issues (e.g., marital satisfaction, career decision making, conflict resolution, and physical health) as well as to examine the utility of enhancing perceived problem-solving abilities in remedial and preventive interventions.

Because problem-solving appraisal is learned, this implies that it is amenable to change; this provides hope for millions of people to bring positive change to their lives through the integration of problem-solving and positive psychology. Indeed, there seem to be many exciting possibilities in future applied interventions to build on people's strengths in problem-solving appraisal to enhance life satisfaction and well-being.

Questions about the Future of Problem-Solving Appraisal

1. To what extent does the Problem Solving Inventory generalize to other cultural contexts in other countries? Why?

2. What does applied problem solving look like in non white groups within the United States, and around the globe?

3. What are the critical events that shape problem-solving appraisal from childhood to adulthood?

References

Anderson, J. R. (1983). *The architecture of cognition.* Cambridge, MA: Harvard University Press.

Antonovsky, A. (1979). *Health, stress, and coping.* San Francisco: Jossey-Bass.

Bandura, A. (1986). *Social foundations of the thought and action: A social cognitive theory.* Englewood Cliffs, NJ: Prentice-Hall.

Baumgardner, A. H., Heppner, P. P., & Arkin, R. M. (1986). Role of casual attribution in personal problem solving. *Journal of Personality and Social Psychology, 50,* 636–643.

Bonner, R. L., & Rich, A. R. (1987). Toward a predictive model of suicide ideation and behavior: Some preliminary data in college students. *Suicide and Life-Threatening Behavior, 17,* 50–63.

Bonner, R. L., & Rich, A. R. (1990). Psychosocial vulnerability, life stress, and suicide ideation in a jail population: A cross-validation study. *Suicide and Life-Threatening Behavior, 20,* 213–224.

Bonner, R. L., & Rich, A. R. (1992). Cognitive vulnerability and hopelessness among correctional inmates: A state of mind model. *Journal of Offender Rehabilitation, 17*(3–4), 113–122.

Butler, L., & Meichenbaum, D. (1981). The assessment of interpersonal problem-solving skills. In P. Kendall & S. D. Hollon (Eds.), *Assessment strategies for cognitive-behavioral interventions* (pp. 197–225). New York: Academic Press.

Chartrand, J. M., Rose, M. L., Elliott, T. R., Marmarosh, C., & Caldwell, S. (1993). Peeling back the onion: Personality, problem solving, and career decision-making style correlates of career indecision. *Journal of Career Assessment, 1,* 66–82.

Cheng, S. K., & Lam, D. J. (1997). Relationships among life stress, problem solving, self-esteem, and dysphoria in Hong Kong adolescents: Test of a model. *Journal of Social and Clinical Psychology, 16,* 343–355.

Cook, S. W., & Heppner, P. P. (1997). A psychometric study of three coping measures. *Educational and Psychological Measurement, 57,* 906–923.

D'Zurilla, T. J. (1986). *Problem-solving therapy: A social competence approach to clinical intervention.* New York: Springer.

D'Zurilla, T. J., & Goldfried, M. R. (1971). Problem solving and behavior modification. *Journal of Abnormal Psychology, 78,* 107–126.

D'Zurilla, T. J., & Nezu, A. (1982). Social problem solving in adults. In P. C. Kendall (Ed.), *Advances in cognitive-behavioral research and therapy* (Vol. 1). New York: Academic Press.

D'Zurilla, T. J., & Nezu, A. (1999). *Problem-solving therapy: A social competence approach to clinical intervention* (2nd ed.). New York: Springer.

Dixon, W. A., Heppner, P. P., & Rudd, D. M. (1994). Problem-solving appraisal, hopelessness, and suicide ideation: Evidence for a mediational model. *Journal of Counseling Psychology, 41,* 91–98.

Elliott, T. R. (1992). Problem-solving appraisal, oral contraceptive use, and menstrual pain. *Journal of Applied Social Psychology, 22,* 286–297.

Elliott, T. R., Godshall, F. J., Herrick, J. M., Witty, T. E., & Spruell, M. (1991). Problem-solving appraisal and psychological adjustment following spinal cord injury. *Cognitive Therapy and Research, 15,* 387–398.

Elliott, T. R., Herrick, S. M., & Witty, T. E. (1992). Problem-solving appraisal and the effects of social support among college students and persons with physical disabilities. *Journal of Counseling Psychology, 39,* 219–226.

Elliott, T. R., & Marmarosh, C. (1994). Problem-solving appraisal, health complaints, and health related expectancies. *Journal of Counseling and Development, 72,* 531–537.

Elliott, T. R., Pickelman, H., & Richeson, C. (1992). *Negative affectivity, problem-solving appraisal, and post-partem depression.* Paper presented at the annual meeting of the Society of Behavioral Medicine, New York.

Flores, L. F., Ojeda, L., Huang, Y., Gee, D., & Lee, S. (2006). The relation of acculturation, problem-solving appraisal, and career decision-making self-efficacy to Mexican American high school students' educational goals. *Journal of Counseling Psychology, 53,* 259–260.

Gambrill, E. (2005). *Critical thinking in clinical practice* (2nd ed.). Hoboken, NJ: Wiley.

Godshall, F. J., & Elliott, T. R. (1997). Behavioral correlates of self-appraised problem-solving ability: Problem-solving skills and health-compromising behaviors. *Journal of Applied Social Psychology, 27,* 929–944.

Heppner, P. P. (1978). The effect of client perceived need and counselor role on clients' behaviors. *Journal of Counseling Psychology, 25,* 514–519.

Heppner, P. P. (1988). *The problem-solving inventory.* Palo Alto, CA: Consulting Psychologist Press.

Heppner, P. P., & Baker, C. E. (1997). Applications of the problem solving inventory. *Measurement and Evaluation in Counseling and Development, 29,* 229–241.

Heppner, P. P., Baumgardner, A. H., Larson, L. M., & Petty, R. E. (1988). The utility of problem-solving training that emphasizes self-management principles. *Counseling Psychology Quarterly, 1,* 129–143.

Heppner, P. P., Hibel, J., Neal, G. W., Weinstein, C. L., & Rabinowitz, F. E. (1982). Personal problem solving: A descriptive study of individual differences. *Journal of Counseling Psychology, 29,* 580–590.

Heppner, P. P., & Hillerbrand, E. T. (1991). Problem-solving training: Implications for remedial and preventive training. In C. R. Snyder & D. R. Forsyth (Eds.), *Handbook of social psychology: The healthy perspective* (pp. 681–698). Elmsford, NY: Pergamon.

Heppner, P. P., & Krauskopf, C. J. (1987). An information processing approach to personal problem solving. *The Counseling Psychologist, 15,* 371–447.

Heppner, P. P., & Petersen, C. H. (1982). The development and implications of a personal problem solving inventory. *Journal of Counseling Psychology, 29,* 66–75.

Heppner, P. P., Pretorius, T. B., Wei, M., Lee, D.-G., & Wang, Y. (2002). Examining the generalizability of problem-solving appraisal in black South Africans. *Journal of Counseling Psychology, 49,* 484–498.

Heppner, P. P., Reeder, B. L., & Larson, L. M. (1983). Cognitive variables associated with personal problem-solving appraisal: Implications for counseling. *Journal of Counseling Psychology, 30,* 537–545.

Heppner, P. P., & Wang, Y. (2003). Problem-solving appraisal. In S. J. Lopez & C. R. Snyder (Eds.), *Positive psychological assessment: A handbook of models and measures* (pp. 127–138). Washington, DC: American Psychological Association.

Heppner, P. P., Walther, D. J., & Good, G. E. (1995). The differential role of instrumentality, expressivity, and social support in predicting problem-solving appraisal in men and women. *Sex Roles, 32,* 91–108.

Heppner, P. P., Witty, T. E., & Dixon, W. A. (2004). Problem-solving appraisal and human adjustment: A review of 20 years of research using the Problem Solving Inventory. *The Counseling Psychologist, 32,* 344–428.

Holland, J. L., & Holland, J. E. (1977). Vocational indecision: More evidence and speculation. *Journal of Counseling Psychology, 24,* 404–414.

Janis, I. L., & Mann, L. (1977). *Decision making: A psychological analysis of conflict, choice, and commitment.* New York: Free Press.

Kendall, P. C., & Fischler, G. L. (1984). Behavioral and adjustment correlates of problem solving: Validational analyses of interpersonal cognitive problem-solving measures. *Journal of Child Development, 55,* 227–243.

LaPorte, L., Sabourin, S., & Wright, J. (1988). L'inventaire de resolution de problemes personels: Une perspective metocognitive. *International Journal of Psychology, 23,* 569–581.

Larson, L. M., Allen, S. J., Imao, R. A. K., & Piersel, W. (1993). Self-perceived effective and ineffective problem solvers' differential view of their partners' problem-solving styles. *Journal of Counseling and Development, 71,* 528–532.

Larson, L. M., & Heppner, P. P. (1989). Problem-solving appraisal with male alcoholics. *Journal of Counseling Psychology, 36,* 73–78.

Larson, L. M., Piersel, W. C., Imao, R. A. K., & Allen, S. J. (1990). Significant predictors of problem-solving appraisal. *Journal of Counseling Psychology, 37,* 482–490.

Larson, L. M., Potenza, M. T., Wennstedt, L. W., & Sailors, P. J. (1995). Personal problem solving in a simulated setting: Do perceptions accurately reflect behavior? *Cognitive Therapy and Research, 19,* 241–257.

Lazarus, R. S., & Folkman, S. (1984). *Stress, appraisal, and coping.* New York: Springer.

MacNair, R. R., & Elliott, T. R. (1992). Self-perceived problem-solving ability, stress appraisal, and coping over time. *Journal of Research in Personality, 26,* 150–164.

Maier, N. R. F. (1970). *Problem solving and creativity.* Belmont, CA: Brooks/Cole.

Marcotte, D., Alain, M., & Gosselin, M.-J. (1999). Gender differences in adolescent depression: Gender-typed characteristics or problem-solving skills deficits? *Sex Roles, 41,* 31–48.

Neal, G. W., & Heppner, P. P. (1986). Problem solving self-appraisal, awareness, and utilization of campus helping resources. *Journal of Counseling Psychology, 33,* 39–44.

Neville, H. A., Heppner, P. P., & Wang, L. (1997). Relations among racial identity attitudes, perceived stressors, and coping styles in African American college students. *Journal of Counseling and Development, 75,* 303–311.

Newell, A., Shaw, J. C., & Simon, H. A. (1963). GPS, a program that simulates human thought. In E. A. Feigenbaum & J. Feldman (Eds.), *Computers and thought* (pp. 39–70). New York: McGraw-Hill.

Nezu, A. M. (1986). Efficacy of a social problem solving therapy approach for unipolar depression. *Journal of Consulting and Clinical Psychology, 54,* 196–202.

Nezu, A., & D'Zurilla, T. J. (1979). An experimental evaluation of the decision-making process in social problem solving. *Cognitive Therapy and Research, 3,* 269–277.

Nezu, A. M., Nezu, C. M., & Perri, M. G. (1989). *Problem-solving therapy for depression: Therapy, research, and clinical guidelines.* New York: Wiley.

Nezu, A. M., & Ronan, G. F. (1988). Social problem solving as a moderator of stress-related depressive symptoms: A prospective analysis. *Journal of Counseling Psychology, 35,* 134–138.

Platt, J. J., Husband, S. D., Hermalin, Cater, J., & Metzger, D. (1993). A cognitive problem-solving employment readiness intervention for methadone clients. *Journal of Cognitive Psychotherapy: An International Quarterly, 7,* 21–33.

Pretorius, T. B., & Diedricks, M. (1994). Problem-solving appraisal, social support and stress–depression relationship. *South African Journal of Psychology, 24,* 86–90.

Rath, J. F., Hennessy, J. J., & Diller, L. (2003). Social problem solving and community integration in postacute rehabilitation outpatients with traumatic brain injury. *Rehabilitation Psychology, 48,* 137–144.

Reid, J. K., & Dixon, W. A. (2000). The relationships among grief experience, problem-solving appraisal, and depression: An exploratory study. *Journal of Personal and Interpersonal Loss, 5,* 77–93.

Rudd, M. D., Rajab, H., & Dahn, P. F. (1994). Problem-solving appraisal in suicide ideators and attempters. *American Journal of Orthopsychiatry, 64,* 136–149.

Sahin, N., Sahin, N. H., & Heppner, P. P. (1993). Psychometric properties of the Problem Solving Inventory (PSI) in a group of Turkish university students. *Cognitive Therapy and Research, 17,* 379–396.

Schotte, D., & Clum, G. A. (1982). Suicide ideation in a college population: A test of a model. *Journal of Consulting and Clinical Psychology, 50,* 690–696.

Schotte, D., & Clum, G. A. (1987). Problem-solving skills in suicidal psychiatric patients. *Journal of Consulting and Clinical Psychology, 55,* 49–54.

Shorkey, C. T., McRoy, R. E., & Armendariz, J. (1985). Intensity of parental punishments and problem-solving attitudes and behaviors. *Psychological Reports, 56,* 283–286.

Shure, M. B. (1982). Interpersonal problem solving: A cog in the wheel of social cognition. *Social-Cognitive Development in Context.* New York: Guilford.

Shure, M. B., & Spivack, G. (1972). Means-ends thinking, adjustment and social class among elementary-school age children. *Journal of Consulting and Clinical Psychology, 38,* 348–353.

Skinner, B. F. (1974). *About Behaviorism.* New York: Knopf.

Slavkin, S. L., Heimberg, R. G., Winning, C. D., & McCaffrey, R. J. (1992). Personal and parental problem drinking: Effects on problem-solving performance and self-appraisal. *Addictive Behaviors, 17,* 191–199.

Snyder, C. R., Michael, S., & Cheavens, J. (1999). Hope as a psychotherapeutic foundation for nonspecific factors, placebos, and expectations. In M. A. Huble, B. Duncan, & S. Miller (Eds.), *Heart and soul of change* (p. 200). Washington, DC: American Psychological Association.

Tableman, B., Marciniak, D., Johnson, D., & Rodgers, R. (1982). Stress management for women on public assistance. *American Journal of Community Psychology, 10,* 357–367.

Urban, H., & Ford, H. (1971). Some historical and conceptual perspectives of psychotherapy and behavioral change. In A. Bergin & S. Garfield (Eds.), *Handbook of psychotherapy and behavior change* (pp. 3–35). New York: Wiley.

Walker, L. O., & Johnson, L. B. (1986). Preschool children's socio-emotional development: Endogenous and environmental antecedents in early infancy. *Final Report to the Hogg Foundation for Mental Health.* As cited in Heppner, P. P. (1988). *The problem* solving inventory: Manuel. Palo Alto, CA: Consulting Psychologists Press, Inc.

Wickelgren, W. (1974). *How to solve problems*. San Francisco: Freeman.

Williams, T. G., & Kleinfelter, K. T. (1989). Perceived problem-solving skills and drinking patterns among college students. *Psychological Reports, 65*, 1235–1244.

Witty, T. E., & Bernard, C. B. (1995). *Problem-solving appraisal and psychological adjustment of chronic low back pain patients*. Paper presented at the annual meeting of American Psychological Association, Los Angeles.

Wright, D. M., & Heppner, P. P. (1991). Coping among non-clinical college age children of alcoholics. *Journal of Counseling Psychology, 38*, 465–472.

Self-Determination

Michael L. Wehmeyer, Todd D. Little, *and* Julie Sergeant

Abstract

Self-determination is a general psychological construct within the organizing structure of theories of human agency which refers to self- (vs. other-) caused action—to people acting volitionally, based on their own will. Human agency refers to the sense of personal empowerment involving both knowing and having what it takes to achieve goals. Human agentic theories share the meta-theoretical view that organismic aspirations drive human behaviors. An organismic perspective of self-determination that views people as active contributors to, or "authors" of their behavior, where behavior is self-regulated and goal-directed, provides a compelling foundation for examining and facilitating the degree to which people become self-determined and the impact of that on the pursuit of optimal human functioning and well-being. Further, an organismic approach to self-determination requires an explicit focus on the interface between the self and context. This chapter discusses the self-determination construct within an organismic perspective, surveys the construct's history and usage in philosophy and psychology, and summarizes four overarching theories of self-determination that are applicable to the field of positive psychology, as well as examining a number of complementary views of human agency as a process of self-determination. Finally, research implications based upon existing knowledge and research in self-determination and positive psychology are identified.

Keywords: causal agency, human agency, self-determination, self-determination theory, volitional action

Self-Determination and Human Agency

Positive psychology is the pursuit of understanding optimal human functioning and well-being. Ryan and Deci (2000a) asserted that in this pursuit for understanding optimal human functioning and well-being, researchers must take into account the agentic nature of human action. This chapter introduces self-determination as a general psychological construct within the organizing structure of theories of human agency. Human agency is "the sense of personal empowerment, which involves both knowing and having what it takes to achieve one's goals" (Little, Hawley, Henrich, & Marsland, 2002, p. 390). An agentic person is the

origin of his or her actions, has high aspirations, perseveres in the face of obstacles, sees more and varied options for action, learns from failures, and overall, has

a greater sense of well being. In contrast, a non-agentic individual can be a pawn to unknown extra-personal influences, has low aspirations, is hindered with problem-solving blinders, often feels helpless and, overall, has a greater sense of ill-being.
(Little et al., 2002, p. 390)

Human agentic theories "share the meta-theoretical view that organismic aspirations drive human behaviors" (Little, Snyder, & Wehmeyer, 2006, p. 61). An organismic perspective views people as active contributors to, or "authors" of their behavior, where behavior is described as self-regulated and goal-directed "action." Unlike stimulus-response accounts of behavior, actions are defined as purposive and self-initiated activities (Brandtstädter, 1998; Chapman, 1984; Harter, 1999). As outlined by Little et al. (2006), human agentic actions are

1. motivated by biological and psychological needs (Deci & Ryan, 2002; Hawley, 1999; Hawley & Little, 2002; Little et al., 2002);

2. directed toward self-regulated goals that service short- and long-term biological and psychological needs;

3. propelled by understandings of links among agents, means, and ends (Chapman, 1984; Little, 1998; Skinner, 1995, 1996), and guided by general action-control behaviors that entail self-chosen forms and functions (Little, Lopez, & Wanner, 2001; Skinner & Edge, 2002; Vanlede, Little, & Card, 2006);

4. those that precipitate self-determined governance of behavior and development, which can be characterized as hope-related individual differences;

5. triggered, executed, and evaluated in contexts that provide supports and opportunities, as well as hindrances and impediments to goal pursuit.

Further, an organismic approach to self-determination requires an explicit focus on the interface between the self and context (Little et al., 2002). Organisms influence and are influenced by the contexts in which they live and develop. Through this person–context interaction people become agents of their own action.

Self-Determination in Philosophy

The construct's origins lie in philosophy and discourse about the doctrines of "determinism" and "free will." Determinism is the philosophical doctrine positing that events, such as human behavior, are effects of preceding causes. John Locke (1690) provided a synopsis of the "free will problem":

> this proposition "men can determine themselves" is drawn in or inferred from this, "that they shall be punished in the other world." For here the mind, seeing the connexion [sic] there is between the idea of men's punishment in the other world and the idea of God punishing; between God punishing and the justice of the punishment; between justice of punishment and guilt; between guilt and a power to do otherwise; between a power to do otherwise and freedom; and between freedom and self-determination, sees the connexion [sic] between men and self-determination.

Locke was a soft determinist; that is, someone who saw both causality and volition or will at work in human behavior. According to Locke, the human mind has the "active" power of beginning or ceasing its own operations as activated by a preference. The exercise of that power is volition or will. Freedom or liberty is "the power to act on our volition, whatever it may be, without any external compulsion or restraint" (Locke, 1690). Human beings act freely insofar as they are capable of translating their mental preferences into actual performance of the action in question (Kemerling, 2000–2001). Freedom is conceptualized as the human capacity to act (or not) as we choose or prefer, without any external compulsion or restraint.

Locke's proposals about the causes of human action as both caused and volitional are important to an organismic theory of self-determination, as is his soft deterministic distinction that it is the "agent" (the person) who is free to act, not the action itself (since it is "caused" by perception or sensation).

Self-Determination in Personality Psychology

In *Foundations for a science of personality* (1941), Angyal proposed that an essential feature of a living organism is its autonomy, where autonomous means self-governing or governed from inside. According to Angyal, an organism "lives in a world in which things happen according to laws which are heteronomous (e.g., governed from outside) from the point of view of the organism" (p. 33), and that "organisms are subjected to the laws of the physical world, as is any other object of nature, with the exception that it can oppose self-determination to external determination" (p. 33).

Angyal (1941) suggested that the "science of personality" is the study of two essential determinants to human behavior: autonomous determinism (self-determination) and heteronomous determinism (other-determined). Angyal placed primary importance for laying the foundation for a science of personality in the fact that a central process of an organism is the movement toward autonomous determination, noting that "without autonomy, without self-government, the life process could not be understood" (p. 34).

Further, Angyal's (1941) use of the term moved away from the hard determinism that dominated psychology, led by Skinner and operant psychologists, toward a soft determinism that considered the importance of both actor and context. This trend has continued in efforts to explain human agency, as evidenced by Bandura's (1997) discussion concerning determinism and human agency:

> When viewed from a sociocognitive perspective, there is no incompatibility between freedom and determinism. Freedom is not conceived negatively as exemption from social influences or situational constraints. Rather it is defined positively as the exercise of self-influence to bring about desired results. (p. 7)

Self-determination, as a psychological construct, refers to self- (vs. other-) caused action—it refers to people acting volitionally, based on their own will. Volition is the capability of conscious choice, decision, and "intention" (Gove, 1967). Volitional behavior, then, implies intent. Self-determined behavior is volitional, intentional, and self-caused or self-initiated.

Theories of Self-Determination
Self-Determination Theory

The most visible application of self-determination as a psychological construct has been "self-determination theory" (SDT; Deci & Ryan, 2002), proposed to explain facets of personality and behavioral self-regulation through interactions between innate and environmental determinants within social contexts (Ryan & Deci, 2000a). With its basis in various subtheories (for details see Ryan & Deci, 2002), SDT brings together innate human tendencies, social contexts, and the motivators for human action to illustrate how congruence between one's basic needs and core values spur individual agency that, ultimately, results in overall well-being.

SDT proposed three basic psychological needs—competence, autonomy, and relatedness—that are either supported or challenged by social contexts (see Little et al., 2002, for a discussion of how these psychological needs mesh with evolutionary-based biological needs). Much of the research stemming from SDT has focused on ways the social environment creates barriers to the integration of these psychological needs (Ryan & Deci, 2002). The context also contributes to intrinsic and extrinsic motivators that are self-regulated at either conscious or unconscious levels. This perspective views the process of self-regulation as an organizational function that "coordinates" systemic behaviors and serves as a foundation for autonomy and the sense of self (Ryan & Deci, 2004).

Early work on SDT focused on the role of social contexts in supporting or thwarting intrinsic motivation and found that conditions fostering autonomy and competence were positively associated with intrinsic motivation. When extrinsically motivated behaviors were acted on, individuals were more likely to integrate the behavior with core values when the social context supported autonomy, competence, and relatedness (Ryan & Deci, 2000a). Recent SDT research has examined the relationship between implicit/explicit motives (conscious or unconscious) and intrinsic/extrinsic motivation (Ryan & Deci, 2004).

As noted, three basic psychological needs (i.e., autonomy, competence, and relatedness) are the driving forces in SDT. Satisfying these needs enhance well-being and contribute to the efficacy of other model components (Deci & Ryan, 2000). Within SDT, autonomous actions express integrity and are based on one's core or "higher-order values" (Ryan & Deci, 2004). Sometimes, outside influences (e.g., social context) force values to conflict and a choice must be made that reflects the true self. Intrinsic and extrinsic motivation plays a role here and these motivators are not simply polar opposites (see Walls & Little, 2005). Instead, the rationale and outcome of negotiating and integrating the demands of intrinsic and extrinsic sources of motivation determines the autonomy of an action (Ryan & Deci, 2004). Thus, an autonomous action is one in which the rationale behind an action response (behavior) to an extrinsic pressure reflects one's core values. Research stemming from SDT has identified conditions that facilitate autonomy and the effect of autonomy on daily functioning and daily life experiences. For example, Sheldon, Ryan, Deci, and Kasser (2004) demonstrated that autonomous motives (e.g., personal identification and enjoyment) and controlled motives (e.g., external rewards and guilt) were associated with higher and lower levels of well-being, respectively.

In SDT, the inherent psychological need for competence refers to the motivation to be effective within environments, which, in turn, stems from the theory of effectence motivation that describes an innate drive for environmental mastery (Deci & Ryan, 2000; White, 1959). This drive leads to behavioral responses that sustain and augment individual capabilities (Ryan & Deci, 2002). The psychological need for relatedness is the sense of connectedness and belonging with others. This sense is distinct from the status of role identification or group membership, as the focus is on personal perceptions of relatedness instead of goal outcomes (Reis, Sheldon, Gable, Roscoe, & Ryan, 2000). Variously, competence, relatedness, and autonomy needs may complement each other, or they may conflict (Deci & Ryan, 2000). More information on SDT research and instruments to assess it can be found at http://www.psych.rochester.edu/SDT/index.html and http://www.agencylab.ku.edu.

Functional Self-Determination Theory

Wehmeyer and colleagues (Wehmeyer, 1996, 2001, 2005) proposed a functional theory of self-determination (fSDT), in which self-determination is conceptualized as a dispositional characteristic that is

A functional model of self-determination

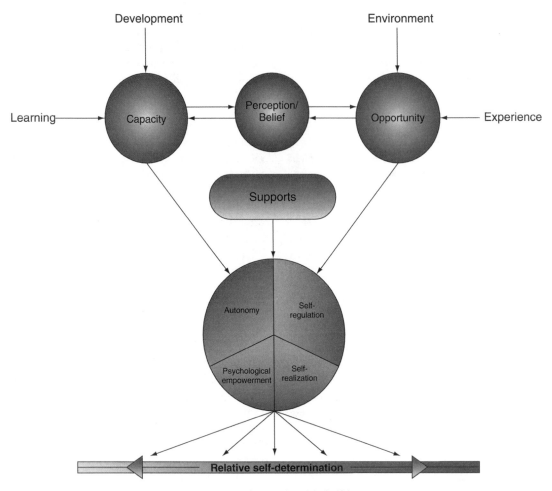

Fig. 33.1 Wehmeyer's functional model of self-determination.

based on the "function" a behavior serves for the individual (Figure 33.1). Self-determined behavior refers to "volitional actions that enable one to act as the primary causal agent in one's life and to maintain or improve one's quality of life" (Wehmeyer, 2005, p. 117). Broadly defined, "causal agency" implies that it is the individual who makes or causes things to happen in his or her life. Causal agency implies more, however, than just causing action; it implies that the individual acts with an eye toward "causing" an effect to "accomplish" a "specific end" or to "cause" or "create change." Bandura (1997) noted the following:

> In evaluating the role of intentionality in human agency, one must distinguish between the personal production of action for an intended outcome, and the effects that carrying out that course of action produce. Agency refers to acts done intentionally. (p. 3)

All of the theoretical perspectives represented here differentiate between self-determination as self-"caused" action and self-determination as "controlling" one's behavior. As Deci (2004) observed, "the concept of personal control ... refers to having control over outcomes" (p. 23). Control is defined as "authority, power, or influence over events, behaviors, situations, or people" (VandenBos, 2007, p. 228). Self-determination is not control over events or outcomes, but the degree to which behavior is volitional and the person is the causal agent.

According to fSDT, self-determined "actions" are identified by four "essential characteristics": (a) the person acts "autonomously"; (b) the behavior is "self-regulated"; (c) the person initiates and responds to the event(s) in a "psychologically empowered" manner; and (d) the person acts in a "self-realizing" manner. These essential characteristics refer not to the specific behavior performed, but to the "function" (e.g., purpose) the behavior serves for the individual; that is, whether the action enabled the person to act as a causal agent.

fSDT's use of behavioral autonomy draws from two sources: autonomy as synonymous with individuation and autonomy as roughly synonymous with independence. Developmental psychologists view the process of individuation, or the formation of the person's individual identity (Damon, 1983), as a critical component of social and personality development. Sigafoos, Feinstein, Damond, and Reiss (1988) defined individuation as "a progression from dependence on others for care and guidance to self-care and self-direction" (p. 432), the outcome of which is autonomous functioning or, when describing the actions of individuals achieving this outcome, behavioral autonomy.

Self-regulation is "a complex response system that enables individuals to examine their environments and their repertoires of responses for coping with those environments to make decisions about how to act, to act, to evaluate the desirability of the outcomes of the action, and to revise their plans as necessary" (Whitman, 1990, p. 373). Self-regulated behaviors include using the self-management strategies (including self-monitoring, self-instruction, self-evaluation, and self-reinforcement), goal setting and attainment behaviors, problem-solving and decision-making behaviors, and observational learning strategies.

Psychological empowerment is a construct emanating from the community psychology literature and refers to the multiple dimensions of perceived control (Zimmerman, 1990). Zimmerman and Rappaport (1988) forwarded the construct of psychological empowerment to account for the multidimensional nature of perceived control, which, according to these authors, had been previously treated as if it were a univariate construct (cf. Little, 1998; Skinner, 1995). Thus, according to Zimmerman, through the process of learning and using problem-solving skills and achieving perceived or actual control in one's life (e.g., learned hopefulness), individuals develop a perception of psychological empowerment that enables them to achieve desired outcomes.

Self-realization, a construct proposed by Gestalt psychologists to refer to the intrinsic purpose in a person's life, also has more global meaning related to the "tendency to shape one's life course into a meaningful whole" (Angyal, 1941, p. 355). People who are self-determined are self-realizing in that they use

a comprehensive, and reasonably accurate, knowledge of themselves—their strengths and limitations—to act in such a manner as to capitalize on this knowledge. This self-knowledge and self-understanding forms through experience with and interpretation of one's environment and is influenced by evaluations of significant others, reinforcement, and attributions of one's own behavior (Little, 1998).

The primary research focus of fSDT has been on people with intellectual disability, although the theory itself is not specific to people with disabilities. Various measures of self-determination from this perspective have been developed for both disabled populations (e.g., Wehmeyer & Kelchner, 1995; Wehmeyer, Kelchner, & Richards, 1996; available at http://www.beachcenter.org) and nondisabled populations (Wehmeyer, Lopez, & Shogren, 2005). Moreover, basic tenets of the theory have been validated (e.g., Wehmeyer & Schwartz, 1997, 1998).

Self-Determination as Self-Regulated Problem Solving

In another theoretical model derived from research in education, Mithaug suggested that "self-determination is a form of self-regulation—one that is unusually effective and markedly free of external influence" (Mithaug, Campeau, & Wolman, 1992, p. iii) in which people who are self-determined regulate their choices and actions more successfully than others (Mithaug, 1993, 1996a, 1996b, 1998). Mithaug suggested that individuals are often in flux between existing states and "goal" or desired states. When a discrepancy between what one has and wants occurs, an incentive for self-regulation and action may be operative. With the realization that a discrepancy exists, the individual may set out to achieve the goal or desired state. Because of a previous history of failure, however, individuals may set expectations that are too low or, in some cases, too high.

The ability to set appropriate expectations is based on the individual's success in matching his or her "capacity" with present "opportunity." Capacity is the individual's assessment of existing resources (e.g., skills, interests, and motivation), and opportunity refers to aspects of the situation that allow the individual to achieve the desired gain. Mithaug referred to optimal prospects as "just-right" matches in which individuals are able to correctly match their capacity (i.e., skills and interests) with existing opportunities (e.g., potential jobs). The experience generated during self-regulation, then, becomes a function of the interaction between the person's capacity and opportunity (Mithaug, 1996a). As Mithaug notes, "the more competent we are, the fewer errors we make, and the less time we take, the greater the gain we produce" (p. 156).

Mithaug (1998) also noted that self-determination always occurs in a social context and suggested that the social nature of the concept is worth reviewing because the distinction between self-determination and other-determination is nearly always in play when assessing an individual's prospects for controlling their life in a particular situation. Mithaug and colleagues (Mithaug, Wehmeyer, Agran, Martin, & Palmer, 1998; Wehmeyer, Palmer, Agran, Mithaug, & Martin, 2000) have applied aspects of this theoretical framework to develop an instructional model that enables teachers to increase student self-determination by preparing students to become self-regulated problem solvers. Mithaug et al. have also developed a measure of self-determination—the AIR Self-Determination Scale (Wolman, Campeau, Dubois, Mithaug, & Stolarski, 1994)—which includes student, teacher, and parent report versions. The scale was normed with 450 students, 80% of whom had a disability, most with a cognitive disability. The validated measures yield indicators of opportunity and capacity to self-determine (available at http://www.ou.edu/zarrow/sdetermination.html).

Causal Agency Theory

Recently, Wehmeyer and Mithaug (2006) proposed "causal agency theory" (CAT) to explain how people become self-determined. CAT attempts to predict how and why people act in such a way as to become "self"- versus "other"-determined. Wehmeyer and Mithaug refer to the "class of behavioral events" that CAT attempts to explain as "causal events," "causal behavior," or "causal actions." These function as a means for the person (the causal agent) to achieve valued goals and, ultimately, become more self-determined.

According to CAT there are a number of "operators" at work that lead to self-determined behavior (Figure 33.2). These operators involve the capability to perform causal actions or behaviors, subdivided into causal capacity and agentic capacity, and

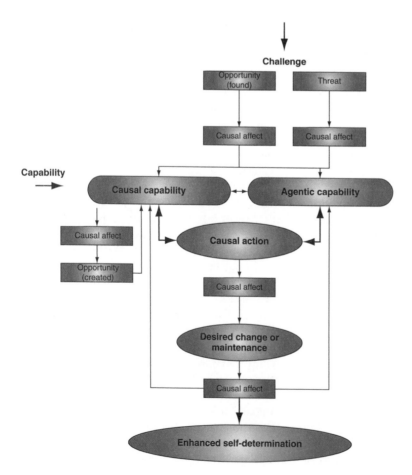

Fig. 33.2 Causal agency theory: overview.

challenges to the organism's self-determination, through causal opportunities or causal threats, which serve as a catalyst to action.

CAPABILITY

Capability refers to having requisite mental or physical capacity to accomplish a particular task. Two types of capabilities are important to causal agency: "causal capability" and "agentic capability." "Causal capability" refers to the mental or physical capacities that enable a person to cause something to happen. These capacities include "causal capacities," the knowledge and behavioral skills necessary to express causal capability, and "causal perceptions," the perceptions and beliefs about oneself and one's environment that are necessary to express causal capability. "Agentic capability" refers to the mental or physical capacity that enables a person to direct causal action. Agency capability also has two components: "agentic capacity," the knowledge and skills needed to direct causal action, including self-regulatory and self-management knowledge and the skills that enable persons to address goal states; and "agentic perceptions," the beliefs about oneself and one's environment that enable one to act.

Wehmeyer and Mithaug (2006) proposed that people are "caused" to implement causal and agentic capabilities in response to challenges that serve as catalysts for causal behavior. A challenge is any circumstance under which one has to engage in the full use of one's abilities or resources to resolve a problem or threat or to achieve a goal or objective. Specifically, causal actions or behaviors are provoked in the organism by two classes of challenges to self-determination: opportunities or threats. "Opportunity" refers to situations or circumstances that provoke the organism to engage in causal action to achieve a planned, desired outcome. Opportunity implies that the situation or circumstance provides a chance for the person to create change or make something happen based upon his or her individual "causal capability," including both causal capacity and causal perceptions. If a person has the "causal capability" to act on the situation or circumstance, that situation or circumstance can be construed as an opportunity. Opportunities can be "found" (unanticipated, happened upon through no effort of one's own) or "created" (the person acts to create a favorable circumstance).

The second challenge condition involves situations or circumstances that threaten the organism's self-determination and provoke the organism to exercise causal action to maintain a preferred outcome or to create change that is consistent with one's own values, preferences, or interests, and not the values, preferences, or interests of others. Wehmeyer and Mithaug (2006) also proposed a third operant in CAT: "causal affect." Causal affects are those emotions, feelings, and other affective components that regulate human behavior, including causal behaviors. For example, emotions (a response involving physiological changes as a preparation for action) are often evoked in response to a challenge, be it opportunity (joy or excitement) or threat (anger or anxiety) that serves to heighten or limit the organism's capacity to respond to the challenge.

People who are causal agents respond to challenges (opportunities or threats) to their self-determination by employing causal and agentic capabilities that result in causal action and allow them to direct their behavior to achieve a desired change or maintain a preferred circumstance or situation. Causal capability and agentic capability work together in a complex way to achieve the desired change or maintenance. Briefly, in response to challenges, causal agents use a "goal generation process" leading to the identification and prioritization of needed actions. The person then frames the most urgent action need in terms of a goal state, and engages in a "goal discrepancy analysis" to compare current status with goal status. The outcome of this discrepancy analysis is a "goal discrepancy problem" to be solved. The person next engages in a "capacity challenge discrepancy analysis" in which capacity to solve the goal discrepancy problem is evaluated. The person maximizes adjustment in capacity (e.g., acquires new or refines existing skills and knowledge) or adjusts the challenge presented to create a "just-right match" between capacity and challenge to optimize the probability of solving the goal discrepancy problem.

Next, the person creates a discrepancy reduction plan by setting causal expectations, making choices and decisions about strategies and methods to reduce the discrepancy between the current status and goal status. When sufficient time has elapsed, the person will engage in a second goal discrepancy analysis, using information gathered through self-monitoring, to self-evaluate progress toward reduction of the discrepancy between current and goal status. If progress is satisfactory, they will continue implementing the discrepancy reduction plan. If not satisfactory, the person either reconsiders the discrepancy reduction plan and modifies that component or returns to the goal generation process to reexamine the overall goal and its priority and, possibly, cycle through the process with a revised or new goal.

Complementary Views

Numerous scholars and theorists provide complementary views of human agency as a process of self-determination. Recent discussions of self-efficacy, for example, clearly draw upon key concepts that underlie self-determination (e.g., Bandura, 1997). Similarly, other theoretical perspectives examine self-determined behavior at either higher or lower levels of analysis. At the lower level, for example, action-control theory examines the perceptions of control from the perspective of behavior as self-determined action (e.g., Chapman, 1984; Little, 1998). At the higher level of analysis, the late Rick Snyder's body of work (e.g., Snyder, 2000) on hope theory emanates from a perspective of self-determined behavior whereby hope is conceptualized as the confluence of agency and pathways thinking—both of which are hallmarks of self-determined behavior. For reviews and integrations of these and related theories see, for example, Bandura, 1997; Freund and Riediger, 2006; Hawley and Little, 2002; Little et al., 2002; Little et al., 2006; Walls and Kollatt, 2006.

Conclusions

That self-determination is a critical construct to the study of a positive psychology seems self-evident to us. An organismic perspective of self-determination that views people as active contributors to, or "authors" of their behavior, where behavior is self-regulated and goal-directed, provides a compelling foundation for examining and facilitating the degree to which people become "causal agents" in their lives. The theoretical frameworks reviewed in this chapter provide both compelling evidence to support the relevance of the construct to positive psychology, as well as multiple perspectives from which to consider further research or intervention development.

Research stemming from SDT strives to differentiate between proactive and reactive psychological processes. Proactive processes are those that support growth of human potential; reactive processes (in terms of their lack of support for growth and well-being) are defensive, subsequent to threats toward basic needs (Ryan & Deci, 2000b). This approach to proactive and reactive processes corresponds with the tenets of positive psychology, and as the theory is applied in a broader range of settings and with more diverse populations, the field of positive psychology will advance concurrently.

Research stemming from the fSDT and Mithaug's self-regulated learning theory, as well as the more recent CAT, emphasize the interaction between opportunity and capacity in self-determined action, and the role of self-regulated problem solving and goal discrepancy analysis to achieve greater self-determination. Recent research by Shogren, Lopez, Wehmeyer, Little, and Pressgrove (2006) explores the interrelationships among self-determination and other positive psychology constructs, including hope, well-being, and life satisfaction, in students with and without cognitive disabilities.

Future Research

In the future, it will be important to evaluate the relationships of self-determination with other positive psychology constructs and the contributions to, singly and combined, more positive adult outcomes and optimal psychological functioning. Further, we believe that research and model development in self-determination will and should continue to be focused on marginalized populations—populations such as people with disabilities, people who are aging and elderly, people from minority ethnic or socio-economically disadvantaged groups, and so forth—not due to historic reasons of deficits focused, but because of the salience and importance of enhanced self-determination to these populations to achieve optimal functioning and outcomes. Finally, our contention is that promoting self-determination should be a major focus of both the educational and the lifelong learning process.

Questions about the Future of Topic

1. To what degree does self-determination interact with other positive psychological constructs to predict optimal human functioning and well-being?

2. How does self-determination fit into models of human agentic behavior and other organismic theories of human action?

3. What interventions enhance personal self-determination?

Acknowledgments

This work was supported in part by grants from the NIH to the University of Kansas through the Mental Retardation and Developmental Disabilities Research Center (5 P30 HD002528), the Center for Biobehavioral Neurosciences in Communication Disorders (5 P30 DC005803), and an NFGRF grant (2301779) from the University of Kansas to the second author. The views expressed herein are not necessarily those of the sponsoring agencies.

References

Angyal, A. (1941). *Foundations for a science of personality.* Cambridge, MA: Harvard University Press.

Bandura, A. B. (1997). *Self-efficacy: The exercise of control.* New York: W. H. Freeman and Co.

Brandtstädter, J. (1998). Action perspectives on human development. In R. M. Lerner (Ed.), *Theoretical models of human development: Vol. 1. Handbook of child psychology* (5th ed., pp. 807–863). New York: Wiley.

Chapman, M. (1984). Intentional action as a paradigm for developmental psychology: A symposium. *Human Development, 27*(3–4), 113–144.

Damon, W. (1983). *Social and personality development.* New York: W. W. Norton and Co.

Deci, E. L. (2004). Promoting intrinsic motivation and self-determination in people with mental retardation. In H. Switzky, L. Hickson, R. Schalock, & M. L. Wehmeyer, (Eds.) *Personality and motivational systems in mental retardation: Vol. 28. International review of research in mental retardation* (pp. 1–31). San Diego, CA: Academic Press.

Deci, E. L. & Ryan, R. M. (2000). The "what" and "why" of goal pursuits: Human needs and the determination of behavior. *Psychological Inquiry, 11,* 227–268.

Deci, E. L., & Ryan, R. M. (2002). *Handbook of self-determination research.* Rochester, NY: University of Rochester Press.

Freund, A. M., & Riediger, M. (2006). Goals as building blocks of personality and development in adulthood. In. D. K. Mroczek & T. D. Little (Eds.), *Handbook of personality development* (pp. 353–372). Mahwah, NJ: LEA.

Gove, P. B. (Ed.). (1967). *Webster's third new international dictionary of the English language, unabridged.* Springfield, MA: Merriam-Webster.

Harter, S. (1999). *The construction of the self: A developmental perspective.* New York: Guilford.

Hawley, P. H. (1999). The ontogenesis of social dominance: A strategy-based evolutionary perspective. *Developmental Review, 19,* 91–132.

Hawley, P. H., & Little, T. D. (2002). Evolutionary and developmental perspectives on the agentic self. In D. Cervone & W. Mischel (Eds.), *Advances in personality science.* New York: Guilford.

Kemerling, G. (2000–2001). *John Locke. Philosophy pages.* Retrieved on October 17, 2006, from http://www.philosophypages.com/locke/g0.htm

Little, T. D. (1998). Sociocultural influences on the development of children's action-control beliefs. In J. Heckhausen & C. S. Dweck (Eds.), *Motivation and self-regulation across the life span* (pp. 281–315). New York: Cambridge University Press.

Little, T. D., Hawley, P. H., Henrich, C. C., & Marsland, K. (2002). Three views of the agentic self: A developmental synthesis. In E. L. Deci & R. M. Ryan (Eds.), *Handbook of self-determination research* (pp. 389–404). Rochester, NY: University of Rochester Press.

Little, T. D., Lopez, D. F., & Wanner, B. (2001). Children's action-control behaviors (Coping): A longitudinal validation of the behavioral inventory of strategic control. *Anxiety, Stress, and Coping, 14,* 315–336.

Little, T. D., Snyder, C. R., & Wehmeyer, M. (2006). The agentic self: On the nature and origins of personal agency across the lifespan. In D. K. Mroczek & T. D. Little (Eds.), *Handbook of personality development* (pp. 61–80). Mahwah, NJ: LEA.

Locke, J. (1690). *An essay on human understanding.* Retrieved on December 29, 2001, from http://www.ilt.columbia.edu/projects/digitexts/locke/understanding/title.html

Mithaug, D. E. (1993). *Self-regulation theory: How optimal adjustment maximizes gain.* Westport, CT: Praeger.

Mithaug, D. (1996a). *Equal opportunity theory.* Thousand Oaks, CA: Sage.

Mithaug, D. (1996b). The optimal prospects principle: A theoretical basis for rethinking instructional practices for self-determination. In D. J. Sands & M. L. Wehmeyer (Eds.), *Self-determination across the life span: Independence and choice for people with disabilities* (pp. 147–165). Baltimore: Paul H. Brookes.

Mithaug, D. (1998). Your right, my obligation? *Journal of the Association for Persons with Severe Disabilities, 23,* 41–43.

Mithaug, D., Campeau, P., & Wolman, J. (1992). Self-determination assessment project. Unpublished grant proposal.

Mithaug, D., Wehmeyer, M. L., Agran, M., Martin, J., & Palmer, S., (1998). The self-determined learning model of instruction: Engaging students to solve their learning problems. In M. L. Wehmeyer & D. J. Sands (Eds.), *Making it happen: Student involvement in educational planning, decision-making and instruction* (pp. 299–328). Baltimore: Brookes Publishers.

Reis, H. T., Sheldon, K. M., Gable, S. L., Roscoe, J., & Ryan, R. M. (2000). Daily well-being: The role of autonomy, competence, and relatedness. *Personality and Social Psychology Bulletin, 26,* 419–435.

Ryan, R. M., & Deci, E. L. (2000a). Self-determination theory and the facilitation of intrinsic motivation, social development, and well-being. *American Psychologist, 55,* 68–78.

Ryan, R. M., & Deci, E. L. (2000b). The darker and brighter sides of human existence: Basic psychological needs as a unifying concept. *Psychological Inquiry, 11,* 319–338.

Ryan, R. M., & Deci, E. L. (2002). An overview of self-determination theory: An organismic-dialectical perspective. In E. L. Deci & R. M. Ryan (Eds.), *Handbook of self-determination research* (pp. 3–36). Rochester, NY: University of Rochester Press.

Ryan, R. M., & Deci, E. L. (2004). Autonomy is no illusion: Self-determination theory and the empirical study of authenticity, awareness, and will. In J. Greenberg, S. L. Koole, & T. Pyszczynski (Eds.), *Handbook of experimental existential psychology* (pp. 449–479). New York: Guilford.

Sigafoos, A. D., Feinstein, C. B., Damond, M., & Reiss, D. (1988). The measurement of behavioral autonomy in adolescence: The Autonomous Functioning Checklist. *Adolescent Psychiatry, 15,* 432–462.

Sheldon, K. M., Ryan, R. M., Deci, E. L., & Kasser, T. (2004). The independent effects of goal contents and motives on well-being: It's both what you pursue and why you pursue it. *Personality and Social Psychology Bulletin, 30,* 475–486.

Shogren, K. A., Lopez, S. J., Wehmeyer, M. L., Little, T. D., & Pressgrove, C. L. (2006). The role of positive psychology constructs in predicting life satisfaction in adolescents with and without cognitive disabilities: An exploratory study. *Journal of Positive Psychology, 1,* 37–52.

Skinner, E. A. (1995). *Perceived control, motivation, and coping.* Beverly Hills, CA: Sage.

Skinner, E. A. (1996). A guide to constructs of control. *Journal of Personality and Social Psychology, 71*(3), 549–570.

Skinner, E. A., & Edge, K. (2002). Self-determination, coping, and development. In E. L. Deci & R. M. Ryan (Eds.), *Handbook of self-determination research* (pp. 297–338). Rochester, NY: University of Rochester Press.

Snyder, C. R. (2000). *Handbook of hope: Theory, measures, and applications*. San Diego, CA: Academic Press.

VandenBos, G. R. (Ed.). (2007). *APA dictionary of psychology*. Washington, DC: APA.

Vanlede, M., Little, T. D., & Card, N. A. (2006). Action-control beliefs and behaviors as predictors of change in adjustment across the transition to middle school. *Anxiety, Stress, and Coping, 19*, 111–127.

Walls, T. A., & Kollatt, S. H. (2006). Agency to agentic personalities: The early to middle childhood gap. In. D. K. Mroczek & T. D. Little (Eds.), *Handbook of personality development* (pp. 231–244). Mahwah, NJ: LEA.

Walls, T. A., & Little, T. D. (2005). Relations among personal agency, motivation, and school adjustment in early adolescence. *Journal of Educational Psychology, 97*, 23–31.

Wehmeyer, M. L. (1996). Self-determination as an educational outcome: Why is it important to children, youth and adults with disabilities? In D. J. Sands & M. L. Wehmeyer (Eds.), *Self-determination across the life span: Independence and choice for people with disabilities* (pp. 15–34). Baltimore: Paul H. Brookes.

Wehmeyer, M. L. (2001). Self-determination and mental retardation. In L. M. Glidden (Ed.), *International review of research in mental retardation* (Vol. 24, pp. 1–48). San Diego, CA: Academic Press.

Wehmeyer, M. L. (2005). Self-determination and individuals with severe disabilities: Reexamining meanings and misinterpretations. *Research and Practice in Severe Disabilities, 30*, 113–120.

Wehmeyer, M. L., & Kelchner, K. (1995). *The Arc's Self-Determination Scale*. Arlington, TX: The Arc National Headquarters.

Wehmeyer, M. L., Kelchner, K., & Richards. S. (1996). Essential characteristics of self-determined behaviors of adults with mental retardation and developmental disabilities. *American Journal on Mental Retardation, 100*, 632–642.

Wehmeyer, M. L., Lopez, S., & Shogren, K. (2005). *The adolescent self-determination scale*. Lawrence, KS: Author.

Wehmeyer, M. L., & Mithaug, D. (2006). Self-determination, causal agency, and mental retardation. In H. Swtizky (Ed.), *International review of research in mental retardation: Vol. 31. Current perspectives on individual differences in personality and motivation in persons with mental retardation and other developmental disabilities* (pp. 31–71). San Diego, CA: Academic Press.

Wehmeyer, M. L., Palmer, S. B., Agran, M., Mithaug, D. E., & Martin, J. (2000). Teaching students to become causal agents in their lives: The self-determining learning model of instruction. *Exceptional Children, 66*, 439–453.

Wehmeyer, M. L., & Schwartz, M. (1997). Self-determination and positive adult outcomes: A follow-up study of youth with mental retardation or learning disabilities. *Exceptional Children, 63*, 245–255.

Wehmeyer, M. L., & Schwartz, M. (1998). The relationship between self-determination, quality of life, and life satisfaction for adults with mental retardation. *Education and Training in Mental Retardation and Developmental Disabilities, 33*, 3–12.

White, R. W. (1959). Motivation reconsidered: The concept of competence. *Psychological Review, 66*, 297–333.

Whitman, T. L. (1990). Self-regulation and mental retardation. *American Journal on Mental Retardation, 94*, 347–362.

Wolman, J., Campeau, P., Dubois, P., Mithaug, D., & Stolarski, V. (1994). *AIR self-determination scale and user guide*. Palo Alto, CA: American Institute for Research.

Zimmerman, M. A. (1990). Toward a theory of learned hopefulness: A structural model analysis of participation and empowerment. *Journal of Research in Personality, 24*, 71–86.

Zimmerman, M. A., & Rappaport, J. (1988). Citizen participation, perceived control, and psychological empowerment. *American Journal of Community Psychology, 16*, 725–750.

Curiosity and Interest: The Benefits of Thriving on Novelty and Challenge

Todd B. Kashdan *and* Paul J. Silvia

Abstract

An imbalance exists between the role of curiosity as a motivational force in nearly all human endeavors and the lack of scientific attention given to the topic. In recent years, however, there has been a proliferation of concepts that capture the essence of curiosity—recognizing, seeking out, and showing a preference for the new. In this chapter, we combine this work to address the nature of curiosity, where it fits in the larger scheme of positive emotions, the advantages of being curious in social relationships, links between curiosity and elements of well-being, and how it has been used in interventions to improve people's quality of life. Our emphasis is on methodologically sophisticated findings that show how curiosity operates in the laboratory and everyday life, and how, under certain conditions, curiosity can be a profound source of strength or a liability. People who are regularly curious and willing to embrace the novelty, uncertainty, and challenges that are inevitable as we navigate the shoals of everyday life are at an advantage in creating a fulfilling existence compared with their less curious peers. Our brief review is designed to bring further attention to this neglected, underappreciated, human universal.

Keywords: curiosity, interest, meaning, motivation, positive emotions, well-being

In the early days of motivation psychology, human activity was explained by relentless, hydraulic drives. The goal of action, theorists argued, was to reduce intense sensations and achieve a state of quiet, still inertia. Novelty, complexity, and challenge were sources of drive and thus stimuli to be avoided (Hull, 1952). It quickly became obvious, however, that people are never inert. There's more to motivation than reducing drives and filling deficits: People seek out complex and challenging activities, intriguing people, and novel ideas. Curiosity and interest—the core of intrinsically motivated action—are things that classic motivation theories never explained well. Seeking new experiences, preferring complexity over simplicity, and engaging in actions out of intrinsic interest are hallmarks of human action, and they lead psychology to the study of how and why people thrive on novelty and challenge.

This chapter examines what modern psychology knows and doesn't know about curiosity and interest. Researchers from many areas of psychology have explored the nature, functions, and consequences of being curious. After reviewing this work, we will turn to the uncertain, complex problems that interest contemporary curiosity researchers. At the start, we should note that we'll use "curiosity" and "interest" as synonyms: both refer to a positive motivational-emotional state associated with exploration. In everyday speech, people tend to use "curious" for upcoming events and "interested" for current events, but this doesn't reflect a conceptual difference. Some researchers have proposed differences between curiosity and interest—such as curiosity is aversive but interest is pleasant (e.g., Hidi & Berndorff, 1998)—but so far no research has shown that they differ (Silvia, 2006, pp. 190–191).

What Is Curiosity?

Given over a century of psychological study of curiosity, it is no surprise to find diverse models of what curiosity is (Kashdan, 2004; Silvia, 2006). The oldest tradition views curiosity as an appetitive, approach-oriented motivational state (Arnold, 1910; Dewey, 1913). Berlyne (1971), for example, proposed that new, complex, and surprising things activate a reward system that generates positive affect. This reward system motivates novelty seeking and rewards exploring novel things. Intense novelty and complexity activate a counterpoised aversion system, which motivates avoidance. The intrinsic motivation tradition—associated with social-personality psychology—traces interest to the operation of organismic needs, particularly needs related to autonomy, relatedness, and competence (Deci, 1992; Ryan & Deci, 2000). When interested, people pursue actions for their own sake instead of for rewards. A tradition rooted in emotion psychology views interest as an emotion (Izard, 1977; Silvia, 2006; Tomkins, 1962). Interest should thus entail facial and vocal expressions, subjective experience, motivational qualities, and adaptive functions across the life span (see Silvia, 2006, chap. 1).

Perhaps, most important are the commonalities among these theoretical approaches. All theories of curiosity agree that curiosity is an approach-oriented motivational state associated with exploration. When curious, people ask questions (Peters, 1978), manipulate interesting objects (Reeve & Nix, 1997), read deeply (Schiefele, 1999), examine interesting images (Silvia, 2005), and persist on challenging tasks (Sansone & Smith, 2000). In short, all theories agree that curiosity's immediate function is to learn, explore, and immerse oneself in the interesting event. In the long term, curiosity serves a broader function of building knowledge and competence. Exploring new events fosters learning new things, meeting new people, and developing new skills.

Curiosity can be defined as the recognition, pursuit, and intense desire to explore novel, challenging, and uncertain events. When curious, we are fully aware and receptive to whatever exists and might happen in the present moment. Curiosity motivates people to act and think in new ways and investigate, be immersed, and learn about whatever is the immediate interesting target of their attention. This definition captures the exploratory striving component and the mindful immersion component. By focusing on the novelty and challenge each moment has to offer, there is an inevitable (however slight) stretching of information, knowledge, and skills. When we are curious, we are doing things for their own sake, and we are not being controlled by internal or external pressures concerning what we should or should not do.

Interest and the Family of Positive Emotions

Although central to positive experience and development, curiosity is not merely another word for happiness, enjoyment, well-being, or positive affect. Curiosity and happiness are distinct positive experiences: they have different functions, causes, and consequences. Silvan Tomkins (1962), writing before the advent of research on positive emotions, proposed that interest and enjoyment play different roles in human development. Interest motivates people to try new things, explore complex ideas, meet intriguing people, and do novel actions. Enjoyment, in contrast, motivates people to form attachments to familiar things and to reinforce activities that were enjoyable before. Tomkins pointed out that these functions can conflict: Interest motivates people to spend their vacation traveling in a new place, whereas enjoyment motivates people to revisit the place they liked last year.

Consistent with Tomkins' view, experiments have found different sources of interest and enjoyment (see Silvia, 2006, pp. 25–29). The dimension of novelty versus familiarity strongly discriminates interest and happiness. In studies of pictures, music, stories, anagrams, and games, interesting things are rated as new, complex, dynamic, and challenging, but enjoyable things are rated as familiar, calming, stable, and resolved (Berlyne, 1971, pp. 213–220; Iran-Nejad, 1987; Russell, 1994). In a recent study of emotional responses to art, Turner and Silvia (2006) found that ratings of interest and enjoyment were unrelated. Disturbing and complex works of art were interesting, whereas calming and simple works of art were enjoyable.

Finally, interest and enjoyment have different consequences. Interest strongly predicts exploratory action, such as how long people visually explore images, how long they listen to music, and how much time they spend on games and tasks. Unlike interest, enjoyment modestly predicts exploratory action. In a study of music, Crozier (1974, experiment 4) found that interest explained 78% of the variance in how long people listened to music, whereas enjoyment explained merely 10%. In a study of visual art (Berlyne, 1974), interest explained 43% of the variance in viewing time, whereas enjoyment explained 14%.

Perhaps, curiosity ought to be placed into a different category of emotion. Positive emotions, according to Lazarus (1991), come from appraising an event as congruent with one's goals. To be interested in something, however, people need not appraise the event as goal-congruent: people are often interested in unpleasant, unfamiliar, and possibly unrewarding activities (Turner & Silvia, 2006). As an alternative, we could place curiosity and interest within the category of "knowledge emotions." Suggested by Keltner and Shiota (2003), this category contains emotions associated with learning and thinking, such as interest, surprise, confusion, and awe. This category highlights curiosity's functional role in building knowledge, skills, and relationships, and it emphasizes the subtle ways in which curiosity contributes to well-being (Kashdan & Steger, 2007).

Is Curiosity Aversive?

One tradition of curiosity research views curiosity as aversive, as a mental itch that must be scratched. Dating to drive reduction models of curiosity (see Fowler, 1965), this approach assumes that curiosity is an aversive experience that motivates its own reduction. Building on Loewenstein's (1994) model of aversive curiosity, Litman (2005) has proposed two facets to curiosity: curiosity as a feeling of interest, and curiosity as a feeling of deprivation. The difference is whether people seek information out of interest or out of frustration at not knowing. These two factors emerge as distinct (although highly related) latent factors in correlational research (Litman & Silvia, 2006). Litman's model raises some interesting questions about curiosity. If curiosity is defined as "wanting to know," then interest and deprivation represent two reasons for wanting to know. If curiosity is defined as a positive motivational-emotional state, then Litman's interest facet is what we mean by curiosity, and Litman's deprivation facet is a different, incurious reason for wanting to know. This is an intriguing program of research, but besides one quasi-experimental study (Litman, Hutchins, & Russon, 2005) it has yet to move beyond correlating global self-report measures with other global measures. Research should examine whether the deprivation facet of curiosity has incremental validity beyond processes, such as rumination, neuroticism, and worry. Complex designs are needed to examine the degree to which aversion motivates variants of curiosity and how this process unfolds differently in people's lives.

Individual Differences in Curiosity

Research on state curiosity inspired a wave of research on individual differences related to curiosity. Psychologists have examined global, higher-order traits associated with curiosity; openness to experience (McCrae, 1996) and sensation seeking (Zuckerman, 1994) are good examples. Other models of curiosity examine lower-order, specific traits. "Trait curiosity" models, which propose individual differences in levels of novelty seeking and exploration, have had a recent flurry of attention (Kashdan, Rose, & Fincham, 2004). According to these mid-range models, trait curiosity explains variance not accounted for by higher-order factors like openness and sensation seeking, so trait curiosity is an appropriate level for examining curiosity. And still other models examine facets of trait curiosity, such as perceptual curiosity (Collins, Litman, & Spielberger, 2004), epistemic curiosity (Litman & Spielberger, 2003), and sensory curiosity (Litman, Collins, & Spielberger, 2005). Trait curiosity models typically assume a spectrum of variation in stable tendencies to experience or express curiosity. A tacit assumption is that states and traits are psychologically equivalent (see Fleeson, 2001): Trait curiosity manifests in the frequency or intensity of state experience (Silvia, 2008).

Recent Discoveries and Unknown Territory
Curiosity in the Social World

Although most research on curiosity has focused on responses to nonsocial stimuli (e.g., preferences for bizarre compared to common pictures, surprise endings to stories), it is reasonable to apply curiosity and exploration to other people and social situations. First, social situations are often ambiguous and challenging. These qualities are the reason that social situations offer great opportunities for self-expansion. Partners who offer greater self-expansion opportunities to us are more desirable. The desirable process of self-expansion often transfers over into the relationship itself, enhancing feelings of connectedness and behaviors that work toward the development of meaningful relationships. Second, when people feel that their primary relationship partner is secure and responsive, a typical response is the willingness to seek out possible growth opportunities by exploring, learning, and taking risks (even in the presence of uncomfortable feelings; Ainsworth, Blehar, Waters, & Wall, 1978; Bowlby, 1969). Third, feelings of curiosity may build social bonds by promoting behaviors, such as engagement, responsiveness, and flexibility to others' varied perspectives. These curiosity-relevant behaviors are desirable in interpersonal transactions and the formative stages of relationship development (Kashdan & Fincham, 2004; McCrae, 1996). People who are more curious have been shown to experience more positive social outcomes (Kashdan & Roberts, 2004; Peters, 1978). People with greater curiosity are more receptive to the ambiguity of social activity, and they enjoy growth opportunities as a function of sharing novel events with other people and discovering new information from them. When something interesting happens to us, sharing it with other people (who are good listeners) can transform memories of the event. Describing an interesting event to others serves to strengthen our own curiosity and make it more salient (Thoman, Sansone, & Pasupathi, 2007). The intrinsic value and motivation for a given activity can be increased through this socialization process. Future work may show that the regulatory benefits of other people extend more broadly to the development of long-term interests (Silvia, 2006, chap. 5).

Fourth, research in educational settings has shown that perceptions of threat and supportiveness affect whether people feel curious, explore, and derive the benefits of these behaviors. In general, students with greater curiosity have more academic success than less curious peers (Hidi & Berndorff, 1998; Schiefele, Krapp, & Winteler, 1992). Yet, there are crucial contextual factors that moderate whether curious students thrive academically. Even though students high in trait curiosity initiate 3 times as many classroom questions compared to their less curious peers, both groups become more inhibited when teachers are perceived as threatening (Peters, 1978). In a large study of students in Hong Kong, adolescents with greater trait curiosity who perceived their schools to be academically challenging had the greatest grades and performance on national achievement tests, whereas students with greater trait curiosity in less challenging schools had the worst academic outcomes (Kashdan & Yuen, 2007).

Overall, there is evidence that people differ in the recognition and sensitivity to nonsocial and social stimuli appraised as novel, complex, uncertain, or growth oriented, with particularly curious people deriving more immediate and lasting psychological and social benefits. But there are boundary conditions to these relations, including how people habitually relate to other people and characterize caregivers, romantic partners, friends, teachers, and the degree of fit with institutional settings. Social anxiety, perceiving people as threatening or nonresponsive, insecure relationships, and being situated in less enriching environments can disable curiosity and exploratory tendencies. Despite the appeal of simplistic models of the benefits of curiosity, there are important social and institutional moderating variables that require careful theoretical and empirical consideration. There has been impressive evidence for examining "curiosity in context" to understand the conditions leading to favorable and unfavorable consequences.

Curiosity and Well-Being

The question of how to develop sustainable increases in well-being is important to humans living amid everyday challenges and suffering and to health professionals interested in intervention. There are several processes that hinder the ability to maintain anything more than short-term changes in well-being, including substantial genetic contributions (Lykken & Tellegen, 1996) and people's profound ability to adapt to changes in life circumstances (and return to relatively stable baseline levels; Brickman, Coates, & Janoff-Bulman, 1978). As a result, nearly all gains in well-being are temporary because the benefits of positive life circumstances tend to be short-lived.

The functions of curiosity make it an ideal candidate to signaling and producing well-being. Curiosity has been defined as one of the fundamental mechanisms of the biologically based reward sensitivity system (Depue, 1996) and intrinsic motivation (Ryan & Deci, 2000), which have profound influences on well-being. Upon seeking and investing effort in novel and challenging activities, people with greater curiosity expand their knowledge, skills, goal-directed efforts, and sense of self (e.g., Ainley, Hidi, & Berndorff, 2002). Feeling curious also appears to increase tolerance for distressing states of self-awareness that result from trying new things and behaving in ways outside of one's comfort zone (Kashdan, 2007; Spielberger & Starr, 1994).

Curiosity motivates people to explore the world and challenge themselves, and it is relevant to obtaining life fulfillments. Using cross-sectional and laboratory research designs, people scoring higher on trait curiosity consistently report greater psychological well-being (Naylor, 1981; Park, Peterson, & Seligman, 2004; Vittersø, 2003). In terms of physical well-being, 3-year-old children with greater curiosity and exploratory tendencies demonstrate greater intelligence at age 11 (Raine, Reynolds, Venables, & Mednick, 2002), and older adults in their early seventies with greater curiosity live longer over a 5-year span than their less curious peers (Swan & Carmelli, 1996).

One theoretical model suggests that people with greater curiosity are more selective of and responsive to activities that are personally and socially enriching, leading to the building of durable psychological resources (for review see Silvia, 2006). Recent work suggests that people with greater curiosity are more reactive to events that offer opportunities for growth, competence, and high levels of stimulation. Over the course of 21 days, people with greater trait curiosity reported more frequent growth-oriented events (such as persisting at goals in the face of obstacles and expressing gratitude to benefactors), greater daily curiosity, and greater sensitivity to these daily events and states (Kashdan & Steger, 2007). In addition, for people with greater trait curiosity, greater daily curiosity was more likely to persist into the next day and, in turn, greater daily curiosity led to persistent elevations in perceived meaning and purpose in life. People with less trait curiosity reported greater sensitivity to hedonistic events and states (such as having sex purely for pleasure and binge drinking), but the benefits were short-lived. The effects of curiosity were not attributable to daily negative affect, trait positive affect, or Big Five personality traits. These results suggest that the neglected interplay of trait and state curiosity may be important in the development and sustainability of particular types of well-being (eudaemonia, meaning in life). Also, these data suggest that feelings of curiosity are particularly reactive to novelty and growth potential as opposed to indiscriminate, positively valenced stimuli.

Although the results in this area of study are appealing, incremental validity and the mechanisms that link curiosity to well-being require further study. After all, the list of constructs associated with well-being is enormous, and it will be important to evaluate whether theoretical models of curiosity provide insight into why curiosity is particularly beneficial. Moreover, there are a number of discrepancies that need to be resolved. For example, some research suggests that the pleasures of curiosity are derived from resolving ambiguity and uncertainty (Beswick, 1971; Loewenstein, 1994), whereas other work finds that the process of discovery and meaning making is intrinsically enjoyable (Feist, 1994) and that positive emotions can be sustained by intentionally attending to the lingering uncertainty in a given situation (Wilson, Centerbar, Kermer, & Gilbert, 2005). The resolution may arise from the inclusion of other variables such as feelings of perceived competence during a given task, whether important environmental contingencies depend on the outcome (e.g., betting a paycheck on a single football game or having a deadline to review a mystery novel), and individual differences in trait curiosity and tolerance for ambiguity.

Clinical Uses of Curiosity

Despite factors that work against the development of increased well-being (e.g., genetic factors or hedonic adaptation), making efforts toward intrinsically valued goals and pursuits may disrupt these stabilizing processes (Hayes, Strosahl, & Wilson, 1999). Arguably, the disposition and state most aligned with these activities is curiosity, which involves active tendencies to seek out, savor, and probe novel distinctions in each moment with an eye toward change and complexity as opposed to stability and familiarity. By focusing on novelty and challenge, people who feel curious challenge their views of self, others, and the world with an inevitable stretching of information, knowledge, and skills. This movement toward intrinsically valued directions appears to be a pathway to the building of meaning in life, with the simultaneous presence of a positive present (mindful engagement, sense of meaningfulness) and future time orientation (search for meaning, planning long-term goals with minimal worry about obstacles). Intuitively, it seems useful to examine changes in trait curiosity and curiosity experiences as an index of engagement, progress, and desired outcomes during the course of intervention efforts.

Although clinical efforts recently have incorporated positive psychological constructs such as positive affect, pleasant events, and optimism, there is insufficient theoretical and empirical attention to curiosity. For people suffering from psychological disorders, intrusive thoughts and anhedonic processes can blunt the experience and expression of appetitive activity. Of particular interest is whether facilitating curiosity can build the self-regulatory resources to withstand the avoidance and disengagement that tends to occur following episodes of extreme anxiety and depression, and whether it can be a backdoor route to approaching, processing, and making meaning of difficult emotional material. In addition, humans are constantly confronted with approach-avoidance conflicts between desired outcomes and contact with unwanted negative feelings, thoughts, and bodily sensations. Using more sophisticated modeling of complex emotional reactions and decisions, scientists can begin to examine whether facilitating curiosity can increase how often people select approach behavior in response to these internal conflicts. Related to this perspective, many clients are ambivalent about whether to make changes in their behavior (e.g., eating junk food) despite unhealthy consequences (e.g., obesity) and many beneficial reasons for change (e.g., mortality or physical stamina). It is useful to elicit nonjudgmental information on the reasons for and against changing versus staying the same, ask whether and how behavior conflicts with values, and highlight and elicit curiosity in any inconsistencies (see work on motivational interviewing; Miller & Rollnick, 2002). As an intervention, it may be useful to help people elaborate their core values and provide feedback from assessments of everyday experiences and event reactivity. In the pursuit of sustainable sources of pleasure and meaning, these exercises may increase the degree to which behavioral patterns and goal pursuits are congruent with intrinsic values and dominant behavioral tendencies (Sheldon & Elliot, 1999). These techniques and the supportive literature have yet to be considered and adopted by the majority of clinical researchers and practitioners. This is unfortunate because the recovery rates for empirically supported treatments for emotion disturbances tend to be no higher than 40–50% (Westen & Bradley, 2005), suggesting the need for refinements and novel directions, such as targeting intrapersonal curiosity and exploratory tendencies.

A Brief Agenda for the Future Study of Curiosity

Despite over a century of scientific theory and research, there is much that remains to be examined about curiosity. Let us boldly emphasize a few challenges potentially worthy of funding and endless hours of contemplation and execution. First, without question, there is a need for more innovative assessment strategies. We suggest a triangulation approach among self-report technologies, unobtrusive measures, and slices of ecological behavior. Rather than simply asking people face-valid questions, scientists also can examine differential activation of biological processes linked to reward sensitivity and exploratory behavior (e.g., dopaminergic agents, left prefrontal cortex asymmetry) in response to stimuli characterized by novelty, complexity, and uncertainty. In addition, experience-sampling approaches provide repeated measurements of what people do from moment-to-moment in the contexts in which they find themselves. This approach can be a useful means of discovering what curious people do and how people become curious during everyday life. People with greater trait curiosity should seek out more frequent novel and challenging events and react to these events with an orientation characterized by openness and exploration,

which in turn promotes the growth of knowledge, competence, and well-being. These different assessment strategies can be merged to differentiate people who differ in dispositional or hardwired curiosity. Additionally, this approach can shed light on the construct specificity of curiosity from other discrete positive affects and dimensions of temperament and character, and the antecedents and consequences of feeling curious at a particular moment in time.

Second, the mechanisms linking curiosity to hardened outcomes, such as mortality, academic and work productivity, creativity, and physical health and illness, have yet to be clearly delineated. For example, why should highly curious people live longer than their less curious peers (Swan & Carmelli, 1996)? Several hypotheses can be generated, such as the process of neurogenesis stemming from continued novel and intellectual pursuits, a nondefensive willingness to try less traditional treatments and health strategies, or the psychological benefits of evaluating stressors as challenges and being guided by exploration as opposed to avoidance (e.g., less overactive hypothalamic-pituitary-adrenal axis). An examination of cognitive, behavioral, social, and biological levels of analysis will lead to promising avenues of when and how curiosity leads to desirable outcomes. To better understand the process of how curiosity leads to an expansion of resources or growth, each of these levels of analysis will require an examination of how these mechanisms unfold over time.

Third, the refinements in assessment and basic research should be in the service of working toward the discovery of how to cultivate curiosity in meaningful life domains. Of particular importance is finding alternative ways to aid people suffering from fear, apathy, intolerance of uncertainty, and lives controlled by avoidance and other forms of overregulation. We argue that the facilitation of curiosity may be a useful supplement to treatments designed to increase self-awareness and introspection, cope with and derive meaning from difficult emotional material, and increase recognition, receptiveness, and reactivity to the reward cues that are often ignored or avoided in everyday life. In the ideal, research on curiosity will no longer be the province of social, personality, and developmental psychologists, but will include allied health professionals invested in applying knowledge to prevention and treatment.

Conclusions

There is mounting evidence that curiosity is important to understanding lives that are well lived. The best way to understand this is to imagine what life would be like without the experience of curiosity. There would be no exploration of the self and world, introspection, search for meaning in life, aesthetic appreciation, scientific pursuits, innovation, and, to some degree, personal growth. When confronted with novelty and challenge, the dominant response tendencies are related to curiosity and anxiety. The literature on anxiety is enormous, but the recognition and study of curiosity has been relatively neglected. We sought to describe some of the basic qualities of curiosity, show how it is unique from other positive emotions, traits, and processes, provide support for how curiosity relates to flourishing in fundamental life domains, suggest some of the social-cognitive and environmental factors that affect curiosity and its benefits, and reveal how much remains to be discovered. To understand how people thrive in general and in particular situations, the multitude of strengths and resources described in this handbook should be studied in tandem and not in isolation. In this science of human flourishing, curiosity can no longer be ignored.

Three Questions for the Future

1. Why are some people more curious than other people?

2. How can clinicians, counselors, and coaches use curiosity and novelty to enhance everyday life and prevent degenerative conditions, such as Alzheimer's disease?

3. How does curiosity influence other constructs in positive psychology, such as meaning in life, maturity, wisdom, spirituality, creativity, and healthy relationships?

References

Ainley, M., Hidi, S., & Berndorff, D. (2002). Interest, learning and the psychological processes that mediate their relationship. *Journal of Educational Psychology, 94,* 545–561.

Ainsworth, M. D. S., Blehar, M. C., Waters, E., & Wall, S. (1978). *Patterns of attachment: A psychological study of the strange situation.* Hillsdale, NJ: Erlbaum.

Arnold, F. (1910). *Attention and interest: A study in psychology and education.* New York: Macmillan.

Berlyne, D. E. (1971). *Aesthetics and psychobiology.* New York: Appleton-Century-Crofts.

Berlyne, D. E. (1974). Verbal and exploratory responses to visual patterns varying in uncertainty and in redundancy. In D. E. Berlyne (Ed.), *Studies in the new experimental aesthetics* (pp. 121–158). Washington, DC: Hemisphere.

Beswick, D. G. (1971). Cognitive process theory of individual differences in curiosity. In H. I. Day, D. E. Berlyne, & D. E. Hunt (Eds.), *Intrinsic motivation: A new direction in education* (pp. 156–170). New York: Holt, Rinehart, & Winston.

Bowlby, J. (1969). *Attachment and loss: Attachment.* New York: Basic Books.

Brickman, P., Coates, D., & Janoff-Bulman, R. (1978). Lottery winners and accident victims: Is happiness relative? *Journal of Personality and Social Psychology, 8,* 917–927.

Collins, R. P., Litman, J. A., & Spielberger, C. D. (2004). The measurement of perceptual curiosity. *Personality and Individual Differences, 36,* 1127–1141.

Crozier, J. B. (1974). Verbal and exploratory responses to sound sequences varying in uncertainty level. In D. E. Berlyne (Ed.), *Studies in the new experimental aesthetics* (pp. 27–90). Washington, DC: Hemisphere.

Deci, E. L. (1992). The relation of interest to the motivation of behavior: A self-determination theory perspective. In K. A. Renninger, S. Hidi, & A. Krapp (Eds.), *The role of interest in learning and development* (pp. 43–70). Hillsdale, NJ: Lawrence Erlbaum.

Depue, R. A. (1996). A neurobiological framework for the structure of personality and emotion: Implications for personality disorders. In J. F. Clarkin & M. F. Lenzenweger (Eds.), *Major theories of personality disorder* (pp. 347–391). New York: Guilford.

Dewey, J. (1913). *Interest and effort in education.* Boston: Riverside.

Feist, G. J. (1994). Affective consequences of insight in art and science students. *Cognition and Emotion, 8,* 489–502.

Fleeson, W. (2001). Toward a structure- and process-integrated view of personality: Traits as density distributions of states. *Journal of Personality and Social Psychology, 80,* 1011–1027.

Fowler, H. (1965). *Curiosity and exploratory behavior.* New York: Macmillan.

Hayes, S. C., Strosahl, K., & Wilson, K. G. (1999). *Acceptance and commitment therapy: An experimental approach to behavior change.* New York: Guilford.

Hidi, S., & Berndorff, D. (1998). Situational interest and learning. In L. Hoffman, A. Krapp, K. A. Renninger, & J. Baumert (Eds.), *Interest and learning* (pp. 74–90). Kiel, Germany: IPN.

Hull, C. L. (1952). *A behavior system.* New Haven, CT: Yale University Press.

Iran-Nejad, A. (1987). Cognitive and affective causes of interest and liking. *Journal of Educational Psychology, 79,* 120–130.

Izard, C. E. (1977). *Human emotions.* New York: Plenum.

Kashdan, T. B. (2004). Curiosity. In C. Peterson & M. E. P. Seligman (Eds.), *Character strengths and virtues: A handbook and classification* (pp. 125–141). New York: Oxford University Press.

Kashdan, T. B. (2007). Social anxiety spectrum and diminished positive experiences: Theoretical synthesis and meta-analysis. *Clinical Psychology Review, 27,* 348–365.

Kashdan, T. B., & Fincham, F. D. (2004). Facilitating curiosity: A social and self-regulatory perspective for scientifically based interventions. In P. A. Linley & S. Joseph (Eds.), *Positive psychology in practice* (pp. 482–503). Hoboken, NJ: Wiley.

Kashdan, T. B., & Roberts, J. E. (2004). Trait and state curiosity in the genesis of intimacy: Differentiation from related constructs. *Journal of Social and Clinical Psychology, 23,* 792–816.

Kashdan, T. B., Rose, P., & Fincham, F. D. (2004). Curiosity and exploration: Facilitating positive subjective experiences and personal growth opportunities. *Journal of Personality Assessment, 82,* 291–305.

Kashdan, T. B., & Steger, M. F. (2007). Curiosity and pathways to well-being and meaning in life: Traits, states, and everyday behaviors. *Motivation and Emotion, 31,* 159–173.

Kashdan, T.B., & Yuen, M. (2007). Whether highly curious students thrive academically depends on the learning environment of their school: A study of Hong Kong adolescents. *Motivation and Emotion, 31*, 260–270.

Keltner, D., & Shiota, M. N. (2003). New displays and new emotions: A commentary on Rozin and Cohen (2003). *Emotion, 3*, 86–91.

Lazarus, R. S. (1991). *Emotion and adaptation.* New York: Oxford University Press.

Litman, J. A. (2005). Curiosity and the pleasures of learning: Wanting and liking new information. *Cognition and Emotion, 19*, 793–814.

Litman, J. A., Collins, R. P., & Spielberger, C. D. (2005). The measurement of sensory curiosity. *Personality and Individual Differences, 39*, 1123–1133.

Litman, J. A., Hutchins, T. L., & Russon, R. K. (2005). Epistemic curiosity, feeling-of-knowing, and exploratory behavior. *Cognition and Emotion, 19*, 559–582.

Litman, J. A., & Silvia, P. J. (2006). The latent structure of trait curiosity: Evidence for interest and deprivation curiosity dimensions. *Journal of Personality Assessment, 86*, 318–328.

Litman, J. A., & Spielberger, C. D. (2003). Measuring epistemic curiosity and its diversive and specific components. *Journal of Personality Assessment, 80*, 75–86.

Loewenstein, G. (1994). The psychology of curiosity: A review and reinterpretation. *Psychological Bulletin, 116*, 75–98.

Lykken, D., & Tellegen, A. (1996). Happiness is a stochastic phenomenon. *Psychological Science, 7*, 186–189.

McCrae, R. R. (1996). Social consequences of experiential openness. *Psychological Bulletin, 120*, 323–337.

Miller, W., & Rollnick, S. (2002). *Motivational interviewing: Preparing people for change.* New York: Guilford.

Naylor, F. D. (1981). A state-trait curiosity inventory. *Australian Psychologist, 16*, 172–183.

Park, N., Peterson, C., & Seligman, M. E. P. (2004). Strengths of character and well-being. *Journal of Social and Clinical Psychology, 23*, 603–619.

Peters, R. A. (1978). Effects of anxiety, curiosity, and perceived instructor threat on student verbal behavior in the college classroom. *Journal of Educational Psychology, 70*, 388–395.

Raine, A., Reynolds, C., Venables, P. H., & Mednick, S. A. (2002). Stimulation-seeking and intelligence: A prospective longitudinal study. *Journal of Personality and Social Psychology, 82*, 663–674.

Reeve, J., & Nix, G. (1997). Expressing intrinsic motivation through acts of exploration and facial displays of interest. *Motivation and Emotion, 21*, 237–250.

Russell, P. A. (1994). Preferability, pleasingness, and interestingness: Relationships between evaluative judgments in empirical aesthetics. *Empirical Studies of the Arts, 12*, 141–157.

Ryan, R. M., & Deci, E. L. (2000). Self-determination theory and the facilitation of intrinsic motivation, social development, and well-being. *American Psychologist, 55*, 68–78.

Sansone, C., & Smith, J. L. (2000). Interest and self-regulation: The relation between having to and wanting to. In C. Sansone & J. M. Harackiewicz (Eds.), *Intrinsic and extrinsic motivation* (pp. 341–372). San Diego, CA: Academic Press.

Schiefele, U. (1999). Interest and learning from text. *Scientific Studies of Reading, 3*, 257–279.

Schiefele, U., Krapp, A., & Winteler, A. (1992). Interest as a predictor of academic achievement: A meta-analysis of research. In K. A. Renninger, S. Hidi, & A. Krapp (Eds.), *The role of interest in learning and development* (pp. 183–212). Hillsdale, NJ: Erlbaum.

Sheldon, K. M., & Elliot, A. J. (1999). Goal striving, need-satisfaction, and longitudinal well-being: The self-concordance model. *Journal of Personality and Social Psychology, 76*, 482–497.

Silvia, P. J. (2005). What is interesting? Exploring the appraisal structure of interest. *Emotion, 5*, 89–102.

Silvia, P. J. (2006). *Exploring the psychology of interest.* New York: Oxford University Press.

Silvia, P. J. (2008). Appraisal components and emotion traits: Examining the appraisal basis of trait curiosity. *Cognition and Emotion, 22*, 94–113.

Spielberger, C. D., & Starr, L. M. (1994). Curiosity and exploratory behavior. In H. F. O'Neil, Jr., & M. Drillings (Eds.), *Motivation: Theory and research* (pp. 221–243). Hillsdale, NJ: Erlbaum.

Swan, G. E., & Carmelli, D. (1996). Curiosity and mortality in aging adults: A 5-year follow-up of the Western Collaborative Group Study. *Psychology and Aging, 11*, 449–453.

Thoman, D. B., Sansone, C., & Pasupathi, M. (2007). Talking about interest: Exploring the role of social interaction for regulating motivation and the interest experience. *Journal of Happiness Studies, 8*, 335–370.

Tomkins, S. S. (1962). *Affect, imagery, consciousness: Vol. 1. The positive affects.* New York: Springer.

Turner, S. A., Jr., & Silvia, P. J. (2006). Must interesting things be pleasant? A test of competing appraisal structures. *Emotion, 6*, 670–674.

Vitterso, J. (2003). Flow versus life satisfaction: A projective use of cartoons to illustrate the difference between the evaluation approach and the intrinsic motivation approach to subjective quality of life. *Journal of Happiness Studies, 4*, 141–167.

Westen, D., & Bradley, R. (2005). Empirically supported complexity. *Current Directions in Psychological Science, 14*, 266–271.

Wilson, T. D., Centerbar, D. B., Kermer, D. A., & Gilbert, D. T. (2005). The pleasures of uncertainty: Prolonging positive moods in ways people do not anticipate. *Journal of Personality and Social Psychology, 88*, 5–21.

Zuckerman, M. (1994). *Behavioral expressions and biosocial bases of sensation seeking.* New York: Cambridge University Press.

Courage

Cynthia L. S. Pury *and* Shane J. Lopez

Abstract

Courage is the well-praised but little-researched virtue of voluntarily facing personal risk to pursue worthy goals. This chapter reviews research on courage and its relationship to fear, morally relevant internal states, efficacy, character development, social influence, altruism, self-regulation, and gender differences, as well as potential measures of courage and applications. The development of additional performance measures of courageous behavior is needed to inform models of courageous behavior, and, ultimately, courage-related interventions.

Keywords: bravery, courage, human strengths, valor, values

Courage has been praised by philosophers as a key virtue, perhaps even *the* key virtue, necessary for the full expression of all other virtues (e.g., Johnson [quoted in Boswell, 1791/2004]). For Aristotle (ca. 350 BCE/1999), courage lies between the extremes of cowardice and rashness. Individual situation and abilities determine cowardice and rashness, thus leading to the same action being courageous for one person and cowardly or rash for another. Stoic philosophers wrote about the courage to choose to maintain integrity in the face of life's difficulties. The existentialist tradition examines courage as the act of facing freedom with full awareness of our responsibility (Putman, in press).

The types of people and actions praised as courageous change as society changes. For example, steadfast support of a lost or doomed cause was considered quite heroic in the early twentieth century, but may be a sign of inflexibility today (Barczewski, 2008; Knight & Saal, 1986).

Despite changes in the types of actions praised for courage, courage itself is valued universally across cultures (e.g., Dahlsgaard, Peterson, & Seligman, 2005). It is also of societal interest: Google hits of web pages for the terms "courage," "bravery," or "heroism" (about 795,000) are nearly as common as those for the terms "fear," "anxiety," or "avoidance" (about 1,190,000): a ratio of approximately 2:3.

Interest from psychologists has been more limited. As indexed by PsychINFO on March 27, 2008, "courage," "bravery," or "heroism" are keywords for 128 peer-reviewed entries, whereas "fear," "anxiety," or "avoidance" are keywords for 45,446 peer-reviewed entries: a ratio of approximately 1:355. Research on courage has gained momentum: over half of all peer-reviewed studies on courage have been published since 2001.

Early Courage Research

Lord (1918) applied the psychological principles of his time to understand courage, which he proposed occurs when the instinct of fear is overridden by another, stronger instinct or sentiment. He describes multiple types of courageous action, based on the opposing instinct or sentiment. In what he called "simpler and lower forms" of courage, the opposing force is an instinct: anger, sex, or self-assertion. In higher forms of courage, the opposing force is an acquired sentiment: like love, honor, or duty. Courageous acts taken for patriotism, a more abstract concept, were regarded by Lord as higher still, with the highest forms representing a mature philosophy of life, honor of self-respect, religious faith, and the dignity of persons. The penultimate form of courage, the "courage of despair," involves the pursuit of a lost cause to which one is supremely loyal and self-identified (and fits Barczewski's [2008] description of Lord's era). Influenced by World War I, Lord discusses the role of courage in training soldiers and treating shell shock, and argues German soldiers were pursuing a baser sentiment than Allied soldiers and were hence less courageous.

Other early work also focused on military courage. Gee (1931) sampled United States Army records from World War I for bravery citations and found five categories. "Individual bravery" is acting alone during battle, such as charging a machine gun nest. "Voluntary collective bravery" is voluntary membership in a group on a dangerous mission. "Line of duty bravery" is accomplishing assigned duties while under attack. "Altruistic bravery" is saving others despite risk to self. Finally, "bravery under physical duress" is carrying on with a mission despite wounds.

Shaffer (1947) defined courage as a reduction of fear and used retrospective surveys of aerial combat fliers during World War II. He found three categories of beliefs or actions that increased courage: confidence in equipment, crew, and leaders; effective activity; and social stimulation. External rewards or a broader moral commitment to the war did not reduce fear; however similar beliefs did make missions easier.

Deutsch (1961) presents a model of social courage, what most today would call moral courage, as inner conviction divided by punishment potential. Courage can be changed by changing inner conviction, punishment potential, or the perception of either. Deutsch also proposed both external forces and individual differences might account for differences in courageous behavior: a later study found that teacher ratings of moral courage, such as standing up for a just but unpopular cause, correlates with moral judgment in children (Gibbs, Clark, Joseph, Green, Goodrick, & Makowski, 1986).

Rachman (1990) returned the focus of courage research to the behaviors of military personnel and professionals in high-risk occupations. His work is discussed in a subsequent section on negative emotional states associated with courage.

Features and Types of Courage

A variety of definitions of courage include describe it as taking an action despite internal or external opposition (e.g., Lopez, O'Byrne, &

Petersen, 2003; Peterson & Seligman, 2004; Worline & Steen, 2004). The greater the opposition, the more likely the action is to be appraised as courageous, but the less likely the action is to occur in the first place (see Miller, 2002). Thus, in evaluating courage theory and research, particularly when evaluating opposing states or traits, such as fear, it is important to distinguish the likelihood of the actor behaving courageously from the likelihood of an observer appraising action as courageous.

Empirical attempts to define courage have concentrated on two major areas: determining the defining features that all courageous actors or persons have in common, and delineating different types or brands of courage.

Necessary Features of Courage

Rate, Clarke, Lindsay, & Sternberg (2007) investigated implicit definitions of courage using a variety of techniques. First, participants listed behaviors of ideally courageous others (Study 1). These behaviors then were rated by a second sample on how "distinctively characteristic" they were of a courageous person (Study 2). The top characteristics identified in Study 2 then were used in a card-sorting task to identify major dimensions of courageous behavior (Study 3). Finally, these dimensions were used to create vignettes to ensure that the dimensions identified are used by individuals in judging behavior to be courageous (Study 4). Rate et al. thus proposed four defining features of courage for adults. The first two are variations on intentional behavior: "willfulness and intentionality" and "mindful deliberation." The third was "objective substantial risk to the actor," and the fourth "a noble or worthy end." "Fear" occupied an unusual and perhaps intermediary role: although "acting despite fear" emerged as a relevant dimension in Studies 2 and 3, it was strongly correlated with risk to the actor in Study 4 and thus did not uniquely predict ratings of courageousness. Other research suggests that children may have a simpler picture of courage that increases in complexity with age (e.g., Szagun & Schäuble, 1997).

Types of Courage

While Rate et al.'s (2007) research examines common core features for all courageous acts, other research has focused on differentiating types of courageous actions. The most commonly mentioned types of courage are physical courage, or facing physical risks and dangers; and moral courage, or standing up for a moral principle in the face of social opposition (Lopez et al., 2003). A more recently added third type is variously called "vital courage" (Finfgeld, 1999) or "psychological courage" (Putman, 2004). Both vital and psychological courage involve transcendence of personal limitations, although vital courage also can involve very real physical risks associated with medical illnesses. Each of these three types of courage has a different pattern of risks and difficulties; physical courage involves physical risks and difficulties, moral courage involves a risk to one's social image, and both moral and psychological courage involve internal struggles (Pury, Kowalski, & Spearman, 2007).

Level of risk can also be used to differentiate courageous acts. Extreme risk to life and limb in pursuit of social values is commonly called "heroism" (Becker & Eagly, 2004; Smirnov, Arrow, Kennett, & Orbel, 2007). The extent to which the mechanisms of heroism differ from other types of courage is unknown.

Courage can also be classified by motivation. "Civil courage" is brave action on behalf of moral norms taken without regard to risk to the actor (Greitemeyer, Osswald, Fischer, & Frey, 2007). "Military courage" is risking one's life for the group in a military context (e.g., Castro, 2006; Smirnov et al., 2007). "Existential courage" (e.g., Larsen & Giles, 1976) is expressing authenticity in the face of threat to one's survival or social standing.

In the Values in Action system (VIA: Peterson & Seligman, 2004b), the universal virtue of courage is characterized by "bravery," or not avoiding threat; "persistence," or finishing what one starts; "integrity," or acting authentically; and "vigor," or approaching situations with energy. Empirically, persistence, bravery, and integrity seem to be common to a wide variety of courageous actions, while vigor is not (Pury & Kowalski, 2007).

There are at least two types of appraisal of courage based on reference group: "personal courage," or actions that are courageous for the specific actor; and "general courage," or actions that would be courageous if performed by anyone (Pury et al., 2007).

Psychological States and Processes Associated with Courage
Negative Emotional States

Many accounts describe courage as acting in opposition to a variety of emotional forces, particularly those of fear. Rachman (1990) examined subjective and physiological fear responses in courageous populations, such as decorated bomb disposal operators. Highly courageous samples commonly had lower subjective and physiological fear responses

to laboratory stressors than less courageous samples (e.g., Cox, Hallam, O'Connor, & Rachman, 1983; O'Connor, Hallam, & Rachman, 1985). If courage is behavioral approach in the face of subjective or physiological fear, individuals engaging in societally labeled courageous actions might better be called "fearless" than courageous. This fearlessness develops similarly to the reduction of fear in exposure therapy; trainees for objectively dangerous military jobs show a reduction in fear and an increase in confidence as training progresses (Rachman, 1990).

The extent to which fear is a part of appraisal of courage may vary with the reference group. Fear has a positive correlation with personal courage and is unrelated to appraisal of the general courage of an action (Pury et al., 2007).

Fear may not be the only emotional state associated with courage: Castro (2006) defines courage as overcoming a threat that may be accompanied by fear, sadness, or anger. Whatever the emotional state, however, it has a competing action tendency with the courageous action.

Morally Relevant States

Historically, both Lord and Deutsch propose an additional internal state in courage—an instinct or sentiment for Lord and an inner conviction for Deutsch—that overcomes fear. More recently, Rate et al. (2007) found lay definitions of courage included the pursuit of a noble goal. Although Rate et al. did not specifically mention the experience of any specific internal states associated with the goal, recent psychological research highlights the emotional nature of moral judgments (e.g., Haidt, 2001; Tangney, Stuewig, & Mashek, 2007). Moral emotions may be a part of at least some courageous actions; the experience of civil courage, for example, commonly includes feelings of indignation and empathy (Greitemeyer et al., 2007). In a process model of the subjective experience of courage, Hannah, Sweeny, and Lester (2007) propose that a variety of internal characteristics influence courageous behavior: inner convictions or values, duty, selflessness, integrity, honor, valor, loyalty, and independence.

Morally relevant goals may appear very different to the actor and to the observer. Silke (2004) reviews academic interviews of some former terrorists. In these accounts, he argues, terrorists describe themselves as soldiers rather than as criminals. They describe overcoming their own fears to complete risky actions—actions that they believe are justified and morally appropriate. These descriptions, Silke argues, contain all of the necessary features of courage save for perhaps the readers' agreement in the justness of the cause.

Efficacy-Relevant States

Hannah et al.'s (2007) model also includes somewhat transient states, such as self-, collective, and means efficacy; hope; resiliency; and positive emotions. Other research reveals that courageous actions are commonly associated with feelings of confidence (Pury et al., 2007; Rachman, 1990). This confidence is positively correlated with ratings of the general courage of the action and has no correlation with the personal courage of the action, while fear is correlated with personal courage and has no correlation with general courage (Pury et al., 2007).

Another efficacy-relevant state, hope, or the ability to develop pathways to reach a desired goal and one's perceived agency to reach those goals (Snyder, 2002), has been correlated with courage in both theory (Hannah et al., 2007) and empirical observation (Kowalski et al., 2006; Pury & Kowalski, 2007).

Character Development

Believing that one has acted with courage may increase the chance of future courageous actions. Boyd and Ross (1994) report anecdotal evidence showing benefits in self-perception and inner resources following describing a past courageous action. Finfgeld (1999) proposes labeling oneself a courageous person promotes vital courage and personal growth. In the battlemind model of courage (Castro, 2006), courageous actions lead to the development of self-confidence and selfless love, which then lead to further courageous behavior. Similarly, Hannah et al. (2007) propose that retroactively labeling one's action as courageous leads to changes in the positive states, values, and beliefs that make future courageous behavior more likely.

Social Influence

Zimbardo's (2007) contextual model of heroism proposes that strong situational determinants, primarily from negative social forces, can blind actors to inherently immoral action. When in the midst of such social forces, individuals will be less likely to see anything amiss with behavior that receives the formal or informal sanction of the group. Persons acting with apparent moral courage to end immoral group behavior, then, are most likely to be those who, in some way, are outside of the social forces of the group.

The well-known bystander effect (e.g., Latané & Nida, 1981), in which people are less likely to intervene on others' behalf when in a group than when alone, disappears when the threat to the potential victim and the actor is more extreme (Fischer, Greitemeyer, Pollozek, & Frey, 2006). The presence of a more extreme threat to the actor may change the behavior from one of simple altruism to one of civil courage (Greitemeyer et al., 2007), thus suggesting that this common social influence may not work for at least some types of courageous behavior.

Some social forces might reinforce courage: Hannah et al.'s (2007) model proposes that positive social forces, such as interdependence, social identity, cohesion, and informational influence, can promote courageous behavior. Consistent data were reported by Shaffer's (1947) observation of the importance of duty to fellow crew members and observation of calm behavior in others in courageous behavior of World War II flyers.

Finally, observing courageous behavior in others creates its own social influence. Worline (2004) found that observation of the courageous behaviors of others in the workplace leads observers to three discernible outcomes. Observers report feelings of inspiration and the possibility of change. Observers also report actual organizational change through what Worline terms "creative fractures," when the moral beauty of a courageous action inspires others to make changes. In a laboratory study, Nemeth and Chiles (1988) used a modified Asch paradigm in which participants were asked to name colors among confederates who sometimes, as a group, gave incorrect responses. Participants who had been exposed to an earlier group in which a lone confederate offered dissenting (and incorrect) answers were more likely to dissent themselves.

Altruism

Courageous actions are commonly taken to benefit another. Kindness (Fagin-Jones & Midlarsky, 2007; Pury & Kowalski, 2007) and altruistic motivations (Becker & Eagly, 2004) frequently co-occur with courageous actions and actors. It should be noted, however, that not all actions described as courageous benefit others; only those that do are likely to be high in kindness.

Additionally, courageous actions seem to be more than mere altruism. In a direct comparison between altruistic actions and civilly courageous actions, Greitemeyer, Fischer, Kastenmüller, and Frey (2006) compared participant recollections of taking or failing to take an altruistic action and taking or failing to take a civilly courageous action. Actions requiring civil courage were perceived more quickly, were riskier and less dependent on skills, and generated more morally relevant emotions. Moreover, actual intervention was predicted by judgment of responsibility, intervention skills, negative consequences of action, societal moral norms, and anger for civil courage; and by perception speed and empathy for altruistic action. Thus, while altruism and its associated strength of kindness might be commonly expressed in courageous actions, taking a courageous action may be different from taking a purely altruistic low-risk action.

Self-Regulation

Serkerka and Bagozzi (2007) propose a self-regulation model of moral courage within an organization. In their model, moral courage is a response to an ethical challenge, which is processed using anticipated emotions, self-efficacy, subjective and group norms, and affect toward the means. This processing leads to a desire to act, which combines with self-regulation to lead to a decision to act and then to the action itself. The self-regulatory processes may be automatic, or they may be conscious and influenced by self-consciousness and social identity.

Gender Differences

Although men are disproportionately represented in some citations for extreme physical courage, such as the Carnegie Hero Medal, empirical investigations of other types of heroism (Becker & Eagly, 2004) and subjective reports of courageous action (Pury et al., 2007) reveal fewer gender differences. The gender differences that have been observed seem to be due to instrumental requirements for upper body strength and speed, favoring males; empathic concern, favoring females; and role differentiation. Occupational roles protecting the community and society, and informal roles protecting the family unit favor males; informal roles of kin or social relationship aiding specific individuals, and formal occupational roles in which the risks are not a direct outcome of the role (e.g., a Peace Corps volunteer in a dangerous country) favor females (Becker & Eagly, 2004).

Measurement of Courage
Self-Report Scales

Few scales have been developed to measure courageous behavior. The Values in Action inventory of strengths (VIA-IS, Peterson & Seligman, 2004a) includes strengths of courage. The entire VIA-IS measures the 24 different strengths in the VIA system that load onto the six VIA virtues,

including courage. Internal consistency appears adequate (e.g., Linley et al., 2007; Park, Peterson, & Seligman, 2004; Peterson & Seligman, 2004a) and is similar across American, English, and Japanese samples (Linley et al., 2007; Shimai, Otake, Park, Peterson, & Seligman, 2006). Strengths show expected cultural differences (e.g., Shimai et al., 2006; Linley, et al., 2007), as well as sensitivity to demographic variables of gender and age (e.g., Linley et al., 2007) and to historical events (Peterson & Seligman, 2003). The measure is commonly scored ipsatively, with the rank ordering of strengths within persons reported (e.g., Park et al., 2004; Shimai et al., 2006). However, only three of the four strengths, which comprise the composite virtue of courage—persistence, bravery, and integrity—were found to be descriptive of a variety of courageous acts, whereas vitality was not particularly descriptive (Pury & Kowalski, 2007). In the same study, two strengths—hope and kindness—also emerged as highly descriptive of courageous action, although the VIA system assigns those two strengths as components of the superordinate values of transcendence (hope) and humanity (kindness). Thus, investigators using the VIA-IS strengths of courage might also include the measures of hope and kindness.

Self-reports of willingness to act in a variety of specific circumstances are used by two different scales measuring courage. The Woodard–Pury Courage Scale (WPCS-23; Woodard, 2004; Woodard & Pury, 2007) consists of 23 items and four factors: willingness to act for one's job or self-interest (e.g., "I would accept an important project at my place of employment even though it would bring intense public criticism and publicity"); willingness to act for one's beliefs (e.g., "If called upon during times of national emergency, I would give my life for my country"); willingness to act despite or on behalf of specific others (e.g., "Intense social pressure would not stop me from doing the right thing"); and willingness to act within a family ("I could approach someone whose family members had just been killed, knowing they were feeling overwhelming grief"). Participants are asked to what extent they would agree or disagree, then asked how much fear they would feel in that situation. Although the original scoring measured courage as the product of willingness to act and fear for each situation (Woodard, 2004), the revised scoring is based solely on willingness to act (Woodard & Pury, 2007). The WPCS-23 appears to have good internal consistency and preliminary validity (Woodard & Pury, 2007).

The Munich Civil Courage Instrument (MuZI: Kastenmüller, Greitemeyer, Fischer, & Frey, 2007) takes a similar approach to measuring civil courage. Respondents indicate their intention to intervene in three types of situations in which others are threatening social beliefs: negative slogans (e.g., "In the pedestrian area right-wing extremists shout slogans against disabled and homosexual people"); in the workplace (e.g., "Some of your colleagues try to isolate another colleague"); and physical violence (e.g., "In the subway a young woman is bothered by two right-wing extremists"). It has adequate reliability and validity (Kastenmuller et al., 2007). The MuZI is available only in German at the present.

Finally, the Courage Measure (CM) consists of 12 self-report items (Norton & Weiss, in press). Unlike the WPCS or the MuZI, the CM asks participants to rate their propensity to act in the face of fear generally, with no mention of specific situations or specific risks. Sample items include "I tend to face my fears" and "Even if something scares me, I will not back down." The scale has a single factor with good internal consistency. Moreover, CM scores gathered immediately before a behavioral approach test in participants high in spider fear predicted performance. CM scores collected approximately three weeks earlier, however, did not (P. J. Norton, personal communication, September 22, 2008; Norton & Weiss, in press).

Other Courage Measurement Procedures

Because the types of risky situations calling for courage are uncommon and ethical laboratory replication is difficult, narrative data are commonly collected (e.g., Finfgeld, 1999; Greitemeyer et al., 2006 Study 2; Pury et al., 2007; Pury & Kowalski, 2007; Worline, 2004). While such data provide rich contextual details and are suitable for exploratory approaches, they also face the limits of self-report. As commonly used—asking participants for exemplars of courageous action—they likely measure people's appraisals of courage in addition to actual behavior.

Life data have been used to find samples of individuals who have taken moderately to extremely dangerous actions, such as living kidney-donors (Becker & Eagly, 2004), volunteers in violent countries (Becker & Eagly, 2004), Holocaust rescuers (Becker & Eagly, 2004; Fagin-Jones & Midlarsky, 2007), and winners of medals for bravery (Becker & Eagly, 2004; Cox et al., 1983); or who are employed in dangerous occupations (O'Connor et al., 1985). These samples are may be difficult to

procure, and to date have been limited to physical courage. Like narrative data, experimental control is not possible.

Vignettes

A variety of researchers have asked participants to rate the courageousness of a set of carefully controlled vignettes (e.g., Study 1, Greitemeyer et al., 2006; Rate et al., 2007; Szagun, 1992). While this procedure offers excellent experimental control, it measures appraisals rather than action.

Laboratory Situations

Few studies have utilized a controlled, standardized procedure to bring courageous action into a laboratory setting. Cox et al. (1983) exposed participants to an increasingly insolvable problem, with electric shock as punishment for an incorrect answer. Fischer et al.'s (2006) participants believed they were watching a live video feed in which a female student was harassed by either a threatening or nonthreatening male student, and time to intervention was recorded. Nemeth and Chiles (1988) created a modified Asch paradigm, with participants resisting social pressure to report their own perceptual experience instead of the group's experience. Norton and Weiss (in press) asked participants who were high in spider fear to get as close to a display of taxidermied spiders as comfort allowed. Each effort examined a different associated factor of courage, and no consistent efforts have been made to develop a model based on multiple types of observable performance.

Future Directions

Courage is a basic psychological phenomenon that warrants further investigation before applications to practice can be developed. To date, underpinnings of courage are a mystery because the examination of courage in a controlled setting is quite challenging. Three other gaps in courage research also need further attention.

Very little research has been done on the longer-term link between courage and life outcomes. Preliminary data suggest that the picture may not be entirely positive: interviews of former militia members and bomb disposal technicians about their own courageous behaviors found few if any personal benefits to courageous acts (Walshe & Briner, 2008). The important goals pursued by these samples, however, may have been societal rather than personal. It may be that courageous actions taken specifically to pursue important life outcomes at an individual level, such as education, medical or fertility treatment, career advancement, or even aiding a loved one rather than unknown others, will lead to an increased likelihood of personal benefit.

As we build a better sense of the factors and products associated with courage, the role that culture plays in the manifestations of courage needs to be considered. Currently, there is extremely limited cross-cultural data on courage. While Dahlsgaard et al. (2005) found that courage was not explicitly mentioned in three Eastern traditions (Confucianism, Taoism, and Buddhism), traditional Chinese medicine does suggest a specific bodily location for courage, the gallbladder (Yu, 2003). Smirnov et al. (2007) describe military heroism as an evolved trait based on our evolutionary ancestors' warlike past: thus, prior cultural conditions may have shaped our genetic propensity today.

Finally, it is becoming clear that learning about courageous actions of others may inspire courageous actions in the observer (e.g., Nemeth & Chiles, 1988; Worline, 2004). As these honors continue, they might be expanded to include more awards for moral and perhaps even psychological courage in pursuit of socially valued goals. The proximal and distal effects of such awards on behavior should be considered.

Conclusion

Recent studies on the psychological processes involved in courageous action provide a promising foundation. To date, these efforts have concentrated on the development of shared, empirically supported definitions of courage, typologies of courage, and related features. Measures of individual differences in courage and of courageous behavior are being refined and models are being developed and tested. We expect a bright future for courage research, including applications to practice, once the definitions, measures, and models gain empirical support.

References

Aristotle (1999). *Nicomachean ethics* (Trans. M. Ostwald). Upper Saddle River, NJ: Prentice-Hall (Original work published ca. 350 BCE).

Barczewski, S. (2008). *Antarctic destinies: Scott, Shackleton and the changing face of heroism.* London: Continuum Books.

Becker, S. W., & Eagly, A. H. (2004). The heroism of women and men. *American Psychologist, 59,* 163–178.

Boswell, J. (1791/2004). *The life of Samuel Johnson LL.D.* C. G. Osgood (Ed.). Retrieved 3/18/2008 from http://ebooks.adelaide.edu.au/b/boswell/james/osgood/chapter29.html

Boyd, J., & Ross, K. (1994). The courage tapes: A positive approach to life's challenges. *Journal of Systemic Therapies, 13,* 64–69.

Castro, C. (2006). Military courage. In T. W. Britt, A. B. Adler, & C. Castro (Eds.), *Military life: The psychology of serving in peace and combat: Vol. 4. Military culture* (pp. 60–78). Westport, CT: Praeger Security International.

Cox, D., Hallam, R., O'Connor, K., & Rachman, S. (1983). An experimental analysis of fearlessness and courage. *British Journal of Psychology, 74,* 107–117.

Dahlsgaard, K., Peterson, C., & Seligman, M. (2005). Shared virtue: The convergence of valued human strengths across culture and history. *Review of General Psychology, 9,* 203–213.

Deutsch, M. (1961). Courage as a concept in social psychology. *Journal of Social Psychology, 55,* 49–58.

Fagin-Jones, S., & Midlarsky, E. (2007). Courageous altruism: Personal and situational correlates of rescue during the Holocaust. *Journal of Positive Psychology, 2,* 136–147.

Finfgeld, D. (1999). Courage as a process of pushing beyond the struggle. *Qualitative Health Research, 9,* 803–814.

Fischer, P., Greitemeyer, T., Pollozek, F., & Frey, D. (2006). The unresponsive bystander: Are bystanders more responsive in dangerous emergencies? *European Journal of Social Psychology, 36,* 267–278.

Gee, W. (1931). Rural–urban heroism in military action. *Social Forces, 10,* 102–111.

Gibbs, J. C., Clark, P. M., Joseph, J. A., Green, J. L., Goodrick, T. S., & Makowski, D. G. (1986). Relations between moral judgment, moral courage, and field independence. *Child Development, 57,* 185–193.

Greitemeyer, T., Fischer, P., Kastenmüller, A., & Frey, D. (2006). Civil courage and helping behavior: Differences and similarities. *European Psychologist, 11,* 90–98.

Greitemeyer, T., Osswald, S., Fischer, P., & Frey, D. (2007). Civil courage: Implicit theories, related concepts, and measurement. *Journal of Positive Psychology, 2,* 115–119.

Haidt, J. (2001). The emotional dog and its rational tail: A social intuitionist approach to moral judgment. *Psychological Review, 108,* 814–834.

Hannah, S., Sweeney, P., & Lester, P. (2007). Toward a courageous mindset: The subjective act and experience of courage. *Journal of Positive Psychology, 2,* 129–135.

Kastenmüller, A., Greitemeyer, T., Fischer, P., & Frey, D. (2007). Das Münchner Zivilcourage-Instrument (MüZI): Entwicklung und Validierung (The Munich Civil Courage Instrument (MüZI): Development and validation). *Diagnostica, 53,* 205–217.

Knight, P., & Saal, F. (1986). Heroism is no substitute for success: Effects of strategy and outcome on perceptions of performance. *Journal of Occupational Psychology, 59,* 81–92.

Kowalski, R. M., Pury, C. L. S., Sporrer, L., Hunter, E., Gorney, A., Baker, M., et al. (2006, November). *Courage and hope: Pathways to action.* Paper presented at the annual meeting of the Society of Southeastern Social Psychologists, November 10–11, Knoxville, TN.

Larsen, K., & Giles, H. (1976, August). Survival or courage as human motivation: Development of an attitude scale. *Psychological Reports, 39*(1), 299–302.

Latané, B., & Nida, S. (1981). Ten years of research on group size and helping. *Psychological Bulletin, 89,* 308–324.

Linley, P., Maltby, J., Wood, A., Joseph, S., Harrington, S., Peterson, C., et al. (2007, July). Character strengths in the United Kingdom: The VIA inventory of strengths. *Personality and Individual Differences, 43,* 341–351.

Lopez, S., O'Byrne, K., & Petersen, S. (2003). Profiling courage. *Positive psychological assessment: A handbook of models and measures* (pp. 185–197). Washington, DC: American Psychological Association.

Lord, H. G. (1918). *The psychology of courage.* Boston: John W. Luce.

Miller, W. (2002). *The mystery of courage.* Cambridge, MA: Harvard University Press.

Nemeth, C., & Chiles, C. (1988). Modelling courage: The role of dissent in fostering independence. *European Journal of Social Psychology, 18,* 275–280.

Norton, P. J., & Weiss, B. J. (in press). The role of courage on behavioral approach in a fear-eliciting situation: A proof-of-concept pilot study. *Journal of Anxiety Disorders.* Available online 12 July 2008, ISSN 0887-6185, DOI: 10.1016/j.janxdis.2008.08.002. (http://www.sciencedirect.com/science/article/B6VDK-4SYTC7G-1/2/a03c4ed41492f5b78e0a03c4fdbb1846)

O'Connor, K., Hallam, R., & Rachman, S. (1985). Fearlessness and courage: A replication experiment. *British Journal of Psychology, 76,* 187–197.

Park, N., Peterson, C., & Seligman, M. (2004). Strengths of character and well-being. *Journal of Social and Clinical Psychology, 23,* 603–619.

Peterson, C., & Seligman, M. (2003). Character strengths before and after September 11. *Psychological Science, 14,* 381–384.

Peterson, C., & Seligman, M. E. P. (2004a). Assessment and applications. In C. Peterson & M. E. P. Seligman (Eds.) *Character strengths and virtues: A handbook and classification.* (pp. 625–644) Washington, DC: American Psychological Association.

Peterson, C., & Seligman, M. E. P. (2004b). Strengths of courage: Introduction. In C. Peterson & M. E. P. Seligman (Eds.) *Character strengths and virtues: A handbook and classification.* (pp. 197–212) Washington, DC: American Psychological Association.

Pury, C. L. S., & Kowalski, R. (2007). Human strengths, courageous actions, and general and personal courage. *Journal of Positive Psychology, 2,* 120–128.

Pury, C. L. S., Kowalski, R. M., & Spearman, M. J. (2007). Distinctions between general and personal courage. *Journal of Positive Psychology, 2,* 99–114.

Putman, D. (2004). *Psychological courage.* Lanham, MD: University Press of America.

Putman, D. (in press). The philosophical roots of the concept of courage. In C. L. S. Pury & S. J. Lopez (Eds.), *The psychology of courage.* New York: APA Books.

Rachman, S. (1990). *Fear and courage* (2nd ed.). New York: W. H. Freeman/Times Books/Henry Holt.

Rate, C., Clarke, J., Lindsay, D., & Sternberg, R. (2007). Implicit theories of courage. *Journal of Positive Psychology, 2,* 80–98.

Serkerka, L. E., & Bagozzi, R. P. (2007). Moral courage in the workplace: Moving to and from the desire and decision to act. *Business Ethics: A European Review, 16,* 132–149.

Shaffer, L. (1947). Fear and courage in aerial combat. *Journal of Consulting Psychology, 11,* 137–143.

Shimai, S., Otake, K., Park, N., Peterson, C., & Seligman, M. (2006). Convergence of character strengths in American and Japanese young adults. *Journal of Happiness Studies, 7,* 311–322.

Silke, A. (2004). Courage in dark places: Reflections on terrorist psychology. *Social Research, 74,* 177–198.

Smirnov, O., Arrow, H., Kennett, D., & Orbell, J. (2007). Ancestral war and the evolutionary origins of "heroism." *Journal of Politics, 69,* 927–940.

Snyder, C. R. (2002). Hope theory: Rainbows in the mind. *Psychological Inquiry, 13,* 249–275.

Spence, G., & Grant, A. (2007). Professional and peer life coaching and the enhancement of goal striving and well-being: An exploratory study. *Journal of Positive Psychology, 2,* 185–194.

Szagun, G. (1992). Age-related changes in children's understanding of courage. *The Journal of Genetic Psychology, 153,* 405–420.

Szagun, G., & Schäuble, M. (1997). Children's and adults' understanding of the feeling experience of courage. *Cognition and Emotion, 11,* 291–306.

Tangney, J., Stuewig, J., & Mashek, D. (2007). Moral emotions and moral behavior. *Annual Review of Psychology, 58,* 345–372.

Walshe, N. D., & Briner, R. (2008). *Diffusing the courage myth: Lessons from those who know best.* Paper presented at the 2008 Academy of Management Meeting, August 8–13, Anaheim, CA.

Woodard, C. (2004). Hardiness and the concept of courage. *Consulting Psychology Journal: Practice and Research, 56,* 173–185.

Woodard, C., & Pury, C. (2007). The construct of courage: Categorization and measurement. *Consulting Psychology Journal: Practice and Research, 59,* 135–147.

Worline, M. C. (2004). *Dancing the cliff edge: The place of courage in social life.* Doctoral dissertation, The University of Michigan.

Worline, M. C., & Steen, T. A. (2004). Bravery. In C. Peterson & M. E. P. Seligman (Eds.), *Character strengths and virtues: A handbook and classification.* (pp. 213–228) Washington, DC: American Psychological Association.

Yu, N. (2003). Metaphor, body, and culture: The Chinese understanding of gallbladder and courage. *Metaphor and Symbol, 18*(1), 13–31.

Zimbardo, P. (2007). *The Lucifer effect: Understanding how good people turn evil.* New York: Random House.

PART 6

Interpersonal Approaches

Relationship Connection: A Redux on the Role of Minding and the Quality of Feeling Special in the Enhancement of Closeness

John H. Harvey *and* Brian G. Pauwels

Abstract

Achieving constructive relationship connections is an important step as an objective of positive psychology. In the context of a culture of dissolution in close relationships, minding serves as an antidote to the demise of feelings of closeness over time. In this paper, we argue that minding the close relationship is a powerful pathway to developing and enhancing closeness. Minding is a combination of thought and behavior patterns that interact to create stability and feelings of closeness. Minding is formally defined as a reciprocal knowing process that occurs nonstop throughout the history of the relationship and that involves a complex package of interrelated thoughts, feelings, and behaviors. The components of minding are knowing and being known, achieved through reciprocal self-disclosure; attribution that is realistic about causality, but that also gives one's partner the benefit of doubt in questionable circumstances; acceptance of what one discovers in the knowing process and respect for one's partner revealed in this process; and reciprocity and continuity. The final component emphasizes the fact that minding must be done by both partners and that it is a never-ending process. The paper also describes other contemporary conceptions to which minding is closely related and addresses future direction for research on the minding process.

Keywords: acceptance and respect, knowing and being known, minding, reciprocity

Minding as Relationship Connection

Paul Newman on the secret to his long, lasting marriage to Joanne Woodward: "Lust, respect, and determination".

(on *The Larry King Show*, CNN, February 28, 1998)

Lust, respect, and determination are strongly implied components of the processes that we will outline in this chapter as vital to relationship maintenance and enhancement. In this chapter, we present and reconsider parts of our earlier writing (Harvey, Pauwels, & Zickmund, 2001) about the concept of relationship connection as a vital part of positive psychology. In this context, relationship connection will refer to ways in which people can enhance their closeness with others with whom they have romantic relationships.

How can romantic couples maintain and enhance closeness? By closeness, we mean mutual satisfaction and behavior that contributes to one another's goals and hopes in life. While our ideas have been developed in the context of close, romantic relationships, they also have relevance to friendships and family relationships. In this chapter, we will explore the role of the mind, thinking, and related emotions in making relationships work and work better over a developmental course. The goal is to explain how people sometimes come to feel very special in relationships, a *sine qua non* of satisfaction and closeness.

Kelley et al. (1983) defined close relationship as "one of strong, frequent, and diverse interdependence [between two people] that lasts over a considerable period of time" (p. 38). Kelley et al.

conceived interdependence as the extent to which two people's lives are closely intertwined, in terms of their behavior toward one another and thoughts and feelings about one another. They also viewed the time factor as involving months or years rather than days. The conception of relationship connection to be articulated in this chapter views interdependence as a key aspect of relationship connection.

"Minding the close relationship" is a theory (Harvey & Omarzu, 1997, 1999) aimed at exploring a powerful pathway to developing and enhancing closeness over time. This theory gives considerable attention to how people focus and give thought to their relationships. "Minding" is a combination of thought and behavior patterns that interact to create stability and feelings of closeness in a relationship. We define minding as "a reciprocal knowing process that occurs nonstop throughout the history of the relationship and that involves a complex package of interrelated thoughts, feelings, and behaviors." There are five specific components of minding, which are described in sections below. Before describing these components, the general idea of minding in psychology deserves attention.

The Popularity of Minding-Like and Positive Psychology Concepts in Contemporary Psychology

Ideas highly related to minding have been around psychology for decades and are quite contemporary in the field. Langer (1978, 1989) was one of the first scholars to describe the differential effects of mindful and mindless activities in daily life. Langer argued that mindlessness may be the preferred mode of interacting with one's environment and mindlessness may be much more common than more thoughtful action in many contexts of human action. Langer's ideas have been tested in various compliance behavior settings (e.g., making copies on a copier, showing how easily people obey instructions from others that are not in their best interests). A major implication of Langer's ideas is that people frequently in daily life give up control and become dependent on scripts. These ideas are readily applicable to relationship situations in which people engage in many acts of incompetence in their relations with close others, including failure to appreciate others' needs and stresses, taking others for granted, and inability to perceive how their own behavior makes other feel in different arenas of action.

Rubinstein and Firstenberg (1999) developed a major application of mindfulness ideas in relating them to organizational behavior. In minding an organization, all the parties involved in a project get together from the start to explore the issues. Each part of the organization knows what the others are doing and is committed to creating a cohesive unit that maintains a unified focus for the future, shares information, articulates and learns from individual errors of its members, continually seeks to strengthen its powers of perception, and is able to express itself creatively in a variety of ways. As will be seen below, these mindful steps parallel the patterns of minding a close relationship.

Germer (2005) provides a review of the centrality of mindfulness ideas in contemporary psychology. For example, there has been a surge of literature on mindfulness and acceptance-based behavioral treatment (Baer, 2003). These approaches cultivate a relaxed, nonadversarial relationship to symptoms, in which disturbing thoughts and feelings are allowed to come and go. Forgiveness and acceptance are major tenets in these approaches. In another development, the field of neuroplasticity has developed as an inquiry about the ability of the mind to shape the brain via meditation (Schwartz & Begley, 2002). More generally, mindfulness has been recognized as health practices, such as the search for information and evaluation of diverse opinions by patient-consumers. As implied by Langer's original writing, the idea is to be less robot-like, less script oriented in relying on authorities' dictums about one's health (Germer, 2005).

This chapter on mindfulness relates closely to our conception of minding the close relationship and to the major precepts of positive psychology. Positive psychology emphasizes the more prosocial aspects of human functioning (e.g., caring about others' losses and pain and altruistic acts designed to help others in need). As will be seen in the minding articulation, there is a relentless focus on gaining information about others and taking actions designed to reflect a positive response to information gained.

Minding the Close Relationship Components
Knowing and Being Known

The first component of minding refers to behaviors aimed at knowing one's partner. These include questioning your partner about his or her thoughts, feelings, and past experiences, as well as disclosing appropriately about yourself (Altman & Taylor, 1973). This search to know a partner can lead to and includes intuition. Partners often "read between the lines" to know that something is wrong with the other; often the knowledge they have about each other makes it easier for them to pick up nonverbal cues. Knowledge about a partner can facilitate this ability to see beneath surface behaviors to the emotions and motivations below.

In well-minded relationships, each partner will recognize that people change in many ways over time. These changes can involve their physical bodies and their psychological compositions; they can be ever so subtle. Minding partners will also recognize that continuous change makes the process of knowing each other a major challenge. It takes energy and time for both partners to find the right forum to discuss certain issues and to feel comfortable being open and expressive.

Most importantly, the focus in minding is on "wanting to know" about one's partner. There is great motivation to know about the other's background, hopes, fears, uncertainties, and what keeps him or her awake at night. There is often emphasis placed on "good communication" in a relationship, sometimes stressing the ability to express one's feelings often and fully. Minding theory acknowledges that accurate and frequent communication is important, but it changes the emphasis on one's own self-expression to an emphasis on the active seeking of the other's self-expression or information. It is this overt desire to really know another person that, we believe, creates an atmosphere that allows more open disclosure and "good communication."

Attribution

The second component is the attributional activity that partners engage in regarding their partner's behavior. Attributions refer to the interpretations or explanations that people make for events in their lives (to the personal dispositions of self or other, or to the environment, or to an interaction of dispositions and the environment). Attribution has been a central concept in the close relationship field for decades (Harvey, 1987). One of Heider's (1958, 1976) invaluable contributions was to describe human attributional patterns. He suggested that attribution was a broad, pervasive type of activity that occurred almost anytime a person interacted with or encountered an event in his or her environment.

Relationship-enhancing attributions tend to be those that attribute positive behaviors to dispositional causes (e.g., "He came home early to spend time with me"; "She called me at work because she cares about me"). Negative behaviors, on the other hand, are attributed more often to external causes (e.g., "She yelled at me because she's stressed at work"; "He is late for our date because his car broke down").

In well-minded relationships, partners will recognize how easy it is to be mistaken about a partner's behavior, feelings, intentions, and motivations, and how important it is to feel firm about attributions regarding behavior of their partner in different situations. Flexibility and willingness to reexamine attributions about one's partner and the relationship characterize well-minded relationships.

Recent theorizing regarding folk explanations of human behavior may provide a more fine-grained analysis of which particular kinds of attributions made by couples are associated with relationship satisfaction. For example, Malle (1999, 2004) asserts that when explaining another's behavior, a key judgment made early in the explanation process is whether the other behaved intentionally or unintentionally. For behaviors judged to be intentional in nature, an individual can potentially use three modes of explanation for understanding the other's behavior: reasons, causal history of reasons, or enabling factors (Malle, 2004).

Applying Malle's analysis to close relationships, a partner may explain the other's behavior by focusing on what are perceived as the other's potential specific "reasons" for acting (e.g., "He bought me flowers because he deliberately wanted to make me feel good"), which is the partner's best guess as to what was in the mind of the other as the other was acting.

Additionally, a partner may consider what Malle calls the other's "causal history of reasons." These are factors that may have contributed to the other's specific reasons for acting (e.g., "He grew up in a family environment, which was pretty generous, so of course he's generous also"). For example, the partner attributes the other's behavior to previous events (family background) or personality characteristics (a generally generous disposition) that led to the other's reasons for giving flowers on this particular occasion.

Finally, "enabling factors" which allowed the other's behavior to occur (e.g., "Since he got the promotion at his job, he can afford to buy gifts more easily") may be considered by a partner as he or she attempts to understand the other's behavior. In this type of judgment, the partner is attempting not so much to understand the other's motivation for behaving a certain way but rather trying to discern how such a behavior was made possible (Malle, 2004).

Future research will have to determine whether the specific distinctions between these three modes of explanation (see Malle, 2004, for an extensive discussion) provide greater utility, compared to the classic attribution frameworks inspired by Heider, for predicting which explanation patterns are associated with greater satisfaction within close relationships.

Acceptance and Respect

Two prototypical features of love are acceptance and respect (Fehr, 1988). However, one of the potentially challenging consequences of minding a relationship is that we may, in the process of discovering information about the other, identify aspects of the other which are less than ideal. A key component of the minding process is to generally accept what we come to know about our close other through this process and to respect the other based on this knowledge. If we have doubts or cannot accept major parts of who our partners are, then minding is much more difficult to implement. Ickes (1996) emphasized the importance of empathy and empathic accuracy, and we place it at the center of acceptance and respect in close relationships.

Consistent with this perspective, researchers who follow couples over time and study their interactions have found that those who display positive types of social behavior together are more satisfied with their relationships (Gottman, 1994, 1995; Jacobson & Christensen, 1996). These positive behaviors include listening respectfully to another's opinions, working out compromises that accept another's needs, paying attention to the other during conflicts, and accepting the other's responses. All these kinds of behaviors are illustrative of respect for the other and acceptance of the other's feelings and thoughts. Less happy couples, on the other hand, tend to display less respectful behavior toward each other, such as verbal attacks, withdrawal, or criticism of the other's ideas.

Gottman (1994, 1995) has done extensive work with couples, observing their interactions and conflicts in a controlled experimental setting. Gottman has described factors, what he refers to as the "Four Horsemen of the Apolycalpse" factors that which he perceives to be the signs of a relationship headed for failure: pervasive criticism, contempt, stonewalling, and defensiveness. Gottman argues that discussion of complaints and disagreements in a relationship can be a healthy, good thing. Criticism, on the other hand, is not. He distinguishes between criticism and complaint by identifying criticism as an attack on the other's personality or character. While a legitimate complaint involves a description of behavior, "doing" something negative, destructive criticism blames a partner for "being" a certain way. He also maintains that while healthy complaints focus on a specific instance of behavior, criticism is more global and therefore more difficult for the criticized partner to handle.

When contempt (read lack of respect) creeps into a relationship, it signals a level of unhappiness and dissatisfaction that, Gottman's research indicates, often results in the dissolution of the relationship. In Gottman's hierarchy of relationship problems, contempt is stronger than criticism because it involves the intent to insult one's partner. Contempt boils down to a lack of respect or admiration for the partner and can lead to a third destructive factor: avoidance.

Gottman pinpoints avoidance or defensive behavior as contributing to relationship breakdown in what he terms "stonewalling." Stonewalling is virtually avoiding communication with a partner, either by physically distancing oneself so that communication is impossible or by emotionally withdrawing until it seems futile for the other partner to try. To withdraw or avoid contact with a partner in this way also signals a lack of respect for the partner's desire to engage in discussion or social interaction. It is tantamount to ignoring one's partner, which is an effective silent way of conveying disapproval or lack of acceptance.

Gottman's program of research into close relationships makes clear that almost all couples display negative patterns of interaction at one time or another. One way of avoiding destructive effects is to concentrate on keeping negative interactions specific and "complaint"-oriented (focused on behaviors). The second key to handling negative interactions, Gottman says, is to consistently express more positive than negative communications toward each other. Minding emphasizes the positive forms of interaction by specifically incorporating respect and acceptance into its principles. Couples who are minding their relationship well will be alert to the potential corrosion of a continued period of negativity in communication, feelings, and family atmosphere. They will be aware of the destructive power of criticism, contempt, and avoidance. They will recognize that each partner needs to have a voice and feel affirmed in the behavior and decisions that characterize the relationship (Rusbult, Zembrodt, & Gunn, 1982).

The recent burgeoning empirical work on the notion of forgiveness may illuminate the factors that promote acceptance, the positive benefits of acceptance within a relationship, and ultimately perhaps the limits to acceptance. For example, Finkel, Rusbult, Kumashiro, and Hannon (2002) demonstrate that the level of commitment within a relationship may be causally related to the degree of forgiveness within that relationship, with commitment levels influencing the manner in which one partner cognitively interprets the perceived transgressions of the other. Presumably, partners within a relationship that has been well-minded and resulted in a higher degree of commitment will be better equipped to offer forgiveness to each other when upsetting information is discovered.

In addition, related work by Hoyt, Fincham, McCullough, Maio, and Davila (2005) suggests that a full understanding of forgiveness must ultimately take into account not only the transgression being considered in a specific event but also the stable characteristics of the forgiver and the transgressor, as well as the features of the relationship itself. We would suggest that individuals in a well-minded relationship would more readily take into account the history of that relationship when deciding whether forgiveness can be offered, essentially using that relationship knowledge as a context for evaluating the severity of the offense and the consequences of offering (or withholding) forgiveness.

Clearly, even the best minded and satisfying relationships will encounter events that cause at least moments of irritation, frustration, confusion, and perhaps even mistrust. A positive psychology perspective on relationships must therefore not only seek to understand how good relationships can be improved, but understand the factors that allow relationships to survive and even thrive when challenges inevitably occur.

The search for knowledge about a potential partner begins quickly, and problems may be uncovered before serious commitments are made. This allows partners time to reflect on whether they are capable of accepting the implications of such negative information. It allows them to search for enhancing attributions and to build those attributions into their overall cognitive schemas about the partner and the relationship. It also allows partners to disengage from a relationship early on, before too much time and emotion have been invested. This knowledge search requires that partners open up to each other, disclose personal backgrounds, and share experiences.

A climate of acceptance not only increases disclosure, it also reduces fears of overall rejection in partners. Fearing or perceiving rejection by a partner can lead to feelings of insecurity and unhappiness in a relationship. People who are more sensitive to rejection seem to have less committed relationships and to feel less secure and satisfied with their relationships.

One of the key benefits of minding is that the emphasis on seeking knowledge about a partner helps to uncover negative information early, before commitment is made. Nevertheless, sometimes secrets may come out late in relationships. It is conceivable that a partner might have originally withheld the information because it was embarrassing or because it did not seem relevant to the current relationship. Or, perhaps a couple's relationship was not well minded in the past but the couple is seeking to improve, and it is through the new minding behaviors that this information finally comes out. For example, what if, after having been married 5 years, you discover that your husband had committed a serious crime? What are the limits of acceptance in such a case?

Such a revelation in a well-established relationship may lead to some serious discussion about why the information was withheld and possibly to some reevaluation of the attributions previously made about the partner. But it need not be "fatal" to the relationship because of the restorative value of such discussion and the acceptance and respect both accorded and attributed by the partners to one another. For example, Fincham, Paleari, and Regalia (2002) found that the overall quality of long-term marriages was associated with the types of attributions made by individuals within the marriage, which consequently influenced the degree of forgiveness for transgressions. This suggests that the continuance of the relationship will be facilitated if there is a history of trust and positive attributions developed through the minding process.

Are there realistic limits to acceptance, or is it all-encompassing? How would minding theory recommend dealing with negative information about a partner or a potential partner? Obviously, acceptance is not intended to be absolute. It is built into minding that as much as possible is discovered as early as possible so that potentially disastrous relationships can be avoided altogether.

Reciprocity in Minding

Minding cannot long involve just one member of a couple engaged in the requisite behavioral patterns we have outlined. There needs to be a sense of equity in relationships, such that each partner receives benefits from the relationship roughly equal to the amount he or she contributes to the relationship. When a person gives more than he or she receives, this could lead to a sense of being underappreciated or "used." Conversely, someone who gives little to a relationship but receives much from the other may conceivably develop equally uncomfortable feelings of guilt or obligation. An inequitable relationship situation can thus affect long-term relationship stability and satisfaction.

This idea of equity is translated in minding theory into the idea of reciprocity: each partner's active participation and involvement in relationship-enhancing thoughts and behaviors. One partner may stimulate, or trigger, the other partner's involvement, but that reciprocity must not be long delayed, lest the more constructively active partner feel betrayed and lose interest in preserving the relationship. Each partner will be involved in the process, even if part of the time their representative behaviors are carried out in a scripted manner (Schank & Abelson, 1977).

Continuity and Minding

This component relates to a criterion for closeness articulated by Kelley and colleagues in a 1983 book: "the close relationship is one of strong, frequent, and diverse interdependence that lasts over a considerable period of time" (p. 38). Since people and situations change, the knowledge gained about a partner through minding cannot remain static. This is a point that Kelley (1967) also made about attributions mirroring the data appropriately, accurately reflecting the behavior or situation. Each and every person represents an intricate set of experiences, personal qualities, dispositions, hopes, plans, and potential reactions to environmental stimuli. Being and staying close to any person over an extended period requires personal planning and action aimed at acquiring and updating knowledge on a regular basis (Acitelli & Holmberg, 1993).

We agree that the amount of time a couple has been together does not necessarily correlate to how well that couple is minding. One couple may be minding well after knowing each other a few weeks, while another couple may fail to achieve a high state of minding after 30 years. Because of the complex nature of relationships, however, a relatively complex, time-consuming process is necessary to understand and describe them.

This line of reasoning is consistent with the classic treatment of mind and the structure of behavior by Miller, Galanter, and Pribram (1960). These theorists discussed the interaction of plans with behaviors designed to test those plans. Such sequences take periods of time to unfold. Miller and colleagues proposed sequences of "tests–operations–tests–exits" in which plans are checked out against real-world circumstances. This type of sequence can be followed in the minding process as well.

People develop plans to become closer to others. As has been suggested in the minding sequence, people thus come to know and be known by, to attribute qualities to, and to accept and respect their partner over some period of time. Throughout this process, individuals are constantly "testing" their thoughts and beliefs about their partners, as well as their overall level of closeness and satisfaction with their relationships. When the tests detect a problem or discrepancy, a new "minding operation" can be directed at correcting it. All of this involves the checking of the "plan to be close" with which each partner starts.

Minding Behaviors

Minding behaviors, per se, were not given ample attention in earlier formulations of minding theory. As suggested by Halford and Behrens (1997), there is a set of behaviors that is strongly related to marital satisfaction. Paraphrased from Halford and Behren's analysis, these behaviors include the following:

1. *Affection*: For example, this may be represented by saying, "I love you," by giving a hug or kiss to the partner, or enjoying a laugh together and saying that you enjoy a partner's company.
2. *Respect*: Listening to a partner's opinion reflects respect, as does introducing a partner to others with pride.
3. *Support and assistance*: This may be represented by doing errands for a partner, or something to save a partner's time and energy.
4. *Shared quality time*: This may be represented by specifically designating a time to do something together and inquiring about one another's well-being. Working together on a project also may reflect this behavior.
5. *Appreciation*: This may be represented simply by saying, "Thank you." Also, in the presence of a partner, telling others how much you appreciate something your partner does may give the partner a greater sense that you are grateful for his or her positive acts.

From a minding standpoint, these are important acts. Minding emphasizes behavior, behavior that is well-conceived in its plan and purpose for the enhancement of the relationship. Each of the foregoing behaviors may reflect minding and consequent behavioral patterns. What is as important as the specific behaviors, however, is each partner's acts of knowing and understanding that goes into them.

Conclusions and Directions for Further Work

Minding theory is a prime example of the positive psychology movement. It emphasizes continuity in relating and how constant vigilance is necessary to produce this precious state of humans' relations. It emphasizes a detailed grid of thought coordinated with behavior that taken seriously will contribute to human bonds that transcend time and space and that affect others, such as children, relatives, and friends, in ways that celebrate closeness and the mutuality of the human condition.

Are certain people better minders of their close relationships than others? Harvey and Omarzu (1997, 1999) have speculated that minding is a skill that can be taught. It should be a skill reflected in individual differences that can be measured, similar to intimacy motivation in general (McAdams, 1989). Minding is a combination of cognitive, emotional, motivational, and behavioral skill. Recent research (Omarzu, Whalen, & Harvey, 2001) has led to a minding scale that would differentiate persons who mind well versus those who do not. Illustrative items were: "You should avoid telling a loved one too much personal detail about your past," "There is no reason to discuss your past relationships with a new love," "It is important to keep some mystery about yourself in a relationship," "The people that we love are really strangers to us."

Other work is directed at differentiating minding theory from general intimacy theory of close relationships (Prager, 1995; Reis & Patrick, 1996), and from major contemporary conceptions of how people achieve and maintain closeness. For example, minding is similar to the detailed cognitive-behavioral logic presented by Beck (1988) in his influential book *Love is never enough*. Minding also resonates with the arguments of Schwartz (1994) in articulating the conditions of "peer marriage" (that is premised on friendship) and Wallerstein and Blakeslee (1995) in formulating what constitutes a "good marriage." To the extent that these theories are process-oriented and emphasize a never-ending diligence in addressing central aspects of a close relationship, they bear considerable overlap with minding theory. Minding theory, however, can be readily differentiated from other prominent positions on relationship closeness, such as the emphasis on the value of positive illusions (e.g., Murray, Holmes & Griffin, 1996). As suggested in the discussion of attribution above, minding embraces a strong reality orientation and dialog about faults that one or both partner(s) might not wish to address. Minding theory does suggest that we need to recognize our faults in relationships, and as best we can, work to redress those faults, or not let them interfere with our achievement of closeness.

Harold Kelley (1979) concluded his analysis of the structures and processes of personal relationships with the following eloquent observation about the difficult quest each human faces in trying to connect intimately with another mind:

> The unavoidable consequence of human social life is a realization of the essentially private and subjective nature of our experience of the world, coupled with a strong wish to break out of that privacy and establish contact with another mind. Personal relationships hold out to their members the possibility, though perhaps rarely realized in full, of establishing such contact. (1979, p. 169)

The processes embraced by minding theory offer us as humans the best means by which we can attempt to break out of our private, subjective experience and connect intimately with another human mind and life. Minding makes people feel special. Nothing else does it better. Minding makes our relationships meaningful. Minding helps us solve problems and plan. Minding bonds and over time creates and sustains a sense of connection between two minds and lives.

Questions for Future Exploration

1. How does the process of minding change for a couple with the birth of children?
2. Are there personality or temperament qualities that make some people more adroit at minding their close relationships than are other people?
3. How is minding transformed at the nonverbal level as couples spend many years together and experience many similar events in their relationship?

References and Recommended Reading

Acitelli, L. K., & Holmberg, D. (1993). Reflecting on relationships. The role of thoughts and memories. In D. Perlman & W. H. Jones (Eds.), *Personal relationships* (Vol. 4, pp. 71–100). London: Kingsley.

Altman, I., & Taylor, D. (1973). *Social penetration: The development of interpersonal relationships.* New York: Holt, Rinehart & Winston.

Baer, R. (2003). Mindfulness training as a clinical intervention. *Clinical Psychology: Science and Practice, 10,* 125–142.

*Beck, A. (1988). *Love is never enough.* New York: Harper & Row.

Fehr, R. (1988). Prototype analysis of the concepts of love and commitment. *Journal of Personality and Social Psychology, 55,* 557–579.

Fincham, F. D., Paleari, F. G., & Regalia, C. (2002). Forgiveness in marriage: The role of relationship quality, attributions, and empathy. *Personal Relationships, 9,* 27–37.

Finkel, E. J., Rusbult, C. E., Kumashiro, M., & Hannon, P. A. (2002). Dealing with betrayal in close relationships: Does commitment promote forgiveness? *Journal of Personality and Social Psychology, 82*(6), 956–974.

Germer, C. K. (2005). Mindfulness. In C. K. Germer, R. D. Siegel, & P. R. Fulton (Eds.), *Mindfulness and psychotherapy* (pp. 3–27). New York: Guilford.

Gottman, J. (1994). *What predicts divorce? The relationship between marital processes and marital outcomes.* Hillsdale, NJ: Erlbaum.

*Gottman, J. (1995). *Why marriages succeed or fail.* New York: Fireside.

Halford, W. K., & Behrens, B. C. (1997). Prevention of marital difficulties. In P. Cotton, & H. Jackson (Eds.), *Early intervention and prevention in mental health* (pp. 21–58). Sydney: Australian Psychological Association.

Harvey, J. H. (1987). Attributions in close relationships: Research and theoretical developments. *Journal of Social and Clinical Psychology, 5,* 8–20.

Harvey, J. H., & Omarzu, J. (1997). Minding the close relationship. *Personality and Social Psychology Review, 1,* 223–239.

*Harvey, J. H., & Omarzu, J. (1999). *Minding the close relationship: A theory of relationship enhancement.* New York: Cambridge University Press.

Harvey, J. H., Pauwels, B. G., & Zickmund, S. (2001). The role of minding in the enhancement of closeness. In C. R. Snyder & S. Lopez (Eds.), *Handbook of positive psychology* (1st ed., pp. 675–691). New York: Oxford University Press.

Heider, F. (1958). *The psychology of interpersonal relationships.* New York: Wiley (Reprinted by Erlbaum).

Heider, F. (1976). A conversation with Fritz Heider. In J. H. Harvey, W. J. Ickes, & R. F. Kidd (Eds.), *New directions in attribution research* (Vol. 1, pp. 1–10). Hillsdale, NJ: Erlbaum.

Hoyt, W. T., Fincham, F. D., McCullough, M. E., Maio, G., & Davila, J. (2005). Responses to interpersonal transgressions in families: Forgivingness, forgivability, and relationship-specific effects. *Journal of Personality and Social Psychology, 89*(3), 375–394.

Ickes, W. (Ed.). (1996). *Empathic accuracy.* New York: Guilford.

Jacobson, N. S., & Christensen, A. (1996). *Integrative couple therapy: Promoting acceptance and change.* New York: Norton.

Kelley, H. H. (1967). Attribution theory in social psychology. In D. Levine (Ed.), *Nebraska symposium on motivation* (Vol. 15, pp. 192–240). Lincoln: University of Nebraska Press.

Kelley, H. H. (1979). *Personal relationships: Their structures and processes.* Hillsdale, NJ: Erlbaum.

Kelley, H. H., Berscheid, E., Christensen, A., Harvey, J. H., Huston, T., Levinger, G., et al. (1983). *Close relationships.* San Francisco: Freeman.

Langer, E. J. (1989). *Mindfulness.* Reading, MA: Addison-Wesley.

Langer, E. J. (1978). Rethinking the role of thought in social interaction. In J. H. Harvey, W. J. Ickes, & R. F. Kidd (Eds.), *New directions in attribution research* (Vol. 2, pp. 25–35). Hillsdale, NJ: Erlbaum.

McAdams, D. P. (1989). *Intimacy: The need to be close.* New York: Doubleday.

Malle, B. F. (1999). How people explain behavior: A new theoretical framework. *Personality and Social Psychology Review, 3,* 23–48.

Malle, B. F. (2004). *How the mind explains behavior.* Cambridge, MA: MIT Press.

Miller, G. A., Galanter, E., & Pribram, K. H. (1960). *Plans and the structure of behavior.* New York: Holt, Rinehart and Winston.

Murray, S. L., Holmes, J. G., & Griffin, D. W. (1996). The benefits of positive illusions: Idealization and the construction of satisfaction in close relationships. *Journal of Personality and Social Psychology, 1,* 79–98.

Omarzu, J., Whalen, J., & Harvey, J. H. (2001). How well do you mind your relationship? A preliminary scale to test the minding theory of relating. In J. H. Harvey & A. Wenzel (Eds.), *Close romantic relationships: Maintenance and enhancement* (pp. 345–355). Mahwah, NJ: Lawrence Erlbaum.

Prager, K. J. (1995). *The psychology of intimacy.* New York: Guilford.

Reis, H. T., & Patrick, B. C. (1996). Attachment and intimacy: Component processes. In E. T. Higgins & A. Kruglanski (Eds.), *Social psychology: Handbook of basic principles* (pp. 523–563). New York: Guilford.

Rubinstein, M. F., & Firstenberg, I. R. (1999). *The minding organization.* New York: Wiley.

Rusbult, C. E., Zembrodt, I. M., & Gunn, L. K. (1982). Exit, voice, loyalty, and neglect: Responses to dissatisfaction in romantic involvements. *Journal of Personality and Social Psychology, 43,* 1230–1242.

Schank, R. C., & Abelson, R. P. (1977). *Scripts, plans, goals, and understanding.* Hillsdale, NJ: Erlbaum.

*Schwartz, P. (1994). *Peer marriage.* New York: Free Press.

Schwartz, J., & Begley, S. (2002). *The mind and the brain: Neuroplasticity and the power of the mental force.* New York: Harper Collins.

*Wallerstein, J., & Blakeslee, S. (1995). *The good marriage.* New York: Warner.

Compassion

Eric J. Cassell

Abstract

This chapter reviews historical and modern perspectives on the positive emotion of compassion. From the time of Aristotle, compassion has been defined as an emotion experienced when individuals witness another person suffering through serious troubles, which are not self-inflicted and that we can picture ourselves experiencing. Compassion at its core is, therefore, a process of connecting by identifying with another person. The identification with others generated from compassion can then provide the motivation to do something to relieve the suffering of others. Compassion is, therefore, an emotion that is vital to the practice of medicine, psychology, and other helping professions. The chapter concludes by proposing that one future topic for the field of positive psychology will be to develop interventions and educational programs that instill compassion in helping professionals.

Keywords: compassion, positive emotions, relationships, suffering

Philoktetes has been given a magical bow by the demigod Herakles. On the way to the war against Troy, in the company of Odysseus and his crew, a sacred serpent bites Philoktetes. The divinely inflicted wound is unbearably painful and foul smelling. Because his cries of agony and the smell are intolerable, the crew stops at the island of Lemnos and casts Philoktetes away. Discovering after 10 years of war that Troy cannot be beaten without Philoktetes and his bow, Odysseus returns to get him. Philoktetes has suffered alone on the barren island in the intervening years when the crew searches him out near the mouth of his cave. The chorus speaks:

> I pity him for all his woes,
> For his distress, for his loneliness,
> With no countryman at his side;
> He is accursed, always alone,
> Brought down by bitter illness;
> He wanders, distraught,
> Thrown off balance by simple needs.
> How can he withstand such ceaseless misfortune?
> (Sophokles, 1986, p. 17)

The chorus seems to be describing the same feeling that has been evoked by so many scenes of the last century: the crying baby sitting alone on the railroad tracks in 1930s' Manchuria surrounded by the destruction of war; dead or living dead victims of the Holocaust; the killing fields of Cambodia; starving children in Africa; wounded or dead children being carried from the wreckage of the Oklahoma bombing; the dead at Columbine High School and the terrified parents waiting to find out if their child is alive; the benumbed parents of the killers; and on and on it goes. Our hearts go out, we say, to the victims of these horrors. We feel compassion, pity, and sadness for them, sympathy for their terrible state, or indignation at the injustice of their fate. On a more personal level, people decry the coldness of modern technological medicine and look for physicians, seemingly rare, who have both scientific knowledge and the capacity to empathize with their patients. When they are sick and when they are well, people search for compassionate partners, caregivers, psychologists, therapists, physicians, and others who can meet their need for succorance.

What actually is compassion, and where does it come from? Is it an emotion similar to grief, sadness, or joy? Is it a duty, or a virtue, a personality characteristic, or simply a feeling common to humankind (and even some animals), or is it all four? It appears to be an emotion that is specifically social or communal, in the same family, perhaps, with the feeling of patriotism or group-specific feeling (communitas, team spirit). Because of this complexity, it has been the subject of debate from the beginnings of Western culture, and it has played a part in major Eastern religions. Compassion has figured in the disputes about reason versus the passions and in controversies about the proper role of medicine and the behavior of physicians.

Basic Requirements for Compassion

As in so many other aspects of human nature, it is useful to start with Aristotle. "Compassion" is the word most often used in connection with the emotion evoked by the sufferings of others. Aristotle (1984, 1385b: 15–18), however, used the word "pity" to stand for "a feeling of pain at an apparent evil, destructive or painful, which befalls one who doesn't deserve it, and which we might expect to befall ourselves or some friend of ours, and moreover befall us soon." Reading these words today, most might say that Aristotle was speaking of compassion. Which word is used is less important than recognizing that such feelings exist and have been commented on since antiquity. (It is possible, however, that the emotions marked by the different words— e.g., compassion, pity, sympathy—might be somewhat different.) Whereas we have feelings of compassion for suffering strangers, for those closest to us the feelings are different. Again, Aristotle (1984, 1386a: 19–22) comments: "The people we pity are those whom we know, if only they are not very closely related to us. For this reason Amasis did not weep, they say, at the sight of his son being led to death, but did weep when he saw his friend begging; the latter sight was pitiful, the former terrible and the terrible, is different than the pitiful."

Since Aristotle, it has been generally accepted that there are three requirements for compassion: First, we must feel that the troubles that evoke our feelings are serious; second, we require that the sufferers' troubles not be self-inflicted—that they be the result of an unjust fate; and finally, it is believed that for compassion to be evoked, we must be able to picture ourselves in the same predicament.

If only serious troubles evoke our compassion, who is to judge the seriousness? Compassion is our

feeling, not that of the persons who evoke it. As long as the suffering arises from war, murder, mayhem, rape, or nature's random destruction, little question arises because both onlookers and victims know that awful things have happened. What of the children, however, who have grown up amid war and know no different, or families denied opportunity or education because of oppression? They, too, may make us cry in compassion, although they do not know themselves to be suffering. In like manner, the plight of a person with dementia who has no awareness of difficulty may evoke compassion even from strangers. To make the point more strongly that compassion is a unilateral emotion, remember that it is most commonly brought forth in settings in which the sufferer(s) have no awareness of the feelings they are evoking in others. They are usually not proximate in space and perhaps not even in time so that, for example, reading about the sufferings of people in the past may bring sadness at their difficulty.

The requirement that the suffering not be self-inflicted demands that the objects of compassion be seen as victims. Michel Foucault's (1979) book on the history of punishment opens with a graphic description of a man who was convicted of regicide being drawn and quartered. The ghastly spectacle went on for a whole day and seems to have been— like the famous executions by guillotine after the French Revolution—an occasion for public entertainment rather than for compassion. The man and the beheaded royalty were seen as having brought their punishment on themselves and, thus, not due sympathy or compassion. Another example is a description by a New York City subway motorman of his reaction to people being run over by his train. In describing the first two times in which a person was killed by a train he was operating (1987 and 1988), Mr. Anthanio, the motorman, seemed more irritated than disturbed: "It was their own fault, you might even say foolishness, that landed them on the tracks in the first place. One man was drunk. The other fellow turned out to have been on drugs." But when a third accident occurred (1989), the motorman did not see the repairmen on the tracks until it was too late. His reactions were very different than in the first two accidents. In his words, "The look on their faces; it was like looking into a mask of horror" (*New York Times*, 2000, p. B1). Indeed, it took Mr. Anthanio almost 2 years to get over this last accident.

The final requirement for compassion and its cognate feelings is said to be identification with the sufferer. Aristotle (1984, 1386a: 25–28) again says:

"Also we pity those who are like us in age, character, disposition, social standing, or birth; for in all these cases it appears more likely that the same misfortune may befall us also. Here too we have to remember the general principle that what we fear for ourselves excites our pity when it happens to others." This comes closer to the social nature of compassion and at the same time to the inescapably social nature of being human. The paradox of compassion, like that of love, is that it is private, born of personal subjectivity, and social. To understand compassion, then, requires a better understanding of identification: how we know that someone is like us.

Compassion's Core: Connecting and Identifying with Others

At its core, compassion is a process of connecting by identifying with another person. The roots of this identification process can be found in more than one place. First, research with infants has shown that even in the first days of their lives they begin to mirror the facial expressions and simple bodily movements of the mother. They are seeing themselves in the other and the other in themselves. This, of course, shows the newborn infant to be more responsive to its caregivers and its environment than previously had been believed and places the onset of identification at the earliest age (Meltzoff, 1985; Meltzoff & Kuhl, 1989; Meltzoff & Moore, 1977; Stern, 1985; Trevarthen, 1988). For George Herbert Mead (1934), in fact, the "self" arises and is developed through the social experience of others; there is no self or self-definition without others. There is reason to believe that the child also is able to mirror, to absorb through feelings, the emotional state of the parent so that identification continues into the domain of feelings.

We see the same attempts at synonymy in older children and teenagers as they dress alike and adopt new styles of clothing, language, or behavior in a neighborhood or nation almost simultaneously. Often, the new fashion copies a popular athlete or entertainer. In adults, this apparently general desire to identify with others (especially those who are admired) is promoted by and is the basis of the fashion industry.

In the eighteenth century, it was considered essential, if you wanted to understand human behavior, to know about four human characteristics: self-esteem, the desired to be approved of, emulativeness (the desire to equal or surpass), and the desire to be like those one admires (Lovejoy, 1961). These features, it would seem, are as much in evidence today. For example, uniqueness seeking (the modern expression of emulativeness) has been well described and supported (see Lynn & Snyder, chap. 47; Snyder & Fromkin, 1980). It is clear from this work that the desire to be unique sits in tension with the other social needs, with its place on the spectrum determined by era, culture, and personality.

The identification with others occurs below the level where uniqueness seeking or its congeners are determined. Consider, for example, the sometimes profound physical as well as psychological effects of abandonment. As we look more closely, we see that virtually all aspects of everyday life—how life is conducted in a specific environment and among others generally unknown to us—is firmly governed by a dense set of "rules" with a closely written script, the presence of which we are mostly unaware. These strictures are not merely what is called etiquette, the conventional rules of personal behavior observed in the intercourse of polite society; they cover virtually every facet of existence—how clothing is worn, the rules of speech, walking on the street and other responses to gravity, facial expression, posture in relation to others (e.g., sitting in a classroom), telephone calls, love letters, the expressions of emotion, eating in all its dimensions, and maintenance of personal hygiene, among countless others. Because we believe in, indeed, are proud of our right to choose, how can such a lack of freedom be suggested? Unquestionably, there is considerable freedom of choice, but it is virtually always choice at a higher level of behavior, and even there within relatively narrow limits and at times more apparent than real. The social nature of the self and the identification with others is quite compatible with individuality (Mead, 1934). The fact of choice that we cherish and which we defend with vigor occurs largely within consciousness (although also in the domain of the unconscious), which, like consciousness itself, as Alfred North Whitehead once pointed out, is a mere flickering on the surface. The level of identification I am describing is virtually invisible.

One of the many consequences of the ubiquity of social regulation that is of special importance to understanding compassion is that individuals from widely diverse circumstances share an essentially and recognizably similar humanity with each other. This accounts for the fact that identification is possible even with people from different nations and disparate cultures. A connection thus exists between almost all; the pain of compassion can be brought about by the sufferings of any of the earth's inhabitants. John Donne (1624/1994) expressed this in his well-known meditation, "No man is an island entire of itself; every man is a piece of the continent, a part of the main; if a clod be washed away by the sea, Europe is the less as well as if a premonitory were, as well as if a manor of thy friends or thine own were; any man's death diminishes me, because I am involved in mankind" (p. 441).

Another possible source of identification has been labeled "spirit." Events sometimes reinforce the belief that the connection that underlies compassion cannot be accounted for solely by universal identification borne of the social forces described earlier. For example, in the same period in the late 1960s in which social upheaval attributed to the Vietnam War was occurring in the United States, student uprisings and general agitation also were taking place in France and Germany, where the war was perceived as being relatively unimportant because it involved the United States. Similarly, a turn to religious fundamentalism occurred simultaneously in very different cultures throughout the world in the late 1970s. For the nineteenth-century German philosopher G. W. F. Hegel (1977), such events would be examples of the fact that all humans are bound together through the universal category of spirit. Each human both shares and is a part, and this spirit, despite its immense complexities and attendant philosophical disputes, provides a way to explain how all of us (unknowingly) actively participate in a universal humanity that has concrete existence (Olson, 1992). Earlier in Meditation XVII, Donne (1624/1994) writes, "The Church is catholic, universal, and so are all her actions. When she baptizes a child, that action concerns me; for that child is thereby connected to that Head which is my Head too, and engrafted into that Body, whereof I am a member. All mankind is of one Author" (p. 441). This a religious statement of Hegel's secularized concept. Whether through spirit or through the shared experience of living, we know others to be as we are, so that when something happens to them, whether in Oklahoma City or Eritrea, we can identify with their sufferings. When it seems that there might be, at first sight, little conscious basis for identification with sufferers, then the pure bodily source of the suffering pulls compassion from us because everyone has a similar body. The sight of people whose limbs have been hacked off has sad meaning to all. Similarly, when children are involved, identification with the helplessness of a child or parental loss is universal.

Our body of knowledge about others provides a further basis for identification. Martha Nussbaum (1996), in a rich examination of compassion as classical authors discuss it, points out that the identification with others reveals one's own weaknesses and potential for injury. Nussbaum quotes Rousseau's Emile:

> Why are kings without pity for their subjects? Because they count on never being human beings. Why are the rich so hard toward the poor? Because they have no fear of being poor. Why does a noble have such contempt for a peasant? It is because he will never be a peasant. Do not, therefore, accustom your pupil to regard the sufferings of the unfortunate and the labors of the poor from the height of his glory; and do not hope to teach him pity if he considers them alien to him. Make him understand well that the fate of these unhappy people can be his, that all of their ills are there in the ground beneath his feet, that countless unforeseen and inevitable events can plunge him into them from one moment to the next. Teach him to count on neither birth nor health nor riches. Show him all the vicissitudes of fortune.
> (Rousseau, 1976, p. 224)

This suggests that the third route to identification with others is through knowledge of the human condition. In Buddhism, the statement that Buddha has infinite knowledge and compassion links the two: "Wisdom is the bliss of seeing through the delusion of self-preoccupation to reveal the underlying dimension of freedom. Compassion is the expression of such bliss to others. Compassion is the sensitivity to others' suffering. It sees them imprisoned in self-involvement, and reaches out to show them the way to freedom" (Thurman, 1997, p. 17).

The more one knows about others, the less quickly one will assign blame to those others for their misfortunes. The frailties and failings of people can be seen in anyone so that when people suffer from what appear to be their own actions, their fate nevertheless may have been beyond their conscious control. Thus, experienced health professionals are less likely to condemn or censure and more likely to feel compassion because they have seen and known how fraught with difficulties are people's lives. So also the clergy may pity and forgive where others would censure. In the episode of torture described by Foucault (1979), only the priest extends his kindness to the suffering man.

It is common experience that people differ in the depth or intensity of their compassion. What brings tears to the eyes of one is a matter of indifference to another. The differences appear to be explained by the varying degree of experienced identification with the suffering other. For Arthur Schopenhauer (who was greatly influenced by Buddhism), such identification required transcending preoccupation with the centrality of the self (the *principium individionis*). The suffering he sees in others touches him almost as much as does his own. He, therefore, tries to strike a balance between the two, denies himself pleasures, and undergoes privations in order to alleviate another's suffering. He perceives that the distinction between himself and others, which "to the wicked man is so great a gulf, belongs only to fleeting, deceptive phenomenon" (Schopenhauer, 1969, p. 372). Compassion, empathy, pity, and charity all require the ability to identify with another, to see in the plight of another what might cause distress in oneself. For compassion, because often it is felt toward strangers, even aliens, the act of identification requires bridging the gap between the self and another when there is no direct connection with the other—or, put another way, when the connection to the other is merely conceptual.

Disconnecting: When Compassion Is Absent

> History tells us that it is by no means a matter of course for the spectacle of misery to move men to pity; even during the long centuries when the Christian religion of mercy determined moral standards of Western civilization, compassion operated outside the political realm and frequently outside the established hierarchy of the Church.
>
> (Arendt, 1963, p. 65)

In the same manner that identification is required to understand compassion, its complete absence may require disidentification—undoing or veiling the identification with individuals or groups so as to make them alien. It is well known that in many traditional and non-Western societies the category of person was extended only to members of the tribe or social group and that those outside this category were considered alien—not of one's own. In some tribal languages, a person is someone who is a member of the tribe; others are not persons and are not due the recognition due to humans—an idea that may be exemplified in contemporary African intertribal brutalities (Mauss, 1985). Compassion may not be extended to aliens. The horrors and brutality perpetrated against the Indians by America's settlers and against the settlers by the Indians fall in this category. From the behavior of soldiers killing in battle to those who commit atrocities, an essential step seems to be to define the object of murder or brutality as "not being us."

The repeated instances of brutality so common in the twentieth century appear to have demonstrated this truth. An important element of Nazism was defining Germans by use of the term "Aryan," with its nineteenth-century connotations of nationalism, which permitted the Nazis to define Jews as alien, despicable, beyond the pale, and outside the boundaries of human. (All of which makes more remarkable, considering its time, the Old Testament injunction to compassion in Leviticus 19:34: "The stranger who sojourns among you shall be to you as one born among you and you shall love him as yourself; for you were strangers in the land of Egypt: I am the Lord your God.")

The sometimes awful actions of people lacking compassion and a sense of identification with others raise the idea, associated with Thomas Hobbes, that the life of humans in a state of nature (the absence of society) is solitary, poor, nasty, brutish, and short. Hobbes (1651/1962) believed that this facet of human nature—that humankind is brutal—was held in check by self-interest and humankind's universal fear of death. Schopenhauer (1969), two centuries later, agreed with the importance of self-interest as one of the three basic motives of human behavior. He also identified gratuitous malice as one of the basic human traits. For humans are the only animals to cause pain to others without any further purpose than just to cause it. Other animals never do this except to satisfy their hunger or in the rage of combat. The appalling record of human life, of human suffering and infliction of pain by humans, is relieved only when the third motive, sympathy or compassion, appears. As Alisdair MacIntyre (1966) points out in his discussion of Schopenhauer:

> To feel compassion is to put oneself imaginatively in the place of the sufferer and to alter one's actions appropriately either by desisting from what would have caused pain or by devoting oneself to its relief. But the exhibiting of compassion has yet a further significance. In a moment of compassion we extinguish self-will. We cease to strive for our own existence; we are relieved from the burden of individuality and we cease to be the playthings of Will. (p. 22)

Compassion as Evidence for the Nature of Humankind

Why is it necessary in a discussion of compassion to raise these philosophical issues? Because if compassion is a social emotion having to do with the relationships of people to each other, then it must raise philosophical, political, and ideological questions. Because the existence of compassion goes to the heart of what it means to be human, its significance has been argued over the centuries. What a particular speaker says about compassion stands a good chance of being influenced by where that person stands on the political spectrum. Hobbes' (1651/1962) pessimistic position about human nature was influenced by belief in original sin and the corrupt state of humankind after the Fall. This view was held throughout the many centuries of the Middle Ages in which scholasticism and the profound influence of the Church prevailed. The rise of humanism in the late sixteenth century, easily seen in the works of Montaigne and Shakespeare, began to build a kinder, more "liberal" view. By the latter part of the seventeenth century and certainly in the eighteenth century, as manifested by the Enlightenment, interest in the innate "moral sense" and indications of the essential goodness of humankind began to be widespread. It is easily seen why the evidence produced by the emotion of compassion was important to these theorists. Here, for example, is Adam Smith (1759/1976) in his eighteenth-century *Theory of moral sentiments*:

> How selfish so ever man may be supposed, there are evidently some principles in his nature, which interest him in the fortunes of others, and render their happiness necessary to him, though he derives nothing from it except the pleasure of seeing it. Of this kind is pity or compassion, the emotion we feel for the misery of others when we see it, or are made to conceive it in a very lively manner. (p. 9)

Well into the nineteenth century, debate continued as to whether democracy and capitalism, where the market economy reigned, would decrease the impact of compassion because of the importance of self-interest in such an environment or increase it because of the sheer number of people with which one might identify. Alexis de Tocqueville (1955), in his famous study of young America, noted that compassion seemed to be characteristic of a democratic society. Considering the political struggles of the twentieth century, it is not surprising that the controversy continues (Arons, 1993; Sznaider, 1998). In the contemporary world, communities and individuals mark themselves on the evidence of their compassion. Appeals for philanthropy frequently are couched in such terms. On the other hand, in a study of attitudes toward public assistance for victims of severe floods, the political ideology (self-defined) of the respondents was related to their answers to questions about the appropriateness of monetary help. Even in the context of a natural disaster, respondents sought out information about the victims' personal responsibility (e.g., whether they had purchased flood insurance). Liberals were more likely to provide humanitarian aid to the "irresponsible" than were conservatives. Conservatives consistently held individuals more responsible for their plight and for resolving it. The reactions of each group to the needs of flood-damaged communities were generally in line with their responses to needy individuals (Skitka, 1999).

The place of compassion as a motivation for individual or societal behavior and as one of the foundations for civil society is a continual topic of debate (Brown, 1996). The debate continues (since Kant) as to whether compassion is a passion and, thus, in opposition to reason or whether it is an emotion, albeit an inherently rational one (Nussbaum, 1996). Some physicians, psychologists, and scientists may become impatient with these discussions, viewing them as philosophical time wasting. This is a pity, however, because such discussions would not go on for centuries if they were trivial. Furthermore, the thinking of philosophers often determines the attitude of the rest of society. Witness the long-lasting impact, not gone to this day (sadly), of René Descartes's seventeenth-century notions of duality of mind and body.

Compassion and the Nature of Suffering

Emotions and feelings are similar to adjectives that spontaneously comment on and modify the facts of experience as they flow by. In this regard, compassion is more complex than other emotions. It demands knowledge of the suffering of others and moves the compassionate person to action (see Batson, Ahmad, & Lishner, this volume). Previously, I noted that compassion requires knowing that others are suffering, identification with the sufferer, and, especially where compassion is felt, knowledge of what the sufferer is experiencing. How is such knowledge acquired, and how does one know that someone suffers?

It is necessary to pause and look at the nature of suffering (Cassell, 1982). It is common to identify suffering with pain or other physical symptoms. They certainly may start the chain of events leading to suffering, but the more proximate and crucial sources of suffering are what the person believes the symptoms mean and what is expected will happen (in the future) if the symptoms continue. Bodies may have physical symptoms, but they do not have a sense of the future and are not concerned with the meaning of things. Bodies do not suffer; only persons do. Suffering is above all highly personal, an affliction of persons. It occurs when persons perceive their impending destruction or loss of integrity as persons, and it continues until the threat of disintegration has passed or until the integrity of the person can be restored in some other manner. Most generally, then, suffering can be defined as the state of severe distress associated with events that threaten the intactness of person. Suffering is not only psychological, or social, or physical; it denies the utility of thinking only in such categories if it is to be understood because suffering involves all aspects of the person.

Let's consider the word "person." We all know ourselves to be persons, but as definitions are attempted, the word's complexity becomes apparent. Persons, for example, think of themselves as more than merely individuals, even though that is a common synonym. One reason it is difficult to define what someone means when he or she says "I am a person" is that the meaning has changed through history. For example, the idea that persons are individual and unique did not enter Western civilization until about the eleventh century, and only in the twentieth century were persons widely acknowledged to have rich interior and unconscious lives. Persons, then, are not only minds, not only selves, not just bodies, and are not simply boundaried like other objects of science. Persons are the entire complex trajectory through time and space of the wholes that are made up of their pasts and believed-in futures, their family and their family's past, their bodies and their relationships with their bodies, relationships with others, day-to-day behaviors and activities, roles, inculcated culture and society, their political dimension, their secret lives (the conscious hopes, aspirations, fantasies, and secret relationships that are wished for or actual, and much more, as in the movie *The secret life of Walter Mitty*), their unconscious, and their spiritual dimension. Suffering may occur in relation to any aspect of the person. For example, sickness, war, or poverty may disrupt persons' relationships to significant others or to the roles or works of a lifetime, thus destroying the persons they know themselves to be. Because everyone is different and distinct from others, suffering always is individual and unique. Suffering is also marked by self-conflict, profound loss of or change in central purpose, and resistance to the loss of personal intactness. Suffering can occur as much from psychological and social insults as from

physical ones, and it appears as often in acute as in chronic illness (Cassell, 1985a).

Knowing That Others Are Suffering

The challenge of knowing that someone else is suffering (and why) is particularly difficult because the quintessential fact about suffering is that it is lonely. The loneliness, which further adds to the suffering, results from its highly personal and individual nature. The most underutilized method of discovering that people are suffering is to ask them. Sufferers themselves may not know that they suffer, however, and may point instead to their diseases or other external circumstances rather than to their disintegrations as people. The early stages of their suffering may be mute and unutterable. Later, the sufferers may become expressive, lamenting what is happening and repeatedly telling the story of their disease or victimization as though looking for someone to help in their search for a new story in which they once again become complete (Reich, 1987). Or one might know the sufferer so well as an individual that the roots of his or her suffering are laid bare. This seems improbable, however, in that we rarely even know ourselves this well.

We often claim to know of another's suffering because of the compassion we have in identifying with that sufferer. (e.g., "What has happened to that (or those) person(s) is so terrible that if it happened to me I certainly would suffer." "Such sickness, loss, or injury is so awful that I never would be able to stand it." "How can the victims of so much disease, destruction, and death not be suffering?" "My heart goes out to them.") There can be no other way of knowing suffering when groups are involved, or when those persons experiencing compassion are separated in time or space from the victims. This "blind" compassion has two difficulties. It may not appreciate that others suffer even if the onlookers do not believe the cause is great enough, or onlookers may believe suffering is present when, in fact, victims have risen above the injury—have grown through their experience and thus are no longer suffering (see chaps 60 and 61). Or the compassionate onlooker may not realize that the victims see the injuries as an opportunity to identify with a larger cause, thus relieving their suffering by giving it meaning just as the saints identified with the suffering of Christ.

On an individual level, the compassionate can be aware of the sights and sounds of the sufferer, and they can feel the pain, sadness, anxiety, and anger through the direct transfer of feelings. More intimately, the compassionate share the same universe with the sufferer—dark and light, air, gravity, and noise and quiet. Also shared are worlds of common values, ideas, beliefs, and aesthetics. We know each other through proximity. Our knowledge of others is a central and constantly expanding feature of life. In other words, we share community—a "we-ness" where all are joined—and from which the absence of the sufferer who is withdrawn into the suffering can be recognized. Thus, compassion is realized through all these methods—identification, knowledge of behaviors, the sights and sounds of suffering, the transfer of feelings, awareness of the change in goals and purposes of sufferers, and the sense of absence of the sufferer from the group—and through their mutual reinforcement.

Compassion and Medicine

Compassion is called for by Item 1 of the American Medical Association's (1981) *Principles of medical ethics*: "A physician shall be dedicated to providing competent medical services with compassion and respect for human dignity." Some still debate whether it is more important to have a competent or a compassionate physician, as though the two qualities are in conflict, mirroring the dispute over the (supposed) opposition between reason and emotion. Most believe, however, that compassion should be an inherent part of medicine and that physicians should be compassionate (Barber, 1976).

It is possible now to tease apart the question raised initially: Is compassion a human emotion, a personality characteristic (different persons have it in varying degrees), a duty, or a virtue? Compassion is the feeling aroused by an acknowledged awareness that others are suffering. The feeling depends on the ability inherent in humans (and some animals) to make a connection with others so as to be aware of their suffering. Compassion necessitates identification with the sufferer(s), and it allows for an evaluation of the magnitude of the suffering. Absent such identification, the sufferer can be considered alien, and no connection will be formed. (In its absence, brutality may become permissible.) The ability to connect and identify with others is of varying degrees, with the feeling of compassion varying in intensity with the nature of the person and the circumstance. Compassion is an emotion, and its magnitude is a function of personality characteristics (among other things).

Generally, felt compassion evokes the desire to do something to relieve the sufferer(s). The wish to be helpful is not compassion itself, but it suggests that compassion, similar to other emotions (anger, for example), may motivate behaviors that reduce the tension brought on by the emotion. There can be no objection to someone feeling compassion, but there may be problems associated with the action that might follow. This is why it has been said that unfettered compassion may be as dangerous as an untrained scalpel.

I noted previously that the words "pity" and "sympathy" (and even "empathy") often are used synonymously with "compassion," especially in discussions from antiquity. Understanding of emotion has evolved greatly in Western history, especially in the last two centuries. (For example, presently I do not believe many would agree with Aristotle (1984, 1370b: 15) when he said, "We feel comparatively little anger or none at all, with those who are much our superiors in power.") Whereas both sympathy and pity require some sense of connection to the victim, sympathy acknowledges fellow feelings for an equal, but pity (similar to mercy) has come to connote an emotion directed downward. The victim may play no active part in the onset of these social emotions; moreover, recipients may resent the expression of compassion, "not want your sympathy," or resent the status connotations of pity. Part of the difficulty in understanding emotion is failing to make the distinctions between an emotion, its state of being, and its associated behavior. This is the difference, for example, between a flash of anger, being angry, and acting angrily. Hearing that some children were killed in a school bus accident, I may feel a surge of compassion for their parents. Seeing very sick patients struggling to maintain their dignity despite their impairments may fill my being with compassion so that I am in a state of compassion. In that state, I may act compassionately, my actions guided not only by my technical knowledge but also by my awareness through identification with the patients and my knowledge of sickness in general, so that in my actions I enhance the patients' feelings of self-worth and adult humanity. It follows that a person may feel compassion but neither become compassionate nor act compassionately.

These distinctions help clarify whether one can say that a universal human emotion that is, in part, a personality characteristic also can be a virtue and required as a duty. One cannot demand that someone feel a surge of compassion as a consequence of something that befalls another individual or group. It might be possible to change things by showing people why the victims deserve their compassion, pity, or sympathy, but evocation of the emotion itself is beyond conscious control. But maintaining oneself in an emotional state can be learned. It can be shown that the discomforts of compassion, for example, the feeling of an uncomfortable urgency to do something when that is not possible, are tolerable as is the emotion itself. In fact, one can help a student discover that the sustained emotion can be an uplifting experience. The state of compassion is a virtuous one, and it can lead to virtuous action. It is, in general, a virtue we should like the citizens of a democratic nation to exhibit as they show appropriate compassion to their fellows from any part of the country (or the globe, for that matter).

Compassion should be desirable in all helpers—whatever their profession. Because I am a physician, I would like to share observations about my field. Compassion is a virtue that has come to be expected of physicians involved in patient care because it is directly related to the recognition and treatment of suffering. Physicians concerned only with the manifestations of disease or the exercise of their technologies may fail to address the suffering that always has its locus in the person rather than only in the body. In not being aware of or dealing with suffering, the physician has failed his or her duties.

The central duties of physicians are the fiduciary responsibility to put the patient's interests first, including the duty not to harm, to deliver proper care, and to maintain confidentiality. Compassion figures in each of these duties because it heightens awareness of the patients' interests; increases the probability that care will be tuned to this patient's needs (and that physicians will maintain their knowledge and skills); and promotes the intimacy of knowledge about each patient that physicians require (Dougherty & Purtillo, 1995).

Compassion and Love

One of the routes to compassion noted previously was knowledge of humankind, a knowledge that also seemed to be the basis of the Buddhist association of wisdom and compassion. Yet the important place of compassion in the healing professions and our belief that it is both a virtue and a duty for caregivers raise the possibility that compassion is not merely a result of knowledge of the suffering of patients, but that it is a basis for that knowledge, and not simply, as Loewy (1998) suggests, because curiosity causes caregivers to discover things about another that then arouse compassion. As I hear my patient recount the story of his illness and all its pain and sadness and see the sickness speaking from his features, my compassion is aroused. I become connected to the patient; we have begun to fuse. I am no longer in an ordinary social interaction where the "distance" between the participants is maintained and where attempts to get closer than the particular culture allows may be perceived as a breach of social convention. When that happens, I begin to listen, look, and intuit with greater intensity, and more information flows toward me. If I make myself conscious of what is happening, I can begin to feel the patient's emotions, and even my hand palpating the abdomen appears to receive more information than it otherwise would. Despite our closeness, and despite the fact that the patient's experience has begun to be part of my experience, we are doctor and patient, not friends (no matter how friendly we may be). If the patient dies, my experience of loss will be real but limited and brief. Armed with the information my compassion has facilitated, my actions will be more appropriate to the needs of my patient for skilled medical care.

Where else does such closeness exist? Even dear friends are rarely so intimate, although the possibility exists. In love? Relationships of love are marked by the closeness of the connection between the loving parties. Here, too, one may experience the feelings of the beloved, know what he or she is thinking. Is this the love (agape) of God for humankind, all-accepting and all-forgiving? No. Nor is it personal love that seeks enduring and intensifying connection and attachment with its object, through which each will become more than she or he was without this love. It is a kind of love whose desire is to help, to do things for its object, and to obtain the knowledge and information necessary for right action. But it is love nonetheless. In a phrase coined by Pope Gregory the Great in the sixth century, "amor ipse notitia est" (love itself is a form of knowledge). "All love (caritas) is compassion or sympathy," said Schopenhauer (1969, p. 374).

Compassion, whose existence testifies to the inherent closeness possible between individuals, is a social emotion with a wide spectrum. At one end is the emotion evoked by the suffering of strangers with whom some identification is possible, and at the other end is the feeling whose effects make it cognate with personal love. Little wonder that it has been the subject of so much discussion and debate in such diverse circles over the last 25 centuries.

A Physician's Compassion and Positive Psychology

For most of the history of Western medicine, the effectiveness of physicians has been identified with their knowledge of medical science, so much so that in the last 50 years it has come to seem as though the knowledge itself makes patients better. Currently, even though people sometimes know a great deal about medications, technology, and medical care, when they are really sick, they need doctors. They require doctors for more than just their technical skills because it is physicians themselves who are the instruments of care. Their knowledge of patients and the therapeutic relationship are the conduit through which the appropriate science and technology are applied. Compassion is the emotion that starts the process of bringing physicians close to their patients, causes them to make the healing connection, and drives their desire to help. What do physicians actually know (if, in fact, they do), and where in them is this knowledge? At their best, they understand the effect of sickness on normal human behavior; they know that the land of the sick is different than that of the well (Cassell, 1985b). They know how to find the path to healing that the therapeutic relationship makes possible, to relieve suffering even when pain or other symptoms will not yield to treatment, and to help rebuild the relationships of the sick and their significant others. They understand the importance and the method of restoring hope and returning the ability to act to the sick when hopelessness and helplessness threaten destruction (Snyder, 2000).

Even when physicians know these things, unfortunately, their knowledge is usually untaught, unvoiced, and wordless, learned by experience and intuition over many years. This body of information is too vital to the proper care of the sick to remain the tacit (and spotty) possession of only some physicians. It should be part of medical education. Who knows enough to teach it, however, even if a place were to be made in the medical curriculum? The kind of knowledge of human behavior, of which I have mentioned only a few examples, is in the domain of positive psychology—the subject of this volume. It must continue to be studied scientifically and taught systematically. It is crucial to medicine's progress.

Questions for the Future

1. How does the experience of compassion relate to other prosocial positive emotions, such as gratitude?

2. Does the experience and expression of compassion vary across cultures and countries?

3. How can medical schools adapt their curricula so as to ensure that physicians are compassionate providers of medical care?

References

American Medical Association. (1981). *Principles of medical ethics*. Chicago: Author.

Arendt, H. (1963). *On revolution*. New York: Viking.

Aristotle. (1984). *Rhetoric. Complete works* (Vol. 2, Ed. J. Barnes). Princeton, NJ: Princeton University Press.

Arons, M. (1993). Philosophy, psychology, and the moral crisis: Reflections on compassion "between tradition and another beginning." *Humanistic Psychologist, 21*, 296–324.

Barber, B. (1976). Compassion in medicine: Toward new definitions and new institutions. *New England Journal of Medicine, 295*, 939–943.

Brown, L. M. (1996). Compassion and societal well-being. *Pacific Philosophical Quarterly, 77*, 216–224.

Cassell, E. J. (1982). The nature of suffering and the goals of medicine. *New England Journal of Medicine, 306*, 639–645.

Cassell, E. J. (1985a). *The healers art*. Cambridge, MA: The MIT Press.

Cassell, E. J. (1985b). *The nature of suffering*. New York: Oxford University Press.

de Tocqueville, A. (1955). *Democracy in America* (Trans. H. Reeve). London: Oxford University Press.

Donne, J. (1624/1994). *Devotions upon emergent occasions: The complete poetry and selected prose of John Donne*. New York: Modern Library.

Dougherty, C. J., & Purtillo, R. (1995). Physicians' duty of compassion. *Cambridge Quarterly of Healthcare Ethics, 4*, 426–433.

Foucault, M. (1979). *Discipline and punish* (Trans. A. Sheridan). New York: Vintage.

Hegel, G. W. F. (1977). *Phenomenology of spirit* (Trans. A. V. Miller). New York: Oxford University Press.

Hobbes, T. (1651/1962). *Leviathan* (Ed. T. Oakeshott). New York: Oxford University Press.

Loewy, E. H. (1998). Curiosity, imagination, compassion, science, and ethics: Do curiosity and imagination serve a central function? *Health Care Analysis, 6*, 286–294.

Lovejoy, A. (1961). *Reflections on human nature*. Baltimore: Johns Hopkins University Press.

MacIntyre, A. (1966). *A short history of ethics*. New York: Macmillan.

Mauss, M. (1985). A category of the human mind: The notion of person; The notion of self. In M. Carrithers, S. Collins, & S. Lukes (Eds.), *The category of the person: Anthropology, philosophy, history* (Trans. W. D. Halls, pp. 1–25). New York: Cambridge University Press.

Mead, G. H. (1934). *Mind, self, and society: From the standpoint of a social behaviorist*. Chicago: University of Chicago Press.

Meltzoff, A. (1985). The roots of social and cognitive development: Models of man's original nature. In T. M. Field & N. A. Fox (Eds.), *Social perception in infants* (pp. 1–30). Norwood, NJ: Ablex.

Meltzoff, A., & Kuhl, P. K. (1989). Infant perception of faces and speech sound: Challenges to developmental theory. In P. R. Zelazo & R. G. Barr (Eds.), *Challenges to developmental paradigms* (pp. 67–91). Hillsdale, NJ: Erlbaum.

Meltzoff, A., & Moore, M. K. (1977). Imitation of facial and manual gestures by human neonates. *Science, 198*, 75–78.

New York Times. (2000, June 13), p. B1.

Nussbaum, M. (1996). Compassion: The basic social emotion. *Social Philosophy and Policy, 13*, 27–58.

Olson, A. M. (1992). *Hegel and the spirit*. Princeton, NJ: Princeton University Press.

Reich, W. (1987). Models of point suffering: Foundations for an ethic compassion. *Acta Neurochirurgica* (Suppl. 38), 117–122.

Rousseau, J. J. (1976). *Emile* (A. Bloom, Trans.). New York: Basic Books.

Schopenhauer, A. (1969). *The world as will and representation* (Vol. 1, Trans. E. F. J. Payne). New York: Dover.

Skitka, L. J. (1999). Ideological and attributional boundaries on public compassion: Reactions to individuals and communities affected by a natural disaster. *Personality and Social Psychology Bulletin, 25*, 793–808.

Smith, A. (1759/1976). *The theory of moral sentiments.* Indianapolis, IN: Liberty Classics.

Snyder, C. R. (Ed.). (2000). *The handbook of hope: Theory, measures, and applications.* New York: Academic Press.

Snyder, C. R., & Fromkin, H. L. (1980). *Uniqueness: The human pursuit of difference.* New York: Plenum.

Sophokles. (1986). *Philoktetes* (Trans. G. McNamee). Port Townsend, WA: Copper Canyon Press.

Stern, D. N. (1985). *The interpersonal world of the infant.* New York: Basic Books.

Sznaider, N. (1998). The sociology of compassion: A study in the sociology of morals. *Cultural Values, 2*, 117–119.

Thurman, R. A. F. (1997). Wisdom and compassion: The heart of Tibetan culture. In M. M. Rhie & R. A. F. Thurman (Eds.), *Wisdom and compassion: The sacred art of Tibet* (pp. 17–19). New York: Tibet House.

Trevarthen, C. (1988). Universal cooperative motives: How infants begin to know the language and culture of their parents. In G. Jahoda & I. M. Lewis (Eds.), *Acquiring culture: Cross cultural studies in child development* (pp. 37–90). London: Croom Helm.

Adult Attachment Security: The Relational Scaffolding of Positive Psychology

Frederick G. Lopez

Abstract

For over three decades, attachment theory has served as a versatile and generative framework for studying how the dynamics of close, enduring emotional bonds with others (i.e., attachments) affect psychosocial growth and development across the life span. Indeed, in recent years, a substantial literature on adult attachment has emerged that has probed the nature, correlates, and consequences of security in one's intimate adult relationships. Although this literature initially emphasized the adverse impacts of attachment insecurity on human functioning, contemporary studies are increasingly adopting a positive psychological perspective that explores the contributions of secure adult relationships to the promotion and maintenance of healthy and adaptive behavior within and across multiple life domains. This chapter highlights this shift in emphasis by first considering how the positive psychology roots of attachment theory, as well as advances in the conceptualization and measurement of adult attachment security, support these initiatives. Following this, a selection of recent studies specifically examining associations between adult attachment security and such relevant constructs as hope, optimism, positive affect, parenting and caregiving competence, academic and career-related motivation, altruistic behavior, and existential well-being are reviewed. Taken together, findings from this emergent literature suggest that adult attachment security can serve as a major organizational construct in the continuing development of positive psychology. Finally, some potentially fruitful directions for future research on the synergistic contributions of adult attachment security to human competence and well-being are briefly discussed.

Keywords: adults, attachment, positive psychology, well-being, review

All of us, from the cradle to the grave, are happiest when
life is organized as a series of excursions, long or short,
from the secure base provided by our attachment figures.
—(*Bowlby*, 1988, p. 62)

Positive psychology is principally concerned with the scientific study of human strengths and potentials and with the nature of human effectiveness, striving, and flourishing (Sheldon & King, 2001). Given these broad inquiry goals, no comprehensive discussion of positive psychology could possibly ignore the central role and contributions of secure intimate adult relationships. For over three decades, attachment theory (Bowlby, 1969/1982) has proven to be a robust and heuristic framework for understanding how these relationships contribute to adaptive adult functioning, mental health, and well-being. Not surprisingly, much of this literature has adopted a "negative focus" by emphasizing how "insecure" adult attachments operate as risk factors for emotional disturbance, maladjustment, and problematic development, or by limiting a consideration of the power of attachment security to its stress-buffering effects. Recently, however, some writers (Lopez & Brennan, 2000; Mikulincer & Shaver, 2005) have proposed that adult attachment security may serve as more than just a protective factor; indeed, as Bowlby originally envisioned, it may function as the very scaffolding supporting optimal human growth and development.

My chapter advances this basic argument in several ways. First, the positive psychological underpinnings of attachment theory and of the generative, self-organizing power of attachment security will be explored in broad-brush strokes. As part of this discussion, conceptual issues regarding the measurement of adult attachment security also will be briefly reviewed. Next, I will selectively review recent studies that have specifically examined associations between adult attachment security and such positive psychology constructs as hope, optimism, and positive affect, healthy relationships and effective parenting, academic achievement and motivation, career development and job satisfaction, the expression of altruistic, prosocial, and "self-transcendence" values, and the experience of posttraumatic growth. I will then draw some general conclusions and comment on future directions for research that may have relevant implications for practice.

The Positive Psychology Underpinnings of Attachment Theory
Theoretical Background

Perhaps more so than any other twentieth-century social science theorist, John Bowlby believed in the formative power of healthy relationships in guiding the optimal course of human psychological growth and development across the life span. Bowlby argued that our human propensity to form and maintain enduring affectional bonds, or attachments, with others functioned as an innate, independent, and biologically anchored motivational system, designed by evolution to protect the species from external threat and predation. He further proposed that natural selection had forged interdependent links between the attachment or proximity-seeking system and each of two other positive motivational systems crucial to human survival and reproduction: exploration and caregiving.

More specifically, Bowlby conjectured that, from birth onward, the infant's attachment system is both responsive and reactive to the caregiving affordances (or lack thereof) in his or her immediate relational context. The infant's experience of fear, illness, discomfort, fatigue, or other distressing emotions typically activates the attachment system and motivates a search for the attachment or caregiving figure. When the infant's bids for care, comfort, and tension

reduction are apprehended and appropriately satisfied by primary caregivers, the infant's attachment system returns to a quiescent state, thus permitting him or her to engage in unfettered exploratory activities until a subsequent experience of threat or distress again activates the need for proximity and protection. To the extent that the infant–caregiver relationship reflected this ongoing and recursive dynamic, the relationship itself was presumed to advance the infant's acquisition of affect self-regulatory competencies as well as to serve as a "secure base" for progressive exploration and environmental mastery.

Bowlby further argued that, whereas the infant's affect regulation was initially a property of the relationship with the caregiver, the interactional patterns established during this early period would, within the first year of life, become cognitively represented by the child as an "internal working model" of self and other, or IWM (Bowlby, 1988, p. 165). This complex schema integrated self-perceptions of lovability and appraisals of the dependability of caregivers along with interactional strategies for managing the experience of insecurity. Once formed, the IWM was presumed to serve as a cognitive template that guided patterns of affective self-regulation and interpersonal behavior in current and future relationships (Bowlby, 1988). Bowlby sometimes used a railway metaphor to figuratively capture these ideas: He argued that from birth onward, a range of potential lines or "tracks" of healthy development existed for all persons and that the continuing experience of attachment security helped to keep the engine of organismic growth "on track" along one of these positive trajectories. By contrast, the intense or protracted experience of attachment insecurity, defined by the repeated neglect or rejection by available caregivers, would likely result in a problematic working model that could detour the course of development along a less favorable pathway.

Today, there is broad empirical support for Bowlby's fundamental contention that relationships serve as a primary context for development (see Reis, Collins, & Berscheid, 2000). Although a rich source of this support has been theory-driven research on infant and early childhood development (e.g., Chorpita & Barlow, 1998; Sroufe, Egeland, Carlson, & Collins, 2005), the burgeoning contemporary literature on adult attachment has dramatically expanded our appreciation of the developmental power of attachment security in promoting human effectiveness and resilience (e.g., Lopez & Brennan, 2000; Mikulincer & Shaver, 2004). In the sections to follow, I will selectively review recent studies from this literature that focus particular attention on the positive functioning and growth-promoting correlates and consequences of adult attachment security. However, because this literature has been informed by two distinct assessment traditions, I will first comment briefly on some important measurement issues.

Measurement Issues

In an earlier chapter (Lopez, 2003), I reviewed several of the more prominent measures of adult attachment security and commented on some of the issues associated with construct assessment. Both interview-based and self-report measures have been developed to assess adult attachment security. The most prominent interview-based measure, the Adult Attachment Interview (AAI; George, Kaplan, & Main, 1985), is an approximately hour-long semi-structured interview with standard questions probing respondents' early experiences of caregiving from parents and other adult figures. Interviews are subsequently transcribed, and independent raters follow an established coding system (Main & Goldwyn, 1984) to classify respondents into one of several attachment "states of mind" by assessing the discourse quality of their narratives: Persons classified as "secure/autonomous" evidence a capacity to respond reflectively and coherently to these probing questions regardless of the emotional content they might trigger (i.e., they are "free to evaluate" their attachment-related experiences), whereas the narratives of "preoccupied" persons demonstrate disabling entanglements with the negative affects associated with these reminiscences. By contrast, persons classified as "dismissing" exhibit a marked difficulty in accessing and elaborating upon attachment-related memories and a tendency to deny painful experiences described in provided examples, whereas persons classified as "unresolved/disorganized" respond to the same set of questions with protracted silences, bizarre lapses in logical reasoning, or eulogistic speech. AAI transcripts can also be coded to yield an overall, continuously scaled "coherence of narrative" score as well as continuous scores on two independent dimensions: "security/anxiety" (or the degree to which the person exhibits an autonomous state of mind vs. one compromised by anxiety) and "hyperactivation/deactivation" (or the extent to which the person is disposed to overfocus on vs. divert attention away from attachment-related concerns).

Self-report measures of adult attachment security generally assess respondents' typical cognitive, affective, and behavioral responses to the demands of intimate peer relationships. Some of these measures are designed to classify respondents into one of three

(secure, anxious, avoidant; Hazan & Shaver, 1987) or four (secure, preoccupied, dismissing, fearful; Bartholomew & Horowitz, 1991) "adult attachment style" prototypes or categories, whereas others produce dimensional "adult attachment orientation" scores. For example, the Experiences in Close Relationships Scale (Brennan, Clark, & Shaver, 1998) yields scores on two factors—Anxiety and Avoidance—that appear to underlie much of the variance in adult attachment organization. The Anxiety dimension taps strong fears of rejection or abandonment by romantic partners and intense desires to maintain proximity; the Avoidance dimension reflects discomfort with closeness and intimacy and strong desires to maintain emotional and behavioral self-sufficiency. Each of the four adult attachment styles has been conceptualized as occupying distinct locations on this two-dimensional space (Bartholomew & Shaver, 1998): "secure" persons report low levels of both Anxiety and Avoidance whereas "fearful" persons score high on both dimensions. Persons with a "preoccupied" style acknowledge low levels of Avoidance and high levels of Anxiety, whereas those with a "dismissing" style exhibit the opposite pattern (i.e., high Avoidance, low Anxiety).

As the AAI and self-report measures respectively focus attention on different facets of adult attachment organization (e.g., memories of caregiving from parental figures vs. current dispositions toward/expectations of romantic partners), it is not surprising that these different assessment approaches have produced at best only modest classification correspondences (Bartholomew & Shaver, 1998). Nonetheless, Shaver, Belsky, and Brennan (2000) found that continuous AAI ratings of "coherence of narrative" were moderately correlated with dimensions of self-reported adult attachment. Elsewhere, Collins, Guichard, Ford, and Feeney (2004) argued that because each assessment tradition offers distinctive yet potentially complementary perspectives on the larger construct of adult attachment security, an integrative consideration of adult attachment literature should be pursued. Consistent with their recommendation, in the sections to follow, I will highlight key findings from both assessment traditions that address the positive psychological correlates and consequences of adult attachment security.

Research Findings
Adult Attachment Security: Harnessing the Power of Positive Affect

Positive psychology researchers recognize that the experience of positive affect is more than a desired end state; more importantly, these experiences uniquely trigger temporary thought–action sequences that can "broaden and build" the repertoire of human competencies, resources, and adaptations (Fredrickson, 2001). Adult attachment security, whether assessed through interview or self-report methods, or contextually activated via experimental laboratory procedures, has been consistently linked to positive emotions across a number of independent studies (e.g., Magai, Hunziker, Mesias, & Culver, 2000; Mikulincer & Sheffi, 2000; Rowe & Carnelley, 2003; Shorey, Snyder, Xiangdong-Yang, & Lewin, 2003), leading some researchers to conclude that the experience of attachment security provides the basic relational platform supporting Fredrickson's "broaden and build" theory of positive emotions (Mikulincer & Shaver, 2005).

For instance, Magai et al. (2000) found that AAI transcripts coded for attachment style using Bartholomew and Horowitz's four-category system were related to biases in decoding photographed facial expressions displaying such emotions as interest, joy, fear, surprise, and shame. Unlike their insecure peers, secure persons more readily discerned facial expressions of joy and were less likely to distract themselves from perceiving negative emotions. Mikulincer and Sheffi (2000) further demonstrated that self-reported adult attachment styles moderated cognitive reactions to the laboratory induction of positive affect. More specifically, persons with secure styles responded to positive affect inductions with enhanced performance on cognitive categorization and creative problem-solving tasks. Interestingly, persons with anxious attachment styles evidenced the opposite pattern, whereas the cognitive processes of persons with avoidant styles appeared largely unaffected by these favorable mood inductions. In a study that experimentally "primed" participants to imagine different attachment styles, Rowe and Carnelley (2003) found that persons primed with a secure style subsequently reported more positive and less negative interpersonal expectations than did participants primed with insecure styles.

There is also evidence linking adult attachment security to indices of hope and dispositional optimism, to more flexible cognitive processes, and to better integrated and more resilient perceptions of self-worth. Therefore, secure attachment schema may additionally serve to elaborate and channel the experience of positive affect along constructive pathways by functioning as chronically accessible cognitive structures that effectively manage the intrusion of negative self and other appraisals. For instance, adults with secure attachment orientations demonstrated lower scores on a measure of dispositional pessimism (Heinonen, Raikkonen, Keltigangas-Jarvinen, & Strandberg, 2004) and were less likely to form either hasty or rigid social judgments of others (Green-Hennessy & Reis, 1998; Zhang & Hazan, 2002). Also in keeping with Bowlby's theoretical claims, secure attachments to supportive and responsive adults have been related to hopeful goal-directed thinking and mental health (Shorey et al., 2003) and to demonstrable growth in the acquisition of active and internal coping capabilities from adolescence to early adulthood (Seiffge-Krenke & Beyers, 2005). Elsewhere, relative to their peers with insecure adult attachment styles, secure adults appear to base their self-esteem on "noncontingent" sources of self-worth (Park, Crocker, & Mikelson, 2004); exhibit more balanced, complex, and cohesive self-structures (Banai, Mikulincer, & Shaver, 2005; Kim, 2005); and evince more self-reflective, meta-cognitive abilities (Fonagy & Target, 1997).

Adult Attachment Security, Exploration, and Academic Motivation

Consistent with theoretical expectations, there is evidence that the ensemble of affect self-regulatory and meta-cognitive skills associated with adult attachment security further scaffolds optimal development by stimulating positive approach and mastery-oriented curiosity, exploration, and task engagement behaviors in various performance and learning contexts. Persons self-reporting a secure attachment orientation (or experimentally "primed" to consider one) are more likely than those with insecure orientations to endorse mastery goals and to demonstrate a greater desire and openness to exploring novel stimuli (Elliot & Reis, 2003; Green & Campbell, 2000). There is also evidence that the links between attachment security and positive exploratory attitudes and behaviors are effectively mediated by appraisals of threat construal and competence valuation. The pattern of these findings suggests that the internalization of secure attachment schema, whether chronically available or contextually activated, enables the natural unfolding of "appetitive" exploratory dispositions unfettered by fears of failure or negative evaluation (Elliot & Reis, 2003, p. 328). In line with this view, adult attachment security has been related to college students' greater curiosity and comfort with academic social interactions, whereas attachment insecurity has been correlated with academic performance anxieties and lower levels of exploratory behavior (Aspelmeier & Kerns, 2003), with higher levels of maladaptive perfectionism (Rice, Lopez, & Vergara, 2005), and with a "disorganized and unfocused approach to academic work" (Aspelmeier & Kerns, 2003, pp. 24–25), particularly among men.

In short, adult attachment security appears to function as a valuable inner resource in academic learning environments and especially during critical periods (e.g., the high school-to-college transition) wherein significant changes in contexts and expectations may confront the learner with multiple adjustment-related challenges and uncertainties. For example, in one short-term longitudinal study, Lopez and Gormley (2002) found that self-reported adult attachment styles were moderately stable among entering university freshmen and that, relative to their peers who reported insecure or unstable attachment styles, participants who maintained a stable, secure attachment style over the 6-month assessment interval exhibited consistently high levels of self-confidence, positive affect (i.e., low depression scores), and ego integration (i.e., low "splitting" scores). More recently, Larose, Bernier, and Tarabulsy (2005) followed a group of students from the end of high school through the end of their first semester of college using the AAI to assess their level of attachment security and tracking changes in their academic performance and learning dispositions (e.g., ability to concentrate, willingness to seek help from peers and instructors, time management, examination anxiety). These researchers found that, compared against their peers classified as insecure, secure students demonstrated significantly more favorable learning dispositions and performance levels.

Career Exploration and Decision Making, Work Satisfaction, and Work–Family Balance

Work is a major life domain with great potential for advancing self-determination, social connectedness, and life satisfaction during adulthood (Blustein, 2006) and, as such, represents another significant venue for examining the positive scaffolding contributions of adult attachment security. The established associations between adult attachment security and favorable exploratory attitudes and learning dispositions would logically forecast positive trajectories of work and career adjustment. Preparation for and entry and adaptive persistence in adult work and ongoing career development tasks also pose multiple demands and uncertainties that challenge a person's capacities to cope with stress and to balance the often competing requirements of

work and family roles. Attachment theory–driven research in work-related domains, although sparse, yields support for the view that adult attachment security indeed promotes the individual's constructive engagement in these myriad activities.

Adult attachment security has been related to favorable early indices of career development, such as lower levels of indecisiveness and fewer commitment fears, and to higher levels of vocational self-concept crystallization (Tokar, Withrow, Hall, & Moradi, 2003; Wolfe & Betz, 2004). Similarly, relative to their less secure peers, persons reporting a secure adult attachment style were found to have a confident approach to work, be relatively free of performance-related fears, demonstrate balanced concerns for relationship and work issues, and to report higher levels of job satisfaction (Hazan & Shaver, 1990). In addition, workers with secure adult attachment orientations were found to report lower levels of work stress and stronger perceptions of supervisor support than did their less secure peers (Schirmer & Lopez, 2001). Secure adult attachment styles were also negatively correlated with work burnout across several distinct cultural groups (Pines, 2004).

Findings from other studies indicate that persons with secure adult attachment styles and orientations report a stronger orientation toward balancing and investing in multiple life roles (Lopez & Fons-Scheyd, 2006) and indeed appear more successful than their less secure counterparts in negotiating the sometimes competing demands of work and family obligations (Sumer & Knight, 2001; Vasquez, Durik, & Hyde, 2002).

The Secure Pathway toward Mature Interdependence

Challenging the conventional psychoanalytic wisdom of his day, Bowlby argued that rather than reinforcing unhealthy infantile dependencies, the consistent parental responsiveness to the child's innate needs for proximity and protection would advance the child's internalized valuing of intimate connections and the corresponding development of a healthy, mature interdependence in adult life (Bowlby, 1969/1982). The available research on adult attachment now not only provides substantial support for this key proposition, it also establishes clear links between secure adult attachment orientations and specific appraisal processes and social competencies deemed crucial to the construction and maintenance of intimate adult relationships. Even more impressively, this literature demonstrates that adult attachment security consistently predicts relationship quality better than do basic personality traits (Noftle & Shaver, 2006).

Relative to their insecure peers, persons with secure adult attachment orientations exhibit higher-quality patterns of self-disclosure with their partners (Keelan, Dion, & Dion, 1998; Mikulincer & Nachson, 1991), greater openness to and valuing of social feedback (Brennan & Bosson, 1998), higher levels of respect, perspective taking, empathic concern for their intimate partners (Frei & Shaver, 2002; Joireman, Needham, & Cummings, 2001), and stronger endorsement of nondeceptive, authentic exchanges with them (Lopez & Rice, 2006). In addition, persons with secure attachment orientations are more likely to view their partners as meeting desired performance standards and expectations (Lopez, Fons-Scheyd, Morua, & Chaliman, 2006), to report engaging their partners in collaborative forms of problem solving (Corcoran & Mallinckrodt, 2000), and to forgive partner transgressions (Lawler-Row, Younger, Piferi, & Jones, 2006).

In laboratory experiments as well as observational studies using diary methodologies, direct associations between adult attachment security and actual support-giving behaviors and more psychologically rewarding interactions with others have also been established (Collins & Feeney, 2000; Feeney & Collins, 2001; Kafetsios & Nezlek, 2002). Using a prospective design, Scharf, Mayseless, and Kivenson-Baron (2004) found that when compared to their less secure counterparts, late adolescents initially classified as secure/autonomous using the AAI were deemed by both parents and friends as demonstrating a greater capacity for mature intimacy 3 years later, once again lending support for Bowlby's assertion that attachment security favorably shapes the individual's developmental trajectory. There is also evidence that the unique constellation of benign appraisal processes and competent communication skills associated with secure adult attachment styles and orientations appears to have constructive reciprocal impacts on relationship problem solving and conflict resolution in dating couples (Creasey & Hesson-McInnis, 2001), forecasts relationship adjustment and satisfaction among young married couples (Cobb, Davila, & Bradbury, 2001; Gallo & Smith, 2001), and contributes to more favorable family dynamics (Mikulincer, Florian, Cowan, & Cowan, 2002).

Attachment Security and Effective Parenting across the Life Span

The strong interdependence between attachment security and intimate social competencies has been more specifically demonstrated in the context of positive parenting attitudes and behaviors that, among other things, are to likely scaffold optimal psychological development by enhancing personal satisfaction with parenting roles and outcomes, by maintaining supportive family relationships and intergenerational ties, and by adaptively coping with family-related stresses across the life span. Unlike their peers with secure styles, both male and female college students with avoidant attachment styles reported less desire to become parents and were more likely to endorse use of harsh discipline practices with young children (Rholes, Simpson, Blakely, Lanigan, & Allen, 1997). Elsewhere, first-time parents with avoidant attachment styles were found to report greater parenting-related stress and to view the parenting role as less satisfying and meaningful (Rholes, Simpson, & Friedman, 2006). In an earlier study, Rholes, Simpson, and Blakely (1995) found that mothers who reported more avoidant attachment styles acknowledged less emotional engagement with their young children and were rated by observers as offering less support to these children as they were attempting to learn a new task. In stark contrast with avoidant (dismissing) mothers, mothers classified as secure on the AAI demonstrated the most open and flexible mind-set in dealing with their own and their toddlers' emotions (DeOliveira, Moran, & Pederson, 2005).

There is also evidence that mothers reporting high levels of attachment insecurity may be at particular risk for negative mental health and marital outcomes when they must care for infants with significant medical problems such as congenital heart defects (Berant, Mikulincer, & Florian, 2001, 2003). In these 1-year longitudinal studies, the significant relationships between attachment avoidance and marital/mental health outcomes appeared mediated by poor marital coping and negative appraisals of the parenting role.

Lastly, adult attachment security also appears to facilitate the developmentally appropriate reversal of caregiving roles between adults and their aging parents during the latter stages of the family life cycle. In their review of this particular literature, Bradley and Cafferty (2001) concluded that when compared to their less secure peers, securely attached adult children reported lower caregiving burden and engaged in more frequent caregiving behaviors when tending to their elderly parents. Consistent with this conclusion, Sorensen, Webster, and Roggman (2002) subsequently found that, even after controlling for adults' actual preparation activities in caring for their aged parents, higher levels of attachment security among these adults uniquely predicted their feelings of preparedness.

Secure Worldviews: Self-Transcendence Values and Posttraumatic Growth

Research on adult attachment security has also been recently extended to broader domains of inquiry such as civic responsibility and existential well-being, thus further enhancing its relevance to positive psychology's wide-ranging interests in human effectiveness and resilience. These domains include the emergence of global prosocial values, enhanced tolerance of cultural differences, and the experience of posttraumatic recovery and growth.

In a series of three experimental studies, Mikulincer et al. (2003) specifically examined causal links between attachment security (both dispositional and contextually induced) and the endorsement of "self-transcendence values" (p. 299). Across these studies, adult attachment security—most notably, low levels of avoidance—was significantly associated with greater concerns for social justice and others' welfare. A follow-up naturalistic study of community-related volunteerism using participants from three different countries (United States, the Netherlands, Israel) similarly found that attachment avoidance was negatively related to volunteerism behaviors (i.e., caring for the elderly, giving blood), whereas high levels of attachment anxiety were associated with egoistic (as opposed to genuinely altruistic) motives for volunteering (Gillath et al., 2005). In an independent series of studies using adult participants from the United States and Israel, the same team of researchers consistently found that the experimental "priming" of attachment security promoted greater expressions of compassion and willingness to help a person in distress, even when participants' scores on measures of self-esteem and neuroticism were controlled (Mikulincer, Shaver, Gillath, & Nitzberg, 2005).

Adult attachment security has also been associated with fewer negative reactions to "out-groups" (Mikulincer & Shaver, 2001) and to more optimal levels of intercultural adjustment within a group of recent Dutch emigrants (Bakker, Van Oudenhoven, & Van Der Zee, 2004). In line with the above findings, these results suggest that the beneficial impacts of adult attachment security may extend beyond the domains of intimate family and peer relationships to favorably affect the construction of broad, flexible worldviews that promote resilience and existential well-being. Hart, Shaver, and Goldenberg (2005) have pursued this idea by arguing that attachment security should be considered (along with self-esteem and world-view processes) as part of a tripartite security system for managing the existential experience of terror. Across their four studies, findings suggested that adult attachment security was not only a distinct defense system; it was one that, for most persons, was preferentially used over other defenses in managing the experience of terror. Relevant to this speculation, Fraley, Fazzari, Bonnano, and Dekel (2006) found that compared to their less secure peers, securely attached New Yorkers living close to the World Trade Center on September 11, 2001, subsequently exhibited fewer symptoms of posttraumatic distress and were more likely to be viewed by friends and relatives as evidencing increased adjustment after the terrorist attacks on that fateful day.

Conclusions and Directions for Future Research

This chapter sought to advance the argument that adult attachment security be considered the relational scaffolding of positive psychology. Toward this end, I selectively reviewed recent studies of the contributions of secure adult attachment styles and orientations to positive functioning and outcomes across several important life domains. These studies represent an impressively diverse range of samples (e.g., college students, married couples, adult workers), research designs (e.g., correlational, experimental, naturalistic, longitudinal), and methods of assessing adult attachment security (e.g., self-report, interview, experimental "priming") as well as multiple indicators of adaptive dispositions and performance behaviors. More importantly, these studies have yielded consistent evidence that relative to their insecurely attached peers, secure adults possess greater capacities for affective self-regulation, more flexible, integrative, and reflective information-processing capabilities, and broader repertoires of social competencies. Taken together, the assembled evidence leads to an overarching and convergent conclusion: As Bowlby originally envisioned, the acquisition and internalization of a secure adult attachment orientation appears to play a crucial role in promoting and maintaining healthy and optimal human development across the life span. Why is this the case? In this closing section, I briefly consider some integrative models for understanding this critical linkage and for pursuing new research directions that may have particularly relevant implications for therapeutic practice.

In an earlier review (Lopez & Brennan, 2000), I initially speculated that the myriad positive life outcomes associated with the experience of adult attachment security argued in favor of conceptualizing attachment security, not simply as an individual differences variable, but as a unique person–context relation that scaffolds optimal development by promoting active, creative, and synergistically transformative exchanges with one's immediate developmental context. The evidence reviewed in this chapter further corroborates this view and, in the intervening years, some new integrative models for probing this relation have emerged. For instance, Zayas, Shoda, and Ayduk (2002) have offered a "personality-in-context" perspective for understanding how stable, chronically accessible relational schema may affect the course of human development by specifically influencing how persons preferentially select social contexts, elicit or evoke particular reactions from others therein, and intentionally modify, change, and influence others in these contexts. Elsewhere, Murray and Derrick (2005) have proposed a framework for examining how the ongoing experience of felt security activates self-fulfilling "microprocesses" that are instrumental for healthy relationship development and change. In a similar vein, Mikulincer and Shaver (2004) have advanced a model for conceptualizing how attachment security progressively enhances greater autonomy and self-regulation by facilitating the cognitive retrieval and deployment of self-soothing and self-care competencies in response to security-related threats. Indeed, from a eudaemonic view of well-being, the appropriate management of such threats is an essential prerequisite of healthy psychological growth and subjective well-being (Lent, 2004).

Although a more extensive discussion of these emergent process-related models is beyond the scope of this chapter, I believe they open up a number of potentially fruitful avenues for future inquiry. For instance, they may guide future efforts at clarifying both the cognitive and interpersonal dynamics, undergirding the maintenance of genuine (stable) self-esteem and authentic, growth-promoting relationships with others (Lent & Lopez, 2002). In this regard, more correlational and experimental studies (and especially those involving repeated measures) of attachment-related processes among intimate adult couples are clearly needed. Such research is inherently more complex and the assumptions of many conventional statistical methods are not amenable to the careful analyses of these processes. Fortunately, recently developed analytic tools that adjust for the nonindependence of data sources (Actor–Partner Interaction Model [APIM]; Cook & Kenny, 2005) are now available and should be seriously considered.

Also needed are more cross-cultural studies of the impacts of adult attachment security. Although Bowlby emphasized the universality of the attachment system, others (Rothbaum, Weisz, Pott, Miyake, & Morelli, 2000) have challenged this assumption, particularly among persons from non-Western cultures. Furthermore, some preliminary research (Wang & Mallinckrodt, 2006) suggests that college students from Western and non-Western cultures may hold different concepts of "ideal attachment." In short, cultural schemata and attachment schemata may interact in complex ways in predicting relationship processes and outcomes. Relatedly, as some of the recent studies cited in this review suggest, continued inquiry of attachment-related dynamics within broader social systems such as schools and workplaces may hold promise in clarifying how structural features of these social contexts may interact with incumbents' adult attachment orientations to promote or impede their performance and adaptation.

Last, but certainly not least, is the need for continued inquiry of attachment dynamics within therapeutic relationships. Preliminary studies have demonstrated that client and therapist attachment orientations are related to different patterns of interpersonal problems (Shorey & Snyder, 2006), to countertransference reactions among counselor trainees (Mohr, Gelso, & Hill, 2005), as well as to session quality (Mallinckrodt, Porter, & Kivlighan, 2005), and the formation of early working alliances (Sauer, Lopez, & Gormley, 2003). In addition, attachment-focused group treatments have been shown to be effective (Kilmann, Urbaniak, & Parnell, 2006). Despite these encouraging findings, until recently, attachment theory has had little impact on clinical theory and practice (Lopez, 2009).

The evidence reviewed in this chapter strongly suggests that, beyond reducing current distress, therapeutic efforts to enhance the experience of adult attachment security may activate a number of healing and growth-promoting cognitive, affective, and interpersonal processes. Although much work remains to be done, if present trends hold, continued advancements within this and other lines of inquiry will one day decisively establish Bowlby's conviction that the psychology of a happy, rewarding, and fulfilling life is ultimately the co-constructed story of our secure attachments with others.

Questions about the Future of the Topic

1. What are the specific mediational mechanisms and processes by which the experience of adult attachment security promotes adaptive and healthy behavioral outcomes in particular life domains?

2. How can adult attachment security be strengthened in intimate relationships as well as in adult work, higher education, and therapeutic relationships as a means of enhancing human effectiveness, resilience, and optimal functioning?

3. Are there important cultural variations in the experience and expression of adult attachment security, and, if so, how do these variations affect the positive psychological growth and development of persons in different cultural groups?

References

Aspelmeier, J. E., & Kerns, K. A. (2003). Love and school: Attachment/exploration dynamics in college. *Journal of Social and Personal Relationships, 20*, 5–30.

Bakker, W., Van Oudenhoven, J. P., & Van der Zee, K. I. (2004). Attachment styles, personality, and Dutch emigrants' intercultural adjustment. *European Journal of Personality, 18*, 387–404.

Banai, E., Mikulincer, M., & Shaver, P. R. (2005). "Selfobject" needs in Kohut's self psychology: Links with attachment, self-cohesion, affect regulation, and adjustment. *Psychoanalytic Psychology, 22*, 224–240.

Bartholomew, K., & Horowitz, L. M. (1991). Attachment styles among young adults: A test of a four category model. *Journal of Personality and Social Psychology, 61*, 226–244.

Bartholomew, K., & Shaver, P. R. (1998). Methods of assessing adult attachment: Do they converge? In J. A. Simpson & W. S. Rholes (Eds.), *Attachment theory and close relationships* (pp. 25–45). New York: Guilford.

Berant, E., Mikulincer, M., & Florian, V. (2001). Attachment style and mental health: A 1-year follow-up study of mothers of infants with congenital heart disease. *Personality and Social Psychology Bulletin, 27*, 956–968.

Berant, E., Mikulincer, M., & Florian, V. (2003). Marital satisfaction among mothers of infants with congenital heart disease: The contributions of illness severity, attachment style, and the coping process. *Anxiety, Stress, and Coping, 16*, 397–415.

Blustein, D. L. (2006). *The psychology of working*. Mahwah, NJ: Lawrence Erlbaum.

Bowlby, J. (1969/1982). *Attachment and loss: Vol. 1. Attachment* (2nd ed.). New York: Basic Books.

Bowlby, J. (1988). *A secure base: Parent–child attachments and healthy human development*. New York: Basic Books.

Bradley, J. M., & Cafferty, T. P. (2001). Attachment among older adults: Current issues and directions for future research. *Attachment and Human Development, 3*, 200–221.

Brennan, K. A., & Bosson, J. K. (1998). Attachment-style differences in attitudes toward and reactions to feedback from romantic partners: An exploration of the relational bases of self-esteem. *Personality and Social Psychology Bulletin, 24*, 699–714.

Brennan, K. A., Clark, C. L., & Shaver, P. R. (1998). Self-reported measurement of adult attachment. In J. A. Simpson & W. S. Rholes (Eds.), *Attachment theory and close relationships* (pp. 46–76). New York: Guilford.

Chorpita, B. E., & Barlow, D. H. (1998). The development of anxiety: The role of control in the early environment. *Psychological Bulletin, 124*, 3–21.

Cobb, R. J., Davila, J., & Bradbury, T. N. (2001). Attachment security and marital satisfaction: The role of positive perceptions and social support. *Personality and Social Psychology Bulletin, 27*, 1131–1143.

Collins, N. L., & Feeney, B. C. (2000). A safe haven: An attachment theory perspective on support seeking and caregiving in intimate relationships. *Journal of Personality and Social Psychology, 78*, 1053–1073.

Collins, N. L., Guichard, A. C., Ford, M., & Feeney, B. C. (2004). Working models of attachment: New developments and emerging themes: In W. S. Rholes & J. A. Simpson (Eds.), *Adult attachment: Theory, research, and clinical implications* (pp. 196–239). New York: Guilford.

Cook, W. L., & Kenny, D. A. (2005). The Actor–Partner Interdependence Model: A model of bidirectional effects in developmental studies. *International Journal of Behavioral Development, 29*, 101–109.

Corcoran, K. O., & Mallinckrodt, B. (2000). Adult attachment, self-efficacy, perspective taking and conflict resolution. *Journal of Counseling and Development, 78*, 478–489.

Creasey, G., & Hesson-McInnis, M. (2001). Affective responses, cognitive appraisals, and conflict tactics in late adolescent romantic relationships: Associations with attachment orientations. *Journal of Counseling Psychology, 48*, 85–96.

DeOliveira, C. A., Moran, G., & Pederson, D. R. (2005). Understanding the link between maternal adult attachment classifications and thoughts and feelings about emotions. *Attachment and Human Development, 7*, 153–170.

Elliot, A. J., & Reis, H. T. (2003). Attachment and exploration in adulthood. *Journal of Personality and Social Psychology, 85*, 317–331.

Feeney, B. C., & Collins, N. L. (2001). Predictors of caregiving in adult intimate relationships: An attachment theoretical perspective. *Journal of Personality and Social Psychology, 80*, 972–994.

Fonagy, P., & Target, M. (1997). Attachment and reflective function: Their role in self-organization. *Development and Psychopathology, 9*, 679–700.

Fraley, R. C., Fazzari, D. A., Bonanno, G. A., & Dekel, S. (2006). Attachment and psychological adaptation in high exposure survivors of the September 11th attack on the World Trade Center. *Personality and Social Psychology Bulletin, 32*, 538–551.

Fredrickson, B. L. (2001). The role of positive emotions in positive psychology. *American Psychologist, 56*, 218–226.

Frei, J. R., & Shaver, P. R. (2002). Respect in close relationships: Prototype definition, self-report assessment, and initial correlates. *Personal Relationships, 9*, 121–139.

Gallo, L. C., & Smith, T. W. (2001). Attachment style in marriage: Adjustment and responses to interaction. *Journal of Social and Personal Relationships, 18*, 263–289.

George, C., Kaplan, N., & Main, M. (1985). The Adult Attachment Interview. Unpublished protocol, Department of Psychology, University of California at Berkeley, Berkeley, CA.

Gillath, O., Shaver, P. R., Mikulincer, M., Nitzberg, R. E., Erez, A., & van IJzendoorn, M. H. (2005). Attachment, caregiving, and volunteering: Placing volunteerism in an attachment-theoretical framework. *Personal Relationships, 12*, 425–446.

Green, J. D., & Campbell, W. K. (2000). Attachment and exploration in adults: Chronic and contextual accessibility. *Personality and Social Psychology Bulletin, 26*, 452–461.

Green-Hennessy, S., & Reis, H. T. (1998). Openness in processing social information among attachment types. *Personal Relationships, 5*, 449–466.

Hart, J., Shaver, P. R., & Goldenberg, J. L. (2005). Attachment, self-esteem, worldviews, and terror management: Evidence of a tripartite security system. *Journal of Personality and Social Psychology, 88*, 999–1013.

Hazan, C., & Shaver, P. R. (1987). Romantic love conceptualized as an attachment process. *Journal of Personality and Social Psychology, 52*, 511–524.

Hazan, C., & Shaver, P. R. (1990). Love and work: An attachment-theoretical perspective. *Journal of Personality and Social Psychology, 59*, 270–280.

Heinonen, K., Raikkonen, K., Keltikangas-Jarvinen, L., & Strandberg, T. (2004). Adult attachment dimensions and recollections of childhood family context: Associations with dispositional optimism and pessimism. *European Journal of Personality, 18*, 193–207.

Joireman, J. A., Needham, T. L., & Cummings, A-L. (2001). Relationships between dimensions of attachment and empathy. *North American Journal of Psychology, 3*, 63–80.

Kafetsios, K., & Nezlek, J. B. (2002). Attachment styles in everyday social interaction. *European Journal of Social Psychology, 32*, 719–735.

Keelan, J. P., Dion, K. K., & Dion, K. L. (1998). Attachment style and relationship satisfaction: Test of a self-disclosure explanation. *Canadian Journal of Behavioral Science, 30*, 24–35.

Kilmann, P. R., Urbaniak, G. C., & Parnell, M. M. (2006). Effects of attachment-focused versus relationship skills-focused group interventions for college students with insecure attachment patterns. *Attachment and Human Development, 8*, 47–62.

Kim, Y. (2005). Emotional and cognitive consequences of adult attachment: The mediating effect of the self. *Personality and Individual Differences, 39*, 913–923.

Larose, S., Bernier, A., & Tarabulsy, G. M. (2005). Attachment state of mind, learning dispositions, and academic performance during the college transition. *Developmental Psychology, 41*, 281–289.

Lawler-Row, K. A., Younger, J. W., Piferi, R. L., & Jones, W. H. (2006). The role of adult attachment style in forgiveness following an interpersonal offense. *Journal of Counseling and Development, 84*, 493–502.

Lent, R. W. (2004). Toward a unifying theoretical and practical perspective on well-being and psychosocial adjustment. *Journal of Counseling Psychology, 51*, 482–509.

Lent, R. W., & Lopez, F. G. (2002). Cognitive ties that bind: Toward a tripartite model of efficacy beliefs in growth-promoting relationships. *Journal of Social and Clinical Psychology, 21*, 256–286.

Lopez, F. G. (2003). The assessment of adult attachment security. In S. J. Lopez & C. R. Snyder (Eds.), *Positive psychological assessment: A handbook of models and measures* (pp. 285–299). Washington, DC: APA Press.

Lopez, F. G. (2009). Clinical correlates of adult attachment organization. In J. H. Obegi & E. Berant (Eds.), *Attachment theory and research in clinical work with adults* (pp. 94–117). New York: Guilford.

Lopez, F. G., & Brennan, K. A. (2000). Dynamic processes underlying adult attachment organization: Toward an attachment-theoretical perspective on the healthy and effective self. *Journal of Counseling Psychology, 47*, 283–300.

Lopez, F. G., & Fons-Scheyd, A. (2006, July). *Adult attachment orientations as predictors of role balance and role overload among emerging adults.* Paper presented at the 26th International Congress of Applied Psychology, Athens, Greece.

Lopez, F. G., Fons-Scheyd, A., Morua, W., & Chaliman, R. (2006). Dyadic perfectionism as a predictor of relationship continuity and distress among college students. *Journal of Counseling Psychology, 53*, 543–549.

Lopez, F. G., & Gormley, B. (2002). Stability and change in adult attachment style over the first-year college transition: Relations to self-confidence, coping, and distress patterns. *Journal of Counseling Psychology, 49*, 355–364.

Lopez, F. G., & Rice, K. G. (2006). Preliminary development and validation of a measure of relationship authenticity. *Journal of Counseling Psychology, 53*, 362–371.

Magai, C., Hunziker, J., Mesias, W., & Culver, L. C. (2000). Adult attachment styles and emotional biases. *International Journal of Behavioral Development, 24*, 301–309.

Main, M., & Goldwyn, R. (1984). Adult attachment scoring and classification system. Unpublished manuscript, University of California at Berkeley, Berkeley, CA.

Mallinckrodt, B., Porter, M. J., & Kivlighan, D. M. (2005). Client attachment to therapist, depth of in-session exploration, and object relations in brief psychotherapy. *Psychotherapy: Theory, Research, Practice, Training, 42*, 85–100.

Mikulincer, M., Florian, V., Cowan, P. A., & Cowan, C. P. (2002). Attachment security in couple relationships: A systemic model and implications for family dynamics. *Family Process, 41*, 405–434.

Mikulincer, M., Gillath, O., Sapir-Lavid, Y., Yaakobi, E., Arias, K., Tal-Aloni, L., et al. (2003). Attachment theory and concern for others' welfare: Evidence that activation of the sense of secure base promotes endorsement of self-transcendence values. *Basic and Applied Social Psychology, 25*, 299–312.

Mikulincer, M., & Nachson, O. (1991). Attachment styles and patterns of self-disclosure. *Journal of Personality and Social Psychology, 61*, 321–331.

Mikulincer, M., & Shaver, P. R. (2001). Attachment theory and intergroup bias: Evidence that priming the secure base schema attenuates negative reactions to outgroups. *Journal of Personality and Social Psychology, 81*, 97–115.

Mikulincer, M., & Shaver, P. R. (2004). Security-based self-representations in adulthood: Contents and processes. In W. S. Rholes & J. A. Simpson (Eds.), *Adult attachment: Theory, research, and clinical implications* (pp. 159–195). New York: Guilford.

Mikulincer, M., & Shaver, P. R. (2005). Mental representations of attachment security: Theoretical foundation of a positive social psychology. In M. Baldwin (Ed.), *Interpersonal cognition* (pp. 233–266). New York: Guilford.

Mikulincer, M., Shaver, P. R., Gilliath, O., & Nitzberg, R. A. (2005). Attachment, caregiving, and altruism: Boosting attachment security increases compassion and helping. *Journal of Personality and Social Psychology, 89*, 817–839.

Mikulincer, M., & Sheffi, E. (2000). Adult attachment style and cognitive reactions to positive affect: A test of mental categorization and creative problem solving. *Motivation and Emotion, 24*, 149–174.

Mohr, J. J., Gelso, C. J., & Hill, C. E. (2005). Client and counselor trainee attachment as predictors of session evaluation and countertransference behavior in first counseling sessions. *Journal of Counseling Psychology, 52*, 298–309.

Murray, S. L., & Derrick, J. (2005). A relationship-specific sense of felt security: How perceived regard regulates relationship-enhancement processes. In M. Baldwin (Ed.), *Interpersonal cognition* (pp. 153–179). New York: Guilford.

Noftle, E. E., & Shaver, P. R. (2006). Attachment dimensions and the Big Five personality traits: Associations and comparative ability to predict relationship quality. *Journal of Research in Personality, 40*, 179–208.

Park, L. E., Crocker, J., & Mickelson, K. D. (2004). Attachment styles and contingencies of self-worth. *Personality and Social Psychology Bulletin, 30*, 1243–1254.

Pines, A. M. (2004). Adult attachment styles and their relationship to burnout: A preliminary, cross-cultural investigation. *Work and Stress, 18*, 66–80.

Reis, H. T., Collins, W. A., & Berscheid, E. (2000). The relationship context of human behavior and development. *Psychological Bulletin, 126*, 844–872.

Rholes, W. S., Simpson, J. A., & Blakely, B. S. (1995). Adult attachment styles and mothers' relationships with their young children. *Personal Relationships, 2*, 35–54.

Rholes, W. S., Simpson, J. A., Blakely, B. S., Lanigan, L., & Allen, E. A. (1997). Adult attachment styles, the desire to have children, and working models of parenthood. *Journal of Personality, 65*, 357–385.

Rholes, W. S., Simpson, J. A., & Friedman, M. (2006). Avoidant attachment and the experience of parenting. *Personality and Social Psychology Bulletin, 32*, 275–285.

Rice, K. G., Lopez, F. G., & Vergara, D. (2005). Parental/social influences on perfectionism and adult attachment orientations. *Journal of Social and Clinical Psychology, 24*, 362–371.

Rothbaum, F., Weisz, J., Pott, M., Miyake, K., & Morelli, G. (2000). Attachment and culture: Security in the United States and Japan. *American Psychologist, 55*, 1093–1104.

Rowe, A., & Carnelley, K. B. (2003). Attachment style differences in the processing of attachment-relevant information: Primed-style effects on recall, interpersonal expectations, and affect. *Personal Relationships, 10*, 59–75.

Sauer, E. M., Lopez, F. G., & Gormley, B. (2003). Respective contributions of therapist and client adult attachment orientations to the development of the early working alliance: A hierarchical linear modeling analysis. *Psychotherapy Research, 13*, 371–382.

Scharf, M., Mayseless, O., & Kivenson-Baron, I. (2004). Adolescents' attachment representations and developmental tasks in emerging adulthood. *Developmental Psychology, 40*, 430–444.

Schirmer, L. L., & Lopez, F. G. (2001). Probing the social support and work strain relationship among adult workers: Contributions of adult attachment orientations. *Journal of Vocational Behavior, 59*, 17–33.

Seiffge-Krenke, I., & Beyers, W. (2005). Coping trajectories from adolescence to young adulthood: Links to attachment state of mind. *Journal of Research on Adolescence, 15*, 561–582.

Shaver, P. R., Belsky, J., & Brennan, K. A. (2000). The Adult Attachment Interview and self-reports of romantic attachment: Associations across domains and methods. *Personal Relationships, 7*, 25–43.

Sheldon, K. M., & King, L. (2001). Why positive psychology is necessary. *American Psychologist, 56*, 216–217.

Shorey, H. S., & Snyder, C. R. (2006). The role of adult attachment styles in psychopathology and psychotherapy outcomes. *Review of General Psychology, 10*, 1–20.

Shorey, H. S., Snyder, C. R., Xiangdong, Y., & Lewin, M. R. (2003). The role of hope as a mediator in recollected parenting, adult attachment, and mental health. *Journal of Social and Clinical Psychology, 22*, 685–715.

Sorensen, S., Webster, J. D., & Roggman, L. A. (2002). Adult attachment and preparing to provide care to older relatives. *Attachment and Human Development, 4*, 84–106.

Sroufe, L. A., Egeland, B., Carlson, E. A., & Collins, W. A. (2005). *The development of the person.* New York: Guilford.

Sumer, H. C., & Knight, P. A. (2001). How do people with different attachment styles balance work and family? A personality perspective on work–family linkage. *Journal of Applied Psychology, 86*, 653–663.

Tokar, D. A., Withrow, J. R., Hall, R. J., & Moradi, B. (2003). Psychological separation, attachment security, vocational self-concept crystallization, and career indecision: A structural equation analysis. *Journal of Counseling Psychology, 50*, 3–19.

Vasquez, K., Durik, A. M., & Hyde, J. S. (2002). Family and work: Implications of adult attachment styles. *Personality and Social Psychology Bulletin, 28*, 874–886.

Wang, C. C., & Mallinckrodt, B. S. (2006). Differences between Taiwanese and U.S. cultural beliefs about ideal attachment. *Journal of Counseling Psychology, 53*, 192–204.

Wolfe, J. B., & Betz, N. E. (2004). The relationships of attachment variables to career decision-making self-efficacy and fear of commitment. *Career Development Quarterly, 52*, 363–369.

Zayas, V., Shoda, Y., & Ayduk, O. N. (2002). Personality in context: An interpersonal systems perspective. *Journal of Personality, 70*, 851–900.

Zhang, F., & Hazan, C. (2002). Working models of attachment and person perception processes. *Personal Relationships, 9*, 225–235.

Empathy and Altruism

C. Daniel Batson, Nadia Ahmad, *and* David A. Lishner

Abstract

Do we humans ever, in any degree, care about others for their sakes and not simply for our own? Psychology has long assumed that everything humans do, no matter how nice and noble, is motivated by self-interest. However, research over the past three decades suggests that this assumption is wrong. This research has focused on the empathy–altruism hypothesis, which claims that empathic concern—an other-oriented emotional response elicited by and congruent with the perceived welfare of a person in need—produces altruistic motivation—motivation with the ultimate goal of increasing another's welfare. Results of the over 30 experiments designed to test this hypothesis against various egoistic alternatives have proved remarkably supportive, leading to the tentative conclusion that feeling empathic concern for a person in need does indeed evoke altruistic motivation to see that need relieved. Sources of altruistic motivation other than empathy also have been proposed, but as yet, there is not compelling research evidence to support these proposals. Two additional forms of prosocial motivation have also been proposed: collectivism and principlism. Collectivism—motivation with the ultimate goal of benefiting some group or collective as a whole—has been claimed to result from group identity. Principlism—motivation with the ultimate goal of upholding some moral principle—has long been advocated by religious teachers and moral philosophers. Whether either is a separate form of motivation, independent of and irreducible to egoism, is not yet clear. Research done to test for the existence of empathy-induced altruism may serve as a useful model for future research testing for the existence of collectivism and principlism. Theoretical and practical implications of the empathy–altruism hypothesis are briefly considered.

Keywords: altruism, collectivism, egoism, empathy, principlism

Altruism refers to a specific form of motivation for benefiting another. Although some biologists, economists, and psychologists speak of altruism as a type of helping behavior, this use fails to consider the motivation for the behavior, which is crucial for altruism. To the degree that one's ultimate goal in benefiting another is to increase the other's welfare, the motivation is altruistic. To the degree that the ultimate goal is to increase one's own welfare, the motivation is egoistic. Accordingly, we shall use the term "altruism" to refer to "a motivational state with the ultimate goal of increasing another's welfare." We shall use the term "helping" to refer to "behavior that benefits another, regardless of the ultimate goal."

A Basic Question: Is Altruism Part of Human Nature?

Does altruism exist? Clearly, humans devote much time and energy to helping others. We send money to rescue famine victims halfway around the world—or to save whales. We stay up all night to comfort a friend who has just suffered a broken relationship. We stop on a busy highway to help a stranded motorist change a flat tire.

Proponents of universal egoism claim that everything we do, no matter how noble and beneficial to others, is really directed toward the ultimate goal of self-benefit. Some self-benefits of helping are obvious, as when we get material rewards and public praise or when we escape public censure. But even when we help in the absence of external rewards, we still may benefit. We may feel good about ourselves for being kind and caring or escape the guilt and shame we might feel if we did not help. We may do a friend a favor because we do not want to lose the friendship or because we expect to see the favor reciprocated. Seeing someone in distress may cause us to feel distress, and we may act to relieve that person's distress as an instrumental means to relieve our own.

Even heroes and martyrs can benefit from their acts of apparent selflessness. Consider the soldier who saves his comrades by diving on a grenade or a man who dies after relinquishing his place in a rescue craft. These persons may have acted to escape anticipated guilt and shame for letting others die. They may have acted to gain the admiration and praise of those left behind—or benefits in an anticipated afterlife. Perhaps they simply misjudged the situation, not thinking that their actions would cost them their lives. To suggest that heroic acts could be motivated by self-benefit may seem cynical, but the possibility must be faced if we are to responsibly address the question of whether altruism exists.

Altruism's proponents do not deny that the motivation for helping is often egoistic. However, they claim more. They claim that at least some of us, to some degree, under some circumstances, help with an ultimate goal of benefiting the person in need. They point out that even though we get self-benefits for helping, these benefits may not be the reason we helped. Rather than our ultimate goal (i.e., the state we are seeking), they may be unintended consequences.

Universal egoism has elegance and parsimony on its side in this debate. It is simpler to explain all human behavior in terms of self-benefit than to postulate a motivational pluralism in which both self-benefit and another's benefit can serve as ultimate goals. Perhaps for this reason, the majority view among Renaissance and post-Renaissance philosophers, as well as contemporary biologists, economists, and psychologists, is that we are, at heart, purely egoistic—we care for others only to the extent that their welfare affects ours (see Mansbridge, 1990; Wallach & Wallach, 1983, for reviews).

Elegance and parsimony are important criteria in developing scientific explanations. However, adequate and accurate explanations are even more important. If altruistic motivation is within the human repertoire, then the picture of who we are as a species and what we are capable of doing is quite different than if it is not. So we need to know if altruism exists, even if this knowledge flies in the face of conventional wisdom and plays havoc with our assumptions about human nature. If altruism exists, it should provide an important cornerstone for positive psychology.

Empathic Emotion: A Possible Source of Altruistic Motivation

In both earlier philosophical writings and in more recent psychological works, the most frequently mentioned possible source of altruistic motivation is an other-oriented emotional reaction to seeing another person in need. This emotional reaction has variously been called "empathy" (Batson, 1987; Krebs, 1975; Stotland, 1969), "sympathy" (Eisenberg & Strayer, 1987; Heider, 1958; Wispé, 1986, 1991), "sympathetic distress" (Hoffman, 1981), "tenderness" (McDougall, 1908), and "pity" or "compassion" (Hume, 1740/1896; Smith, 1759/1853). We shall call this other-oriented emotion "empathy." It has been named as a source—if not the source—of altruism by philosophers ranging from Aquinas to Rousseau to Hume to Adam Smith, and by psychologists ranging from William McDougall to contemporary researchers such as Hoffman, Krebs, and Batson.

Formally, we define empathy as "an other-oriented emotional response elicited by and congruent with the perceived welfare of someone else." Four points may help clarify this definition. First, "congruent" here refers to the valence of the emotion—positive when the perceived welfare of the other is positive, negative when the perceived welfare is negative—not to the specific content of the emotion. One might, for example, feel sad or sorry for someone who is upset and afraid. Second, although this definition is broad enough to include feeling empathic joy at another's good fortune (Smith, Keating, & Stotland, 1989; Stotland, 1969), it is the empathic emotion felt when another is perceived to be in need that is hypothesized to evoke altruistic motivation.

Third, empathic emotion as defined is not a single, discrete emotion but includes a whole constellation of feelings. It can include feelings of sympathy, compassion, soft-heartedness, tenderness, and the like—feelings that are inherently other-oriented. It can also include feelings of sorrow and sadness, of upset and distress, of concern and grief—feelings that can be, but are not always, other-oriented. Fourth, empathic feelings are other-oriented in the sense that they involve feeling *for* the other—feeling sorry for, distressed for, concerned for the other. It is also possible to feel sorrow, distress, or concern that is not oriented toward the other, as when something bad happens directly to us. Both other-oriented and self-oriented versions of these emotions may be described as feeling sorry or sad, upset or distressed, concerned or grieved. This breadth of usage invites confusion. The relevant psychological distinction must be based not on whether these terms are used but on whose welfare is the focus of the emotional response. Is one feeling sad, distressed, or concerned for the other, or feeling these emotions more directly?

The other-oriented emotional response we are calling empathy should be distinguished from a number of related but conceptually distinct psychological states, each of which has at one time or another also been called empathy. These include (a) inferring another's internal state, (b) assuming the posture of an observed other, (c) coming to feel as another person feels, (d) intuiting or projecting oneself into another's situation, (e) imagining how another is feeling, (f) imagining how one would think and feel in another's place, and (h) being personally upset by another person's suffering (see Batson, Ahmad, Lishner, & Tsang, 2002, for a more complete discussion of each of these states).

Other-oriented empathic emotion has often been thought to be the product of (a) perceiving another as in need and (b) adopting the other's perspective (i.e., imagining how the other is feeling). These two factors frequently have been combined to produce empathy in laboratory research (see Batson, 1991, for a partial review). However, when we encounter a person in need in daily life without having been instructed to imagine how that person feels, as we often do, the antecedents of empathy are likely to be (a) perceiving the other as in need and (b) noninstrumental valuing of the other's welfare. Valuing the other's welfare not only produces a lively response to events that affect this person's welfare, much as we might respond to events that affect our own welfare; it also produces vigilance. We are on the lookout for events that might affect this person's welfare. As a result, valuing the other leads us spontaneously to adopt his or her perspective. We are predisposed to imagine how this person thinks and feels about events because his or her pleasure and pain have become part of our own value structure.

Empathic Emotion as Situational, Not Dispositional

The empathic emotion that has been proposed to be a source of altruistic motivation is a response to the plight of a specific individual (or individuals) in a specific need situation. It does not refer to a general disposition or personality trait. There may well be individual differences in the ability and inclination to experience empathic emotion (see Davis, 1994, for a discussion), but attempts to measure these individual differences by standard retrospective self-report questionnaires seem suspect at best. Such questionnaires are more likely to tap a desire to see oneself and to be seen by others as empathic rather than to provide a valid measure of one's proclivity to actually be empathic.

Testing the Empathy–Altruism Hypothesis

The claim that feeling empathic emotion for someone in need evokes altruistic motivation to relieve that need has been called the "empathy–altruism hypothesis" (Batson, 1987, 1991). According to this hypothesis, the more the empathy felt for a person in need, the more is the altruistic motivation to see the need relieved.

Considerable evidence supports the idea that feeling empathy for a person in need leads to increased helping of that person (Coke, Batson, & McDavis, 1978; Dovidio, Allen, & Schroeder, 1990; Krebs, 1975; see Batson, 1991, and Eisenberg & Miller, 1987, for reviews). To observe an empathy–helping relationship, however, tells us nothing about the nature of the motivation that underlies this relationship. Increasing the other person's welfare could be an ultimate goal, an instrumental goal sought as a means to the ultimate goal of gaining one or more self-benefits, or both. That is, the motivation could be altruistic, egoistic, or both.

Three general classes of self-benefits can result from helping a person for whom one feels empathy. Helping enables one to (a) reduce one's empathic arousal, which may be experienced as aversive; (b) avoid possible social and self-punishments for failing to help; and (c) gain social and self-rewards for doing what is good and right. The empathy–altruism hypothesis does not deny that these self-benefits of empathy-induced helping exist. It claims, however, that with regard to the motivation evoked by empathy, these self-benefits are unintended consequences of reaching the ultimate goal of reducing the other's need. Advocates of egoistic alternatives to the empathy–altruism hypothesis disagree; they claim that one or more of these self-benefits is the ultimate goal of empathy-induced helping. In the past several decades, more than 30 experiments have tested these three egoistic alternatives to the empathy–altruism hypothesis.

1. Aversive-Arousal Reduction

The most frequently proposed egoistic explanation of the empathy-helping relationship is aversive-arousal reduction. According to this explanation, feeling empathy for someone who is suffering is unpleasant, and empathically aroused individuals help in order to eliminate their empathic feelings. Benefiting the person for whom empathy is felt is simply a means to this self-serving end.

Researchers have tested the aversive-arousal reduction explanation against the empathy–altruism hypothesis by varying the ease of escape from further exposure to a person in need without helping. Because empathic arousal is a result of witnessing the person's suffering, either terminating this suffering by helping or terminating exposure to it by escaping should reduce one's own aversive arousal. (To be effective, the escape must be psychological not simply physical—that is, escape from anticipated as well as experienced aversive arousal.) Escape does not, however, enable one to reach the altruistic goal of relieving the other's distress. Therefore, the aversive-arousal explanation predicts elimination of the empathy-helping relationship when escape is easy; the empathy–altruism hypothesis does not. Results of experiments testing these competing predictions have consistently supported the empathy–altruism hypothesis, not the aversive-arousal reduction explanation. These results cast serious doubt on this popular egoistic explanation (see Batson, 1991; Stocks, 2005, for reviews of these experiments).

2. Empathy-Specific Punishment

A second egoistic explanation claims that people are socialized to feel obligation to help those for whom they feel empathy; failing to help such a target results in feelings of shame and guilt. As a result, when people feel empathy, they are faced with impending social or self-censure beyond any general punishment associated with failure to help. They say to themselves, "What will others think—or what will I think of myself—if I don't help when I feel like this?" and then they help out of an egoistic desire to avoid these empathy-specific punishments. Once again, experiments designed to test this explanation have consistently failed to support it; results have instead consistently supported the empathy–altruism hypothesis (again, see Batson, 1991).

3. Empathy-Specific Reward

The third major egoistic explanation claims that people learn through socialization that special rewards in the form of praise, honor, and pride are attendant on helping a person for whom they feel empathy. As a result, when people feel empathy, they think of these rewards and help out of an egoistic desire to gain them.

A general form of this explanation has been tested in several experiments and received no support (studies 1 & 5, Batson et al., 1988; Batson & Weeks, 1996), but two variations have been proposed for which at least some support has been claimed. Best known is the negative-state relief explanation proposed by Cialdini et al. (1987), who suggested that the empathy experienced when witnessing another person's suffering is a negative affective state—a state of temporary sadness or sorrow—and the person feeling empathy helps in order to relieve this negative state.

At first glance, this negative-state explanation may appear to be the same as the aversive-arousal reduction explanation. Both explanations begin with the proposition that feeling empathy for someone in need involves a negative affective state. Yet, from this common starting point, they diverge. The aversive-arousal reduction explanation claims that the goal of helping is to eliminate the negative state; the negative-state relief explanation claims that the goal of helping is to gain mood-enhancing self-rewards that one has learned are associated with helping.

Although the negative-state relief explanation received some initial support (Cialdini et al., 1987; Schaller & Cialdini, 1988), subsequent researchers have found that this support was likely due to procedural artifacts (e.g., distractions). Experiments avoiding these artifacts have consistently supported the empathy–altruism hypothesis (Batson et al., 1989; Dovidio et al., 1990; Schroeder, Dovidio, Sibicky, Matthews, & Allen, 1988). It now seems clear that the motivation to help evoked by empathy is not directed toward the egoistic goal of negative-state relief.

A second variation on the empathy-specific reward explanation was proposed by Smith et al. (1989). They hypothesized that, rather than helping to gain the rewards of seeing oneself or being seen by others as a helpful person, empathically aroused individuals help in order to feel joy at the needy individual's relief: "It is proposed that the prospect of empathic joy, conveyed by feedback from the help recipient, is essential to the special tendency of empathic witnesses to help. . . . The empathically concerned witness ... helps in order to be happy" (Smith et al., 1989, p. 641).

Some early self-report data were supportive, but more rigorous experimental evidence has failed to support this empathic–joy hypothesis. Instead, experimental results have consistently supported the empathy–altruism hypothesis (Batson et al., 1991; Smith et al., 1989). The empathic–joy hypothesis, like other versions of the empathy-specific reward explanation, seems unable to account for the empathy–helping relationship.

A Tentative Conclusion

Reviewing the empathy–altruism research, as well as some recent literature in sociology, economics, political science, and biology, Piliavin and Charng (1990) observed:

> There appears to be a "paradigm shift" away from the earlier position that behavior that appears to be altruistic must, under closer scrutiny, be revealed as reflecting egoistic motives. Rather, theory and data now being advanced are more compatible with the view that true altruism—acting with the goal of benefiting another—does exist and is a part of human nature. (p. 27)

Pending new evidence or a plausible new egoistic explanation of the existing evidence, this observation seems correct. It appears that the empathy–altruism hypothesis should—tentatively—be accepted as true.

Other Possible Sources of Altruistic Motivation

Several sources of altruistic motivation other than empathic emotion have been proposed, including an "altruistic personality" (Oliner & Oliner, 1988), principled moral reasoning (Kohlberg, 1976), and internalized prosocial values (Staub, 1974, 1989). There is some evidence that each of these potential sources is associated with increased motivation to help, but it is not yet clear that this motivation is altruistic. It may be, or it may be an instrumental means to the egoistic ultimate goals of maintaining one's positive self-concept or avoiding guilt (Batson, 1991; Batson, Bolen, Cross, & Neuringer-Benefiel, 1986; Carlo, Eisenberg, Troyer, Switzer, & Speer, 1991; Eisenberg et al., 1989). More and better research exploring these possibilities is needed.

Two Other Possible Prosocial Motives

Thinking beyond the egoism–altruism debate that has been a focus of attention and contention for the past three decades, there may be other forms of prosocial motivation for which the ultimate goal is neither to benefit self nor to benefit another individual. Two forms seem especially worthy of consideration: collectivism and principlism.

Collectivism

"Collectivism" is motivation to benefit a particular group as a whole. The ultimate goal is to increase the welfare of the group not to increase one's own welfare or that of specific others. Robyn Dawes and his colleagues put it succinctly: "Not me or thee but we" (Dawes, van de Kragt, & Orbell, 1988). They suggested that collectivist motivation is a product of group identity (Tajfel, 1981; Turner, 1987).

As with altruism, what looks like collectivism actually may be a subtle form of egoism. Perhaps attention to group welfare is simply an expression of enlightened self-interest. After all, if one recognizes that ignoring group needs and the public good in headlong pursuit of self-benefit will lead to less self-benefit in the long run, then one may decide to benefit the group as a means to maximize overall self-benefit. Certainly, appeals to enlightened self-interest are commonly used by politicians and social activists to encourage response to societal needs: They warn of the long-term consequences for oneself and one's children of pollution and squandering natural resources; they remind that if the plight of the poor becomes too severe, the well-off may face revolution. Such appeals seem to assume that collectivism is simply a form of egoism.

Principlism

Most moral philosophers argue for the importance of a prosocial motive other than egoism. Most since Kant (1785/1898) shun altruism and collectivism as well. Philosophers reject appeals to altruism, especially empathy-induced altruism, because feelings of empathy, sympathy, and compassion are judged to be too fickle and too circumscribed. Empathy is not felt for everyone in need, at least not in the same degree. They reject appeals to collectivism because group interest is bounded by the limits of the group. Collectivism not only permits but may even encourage doing harm to those outside the group. Given these problems with altruism and collectivism, moral philosophers typically advocate prosocial motivation with an ultimate goal of upholding a universal and impartial moral principle, such as justice (Rawls, 1971). This moral motivation has been called "principlism" (Batson, 1994).

As with altruism and collectivism, we need to understand the nature of principlism as a prosocial motive. Is acting with an ultimate goal of upholding a moral principle possible, or do we act in accord with moral principles only as an instrumental means to reach the ultimate goal of self-benefit? Certainly, there are conspicuous self-benefits to be gained from acting morally. One can gain the social and self-rewards of being seen and seeing oneself as a good person. One also can avoid the social and self-punishments of shame and guilt for failing to do the right thing. As Freud (1930) suggested, society may inculcate moral principles in the young in order to bridle their antisocial impulses by making it in their best personal interest to act morally (also see Campbell, 1975).

If the desire to uphold justice (or some other moral principle) is simply an instrumental goal on the way to the ultimate goal of self-benefit, then this desire is a subtle and sophisticated form of egoism. Alternatively, if upholding the principle is an ultimate goal and ensuing self-benefits are unintended consequences, then principlism can be considered a fourth type of prosocial motivation, independent of egoism, altruism, and collectivism.

Toward a General Model of Prosocial Motivation

Staub (1989) and Schwartz (1992) have for many years emphasized the importance of values as determinants of prosocial behavior. Batson (1994) has proposed a general model that links prosocial values and motives: The value underlying egoism is enhanced personal welfare; the value underlying altruism is the enhanced welfare of one or more individuals as individuals; the value underlying collectivism is enhanced group welfare; and the value underlying principlism is upholding a moral principle. Four experiments have provided evidence for the predicted link between empathic emotion—a source of altruistic motivation—and valuing another individual's welfare (Batson, Turk, Shaw, & Klein, 1995); the other value–motive links await test.

Prosocial values are usually assumed to be mutually supportive and cooperative; concerns for the welfare of others and of society are assumed to be moral (Hoffman, 1989; Staub, 1989). If, however, the different values evoke different ultimate goals and therefore different motives, they may at times conflict rather than cooperate. For example, concern for the welfare of a specific other person (altruism) may conflict not only with self-interest but also with concern for the welfare of the group as a whole (collectivism) or concern to uphold a moral principle (principlism). Evidence of such conflicts has been

found (Batson, Batson et al., 1995; Batson, Klein, Highberger, & Shaw, 1995; Batson et al., 1999).

To entertain the possibility of multiple prosocial motives (egoism, altruism, collectivism, and principlism) based on multiple prosocial values (self, other, group, principle) begs for a better understanding of cognitive representation of the self–other relationship. Several representations have been proposed. Concern for another's welfare may be a product of (a) a sense of we-ness based on cognitive unit formation or identification with the other's situation (Hornstein, 1982; Lerner, 1982); (b) the self expanding to incorporate aspects of the other (Aron & Aron, 1986); (c) responding to aspects of the self seen in the other (Cialdini, Brown, Lewis, Luce, & Neuberg, 1997); (d) empathic feeling for the other, who remains distinct from self (Batson & Shaw, 1991; Jarymowicz, 1992); (e) the self being redefined at a group level, where me and thee become interchangeable parts of a self that is we (Dawes et al., 1988; Turner, 1987); or (f) the self dissolving in devotion to something outside itself, whether another person, a group, or a principle (James, 1910/1982).

Most of these proposals seem plausible, but not all can be true, at least not at the same time. Based on research to date, it appears that neither empathic feelings nor their effect on helping are a product of any of the various forms of self–other merging or overlap—we-ness, self-expansion, self-projection, or group-level self-definition (Batson, Sager et al., 1997; Cialdini et al., 1997). Recent neuroimaging research further supports this conclusion (e.g., Jackson, Meltzoff, & Decety, 2005; Lamm, Batson, & Decety, 2007; Lawrence et al., 2006).

In apparent contradiction to this conclusion, Maner et al. (2002) claimed to provide evidence that once the effects of self–other overlap and negative affect are removed, there is no longer a positive relation between empathy and helping. In their research, however, they included only empathic emotions in their global measure of negative affect (feeling "sympathetic," "compassionate," and "soft-hearted," as well as three sadness items that in response to the need situation they used likely tapped feeling sadness *for* the person in need—"sad," "low-spirited," and "heavy-hearted"). As a result, when controlling for negative affect, they actually removed the effect of empathic feelings. It is not very surprising (and also not very informative) to find that once the effect of empathy is removed, there is no longer a relation between empathy and helping. More and better research is needed if we are to understand the role various cognitive representations of the self–other relationship play in responses to others in need.

Theoretical Implications of the Empathy–Altruism Relationship

Returning to the empathy-altruism relationship, it is clear that this relationship has broad theoretical implications. Universal egoism—the assumption that all human behavior is ultimately directed toward self-benefit—has long dominated not only psychology but other social and behavioral sciences as well (Campbell, 1975; Mansbridge, 1990; Wallach & Wallach, 1983). If individuals feeling empathy act, at least in part, with an ultimate goal of increasing the welfare of another, then the assumption of universal egoism must be replaced by a more complex view of motivation that allows for altruism as well as egoism. Such a shift in our view of motivation requires, in turn, a revision of our underlying assumptions about human nature and human potential. It implies that we humans may be more social than we have thought: Other people can be more to us than sources of information, stimulation, and reward as we each seek our own welfare. We have the potential to care about their welfare as well.

The empathy–altruism relationship also forces us to face the question of why empathic feelings exist. What evolutionary function might they serve? Admittedly speculative, the most plausible answer relates empathic feelings to parenting among higher mammals, in which offspring live for some time in a very vulnerable state (Bell, 2001; de Waal, 1996; Hoffman, 1981; McDougall, 1908; Zahn-Waxler & Radke-Yarrow, 1990). Were parents not intensely interested in the welfare of their progeny, these species would quickly die out. Empathic feelings for offspring and the resulting altruistic motivation may promote one's reproductive potential not by increasing the number of offspring but by increasing the chance of their survival.

Of course, empathic feelings extend well beyond one's own children. People can feel empathy for a wide range of targets (including nonhumans), as long as there is no preexisting antipathy (Batson, 1991; Batson, Lishner, Cook, & Sawyer, 2005; Krebs, 1975; Shelton & Rogers, 1981). From an evolutionary perspective, this extension is usually attributed to cognitive generalization whereby one "adopts" others, making it possible to evoke the primitive and fundamental impulse to care for progeny when these adopted others are in need (Batson, 1987; Hoffman, 1981; MacLean, 1973). Such cognitive generalization may be facilitated by human cognitive capacity, including symbolic thought and the lack of evolutionary advantage for sharp discrimination of empathic feelings in early human small hunter-gatherer bands. In these bands, those in need were often one's children or close kin, and one's own welfare was tightly tied to the welfare even of those who were not close kin (Hoffman, 1981).

William McDougall (1908) long ago described these links in his depiction of the "parental instinct." As with all McDougall's theorized instincts, the parental instinct involved cognitive, affective, and conative (motivational) components: Cues of distress from one's offspring, including cognitively adopted offspring (e.g., a pet), evoke what McDougall called "the tender emotion" (empathy), which in turn produces altruistic motivation. Although few psychologists would wish to return to McDougall's emphasis on instincts, his attempt to integrate (a) valuing based on cognitive generalization of the perception of offspring in distress; (b) empathic (sympathetic, compassionate, tender) emotional response; and (c) goal-directed altruistic motivation seems at least as much a blueprint for the future as a curio from the past.

Practical Implications of the Empathy–Altruism Relationship

The empathy–altruism relationship also has broad practical implications. Given the power of empathic feelings to evoke altruistic motivation, people may sometimes suppress or avoid these feelings. Loss of the capacity to feel empathy for clients may be a factor, possibly a central one, in the experience of burnout among case workers in the helping professions (Maslach, 1982). Aware of the extreme effort involved in helping or the impossibility of helping effectively, these case workers—or nurses caring for terminal patients, or even pedestrians confronted by the homeless—may try to avoid feeling empathy in order to avoid the resulting altruistic motivation (Shaw, Batson, & Todd, 1994; Stotland, Mathews, Sherman, Hansson, & Richardson, 1978).

Nor should we expect empathy-induced altruism to always produce prosocial effects. It may lead one to increase the welfare of those for whom empathy is felt at the expense of other potential prosocial goals. Research suggests that individuals are willing to act against the greater collective good or to violate their own moral principles of fairness and justice if doing so will benefit a person for whom empathy is felt (Batson et al., 1999; Batson, Batson et al., 1995; Batson, Klein et al., 1995).

More positively, research suggests that empathically aroused individuals may focus on the long-term welfare rather than just the short-term welfare of those in need, providing more sensitive care (Sibicky, Schroeder, & Dovidio, 1995). The empathy–altruism relationship also makes possible the use of empathy-based socialization practices to enhance prosocial behavior. Empathy-based socialization is very different from current practices directed toward inhibition of egoistic impulses through shaping, modeling, and internalized guilt (see Batson, 1991, for some suggestions). Further, therapeutic programs built around facilitating altruistic impulses by encouraging perspective taking and empathic feelings might enable individuals to develop more satisfactory interpersonal relations, especially long-term relationships. There may be personal health benefits as well (Luks, 1988; Williams, 1989).

At a societal level, experiments have indicated that empathy-induced altruism can be used to improve attitudes toward stigmatized outgroups. Empathy inductions have been used to improve racial attitudes, as well as attitudes and action toward people with AIDS, the homeless, and even convicted murderers and drug dealers (Batson, Chang, Orr, & Rowland, 2002; Batson, Polycarpou et al., 1997; Dovidio, Gaertner, & Johnson, 1999). Empathy-induced altruism has also been found to increase cooperation in a competitive situation (a Prisoner's Dilemma)—even when one knows that the person for whom one feels empathy has acted competitively (Batson & Ahmad, 2001; Batson & Moran, 1999).

Conclusion

Why do people help others, often at considerable cost to themselves? What does this behavior tell us about the human capacity to care, about the degree of interconnectedness among us, about how social an animal we humans are? These classic philosophical questions have resurfaced in the behavioral and social sciences in the past several decades. Psychological research has focused on the empathy–altruism hypothesis, which claims that empathic emotion produces altruistic motivation—motivation with the ultimate goal of increasing another's welfare.

Results of the over 30 experiments designed to test this hypothesis against various egoistic alternatives have proved remarkably supportive, leading to

the tentative conclusion that feeling empathy for a person in need does indeed evoke altruistic motivation to see that need relieved. Sources of altruistic motivation other than empathy also have been proposed, but as yet, there is not compelling research evidence to support these proposals.

Thinking beyond the egoism–altruism debate, two additional forms of prosocial motivation deserve consideration: collectivism and principlism. Collectivism—motivation with the ultimate goal of benefiting some group or collective as a whole—has been claimed to result from group identity. Principlism—motivation with the ultimate goal of upholding some moral principle—has long been advocated by religious teachers and moral philosophers. Whether either is a separate form of motivation, independent of and irreducible to egoism, is not yet clear. Research done to test the independent status of empathy-induced altruism may serve as a useful model for future research assessing the independent status of collectivism and principlism.

We know more now than a few years ago about why people help. As a result, we know more about human motivation, and even about human nature. These are substantial gains. Still, many questions remain about the emotional and motivational resources that could be tapped to build a more caring, humane society. Providing answers to these questions is, we believe, an important agenda item for positive psychology.

Three Questions for the Future

1. If empathic concern produces altruistic motivation (as the empathy–altruism hypothesis claims), then what produces empathic concern?

2. Can we give a plausible account of the evolution of empathy-induced altruism? (Inclusive fitness, reciprocal altruism, and group selection all fail to do so.)

3. Can we develop practical procedures that use what we have learned about the psychological implications of the empathy–altruism hypothesis to create a more humane, caring society?

References and Recommended Reading

Aron, A., & Aron, E. N. (1986). *Love and the expansion of self: Understanding attraction and satisfaction.* Washington, DC: Hemisphere.

Batson, C. D. (1987). Prosocial motivation: Is it ever truly altruistic? In L. Berkowitz (Ed.), *Advances in experimental social psychology* (Vol. 20, pp. 65–122). New York: Academic Press.

Batson, C. D. (1991). *The altruism question: Toward a social-psychological answer.* Hillsdale, NJ: Erlbaum.

Batson, C. D. (1994). Why act for the public good? Four answers. *Personality and Social Psychology Bulletin, 20*, 603–610.

Batson, C. D., & Ahmad, N. (2001). Empathy-induced altruism in a Prisoner's Dilemma II: What if the target of empathy has defected? *European Journal of Social Psychology, 31*, 25–36.

Batson, C. D., Ahmad, N., Lishner, D. A., & Tsang, J. (2002). Empathy and altruism. In C. R. Snyder & S. J. Lopez (Eds.), *Handbook of positive psychology* (pp. 485–498). New York: Oxford University Press.

Batson, C. D., Ahmad, N., Yin, J., Bedell, S. J., Johnson, J. W., Templin, C. M., et al. (1999). Two threats to the common good: Self-interested egoism and empathy-induced altruism. *Personality and Social Psychology Bulletin, 25*, 3–16.

Batson, C. D., Batson, J. G., Griffitt, C. A., Barrientos, S., Brandt, J. R., Sprengelmeyer, P., et al. (1989). Negative-state relief and the empathy-altruism hypothesis. *Journal of Personality and Social Psychology, 56*, 922–933.

Batson, C. D., Batson, J. G., Slingsby, J. K., Harrell, K. L., Peekna, H. M., & Todd, R. M. (1991). Empathic joy and the empathy-altruism hypothesis. *Journal of Personality and Social Psychology, 61*, 413–426.

Batson, C. D., Batson, J. G., Todd, R. M., Brummett, B. H., Shaw, L. L., & Aldeguer, C. M. R. (1995). Empathy and the collective good: Caring for one of the others in a social dilemma. *Journal of Personality and Social Psychology, 68*, 619–631.

Batson, C. D., Bolen, M. H., Cross, J. A., & Neuringer-Benefiel, H. E. (1986). Where is the altruism in the altruistic personality? *Journal of Personality and Social Psychology, 50*, 212–220.

Batson, C. D., Chang, J., Orr, R., & Rowland, J. (2002). Empathy, attitudes, and action: Can feeling for a member of a stigmatized group motivate one to help the group? *Personality and Social Psychology Bulletin, 28*, 1656–1666.

Batson, C. D., Dyck, J. L., Brandt, J. R., Batson, J. G., Powell, A. L., McMaster, M. R., et al. (1988). Five studies testing two new egoistic alternatives to the empathy-altruism hypothesis. *Journal of Personality and Social Psychology, 55*, 52–77.

Batson, C. D., Klein, T. R., Highberger, L., & Shaw, L. L. (1995). Immorality from empathy-induced altruism: When compassion and justice conflict. *Journal of Personality and Social Psychology, 68*, 1042–1054.

Batson, C. D., Lishner, D. A., Cook, J., & Sawyer, S. (2005). Similarity and nurturance: Two possible sources of empathy for strangers. *Basic and Applied Social Psychology, 27*, 15–25.

Batson, C. D., & Moran, T. (1999). Empathy-induced altruism in a Prisoner's Dilemma. *European Journal of Social Psychology, 29*, 909–924.

Batson, C. D., Polycarpou, M. P., Harmon-Jones, E., Imhoff, H. J., Mitchener, E. C., Bednar, L. L., et al. (1997). Empathy and attitudes: Can feeling for a member of a stigmatized group improve feelings toward the group? *Journal of Personality and Social Psychology, 72*, 105–118.

Batson, C. D., Sager, K., Garst, E., Kang, M., Rubchinsky, K., & Dawson, K. (1997). Is empathy-induced helping due to self-other merging? *Journal of Personality and Social Psychology, 73*, 495–509.

Batson, C. D., & Shaw, L. L. (1991). Evidence for altruism: Toward a pluralism of prosocial motives. *Psychological Inquiry, 2*, 107–122.

Batson, C. D., Turk, C. L., Shaw, L. L., & Klein, T. R. (1995). Information function of empathic emotion: Learning that we value the other's welfare. *Journal of Personality and Social Psychology, 68*, 300–313.

Batson, C. D., & Weeks, J. L. (1996). Mood effects of unsuccessful helping: Another test of the empathy-altruism hypothesis. *Personality and Social Psychology Bulletin, 22*, 148–157.

Bell, D. C. (2001). Evolution of parental caregiving. *Personality and Social Psychology Review, 5*, 216–229.

Campbell, D. T. (1975). On the conflicts between biological and social evolution and between psychology and moral tradition. *American Psychologist, 30*, 1103–1126.

Carlo, G., Eisenberg, N., Troyer, D., Switzer, G., & Speer, A. L. (1991). The altruistic personality: In what contexts is it apparent? *Journal of Personality and Social Psychology, 61*, 450–458.

Cialdini, R. B., Brown, S. L., Lewis, B. P., Luce, C., & Neuberg, S. L. (1997). Reinterpreting the empathy-altruism relationship: When one into one equals oneness. *Journal of Personality and Social Psychology, 73*, 481–494.

Cialdini, R. B., Schaller, M., Houlihan, D., Arps, K., Fultz, J., & Beaman, A. L. (1987). Empathy-based helping: Is it selflessly or selfishly motivated? *Journal of Personality and Social Psychology, 52*, 749–758.

Coke, J. S., Batson, C. D., & McDavis, K. (1978). Empathic mediation of helping: A two-stage model. *Journal of Personality and Social Psychology, 36*, 752–766.

Davis, M. H. (1994). *Empathy: A social psychological approach*. Madison, WI: Brown & Benchmark.

Dawes, R., van de Kragt, A. J. C., & Orbell, J. M. (1988). Not me or thee but we: The importance of group identity in eliciting cooperation in dilemma situations: Experimental manipulations. *Acta Psychologica, 68*, 83–97.

de Waal, F. B. M. (1996). *Good natured: The origins of right and wrong in humans and other animals*. Cambridge, MA: Harvard University Press.

Dovidio, J. F., Allen, J. L., & Schroeder, D. A. (1990). The specificity of empathy-induced helping: Evidence for altruistic motivation. *Journal of Personality and Social Psychology, 59*, 249–260.

Dovidio, J. F., & Gaertner, S. L., & Johnson, J. D. (1999, October). *New directions in prejudice and prejudice reduction: The role of cognitive representations and affect*. Paper presented at the annual meeting of the Society of Experimental Social Psychology, St. Louis, MO.

Eisenberg, N., & Miller, P. (1987). Empathy and prosocial behavior. *Psychological Bulletin, 101*, 91–119.

Eisenberg, N., Miller, P. A., Schaller, M., Fabes, R. A., Fultz, J., Shell, R., et al. (1989). The role of sympathy and altruistic personality traits in helping: A re-examination. *Journal of Personality, 57*, 41–67.

Eisenberg, N., & Strayer, J. (Eds.) (1987). *Empathy and its development*. New York: Cambridge University Press.

Freud, S. (1930). *Civilization and its discontents* (Trans. J. Riviere). London: Hogarth.

Heider, F. (1958). *The psychology of interpersonal relations*. New York: Wiley.

Hoffman, M. L. (1981). Is altruism part of human nature? *Journal of Personality and Social Psychology, 40*, 121–137.

Hoffman, M. L. (1989). Empathic emotions and justice in society. *Social Justice Research, 3*, 283–311.

Hornstein, H. A. (1982). Promotive tension: Theory and research. In V. Derlega & J. Grzelak (Eds.), *Cooperation and helping behavior: Theories and research* (pp. 229–248). New York: Academic Press.

Hume, D. (1740/1896). *A treatise of human nature* (Ed. L. A. Selby-Bigge). Oxford: Oxford University Press.

Jackson, P. L., Meltzoff, A. N., & Decety, J. (2005). How do we perceive the pain of others?: A window into the neural processes involved in empathy. *NeuroImage, 24*, 771–779.

James, W. (1910/1982). The moral equivalent of war. In F. H. Burkhardt (Ed.), *The works of William James: Essays in religion and morality* (pp. 162–173). Cambridge, MA: Harvard University Press.

Jarymowicz, M. (1992). Self, we, and other(s): Schemata, distinctiveness, and altruism. In P. M. Oliner, S. P. Oliner, L. Baron, L. A. Blum, D. L. Krebs, & M. Z. Smolenska (Eds.), *Embracing the other: Philosophical, psychological, and historical perspectives on altruism* (pp. 194–212). New York: New York University Press.

Kant, I. (1785/1898). *Kant's Critique of Practical Reason and other works on the theory of ethics* (4th ed., Trans. T. K. Abbott). New York: Longmans, Green & Co.

Kohlberg, L. (1976). Moral stages and moralization: The cognitive-developmental approach. In T. Lickona (Ed.), *Moral development and behavior: Theory, research, and social issues* (pp. 31–53). New York: Holt, Rinehart, & Winston.

Krebs, D. L. (1975). Empathy and altruism. *Journal of Personality and Social Psychology, 32*, 1134–1146.

Lamm, C., Batson, C. D., & Decety, J. (2007). The neural substrate of human empathy: Effects of perspective taking and cognitive appraisal. *Journal of Cognitive Neuroscience, 19*, 42–58.

Lawrence, E. J., Shaw, P., Giampietro, V. P., Surguladze, S., Brammer, M. J., & David, A. S. (2006). The role of "shared representations" in social perception and empathy: An fMRI study. *NeuroImage, 29*, 1173–1184.

Lerner, M. J. (1982). The justice motive in human relations and the economic model of man: A radical analysis of facts and fictions. In V. J. Derlega & J. Grzelak (Eds.), *Cooperation and helping behavior: Theories and research* (pp. 249–278). New York: Academic Press.

Luks, A. (1988). Helper's high. *Psychology Today, 22*(10), 39–42.

McDougall, W. (1908). *An introduction to social psychology*. London: Methuen.

MacLean, P. D. (1973). *A triune concept of the brain and behavior*. Toronto, ON: University of Toronto Press.

Maner, J. K., Luce, C. L., Neuberg, S. L., Cialdini, R. B., Brown, S., & Sagarin, B. J. (2002). The effects of perspective taking on helping: Still no evidence for altruism. *Personality and Social Psychology Bulletin, 28*, 1601–1610.

Mansbridge, J. J. (Ed.). (1990). *Beyond self-interest*. Chicago: University of Chicago Press.

Maslach, C. (1982). *Burnout: The cost of caring*. Englewood Cliffs, NJ: Prentice-Hall.

Oliner, S. P., & Oliner, P. M. (1988). *The altruistic personality: Rescuers of Jews in Nazi Europe*. New York: The Free Press.

Piliavin, J. A., & Charng, H.-W. (1990). Altruism: A review of recent theory and research. *American Sociological Review, 16*, 27–65.

Rawls, J. (1971). *A theory of justice*. Cambridge, MA: Harvard University Press.

Schaller, M., & Cialdini, R. B. (1988). The economics of empathic helping: Support for a mood-management motive. *Journal of Experimental Social Psychology, 24*, 163–181.

Schroeder, D. A., Dovidio, J. F., Sibicky, M. E., Matthews, L. L., & Allen, J. L. (1988). Empathy and helping behavior: Egoism or altruism? *Journal of Experimental Social Psychology, 24*, 333–353.

Schwartz, S. H. (1992). Universals in the content and structure of values: Theoretical advances and empirical tests in 20 countries. In M. P. Zanna (Ed.), *Advances in experimental social psychology* (Vol. 25, pp. 1–65). San Diego, CA: Academic Press.

Shaw, L. L., Batson, C. D., & Todd, R. M. (1994). Empathy avoidance: Forestalling feeling for another in order to escape the motivational consequences. *Journal of Personality and Social Psychology, 67*, 879–887.

Shelton, M. L., & Rogers, R. W. (1981). Fear-arousing and empathy-arousing appeals to help: The pathos of persuasion. *Journal of Applied Social Psychology, 11*, 366–378.

Sibicky, M. E., Schroeder, D. A., & Dovidio, J. F. (1995). Empathy and helping: Considering the consequences of intervention. *Basic and Applied Social Psychology, 16*, 435–453.

Smith, A. (1759/1853). *The theory of moral sentiments*. London: Alex Murray.

Smith, K. D., Keating, J. P., & Stotland, E. (1989). Altruism reconsidered: The effect of denying feedback on a victim's status to empathic witnesses. *Journal of Personality and Social Psychology, 57*, 641–650.

Staub, E. (1974). Helping a distressed person: Social, personality, and stimulus determinants. In L. Berkowitz (Ed.), *Advances in experimental social psychology* (Vol. 7, pp. 293–341). New York: Academic Press.

Staub, E. (1989). Individual and societal (group) values in a motivational perspective and their role in benevolence and harmdoing. In N. Eisenberg, J. Reykowski, & E. Staub (Eds.), *Social and moral values: Individual and societal perspectives* (pp. 45–61). Hillsdale, NJ: Erlbaum.

Stocks, E. L. (2005). Empathy and the motivation to help: Is the ultimate goal to relieve the victim's suffering or to relieve one's own? Unpublished PhD dissertation, University of Kansas.

Stotland, E. (1969). Exploratory investigations of empathy. In L. Berkowitz (Ed.), *Advances in experimental social psychology* (Vol. 4, pp. 271–313). New York: Academic Press.

Stotland, E., Mathews, K. E., Sherman, S. E., Hansson, R. O., & Richardson, B. Z. (1978). *Empathy, fantasy, and helping*. Beverly Hills, CA: Sage.

Tajfel, H. (1981). *Human groups and social categories: Studies in social psychology*. Cambridge: Cambridge University Press.

Turner, J. C. (1987). *Rediscovering the social group: A self-categorization theory*. London: Basil Blackwell.

Wallach, M. A., & Wallach, L. (1983). *Psychology's sanction for selfishness: The error of egoism in theory and therapy*. San Francisco: W. H. Freeman.

Williams, R. (1989). *The trusting heart: Great news about type A behavior*. New York: Random House.

Wispé, L. (1986). The distinction between sympathy and empathy: To call forth a concept a word is needed. *Journal of Personality and Social Psychology, 50*, 314–321.

Wispé, L. (1991). *The psychology of sympathy*. New York: Plenum.

Zahn-Waxler, C., & Radke-Yarrow, M. (1990). The origins of empathic concern. *Motivation and Emotion, 14*, 107–130.

Forgiveness

Michael E. McCullough, Lindsey M. Root, Benjamin A. Tabak, *and* Charlotte van Oyen Witvliet

Abstract

We posit that humans have a propensity to forgive, under certain circumstances, that is every bit as intrinsic to human nature as the tendency to seek revenge when harmed. The human tendency to forgive is reliably elicited by social and environmental factors that lead victims to view their transgressors as worthy of care, potentially valuable to the victim in the future, and safe. The victim's personality characteristics may also influence the likelihood of viewing transgressors as careworthy, valuable, and safe. Using these categories, we review recent developments in the scientific study of the social and personality factors that promote forgiveness. We also review developments in the measurement of forgiveness, the links of forgiveness to health and well-being, and quantitative evidence regarding the effectiveness of interventions for promoting forgiveness.

Keywords: conflict, evolution, forgiveness, health, revenge

Human nature—as understood through the lenses of evolutionary biology, moral philosophy, and theology—contains the capacity for evil and for good, for harming and for helping, and for offending or retaliating and for forgiving or reconciling. Most people can recall a time within the previous year when they strongly desired vengeance against someone who harmed them. Such revenge desire has an appetitive feeling, which when satisfied, yields contentment (Crombag, Rassin, & Horselenberg, 2003; de Quervain et al., 2004), although this short-term contentment may be offset by its tendency to create physiological arousal and subjective distress (Witvliet, Ludwig, & VanderLaan, 2001). Nevertheless, revenge occurs across species (Aureli, Cozzolino, Cordischi, & Scucchi, 1992; Dugatkin, 1988), and people in virtually every culture have used revenge to control aggression (Daly & Wilson, 1988) and to prompt cooperation among unrelated individuals (Axelrod, 1984; Boyd & Richerson, 1992)—evidence hinting that the desire for revenge is the result of adaptive design (Schmitt & Pilcher, 2004).

Rather than becoming locked in interminable cycles of revenge and counter-revenge, however, people often seek to overcome social conflict and aggression in more positive ways. Peacemaking is an active process—not simply an absence of aggression (Fry, 2006). Humans and other social animals often work actively to restore positive, cooperative relationships with some of the individuals in their social networks following aggression and conflict (Aureli & de Waal, 2000). One of the tools for doing so is forgiveness. Some evidence suggests that the capacity to forgive may arise by natural selection (Hruschka & Henrich, 2006; Nowak & Sigmund, 1993). We hypothesize that the capacity to forgive is every bit as intrinsic to human nature as our penchant for revenge (McCullough, 2008).

Scientific theory and research on forgiveness have burgeoned in the last decade. This chapter addresses scientific developments on this topic since the chapter we wrote for the previous edition of this handbook (McCullough & Witvliet, 2000).

Measuring Forgiveness

Forgiveness involves overcoming one's relationship-destructive responses toward a transgressor with relationship-appropriate prosocial responses. In the years since our earlier review, self-report scales for measuring forgiveness for specific offenses and individual differences in the disposition to forgive have remained popular (e.g., McCullough et al., 1998; Rye et al., 2001; Subkoviak, Enright, Wu, & Gassin, 1995). A revision to the TRIM has added a benevolence scale to account for prosocial motivation in addition to the previous scales assessing levels of revenge and avoidance (McCullough, Root, & Cohen, 2006). Newer scales include the Heartland Forgiveness Scale (Thompson et al., 2005), the Tendency to Forgive Scale (Brown, 2003), and a Marital Functioning Scale (Gordon & Baucom, 2003). In addition to a single measurement period, forgiveness of a specific transgression can be measured as a time-bound construct. This work uses multilevel modeling to describe the natural longitudinal trajectory of people's responses to a transgressor over time (McCullough, Fincham, & Tsang, 2003).

Measurement has also expanded to include implicit and behavioral indices. For example, Karremans, Van Lange, and Holland (2005) examined word stem tasks, pronoun choices, and charitable donations as correlates of forgiveness. Other approaches include the Prisoner's Dilemma and similar games (Axelrod, 1984), as well as asking participants to anonymously provide feedback about an offender and to report their willingness to do the offender a favor after a laboratory offense (Zechmeister, Garcia, Romero, & Vas, 2004). Investigation into the neural correlates of retaliation (de Quervain et al., 2004; Singer et al., 2006) has also begun.

Antecedents of Forgiveness

Researchers have made much progress in identifying variables that facilitate forgiveness. One way to organize these variables is to consider three basic psychological conditions that we theorize to play some role in motivating forgiveness: "careworthiness," "expected value," and "safety" (McCullough, 2008). Transgressors are "careworthy" when the victim perceives that the transgressor is an appropriate target for moral concern. Transgressors have expected value when a victim anticipates that the relationship will have future utility. Transgressors seem safe when they seem unwilling or unable to harm their victims again. Personality correlates of forgiveness also may influence forgiveness via their ability to influence perceived careworthiness, expected value, and safety.

Careworthiness

Forgiveness is likely built upon some of the same scaffolding used to generate care for others. For example, people more readily forgive people to whom they feel close and for whom they feel empathy (McCullough et al., 1998; McCullough, Worthington, & Rachal, 1997; Zechmeister & Romero, 2002). Empathy promotes a desire to reduce other people's suffering (Batson, Ahmad, Lishner, & Tsang, 2002) and likewise promotes forgiveness in relationships between coworkers, friends, and romantic partners, and even between perpetrators of crimes and their victims (Berry, Worthington, Wade, Witvliet, & Keifer, 2005; Eaton & Struthers, 2006). Likewise, empathy reduces the motivation to retaliate (Batson & Ahmad, 2001), perhaps by interfering with the brain's usual tendency to perceive revenge seeking as appetitive (Singer et al., 2006), and by interrupting the approach motivation that underlies efforts to retaliate (Harmon-Jones, Vaughn-Scott, Mohr, Sigelman, & Harmon-Jones, 2004).

Expected Value

When people have positive expectations for an upcoming social interaction, the brain signals that rewards are forthcoming (Knutson & Wimmer, 2006). The expectation of upcoming rewards, in turn, shapes how they treat their interaction partners. Relationships holding reward value (indexed by feelings of commitment) generate more motivation to forgive (Finkel, Rusbult, Kumashiro, & Hannon, 2002). The importance of expected value may explain why people tend to want some form of compensation prior to forgiving (Boehm, 1987; Bottom, Gibson, Daniels, & Murnighan, 2002): Compensation signals that a transgressor has the potential to be valuable to the victim in the future.

Safety

People more readily forgive people whom they trust and are less prone to forgive people who have harmed them deeply and therefore seem more dangerous (Hoyt, Fincham, McCullough, Maio, & Davila, 2005; McCullough & Hoyt, 2002). Trust and safety are enhanced when transgressors seem unwilling to harm again, such as when they have repented or expressed remorse (Bottom et al., 2002; Gold & Weiner, 2000). Transgressors' expressions of sympathy for a victim's suffering and a sincere desire to uphold a society's moral standards signal decreased risk of harming the victim again (Gold & Weiner, 2000; Nadler & Liviatan, 2006; Zechmeister et al., 2004). Displays like blushing, which apparently facilitate forgiveness after some transgressions (de Jong, Peters, & de Cremer, 2003), may serve a similar function by signaling an eagerness to distance oneself from one's previous transgressions. In a related vein, people more readily forgive transgressors whose behavior was unintentional, unavoidable, or committed without awareness of its potential negative consequences (Eaton & Struthers, 2006; Gordon, Burton, & Porter, 2004).

Another way to prompt the perception of safety is to create physical and emotional barriers preventing the transgressor from harming the victim, perhaps through intervening with justice or barring reconciliation. In those cases in which reconciliation accompanies forgiveness, reconciliation rituals sometimes involve the surrender of weapons (Boehm, 1987).

Forgiveness and Personality

Four personality predictors of forgiveness—neuroticism, agreeableness, narcissism, and religiousness—merit extended treatment here. To explain how such personality–forgiveness associations arise, personality traits (e.g., traits like neuroticism and agreeableness) can be conceptualized as filters that shape one's perceptions of the transgressor (McCullough & Hoyt, 2002)—particularly, perceptions of the transgressor's careworthiness, value, and safety.

For example, an explanation for the inverse relationship of neuroticism and forgiveness (Brose, Rye, Lutz-Zois, & Ross, 2005) is that neuroticism makes transgressions feel more severe (McCullough & Hoyt, 2002). When people feel as though they have already endured a lot of pain, they may view forgiveness as compromising their safety or requiring psychological energy they don't have. Furthermore, because neuroticism makes transgressions seem more painful, it may also limit perception that the relationship with the transgressor will have value in the future, which would make the prospect of a renewed relationship with the transgressor less motivating.

Agreeableness may make it easier for victims to experience empathy and trust for their transgressors, thereby making transgressors seem more careworthy

and safer (and therefore, more forgivable). In addition, highly agreeable people might anticipate that a relationship with a transgressor possesses future value. Depue and Morrone-Strupinsky (2005) argued that agreeableness (which they called "affiliation") arises from a neural architecture by which affiliative stimuli (e.g., neural representations of particular individuals) stimulate opioid release. By this reasoning, affiliative people may find it easier to forgive a transgressor because they are more likely to perceive that the relationship is likely to lead to future fulfillment. This may also help to explain why the "warmth" facet of extraversion, which measures the ability to derive pleasure from social interaction, has been linked with the propensity to forgive (Brose et al., 2005).

Narcissism is another personality variable that is negatively associated with forgiveness (Eaton, Struthers, & Santelli, 2006)—in particular, its entitlement facet (Exline, Baumeister, Bushman, Campbell, & Finkel, 2004). After a transgression, narcissistically entitled individuals require more punishment of the transgression and compensation prior to forgiving (Exline et al., 2004). Narcissists' unwillingness to forgive may be further exacerbated by the fact that they tend to denigrate the value and/or careworthiness of other people, and are more easily offended (McCullough, Emmons, Kilpatrick, & Mooney, 2003). These factors may conspire to cause narcissistically entitled people to perceive that forgiveness has many potential costs and few potential benefits.

Finally, self-reports of forgiveness have been consistently related to higher levels of religiousness (McCullough, Bono, & Root, 2005; Tsang, McCullough, & Hoyt, 2005). Recent research not only linked intrinsic religious motivation with lower scores on self-reported vengefulness (and extrinsic religious motivation was associated with higher levels), but also suggested that some aspects of traditional religiousness may be associated with behavioral retaliation (Greer, Berman, Varan, Bobrycki, & Watson, 2005).

Understandings of what forgiveness means and requires are profoundly shaped by people's core beliefs and values (Mahoney, Rye, & Pargament, 2005). On a broad scale, people who self-identify as religious—rather than "spiritual"—consistently score as having more forgiving personalities than those who self-identify as spiritual—rather than "religious" (DeShea, Tzou, Kang, & Matsuyuki, 2006). In comparing religions, Cohen, Malka, Rozin, and Cherfas (2006) found that Protestant

Christians and Jews differed in their understanding of and approaches to forgiveness, with Jews more likely to believe that some offenses are unforgivable, and to endorse theological reasons for this belief. Future investigations on the religion–forgiveness issue should probably examine not only self-reports but also behavioral measures and might do well to consider whether religion obtains its relations to forgiveness by influencing victims' perceptions of the transgressors careworthiness, expected value, and safety.

Associations of Forgiveness with Health and Well-Being

Forgiveness tends to be positively associated with psychological well-being, physical health, and desirable relationship outcomes (Worthington & Scherer, 2004). For example, people who tend to forgive others score lower on measures of anxiety, depression, and hostility (Brown, 2003; Thompson et al., 2005). People with a strong propensity to forgive (or a weak propensity to seek revenge when harmed by others) experience a reduced risk for nicotine dependence disorders, substance abuse disorders, depressive disorders, and several anxiety disorders (Kendler et al., 2003). Forgiveness has also been associated with better psychological well-being, operationalized as high positive emotion, low negative emotion, high satisfaction with life, and low self-reported physical health symptoms (Bono & McCullough, 2006).

Several recent studies have demonstrated that when people entertain forgiving imagery of a transgression they have suffered or describe such a transgression, they experience less cardiovascular reactivity (e.g., blood pressure and heart rate) than when they ruminate or entertain grudge-related imagery (Witvliet et al., 2001) or describe a transgression that they have not forgiven (Lawler et al., 2003).

Forgiveness might influence such outcomes via several mechanisms. Witvliet and McCullough (2007) have presented a theory of forgiveness and emotion that linked attention, motivation, subjective emotional experience, physiology, and behavior in a neurovisceral integration model (Thayer & Lane, 2000). Insofar as forgiveness is a "cause" of mental or physical health, it is at least in part because genuine forgiveness inhibits inappropriate responses and facilitates beneficial emotion regulation processes. Forgiveness provides an alternative to maladaptive psychological responses such as rumination and suppression, which appear to have negative consequences for mental and physical health

(McCullough, Orsulak, Brandon, & Akers, 2007; Witvliet & McCullough, 2007). Forgiveness may also function as an alternative to behaviors such as smoking and alcohol/drug use (Kendler et al., 2003) for coping with negative emotions and social experiences. Genuine forgiveness also facilitates beneficial emotion regulation processes, including the ability to process information that can promote compassion and the adoption of merciful thoughts, feelings, and behaviors that are associated with more positive and relaxed psychophysiological profiles (Witvliet et al., 2001).

Forgiveness also influences social support, a robust predictor of mental and physical health (House, Landis, & Umberson, 1988). Inasmuch as people who readily forgive their transgressors are better at maintaining positive relations with relationship partners (McCullough et al., 1998), they may be better at reaping the benefits of social support, experiencing relational closeness, commitment, willingness to accommodate, willingness to sacrifice, and cooperation following a transgression (Karremans & Van Lange, 2004; McCullough et al., 1998; Tsang, McCullough, & Fincham, 2006). By contrast, failures to forgive close relationship partners can lead to "psychological tension" associated with the ambivalence that comes from a failure to extend benevolent behavior to an important relationship partner (Karremans, Van Lange, Ouwerkerk, & Kluwer, 2003). This psychological tension may potentially reduce life satisfaction and state self-esteem, while increasing negative affect. In addition, activating the concept of forgiveness makes people more focused on other people, more likely to engage in volunteering, and more likely to contribute to a charity—pro-relationship motivation that extends beyond the forgiver's relationship with a specific offender (Karremans et al., 2005).

The fact that forgiveness leads to increased relationship motivation has its drawbacks. For example, the tendency for forgiveness to lead to restored relationships may be one of the dynamics by which intimate partner violence is perpetuated (Gordon et al., 2004). Nevertheless, the preponderance of data suggests that forgiveness may be a wellspring of new, and renewed, motivation to affiliate with and care for other people, which may explain some of the links between forgiveness and health.

Careful work needs to be done to address potential confounding variables that might create the appearance of a substantive relationship between measures of forgiveness and measures of well-being. For example, high neuroticism is a predictor of a low tendency to forgive others, as well as many psychiatric disorders and lower psychological well-being (Hettema, Neale, Myers, Prescott, & Kendler, 2006). On the other hand, the association of forgiveness and well-being cannot be solely due to static personality processes (Bono, McCullough, & Root, 2008) because within-subjects research shows that on days when people are more forgiving than is typical for them, they also have better subjective well-being (measured in terms of low negative affect, high positive affect, high satisfaction with life, and low rates of self-reported physical health symptoms). Nevertheless, closer attention to third variables is sorely needed now that basic work has established that forgiveness is indeed associated with many indices of health and well-being.

Interventions

Intervention research demonstrates the benefits of incorporating forgiveness into psychological treatment. Several theoretical models have guided intervention studies, including Enright et al.'s process model (Enright & Coyle, 1998), Worthington's (2001) REACH model, and others (e.g., Gordon, Baucom, & Snyder, 2005; Rye et al., 2005).

Two recent meta-analytic reviews summarize the existing intervention studies. Baskin and Enright (2004) categorized nine forgiveness interventions from six studies into three groups: (a) decision-based interventions, (b) group process interventions, and (c) individual process interventions. Effect sizes (ESs), which were completed for each intervention, revealed that the average person who participated in decision-based groups did not achieve more forgiveness than those who did not participate ($d = -0.04$). The average person in a group process intervention did as well or better than 75% of the control group ($d = 0.82$), whereas the average person in an individual process intervention did as well or better than 95% of the control group ($d = 1.66$). In addition, those in the group process and individual interventions also improved on other mental health variables (e.g., anxiety, depression, self-esteem), with the same pattern of results ($d = 0.16$, 0.59, and 1.42, respectively).

Wade, Worthington, and Meyer's (2005) meta-analysis incorporated 65 group intervention conditions from 27 studies. They contrasted forgiveness interventions (i.e., theoretically grounded forgiveness interventions and forgiveness-oriented comparison interventions), alternate treatment conditions (e.g., support groups, leadership interventions), and no-treatment conditions (e.g., wait-list control groups). An ES was computed for each condition by estimating the amount of pre–post gain in forgiveness that participants experienced on average, expressed as standard change units. The theoretically grounded forgiveness interventions were the most effective in increasing forgiveness ($ES = 0.56$) but were not statistically superior to forgiveness-oriented comparison interventions ($ES = 0.43$). Alternative treatments ($ES = 0.26$) were significantly less effective than theoretically grounded treatments but not less effective than forgiveness-oriented comparison interventions. Additionally, any intervention was more effective than a no-treatment control group ($ES = 0.10$). Wade et al. also found that the amount of time spent empathizing with the offender, committing to forgive, and the use of strategies like relaxation and anger management were significantly related to outcome.

These studies show that forgiveness interventions promote forgiveness better than no-treatment conditions and interventions that are not expected to produce strong effects. However, they do not adequately explore the extent to which forgiveness interventions are more effective than established treatments that do not explicitly promote forgiveness: Many of the comparison groups used were attention-only controls, rather than alternative interventions. As Baskin and Enright (2004) commented, more rigorous standards are necessary before forgiveness interventions are able to meet criteria for empirically supported treatments. This should be a focus for future forgiveness intervention research (Root & McCullough, in press). Bono and McCullough (2006) also encouraged the explicit integration of cognitive factors (e.g., attributions, empathy, perspective taking, rumination) that appear to influence forgiveness, which would likely improve the effectiveness of such interventions.

A review of forgiveness interventions would be incomplete without describing interventions designed to address larger-scale social problems through forgiveness. Staub, Pearlman, Gubin, and Hagengiama (2005) documented that actors in the 1994 Rwandan genocide could be helped to forgive and to experience reductions in the symptoms of trauma by participating in psychoeducational groups. Forgiveness interventions have been effective in promoting forgiveness among victims of convicted criminals as well. Sherman et al. (2005) conducted several randomized trials to evaluate the efficacy of that face-to-face restorative justice meetings between convicted criminals and their victims. Victims who participate in restorative justice conferences with the offenders who have robbed, burglarized, or assaulted them are 23 times more likely than are people who participate only in conventional justice proceedings to feel that they have received a sincere apology from their offenders, 4 times less likely to experience a lingering desire for revenge, and 2.6 times as likely to report that they have forgiven their offenders (although the effects of these conferences on forgiveness seem to be more pronounced in some settings than in others). We admire efforts like these to evaluate interventions that are designed to promote forgiveness as a partial solution to difficult social problems.

Conclusion

Ten years ago, researchers could easily keep abreast of all of the major theoretical and empirical developments on forgiveness. That era is over. Forgiveness has become a legitimate topic for research in the social and life sciences. As a result, the knowledge base is growing admirably—and quickly. Attention is expanding beyond granting interpersonal forgiveness to other topics including (a) seeking forgiveness, (b) self-forgiveness, and (c) resolving anger toward God.

Our understanding of forgiveness gets clearer with each passing year. Forgiveness is associated with emotional stability, agreeableness, a focus on others, and religious commitment. Forgiveness is aided by apology, restitution, and sincere remorse, which may influence forgiveness by making transgressors seem worthy of care, valuable, and safe. Forgiveness can be encouraged through individual

and group interventions, and it is associated with happiness, well-being, physiological indicators of resilience, and positive interpersonal outcomes.

Despite the positives, forgiveness can be difficult—especially in cases of severe, potentially life-changing harms. Insofar as the world needs more forgiveness (and we think it does), one challenge for future research is to explore interventions and societal institutions that can help people safely and effectively extend their natural abilities to forgive into interpersonal and social predicaments in which revenge might be a more natural or preferred behavioral inclination. If researchers and policy reformers can develop interventions to help crime victims safely and voluntarily forgive (even violent) perpetrators, and to help Rwandan Tutsis and Hutus to forgive each other, then perhaps there is hope for the rest of us.

Questions for Future Research

1. How can research demonstrating that revenge is driven by appetitive motivation, and is associated with contentment, be reconciled with research showing that unwillingness to forgive is associated with negative affect and negative psychological outcomes?

2. Knowing that forgiveness is related cross-sectionally to a variety of positive outcomes, how can research proceed in evaluating the causal status of those links?

3. Are clinical interventions for promoting forgiveness comparable in their effectiveness to bona fide treatments for addressing mental disorders?

Appendix A   Trim 18–R

For the following questions, please indicate your current thoughts and feelings about the person who hurt you; that is, we want to know how you feel about that person **right now**. Next to each item, circle the number that best describes your current thoughts and feelings.

	Strongly Disagree 1	Disagree 2	Neutral 3	Agree 4	Strongly Agree 5
1. I'll make him/her pay.	1	2	3	4	5
2. I am trying to keep as much distance between us as possible.	1	2	3	4	5
3. Even though his/her actions hurt me, I have goodwill for him/her.	1	2	3	4	5
4. I wish that something bad would happen to him/her.	1	2	3	4	5
5. I am living as if he/she doesn't exist, isn't around.	1	2	3	4	5

6. I want us to bury the hatchet and move forward with our relationship.	1	2	3	4	5
7. I don't trust him/her.	1	2	3	4	5
8. Despite what he/she did, I want us to have a positive relationship again.	1	2	3	4	5
9. I want him/her to get what he/she deserves.	1	2	3	4	5
10. I am finding it difficult to act warmly toward him/her.	1	2	3	4	5
11. I am avoiding him/her.	1	2	3	4	5
12. Although he/she hurt me, I am putting the hurts aside so we can resume our relationship.	1	2	3	4	5
13. I'm going to get even.	1	2	3	4	5
14. I have given up my hurt and resentment.	1	2	3	4	5
15. I cut off the relationship with him/her.	1	2	3	4	5
16. I have released my anger so I can work on restoring our relationship to health.	1	2	3	4	5
17. I want to see him/her hurt and miserable.	1	2	3	4	5
18. I withdraw from him/her.	1	2	3	4	5

Scoring Instructions
Avoidance Motivations:
Add up the scores for items 2, 5, 7, 10, 11, 15 and 18
Revenge Motivations:
Add up the scores for items 1, 4, 9, 13, and 17
Benevolence Motivations:
Add up the scores for items 3, 6, 8, 12, 14, and 16

References

Aureli, F., Cozzolino, R., Cordischi, C., & Scucchi, S. (1992). Kin-oriented redirection among Japanese macaques: An expression of a revenge system? *Animal Behaviour, 44,* 283–291.

Aureli, F., & de Waal, F. B. M. (2000). *Natural conflict resolution.* Berkeley, CA: University of California Press.

Axelrod, R. (1984). *The evolution of cooperation.* New York: Basic Books.

Baskin, T. W., & Enright, R. D. (2004). Intervention studies on forgiveness: A meta-analysis. *Journal of Counseling and Development, 82,* 79–90.

Batson, C. D., & Ahmad, N. (2001). Empathy-induced altruism in a Prisoner's Dilemma II: What if the target of empathy has defected? *European Journal of Social Psychology, 31,* 25–36.

Batson, C. D., Ahmad, N., Lishner, D. A., & Tsang, J. (2002). Empathy and altruism. In C. R. Snyder & S. J. Lopez (Eds.), *Handbook of positive psychology* (pp. 485–498). New York: Oxford University Press.

Berry, J. T., Worthington, E. L., Wade, N. G., Witvliet, C. v. O., & Keifer, R. (2005). Forgiveness, moral identity, and perceived justice in crime victims and their supporters. *Humboldt Journal of Social Relations, 29,* 136–162.

Boehm, C. (1987). *Blood revenge: The enactment and management of conflict in Montenegro and other tribal societies* (2nd ed.). Philadelphia: University of Pennsylvania Press.

Bono, G., & McCullough, M. E. (2006). Positive responses to benefit and harm: Bringing forgiveness and gratitude into cognitive therapy. *Journal of Cognitive Psychotherapy, 20,* 147–158.

Bono, G., McCullough, M. E., & Root, L. M. (2008). Forgiveness, feeling connected to others, and well-being: Two longitudinal studies. *Personality and Social Psychology Bulletin, 34,* 182–195.

Bottom, W. P., Gibson, K., Daniels, S. E., & Murnighan, J. K. (2002). When talk is not cheap: Substantive penance and expressions of intent in rebuilding cooperation. *Organization Science, 13,* 497–513.

Boyd, R., & Richerson, P. J. (1992). Punishment allows the evolution of cooperation (or anything else) in sizable groups. *Ethology and Sociobiology, 13,* 171–195.

Brose, L. A., Rye, M. S., Lutz-Zois, C., & Ross, S. R. (2005). Forgiveness and personality traits. *Personality and Individual Differences, 39,* 35–46.

Brown, R. P. (2003). Measuring individual differences in the tendency to forgive: Construct validity and links with depression. *Personality and Social Psychology Bulletin, 29,* 759–771.

Cohen, A. B., Malka, A., Rozin, P., & Cherfas, L. (2006). Religion and unforgivable offenses. *Journal of Personality, 74,* 85–117.

Crombag, H., Rassin, E., & Horselenberg, R. (2003). On vengeance. *Psychology, Crime and Law, 9,* 333–344.

Daly, M., & Wilson, M. (1988). *Homicide.* New York: Aldine de Gruyter.

de Jong, P. J., Peters, M. L., & de Cremer, D. (2003). Blushing may signify guilt: Revealing effects of blushing in ambiguous social situations. *Motivation and Emotion, 27,* 225–249.

de Quervain, D. J.-F., Fischbacher, U., Treyer, V., Schellhammer, M., Schnyder, U., Buck, A., et al. (2004). The neural basis of altruistic punishment. *Science, 305,* 1254–1258.

Depue, R. A., & Morrone-Strupinsky, J. V. (2005). A neurobehavioral model of affiliative bonding: Implications for conceptualizing a human trait of affiliation. *Behavioral and Brain Sciences, 28,* 313–350.

DeShea, L., Tzou, J., Kang, S., & Matsuyuki, M. (2006, January). *Trait forgiveness II: Spiritual vs. religious college students and the Five-Factor Model of personality.* Poster presented at the annual conference of the Society for Personality and Social Psychology, Palm Springs, CA.

Dugatkin, L. A. (1988). Do guppies play tit-for-tat during predator inspection visits? *Behavioral Ecology and Sociobiology, 25,* 395–399.

Eaton, J., & Struthers, C. W. (2006). The reduction of psychological aggression across varied interpersonal contexts through repentance and forgiveness. *Aggressive Behavior, 32,* 195–206.

Eaton, J., Struthers, C. W., & Santelli, A. G. (2006). Dispositional and state forgiveness: The role of self-esteem, need for structure, and narcissism. *Personality and Individual Differences, 41,* 371–380.

Enright, R. D., & Coyle, C. T. (1998). Researching the process model of forgiveness within psychological interventions. In E. L. Worthington (Ed.), *Dimensions of forgiveness: Psychological research and theological perspectives* (pp. 139–161). Philadelphia: Templeton Foundation Press.

Exline, J. J., Baumeister, R. F., Bushman, B. J., Campbell, W. K., & Finkel, E. J. (2004). Too proud to let go: Narcissistic entitlement as a barrier to forgiveness. *Journal of Personality and Social Psychology, 87,* 894–912.

Finkel, E. J., Rusbult, C. E., Kumashiro, M., & Hannon, P. A. (2002). Dealing with a betrayal in close relationships: Does commitment promote forgiveness? *Journal of Personality and Social Psychology, 82,* 956–974.

Fry, D. P. (2006). *The human potential for peace.* New York: Oxford University Press.

Gold, G. J., & Weiner, B. (2000). Remorse, confession, group identity, and expectancies about repeating a transgression. *Basic and Applied Social Psychology, 22,* 291–300.

Gordon, K. C., & Baucom, D. H. (2003). Forgiveness and marriage: Preliminary support for a measure based on a model of recovery from a marital betrayal. *American Journal of Family Therapy, 31,* 179–199.

Gordon, K. C., Baucom, D. H., & Snyder, D. K. (2005). Forgiveness in couples: Divorce, infidelity, and couples therapy. In E. L. Worthington (Ed.), *Handbook of forgiveness* (pp. 423–439). New York: Routledge.

Gordon, K. C., Burton, S., & Porter, L. (2004). Predicting the intentions of women in domestic violence shelters to return to partners: Does forgiveness play a role? *Journal of Family Psychology, 18,* 331–338.

Greer, T., Berman, M., Varan, V., Bobrycki, L., & Watson, S. (2005). We are a religious people; we are a vengeful people. *Journal for the Scientific Study of Religion, 44,* 45–57.

Harmon-Jones, E., Vaughn-Scott, K., Mohr, S., Sigelman, J., & Harmon-Jones, C. (2004). The effect of manipulated sympathy and anger on left and right frontal cortical activity. *Emotion, 4,* 95–101.

Hettema, J. M., Neale, M. C., Myers, J. M., Prescott, C. A., & Kendler, K. S. (2006). A population-based twin study of the relationship between neuroticism and internalizing disorders. *American Journal of Psychiatry, 163,* 857–864.

House, J. S., Landis, K. R., & Umberson, D. (1988). Social relationships and health. *Science, 241,* 540–545.

Hoyt, W. T., Fincham, F., McCullough, M. E., Maio, G., & Davila, J. (2005). Responses to interpersonal transgressions in families: Forgivingness, forgivability, and relationship-specific effects. *Journal of Personality and Social Psychology, 89,* 375–394.

Hruschka, D. J., & Henrich, J. (2006). Friendship, cliquishness, and the emergence of cooperation. *Journal of Theoretical Biology, 239,* 1–15.

Karremans, J. C., & Van Lange, P. A. M. (2004). Back to caring after being hurt: The role of forgiveness. *European Journal of Social Psychology, 34,* 207–227.

Karremans, J. C., Van Lange, P. A. M., & Holland, R. W. (2005). Forgiveness and its associations with prosocial thinking, feeling, and doing beyond the relationship with the offender. *Personality and Social Psychology Bulletin, 31,* 1315–1326.

Karremans, J. C., Van Lange, P. A. M., Ouwerkerk, J. W., & Kluwer, E. S. (2003). When forgiving enhances psychological well-being: The role of interpersonal commitment. *Journal of Personality and Social Psychology, 84,* 1011–1026.

Kendler, K. S., Liu, X., Gardner, C. O., McCullough, M. E., Larson, D. B., & Prescott, C. A. (2003). Dimensions of religiosity and their relationship to lifetime psychiatric and substance use disorders. *American Journal of Psychiatry, 160,* 496–503.

Knutson, B., & Wimmer, G. E. (2006). Reward: Neural circuitry for social valuation. In E. Harmon-Jones & P. Winkielman (Eds.), *Fundamentals of social neuroscience.* New York: Guilford.

Lawler, K. A., Younger, J. W., Piferi, R. L., Billington, E., Jobe, R., Edmondson, K., et al. (2003). A change of heart: Cardiovascular correlates of forgiveness in response to interpersonal conflict. *Journal of Behavioral Medicine, 26,* 373–393.

McCullough, M. E. (2008). *Beyond revenge: The evolution of the forgiveness instinct.* San Francisco: Jossey-Bass.

McCullough, M. E., Bono, G. B., & Root, L. M. (2005). Religion and forgiveness. In R. Paloutzian & C. Park (Eds.), *Handbook of the psychology of religion and spirituality* (pp. 394–411). New York: Guilford.

McCullough, M. E., Emmons, R. A., Kilpatrick, S. D., & Mooney, C. N. (2003). Narcissists as "victims": The role of narcissism in the perception of transgressions. *Personality and Social Psychology Bulletin, 29,* 885–893.

McCullough, M. E., Fincham, F. D., & Tsang, J. (2003). Forgiveness, forbearance, and time: The temporal unfolding of transgression-related interpersonal motivations. *Journal of Personality and Social Psychology, 84,* 540–557.

McCullough, M. E., & Hoyt, W. T. (2002). Transgression-related motivational dispositions: Personality substrates of forgiveness and their links to the Big Five. *Personality and Social Psychology Bulletin, 28,* 1556–1573.

McCullough, M. E., Orsulak, P., Brandon, A., & Akers, L. (2007). Rumination, fear, and cortisol: An *in vivo* study of interpersonal transgressions. *Health Psychology, 26,* 126–132.

McCullough, M. E., Rachal, K. C., Sandage, S. J., Worthington, E. L., Brown, S. W., & Hight, T. L. (1998). Interpersonal forgiving in close relationships: II. Theoretical elaboration and measurement. *Journal of Personality and Social Psychology, 75,* 1586–1603.

McCullough, M. E., Root, L. M., & Cohen, A. D. (2006). Writing about the personal benefits of a transgression facilitates forgiveness. *Journal of Consulting and Clinical Psychology, 74,* 887–897.

McCullough, M. E., & Witvliet, C. v. O. (2000). The psychology of forgiveness. In C. R. Snyder & S. J. Lopez (Eds.), *Handbook of positive psychology* (pp. 446–458). New York: Oxford.

McCullough, M. E., Worthington, E. L., & Rachal, K. C. (1997). Interpersonal forgiving in close relationships. *Journal of Personality and Social Psychology, 73,* 321–336.

Mahoney, A., Rye, M. S., & Pargament, K. I. (2005). When the sacred is violated: Desecration as a unique challenge to forgiveness. In E. L. Worthington (Ed.), *Handbook of forgiveness* (pp. 57–71). New York: Routledge.

Nadler, A., & Liviatan, I. (2006). Intergroup reconciliation: Effects of adversary's expressions of empathy, responsibility, and recipients' trust. *Personality and Social Psychology Bulletin, 32,* 459–470.

Nowak, M., & Sigmund, K. (1993). A strategy of win-stay, lose-shift that outperforms tit-for-tat in the Prisoner's Dilemma game. *Nature, 364,* 56–58.

Root, L. M., & McCullough, M. E. (in press). Low cost interventions for promoting forgiveness. In L. L'Abate, D. D. Embry, & M. S. Baggett (Eds.), *Handbook of low-cost interventions to promote physical and mental health.* New York: Springer-Verlag.

Rye, M. S., Loiacono, D. M., Folck, C. D., Olszewski, B. T., Heim, T. A., & Madia, B. P. (2001). Evaluation of the psychometric properties of two forgiveness scales. *Current Psychology, 20,* 260–277.

Rye, M. S., Pargament, K. I., Pan, W., Yingling, D. W., Shogren, K. A., & Ito, M. (2005). Can group interventions facilitate forgiveness of an ex-spouse? A randomized clinical trial. *Journal of Consulting and Clinical Psychology, 73,* 880–892.

Schmitt, D. P., & Pilcher, J. J. (2004). Evaluating evidence of psychological adaptation: How do we know one when we see one? *Psychological Science, 15,* 643–649.

Sherman, L. W., Strang, H., Angel, C., Woods, D., Barnes, G. C., Bennett, S., et al. (2005). Effects of face-to-face restorative justice on victims of crime in four randomized, controlled trials. *Journal of Experimental Criminology, 1,* 367–395.

Singer, T., Seymour, B., O'Doherty, J. P., Stephan, K. E., Dolan, R. J., & Frith, C. D. (2006). Empathic neural responses are modulated by the perceived fairness of others. *Nature, 439,* 466–469.

Staub, E., Pearlman, L. A., Gubin, A., & Hagengimana, A. (2005). Healing, reconciliation, forgiving, and the prevention of violence after genocide or mass killing: An intervention and its experimental evaluation in Rwanda. *Journal of Social and Clinical Psychology, 24,* 297–334.

Subkoviak, M. J., Enright, R. D., Wu, C., & Gassin, E. A. (1995). Measuring interpersonal forgiveness in late adolescence and middle adulthood. *Journal of Adolescence, 18,* 641–655.

Thayer, J. F., & Lane, R. D. (2000). A model of neurovisceral integration in emotion regulation and dysregulation. *Journal of Affective Disorders, 61,* 201–216.

Thompson, L. Y., Snyder, C. R., Hoffman, L., Michael, S. T., Rasmussen, H. N., Billings, L. S., et al. (2005). Dispositional forgiveness of self, others, and situations. *Journal of Personality, 73,* 313–359.

Tsang, J., McCullough, M. E., & Fincham, F. (2006). The longitudinal association between forgiveness and relationship closeness and commitment. *Journal of Social and Clinical Psychology, 25,* 448–472.

Tsang, J., McCullough, M. E., & Hoyt, W. T. (2005). Psychometric and rationalization accounts for the religion–forgiveness discrepancy. *Journal of Social Issues, 61,* 785–805.

Wade, N. G., Worthington, E. L., & Meyer, J. E. (2005). But do they work? A meta-analysis of group interventions to promote forgiveness. In E. L. Worthington (Ed.), *Handbook of forgiveness* (pp. 423–439). New York: Routledge.

Witvliet, C. v. O., Ludwig, T. E., & Vander Laan, K. L. (2001). Granting forgiveness or harboring grudges: Implications for emotion, physiology, and health. *Psychological Science, 12,* 117–123.

Witvliet, C. v. O., & McCullough, M. E. (2007). Forgiveness and health: A review and theoretical exploration of emotion pathways. In S. G. Post (Ed.), *Altruism and health: Perspectives from empirical research* (pp. 259–276). New York: Oxford University Press.

Worthington, E. L. (2001). *Five steps to forgiveness: The art and science of forgiving.* New York: Crown.

Worthington, E. L., & Scherer, M. (2004). Forgiveness as an emotion-focused coping strategy that can reduce health risks and promote health resilience: Theory, review, and hypotheses. *Psychology and Health, 19,* 385–405.

Zechmeister, J. S., Garcia, S., Romero, C., & Vas, S. N. (2004). Don't apologize unless you mean it: A laboratory investigation of forgiveness and retaliation. *Journal of Social and Clinical Psychology, 23,* 532–564.

Zechmeister, J. S., & Romero, C. (2002). Victim and offender accounts of interpersonal conflict: Autobiographical narratives of forgiveness and unforgiveness. *Journal of Personality and Social Psychology, 84,* 675–686.

Furthering the Science of Gratitude

Philip C. Watkins, Michael Van Gelder, *and* Araceli Frias

Abstract

In this chapter, we sought to strengthen the science of gratitude. We suggest effective approaches for studying gratitude, present a theoretical framework for researching gratitude, review recent gratitude research, and suggest directions and questions for future research, all in an attempt to encourage research on this important virtue. After presenting a brief historical background of gratitude, we define state and trait gratitude and describe several useful measurement tools. We review research that has examined traits that are associated with gratitude and show that grateful individuals have many salutary traits. We then overview research strategies that have been used to investigate gratitude and pay particular attention to successful experimental manipulations of gratitude. A number of studies have investigated the advantages of gratitude. Not only is gratitude strongly associated with happiness, but experimental studies have shown that gratitude actually enhances happiness. We propose several mechanisms whereby gratitude might enhance happiness. Gratitude may support happiness through enhancing enjoyment of benefits, relationships, self-esteem, and coping ability. Grateful processing of pleasant events may also enhance the accessibility of pleasant memories. Conversely, gratitude may support happiness by inhibiting envy and preventing depression. We conclude by presenting some concerns and prospects for the future of gratitude research. Continued understanding of this important emotion and virtue will do much to advance our understanding of the critical components of the good life.

Keywords: appreciation, gratitude, happiness, subjective well-being, thank

Furthering the Science of Gratitude

Although gratitude is yet understudied, we will not bemoan its neglect here (see Solomon, 2004). Currently, there are only a few researchers who have devoted their research programs to gratitude, but recent texts and reviews have begun to give gratitude its just due (Emmons, 2007; Emmons & McCullough, 2004; McCullough, Kilpatrick, Emmons, & Larson, 2001; Watts, Dutton, & Guilford, 2006). The primary aim of this chapter is to further the science of gratitude. We will "stand on the shoulders" of previous excellent reviews (Emmons & Shelton, 2002; McCullough et al., 2001) to give the reader a current perspective of research in the field. To accomplish our goal, we will define gratitude and describe what we believe to be effective gratitude measurement techniques. We

will then describe research methodologies that have been successful in furthering our knowledge of gratitude. Finally we will review research showing how gratitude is an important component of the good life.

What Is Gratitude?
Historical Background

Virtually every language has an equivalent for gratitude, and all major religions have encouraged expressions of gratitude (Emmons & Crumpler, 2000). Although expressing gratitude had its occasional detractors (e.g., Aristotle), these only serve as stark contrasts to how much humankind has valued giving thanks throughout history. In the United States, for example, gratitude has been institutionalized through its national Thanksgiving holiday. Moving Thanksgiving proclamations by Presidents Washington and Lincoln remind us of the importance that gratitude has held in the past. Expressions of gratitude may vary across the world, but gratitude appears to serve as a virtue in all cultures, and it is difficult to think of any societies that think of gratitude as a vice. Illustrating this point, some work has shown that people in the South Indian culture rarely express verbal thanks for a benefit but almost always express their gratitude with some kind of return favor (Appadurai, 1985). Some scholars have submitted that major moments in history have been essentially focused on gratitude. For example, Gerrish (1992) argued that the reformation theologies of Luther and Calvin were primarily Eucharistic—theologies that focused on grace and gratitude.

The history of the English words "grateful" and "thankful" is not only interesting but also informative. The "grate" that a person is full of when feeling grateful is derived from the Latin *gratus* which means thankful and pleasing (Ayto, 1990). All associations with *gratus* are positive, and research has confirmed that grateful emotion should be placed firmly within the positive affects (McCullough, Emmons, & Tsang, 2002; Watkins, Woodward, Stone, & Kolts, 2003) and the moral emotions (McCullough et al., 2001). "Grace" is also derived from *gratus*, and thus gratitude has close associations with unmerited favor. Although some research has indirectly investigated the association between grace and gratitude, in our view, more research should investigate this relationship. We propose that some of the most intense experiences of gratitude result from an experience of grace.

"Thank" has an even longer history in English than does grateful, originating before the twelfth century (Ayto, 1990). The word is derived from "thoughtfulness," which then evolved into "favorable thought." Clearly, feeling grateful involves "favorable thought" toward one's benefactor, and because gratitude involves thoughtfulness about the benefits one receives from others, some have argued that gratitude is essentially an empathic emotion (Lazarus & Lazarus, 1994). How accurately must a beneficiary understand the state of mind of his or her benefactor in order to feel grateful? This would be an interesting question for future research.

Defining State Gratitude

In order for a science of gratitude to proceed we must have a clear definition and means of measuring the construct. We offer the following definition: An individual experiences the emotion of gratitude (i.e., state gratitude) when they affirm that something good has happened to them when and they recognize that someone else is largely responsible for this benefit (derived from Emmons, 2004). In our definition, "someone else" could be a supernatural force as well as human benefactors. The perceived benefit may be the awareness of the absence of some negative event (e.g., when your plane lands safely in the midst of a severe lightning storm). Although people may feel grateful toward impersonal forces and objects (e.g., "I feel so grateful that fate was with me on that plane trip"), we submit that in these cases people are implicitly appraising intentional benevolence on the part of the impersonal benefactor. An interesting avenue of research would be to investigate experiences of gratitude when no obvious human benefactor is evident (Watkins, Gibler, Mathews, & Kolts, 2005).

Following Adam Smith (1790/1976), McCullough and colleagues (2001) have argued convincingly that gratitude may be seen as a moral affect. They proposed that gratitude serves as a "moral barometer" (it tells the beneficiary that the moral climate has changed in her favor—someone has benefited her), a "moral motivator" (it encourages prosocial behavior), and a "moral reinforcer" (when someone expresses gratitude, it encourages their benefactors to act favorably toward them in the future). This approach has provided researchers with a useful organization of previous gratitude research findings, as well as providing direction for future work.

How can one assess the emotion of gratitude? It appears that a simple but effective way of measuring the state of gratitude is having individuals respond to three adjectives (grateful, thankful, and appreciative; McCullough et al., 2002). Here individuals simply indicate their extent of feeling for these descriptors on a Likert-type scale ranging from "not at all" to "extremely." In measuring grateful affect, one question that arises is whether one should direct the queries toward the benefit and/or benefactor. In this regard, we recommend investigators consider carefully whether their research demands a more general assessment of grateful affect (i.e., "how grateful do you feel?"), or whether the queries should be directed toward gratitude for the benefit and/or benefactor ("how grateful do you feel about . . .?", "how grateful do you feel toward . . .?").

Grateful emotion clearly covaries with other positive emotions (Watkins, Scheer, Ovnicek, & Kolts, 2006). Although feeling thankful is sometimes negatively associated with negative affect, several studies have shown that state gratitude correlates more strongly with positive affect (McCullough et al., 2002; Watkins, Woodward et al., 2003). Some have proposed that gratitude should be related to aesthetic emotions such as awe (e.g., Keltner & Haidt, 2003), and we have found some support for this idea (Watkins, Gibler et al., 2005). In this study, participants either viewed photographs of beautiful nature scenes or pictures of neutral objects. Participants viewing the nature scenes were randomly assigned to judge the beauty of the scene or the geographic location. We found that gratitude was most enhanced in the beauty appreciation condition.

When considering the construct of gratitude, it is important to discriminate gratitude from other emotional states. For example, many in the social sciences have assumed that gratitude was synonymous with indebtedness (feeling obligated to repay). However, several studies have now provided evidence that these should be viewed as distinct (but sometimes related) states. For example, in two studies, we were able to dissociate gratitude from indebtedness (Watkins, Scheer et al., 2006). We found that as the benefactor's expectations of reciprocity increased, gratitude in the beneficiary decreased, but indebtedness increased. In addition, the thought/action tendencies of gratitude were distinct from that of indebtedness.

Trait Gratitude

As with other emotions, when investigating gratitude, it is important to determine whether one is studying gratitude at the level of emotional state or affective trait (Rosenberg, 1998). Up to this point, we have described the emotional state of gratitude. However, it is also important to consider gratitude as an affective trait. Trait gratitude refers to one's disposition for gratitude. If an individual is high in trait gratitude, then they should experience gratitude more easily and more frequently than one who is not a grateful person. The disposition of gratitude more closely approximates what we mean when we discuss the virtue of gratitude.

To our knowledge, there are three well-developed measures of dispositional gratitude. McCullough et al. (2002) developed the GQ-6, a short (six items) but reliable measure of trait gratitude. It is quite clear to participants that the GQ-6 is tapping gratitude, so researchers who are concerned with issues of self-presentation may wish to use a more subtle measure, such as the GRAT appears to be (Watkins,

Woodward et al., 2003). The GRAT is a longer measure that attempts to assess three lower-order characteristics of the grateful person. We have proposed (with some support) that grateful individuals should have a sense of abundance (or negatively, a lack of a sense of deprivation), a sense of simple appreciation (they appreciate the day-to-day pleasures available to most individuals), and an appreciation of others. Thus the GRAT focuses on these facets of trait gratitude. A third reliable gratitude measure that probably assesses gratitude at the trait level would be the gratitude subscale of the Values in Action scale (Peterson & Seligman, 2004). If one were interested in assessing gratitude in the context of other virtues, this scale would appear to be ideal. Both the GRAT and the GQ-6 appear to have excellent psychometrics, and more recently, we have developed a revised version of the GRAT (GRAT-R) and a shorter 16-item version, that offer several improvements over the original (Thomas & Watkins, 2003). One may also assess appreciation more generally (Adler & Fagley, 2005), but this factor does not appear to be distinct from dispositional gratitude (Wood, Maltby, Stewart, & Joseph, 2008).

Although these instruments appear to be effective measures of gratitude, they suffer from the same problems as all self-report measures, and with socially desirable traits such as gratitude, this could pose a significant problem for some research protocols. Thus, in some studies, informant reports (cf. McCullough et al., 2002) or behavioral markers of gratitude, such as verbal expressions of thanks or reciprocity behavior, may be preferred. The development of an implicit gratitude measure also would be a useful advance. In every case the researcher needs to determine her measurements carefully in the context of the purpose of the research.

Characteristics of Grateful People

What personality traits are most likely to describe a grateful (or an ungrateful) person? In a nutshell, gratitude appears to be a positive trait. Grateful individuals tend to be agreeable, emotionally stable, self-confident but less narcissistic, and non-materialistic (McComb, Watkins, & Kolts, 2004; McCullough et al., 2002; McLeod, Maleki, Elster, & Watkins, 2005; Watkins, Woodward et al., 2003). Given that major religions have discouraged narcissism and materialism, this raises the issue of the spirituality of grateful people, and indeed, gratitude does appear to be positively associated with spirituality. For example, grateful people have been found to show more intrinsic religious motivation, but less extrinsic religiosity (Watkins, Woodward et al., 2003). Grateful people say that religion is more important to them and also report that they attend more religious services, read the Scriptures more frequently, pray more, and report a closer relationship with God than less grateful individuals (McCullough et al., 2002). Because experiences of grace are often significant to religious individuals, it may be important to investigate the relationship of grace and gratitude in this context. Although there is considerable research on the salubrious effects of forgiving another (for a review, see Exline & Baumeister, 2000), very little research to date has investigated the impact of being forgiven by another. We submit that gratitude is likely to result from experiences of grace and forgiveness.

Although several studies have investigated the characteristics of grateful people, we have little, if any, data informing us as to how people come to be grateful. Many questions remain about relationships between gratitude and other personality traits. For example, are people grateful because they are agreeable, or does being a grateful person contribute to one's agreeableness? Perhaps even more profound questions arise out of the gratitude and religiosity associations. One would think that because most religions promote gratitude, the direction of causation would be from religiosity to gratitude. However, because positive affect enhances one's ability to see meaningful relationships and thus meaning in life (King, Hicks, Krull, & Del Gaiso, 2006), it is quite possible that gratitude enhances religiosity. In fact, it appears that intense experiences of gratitude were instrumental in the religious conversion of G. K. Chesterton (1908/1986):

> Here I am only trying to describe the enormous emotions which cannot be described. And the strongest emotion was that life was as precious as it was puzzling. . . . The test of all happiness is gratitude; and I felt grateful, though I hardly knew to whom. Children are grateful when Santa Claus puts in their stockings gifts of toys or sweets. Could I not be grateful to Santa Claus when he put in my stockings the gift of two miraculous legs? We thank people for birthday presents of cigars and slippers. Can I thank no one for the birthday present of birth?
>
> (p. 258)

Future research investigating grateful experiences when no human benefactor is evident should produce intriguing results (cf. Watkins, Gibler et al., 2005).

Gratitude Research Methodologies

Virtually all of the studies discussed thus far are plagued by the problem associated with much positive psychology research: the use of correlational designs. More definitive knowledge would be gained about the causes and consequences of gratitude with experimental research. If we are to conduct experimental studies of gratitude, we must have techniques that reliably manipulate gratitude in the lab. Several researchers have used a "count your blessings" approach, where participants in the gratitude condition were encouraged to list several things they were thankful for. For example, in the first week or so of fall quarter we asked students in our gratitude condition to recall things they did over the summer that they were grateful for (study 3, Watkins, Woodward et al., 2003). These students reported more gratitude for their summer than students who listed things they wanted to do over the summer but couldn't. Emmons and McCullough (2003) asked their participants to list up to five blessings they were thankful for, and this also impacted their gratitude. Although the concern of Emmons and McCullough was more long-term impact of counting one's blessings, Dunn and Schweitzer (2005) successfully used a similar procedure to manipulate gratitude in the lab. They first asked their participants to list three to five things that made them most grateful. Participants were then asked to describe in detail the one situation that made them most grateful. This appears to be a low-cost manipulation that produces reliable changes in gratitude.

We have also asked participants to think about someone they were grateful for, and this produced reliable effects on positive affect (study 4, Watkins, Woodward et al., 2003). Somewhat surprisingly, people who "thought" about their benefactor showed more enhanced positive affect than those who "wrote" about their benefactor. This raises the important issue of how one might best cognitively process their blessings or benefactor to enhance gratitude. For example, simply listing as many blessings as possible may not create the kind of cognitive processing that maximizes gratitude. Similarly, recent data from Lyubomirsky's lab (Lyubomirsky, Sousa, & Dickerhoof, 2006) suggest that thinking about a positive event in a reliving—repetitive—manner enhanced emotional well-being more than writing or thinking analytically about positive events. Can one overanalyze a grateful event? Lyubomirsky's studies (see chap. 63) suggest that analytic thinking might be detrimental to gratitude, and this has important implications for gratitude interventions.

Finally, several researchers have attempted to manipulate gratitude by having a confederate provide the participant with some benefit (e.g., Tsang, 2006). For example, Bartlett and DeSteno (2006) had participants complete a tedious task, only to find out that the computer had malfunctioned and the participant would have to start over. However, a confederate discovers the problem (they simply plug in the computer monitor), and the participant is allowed to continue without wasting their previous work. Not surprisingly, this manipulation produced significant gratitude toward the confederate. Other approaches such as vignettes (e.g., Watkins, Scheer et al., 2006) and qualitative studies of gratitude exemplars should also provide advances in our understanding of gratitude.

The Good of Gratitude

In this recent wave of gratitude research, investigators have operated from the premise that gratitude was important to the good life. Most of this research was focused on the potential of gratitude to enhance happiness. Hence, early research asked the question, "Are grateful people happy people?" Correlations of trait gratitude with emotional well-being confirmed that grateful people do tend to be happy people. Both the GQ-6 and the GRAT show moderate to strong relationships with happiness measures (McCullough et al., 2002; Watkins, Woodward et al., 2003). Furthermore, Park, Peterson, and Seligman (2004) found that of the 24 Values in Action strengths, gratitude fell behind only hope and zest in predicting subjective well-being. More recently, we have found that trait gratitude predicts increased happiness 1 month later (Spangler, Webber, Xiong, & Watkins, 2008).

It has been known that personality traits are much stronger predictors of happiness than demographic variables (Diener, Suh, Lucas, & Smith, 1999). Thus, several studies have compared trait gratitude with other well-known personality predictors of happiness (McComb et al., 2004; McCullough et al., 2002; Wood, Joseph, & Maltby, 2008). In each case, gratitude predicted happiness above and beyond Big Five traits, and gratitude was shown to be the strongest trait predictor of happiness. This pattern of results appears to hold not only with self-report measures, but with informant reports as well (McCullough et al., 2002). Although the relationship between gratitude and subjective well-being seems clear, one remaining question revolves around the source of one's gratitude. Watts et al. (2006) ask whether to whom one is grateful should make a difference in one's happiness. To our knowledge, this question has yet to be resolved.

Although these results provide support for the theory that gratitude enhances happiness, the correlational nature of these studies leaves the question of causation open. It is quite possible that gratitude is simply the happy consequence of being happy or that both happiness and gratitude result from a third variable such as reward sensitivity. Fortunately, several experimental studies have added credence to the idea that gratitude actually causes happiness. In two studies, we found that gratitude manipulations enhanced mood state (studies 3 and 4, Watkins, Woodward et al., 2003). In three studies, Emmons and McCullough (2003) found that a simple practice of counting one's blessings enhanced several subjective well-being measures compared to control conditions. Froh and colleagues found that this intervention was also effective with adolescents (Froh, Sefick, & Emmons, 2008). Lyubomirsky, Sheldon, and Schkade (2005) replicated these results with one important caveat. They found that more is not necessarily better when it comes to counting your blessings. Individuals who counted their blessings once a week showed more improvement in life satisfaction than did those who engaged in this practice three times per week. Many questions remain as to the most productive ways to utilize gratitude exercises, and the effectiveness of gratitude interventions is likely to be moderated by individual differences as well.

Perhaps one of the most powerful gratitude interventions to date is the treatment investigated by Seligman, Steen, Park, and Peterson (2005). In this exercise, individuals wrote a letter of gratitude to a person they felt had benefited them but whom they had "not properly thanked" (p. 416). They then delivered the letter to their benefactor. This intervention resulted in strong increases in happiness and decreases in depression compared to the placebo condition. In fact, the immediate impact of this intervention appeared to be superior to other positive psychology interventions. Although significant treatment gains were maintained 1 month post-intervention, by 6 months, happiness and depression scores had returned to baseline. While the temporality of this gratitude intervention might seem discouraging, we believe this result should be expected, and we will comment further on this issue later in this chapter.

In sum, both correlational and experimental results support the proposition that gratitude enhances the good life. Thus, it does not appear that gratitude is simply an epiphenomenon of happiness. However, positive affect research would lead us to believe that feeling good should increase the likelihood of feeling grateful. When individuals are happy, they are better able to notice and remember good things in their environment (e.g., Isen, Shalker, Clark, & Karp, 1978) and are more likely to attribute good intentions to their benefactors (Isen, Niedenthal, & Cantor, 1992). Gratitude research suggests that both of these factors should enhance the experience of gratitude (McCullough et al., 2001). However, the experimental research reviewed previously suggests that gratitude also enhances happiness. Perhaps then, happiness enhances gratitude, but gratitude in turn enhances happiness, resulting in a "cycle of virtue" (Watkins, 2004). Future investigations of this upward spiral would benefit our understanding of gratitude and the good life.

We would now like to suggest several mechanisms that help explain how gratitude contributes to happiness. First, we propose that gratitude directly enhances positive affect. We submit that gratitude enhances one's enjoyment of benefits. Chesterton observed, "gratitude produced . . . the most purely joyful moments that have been known to man" (1924/1989, p. 78). His reasoning was, "All goods look better when they look like gifts." Is a benefit experienced more positively when it is accepted as a gift? To our knowledge, this question has not been directly investigated, but various studies show that one is more likely to feel grateful when one thinks that a benefit was intentionally given for one's well-being (McCullough et al., 2001). C. S. Lewis (1958) also argued that the expression of gratitude (or praise) enhanced one's enjoyment of a benefit:

> I think we delight to praise what we enjoy because the praise not merely expresses but completes the enjoyment; it is its appointed consummation. It is not out of compliment that lovers keep on telling one another how beautiful they are; the delight is incomplete until it is expressed. (p. 95)

Experimental work reviewed previously tends to indirectly support Lewis's proposition, but we believe that research could more specifically target Lewis's theory here. It is also likely that individual differences play a role. Although it may be true that most people would enjoy a benefit if it is a gift rather than a simple good, those who tend to easily feel indebted actually may enjoy a gift less than a mere benefit.

Gratitude may also directly benefit mood by directing one's focus to good things that one has and away from things they lack, thus preventing unpleasant emotional states involved with upward social comparison and envy. Trait envy and materialism are negatively associated with trait gratitude (McCullough et al., 2002). However, more research needs to directly address the issue of whether gratitude actually tends to direct one's attention to benefits they have and away from benefits they lack.

Gratitude could also promote happiness by enhancing one's social relationships. It appears that one of the most reliable predictors of happiness is stable social relationships (Diener et al., 1999). Thus, if gratitude supports quality relationships, it should support happiness as well. Informants see grateful people as more likable (Watkins, Martin, & Faulkner, 2003); grateful expressions engender more social reward (McCullough et al., 2001). Some have proposed that gratitude should enhance social bonding (Fredrickson, 2004), and recent evidence has emerged to support this theory (Algoe, Haidt, & Gable, 2008). Furthermore, several experiments have shown that gratitude promotes prosocial behavior. We found that gratitude is associated with prosocial action tendencies, while inhibiting antisocial urges (Watkins, Scheer et al., 2006). In two studies Bartlett and DeSteno (2006) found that gratitude inductions enhanced an individual's likelihood to engage in prosocial behavior toward a benefactor or a stranger. What is notable about these studies is that gratitude increased helping efforts even when the task was unpleasant. Furthermore, they showed that gratitude was more likely to increase helping than another positive affect: amusement (see also Tsang, 2006). In a series of studies, Dunn and Schweitzer (2005) showed that experimental inductions of gratitude enhanced trust. Because trust is an important quality in healthy relationships, we believe this finding has implications for how gratitude might enhance happiness through supportive relationships. Thus, gratitude may enhance happiness because it is a prosocial trait.

It is also possible that gratitude may support happiness by enhancing adaptive coping. By focusing on positive consequences resulting from a difficult experience that one may be grateful for, one may be able to make sense of stressful events. Several studies have shown that grateful people report more adaptive coping techniques (e.g., Neal, Watkins, & Kolts, 2005), and other studies have found that grateful individuals report less posttraumatic symptoms following a trauma than less grateful people (e.g., Kashdan, Uswatte, & Julian, 2006). Gratitude for God also appears to be a buffer for the impact of stress on illness in elders (Krause, 2006). Moreover, the unpleasantness of negative memories tends to fade faster for grateful than for less grateful individuals (Watkins, Grimm, & Kolts, 2004). This evidence is largely descriptive, but recently we found in an experimental design that grateful processing of troubling memories helps bring closure, decrease the unpleasant impact, and decrease the intrusiveness of these recollections (Watkins, Cruz, Holben, & Kolts, 2008).

Finally, we propose that gratitude has a beneficial effect on subjective well-being by increasing the accessibility of positive memories. C. S. Lewis (1996, p. 73) wrote, "A pleasure is only full grown when it is remembered." A multitude of positive events from one's past would not be likely to benefit one's subjective well-being unless one were able to easily recollect these events. In fact, several studies have found that happy people are more able to recall pleasant events from their past (e.g., Seidlitz & Diener, 1993). Memory processes should be important to gratitude as well. We propose that encoding and reflecting on pleasant events with gratitude should enhance a positive memory bias, which in turn should support one's happiness. Watkins (2004) has provided an information processing rationale for this hypothesis, and some evidence supports this idea. In several studies, we have found that gratitude is associated with a positive memory bias (Watkins, Gilber et al., 2005). Not only are grateful individuals able to recollect more pleasant events than their less grateful counterparts, recollecting both positive and negative memories has a more positive emotional impact on grateful than less grateful people. Recently, we have found that trait gratitude predicts positive memory bias 1 month later, and this relationship was found to be independent of depression, positive affect, and happiness (Watkins, Van Gelder, & Maleki, 2006). Although these results are promising, experimental work would more directly address our notion that grateful processing enhances the accessibility of positive memories. In sum, grateful people appear to reflect more favorably on their past, and easily retrievable positive memories should enhance one's emotional well-being. If gratitude actually enhances a positive memory bias, gratitude may also support happiness by mitigating depression (Wood, Maltby, Gillett, Linley, & Joseph, 2008). Depression is associated with a negativistic memory bias, and having a ready collection of positive memories may help reverse the mood and memory vicious cycle in depression (Watkins, Grimm, Whitney, & Brown, 2005). Although these initial results are promising, many questions remain as to whether gratitude actually enhances the accessibility of positive memories, and if so, how gratitude might produce this bias.

Conclusions

Although much work remains to be done, it seems clear that gratitude is an important component of the good life. "I would maintain that thanks are the highest form of thought"; wrote Chesterton (1917, *The Age of the Crusades*, para. 2), "and that gratitude is happiness doubled by wonder." Not only is gratitude strongly associated with happiness, experimental manipulations of gratitude have enhanced emotional well-being. However, as pointed out previously, the impact of gratitude interventions appears to be somewhat transitory. We would not expect one gratitude visit to permanently increase one's happiness, and it is impressive to us that this gratitude intervention still shows significant effects on happiness 1 month later. One exercise of counting one's blessings or one gratitude visit is not likely to impact long-term happiness. Rather, we submit that it should be a more regular practice of gratitude that will result in long-range increases in happiness. How "regular" these exercises need to be probably depends on the person and the type of gratitude practice one engages in, and this should be the focus of future research. However, Lyubomirsky et al.'s work (2005) reminds us that more is not necessarily better when it comes to practices of gratitude. This raises the question of whether one can actually practice their way into being a more grateful person. We believe that the trait of gratitude can be enhanced, but this hope must be tested by future research. In this regard, we are also concerned that gratitude may be pursued in an extrinsic or instrumental fashion. For example, if an individual expresses gratitude only to feel better, might this approach backfire? Although gratitude clearly has social benefits, there is some research suggesting that those benefits will not be achieved if it is suspected that the person expressing gratitude is only doing so to receive more benefits (Carey, Clicque, Leighton, & Milton, 1976). Analogously, although gratitude has emotional benefits, we submit that if one focuses on those benefits, these emotional benefits will be mitigated. Authentic gratitude is an other-focused emotion and as such entails focus on the giver, not on one's own emotional condition.

Through this chapter, we hope to encourage more gratitude research. To accomplish this aim, we have described the construct of gratitude, the measurement of gratitude, and fruitful research methods for investigating gratitude. We have presented research supporting the importance of this construct, namely because gratitude appears to be important to the good life. We have also attempted to provide a theoretical framework for investigating the gratitude/happiness relationship. Hopefully this will encourage more to embark on gratitude research and further advancement will be seen. Henry Ward Beecher (n.d., para. 1) concluded, "Gratitude is the fairest blossom which springs from the soul." We hope that through this chapter we have planted seeds that will yield a harvest of research furthering our understanding of gratitude.

Three Questions for Future Gratitude Research

1. Can interventions be developed that enhance the trait of gratitude?

2. Why does gratitude enhance happiness?

3. How does the trait of gratitude develop in a person? How does a person become grateful?

References

Adler, M. G., & Fagley, N. S. (2005). Appreciation: Individual differences in finding value and meaning as a unique predictor of subjective well-being. *Journal of Personality, 73*, 79–113.

Algoe, S. B., Haidt, J., & Gable, S. L. (2008). Beyond reciprocity: Gratitude and relationships in everyday life. *Emotion, 8*, 425–429.

Appadurai, A. (1985). Gratitude as a social mode in south India. *Ethos, 13*, 236–245.

Ayto, J. (1990). *Dictionary of word origins*. New York: Arcade.

Bartlett, M. Y., & DeSteno, D. (2006). Gratitude and prosocial behavior. *Psychological Science, 17*, 319–325.

Beecher, H. W. (n.d.). *Henry Ward Beecher*. Retrieved July 28, 2006, from Wisdom Quotes, hppt://www.wisdomquotes.com/002943.html

Carey, J. R., Clicque, S. H., Leighton, B. A., & Milton, F. (1976). A test of positive reinforcement of customers. *Journal of Marketing, 40*, 98–100.

Chesterton, G. K. (1908/1986). Orthodoxy. In D. Dooley (Ed.), *G. K. Chesterton: Collected works* (pp. 209–366). San Francisco: Ignatius Press.

Chesterton, G. K. (1917). *A short history of England*. Retrieved July 28, 2006, from http://www.dur.ac.uk/martin.ward/gkc/books/history.txt

Chesterton, G. K. (1924/1989). *Saint Francis of Assisi*. New York: Image Books/Doubleday.

Diener, E., Suh, E. M., Lucas, R. E., & Smith, H. L. (1999). Subjective well-being: Three decades of progress. *Psychological Bulletin, 125*, 276–302.

Dunn, J. R., & Schweitzer, M. E. (2005). Feeling and believing: The influence of emotion on trust. *Journal of Personality and Social Psychology, 88*, 736–748.

Emmons, R. A. (2004, July). Gratitude is the best approach to life. In L. Sundarajan (Chair), *Quest for the good life: Problems/promises of positive psychology*. Symposium presented at the Annual Convention of the American Psychological Association, Honolulu, HI.

Emmons, R. A. (2007). *Thanks!: How the new science of gratitude can make you happier*. New York: Houghton Mifflin.

Emmons, R. A., & Crumpler, C. A. (2000). Gratitude as human strength: Appraising the evidence. *Journal of Social and Clinical Psychology, 19*, 56–69.

Emmons, R. A., & McCullough, M. E. (2003). Counting blessings versus burdens: An empirical investigation of gratitude and subjective well-being in daily life. *Journal of Personality and Social Psychology, 84*, 377–389.

Emmons, R. A., & McCullough, M. E. (2004). *The psychology of gratitude*. New York: Oxford University Press.

Emmons, R. A., & Shelton, C. (2002). Gratitude and the science of positive psychology. In C. R. Snyder & S. J. Lopez (Eds.), *Handbook of positive psychology* (pp. 459–471). New York: Oxford University Press.

Exline, J. J., & Baumeister, R. F. (2000). Expressing forgiveness and repentance: Benefits and barriers. In M. E. McCollough, K. E. Pargament, & C. E. Thorsen (Eds.), *Forgiveness: Theory, research, and practice* (pp. 133–155). New York: Guilford.

Fredrickson, B. L. (2004). Gratitude, like other positive emotions, broadens and builds. In R. A. Emmons & M. E. McCullough (Eds.), *The psychology of gratitude* (pp. 145–166). New York: Oxford University Press.

Froh, J. J., Sefick, W. J., & Emmons, R. A. (2008). Counting blessings in early adolescents: An experimental study of gratitude and subjective well-being. *Journal of School Psychology, 46*, 213–233.

Gerrish, B. A. (1992). *Grace and gratitude: The Eucharistic theology of John Calvin*. Eugene, OR: Wipf and Stock Publishers.

Isen, A. M., Niedenthal, P. M., & Cantor, N. (1992). An influence of positive affect on social categorization. *Motivation and Emotion, 16*, 65–78.

Isen, A. M., Shalker, T. E., Clark, M., & Karp, L. (1978). Affect, accessibility of material in memory, and behavior: A cognitive loop? *Journal of Personality and Social Psychology, 36*, 1–12.

Kashdan, T. B., Uswatte, U., & Julian, T. (2006). Gratitude and eudaimonic well-being in Vietnam War veterans. *Behaviour Research and Therapy, 44*, 177–199.

Keltner, D., & Haidt, J. (2003). Approaching awe, a moral, spiritual, and aesthetic emotion. *Cognition and Emotion, 17*, 297–314.

King, L. A., Hicks, J. A., Krull, J. L., & Del Gaiso, A. K. (2006). Positive affect and the experience of meaning in life. *Journal of Personality and Social Psychology, 90*, 179–196.

Krause, N. (2006). Gratitude toward God, stress, and health in late life. *Research on Aging, 28*, 163–183.

Lazarus, R., & Lazarus, B. (1994). *Passion and reason*. New York: Oxford University Press.

Lewis, C. S. (1958). *Reflections on the Psalms*. New York: Harcourt, Brace and Co.

Lewis, C. S. (1996). *Out of the silent planet*. New York: Scribner Paperback Fiction.

Lyubomirsky, S., Sheldon, K. M., & Schkade, D. (2005). Pursuing happiness: The architecture of sustainable change. *Review of General Psychology, 9*, 111–131.

Lyubomirsky, S., Sousa, L., & Dickerhoof, R. (2006). The costs and benefits of writing, talking, and thinking about life's triumphs and defeats. *Journal of Personality and Social Psychology, 90,* 692–708.

McComb, D., Watkins, P., & Kolts, R. (2004, May). *Personality predictors of happiness: The importance of gratitude.* Presentation to the 84th Annual Convention of the Western Psychological Association, Phoenix, AZ.

McCullough, M. E., Emmons, R. A., & Tsang, J. (2002). The grateful disposition: A conceptual and empirical topography. *Journal of Personality and Social Psychology, 82,* 112–127.

McCullough, M. E., Kilpatrick, S. D., Emmons, R. A., & Larson, D. B. (2001). Is gratitude a moral affect? *Psychological Bulletin, 127,* 249–266.

McLeod, L., Maleki, L., Elster, B., & Watkins, P. (2005, April). *Does narcissism inhibit gratitude?* Presentation to the 85th Annual Convention of the Western Psychological Association, Portland, OR.

Neal, M., Watkins, P. C., & Kolts, R. (2005, August). *Does gratitude inhibit intrusive memories?* Presentation to the Annual Convention of the American Psychological Association, Washington, DC.

Park, N., Peterson, C., & Seligman, M. E. P. (2004). Strengths of character and well-being. *Journal of Social and Clinical Psychology, 23,* 603–619.

Peterson, C., & Seligman, M. E. P. (2004). *Character strengths and virtues: A handbook and classification.* New York: American Psychological Association and Oxford University Press.

Rosenberg, E. (1998). Levels of analysis and the organization of affect. *Review of General Psychology, 2,* 247–270.

Seidlitz, L., & Diener, E. (1993). Memory for positive versus negative life events: Theories for the differences between happy and unhappy persons. *Journal of Personality and Social Psychology, 64,* 654–664.

Seligman, M. E. P., Steen, T. A., Park, N., & Peterson, C. (2005). Positive psychology progress: Empirical validation of interventions. *American Psychologist, 60,* 410–421.

Smith, A. (1790/1976). *The theory of moral sentiments* (6th ed.). Oxford: Clarendon Press.

Solomon, R. C. (2004). Foreword. In R. A. Emmons & M. E. McCullough (Eds.), *The psychology of gratitude* (pp. v–xi). New York: Oxford University Press.

Spangler, K., Webber, A., Xiong, I., & Watkins, P. C. (2008, April). *Gratitude predicts enhanced happiness.* Presentation to the National Conference on Undergraduate Research, April, 2008, Salisbury, MD.

Thomas, M., & Watkins, P. (2003, May). *Measuring the grateful trait: Development of the revised GRAT.* Presentation to the 83rd Annual Convention of the Western Psychological Association, Vancouver, BC.

Tsang, J. (2006). Gratitude and prosocial behaviour: An experimental test of gratitude. *Cognition and Emotion, 20,* 138–148.

Watkins, P. C. (2004). Gratitude and subjective well-being. In R. A. Emmons & M. E. McCullough (Eds.), *The psychology of gratitude* (pp. 167–192). New York: Oxford University Press.

Watkins, P. C., Cruz, L., Holben, H., & Kolts, R. L. (2008). Taking care of business? Grateful processing of unpleasant memories. *Journal of Positive Psychology, 3,* 87–99.

Watkins, P. C., Gibler, A., Mathews, M., & Kolts, R. (2005, August). *Aesthetic experience enhances gratitude.* Paper presented to the Annual Convention of the American Psychological Association, Washington, DC.

Watkins, P. C., Grimm, D. L., & Kolts, R. (2004). Counting your blessings: Positive memories among grateful persons. *Current Psychology, 23,* 52–67.

Watkins, P. C., Grimm, D. L., Whitney, A., & Brown, A. (2005). Unintentional memory bias in depression. In A. V. Clark (Ed.), *Mood state and health* (pp. 59–86). Hauppage, NY: Nova Science.

Watkins, P. C., Martin, B. D., & Faulkner, G. (2003, May). *Are grateful people happy people? Informant judgments of grateful acquaintances.* Presentation to the 83rd Annual Convention of the Western Psychological Association, Vancouver, BC.

Watkins, P. C., Scheer, J., Ovnicek., M., & Kolts, R. D. (2006). The debt of gratitude: Dissociating gratitude and indebtedness. *Cognition and Emotion, 20,* 217–241.

Watkins, P. C., Van Gelder, M., & Maleki, L. (2006, August). *Counting (and recalling) blessings: Trait gratitude predicts positive memory bias.* Presentation to the Annual Convention of the American Psychological Association, New Orleans, LA.

Watkins, P. C., Woodward, K., Stone, T., & Kolts, R. D. (2003). Gratitude and happiness: The development of a measure of gratitude and its relationship with subjective well-being. *Social Behavior and Personality, 31,* 431–452.

Watts, F., Dutton, K., & Guilford, L. (2006). Human spiritual qualities: Integrating psychology and religion. *Mental Health, Religion and Culture, 9,* 277–289.

Wood, A. M., Joseph, S., & Maltby, J. (2008). Gratitude uniquely predicts satisfaction with life: Incremental validity above the domains and facets of the five factor model. *Personality and Individual Differences, 45,* 49–54.

Wood, A. M., Maltby, J., Gillett, R., Linley, P. A., & Joseph, S. (2008). The role of gratitude in the development of social support, stress, and depression: Two longitudinal studies. *Journal of Research in Personality, 42,* 854–871.

Wood, A. M., Maltby, J., Stewart, N., & Joseph, S. (2008). Conceptualizing gratitude and appreciation as a unitary personality trait. *Personality and Individual Differences, 44,* 621–632.

Love

Clyde Hendrick *and* Susan S. Hendrick

Abstract

The development of relationship science is integral to the development of positive psychology. The scientific study of love is of central importance to relationship science and is, therefore, very important for positive psychology. This chapter focuses primarily on the history and science of romantic love. One historical view is that romantic love, and especially "love marriage," developed only in the past few centuries. Other scholars (e.g., Hatfield) have argued that passionate love is a human universal, existing across time and cultures. So this issue is open. The study of love divides into naturalistic/biological approaches (such as passionate vs. companionate love, attachment, and the evolution of love) and psychological/social approaches. The latter include prototypes of love, self-expansion theory, triangular theory, and love styles. Measures used to assess these various approaches are discussed briefly. There is much research on love, forcing selective coverage of topics, including communication of love, love styles, cross-cultural aspects of love, love and sexuality, love and happiness/well-being, and a new entry into the variable mix: love and respect. Clinical psychology and even psychoanalysis have recognized the centrality of a successful love relationship for the full development and emotional stability of *most* people. Love stands at the center of many aspects of human life. It is time that all of psychology, and the funding agencies, fully recognize the centrality and power of love. Until that happens, romantic love *is* the giant elephant that is unseen in psychology's living room.

Keywords: evolution, love styles, measurement, respect, sexuality

We review briefly the progress of the study of love over the past four decades and briefly discuss love's role in positive psychology. Traditionally, a respectable hard-nosed psychologist simply would not study a "soft" topic such as love. It took courage for Berscheid and Walster (1969) to introduce romantic love into the study of interpersonal attraction, for Rubin (1970) to distinguish loving from liking, and for Harlow (1974) to extend the study of love to nonhuman species.

These and other research pioneers in the study of love paved the way for today's flourishing research on love within the larger discipline of relationship science (Berscheid, 2000). Our goal is to convey some of the interest and drama of this new discipline. We begin with a historical overview of the meaning of love, then consider current scientific models and methods for measuring love. We provide a sample of current research findings and conclude with suggestions regarding future direction of the field.

History of Romantic Love

A comprehensive philosophical history of love was written by Irving Singer (1984). Very early, conceptual thought about love was largely linked to abstract virtues (e.g., "the good") or to gods. Singer discerned four broad conceptual traditions: "Eros" (desire for the good or the beautiful); "Philia" (friendship love); "Nomos" (submission to a god's will; in human terms, obedience to the desires of a loved one); and "Agape" (a divine bestowal of love upon creation). Over the centuries, various writers worked with these disparate conceptions, attempting to synthesize and translate them into human terms.

Some have questioned whether romantic/passionate love even existed before the last few centuries. On the other hand, Hatfield (1988) proposed that passionate love, as an intense attraction, has existed in all cultures and historical eras and is essentially a "human universal." Passionate love of *and* marriage to the same person, however, is a relatively recent cultural invention. Throughout much of human history, marriage for love was unknown. As it developed during the Middle Ages, courtly love involved a highly stylized ritual and, as such, may have been a historical harbinger of change from the tradition of arranged marriages. Courtly love idealized the love felt toward another person, a love of intense passion between a man and a woman who generally were not married to each other.

Slowly, this notion of passionate love between man and woman, within a courtship context, led to "love marriages," often to the consternation of those who held to traditional norms. The growth of love marriages spread widely in the Western world in the eighteenth century. Detailed histories are available (e.g., Murstein, 1974). The perceived link between love and marriage is still undergoing dynamic change. Simpson, Campbell, and Berscheid (1986) examined college students' perceptions of the importance of love as a basis for marriage, in data collected over a 30-year period. Students over time reported romantic love as being an increasingly important basis for marriage. Students also viewed remaining in love as necessary for continuing the marriage. More recently, an American sample of men and women expressed a stronger link between love and marriage than did a Chinese sample "and also believed that passionate love was a more important prerequisite for entering marriage" (Sprecher & Toro-Morn, 2002, p. 139). Consistent with these findings, love and marriage were more strongly linked for college students from Western/Westernized nations than students from Eastern nations (Levine, Sato, Hashimoto, & Verma, 1995). Given this linking of love with marriage, the increased divorce rate may be driven by the view that when the passions die, so, too, do marriages or other intimate partnered relationships.

If the passion aspect of love is not sufficient to bond partners, perhaps the addition of other love components such as friendship would strengthen the bond. If one also could be good friends, perhaps even best friends, with one's passionate lover, then perhaps the "relationship" could survive the turbulent comings and goings of passion. There is some evidence that such cultural change is under way. The old adage that "you can't be friends with the one you love" is no longer true. Many young couples now seek partners who are good companions as well as good lovers. In a study by S. Hendrick and Hendrick (1993), college students wrote essays about their romantic relationships or about their closest friendship. Not only was friendship the dominant theme in describing romantic relationships but almost half of the participants spontaneously named their romantic partner as their closest friend. Consistent with these findings, Sprecher and Regan (1998) found that "both" companionate love and passionate love were related to commitment and relationship satisfaction. Friendship, along with passion, is thus an important ingredient of romantic love.

Models for Explaining Love

There are many perspectives on the study of love. Theories of love are disparate and difficult to classify. Nevertheless, they can be grouped under two broad headings: naturalistic/biological and psychological/social. Naturalistic approaches are rooted in the body, in emotion, and in our evolutionary heritage—especially as evolution relates to sexuality. We consider passionate and companionate love, attachment processes, and the evolution of love. In the psychological/social approach, there are concepts such as cognition (e.g., prototypes), social motives, interaction and communication, and various classifications of love.

Naturalistic/Biological Approaches
Passionate and Companionate Love

Berscheid and Walster (1978) defined passionate love as a state of total absorption of two lovers, with mood swings between ecstasy and anguish. Companionate love is the affection felt by two people whose lives are deeply intertwined. Thus, love begins in the heat of passion but eventually cools into the quiet glow of companionship. This contrast of passion versus companionship received its fullest development from Walster and Walster (1978). More recently, Hatfield (1988) viewed the two types of love as coexisting in a relationship rather than as being sequential. Hatfield also noted that people appear to want both passion and companionship in their love relationships. This theme of including both within the love bond was noted previously and has been echoed by other scholars (e.g., Noller, 1996).

Attachment

The attachment Zeitgeist has been influential in several areas of psychology (e.g., developmental, social). It developed out of the work of Bowlby (1969), who studied the types of relationships (e.g., secure, anxious, avoidant) that infants form with their caregivers. These early attachments are posited to be causally related to subsequent relationships. For example, Hazan and Shaver (1987) applied attachment theory to adult love relationships, noting that it provides an explanation for both the joys and the sorrows manifested in adult love. The evidence regarding the relationship between childhood and adult attachment styles is mixed, with questions of attachment "stability" awaiting further research (Feeney & Noller, 1996). More recently, attachment theory and research have moved beyond their early linkages with love theory and research to explore such wide-ranging topics as parents' attachment styles and their influences on children (Feeney, 2006), volunteerism (Gillath et al., 2005), emotions (Mikulincer & Shaver, 2005), and attachment networks (Doherty & Feeney, 2004).

Evolution of Love

Mellen (1981) argued that the survival of the human species necessitated an emotional bond between breeding pairs of partners so that both partners would attend to their helpless infants. Pairs without such bonds lost the evolutionary race through higher infant mortality. Such primitive emotional bonding was hypothesized to be the beginning of love. Related themes have been further developed by evolutionary psychologists. For example, Buss (1988) defined love as consisting of behaviors enacted by both females and males that strengthen the bonding function and ultimately serve to perpetuate the species. Building on Trivers' (1972) differential parental investment model, in which males seek to mate with many females, whereas females mate more selectively and nurture their few offspring, evolutionary psychologists have hypothesized selected gender differences in courtship and mating strategies. Some research supports this evolutionary approach (e.g., Buss & Kenrick, 1998), although there are also vigorous counterarguments (Eagly & Wood, 1999). An extended discussion of evolution as a basis for psychological theory more generally may be found in

C. Hendrick (2005). The role of evolution in sex and romantic love is presented in C. Hendrick and Hendrick (2004).

Psychological/Social Approaches
Prototypes of Love

Fehr (1994) construed love as a prototype or "best example," defined by its best or most representative set of features. Focusing on love in general, Fehr discovered that respondents rated companionate love as most typical of love, with maternal love, parental love, and friendship as the best examples. Passionate and sexual love received lower prototypicality ratings. Regan, Kocan, and Whitlock (1998), in a prototype study of romantic love in which participants rated the central features of romantic love, found that passion was among the list of central features, but it still ranked below several companionate features (e.g., honesty, trust). Within this research paradigm, it appears that the most general concept of love is that of companionship. Romantic love is conceived as companionate love plus passion.

Self-Expansion

Aron and Aron (1996), based on Eastern traditions concerning the concept of self, proposed that humans have a basic motive for self-expansion. This growth of self may incorporate physical possessions, as well as power and influence. Falling in love creates a rapid expansion of self-boundaries and therefore is pleasurable. When two people are falling in love, they can mutually incorporate one another into the expansion process (see also Aron, Norman, Aron, McKenna, & Heyman, 2000). In this way, "you and me" becomes "us."

Love Triangles

In his triangular theory of love, Sternberg (1986) proposed that love is a mix of intimacy, passion, and commitment. A relationship may be high or low on each concept, with eight types of love being possible. For example, the presence of all three components is named "consummate love," the absence of all three is "nonlove," and so on. More recently, Sternberg focused on love as a social construction, varying across time and cultures. Consistent with this view, Sternberg (1998) proposed that love is also a personal form of social construction, a story that each individual creates by living it.

Love Styles

In developing a typology of ways that people love, Lee (1973) used the metaphor of a color wheel for his "colors" of love. As with color, there were primary love styles and secondary, and even tertiary, mixes. Considerable research on love styles has built on Lee's theory (e.g., C. Hendrick & Hendrick, 1986). Attention has focused on six relatively independent styles of love. "Eros" is passionate love, where the lover idealizes the partner, has definite preferences for physical characteristics in a partner, and pursues love with intensity. "Ludus" is love played as a game, for mutual enjoyment, without the intensity of Eros. Ludus is short on commitment, and the "game of love" can occur with multiple partners simultaneously. "Storge" is friendship love and is analogous to companionate love, discussed previously. "Pragma" is practical love; it involves "shopping" for a mate with a list of desired qualities in hand (e.g., computer matching). "Mania" is "manic" love. A manic lover desperately wants love but often finds that it is painful. Thus, "stormy passion" is an apt descriptor, and a cycle of jealousy, dramatic breakups, and equally dramatic reconciliations characterize this love style. "Agape" is selfless and giving love where the person is fully concerned with the partner's welfare. A wide range of research supports the love styles approach to the study of love (see C. Hendrick & Hendrick, 2006, for a review).

Measurement of Love

Various paper-and-pencil questionnaires measure one or more types of love. Some of the more popular of these measures include Rubin's (1970) scales that assess loving and liking; Hatfield and Sprecher's (1986) Passionate Love Scale; a variety of instruments to measure attachment based on Hazan and Shaver's (1987) seminal study; Fehr's (1993) various prototype measures of love; Davis and Todd's (1985) Relationship Rating Form; and Sternberg's (1986) Triangular Theory of Love Scale.

Our own measure of love, the Love Attitudes Scale (LAS), is based on Lee's (1973) typological approach to love. We construed the six types of love as six variables and developed a set of six subscales (C. Hendrick & Hendrick, 1986). The subscales of the LAS have good psychometric properties (e.g., factor structure and loadings, alphas, test–retest reliabilities) and are relatively independent of each other. Refinements of the LAS include a relationship-specific version (C. Hendrick & Hendrick, 1990) and a rigorously validated short form with four items per subscale (C. Hendrick, Hendrick, & Dicke, 1998).

Current Research on Love

Theories of love have led to considerable empirical research in recent decades. In this section, we explore current love research, including how people communicate love, love styles, love across cultures, love's links with sexuality, love and respect, and love's relationship to happiness.

Communicating Love

Hecht, Marston, and Larkey (1994) developed a typology of "love ways," which included both verbal and nonverbal methods of showing love to a partner. They identified five different ways (or styles) of love (active/collaborative, committed, intuitive, secure, and traditional), each of which used somewhat different methods of communicating.

Love is communicated in complex ways. For example, research on the positive illusions that love partners hold about each other and their relationship (e.g., Murray & Holmes, 1997) suggests that such illusions actually may influence relationship outcomes positively. In related research, Meeks, Hendrick, and Hendrick (1998) assessed both love variables and communication for college dating couples. They found that both love and communication, including the ability to handle conflict constructively, were predictive of relationship satisfaction. Consistent with the research of Murray and Holmes (1997), perceptions of partners' disclosure were more predictive of relationship satisfaction than partners' actual levels of disclosure.

Love Styles

As noted previously, the love styles capture multidimensional aspects of love. These six different love styles have been used to explore many aspects of love, including gender differences, relationship satisfaction, and love and friendship.

Gender differences in love styles occur in most studies, with men typically reporting more game-playing (ludic) love and women more friendship-oriented (storgic) and practical (pragmatic) love (C. Hendrick & Hendrick, 1986). More recently, men also have reported more altruistic (agapic) love (C. Hendrick et al., 1998). Game-playing love has been shown to be negatively related to relationship satisfaction (S. Hendrick, Hendrick, & Adler, 1988). Women may be more friendship oriented and practical than men, but these love styles are not related strongly to satisfaction. On the other hand, women and men differ little on passionate love, which *is* related strongly to relationship satisfaction. In fact, passion is very predictive of relationship satisfaction across both age and cultures (Contreras, Hendrick, & Hendrick, 1996).

Love across Cultures

Although some scholars note that love needs to be understood within a cultural context, others believe that most fundamental aspects of love transcend place and time. Cho and Cross (1995) found that the themes of passionate love, obsessive love, casual love, devoted love, and free choice of a mate were present in Chinese literature dating back thousands of years.

In other research, European American, Japanese American, and Pacific Islander residents of Hawaii were similar on several aspects of love and relationships (Doherty, Hatfield, Thompson, & Choo, 1994). Sprecher et al. (1994) found similar love attitudes and experiences when they studied American, Japanese, and Russian approaches to love. More recently, Sprecher and Toro-Morn (2002) found that an American sample was less pragmatic and less manic than a Chinese sample. Yet these differences are typically not large. Humans are indeed more the same than we are different.

Love and Sexuality

Scholars of relationships typically have either separated love from sexuality or have tried to subsume one by the other. Aron and Aron (1991) visualized scholarship on the two topics as a continuum, with the idea that sex can be subsumed under love at one end of the continuum and the idea that love can be subsumed under sex at the other end of the continuum. Some scholars view the two aspects of human experience as linked, however, with both sex and love having important and related roles in intimate, partnered relationships. Regan and Berscheid (1999), for example, noted that sexual desire is a fundamental component of romantic love. In our work, we have found positive relationships between love (as measured by the LAS) and sex (as measured by the Sexual Attitudes Scale; C. Hendrick, Hendrick, & Reich, 2006). For example, greater erotic and altruistic love are related to more idealistic sexuality (the Communion subscale of the Sexual Attitudes Scale), whereas game-playing love is related positively to casual and biologically oriented sexuality (Permissiveness and Instrumentality subscales).

We (S. Hendrick & Hendrick, 2002) proposed that people link love and sex (broadly construed as more than just intercourse) in their romantic relationships and asked people to describe these links. Several themes emerged, including love being the most important thing in the relationship and coming before sex in both significance and sequencing. Another significant theme was that sex was viewed as a profoundly important way of demonstrating love.

In a large-scale study of sexual behavior in the United States, Laumann, Gagnon, Michael, and Michaels (1994) found that respondents who expressed the greatest physical pleasure and emotional satisfaction in their relationships were those in partnered, monogamous relationships. Although love was not discussed directly, it surely was implied.

Researchers may have been slow to link sex with love, but based on our personal, empirical, and clinical experience, we know the two are related. While it is possible to experience love without sexual/physical intimacy or to experience sex without love, for most of us, most of the time, love and sex are linked.

Love and Respect

Until recently, little work has explored respect as a potentially important influence in romantic relationships and a co-contributor with love to relationship satisfaction. This situation is changing. As noted couple researcher John Gottman (1994) stated, most couples desire "just two things from their marriage—love and respect" (p. 18).

Frei and Shaver (2002) used a prototype approach in one study and conducted two additional studies to identify the central features of respect and to develop a scale based on those features. Their 45-item Respect for Partner Scale, along with a measure of love (Rubin, 1970), was a strong predictor of relationship satisfaction.

We (S. Hendrick & Hendrick, 2006a) crafted a respect scale based on the six dimensions of respect delineated by Lawrence-Lightfoot (2000), including attention, curiosity, dialog, empowerment, healing, and self-respect. Our six-item Respect Toward Partner Scale was correlated with love (and other variables) across three studies, two with college students and one with employed adults. Respect was significantly and positively correlated with passionate (erotic) love and altruistic (agapic) love across all three studies and with friendship (storgic) love across two studies. It was also correlated negatively and significantly with game-playing (ludic) love across two studies. Frei and Shaver's (2002) respect scale was used in one of the three studies and correlated significantly with five of the six love styles (positively with Eros, Pragma, and Agape and negatively with Ludus and Mania). In addition, both Eros and the Respect Toward Partner Scale were strong predictors of relationship satisfaction (S. Hendrick & Hendrick, 2006b). The items comprising the Respect Toward Partner Scale are provided in the Appendix. We foresee continued theoretical and empirical exploration of love and respect and their individual and shared influences in romantic relationships.

Love and Happiness/Well-Being

Love clearly is important to the human condition, as is being in a relationship. Baumeister and Leary (1995) argued persuasively that humans are a group species that has a "need to belong." Consistent with this thesis, Myers and Diener (1995), in discussing happiness, noted, "Throughout the Western world, married people of both sexes report more happiness than those never married, divorced, or separated" (p. 15). Still other research results confirm this finding. A series of studies of perceptions between love and sex (S. Hendrick & Hendrick, 2002) also examined the links between happiness and several relationship variables. In one large sample, people who were in love were significantly happier than people not in love; also, happiness scores were correlated positively with passionate love, friendship love, and relationship satisfaction.

Future Directions

Love is important to positive psychology and is an intrinsic part of the field of close relationships. Clinical psychology has discovered that knowledge about romantic love is important for practicing therapists (e.g., Bergner, 2000). Even psychoanalysts now take romantic love seriously. Mitchell's (2002) volume *Can love last?* was considered so important to the field that it drew several commentaries (e.g., Ogden, 2004). Other disciplines are now similarly engaged in studying romantic love.

The study of love needs to become a priority for researchers and funding agencies in "the near future." One need only look around to understand that love already is a priority for much of humanity. Scientists have begun once again to view humans as whole persons, not as a set of disconnected variables. Along with this holistic approach must come an awareness that people's intimate relationships, most particularly their love relationships, are an essential aspect of life.

One aspect of this recognition of the interweaving of mind and body is an appreciation for the (often) shared context of love and sexuality. As noted previously, rather than trying to subsume sex within love or love within sex, we prefer to view the two as coequals in partnered intimate relationships. And sex needs to be "very broadly" defined in future research to include all forms of physical affection rather than only sexual intercourse. Humans may be hardwired for intercourse, but they are even more fundamentally hardwired for physical touch. Babies require touching. Premature infants who are touched gain weight more rapidly (Field, 1998). People with pets (whom they presumably touch) show health benefits (Vormbrock & Grossber, 1988). All these manifestations of the need to touch and be touched speak to the importance of physical contact.

In addition to linking love with sex and construing sexuality more broadly, in future research we should more fully engage the issue of sexuality in aging. The aging of the U. S. population, the lengthening life span, and the Viagra phenomenon have not so much changed sexuality in later life as made it more visible. Both academic writing (Levy, 1994) and popular articles make clear that later-life sexuality is physically and emotionally satisfying, limited less by age than by the availability of a suitable partner. And for the aged, as for the young, "Sexual intercourse isn't everything. Just being together is an essential part of intimacy" (Mathias-Riegel, 1999, p. 48). It can be hoped that stereotypes about sex and aging are slowly changing. Any research that enriches our knowledge about love, sex, and aging should be popularized and disseminated widely. Love and sex span all of life.

Love and sex at any age are affected negatively by stress, one of positive psychology's worst enemies. " 'Less stress' and 'more free time' are the top things 45–59-year-olds say would most improve their sex life" (Jacoby, 1999, p. 43). And Herbert Benson (1996) noted that "the vast majority of the medical complaints brought to doctors' offices are stress- and belief-related" (p. 292). If we can help people to simplify their lives, thus reducing their stress levels, it is very likely that people's relationships (including love and sex) would be enriched greatly. Moreover, the positive aspects of their lives would be enriched accordingly.

In the introduction, we noted that love, sex, friendship, and marriage are increasingly linked in romantic relationships. We also have argued for the integrated study of love and sexuality throughout life span. We wish to close by generalizing our argument: Love should be studied as a central concept with links to many other positive psychological concepts. In this way, a systematic approach to a positive psychology can be developed.

Questions about the Future

1. Will the broad disciplines that constitute psychology come to recognize the power and centrality of love for human relationships?

2. Will funding agencies ever recognize love as a topic worthy of serious research funding?

3. Will the study of love become a central issue in the development of positive psychology?

References

Aron, A., & Aron, E. N. (1991). Love and sexuality. In K. McKinney & S. Sprecher (Eds.), *Sexuality in close relationships* (pp. 25–48). Hillsdale, NJ: Erlbaum.

Aron, A., Norman, C. C., Aron, E. N., McKenna, C., & Heyman, R. E. (2000). Couples' shared participation in novel and arousing activities and experienced relationship quality. *Journal of Personality and Social Psychology, 78*, 273–284.

Aron, E. N., & Aron, A. (1996). Love and expansion of the self: The state of the model. *Personal Relationships, 3*, 45–58.

Baumeister, R. F., & Leary, M. R. (1995). The need to belong: Desire for interpersonal attachments as a fundamental human motivation. *Psychological Bulletin, 117*, 497–529.

Benson, H. (1996). *Timeless healing: The power and biology of belief.* New York: Scribner's.

Bergner, R. M. (2000). Love and barriers to love: An analysis for psychotherapists and others. *American Journal of Psychotherapy, 54*, 1–17.

Berscheid, E. (2000). Foreword: Back to the future and forward to the past. In C. Hendrick & S. S. Hendrick (Eds.), *Close relationships: A sourcebook* (pp. ix–xxi). Thousand Oaks, CA: Sage.

Berscheid, E., & Walster, E. H. (1969). *Interpersonal attraction.* Reading, MA: Addison-Wesley.

Berscheid, E., & Walster, E. H. (1978). *Interpersonal attraction* (2nd ed.). Reading, MA: Addison-Wesley.

Bowlby, J. (1969). *Attachment and loss: Vol. 1. Attachment.* New York: Basic Books.

Buss, D. M. (1988). Love acts: The evolutionary biology of love. In R. J. Sternberg & M. L. Barnes (Eds.), *The psychology of love* (pp. 100–117). New Haven, CT: Yale University Press.

Buss, D. M., & Kenrick, D. T. (1998). Evolutionary social psychology. In D. T. Gilbert, S. T. Fiske, & G. Lindzey (Eds.), *The handbook of social psychology* (Vol. 2, 4th ed., pp. 982–1026). Boston: McGraw-Hill.

Cho, W., & Cross, S. E. (1995). Taiwanese love styles and their association with self-esteem and relationship quality. *Genetic, Social, and General Psychology Monographs, 121*, 283–309.

Contreras, R., Hendrick, S. S., & Hendrick, C. (1996). Perspectives on marital love and satisfaction in Mexican American and Anglo couples. *Journal of Counseling and Development, 74*, 408–415.

Davis, K. E., & Todd, M. J. (1985). Assessing friendship: Prototypes, paradigm cases and relationship description. In S. Duck & D. Perlman (Eds.), *Understanding personal relationships: An interdisciplinary approach* (pp. 17–38). London: Sage.

Doherty, N. A., & Feeney, J. A. (2004). The composition of attachment networks throughout the adult years. *Personal Relationships, 11*, 469–488.

Doherty, R. W., Hatfield, E., Thompson, K., & Choo, P. (1994). Cultural and ethnic influences on love and attachment. *Personal Relationships, 1*, 391–398.

Eagly, A. H., & Wood, W. (1999). The origins of sex differences in human behavior. *American Psychologist, 54*, 408–423.

Feeney, J. A. (2006). Parental attachment and conflict behavior: Implications for offsprings' attachment, loneliness, and relationship satisfaction. *Personal Relationships, 13*, 19–36.

Feeney, J. A., & Noller, P. (1996). *Adult attachment.* Thousand Oaks, CA: Sage.

Fehr, B. (1993). How do I love thee? Let me consult my prototype. In S. Duck (Ed.), *Individuals in relationships* (pp. 87–120). Newbury Park, CA: Sage.

Fehr, B. (1994). Prototype-based assessment of laypeople's views of love. *Personal Relationships, 1*, 309–331.

Field, T. M. (1998). Touch therapies. In R. R. Hoffman, M. F. Sherrick, & J. S. Warm (Eds.), *Viewing psychology as a whole* (pp. 603–624). Washington, DC: American Psychological Association.

Frei, J. R., & Shaver, P. R. (2002). Respect in close relationships: Prototype definition, self-report assessment, and initial correlates. *Personal Relationships, 9*, 121–139.

Gillath, O., Shaver, P. R., Mikulincer, M., Nitzberg, R. E., Erez, A., & Van IJzendoorn, M. H. (2005). Attachment, caregiving, and volunteering: Placing volunteerism in an attachment-theoretical framework. *Personal Relationships, 12*, 425–446.

Gottman, J. M. (1994). *Why marriages succeed or fail.* New York: Simon & Schuster.

Harlow, H. F. (1974). *Learning to love.* New York: Jason Aronson.

Hatfield, E. (1988). Passionate and companionate love. In R. J. Sternberg & M. L. Barnes (Eds.), *The psychology of love* (pp. 191–217). New Haven, CT: Yale University Press.

Hatfield, E., & Sprecher, S. (1986). Measuring passionate love in intimate relations. *Journal of Adolescence, 9*, 383–410.

Hazan, C., & Shaver, P. (1987). Romantic love conceptualized as an attachment process. *Journal of Personality and Social Psychology, 52*, 511–524.

Hecht, M. L., Marston, P. J., & Larkey, L. K. (1994). Love ways and relationship quality. *Journal of Social and Personal Relationships, 11*, 25–43.

Hendrick, C. (2005). Evolution as a foundation for psychological theories. In S. Strack (Ed.), *Handbook of personology and psychopathology* (pp. 3–23). Hoboken, NJ: Wiley.

Hendrick, C., & Hendrick, S. S. (1986). A theory and method of love. *Journal of Personality and Social Psychology, 50*, 392–402.

Hendrick, C., & Hendrick, S. S. (1990). A relationship-specific version of the Love Attitudes Scale. *Journal of Social Behavior and Personality, 5*, 230–254.

Hendrick, C., & Hendrick, S. S. (2004) Sex and romantic love: Connects and disconnects. In J. H. Harvey, A. Wenzel, & S. Sprecher (Eds.), *The handbook of sexuality in close relationships* (pp. 159–182). Mahwah, NJ: Erlbaum.

Hendrick, C., & Hendrick, S. S. (2006). Styles of romantic love. In R. J. Sternberg & K. Weis (Eds.), *The psychology of romantic love* (2nd ed., pp. 149–170). New Haven, CT: Yale University Press.

Hendrick, C., Hendrick, S. S., & Dicke, A. (1998). The Love Attitudes Scale: Short form. *Journal of Social and Personal Relationships, 15*, 147–159.

Hendrick, C., Hendrick, S. S., & Reich, D. A. (2006). The Brief Sexual Attitudes Scale. *The Journal of Sex Research, 43*, 76–86.

Hendrick, S. S., & Hendrick, C. (1993). Lovers as friends. *Journal of Social and Personal Relationships, 10*, 459–466.

Hendrick, S. S., & Hendrick, C. (2002). Linking romantic love and sex: Development of the Perceptions of Love and Sex Scale. *Journal of Social and Personal Relationships, 19*, 361–378.

Hendrick, S. S., & Hendrick, C. (2006a). Measuring respect in close relationships. *Journal of Social and Personal Relationships, 23*, 881–899.

Hendrick, S. S., & Hendrick, C. (2006b, November). *Respect: An important predictor of relationship satisfaction.* Paper presented at the Annual Conference of the National Council on Family Relations, Minneapolis, MN.

Hendrick, S. S., Hendrick, C., & Adler, N. L. (1988). Romantic relationships: Love, satisfaction, and staying together. *Journal of Personality and Social Psychology, 54*, 980–988.

Jacoby, S. (1999, September–October). Great sex: What's age got to do with it? *Modern Maturity, 42w*, 41–45, 91.

Laumann, E. O., Gagnon, J. H., Michael, R. T., & Michaels, S. (1994). *The social organization of sexuality: Sexual practices in the United States.* Chicago: University of Chicago Press.

Lawrence-Lightfoot, S. (2000). *Respect.* Cambridge, MA: Perseus Books.

Lee, J. A. (1973). *The colors of love: An exploration of the ways of loving.* Don Mills, ON: New Press.

Levine, R., Sato, S., Hashimoto, T., & Verma, J. (1995). Love and marriage in 11 cultures. *Journal of Cross-cultural Psychology, 26*, 554–571.

Levy, J. A. (1994). Sex and sexuality in later life stages. In A. S. Rossi (Ed.), *Sexuality across the life course* (pp. 287–309). Chicago: University of Chicago Press.

Mathias-Riegel, B. (1999, September–October). Intimacy 101: A refresher course in the language of love. *Modern Maturity, 42w*, 46–49, 84.

Meeks, B. S., Hendrick, S. S., & Hendrick, C. (1998). Communication, love, and relationship satisfaction. *Journal of Social and Personal Relationships, 15*, 755–773.

Mellen, S. L. W. (1981). *The evolution of love.* San Francisco: Freeman.

Mikulincer, M., & Shaver, P. R. (2005). Attachment theory and emotions in close relationships: Exploring the attachment-related dynamics of emotional reactions to relational events. *Personal Relationships, 12*, 149–168.

Mitchell, S. A. (2002). *Can love last? The fate of romance over time.* New York: Norton.

Murray, S. L., & Holmes, J. G. (1997). A leap of faith? Positive illusions in romantic relationships. *Personality and Social Psychology Bulletin, 23*, 586–604.

Murstein, B. I. (1974). *Love, sex, and marriage through the ages.* New York: Springer.

Myers, D. G., & Diener, E. (1995). Who is happy? *Psychological Science, 6*, 10–19.

Noller, P. (1996). What is this thing called love? Defining the love that supports marriage and family. *Personal Relationships, 3*, 97–115.

Ogden, T. H. (2004). The fate of romance over time. *Psychoanalytic Dialogues, 14*, 373–379.

Regan, P. C., & Berscheid, E. (1999). *Lust: What we know about human sexual desire.* Thousand Oaks, CA: Sage.

Regan, P. C., Kocan, E. R., & Whitlock, T. (1998). Ain't love grand! A prototype analysis of the concept of romantic love. *Journal of Social and Personal Relationships, 15*, 411–420.

Rubin, Z. (1970). Measurement of romantic love. *Journal of Personality and Social Psychology, 16*, 265–273.

Simpson, J. A., Campbell, B., & Berscheid, E. (1986). The association between romantic love and marriage: Kephart (1967) twice revisited. *Personality and Social Psychology Bulletin, 12*, 363–372.

Singer, I. (1984). *The nature of love: Vol. 1. Plato to Luther* (2nd ed.). Chicago: University of Chicago Press.

Sprecher, S., Aron, A., Hatfield, E., Cortese, A., Potapova, E., & Levitskaya, A. (1994). Love: American style, Russian style, and Japanese style. *Personal Relationships, 1*, 349–369.

Sprecher, S., & Regan, P. C. (1998). Passionate and companionate love in courting and young married couples. *Sociological Inquiry, 68*, 163–185.

Sprecher, S., & Toro-Morn, M. (2002). A study of men and women from different sides of earth to determine if men are from Mars and women are from Venus in their beliefs about love and romantic relationships. *Sex Roles, 46*, 131–147.

Sternberg, R. J. (1986). A triangular theory of love. *Psychological Review, 93*, 119–135.

Sternberg, R. J. (1998). *Love is a story.* New York: Oxford University Press.

Trivers, R. L. (1972). Parental investment and sexual selection. In B. Campbell (Ed.), *Sexual selection and the descent of man* (pp. 136–179). Chicago: Aldine.

Vormbrock, J. K., & Grossberg, J. M. (1988). Cardiovascular effects of human—pet dog interactions. *Journal of Behavioral Medicine, 11*, 509–517.

Walster, E., & Walster, G. W. (1978). *A new look at love.* Reading, MA: Addison-Wesley.

Appendix: Respect toward Partner Scale

1. I respect my partner.
2. I am interested in my partner as a person.
3. I am a source of healing for my partner.
4. I honor my partner.
5. I approve of the person my partner is.
6. I communicate well with my partner.

Note. For purposes of analyses, the items are scored on a 1 (Strongly Agree) to 5 (Strongly Disagree) basis. The set of items is averaged to produce a scale score.

For Richer ... in Good Times ... and in Health: Positive Processes in Relationships

Natalya C. Maisel *and* Shelly L. Gable

Abstract

Although psychologists have learned a great deal about negative and harmful processes in relationships, they have focused less on understanding the positive and beneficial processes in relationships. Of course, almost every close relationship offers the promise of both meaningful rewards and substantial risks, such as support, intimacy, companionship, conflict, rejection, and criticism. In this chapter, we attempt to highlight the complexities involved in relationships, with an emphasis on positive processes, with the goal of creating a picture that represents the dynamic reality of the social world. We first discuss the important role that intimate relationships play in human life and their strong links with health and well-being. We then highlight research on the positive processes in relationships, such as positive emotional expressions, shared novel experiences, intimacy, and the benefits of sharing positive events. This work complements previous literature which has tended to focus on the potential pitfalls in relationships. For example, displaying low levels of negative emotions may not be enough to create a strong relationship—expressions of positive emotions are also beneficial. Finally, we point to future directions in the positive psychology of relationships, such as a greater focus on biology and health (e.g., examining hormones that promote bonding), and the need to examine other types of relationships, such as friendships.

Keywords: capitalization, emotions, interpersonal, intimacy, relationships

We know a great deal about processes that go awry in relationships, but we are still at the early stages of arriving at a nuanced understanding of what makes them work. In this chapter, we attempt to highlight the complexities involved in relationships (including the positive processes), with the goal of creating a picture that represents the dynamic reality of the social world.

We begin by making the obvious but still important point that intimate relationships constitute not just "an aspect of life" but one of the most important aspects of life. Next, we briefly review the literature on close relationships, which has tended to focus on negative and aversive processes, such as conflict and criticism. We then make a case for the importance of focusing on appetitive processes in relationships, such as positive emotional expressions, intimacy processes, and the benefits of sharing positive events. We review some of these exciting areas of research and suggest possible future directions for the positive psychology of interpersonal relationships.

Relationships, Health, and Psychological Well-Being

A large body of research has demonstrated that close relationships have a profound impact on health and well-being. For example, Berkman and Syme (1979) found that having a large social network was related to a decreased risk of mortality. In their review, House, Landis, and Umberson (1988) found that a lack of strong social ties was a mortality risk factor on the order of smoking and high blood pressure. More recently, Uchino, Cacioppo, and Kiecolt-Glaser (1996) reviewed 81 studies on social support and social integration and found a consistent association between social ties and increased positive physiological functioning of the cardiovascular, endocrine, and immune systems. Close relationships, the most important of our "social ties," are not only related to health and mortality, they also have been shown to have a strong association to subjective reports of happiness and life satisfaction (e.g., Diener & Seligman, 2002). Indeed, the need to connect with others has been proposed as a central motivation for human beings (Baumeister & Leary, 1995).

Although it is clear that having close social ties is important for health and well-being, research also has highlighted the negative consequences of interpersonal relationships (e.g., Rook, 1984). For example, losing a partner through death or divorce can be quite devastating, and such losses are often associated with large decreases in well-being (e.g., Stroebe, Stroebe, Abakoumkin, & Schut, 1996). Researchers have noted that negative social relationships can be a major source of stress and pain (e.g., Kiecolt-Glaser, 1999; Seeman, 2001). Although early epidemiological studies focused mainly on whether people were socially connected, researchers soon realized that the "quality" of these relationships must also be taken into account. For example, marriage seems to be related to positive health and psychological outcomes only if the marriage is happy and nondistressed (e.g., Kiecolt-Glaser & Newton, 2001). In short, the data suggest that having social bonds and close relationships are necessary for health and well-being. However, there is also risk involved; if these relationships are filled with negative emotions and conflict, they are detrimental to health and well-being.

Appetitive and Aversive Processes in Relationships

As noted above, although relationships are often a source of pleasure and joy, they can also be a major source of stress. A great deal of research in the field of close relationships has focused on these negative processes in relationships; however, more recently, researchers have begun to investigate the independent effects of negative and positive processes in relationships (e.g., Kiecolt-Glaser & Newton, 2001; Reis & Gable, 2003; Uchino, Holt-Lunstad, Uno, & Flinders, 2001). One particularly useful framework for making the distinction between these positive and negative aspects of relationships is a focus on appetitive and aversive dimensions of motivation, which differentiates between moving "toward" rewarding and desired outcomes (appetitive processes) and moving "away" from punishing and undesired outcomes (aversive processes;

e.g., Carver, 1996). The appetitive dimension regulates approach-oriented behavior (e.g., focusing on potentially rewarding stimuli), whereas the aversive dimension regulates avoidance-oriented behavior (e.g., focusing on potentially punishing stimuli; see Gable, 2006).

This focus on appetitive and aversive processes has a long history of inquiry across various domains, and recent work suggests that separate biological systems underlie the two processes (see Elliot & Covington, 2001). Specifically, research on the brain has found that individual differences in behavioral activation system (BAS) and behavioral inhibition system (BIS) scores (e.g., Gray, 1987) differentially predicted prefrontal cortex activity, such that participants with higher BAS showed more resting activity in the left prefrontal cortex and participants with higher BIS showed more resting activity in the right prefrontal cortex (Sutton & Davidson, 1997). Moreover, the appetitive and aversive systems are seen as largely independent, as shown by Gable, Reis, and Elliot (2003) in the domains of motivation, affect, personality, attitude formation, and more. The distinction between the two systems can also be usefully applied to the research on interpersonal relationships.

Aversive Processes in Relationships

Research that has focused on the presence or absence of aversive social relationship behaviors, such as anger, violence, and conflict, has played an extremely important role in shedding light on interpersonal relationships (e.g., Bradbury, Fincham, & Beach, 2000). Studies of videotaped interactions between partners have highlighted negative patterns, such as demand-withdrawal patterns, where criticism and defensiveness create a detrimental cycle of handling conflict in relationships (e.g., Christensen & Heavey, 1990). Gottman's (1998) program of research has highlighted several predictors of divorce, such as contempt, negative affect reciprocity, stonewalling, belligerence, and criticism. In fact, conflict and negative affect management in relationships have been thought to be two of the most important factors influencing relationship satisfaction and stability (Christensen & Walczynski, 1997; Gottman, Coan, Carrere, & Swanson, 1998).

In addition to examining the presence of negative processes in relationships (e.g., conflict, criticism), researchers have examined the absence of negatives (e.g., trust, security). Research on trust in relationships has emphasized the importance of predictability and dependability in relationships, and trust in couples has been associated with a number of important relationship outcomes (Rempel, Ross, & Holmes, 2001). A related construct in this literature is "felt security" (e.g., Holmes, 2002). Research has demonstrated that feeling secure in one's relationships helps protect against the threat of rejection and leads to feeling more loved and accepted by one's partner (e.g., Murray, 2005). The research on criticism, conflict, trust, security, and other processes has been invaluable for our understanding of relationships. However, the importance of appetitive processes in relationships should not be overlooked, and we review some of these appetitive processes next.

Appetitive Processes in Relationships
Positive Emotions and Relationships

The bulk of research on emotions has focused on negative emotions, such as sadness, anger, and fear (see Fredrickson, 1998). However, in recent years, theorists have begun to examine the impact of positive emotions. Fredrickson (1998), in her broaden-and-build model of positive emotions, proposed that positive emotions serve adaptive functions, including promoting prosocial behavior and motivating people to build social resources. Although the focus of positive emotions was initially "intra"-personal, such as how these emotions could increase our attention capacity (e.g., Fredrickson, 2001), researchers have also begun to tackle the interpersonal or relational nature of these emotions (e.g., Shiota, Campos, Keltner, & Hertenstein, 2004).

Importantly, positive and negative emotions are largely independent dimensions that should not just be thought of as opposite ends of a single pole (e.g., Watson, Clark, & Tellegen, 1988). Along these lines, Updegraff, Gable, and Taylor (2004) found that people differed in terms of the frequency and impact of positive emotions in their daily lives. Specifically, they found that people who were higher in approach-oriented motivation tended to experience more positive emotions daily and tended to base more of their day-to-day subjective well-being on their positive emotional experiences. These effects were separate from the impact of any negative emotions, which is consistent with research demonstrating that trait-level positive and negative affect loaded onto separate appetitive and aversive dimensions (e.g., Gable et al., 2003).

What might be the interpersonal consequences of focusing more on positive emotional experiences? Research has demonstrated that people who

generally reported greater positive affect were better at social interactions and had interactions of higher quality, whereas negative affect did not predict either of these outcomes (Berry & Hansen, 1996). In addition, Berry, Willingham, and Thayer (2000) conducted a daily diary study on friendship dyads and found that high positive affect was related to feelings of closeness, whereas high negative affect was related to feelings of irritation and occurrences of conflict in the relationship. As noted above, ignoring the appetitive processes (in this case, positive affect) would mean that a great deal of information about relationships is lost.

Many positive emotions are inherently social in nature. When one experiences emotions such as gratitude, compassion, and love, there is almost always an interpersonal target of these emotions. Emotions such as joy may trigger play behavior that solidifies relationships (Fredrickson, 2001). Even pride can have interpersonal consequences as it may motivate people to tell close others about their achievement, which can strengthen interpersonal connections (Lewis, 1993). Studies have demonstrated that when people experience positive emotions together, such as amusement and excitement, these shared experiences can result in potentially long-lasting social bonds (see Fredrickson, 2001). Additionally, the positive emotion of gratitude is associated with more prosocial activity and more empathy for others (e.g., McCullough, Emmons, & Tsang, 2002). Other important positive emotions in relationships are love and desire. In the current volume, there are excellent chapters on the topics of gratitude (see chap. 41) and love (see chap. 42) to which we refer the reader.

Social Support and Capitalization

Researchers often posit that the associations among social ties and positive outcomes in health and well-being have a great deal to do with social support, which refers to the aid, assistance, and emotional support we receive from friends, family members, and others (e.g., Barrera, Sandler, & Ramsay, 1981). Several observational coding guides for behavioral responses to social support disclosures have been developed which shed more light on the actual interaction processes of couples (e.g., Cutrona & Suhr, 1992). Additionally, researchers have attempted to uncover what support behaviors are helpful under different circumstances (e.g., Cutrona & Russell, 1990). Social support in close relationships tends to involve a complicated interaction between individual differences (e.g., attachment style), contextual factors (e.g., mood, severity of the stressor), relationship factors (e.g., satisfaction), and the actual support that is provided (e.g., Lakey, McCabe, Fisicaro, & Drew, 1996).

The classic focus of social support research has been on the disclosure of negative and stressful events to others. A much newer addition to the social support literature is the idea of capitalization, which is the process of sharing positive events with others and gaining additional benefits from this disclosure (Gable, Reis, Impett, & Asher, 2004). Extending Langston's (1994) research on the positive consequences of sharing positive experiences, Gable and colleagues (2004) have provided evidence for the importance of considering these positive event disclosures. These researchers conducted several studies demonstrating that people derive additional benefits, such as increased daily positive affect and daily well-being, when they share positive events with other people. These increases in positive affect and well-being are significant even when controlling for the benefits produced by the positive event itself. Additionally, this research suggests that capitalization interactions provide an important opportunity for people in relationships to foster intimacy and closeness through supportive exchanges without the drawback of risking one's self-esteem or self-worth, as one might do when seeking support for a negative event (e.g., Bolger, Zuckerman, & Kessler, 2000).

Capitalization is a very common occurrence; Gable and colleagues (2004) found that people report sharing positive events with others on approximately 80% of days out of a 10-day period. Thus, the way that people "respond" to these positive event disclosures in everyday life is an important new area of research. For example, the benefits of capitalization were greatest when the person hearing the news reacted actively and constructively (e.g., enthusiastic, genuine responses; Gable et al., 2004). To further examine these reactions to capitalization attempts, Gable, Gonzaga, and Strachman (2006) examined responses to positive event disclosures in the lab. As predicted, active and constructive responses were significantly related to positive post-interaction reports and to other relationship well-being measures. Finally, another line of research on the importance of positive events includes the research on savoring, which describes one's ability to focus on and attend to positive emotions and experiences (Bryant, 1989). More recent studies have randomly assigned people to positive reminiscence conditions, and results indicated that positive

reminiscences lead to greater savoring and increased reports of happiness (e.g., Bryant, Smart, & King, 2005).

Intimacy and Responsiveness

Another body of research that has focused on appetitive processes in relationships is the literature on intimacy and perceived partner responsiveness (e.g., Reis & Patrick, 1996). Humans not only have a need to belong, but they are also highly motivated to seek out intimacy with close others (Reis & Shaver, 1988). Reis and Shaver's model of intimacy begins with a person's self-disclosure to a romantic partner. His or her partner then interprets this disclosure (through the filter of individual differences and contextual factors) and responds to the disclosure. Finally, the disclosing person interprets his or her partner's response (again, through the filter of factors such as goals, personality traits, and context), and the outcome may be "perceived partner responsiveness," or the feeling that one is understood, validated, and cared for by one's partner (Reis & Patrick, 1996).

Self-disclosure and responsiveness are thus central aspects of intimacy. Although much attention in the past has been given to self-disclosure, disclosure alone is not enough to create intimacy (Reis & Patrick, 1996). A number of studies have now outlined the importance of perceived responsiveness to the self (e.g., Reis, Clark, & Holmes, 2004), including its association to relationship satisfaction (e.g., Reis & Patrick, 1996) and felt security (e.g., Holmes, 2002). Laurenceau, Barrett, and Pietromonaco (1998) used an event-contingent diary design to examine the effects of disclosure and responsiveness on evaluations of intimacy. They found perceived partner responsiveness to be a strong mediator of the link between self-disclosure and intimacy. Similarly, one study by Manne and colleagues (2004) examined couples where one partner had cancer and found that perceived partner responsiveness mediated the positive association between self-disclosure and increases in intimacy. An important next step in the literature on intimacy and responsiveness may be to see how widely applicable this process is across various types of interpersonal interactions (e.g., when partners share personal goals with each other; Feeney, 2004).

Shared Novel Experiences

Another important appetitive process in relationships is self-expansion (e.g., Aron, Aron, Tudor, & Nelson, 1991), which refers to the process of including a close other in one's conception of the self. This self-expansion process can include taking in a close other's "resources, perspectives and characteristics" (Aron et al., 1991, p. 243). Work by Aron and colleagues (e.g., Aron, Norman, Aron, McKenna, & Heyman, 2000) has demonstrated that partners' participation in novel, arousing experiences together can increase relationship satisfaction, presumably because these experiences offer opportunities for continued expansion. The importance of considering appetitive processes in relationships is especially clear in this body of research—partners who are motivated to engage in fun and exciting activities together, such as outdoor sports and travel, also tend to have high levels of marital satisfaction (e.g., Hill, 1988).

Experimental studies have also demonstrated that creating a novel and physiologically arousing task that couples participate in together leads to increases in relationship satisfaction (Aron et al., 2000). Further investigation into this effect has suggested that high positive affect (and not decreased negative affect) might be the mediating factor between these novel tasks and increased relationship satisfaction (see Strong & Aron, 2006). Other studies have since extended some of these findings in married couples to other relationships. Fraley and Aron (2004) found that closeness between strangers was increased through a shared humorous experience. Continued research on the ways that couples keep their relationships fun and exciting may prove to be a very beneficial strategy for guarding against decreased satisfaction.

Future Directions
Biology and Interpersonal Relationships

Researchers have begun to explore the biological systems underlying appetitive and aversive social processes. For example, Panksepp has proposed that an underlying reward system in the brain is thought to "mediate specific behavioral sequences related to appetitive engagements with the world" (Panksepp, Knutson, & Burgdorf, 2002, p. 462). This "seeking system" for social rewards is proposed to be distinct from a separation-distress system. Additionally, further research on the brain using electroencephalograms (EEGs) has supported the idea that different parts of the brain are activated when humans are approaching rewarding stimuli versus when they are avoiding punishing stimuli (e.g., Pizzagalli, Sherwood, Henriques, & Davidson, 2005). Research on the biological basis of affiliative behavior in humans is growing as well.

The hormone oxytocin appears to reduce anxiety and increase one's willingness to trust others and engage in prosocial behavior (Bartz & Hollander, 2006). As researchers explore the links between interpersonal relationships and biology in greater detail, neuroscience may be a productive new avenue of research (e.g., Fisher, Aron, Mashek, Li, & Brown, 2002).

Positive Emotions and Health

As noted previously, positive emotions have been shown to have a number of beneficial consequences for intrapersonal and interpersonal well-being. One burgeoning area of research in the field of positive emotions is examining the link between positive emotions and health. Relatively few studies to date have tackled this question directly, although there is evidence that positive emotions and dispositional positive affect are related to better health. For example, Harker and Keltner (2001) found that women who showed more positive affect in their college yearbook photos also reported better emotional and physical health 30 years later. In another interesting study, Danner, Snowdon, and Friesen (2001) coded autobiographies from Catholic nuns written when the women were in their early twenties. These researchers found a significant relationship between high positive emotional content in the autobiographies of the women and increased longevity. Research on positive emotions and health would likely benefit from an increasing focus on interpersonal relationships. Social relationships may prove to be one of the pathways through which positive emotions influence health. For example, people who are higher on trait levels of positive affect and agreeableness tend to have better social relationships (Watson, Clark, McIntyre, & Hamaker, 1992), which may then lead to improved health and well-being.

Other Relationships

Our review of the positive psychology of relationships has tended to focus on romantic relationships and the adult pair bond. Of course, there are many fascinating areas of research that focus on other types of relationships, which we have not had space to go into great detail here. The literature on the parent–child relationship is also beginning to focus on the positive psychology of relationships. In the past, much of the research on parents and children has focused on the outcomes of the children, and when researchers examined the outcomes of the parents, they often focused on the stress caused by the transition to parenthood. In particular, having children is thought to cause a significant decline in marital quality (e.g., Schulz, Cowan, & Cowan, 2006). But what are the benefits of having children? More research is needed to examine the factors that create positive parent–child relationships and the factors that help ease the adjustment to parenting (e.g., Demo & Cox, 2000).

Friendship relationships are another area of research where positive psychology can have a significant impact. The research cited on social support and social networks highlights the importance of friendship to health and well-being. Although there has not been a great deal of scholarship concerning friendships in adulthood, the research to date does suggest that relationships with friends have a number of important implications for health and well-being (see Bagwell et al., 2005). Interventions targeted at helping the elderly improve their friendship networks have been shown to decrease loneliness and increase well-being (e.g., Stevens & van Tilburg, 2000). Additionally, recent studies have begun to examine the effect of giving support in close relationships. For example, Brown, Nesse, Vinokur, and Smith (2003) examined mortality status in older individuals over a 5-year time period, and they found that providing emotional support to one's spouse was related to reduced mortality. Having a friendship network also might provide people with multiple opportunities to provide support, which may have a number of beneficial effects.

Concluding Comments

By focusing on appetitive relationship processes, such as positive emotions, capitalization, perceived partner responsiveness, and novel experiences, researchers are beginning to get a more complete picture about what makes relationships work. As this review of future directions indicates, there are still many unanswered questions regarding appetitive processes in interpersonal relationships. As both the fields of positive psychology and close relationships advance, we hope that researchers will continue to examine how the presence of positives in relationships can affect relationship well-being as well as individual functioning.

Questions about the Future of the Topic

1. How do couples maintain appetitive processes over time?

2. In addition to interventions aimed at reducing negative behaviors in relationships, are interventions to increase positive behaviors effective?

3. Under which circumstances are appetitive and aversive processes most important for interpersonal relationships?

References

Aron, A., Aron, E. N., Tudor, M., & Nelson, G. (1991). Close relationships as including other in the self. *Journal of Personality and Social Psychology, 60*(2), 241–253.

Aron, A., Norman, C. C., Aron, E. N., McKenna, C., & Heyman, R. E. (2000). Couples' shared participation in novel and arousing activities and experienced relationship quality. *Journal of Personality and Social Psychology, 78*(2), 273–284.

Bagwell, C. L., Bender, S. E., Andreassi, C. L., Kinoshita, T. L., Montarello, S. A., & Muller, J. G. (2005). Friendship quality and perceived relationship changes predict psychosocial adjustment in early adulthood. *Journal of Social and Personal Relationships, 22*(2), 235–254.

Barrera, M., Sandler, I. N., & Ramsay, T. B. (1981). Preliminary development of a scale of social support: Studies on college students. *American Journal of Community Psychology, 9*(4), 435–447.

Bartz, J. A., & Hollander, E. (2006). The neuroscience of affiliation: Forging links between basic and clinical research on neuropeptides and social behavior. *Hormones and Behavior, 50*(4), 518–528.

Baumeister, R. F., & Leary, M. R. (1995). The need to belong: Desire for interpersonal attachments as a fundamental human motivation. *Psychological Bulletin, 117*(3), 497–529.

Berkman, L. F., & Syme, S. L. (1979). Social networks, host resistance and mortality: A nine-year follow-up of Alameda County residents. *American Journal of Epidemiology, 109*, 186–204.

Berry, D. S., & Hansen, J. S. (1996). Positive affect, negative affect, and social interaction. *Journal of Personality and Social Psychology, 71*(4), 796–809.

Berry, D. S., Willingham, J. K., & Thayer, C. A. (2000). Affect and personality as predictors of conflict and closeness in young adults' friendships. *Journal of Research in Personality, 34*(1), 84–107.

Bolger, N., Zuckerman, A., & Kessler, R. C. (2000). Invisible support and adjustment to stress. *Journal of Personality and Social Psychology, 79*(6), 953–961.

Bradbury, T. N., Fincham, F. D., & Beach, S. R. H. (2000). Research on the nature and determinants of marital satisfaction: A decade in review. *Journal of Marriage and the Family, 62*(4), 964–980.

Brown, S. L., Nesse, R. M., Vinokur, A. D., & Smith, D. M. (2003). Providing social support may be more beneficial than receiving it: Results from a prospective study of mortality. *Psychological Science, 14*(4), 320–327.

Bryant, F. B. (1989). A four-factor model of perceived control: Avoiding, coping, obtaining, and savoring. *Journal of Personality, 57*(4), 773–797.

Bryant, F. B., Smart, C. M., & King, S. P. (2005). Using the past to enhance the present: Boosting happiness through positive reminiscence. *Journal of Happiness Studies, 6*(3), 227–260.

Carver, C. S. (1996). Emergent integration in contemporary personality psychology. *Journal of Research in Personality, 30*, 319–334.

Christensen, A., & Heavey, C. L. (1990). Gender and social structure in the demand/withdraw pattern of marital conflict. *Journal of Personality and Social Psychology, 59*(1), 73–81.

Christensen, A., & Walczynski, P. T. (1997). Conflict and satisfaction in couples. In R. J. Sternberg & M. Hojjat (Eds.), *Satisfaction in close relationships* (pp. 249–274). New York: Guilford.

Cutrona, C. E., & Russell, D. W. (1990). Type of social support and specific stress: Toward a theory of optimal matching. In B. R. Sarason, I. G. Sarason, & G. R. Pierce (Eds.), *Social support: An interactional view* (pp. 319–366). Oxford: Wiley.

Cutrona, C. E., & Suhr, J. A. (1992). Controllability of stressful events and satisfaction with spouse support behaviors. *Communication Research, 19*(2), 154–174.

Danner, D. D., Snowdon, D. A., & Friesen, W. V. (2001). Positive emotions in early life and longevity: Findings from the nun study. *Journal of Personality and Social Psychology, 80*(5), 804–813.

Demo, D. H., & Cox, M. J. (2000). Families with young children: A review of research in the 1990s. *Journal of Marriage and the Family, 62*(4), 876–895.

Diener, E., & Seligman, M. E. P. (2002). Very happy people. *Psychological Science, 13*(1), 81–84.

Elliot, A. J., & Covington, M. V. (2001). Approach and avoidance motivation. *Educational Psychology Review, 13*(2), 73–92.

Feeney, B. C. (2004). A secure base: Responsive support of goal strivings and exploration in adult intimate relationships. *Journal of Personality and Social Psychology, 87*(5), 631–648.

Fisher, H. E., Aron, A., Mashek, D., Li, H., & Brown, L. L. (2002). Defining the brain systems of lust, romantic attraction, and attachment. *Archives of Sexual Behavior, 31*(5), 413–419.

Fraley, B., & Aron, A. (2004). The effect of a shared humorous experience on closeness in initial encounters. *Personal Relationships, 11*(1), 61–78.

Fredrickson, B. L. (1998). What good are positive emotions? *Review of General Psychology, 2*(3), 300–319.

Fredrickson, B. L. (2001). The role of positive emotions in positive psychology: The broaden-and-build theory of positive emotions. *American Psychologist, 56*(3), 218–226.

Gable, S. L. (2006). Approach and avoidance social motives and goals. *Journal of Personality, 74*(1), 175–222.

Gable, S. L., Gonzaga, G. C., & Strachman, A. (2006). Will you be there for me when things go right? Supportive responses to positive event disclosures. *Journal of Personality and Social Psychology, 91*(5), 904–917.

Gable, S. L., Reis, H. T., & Elliot, A. J. (2003). Evidence for bivariate systems: An empirical test of appetition and aversion across domains. *Journal of Research in Personality, 37*(5), 349–372.

Gable, S. L., Reis, H. T., Impett, E. A., & Asher, E. R. (2004). What do you do when things go right? The intrapersonal and interpersonal benefits of sharing positive events. *Journal of Personality and Social Psychology, 87*(2), 228–245.

Gottman, J. M. (1998). Psychology and the study of marital processes. *Annual Review of Psychology, 49*, 169–197.

Gottman, J. M., Coan, J., Carrere, S., & Swanson, C. (1998). Predicting marital happiness and stability from newlywed interactions. *Journal of Marriage and the Family, 60*(1), 5–22.

Gray, J. A. (1987). *The psychology of fear and stress* (2nd ed.). New York: Cambridge University Press.

Harker, L., & Keltner, D. (2001). Expressions of positive emotion in women's college yearbook pictures and their relationship to personality and life outcomes across adulthood. *Journal of Personality and Social Psychology, 80*(1), 112–124.

Hill, M. S. (1988). Marital stability and spouses' shared time: A multidisciplinary hypothesis. *Journal of Family Issues, 9*(4), 427–451.

Holmes, J. G. (2002). Interpersonal expectations as the building blocks of social cognition: An interdependence theory perspective. *Personal Relationships, 9*(1), 1–26.

House, J. S., Landis, K. R., & Umberson, D. (1988). Social relationships and health. *Science, 241*, 540–545.

Kiecolt-Glaser, J. K. (1999). Stress, personal relationships, and immune function: Health implications. *Brain, Behavior and Immunity, 13*(1), 61–72.

Kiecolt-Glaser, J. K., & Newton, T. L. (2001). Marriage and health: His and hers. *Psychological Bulletin, 127*(4), 472–503.

Lakey, B., McCabe, K. M., Fisicaro, S., & Drew, J. B. (1996). Environmental and personal determinants of support perceptions: Three generalizability studies. *Journal of Personality and Social Psychology, 70*(6), 1270–1280.

Langston, C. A. (1994). Capitalizing on and coping with daily-life events: Expressive responses to positive events. *Journal of Personality and Social Psychology, 67*(6), 1112–1125.

Laurenceau, J., Barrett, L. F., & Pietromonaco, P. R. (1998). Intimacy as an interpersonal process: The importance of self-disclosure, partner disclosure, and perceived partner responsiveness in interpersonal exchanges. *Journal of Personality and Social Psychology, 74*(5), 1238–1251.

Lewis, M. (1993). Self-conscious emotions: Embarassment, pride, shame, and guilt. In M. Lewis & J. M. Haviland (Eds.), *Handbook of emotions* (pp. 563–573). New York: Guilford.

Manne, S., Ostroff, J., Rini, C., Fox, K., Goldstein, L., & Grana, G. (2004). The interpersonal process model of intimacy: The role of self-disclosure, partner disclosure, and partner responsiveness in interactions between breast cancer patients and their partners. *Journal of Family Psychology, 18*(4), 589–599.

McCullough, M. E., Emmons, R. A., & Tsang, J. (2002). The grateful disposition: A conceptual and empirical topography. *Journal of Personality and Social Psychology, 82*(1), 112–127.

Murray, S. L. (2005). Regulating the risks of closeness: A relationship-specific sense of felt security. *Current Directions in Psychological Science, 14*(2), 74–78.

Panksepp, J., Knutson, B., & Burgdorf, J. (2002). The role of brain emotional systems in addictions: A neuro-evolutionary perspective and new "self-report" animal model. *Addiction. Special Issue: Evolutionary Psychobiological Approaches to Addiction, 97*(4), 459–469.

Pizzagalli, D. A., Sherwood, R. J., Henriques, J. B., & Davidson, R. J. (2005). Frontal brain asymmetry and reward responsiveness. A source-localization study. *Psychological Science, 16*(10), 805–813.

Reis, H. T., Clark, M. S., & Holmes, J. G. (2004). Perceived partner responsiveness as an organizing construct in the study of intimacy and closeness. In D. J. Mashek & A. P. Aron (Eds.), *Handbook of closeness and intimacy* (pp. 201–225). Mahwah, NJ: Lawrence Erlbaum.

Reis, H. T., & Gable, S. L. (2003). Toward a positive psychology of relationships. In C. L. M. Keyes & J. Haidt (Eds.), *Flourishing: Positive psychology and the life well-lived* (pp. 129–159). Washington, DC: American Psychological Association.

Reis, H. T., & Patrick, B. C. (1996). Attachment and intimacy: Component processes. In E. T. Higgins & A. W. Kruglanski

(Eds.), *Social psychology: Handbook of basic principles* (pp. 523–563). New York: Guilford.

Reis, H. T., & Shaver, P. (1988). Intimacy as an interpersonal process. In S. Duck & D. F. Hay (Eds.), *Handbook of personal relationships: Theory, research and interventions* (pp. 367–389). Oxford: Wiley.

Rempel, J. K., Ross, M., & Holmes, J. G. (2001). Trust and communicated attributions in close relationships. *Journal of Personality and Social Psychology, 81*(1), 57–64.

Rook, K. S. (1984). The negative side of social interaction: Impact on psychological well-being. *Journal of Personality and Social Psychology, 46*(5), 1097–1108.

Schulz, M. S., Cowan, C. P., & Cowan, P. A. (2006). Promoting healthy beginnings: A randomized controlled trial of a preventive intervention to preserve marital quality during the transition to parenthood. *Journal of Consulting and Clinical Psychology, 74*(1), 20–31.

Seeman, T. (2001). How do others get under our skin? Social relationships and health. In C. D. Ryff & B. H. Singer (Eds.), *Emotion, social relationships, and health* (pp. 189–210). New York: Oxford University Press.

Shiota, M. N., Campos, B., Keltner, D., & Hertenstein, M. J. (2004). Positive emotion and the regulation of interpersonal relationships. In P. Philippot & R. S. Feldman (Eds.), *The regulation of emotion* (pp. 127–155). Mahwah, NJ: Lawrence Erlbaum.

Stevens, N., & van Tilburg, T. (2000). Stimulating friendship in later life: A strategy for reducing loneliness among older women. *Educational Gerontology. Special Issue: International research and practice, 26*(1), 15–35.

Stroebe, W., Stroebe, M., Abakoumkin, G., & Schut, H. (1996). The role of loneliness and social support in adjustment to loss: A test of attachment versus stress theory. *Journal of Personality and Social Psychology, 70*(6), 1241–1249.

Strong, G., & Aron, A. (2006). The effect of shared participation in novel and challenging activities on experienced relationship quality: Is it mediated by high positive affect? In K. D. Vohs & E. J. Finkel (Eds.), *Self and relationships: Connecting intrapersonal and interpersonal processes* (pp. 342–359). New York: Guilford.

Sutton, S. K., & Davidson, R. J. (1997). Prefrontal brain asymmetry: A biological substrate of the behavioral approach and inhibition systems. *Psychological Science, 8*(3), 204–210.

Uchino, B. N., Cacioppo, J. T., & Kiecolt-Glaser, J. K. (1996). The relationship between social support and physiological processes: A review with emphasis on underlying mechanisms and implications for health. *Psychological Bulletin, 119*(3), 488–531.

Uchino, B. N., Holt-Lunstad, J., Uno, D., & Flinders, J. B. (2001). Heterogeneity in the social networks of young and older adults: Prediction of mental health and cardiovascular reactivity during acute stress. *Journal of Behavioral Medicine, 24*(4), 361–382.

Updegraff, J. A., Gable, S. L., & Taylor, S. E. (2004). What makes experiences satisfying? The interaction of approach-avoidance motivations and emotions in well-being. *Journal of Personality and Social Psychology, 86*(3), 496–504.

Watson, D., Clark, L. A., McIntyre, C. W., & Hamaker, S. (1992). Affect, personality, and social activity. *Journal of Personality and Social Psychology, 63*(6), 1011–1025.

Watson, D., Clark, L. A., & Tellegen, A. (1988). Development and validation of brief measures of positive and negative affect: The PANAS scales. *Journal of Personality and Social Psychology, 54*(6), 1063–1070.

PART 7

Self-Based Approaches

What's Positive About Self-Verification?

Rebecca J. North *and* William B. Swann, Jr.

Abstract

Self-verification theory assumes that people work to preserve their self-views by seeking to confirm them. As is the case with other processes advocated by positive psychology, self-verification is presumed to be a fundamentally adaptive process. Intrapsychically, self-verification strivings maintain psychological coherence, reduce anxiety, improve physical health, and may foster authenticity. Interpersonally, they encourage people to gravitate toward honest relationship partners, foster trust and intimacy in relationships, and ensure predictability in one's behavior, which further promotes trust. Although self-verification is adaptive overall, it may lead to the perpetuation of negative self-views. Nevertheless, identifying the underlying processes in self-verification may lend insight into how to raise self-esteem. It is posited that to help raise the self-esteem of someone with a negative self-view, one should first provide the person with self-verification and subsequently provide positive feedback that challenges the negative self-views. In these and other instances, understanding the self-verification process more deeply may also shed light on how to define and build happiness.

Keywords: acceptance, happiness, positivity, self-esteem, self-verification

The original title of John Steinbeck's acclaimed novel *Of Mice and Men* was "Something That Happened" (Shillinglaw, 1994). This title reflects Steinbeck's life philosophy of accepting things as they are without judgment (Shillinglaw, 1994), an approach he called "is thinking." He once wrote that this mode of thinking "concerns itself primarily not with what should be, or could be, or might be, but rather with what actually 'is' . . ." (Steinbeck, 1951). Steinbeck thought "is thinking" was adaptive because it fostered understanding and acceptance. Self-verification theory is very much in the spirit of "is thinking," as it asserts that people are motivated to seek confirmation of their positive—and negative—self-views (Swann, 1983). Self-verifiers, therefore, prefer to be around "is thinkers," people who see them as they believe they "actually" are, not as they want to be, should be, or could be. In this chapter, we contend that, like "is thinking," self-verification is also adaptive, both for the reasons

that Steinbeck identified and because of other intrapsychic and interpersonal benefits associated with self-verification. We describe these benefits in the course of providing a brief overview of self-verification theory.

What Is Self-Verification?

Self-verification theory begins with the assumption that once people form their self-views, these self-views come to provide them with a powerful sense of coherence and a related capacity to predict and control their worlds (Cooley, 1902; Mead, 1934). Because self-views serve these critically important functions, people become invested in maintaining them, even if their self-views happen to be negative (Swann, 1983). As a result, when given the opportunity, people will choose to interact with others who see them as they see themselves. Specifically, just as people with positive self-views prefer interaction partners who see them positively, people with negative self-views prefer interaction partners who appraise them negatively (e.g., Hixon & Swann, 1993; Robinson & Smith-Lovin, 1992; Swann, Hixon, Stein-Seroussi, & Gilbert, 1990; Swann, Pelham, & Krull, 1989).

Not only does self-verification theory predict the relationship partners people choose, it also predicts how happy people are in those relationships and whether they remain in the relationships. Research has shown that people experience greater relationship quality and more intimacy in romantic relationships when partners verify their self-views (De La Ronde & Swann, 1998; Swann, De La Ronde, & Hixon, 1994). Conversely, people tend to withdraw from relationships in which the relationship partner fails to provide self-verification. For example, Swann and Pelham (2002) found that college students with negative self-views who had roommates who appraised them positively made plans to find a new roommate. In a similar way, married people with negative self-views became less intimate with partners who saw them in a more positive way than they saw themselves (e.g., Burke & Stets, 1999; De La Ronde & Swann, 1998; Murray, Holmes, & Griffin, 2000; Ritts & Stein, 1995; Schafer, Wickrama, & Keith, 1996; Swann et al., 1994) and even separated from or divorced overly positive, nonverifying partners (e.g., Cast & Burke, 2002).

Self-verification theory's prediction that people who have positive self-views gravitate toward others who see them in a positive light is hardly surprising, as it squares well with self-enhancement theory's assumption that people want to think well of themselves (Jones, 1973). The symmetric proposition—that people with negative self-views prefer partners who view them negatively—is less obvious to most people, however. Nevertheless, as we shall show, the notion that the self-verification strivings of people with negative self-views prevail over their self-enhancement strivings is more understandable when one recognizes that for people with negative self-views, negative evaluations are reassuring and credible; unexpectedly, positive evaluations can be profoundly disquieting and anxiety provoking. In this way, receiving self-verification provides psychological coherence, a feeling that one's self and the world are as one thinks they are. Psychological coherence, however, is just one benefit of self-verification. We will illustrate in this chapter that irrespective of the type of self-view one has, receiving confirmation of one's self-view, as in the case of self-verification, is associated with a host of intrapsychic and interpersonal benefits.

Self-Verification Theory and Positive Psychology

How is self-verification relevant to positive psychology? Positive psychology is the study of "what works" and "what is right" with human functioning (Sheldon & King, 2001); it specifically focuses on the adaptive aspects of human behavior. In keeping with such priorities, we suggest that self-verification is adaptive, serving many positive purposes for the individual. In this chapter, we first consider how self-verification is adaptive intrapsychically, that is, for the individual him- or herself, and then we will reflect on how it is adaptive interpersonally, that is, in social relationships. Additionally, we will address limitations in this argument by considering instances in which self-verification may not be adaptive. Finally, we will explore how an understanding of self-verification strivings can shed light on how to avert or remedy such maladaptive outcomes.

How Is Self-Verification Adaptive Intrapsychically?

Self-verification is adaptive intrapsychically for the role it plays in fostering psychological coherence, reducing anxiety, improving physical health, and cultivating authenticity. That said, we hasten to add that although most of the foregoing variables have been linked empirically to self-verification, the last one—authenticity—has not. It will remain for future researchers to test our suggestion that self-verification fosters authenticity.

Self-verification promotes psychological coherence. Psychological coherence, a sense that things are as people think they are, is a key positive outcome associated with self-verification; it has been identified as an important source of emotional comfort (Swann, Chang-Schneider, & Angulo, 2007). Self-verification strivings foster psychological coherence because they lead to the validation of self-views. People choose not to interact with individuals who do not confirm their self-views and thus avoid the feelings of a lack of psychological coherence that would result. Comments of self-verifiers from a study of Swann, Stein-Seroussi, and Giesler (1992) provide evidence that psychological coherence is associated with the self-verification process and is desirable to people. When self-verifiers with negative self-views were asked to explain why they chose to interact with a confederate who evaluated them negatively, one participant said, "Yeah, I think that's pretty close to the way I am. [The negative evaluator] better reflects my own view of myself, from experience." Not only is psychological coherence desirable, but as the following comment from another participant illustrates, psychological coherence is so important to people that it trumps desire for positive appraisals from others. One participant with a negative self-view explained why he or she chose to interact with a confederate who viewed him or her negatively in the following way: "I like the [favorable] evaluation but I am not sure that it is, ah, correct maybe. It *sounds* good, but [the negative evaluator] . . . seems to know more about me. So, I'll choose [the negative evaluator]." Psychological coherence is appealing and comforting to people, and it is a central intrapsychic benefit of self-verification.

Self-verification reduces anxiety. Self-verification not only provides feelings of psychological coherence, it actually reduces anxiety (for a review, see Swann, Chang-Schneider, & Angulo, 2007). That is, research has shown that verifying feedback leads to lower levels of anxiety than nonverifying feedback. Mendes and Akinola (2006), for example, observed people's cardiovascular responses to positive and negative evaluations, which could be either self-verifying or nonverifying. When people with negative self-views received positive feedback, they were physiologically "threatened" (avoidant and distressed). When they received negative feedback, they were physiologically "galvanized" (i.e., cardiovascularly aroused but in a positive way related to approach motivation). People with positive self-views reacted in opposite ways to the positive and negative feedback. Similarly, Wood, Heimpel, Newby-Clark, and Ross (2005) compared the reactions to success experiences of high- versus low-self-esteem participants. High-self-esteem individuals reacted favorably to success, but low-self-esteem individuals became anxious, apparently because the feedback was not consistent with their self-views (cf. Lundgren & Schwab, 1977). Similarly, Ralph and Mineka (1998) observed students' reactions to receiving grades on a midterm examination and found that students with low self-esteem experienced the greatest increase in overall distress, including anxious and depressive symptoms, after they received grades that were considered successful to them. That is to say, low-self-esteem participants responded with more distress to grades that they deemed acceptable than they did to grades that they considered to be failures. Events that are not self-verifying, therefore, increase anxiety even if they are positive, just as self-verifying events and feedback reduce anxiety even if they happen to be negative.

Self-verification improves health. Since positive but nonverifying events have been shown to cause stress for people with negative self-views, over an extended period of time these types of experiences can be detrimental to physical health. There is some support for this self-verification hypothesis. For instance, in a pair of prospective studies, Brown and McGill (1989) assessed the impact of positive life events on health outcomes for high- and low-self-esteem people. For participants with high self-esteem, positive life events (e.g., getting very good grades, improvement in living conditions) predicted increases in health. For participants with low self-esteem, positive life events predicted "decreases" in health. Shimizu and Pelham (2004) replicated and extended this finding. They found that positive life events predicted increased illness for low-self-esteem individuals. This pattern emerged even when controlling for negative affectivity, thus undermining an alternative hypothesis that negative affect influenced both self-reported self-esteem and reports of physical symptoms. Apparently, for people with negative self-views, the gap between positive life events and a chronically negative identity may be sufficiently psychologically threatening that it undercuts physical health (cf. Iyer, Jetten, & Tsivrikos, 2008).

Self-verification and authenticity. Self-verification may foster authenticity, which can be defined as "the unobstructed operation of one's true, or core, self in one's daily enterprise" (Kernis, 2003, p. 1). Research has shown that when an individual's inner experience is validated, authenticity is enhanced (Kernis); research related to self-verification has illustrated that people choose to interact with others who validate their self-views, or inner experience, suggesting that self-verification may promote authenticity. Adding further strength to this argument, Leary (2003) posits that authentic actions arise when people believe they can be accepted by being themselves. Deci and Ryan (1995) argue that authenticity in children emerges when caregivers love the children for being who they are. In a similar way, Harter, Marold, Whitesell, and Cobbs (1996) found that among adolescents, higher quality of support from classmates (scores range from conditional to unconditional) predicted more true-self behavior (defined as acting in ways that are the "real me"). Since self-verifiers seek relationships with others who see them as they see themselves, they surround themselves with relationship partners who are with them based on who they feel they actually are (i.e., "is thinkers"). Such a social environment may promote authenticity (cf. Deci & Ryan, 1995; Harter et al., 1996; Leary, 2003).

A process that promotes authenticity is beneficial because authenticity is, itself, a character strength

(Peterson & Seligman, 2004). Authenticity is also related to other positive psychological outcomes, such as more positive affect (Harter et al., 1996) and greater psychological well-being (Sheldon, Ryan, Rawsthorne, & Ilardi, 1997). In turn, a lack of authenticity has been associated with negative psychological outcomes, such as neuroticism (Horney, 1950) and narcissistic disorders (Bleiberg, 1984).

Strengthening the connection between self-verification and authenticity is research showing that an absence of self-verification processes is associated with inauthenticity. Horney (1950) found that neurotics strive to have others see them in a more positive way than they see themselves, reflective of a lack of self-verification strivings and inauthenticity. Specifically, neurotics often create an all-powerful, idealized image of the self to compensate for feelings of weakness and inadequacy; they subsequently portray this idealized self to others in an effort to gain approval, and, consequently, they lose touch with the real self (Horney, 1950). To illustrate this point, consider the example of a person who is a phenomenal artist, a mediocre athlete, and grumpy in the mornings. According to Horney, if this person is neurotic, he or she may promote an idealized self to gain approval from others. Instead of choosing to interact with others who see this individual as he or she is, the person might choose to interact with people who see him or her as a phenomenal artist, a superb athlete, and always cheery in the mornings. This would foster *in*authenticity. Similarly, Bleiberg (1984) found that narcissistic disorders, an extreme form of inauthenticity, can emerge among children when caregivers do not accept the true self of a child; narcissistic children attempt to create idealized selves to meet the expectations of the caregivers, thereby experiencing "alienation from authenticity" (p. 510). Kernis (2003) also contends that failing to validate the legitimacy of the inner experience of a child is detrimental to the development of authenticity. Therefore, when self-verification strivings are absent and people have relationships with others who do not see them as they see themselves, inauthenticity may emerge. In the worst case scenarios, this inauthenticity may even result in neuroses and narcissistic disorders.

How Is Self-Verification Adaptive Interpersonally?

Self-verification strivings are adaptive interpersonally because they encourage people to enter into relationships with honest "is thinking" relationship partners, thereby leading to greater intimacy and trust in relationships. Furthermore, self-verification is associated with greater predictability in people's behavior, which allows interactions to flow smoothly and is also related to greater trust in relationships (Rempel, Holmes, & Zanna, 1985). Empirical findings support the relationship between intimacy and self-verification, predictability in behavior and self-verification, and, in turn, harmonious social interactions and self-verification. As was the case with the authenticity argument in the previous section, the connection drawn between trust and self-verification has yet to be tested empirically. Here again, we hope that our speculations will offer a theoretical foundation for future empirical research in the area.

INTIMACY

Self-verification strivings are associated with greater intimacy in relationships. Swann et al. (1994) offer empirical support for the connection between self-verification and intimacy in a study of married couples. They found that participants reported having more intimacy when their spouses saw them as they saw themselves; this finding held for people with positive self-views and for people with negative self-views. Even among people with positive self-views, those whose spouses viewed them in an "extremely" favorable way tended to withdraw from the relationship. Furthermore, a recent meta-analysis of self-verification in marriage relationships supported the robustness of the tendency for people whose spouses viewed them in a self-verifying way to enjoy superior relationship quality (Chang-Schneider & Swann, 2009), irrespective of whether people had positive or negative self-views. Furthermore, Cassidy (2001) posits that intimacy "is making one's innermost known, sharing one's core, one's truth, one's heart, with another" (p. 122); this is the essence of self-verification—seeking out relationship partners who see you as you believe you truly are. Cassidy explains further that the ability to have intimacy is related to secure attachment in childhood, and secure attachment "is thought to be associated with validating the truth of the child's experiences" (p. 143). The connection here is drawn between intimacy and the validation of inner experience, which is a part of the self-verification process.

Feeling understood, a key part of intimacy (Cassidy, 2001; Reiss & Shaver, 1988), might be responsible for the connection between self-verification and intimacy. Comments from self-verifiers provide evidence that feeling understood drives self-verification. In one study (Swann et al., 1992), self-verifiers with negative self-views were asked to explain why they chose to interact with a confederate who evaluated them negatively. One participant said, "Well, I mean, after examining all of this I think [the negative evaluator] pretty much has me pegged." Another participant mentioned, "Since [the negative evaluator] seems to know my position and how I feel sometimes, maybe I'll be able to get along with him." The satisfaction of feeling understood, an integral part of intimacy, attracts people to relationship partners who confirm their self-views.

Another possible pathway to greater intimacy might be related to the way in which self-verification strivings can help people to identify relationship partners they believe to be honest. Choosing interaction partners who see people as they see themselves could be equivalent to choosing interaction partners who are deemed to be honest. Consistent with this notion, previous studies have shown that people endorse the validity of feedback only insofar as it confirms their self-conceptions (Crary, 1966; Markus, 1977). Identifying honest relationship partners could increase intimacy in one's life because honesty in relationships breeds intimacy (Lerner, 1993). Lerner argues that "closeness requires honesty" and that "truth telling" is "the foundation of . . . intimacy" (p. 15). Although it might be somewhat tempting to surround ourselves with others who see a glorified version of who we actually are, doing so does not bring intimacy into our lives; ultimately, it is not satisfying. To opt for the alternative of being around others who see us as we feel we actually are not only creates deep intimacy but is rewarding and validating at the deepest level.

HARMONIOUS SOCIAL INTERACTIONS

The behavior of both the self-verifier and his or her interaction partners becomes more predictable through the self-verification process, which allows social interactions to flow more smoothly. The process is negotiated like this: The self-verifier acts in predictable, consistent ways to communicate a stable self-view to others, and through a process of surrounding him- or herself with others who consistently confirm that self-view, the interaction partners' behavior becomes predictable too. This mutual predictability facilitates more harmonious social relations. One can imagine that if a relationship partner did not have a stable self-view and assumed distinct personalities on different days, that would put a strain on social relationships. The importance of acting in predictable ways is particularly salient in considering the

evolutionary perspective, where mutual predictability among small hunter-gatherer groups would have facilitated a more effective division of labor and better promoted survival (Goffman, 1959; Swann, Chang-Schneider, & Angulo, 2007). Predictability in a person's behavior is a highly valued characteristic in relationship partners (Athay & Darley, 1981; Rempel et al., 1985).

TRUST

Greater predictability in people's behavior, which results from the self-verification process, not only allows social interactions to flow more smoothly, but it also enhances trust. Rempel et al. (1985) characterized predictability of a relationship partner's behavior as one of the three components of their model of trust, along with dependability and faith. Other literature has similarly articulated that predictability is a key aspect of trust (Tyler, 2001). The centrality of predictability in establishing trust can be illustrated in student–teacher relationships. Imagine an elementary school teacher who has a policy that when students answer questions without raising their hands three times, students will miss recess. If this teacher's response to students failing to raise their hands is predictable (i.e., he or she keeps to the policy), this breeds trust in the student–teacher relationship. Alternatively, acting in unpredictable ways by failing to stick to the policy altogether or enforcing the policy arbitrarily erodes trust. In essence, the self-verification process leads to greater predictability in people's behavior which leads to more trust.

Another way in which self-verification strivings might enhance trust is by encouraging people to seek out interaction partners they deem to be honest, a positive consequence of self-verification discussed in the previous section on intimacy. Honesty in the relationship, in turn, fosters trust (Lerner, 1993). Shrauger and Lund (1975) offer further evidence of the connection between self-verification and the identification of honest interaction partners; they found that people expressed greater confidence in an evaluator's perceptiveness when the evaluator's impression confirmed their self-conceptions. Self-verification leads to finding honest interaction partners, and honesty leads to trust.

In sum, self-verification is adaptive for relationships in that it encourages people to identify and prefer honest relationship partners, fostering intimacy and trust in relationships; it also encourages predictability in behavior, which leads to more harmonious social interactions and further promotes trust. But if the self-verification process is adaptive for most people most of the time, like any adaptive process, there may be instances in which it is maladaptive. In the next section of this chapter, we consider some such instances.

When Is Self-Verification Maladaptive?

Although self-verification has many benefits for people with positive and negative self-views, it does contribute to the perpetuation of these self-views, which may be problematic for people whose self-views are negative. Although some have challenged the notion that higher self-esteem is better (Kernis, 2003) and asserted that higher self-esteem is not always related to greater well-being (Ryan & Brown, 2003), much research linking low self-esteem to depression (Murrell, Meeks, & Walker, 1991; Reinherz, Giaconia, Pakiz, & Silverman, 1993; Roberts, Gotlib, & Kassel, 1996; Robinson, Garber, & Hillsman, 1995; Trzesniewski et al., 2006) and high self-esteem to happiness (Diener & Diener, 1995; Furnham & Cheng, 2000; Shackelford, 2001) provides reason to see the perpetuation of low self-esteem via self-verification as potentially maladaptive (see also Swann, Chang-Schneider, & McClarty, 2007).

To be sure, all people possess flaws and limitations that are difficult, if not impossible, to change. For example, some people are less artistic, physically strong, or musical than others, and adopting overly positive, inaccurate assessments of their capacities can inhibit personal growth and flourishing. Nevertheless, the self-views associated with low self-esteem and depression may often be unfounded, as the basis for concluding that one is "worthless" is often quite subjective and arbitrary. Consider the example of depressed individuals who often have inaccurate, negative beliefs about their competence and likability. Self-verification predicts these individuals will choose to interact with others who see them negatively, even though the negative views are not accurate, because these relationships maintain psychological coherence, a sense that things are as one thinks they are. This cycle will perpetuate the negative, false self-views of these individuals in a way that may prevent them from realizing their true capabilities and attaining happiness.

If self-verification can be maladaptive for low-self-esteem individuals (comprising approximately one-third of the population; Swann, 1987), finding a way to effectively raise self-esteem seems necessary. Although self-verification does not, itself, raise self-esteem, understanding how it operates provides valuable information in understanding how to increase self-esteem. Additionally, self-verification may aid the process of raising self-esteem by stabilizing an individual's self-view, thereby creating a firm, safe foundation ready for meaningful change. As we explain next, the process of self-verification can be seen as a necessary but not sufficient step for raising self-esteem.

What Can Self-Verification Reveal about Raising Self-Esteem?

Attempting to raise others' self-esteem by simply telling individuals with negative self-views that they are wrong about themselves is unlikely to bear fruit. That is, this strategy is unlikely to be successful because research related to self-verification shows that people work to preserve their self-views, and people will either avoid interaction partners who do not verify their self-views or will withdraw emotionally from the relationship. People's self-views are deeply rooted and provide psychological coherence, so attempting to completely overhaul them will be discordant with people's deeply held convictions and will be disconcerting, confusing, and, consequently, unproductive. Steinbeck would call the approach of attempting to raise another's self-esteem through sheer persuasion "teleological thinking," as opposed to "is thinking" (also called "non-teleological thinking"), discussed previously. Teleological thinking is based not on what *is* but on what *could be* or *should be* (Steinbeck, 1951). Steinbeck warns that effective change cannot come from teleological thinking. He gave the following counsel: "In their sometimes intolerant refusal to face facts as they are, teleological notions may substitute a fierce but ineffectual attempt to change conditions which are assumed to be undesirable, in place of the understanding-acceptance which would pave the way for a more sensible attempt at any change" (Steinbeck, 1951, p. 138). He, therefore, advises that change is better effected through "is thinking." If, however, "is thinking" is concerned with accepting things as they are, how can this lead to change?

The answer is that validating others' self-views, as occurs in self-verification and is a characteristic of "is thinking," is a necessary first step in this slow process of change. It provides fertile soil for change by fostering stability, coherence, and a sense of feeling understood and accepted. Deci and Ryan (1995) support this notion by positing that fostering self-esteem in another entails "valuing the other for who he or she is and taking that other's frame of reference ... it means beginning by accepting and relating to the self of the other. It is precisely the acceptance of *self*—first by others and then by one-self—that supports the development and maintenance of true self-esteem" (p. 46). This type of acceptance is analogous to Carl Rogers' (1961) notion of "unconditional positive regard," the concept that therapists could facilitate personal growth and successful change in clients by providing an atmosphere of unconditional acceptance. Rogers elaborated on this concept in his book, *On Becoming a Person*, in which he wrote: "So I find that when I can accept another person, which means specifically accepting the feeling and attitudes and beliefs that he has as a real and vital part of him, then I am assisting him to become a person" (p. 21). He underscored the somewhat counterintuitive relationship between acceptance and change when he wrote, "the curious paradox is that when I accept myself as I am, then I change" (Rogers, 1961, p. 17). Accepting what another is actually feeling, as opposed to what one thinks the individual should feel or could feel, is a necessary first step to change. In this way, self-verification constitutes a necessary first step in the process of raising self-esteem, but it is not sufficient.

Positive feedback, which challenges negative self-views, must accompany verification but must come in manageable doses. Research has shown that positive feedback from an interaction partner can encourage an individual to internalize a new self-view (Jones, Gergen, & Davis, 1962), so positive comments have the potential to raise self-esteem, but they must be carried out in combination with verification. A study by Finn and Tonsager (1992) revealed that integrating verification and positivity does, in fact, raise self-esteem. College students who received feedback about a problem-focused personality test in a supportive environment experienced an increase in self-esteem, even though the feedback was often negative. Finn and Tonsager believe that the results are due to the combination of "creating a positive emotional tone, while verbally offering self-confirmatory (and often negative) feedback" (p. 285). In essence, Finn and Tonsager found that this combination of accepting another's reality or truth while slowly and gently infusing positivity raises self-esteem.

In a similar way, combining an acceptance of one's current reality with positive change is evident in various types of therapies. In Acceptance and Commitment Therapy (ACT), clients are taught not to try to control thoughts or feelings but to observe them nonjudgmentally and to accept them, while changing behaviors in beneficial ways to better their lives (Hayes, 1994). In Dialectical Behavior Therapy (DBT), the dialectic between acceptance and change is also central (Baer, 2003). Clients are taught to accept themselves completely, while working to change their behaviors and environments to improve their lives (Baer, 2003). Acceptance and positivity, this combination in this sequence, may serve as a road map for raising self-esteem.

What Can Self-Verification Reveal about Happiness?

Understanding the self-verification process may offer insight not only into raising self-esteem but also into building and even defining happiness. We contend that encouraging people to accept themselves, in effect offering themselves self-verification, is a key component of happiness.

Our argument is based on the assumption that self-acceptance, including acceptance of one's vulnerabilities, imperfections, and the full range of one's emotions, is an integral part of happiness. This perspective differs from many contemporary conceptualizations of happiness, which define happiness as the frequency of positive emotions and infrequency of negative emotions (for a review, see Lyubomirsky, King, & Diener, 2005). In contrast, we suggest that happiness is more aptly described as a compassionate embracing or acceptance of a fuller range of emotions, rather than one's overall amount of positive emotions or net value of positive minus negative emotions.

The belief that happiness encompasses a wide range of feelings and emotions has been articulated by Matthieu Ricard (2003) in his book *Happiness: A Guide to Developing Life's Most Important Skill*. He writes: "we so often confuse genuine happiness with merely seeking enjoyable emotions," but happiness is about learning how to "reduce the gap between appearances and reality" (pp. 26, 23). That is to say, it is about acceptance. He added: "There exists a way of being that underlies and suffuses all emotional states, that embraces all joys and sorrows that come to us. . . . The Sanskrit word for this state of being is *sukha*" (p. 25). In these quotations, Ricard underscores the significance of acceptance, specifically accepting all emotions—in essence, accepting ourselves. He elaborates on this concept of *sukha* when he writes: "*Sukha* is the state of lasting well-being that manifests itself when we have freed ourselves of mental blindness and afflictive emotions. It is also the wisdom that allows us to see the world as it is, without veils or distortions. It is, finally, the joy of moving toward inner freedom and the loving-kindness that radiates toward others" (p. 25). Again, Ricard echoes the notion that happiness is not about attempting to reframe all emotions as positive ones or "merely seeking enjoyable emotions"; it is associated with the warm welcoming of "the world as it is."

Equally important to self-acceptance is acceptance by others. For example, research on the impact of social support in the face of traumatic events has shown that significant others frequently respond to a loved one who is a trauma victim by forcing cheerfulness and displaying an optimistic facade (Wortman & Dunkel-Schetter, 1979, 1987). Forced cheerfulness, however, minimizes the victim's situation, which may make the victim feel abandoned or rejected (Dakof & Taylor, 1990). In a similar way, Dakof and Taylor (1990) found that minimization of trauma by social support providers (i.e., family, physicians, and nurses) was one of the most frequent complaints of cancer victims. Furthermore, Ingram, Betz, Mindes, Schmitt, and Smith (2001) found that forcing optimism or downplaying an individual's concerns (e.g., saying the victim "should look on the bright side") is such a common and unsupportive response that it was one of the four main factors upon which these authors loaded all negative, unsupportive responses to difficult life events. This type of reaction was not only characterized by victims as being unsupportive, it was also associated with depressive symptoms.

Ironically, the implicit belief that happiness can be achieved by shoehorning all experiences into positive ones may have the opposite of the effect intended. When a person does not feel that their negative feelings are validated or accepted by others in the social support network, their physical and mental health suffers. In short, acceptance is essential to enduring happiness at both an intrapsychic and interpersonal level, but it is often overlooked in the definition and measurement of happiness. Our theoretical perspective suggests that a more expansive definition of happiness, as well as appropriate measures, is needed to reflect a richer understanding of the nature and origins of the construct.

Conclusion

Self-verification theory assumes that individuals work to maintain their self-views by seeking confirmation of them irrespective of whether their self-views are positive or negative. This process is related to positive psychology because it is presumed to be fundamentally adaptive, providing many intrapsychic and interpersonal benefits. In fact, self-verification

strivings facilitate the development of some of the most intrinsically rewarding aspects of life; prominent among them are authenticity of self and intimacy in relationships.

To be sure, although self-verification strivings are fundamentally adaptive, they may perpetuate inaccurate self-views which will be particularly problematic if they are inappropriately negative. Nevertheless, in such instances, it is the erroneous nature of the initial self-view rather than the process of self-verification that is the root of the problem. Once a self-view is formed, the individual places a psychological premium on its verification, and any attempts to deny it result in defensive reactions that can have unproductive consequences.

Understanding the critical importance of self-verification processes offers insights into how to raise self-esteem. We suggest that to help raise the self-esteem of someone with a negative self-view, one should first offer the person self-verification and only then provide positive feedback that challenges the negative self-views. This ordered combination of acceptance plus positivity will theoretically engender positive self-views without evoking defensiveness. Once such positive self-views are in place, the process of self-verification can resume anew, but this time it will be in the service of promoting personal and social realities that are both truthful and adaptive. From this vantage point, people will become like Steinbeck's "is thinkers" in a deeper sense, as they think about themselves in a new, more meaningful, more complete, and more sustaining way.

But understanding self-verification not only offers insight into how to raise self-esteem, it also offers a new perspective on the optimal strategy for enhancing and even defining happiness. In particular, self-verification theory underscores the importance of accepting oneself fully, including vulnerabilities, imperfections, and the full range of one's emotions, and suggests that such acceptance may be crucial to happiness. From this perspective, the key to happiness may reside not in continually striving to improve the reality of who one is but in embracing the reality and incorporating it more fully into one's self-view, relationships, and work—into one's life.

Questions about the Future of the Topic

1. If happiness is best attained through self-acceptance, it becomes important to develop ways of bolstering self-acceptance. How would you go about this?

2. Recent research has questioned the cross-cultural generality of some motives, such as the desire for positive evaluations. Might self-verification strivings also be limited to Westerners?

3. Finn and Tonsager were successful in changing the self-views of people with low self-esteem. Do you think that their findings would generalize to people with depression? Why or why not?

References

Athay, M., & Darley, J. M. (1981). Towards an interpersonal action-centered theory of personality. In N. Cantor & J. Kihlstrom (Eds.), *Personality, cognition and social interactions* (pp. 281–307). Hillsdale, NJ: Erlbaum.

Baer, R. A. (2003). Mindfulness training as a clinical intervention: A conceptual and empirical review. *Clinical Psychology: Science and Practice, 10,* 125–143.

Bleiberg, E. (1984). Narcissistic disorders in children. *Bulletin of the Menninger Clinic, 48,* 501–517.

Brown, J. D., & McGill, K. J. (1989). The cost of good fortune: When positive life events produce negative health consequences. *Journal of Personality and Social Psychology, 55,* 1103–1110.

Burke, P. J., & Stets, J. E. (1999). Trust and commitment through self-verification. *Social Psychology Quarterly, 62,* 347–360.

Cassidy, J. (2001). Truth, lies, and intimacy: An attachment perspective. *Attachment and Human Development, 3,* 121–155.

Cast, A. D., & Burke, P. J. (2002). A theory of self-esteem. *Social Forces, 80,* 1041–1068.

Chang-Schneider, C., & Swann, W. B., Jr. (2009). Self-verification in marital relationships: A meta-analytic review. Manuscript in preparation, University of Texas at Austin.

Cooley, C. S. (1902). *Human nature and the social order.* New York: Scribner's.

Crary, W. G. (1966). Reactions to incongruent self-experiences. *Journal of Consulting Psychology, 30,* 246–252.

Dakof, G. A., & Taylor, S. E. (1990). Victims' perceptions of social support: What is helpful from whom? *Journal of Personality and Social Psychology, 58,* 80–89.

Deci, E. L., & Ryan, R. M. (1995). Human autonomy: The basis for true self-esteem. In M. H. Kernis (Ed.), *Efficacy, agency, and self-esteem* (pp. 31–46). New York: Plenum.

De La Ronde, C., & Swann, W. B., Jr. (1998). Partner verification: Restoring shattered images of our intimates. *Journal of Personality and Social Psychology, 75,* 374–382.

Diener, E., & Diener, M. (1995). Cross-cultural correlates of life satisfaction and self-esteem. *Journal of Personality and Social Psychology, 68,* 653–663.

Finn, S. E., & Tonsager, M. E. (1992). Therapeutic impact of providing MMPI-2 feedback to college students awaiting therapy. *Journal of Psychological Assessment, 4,* 278–287.

Furnham, A., & Cheng, H. (2000). Lay theories of happiness. *Journal of Happiness Studies, 1,* 227–246.

Goffman, E. (1959). *The presentation of self in everyday life.* Garden City, NY: Doubleday-Anchor.

Harter, S., Marold, D. B., Whitesell, N. R., & Cobbs, G. (1996). A model of the effects of parent and peer support on adolescent false self behavior. *Child Development, 67,* 360–374.

Hayes, S. C. (1994). Content, context, and the types of psychological acceptance. In S. C. Hayes, N. S. Jacobson, V. M. Follette, & M. J. Dougher (Eds.), *Acceptance and change: Content and context in psychotherapy* (pp. 13–32). Reno, NV: Context and Press.

Hixon, J. G., & Swann, W. B., Jr. (1993). When does introspection bear fruit? Self-reflection, self-insight, and interpersonal choices. *Journal of Personality and Social Psychology, 64,* 35–43.

Horney, K. (1950). *Neurosis and human growth.* New York: Norton.

Ingram, K. M., Betz, N. E., Mindes, E. J., Schmitt, M. M., & Smith, N. G. (2001). Unsupportive responses from others concerning a stressful life event: Development of the unsupportive interactions inventory. *Journal of Social and Clinical Psychology, 20,* 173–207.

Iyer, A., Jetten, J., & Tsivrikos, D. (2008). Torn between identities: Predictors of adjustment to identity change. In F. Sani (Ed.), *Self-continuity: Individual and collective perspectives* (pp. 187–197). New York: Psychology Press

Jones, E. E., Gergen, K. J., & Davis, K. E. (1962). Some determinants of reactions to being approved or disapproved as a person. *Psychological Monographs, 76,* 117.

Jones, S. C. (1973). Self and interpersonal evaluations: Esteem theories versus consistency theories. *Psychological Bulletin, 79,* 185–199.

Kernis, M. H. (2003). Toward a conceptualization of optimal self-esteem. *Psychological Inquiry, 14,* 1–26.

Leary, M. R. (2003). Interpersonal aspects of optimal self-esteem and the authentic self. *Psychological Inquiry, 14,* 52–54.

Lerner, H. G. (1993). *The dance of deception.* New York: HarperCollins.

Lundgren, D. C., & Schwab, M. R. (1977). Perceived appraisals by others, self-esteem, and anxiety. *The Journal of Psychology, 97,* 205–213.

Lyubomirsky, S., King, L., & Diener, E. (2005). The benefits of frequent positive affect: Does happiness lead to success? *Psychological Bulletin, 131,* 803–855.

Markus, H. (1977). Self-schemas and processing information about the self. *Journal of Personality and Social Psychology, 35,* 63–78.

Matthieu, R. (2003). *Happiness: A guide to developing life's most important skill.* Translated by Jesse Browner. New York: Little, Brown, and Company.

Mead, G. H. (1934). *Mind, self and society.* Chicago: University of Chicago Press.

Mendes, W. B., & Akinola, M. (2006). Getting what you expected: How self-verifying information reduces autonomic and hormonal responses related to threat. Unpublished manuscript, Harvard University, Cambridge, MA.

Murray, S. L., Holmes, J. G., & Griffin, D. W. (2000). Self-esteem and the quest for felt security: How perceived regard regulates attachment processes. *Journal of Personality and Social Psychology, 78,* 478–498.

Murrell, S. A., Meeks, S., & Walker, J. (1991). Protective functions of health and self-esteem against depression in older adults facing illness or bereavement. *Psychology and Aging, 6,* 352–360.

Peterson, C., & Seligman, M. E. P. (2004). *Character strengths and virtues: A handbook and classification.* New York: Oxford University Press.

Ralph, J. A., & Mineka, S. (1998). Attributional style and self-esteem: The prediction of emotional distress following a midterm exam. *Journal of Abnormal Psychology, 107,* 203–215.

Reinherz, H. Z., Giaconia, R. M., Pakiz, B., & Silverman, A. B. (1993). Psychosocial risks for major depression in late adolescence: A longitudinal community study. *Journal of the American Academy of Child and Adolescent Psychiatry, 32,* 1155–1163.

Reiss, H. T., & Shaver, P. R. (1988). Intimacy as an interpersonal process. In S. W. Duck (Ed.), *Handbook of personal relationships* (pp. 367–389). New York: Wiley.

Rempel, J. K., Holmes, J. G., & Zanna, M. P. (1985). Trust in close relationships. *Journal of Personality and Social Psychology, 49,* 95–112.

Ritts, V., & Stein, J. R. (1995). Verification and commitment in marital relationships: An exploration of self-verification theory in community college students. *Psychological Reports, 76,* 383–386.

Roberts, J. E., Gotlib, I. H., & Kassel, J. D. (1996). Adult attachment security and symptoms of depression: The mediating roles of dysfunctional attitudes and low self-esteem. *Journal of Personality and Social Psychology, 70,* 310–320.

Robinson, D. T., & Smith-Lovin, L. (1992). Selective interaction as a strategy for identity maintenance: An affect control model. *Social Psychology Quarterly, 55,* 12–28.

Robinson, N. S., Garber, J., & Hilsman, R. (1995). Cognitions and stress: Direct and moderating effects on depressive versus externalizing symptoms during the junior high school transition. *Journal of Abnormal Psychology, 104,* 453–463.

Rogers, C. (1961). *On becoming a person: A therapist's view of psychotherapy.* New York: Houghton Mifflin.

Ryan, R. M., & Brown, K. W. (2003). Why we don't need self-esteem: On fundamental needs, contingent love, and mindfulness. *Psychological Inquiry, 14,* 71–76.

Schafer, R. B., Wickrama, K. A. S., & Keith, P. M. (1996). Self-concept disconfirmation, psychological distress, and marital happiness. *Journal of Marriage and the Family, 58,* 167–177.

Shackelford, T. K. (2001). Self-esteem in marriage. *Personality and Individual Differences, 30,* 371–390.

Sheldon, K., & King, L. (2001). Why positive psychology is necessary. *American Psychologist, 56,* 216–217.

Sheldon, K. M., Ryan, R. M., Rawsthorne, L. J., & Ilardi, B. (1997). Trait self and true self: Cross-role variation in the Big-Five personality traits and its relations with psychological authenticity and subjective well-being. *Journal of Personality and Social Psychology, 73,* 1380–1393.

Shillinglaw, S. (1994). Introduction. In J. Steinbeck, *Of mice and men.* New York: Penguin.

Shimizu, M., & Pelham, B. W. (2004). The unconscious cost of good fortune: Implicit and explicit self-esteem, positive life events, and health. *Health Psychology, 23,* 101–105.

Shrauger, J. S., & Lund, A. (1975). Self-evaluation and reactions to evaluations from others. *Journal of Personality, 43,* 94–108.

Steinbeck, J. (1951). *The log from the Sea of Cortez.* New York: The Viking Press.

Swann, W. B., Jr. (1983). Self-verification: Bringing social reality into harmony with the self. In J. Suls & A. G. Greenwald (Eds.), *Psychological perspectives on the self* (Vol. 2, pp. 33–66). Hillsdale, NJ: Erlbaum.

Swann, W. B., Jr. (1987). Identity negotiation: Where two roads meet. *Journal of Personality and Social Psychology, 53,* 1038–1051.

Swann, W. B., Jr., Chang-Schneider, C., & Angulo, S. (2007). Self-verification in relationships as an adaptive process. In J. Wood, A. Tesser, & J. Holmes (Eds.), *Self and relationships.* New York: Psychology Press.

Swann, W. B., Jr., Chang-Schneider, C., & McClarty, K. L. (2007). Do people's self-views matter? Self-concept and self-esteem in everyday life. *American Psychologist, 62,* 84–94.

Swann, W. B., Jr., De La Ronde, C., & Hixon, J. G. (1994). Authenticity and positivity strivings in marriage and courtship. *Journal of Personality and Social Psychology, 66,* 857–869.

Swann, W. B., Jr., Hixon, J. G., Stein-Seroussi, A., & Gilbert, D. T. (1990). The fleeting gleam of praise: Behavioral reactions to self-relevant feedback. *Journal of Personality and Social Psychology, 59,* 17–26.

Swann, W. B., Jr., & Pelham, B. (2002). Who wants out when the going gets good? Psychological investment and preference for self-verifying college roommates. *Self and Identity, 1,* 219–233.

Swann, W. B., Jr., Pelham, B. W., & Krull, D. S. (1989). Agreeable fancy or disagreeable truth? Reconciling self-enhancement and self-verification. *Journal of Personality and Social Psychology, 57,* 782–791.

Swann, W. B., Jr., Stein-Seroussi, A., & Giesler, B. (1992). Why people self-verify. *Journal of Personality and Social Psychology, 62,* 392–401.

Trzesniewski, K. H., Donnellan, M. B., Moffitt, T. E., Robins, R. W., Poulton, R., & Caspi, A. (2006). Low self-esteem during adolescence predicts poor health, criminal behavior, and limited economic prospects during adulthood. *Developmental Psychology, 42,* 381–390.

Tyler, T. R. (2001). Why do people rely on others? Social identity and social aspects of trust. In K. S. Cook (Ed.), *Trust in society* (Vol. 2, pp. 285–306). New York: Russell Sage Foundation.

Wood, J. V., Heimpel, S. A., Newby-Clark, I., & Ross, M. (2005). Snatching defeat from the jaws of victory: Self-esteem differences in the experience and anticipation of success. *Journal of Personality and Social Psychology, 89,* 764–780.

Wortman, C. B., & Dunkel-Schetter, C. (1987). Conceptual and methodological issues in the study of social support. In A. Baum & J. Singer (Eds.), *Handbook of psychology and health* (pp. 63–108). Hillsdale, NJ: Erlbaum.

Wortman, C. B., & Dunkel-Schetter, C. (1979). Interpersonal relationships and cancer: A theoretical analysis. *Journal of Social Issues, 35,* 120–155.

Reality Negotiation

Raymond L. Higgins *and* Matthew W. Gallagher

Abstract

This chapter presents an overview of the development and status of the reality negotiation construct and relates it to a variety of coping processes. The reality negotiation construct follows from the social constructionist tradition and first appeared in discussions of how excuses protect self-images by decreasing the causal linkage to negative outcomes. The reality negotiation construct was later expanded to include a discussion of how the process of hoping may be used to increase perceived linkage to positive outcomes. In the two decades since these constructs were first introduced, four individual differences measures have been developed, and the effects of these reality negotiation techniques have been studied extensively. Reality negotiation techniques can be both maladaptive and adaptive and have been shown to be associated with coping and social support in a variety of populations. The chapter concludes by highlighting a few areas in which reality negotiation research could expand to further its relevance and applicability to the field of positive psychology.

Keywords: coping, excuses, hope, self-handicapping

Reality Negotiation Defined

The reality negotiation (RN) construct first appeared in Snyder and Higgins's (1988a, 1988b) discussions of how excuses protect self-images. These authors proposed that people continually assess their degree of causal linkage to self-relevant outcomes and employ attribution and appraisal strategies to manipulate the extent of those linkages (Higgins & Snyder, 1991).

Thinking about RN initially emphasized shifting causal attributions for "negative" outcomes from "sources that are relatively more central to the person's sense of self to sources that are relatively less central" (Snyder & Higgins, 1988b, p. 23), a definition that incorporated only a (causal) linkage dimension. In 1989, Snyder introduced a valence dimension along with his construct of "hoping" (see chap. 30). In contrast to excuses, hoping was seen as a process of "increasing" causal linkages to "positive" outcomes. Subsequently, the RN construct has incorporated both linkage and valence

dimensions, contrasting excusing (self-esteem maintenance) and hoping (self-esteem enhancement) processes.

This linkage–valence framework has been represented as a two-dimensional matrix wherein "linkage to outcome" (none to total) formed the *X*-axis and "valence of outcome" (positive to negative) formed the *Y*-axis. Accordingly, an individual's relation to any given outcome can be mapped onto this matrix. People wishing to enhance or preserve a positive image would likely work to "decrease" linkages to negative outcomes, to "decrease" the negativity of those outcomes, or both. When faced with positive outcomes, people might be expected to work toward "increasing" their causal linkages and/or toward "increasing" their positive valence. In contrast, people with negative self-theories might try to distance themselves from positive outcomes (Barone, Maddux, & Snyder, 1997; Snyder & Higgins, 1997).

Reality Negotiation in Context

The RN construct follows from the social constructivist tradition (Barone et al., 1997) of such philosophers as Hegel (1807/1967), Kant (1781/1965), and Vaihinger (1925) and from the work of authors who viewed self-esteem maintenance as a fundamental human motive (e.g., Maslow, 1968; Rogers, 1951). As noted previously, however, its contemporary roots lay in work on excuses (Higgins & Snyder, 1989; Snyder, Higgins, & Stucky, 1983) as well as evidence for the self-serving nature of causal attributions (Arkin, Cooper, & Kolditz, 1980; Miller, 1976; Zuckerman, 1979).

The "negotiation" component of the construct derives from the interactive nature of sequences wherein protagonists and audiences work to achieve mutual understandings of events (Higgins & Snyder, 1989; Snyder & Higgins, 1988a, 1988b). For example, students may tell one another that an examination was unfair in order to lessen the impact of negative performances. As Snyder et al. (1983) observed, however, even "private" excuses (i.e., those not proffered to external audiences) require negotiation between protagonists and their "mental representations" of others' judgments. The term "revolving self-images" (Snyder et al., 1983, p. 38) was coined to convey the idea that self-images reflect the values of role models and caregivers and that even private excuses involve attention to both internal and external audience concerns.

Individual Differences in Reality Negotiation

To date, four individual differences measures have been developed specifically to tap RN tendencies. Both trait (Snyder et al., 1991) and state (Snyder et al., 1996) versions of the Hope Scale have been developed. These tap motivation and perceived ability to achieve goals and correlate positively with measures related to self-presentation, coping, and health (for reviews, see Snyder, 2002; Snyder, Cheavens, & Michael, 1999; chap. 30). Hope is also posited to underlie the capacity for positive psychological change (Snyder, 2002; Snyder, Ilardi, Michael, & Cheavens, 2000). The items from these adult-oriented scales also have been adapted for use with children (The Children's Hope Scale; Snyder et al., 1997).

The only measure specifically designed to assess RN is the Linkage Into Valenced Elements Scale (LIVE; Snyder & Samuelson, 1998). The LIVE samples from eight life arenas (i.e., appearance, health, intelligence, school, job, leisure, personality, relationships) and refers to both positive (e.g., intellectual ability) and negative (e.g., poor academic performance) characteristics. Respondents use rating scales (1 = "not at all" to 9 = "totally") to indicate the extent to which they are causally linked to the outcomes represented in the items. There are currently no published data relating to the validity or psychometric properties of the LIVE. Samuelson (1996), however, tested an earlier, 80-item version with college students and found support for its construct validity, including a positive correlation with the trait Hope Scale.

Measures of performance, values, causal attributions, goal directedness, or perceived control potentially relate to individual differences in RN. A few measures, however, have been directly associated with RN. Most notably, The Self-Handicapping Scale (Jones & Rhodewalt, 1982; see also Higgins, Snyder, & Berglas, 1990) stands out as an index of linkage-weakening excuse tactics such as preemptively labeling a task unfair or too difficult (see Rhodewalt & Tragakis, 2002, for review).

Because excuses are prompted by threats to self-esteem, differences in self-esteem have been related to differences in RN. Levels of self-esteem also relate to differences in the use of downward social comparison (a valence-shifting tactic; Aspinwall & Taylor, 1993); in the use of self-enhancement (linkage-shifting) strategies (Baumeister, Tice, & Hutton, 1989); and in the use of excuses (Tice & Baumeister, 1984). Differences in self-handicapping vary with self-esteem (Zuckerman, Kieffer, & Knee, 1998), with self-esteem uncertainty (Harris & Snyder, 1986), and with self-esteem instability (Kernis, Grannemann, & Barclay, 1992).

Measures of depression and negative affect are also associated with RN. Depressed individuals, for example, tend to make internalizing (linkage-increasing) rather than externalizing (linkage-weakening) attributions for negative events (for review, see Burns & Seligman, 1991). Relatedly, dispositional (linkage-increasing) attributions for failure appear to be more typical of depression than are attributions to behaviors (Anderson, Miller, Riger, Dill, & Sedikides, 1994). Neuroticism also has been associated with greater self-handicapping tendencies (Ross, Canada, & Rausch, 2002), and negative mood has been associated with higher levels of trait self-handicapping over time (Zuckerman et al., 1998).

Reality Negotiation: An Overview
Reality Negotiation as an Automatic Process

RN processes are thought to be so automatic that the individual is often unaware of them (Higgins & Snyder, 1989). Self-schemata render certain information more easily expected and recognized (Bargh & Pratto, 1986; Markus & Wurf, 1987), as well as more readily recalled (Higgins et al., 1982). Information that confirms expectations is unlikely to stimulate effortful, conscious processing (Higgins, 1989; Jones, 1990).

Active processing of information becomes more likely as it becomes increasingly unexpected or schema discrepant (Hastie, 1984; Pyszczynski & Greenberg, 1981). Dealing with external audiences may also push negotiations into awareness (Higgins & Snyder, 1989; Snyder & Higgins, 1988a, 1988b).

Linkage-Focused Reality Negotiation

Excuses are strategies for shifting causal attributions for negative outcomes away from the core (e.g., "good" and "in control") sense of self. Some excuses (e.g., denial) aim to completely sever causal linkages. Most, however, shift attributions from one internal source to another, less central, internal source. Many of them are addressed in Kelley's (1967, 1971) theory of attribution.

"Consistency-lowering" excuses frustrate dispositional attributions by implicating lack of effort (Miller, 1976), lack of intention (Rotenberg, 1980), or unforeseeable consequences. "Consensus-raising" excuses deflect dispositional attributions by advancing situational causes (e.g., task difficulty) over personal causes (e.g., ability). Both consistency-lowering and consensus-raising excuses weaken but do not sever causal linkages (Miller, 1976; Zuckerman, 1979).

Kelley's (1971) attribution principles also apply to anticipatory excuses. For example, not preparing may establish a consistency-lowering excuse in the event of future failure. Anticipatory consensus-raising excuses might involve strategies such as pronouncing an upcoming task unfair (Smith, Snyder, & Handelsman, 1982). Such "self-handicapping" strategies (Berglas & Jones, 1978; Higgins et al., 1990; Jones & Berglas, 1978) capitalize on Kelley's "discounting" principle: When outcomes are associated with more than one possible cause, attributions to any one cause are weakened. Self-handicaps may also capitalize on Kelley's principle of "augmentation." When individuals succeed "despite" being handicapped, ability attributions may actually be strengthened (Feick & Rhodewalt, 1997; Rhodewalt, Morf, Hazlett, & Fairfield, 1991).

At the other end of the RN spectrum is the process of hoping (Snyder, 1989; chap. 30). Hope, which involves increasing linkages to both past and future positive outcomes, has been defined as "the perceived capability to derive pathways to desired goals, and motivate oneself via agency thinking to use those pathways" (Snyder, 2002, p. 249). Within the context of RN, agency thinking motivates efforts toward positive goals, whereas the pathways component provides the directions for achieving them. Positive linkage-focused RN is considered a developmental antecedent to high levels of hope (see Snyder, 2002, for review).

Valence-Focused Reality Negotiation

Valence-shifting strategies aim to detoxify threatening outcomes. One strategy is to discredit the information (Aronson & Worchel, 1966). Blaming victims or invoking exonerative moral reasoning (e.g., "It was for her own good") may also soften perceived negativity (Lerner, 1980). Minimizing outcomes (e.g., "It's not as bad as it looks"; Snyder, Irving, Sigmon, & Holleran, 1992) or redefining them ("lies" become "white lies") may also negotiate less threatening outcomes.

Another valence-shifting tactic is to find meaning in adversity. Finding benefits or "meaning" in misfortune may help restore a positive sense of self (Nolen-Hoeksema & Davis, 2002; Tennen & Affleck, 2002).

Additional valence-focused strategies include selectively attending to positive outcomes in order to maintain and present a favorable self-image. Such impression management can help preserve desired images when interacting with others. It may also increase levels of hope by enhancing perceptions of past successes (Roth, Harris, & Snyder, 1988; Snyder, 1989).

Reality Negotiation as Coping

RN mechanisms that support "negative" self-images may also be adaptive. Brown and McGill (1989) reported that desirable life changes were actually associated with "increased" illness among low-esteem individuals. Presumably, the positive changes led to stressful identity disruption. That an event's stressfulness may derive from its demand for personal redefinition finds support in studies (Hammen, Marks, Mayol, & DeMayo, 1985; Swann, Hixon, & De La Ronde, 1992; Swann, Wenzlaff, Krull, & Pelham, 1992) that highlight the importance of self-consistency in maintaining a sense of predictability and control (see also Swann & Pelham, 2002).

Although the preceding remarks emphasize RN's role in promoting self-theory stability, it would be a mistake to equate stability with stasis. RN aims to manage the pace and flow of change. According to Higgins and Leibowitz (1999), RN "aids in coping, *not because the resulting products are inherently self-enhancing or self-verifying, but rather because the individual experiences a degree of control over the self-definitional implications of the person-data transaction*" (p. 30). Maintaining a continuous and integrated sense of self helps people unfold their lives in an orderly manner.

RN can also affect coping through the maintenance and generation of positive self-images. Hope theory (Snyder, 2002) posits that high levels of hope should be associated with more adaptive coping. In fact, high hope has been associated with improved adjustment and coping with spinal cord injuries (Elliot, Witty, Herrick, & Hoffman, 1991), burn injuries (Barnum, Snyder, Rapoff, Mani, & Thompson, 1998), and arthritis (Laird, 1992). High hope is also correlated with better overall psychological adjustment (Kwon, 2002). The benefits of hopeful thinking are not limited to improved reactions to physical illness, however. For example, higher hope women are more knowledgeable about cancer facts and also report stronger intentions to engage in cancer prevention (Irving, Snyder, & Crowson, 1998). RN in the form of hope may therefore actually help prevent circumstances that necessitate coping.

Reality Negotiation: Who Controls the Process?

Early discussions of RN acknowledged the role of external audiences but emphasized the individual. A more dynamic vision (Higgins & Leibowitz, 1999; Snyder & Higgins, 1997) argues that, through the efforts of socialization agents, individuals learn to value and promote self-theories that buttress larger social interests. Higgins and Leibowitz (1999) reasoned that socialization agents shape individual interpretations of reality in order to advance *the social agents'* image maintenance goals. One's standing as a "good parent," for example, derives from one's children embodying culturally favored values. This perspective raises interesting questions about who ultimately controls the RN process.

Socialization agents encourage individuals to affiliate with group-approved goals and values and shape the very content of their self-theories (Markus & Cross, 1990). Group memberships provide performance standards and frames from which to evaluate "reality." It is important to recognize, however, that protagonist/audience relationships are reciprocal. Individuals affiliate with groups that support their self-definitional interests, thereby endowing the groups with an interest in the individual's outcomes. It often happens, for example, that one's actions have implications for a wider audience's image. The notorious acts of torture at the Abu Ghraib prison in Iraq illustrate how the acts of a few can tarnish the image of an entire country. Similarly, the 2006 scandal involving U.S. representative Mark Foley's email liaisons with male congressional pages illustrates how the acts of an individual can alter the fortunes of an entire political party.

In September 2006, it was reported ("Florida Congressman quits," 2006) that Foley had sent sexually explicit instant messages and emails to congressional pages. Immediately thereafter, Foley and other Republican party members engaged in a series of RN tactics to minimize the scandal's effects on the upcoming midterm elections. Foley offered a series of excuses: He was an alcoholic, he was molested as a teenager, and he was homosexual. These confessions were made in an attempt to lessen Foley's responsibility for his actions.

Simultaneously, Republican party spokesmen attempted to lessen the perceived negativity of Foley's actions. White House Press Secretary Tony Snow, for example, described Foley's emails as merely "naughty emails." House Speaker Dennis Hastert recast the episode as dirty politics, claiming that the "Democrats . . . put this thing forward to try to block us." By (falsely) claiming the scandal was revealed by political opponents, Hastert attempted to make Foley's actions appear relatively less negative than those of political opponents who may have acted for political gain. Each of these efforts illustrates the interplay between individual and group identities. Another arena, that of coping with serious health problems, also illuminates the interactive workings of RN.

Reality Negotiation and Social Support

When faced with illness or disability, people search for causes (Taylor, 1983). Doing so may help them preserve their sense of being in control (Higgins & Snyder, 1991). For example, "self-blame" has been associated with better adjustment to spinal cord injury (Bulman & Wortman, 1977), breast cancer (Timko & Janoff-Bulman, 1985), and renal failure

(Witenberg et al., 1983). The causes people identify may also help them preserve important social support resources (Higgins & Leibowitz, 1999).

The idea that finding meaning in suffering may have emotional or coping benefits is not new. Benefit finding has been shown to aid coping with such problems as myocardial infarction (Affleck, Tennen, Croog, & Levine, 1987), amputation (Dunn, 1996), breast cancer (Taylor, Lichtman, & Wood, 1984), and rheumatoid arthritis (Tennen, Affleck, Urrows, Higgins, & Mendola, 1992; also see Nolen-Hoeksema & Davis, 2002; Tennen & Affleck, 2002). Higgins and Leibowitz (1999) speculated that benefit finding (valence negotiation) may assist coping by helping to secure access to social supports.

Audiences often experience vicarious threat (Silver, Wortman, & Crofton, 1990) and engage in defensive attributional distortions (e.g., victim blaming) when confronted with suffering, and victims of illness or disability often must accommodate their audiences' emotional needs. Those who attribute their suffering to personal faults or failings not only may boost their own sense of control, they also may salve their fellow travelers' control aspirations.

Such self-blame, however, also may disrupt social supports. For example, compared with those who are not seen as responsible, sufferers who are seen as responsible may experience more negative social reactions (Herbert & Dunkel-Schetter, 1992). This double-edged quality of self-blame may help explain why sufferers' searches for causation fade over time as maintaining access to material and interpersonal resources increases in importance (Schulz & Decker, 1985). In effect, people shift from negotiating a relationship with the initial trauma to negotiating a relationship with the ongoing demands of living.

Economic models of social support are based on equitable resource exchange, yet ill or disabled individuals often elicit social support despite being involved in objectively inequitable exchanges (Antonucci & Jackson, 1990). An RN perspective may help explain such findings by implicating ways in which the ill or disabled *are* positioned to contribute to such relationships. Higgins and Leibowitz (1999), for example, cited the importance of addressing the emotional needs of social support providers. These individuals seek to be helpful and may withdraw and/or react negatively if their efforts are not rewarded by improvement (Silver et al., 1990). Individuals who negotiate a view of their helper's efforts as "helpful" are most likely to continue receiving support.

Social support providers also need to have their own personal illusions of control affirmed. A sufferer's self-blame may bolster a helper's sense of being in control of their own fate. Similarly, finding meaning, spiritual enlightenment, or renewed purpose in suffering may detoxify helpers' assessments of the patients' condition, possibly alleviating anxieties about their own vulnerability. In effect, an RN perspective suggests that sufferers may often preserve their access to social support resources by negotiating more benign views of their plights.

Such social support dynamics may even be present in professional helping relationships. In discussing RN within nursing settings, Ersek (1992) cited problems that arise when patients cling to unrealistically hopeful beliefs about their conditions. Ersek reported that nurses may become alienated from patients who are unwilling to adopt "realistic" outlooks. According to Ersek, it may actually be critical for health care "institutions" to endorse nurses' views of patients' reality at such times in order to preserve the nurses' ability to continue providing effective and professional services.

New Directions

In this chapter, we have attempted to briefly explicate the workings of the RN process and to illustrate the RN construct's evolution from one emphasizing efforts to minimize the self-definitional implications of negative outcomes to one that also embraces RN in the service of furthering individuals' positive goal strivings. In doing so, we have selected examples that illustrate the inherently "interpersonal" nature of RN and how, in all but strictly "private" instances, the outcomes of RN sequences have implications not only for the actors, but also for the social groups with which they associate.

Whether it be in the form of retrospective excuses (Higgins & Snyder, 1989), self-handicapping (Higgins et al., 1990), or hope (Snyder, 2002), RN-related research has flourished in the past 20 years. There remain, however, a number of areas in which research is lacking. One noticeable absence is research examining the potential effects of such demographic variables as age, race, and income. While not unique to research on RN, the tendency to use convenience samples of Caucasian, middle-class college students potentially limits the generalizability of findings. RN research could also benefit from longitudinal investigations of RN across the life span. There is, for example, a dearth of research relating RN to the self-theory challenges posed by aging.

Nearly two decades of research now indicates that hopeful thinking is associated with a positive sense of self and is advantageous in a range of life domains (Snyder, 2002). Unfortunately, there is much less research examining how to help people move from the defensive avoidance of negative self-images toward the active pursuit of positive, self-affirming goals. Producing research aimed at illuminating those pathways will be a worthy objective for the next decade of RN and positive psychology research.

Questions for the Future

1. How does the use of RN strategies such as excuses and hoping vary across cultures?

2. Are there age-related differences in terms of how frequently people use different RN techniques?

3. Can interventions be developed to facilitate the use of adaptive RN techniques?

References

Affleck, G., Tennen, H., Croog, S., & Levine, S. (1987). Causal attribution, perceived benefits, and morbidity after a heart attack: An 8-year study. *Journal of Consulting and Clinical Psychology, 55,* 29–35.

Anderson, C. A., Miller, R. S., Riger, A. L., Dill, J. C., & Sedikides, C. (1994). Behavioral and characterological attributional styles as predictors of depression and loneliness: Review, refinement, and test. *Journal of Personality and Social Psychology, 66,* 549–558.

Antonucci, T. C., & Jackson, J. S. (1990). The role of reciprocity in social support. In B. R. Sarason, I. G. Sarason, & G. R. Pierce (Eds.), *Social support: An interactional view* (pp. 173–189). New York: Wiley.

Arkin, R. M., Cooper, H., & Kolditz, T. (1980). A statistical review of the literature concerning the self-serving attribution bias in interpersonal influence situations. *Journal of Personality, 48,* 435–448.

Aronson, E., & Worchel, P. (1966). Similarity vs. liking as determinants of interpersonal attractiveness. *Psychonomic Science, 5,* 157–158.

Aspinwall, L. G., & Taylor, S. E. (1993). Effects of social comparison direction, threat, and self-esteem on affect, self-evaluation, and expected success. *Journal of Personality and Social Psychology, 64,* 708–722.

Bargh, J. A., & Pratto, F. (1986). Individual construct accessibility and perceptual selection. *Journal of Experimental Social Psychology, 22,* 293–311.

Barnum, D. D., Snyder, C. R., Rapoff, M. A., Mani, M. M., & Thompson, R. (1998). Hope and social support in the psychological adjustment of pediatric burn survivors and matched controls. *Children's Health Care, 27,* 15–30.

Barone, D. F., Maddux, J. E., & Snyder, C. R. (1997). *Social cognitive psychology: History and current domains.* New York: Plenum.

Baumeister, R. F., Tice, D. M., & Hutton, D. G. (1989). Self-presentational motivations and personality differences in self-esteem. *Journal of Personality, 57,* 547–579.

Berglas, S., & Jones, E. E. (1978). Drug choice as a self-handicapping strategy in response to noncontingent success. *Journal of Personality and Social Psychology, 36,* 405–417.

Brown, J. D., & McGill, K. L. (1989). The cost of good fortune: When positive life events produce negative health consequences. *Journal of Personality and Social Psychology, 57,* 1103–1110.

Bulman, R. J., & Wortman, C. B. (1977). Attributions of blame and coping in the "real world": Severe accident victims react to their lot. *Journal of Personality and Social Psychology, 35,* 351–363.

Burns, M. O., & Seligman, M. E. P. (1991). Explanatory style, helplessness, and depression. In C. R. Snyder & D. R. Forsyth (Eds.), *Handbook of social and clinical psychology: The health perspective* (pp. 267–284). New York: Pergamon.

Dunn, D. S. (1996). Well-being following amputation: Salutary effects of positive meaning, optimism, and control. *Rehabilitation Psychology, 41,* 285–302.

Elliott, T. R., Witty, T. E., Herrick, S., & Hoffman, J. T. (1991). Negotiating reality after physical loss: Hope, depression, and disability. *Journal of Personality and Social Psychology, 61,* 608–613.

Ersek, M. (1992). Examining the process and dilemmas of reality negotiation. *IMAGE: Journal of Nursing Scholarship, 24,* 19–25.

Feick, D. L., & Rhodewalt, F. (1997). The double-edged sword of self-handicapping: Discounting, augmentation, and the protection and enhancement of self-esteem. *Motivation and Emotion, 21,* PG147–163.

Florida congressman quits following disclosure of e-mails to male page. (2006, September 29). *USA Today.* Retrieved November 12, 2006, from http://www.usatoday.com

Hammen, C. L., Marks, T., Mayol, A., & DeMayo, A. R. (1985). Depressive self-schemas, life stress, and vulnerability to depression. *Journal of Abnormal Psychology, 94,* 308–319.

Harris, R. N., & Snyder, C. R. (1986). The role of uncertain self-esteem in self-handicapping. *Journal of Personality and Social Psychology, 51,* 451–458.

Hastie, R. (1984). Causes and effects of causal attribution. *Journal of Personality and Social Psychology, 46,* 44–56.

Hegel, G. W. (1807/1967). *The phenomenology of mind* (Trans. J. B. Baillie). New York: Harper and Row.

Herbert, T. B., & Dunkel-Schetter, C. (1992). Negative social reactions to victims: An overview of responses and their determinants. In L. Montada, S.-H. Filipp, & M. J. Lerner (Eds.), *Life crises and experiences of loss in adulthood* (pp. 497–518). Hillsdale, NJ: Erlbaum.

Higgins, E. T. (1989). Knowledge accessibility and activation: Subjectivity and suffering from unconscious sources. In J. S. Uleman & J. A. Bargh (Eds.), *Unintended thought: Limits of awareness, intention, and control* (pp. 75–123). New York: Guilford.

Higgins, E. T., King, G. A., & Mavin, G. H. (1982). Individual construct accessibility and subjective impressions and recall. *Journal of Personality and Social Psychology, 43,* 35–47.

Higgins, R. L., & Leibowitz, R. Q. (1999). Reality negotiation and coping: The social construction of adaptive outcomes. In C. R. Snyder (Ed.), *Coping: The psychology of what works* (pp. 20–49). New York: Oxford University Press.

Higgins, R. L., & Snyder, C. R. (1989). Excuses gone awry: An analysis of self-defeating excuses. In R. C. Curtis (Ed.), *Self-defeating behaviors: Experimental research, clinical impressions, and practical implications* (pp. 99–130). New York: Plenum.

Higgins, R. L., & Snyder, C. R. (1991). Reality negotiation and excuse-making. In C. R. Snyder & D. R. Forsyth (Eds.), *Handbook of social and clinical psychology: The health perspective* (pp. 79–95). Elmsford, NY: Pergamon.

Higgins, R. L., Snyder, C. R., & Berglas, S. (1990). *Self-handicapping: The paradox that isn't.* New York: Plenum.

Irving, L. M., Snyder, C. R., & Crowson, J. J., Jr. (1998). Hope and the negotiation of cancer facts by college women. *Journal of Personality, 66,* 195–214.

Jones, E. E., & Berglas, S. (1978). Control attributions about the self through self-handicapping strategies: The appeal of alcohol and the role of underachievement. *Personality and Social Psychology Bulletin, 4,* 200–206.

Jones, E. E., & Rhodewalt, F. (1982). *The Self-Handicapping Scale.* (Available from F. Rhodewalt, Department of Psychology, University of Utah.)

Jones, R. A. (1990). Expectations and delay in seeking medical care. *Journal of Social Issues, 46,* 81–95.

Kant, I. (1781/1965). *Critique of pure reason* (unabridged ed.; Trans. N. K. Smith). New York: St. Martin's Press.

Kelley, H. H. (1967). Attribution theory in social psychology. In D. Levine (Ed.), *Nebraska Symposium on Motivation* (Vol. 15, pp. 192–238). Lincoln: University of Nebraska Press.

Kelley, H. H. (1971). *Attribution in social interaction.* New York: General Learning Press.

Kernis, M. H., Grannemann, B. D., & Barclay, L. H. (1992). Stability of self-esteem: Assessment, correlates, and excuse making. *Journal of Personality, 60,* 621–644.

Kwon, P. (2002). Hope, defense mechanisms, and adjustment: Implications for false hope and defensive hopelessness. *Journal of Personality, 70,* 207–231.

Laird, S. (1992). A preliminary investigation into prayer as a coping technique for adult patients with arthritis. Unpublished doctoral dissertation, Department of Psychology, University of Kansas, Lawrence, KS.

Lerner, M. J. (1980). *The belief in a just world: A fundamental delusion.* New York: Plenum.

Markus, H. M., & Cross, S. (1990). The interpersonal self. In L. A. Pervin (Ed.), *Handbook of personality: Theory and research* (pp. 576–608). New York: Guilford.

Markus, H. M., & Wurf, E. (1987). The dynamic self-concept: A social psychological perspective. *Annual Review of Psychology, 38,* 299–337.

Maslow, A. (1968). *Toward a psychology of being* (2nd ed.). New York: Van Nostrand.

Miller, D. T. (1976). Ego involvement and attribution for success and failure. *Journal of Personality and Social Psychology, 34,* 901–906.

Nolen-Hoeksema, S., & Davis, C. G. (2002). Positive responses to loss: Perceiving benefits and growth. In C. R. Snyder & S. J. Lopez (Eds.), *Handbook of positive psychology* (pp. 598–607). New York: Oxford University Press.

Pyszczynski, T. A., & Greenberg, J. (1981). Role of disconfirmed expectancies in the instigation of attributional processing. *Journal of Personality and Social Psychology, 40,* 31–38.

Rhodewalt, F., Morf, C., Hazlett, S., & Fairfield, M. (1991). Self-handicapping: The role of discounting and augmentation in the preservation of self-esteem. *Journal of Personality and Social Psychology, 61,* 122–131.

Rhodewalt, F., & Tragakis, M. (2002). Self-handicapping and the social self: The cost and rewards of interpersonal self-construction. In J. P. Forgas & K. D. Williams (Eds.), *The social self: Cognitive, interpersonal, and intergroup perspectives* (pp. 121–140). New York: Psychology Press.

Rogers, C. R. (1951). *Client-centered therapy: Its current practice, implications, and theory.* Boston: Houghton Mifflin.

Ross, S. R., Canada, K. E., & Rausch, M. K. (2002). Self-handicapping and the Five Factor Model of personality: Mediation between Neuroticism and Conscientiousness. *Personality and Individual Differences, 32,* 1173–1184.

Rotenberg, K. (1980). Children's use of intentionality in judgments of character and disposition. *Child Development, 51,* 282–284.

Roth, D. L., Harris, R. N., & Snyder, C. R. (1988). An individual differences measure of attributive and repudiative tactics of favorable self-presentation. *Journal of Social and Clinical Psychology, 6,* 159–170.

Samuelson, B. E. A. (1996). Measuring linkage into valenced elements: The LIVE scale. Unpublished master's thesis, University of Kansas, Lawrence, KS.

Schulz, R., & Decker, S. (1985). Long-term adjustment to physical disability: The role of social support, perceived control and self-blame. *Journal of Personality and Social Psychology, 48,* 1162–1172.

Silver, R. C., Wortman, C. B., & Crofton, C. (1990). The role of coping in support provision: The self-representational dilemma of victims of life crises. In B. R. Sarason, I. G. Sarason, & G. R. Pierce (Eds.), *Social support: An interactional view* (pp. 397–426). New York: Wiley.

Smith, T. W., Snyder, C. R., & Handelsman, M. M. (1982). On the self-serving function of an academic wooden leg: Test anxiety as a self-handicapping strategy. *Journal of Personality and Social Psychology, 42,* 314–321.

Snyder, C. R. (1989). Reality negotiation: From excuses to hope and beyond. *Journal of Social and Clinical Psychology, 8,* 130–157.

Snyder, C. R. (2002). Hope theory: Rainbows in the mind. *Psychological Inquiry, 13,* 249–275.

Snyder, C. R., Cheavens, J., & Michael, S. T. (1999). Hoping. In C. R. Snyder (Ed.), *Coping: The psychology of what works* (pp. 205–229). New York: Oxford University Press.

Snyder, C. R., Harris, C., Anderson, J. R., Holleran, S. A., Irving, L. M., Sigmon, S. T., et al. (1991). The will and the ways: Development and validation of an individual-differences measure of hope. *Journal of Personality and Social Psychology, 60,* 570–585.

Snyder, C. R., & Higgins, R. L. (1988a). Excuse attributions: Do they work? In S. L. Zelen (Ed.), *Self-representation: The second attribution-personality theory conference* (pp. 50–122). New York: Springer-Verlag.

Snyder, C. R., & Higgins, R. L. (1988b). Excuses: Their effective role in the negotiation of reality. *Psychological Bulletin, 104,* 23–35.

Snyder, C. R., & Higgins, R. L. (1997). Reality negotiation: Governing one's self and being governed by others. *General Psychology Review, 1,* 336–350.

Snyder, C. R., Higgins, R. L., & Stucky, R. J. (1983). *Excuses: Masquerades in search of grace.* New York: Wiley-Interscience.

Snyder, C. R., Hoza, B., Pelham, W. E., Rapoff, M., Ware, L., Danovsky, M., et al. (1997). The development and validation of the Children's Hope Scale. *Journal of Pediatric Psychology, 22,* 399–421.

Snyder, C. R., Ilardi, S., Michael, S. T., & Cheavens, J. (2000). Hope theory: Updating a common process for psychological change. In C. R. Snyder & R. E. Ingram (Eds.), *Handbook of* psychological change: *Psychotherapy processes and practices for the 21st century* (pp. 128–150). New York: Wiley.

Snyder, C. R., Irving, L. R., Sigmon, S. T., & Holleran, S. (1992). Reality negotiation and valence/linkage self theories: Psychic showdown at the "I'm OK" corral and beyond. In L. Montrada, S.-H. Filipp, & M. J. Lerner (Eds.), *Life crises and experiences of loss in adulthood* (pp. 275–297). Hillsdale, NJ: Erlbaum.

Snyder, C. R., & Samuelson, B. E. A. (1998). *Development and validation of the LIVE Scale: Linkage into valenced elements.* Unpublished manuscript, University of Kansas, Lawrence, KS.

Snyder, C. R., Sympson, S. C., Ybasco, F. C., Borders, T. F., Babyak, M. A., & Higgins, R. L. (1996). Development and validation of the State Hope Scale. *Journal of Personality and Social Psychology, 70,* 321–335.

Swann, W. B., Jr., Hixon, J. G., & De La Ronde, C. (1992). Embracing the bitter "truth": Negative self-concepts and marital commitment. *Psychological Science, 3,* 118–121.

Swann, W. B., & Pelham, B. W. (2002). The truth about illusions: Authenticity and positivity in social relationships. In C. R. Snyder & S. J. Lopez (Eds.), *Handbook of Positive Psychology* (pp. 366–381). New York: Oxford University Press.

Swann, W. B., Jr., Wenzlaff, R. M., Krull, D. S., & Pelham, B. W. (1992). Allure of negative feedback: Self-verification strivings among depressed persons. *Journal of Abnormal Psychology, 101,* 293–306.

Taylor, S. E. (1983). Adjustment to threatening events: A theory of cognitive adaptation. *American Psychologist, 38,* 1161–1173.

Taylor, S. E., Lichtman, R. R., & Wood, J. V. (1984). Attributions, beliefs about control, and adjustment to breast cancer. *Journal of Personality and Social Psychology, 46,* 489–502.

Tennen, H., & Affleck, G. (2002). Benefit-finding and benefit-reminding. In C. R. Snyder & S. J. Lopez (Eds.), *Handbook of Positive Psychology* (pp. 584–597). New York: Oxford University Press.

Tennen, H., Affleck, G., Urrows, S., Higgins, P., & Mendola, R. (1992). Perceiving control, construing benefits, and daily processes in rheumatoid arthritis. *Canadian Journal of Behavioral Science, 24,* 186–203.

Tice, D. M., & Baumeister, R. F. (1984). *Self-handicapping, self-esteem, and self-presentation.* Paper presented at the meeting of the Midwestern Psychological Association, Chicago.

Timko, C., & Janoff-Bulman, R. (1985). Attributions, vulnerability and psychological adjustment: The case of breast cancer. *Health Psychology, 4,* 521–546.

Vaihinger, H. (1925). *The philosophy of "as if"* (Trans. C. K. Ogden). New York: Harcourt Brace.

Witenberg, S. H., Blanchard, E. B., Suls, J., Tennen, H., McCoy, G., & McGoldrick, M. D. (1983). Perceptions of control and causality as predictors of compliance and coping in hemodialysis. *Basic and Applied Social Psychology, 4,* 319–336.

Zuckerman, M. (1979). Attribution of success and failure revisited, or: The motivational bias is alive and well in attribution theory. *Journal of Personality, 47,* 245–287.

Zuckerman, M., Kieffer, S. C., & Knee, C. R. (1998). Consequences of self-handicapping: Effects on coping, academic performance, and adjustment. *Journal of Personality and Social Psychology, 74,* 1619–1628.

Humility

June Price Tangney

Abstract

Although humility is commonly equated with a sense of unworthiness and low self-regard, true humility is a rich, multifaceted construct that is characterized by an accurate assessment of one's characteristics, an ability to acknowledge limitations, and a "forgetting of the self." In this chapter, I describe current conceptions of humility, discuss the challenges in its measurement, and review the scant empirical work addressing it directly and indirectly. I will also discuss briefly interventions for enhancing humility.

Keywords: humility, modesty, pride, virtue

History of the Psychology of Humility: Still at the Point of Humble Beginnings

Scientific study of humility is still in its infancy. A review of the empirical literature from the last 20 years yields only a handful of research studies with any consideration of this long-revered construct. Furthermore, in virtually every case where humility is addressed, it has been tangential to the main research focus.

Why has humility been neglected so long? Two factors come readily to mind. First, the concept of humility is linked to values and religion in many people's minds. As a field, for many years, mainstream psychology steered clear of such value-laden topics as religion, virtue, and (with the exception of Kohlberg's work on "forms" of moral "thinking") morality. In their zeal to establish psychology as a bona fide "science," psychological scientists embraced notions of objectivity and fact. Indeed, it is worth noting that the virtues *as a group* have been relatively neglected in psychology. Until very recently, wisdom, gratitude, and forgiveness, for example, all represented "black holes" in the literature based on a century of psychological science.

A second factor undoubtedly contributing to the neglect of humility is the lack of a well-established measure of this construct. If you can't measure it,

you can't study it. Psychology and the sciences in general are chock-full of examples of how an advance in measurement can lead to a dramatic expansion in empirical research. For example, after years of neglect, the scientific study of shame virtually exploded in the early 1990s—shortly after the development of several psychometrically sound, easily administered measures of individual differences in proneness to shame (Harder & Lewis, 1987; Hoblitzelle, 1987; Tangney, 1990). As discussed in greater detail later, measurement remains a significant challenge in the area of humility.

Contrasting Conceptions of Humility

Another challenge facing psychological scientists interested in humility centers on the varying definitions of the construct. For many, humility simply means holding oneself in low regard. For example, in the *Oxford English Dictionary* (1998), humility is defined as "the quality of being humble or having a lowly opinion of oneself; meekness, lowliness, humbleness: the opposite of 'pride' or 'haughtiness.'" In other dictionaries, humility is defined largely as a state of being "humble," which in turn is defined, for example, by *Funk & Wagnalls Standard College Dictionary* (1963) as "lowly in kind, state, condition, etc.; of little worth; unimportant; common . . . .

Lowly in feeling; lacking self-esteem; having a sense of insignificance, unworthiness, dependence, or sinfulness; meek; penitent" (p. 653). From this "low self-esteem" perspective, humility certainly does not stand out as one of the more attractive virtues. For example, most of us would have difficulty appreciating a friend's efforts to strengthen our character by "humbling" us (e.g., making us lower in state or condition, reducing possessions or esteem, abasing us).

The "low self-esteem" conception of humility is prevalent not only in dictionaries but also in the psychological literature (e.g., Klein, 1992; Knight & Nadel, 1986; Langston & Cantor, 1988; Weiss & Knight, 1980), as well as in common parlance. Nonetheless, it is clear that when "experts" (e.g., philosophers, theologians, sociologists, psychologists, and other "wise" persons) delve into the broader significance of humility, they have a different—and much richer—notion of this construct. Emmons (1998) clearly articulated this alternative view of humility by stating:

> Although humility is often equated in people's minds with low self-regard and tends to activate images of a stooped-shouldered, self-deprecating, weak-willed soul only too willing to yield to the wishes of others, in reality humility is the antithesis of this caricature. To be humble is not to have a low opinion of oneself, it is to have an accurate opinion of oneself. It is the ability to keep one's talents and accomplishments in perspective (Richards, 1992), to have a sense of self-acceptance, an understanding of one's imperfections, and to be free from arrogance and low self-esteem. (Clark, 1992, p. 33)

Templeton (1997) presents a similar conceptualization of humility:

> Humility is not self-deprecation. To believe that you have no worth, or were created somehow flawed or incompetent, can be foolish. Humility represents wisdom. It is knowing you were created with special talents and abilities to share with the world; but it can also be an understanding that you are one of many souls created by God, and each has an important role to play in life. Humility is knowing you are smart, but not *all-knowing*. It is accepting that you have personal power, but are not omnipotent.... Inherent in humility resides an open and receptive mind ... it leaves us more open to learn from others and refrains from seeing issues and people only in blacks and whites. The opposite of humility is arrogance—the belief that we are wiser or better than others. Arrogance promotes separation rather than community. It looms like a brick wall between us and those from whom we could learn. (pp. 162–163)

For many, there is a religious dimension to humility—the recognition that "God infinitely exceeds anything anyone has ever said of Him, and that He is infinitely beyond human comprehension and understanding" (Templeton, 1997, p. 30; see also Schimmel, 1997). Here, too, the emphasis is not on human sinfulness, unworthiness, and inadequacy but rather on the notion of a higher, greater power and the implication that, although we may have considerable wisdom and knowledge, there always are limits to our perspective. Humility carries with it an open-mindedness, a willingness to admit mistakes and seek advice, and a desire to learn (Hwang, 1982; Templeton, 1997).

Also inherent in the state of humility is a relative lack of self-focus or self-preoccupation. Templeton (1997) refers to a process of becoming "unselved," which goes hand in hand with the recognition of one's place in the world. A person who has gained a sense of humility is no longer phenomenologically at the center of his or her world. The focus is on the larger community, of which he or she is one part. From this perspective, the excessively self-deprecating person can be seen, in some important respects, as *lacking* humility. Consider the person who repeatedly protests, "Oh, *I*'m not really very good in art. *I* never did very well in art class at school. Oh, *this* little painting that *I* did really is nothing. *I* just whipped it together last night. It (*my* painting) is really nothing." Such apparently humble protests betray a marked self-focus. The person remains at the center of attention, with the self as the focus of consideration and evaluation.

In relinquishing the very human tendency toward an egocentric focus, persons with humility become ever more open to recognizing the abilities, potential, worth, and importance of others. One important consequence of becoming "unselved" is that we no longer have the need to enhance and defend an all-important self at the expense of our evaluation of others (Halling, Kunz, & Rowe, 1994). Our attention shifts outward, and our eyes are opened to the beauty and potential in those around us. As Means, Wilson, Sturm, Biron, and Bach (1990) observed, humility "is an increase in the valuation of others and not a decrease in the valuation of oneself" (p. 214). Myers (1979) effectively captured these latter two elements of humility, stating:

> The true end of humility is not self-contempt.... To paraphrase C. S. Lewis, humility does not consist in

handsome people trying to believe they are ugly, and clever people trying to believe they are fools . . . . True humility is more like self-forgetfulness . . . . It leaves people free to esteem their special talents and, with the same honesty, to esteem their neighbor's. Both the neighbor's talents and one's own are recognized as gifts and, like one's height, are not fit subjects for either inordinate pride or self-deprecation. (p. 38)

In the theological, philosophical, and psychological literatures, therefore, humility is portrayed as a rich, multifaceted construct, in sharp contrast to dictionary definitions that emphasize a sense of unworthiness and low self-regard. Specifically, the key elements of humility seem to include

- an accurate assessment of one's abilities and achievements (*not* low self-esteem, self-deprecation)
- an ability to acknowledge one's mistakes, imperfections, gaps in knowledge, and limitations (often vis-à-vis a "higher power")
- openness to new ideas, contradictory information, and advice
- keeping one's abilities and accomplishments—one's place in the world—in perspective (e.g., seeing oneself as just one person in the larger scheme of things)
- a relatively low self-focus, a "forgetting of the self," while recognizing that one is but part of the larger universe
- an appreciation of the value of all things, as well as the many different ways that people and things can contribute to our world.

What Humility Is Not

Humility is a rich psychological construct that is related to, but conceptually distinct from, familiar constructs such as narcissism, modesty, and self-esteem. Clearly, from the foregoing discussion, humility is *not* low self-esteem (Ryan, 1983), nor is it an underestimation of one's abilities, accomplishments, or worth. Furthermore, as explained subsequently, humility is related to, but distinct from, modesty and narcissism.

The concept of modesty focuses primarily on a moderate estimate of personal merits or achievements. As such, "modesty" does not capture other key aspects of humility such as a "forgetting of the self" and an appreciation of the variety of ways in which others can be "worthy." Rather, use of the term "modesty" often extends into issues of propriety in behavior and dress, where the notion of humility is less relevant. Thus, modesty is both too narrow, missing fundamental components of

humility, and too broad, relating also to bodily exposure and other dimensions of propriety. One might view modesty—in the sense of an accurate, unexaggerated estimation of one's strengths—as a component of humility. But it does not tell the whole story.

The construct of narcissism is perhaps most closely related to humility. People who are narcissistic clearly lack humility. It is not clear, however, that an *absence* of narcissism can be equated with the *presence* of humility. In conceptualizing narcissism, social psychologists tend to focus on grandiosity, an exaggerated sense of self-importance, and an overestimation of one's abilities. But there's much more to the clinical conceptions of narcissism. Clinical theorists, drawing on a long history of "object relations," typically use the term "narcissism" to refer to a distinctly pathological form of self-focus and fluctuating self-regard, which stems from fundamental defects in the self-system (e.g., Kohut, 1971). When clinicians refer to a person with narcissism, they generally have in mind a seriously disturbed individual who exhibits pervasive adjustment difficulties that go hand in hand with a *DSM-IV* (American Psychiatric Association, 1994) diagnosis of personality disorder. This is not simply an overconfident, conceited dolt, but rather someone with a damaged sense of self. Attempts to shore up the self with unrealistic fantasies of grandiosity inevitably alternate with a grinding sense of emptiness and self-loathing. Other hallmarks of narcissism include a pervasive self-focus and a corresponding inability to focus on and empathize with others.

Narcissistic individuals clearly lack many of the essential components of humility. But it is not clear that people who score low on a measure of narcissism necessarily embody humility. People low on narcissism may or may not make accurate assessments of their abilities and achievements. For example, low-self-esteem, self-deprecating individuals are neither narcissistic nor paragons of humility. Similarly, people without narcissistic tendencies may or may not have the wisdom to keep their places in the world in perspective (e.g., seeing themselves as one person in the larger scheme of things). They may or may not have a deep appreciation for the unique gifts and talents of others.

In defining complex constructs such as humility, as well as in developing measurement instruments, it is important to specify how the focal construct differs from other related but distinct concepts. As underscored by Campbell and Fiske (1959), "discriminant validity" is a critical component of measurement validation. It is important to know not only that a measure correlates well (positively or negatively) with (measures of) other relevant constructs in a theoretically meaningful way. It is also important to demonstrate that the measure *does not* correlate too highly with (or behave identically to) established measures of some other construct.

Measures that are *confounded* by items tapping other nonfocal constructs not only present conceptual ambiguity but also impede science by blurring the boundaries between constructs, inadvertently precluding the possibility of studying functional relations *among* them. For example, in the case of forgiveness, it is impossible to examine meaningfully the functional relationship between empathy and forgiveness if one uses a forgiveness measure that includes items tapping empathy. In short, it is important to decide where to draw the conceptual line.

Measurement of Humility: Two Levels of Measurement, Two Levels of Questions

Halling et al. (1994) observed that doing research on humility is humbling. Quite possibly, the quest for a reliable and valid measure of humility is the most humbling aspect of research on this topic. By its very nature, the construct of humility poses some special challenges in the area of measurement. As a consequence, psychological scientists have yet to develop a well-validated tool for assessing humility. This is a glaring gap in the literature, because without a solid assessment method, the science pretty much comes to a halt. It is also worth noting that psychologists are most likely to develop strong, meaningful measures when those measures are informed by theory. Although we have some clear definitions of humility, comprehensive theories or models need to be developed and refined, which in turn would form a solid foundation for assessment.

Theoretically, humility could be assessed at two distinct levels—at the level of *states* and at the level of *dispositions*. A *dispositional* assessment would focus on stable, individual differences in humility. In this context, humility would be viewed as a component of one's personality, as a relatively enduring disposition that a person brings to many different kinds of situations. In contrast, a *state* measure would focus on feelings or experiences of humility "in the moment." Personality and individual differences aside, most of us have humility in some situations but not in others.

Regarding dispositional humility, a few options presently are available to researchers, but each has

significant drawbacks. In several earlier studies, humility has been operationalized as low self-esteem (e.g., Weiss & Knight, 1980), but this is clearly inconsistent with broader conceptualizations of humility. In fact, theoretically, scores on self-esteem measures such as the Rosenberg (1965) and Janis and Fields (1956) scales should be positively correlated with (although not identical to) individual differences in humility. Consider the types of items included on the Rosenberg Self-Esteem Scale (rated on a scale of 1–5, from "always false" to "always true"): "I feel that I'm a person of worth, at least on an equal plane with others" and "I feel I have a number of good qualities." The person with a true sense of humility would be expected to endorse such items positively, not negatively.

Taking a different approach, Farh, Dobbins, and Cheng (1991) and Yu and Murphy (1993) operationalized workers' "modesty" by comparing self-ratings to ratings made of them by knowledgeable others (e.g., supervisors and coworkers). Those who rated themselves lower than their supervisors were viewed as showing a "modesty bias." Here, too, there are some conceptual ambiguities with such "self versus knowledgeable other" comparisons. Given that humility theoretically entails an *accurate* assessment of one's abilities, one could argue that high humility should be indexed by high levels of *agreement* between self and other, not self-deprecating discrepancies.

Emmons (personal communication, December 4, 1998) attempted to develop a self-report measure of humility. Using a forced-choice format to circumvent social desirability biases, Emmons developed an array of theoretically derived items tapping the diverse components of humility described previously. The measure is well crafted in design and content. Unfortunately, Emmons's initial analyses of the measure's internal reliability were disappointing, and he is now rather skeptical that this construct can be adequately assessed via self-report.

With regard to experiences of humility "in the moment," currently there is no established self-report measure of state humility. But Exline, Bushman, Faber, and Phillips (2000) recently developed a technique for experimentally inducing a sense of humility by asking people to write about "a time when they felt humble or experienced a sense of humility" versus "a time when they felt important or had a sense of importance." Based on results from an initial study, some complications arise in using this technique to prime humility. Specifically, people receiving humility instructions wrote two very different types, of narratives. The majority of persons described instances in which they felt "bad about themselves" for doing something stupid or wrong. For this group, the instructions seemed to prime a sense of humiliation or shame rather than a sense of humility. A smaller subset of respondents described events that seemed more directly relevant to the experience of humility—for example, situations that evoked a "forgetting of the self" or that caused respondents to see themselves in a broader context. Thus, in using the Exline et al. (2000) priming technique, it is important to distinguish between stories involving humiliation versus humility themes. In addition, some modifications to the instructions may be necessary in order to more consistently elicit stories of "true" humility rather than shaming experiences.

No doubt, psychologists will continue efforts to develop psychometrically sound measures of both state and dispositional humility in the years to come. It is worth noting that researchers generally rely on self-report methods for assessing personality traits. In the case of humility, however, there is a potentially serious catch. To the degree that a key component of humility is a "forgetting of the self," self-reflection and self-report of one's level of humility may be oxymoronic. What do we make of a person who views him- or herself as someone with "unusually high humility"? As Halling et al. (1994) point out, "One can reflect on one's own experience of fear, isolation, or self-rejection, but the attention during the experience of humility is directed toward others" (p. 121). Similarly, Singh (1967) observed that "true humility is freedom from all consciousness of self, which includes freedom from the consciousness of humility. The truly humble man never knows that he is humble" (p. 4).

There are good reasons for psychologists' preference for self-report measures of personality traits. Traits such as humility are not easily inferred from quick observation. Also, systematic behavioral observational methods are cumbersome and time consuming. So there is a strong preference for paper-and-pencil questionnaires that require little time and training to administer and score. But humility may represent a rare personality construct that is simply unamenable to direct self-report methods. Thus, the present bottom line is that the measurement of humility remains an unsolved challenge in psychology.

Psychological and Social Implications of Humility: Relevant Empirical Research

Researchers have yet to directly address the psychology of humility and develop a theory-based, reliable, and valid measure. Some insights can be gleaned, however, from related areas of psychological research. In this section, I provide a brief review of relevant findings from related literatures.

Basic research on the self and its operations suggests that humility may be a relatively rare human characteristic. The pervasiveness of "self-enhancement biases" is underscored in the social psychological literature (Baumeister, 1998; Greenwald, 1980). From this literature, we learn that the self is remarkably resourceful at accentuating the positive and deflecting the negative. For example, research consistently shows that people are inclined to take credit for "their" successes but blame other factors for "their" failures and transgressions (Baumeister, Stillwell, & Wotman, 1990; Snyder, Higgins, & Stucky, 1983; Zuckerman, 1979). As another example, people are more likely to notice, think about, and remember positive information about themselves, with negative information being "lost in the shuffle" (Mischel, Ebbesen, & Zeiss, 1976). Indeed based on this self-enhancement literature, one might infer that humility is quite antithetical with human nature.

Nonetheless, people apparently can control the degree to which they self-enhance in response to situational demands. On this point, Tice, Butler, Muraven, and Stillwell (1995) demonstrated that people adjust their self-enhancement according to the nature of the social setting, showing more modesty in the company of friends than strangers.

Whether with friends or strangers, some degree of humility may be beneficial. The benefits of modesty—especially "moderate" modesty—have been underscored in numerous studies (Baumeister & Ilko, 1995; Bond, Leung, & Wan, 1982; Forsyth, Berger, & Mitchell, 1981; Jones & Wortman, 1973; Robinson, Johnson, & Shields, 1995). People *like* and feel less threatened by others who are modest about their achievements, whereas boastful, arrogant behavior often results in social disapproval. The benefits of modesty seem to extend beyond positive evaluation in purely social contexts. In answer to the objection that "you can't get ahead without tooting your own horn," Wosinska, Dabul, Whetstone-Dion, and Cialdini (1996) have provided some evidence that modesty can be attractive in work contexts, as well.

Likewise, tendencies toward self-enhancement, grandiosity, and narcissism bode poorly for long-term adjustment, especially in the interpersonal realm (Ehrenberg, Hunter, & Elterman, 1996; Means et al., 1990). Although much has been written about the benefits of various "positive illusions" (Brown, 1993; Taylor & Brown, 1988, 1994), researchers have also shown repeatedly that tendencies toward self-enhancement are problematic. Specifically, psychological *mal*adjustment is associated with the degree to which people rate themselves more favorably than others rate them (Asendorpf & Ostendorf, 1998; Colvin, Block, & Funder, 1995). Perez, Vohs, & Joiner (2005) also found that people who are immodest (relative to how others rate them) are more inclined toward physical aggression than are their more modest peers. Along the same lines, researchers have shown that narcissistic individuals are sensitive to interpersonal slights, quick to anger, and less inclined to forgive others (Exline & Baumeister, 2000; Exline, Campbell, Baumeister, Joiner, & Krueger, in press; Sandage, Worthington, Hight, & Berry, 2000; Tangney, Boone, Fee, & Reinsmith, 1999). From these findings, one might infer that a sense of humility inhibits anger and aggression and fosters forgiveness.

In one of the few studies to explicitly address the psychology of humility, Exline et al. (2000) found results suggestive of a link between humility and forgiveness. People who were successfully primed to experience humility (e.g., who wrote personal accounts of a non-self-deprecating humility experience) were slower to retaliate in response to provocation on a laboratory task. In contrast, individuals primed to feel morally superior judged another person's transgression more harshly and as less forgivable.

Humility not only implies an accurate assessment of oneself (neither unduly favorable nor unfavorable) but also entails a "forgetting of the self," an outwardly directed orientation toward a world in which one is "just one part." This process of becoming "unselved" may have significant psychological and physical benefits. Clinicians have long noted the links between excessive self-focus and a broad range of psychological symptoms, including anxiety, depression, social phobias, and so on. As Baumeister (1991) argues, there are many advantages to "escaping the self," not the least of which is a relief from the burden of self-preoccupation (Halling et al., 1994) and the Western imperative to defend the vulnerable self. Even in the area of

physical health, researchers suggest that excessive self-focus is a risk factor for coronary heart disease (Fontana, Rosenberg, Burg, Kerns, & Colonese, 1990; Scherwitz & Canick, 1988).

Interventions to Enhance Humility?

Psychologists have not developed interventions aimed specifically at promoting humility, although many therapies include components that may do so. A focus on "humility promotion" is most likely to be observed in the treatment of narcissistic personality disorder. For example, cognitive-behavioral therapy of the disorder may include efforts to reduce the client's egocentric bias—correcting cognitive distortions regarding the centrality and importance of the self relative to others, reducing self-serving biases, and so forth. Beyond the treatment of narcissism per se, many psychotherapies inevitably touch on philosophical and existential issues centrally relevant to a sense of humility. Insight-oriented, humanistic, and existential therapies are especially likely to include examination and exploration of one's place in the world. Finally, a common goal in virtually all "talk" therapies is to help clients develop a realistic assessment and acceptance of both their strengths and their weaknesses.

Outside of the therapist's office, parents, teachers, heroes, and community leaders all play a role in modeling (or not modeling) a sense of humility for the subsequent generation. Throughout their early years, children learn important lessons about themselves, the world, and their place in the world. As they mature, a sense of humility may be further fostered by exposure to different peoples and cultures, by life-changing events (a life-threatening illness, a serious accident, birth of a child, dissolution of a marriage), by religious beliefs, or via other types of "transcendental" experiences.

Future Directions

As one of the classic virtues, humility has a well-deserved place in positive psychology. Although little research has directly examined causes and consequences of humility, psychological science provides a good deal of indirect evidence supporting its presumed value. Consistent with age-old wisdom, a sense of humility appears beneficial for both the individual and his or her social group. But this is nearly virgin territory, and many intriguing questions remain. In what specific domains is a sense of humility adaptive? And via what mechanisms? Are there circumstances in which humility is a liability? Are there important gender and/or cultural differences in the meaning and implications of humility? How can parents, teachers, and therapists foster an adaptive sense of humility? Certainly at the top of the research agenda is the need for continued efforts to develop a well-articulated theoretical framework and associated psychological measures of both state and dispositional humility. Armed with a solid conceptual and measurement base, scientists will no doubt develop a clearer picture of this long-neglected source of human strength.

Questions for Future Study

1. What are the developmental origins of humility?

2. In what contexts is humility most adaptive?

3. What behaviors or psychological processes mediate the effects of humility?

Acknowledgments

Many thanks to members of our "humility" reading group—Luis ClaviJo, Rosangela Di Manto, Andy Drake, Ronda Fee, Ramineh Kangarloo, Jean No, and Justin Reznick—for their invaluable insights, and to Bob Emmons for his wisdom and advice. Preparation of this chapter was supported in part by a grant from the John Templeton Foundation. Portions were adapted from Tangney (2000).

References

American Psychiatric Association. (1994). *Diagnostic and statistical manual of mental disorders* (4th ed.). Washington, DC: Author.

Asendorpf, J. B., & Ostendorf, F. (1998). Is self-enhancement healthy? Conceptual, psychometric, and empirical analysis. *Journal of Personality and Social Psychology, 74*, 955–966.

Baumeister, R. F. (1991). *Escaping the self: Alcoholism, spirituality, masochism, and other flights from the burden of selfhood.* New York: Basic Books.

Baumeister, R. F. (1998). The self. In D. T. Gilbert, S. T. Fiske, & G. Lindzey (Eds.), *The handbook of social psychology* (4th ed., pp. 680–740). New York: McGraw-Hill.

Baumeister, R. F., & Ilko, S. A. (1995). Shallow gratitude: Public and private acknowledgement of external help in accounts of success. *Basic and Applied Social Psychology, 16*, 191–209.

Baumeister, R. F., Stillwell, A., & Wotman, S. R. (1990). Victim and perpetrator accounts of interpersonal conflict: Autobiographical narratives about anger. *Journal of Personality and Social Psychology, 59*, 994–1005.

Bond, M. H., Leung, K., & Wan, K. C. (1982). The social impact of self-effacing attributions: The Chinese case. *Journal of Social Psychology, 118*, 157–166.

Brown, J. D. (1993). Coping with stress: The beneficial role of positive illusions. In A. P. Turnbull, J. M. Patterson, S. K. Behr, D. L. Murphy, J. G. Marquis, & M. J. Blue-Banning (Eds.), *Cognitive coping, families, and disability* (pp. 123–137). Baltimore: Paul H. Brookes.

Campbell, D. T., & Fiske, D. W. (1959). Convergent and discriminant validation by the multitrait-multimethod matrix. *Psychological Bulletin, 56*, 81–105.

Clark, A. T. (1992). Humility. In D. H. Ludlow (Ed.), *Encyclopedia of Mormonism* (pp. 663–664). New York: Macmillan.

Colvin, C. R., Block, J., & Funder, D. C. (1995). Overly positive self-evaluations and personality: Negative implications for mental health. *Journal of Personality and Social Psychology, 68*, 1152–1162.

Ehrenberg, M. F., Hunter, M. A., & Elterman, M. F. (1996). Shared parenting agreements after marital separation: The roles of empathy and narcissism. *Journal of Consulting and Clinical Psychology, 64*, 808–818.

Emmons, R. A. (1998). The psychology of ultimate concern: Personality, spirituality, and intelligence. Unpublished manuscript, University of California at Davis.

Exline, J. J., & Baumeister, R. F. (2000). [Narcissism, grudges, and forgiveness]. Unpublished raw data, Case Western Reserve University.

Exline, J. J., Bushman, B., Faber, J., & Phillips, C. (2000, February). Pride gets in the way: Self-protection works against forgiveness. In J. J. Exline (Chair), *Ouch! Who said forgiveness was easy?* Symposium conducted at the annual meeting of the Society for Personality and Social Psychology, Nashville, TN.

Exline, J. J., Campbell, W. K., Baumeister, R. F., Joiner, T., & Krueger, J. (2004). Humility and modesty. In C. Peterson & M. Seligman, *The Values In Action (VIA) classification of strengths* (pp. 461–475). Cincinnati, OH: Values in Action Institute.

Farh, J. L., Dobbins, G. H., & Cheng, B. S. (1991). Cultural relativity in action: A comparison of self-ratings made by Chinese and U.S. workers. *Personnel Psychology, 44*, 129–147.

Fontana, A. F., Rosenberg, R. L., Burg, M. M., Kerns, R. D., & Colonese, K. L. (1990). Type A behavior and self-referencing: Interactive risk factors? *Journal of Social Behavior and Personality, 5*, 215–232.

Forsyth, D. R., Berger, R. E., & Mitchell, T. (1981). The effect of self-serving versus other-serving claims of responsibility on attraction and attributions in groups. *Social Psychology Quarterly, 44*, 59–64.

Funk & Wagnalls. (1963). *Standard college dictionary.* New York: Harcourt, Brace and World.

Greenwald, A. G. (1980). The totalitarian ego: Fabrication and revision of personal history. *American Psychologist, 35*, 603–618.

Halling, S., Kunz, G., & Rowe, J. O. (1994). The contributions of dialogal psychology to phenomenological research. *Journal of Humanistic Psychology, 34*, 109–131.

Harder, D. W., & Lewis, S. J. (1987). The assessment of shame and guilt. In J. N. Butcher & C. D. Spielberger (Eds.), *Advances in personality assessment* (Vol. 6, pp. 89–114). Hillsdale, NJ: Erlbaum.

Hoblitzelle, W. (1987). Attempts to measure and differentiate shame and guilt: The relation between shame and depression. In H. B. Lewis (Ed.), *The role of shame in symptom formation* (pp. 207–235). Hillsdale, NJ: Erlbaum.

Hwang, C. (1982). Studies in Chinese personality: A critical review. *Bulletin of Educational Psychology, 15*, 227–242.

Janis, I. L., & Fields, P. B. (1956). A behavioral assessment of persuasibility: Consistency of individual differences. *Sociometry, 19*, 241–259.

Jones, E. E., & Wortman, C. (1973). *Ingratiation: An attributional approach.* Morristown, NJ: General Learning Press.

Klein, D. C. (1992). Managing humiliation. *Journal of Primary Prevention, 12*, 255–268.

Knight, P. A., & Nadel, J. I. (1986). Humility revisited: Self-esteem, information search, and policy consistency. *Organizational Behavior and Human Decision Processes, 38*, 196–206.

Kohut, H. (1971). *The analysis of the self.* New York: International Universities Press.

Langston, C. A., & Cantor, N. (1988). Social anxiety and social constraint: When making friends is hard. *Journal of Personality and Social Psychology, 56*, 649–661.

Means, J. R., Wilson, G. L., Sturm, C., Biron, J. E., & Bach, P. J. (1990). Theory and practice: Humility as a psychotherapeutic formulation. *Counseling Psychology Quarterly, 3*, 211–215.

Mischel, W., Ebbesen, E. B., & Zeiss, A. R. (1976). Determinants of selective memory about the self. *Journal of Consulting and Clinical Psychology, 44*, 92–103.

Myers, D. G. (1979). *The inflated self: Human illusions and the biblical call to hope.* New York: Seabury.

Oxford English Dictionary. (1998). [On-line]. Available at http://etext.virginia.edu/etcbin/oedbin/oed-id?id=191647477

Perez, M., Vohs, K. D., & Joiner, T. E. (2005). Discrepancies between self and other esteem as correlates of aggression. *Journal of Social & Clinical Psychology, 24*, 607–620.

Richards, N. (1992). *Humility.* Philadelphia: Temple University Press.

Robinson, M. D., Johnson, J. T., & Shields, S. A. (1995). On the advantages of modesty: The benefits of a balanced self-presentation. *Communication Research, 22*, 575–591.

Rosenberg, M. (1965). *Society and the adolescent self-image.* Princeton, NJ: Princeton University Press.

Ryan, D. S. (1983). Self-esteem: An operational definition and ethical analysis. *Journal of Psychology and Theology, 11*, 295–302.

Sandage, S. J., Worthington, E. L., Jr., Hight, T. L., & Berry, J. W. (2000). Seeking forgiveness: Theoretical context and an initial empirical study. *Journal of Psychology and Theology, 28*, 21–35.

Scherwitz, L., & Canick, J. C. (1988). Self-reference and coronary heart disease risk. In B. K. Houston & C. R. Snyder (Eds.), *Type A behavior pattern: Research, theory, and intervention* (pp. 146–167). New York: Wiley.

Schimmel, S. (1997). *The seven deadly sins.* New York: Oxford University Press.

Singh, S. K. (1967). *Untitled* [On-line]. Available: www.humboldt1.com/∼jiva/humility.html

Snyder, C. R., Higgins, R. L., & Stucky, R. (1983). *Excuses: Masquerades in search of grace.* New York: Wiley-Interscience.

Tangney, J. P. (1990). Assessing individual differences in proneness to shame and guilt: Development of the self-conscious affect and attribution inventory. *Journal of Personality and Social Psychology, 59*, 102–111.

Tangney, J. P. (2000). Humility: Theoretical perspectives, empirical findings, and directions for future research. *Journal of Social and Clinical Psychology, 19*, 70–82.

Tangney, J. P., Boone, A. L., Fee, R., & Reinsmith, C. (1999). *Individual differences in the propensity to forgive: Measurement and implications for psychological and social adjustment.* Fairfax, VA: George Mason University.

Taylor, S. E., & Brown, J. D. (1988). Illusion and well-being: A social psychological perspective on mental health. *Psychological Bulletin, 103*, 193–210.

Taylor, S. E., & Brown, J. D. (1994). Positive illusions and well-being revisited: Separating fact from fiction. *Psychological Bulletin, 116*, 21–27.

Templeton, J. M. (1997). *Worldwide laws of life.* Philadelphia: Templeton Foundation Press.

Tice, D. M., Butler, J. L., Muraven, M. B., & Stillwell, A. M. (1995). When modesty prevails: Differential favorability of self-presentation to friends and strangers. *Journal of Personality and Social Psychology, 69*, 1120–1138.

Weiss, H. M., & Knight, P. A. (1980). The utility of humility: Self-esteem, information search, and problem-solving efficiency. *Organizational Behavior and Human Performance, 25*, 216–223.

Wosinska, W., Dabul, A. J., Whetstone-Dion, R., & Cialdini, R. B. (1996). Self-presentational responses to success in the organization: The costs and benefits of modesty. *Basic and Applied Social Psychology, 18*, 229–242.

Yu, J., & Murphy, K. R. (1993). Modesty bias in self-ratings of performance: A test of the cultural relativity hypothesis. *Personnel Psychology, 46*, 357–363.

Zuckerman, M. (1979). Attribution of success and failure revisited; or The motivational bias is alive and well in attribution theory. *Journal of Personality, 47*, 245–287.

The Motive for Distinctiveness:
A Universal, but Flexible Human Need

Vivian L. Vignoles

Abstract

Existential and evolutionary reasoning converge to suggest that humans in all historical and cultural settings will have an enduring and universal need to distinguish themselves from others and their ingroups from outgroups. European and North American studies suggest that people use a variety of positive and negative strategies to maintain their distinctiveness and that these strategies tend to be intensified when distinctiveness is threatened or undermined. Yet, there also appear to be significant individual and cultural differences in distinctiveness seeking, as evidenced by "need for uniqueness" measures; an important question is to what extent these measures capture true variation in the strength of the underlying need for distinctiveness, as opposed to variation in the perceived value of particular forms of distinctiveness or in the particular ways in which feelings of distinctiveness can be achieved. Research suggests that distinctiveness seeking is not reducible to the effects of other identity motives, such as self-esteem concerns; however, the relationship between motives for distinctiveness and belonging is an important avenue for further research. Given that distinctiveness seeking appears to be a fundamental human need, positive psychologists should focus on trying to channel the effects of this motive into more productive routes (e.g., creativity) rather than harmful ones (e.g., discrimination against outgroups). To the extent that benign and beneficial forms of distinctiveness seeking are available, valued, and encouraged in society, more harmful responses potentially may be reduced.

Keywords: culture, distinctiveness, identity, motivation, uniqueness

> BRIAN: Look. You've got it all wrong. You don't need to follow me. You don't need to follow anybody! You've got to think for yourselves. You're all individuals!
>
> FOLLOWERS: Yes, we're all individuals!
>
> BRIAN: You're all different!
>
> FOLLOWERS: Yes, we are all different!
>
> —*Monty Python's Life of Brian* (*Goldstone & Jones*, 1979)

I will argue here that human beings in all historical periods and in all cultures have needed, need, and will need to see themselves as distinctive. This need motivates people to differentiate themselves from other individuals and their ingroups from relevant outgroups, and it is implicated in many both positive and negative outcomes for individuals and for their societies.

At first sight, such an argument may seem misguided to many readers. Frequently, it is claimed that distinctiveness seeking is a relatively recent historical phenomenon, arising from the development of individualistic cultural values in modern "Western" societies (e.g., Snyder & Fromkin, 1980; Triandis, 1995). According to this account, what seems like a basic psychological need is actually a manifestation of individuals' internalization of normative cultural values: modern "Western" individuals are like the followers of Brian in the Monty Python film, declaring their uniqueness in order to fit in.

In contrast, I will argue that it is one thing to "value" particular forms of distinctiveness and another thing to have an underlying "motive" or "need" to establish and maintain some sense of what distinguishes oneself from others. For one thing, people are generally aware of their values, whereas they may or may not be aware of their motives. Thus, when an Anglican curate I was interviewing about distinctiveness among members of the clergy declared, "I don't care if I'm distinctive or not," he was clearly denying the value of distinctiveness, but his denial also could be interpreted as an attempt to distinguish himself both from the individualistic values of British society and from his perception of my values. Perhaps he needed to be distinctive more than he knew. An important part of my argument will be that there are many ways of being distinctive and that not all of these involve emphasizing one's difference from others.

Why Should People Need To Be Distinctive?

The fact that certain forms of distinctiveness are positively valued in individualistic cultures explains why many people might "value" these forms of distinctiveness but does not explain why people should "need" distinctiveness—except in the sense that they also may need self-esteem, which would be enhanced by seeing oneself in a way which is culturally valued (e.g., Pyszczynski, Greenberg, Solomon, Arndt, & Schimel, 2004). Why, then, should people need to be distinctive?

Vignoles, Chryssochoou, and Breakwell (2000) argued that establishing some form of distinctiveness is a logical precondition for the existence of a coherent sense of identity in any cultural meaning system. A notable feature of all meaning systems is that concepts are defined in relation to each other, involving a process of differentiation. This was illustrated by Saussure: "If I am to explain to someone the meaning of *stream* I must tell him about the difference between a stream and a river, a stream and a rivulet, etc." (cited by Culler, 1976, p. 24). The same principle applies to the concept of oneself. For example, the statement "I am British" clearly implies that I have something in common with others whom I would describe as British, but equally it implies a distinction from those whom I would not describe as British. Without such a distinction, it is not clear how "Britishness" would be a meaningful concept. More generally, I cannot have a meaningful sense of who I am without some sense of distinctiveness from who I am not. This suggests that the need for distinctiveness will be universal—not for any biological reason, but in the sense that distinctiveness seeking will be a necessary feature of the human condition. Thus, the motive for distinctiveness might be described as an "existential need."

Arguably, distinctiveness seeking may also have some evolutionary basis. Burris and Rempel (2004) propose that there are survival benefits in maintaining at least certain forms of distinctiveness. They argue that three "boundaries" are especially important to human survival. At the most basic level, in common with even the most simple living organisms, individuals differentiate that which is "self" (in the bodily sense) from that which is "nonself": what is inside one's skin must be protected, whereas what is outside may be eaten or may be a predator. Second, as social animals, humans differentiate friend from foe (and from food), or ingroups from outgroups: One can generally count on ingroup members not to pose a threat and to help with basic survival needs, whereas this is not true of outgroup members. Third, as animals with a capacity for symbolic representation, humans differentiate "mine" from "not-mine," using identity markers (places, possessions, etc.) to define their spatial and symbolic territory.

Crucially, both existential and evolutionary arguments suggest that distinctiveness is important in its own right and not solely because it is valued within a particular cultural worldview. Thus, the motive for distinctiveness is separated theoretically from self-esteem concerns. Nevertheless, the distinctiveness motive influences identity construction in concert with other identity motives, including pressures for self-esteem, continuity, meaning, efficacy, and belonging (Vignoles, Regalia, Manzi, Golledge, & Scabini, 2006). Later, I will discuss relationships between distinctiveness and other identity motives.

Evidence for Distinctiveness Seeking Processes

Studies conducted in Europe and North America have cataloged various ways in which people construct and maintain individual distinctiveness. For example, research participants typically remember information better if it distinguishes the self from others (Leyens, Yzerbyt, & Rogier, 1997), are most likely to mention their more distinctive attributes when asked to describe themselves (McGuire & Padawer-Singer, 1976), consider their more distinctive attributes as especially self-defining (Turnbull, Miller, & McFarland, 1990; Vignoles et al., 2006), and describe themselves as less similar to others than others are to themselves (Codol, 1987). Similarly, people use a variety of strategies to enhance and protect the distinctiveness of their group identities, including ingroup stereotyping (van Rijswijk, Haslam, & Ellemers, 2006), derogating ingroup imposters and deviants (Jetten, Summerville, Hornsey, & Mewse, 2005; Marques & Páez, 1994), and discriminating against outgroups (Jetten, Spears, & Postmes, 2004).

When feelings of distinctiveness are threatened or undermined, people typically report reduced psychological well-being and attempt in various ways to restore distinctiveness. In experimental studies, participants made to feel excessively similar to others report more negative emotions (Fromkin, 1972), are faster to recognize uniqueness-related words as self-descriptive (Markus & Kunda, 1986), show a greater preference for uncommon experiences and scarce information (Fromkin, 1970; Powell, 1974), reduce their physical proximity to others (Snyder & Endelman, 1979), and increase their identification with distinctive groups (Pickett, Silver, & Brewer, 2002; for additional findings, see Lynn & Snyder, 2002). Adolescents in highly "enmeshed" families—where differentiation between family members is impeded—are especially prone to a variety of psychological and social problems, including anxiety, depression, social withdrawal, and aggressive behavior (Barber & Buehler, 1996). When the distinctiveness of a group identity is threatened, group members are more likely to engage in behavioral forms of intergroup differentiation (Jetten et al., 2004) and to condone and practice derogatory behavior toward outgroup members (Maass, Cadinu, Guarnieri, & Grasselli, 2003; Ojala & Nesdale, 2004). Similarly, attempts to reduce intergroup conflict by activating a superordinate identity are only successful where subgroup distinctiveness is maintained (Hornsey & Hogg, 2000), and affirming between-group differences can lead to reductions in prejudice (Zárate & Garza, 2002).

Some have argued that needs for individual and group distinctiveness are separate motives (Spears, Jetten, & Scheepers, 2002). Nevertheless, several strands of research show trade-offs between perceptions of interpersonal and intergroup differentiation, implying that these are alternative means of satisfying the same underlying motive. People describe their ingroups as more heterogeneous and themselves as less stereotypical of their ingroups when the ingroup is larger—enhancing individual distinctiveness when less group distinctiveness is available (Brewer, 1993; Brewer & Weber, 1994). Threats to group distinctiveness can lead to reduced self-stereotyping—again enhancing individual distinctiveness—although only among lower identifiers (Spears, Doosje, & Ellemers, 1997). Conversely, threats to individual distinctiveness can lead to increased identification with distinctive groups and tightening of ingroup boundaries (Brewer & Pickett, 1999; Pickett, Silver, & Brewer, 2002).

Individual Differences in Distinctiveness Seeking

Even if all people need some degree of distinctiveness, it remains likely that individuals may differ in the strength of the distinctiveness motive. Snyder and Fromkin (1977, 1980) developed a Need For Uniqueness (NFU) scale, with factors reflecting lack of concern for the reactions of others, desire not to always follow rules, and willingness to defend one's beliefs publicly. Although widely used, this measure has been criticized for focusing exclusively on public and socially risky forms of uniqueness. Hence, Lynn and Harris (1997b) developed a shorter measure of Self-Attributed Need for Uniqueness (SANU), in which respondents rate directly how strongly they need to be unique.

Scores on these measures predict affective responses to similarity feedback, signature sizes, unusual word associations, and membership of and identification with relatively distinctive and autonomous groups (Riketta, 2008; Snyder & Fromkin, 1977, 1980). Higher scorers show not only greater creativity (Dollinger, 2003) but also greater cultural estrangement—mediated by perceived discrepancies between personal and societal values (Bernard, Gebauer, & Maio, 2006). High NFU scorers typically show little concern for social acceptance, scoring low on measures of public self-consciousness, social anxiety, and shyness, although it is unknown if these results would generalize to high SANU scorers (reviewed by Lynn & Snyder, 2002).

Many studies have focused on the role of consumer goods and choices as sources of uniqueness. Participants scoring higher in NFU and/or SANU show a greater preference for scarce and customized products, are more innovative consumers, prefer to shop in more unusual venues, prefer less popular products—if the products in question are visible (reviewed by Lynn & Snyder, 2002), and see the same product as more desirable if it is more expensive (Amaldoss & Jain, 2005). Two groups of researchers have developed measures of individual differences in the pursuit of uniqueness through consumption, which are expected to account for many of these findings (Lynn & Harris, 1997a; Tian, Bearden, & Hunter, 2001; see also Lynn & Harris, 1997b).

Especially interesting is research into responses to advertising. Simonson and Nowlis (2000) found that high NFU scorers were more resistant to advertising tactics when making brand choices, but only when asked to give reasons for their choices. This suggests that NFU may predict conscious, reasoned decision making, perhaps especially when one is accountable to others, but may be less relevant to unconscious, emotional, and private choices. This raises a crucial question about the extent to which people are aware of their distinctiveness needs. Both scales—most obviously the SANU—measure people's explicit beliefs about their need for distinctiveness, but beliefs about one's needs may not correspond to one's actual needs, as noted previously. Arguably, these scales may be measuring the conscious value placed on uniqueness and difference, rather than on the respondent's underlying psychological needs.

Vignoles and Moncaster (2007) created "implicit measures" of individual differences in the strengths of identity motives, adapting the method of Vignoles et al. (2006). According to this method, people with a strong need for distinctiveness should perceive as most central and self-defining those aspects of their identities which they consider to distinguish them most from others; this tendency should be weaker among those with a weaker need for distinctiveness. Hence, within-participant correlations between distinctiveness and perceived centrality ratings of multiple identity aspects can be used to measure individual differences in strength of the distinctiveness motive.

Initial studies show that these implicit measures are unrelated to explicit measures such as NFU and SANU; nevertheless, they show meaningful relationships with several outcomes. Vignoles and Moncaster (2007) found an interaction effect of distinctiveness motivation and British national identification in predictions of national favoritism: Among higher identifiers, the strength of the

distinctiveness motive was positively correlated with discrimination against members of a national outgroup. Petavratzi (2004) studied effects of SANU and implicit need for distinctiveness on preferences for more or less distinctive romantic partners. SANU did not predict partner preferences, but the implicit measure did: Participants with lower distinctiveness motivation did not distinguish between more and less distinctive partners in their preferences, but those with higher distinctiveness motivation tended to prefer the more distinctive partners. Although still in its infancy, research into implicit measures of motive strength seems an important avenue for future development.

Distinctiveness Seeking in Historical and Cultural Context

Theorists have suggested that distinctiveness seeking is a recent historical development tied to the rise of individualistic values in Western nations (Snyder & Fromkin, 1980) and that the motive for distinctiveness may be weaker or absent among people living in collectivist cultures (Triandis, 1995). Yet, there is little direct evidence for either claim. Yamaguchi, Kuhlman, and Sugimori (1995) reported somewhat lower mean NFU scores among Japanese and Korean undergraduates compared to Americans, although statistical significance was not tested. Burns and Brady (1992) found significantly lower mean NFU scores among Malaysian than U.S. business students; however, this difference was reflected only on the "lack of concern for others" subscale, suggesting a cultural difference in concern for social acceptance, rather than need for uniqueness per se. Tafarodi, Marshall, and Katsura (2004) found no difference between Japanese and Canadian undergraduates in overall NFU scores, although Japanese participants scored lower on items reflecting "desire to be different." These findings provide relatively weak evidence for cultural variation in the distinctiveness motive, especially given the concerns raised previously about interpreting self-report measures of distinctiveness seeking. Moreover, claims of cultural and historical specificity seem inconsistent with the existential and evolutionary arguments reviewed previously, which suggested that the distinctiveness motive should be universal.

A possible way out of this theoretical dilemma has been suggested by Vignoles et al. (2000). They proposed that distinctiveness can be constructed in various ways: through difference, separateness, or social position (see Figure 47.1). In psychological research, distinctiveness is usually operationalized as

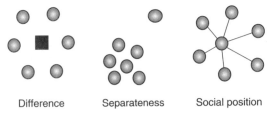

Difference   Separateness   Social position

Fig. 47.1 Sources of distinctiveness (adapted from Vignoles et al., 2002).

"difference"—distinctiveness in qualities such as abilities, opinions, personality, and appearance. In contrast, "social position" refers to distinctiveness in one's place within social relationships, including kinship ties, friendships, roles, and social status. "Separateness" refers to distinctiveness in terms of distance from others, encompassing physical and symbolic boundaries, and feelings of privacy, independence, and isolation. In any given situation, these different "sources of distinctiveness" will be supported best by different cognitions and behaviors: Social position will often be best maintained by conforming to expectations of one's role, difference by deviating from the same expectations, and separateness by detaching oneself either psychologically or physically from the situation. Hence, Vignoles et al. suggested that distinctiveness may be a necessary goal of identity processes in all cultures but that different sources of distinctiveness will be emphasized in identity depending on cultural beliefs, norms, and values (for a related argument, see Tafarodi et al., 2004). Although all three sources will be detectable within most or all cultural systems, difference and separateness will be emphasized and valued more in individualistic contexts, whereas social position will be emphasized and valued more in collectivist contexts. Thus, the same underlying motive can lead to different and even opposite cognitions and behaviors according to the cultural context.

Although there has yet to be a systematic cross-cultural test of these predictions, preliminary evidence comes from a "case study" of a particular cultural group. Among a sample of parish priests in the UK, Vignoles, Chryssochoou, and Breakwell (2002) investigated implications for identity construction and subjective well-being of the three sources of distinctiveness. The priests scored lower in independent self-construal and higher in interdependent self-construal compared with baseline statistics from American, Australian, Japanese, and Korean student samples, suggesting that they

shared in a relatively collectivistic cultural meaning system, despite residing in an individualistic nation. Thus, it was predicted that social position would be an especially salient and beneficial form of distinctiveness among these participants. Results showed that each of the three sources of distinctiveness made an independent contribution to the priests' global concepts of distinctiveness. However, consistent with expectations for a relatively collectivist sample, only social position was emphasized in identity, and this was associated with more positive and less negative affect; difference was not related to identity definition or affect; separateness was unrelated to identity definition and was associated with greater negative and less positive affect.

Theorizing about different forms of distinctiveness may also help to address claims that distinctiveness seeking is a relatively recent cultural phenomenon. With the advance of modernity, individuals increasingly have moved from living in small face-to-face communities to conditions of relative anonymity such as are found in large cities (Simmel, 1903/1950). One might speculate that traditional forms of distinctiveness in terms of social position have become harder to sustain as a result, leading to a shift toward constructing distinctiveness in terms of difference and separateness. Hence, perhaps there has been an historical transition, not in the importance of distinctiveness per se, but in how distinctiveness is typically constructed. In this process, perhaps distinctiveness seeking also has become more "problematic" (after Baumeister, 1987). Whereas in previous cultural systems distinctiveness largely would have been "ascribed" from birth by one's place in the social order, identities in the modern world are much more flexible and so distinctiveness must be "achieved" by the active efforts of the individual. Thus, even if distinctiveness always has been needed, with modernization one might expect to see an increase in effortful forms of distinctiveness seeking.

Of course, such historical processes are extremely difficult to study empirically. Nevertheless, some idea can be gained from research by Speller, Lyons, and Twigger-Ross (2002) into effects of the enforced relocation of a traditional coal-mining community in the North of England. In this "natural experiment," villagers were relocated from traditional nineteenth-century terraced housing to new semi-detached housing with front and back gardens. The new housing gave greater privacy to each household and weakened preexisting patterns of social interaction; moreover, the new village included former outsiders as well as members of the original community. Before relocation, villagers appeared to derive a sense of distinctiveness especially from the uniqueness of their community and from their individual social positions within the community. Both of these forms of distinctiveness were harder to sustain in the new environment. However, new signs of differentiation began to emerge, as many villagers increased their separateness by erecting high garden fences and hedges and expressed their differences by personalizing their houses with colorful external decorations. At the same time, villagers shifted toward a more individualistic worldview. Perhaps these changes might be viewed as a microcosm of slower but more widespread historical processes.

Distinctiveness and Other Identity Motives

I noted previously that the distinctiveness motive influences identity construction in concert with other identity motives, including pressures for self-esteem, continuity, meaning, efficacy, and belonging (Vignoles et al., 2006). The distinctiveness motive is separable theoretically from self-esteem concerns, but is this borne out empirically?

A great deal of research attests to the importance of "positive distinctiveness"—the belief that one is better than others—in self-esteem maintenance (Wills, 1981): People show more confidence in the accuracy of social comparisons which distinguish them positively from others (Schwartz & Smith, 1976), overestimate the uniqueness of their positive attributes (Campbell, 1986), and, especially in situations of threat, prefer to compare themselves with others from whom they are positively distinguished (Hakmiller, 1966). Conversely, people also frequently emphasize their similarity to positively valued others (Wheeler, 1966)—apparently sacrificing distinctiveness for self-esteem.

Nevertheless, distinctiveness seeking is not wholly reducible to self-esteem maintenance. Participants in Vignoles and colleagues' (2006) studies of motivated identity construction consistently rated as more central and self-defining those aspects of their identities which distinguished them more from others, and these effects persisted when controlling statistically for similar effects of feelings of self-esteem, continuity, belonging, efficacy, and meaning. Brewer, Manzi, and Shaw (1993) studied effects of "depersonalization" among participants categorized into high- and low-status majority and minority groups. Without depersonalization, participants showed a complex pattern of ingroup evaluations consistent with

self-esteem maintenance; however, when participants were primed with depersonalizing information—frustrating the distinctiveness motive—participants simply evaluated minority ingroups more positively than majority ingroups regardless of status, now apparently prioritizing distinctiveness over self-esteem.

Especially interesting is the relationship between motives for distinctiveness and belonging. Dominant theories of both individual and group distinctiveness have viewed these motives as fundamentally opposed with each other. Uniqueness theory (Snyder & Fromkin, 1980) proposes that degrees of individual similarity to others are encoded at different levels of acceptability, moderate similarity being the most acceptable and very high or very low similarity (i.e., very low or very high distinctiveness) the least acceptable outcomes. In a series of studies, the authors induced feelings of varying levels of similarity in participants, finding convergent evidence for the positive value of moderate distinctiveness across various affective and behavioral outcomes. The preference for moderate over low similarity is explained by the fact that "in many situations, people want not to be unique but to be similar to others" (p. 216).

Similarly, optimal distinctiveness theory (Brewer, 1991, 2003) proposes that social identity processes are driven by two motivational principles, a need for "differentiation" and a need for "inclusion," understood to act in opposition to each other. According to this theory, "optimal distinctiveness" occurs at a point of equilibrium between the two needs, which will normally be a state of moderate distinctiveness. Predictions of optimal distinctiveness theory are similar to those of uniqueness theory, but they have been applied especially to questions of group identity finding support in many contexts (reviewed by Brewer, 2003; Vignoles et al., 2000).

Both theories imply that humans are placed in an inevitable state of identity conflict by the opposition of distinctiveness and belonging needs. However, both theories rely on particular constructions of these motives. In uniqueness theory, distinctiveness is understood as difference, which is opposed with similarity. In optimal distinctiveness theory, distinctiveness is operationalized in terms of group size: The larger the group, the more the inclusion; the smaller the group, the more the differentiation.

When distinctiveness and belonging are operationalized in these ways, empirical support is found for the value of moderate distinctiveness—balancing the two motivational pressures. However, when both motives are conceptualized more fully, a different picture emerges. Although many constructions of distinctiveness and belonging are opposed—difference with similarity, separation with closeness, and exclusiveness with inclusiveness of group membership—this is by no means inevitable. Constructions of distinctiveness in terms of social position are entirely compatible with belonging needs: Positional distinctiveness actually depends on inclusion within social relationships (Vignoles et al., 2000). Similarly, feelings of belonging may be founded on acceptance by others, which actually tends to support individual distinctiveness (Green & Werner, 1996). Moreover, Hornsey and Jetten (2004) review a multitude of ways in which individuals may use group memberships to maintain their distinctiveness while simultaneously affirming belonging.

Although much research supports the co-presence of motives for distinctiveness and belonging, it is harder to find empirical support for their "fundamental opposition." Indeed, some research into optimal distinctiveness theory has shown that identical coping strategies can be used to compensate for threats to distinctiveness or to belonging (e.g., Pickett, Bonner, & Coleman, 2002), which would not be the case if increases in distinctiveness automatically lowered belonging, and vice versa. Nor do more distinctive identity aspects necessarily provide less belonging: Across four studies reported by Vignoles et al. (2006), ratings of identity aspects for satisfaction of these two motives showed correlations from .03 to .36. Thus, feelings of distinctiveness and belonging appear to be independent, or even positively related.

Unpublished analyses of these data show considerable individual variation in the congruence or opposition of motives for distinctiveness and belonging. In one study, within-participant correlations between distinctiveness and belonging ratings ranged from −1.00, suggesting a perfect opposition between the two motives, to +.97, suggesting almost perfect congruence; interestingly, individuals showing greater opposition between the two motives tended to report slightly lower subjective well-being. In another study, individuals showing greater opposition between the two motives tended to score higher on the Narcissistic Personality Inventory. Although exploratory, these findings suggest that those who manage to resolve the potential conflict between distinctiveness and belonging may achieve better psychological adjustment.

Distinctiveness Seeking and Positive Psychology

Lynn and Snyder (2002) proposed that uniqueness seeking is beneficial for the individual and for society, despite the negative connotations of terms such as "deviant" and "abnormal" often used to describe those who differentiate themselves from the majority. Apart from the implications for individual psychological welfare, they proposed that valuing and seeking distinctiveness also has two important social benefits. First, the more people value and pursue different interests and goals, the less competition and conflict there will be for success on a limited range of dimensions, and hence the more likely that every individual can succeed in something valued within society. Second, the more diversity within a society, the greater the range of human resources will be available for it to adapt and survive in the face of difficulties. Hence, they called for greater social acceptance of human differences.

Certainly, the validity and importance of these arguments remain undiminished. Nevertheless, it seems important also to acknowledge that not all distinctiveness seeking has beneficial consequences for the individual or for society. Distinctiveness seeking sometimes can be associated with cultural estrangement, disregard for the feelings of others, and even prejudice and discrimination. Yet, attempts to alleviate such problems by blocking distinctiveness seeking, or denying diversity, are often counterproductive, leading to greater defensiveness and fuelling intergroup conflict. Hence, what seems important is not to encourage or discourage differentiation per se, but to try to channel distinctiveness seeking into productive rather than damaging routes. To the extent that benign and beneficial forms of distinctiveness seeking are available, valued, and encouraged in society, more harmful distinctiveness seeking responses may potentially be reduced.

In one respect, research now offers a considerably more optimistic message than previous thinking about distinctiveness seeking. Whereas previous theories (Brewer, 1991; Snyder & Fromkin, 1980) have typically portrayed distinctiveness and belonging motives as fundamentally opposed, placing individuals in an inevitable position of identity conflict, findings reviewed here suggest that the conflict between distinctiveness and belonging motives is neither fundamental nor inevitable. Seemingly, most people do not experience conflict between these two motives, and those who experience them as compatible experience better psychological adjustment. Although more research is needed, perhaps more positive individual and societal outcomes might be achieved by fostering forms of distinctiveness and belonging which are compatible.

Questions for Future Research

1. What are the different processes underlying implicit and explicit measures of distinctiveness seeking?

2. To what extent, and in what sense, is distinctiveness seeking culturally variable?

3. How can one best reconcile the potential conflict between distinctiveness and belonging needs?

References

Amaldoss, W., & Jain, S. (2005). Pricing of conspicuous goods: A competitive analysis of social effects. *Journal of Marketing Research, 42*, 30–42.

Barber, B. K., & Buehler, C. (1996). Family cohesion and enmeshment: Different constructs, different effects. *Journal of Marriage and the Family, 58*, 433–441.

Baumeister, R. F. (1987). How the self became a problem: A psychological review of historical research. *Journal of Personality and Social Psychology, 52*, 163–176.

Bernard, M. M., Gebauer, J. E., & Maio, G. R. (2006). Cultural estrangement: The role of personal and societal value discrepancies. *Personality and Social Psychology Bulletin, 32*, 78–92.

Brewer, M. B. (1991). The social self: On being the same and different at the same time. *Personality and Social Psychology Bulletin, 17*, 475–482.

Brewer, M. B. (1993). Social identity, distinctiveness, and in-group homogeneity. *Social Cognition, 11*, 150–164.

Brewer, M. B. (2003). Optimal distinctiveness, social identity, and the self. In M. R. Leary & J. P. Tangney (Eds.), *Handbook of self and identity* (pp. 480–491). New York: Guilford.

Brewer, M. B., Manzi, J. M., & Shaw, J. S. (1993). In-group identification as a function of depersonalization, distinctiveness, and status. *Psychological Science, 4*, 88–92.

Brewer, M. B., & Pickett, C. L. (1999). Distinctiveness motives as a source of the social self. In T. R. Tyler, R. M. Kramer, & O. P. John (Eds.), *The psychology of the social self* (pp. 71–87). Mahwah, NJ: Lawrence Erlbaum.

Brewer, M. B., & Weber, J. G. (1994). Self-evaluation effects of interpersonal versus intergroup social comparison. *Journal of Personality and Social Psychology, 66*, 268–275.

Burns, D. J., & Brady, J. (1992). A cross-cultural comparison of the need for uniqueness in Malaysia and the United States. *Journal of Social Psychology, 132*, 487–495.

Burris, C. T., & Rempel, J. K. (2004). "It's the end of the world as we know it": Threat and the spatial-symbolic self. *Journal of Personality and Social Psychology, 86*, 19–42.

Campbell, J. D. (1986). Similarity and uniqueness: The effects of attribute type, relevance, and individual differences in self-esteem and depression. *Journal of Personality and Social Psychology, 50*, 281–294.

Codol, J. P. (1987). Comparability and incomparability between oneself and others: Means of differentiation and comparison

reference points. *European Journal of Cognitive Psychology, 7*, 1–19.

Culler, J. (1976). *Saussure*. Glasgow, UK: Fontana.

Dollinger, S. J. (2003). Need for uniqueness, need for cognition and creativity. *Journal of Creative Behavior, 37*, 99–116.

Fromkin, H. L. (1970). Effects of experimentally aroused feelings of indistinctiveness upon valuation of scarce and novel experiences. *Journal of Personality and Social Psychology, 16*, 521–529.

Fromkin, H. L. (1972). Feelings of interpersonal undistinctiveness: An unpleasant affective state. *Journal of Experimental Research in Personality, 6*, 178–182.

Goldstone, J. (Producer), & Jones, T. (Director). (1979). *Monty Python's Life of Brian* [Motion picture]. UK: Python (Monty) Pictures Limited.

Green, R. J., & Werner, P. D. (1996). Intrusiveness and closeness-caregiving: Rethinking the concept of family enmeshment. *Family Process, 35*, 115–136.

Hakmiller, K. L. (1966). Threat as a determinant of downward comparison. *Journal of Experimental Social Psychology, Supplement, 1*, 32–39.

Hornsey, M. J., & Hogg, M. A. (2000). Assimilation and diversity: An integrative model of subgroup relations. *Personality and Social Psychology Review, 4*, 143–156.

Hornsey, M. J., & Jetten, J. (2004). The individual within the group: Balancing the need to belong with the need to be different. *Personality and Social Psychology Review, 8*, 248–264.

Jetten, J., Spears, R., & Postmes, T. (2004). Intergroup distinctiveness and differentiation: A meta-analytic integration. *Journal of Personality and Social Psychology, 86*, 862–879.

Jetten, J., Summerville, N., Hornsey, M. J., & Mewse, A. J. (2005). When differences matter: Intergroup distinctiveness and the evaluation of impostors. *European Journal of Social Psychology, 35*, 609–620.

Leyens, J. P., Yzerbyt, V. Y., & Rogier, A. (1997). Personality traits that distinguish you and me are better memorized. *European Journal of Social Psychology, 27*, 511–522.

Lynn, M., & Harris, J. (1997a). The desire for unique consumer products: A new individual differences scale. *Psychology and Marketing, 14*, 601–616.

Lynn, M., & Harris, J. (1997b). Individual differences in the pursuit of self-uniqueness through consumption. *Journal of Applied Social Psychology, 27*, 1861–1883.

Lynn, M., & Snyder, C. R. (2002). Uniqueness seeking. In C. R. Snyder & S. J. Lopez (Eds.), *Handbook of positive psychology* (pp. 395–410). London: Oxford University Press.

Maass, A., Cadinu, M., Guarnieri, G., & Grasselli, A. (2003). Sexual harassment under social identity threat: The computer harassment paradigm. *Journal of Personality and Social Psychology, 85*, 853–870.

Markus, H., & Kunda, Z. (1986). Stability and malleability of the self-concept. *Journal of Personality and Social Psychology, 51*, 858–866.

Marques, J. M., & Páez, D. (1994). The "black sheep effect": Social categorization, rejection of ingroup deviates, and perception of group variability. *European Review of Social Psychology, 5*, 37–68.

McGuire, W. J., & Padawer-Singer, A. (1976). Trait salience in the spontaneous self-concept. *Journal of Personality and Social Psychology, 33*, 743–754.

Ojala, K., & Nesdale, D. (2004). Bullying and social identity: The effects of group norms and distinctiveness threat on attitudes towards bullying. *British Journal of Developmental Psychology, 22*, 19–35.

Petavratzi, F. (2004). *Implicit and explicit distinctiveness motivation and romantic partner preferences.* Unpublished BA dissertation, University of Sussex, Brighton, UK.

Pickett, C. L., Bonner, B. L., & Coleman, J. M. (2002). Motivated self-stereotyping: Heightened assimilation and differentiation needs result in increased levels of positive and negative self-stereotyping. *Journal of Personality and Social Psychology, 82*, 543–562.

Pickett, C. L., Silver, M. D., & Brewer, M. B. (2002). The impact of assimilation and differentiation needs on perceived group importance and perceptions of ingroup size. *Personality and Social Psychology Bulletin, 28*, 546–568.

Powell, F. A. (1974). The perception of self-uniqueness as a determinant of message choice and valuation. *Speech Monographs, 41*, 163–168.

Pyszczynski, T., Greenberg, J., Solomon, S., Arndt, J., & Schimel, J. (2004). Why do people need self-esteem? A theoretical and empirical review. *Psychological Bulletin, 130*, 435–468.

Riketta, M. (2008). Who identifies with which group? The motive-feature match principle and its limitations. *European Journal of Social Psychology, 38*, 715–735.

Schwartz, J. M., & Smith, W. P. (1976). Social comparison and the inference of ability difference. *Journal of Personality and Social Psychology, 34*, 1268–1275.

Simmel, G. (1903/1950). The metropolis and mental life (Trans. H. H. Gerth & C. Wright Mills). In K. H. Wolff (Ed.), *The sociology of Georg Simmel* (pp. 409–424). New York: Free Press.

Simonson, I., & Nowlis, S. M. (2000). The role of explanations and need for uniqueness in consumer decision making: Unconventional choices based on reasons. *Journal of Consumer Research, 27*, 49–68.

Snyder, C. R., & Endelman, J. R. (1979). Effects of degree of interpersonal similarity on physical distance and self-reported attraction: A comparison of uniqueness and reinforcement theory predictions. *Journal of Personality, 47*, 492–505.

Snyder, C. R., & Fromkin, H. L. (1977). Abnormality as a positive characteristic: The development and validation of a scale measuring need for uniqueness. *Journal of Abnormal Psychology, 86*, 518–527.

Snyder, C. R., & Fromkin, H. L. (1980). *Uniqueness: The human pursuit of difference.* New York: Plenum.

Spears, R., Doosje, B., & Ellemers, N. (1997). Self-stereotyping in the fact of threats to group status and distinctiveness: The role of group identification. *Personality and Social Psychology Bulletin, 23*, 538–553.

Spears, R., Jetten, J., & Scheepers, D. (2002). Distinctiveness and the definition of collective self: A tripartite model. In A. Tesser, D. A. Stapel, & J. V. Wood (Eds.), *Self and motivation: Emerging psychological perspectives* (pp. 147–171). Washington, DC: APA.

Speller, G., Lyons, E., & Twigger-Ross, C. (2002). A community in transition: The relationship between spatial change and identity processes. *Social Psychological Review, 4*, 39–58.

Tafarodi, R. W., Marshall, T. C., & Katsura, H. (2004). Standing out in Canada and Japan. *Journal of Personality, 72*, 785–814.

Tian, K. T., Bearden, W. O., & Hunter, G. L. (2001). Consumers' need for uniqueness: Scale development and validation. *Journal of Consumer Research, 28*, 50–66.

Triandis, H. C. (1995). *Individualism and Collectivism.* Boulder, CO: Westview Press.

Turnbull, W., Miller, D. T., & McFarland, C. (1990). Population-distinctiveness, identity, and bonding. In J. M. Olson & M. P. Zanna (Eds.), *Self-inference processes: The Ontario symposium* (Vol. 6, pp. 115–133). Hillsdale, NJ: Erlbaum.

van Rijswijk, W., Haslam, S. A., & Ellemers, N. (2006). Who do we think we are? The effects of social context and social identification on in-group stereotyping. *British Journal of Social Psychology, 45*, 161–174.

Vignoles, V. L., Chryssochoou, X., & Breakwell, G. M. (2000). The distinctiveness principle: Identity, meaning and the bounds of cultural relativity. *Personality and Social Psychology Review, 4*, 337–354.

Vignoles, V. L., Chryssochoou, X., & Breakwell, G. M. (2002). Sources of distinctiveness: Position, difference and separateness in the identities of Anglican parish priests. *European Journal of Social Psychology, 32*, 761–780.

Vignoles, V. L., & Moncaster, N. (2007) Identity motives and ingroup favouritism: A new approach to individual differences in intergroup discrimination. *British Journal of Social Psychology, 46*, 91–113.

Vignoles, V. L., Regalia, C., Manzi, C., Golledge, J., & Scabini, E. (2006). Beyond self-esteem: Influence of multiple motives on identity construction. *Journal of Personality and Social Psychology, 90*, 308–333.

Wheeler, L. (1966). Motivation as a determinant of upward comparison. *Journal of Experimental Social Psychology, Supplement 1*, 27–31.

Wills, T. A. (1981). Downward comparison principles in social psychology. *Psychological Bulletin, 90*, 245–271.

Yamaguchi, S., Kuhlman, D. M., & Sugimori, S. (1995). Personality correlates of allocentric tendencies in individualist and collectivist cultures. *Journal of Cross-cultural Psychology, 26*, 658–672.

Zárate, M. A., & Garza, A. A. (2002). In-group distinctiveness and self-affirmation as dual components of prejudice reduction. *Self and Identity, 1*, 235–249.

PART 8

Biological Approaches

A Role for Neuropsychology in Understanding the Facilitating Influence of Positive Affect on Social Behavior and Cognitive Processes

Alice M. Isen

Abstract

This chapter summarizes findings showing that mild positive affect facilitates thinking, problem solving, and social interaction through increased cognitive flexibility and explores a possible role for neuropsychology in understanding these effects. Several lines of research show that mild happy feelings, induced in everyday ways that people often encounter in the course of their daily lives, promote effective thinking and problem solving by enabling flexible thinking that allows the person to respond to the situation in its complex context. Studies have demonstrated that positive affect engenders motives such as kindness, helpfulness, and generosity, but also positive-affect maintenance and fairness to oneself as well as to others. Recent work is showing that one reason this occurs is because positive affect facilitates cognitive flexibility characterized by openness to useful information (even if it is negative in tone), reduced "defensiveness," and the ability to see multiple sides of the situation and switch attention among them. This ability to hold multiple ideas or facets of a situation in mind, in turn, fosters a better ability to solve complex problems, both interpersonal and nonsocial. Another result of this kind of openness to information and cognitive flexibility that is fostered by positive affect is increased enjoyment of variety in safe situations and improved ability to deal with a large, complex decision task or set of material or options. Another, however, is reduced risk taking in dangerous situations, as people—although more optimistic about winning—are also more aware of the negative utility or consequences of a loss. Most recently, research is focusing on positive affect's beneficial effect on self-control of several types, including its facilitation of flexible attention deployment that enables both broadened attention and focus on a target task. This ability is reflected in superior incidental learning and divided attention, without impaired performance on the target task. This chapter summarizes some of these findings and explores a possible role for neuropsychology in understanding these effects, arguing not for the superiority of one level of analysis (behavioral, cognitive, neuropsychological) over others, but for their integration and a search for the ways in which each can contribute to the others.

Keywords: anterior cingulate cortex (ACC), broadened focus, choice overload, cognitive flexibility, complex decision making, creative problem solving, distractibility, dopamine hypothesis, flexible thinking, helpfulness, positive affect, problem solving, risk preference, self-control, socially responsible behavior

A growing body of research indicates that mild positive affect (happy feelings), induced in subtle, common ways that can occur frequently in everyday life, facilitates a broad range of important social behaviors and thought processes. For example, work from approximately the past two decades shows that positive affect leads to greater creativity (e.g., Isen, Daubman, & Nowicki, 1987; see Isen, 1999a, for discussion), improved negotiation processes and outcomes (Carnevale & Isen, 1986), and more thorough, open-minded, flexible thinking and problem solving (e.g., Estrada, Isen, & Young, 1997;

Isen, Rosenzweig, & Young, 1991). And this is in addition to earlier work showing that positive affect promotes generosity and social responsibility in interpersonal interactions (see, for example, Isen, 1987, for review). The literature indicates that, under most circumstances, people who are feeling happy are more likely to do what they want to do, want to do what is socially responsible and helpful and what needs to be done, enjoy what they are doing more, are more motivated to accomplish their goals, and are more open to information and think more clearly.

Although people experiencing positive affect sometimes appear not to perform as well as controls, this seems to occur only in limited circumstances, such as when a task is neither interesting nor important, nor provides any reason to engage it (e.g., Bodenhausen, Kramer, & Susser, 1994; Bodenhausen, Mussweiler, Gabriel, & Moreno, 2001; Isen & Reeve, 2005; Melton, 1995; see Isen, 2000, for discussion). Significantly, recent research now clearly has countered the previously widely held view that positive affect, by its nature, typically leads to oversimplification or superficial cognitive processing and thus impairs systematic processing (for statements of the previously held view, see, for example, Bless, Bohner, Schwarz, & Strack, 1990; Mackie & Worth, 1991; Schwarz & Bless, 1991; for examples of studies countering that view, see, for example, Bless et al., 1996; Erez & Isen, 2002; Estrada et al., 1997; Isen, 1993; Isen & Reeve, 2005; Isen et al., 1991; Johnson & Fredrickson, 2005; Kazen & Kuhl, 2005; Kuhl & Kazen, 1999; Lee & Sternthal, 1999; Roehm & Sternthal, 2001).

The purpose of this chapter is to focus attention on the effects that positive affect has on thinking, problem solving, and social behavior and to explore a possible role for neuropsychology in understanding this influence. Thus, I will summarize these and related findings briefly and then consider what, neurobiologically, may underlie these effects. That is, noting that positive affect promotes cognitive flexibility, for example, one may ask what in the neurobiology of the organism enables cognitive flexibility, the ability to think about material in multiple ways or to switch attention as needed, and what relation such neurobiological processes may have to positive affect. The reasoning is that, if positive affect promotes ability to integrate several different lines of thinking at once, or to switch attention without loss of concentration, and if this kind of flexibility involves certain neuropsychological processes, then positive affect also may involve those neurological processes.

From this reasoning alone, it would not be possible to say whether positive affect caused the neurological process directly, whether something else that regularly accompanies positive affect (e.g., certain cognitive aspects or consequences of the affective state) caused the neurological process, whether the neurological process caused the positive affect, or whether the affect and the neurological process simply occurred together. However, adopting this approach would provide a starting point for exploring a potential neuropsychological link because it would be possible to say at least that positive affect is not incompatible with this neurological process.

Thus, this approach would increase our understanding of positive affect not only by identifying neuropsychological processes that are compatible with positive affect, but also by adding whatever else may be known about those neurological processes. For example, if the neurological process that underlies cognitive flexibility also mediates other cognitive functions, such as working memory (which is hypothesized by the dopamine hypothesis), then one could expect positive affect to be compatible with those functions also, adding to our predictions about positive affect's effects. If, in addition, that neurological process can be related specifically to positive affect in a fundamental way, then our understanding of what else positive affect may be expected to do, and how positive affect may have its effects, could be expanded even further. Let us begin, then, by briefly summarizing some effects of positive affect that are known.

Positive Affect Promotes Improved Functioning
Social Behavior

Considerable research over the past three decades documents the impact of positive affect on social interaction such as helping and generosity (see Isen, 1987, for example, for review). All else equal, people in whom mild positive affect has been induced are more helpful and generous to others (e.g., Aderman, 1972; Cunningham, 1979; Cunningham, Steinberg, & Grev, 1980; Isen, 1970; Isen & Levin, 1972), more sociable and friendly (e.g., Veitch & Griffitt, 1976), and more socially responsible (e.g., Berkowitz, 1972; Berkowitz & Daniels, 1964). For example, in one series of studies, people who were told they had succeeded on a task, or who were offered a cookie, or who found change in the coin return of a public telephone, donated more to a charity collection bin, were more helpful to a stranger who needed help carrying several books and papers, and were more willing to help a passerby who dropped a folder of papers (Isen, 1970; Isen & Levin, 1972). Similarly, positive affect–inducing conditions have been found to reduce interpersonal conflict (e.g., Baron, 1984; Lyubomirsky, King, & Diener, 2005) and to facilitate face-to-face negotiations (Carnevale & Isen, 1986).

In the negotiation study by Carnevale and Isen (1986), positive affect induced by a small gift (a pad of paper) and a few cartoons significantly increased the tendency of bargainers who were face-to-face to reach agreement and to obtain the optimal outcome possible for both parties in the negotiation. In contrast, negotiators in the control condition (no affect induced) bargaining face-to-face most often broke off negotiation without reaching any agreement. Their sessions were also characterized by open hostility and conflict, and the parties reported not enjoying the process. This contrasts markedly with the experiences of those in the positive affect condition, whose sessions were reported to be pleasant and enjoyable. Although some might assume that the improved outcomes for those in the positive affect condition were attributable to social factors, there is reason to believe that cognitive factors also are implicated in the process. This latter issue is explored next.

Flexibility in Thinking

A substantial literature supports the conclusion that positive affect promotes flexible thinking. This includes flexible categorization of neutral material (e.g., Isen, 1987; p. 234; Isen & Daubman, 1984; Isen, Niedenthal, & Cantor, 1992; Kahn & Isen, 1993; Murray, Sujan, Hirt, & Sujan, 1990); more diverse product consideration sets and more diverse and less typical word associations to neutral stimuli (e.g., Isen, Johnson, Mertz, & Robinson, 1985; Kahn & Isen, 1993); and openness to information (e.g., Estrada et al., 1997). In addition, extensive research carried out in a variety of settings and assessing the responses of diverse populations (from young adolescents to practicing physicians and managers in organizations) shows that this flexibility translates into increases in actual creativity as well as in more successful problem solving, such as medical diagnosis, that might not be considered "creative" (e.g., Amabile, Barsade, Mueller, & Staw, 2005; Estrada, Isen, & Young, 1994; Estrada et al., 1997; Greene & Noice, 1988; Hirt, Melton, McDonald, & Harackiewicz, 1996; Isen et al., 1987; Staw & Barsade, 1993; see Isen, 1999a and Amabile et al., 2005, for review and discussion).

One study, conducted over a long period of time in an organization, found that positive affect at work was an antecedent of creative breakthroughs, and also reported that such creative events resulted in positive affect subsequently; these effects were also found to carry over for days (Amabile et al., 2005). However, in addition, as noted, positive affect has also been found to promote flexible thinking and problem solving that, while innovative and facilitated, might not typically be labeled "creative." For example, in one series of studies, medical students and practicing physicians in whom positive affect had been induced showed increased creativity as measured by Remote Associates Test items (Estrada et al., 1994), improved performance on tasks related to medical diagnosis, and more open, flexible consideration of diagnostic alternatives, with significantly less tendency than controls to distort or ignore information that did not fit with a diagnostic hypothesis under consideration (Estrada et al., 1997; Isen et al., 1991).

Note that the "flexibility" that has been observed involves the ability to switch perspectives or focus, see connections among relatable concepts, or hold multiple considerations in mind at once, as needed to solve a problem or to take multiple goals (including long-range goals as well as immediate goals) into consideration (for discussion see, for example, Aspinwall, 1998, 2005; Isen, 2008; Isen & Reeve, 2005). Thus the term "flexible" does not mean completely unconstrained or swinging uncontrollably, or "silly," or relevant only to play or even creativity, as has been assumed by some authors (see, for example, Forgas, 2002; Schwarz, 2002). Rather, it refers to the ability to see connections where connections are possible and reasonable, think about multiple factors and aspects of situations, and switch focus among them as needed to address a problem without losing focus on the problem.

It should be noted that this work showing that positive affect facilitates creative problem solving and flexibility in thinking has involved both verbal and spatial tasks. For example, one series of studies investigating the influence of positive affect on creative problem solving used the Duncker Candle task (Dunker, 1945) and items from the Remote Associates Test (Mednick, Mednick, & Mednick, 1964) as indicators of creative problem solving (e.g., Isen et al., 1987). The Candle Task, in which people are asked to figure out how to attach a candle to the wall using only the materials they are given (a candle, a book of matches, and a box of tacks), is a spatial task; whereas the Remote Associates Test requires people to find a word that fits with each of three other words given in the stem of the item. Thus, the hypothesis put forth by Gray (2001), that positive affect facilitates verbal tasks, but impairs spatial tasks, would not account for all of the data.

Other studies reveal that the decision-making processes of people in whom positive affect has been induced, as compared to those of persons in control conditions, are both more efficient and, simultaneously, more thorough (e.g., Isen & Means, 1983; Isen et al., 1991). For example, in one protocol-analysis study, people choosing a fictitious car for purchase made their choices earlier (although their choices did not differ, on average, from those of the control group) and made the choice more efficiently, by exhibiting, for example, less redundancy in their search processes (Isen & Means, 1983). When this same choice problem was recast as a disease identification task and given to advanced medical student subjects, results again showed that people in the positive affect condition, in contrast with controls, solved the assigned problem earlier (in this case, by identifying the correct patient earlier in their protocols). In this instance, however, the positive affect group did not stop working on the materials once the assigned task was completed, but instead, significantly more than controls, went beyond the assigned task (doing things such as diagnosing the other patients or suggesting treatments), integrated the material more, and showed less confusion in their decision making (Isen et al., 1991).

More recently, a protocol analysis study examining the influence of positive affect on physicians' diagnostic processes showed that doctors in the positive affect condition, as compared to a control, correctly identified the domain of the illness they were attempting to diagnose significantly earlier in their protocols and showed significantly less "anchoring" to an initial hypothesis. That is, they were more open to information—even information that countered what they were currently thinking—as shown by their significantly lower likelihood, compared with doctors in the control condition, to distort or ignore information that did not fit with their existing hypothesis (Estrada et al., 1997). It also was observed, as would be compatible with such a finding, that they were not likely to jump to conclusions, to show premature closure, or to display any evidence of superficial or faulty processing.

FLEXIBLE FOCUS

Another possibility that follows from the flexibility hypothesis is that positive affect enables

people to take a broader focus, while not losing the ability to focus in on details, or a target task, simultaneously. The idea of positive affect's broadening focus has been of interest to the research community in recent years, although it has taken different forms. For example, Fredrickson (1998, 2001) proposed that positive affect enables a person to broaden and build on his or her skills and repertoire and thus enables improved performance and resources for the future.

A different approach was taken by Gasper and Clore (2002), who proposed that positive affect leads to taking a broader perceptual perspective on a visual stimulus but might impair the ability to focus on problems more narrowly, and might lead to less detailed and poorer performance on tasks requiring attention to detail. The paper by Gasper and Clore (2002) actually found, however, no impairment resulting from positive affect—and no broadening, actually either, because the positive affect group did not differ from the control group, but only differed from a negative affect group, which focused more narrowly than the positive or neutral group. The negative affect group did not perform better, however, on a task that allowed observation of detail.

In another approach, some researchers (see Ashby, Isen, & Turken, 1999, for discussion) have reported that positive affect reduces perseveration (the maintenance of a response after conditions have changed so that the response is no longer correct), which could be seen as an aspect of broadened or, more accurately, flexible—perception, as the person must notice the new stimulus and the new conditions that indicate that the new, not the old, response is now appropriate. One recent study, measuring reaction time to respond to displayed items, reported that positive affect does reduce perseveration on incorrect responses, but at the cost of increased distractibility as reflected by reaction time to respond to a correct stimulus when a new, but incorrect, stimulus is introduced (Dreisbach & Goschke, 2004). Those authors argue that for people in positive affect the novel stimulus captures attention and causes a slight but statistically significant delay in reaction time to respond. Error rates between the affect groups were not different.

Other studies have shown that positive affect (and approach motivation) does enable broader focus and does not impair performance by doing so, reporting that people in a mildly positive state can focus broadly or narrowly, depending on what the task requires (e.g., Baumann & Kuhl, 2005; Friedman & Forster, 2005). Several studies have found, in fact, that people in positive affect can perform better when the task requires switching focus or pursuing multiple goals simultaneously (e.g., Derryberry, 1993; Friedman & Forster, 2005; Isen & Shmidt, 2007; see Isen, 2008, for discussion). For example, Derryberry (1993) reported that success on a previous task led people to be able to attend to low-value targets while not missing high-value targets, whereas failure on the previous task caused narrowed focus on high-value targets alone without improved performance on them. For another example, Isen and Shmidt (2007) found that positive affect led to better incidental learning and ability to divide attention, while not impairing performance on the main task that was being performed simultaneously.

It is possible that the discrepancy between the findings reported by Dreisbach and Goschke (2004) and these other authors has to do with the phase of the problem-solving task that was being observed. That is, it may be that in the very early stage (first milliseconds) of consideration of an item, there may be a delay of a few milliseconds that results from considering the new stimulus display. However, as is evident from all the studies described (including Dreisbach and Goschke's own), this consideration of the new display does not result in impaired performance (errors) on the task. Thus, it does not represent "distraction" in the way that term is usually used (inability to concentrate or perform well on a given task). In fact, it may not be that the reaction time measure used by Dreisbach and Goschke (2004) indicates distraction, but rather indicates taking in the new stimulus display/condition. If it were "distraction," one might expect the previously correct response to take a toll as well, but that is labeled "perseveration" and is found to be reduced by positive affect. This issue of distractibility, as well as broadened focus more generally, is one that remains to be resolved and will likely receive continued attention in the literature.

FLEXIBILITY FACILITATES INTERPERSONAL PROBLEM SOLVING AS WELL AS NONSOCIAL PROBLEM SOLVING

The two-person negotiation situation described previously is an example of one kind of interpersonal problem-solving situation in which positive affect may contribute to improved outcomes (and processes). It is important to note that this interpersonal effect of positive affect, in which happy feelings facilitated the bargaining process and outcome, may have occurred not only because of an effect on friendliness

or prosocial inclination, but at least in part because of the cognitive effects of positive feelings—particularly positive affect's influence on cognitive flexibility. This is because success on the bargaining task required reasoning integratively about possibilities and making trade-offs between alternatives. In addition, the task was one in which simple yielding would not lead to a satisfactory outcome (see Pruitt, 1983, for discussion of the task). It also should be noted that people in the positive affect condition were better able to describe the other party's payoff matrix (a fact not disclosed during the session) when asked about it after the session. This suggests that they had been better able than controls to take the other party's perspective during the session, another indicator of the kind of flexibility—ability to see multiple perspectives or aspects of situations, simultaneously—that is being discussed here.

FLEXIBILITY MAY FACILITATE PROSOCIAL INTERACTION MORE DIRECTLY

Flexibility in perspective taking also may underlie the helping findings that have been observed. This follows because such flexibility may allow a person to see another person's perspective as well as his or her own view. This broadening of focus, or possible reduction in self-focus, may play a role in the increased generosity and helpfulness that results from positive affect. For example, in one of the earliest demonstrations of the link between positive affect and helping, Isen (1970) reported a narrowing of the range of attention among participants who had failed, relative to those who had succeeded. The relatively broader range of attention among people in whom positive affect had been induced actually may represent more flexibility in their focus of attention—that is, more ability to switch back and forth between attention to their own needs and those of others, or to consider both views simultaneously. Increased flexibility in thinking may also explain why people who are experiencing positive affect are not simply more compliant and do not stop attending to their own welfare at the same time that they broaden their foci to include the welfare of others (e.g., Isen & Simmonds, 1978).

Similarly, another finding that integrates the impact of positive affect on cognitive flexibility with its influence on prosocial interaction is one reported by Dovidio, Gaertner, Isen, and Lowrance (1995). This study found that people in a positive affect condition were more likely than controls to form an inclusive group representation that linked their own group and another group. This resulted in better evaluations of the outgroup members, more acceptance and liking of the other group, and lower levels of intergroup bias; moreover, a path analysis confirmed the crucial roles of positive affect and of group representation (categorization of the groups) in producing such effects.

This kind of effect was explored further by Urada and Miller (2000), who reported results of four studies investigating the influence of positive affect on crossed categorization. (Crossed categorization refers to situations in which outgroup members share some qualities with ingroup members but differ from them on others.) Their results indicate that positive affect changed the representation and improved the evaluation of outgroup (crossed) members when they shared an important quality with the ingroup, but not when they shared only an unimportant quality. Thus, positive affect results in more flexible consideration of social concepts, as well as of nonsocial concepts. Current research is expanding the exploration of this broadening effect of positive affect and its constructive influence on both cognitive and social processes (e.g., Dovidio, Gaertner, Isen, Rust, & Guerra, 1998; Fredrickson, 1998, 2001; Fredrickson, Mancuso, Branigan, & Tugade, 2000; Isen, 1990; Kahn & Isen, 1993; Urada & Miller, 2000).

FLEXIBILITY ENABLES MORE DETAILED AND
RESPONSIVE CONSIDERATION OF SITUATIONS AND
POSSIBLE OUTCOMES

Throughout the literature on positive affect, the results of studies indicate that positive affect does not act via any simple biasing or distortion of perception or decision making. For example, the experience of positive affect does not lead to general biasing in a positive direction or in a simplifying direction—two hypotheses that were suggested early in the work on positive affect and cognition. Rather, accumulating evidence indicates that positive affect leads people to take in information carefully and fully, consider many aspects of situations simultaneously, and make evaluations and choose behaviors that are responsive to the situation and task demands. Thus, the operative process is the product of thought rather than of simple bias.

For example, studies have shown that positive affect leads to improved evaluation of neutral or ambiguous material but not of clearly positive or negative material (e.g., Erez & Isen, 2002; Isen & Shalker, 1982; Schiffenbauer, 1974). Similarly, a study on the influence of positive affect on word associations showed that positive affect resulted in more extensive and diverse word associations to neutral words, but not to negative or even positive words (Isen et al., 1985). In addition, a study investigating categorization of people into person-type categories found that positive affect influenced perception (classification) of marginal category representatives into positive person categories (such as "bartender" into the category "nurturant people"), but not of marginal category representatives into negative person categories (such as "genius" into the category "unstable people"; Isen et al., 1992).

Similarly, in the studies by Urada and Miller (2000), positive affect influenced the group representation and acceptance of outgroup members who shared an important, but not an unimportant, characteristic with the ingroup. This too indicates that positive affect's influence on thought processes and cognitive organization does not just reflect a global bias, or simplistic or superficial processing, but rather stems from flexible, integrated categorization and a detailed, integrated consideration of the relevant materials to be thought about in the situation.

In yet another example, a study set in an organizational context showed that positive affect influenced task perceptions and satisfaction for an enriched task, but not for an unenriched task (Kraiger, Billings, & Isen, 1989). In the organizational behavior literature, an "enriched task" is one that allows employees an opportunity for some autonomy, diversity of activity, and sense of control and meaningfulness, whereas an unenriched task is one that requires only relatively routine, scripted activity and/or allows little sense of control or meaningfulness. *An important point here is that positive affect cues positive material about items for which positive thoughts exist in the person's mind, and does not simply result in a global perceptual or response bias, as if the person were viewing everything through "rose-colored glasses" or responding thoughtlessly.*

For another example, in the studies of intrinsic motivation and self-control by Isen and Reeve (2005), people in whom mild positive affect had been induced, although showing a preference for working on an enjoyable puzzle task rather than a tedious work task, reduced the amount of time they spent on the enjoyable task, in favor of the work task, significantly more than controls, when they knew that the work needed to be done. Compatibly with the points being made here, people in the positive affect condition showed greater liking of the puzzle task than did controls but not greater liking of the tedious work task.

Even more importantly, the differential responding by people in positive affect to important, versus unimportant, tasks or situations indicates that positive affect promotes detailed consideration of situations and stimuli, including their relative importance or relevance, and flexible responding to situations based on that integrated consideration of factors and possible outcomes (e.g., study 4, Bodenhausen et al., 1994; Bodenhausen et al., 2001; Erez & Isen, 2002; Estrada et al., 1997; Isen & Reeve, 2005; Johnson & Fredrickson, 2005). Several studies have also shown more detailed perception of stimuli, as well, as was described by Johnson and Fredrickson (2005) in showing that positive affect counters the "own-race bias" effect by fostering more detailed perception of faces not usually well differentiated. The studies showing better incidental learning and ability to divide attention while not sacrificing performance on a central or more important task (e.g., Derryberry, 1993; Isen & Shmidt, 2007) also attest to this point.

POSITIVE AFFECT ENABLES IMPROVED COPING

A growing body of work in the coping literature indicates that positive affect may help people to cope with problematic situations (see Aspinwall & McNamara, 2005; Aspinwall & Taylor, 1997; Fredrickson & Joiner, 2002; Taylor & Aspinwall, 1996, for reviews), and this may result, at least in part, from the flexibility engendered by positive affect. Similarly, people in positive affect have been found to be less defensive (Aspinwall, 1998; Reed & Aspinwall, 1998; Trope & Netter, 1994; Trope & Pomerantz, 1998) and less likely to distort or ignore information that does not fit their preconceptions (Estrada et al., 1997), and to show superior coping skills and styles (Aspinwall & Taylor, 1997; Showers & Cantor, 1985; Taylor & Aspinwall, 1996). In a related finding, people relatively high in optimism and hope are known to persist more at tasks and show better management of stress than those low in optimism (see Armor & Taylor, 1998; Scheier & Carver, 1992; Snyder, 1994; Taylor & Aspinwall, 1996, for reviews). The same is true for people experiencing induced mild positive affect (e.g., Erez & Isen, 2002). It should be noted, however, that positive affect leads people to disengage more rapidly from unsolvable tasks if there are solvable tasks to be done and to perform better on the solvable tasks (e.g., Aspinwall & Richter, 1999). This is yet another way in which positive affect fosters improved flexibility and coping.

Positive Affect Reduces Dangerous Risk Taking

The significant interactions between positive affect and other aspects of situations also suggest that affect's role is not simply to influence decisions in a positive direction regardless of the dangers or other factors that may be present. This reflects another way in which positive affect may contribute to adaptive functioning; it leads or enables people to use good judgment and be especially cautious of dangerous risks. In illustration, several studies, to be described next, have shown that positive affect's influence on risk preference, or behavior in risky situations, is characterized by significant interactions between affective state and the amount of potential unpleasantness or danger of the outcome under consideration. This indicates that positive affect's influence on such behavior is complex, the product of thought, rather than simple or impulsive.

A recent paper reported a theoretical model and results at the neurological level that point to a possible mechanism for differentiation of risky from safe situations or dangerous risks from trivial risks (Brown & Braver, 2005), and it is one that allows a role for positive affect. This mechanism implicates activation of the anterior cingulate cortex (ACC) and thus, as will be discussed later, in the context of the dopamine hypothesis, points to a way in which positive affect may be having these complex effects on risk preference that have been observed— through activation of the ACC. That paper suggests that the ACC may function to predict error likelihood or likelihood of negative consequences, based on reinforcement learning, of which conflict and error detection are special cases. Thus, through activation of the ACC, which we suggest accompanies positive affect, people may anticipate the general amount of risk and have an early warning that negative consequences may follow.

SUBJECTIVE PROBABILITY OF WINNING OR LOSING AND UTILITY OF POSSIBLE GAINS OR LOSSES

The work on positive affect and risk taking suggests that the effects of positive affect on risk preference and behavior result from differential effects of positive affect on the subjective probability of losing and the perceived utility (actually, the disutility) of the potential loss. More specifically, although positive affect decreases the subjective probability of losing, it increases the negative utility of the potential loss (e.g., Isen, Nygren, & Ashby, 1988; Johnson & Tversky, 1983; Nygren, Isen, Taylor, & Dulin, 1996). That is, while the probability of losing may seem smaller for those who are feeling happy as compared to control persons, the bad feeling that would result from the potential loss seems greater to the positive affect group. Thus, perhaps seeking to maintain their positive state, such persons are more likely than controls to refrain from taking a large and consequential risk (e.g., Isen & Geva, 1987; Isen & Patrick, 1983). This may result from a greater motive to maintain positive feelings among those in positive affect, as speculated previously (e.g., Isen et al., 1988), but it may actually result from better understanding among people in positive affect that negative consequences may follow in the particular context under consideration, (e.g., Brown & Braver, 2005).

RISK PREFERENCE

Studies on the influence of positive affect on risk preference or choices among gambles having alternative odds and win–loss structures, show that, although positive affect may appear to increase risk taking in a low-risk or hypothetical situation, it actually leads to risk avoidance or decreased risk preference in situations of high, real risk or possible genuine, meaningful loss (e.g., Isen & Geva, 1987; Isen & Patrick, 1983). This significant interaction, like those described previously, indicates that positive affect influences thinking in a complex manner that involves elaboration and evaluation of outcomes, rather than just by biasing responding in a positive direction. This suggests that positive affect fosters thinking about whatever needs to be thought about in the situation and does not lead people to downplay, ignore, or distort potential negative information. In fact, in one study, where a high risk of a genuine loss was involved, people in the positive affect condition, relative to controls, had significantly more thoughts about the potential loss (as reflected in a thought-listing task following the risk measure; Isen & Geva, 1987). This finding in particular is also compatible with the previously described findings of improved coping and reduced defensiveness because it indicates that people in positive affect can deploy their cognitive resources flexibly and attend to the crucial factors in the situation that serve their long-term best interests. Thus, even though, all else equal, people experiencing positive affect prefer not to lose their happy feelings, they are not limited to immediate affect maintenance as a goal (for discussion, see Aspinwall, 2005; Gervey, Igou, & Trope, 2005; Isen, 2003; Isen & Reeve, 2005).

VARIETY SEEKING

A series of potentially related studies has shown that people in positive affect conditions prefer to experience variety, if the options involved are safe and enjoyable. For example, in three studies looking at consumers' choices among snack foods, Kahn and Isen (1993) found that, as long as the products promised to be enjoyable, positive affect led to increased preference for variety (as measured by number of alterations between products [higher], diversity in the set of items considered [larger], and "market share" of the most preferred item [smaller]). ("Market share" refers to the percentage of the total number selected that is captured by one alternative; market share of the most preferred item would be the percentage of choices that goes to the most preferred item, and variety seeking, or preference for variety, would be reflected by the most preferred brand/item's receiving a smaller market share or percentage of the total number of choices.) This was not true, however, when the items were unfamiliar and the description of them (e.g., low salt) suggested that they might taste bad. In that circumstance, the positive affect and control groups did not differ in their degrees of variety seeking. This suggests that the increase in preference for variety that results from positive affect arises because of greater anticipated enjoyment, but that, as found in other contexts, this assessment is quite responsive to the details of the situation.

Recently, another series of studies that relates to liking for variety among people in positive affect has shown that positive affect counters the "choice overload" effect (e.g., Dhar, 1997; Iyengar & Lepper, 2000) and enables people to deal with and enjoy a large set of options. For example, in previous work, it had been found that in general people feel overwhelmed by having to make a selection from a very large set of options (e.g., 24 or 30 options) and frequently, after choosing from among such a set, regret their choice. People in positive affect, however, not only enjoy the process of choosing from a large set, but are more satisfied with their choice than controls who chose from the large set—even though there is no difference in satisfaction between the affect and control groups when choosing from the smaller set (e.g., 6 options; Isen & Spassova, 2008).

To summarize, then, extensive research using varied affect inductions and/or measures of optimism and self-esteem and varied measures of creativity and flexibility supports the conclusion that positive affect fosters cognitive flexibility, creativity, and innovation, and at the same time careful adaptive thinking and reasonable responses. As noted, people in whom positive affect has been induced show more unusual (but still reasonable and sensible) word associations to neutral words, more liking for unusual, nontypical products, and more flexible categorization of neutral words into topic categories and of products into product classes. They also show greater preference for variety among safe, enjoyable alternatives and better ability to deal with and enjoy a large number of alternative options (Isen & Daubman, 1984; Isen & Spassova, 2008; Isen et al., 1985; Kahn & Isen, 1993; Murray et al., 1990; Showers & Cantor, 1985). As described, this effect also applies to people's classification of person types into positive categories (but not into negative categories) and other-group members into ingroups (Dovidio et al., 1995; Isen et al., 1992; Urada & Miller, 2000). Relative to control groups, people in positive affect conditions have better negotiation outcomes and enjoy the task more, where the bargaining situation requires a problem-solving approach and they can take the other person's perspective (Carnevale & Isen, 1986); thus, it seems that the influence of positive affect on flexibility may also play some role in positive affect's improvement of interpersonal interaction (see, for example, Isen, 1999b, for discussion).

Neuropsychological Underpinnings

As noted in the introduction, this chapter also considers some neurological processes that may enable, or (to put it more neutrally) be associated with, these effects of positive affect. One reason for considering this question is to extend our understanding of affect by adding another level of analysis to our inquiry. Several lines of research have recently been using neurological techniques, such as functional magnetic resonance imaging (fMRI), event-related potentials (ERPs), and others, to investigate the influence of affect on cognitive processes and behavior and have found evidence compatible with the behavioral and cognitive effects observed previously. Such studies, then, not only provide converging evidence, using very different types of measures, that confirms in a different way those previously observed effects, but they also advance understanding of the processes involved and suggest additional hypotheses for investigation. For example, Federmeier, Kirson, Moreno, and Kutas (2001), using the ERP technique, and looking specifically at the N400 measure, which is thought to be reflective of semantic relationships, reported that mild positive affect resulted in a change in

organization of semantic memory and the way semantic memory is used, as suggested by the flexibility hypothesis (e.g., Isen, 1993, 2000, 2008) and the empirical work discussed earlier in this chapter, supporting that hypothesis (e.g., Estrada et al., 1994, 1997; Isen & Daubman, 1984; Isen et al., 1992; Isen et al., 1985, 1987). Not only do these findings confirm the earlier work and theorizing, but the technique used also helps in ruling out an alternative interpretation in terms of arousal or motivation alone (Federmeier et al., 2001, p. 151).

However, as is evident from the foregoing example, in making this recommendation to integrate the neurological level of analysis in the work on understanding affect's influence and function, I am not suggesting that the cognitive and behavioral levels of analysis be replaced by the neurological, but rather, that the different kinds of methods and levels of analysis supplement each other. That is, asking about the neuropsychological concomitants of positive affect should not be taken to imply that other levels of analysis are less important or less informative. Rather, I am suggesting using this level of analysis to discover what can be added to our understanding by investigating the neurological processes associated with positive affect or with the processes that have been found to result from positive affect. For example, neuropsychological analyses may suggest new dimensions or variables that are important for understanding the impact of affect on cognition or behavior, or they may suggest additional influences of affect that would be observable at the behavioral or cognitive level but that are not yet recognized.

To address the question of the neurological processes that may be involved in positive affect's influence on cognition and behavior, one can first describe certain effects of positive affect that have been observed and then consider what neurological processes are known to enable or be involved in those cognitive processes. One may begin by making the simple point that such neurological processes must also be present during positive affect. As a first step, all that may be said is that that neurological process is not incompatible with positive affect or that positive affect is not incompatible with that neurological process. Nonetheless, this consideration can provide important information because it suggests that positive affect does not interfere with certain neurological processes and that positive affect may even cause or facilitate those processes. Then, additional questions can be asked about the effects or processes activated by that neurological system.

This, in turn, can extend our understanding of affect and enable us to generate new predictions about expected neurological, cognitive, and behavioral effects of affect. Further, as new information is discovered about the operation of that system, new hypotheses about affect's influence and mechanisms may be generated.

The Dopamine Hypothesis

In the case of positive affect, as has been described in this chapter, one of the most clear, and most distinctive, cognitive effects observed is increased flexibility and improved creativity and problem-solving ability. Thus, initially, one question that may be asked is about the neuropsychological substrate of flexible thinking, the ability to switch focus as needed and/or hold multiple ideas in mind simultaneously. Of course, to be relevant to positive affect, it would be most clear if any neuropsychological process identified also were related, not only to flexibility, but also to positive affect. Thus, beginning with this question of what neurological processes enable or are associated with cognitive flexibility, we also asked whether any such identified processes also are associated with positive affect. Because dopamine in frontal regions of the brain is associated with both cognitive flexibility and reward (which may potentially be related to positive affect), it seemed especially promising to explore the potential role of the dopamine system in the impact of positive affect on thinking (see Ashby et al., 1999).

A large body of literature on the neuropsychology of reward suggests the importance of dopamine in the mediation of reward and particularly in the process of learning from reward (see Ashby et al., 1999, for discussion). We assume that positive affect conditions and the experiencing of reward may share some elements. In addition, the literature indicates that dopamine in the anterior cingulate region of the brain enables cognitive perspective taking or set switching (e.g., Owen et al., 1993; see Ashby et al., 1999). Thus, the neuropsychological work shows, in animal studies, that dopamine is released in the brain in response to reward; and, in both animal and human studies, that dopamine is associated with cognitive flexibility. In addition, reductions in dopamine (e.g., as occur in Parkinson's disease) are associated with humans' diminished performance on tasks requiring them to switch "set." Thus, my colleagues and I have proposed that the influence of positive affect on cognitive processes may be mediated by release of the neurotransmitter dopamine. Direct evidence is yet to be obtained for this

hypothesis; however, based on the data just reviewed, that suggestion seems plausible.

Additional predictions follow from the dopamine hypothesis, as well. For example, because there are dopamine projections into frontal brain regions responsible for processes such as thinking, working memory, and the like, this hypothesis suggests that positive affect should enhance working memory and processes related to thinking, through activation of these brain regions. In contrast, since the visual and auditory areas of the brain are not rich in dopamine receptors, this hypothesis would not predict that positive affect should influence visual or auditory perception (see Ashby et al., 1999, for discussion). The recent paper by Brown and Braver (2005), suggesting that activation of ACC leads to differentiation of dangerous risk situations versus safe situations, supports another hypothesis, the proposition that positive affect should reduce dangerous risk taking (but not trivial risk taking).

Interestingly, the suggestion that the dopamine system is involved in positive affect has also been advanced by Depue and colleagues, although they adopt a somewhat different perspective (e.g., Depue & Collins, 1999; Depue, Luciana, Arbisi, Collins, & Leon, 1994). Their work takes an individual-difference approach and characterizes people in terms of their relatively stable levels of positive emotionality (e.g., as reflected by the personality trait of extraversion). Depue and his colleagues have reported increased levels of brain dopamine activity among people who score relatively high in characteristics such as extraversion. Also consistent with the argument being put forth here, other work has found that people scoring relatively high in measures of dispositional "positivity" (as measured by instruments such as the Positive Affectivity Negative Affectivity Scale [PANAS]; e.g., Watson & Telegen, 1985) also show increases in problem-solving performance (e.g., George & Brief, 1996; Staw & Barsade, 1993).

One might wonder how a trait approach could be compatible with the present suggestion that mildly induced positive affective states can influence the dopamine system, or have their impact on cognition through release of dopamine in the brain. This may seem especially problematic in light of Depue and colleagues' proposition that the dopamine system itself is different in people who are high, rather than low, in the personality characteristic of "extraversion" (e.g., Depue & Collins, 1999). Those authors relate "extraversion" to positive incentive motivation and maintain that some individuals ("extraverts") have a ventral tegmental area dopamine system (VTA-DA) that functions to increase their positive incentive motivation or approach behavior. According to Depue and colleagues, the characteristic VTA dopamine system that sets extraverts apart can come about in any of three ways: through genetic endowment, through "experience-expectant" processes, or through "experience-dependent" processes. Their view holds, however, that regardless of how this development occurs, the requisite VTA dopamine system becomes a stable characteristic by adulthood. Thus, in consideration of Depue's view, it might seem difficult to argue that induced positive affect has its impact through activation of the dopamine system.

There are several potential ways of integrating these two dopamine-related positions, however. First, it may be that effects of positive affect inductions may differ for people with differently developed dopamine systems or for those who are very high or very low in certain dispositional tendencies. However, since the experimental findings show effects of induced affect when people have been randomly assigned to conditions, this cannot be the primary way to integrate these lines of research.

Second, then, it is noteworthy that other authors have taken issue with aspects of Depue's position in ways that make it possible to integrate Depue's findings with the suggestion that induced positive affect can influence the dopamine system. For example, Cabib and Puglisi-Allegra (1999) point out that the functioning of the VTA dopamine system may not be immutable even in adulthood, noting that, at least in animal studies, the dopamine system continues to be very responsive to environmental conditions even in mature organisms. In addition, other authors suggest that the direction of influence between the VTA and behavior/cognition in humans is not necessarily only from dopamine to behavior. For example, Isom and Heller (1999) and Miller (1996) reason and provide many examples in support of their logic that cognitive-behavioral interventions can influence neurobiology. This means that the causal arrow can go in either direction or in both directions. Thus, even if there are individual differences in people's dopamine systems, it is still possible that these systems remain malleable, and that affective experiences may continue to influence both the dopamine system and the cognitive and behavioral effects that are produced. Consequently, it remains plausible that the neurological system is responsive even among adults, that induced positive affect in humans may have its effects through the VTA dopamine system and that these effects can be powerful, even for adults. This position does not deny that the dopamine system or the cognitive and social patterns associated with its functioning may be built up over time, as held by Depue and colleagues, but it does suggest a more flexible, malleable, bidirectional process than is usually assumed.

Additional neuropsychological work, although focusing primarily on other factors, has also yielded results that fit with the suggestion that brain dopamine may play a role in the effects of positive affect on cognition that have been observed. Davidson (1993, 1999), for example, investigating lateralization of brain function, and using positron emission tomography (PET) and fMRI techniques to observe which brain areas are active at the time of processing of different types of materials or stimuli, hypothesized that positive affect is processed in the left frontal and right posterior areas of the brain. Although the suggestion that positive affect is mediated by the dopamine system does not focus specifically on hemispheric lateralization of brain function, it is worth noting that these regions postulated by Davidson to be active in positive affect, especially the left frontal region, are rich in dopamine receptors.

In recent years, several authors have begun to focus on the role of the dopamine system, and particularly the ACC, in cognitive processing associated with affect or predictions of affect (e.g., Brown & Braver, 2005; Bush, Luu, & Posner, 2000; Mohanty et al., 2007; Whalen et al., 1998). Some of this work has focused on general issues such as whether affect and cognition are mediated by different brain regions or separate systems (e.g., Whalen et al., 1998), and subdivisions of the ACC with potentially different cognitive and emotion-related functions have been proposed. Some authors reason from such studies that emotion and cognition are mediated by separate brain systems, but others (e.g., Mohanty et al., 2007) argue for a continuum between them and overlap in their mediation, indicating that at base they are not separate brain systems. For purposes of this chapter, it should be noted, in addition, that when separate functions are identified, it is not clear whether the "emotion" findings apply to positive affect as well as to negative, because most often the "emotion" materials are only negative.

On the other hand, some of the recent research on ACC functioning focuses on what the specific effects are. For example, some work has focused on flexibility in function of the prefrontal cortex (PFC) and the potential roles of dopamine in PFC in cognitive control involving both maintenance and updating of information and gating functions in updating (e.g., Miller & Cohen, 2001; Montague, Hyman, & Cohen, 2004). These processes are potentially important in integrating cognitive and affective processes mediated by positive affect, such as flexibility, which have been proposed in the dopamine hypothesis of positive affect's effects described in this chapter.

Conclusion

As revealed throughout this chapter, positive affect is a source of human strength. Contrary to some of the earlier misconceptions, the experience of positive affect does not generally result in superficial or flawed thought processes, even where careful thinking about serious matters is required. Many studies on cognitive processes such as memory, decision making, and problem solving have shown that positive affect is generally facilitating. For example, it enables flexible thinking and creative problem solving on tasks that otherwise are very difficult, and it promotes thinking that is not only efficient, but also careful, open-minded, and thorough. Furthermore, the experience of positive affect is known to promote social interaction, helpfulness, generosity, and social responsibility—and it does so without undermining attention to a person's own long-term welfare.

Although some earlier papers suggested that positive affect impaired systematic processing either because of draining limited cognitive capacity or interfering with motivation to process carefully (e.g., Bless et al., 1990; Mackie & Worth, 1989), many authors did not find results compatible with that suggestion (e.g., Isen et al., 1991; Smith & Shaffer, 1991; Staw & Barsade, 1993), and still other investigators reported findings pertaining to deployment of attention that would lead to an opposite conclusion (e.g., Derryberry, 1993). More recently, several studies have found that the previously reported impairing effects of positive affect primarily occurred when the task was dull or unpleasant *and* unimportant, and thus not necessarily engaged by people (e.g., Isen & Reeve, 2005; see also Aspinwall, 2005; Isen, 1993, 2000, 2008, for discussion).

As noted earlier, it has been proposed that at least some of the effects of positive affect may depend on the neurotransmitter dopamine (e.g., Ashby et al., 1999; Depue et al., 1994; Depue & Collins, 1999). This hypothesis carries the implication that positive affect may especially influence tasks that are controlled by brain regions containing dopamine receptors. Consequently, this suggestion may lead us to more specific ways of defining the kinds of tasks that may, or may not, be facilitated by positive affect. This may help us to avoid the use of vague terms, such as "heuristic" versus "systematic" processing, which—although useful in other contexts—have sometimes fostered confusion in understanding the impact of affect on cognitive processing (see Isen, 1993, 2000, 2008, for discussion).

Most likely, the full picture will be more complex than seems implied at first. For example, the effects of combinations of different neurotransmitters will have to be considered, and their interactions can be quite complex. There already have been propositions put forth, for example, about the effects of dopamine in the presence of serotonin (where it is thought to result in intelligent switching between responsive engagement and long-term planning), versus where serotonin is blocked (e.g., Katz, 1999). Similarly, even though dopamine may be the primary neurotransmitter associated with extraversion, the presence or absence of serotonin may play an important role in which aspect of extraversion (e.g., sociability vs. impulsiveness) is salient (e.g., Heller, 1997). The work linking affect (especially positive affect) and brain function is still in its early stages, and certainly it will take some time to develop and refine this information.

As this development is pursued, however, the purposive nature of people's thinking and behavior will need to be integrated into our understanding of the effects of various neurotransmitters, singly or in concert. That is, the fact that people's goals influence their interpretations of situations and their behaviors in those situations is supported by so much evidence, that such processes cannot be ignored in subsequent neurological analyses. This means that simple reductionism will not be appropriate; rather, insights from the cognitive, behavioral, and neuropsychological levels of analysis will have to be integrated and recognized as being mutually informative. To illustrate this point, consider the dopamine hypothesis of the mediation of the effects of positive affect on cognition. This hypothesis arose from the observation, at the behavioral and cognitive levels, that positive affect fosters cognitive flexibility and the ability to switch perspectives (together with the understanding that dopamine in the anterior cingulate region of the brain enables flexible perspective taking or set switching). (See also Isom and Heller, 1999, and Miller, 1996 for discussion of the bidirectionality of neurological, cognitive, and social or behavioral influence.)

Finally, it should be emphasized that all of the aforementioned effects of positive affect have resulted from mild, everyday affect inductions, experiences that can occur frequently in daily life. Furthermore, these effects have been observed when people were randomly assigned to experimental conditions. This indicates that these effects, many of which are beneficial and highly sought after (e.g., creative problem solving, helpfulness, improved conflict resolution), can be fostered readily in virtually everyone. Although there may be individual differences among people in abilities and skills underlying these processes, and perhaps even variability in genetic propensity toward them, those are not sufficient to negate the substantial power of simply induced, mild, happy feelings to enhance performance. For this reason, the currently popular foci involving genetic endowments, early-childhood experience, or individual differences developed over many years should not obscure the fact that people respond to their surroundings and that a small positive event can have powerful effects on many important processes. As current brain research is showing, even the brain development itself responds to environmental stimuli throughout the life span. Thus, not only are happy feelings a source of important strength for people, but they constitute one that is potentially available to all of us and those in our charge.

Questions

1. What do the research data suggest regarding the effects of mild positive affect on thinking about a topic of interest: impaired, superficial, impulsive cognitive processing or more flexible, adaptive, appropriate and effective cognitive processing?

2. How can the dopamine hypothesis help to understand the effects of positive affect on cognition and behavior that have been observed?

3. Do the data of this field suggest that one level of analysis (behavioral, cognitive, neuropsychological) is superior to the others in helping to understand the influence of mild positive affect on cognition and behavior?

References

Aderman, D. (1972). Elation, depression and helping behavior. *Journal of Personality and Social Psychology, 24*, 91–101.

Amabile, T. M., Barsade, S. G., Mueller, J. S., & Staw, B. M. (2005). Affect and creativity at work. *Administrative Science Quarterly, 50*, 367–403.

Armor, D. A., & Taylor, S. E. (1998). Situated optimism: Specific outcome expectancies and self-regulation. *Advances in Experimental Social Psychology, 30*, 309–379.

Ashby, F. G., Isen, A. M., & Turken, A. (1999). A neuropsychological theory of positive affect and its influence on cognition. *Psychological Review, 106*, 529–550.

Aspinwall, L. G. (1998). Rethinking the role of positive affect and self-regulation. *Motivation and Emotion, 22*, 1–32.

Aspinwall, L. G. (2005). The psychology of future-oriented thinking: From achievement to proactive coping, adaptation, and aging. *Motivation and Emotion, 29*, 203–235.

Aspinwall, L. G., & McNamara, A. (2005). Taking positive changes seriously: Toward a positive psychology of cancer survivorship and resilience. *Cancer, 104* (11 Suppl.), 2549–2556.

Aspinwall, L. G., & Richter, L. (1999). Optimism and self-mastery predict more rapid disengagement from unsolvable tasks in the presence of alternatives. *Motivation and Emotion, 23*, 221–245.

Aspinwall, L. G., & Taylor, S. E. (1997). A stitch in time: Self-regulation and proactive coping. *Psychological Bulletin, 121*, 417–436.

Baron, R. A. (1984). Reducing organizational conflict: An incompatible response approach. *Journal of Applied Psychology, 69*, 272–279.

Baumann, N., & Kuhl, J. (2005). Positive affect and flexibility: Overcoming the precedence of global over local processing of visual information. *Motivation and Emotion, 29*, 123–134.

Berkowitz, L. (1972). Social norms, feelings, and other factors affecting helping and altruism. In L. Berkowitz (Ed.), *Advances in experimental social psychology* (Vol. 6, pp. 63–108). New York: Academic Press.

Berkowitz, L., & Daniels, L. (1964). Affecting the salience of the social responsibility norm: Effect of past help on response to dependency relationships. *Journal of Abnormal and Social Psychology, 67*, 275–281.

Bless, H., Bohner, G., Schwarz, N., & Strack, F. (1990). Mood and persuasion: A cognitive response analysis. *Personality and Social Psychology Bulletin, 16*, 331–345.

Bless, H., Clore, G. L., Schwarz, N., Golisano, V., Rabe, C., & Wolk, M. (1996). Mood and the use of scripts: Does a happy mood really lead to mindlessness? *Journal of Personality and Social Psychology, 71*, 665–679.

Bodenhausen, G. V., Kramer, G. P., & Susser, K. (1994). Happiness and stereotypic thinking in social judgment. *Journal of Personality and Social Psychology, 66*, 621–632.

Bodenhausen, G. V., Mussweiler, T., Gabriel, S., & Moreno, K. N. (2001). Affective influences on stereotyping and intergroup relations. In J. P. Forgas (Ed.), *Handbook of Affect and Social Cognition* (pp. 319–343). Mahwah, NJ: Erlbaum.

Brown, J. W., & Braver, T. S. (2005). Learned predictions of error likelihood in the anterior cingulate cortex. *Science, 307*, 1118–1121.

Bush, G., Luu, P., & Posner, M. I. (2000). Cognitive and emotional influences in anterior cingulate cortex. *Trends in Cognitive Sciences, 4*, 215–222.

Cabib, S., & Puglisi-Allegra, S. (1999). Of genes, environment, and destiny. *Behavioral and Brain Sciences, 22*, 519.

Carnevale, P. J. D., & Isen, A. M. (1986). The influence of positive affect and visual access on the discovery of integrative solutions in bilateral negotiation. *Organizational Behavior and Human Decision Processes, 37*, 1–13.

Cunningham, M. R. (1979). Weather, mood, and helping behavior: Quasi-experiments in the sunshine Samaritan. *Journal of Personality and Social Psychology, 37*, 1947–1956.

Cunningham, M. R., Steinberg, J., & Grev, R. (1980). Wanting to and having to help: Separate motivations for positive mood and guilt induced helping. *Journal of Personality and Social Psychology, 38*, 181–192.

Davidson, R. J. (1993). The neuropsychology of emotion and affective style. In M. Lewis & J. Haviland (Eds.), *Handbook of emotions* (pp. 143–154). New York: Guilford.

Davidson, R. J. (1999). Neuropsychological perspectives on affective styles and their cognitive consequences. In T. Dalgleish & M. Power (Eds.), *The handbook of cognition and emotion* (pp. 103–123). Sussex, UK: Wiley.

Depue, R. A., & Collins, P. F. (1999). Neurobiology of the structure of personality: Dopamine, facilitation of incentive motivation, and extraversion. *Behavioral and Brain Sciences, 22*, 491–569.

Depue, R. A., Luciana, M., Arbisi, P., Collins, P., & Leon, A. (1994). Dopamine and the structure of personality: Relation of agonist-induced dopamine activity to positive emotionality. *Journal of Personality and Social Psychology, 67*, 485–498.

Derryberry, D. (1993). Attentional consequences of outcome-related motivational states: Congruent, incongruent, and focusing effects. *Motivation and Emotion, 17*, 65–90.

Dhar, R. (1997). Consumer preference for a no-choice option. *Journal of Consumer Research, 24*, 215–231.

Dovidio, J. F., Gaertner, S. L., Isen, A. M., & Lowrance, R. (1995). Group representations and intergroup bias: Positive affect, similarity, and group size. *Personality and Social Psychology Bulletin, 21*, 856–865.

Dovidio, J. F., Gaertner, S. L., Isen, A. M., Rust, M., & Guerra, P. (1998). Positive affect, cognition, and the reduction of intergroup bias. In C. Sedikides, J. Schopler, & C. A. Insko (Eds.), *Intergroup cognition and intergroup behavior* (pp. 337–366). Mahwah, NJ: Erlbaum.

Dreisbach, G., & Goschke, T. (2004). How positive affect modulates cognitive control: Reduced perseveration at the cost of increased distractibility. *Journal of Experimental Psychology: Learning, Memory, and Cognition, 30*, 343–353.

Duncker, K. (1945). On problem-solving. *Psychological Monographs, 58* (Whole No. 5).

Erez, A., & Isen, A. M. (2002). The influence of positive affect on the components of expectancy motivation. *Journal of Applied Psychology, 87*, 1055–1067.

Estrada, C. A., Isen, A. M., & Young, M. J. (1994). Positive affect influences creative problem solving and reported source of practice satisfaction in physicians. *Motivation and Emotion, 18*, 285–299.

Estrada, C. A., Isen, A. M., & Young, M. J. (1997). Positive affect facilitates integration of information and decreases anchoring in reasoning among physicians. *Organizational Behavior and Human Decision Processes, 72*, 117–135.

Federmeier, K. D., Kirson, D. A., Moreno, E. M., & Kutas, M. (2001). Effects of transient, mild mood states on semantic memory organization and use: An event-related potential investigation in humans. *Neuroscience Letters, 305*, 149–152.

Forgas, J. P. (2002). Feeling and doing: Affective influences on interpersonal behavior. *Psychological Inquiry, 13*, 1–29.

Fredrickson, B. L. (1998). What good are positive emotions? *Review of General Psychology, 2*, 300–319.

Fredrickson, B. L. (2001). The role of positive emotions in positive psychology: The broaden-and-build theory of positive emotions. *American Psychologist, 56*, 218–226.

Fredrickson, B. L., & Joiner, T. (2002). Positive emotions trigger upward spirals toward emotional well-being. *Psychological Science, 13*, 172–175.

Fredrickson, B. L., Mancuso, R. A., Branigan, C., & Tugade, M. M. (2000). The undoing effect of positive emotions. *Motivation and Emotion, 24*, 237–258.

Friedman, R. S., & Forster, J. (2005). The influence of approach and avoidance cues on attentional flexibility. *Motivation and Emotion, 29*, 69–81.

Gasper, K., & Clore, G. L. (2002). Attending to the big picture: Mood and global versus local processing of visual information. *Psychological Science, 13*, 34–40.

George, J. M., & Brief, A. P. (1996). Motivational agendas in the workplace: The effects of feelings on focus of attention and work motivation. In L. L. Cummings & B. M. Staw (Eds.), *Research in organizational behavior* (Vol. 18, pp. 75–109). Greenwich, CT: JAI.

Gervey, B., Igou, E. R., & Trope, Y. (2005). Positive mood and future-oriented self-evaluation. *Motivation and Emotion, 29*, 269–296.

Gray, J. R. (2001). Emotion modulation of cognitive control: Approach-withdrawal states double-dissociate spatial from verbal two-back task performance. *Journal of Experimental Psychology: General, 130*, 436–452.

Greene, T. R., & Noice, H. (1988). Influence of positive affect upon creative thinking and problem solving in children. *Psychological Reports, 63*, 895–898.

Heller, W. (1997). Emotion. In M. Banich (Ed.), *Neuropsychology: The neural bases of mental function* (pp. 398–429). Boston: Houghton Mifflin.

Hirt, E. R., Melton, R. J., McDonald, H. E., & Harackiewicz, J. M. (1996). Processing goals, task interest, and the mood-performance relationship: A mediational analysis. *Journal of Personality and Social Psychology, 71*, 245–261.

Isen, A. M. (1970). Success, failure attention and reactions to others: The warm glow of success. *Journal of Personality and Social Psychology, 17*, 107–112.

Isen, A. M. (1987). Positive affect, cognitive processes and social behavior. In L. Berkowitz (Ed.), *Advances in experimental social psychology* (pp. 203–253). New York: Academic.

Isen, A. M. (1990). The influence of positive and negative affect on cognitive organization: Implications for development. In N. Stein, B. Leventhal, & T. Trabasso (Eds.), *Psychological and biological processes in the development of emotion* (pp. 75–94). Hillsdale, NJ: Erlbaum.

Isen, A. M. (1993). Positive affect and decision making. In M. Lewis & J. Haviland (Eds.), *Handbook of emotions* (pp. 261–277). New York: Guilford.

Isen, A. M. (1999a). On the relationship between affect and creative problem solving. In S. Russ (Ed.), *Affect, creative experience, and psychological adjustment* (pp. 3–17). Philadelphia: Taylor & Francis.

Isen, A. M. (1999b). Positive affect. In T. Dalgleish & M. Power (Eds.), *The handbook of cognition and emotion* (pp. 521–539). Sussex, UK: Wiley.

Isen, A. M. (2000). Positive affect and decision making. In M. Lewis & J. Haviland-Jones (Eds.). *Handbook of emotions* (2nd ed., pp. 417–435). New York: Guilford.

Isen, A. M. (2003). Positive affect as a source of human strength. In L. G. Aspinwall & U. Staudinger (Eds.), *A Psychology of Human Strengths* (pp. 179–195). Washington, DC: American Psychological Association.

Isen, A. M. (2008). Some ways in which positive affect influences decision making and problem solving. In M. Lewis, J. Haviland-Jones, & L. F. Barrett (Eds.), *Handbook of Emotions* (3rd ed., pp. 548–573). NY: Guilford.

Isen, A. M., & Daubman, K. A. (1984). The influence of affect on categorization. *Journal of Personality and Social Psychology, 47*, 1206–1217.

Isen, A. M., Daubman, K. A., & Nowicki, G. P. (1987). Positive affect facilitates creative problem solving. *Journal of Personality and Social Psychology, 52*, 1122–1131.

Isen, A. M., & Geva, N. (1987). The influence of positive affect on acceptable level of risk: The person with a large canoe has a large worry. *Organizational Behavior and Human Decision Processes, 39*, 145–154.

Isen, A. M., Johnson, M. M. S., Mertz, E., & Robinson, F. G. (1985). The influence of positive affect on the unusualness of word association. *Journal of Personality and Social Psychology, 48*, 1413–1426.

Isen, A. M., & Levin, P. F. (1972). The effect of feeling good on helping: Cookies and kindness. *Journal of Personality and Social Psychology, 21*, 384–388.

Isen, A. M., & Means, B. (1983). The influence of positive affect on decision-making strategy. *Social Cognition, 2*, 18–31.

Isen, A. M., Niedenthal, P., & Cantor, N. (1992). The influence of positive affect on social categorization. *Motivation and Emotion, 16*, 65–78.

Isen, A. M., Nygren, T. E., & Ashby, F. G. (1988). The influence of positive affect on the perceived utility of gains and losses. *Journal of Personality and Social Psychology, 55*, 710–717.

Isen, A. M., & Patrick, R. (1983). The influence of positive feelings on risk taking: When the chips are down. *Organizational Behavior and Human Performance, 31*, 194–202.

Isen, A. M., & Reeve, J. (2005). The influence of positive affect on intrinsic and extrinsic motivation: Facilitating enjoyment of play, responsible work behavior, and self-control. *Motivation and Emotion, 29*, 297–325.

Isen, A. M., Rosenzweig, A. S., & Young, M. J. (1991). The influence of positive affect on clinical problem solving. *Medical Decision Making, 11*, 221–227.

Isen, A. M., & Shalker, T. E. (1982). Do you "accentuate the positive, eliminate the negative" when you are in a good mood? *Social Psychology Quarterly, 45*, 58–63.

Isen, A. M., & Shmidt, E. (2007). *Positive affect: Broadened focus without increased distractibility.* Paper presented at the Emotions preconference to the annual meeting of the Society for Personality and Social Psychology, Memphis, TN.

Isen, A. M., & Simmonds, S. F. (1978). The effect of feeling good on a helping task that is incompatible with good mood. *Social Psychology Quarterly, 41*, 345–349.

Isen, A. M., & Spassova, G. (2008). *Positive affect reduces the debilitating effects of choice overload.* Paper presented at the annual meeting of the Society for Personality and Social Psychology, Albuquerque, NM.

Isom, J., & Heller, W. (1999). Neurobiology of extraversion: Pieces of the puzzle still missing. *Behavioral and Brain Sciences, 22*, 524.

Iyengar, S. S., & Lepper, M. R. (2000). When choice is demotivating: Can one desire too much of a good thing? *Journal of Personality and Social Psychology, 79*, 995–1006.

Johnson, K. J., & Fredrickson, B. L. (2005). "We all look the same to me": Positive emotions eliminate the own-race bias in face recognition. *Psychological Science, 16*, 875–881.

Johnson, E., & Tversky, A. (1983). Affect generalization, and the perception of risk. *Journal of Personality and Social Psychology, 45*, 20–31.

Kahn, B., & Isen, A. M. (1993). The influence of positive affect on variety-seeking among safe, enjoyable products. *Journal of Consumer Research, 20*, 257–270.

Katz, L. D. (1999). Dopamine and serotonin: Integrating current affective engagement with longer-term goals. *Behavioral and Brain Sciences, 22*, 527.

Kazen, M., & Kuhl, J. (2005). Intention memory and achievement motivation: Volitional facilitation and inhibition as a function of affective contents of need-related stimuli. *Journal of Personality and Social Psychology, 39*, 426–448.

Kraiger, K., Billings, R. S., & Isen, A. M. (1989). The influence of positive affective states on task perceptions and satisfaction. *Organizational Behavior and Human Decision Processes, 44*, 12–25.

Kuhl, J., & Kazen, M. (1999). Volitional facilitation of difficult intentions: Joint activation of intention memory and positive affect removes Stroop interference. *Journal of Experimental Psychology: General, 128*, 382–399.

Lee, A., & Sternthal, B. (1999). The effects of positive mood on memory. *Journal of Consumer Research, 26*, 115.

Lyubomirsky, S., King, L., & Diener, E. (2005). The benefits of frequent positive affect: Does happiness lead to success? *Psychological Bulletin, 131*, 803–855.

Mackie, D. M., & Worth, L. T. (1989). Cognitive deficits and the mediation of positive affect in persuasion. *Journal of Personality and Social Psychology, 57*, 27–40.

Mackie, D. M., & Worth, L. (1991). Feeling good but not thinking straight: The impact of positive mood on persuasion. In J. P. Forgas (Ed.), *Emotion and social judgment* (pp. 201–220). Oxford: Pergamon.

Mednick, M. T., Mednick, S. A., & Mednick, E. V. (1964). Incubation of creative performance and specific associative priming. *Journal of Abnormal and Social Psychology, 69*, 84–88.

Melton, R. J. (1995). The role of positive affect in syllogism performance. *Personality and Social Psychology Bulletin, 21*, 788–794.

Miller, E. K., & Cohen, J. D. (2001). An integrative theory of prefrontal cortex function. *Annual Review of Neuroscience, 24*, 167–202.

Miller, G. A. (1996). How we think about cognition, emotion, and biology in psychopathology. *Psychophysiology, 33*, 615–628.

Mohanty, A., Engels, A. S., Herrington, J. D., Heller, W., Ho, M.-H. R., Banich, M. T., et al. (2007). Differential engagement of anterior cingulate cortex subdivisions for cognitive and emotional function. *Psychophysiology, 44*, 343–351.

Montague, P. R., Hyman, S. E., & Cohen, J. D. (2004). Computational roles for dopamine in behavioural control. *Nature, 431*(7010), 760–767.

Murray, N., Sujan, H., Hirt, E. R., & Sujan, M. (1990). The influence of mood on categorization: A cognitive flexibility interpretation. *Journal of Personality and Social Psychology, 59*, 411–425.

Nygren, T. E., Isen, A. M., Taylor, P. J., & Dulin, J. (1996). The influence of positive affect on the decision rule in risk situations: Focus on outcome (and especially avoidance of loss) rather than probability. *Organizational Behavior and Human Decision Processes, 66*, 59–72.

Owen, A. M., Roberts, A. C., Hodges, J. R., Summers, B. A., Polkey, C. E., & Robbins, T. W. (1993). Contrasting mechanisms of impaired attentional set-shifting in patients with frontal lobe damage or Parkinson's disease. *Brain, 116*, 1159–1175.

Pruitt, D. G. (1983). Strategic choice in negotiation. *American Behavioral Scientist, 27*, 167–194.

Reed, M. B., & Aspinwall, L. G. (1998). Self-affirmation reduces biased processing of health-risk information. *Motivation and Emotion, 22*, 99–132.

Roehm, M., & Sternthal, B. (2001). The moderating effects of knowledge and resources on the persuasive impact of analogies. *Journal of Consumer Research, 28*, 257–272.

Scheier, M. F., & Carver, C. S. (1992). Effects of optimism on psychological well-being: Theoretical overview and empirical update. *Cognitive Therapy and Research, 16*, 201–228.

Schiffenbauer, A. (1974). Effects of observer's emotional state on judgments of the emotional state of others. *Journal of Personality and Social Psychology, 30*, 31–36.

Schwarz, N. (2002). Situated cognition and the wisdom of feelings: Cognitive tuning. In L. F. Barrett & P. Salovey (Eds.), *The wisdom in feeling* (pp. 144–166). New York: Guilford.

Schwarz, N., & Bless, H. (1991). Happy and mindless, but sad and smart? The impact of affective states on analytic reasoning. In J. P. Forgas (Ed.), *Emotion and social judgment* (pp. 55–71). Oxford: Pergamon.

Showers, C., & Cantor, N. (1985). Social cognition: A look at motivated strategies. *Annual Review of Psychology, 36*, 275–305.

Smith, S. M., & Shaffer, D. R. (1991). The effects of good moods on systematic processing: "Willing but not able, or able but not willing?" *Motivation and Emotion, 15*, 243–279.

Snyder, C. R. (1994). *The psychology of hope: You can get there from here.* New York: Free Press.

Staw, B. M., & Barsade, S. G. (1993). Affect and managerial performance: A test of the sadder-but-wiser vs. happier-and-smarter hypotheses. *Administrative Science Quarterly, 38*, 304–331.

Taylor, S. E., & Aspinwall, L. G. (1996). Mediating and moderating processes in psychosocial stress: Appraisal, coping, resistance and vulnerability. In H. B. Kaplan (Ed.), *Psychosocial stress: Perspectives on structure, theory, life-course, and methods* (pp. 71–110). San Diego, CA: Academic Press.

Trope, Y., & Netter, E. (1994). Reconciling competing motives in self-evaluation: The role of self-control in feedback seeking. *Journal of Personality and Social Psychology, 66*, 646–657.

Trope, Y., & Pomerantz, E. M. (1998). Resolving conflicts among self-evaluative motives: Positive experiences as a resource for overcoming defensiveness. *Motivation and Emotion, 22*, 53–72.

Urada, M., & Miller, N. (2000). The impact of positive mood and category importance on crossed categorization effects. *Journal of Personality and Social Psychology, 78*, 417–433.

Veitch, R., & Griffitt, W. (1976). Good news–bad news: Affective and interpersonal effects. *Journal of Applied Social Psychology, 6*, 69–75.

Watson, D. A., & Tellegen, A. (1985). Toward a consensual structure of mood. *Psychological Bulletin, 98*, 219–235.

Whalen, P. J., Bush, G., McNally, R. J., Wilhelm, S., McInerney, S. C., Janike, M. A., et al. (1998). The emotional Stroop counting paradigm: An fMRI probe of the anterior cingulate affective division. *Biological Psychiatry, 44*, 1219–1228.

Toward a Biology of Social Support

Sally S. Dickerson *and* Peggy M. Zoccola

Abstract

The presence of close, supportive ties to others can have a wide range of positive effects on health; certain biological processes may play a key role in linking positive social relationships to salubrious health outcomes. In this chapter, we review the research that connects the presence of strong, supportive social ties to positive physiological functioning, with an underlying emphasis on the implications for health and disease. Cross-sectional and prospective studies demonstrate that high levels of social integration and/or social support are associated with positive biological profiles (e.g., lower levels of neuroendocrine activity, better functioning of the immune system), whereas social isolation and loneliness can have detrimental effects on these parameters. Other research provides evidence for the stress-buffering hypothesis; social support exerts beneficial effects via a downregulation of stress responses, including dampened sympathetic and neuroendocrine activity. Conversely, deficient social relationships or social conflict has been linked with negative biological profiles. Emerging animal and human research suggests that oxytocin and endogenous opioids may underlie some of these physiological and health effects. Further elucidating the pathways through which social support could influence health outcomes could subsequently be used to develop theoretically sound interventions to optimize physiological functioning and health.

Keywords: psychoneuroimmunology, reactivity, social relationships, social support, stress

Toward a Biology of Social Support

Social relationships can have a profound influence on health. A large body of compelling research has demonstrated that the presence of close, supportive ties can have a wide range of positive effects. For example, seminal large-scale, prospective studies have found that having diverse social connections consistently predicts longevity, even when controlling for demographic factors and health behaviors (e.g., Berkman & Syme, 1979; House, Landis, & Umberson, 1988). In fact, the absence of close personal ties is associated with an increased risk of mortality of approximately the same magnitude as other established risk factors such as obesity and smoking (Berkman & Syme, 1979). Other studies have shown that those who are socially well integrated or have high levels of social support show reduced susceptibility to infection (e.g., Cohen, Doyle, Skoner, Rabin, & Gwaltney, 1997),

attenuated rates of cardiovascular disease progression (e.g., Lett et al., 2005), and slower cognitive declines with aging (e.g., Seeman, Lusignolo, Albert, & Berkman, 2001). This research demonstrates a clear association between social ties and positive health outcomes; however, the complex mechanisms through which these effects occur are less understood and are only beginning to be delineated.

Increasing evidence suggests that certain biological processes may play a key role in linking positive social relationships to salubrious health outcomes. In this chapter, we review the research that connects the presence of strong, supportive social ties to positive physiological functioning, with an underlying emphasis on the implications for health and disease. After providing a biological overview of stress and physiological reactivity, we will review cross-sectional and prospective studies that demonstrate high levels of social integration and/or social support are associated with positive biological profiles (e.g., lower levels of neuroendocrine activity, better functioning of the immune system), whereas social isolation and loneliness can have detrimental effects on these parameters. We will then discuss evidence for the stress-buffering hypothesis; social support exerts beneficial effects via a downregulation of stress responses. Finally, we will review the emerging animal and human research that suggests oxytocin and endogenous opioids may underlie some of these physiological and health effects.

Stress-Responsive Systems

Stressful situations are capable of eliciting physiological changes that—if experienced persistently—could have implications for disease. Acute stressors can activate the sympathetic nervous system (SNS), which elicits elevations in heart rate, blood pressure, and secretion of the catecholamines epinephrine and norepinephrine. In response to certain stressful conditions, the hypothalamic-pituitary-adrenal (HPA) axis can also become activated, leading to the release of the hormone cortisol. This integrated pattern of sympathetic and HPA activation is thought to be important in the short term, as it modulates a wide range of somatic functions that may be needed for appropriate responses to stressors (e.g., changes in metabolic activity; for review, see Lovallo, 1997).

However, prolonged activation of the stress-responsive systems can take its toll on the body. Chronic or repeated exposure to stressors—and the resulting exposure to stress hormones—has been associated with a range of negative outcomes, including suppression of certain components of the immune system (e.g., decreased lymphocyte proliferation), damage to hippocampal neurons, and increases in depressive symptomology (e.g., Heim & Nemeroff, 1999; Sapolsky, Romero, & Munck, 2000). Elevated levels of SNS and HPA hormones have been linked with pathophysiological parameters (e.g., high blood pressure, elevated cholesterol levels, greater waist-to-hip ratios), which are risk factors for numerous serious and chronic health conditions (e.g., cardiovascular disease, diabetes; see McEwen & Seeman, 2003, for review). Additionally, there has been growing attention to the role that inflammatory markers may play in linking stressors and health; proinflammatory cytokines can be activated by certain stressful situations (e.g., Segerstrom & Miller, 2004), and elevations in these parameters have been linked with increased mortality risk (Reuben et al., 2002) and the incidence and progression of disease (e.g., Black, 2003).

It follows, then, that psychosocial factors that influence these stress-responsive systems could ultimately influence health outcomes. In particular, social support could be linked with positive health outcomes through alterations in SNS, HPA, and inflammatory activity (as well as modulation of other physiological processes). These alterations could occur in two ways: Social support could directly affect basal or resting levels of these parameters, or it may alter physiological reactivity to or recovery from stressful situations. We review the evidence for these hypotheses below.

Social Connections, Physiological Functioning, and Health

A growing body of research suggests that the quantity and quality of social connections are associated with markers of physiological regulation. Measures of social support have been related to basal levels of cardiovascular activity; for example, a meta-analysis of 21 correlational studies found a small but reliable association between higher levels of social support and lower resting blood pressure levels (Uchino, Cacioppo, & Kiecolt-Glaser, 1996). Community-based population studies have found links between higher levels of social support and lower resting heart rate, cholesterol, blood pressure, norepinephrine levels and markers of systemic inflammation (e.g., Bland, Krogh, Winkelstein, & Trevisan, 1991; Loucks, Berkman, Gruenewald, & Seeman, 2006; Seeman, Berkman, Blazer, & Rowe, 1994; Thomas, Goodwin, & Goodwin, 1985; Unden, Orth-Gomer, & Elofsson, 1991). These relationships persisted even when controlling for health behaviors, chronic health problems, and current physical health.

Other work has looked at the effect of social relationships on immunologic parameters. Inadequate levels of social support and feelings of loneliness have been associated with poorer immune outcomes (e.g., lower levels of natural killer cell activity; Kiecolt-Glaser, Speicher, Holliday, & Glaser, 1984; Kiecolt-Glaser et al., 1984). In contrast, social support has been shown to have a positive influence on functional immune parameters (e.g., blastogenic response to antigen; Uchino et al., 1996). For example, Glaser, Kiecolt-Glaser, Bonneau, Malarkey, and Hughes (1992) examined medical students' responses to a series of hepatitis B inoculations and found that the students reporting greater levels of social support had stronger immune responses to the vaccine. This suggests the individuals with impoverished social support networks could have a delayed antibody response to pathogens, which could put them at risk for illness (Kiecolt-Glaser, 1999).

Cohen and colleagues (1997) showed that individuals with fewer social network ties were more susceptible to the common cold than individuals with more diverse social connections. Furthermore, as the number of social network ties increased, the quantity of viral replications and severity of objective and self-reported symptoms decreased. However, chronic interpersonal stressors also predicted developing a cold (Cohen et al., 1998), suggesting that social ties are beneficial to the extent that they are not conflict ridden. Therefore, while diverse social ties appear to be beneficial in warding off infection, conflicted relationships can have detrimental effects on acute illness incidence.

Social Connections and Reactivity to Stressors

The literature reviewed here illustrates that supportive, diverse ties are associated with superior physiological and health outcomes, whereas social isolation, loneliness, and conflict are associated with more negative health profiles. Other research has examined the stress reactivity hypothesis, which proposes that social relationships enhance health by attenuating physiological responses to stressors.

Social Support and Physiological Reactivity

In a typical laboratory stressor reactivity study, participants are randomly assigned to undergo an acute laboratory stress task (e.g., mental arithmetic, public speaking), either alone or in the presence of a friend or supportive audience. Across a number of studies, participants receiving social support have shown reduced cardiovascular responses to the stressor (Christenfeld et al., 1997; Edens, Larkin, & Abel, 1992; Gerin, Pieper, Levy, & Pickering, 1992; Kamarck, Annunziato, & Amateau, 1995; Kamarck, Manuck, & Jennings, 1990), although some findings are mixed (Allen, Blascovich, Tomaka, & Kelsey, 1991; Christian & Stoney, 2006; Sheffield & Carroll, 1994). A number of studies have been conducted to delineate under what conditions and for whom social support during a stressor may be beneficial.

Social support has been operationalized in many ways in the stress reactivity literature, which could contribute to some of the inconsistent findings. Lepore (1998) provided a useful taxonomy, classifying the studies into "active" and "passive" support paradigms. Active social support involves receiving unambiguous emotional support from a confederate or a friend. Participants who received active support while undergoing an acute stressor typically show an attenuated cardiovascular response compared to those in an alone condition (e.g., Christenfeld et al., 1997; Gerin et al., 1992; Lepore, 1995; Lepore, Allen, & Evans, 1993; Thorsteinsson, James, & Gregg, 1998).

Passive support is defined as the mere presence of a friend or stranger; support is implied by propinquity. While the presence of a friend is assumed to be beneficial, fears of negative evaluation could interfere with support effects (Allen et al., 1991; Lepore, 1998). This was illustrated by a study in which participants performed mental arithmetic alone or in the presence of a close friend (Kors, Linden, & Gerin, 1997). The friend could either monitor the performance (high evaluation) or not (low evaluation). Having a friend present attenuated cardiovascular responses only in the low evaluation condition; evaluation apprehension appeared to counter the benefits of support. The mere presence of a friend (Edens et al., 1992; Kamarck et al., 1990, 1995) or stranger (Fontana, Diegnan, Villeneuve, & Lepore, 1999) effectively buffered cardiovascular reactivity relative to the condition in which the threat of evaluation was removed.

Other studies have shown that the supportive partner does not need to be physically present in order to reduce cardiovascular responses to stressors. Simply thinking about a close friend prior to a stressor can reduce systolic blood pressure responses, in comparison to those who recall an acquaintance before the task (Ratnasignam & Bishop, 2007; Smith, Ruiz, & Uchino, 2004). This suggests that activating mental representations of social support may be sufficient to reduce cardiovascular reactivity to stressors.

Compared to research on cardiovascular reactivity, fewer studies have examined the effects on social support and cortisol responses to stressful situations. However, an emerging literature suggests that social support could dampen HPA responses to acute stressors as well. For example, individuals who had frequent interactions with supportive others during a 10-day period showed reduced cortisol responses to a subsequent laboratory stressor (Eisenberger, Taylor, Gable, Hilmert, & Lieberman, 2007). Other studies have experimentally manipulated social support in the context of a laboratory stressor. Those who received video-relayed emotional support had reductions in cortisol levels and heart rate during a cognitive challenge compared to a no-support condition (Thorsteinsson et al., 1998). Several studies have found that men who were supported by their romantic partners or friends show attenuated cortisol responses to a speech/math stressor compared to no-support conditions (Heinrichs, Baumgartner, Kirschbaum, & Ehlert, 2003; Kirschbaum, Klauer, Filipp, & Hellhammer, 1995). However, studies have demonstrated that the relationship between social support and cortisol reactivity can vary by factors such as gender (Kirschbaum et al., 1995) and culture (Taylor, Welch, Kim, & Sherman, 2007). Taken together, these studies suggest that while social support can generally exert beneficial effects via dampened cortisol reactivity to stressors, this effect can hinge on several factors, including individual characteristics of the support provider and recipient.

While social support during an acute stressor can buffer cardiovascular and neuroendocrine responses, social conflict or antagonistic exchanges can elicit and/or potentiate reactivity. For example, cardiovascular reactivity is heightened when others present act in nonsupportive ways (e.g., conveying boredom/disinterest, directly disagreeing or undermining the participant; Gerin et al., 1992; Lepore et al., 1993; Sheffield & Carroll, 1994). Other research has demonstrated that social evaluation and rejection are capable of eliciting pronounced increases in cortisol. In a meta-analytic review, Dickerson and Kemeny (2004) found that stressors characterized by social-evaluative threat (e.g., presence of an evaluative audience) were associated with greater cortisol responses and delayed times to recovery compared to those without this element. Subsequent empirical studies have corroborated this meta-analytic finding (Dickerson, Mycek, & Zaldivar, 2008; Gruenewald, Kemeny, Aziz, & Fahey, 2004). Other work has shown that couples displaying negative behaviors (e.g., criticism, put-downs) during a discussion of a marital issue had greater sympathetic and HPA responses and decreases in immune functioning compared to those who did not show this negative behavioral pattern (for review, see Kiecolt-Glaser, 1999). Taken together, these studies demonstrate that nonsupportive or antagonistic interactions can elicit and/or exaggerate SNS, HPA, and immune reactivity to an acute stressor, whereas social support can often attenuate the response.

While the majority of the research on social support and physiological reactivity has been conducted in the laboratory, some studies have addressed this question in daily life. Using ambulatory monitoring,

individuals with high levels of social support or who have interactions with close others have shown healthier cardiovascular profiles (e.g., less total peripheral resistance and higher cardiac output, lower blood pressure) compared to lonely individuals or those without strong social connections (e.g., Hawkley, Burleson, & Cacioppo, 2003; Holt-Lunstad, Uchino, Smith, Olson-Cerny, & Nealy-Moore, 2003). Others have shown that high levels of social support can buffer cardiovascular reactivity to negative emotional states in daily life (Ong & Allaire, 2005). Although more research is needed, these promising findings suggest that the association between social support and positive physiological responses often observed in the laboratory may be generalizable to naturally occurring situations.

Individual Differences, Social Support, and Reactivity

Certain individuals may not derive the same physiological benefits from social support as others; gender, personality, or other factors that could shape one's appraisals of, and responses to, support attempts. Therefore, these individual differences may influence subsequent physiological responses. For example, hostility is characterized by negative beliefs about others, including cynicism, mistrust, and denigration, which could prevent highly hostile individuals from utilizing social support in a beneficial way. Lepore (1995) tested this hypothesis by randomly assigning participants scoring high and low on cynicism to deliver a speech alone or with a supportive confederate. Social support buffered cardiovascular reactivity for the low—but not high—cynicism participants. Others have found similar interactions between social support and hostility (e.g., Chen, Gilligan, Coups, & Contrada, 2005). Failure to effectively utilize social support under stressful situations could be one mechanism through which hostility could lead to the increased risk of cardiovascular disease.

Interestingly, many studies have reported interactions between gender, social support, and physiological reactivity. For example, the presence of a supportive male partner under stress can elicit "exaggerated" cardiovascular and cortisol reactivity in women (e.g., Glynn, Christenfeld, & Gerin, 1999; Kirschbaum et al., 1995; Sheffield & Carroll, 1994), which contrasts the pattern of attenuated reactivity often observed for men. Women also appear to be more physiologically responsive to negative marital interactions (e.g., Kiecolt-Glaser, 1999). This pattern of gender differences is particularly intriguing in light of epidemiological studies that show the health-protective effects of social ties are stronger in men than in women (e.g., House et al., 1988). Women typically are more emotionally responsive to conflict and report more negative interactions within relationships (Schuster, Kessler, & Aseltine, 1990). Thus, women might not manifest the same benefits from social relationships because they are more vulnerable to negative social interactions (for review of gender differences and social support, see Taylor et al., 2000).

Taken together, these findings argue against a philosophy that social support is universally beneficial; instead, they suggest a more nuanced perspective. Although social support can buffer physiological stress responses, it does not appear to do so for everyone all the time. Further research examining characteristics of the social support provider and recipient in the context of stress reactivity is clearly warranted.

Additionally, positive social relationships may be particularly important during certain stages of development. Neonatal, infant, and early child development periods are critical windows of time during which social interaction can affect later social behavior and physiology (for review, see Cushing & Kramer, 2005; Repetti, Taylor, & Seeman, 2002). Negative interaction and/or the absence of positive interaction in early development can lead to adverse physiological and behavioral outcomes in humans and animals. Reciprocally, positive social contact and relationships during early postnatal periods in mammals (e.g., nursing, handling, grooming) can have beneficial effects. For example, when rat pups are repeatedly separated from their mothers, they show increased stress vulnerability in adulthood (e.g., increased HPA responses to novel stimuli; Francis, Caldji, Champagne, Plotsky, & Meaney, 1999). Future research should continue to investigate the developmental trajectory of the stress-responsive system and how this can be modulated by social processes.

Physiological Substrates of Affiliative Behavior: Oxytocin and Endogenous Opioids

As already reviewed, the presence of social support has been linked to attenuated physiological stress responses. Accumulating evidence highlights the important function that oxytocin, endogenous opioids, and other neuropeptides may play in understanding the biological mechanisms underlying social support processes. Specifically, a growing body of primarily animal research demonstrates

that oxytocin and endogenous opioids are implicated in the development and maintenance of social bonds, and can attenuate physiological responses under stress. Therefore, these physiological substrates could play a key role in elucidating the complex associations between social support, physiology, and health (see Taylor et al., 2000; Taylor, Dickerson, & Klein, 2002, for review).

Research has demonstrated that oxytocin is associated with many social processes in animals; for example, oxytocin can facilitate social affiliation, parental nurturing behaviors, and the formation of selective mother–infant bonds (for reviews, see Bartz & Hollander, 2006; Carter et al., 2006). There is also evidence that oxytocin can influence stress-regulatory responses. For example, intranasally administered oxytocin in female squirrel monkeys led to reduced adrenocorticotropin hormone (ACTH) responses to an isolation stressor compared to monkeys that received saline (Parker, Buckmaster, Schatzberg, & Lyons, 2005). In another study, newborn rats exposed to higher levels of oxytocin subsequently had lower HPA reactivity in adulthood (Holst, Petersson, & Uvnäs-Moberg, 2002).

Methodological restrictions have limited oxytocin research in humans, but the accumulating evidence complements the findings from the animal literature, demonstrating that oxytocin also attenuates the stress response and is associated with increased social affiliation. One line of research has shown that oxytocin is associated with prosocial emotions (Carter, 1998). For example, intranasally administered oxytocin leads to substantial increases in trust in humans (Kosfeld, Heinrichs, Zak, Fischbacher, & Fehr, 2005), and oxytocin released in response to breastfeeding has been associated with subsequent calmness (Heinrichs, Neumann, & Ehlert, 2002; Nissen, Gustavsson, Widström, & Uvnäs-Moberg, 1998).

Oxytocin has also been associated with stress buffering and anxiolytic effects in humans, particularly when coupled with social support (Heinrichs et al., 2003). In a placebo-controlled, double-blind experiment, participants who received both intranasally administered oxytocin and social support showed lower cortisol and anxiety and increased calmness after an acute psychosocial stressor in the laboratory compared to other participants (Henrichs et al., 2003). In a study of 38 cohabitating couples, greater reported partner support was related to higher plasma oxytocin in men and women in the lab (before and after 10 min of warm contact; Grewen, Girdler, Amico, & Light, 2005).

Additionally, higher oxytocin in women was linked to lower systolic blood pressure during rest after warm contact in lab. Together, these findings suggest that oxytocin may have protective effects on SNS and HPA activity, particularly in a social context.

Endogenous opioids are also implicated in social behaviors and the regulation of the physiological stress response (for review, see Nelson & Panksepp, 1998). Evidence has emerged in both animal and human studies, which demonstrate that opioids are released in response to social contact, and act as reward for social affiliation and aid in social learning (Nelson & Panksepp, 1998; Ribeiro, Kennedy, Smith, Stohler, & Zubieta, 2005). Additionally, opioids can attenuate SNS and HPA responses to stressors in both animal and human models. For example, McCubbin (1993) demonstrated that administration of an opioid antagonist to human subjects prior to a laboratory stressor resulted in increased blood pressure, heart rate, and cortisol responses, compared to those given a placebo injection; this suggests that opioids could play an important role in the downregulation of stress responses.

In summary, research on the role oxytocin and endogenous opioids play in social affiliation has been traditionally confined to animal models but more recently has been examined in humans as well. Evidence from both lines of research demonstrate that oxytocin and endogenous opioids are released in response to social bonding activities and are associated with attenuated physiological stress responses and reductions in anxiety and anxiety-like behaviors in animals and humans. These stress-buffering physiological effects may have longer-term beneficial health implications, and the positive psychological effects may also serve to increase motivation to seek out social contact and support.

Conclusions

There is a wealth of evidence supporting a link between social relationships and health. Across a wide variety of studies, social support and social integration have been associated with positive physiological outcomes, including dampened SNS and HPA activity and increased immune functioning, whereas deficient social relationships or social conflict have been linked with more negative biological profiles. How the body responds to stressful situations appears to be a key factor in understanding the links between social connections and health. Dampening the physiological stress response could be an important pathway through which social

support could promote positive health outcomes. Recent evidence suggests that this could be in part biologically mediated through oxytocin and endogenous opioids. Ongoing research is continuing to delineate these complex and important processes. Further elucidating the pathways through which social support could influence health outcomes could then be used to develop theoretically sound interventions to optimize physiological functioning and health.

Key Questions

1. Different mechanisms linking social support and health are being further delineated; how can we best incorporate research from these various fields (e.g., neuroscience, physiology, psychology) into an integrative model?

2. Are there specific windows during development and/or certain life-span transitions that are particularly salient for understanding how social support can influence health trajectories?

3. How do characteristics of the support provider influence the relationship between social support and health?

References

Allen, K. M., Blascovich, J., Tomaka, J., & Kelsey, R. M. (1991). Presence of human friends and pet dogs as moderators of autonomic responses to stress in women. *Journal of Personality and Social Psychology, 61*, 582–589.

Bartz, J. A., & Hollander, E. (2006). The neuroscience of affiliation: Forging links between basic and clinical research on neuropeptides and social behavior. *Hormones and Behavior, 50*, 518–528.

Berkman, L. F., & Syme, S. L. (1979). Social networks, host resistance, and mortality: A nine-year follow-up study of Alameda County residents. *American Journal of Epidemiology, 109*, 186–204.

Black, P. H. (2003). The inflammatory response is an integral part of the stress response: Implications for atherosclerosis, insulin resistance, type II diabetes and metabolic syndrome X. *Brain Behavior and Immunity, 17*(5), 350–364.

Bland, S. H., Krogh, V., Winkelstein, W., & Trevisan, M. (1991). Social network and blood pressure: A population study. *Psychosomatic Medicine, 53*, 598–607.

Carter, C. S. (1998). Neuroendocrine perspectives on social attachment and love. *Psychoneuroendocrinology, 23*, 779–818.

Carter, C. S., Pournajafi-Nazarloo, H., Kramer, K. M., Ziegler, T. E., White-Traut, R., Bello, D., et al. (2006). Oxytocin: Behavioral associations and potential as a salivary biomarker. *Annals of the New York Academy of Sciences, 1098*, 312–322.

Chen, Y. Y., Gilligan, S., Coups, E. J., & Contrada, R. J. (2005). Hostility and perceived social support: Interactive effects on cardiovascular reactivity to laboratory stressors. *Annals of Behavioral Medicine, 29*, 37–43.

Christenfeld, N., Gerin, W., Linden, W., Sanders, M., Mathur, J., Deich, J. D., et al. (1997). Social support effects on cardiovascular reactivity: Is a stranger as effective as a friend? *Psychosomatic Medicine, 59*, 388–398.

Christian, L. M., & Stoney, C. M. (2006). Social support versus social evaluation: Unique effects on vascular and myocardial response patterns. *Psychosomatic Medicine, 68*, 914–921.

Cohen, S., Doyle, W. J., Skoner, D. P., Rabin, B. S., & Gwaltney, J. M. (1997). Social ties and susceptibility to the common cold. *JAMA, 277*, 1940–1944.

Cohen, S., Frank, E., Doyle, W. J., Skoner, D. P., Rabin, B. S., & Gwaltney, J. M. (1998). Types of stressors that increase susceptibility to the common cold in healthy adults. *Health Psychology, 17*, 214–223.

Cushing, B. S., & Kramer, K. M. (2005). Mechanisms underlying epigenetic effects of early social experience: The role of neuropeptides and steroids. *Neuroscience and Biobehavioral Reviews, 29*, 1089–1105.

Dickerson, S. S., & Kemeny, M. E. (2004). Acute stressors and cortisol responses: A theoretical integration and synthesis of laboratory research. *Psychological Bulletin, 130*(3), 355–391.

Dickerson, S. S., Mycek, P. J., & Zaldivar, F. (2008). Negative social evaluation—but not mere social presence—elicits cortisol responses in the laboratory. *Health Psychology, 27*(1), 116–121.

Edens, J., Larkin, K. T., & Abel, J. L. (1992). The effect of social support and physical touch on cardiovascular reactions to mental stress. *Journal of Psychosomatic Research, 36*, 371–382.

Eisenberger, N. I., Taylor, S. E., Gable, S. L., Hilmert, C. J., & Lieberman, M. D. (2007). Neural pathways link social support to attenuated neuroendocrine stress responses. *NeuroImage, 35*, 1601–1612.

Fontana, A. M., Diegnan, T., Villeneuve, A., & Lepore, S. J. (1999). Nonevaluative social support reduces cardiovascular reactivity in young women during acutely stressful performance situations. *Journal of Behavioral Medicine, 22*, 75–91.

Francis, D. D., Caldji, C., Champagne, F., Plotsky, P. M., & Meaney, M. J. (1999). The role of corticotrophin-releasing factor–norepinephrine systems in mediating the effects of early experience on the development of behavioral and endocrine responses to stress. *Biological Psychiatry, 46*, 1153–1166.

Gerin, W., Pieper, C., Levy, R., & Pickering, T. G. (1992). Social support in social interaction: A moderator of cardiovascular reactivity. *Psychosomatic Medicine, 54*, 324–336.

Glaser, R., Kiecolt-Glaser, J. K., Bonneau, R., Malarkey, W., & Hughes, J. (1992). Stress-induced modulation of the immune response to recombinant hepatitis B vaccine. *Psychosomatic Medicine, 54*, 22–29.

Glynn, L. M., Christenfeld, N., & Gerin, W. (1999). Gender, social support, and cardiovascular responses to stress. *Psychosomatic Medicine, 61*, 234–242.

Grewen, K. M., Girdler, S. S., Amico, J., & Light, K. C. (2005). Effects of partner support on resting oxytocin, cortisol, norepinephrine, and blood pressure before and after warm partner contact. *Psychosomatic Medicine, 67*, 531–538.

Gruenewald, T. L., Kemeny, M. E., Aziz, N., & Fahey, J. L. (2004). Acute threat to the social self: Shame, social self-esteem, and cortisol activity. *Psychosomatic Medicine, 66*, 915–924.

Hawkley, L. C., Burleson, M. H., & Cacioppo, J. T. (2003). Loneliness in everyday life: Cardiovascular activity, psychosocial context, and health behaviors. *Journal of Personality and Social Psychology, 85*, 105–120.

Heinrichs, M., Baumgartner, T., Kirschbaum, C., & Ehlert, U. (2003). Social support and oxytocin interact to suppress cortisol and subjective responses to psychosocial stress. *Biological Psychiatry, 54*, 1389–1398.

Heinrichs, M., Neumann, I., & Ehlert, U. (2002). Lactation and stress: Protective effects of breast-feeding in humans. *Stress, 5*, 195–203.

Heim, C., & Nemeroff, C. B. (1999). The impact of early adverse experiences on brain systems involved in the pathophysiology of anxiety and affective disorders. *Biological Psychiatry, 46*, 1509–1522.

Holst, S., Petersson, K., & Uvnäs-Moberg, M. (2002). Postnatal oxytocin treatment and postnatal stroking of rats reduce blood pressure in adulthood. *Autonomic Neuroscience, 99*, 85–90.

Holt-Lunstad, J., Uchino, B. N., Smith, T. W., Olson-Cerny, C., & Nealy-Moore, J. B. (2003). Social relationships and ambulatory blood pressure: Structural and qualitative predictors of cardiovascular function during everyday social interactions. *Health Psychology, 22*, 388–397.

House, J. S., Landis, K. R., & Umberson, D. (1988). Social relationships and health. *Science, 241*, 540–545.

Kamarck, T. W., Annunziato, B., & Amateau, L. M. (1995). Affiliation moderates the effects of social threat on stress-related cardiovascular responses: Boundary conditions for a laboratory model of social support. *Psychosomatic Medicine, 57*, 183–194.

Kamarck, T. W., Manuck, S. B., & Jennings, R. (1990). Social support reduces cardiovascular reactivity to psychological challenge: A laboratory model. *Psychosomatic Medicine, 52*, 42–58.

Kiecolt-Glaser, J. K. (1999). Stress, personal relationships, and immune function: Health implications. *Brain, Behavior and Immunity, 13*, 61–72.

Kiecolt-Glaser, J. K., Garner, W., Speicher, C., Penn, G. M., Holliday, J., & Glaser, R. (1984). Psychosocial modifiers of immunocompetence in medical students. *Psychosomatic Medicine, 46*, 7–14.

Kiecolt-Glaser, J. K., Speicher, C. E., Holliday, J. E., & Glaser, R. (1984). Stress and the transformation of lymphocytes by Epstein–Barr virus. *Journal of Behavioral Medicine, 7*, 1–12.

Kirschbaum, C., Klauer, T., Filipp, S. H., & Hellhammer, D. H. (1995). Sex-specific effects of social support on cortisol and subjective responses to acute psychological stress. *Psychosomatic Medicine, 57*, 23–31.

Kors, D. J., Linden, W., & Gerin, W. (1997). Evaluation interferes with social support: Effects on cardiovascular stress reactivity in women. *Journal of Social and Clinical Psychology, 16*, 1–23.

Kosfeld, M., Heinrichs, M., Zak, P. J., Fischbacher, U., & Fehr, E. (2005). Oxytocin increases trust in humans. *Nature, 435*, 673–676.

Lepore, S. J. (1995). Cynicism, social support, and cardiovascular reactivity. *Health Psychology, 14*, 210–216.

Lepore, S. J. (1998). Problems and prospects for the social support-reactivity hypothesis. *Annals of Behavioral Medicine, 20*, 257–269.

Lepore, S. J., Allen, K. A., & Evans, G. W. (1993). Social support lowers cardiovascular reactivity to an acute stressor. *Psychosomatic Medicine, 55*, 518–524.

Lett, H. S., Blumenthal, J. A., Babyak, M. A., Strauman, T. J., Robins, C., & Sherwood, A. (2005). Social support and coronary heart disease: Epidemiological evidence and implications for treatment. *Psychosomatic Medicine, 67*, 869–878.

Loucks, E. B., Berkman, L. F., Gruenewald, T. L., & Seeman, T. E. (2006). Relation of social integration to inflammatory marker concentrations in men and women 70 to 90 years. *American Journal of Cardiology, 97,* 1010–1016.

Lovallo, W. R. (1997). *Stress & health: Biological and psychological interactions.* Thousand Oaks, CA: Sage.

McCubbin, J. (1993). Stress and endogenous opioids: Behavioral and circulatory interactions. *Biological Psychology, 35,* 91–122.

McEwen, B. S., & Seeman, T. (2003). Stress and affect: Applicability of the concepts of allostasis and allostatic load. In R. J. Davidson, K. R. Scherer, & H. H. Goldsmith (Eds.), *Handbook of affective sciences* (pp. 1117–1138). Oxford: Oxford University Press.

Nelson, E. E., & Panksepp, J. (1998). Brain substrates of infant–mother attachment: Contributions of opioids, oxytocin, and norepinephrine. *Neuroscience and Biobehavioral Reviews, 22,* 437–452.

Nissen, E., Gustavsson, P., Widström, A., & Uvnäs-Moberg, K. (1998). Oxytocin, prolactin, milk production and their relationship with personality traits in women after vaginal delivery or Cesarean section. *Journal of Psychosomatic Obstetrics and Gynecology, 19,* 49–58.

Ong, A. D., & Allaire, J. C. (2005). Cardiovascular intraindividual variability in later life: The influence of social connectedness and positive emotions. *Psychology and Aging, 20,* 476–485.

Parker, K. J., Buckmaster, C. L., Schatzberg, A. F., & Lyons, D. M. (2005). Intranasal oxytocin administration attenuates the ACTH stress response in monkeys. *Psychoneuroendocrinology, 30,* 924–929.

Ratnasignam, P., & Bishop, G. D. (2007). Social support schemas, trait anger, and cardiovascular responses. *International Journal of Psychophysiology, 63,* 308–316.

Repetti, R. L., Taylor, S. E., & Seeman, T. (2002). Risky families: Family social environments and the mental and physical health of offspring. *Psychological Bulletin, 182,* 330–366.

Reuben, D. B., Chen, A. I., Harris, T. B., Ferrucci, L., Rowe, J. W., Tracy, R. P., et al. (2002). Peripheral blood markers of inflammation predict mortality and functional decline in high-functioning community-dwelling older persons. *Journal of the American Geriatrics Society, 50,* 638–644.

Ribeiro, S. C., Kennedy, S. E., Smith, Y. R., Stohler, C. S., & Zubieta, J. K. (2005). Interface of physical and emotional stress regulation through the endogenous opioid system and mu-opioid receptors. *Progress in Neuro-psychopharmacology and Biological Psychiatry, 29,* 1264–1280.

Sapolsky, R. M., Romero, L. M., & Munck, A. U. (2000). How do glucocorticoids influence stress responses? Integrating permissive, suppressive, stimulatory, and preparative actions. *Endocrine Reviews, 21,* 55–89.

Schuster, T. L., Kessler, R. C., & Aseltine, R. H. (1990). Supportive interactions, negative interactions and depressed mood. *American Journal of Community Psychology, 18,* 423–438.

Seeman, T. E., Berkman, L. F., Blazer, D., & Rowe, J. W. (1994). Social ties and support and neuroendocrine function. MacArthur studies of successful aging. *Annals of Behavioral Medicine, 16,* 95–106.

Seeman, T. E., Lusignolo, T. M., Albert, M., & Berkman, L. (2001). Social relationships, social support, and patterns of cognitive aging in healthy, high-functioning older adults: MacArthur studies of successful aging. *Health Psychology, 20*(4), 243–255.

Segerstrom, S. C., & Miller, G. E. (2004). Psychological stress and the human immune system: A meta-analytic study of 30 years of inquiry. *Psychological Bulletin, 130*(4), 601–630.

Sheffield, D., & Carroll, D. (1994). Social support and cardiovascular reactions to active laboratory stressors. *Psychology and Health, 9,* 305–316.

Smith, T. W., Ruiz, J. M., & Uchino, B. N. (2004). Mental activation of supportive ties, hostility, and cardiovascular reactivity to laboratory stress in young men and women. *Health Psychology, 23,* 476–485.

Taylor, S. E., Dickerson, S. S., & Klein, L. C. (2002). Toward a biology of social support. In C. R. Snyder & S. J. Lopez (Eds.), *The handbook of positive psychology* (pp. 556–569). New York: Oxford University Press.

Taylor, S. E., Klein, L. C., Lewis, B. P., Gruenewald, T. L., Gurung, R. A. R., & Updegraff, J. A. (2000). Biobehavioral responses to stress in females: Tend-and-befriend, not fight-or-flight. *Psychological Review, 107,* 411–429.

Taylor, S. E., Welch, W. T., Kim, H. S., & Sherman, D. K. (2007). Cultural differences in the impact of social support on psychological and biological stress responses. *Psychological Science, 18,* 831–837.

Thomas, P. D., Goodwin, J. M., & Goodwin, J. S. (1985). Effect of social support on stress-related changes in cholesterol level, uric acid level, and immune function in an elderly sample. *American Journal of Psychiatry, 142,* 735–737.

Thorsteinsson, E. B., James, J. E., & Gregg, M. E. (1998). Effects of video-relayed social support on hemodynamic reactivity and salivary cortisol during laboratory-based behavioral challenge. *Health Psychology, 17,* 436–444.

Uchino, B. N., Cacioppo, J. T., & Kiecolt-Glaser, J. K. (1996). The relationship between social support and physiological processes: A review with emphasis on underlying mechanisms and implications for health. *Psychological Bulletin, 119,* 488–531.

Unden, A. L., Orth-Gomer, K., & Elofsson, S. (1991). Cardiovascular effects of social support in the work place: Twenty-four hour ECG monitoring of men and women. *Psychosomatic Medicine, 53,* 50–60.

The Central Role of the Heart in Generating and Sustaining Positive Emotions

Rollin McCraty *and* Robert A. Rees

Abstract

Scientific research has established a significant, complex, and highly sophisticated connection between the human heart and brain. The heart directly influences the activity of higher brain centers involved in perceptual and cognitive processing and in the creation of emotional experience. An important tool that provides a window into the activity occurring between the heart and brain is heart rate variability (HRV), an analytic tool that measures the beat-to-beat changes in heart rate. HRV is generated largely by interaction between the heart and brain via the neural signals flowing through the afferent (ascending) and efferent (descending) pathways of the sympathetic and parasympathetic branches of the autonomic nervous system (ANS).

Research has shown that sustained positive emotions facilitate an emergent global shift in psychophysiological functioning, which is marked by a distinct change in the rhythm of heart activity. This global shift generates a state of optimal functioning, characterized by increased synchronization, harmony, and efficiency in the interactions within and among the physiological, cognitive, and emotional systems. This state is called psychophysiological coherence. As people experience sincere positive feelings, the more ordered information flowing from the heart to the brain acts to facilitate cortical function and improve cognitive performance. These findings may help explain the significant shifts in perception, increased mental clarity, and heightened intuitive awareness many individuals report when practicing heart-centered, positive emotion–refocusing and restructuring techniques.

Keywords: brain, coherence, emotion, heart, HRV

Throughout history, philosophers, poets, and prophets, as well as ordinary people, have associated the heart with positive emotions. In *The Epic of Gilgamesh*, the oldest recorded human story, the heart is seen "as the wellspring of our human emotions" (Godwin, 2001). In most early civilizations, the heart was considered the seat of happiness, joy, ecstasy, and similar emotions (Godwin, 2001; Young, 2003). Only recently has science begun unweaving the mystery of the heart and decoding its many functions beyond pumping blood, including its functional role in generating emotional states, especially positive emotions.

Recent years have seen the emergence of a new understanding of how the brain functions and how the heart and brain interact in a dynamic and complex relationship. Rather than assembling thoughts and feelings from bits of data like a digital computer, the brain is an analog processor that relates whole concepts or patterns to one another and looks for similarities and differences, and relationships between them (Ratey, 2001). This way of understanding brain processes has challenged long-held views of how emotions are generated (LeDoux, 1996). Psychologists once maintained that emotions were purely mental expressions generated by the brain alone. We now know that emotions have as much to do with the body as they do with the brain. A current view widely held among neuroscientists and psychophysiologists is that the emergence of emotional experience results from the ongoing interactions between the brain, the body, and the external environment (Damasio, 2003; Pribram & Melges, 1969). In this chapter, we focus on the key role of the heart in emotional experience and how heart-focused, positive-emotion refocusing techniques can be used to both transform negative emotions in the moment and facilitate an enduring positive change in attitudes and affect.

The Physiology of Positive Emotions

Research at the Institute of HeartMath on how psychophysiological patterns change during stress and various emotional states consistently has found that the rhythmic beating patterns of the heart are reflective of changes in emotional states and that they covary with emotions in real time. Specifically, we examined the natural fluctuations in heart rate, known as heart rate variability (HRV) or heart rhythms. These beat-to-beat changes in heart rate are generated largely by the interaction between the heart and brain via the neural signals flowing through the afferent (ascending) and efferent (descending) pathways of the sympathetic and parasympathetic branches of the autonomic nervous system (ANS). HRV is thus considered a measure of neurocardiac function that reflects heart–brain interactions and ANS dynamics.

Utilizing HRV analysis, we have demonstrated that distinct heart rhythm patterns characterize different emotional states. In general, emotional stress—including emotions such as anger, frustration, and anxiety—leads to heart rhythm patterns that appear incoherent (see Figure 50.1).

Overall, compared to a neutral baseline state, this indicates disorder in the higher-level control systems in the brain and less synchronization in the reciprocal action of the parasympathetic and sympathetic branches of the ANS. This desynchronization in the ANS, if sustained, taxes the nervous system and bodily organs, impeding the efficient synchronization and flow of information throughout the psychophysiological systems. This, in turn, results in cortical inhibition, which impairs cognitive functions and diminishes one's ability to think clearly, discriminate among behavioral choices, and self-regulate emotions (McCraty, Atkinson, Tomasino, & Bradley, 2005; McCraty & Childre, 2004).

In contrast, sustained positive emotions, such as appreciation, compassion, and love, generate a smooth, ordered, sine wave–like pattern in the heart's rhythms. This reflects increased synchronization in higher-level brain systems and in the activity occurring in the two branches of the ANS as well as a shift in autonomic balance toward increased parasympathetic activity. As depicted in Figure 50.1 and also demonstrable by quantitative methods (McCraty et al., 2005; Tiller, McCraty, & Atkinson, 1996), heart rhythms associated with sustained positive emotions are clearly more coherent (autocoherence) than those generated during a neutral or negative emotional experience. During the coherent mode, a harmonious heart rhythm pattern emerges which typically oscillates at around 6 cycles per minute (Figure 50.1; McCraty et al., 2005).

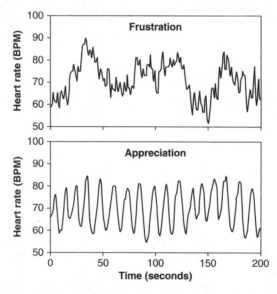

Fig. 50.1 Emotions are reflected in heart rhythm patterns. The heart rhythm pattern shown in the top graph, characterized by its erratic, irregular pattern (incoherence), is typical of negative emotions such as anger or frustration. The bottom graph shows an example of the coherent heart rhythm pattern typically observed when an individual is experiencing sustained, modulated positive emotions.

Further research has revealed that these associations hold true in studies conducted in both laboratory and natural settings and for both spontaneous emotions and intentionally generated feelings (Rein, Atkinson, & McCraty, 1995; Tiller et al., 1996). Importantly, although heart rate and the amount of HRV can covary with emotional changes, we have found that it is the "pattern" of the heart's rhythm that is primarily reflective of the emotional state. Thus, it is the rhythmic pattern, rather than the rate, that is most directly related to emotional dynamics and physiological synchronization, that is, a state in which the body's various functions operate harmoniously in relation to one another (McCraty et al., 2005).

Psychophysiological Coherence and Positive Emotional States

Taking this research further, we observed that when positive states are maintained, through the intentional generation of positive emotions, coherent heart rhythm patterns can be sustained for longer periods, which lead to increased synchronization and entrainment between the heart's rhythm and the activity of multiple bodily systems. Such synchronization is observed between heart rhythms, respiratory rhythms, and blood pressure oscillations; however, other biological oscillators, including very low frequency brain rhythms, craniosacral rhythms, and electrical potentials measured across the skin, can also become synchronized. The coherent state is characterized by increased synchronization between the activity of the heart and brain. Specifically, we have found that the brain's alpha and beta rhythms, as well as lower frequency brain activity, exhibit increased synchronization with the cardiac cycle during this mode. We have introduced the term "psychophysiological coherence" to describe the distinctive set of positive, emotion-driven physiological correlates that consistently are observed in such states across diverse subject populations (McCraty & Childre, 2004). This coherent state reflects a global state of optimal function, characterized by increased synchronization, harmony, and efficiency in the interactions within and among the physiological, cognitive, and emotional systems.

In terms of physiological functioning, coherence is a highly efficient mode that confers a number of benefits to the system, including (a) resetting of baroreceptor (neurons sensitive to changes in pressure) sensitivity, which is related to improved short-term blood pressure control and increased respiratory efficiency (Lehrer et al., 2003); (b) increased vagal afferent traffic (McCraty et al., 2005), which is involved in the inhibition of pain signals and sympathetic outflow (Foreman, 1994); (c) increased cardiac output in conjunction with increased efficiency in fluid exchange, filtration, and absorption between the capillaries and tissues (Siegel et al., 1984); (d) increased ability of the cardiovascular system to adapt to circulatory requirements (Langhorst, Schulz, & Lambertz, 1984); and (e) increased temporal synchronization of cells throughout the body (Langhorst et al., 1984). Together, these benefits result in increased system-wide energy efficiency, metabolic energy savings, and increased harmony in bodily processes.

Psychologically, the coherence mode is associated with a calm, emotionally balanced, yet alert and responsive state that is conducive to improved cognitive and task performance, including problem solving, decision making, long-term memory, and activities requiring perceptual acuity—attentional focus, coordination, and discrimination (McCraty et al., 2005)—a state similar to that known as "flow." These observations between increased physiological efficiency and positive emotions may provide an important aspect of the mechanism that explains the growing number of documented correlations between positive emotions, increased cognitive flexibility, and creativity (see chaps 24 and 48), broadened thought–action repertoires, increased personal resources (see chap. 3), improved health, and increased longevity (Danner, Snowdon, & Friesen, 2001; Levy, Slade, Kunkel, & Kasl, 2002; Ostir, Markides, Black, & Goodwin, 2000).

The Key Role of the Heart in Emotional Experience

As described previously, our findings suggests a fundamental link between emotions and the "patterns" of both efferent and afferent autonomic activity as well as changes in ANS activation, which are clearly reflected in heart rhythm patterns and therefore play a key role in emotional experience. It is important to emphasize, however, that the heart's rhythmic patterns not only "reflect" an individual's emotional state, they also play a direct role in "determining" emotional experience. At the physiological level, as shown in Figure 50.2, afferent input from the heart is conveyed to a number of subcortical regions of the brain that are involved in emotional processing, including the thalamus, hypothalamus, and amygdala.

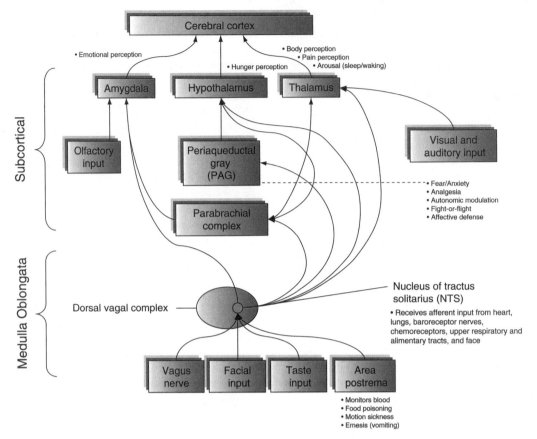

Afferent Pathways

Fig. 50.2 Diagram of the currently known afferent pathways by which information from the heart and cardiovascular system modulates brain activity. Note the direct connections from the NTS to the amygdala, hypothalamus, and thalamus. Although not shown, there is also evidence emerging of a pathway from the dorsal vagal complex that travels directly to the frontal cortex.

Moreover, cardiac afferent input has a significant influence on the activity of these brain centers (Cameron, 2002; Foreman, 1997; Oppenheimer & Hopkins, 1994). For example, activity in the amygdala has been found to be synchronized to the cardiac cycle (Frysinger & Harper, 1990).

These findings and those from our own research led us to ponder the fundamental physiological significance of the covariance between the heart's rhythms and changes in emotion. This question was especially intriguing in light of current views in neuroscience that the contents of feelings are essentially the configurations of bodily states represented in somatosensory maps (Cameron, 2002; Damasio, 2003). As Damasio (2003) states, "The essential content of feeling is the mapping of a particular body state; the substrate of feelings is the set of neural patterns that map the body state and from which a mental image of the body state can emerge"

(p. 88). The essence of this theory of emotion was first proposed by William James (1884).

Pribram's theory of emotion extends the mapping of body states and provides an understanding of how the heart is involved in the processing of emotional experience (Pribram & Melges, 1969). In this theory, the brain is viewed as a complex pattern storage, identification, and matching system. According to Pribram's model, past experience builds within us a set of familiar patterns, which become established in the neural architecture. Inputs to the brain from both the external and internal environments contribute to the maintenance of these patterns. Many processes within the body provide constant rhythmic inputs with which the brain becomes familiar. These include the heart's rhythmic activity; digestive, respiratory and hormonal rhythms; and patterns of muscular tension, particularly facial expressions. These inputs are monitored continuously by the brain and help organize perception, feelings, and behavior. Current inputs are compared to the familiar reference pattern established in the neural maps. When the pattern of the current input is sufficiently different from the familiar reference pattern, a "mismatch" occurs. This mismatch, or "departure from the familiar," is what underlies the generation of feelings and emotions.

Although inputs originating from many different bodily organs and systems are involved in the processes that ultimately determine emotional experience, it is now abundantly clear that the heart plays a particularly important role. The heart is the primary and most consistent source of dynamic rhythmic patterns in the body. Furthermore, the afferent networks connecting the heart and cardiovascular system with the brain are far more extensive than are the afferent systems associated with other major organs (Cameron, 2002). Additionally, the heart is particularly sensitive and responsive to changes in a number of other psychophysiological systems. For example, heart rhythm patterns are modulated continually and rapidly by changes in the activity of either branch of the ANS. Further, the heart's extensive intrinsic network of sensory neurons enables it to detect and respond to variations in hormonal rhythms and patterns (Armour & Ardell, 1994). In addition to functioning as a sophisticated information processing and encoding center (Armour & Kember, 2004), the heart is also an endocrine gland that produces and secretes hormones and neurotransmitters, including oxytocin (Huang et al., 1996). The heart not only pumps blood, but also continually transmits dynamic patterns of neurological, hormonal, pressure, and electromagnetic information to the brain and throughout the body.

An example illustrating the influence of cardiac afferent input on emotional experience is provided from research showing that psychological aspects of panic disorder are often created by an unrecognized cardiac arrhythmia. One study found that the *DSM-IV* criteria for panic disorder were fulfilled in more than two-thirds of patients with sudden-onset arrhythmias. In the majority of cases, once the arrhythmia was discovered and treated, the symptoms of panic disorder disappeared (Lessmeier et al., 1997). When the heart rate variability patterns of such an arrhythmia are plotted, the erratic, incoherent waveform appears quite similar to the heart rhythm pattern produced during strong feelings of anxiety in a healthy person. Because the sudden, large change in the pattern of afferent information is detected by the brain as a mismatch relative to the stable baseline pattern, it consequently results in feelings of anxiety and, since the brain mechanisms involved in self-regulation cannot regain control, it escalates into feelings of panic.

The previous example illustrates the immediate and profound impact that changes in the heart's rhythmic activity can have on one's emotional experience. In this example—as is usually the case—such changes occur unconsciously. One of the most important findings of our research, however, is that changes in the heart's rhythmic patterns can also be "intentionally generated." An intentional shift of focus to the physical area of the heart with the self-induction of a positive emotional state rapidly initiates increased coherence. This, in turn, results in a change in the pattern of afferent cardiac signals sent to the brain, which serves to "reinforce" the self-generated positive emotional shift, making it easier to sustain. Through the consistent use of coherence-building techniques, the coupling between the psychophysiological coherence mode and positive emotions is further reinforced. This subsequently strengthens the ability of a positive feeling shift to initiate a beneficial physiological shift toward increased coherence (with the resulting increase in efficiency and performance) or a physiological shift to facilitate the experience of a positive emotion.

While the process of activating the psychophysiological coherence mode clearly leads to immediate benefits by helping to transform stress in the moment it is experienced, it can also contribute to long-term improvements in emotion regulation abilities and emotional well-being that ultimately affect many aspects of one's life. This is because each time individuals intentionally self-generate a state of coherence, the "new" coherent patterns—and "new" repertoires for responding to challenge—are reinforced in the neural systems. With consistency of practice, these patterns become increasingly familiar to the brain. Thus, these new, healthy patterns become established as a new baseline or reference, which the system then strives to maintain. It is in this way that HeartMath tools facilitate a "repatterning process" whereby the maladaptive patterns that underlie the experience of stress are progressively replaced by healthier physiological, emotional, cognitive, and behavioral patterns as the "automatic" or familiar way of being (McCraty, 2003; McCraty & Childre, 2004).

Positive Emotion–Refocusing Tools and Techniques

The research described here has informed the development of a set of positive emotion–refocusing techniques, known as the HeartMath System (Childre, 1994; Childre & Cryer, 2000; Childre & Martin, 1999; Childre & Rozman, 2002, 2005). The significance of the HeartMath process is that it offers individuals a systematic and reliable means to intentionally shift out of a state of emotional unease or stress into a "new" positive state of emotional calm and stability. This occurs as result of a process in which the individual intentionally creates a new positive emotional state as a future target and activates changes in patterns of psychophysiological activity that enable the system to achieve and maintain that new state.

Studies conducted across diverse populations in laboratory, organizational, educational, and clinical settings have demonstrated that these coherence-building techniques are effective in producing both immediate and sustained reductions in stress and its associated disruptive and dysfunctional emotions together with improvements in many dimensions of psychosocial well-being (McCraty, Atkinson, Tiller, Rein, & Watkins, 1995; McCraty, Atkinson, & Tomasino, 2003; McCraty, Atkinson, Tomasino, Goelitz, & Mayrovitz, 1999; McCraty, Barrios-Choplin, Rozman, Atkinson, & Watkins, 1998; Tiller et al., 1996). Collectively, results indicate that such techniques are easily learned and employed, produce rapid improvements, have a high rate of compliance, can be sustained over time, and are readily adaptable to a wide range of ages and demographic groups.

Such emotion-refocusing techniques are designed to enable people to intervene in the moment when negative and disruptive emotions are triggered, thus interrupting the body's normal stress response and initiating a shift toward increased coherence. This shift facilitates higher cognitive functioning and increased emotional regulation, both of which normally are compromised during stress and negative emotional states.

In addition to such positive emotion–refocusing techniques, which generally are used to address stress in the moment, HeartMath has developed several emotion-restructuring techniques through which individuals hold a positive emotional focus and maintain a state of coherence for longer periods (5–15 minutes or longer, if desired). These emotion-restructuring techniques can be an effective means to diffuse accumulated stress and negative feelings and to facilitate physical, mental, and emotional regeneration. The movement to a more organized pattern of cardiac afferent input that accompanies a coherent heart rhythm is one that the brain associates with feelings of security and

well-being, resulting in a "pattern match" with positive emotional experience. This shift in the pattern of the heart's input to the brain thus serves to reinforce the self-generated positive emotional shift, making it easier to sustain. Through consistent use of HeartMath tools,[1] the coupling between the psychophysiological coherence mode and positive emotions is further reinforced.

Practice of the emotional restructuring techniques is typically accompanied by feelings of deep peacefulness and a sense of inner harmony. By quieting the normal stream of mental dialogue through this process, many users report the spontaneous emergence of increased intuitive clarity and insight relative to problems or troublesome issues.

The process of coupling an intentional shift in attention to the area of the heart with the self-induction of a sincere heartfelt positive emotion appears to excite the system at its resonant frequency, thus facilitating the emergence of the psychophysiological coherence mode (Figure 50.1). This shift to coherence, in turn, results in a change in the pattern of afferent cardiac signals sent to the brain, which is significant because at the physiological level this shift serves to interrupt or prevent the triggering of the body's normal stress response. In addition, the increased physiological efficiency associated with the coherent mode appears to facilitate the body's regulatory and regenerative processes and speed recovery from stress (Luskin, Reitz, Newell, Quinn, & Haskell, 2002; McCraty, Tomasino, Atkinson, & Sundram, 1999; McCraty et al., 2003; McCraty et al., 2005; McCraty et al., 1999; McCraty et al., 1998). This may explain Frederickson's observations that positive emotions can undo the accumulated effects of negative emotions (Fredrickson, Mancuso, Branigan, & Tugade, 2000).

A further outcome of the shift to a state of coherence manifests at the cognitive level as a result of the change in the pattern of cardiac afferent information reaching the brain's higher cognitive centers. Research has shown that changes in input to the brain from the cardiovascular system can modify the brain's electrophysiological activity and lead to changes in perceptual and cognitive processing, leading specifically to increased mental clarity and higher cognitive functions (reviewed in McCraty & Tomasino, 2006; McCraty et al., 2005). The

[1] HeartMath has developed a set of practical, easy-to-use positive emotion–refocusing and restructuring tools and techniques. These include Neutral, Quick Coherence, Freeze-Frame, Heart Lock-In, Attitude Breathing, and Cut-Thru (Childre, 1994; Childre & Martin, 1999; Childre & Rozman, 2002, 2005).

activation of the coherent state thus often results in a change in perception or attitude about a given stressor and the ability to address it from a more objective, discerning, and resourceful perspective.

Heart Rhythm Coherence Feedback Training: Facilitating Coherence

The learning and effective use of these positive emotion–focusing tools can be facilitated by heart rhythm coherence feedback training. The technology designed specifically for this purpose provides real-time physiological feedback that serves as a powerful aid and objective validation in the process of learning to self-generate positive emotions and increase psychophysiological coherence.

Heart rhythm feedback and coherence-building systems known as the emWave PC and emWave Personal Stress Reliever (Quantum Intech, Boulder Creek, CA) allow one to see one's heart rhythm patterns in real time on a computer screen or as series of indicators. They also provide an objective measure of the current level of physiological coherence as well as an accumulated score. The systems also include tutorials that provide instruction in the coherence-building techniques. As users practice the techniques, they can readily see and experience the changes in their heart rhythm patterns, which generally become more ordered and more sine wave–like as they cultivate positive emotional states. The computer-based version includes a series of interactive games, controlled by the user's coherence level, which are designed to reinforce the positive emotion–refocusing skills.

Heart rhythm coherence feedback training and positive emotion–focused, coherence-building techniques are employed in diverse contexts by physicians and other mental health professionals, law enforcement personnel, educators, athletes, executives, and individuals to increase positive emotions and reduce the effect of negative and maladaptive emotions. Applications include managing stress and anger; decreasing anxiety, depression, and fatigue; promoting improved academic, work, and sports performance; reducing physical and psychological health risk factors; and facilitating improvements in health and quality of life in patients with various clinical disorders.

The coherence mode contributes to long-term attitude shifts and improvements in emotional regulation and well-being. When individuals intentionally arrest and override the patterns associated with stress responses by self-generating a positive emotion and activating a state of coherence, a "new" coherent pattern—and "new" repertoires for responding to challenges—are deepened and reinforced in the neural architecture.

The occurrence of such a repatterning process is supported by both physiological and psychological data. At the electrophysiological level, ambulatory recordings demonstrate a greater frequency of spontaneous periods of coherence in the heart rhythm patterns of individuals practiced in the HeartMath techniques, in comparison to the general population. There are also data linking the practice of HeartMath tools to favorable changes in hormonal patterns. Specifically, a significant increase in the DHEA/cortisol ratio was manifest in individuals who consistently used the HeartMath tools for 30 days. This finding, which recently has been independently replicated (Cobain & Butlin, 2002), is evidence of a repatterning process occurring at a fundamental level, given that there is normally little variability in levels of these hormones from month to month (McCraty et al., 1998).

Another important recent finding is that the heart produces as much oxytocin as does the brain (Gutkowska, Jankowski, Mukaddam-Daher, & McCann, 2000). This hormone has been demonstrated to be associative both with countering negative and boosting positive emotional states. Oxytocin, released in the body in such bonding experiences as lactation, romantic and sexual bonding, and positive social affiliation, is also produced in response to stress. As Taylor, Dickerson, and Klein (2005) summarize, "Oxytocin, released in response to stress, appears to induce a state of mild sedation and relaxation, reduce anxiety, decrease sympathetic and HPA activity, and promote affiliative and pro-social behavior under stressful circumstances" (p. 561). Imagine: a hormone that both diminishes negative emotions and magnifies positive ones!

The Heart, Positive Emotions, and Spirituality

George Vaillant (2005, 2006) asked, "Is spirituality just another word for the positive emotions?" and answers his own question by stating, "Spirituality and the positive emotions are virtually synonymous." The heart has long been associated with positive spiritual states. All faith traditions consider the heart the seat of positive emotions, including love, compassion, praise, and joy. From earliest recorded history, humans considered the heart a sacred center of human experience essential not only for the transfer of knowledge and for passing on wisdom, but for achieving and expressing transcendent spiritual feelings. From father to son, mother to daughter, rabbi, shaman, and sage to their followers, and even God to prophets, spiritual feelings were conveyed from heart to heart as well as from heart to mind. Images of the heart show up in the iconography of most ancient cultures. As Louisa Young says, "As soon as mankind knew anything about itself, it knew that it had a heart" (2003, p. xxiii).

The heart is at the heart of all religious traditions. The ancient Hebrews, Greeks, Egyptians, Sumerians, Hindus, Muslims, Christians, and Buddhists all saw the heart as a major force in spiritual birth and rebirth. For ancients, the heart was not merely a metaphor for the home of the spirit; it was seen as being literally so. In fact, many traditional cultures saw the heart as the locus of the intellect, memory, spirit, and regenerative power. In many early texts, we find the idea of offering one's heart to deity. The Bible uses such language as God creating a new heart for those who seek to change their lives, purifying one's heart, and having God's word written on one's heart. Similar ideas are found in Muslim, Buddhist, and other sacred books.

One of the strongest common threads uniting the views of diverse cultures and religious and spiritual traditions throughout human history has been a universal regard for the heart as a point of spiritual influx and as a source of wisdom and positive emotions. According to the Buddha, "There is the heart element or current, which is the center of a being's consciousness, and the very center of its mind. The Buddha referred to it as the 'reflective current of the heart'.... The function of this current is to reflect in the mind the feelings, the passions, and the emotions" (Reiter, 2006, p. 87). It is striking how specific this statement is and how close it comes to capturing the essence of our scientific model of emotion where the rhythms and patterns of heart activity are interpreted by the brain and mind as feelings and emotions.

Such ideas about the heart flourished in Western society until the seventeenth century. However, since then, the heart has been reduced essentially to either a simple pump or a sentimental valentine. We contend that much of the alienation of the spirit in the West is related to the loss of understanding of the heart as a central organ in spiritual transformation. Charles Siebert argues that we may "be suffering a kind of collective heart attack, a modern metaphysical one—pained by the weakening of long-held notions of the heart as the home of the soul and the seat of deep emotions" (Siebert, 1980, p. 54).

One of these notions is that intuitive insight is related to the connection between the heart and spirit. In this context, a number of studies have shown that the body often responds to a future unknown emotionally arousing event 4–7 minutes prior to experiencing the actual event. In a study of the electrophysiology of intuition (McCraty, Atkinson, & Bradley, 2004a, 2004b), which was designed to investigate where and when in the brain and body information about a future event is registered and processed, we discovered, surprisingly, that both the heart and brain appear to receive and respond to intuitive information. Even more surprising was the finding that the heart appears to receive intuitive information before the brain does. The ability of the heart to respond to emotionally relevant information indicates that the heart seems to be tuned to or able to access field of information that is not limited by the boundaries of time and space. This may be the first scientific demonstration which indicates that the heart may indeed be linked to what might be called the higher self or spirit, as all the great religions and ancient civilizations have maintained.

As the research reported here demonstrates, when people engender heart-centered feelings, the resultant coherent heart rhythms reflect an emotional state normally associated with the spiritual—internal harmony, tranquility, a greater capacity for love and compassion, an increased impulse to forgive, and even euphoria and transcendence. Many speak of profound life changes as a result of incorporating such tools and techniques into their personal and professional lives.

We believe that understanding the heart's role in spiritual development and spiritual evolution requires both scientific and humanistic tools and that these will prove complementary. We postulate that the investigation of the heart as the locus or portal of spiritual transformative experience represents a new field of inquiry, one that holds promise of discovery of elemental truths about the interconnectedness of the whole person—body, mind, and spirit. As Jung said, "The utterances of the heart—unlike those of the discriminating intellect—always relate to the whole" (cited in Godwin, 2001, p. 13).

Summary and Conclusion

Most people do not need to be convinced that the heart is intimately and deeply involved in positive emotions since most feel such emotions in or near their hearts. Additionally, most people experience heartfelt emotions in regard to their most significant, enduring, and intimate relations with others. Further, imaginative and artistic expressions of positive emotions in such forms as music, poetry, and dance often are expressed in terms of the heart. Finally, the essence of our spiritual traditions and expressions are heart centered.

The heart, that strange, mysterious organ beating rhythmically at the center of our bodies, which for millennia has inspired the imagination, turns out to be the very core of our being. As Schwartz and Russek state, "Metaphorically the heart is the sun, the pulsing, energetic center of our bio-physical solar system, and the brain is the earth. . . . One implication of the energy cardiology/cardio-energetic revolution is the radical idea that, energetically, the brain revolves around the heart, not the other way around" (cited in Young, 2003, p. 100). Recently, science has begun unraveling the heart's mystery and revealing its hidden power. New discoveries about the heart and its place in our physical, social, and spiritual lives hold the promise not only of reconnecting us to the enlightened understanding about the heart found in ancient cultures but also of revealing new understandings not yet unfolded to our minds or imaginations.

Throughout history and across diverse cultures, religions, and spiritual traditions, the heart has been associated with spiritual influx, wisdom, and emotional experience, particularly with regard to other-centered, positive emotions such as appreciation and love. Current research provides evidence that the heart does indeed play a role in the generation of emotional experience. The model of emotion discussed herein includes the heart, together with the brain, and nervous and hormonal systems, as fundamental components of a dynamic, interactive network from which emotional experience emerges. Further, research has identified new physiological correlates associated with the experience of heartfelt positive emotions. Heart-based, positive emotion–focused techniques designed to help people self-induce and sustain states of positive emotions have proven effective in a variety of settings. The study of the relation of the heart to positive emotions is one of the exciting frontiers in positive psychology.

Questions about the Future of this Topic

1. What discoveries are yet to unfold that will broaden and deepen our understanding of the heart's role in generating emotional and perceptual experience?

2. What explains how the heart can "know" a future emotionally relevant event before it happens?

3. Can the generation of coherent fields facilitate coherence among humans and between humans and other living organisms?

References

Armour, J. A., & Ardell, J. L. (Eds.). (1994). *Neurocardiology*. New York: Oxford University Press.

Armour, J. A., & Kember, G. C. (2004). Cardiac sensory neurons. In J. A. Armour & J. L. Ardell (Eds.), *Basic and clinical neurocardiology* (pp. 79–117). New York: Oxford University Press.

Cameron, O. G. (2002). *Visceral sensory neuroscience: Interoception*. New York: Oxford University Press.

Childre, D. L. (1994). *Freeze-Frame®, fast action stress relief*. Boulder Creek, CA: Planetary.

Childre, D. L., & Cryer, B. (2000). *From chaos to coherence: The power to change performance*. Boulder Creek, CA: Planetary.

Childre, D. L., & Martin, H. (1999). *The HeartMath solution*. San Francisco: Harper San Francisco.

Childre, D. L., & Rozman, D. (2002). *Overcoming emotional chaos: Eliminate anxiety, lift depression and create security in your life*. San Diego, CA: Jodere.

Childre, D. L., & Rozman, D. (2005). *Transforming stress: The HeartMath solution to relieving worry, fatigue, and tension*. Oakland, CA: New Harbinger Publications.

Cobain, M. R., & Butlin, L. (2002). *A psychosocial intervention in the workplace: Endocrine and cardiovascular effects* (No. CW 02 0319). Colworth, UK: Unilever R&D.

Damasio, A. (2003). *Looking for Spinoza: Joy, sorrow, and the feeling brain*. Orlando: Harcourt.

Danner, D. D., Snowdon, D. A., & Friesen, W. V. (2001). Positive emotions in early life and longevity: Findings from the nun study. *Journal of Personality and Social Psychology*, *80*(5), 804–813.

Foreman, R. D. (1994). Vagal afferent modulation of cardiac pain. In M. N. Levey & P. J. Schwartz (Eds.), *Vagal control of the heart: Experimental basis and clinical implications* (pp. 345–368). Armonk, NY: Futura Publishing Co.

Foreman, R. (1997). Organization of visceral input. In T. L. Yaksh, C. Lynch, III, W. M. Zapol, M. Maze, J. F. Biebuyck, & L. J. Saidman (Eds.), *Anesthesia: Biologic foundations* (pp. 663–683). Philadelphia: Lippincott-Raven.

Fredrickson, B. L., Mancuso, R. A., Branigan, C., & Tugade, M. M. (2000). The undoing effect of positive emotions. *Motivation and Emotion*, *24*, 237–258.

Frysinger, R. C., & Harper, R. M. (1990). Cardiac and respiratory correlations with unit discharge in epileptic human temporal lobe. *Epilepsia*, *31*(2), 162–171.

Godwin, G. (2001). *Heart: A personal journey through its myths and meanings*. New York: William Morrow.

Gutkowska, J., Jankowski, M., Mukaddam-Daher, S., & McCann, S. M. (2000). Oxytocin is a cardiovascular hormone. *Brazilian Journal of Medical and Biological Research*, *33*, 625–633.

Huang, M. H., Friend, D. S., Sunday, M. E., Singh, K., Haley, K., Austen, K. F., et al. (1996). An intrinsic adrenergic system in mammalian heart. *Journal of Clinical Investigation*, *98*(6), 1298–1303.

James, W. (1884). What is an emotion? *Mind*, *9*(34), 188–205.

Langhorst, P., Schulz, G., & Lambertz, M. (1984). Oscillating neuronal network of the "common brainstem system." In K. Miyakawa, H. P. Koepchen, & C. Polosa (Eds.), *Mechanisms of blood pressure waves* (pp. 257–275). Tokyo: Japan Scientific Societies Press.

LeDoux, J. (1996). *The emotional brain: The mysterious underpinnings of emotional life.* New York: Simon and Schuster.

Lehrer, P. M., Vaschillo, E., Vaschillo, B., Lu, S. E., Eckberg, D. L., Edelberg, R., et al. (2003). Heart rate variability biofeedback increases baroreflex gain and peak expiratory flow. *Psychosomatic Medicine, 65*(5), 796–805.

Lessmeier, T. J., Gamperling, D., Johnson-Liddon, V., Fromm, B. S., Steinman, R. T., Meissner, M. D., et al. (1997). Unrecognized paroxysmal supraventricular tachycardia: Potential for misdiagnosis as panic disorder. *Archives of Internal Medicine, 157,* 537–543.

Levy, B. R., Slade, M. D., Kunkel, S. R., & Kasl, S. V. (2002). Longevity increased by positive self-perceptions of aging. *Journal of Personality and Social Psychology, 83*(2), 261–270.

Luskin, F., Reitz, M., Newell, K., Quinn, T. G., & Haskell, W. (2002). A controlled pilot study of stress management training of elderly patients with congestive heart failure. *Preventive Cardiology, 5*(4), 168–172.

McCraty, R. (2003). *Heart–brain neurodynamics: The making of emotions,* Publication no. 03-015. Boulder Creek, CA: HeartMath Research Center, Institute of HeartMath.

McCraty, R., Atkinson, M., & Bradley, R. T. (2004a). Electrophysiological evidence of intuition: Part 1. The surprising role of the heart. *Journal of Alternative and Complementary Medicine, 10*(1), 133–143.

McCraty, R., Atkinson, M., & Bradley, R. T. (2004b). Electrophysiological evidence of intuition: Part 2. A system-wide process? *Journal of Alternative and Complementary Medicine, 10*(2), 325–336.

McCraty, R., Atkinson, M., Tiller, W. A., Rein, G., & Watkins, A. D. (1995). The effects of emotions on short-term power spectrum analysis of heart rate variability. *American Journal of Cardiology, 76*(14), 1089–1093.

McCraty, R., Atkinson, M., & Tomasino, D. (2003). Impact of a workplace stress reduction program on blood pressure and emotional health in hypertensive employees. *Journal of Alternative and Complementary Medicine, 9*(3), 355–369.

McCraty, R., Atkinson, M., Tomasino, D., & Bradley, R. T. (2005). *The coherent heart: Heart–brain interactions, psychophysiological coherence, and the emergence of system-wide order,* Publication no. 05-022. Boulder Creek, CA: HeartMath Research Center, Institute of HeartMath.

McCraty, R., Atkinson, M., Tomasino, D., Goelitz, J., & Mayrovitz, H. N. (1999). The impact of an emotional self-management skills course on psychosocial functioning and autonomic recovery to stress in middle school children. *Integrative Physiological and Behavioral Science, 34*(4), 246–268.

McCraty, R., Barrios-Choplin, B., Rozman, D., Atkinson, M., & Watkins, A. D. (1998). The impact of a new emotional self-management program on stress, emotions, heart rate variability, DHEA and cortisol. *Integrative Physiological and Behavioral Science, 33*(2), 151–170.

McCraty, R., & Childre, D. (2004). The grateful heart: The psychophysiology of appreciation. In R. A. Emmons & M. E. McCullough (Eds.), *The psychology of gratitude* (pp. 230–255). New York: Oxford University Press.

McCraty, R., & Tomasino, D. (2006). Emotional stress, positive emotions, and psychophysiological coherence. In B. B. Arnetz & R. Ekman (Eds.), *Stress in health and disease* (pp. 360–383). Weinheim, Germany: Wiley-VCH.

McCraty, R., Tomasino, D., Atkinson, M., & Sundram, J. (1999). *Impact of the HeartMath self-management skills program on physiological and psychological stress in police officers,* Publication no. 99-075. Boulder Creek, CA: HeartMath Research Center, Institute of HeartMath.

Oppenheimer, S., & Hopkins, D. (1994). Suprabulbar neuronal regulation of the heart. In J. A. Armour & J. L. Ardell (Eds.), *Neurocardiology* (pp. 309–341). New York: Oxford University Press.

Ostir, G. V., Markides, K. S., Black, S. A., & Goodwin, J. S. (2000). Emotional well-being predicts subsequent functional independence and survival. *Journal of the American Geriatric Society, 48*(5), 473–478.

Pribram, K. H., & Melges, F. T. (1969). Psychophysiological basis of emotion. In P. J. Vinken & G. W. Bruyn (Eds.), *Handbook of clinical neurology* (Vol. 3, pp. 316–341). Amsterdam: North-Holland.

Ratey, J. J. (2001). *A user's guide to the brain: Perception, attention, and the four theaters of the brain.* New York: Pantheon.

Rein, G., Atkinson, M., & McCraty, R. (1995). The physiological and psychological effects of compassion and anger. *Journal of Advancement in Medicine, 8*(2), 87–105.

Reiter, L. (2006). *Lord Buddha's explanation of the universe: An interpretation of the Abhidharma.* Myrtle Beach, SC: Sheriar.

Siebert, C. (1980). "The rehumanization of the heart," *Harpers,* February, 1980, pp. 53–60.

Siegel, G., Ebeling, B. J., Hofer, H. W., Nolte, J., Roedel, H., & Klubendorf, D. (1984). Vascular smooth muscle rhythmicity. In K. Miyakawa, H. P. Koepchen, & C. Polosa (Eds.), *Mechanisms of blood pressure waves* (pp. 319–338). Tokyo: Japan Scientific Societies Press.

Taylor, S. E., Dickerson, S. S., & Klein, L. C. (2005). Toward a biology of social support. In C. R. Snyder & S. J. Lopez (Eds.), *Handbook of positive psychology* (pp. 556–569). Oxford: Oxford University Press.

Tiller, W. A., McCraty, R., & Atkinson, M. (1996). Cardiac coherence: A new, noninvasive measure of autonomic nervous system order. *Alternative Therapies in Health and Medicine, 2*(1), 52–65.

Vaillant, G. (2005). *Is spirituality just another word for the positive emotions?* Paper presented at the 2005 International Positive Psychology Summit. Retrieved on May 30, 2006, from http://www.gallupippi.com/content/?CI=15784.

Vaillant, G. (2006). *"Alcoholics anonymous: Cult or cure?"* Abstract, international network on personal meaning, July 21–23, 2006. Retrieved May 29, 2006, from http://www.meaning.ca/conference06/index.htm.

Young, L. (2003). *The book of the heart.* New York: Doubleday.

Toughness

Richard A. Dienstbier *and* Lisa M. Pytlik Zillig

Abstract

This chapter presents an overview of the concept of toughness, which at the abstract level is about the harmony of physiological systems, and more concretely is about how the body influences the mind. Toughness theory begins with the recognition that there is a "training effect" for neuroendocrine systems. Following a review of the characteristics of interventions and training programs that can promote toughness, the authors present a model in which the effects of toughness are mediated by neuroendocrine systems such as the pituitary-adrenal-cortical system and the central nervous system. The elements of toughness (e.g., having a greater capacity for arousal and energy when needed) are proposed to promote positive outcomes by facilitating the use of adaptive coping strategies and improving emotional stability. Toughness therefore appears to be a promising concept within positive psychology in that it helps to explain how the dynamic interactions between psychological and somatic processes can promote positive outcomes.

Keywords: coping, hardiness, resilience, toughness

The ancient Greeks had it right; mind and body are integrally connected. In modern psychology, we are catching up. We have begun to explore the mind–body connection, but we have typically approached it by emphasizing the mind's influence on the body—how our emotions and thoughts influence health and physical well-being through processes that range from immune function to neuroendocrine availability. Toughness emphasizes the reciprocal path—how body influences mind. Because the evidence for toughness comes largely from experimental studies in which the researchers have demonstrated positive impacts on mind from manipulations that change the body, in toughness theory we propose that lifestyle choices enhance psychological well-being through observable neuroendocrine mediation.

At an abstract level, toughness is about the harmony between physiological systems and, ultimately, about the correspondences of physiological systems with psychological ones. The anthropologist

Gregory Bateson (1979) observed that when a changed environment forces an organ system to adapt so much that the system nears the limits of its genetic potential, not only is that system strained, but other organ systems with which that system interacts are similarly strained. As an example of cascading negative impacts, consider the downstream impacts of a lifetime of smoking on reducing respiratory efficiency. By leading to reduced physical activity, respiratory insufficiency may ultimately lead to muscular weakness, and then to a higher ratio of fat to lean tissues. Those changes may in turn lead to bone decalcification and perhaps to insulin insensitivity, sugar intolerance, circulatory breakdown, infection, and so on. Based on Bateson's observations, we suggest several principles that underlie toughness theory. The first is that all major physiological systems within an organism interact, so that the state of one system (e.g., the major muscles) will influence most others (e.g., the endocrine and neural systems). The second is that in order to maintain general health, physical systems should be stimulated and used in ways that maintain them near the midpoints of their genetically determined operating potentials. The third principle follows from the first two—similar to most systems, for best results the body must be exposed to environments it was designed to experience, and in general ways the organism must behave in ways that correspond with the ways it was designed to behave.

More specifically, in toughness theory, we emphasize that balances within the neuroendocrine systems are modifiable by lifestyles but also by aging. Those modifications in neuroendocrine systems that result from activities that toughen (i.e., usually increased capacities, responsivity, and sensitivities to hormones, neural modulators, and transmitters), in turn, positively influence a variety of performance, personality, and health outcomes.

In this chapter, we begin with a brief review of the theoretical perspective concerning toughness. We have sequenced the initial section according to the order that various literatures contributed to the toughness concept as it was initially discussed by the first author (Dienstbier, 1989). Subsequently, we will explore research areas that we have not previously related to toughness (e.g., possible impacts of toughening on serotonin levels and the apparent toughening effects of antidepressants). As will be quickly evident, the toughness concept consists of a series of inferences about apparent interrelationships between research and theory from fields ranging from social and clinical psychology to immunology and pharmacology. We are not experts in most of those areas, and we therefore invite suggestions about possible omissions.

Definitions and Physiological Systems

While our thinking about stress has been influenced by Lazarus and colleagues (e.g., Folkman & Lazarus, 1985), the concept of toughness requires a firm distinction between challenges on the one hand, and stressors, including threat and harm/loss, on the other. Challenges are potentially taxing situations appraised as likely to lead to positive outcomes and positive emotions. Threatening situations are similarly taxing, but threats are appraised more pessimistically. Toughness is less relevant to situations experienced as harm/loss, where negative outcomes already have occurred, and where instrumental coping is thought to be useless. As will become evident in our subsequent discussion of the toughness concept, there is a mutually causal relationship between appraisals of challenge versus threat and physiological toughness.

Because the physiological concepts that we will use in this chapter are not complex, we can describe them quite briefly. Reference to central nervous system (CNS) monoamines includes serotonin and the catecholamines noradrenaline, adrenaline, and dopamine. Reference to peripheral catecholamines suggests adrenaline and noradrenaline, associated with arousal of the sympathetic nervous system (SNS); dopamine is not included as a peripheral catecholamine because it is found largely in conjugated or inactive forms in the body (Bove, Dewey, & Tyce, 1984). Arousal of the SNS stimulates various arousal-generating systems in the body including the adrenal medulla, which then secretes adrenaline; this arousal complex is referred to as the "SNS–adrenal medullary system," here accorded the friendly acronym "SAM." Adrenaline contributes to arousal in a variety of ways, especially stimulating the release of glucose into the blood and facilitating the subsequent utilization of glucose and other fuels for energy. SAM arousal occurs in contexts of both positive and negative emotion–evoking circumstances and when physical activity or mental effort is required. It is a system that may cease to provide arousal quickly after the circumstances requiring arousal have passed because the half-life of the catecholamines in the periphery is less than 2 min in humans.

Arousal of the pituitary-adrenal-cortical (PAC) system begins with a hypothalamic hormone (CRH) that stimulates a pituitary hormone (ACTH) that leads to the adrenal cortex secreting the corticosteroids, of which cortisol is primarily important in humans. The stimulation of this system occurs in novel situations and following attributions of threat; the experiences of harm/loss, social tension, helplessness, and lingering depression are also associated with elevated cortisol levels. Like the SAM, cortisol stimulates energy. However, its contribution to energy comes at some costs, such as immune system suppression. And when distressing circumstances end, the arousal fostered by the PAC system is not as easily discontinued as is SAM arousal because the half-life of cortisol in humans is around 90 min.

Elements of the Toughness Model

Toughness theory begins with the recognition that there is a "training effect" for neuroendocrine systems. That is, certain manipulations lead to specific neuroendocrine system modifications that, in turn, mediate specific impacts on personality, performance, and health. While a great deal of experimental animal research supports this model, those causal relationships are supported by research with human participants that is largely, but not exclusively, correlational.

Manipulations That Toughen

At the most general and abstract level, lifestyles, training programs, or laboratory manipulations that lead to the physiological changes called toughness include repeated episodes of challenge/threat followed by recovery periods (hereafter "intermittent challenge/threat"). A single episode of an effective toughening manipulation should tax or stimulate an organism sufficiently to result in noticeable neuroendocrine expenditures or even in short-term neuroendocrine depletion. For animal subjects, toughening manipulations typically include swimming in cold water, running in an exercise wheel, being handled or shocked, or even having neuroendocrines depleted by pharmacological interventions. For humans, well-established toughening manipulations include aerobic exercise and working in cold environments. Less well established but likely toughening activities for humans range from intellectual stimulation through games, socializing, and challenging occupations to humor. Whether an activity leads to toughening depends on the original state of toughness. Thus, one who is bedridden may achieve toughness with regular exposure to humor, whereas far more substantial activities may be required to increase toughness in a young and active 20-year-old. As illustrated by the research reviewed subsequently, a wide variety of intermittently repeated stimuli and activities have been shown to toughen.

The number of repetitions of taxing activity and recovery that lead to toughening undoubtedly depends on the nature of the manipulations and the associated coping activities. However, most effective laboratory programs with animal subjects span periods of at least 2–4 weeks and use 24-hr rhythms of stimulation and rest (e.g., DeBoer, Koopmans, Slangen, & Van der Gugten, 1990). Comparable training programs with humans span longer periods but also typically depend on 24-hr stimulation and rest sequences (e.g., Winder, Hagberg, Hickson, Ehsani, & McLane, 1978).

Some toughening "manipulations" such as living in cold environments may appear to be continuous, but behaviorally adapting organisms may experience them as intermittent (e.g., by periodically retreating to nests or to warm homes). Therefore, such "manipulations" should foster the development of toughness. On the other hand, some situations such as social stressors that appear to be intermittent may be experienced as continuous stressors if individuals ruminate about them. If they are experienced as continuous, such "manipulations" may weaken the organism. Finally, aging is associated with decreasing neuroendocrine capacities. Therefore, unfortunately, aging past young adulthood has weakening effects (Dienstbier, 1992).

Neuroendocrine Mediators

The reason that some manipulations toughen is because repeating taxing (but manageable) episodes with intermittent rest periods leads eventually to the development of compensatory physiological capacities, with greater protection against future neuroendocrine depletion. Thus, the neuroendocrine training effects introduced previously refer to changes in the CNS and in the SAM and PAC systems. That is, toughening manipulations enhance the capacity for various tissues in the CNS to generate the monoamines, especially noradrenaline and serotonin, and enhance the capacity of the body other than CNS (hereafter "periphery") to generate noradrenaline and adrenaline. The increased CNS monoamine capacities result in resistance to depletion of CNS noradrenaline (and probably serotonin) in episodes of extended stress. Increased peripheral catecholamine capacity results in high rates of catecholamine release for extended time periods in the context of long and especially taxing challenge/stress episodes. On the other hand, in shorter and less taxing episodes, decreased neuroendocrine responses are likely because of the increased physiological efficiency of the tough individual.

The increased physiological efficiency in the toughened individual results largely from increases in physiological sensitivity and responsivity to important neuroendocrine systems. For example, the sensitivities to catecholamines of the alpha-receptors and beta-receptors in the CNS are modified, and the physiological responsivity of some peripheral tissue is increased. As an example of peripheral effects, in the toughened individual there is a greater release of glucose by the liver per "dose" of circulating catecholamine (LeBlanc et al., 1977). In turn, to keep arousal from increasing when it is not needed, the increased tissue sensitivity necessitates a reduction in base rates of neuroendocrine secretion, as indicated by reduced "base rates" of peripheral catecholamine secretion, as measured with urinary assays. Those reductions in base rate levels of neuroendocrines often result, in turn, in a net reduction in base rates of some other physical indicators, such as heart rate.

In taxing situations, not all neuroendocrine responses are increased in the toughened individual. For example, much (but not all) research indicates that the increased capacity of the body to secrete catecholamines and the increased responsivity of the body to those neuroendocrines then lead to delay and/or suppression of PAC responses in challenge/threat episodes. And, once coping is no longer required, tough individuals show faster recovery to base rate levels in most indicators of arousal (e.g., as reviewed by Linden, Earle, Gerin, & Christenfeld, 1997). This faster recovery from arousal is evidenced particularly when organisms are subjected to a series of related challenge/stress episodes. Both animal and human research suggests that toughened individuals return to (particularly PAC) base rate levels after fewer episodes than is the case for weaker individuals (e.g., Baade, Ellertsen, Johnsen, & Ursin, 1978).

Personality, Performance, and Health

Our approach to toughness suggests that the physiological mediators listed earlier cause a syndrome of positive changes in personality and performance. However, the causal paths from those neuroendocrine mediators to personality and performance are less well established because these observations depend less on causal research and more on correlational research with human participants. Nevertheless, sufficient research exists to conclude that the pattern of physiological changes (i.e., toughness) corresponds positively with performance in challenging tasks, enhanced learning abilities, emotional stability, resistance to depression in humans (and resistance to "learned helplessness" or behavioral suppression in animals), and positive physical health.

As social-personality psychologists, we are interested mainly in understanding how the physiological pattern of toughness leads to the personality, performance, and health consequences described here, but some speculation embellishes our ideas about those links. To avoid mixing research-based levels of analyses with those that are less so, we will first sketch some of the support for the existence of the nomological network of toughness and will deal with the softer explanations of why and how later. (Readers wishing to see the more complete nomological net and extensive references should contact the first author.)

A Brief History of Toughness

In this section, we describe the paths that led toward this model as it was initially formulated by Dienstbier (1989). Each of the following paragraphs presents a separate literature; together they lead to the major tenets of toughness. We begin with the four-decade-old observation, based on the research of Seymour Levine (1960) and others, that emotional stability in adult animals (usually rats or mice) followed from their exposure as pups to intermittent stimulation, ranging from daily shocking to handling. The adult calmness of those early-stimulated animals seemed especially curious following the most stressful manipulations (i.e., the shocking). Similarly, the observation that those calm animals had "larger" adrenal glands and thus apparently greater arousal capacity fit poorly with classical stress theories and with the finding that such animals tended to be calm and to have reduced stressor-induced PAC responses (Hennessy & Levine, 1979).

While this research on the early experience of animals suggested that increased capacity for arousal was associated with a calm temperament, other literatures of that era suggested the opposite relationship. For example, an examination of the literature on autonomic nervous system balance in humans would lead one to infer that "SNS types" (i.e., those with greater arousal reactivity) would be anxious and neurotic. But "SNS types" should be tolerant of cold temperatures because cold tolerance is associated with the body's ability to stimulate energy through SAM arousal (i.e., through the increased generation of and sensitivity to adrenaline and noradrenaline; e.g., LeBlanc, Dulac, Cote, & Girard, 1975). Following this reasoning, one could predict that cold tolerance and the associated strong and responsive SAM arousal capacity should correspond to anxiety and neuroticism. But in our research, the results demonstrated the opposite relationship: that cold tolerance and hence a strong and responsive SAM arousal capacity corresponded to emotional stability (Dienstbier, LaGuardia, & Wilcox, 1987).

Working with only human participants, researchers at the Karolinska Institute (and elsewhere in Europe) similarly concluded that greater arousal capabilities predicted both positive personality and positive task performance on a variety of tests and tasks both inside and outside of laboratories. Frankenhaeuser and her colleagues (e.g., Frankenhaeuser, 1979) had shown that better performance in even very complex tasks was associated with greater adrenergic responsivity in humans (assaying urinary catecholamines at the end of the task and comparing those with base rates). Furthermore, individuals who showed increased adrenergic responsivity in the context of many tests and tasks were more emotionally stable than were less responsive individuals. However, these more stable individuals also tended to have lower catecholamine base rates.

With several colleagues, the first author explored the growing but often flawed literature on the impact of exercise on temperament. Imperfect or not, a consistent finding in the research was that like early-stimulated animals, people who undertook programs of aerobic training were subsequently more energetic and more emotionally stable (for a review, see Dienstbier, 1984). It followed that an interesting link would be forged with the literatures discussed earlier if we could show that aerobic exercise changed neuroendocrine responses. That link would be particularly strong if those neuroendocrine changes were evident in mentally challenging situations and if they were like those shown by the Scandinavian researchers to characterize their emotionally stable and high-performing participants. Clearly, this hypothesis, that aerobic training would lead to increased catecholamine capacities, ran counter to most physiologically oriented research with humans, especially research on the "Type A" personality. Researchers in that tradition typically hypothesized that following conditioning with regular exercise, positive personality changes and performance enhancement would follow from "reduced" arousal intensity in response to a variety of situations (e.g., Blumenthal et al., 1990). However, it was clear that episodes of exercise elicited high SNS arousal and catecholamine generation, suggesting that repeated cycles of use/depletion followed by recovery would stimulate an increased ability to generate such arousal. In short, we hypothesized a neuroendocrine "training effect." Other researchers already had shown that when aerobically trained participants were tested under physically exhausting conditions, they produced higher catecholamine levels (Hull, Young, & Ziegler, 1984). But our focus was on the relevance of toughness to situations requiring mental coping. In a series of three studies, we found that, when tested on a nonexercise day after a program of aerobic training, our participants responded to an extended mental challenge/threat condition with increased adrenergic arousal (over base rates, in contrast to themselves before training and in contrast to untrained control groups; Dienstbier, LaGuardia, Barnes, Tharp, & Schmidt, 1987). In a study without control participants, Cleroux, Peronnet, and de Champlain (1985) found similar increases

in adrenaline in challenge contexts for eight men following aerobic training; moreover, others have noted faster recovery to base rate levels for aerobically conditioned participants following laboratory challenges (as discussed by Linden et al., 1997).

Even before the era of exercise research described previously, researchers working with animals had advanced and confirmed similar hypotheses regarding CNS adrenergic capacities. In a series of elegant studies, Weiss and colleagues had noted that "learned helplessness" in animals was associated with CNS catecholamine depletion in certain brain regions. To induce resistance to such helplessness, those researchers "toughened up" their animals (a term first applied by Miller, 1980). Long-term increases in CNS catecholamine capacity resulted from manipulations ranging from daily shocking (e.g., Weiss, Glazer, Pohorecky, Brick, & Miller, 1975) and exercise (e.g., Brown et al., 1979) to systematic CNS catecholamine depletion through chemical means (e.g., Glazer, Weiss, Pohorecky, & Miller, 1975). In addition to showing that those manipulations that decreased CNS catecholamines in the short term increased those neuroendocrine capacities in the long term, in some of the studies in that tradition the increased neuroendocrine capacities were shown to be the mediators of the manipulation-induced increases in stress tolerance (i.e., resistance to behavioral suppression; Weiss et al., 1975).

Because of this pattern of compatible findings in research with both animals and human participants and supportive research from other areas, "toughening up" was expanded to the current toughness concept. In the initial discussion of toughness by Dienstbier (1989), the research review showed that each of the toughening manipulations (active and passive intermittent challenges/stressors for young and mature organisms) led to the entire complex of physiological changes (with CNS and peripheral catecholamine enhancement effects and cortisol suppression), and that those physiological mediators were in turn associated with each of the personality/performance variables listed previously in the section on personality, performance, and health.

Limitations of the Model
When and Where Toughness Will Be Evident

Physiological toughening does not lead to identical or equal toughness in all tissues. For example, in the heart, both base rates *and* rates in response to physical and psychological challenge/threats often decline after toughening; and there is evidence that even under maximal workloads, noradrenaline production and turnover in heart tissue are reduced. On the other hand, as with most organs studied, noradrenaline turnover in the livers of toughened animals is greatly enhanced (Mazzeo, 1991). Thus, in those "Type A" studies where it was shown that physical conditioning leads to reduced heart rates in response to physical and psychological challenges and threats, focus was on an aspect of arousal that, although very important, is the exception rather than the prototype.

Demonstrations of increased neuroendocrine capacities from toughness also depend on the researcher's choice of training and testing tasks. This issue is illustrated by Konarska and colleagues in research where blood samples from live animals were used to assess catecholamines. After a few weeks of daily exposure to an intermittent stressor, rats subsequently generated a reduced SAM response in response to the same stressor (reduced blood adrenaline and noradrenaline; Konarska, Stewart, & McCarty, 1989a), whereas they showed increased peripheral catecholamine responses to unfamiliar stressors (Konarska, Stewart, & McCarty, 1989b). While their interpretation was that "sensitization" to unfamiliar stressors results from exposure to intermittent stressors, our interpretation of their findings is closer to the suggestion originally made by Kvetnansky (1980), namely, that toughness training induces physiological adaptation with increased neuroendocrine capacities, but those capacity increases also are accompanied by psychological habituation to now-familiar stressors. Those increased catecholamine capacities in toughened organisms will be evident only when energy demands are unusual, as a result of prolonged extreme stressors or novel ones where responses are inefficient or where searching for solutions occurs.

This interpretation seems particularly applicable to the data of Konarska et al. (1989b) from animals forced at final test to swim (or sink). When tested in very cold water, where extreme energy output is required, toughened animals show higher and much more long-lasting increases in catecholamines than do untoughened animals, whereas in temperate water absolute catecholamine levels were much lower and between-group differences smaller (Konarska, Stewart, & McCarty, 1990). Happily, the toughened animals swam longer, too.

When this interpretation is applied to research with humans, a similar logic holds and can be used to explain apparently inconsistent findings concerning SAM responses to tests following aerobic training or other toughening manipulations. That is, in most aerobic training studies with humans, dependent measures are typically very short-term mental tasks (e.g., 15 min or less). In such test circumstances, trained individuals showed reduced indicators of arousal, including reduced catecholamines (using blood assays; e.g., Blumenthal et al., 1990). As discussed more extensively elsewhere (Dienstbier, 1991), in order to observe the increased catecholamine capacities of toughened humans, it is necessary to use taxing tests that are longer in duration (45 min is probably minimal) and to employ urinary rather than blood assays because the urinary measures provide a more appropriate and accurate measure of long-term neuroendocrine use and turnover (Steptoe, 1987; recall that because the half-life of the catecholamines in humans is less than 2 min, blood measures are of limited usefulness in assessing SAM arousal across longer intervals).

Training That Will Not Toughen

Just as the increased capacities and responsivities that result from toughening are not evident in all test situations, toughening is not accomplished in all programs of intermittent challenges or stressors. For example, it is possible to overwhelm organisms with training that is too intense, extended, or unexpected; even a single episode of a traumatic stressor can be overwhelming.

In the first instance of programs of intermittent stressors that weaken, it has been observed that several weeks of 2 hr daily of restraint stress (as standardized by Kvetnansky) seems to have detrimental impacts on later stress tolerance of rats, sometimes leading to increased catecholamine base rates (McCarty, Horwatt, & Konarska, 1988). Similarly, a combination of unpredictability with great severity may overwhelm the capacity of organisms to recover, leading to weakness rather than toughness (Rodriguez Echandia, Gonzalez, Cabrera, & Fracchia, 1988). Apparent parallels in human research are noted with stress levels that are overwhelming or not truly intermittent, as may be the case with stressors (such as combat) that lead to posttraumatic stress disorders. Similarly, repeated workouts that are too intense to allow complete recovery may cause endurance athletes to experience "staleness," a syndrome that is characterized by increased psychological symptoms of anxiety with increased SNS, catecholamine, and cortisol base rates (e.g., Morgan, Brown, Raglin, O'Connor, & Ellickson, 1987).

Paralleling the observation that animals may be weakened by single episodes of overwhelming stressors, people who were exposed to single early traumatic episodes may display exaggerated PAC responses to acute stressors (Levine & Levine, 1989). For example, maternal death during an individual's childhood has been related to reduced stress resistance in adulthood, resulting in depression (Brown, 1988); similarly, the conditions that lead to posttraumatic stress disorders often result in effects opposite to toughening (e.g., Barlow, Chorpita, & Turovsky, 1996).

Extensions of Toughness Relationships

In this section, we expand the toughness model beyond its original formulations (in Dienstbier, 1989, 1991). Specifically, based on our review of relevant literatures, we suggest that regimes of antidepressant medication and electroconvulsive shock (ECS) should be included with our list of "manipulations" that toughen. These manipulations, in turn, lead to CNS serotonin availability; thus we add serotonin availability to the list of physiological mediators. In addition, learning enhancement should be added to the performance-personality column, because learning improves with several of the physiological changes that constitute toughness.

Antidepressant Medication, ECS, Serotonin, and Receptor Sensitivities

There are many changes induced in the CNS by the manipulations discussed in this section, and there is little certainty about which of these changes are the critical ones for the personality/performance effects noted. Tranquilizers (e.g., chlorpromazine) that prevent episodes of acute stress from depleting neuroendocrines prevent toughening, even in the context of long-term manipulation programs (Adell, Garcia-Marquez, Armario, & Gelpi, 1989). Antidepressant medication and ECS (Weiner, 1984) regimes, however, have toughening impacts on the CNS that are similar to the effects of intermittent stressors. That is, ECS, tricyclic antidepressants such as imipramine, and intermittent stressors all initially stimulate CNS monoamine release, in the long term increasing the availability of catecholamines and serotonin in many brain areas (e.g., increases in adrenaline and noradrenaline in the hypothalamus; Roth, Mefford, & Barchas, 1982). Increased availability leads to resistance to depletion of CNS monoamines during subsequent prolonged stress and apparently stimulates secondary changes in receptor sensitivities, such as the downregulation (decreased

sensitivity) of CNS beta-receptors (as reflected in reduced cyclic AMP responses; Adell et al., 1989; Anisman & Zacharko, 1982; Stone, McEwen, Herrera, & Carr, 1987). All these physiological responses coincide with the positive personality/performance changes that are fostered by these therapeutic regimes (and by other toughening manipulations).

The noradrenaline-activated neurons of the locus ceruleus (LC), which form a major relay area for neural responses during stress, are also altered by the neuroendocrine processes induced by toughening. That is, LC discharge rates are reduced both by increased CNS adrenaline and by decreased CNS levels of CRH (the hypothalamic hormone responsible for activation of PAC arousal; Butler, Weiss, Stout, & Nemeroff, 1990). This circle of relationships is completed by noting that CNS adrenaline and noradrenaline both inhibit the release of CRH (Kvetnansky, 1980; this facilitating impact of CRH on LC firing may be one of the means by which CRH infusion induces anxiety [Bakke, Bogsnes, & Murison, 1990]).

A remaining controversial issue is whether the toughening-induced downregulation of brain monoamine receptors ultimately leads to reduced neural activity (Stone, 1983). Reduced beta-receptor sensitivity is associated with increased monoamine capacities and therefore potentially with increased transmitter discharge and neural responsivity under certain conditions. Another avenue for sustained or increased neural responsivity despite beta-receptor downregulation is suggested by the downregulation of the alpha-2 receptors (which inhibit noradrenaline discharge from neurons); those changes also result from the antidepressant regimes and probably from other toughening manipulations as well (Siever, 1983; Smith & Zelnik, 1983). Inferential evidence of increased neural responsivity despite receptor downregulation is seen in the functioning of peripheral organs, where intermittent stress or prolonged catecholamine administration is known to decrease beta-adrenergic receptor densities and/or cyclic AMP responsivity in heart, brown fat, white fat, and salivary glands with no decrease in function, but rather an increase in organ output in response to catecholamines (Stone, 1983).

Toughening Links to Learning Enhancement

While most of the research on learning enhancement has been done with animal subjects, there are supportive findings from research on learning in older humans. Peripheral catecholamine arousal

(McGaugh, 1990) and/or glucose elevations (Gold, 1986) during or immediately following a learning opportunity lead to vastly improved retention in animals, whereas processes that reduce catecholamines and/or glucose have opposite effects. Because chronic or severe acute stress depletes both the catecholamines and blood glucose, it follows (and is observed) that memory consolidation is disrupted for tasks that follow extreme stress in untoughened animals (Foy, Foy, Levine, & Thompson, 1990). On the other hand, memory facilitation effects follow sugar ingestion in animals (Messier & Destrade, 1988) and in older humans (Manning, Hall, & Gold, 1990). There are four observations that we would make in regard to the relationship of those memory processes to toughness. First, as discussed earlier, toughening increases the storage and synthesis of the neuroendocrines (primarily catecholamines) that stimulate glucose release. Thus, toughening manipulations may impact learning by indirectly changing glucose availability. Remember that glucose is the only source of energy that is used by the CNS, and glucose uptake in the brain is related to localized brain function, differing between brain areas depending on the nature of the learning required (Starter, Bodewitz, & Steckler, 1989; glucose also may regulate CNS function through direct impact on cholinergic functions [Stone, Cottrill, Walker, & Gold, 1988]). Second, as suggested by McGaugh (1990), it is likely that peripheral adrenaline directly stimulates peripheral receptors that, in turn, elicit noradrenaline release within the amygdala, thereby facilitating memory consolidation. Third, there is experimental evidence that aerobic exercise programs with elderly humans lead to enhanced mental performance in a variety of complex tasks (though such improvement could result from factors other than a more responsive catecholamine–glucose axis; Chodzko-Zajko, 1991). Fourth, and finally, there are neurotoxic effects from glucocorticoids acting on the hippocampus. The hippocampus (vital in memory consolidation) becomes damaged in normal animals as they age as a result of the normal activation of the PAC system. A program of toughening from early handling of rodents, however, results in adult animals that sustain lower base rates of PAC arousal and are better able to suppress stress-induced PAC arousal. As they age, those toughened animals show less age- and stress-related hippocampal damage, and they are superior to control animals in resisting aging-related spatial memory impairments (Meaney, Aitken, Viau, Sharma, & Sarrieau, 1989).

How Toughness Leads to Improved Coping and Emotional Stability

Before we elaborate this sequence of relationships, consider a basic model of interaction of mind and body. Cognitions and perceptions often elicit neuroendocrine changes that, in turn, cause end-organ physiological changes that then influence emotional or motivational states. Those state changes, in turn, modify (usually by sensitizing) readiness to perceive or generate relevant perceptions and cognitions. Any one of the elements of this circle may be the beginning of the interacting sequence. The influence of situation-induced physiological changes on the experience of panic discussed by Barlow et al. (1996) fits this model; interactions between mind and body in sequences of sexual arousal similarly fit; and, similarly, food perception or preoccupations that lead to insulin-induced blood glucose decline, and to subsequent increased hunger, may increase readiness to perceive and engage food cues. Our foci involve how perceptions of challenge/threat situations lead to arousal in the physiological systems of concern in this thesis, and how those changes in turn impact the personality/performance variables introduced previously.

The two most important relationships in the following sequence are that perceptions of challenge versus threat differentially impact arousal quality, and that physiological toughness similarly impacts both the quality and quantity of arousal. The Karolinska researchers (e.g., Frankenhaeuser, 1979) and others (e.g., study 1, Tomaka, Blascovich, Kibler, & Ernst, 1997) show that one's interpretation of a situation as challenging leads to arousal of the SAM, whereas perceptions of threat lead to a combination of PAC and SAM arousal. Recent research suggests that negative appraisals leading to PAC arousal occur more reliably for men than for women (e.g., Earle, Linden, & Weinberg, 1999). Even with nonhuman subjects, when active coping behaviors are permitted, leading to the experience of control and the possibility of successful coping, arousal of the PAC system is reduced (Hennessy & Foy, 1989; Levine & Levine, 1989; activation of the PAC system therefore seems relevant to Gray's [1981] behavioral inhibition system, and arousal of the SAM, with its stimulation of energy, relates to Gray's behavioral activation system).

Another key point in our argument is that with SAM arousal, energy will be stimulated by increased catecholamine availability (particularly by adrenaline, acting to stimulate glucagon and the breakdown of glycogen to glucose [glycogenolysis]). In combination with coping skills, if that energy is appraised as sufficient to successfully meet demands (a secondary appraisal, in the Lazarus system), then the (primary) appraisal of a potentially positive outcome is supported. Activities that previously have toughened the organism enhance this effect by increasing the liver's generation and utilization of the catecholamines with increasing glycogenolysis and thus the experience of energy (Mazzeo, 1991; U'Prichard & Kvetnansky, 1980).

On the other hand, consider the negative appraisal that stimulates the PAC system. While that system contributes to the processes of energy generation by increasing tissue sensitivity to the catecholamines (and by other more costly impacts such as facilitating the conversion of lean tissue to energy), such energization comes at some expense. That is, PAC arousal may contribute to the experience of anxiety, particularly via CRH effects in the brain (Butler et al., 1990), and to depression, particularly from cortisol and other corticosteroids (Barnes, 1986). Once those negative mood states have begun, self-focused attention rather than effective coping may result, with the subsequent reinforcement of the original negative appraisal and continued reactivation of PAC arousal. (Activation of that system also is associated with suppression of the immune system [O'Leary, 1990] and with some CNS neural damage [Meaney et al., 1989].)

Stripped of embellishments and references for simplicity, the following summarizes the foregoing:

1. Some of the elements of toughness (e.g., having a greater capacity for arousal and energy when needed, and being resistant to depression) lead to successful experiences rather than to failures.

2. Such a history of successes leads to optimistic appraisals in future situations where either challenge or threat could be perceived (i.e., one of the most common social-psychological manipulations to encourage optimistic predictions is to provide a history of past success).

3. Both optimistic appraisals and physiological toughness lead to activation of SAM-based arousal and associated feelings of energy, with minimal tension due to delayed activation of the PAC system.

4. Feeling energy rather than tension reinforces the optimistic secondary appraisal that coping will be successful, allowing one to focus on instrumental coping.

5. Attention to instrumental coping leads to frequent successes more reliably than does the self-focused attention and emotion-focused coping that tension frequently stimulates.

6. Successful coping leads to acceptance rather than avoidance of future challenges.

7. Acceptance of challenges over the long term leads to toughness.

Another feature of physiological toughness is the reduction in base rates of arousal in both the SAM and PAC systems. Apparently "sustained" arousal induced by either or both systems is eventually experienced as tension. Thus, it is commonplace to use arousal elevation as an indicator of strain (though researchers often are imprecise as to whether it is base rates or situation-induced arousal that they assess). It is these high base rates rather than increased situationally induced SAM responsivity that are associated with the psychosomatic problems often misattributed to responsivity (e.g., Matthews, 1986; Rauste-von Wright, von Wright, & Frankenhaeuser, 1981). Returns to base rates are studied infrequently but are undoubtedly centrally important in determining whether physiological damage results.

Finally, other modern additions to the previous observations from Tomaka, Blascovich, and colleagues (e.g., Tomaka et al., 1997) suggest that challenge appraisals lead to highly increased cardiac output with decreased total peripheral vascular resistance (the kind of arousal also associated with physical exercise). In contrast, threat appraisals are associated not only with moderate cardiac output increases but also with increased peripheral vascular resistance, suggesting physiological desynchronization with the possibility of long-term cardiovascular damage.

Recently, following Epel, McEwen, and Ickovics (1998), we have added "thriving" to the toughness concept. In these researchers' conceptualization of "thriving," neuroendocrine processes are divided into the traditional anabolic (growth and conservation of energy) versus catabolic (arousal and tissue-degrading) processes. Their emphasis is primarily on the catabolic and dysregulating effects of chronically elevated cortisol levels on PAC system balance, and insensitivities that then develop to both insulin and growth hormone.

On the other hand, Epel et al. suggested parallels to the toughness model by emphasizing anabolic "counterregulatory responses" that promote growth and toughening when organisms generate the catabolic responses that result from the experience of manageable challenges and stressors in the rhythms of intermittent exposure described here. In an empirical study, women who showed consistently elevated cortisol to lab stressors that were experienced across several days had lower psychological adjustment on a variety of indices (e.g., spiritual growth and appreciation for life).

Conclusions

Psychologists have traditionally focused on deficit conditions such as helplessness and depression. Those conditions tend to be self-sustaining. That is, the pessimism associated with depression leads to an avoidance of challenges and a corresponding lack of experiences that could have led to growth and an emergence from depression. The lack of energy that depression fosters similarly stimulates the avoidance of potentially restorative physical activity.

On the other hand, our emphasis on the positive psychology of toughness suggests that positive cycles can be similarly self-sustaining. Thus, once an individual becomes tough and thereby experiences the sustained energy (with minimal tension) necessary for successful coping, that person is likely to experience a greater variety of situations as challenging rather than threatening. That combination of optimism and energy should lead to the successes that stimulate further optimism and the acceptance of even more challenges. Toughness will increase with such a rhythm.

Questions for the Future

1. Are there critical periods for the development of toughness?
2. What psychological processes and interventions might best facilitate the development of toughness?
3. Does the efficacy of interventions that promote toughness vary across cultures and countries?

References

Adell, A., Garcia-Marquez, C., Armario, A., & Gelpi, E. (1989). Chronic administration of clomipramine prevents the increase in serotonin and noradrenaline induced by chronic stress. *Psychopharmacology, 99*, 22–26.

Anisman, H., & Zacharko, R. M. (1982). Depression: The predisposing influence of stress. *Behavioral and Brain Sciences, 5*, 89–137.

Baade, E., Ellertsen, B., Johnsen, T. B., & Ursin, H. (1978). Physiology, psychology, and performance. In H. Ursin, E. Baade, & S. Levine (Eds.), *Psychobiology of stress: A study of coping men* (pp. 163–182). New York: Academic Press.

Bakke, H. K., Bogsnes, A., & Murison, R. (1990). Studies on the interaction between ICV effects of CRF and CNS noradrenaline depletion. *Physiology and Behavior, 47*, 1253–1260.

Barlow, D. H., Chorpita, B. F., & Turovsky, J. (1996). Fear, panic, anxiety and disorders of emotion. In D. A. Hope (Ed.), *Nebraska Symposium on Motivation: Perspectives on anxiety,* *panic, and fear* (Vol. 43, pp. 251–328). Lincoln: University of Nebraska Press.

Barnes, D. M. (1986). Steroids may influence changes in mood. *Science, 232*, 1344–1345.

Bateson, G. (1979). *Mind and nature: A necessary unity*. London: Fontana Paperbacks.

Blumenthal, J. A., Fredrikson, M., Kuhn, C. M., Ulmer, R. L., Walsh-Riddle, M., & Appelbaum, M. (1990). Aerobic exercise reduces levels of cardiovascular and sympathoadrenal responses to mental stress in subjects without prior evidence of myocardial ischemia. *American Journal of Cardiology, 65*, 93–98.

Bove, A. A., Dewey, J. D., & Tyce, G. M. (1984). Increased conjugated dopamine in plasma after exercise training. *Journal of Laboratory and Clinical Medicine, 104*, 77–85.

Brown, G. W. (1988). Early loss of parent and depression in adult life. In S. Fisher & J. Reason (Eds.), *Handbook of life stress, cognition and health* (pp. 441–466). Chichester, UK: Wiley.

Brown, B. S., Payne, T., Kim, C., Moore, G., Krebs, P., & Martin, W. (1979). Chronic response of rat brain norepinephrine and serotonin levels to endurance training. *Journal of Applied Physiology: Respiration, Environmental and Exercise Physiology, 46*, 19–23.

Butler, P. D., Weiss, J. M., Stout, J. C., & Nemeroff, C. B. (1990). Corticotropin-releasing factor produces fear-enhancing and behavioral activating effects following infusion into the locus ceruleus. *Journal of Neuroscience, 10*, 176–183.

Chodzko-Zajko, W. J. (1991). Physical fitness, cognitive performance, and aging. *Medicine and Science in Sports and Exercise, 23*, 868–872.

Cleroux, J., Peronnet, F., & de Champlain, J. (1985). Sympathetic indices during psychological and physical stimuli before and after training. *Physiology and Behavior, 35*, 271–275.

DeBoer, S. F., Koopmans, S. J., Slangen, J. L., & Van der Gugten, J. (1990). Plasma catecholamine, corticosterone and glucose responses to repeated stress in rats: Effect of interstressor interval length. *Physiology and Behavior, 47*, 1117–1124.

Dienstbier, R. A. (1984). The effect of exercise on personality. In M. L. Sachs & G. B. Buffone (Eds.), *Running as therapy: An integrated approach*. Lincoln, NE: University of Nebraska Press.

Dienstbier, R. A. (1989). Arousal and physiological toughness: Implications for mental and physical health. *Psychological Review, 96*, 84–100.

Dienstbier, R. A. (1991). Behavioral correlates of sympathoadrenal reactivity: The toughness model. *Medicine and Science in Sports and Exercise, 22*, 846–852.

Dienstbier, R. A. (1992). Mutual impacts of toughening on crises and losses. In L. Montada, S.-H. Filipp, & M. J. Lerner (Eds.), *Life crises and experiences of loss in adulthood* (pp. 367–384). Hillsdale, NJ: Erlbaum.

Dienstbier, R. A., LaGuardia, R. L., Barnes, M., Tharp, G., & Schmidt, R. (1987). Catecholamine training effects from exercise programs: A bridge to exercise–temperament relationships. *Motivation and Emotion, 11*, 297–318.

Dienstbier, R. A., LaGuardia, R. L., & Wilcox, N. S. (1987). The relationship of temperament to tolerance of cold and heat: Beyond "cold hands–warm heart." *Motivation and Emotion, 11*, 269–295.

Earle, T. L., Linden, W., & Weinberg, J. (1999). Differential effects of harassment on cardiovascular and salivary cortisol stress reactivity and recovery in women and men. *Journal of Psychosomatic Research, 46,* 125–141.

Epel, E. S., McEwen, B. S., & Ickovics, J. R. (1998). Embodying psychological thriving: Physical thriving in response to stress. *Journal of Social Issues, 54,* 301–322.

Folkman, S., & Lazarus, R. S. (1985). If it changes it must be a process: Study of emotion and coping during three stages of a college examination. *Journal of Personality and Social Psychology, 48,* 150–170.

Foy, M. R., Foy J. G., Levine, S., & Thompson, R. F. (1990). Manipulation of pituitary-adrenal activity affects neural plasticity in rodent hippocampus. *Psychological Science, 1,* 201–204.

Frankenhaeuser, M. (1979). Psychoneuroendocrine approaches to the study of emotion as related to stress and coping. In H. E. Howe, Jr., & R. A. Dienstbier (Eds.), *Nebraska Symposium on Motivation, 1978: Human emotion* (Vol. 26, pp. 123–161). Lincoln, NE: University of Nebraska Press.

Glazer, H. I., Weiss, J. M., Pohorecky, L. A., & Miller, N. E. (1975). Monoamines as mediators of avoidance-escape behavior. *Psychosomatic Medicine, 37,* 535–543.

Gold, P. E. (1986). Glucose modulation of memory storage processing. *Behavioral and Neural Biology, 45,* 342–349.

Gray, J. A. (1981). *The physiopsychology of anxiety.* Oxford: Oxford University Press.

Hennessy, M. B., & Foy, T. (1989). Nonedible material elicits chewing and reduces the plasma corticosterone response during novelty exposure in mice. *Behavioral Neuroscience, 101,* 237–245.

Hennessy, J. W., & Levine, S. (1979). Stress, arousal, and the pituitary-adrenal system: A psychoendocrine hypothesis. In J. M. Sprague & A. N. Epstein (Eds.), *Progress in psychobiology and physiological psychology* (Vol. 8, pp. 33–67). New York: Academic Press.

Hull, E., Young, S., & Ziegler, M. (1984). Aerobic fitness affects cardiovascular and catecholamine responses to stressors. *Psychophysiology, 21,* 253–260.

Konarska, M., Stewart, R. E., & McCarty, R. (1989a). Habituation of sympathetic-adrenal medullary responses following exposure to chronic intermittent stress. *Physiology and Behavior, 45,* 255–261.

Konarska, M., Stewart, R. E., & McCarty, R. (1989b). Sensitization of sympathetic-adrenal medullary responses to a novel stressor in chronically stressed laboratory rats. *Physiology and Behavior, 46,* 129–135.

Konarska, M., Stewart, R. E., & McCarty, R. (1990). Habituation and sensitization of plasma catecholamine responses to chronic intermittent stress: Effects of stressor intensity. *Physiology and Behavior, 47,* 647–652.

Kvetnansky, R. (1980). Recent progress in catecholamines under stress. In E. Usdin, R. Kvetnansky, & I. J. Kopin (Eds.), *Catecholamines and stress: Recent advances* (pp. 1–7). New York: Elsevier/North Holland.

LeBlanc, J., Boulay, M., Dulac, S., Jobin, M., Labrie, A., & Rousseau-Migneron, S. (1977). Metabolic and cardiovascular responses to norepinephrine in trained and nontrained human subjects. *Journal of Applied Physiology, 42,* 166–173.

LeBlanc, J., Dulac, S., Cote, J., & Girard, B. (1975). Autonomic nervous system and adaptation to cold in man. *Journal of Applied Physiology, 39,* 181–186.

Levine, S. (1960). Stimulation in infancy. *Scientific American, 202,* 80–86.

Levine, R., & Levine, S. (1989). Role of the pituitary-adrenal hormones in the acquisition of schedule-induced polydipsia. *Behavioral Neuroscience, 103,* 621–637.

Linden, W., Earle, T. L., Gerin, W., & Christenfeld, N. (1997). Physiological stress reactivity and recovery: Conceptual siblings separated at birth? *Journal of Psychosomatic Research, 42,* 117–135.

Manning, C. A., Hall, J. L., & Gold, P. E. (1990). Glucose effects on memory and other neuropsychological tests in elderly humans. *Psychological Science, 5,* 307–311.

Matthews, K. A. (1986). Summary, conclusions, and implications. In K. A. Matthews, S. M. Weiss, T. Detre, T. M. Dembroski, B. Falkner, S. B. Manuck, et al. (Eds.), *Handbook of stress, reactivity, and cardiovascular disease* (pp. 461–473). New York: Wiley.

Mazzeo, R. S. (1991). Catecholamine responses to acute and chronic exercise. *Medicine and Science in Sports and Exercise, 23,* 839–845.

McCarty, R., Horwatt, K., & Konarska, M. (1988). Chronic stress and sympathetic-adrenal medullary responsiveness. *Social Science and Medicine, 26,* 333–341.

McGaugh, J. L. (1990). Significance and remembrance: The role of neuromodulatory systems. *Psychological Science, 1,* 15–25.

Meaney, M. J., Aitken, D. H., Viau, V., Sharma, S., & Sarrieau, A. (1989). Neonatal handling alters adrenocortical negative feedback sensitivity and hippocampal Type II glucocorticoid receptor binding in the rat. *Neuroendocrinology, 50,* 597–604.

Messier, C., & Destrade, C. (1988). Improvement of memory for an operant response by post-training glucose in mice. *Behavioral Brain Research, 31,* 185–191.

Miller, N. E. (1980). A perspective on the effects of stress and coping on disease and health. In S. Levine & H. Ursin (Eds.), *Coping and health* (pp. 323–354). New York: Plenum.

Morgan, W. P., Brown, D. R., Raglin, J. S., O'Connor, P. J., & Ellickson, K. A. (1987). Psychological monitoring of overtraining and staleness. *British Journal of Sports Medicine, 27,* 107–114.

O'Leary, A. (1990). Stress, emotion, and human immune function. *Psychological Bulletin, 108,* 363–382.

Rauste-von Wright, M., von Wright, J., & Frankenhaeuser, M. (1981). Relationships between sex-related psychological characteristics during adolescence and catecholamine excretion during achievement stress. *Psychophysiology, 18,* 362–370.

Rodriguez Echandia, E. L., Gonzalez, A. S., Cabrera, R., & Fracchia, L. N. (1988). A further analysis of behavioral and endocrine effects of unpredictable chronic stress. *Physiology and Behavior, 43,* 789–795.

Roth, K. A., Mefford, I. M., & Barchas, J. D. (1982). Epinephrine, norepinephrine, dopamine and serotonin: Differential effects of acute and chronic stress on regional brain amines. *Brain Research, 239,* 417–424.

Siever, L. J. (1983). Mode of action of antidepressant agents: Increased output or increased efficiency? *Behavioral and Brain Sciences, 6,* 558.

Smith, C. B., & Zelnik, T. C. (1983). Alpha-2 adrenergic receptors and the mechanism of action of antidepressants. *Behavioral and Brain Sciences, 6,* 559.

Starter, M., Bodewitz, G., & Steckler, T. (1989). 2-[3*H*] Deoxyglucose uptake patterns in rats exploring a six-arm radial tunnel maze: Differences between experienced and nonexperienced rats. *Behavioral Neuroscience, 103,* 1217–1225.

Steptoe, A. (1987). Invited review: The assessment of sympathetic nervous function in human stress research. *Journal of Psychosomatic Research, 31,* 141–152.

Stone, E. A. (1983). Problems with current catecholamine hypotheses of antidepressant agents: Speculations leading to a new hypothesis. *Behavioral and Brain Sciences, 6,* 535–547.

Stone, E. A., McEwen, B. S., Herrera, A. S., & Carr, K. D. (1987). Regulation of alpha and beta components of noradrenergic cyclic AMP response in cortical slices. *European Journal of Pharmacology, 141,* 347–356.

Stone, W. S., Cottrill, K. L., Walker, D. L., & Gold, P. E. (1988). Blood glucose and brain function: Interactions with CNS cholinergic systems. *Behavioral and Neural Biology, 59,* 325–334.

Tomaka, J., Blascovich, J., Kibler, J., & Ernst, J. M. (1997). Cognitive and physiological antecedents of threat and challenge appraisal. *Journal of Personality and Social Psychology, 73,* 63–72.

U'Prichard, D. C., & Kvetnansky, R. (1980). Central and peripheral adrenergic receptors in acute and repeated immobilization stress. In E. Usdin, R. Kvetnansky, & I. J. Kopin (Eds.), *Catecholamines and stress: Recent advances* (pp. 299–308). New York: Elsevier/North Holland.

Weiner, R. D. (1984). Does electroconvulsive therapy cause brain damage? *Behavioral and Brain Sciences, 7,* 1–53.

Weiss, J. M., Glazer, H. I., Pohorecky, L. A., Brick, J., & Miller, N. E. (1975). Effects of chronic exposure to stressors on avoidance-escape behavior and on brain norepinephrine. *Psychosomatic Medicine, 37,* 522–534.

Winder, W. W., Hagberg, J. M., Hickson, R. C., Ehsani, A. A., & McLane, J. A. (1978). Time course of sympathoadrenal adaptation to endurance exercise training in man. *Journal of Applied Physiology, 45,* 370–376.

PART 9

Positive Institutions

Family-Centered Positive Psychology

Susan M. Sheridan *and* Jennifer D. Burt

Abstract

Throughout the past several decades the economic and cultural conditions of the American family have changed dramatically. These changing family dynamics create challenges for service providers to work with families in a way that supports their healthy functioning and respects their values. The presence of multiple risk factors is generally understood to create discontinuities in interaction rules between home and community environments and contribute to challenges in assuring positive family functioning. Within this chapter, we discuss the characteristics of healthy children and families and how the parent–child relationship can serve as a protective factor for young children at risk. Family-centered positive psychology (FCPP) recognizes the family as a constant in the child's life and strives to support both child well-being and healthy family functioning. Throughout this chapter, families and children are discussed from a strengths-based approach that recognizes the assets and strengths present within the family rather than the deficits or limitations. Family-centered services (FCSs) are a framework for service delivery that is based on the principles of FCPP. In FCSs, service providers strive to create a context within which families may become empowered; assist family members to identify their unique needs and acquire skills and competencies; and identify social networks to promote positive outcomes for the child and family. In this chapter, we describe the primary principles of family-centered care, discuss implications for practice, describe one model of family-centered care that illustrates FCS in practice, and discuss future research directions for FCPP.

Keywords: child well-being, conjoint behavioral consultation, family-centered services, parent–child relationship, positive psychology

Throughout the past several decades the American family has become increasingly diverse. There has been a dramatic decrease in the traditional family, which consists of two biological parents with one parent in the workforce and one parent serving as the caregiver. The population of children living with two parents has decreased from 77% in 1980 to 67% in 2005 (Federal Interagency Forum for Child and Family Statistics, 2006), and the proportion of single-parent families with women as the primary caregiver more than doubled between 1960 and 1988 (Carlson, 1996). Further, the number of unmarried parents grew by 71% in the 1990s, and 36% of all births in 2004 were to unmarried women (Federal Interagency Forum for Child and Family Statistics, 2006).

The cultural and economic conditions of the family have also changed during the past several decades. In 2002, the United States Department of Education reported 60.3% of children were White, non-Hispanic; 17.2% Black, non-Hispanic; 17.1% Hispanic; 4.2% Asian/Pacific Islander; and 1.2% American Indian/Alaska Native. In addition, the number of children in immigrant families has grown rapidly in nearly every state across the country. According to the 2000 census, 1 of every 5 children in the United States is an immigrant, or a child of immigrant parents (Hernandez, 2004), and nearly 20% of children speak a language other than English in the home (Federal Interagency Forum for Child and Family Statistics, 2006). Further, 17% of children under the age of 18 in the United States live in poverty (Federal Interagency Forum for Child and Family Statistics, 2006).

The changing dynamics of the American family creates challenges for service providers to work with families in ways that support their healthy functioning and respect their cultural values. It is generally understood that the presence of multiple risk factors (e.g., poverty status, speaking English as a second language, and female-headed household) creates discontinuities for children and families and contributes to challenges in assuring positive family functioning. However, certain protective factors are also known to create conditions to support healthy development, and the promotion of such buffers may help ameliorate risk and improve child outcomes.

Parent involvement in child learning and development is hypothesized to serve as a protective factor for young children at risk (Fantuzzo, McWayne, Perry, & Childs, 2004; McWayne, Hampton, Fantuzzo, Cohen, & Sekino, 2004; Parker, Boak, Griffin, Ripple, & Perry, 1999). Once children start school, they spend 70% of their waking hours outside of school (Clark, 1990). Given the large percentage of time that children spend with their families, it is critical that child and family well-being is emphasized as a major priority for service delivery providers as children learn and develop in the context of the family (Pianta & Walsh, 1996). The purpose of this chapter is to define qualities of a healthy family and to provide recommendations for service providers to promote child and family well-being.

Healthy Children and Families

Child well-being and health is developed within the context of the family. Pollard and Rosenberg (2003) define child well-being as everything that encompasses the child's physical health and psychological development. "Health" is defined as a condition of complete physical, mental, and social well-being rather than the mere absence of disease (World Health Organization, 1983). These definitions are contrary to traditional psychological and medical approaches that generally focus on disorders, disabilities, and deficits. Further, most research on children and families maintains a deficit focus; it concentrates more on the role of risk factors than assets and protective factors. We argue that understanding the qualities of families and their environments that might explain why some children and families fare better than others in the face of adversity is equally important to address in research and practice. Throughout this chapter, families and children will

be discussed from a strengths-based approach that focuses on assets and strengths present within families rather than deficits or absences of a specific asset. First, we will discuss the role of child and family assets and the parent–child relationship to understand the context necessary to promote child well-being. Then we will discuss a method of service delivery, family-centered services (FCSs), that builds on existing family strengths to promote positive outcomes for children and families.

Assets are the opposite of risk factors in that their presence predicts better outcomes regardless of the level of risk (Masten & Reed, 2002). To promote child well-being, it is critical to develop a thorough understanding of child and family assets as a method to provide services that build on the strengths of the entire family. The Search Institute of Minneapolis (2005) defines 40 developmental assets, both internal and external, that serve as essential tools for healthy child development. External assets consist of the physical experiences available to the child from the world around them (e.g., providing support; providing appropriate boundaries and expectations; creating opportunities for positive, structured activities). These assets are constructed and shaped by the child's caregiver and/or community. For example, a family that provides support to their child demonstrates that the child is loved and accepted by making family dinners a priority, spending time getting to know their child's friends, and asking their child to provide opinions about important family issues.

Internal assets reflect what caregivers do to enhance the child's psychological well-being (e.g., providing opportunities to develop a commitment to learning, instilling positive values and commitments, nurturing social competencies, instilling a sense of self-confidence and positive identity). The internal developmental assets are hypothesized to help children make thoughtful, positive choices and enhance self-confidence (Search Institute, 2005). For example, a family that helps a child develop social competencies allows the child to make mistakes and then helps the child to accept responsibility and learn from the mistake. A parent might also encourage conversations about peer pressure and share stories about his or her own childhood and teenage years. The extent to which children develop into healthy adults is influenced by the presence or absence of both external and internal assets.

A strong, consistent relationship exists between the number of assets present in young people's lives and the extent to which they develop in positive, healthy ways (Search Institute, 2005). Children with more assets present in their life have been found to exhibit leadership skills, maintain positive health, value diversity, and demonstrate positive academic outcomes. Conversely, youth with few assets are at increased risk to engage in high-risk behaviors such as alcohol use, violence, drug use, and sexual activity. The Search Institute of Minneapolis proposed that 31 assets are ideal to increase positive youth outcomes. However, 59% of young people surveyed reported fewer than 20 assets present, suggesting that there is a gap in the number of assets that most youth experience and the number of assets desired for healthy development.

Promoting these assets within the context of the family system is crucial for helping families to build competencies in their children. Building assets is an ongoing process that starts at birth and continues through adolescence and beyond. Importantly, families must provide young people with consistent messages about what is important and expected of them, and these assets should be continually reinforced by families throughout each developmental stage. Service providers can also help parents develop and enhance these assets within the context of a healthy parent–child relationship.

Parent–Child Relationship

The quality of the parent–child relationship sets the stage for later competence (de Ruiter & van Ijzendoorn, 1993; NICHD Early Child Care Research Network, 2002; Parker et al., 1999). In this sense, it is less about what the parent *does* and more about *how* the parent interacts with the child that determines a positive developmental trajectory. Specific parenting behaviors associated with child well-being include (a) warmth and sensitivity (DeKlyen, Speltz, & Greenberg, 1998; Goldberg, 1990; Maccoby & Martin, 1983) and (b) support for autonomy (Coplan, Findlay, & Nelson, 2004; Herrenkohl & Russo, 2001; Smith, Landry, & Swank, 2000). Warm and sensitive parenting is defined as responsiveness to the child's cues and emotional availability to the child (Emde & Robinson, 2000). Parental support for autonomy is characterized by those behaviors that help children to negotiate tasks that challenge their tolerance, self-control, and attention span (Sheridan, Edwards, & Knoche, 2003).

The extent to which these behaviors are present within parent–child interactions appears equally important from early childhood through adolescence.

For example, maternal sensitivity to the child's signals has been found to predict positive cognitive and social outcomes during early childhood (NICHD Early Child Care Research Network, 2002; Parker et al., 1999). During middle childhood, parental warmth and responsiveness is associated with the development of self-esteem, competence, and social responsibility in the child (Collins, Harris, & Sussman, 1995). In adolescence, warm and responsive parenting has been associated with a variety of positive outcomes including self-esteem, identity formation, prosocial behavior, better parent–adolescent communication, and less depression, anxiety, and behavior problems (Hetherington & Martin, 1986; Holmbeck, Paikoff, & Brooks-Gunn, 1995; Maccoby & Martin, 1983). Although the nature of the parent–child relationship changes from early childhood to adolescence, the presence of these parenting behaviors appears to be critical to child well-being. Ecological systems theory provides a conceptual framework for understanding the role of the parent–child relationship and of the family system on promoting and fostering child well-being.

Ecological Theory as a Framework for Understanding and Working with Families

Ecological systems theory proposes that children learn and develop within the context of the many interactions between the child, family, classroom, school, and community (Bronfenbrenner, 1989; Rimm-Kaufman & Pianta, 2000). Central to this theory is the premise that each child and family member is an inseparable part of a larger social network consisting of four interrelated systems (i.e., microsystem, mesosystem, exosystem, and macrosystem). The microsystem is the layer closest to the individual (e.g., home, child care providers, and school) and includes immediate environments in which individuals function. The mesosystems are the connections or relationships between microsystem members (e.g., child–parent, child–school, and school–family). The exosystem describes the larger social system in which microsystems and mesosystems exist, but that does not impact individual functioning in a direct manner. The macrosystem includes cultural values, customs, and laws that influence the interactions throughout all of the systems.

The home setting constitutes a significant influence on a child's development at the microsystemic level. Consistent with ecological theory, family configuration, social support, social class, poverty, and culture are all associated with differences in parenting practices. Factors such as the marital relationship, child temperament, financial and emotional stress, and level of support can have a significant influence on the quality of the parent–child relationship (Cox & Harter, 2003). Thus, to understand and support families, it is essential that broader social and cultural factors be considered as they permeate all family and child experiences.

Interactions between the family and other important systems in a child's life (e.g., school) constitute an important aspect of the mesosystem. These relationships, including parent–child relationships, do not occur in a vacuum (Cox & Harter, 2003). Support and structures from agencies and workplaces within the broader community that support healthy parent–child relationships and asset building represent the effect of the exosystem on the family system (Christenson & Sheridan, 2001). Ensuring access to community resources and social networks has the potential to positively influence family behavior and positive child development. Further, the macrosystem serves as a foundation for promoting a context that influences family beliefs and practices and ultimately child behavior and development. Creating connections with and for families is a key translational implication of ecological theory (i.e., linking theory to practice). Family-centered positive psychology (FCPP), focused on families' assets, strengths, and social networks, provides a framework for translating ecological theory into services.

Family-Centered Positive Psychology

FCPP "is a framework for working with children and families that promotes strengths and capacity building within individuals and systems, rather than one focusing on the resolution of problems or remediation of deficiencies" (Sheridan et al., 2004, p. 7). Within this framework, the family is recognized as a constant within a child's life and services are delivered *with* families, rather than *to* or *for* families, to support both child well-being and healthy family functioning (Garbacz et al., 2006). Promoting well-being in children and families is more than fixing what is wrong with them. It is about identifying and nurturing their strongest qualities and using them to build capacities within the child and family (Seligman & Csikszentmihalyi, 2000). Services that are family-centered focus on assessing a family's needs and strengths from the perspective of the family using a positive, strengths-based approach rather than being concerned with

ameliorating deficits (Dunst, Trivette, Davis, & Cornwell, 1994).

FCSs aim to provide opportunities for parents and other familial caregivers to develop and demonstrate competence and confidence. This is accomplished by helping family members use or develop their own skills and social networks to support their efforts to help their children learn and grow. Major emphasis is placed on "supporting and strengthening family functioning" (Dunst, Trivette, & Deal, 1994, p. 73) from a positive and proactive rather than deficit-based or categorical orientation (McWilliam, Tocci, & Harbin, 1998).

Guiding Principles of Family-Centered Services

FCSs are based on several premises or principles that together form the basis of service delivery. These are (a) family empowerment, (b) acquisition of competencies, (c) identification of family-determined needs, (d) the use of existing family strengths, and (e) promotion of social supports.

FAMILY EMPOWERMENT

Family-centered approaches to working with families create contexts within which families may become empowered. Empowerment involves proactively promoting an individual's sense of control through their ability to use existing strengths (Dempsey & Dunst, 2004). We borrow from Dunst, Trivette, and Deal's (1988) notion of empowerment as a helping model that supports families in proactively identifying needs, mobilizing resources, and accomplishing goals through the development of personal capacities, strengths, and abilities. According to Dunst et al. (1988), "it is not just an issue of whether needs are met but rather that [*sic*] manner in which mobilization of resources and support occurs that is a major determinant of . . . empowering families" (p. 44). The emphasis is on family members' acquisition of competencies necessary for goal attainment. As such, there is a focus on growth-producing behaviors among parents, children, and educators, rather than simply treating existing problems.

ACQUISITION OF NEW SKILLS AND COMPETENCIES

Rather than utilizing strategies to "treat" problems or remediate deficiencies, FCS approaches strive to promote the acquisition of family and child competencies. Alternatively, FCS attends proactively to growth-producing behaviors through its emphasis on strengths, assets, and skills among family members. This, in turn, builds competence and confidence, allowing family members to address a range of presenting challenges in the future. In sum, it is not sufficient to simply "solve" an identified "problem"; it is also necessary to provide assistance to a family so that its members develop increased skills and resources to approach future concerns and needs (Sheridan et al., 2004).

FAMILY-IDENTIFIED RATHER THAN PROFESSIONAL-DETERMINED NEEDS

FCS is responsive to the needs of the family and focuses assessment efforts on those needs that are most essential for the continued growth of the family. FCS models assume that families are in the best position to identify their most important needs, and commitment to change may be greatest when families' needs are self-determined.

USE OF EXISTING FAMILY STRENGTHS

FCS is founded on the belief that all families have strengths and abilities, but environmental or systemic conditions may present difficulties in accessing or using those strengths. The help provider is in a position to assist family members to identify, access, and mobilize their strengths and use them to attain their self-determined goals. The ability of family members to use existing strengths for meeting their needs leads to positive changes in their functioning (Garbarino, 1982).

STRENGTHENING SOCIAL SUPPORTS

FCS models are structured around collaborations and partnerships that access formal and informal supports for family members. The development of positive, proactive linkages and networks help family members mobilize resources that are available to them but that they may have been perceived as inaccessible. Furthermore, the notion of "partnership" implies that family members are co-equal

partners in the identification of needs and goals, selection of strategies and plans, and evaluation of outcomes as programs and resources are utilized (Christenson & Sheridan, 2001; Welch & Sheridan, 1995). Thus, services are not delivered to or for families, but with family members as active partners and participants.

Implications for Practice: Collaborating With versus Treating Families

Various methods for working with families are available, including those that use problem-oriented, prevention-oriented, or strengths-oriented perspectives. We concur with Pollard and Rosenberg (2003) who argued for an integration of these approaches. That is, a model that views the benefits of a strengths-based approach with a problem prevention approach can glean the benefits of each. Structured problem-focused models are useful as frameworks for organizing and delivering services. Prevention models have a broad impact and tend to address potential concerns before they reach crisis levels. Strengths-based approaches build on existing competencies and promote personal investment in growth and development. From a family-centered perspective, "collaborating with" versus "treating" families promotes optimal growth.

Certain professional practices promote an integrated, collaborative approach when working with families. These "helpful helping" behaviors reflect actions that seek to involve the family as active participants in the change process. Alternatively, actions wherein control and decision making reside with the professional limit the opportunity for family members to develop skills and competencies independent of the professional. Examples of practices that are characteristic of "helpful helping" are listed in Table 52.1.

As a result of helpful help-giving practices, families are likely to experience feelings of

---

Table 52.1 Professional practices that promote "helpful helping"

Help giver

Employs active and reflective listening
Helps clients clarify concerns and needs
Proactively offers help in response to help-seeker's needs
Offers help that is congruent and matches the help seeker's appraisal of needs
Promotes acquisition of competencies to meet needs, solve problems, and achieve aspirations
Allows locus of decision making to rest with the family member
Promotes partnerships and parent–professional collaboration as the mechanism for meeting needs

empowerment, increased competency, and positive self-attributions. Effective helping practices are largely defined by notions of "empowerment," wherein families develop personal strengths, capacities, and capabilities in identifying needs, mobilizing resources, and attaining goals (Sheridan et al., 2004). Through a process that creates conditions within which family members become empowered, they develop self-efficacy and a sense of control. This, in turn, maximizes families' abilities to access and activate personal resources and meet personal needs (Dempsey & Dunst, 2004). That is, within this framework, families develop the "confidence and competence" to meet their own needs while help providers work collaboratively to prioritize needs and support family improvements.

Family-centered practices are distinguished by relational and participatory components that together contribute to the effectiveness of help-giving strategies (Dunst, 2002). "Relational components" consist of practices associated with good clinical behaviors and listening skills, and the beliefs toward working with families that are communicated through actions and attitudes. They are important prerequisites to effective family-centered services. "Participatory components" emphasize the nature of services themselves in ways that promote active roles of family members. Services that are participatory are individualized, flexible, and responsive to family needs. They facilitate family–professional partnerships to maximize families' abilities to acquire skills and knowledge, participate in decision making, and develop and implement actions to achieve family-identified goals. Although relational components are commonly utilized within family-oriented models, the simultaneous use of "both" relational and participatory components distinguishes a family-centered approach as an effective "help-giving" model, as they set the stage for family members to be truly empowered.

A collaborative approach to working with families may promote an integrated framework for services. Family involvement in planning, decision making, and intervening on behalf of themselves and their child(ren) has been shown to be related to a host of positive developmental outcomes for children (Henderson & Berla, 1994; Sheridan, Kratochwill, & Elliott, 1990). Models of service delivery in home and community settings that focus on collaboration between family members and professionals provide a unique, strengths-based framework for implementing prevention and intervention programs. From a partnership perspective, ideas, opinions, values, and priorities are shared among parents and professionals (Dunst, Trivette, & Deal, 1988; Hanft, Rush, & Shelden, 2004). These shared inputs determine the direction of decision making, allowing for the mutual creation of intervention strategies that reflect unique contributions from multiple perspectives. Such commitment to the collective process increases participants' ownership of and responsibility for problem solving and implementation of intervention plans (Duke, Showers, & Imber, 1980; Dunst, Trivette, & Deal, 1994).

Consultation-based service delivery models with families provide opportunities to work with families in a collaborative manner. Decades of research in consultation-based service delivery (cf. Sheridan, Clarke, & Burt, 2008; Sheridan, Welch, & Orme, 1996) have yielded substantial empirical evidence supporting a structured, data-based model that involves (a) identifying and prioritizing shared goals, (b) analyzing factors that may influence skill development or performance, (c) developing intervention strategies that can address concerns and achieve goals, and (d) evaluating the effectiveness of chosen strategies. These structured service-delivery models share the dual goals of promoting positive child outcomes, and enhancing skills and competencies of participants (e.g., parents) to address future needs.

One such model for achieving data-based collaboration with families is conjoint behavioral consultation (CBC; Sheridan & Kratochwill, 2008; Sheridan et al., 1996). CBC is a model of service delivery that attempts to develop effective partnerships and social supports for families. It is defined as "a strength-based, cross-system problem-solving and decision-making model wherein parents and other caregivers or service providers work as partners and share responsibility for promoting positive and consistent outcomes related to children's . . . development" (Sheridan & Kratochwill, 2008). In CBC, parents and other caregivers engage collaboratively in a structured problem-solving process with a professional consultant to address the needs of children across settings, such as home and school. Through a series of structured meetings and frequent unstructured, supportive interactions, parents and other caregivers work together with consultants to share information in the identification of children's needs and to develop, implement, and evaluate interventions that address those needs.

Three overarching goals drive CBC services. The first goal is to enhance "positive outcomes for children and families" through mutual planning. The second goal is to promote "parent engagement with children" and "involvement in interventions" within a developmental, culturally sensitive framework. Finally, a collaborative planning process strives to "strengthen relationships and support networks for parents and children" by (a) being responsive to the priorities and concerns of families, (b) developing and enhancing competencies and skills of parents and other caregivers, and (c) strengthening social supports and promoting partnerships and collaboration among participants (Sheridan et al., 2008). Thus, building skills for parents and other caregivers to engage in long-term problem solving and decision making, versus simply learning a discrete set of intervention steps, are important foci of collaborative approaches.

Research on CBC has demonstrated consistently that the consultation-based model is effective in positively enhancing child outcomes across social, behavioral, and academic domains for children in kindergarten through grade 12 (Sheridan, Eagle, Cowan, & Mickelson, 2001; Sheridan et al., 2008). Its usefulness in promoting social skills has been documented for early elementary-aged children (Sheridan et al., 1990) and children with disabilities (Colton & Sheridan, 1998). The effectiveness of CBC in addressing concerns of families and caregivers in early-intervention contexts (Sheridan, Clarke, Knoche, & Edwards, 2006) has also been demonstrated. The advantages of this model lie in its focus on parents as competent partners and the use of children's natural learning opportunities with parents, while retaining an effective, data-based decision-making process (Sheridan et al., 1990, 2001).

Future Research Directions

The dynamic and responsive nature of FCSs provides ample opportunities to operationalize the principles into meaningful practice. However, there has been a dearth of formal models that provide a structure for service delivery. CBC is just one model that can be conceptualized and practiced using family-centered principles. There may be more specific and structured practices that define the practice; however, these have not been investigated in empirical research. That is, FCSs have not been adequately operationalized or defined as an independent variable in intervention research to date. Research is needed that operationally defines FCSs, assesses their potential efficacy in demonstration-level projects, and subsequently subjects them to rigorous empirical investigation.

Related to the need to operationalize FCSs as an independent variable in research is the need to define relevant outcomes. The most meaningful manner to evaluate FCSs has not been identified. That is, the selection of functional and relevant dependent variables should be determined. Similarly, reliable and valid measurement of outcomes is essential but currently imprecise. A multimethod, multisource assessment framework that extends beyond informant reports or self-perceptions, and includes direct measures of family functioning, is necessary.

Finally, there is a need to understand the mechanisms by which FCSs interact with family contexts within overlapping ecological levels. By definition, FCS is responsive to and empowering of unique and relevant family dynamics. Nevertheless, unique family circumstances (e.g., family constellation, composition, experiences, culture) may determine the manner in which FCS is most effectively defined and evaluated. This reality of practice complicates research that strives to operationalize services and outcomes, and is a fruitful area of conceptual and empirical development.

Acknowledgments

This chapter was supported in part by grants awarded to the first author by the Department of Health and Human Services (DHHS), National Institute of Child Health and Human Development (NICHD), Administration for Children and Families (ACF) and Office of the Assistant Secretary for Planning and Evaluation (ASPE), and the U.S. Department of Education (DOE) Office of Special Education and Rehabilitative Services (OSERS); Grant #R01H00436135. The opinions presented are those of the authors and do not reflect official positions or policies of the granting agencies.

Questions about the Topic

1. What is the operational definition of family-centered services and which models of care meet this definition?

2. How can the integrity and quality of family-centered services be assessed?

3. How does the application of family-centered services translate to child and family outcomes (e.g., treatment integrity, child outcomes, parent satisfaction, parenting skills, parent sense of competence)?

References

Bronfenbrenner, U. (1989). Ecological systems theory. *Annals of Child Development, 6*, 187–249.

Carlson, C. (1996). Best practices in working with single-parent and step-family systems. In A. Thomas & J. Grimes (Eds.), *Best practices in school psychology III* (pp. 1097–1110).

Washington, DC: National Association of School Psychologists.

Christenson, S. L., & Sheridan, S. M. (2001). *Schools and families: Creating essential connections for learning*. New York: Guilford.

Clark, R. M. (1990, Spring) . Why disadvantaged students succeed: What happens outside school is critical. *Public Welfare*, 17–23.

Collins, W. A., Harris, M. L., & Sussman, A. (1995). Parenting during middle childhood. In M. H. Bornstein (Ed.), *Handbook of parenting: Vol.1. Children and parenting* (pp. 65–89). Mahwah, NJ: Lawrence Erlbaum.

Colton, D., & Sheridan, S. M. (1998). Conjoint behavioral consultation and social skills training: Enhancing the play behavior of boys with attention deficit-hyperactivity disorder. *Journal of Educational and Psychological Consultation, 9*, 3–28.

Coplan, R. J., Findlay, L. C., & Nelson, L. J. (2004). Characteristics of preschoolers with lower perceived competence. *Journal of Abnormal Child Psychology, 32*, 399–408.

Cox, M. J., & Harter, K. S. M. (2003). Parent–child relationships. In M. Bornstein, L. Davidson, C. Keyes, & K. Moore (Eds.), *Well-being: Positive development across the life course* (pp. 191–203). Mahwah, NJ: Lawrence Erlbaum.

DeKlyen, M., Speltz, M. L., & Greenberg, M. T. (1998). *A license to teach: Raising standards for teaching*. San Francisco: Jossey-Bass.

Dempsey, I., & Dunst, C. J. (2004). Help-giving styles as a function of parent empowerment in families with a young child with a disability. *Journal of Intellectual and Developmental Disability, 29*(1), 50–61.

de Ruiter, C., & van Ijzendoorn, M. H. (1993). Attachment and cognition: A review of the literature. *International Journal of Educational Research, 18*, 525–540.

Duke, D., Showers, B., & Imber, M. (1980). Teachers and shared decision-making: The costs and benefits of involvement. *Educational Administration Quarterly, 16*(1), 93–106.

Dunst, C. J. (2002). Family-centered practices: Birth through high school. *Journal of Special Education, 36*, 139–147.

Dunst, C. J., Trivette, C. M., & Deal, A. (Eds.). (1994). *Supporting and strengthening families: Vol. I. Methods, strategies and practices*. Cambridge, MA: Brookline Books.

Dunst, C. J., Trivette, C. M., Davis, M., & Cornwell, J. C. (1994). Characteristics of effective help-giving practices. In C. J. Dunst, C. M. Trivette, & A. Deal (Eds.), *Supporting and strengthening families: Vol. I. Methods, strategies and practices* (pp. 171–186). Cambridge, MA: Brookline.

Dunst, C. J., Trivette, C. M., & Deal, A. (1988). *Enabling & empowering families: Principles & guidelines for practice*. Cambridge, MA: Brookline.

Emde, R. N., & Robinson, J. (2000). Guiding principles for a theory of early intervention: A developmental-psychoanalytic perspective. In J. Shonkoff & S. Meisels (Eds.), *Handbook of early childhood intervention* (2nd ed., pp. 160–178). Cambridge: Cambridge University Press.

Fantuzzo, J., McWayne, C., Perry, M. A., & Childs, S. (2004). Multiple dimensions of family involvement and their relations to behavioral and learning competencies for urban, low-income children. *School Psychology Review, 33*, 467–480.

Federal Interagency Forum for Child and Family Statistics. (2006). *America's children: Key national indicators of well-being, 2006*. Washington, DC: U.S. Government Printing Office.

Garbacz, S. A., Rohlk, A. M., Swanger, M. S., Woods, K. E., Black, K. A., & Sheridan, S. M. (2006, March). *Conjoint behavioral consultation: The effectiveness of a partnership orientation*. Paper presented at the annual meeting of the National Association of School Psychologists, Anaheim, CA.

Garbarino, J. (1982). *Children and families in the social environment*. New York: Aldine.

Goldberg, S. (1990). Attachment in infants at risk: Theory, research, and practice. *Infants and Young Children, 2*(4), 11–20.

Hanft, B., Rush, D., & Shelden, M. (2004). *Coaching families and colleagues in early childhood intervention*. Baltimore: Paul Brookes Publishing Co.

Henderson, A. T., & Berla, N. (Eds.). (1994). *A new generation of evidence: The family is critical to student achievement*. Washington, DC: Center for Law and Education (ERIC Document Reproduction Service No. ED3750968).

Hernandez, D. J. (2004). *Demographic change and the life circumstances of immigrant families*. Washington, DC: Foundation for Child Development.

Herrenkohl, R. C., & Russo, M. J. (2001). Abusive early child rearing and early childhood aggression. *Child Maltreatment, 6*, 3–16.

Hetherington, E. M., & Martin, B. (1986). Family factors and psychopathology in children. In H. C. Quay & J. S. Werry (Eds.), *Psychopathology disorders of childhood* (3rd ed., pp. 332–390). New York: Wiley.

Holmbeck, G. N., Paikoff, R. L., & Brooks-Gunn, J. (1995). Parenting adolescents. In: M. Bornstein (Ed.), *Handbook of parenting*(Vol. 1, pp. 91–118). Hillsdale, NJ: Erlbaum.

Maccoby, E. E., & Martin, J. A. (1983). Socialization in the context of the family: Parent–child interaction. In E. M. Hetherington (Ed.), *Handbook of child psychology: Vol. 4. Socialization, personality, and social development* (pp. 469–546). New York: Wiley.

Masten, A. S., & Reed, M.-G. J. (2002). Resilience in development. In C. R. Snyder & S. J. Lopez (Eds.), *Handbook of positive psychology* (pp. 74–88). New York: Oxford University Press.

McWayne, C., Hampton, V., Fantuzzo, J., Cohen, H. L., & Sekino, Y. (2004). A multivariate examination of parent involvement and the social and academic competencies of urban kindergarten children. *Psychology in the Schools, 41*, 363–377.

McWilliam, R. A., Tocci, L., & Harbin, G. L. (1998). Family-centered services: Service providers' discourse and behavior. *Topics in Early Childhood Special Education, 18*, 206–221.

NICHD Early Child Care Research Network. (2002). Parenting and family influences when children are in child care: Results from the NICHD Study of Early Child Care. In J. G. Borkowski & S. L. Ramey (Eds.), *Parenting and the child's world: Influences on academic, intellectual, and social-emotional development* (pp. 99–123). Mahwah, NJ: Lawrence Erlbaum.

Parker, F. L, Boak, A. Y., Griffin, K. W., Ripple, C., & Perry, L. (1999). Parent–child relationship, home learning environment, and school readiness. *School Psychology Review, 28*, 413–425.

Pianta, R. C., & Walsh, D. S. (1996). *High-risk children in schools: Constructing sustaining relationships*. New York: Routledge.

Pollard, E. L., & Rosenberg, M. L. (2003). The strength-based approach to child well-being: Let's begin with the end in mind. In M. Bornstein, L. Davidson, C. Keyes, & K. Moore (Eds.), *Well-Being: Positive development across the life course* (pp. 13–21). Mahwah, NJ: Lawrence Erlbaum.

Rimm-Kaufman, S. E., & Pianta, R. C. (2000). An ecological perspective on the transition to kindergarten: A theoretical framework to guide empirical research. *Journal of Applied Developmental Psychology, 21*, 491–511.

Search Institute. (2005). *40 developmental assets for early childhood.* Retrieved June 6, 2006, from http://www.search-institute.org/research/40AssetsEC.pdf

Seligman, M. E. P., & Csikszentmihalyi, M. (2000). Positive psychology. *American Psychologist, 56*, 216–217.

Sheridan, S. M., Clarke, B. L., & Burt, J. D. (2008). Conjoint behavioral consultation: What do we know and what do we need to know? In W. P. Erchul & S. M. Sheridan (Eds.), *Handbook of research in school consultation: Empirical foundations for the field* (pp. 171–202). Mahwah, NJ: Lawrence Erlbaum.

Sheridan, S. M., Clarke, B. L., Knoche, L. L., & Edwards, C. P. (2006). The effects of conjoint behavioral consultation in early childhood settings. *Early Education and Development, 17*, 593–617.

Sheridan, S. M., Eagle, J. W., Cowan, R. J., & Mickelson, W. (2001). The effects of conjoint behavioral consultation: Results of a four-year investigation. *Journal of School Psychology, 39*, 361–385.

Sheridan, S. M., Edwards, C. P., & Knoche, L. L. (2003, November). *Parent engagement and child learning birth to five.* Paper presented at the semi-annual meeting of the Interagency School Readiness Consortium, Washington, DC.

Sheridan, S. M., & Kratochwill, T. R. (2008). *Conjoint behavioral consultation: Promoting family–school connections and interventions.* New York: Springer.

Sheridan, S. M., Kratochwill, T. R., & Elliott, S. N. (1990). Behavioral consultation with parents and teachers: Delivering treatment for socially withdrawn children at home and school. *School Psychology Review, 19*, 33–52.

Sheridan, S. M., Warnes, E., Brown, M., Schemm, A., Cowan, R. J., & Clarke, B. L. (2004). Family-centered positive psychology: Building on strengths to promote student success. *Psychology in the Schools, 41*, 7–17.

Sheridan, S. M., Welch, M., & Orme, S. (1996). Is consultation effective? A review of outcome research. *Remedial and Special Education, 17*, 341–354.

Smith, K. E., Landry, S. H., & Swank, P. R. (2000). The influence of early patterns of positive parenting on children's preschool outcomes. *Early Education and Development, 11*, 147–169.

United States Department of Education, National Center for Education Statistics. (2002). *Mini digest of education statistics, 2002* [Data file]. Retrieved March 15, 2004, from Links to Educational Resources: http://usinfo.state.gov/usa/infousa/educ/edlinks.htm

Welch, M., & Sheridan, S. M. (1995). *Educational partnerships: Serving students at-risk.* San Antonio, TX: Harcourt-Brace Jovanovich.

World Health Organization. (1983). *A WHO report on social and biological effects on perinatal mortality, 1.* Statistical Publishing House, Budapest, Hungary, 1978. Reissued by *Saudi Medical Journal*, 1983, *4*, Suppl. 1.

Positive Schools

E. Scott Huebner, Rich Gilman, Amy L. Reschly, *and* Russell Hall

Abstract

This chapter defines positive schools as ones in which students experience predominantly positive subjective well-being in the form of positive emotions and positive attitudes toward school (i.e., school satisfaction). Following a definition of positive subjective well-being, measurement issues are discussed. Subsequently, research on the correlates of positive school satisfaction is discussed, including presumed antecedents and consequences of individual differences in school satisfaction among children of elementary and secondary school age. Key features of positive schools are identified and several examples of empirically validated, school-based intervention programs that influence students' subjective well-being are given. Finally, implications for future research are discussed.

Keywords: children, engagement, schooling, school satisfaction, well-being

Positive psychology research has been organized into three overarching themes: positive emotions, positive traits, and positive institutions (Seligman & Csikszentmihalyi, 2000). The first theme focuses on persons' subjective well-being (SWB), which incorporates frequent positive affect (PA; e.g., joy, excitement), infrequent negative affect (NA; e.g., sadness, anxiety), and satisfaction with life overall and with specific domains, such as family life and schooling (Diener, Emmons, Larsen, & Griffin, 1985). The second theme focuses on character traits (e.g., citizenship, altruism, work ethic), and the third involves institutions, such as schools and families. Basic research related to individual differences in SWB and character traits of children (and adults) has increased during the last few decades; however, research on SWB and "schooling" has lagged behind. Likewise, school reform efforts have deemphasized the importance of SWB. Rather, attention has been directed mostly to cognitive outcomes, especially academic achievement (Rutter & Maughan, 2002).

Studies of positive psychology (including SWB) and schooling have been limited (Snyder & Lopez, 2007). The majority of the data collected on school-age children has emphasized "negative" indicators of SWB (e.g., NA, psychological symptoms); there has been a dearth of data involving positive indicators. However, an interest in positive youth development has initiated the construction of positive measures of SWB in children and youth (Roberts, Brown, Johnson, & Reinke, 2002).

Research with adults has demonstrated that frequent PA is predictive of success in numerous life domains, including marriage, friendships, income, vocational success, and physical and mental health (see Lyubomirsky, King, & Diener, 2005). The findings are consistent with Frederickson's (2001) "broaden and build" model, which posits that PA expands individuals' thought and action repertoires (e.g., play, explore), promoting adaptive behavior. In contrast, NA is thought to narrow people's reactions (e.g., fight, flight) to immediate threats. Across time, PA thus enhances adaptive behavior through the construction of a wide array of personal resources, positive social relationships, flexible coping behaviors, and learning opportunities whereas frequent NA reduces environmental exploration and personal resilience. Little research has explored connections between adults' positive SWB (including PA) and educational experiences; however, the extant literature suggests that individuals who experience frequent positive emotions would be most likely to be successful in the educational arena as well, given that they are emotionally "prepared" to explore, solve problems, and succeed at new learning tasks (Lewis, Huebner, Reschly, & Valois, in press; Lyubomirsky et al., 2005; Reschly, Huebner, Appleton, & Antaramian, 2008).

Although there is a fairly substantial body of research on the adaptive functions of positive SWB in adults, little research has been conducted with children and youth. Even less research has been conducted regarding the relationships between positive SWB and the functioning of children in "schools." The purpose of this chapter is to summarize the knowledge and implications related to personal and contextual (e.g., school) variables that contribute to children's SWB in school settings. In the first section, a conceptualization of positive schools and a brief overview of measurement techniques are provided. The second section summarizes key features of positive schools that can be derived from the literature. Finally, examples of "formal," evidence-based, school-based interventions influencing SWB in school-age children are provided.

Conceptualization and Measurement of Positive School Experiences

A substantial body of research links SWB via NA (e.g., sadness, anxiety) with decreased academic performance (e.g., Roeser, Eccles, & Strobel, 1998). However, little research has explored whether PA enhances academic success or school behavior. Because there are few studies of students' individual differences in PA in schools, this review focuses primarily on life satisfaction (LS), specifically satisfaction with school experiences.

School satisfaction (SS) is defined as a student's judgment of the positivity of his or her school experiences "as a whole" (Huebner, 1994). Similar to global LS, SS is a construct that reflects both a cognitive judgment and related affect, such as the frequency of positive and negative emotions (cf. Diener et al., 1985; Huebner & McCullough, 2001). Given the relatively small body of literature on SS, studies of variables (e.g., school bonding, flow) related to SS are included at times.

Research supports the importance of individual differences in students' SS. Huebner and Gilman (2006) showed that high levels of SS are associated

with school-related benefits above and beyond "average" and "below average" levels, such as higher GPAs, a greater sense of agency, and fewer psychological symptoms. Also, higher SS is associated with fewer adolescent problem behaviors (DeSantis King, Huebner, Suldo, & Valois, 2006). Most importantly, SS has been shown to be a precursor of student engagement behaviors and academic progress, in students as young as kindergarteners (Ladd, Buhs, & Seid, 2000).

SS has been investigated primarily within the context of multidimensional models of LS. For example, Huebner (1994) developed a hierarchical model for children and youth, including general LS as the higher-order factor along with five lower-order domains: family, friends, school, self, and living environment. The relative importance of SS, relative to the other domains, is illustrated by two large-scale studies, one with middle schoolers (Huebner, Valois, Paxton, & Drane, 2005) and one with high schoolers (Huebner, Drane, & Valois, 2000). Both studies revealed that students were more likely to be "dissatisfied" with school than family, friends, self, living environment, or their overall lives. Nearly a quarter of the 5,545 students in the high school study reported dissatisfaction with school, with 9% describing their experiences as "terrible." Similar findings have also been noted among students in Ireland, Croatia, and South Korea (Gilman et al., 2008). These findings suggest that a sizeable number of students in the United States and elsewhere experience a negative quality of school life.

Studies of children's perceptions of the quality of their life experiences, including SS, necessitate psychologically sound measurement tools. The development of reliable and valid SWB measures (especially measures of PA) appropriate for children and youth has lagged behind that of adults (Gilman & Huebner, 2003). Nevertheless, measures of LS and SS exist that are appropriate for research. For example, the Students' Life Satisfaction Scale (SLSS: Huebner, 1991) and the Multidimensional Students' Life Satisfaction Scale (MSLSS) (Huebner, 1994; Huebner, Laughlin, Ash, & Gilman, 1998) have been validated for students in grades 3–12. The SLSS is based on a unidimensional model (cf. Diener et al., 1985) that reflects domain-free LS (e.g., "I am satisfied with my life 'overall' ") whereas the MSLSS is based on a multidimensional model incorporating multiple major domains (e.g., family, school). These measures enable the assessment of satisfaction levels above neutral (e.g., mildly vs. moderately satisfied), encompassing a more comprehensive range of experiences compared to psychopathology-based measures (e.g., depression, anxiety). Differentiations in the higher ranges are useful because they reveal variations in adjustment that are not captured by measures of psychopathology (Gilman & Huebner, 2006; Suldo & Huebner, 2006).

The MSLSS School subscale represents a unidimensional construct, that is, satisfaction with school experiences "as a whole." Student responses reflect their own criteria, rather than those of the researchers (e.g., teacher relations, curricula, facilities). Students thus individually "weight" the criteria that determine their overall subjective experience of schooling without being limited to specific, a priori facets (Diener et al., 1985). In addition to the MSLSS, measures of global SS are included within some well-validated instruments of a more general nature, such as the Behavior Assessment System for Children (Reynolds & Kamphaus, 2004) and the Quality of School Life Scale (Epstein & McPartland, 1976).

From this "quality of life" perspective, a positive school is defined as a school whose students report generally positive emotions and SS. This perspective is thus differentiated from school climate research, in which researchers typically preselect key environmental features (see Lehr & Christenson, 2002, for a review of the school climate literature). Although multidimensional measures of quality of school life and school climate exist, researchers have not agreed upon the critical features.

Measures of global SS and related constructs (e.g., PA) thus provide a global evaluation of students' perceived goodness of fit between their needs and values and their educational environments. This broad evaluation perspective is consistent with scholars who have issued calls for assessments of the impact on quality of life of all human "interventions" including public schooling.

Correlates of School Satisfaction

The SS literature remains in an early stage of development; however, preliminary evidence supports a synthesis of the literature. This review will first summarize research investigating student-level correlates of SS, including demographic, personality, and behavioral characteristics. The review will then describe contextual factors, more specifically teacher–classroom and school variables that promote or hinder SS.

Student-Level Correlates

Demographic characteristics. Similar to what has been reported in the larger LS literature, variance accounted for by demographic variables is small, generally ranging from about 2% (Ainley, Foreman, & Sheret, 1991) to 7% (Karatzias, Power, Flemming, Lennan, & Swanson, 2002), depending on the variables studied, sample compositions, and measures used. Studies of gender differences have yielded equivocal findings, with some studies revealing no gender differences (Bulcock, Whitt, & Beebe, 1991; Huebner, Ash, & Laughlin, 2001; Huebner & Gilman, 2006; Katja, Paivi, Marja-Terttu, & Pekka, 2002) whereas others finding that girls reported significantly higher SS than boys (Eamon, 2002; Karatzias et al., 2002; Okun, Braver, & Weir, 1990; Verkuyten & Thijs, 2002). Nevertheless, the effect size of these differences was 0.20 or less. Studies investigating age differences also report small effect sizes (Karatzias et al., 2002). Several large-scale studies investigating race differences among American samples have reported no differences between African American and Caucasian students' SS (e.g., Eamon, 2002; Epstein & McPartland, 1976) or between Native Americans, Hispanic Americans, and Asian Americans (Okun et al., 1990). Finally, cross-national differences have been noted. A recent study of adolescents in America, Ireland, Croatia, Korea, and China found that students from Western countries reported lower SS than their counterparts from Eastern countries (Gilman et al., 2008). However, effect sizes were also "low."

Personality characteristics. Compared to demographics, personality characteristics contribute greater variance to students' SS. For example, self-esteem relates positively to SS, with effect sizes reported as high as 0.48 (Karatzias et al., 2002). Further, although SS is related to higher grades (Huebner & Gilman, 2006), high grades alone are not enough to explain SS (Epstein & McPartland, 1976). One important variable in comprehensive explanatory models is academic self-efficacy, which mediates the relationship between school performance and SS (Verkuyten & Thijs, 2002). Other personality correlates include hope (Huebner & Gilman, 2006), PA (Karatzias et al., 2002), and intrinsic motivation (Gilman & Anderman, 2006). Conversely, SS relates negatively to depression (Eamon, 2002), anxiety (Epstein & McPartland, 1976; Huebner & Gilman, 2006), NA (Karatzias et al., 2002), and external locus of control (Gilman & Anderman, 2006). In general, these findings demonstrate that comprehensive models of SS must include personality variables.

Behavioral characteristics and life experiences. Beyond personality correlates, SS has been associated with important school and personal behaviors. For example, students who report higher levels of SS tend to be more involved in extracurricular activities (Gilman, 2001) and socially competent (Eamon, 2002). They are also less likely to drop out (Ekstrom, Goertz, Pollack, & Rock, 1986), or participate in risk behaviors, such as using alcohol or drugs (Katja et al., 2002). Lower SS is also related to interpersonal difficulties (Gilman & Anderman, 2006) and mental health problems (Baker, 1998).

SS can be related to events outside of students' control. For example, Huebner et al. (2001) reported that nonschool events were significant predictors of SS, with chronic negative life experiences contributing variance above acute negative life events. Positive life experiences also contribute variance to SS. For example, Huebner and McCullough (2000) reported that positive nonschool events (e.g., hobbies, dating, spending time with family) predicted variance in SS beyond that of negative events. Positive social resources in particular appear to contribute important variance (Huebner et al., 2001).

Specific groups. Little research has examined the SS of members of specific groups. Further, relationships may be mediated by the nature and quality of resources provided to the student. For example, Zeidner and Schleyer (1999) found that students in gifted classes reported higher SS than gifted youth in regular classes. Ash and Huebner (1998) observed that gifted youths' SS contributed a greater portion of variance to their overall LS than that of nongifted youth. Both studies suggest that contextual factors may differentially influence SS.

Studies of students with disabilities have been rare, although extant findings indicate significant differences between SS reports of disabled versus nondisabled students. For example, one study of youth representing a variety of disabilities (physical, sensory, learning, etc.) found that, collectively, such students reported significantly lower SS than nondisabled peers (Hogan, McLellan, & Bauman, 2000). Conversely, Brantley, Huebner, and Nagle (2002) found that adolescents with mild mental disabilities (MMDs) reported significantly higher SS than nondisabled peers. Again, one explanation for these contradictory findings may involve differences in educational resources provided to children with disabilities. For example, in the Brantley et al. study, classroom placement appeared to influence the level of satisfaction held by MMD students, as students in self-contained settings reported significantly higher SS than disabled peers who spent 3 or more hours in a regular education setting. Similar findings also were noted with deaf/hard-of-hearing youth, where higher SS was reported by those in totally segregated environments, in comparison to those attending day school (Gilman, Easterbrooks, & Frey, 2004).

Contextual Factors

Teacher–classroom variables. Research consistently shows that the types of supports and structure that are afforded by teachers are related to students' engagement and participation in school (Furrer & Skinner, 2003; Wentzel, 1998), which in turn may facilitate positive SWB, including SS (Baker, 1998; Baker, Terry, Bridger, & Winsor, 1997). For example, teachers who provide a high degree of clarity in developing and enforcing classroom rules, and who create a predictable classroom structures, facilitate SS (see Baker, Dilly, Aupperlee, & Patil, 2003). Other classroom contextual factors that may contribute to high SS include establishing curricula that promote choice and autonomy (Karatzias et al., 2002), promoting a task-oriented classroom ethos (Baker, 1998), providing ample praise for appropriate behaviors (Baker, 1999), and emphasizing goals that promote future academic aspirations (Malin & Linnakyla, 2001). By the same token, teachers who establish class structures that are overly controlling or give more attention to misbehaviors rather than good behaviors can diminish students' SS (Baker, 1999; Carey & Bourbon, 2005).

Factors that contribute to social acceptance and peer support also contribute to SS (see Baker et al., 2003, for a review). Students whose teachers are able to promote positive peer interactions report positive attitudes toward their teachers and overall SS (Baker, 1998; Verkuyten & Thijs, 2002). Further, schools that actively encourage students to participate in school-related activities (e.g., sports, student government) also report higher SS than students in schools that offer little encouragement (Berntsson & Gustafsson, 2000). Some evidence suggests that the benefits of such encouragement may generalize to non-school-related activities (e.g., active involvement in church and community-related interests; Gilman, 2001).

Finally, the relevance of classroom instructional methods has been underscored. A recent study examined a variety of school courses from the perspective of flow theory (Shernoff, Csikszentmihalyi,

Schneider, & Shernoff, 2003). In brief, "flow" is a state of deep absorption in an intrinsically interesting activity that contains challenges and skills that neither exceed nor underutilize an individual's abilities (see chap. 18). Shernoff et al. found that the most engaging and satisfying moments for students occurred during instructional tasks that incorporated group work activities or individual activities that involved active learning, as opposed to a lecture format. Although additional studies are needed, these particular results provide a unique perspective on the type of instructional methods that may best foster meaningful and satisfying classroom learning experiences.

School variables. To date, limited research has examined relationships between school structure variables and SS. Extant research has yielded equivocal results. For example, the relationship between school size and SS is nonsignificant in some studies (Verkuyten & Thijs, 2002), but significant in others (Bowen, Bowen, & Richman, 2000; Malin & Linnakyla, 2001). Among the significant findings, Bowen et al. reported SS declines in schools with populations of 1,000 students or more, whereas Malin and Linnakyla found a gender effect, with girls in large classrooms reporting lower SS than boys. These differences may be due to the sample composition (Dutch vs. Finnish vs. American children), educational philosophy of the nations represented by these samples, and/or the measures used to assess SS.

Continuity of contact between teachers and students may also be important. For example, the practice of teachers following their students from one year to the next (i.e., "looping") has evidenced greater teacher and parent satisfaction (Felner et al., 1993).

Characteristics of Positive Schools

The research reviewed herein reveals general support for a positive psychology perspective in which schools can be viewed as empowering institutions that promote positive SWB, as indicated by SS and related variables, and the development of psychosocial strengths, in addition to academic learning. As such, positive schools can move away from problem-centered approaches to "wellness" approaches, which focus on "maximizing children's chances to manifest and exploit their abilities and interests" (Cowen, 1997, p. ix). This thinking is in line with the assertion of Roberts et al. (2002) that positive psychology needs to take a developmental perspective, recognizing that childhood may be the optimal

time to promote healthy SWB. Such efforts are expected to be especially attractive to school personnel who work to design optimal environments for children with special needs, as well as "all" children (Snyder & Lopez, 2002). Given this perspective, personnel can expand their roles beyond the traditional "repair" modes emphasized in psychology, special education, medicine, and so on (Gilman & Huebner, 2003).

More specifically, this research has implications for the delivery of psychologically healthy educational environments for children. Although much additional research is needed, several key attributes of positive schools can be hypothesized from the SS literature. These attributes include monitoring SS and related SWB variables, individualizing experiences for students, providing supportive interpersonal relationships, and increasing the active engagement of students.

First, positive schools appreciate the importance of SWB to students' academic success. Positive schools recognize that they must be inhabited by emotionally healthy students. They implement systematic plans to frequently assess students' SWB, including SS and emotions. Because aspects of SWB appear to be among the determinants of academic and behavioral performance, as well as "indicators" of positive outcomes, data regarding the levels and fluctuations in students' SWB should prove useful in efforts to promote the "psychological health" of schools. Beyond school-wide efforts, students who show low or decreased levels of SWB could be targeted for group or individual interventions. Staff members realize that by promoting SWB in their schools, they are supporting an important protective factor against the development of behavior problems.

Second, positive schools work with individual differences in personality, abilities, and interests to maximize the goodness of fit between school experiences and students' needs. Their efforts include attention to students' unique personal strengths and environmental assets. As noted previously, this situation applies not only to "normal" students but also to students with special needs and at-risk students. The articulation of personal strengths and environmental supports can balance the identification of "deficits" so that such students can be understood and educated in a more holistic manner. Students are more likely to be satisfied with their schooling if they are treated as persons with strengths, who are inherently capable of growth. Such positive SWB should hopefully set an "upward spiral" of success into motion (Frederickson, 2001).

Third, positive schools facilitate supportive teacher and peer relationships. They intentionally design school settings to maintain high levels of positive interactions among "all" participants. For example, school-wide positive behavior support programs have been developed, which focus on the development and maintenance of positive teacher–student and student–student interactions in an environment rich with reinforcers (Lewis, Sugai, & Colvin, 1998).

Fourth, positive school settings emphasize instructional tasks that enhance student involvement through offering appropriately challenging, interesting, and voluntary activities. Csikszentmihalyi and Schneider (2000) provide useful recommendations pertinent to educational policy for secondary schools. These recommendations include the development of curricula that emphasize creativity and emotional intelligence and increased provision of instructional activities that are intellectually engaging (vs. passive), social in nature (e.g., activities with peers), and intrinsically motivating—underscoring the importance of lifelong learning for students, clarifying the links between time management and vocational preparation, and leading to greater parental involvement in teenagers' lives.

The final implication of this research relates to program planning and evaluation efforts. Students are the recipients of a wide variety of psychosocial, educational, and medical "programs" as individuals and members of groups. SS research, which is embedded within the larger SWB literature, underscores the importance of monitoring the effects of universal interventions (e.g., public school programs) as well as selected interventions (e.g., individualized programs for students with special needs, medication treatments for adolescents with depression). In all cases, school programs should be evaluated from the ethical perspective of at least "do no harm" to the longer-term quality of life and SWB of their child clients. The development of an SWB research base and associated measures appropriate for children of a wide age and ability range provides the opportunity to evaluate programs from a more comprehensive perspective than usual, that is, with respect to their impact upon recipients' subjective quality of life, in addition to more traditional indicators (e.g., behavior problems, academic performance).

Few formal classroom intervention programs have targeted and/or demonstrated effects on SWB. In a review of empirically validated, school-based social-emotional programs, Zins, Bloodworth, Weissberg, and Walberg (2004) identified two large-scale, formal programs that increased positive attitudes toward school among students. The first program was the Child Development Project (Solomon, Battistich, Watson, Schaps, & Lewis, 2000), which conceptualized schools as caring communities of learners. This project utilized cooperative learning, proactive classroom management, prosocial norms, classroom and school-wide community building activities, parent–student activities, and a language arts program that emphasized critical thinking about social and ethical issues. The second program was the Seattle Social Development Project (Hawkins, Catalano, Kosterman, Abbott, & Hill, 1999), which was a multiyear school-based program infused throughout the elementary school curriculum. This project also was multifaceted, incorporating proactive classroom management, active student involvement, interpersonal problem-solving training, cooperative learning activities, and varied reading instruction approaches. Systematic evaluations of these projects converge to demonstrate that academic and social-emotional goals and activities can be integrated successfully in classrooms, with positive effects in both the affective and academic realms. More detailed descriptions of these programs can be found on the Web site for the Center for Academic and Social-Emotional Learning (CASEL), http://www.casel.org.

Conclusion

Positive psychology offers a valuable perspective for school policy. In contrast to a traditional problem-oriented focus, positive psychology provides a "wellness" focus that has the potential to expand conceptualizations of schooling, students, and educational processes (Cowen, 1997). From this perspective, positive schools seek to orient their goals toward promoting students' SWB as well as their cognitive and academic competencies. Furthermore, SWB is conceptualized as more than the absence of "problems." Thus, positive schools attempt to facilitate optimal functioning among all students, recognizing that "all" students have strengths. Notably, students' environments, including their school environments, also exhibit some protective factors, which influence SWB. The existing research illuminates the broad outlines of the characteristics of positive schools, that is, schools that facilitate student SWB.

Future research is needed to delineate the specific, core components and psychosocial mechanisms associated with positive school environments.

To date, there is noteworthy lack of studies of broader environmental contexts, such as neighborhood, community, media, and interactional systems (e.g., home–school connections, school–community connections). Using Bronfenbrenner's (1979) conceptualization, the mesosystem, exosystem, and macrosystem have been largely ignored. Research addressing linkages between these systems and student SWB will likely provide a more comprehensive perspective and understanding of the determinants, correlates, and consequences of individual differences in students' school performance.

Three Key Questions about the Future of This Topic

1. Is the positive school-related subjective well-being–academic performance relationship reciprocal in nature?

2. What are the psychosocial mediators and moderators of the school-related subjective well-being–academic performance relationship?

3. What larger ecosystemic factors (e.g., macrosystem) relate to students' school-related subjective well-being?

References

Ainley, J., Foreman, J., & Sheret, M. (1991). High school factors that influence students to remain in school. *Journal of Educational Research, 85*, 69–80.

Ash, C., & Huebner, E. S. (1998). Life satisfaction reports of gifted middle-school children. *School Psychology Quarterly, 13*, 310–321.

Baker, J. A. (1998). The social context of school satisfaction among urban, low-income, African-American students. *School Psychology Quarterly, 13*, 25–44.

Baker, J. A. (1999). Teacher–student interaction in urban at-risk classrooms: Differential behavior, relationship quality, and student satisfaction with school. *The Elementary School Journal, 100*, 57–70.

Baker, J. A., Dilly, L. J., Aupperlee, J. L., & Patil, S. A. (2003). The developmental context of school satisfaction: Schools as psychologically healthy environments. *School Psychology Quarterly, 18*, 206–221.

Baker, J. A., Terry, T., Bridger, R., & Winsor, A. (1997). Schools as caring communities: A relational approach to school reform. *School Psychology Review, 26*, 586–602.

Berntsson, L., & Gustafsson, J. E. (2000). Determinants of psychosomatic complaints in Swedish schoolchildren aged seven to twelve years. *Scandinavian Journal of Public Health, 28*, 283–293.

Bowen, G. L., Bowen, N. K., & Richman, J. M. (2000). School size and middle school students' perceptions of the school environment. *Social Work in Education, 22*, 69–82.

Brantley, A., Huebner, E. S., & Nagle, R. J. (2002). Multidimensional life satisfaction reports of adolescents with mild mental disabilities. *Mental Retardation, 40*, 321–329.

Bronfenbrenner, U. (1979). *The ecology of human development.* Cambridge, MA: Harvard University Press.

Bulcock, J. W., Whitt, M. E., & Beebe, M. J. (1991). Gender differences, student well-being, and high school achievement. *Alberta Journal of Educational Research, 37*, 209–224.

Carey, T. A., & Bourbon, W. T. (2005). Countercontrol: What do the children say? *School Psychology International, 26*, 595–615.

Cowen, E. (1997). Foreword. In R. P. Weissberg, T. P. Gullotta, R. L. Hampton, B. A. Ryan, & G. R. Adams (Eds.), *Enhancing children's wellness* (Vol. 8, pp. ix–xi). Thousand Oaks, CA: Sage.

Csikszentmihalyi, M., & Schneider, B. (2000). *Becoming adult: How teenagers prepare for the world of work.* New York: Basic Books.

DeSantis King, A., Huebner, E. S., Suldo, S. M., & Valois, R. F. (2006). An ecological view of school satisfaction in adolescence: Linkages between social support and behavior problems. *Applied Research in Quality of Life, 1*, 279–295.

Diener, E., Emmons, R. A., Larsen, R. J., & Griffin, S. (1985). The Satisfaction with Life Scale. *Journal of Personality Assessment, 49*, 71–75.

Eamon, M. K. (2002). Influences and mediators of the effect of poverty on youth adolescent depressive symptoms. *Journal of Youth and Adolescence, 31*, 231–242.

Ekstrom, R. B., Goertz, M. E., Pollack, J. M., & Rock, D. A. (1986). Who drops out of high school and why? Findings from a national study. *Teachers College Record, 87*, 356–373.

Epstein, J., & McPartland, J. M. (1976). The concept and measurement of the quality of school life. *American Educational Research Journal, 13*, 15–30.

Felner, R. D., Brand, S., Adan, A. M., Mulhall, P. F., Flowers, N., Sartain, B., et al. (1993). Restructuring the ecology of the school as an approach to prevention during school transitions: Longitudinal follow-ups and extensions of the School Transitional Environment Project (STEP). *Prevention in Human Services, 10*, 103–136.

Frederickson, B. L. (2001). The role of positive emotions in positive psychology: The broaden-and-build theory of positive emotions. *American Psychologist, 56*, 218–226.

Furrer, C., & Skinner, E. (2003). Sense of relatedness as a factor in children's academic engagement and performance. *Journal of Educational Psychology, 95*, 148–162.

Gilman, R. (2001). The relationship between life satisfaction, social interest, and frequency of extracurricular activities among adolescent students. *Journal of Youth and Adolescence, 30*, 749–767.

Gilman, R., & Anderman, E. M. (2006). The relationship between relative levels of motivation and intrapersonal, interpersonal, and academic functioning among older adolescents. *Journal of School Psychology, 44*, 375–391.

Gilman, R., Easterbrooks, S. R., & Frey, M. (2004). A preliminary study of multidimensional life satisfaction among deaf/hard-of-hearing youth across environmental settings. *Social Indicators Research, 66*, 143–164.

Gilman, R., & Huebner, E. S. (2003). A review of life satisfaction research with children and adolescents. *School Psychology Review, 18*, 192–205.

Gilman, R., & Huebner, E. S. (2006). Characteristics of adolescents who report very high life satisfaction. *Journal of Youth and Adolescence, 31*, 311–319.

Gilman, R., Huebner, E. S., Tian, L., Park, N., O'Byrne, J., Schiff, M., et al. (2008). Cross-national adolescent multidimensional life satisfaction reports: Analyses of mean scores and response style differences. *Journal of Youth and Adolescence, 37,* 142–154.

Hawkins, J. D., Catalano, R. F., Kosterman, R., Abbott, R., & Hill, K. G. (1999). Preventing adolescent health risk behaviors by strengthening protection during childhood. *Archives of Pediatric Medicine, 153,* 226–234.

Hogan, A., McLellan, L., & Bauman, A. (2000). Health promotion needs of young people with disabilities: A population study. *Disability and Rehabilitation, 22,* 352–357.

Huebner, E. S. (1991). Initial development of the Students' Life Satisfaction Scale. *School Psychology International, 6,* 103–111.

Huebner, E. S. (1994). Preliminary development and validation of a multidimensional life satisfaction scale for children. *Psychological Assessment, 6,* 149–158.

Huebner, E. S., Ash, C., & Laughlin, J. E. (2001). Life experiences, locus of control, and school satisfaction in adolescence. *Social Indicators Research, 55,* 167–183.

Huebner, E. S., Drane, W., & Valois, R. F. (2000). Levels and demographic correlates of adolescent life satisfaction reports. *School Psychology International, 21,* 281–292.

Huebner, E. S., & Gilman, R. (2006). Students who like and dislike school. *Applied Research in Quality of Life, 2,* 139–150.

Huebner, E. S., Laughlin, J. E., Ash, C., & Gilman, R. (1998). Further validation of the Multidimensional Students' Life Satisfaction Scale. *Journal of Psychoeducational Assessment, 16,* 118–134.

Huebner, E. S., & McCullough, G. (2000). Correlates of school satisfaction among adolescents. *Journal of Educational Research, 93,* 331–335.

Huebner, E. S., Valois, R. F., Paxton, R. J., & Drane, J. W. (2005). Middle school students' perception of quality of life. *Journal of Happiness Studies, 6,* 15–24.

Karatzias, A., Power, K. G., Flemming, J., Lennan, F., & Swanson, V. (2002). The role of demographics, personality variables and school stress on predicting school satisfaction/dissatisfaction: Review of the literature and research findings. *Educational Psychology, 22,* 33–50.

Katja, R., Paivi, A.-K., Marja-Terttu, T., & Pekka, L. (2002). Relationships among adolescent subjective well-being, health behavior, and school satisfaction. *Journal of School Health, 72,* 243–249.

Ladd, G. W., Buhs, E. S., & Seid, M. (2000). Children's initial sentiments about kindergarten: Is school liking an antecedent of early classroom participation and achievement? *Merrill-Palmer Quarterly, 46,* 255–278.

Lehr, C. A., & Christenson, S. (2002). Best practices in promoting a positive school climate. In A. Thomas & J. Grimes (Eds.), *Best practices in school psychology IV* (pp. 929–947). Bethesda, MD: National Association of School Psychologists.

Lewis, A. D., Huebner, E. S., Reschly, A. L., & Valois, R. F. (in press). The incremental validity of positive emotions in predicting school functioning. *Journal of Psychoeducational Assessment.*

Lewis, T. J., Sugai, G., & Colvin, G. (1998). Reducing problem behavior through a school-wide system of effective behavioral support: Investigation of a schoolwide social skills training program and contextual interventions. *School Psychology Review, 27,* 446–459.

Lyubormirsky, S., King, L. A., & Diener, E. (2005). The benefits of frequent positive affect: Does happiness lead to success? *Psychological Bulletin, 131,* 803–855.

Malin, A., & Linnakyla, P. (2001). Multilevel modeling in repeated measures of the quality of Finnish school life. *Scandinavian Journal of Educational Research, 45,* 145–166.

Okun, M. A., Braver, M. W., & Weir, R. M. (1990). Grade level differences in school satisfaction. *Social Indicators Research, 22,* 419–427.

Reschly, A. L., Huebner, E. S., Appleton, J. J., & Antaramian, S. (2008). Engagement as flourishing: The contribution of positive emotions and coping to adolescents' engagement at school and with learning. *Psychology in the Schools, 45,* 419–431.

Reynolds, C. R., & Kamphaus, R. W. (2004). *Manual: Behavior Assessment System for Children.* Circle Pines, MN: American Guidance Service.

Roberts, M. C., Brown, K. J., Johnson, R. J., & Reinke, J. (2002). Positive psychology for children: Development, prevention, and promotion. In C. R. Snyder & S. J. Lopez (Eds.), *Handbook of positive psychology* (pp. 663–675). Oxford: Oxford University Press.

Roeser, R. W., Eccles, J. S., & Strobel, K. (1998). Linking the study of schooling and mental health: Selected issues and empirical illustrations at the level of the individual. *Educational Psychologist, 33,* 153–176.

Rutter, M., & Maughan, B. (2002). School effectiveness findings 1979–2002. *Journal of School Psychology, 40,* 451–475.

Seligman, M. E. P., & Csikszentmihalyi, M. (2000). Positive psychology: An introduction. *American Psychologist, 55,* 5–14.

Shernoff, D. J., Csikszentmihalyi, M., Schneider, B., & Shernoff, E. S. (2003). Student engagement in high school classrooms from the perspective of flow theory. *School Psychology Quarterly, 18,* 158–176.

Solomon, D., Battistich, V., Watson, M., Schaps, E., & Lewis, C. (2000). A six-district study of educational change: Direct and mediated effects of the Child Development Project. *Social Psychology of Education, 4,* 3–51.

Snyder, C. R., & Lopez, S. J. (2002). The future of positive psychology: A declaration of independence. In C. R. Snyder & S. J. Lopez (Eds.), *Handbook of positive psychology* (pp. 751–768). Oxford: Oxford University Press.

Snyder, C. R., & Lopez, S. J. (2007). *Positive psychology: The scientific and practical explorations of human strengths.* Thousand Oaks, CA: Sage.

Suldo, S. M., & Huebner, E. S. (2006). Is extremely high life satisfaction advantageous during adolescence? *Social Indicators Research, 78,* 179–203.

Verkuyten, M., & Thijs, J. (2002). School satisfaction of elementary school children: The role of performance, peer relations, ethnicity and gender. *Social Indicators Research, 59,* 203–228.

Wentzel, K. R. (1998). Social relationships and motivation in middle school: The role of parents, teachers, and peers. *Journal of Educational Psychology, 90,* 202–209.

Zeidner, M., & Schleyer, E. J. (1999). The effects of educational context on individual difference variables, self-perceptions of giftedness, and school attitudes in gifted adolescents. *Journal of Youth and Adolescence, 28,* 687–703.

Zins, J. E., Bloodworth, M. R., Weissberg, R. P., & Walberg, H. J. (2004). The scientific base linking social and emotional learning to school success. In J. E. Zins, R. P. Weissberg, M. C. Wang, & H. J. Walberg (Eds.), *Building academic success on social and emotional learning: What does the research say?* (pp. 3–22). New York: Teachers College Press.

Positive Psychology on Campus

Laurie A. Schreiner, Eileen Hulme, Roderick Hetzel, *and* Shane J. Lopez

Abstract

This chapter synthesizes the research from positive psychology on fulfilled individuals and thriving communities with the research from higher education on student success and institutional effectiveness, in order to build a bridge from one discipline to the other. Principles from positive psychology are applied in practical ways to the daily work of faculty, staff, and administrators in four key areas: (a) teaching and learning, (b) academic advising, (c) student leadership development, and (d) promoting students' psychological well-being. Self-determination theory and the talent development approach are synthesized into practical applications for the teaching and learning process with an emphasis on engaged learning and strengths-based education. Specific strategies for academic advisors are outlined in order to increase the likelihood of engaged learners persisting to graduation. Authentic leadership principles are applied to student leadership development programs, with an emphasis on emotional intelligence, mindfulness, the importance of a growth mind-set, and strengths-based approaches to leadership development. Finally, positive psychology principles are applied to counseling and psychotherapy services, preventive outreach, and consultation services to the broader campus community in order to build students' psychological well-being.

Keywords: higher education, leadership, positive psychology, strengths, students

Colleges and universities face a critical period in their histories—a time when it is not enough to simply graduate engineers, lawyers, and business managers. "The primary goal of higher education is not merely the successful completion of college degrees. It is the formation of a generation of people that clearly understand their unique contribution and genuinely desire to use this uniqueness for the common good" (Shushok & Hulme, 2006, p. 2). Graduating individuals who can use their strengths to find meaning in life and serve the greater good through their work is now the challenge. Society hungers for individuals who can become positive, authentic leaders of engaged organizations, communities, and schools.

The field of positive psychology offers the opportunity to turn the academic focus to helping students explore what makes life worth living. In Seligman and Csikszentmihalyi's (2000) words, the "fulfilled individual and the thriving community" (p. 5) are the targets of attention in positive psychology. Higher education targets these same areas, affirming as its goals student success and institutional effectiveness. Student success is broadly defined by Kuh, Kinzie, Schuh, and Whitt (2005) as "satisfaction, persistence, and high levels of learning and personal development" (p. xiv), whereas institutional effectiveness is conceptualized as the value added to students' lives by their college experience. The challenge is for positive psychology to inform the field of higher education by applying its principles to the work of faculty, staff, and administrators on college campuses.

This chapter serves as an initial attempt to synthesize the research from positive psychology with the research from higher education, to build a bridge from one discipline to the other. Applying the best principles and practices from both fields can increase the likelihood of not only student success ("the fulfilled individual") but also institutional effectiveness ("the thriving community"). Many concepts from positive psychology are mirrored in higher education literature using different terminology; we apply those concepts to the daily work of individual faculty and staff and the programs they create. Our goal is to provide practical suggestions congruent with the best of positive psychology and higher education theory. We hope that individuals can readily implement these proposed strategies in their teaching and advising, as well as programmatically in student leadership development and university counseling center services.

Applying Positive Psychology to Teaching and Learning

Motivating students to take responsibility for their own learning process stands as the primary challenge for educators (Perry, Hall, & Ruthig, 2005; Pintrich & Zusho, 2002). Instructors are faced with the increasingly daunting task of engaging students in learning, as a wider spectrum of prior learning experiences and diversity of talents characterizes today's college students. The talent development approach (Kuh et al., 2005), which acknowledges and capitalizes on the strengths students bring to the learning environment, provides a foundation for student success in its recognition that all students can learn under the right conditions. Applying positive psychology principles derived from self-determination theory (Ryan & Deci, 2000) could provide educators with tools for a more positive impact on students' motivation, leading to higher levels of engagement that enable students to succeed and persist to graduation.

The Conceptual Framework: Self-Determination Theory and Engaged Learning

Self-determination theory (Ryan & Deci, 2000) provides a conceptual framework that can assist educators who desire to increase students' authentic motivation. Authentic motivation denotes motivation that is self-authored, that is, self-initiated and self-regulated (Baxter Magolda, 1999; Ryan & Deci, 2000). In contrast to extrinsic motivation, this motivation results in higher levels of "interest, excitement, and confidence, which in turn is manifest both as enhanced performance, persistence, and creativity... and as heightened vitality..., self-esteem..., and general well-being..." (Ryan & Deci, 2000, p. 69). We use the term "authentic motivation" throughout this chapter to incorporate

such concepts as intrinsic motivation, internalized motivation, self-authorship, and self-determination.

When students are authentically motivated, they are more likely to engage in the learning process (Connell & Wellborn, 1991). Such engagement produces higher levels of academic performance as well as the kind of content mastery that lasts beyond the final exam; it also facilitates student growth and development, leading to psychological well-being and persistence to graduation (Kuh et al., 2005). Throughout this chapter we use the term "engaged learning" to encompass the concepts of self-regulated learning (Pintrich & Zusho, 2002), vital engagement (Nakamura & Csikszentmihalyi, 2003), deep learning (Tagg, 2003), and student engagement (Kuh et al., 2005). Environments that support students' needs for autonomy, competence, and relatedness provide contexts that can engage students and contribute to their development and optimal functioning (Ryan & Deci, 2000). Throughout this chapter we use the conceptual framework of self-determination theory (authentic motivation + engaged learning) as the basis for our practical suggestions to faculty and staff.

The Talent Development Approach: Strengths-Based Education

Congruent with the principles of self-determination theory (Ryan & Deci, 2000) in positive psychology is the talent development approach in higher education (Kuh et al., 2005), an approach that is recommended as one of the best strategies for creating an environment that facilitates engaged learning and student success. A talent development approach "refers to the notion that every student can learn under the right conditions" (p. 77). Institutional commitment to talent development "arranges resources and learning conditions to maximize student potential so that students leave college different in desired ways from how they started" (p. 77).

Implicit within the talent development approach is a philosophy that capitalizing on one's areas of greatest talent is likely to lead to greater success than investing comparable time and effort to remediate areas of weakness (Clifton & Harter, 2003). The term "strengths-based" that is used throughout this chapter denotes higher education's emphasis on talent development and positive psychology's focus on strengths and virtues. Strengths-based approaches to the tasks and goals of higher education assume that students have talents that they bring to the academic environment. These talents, defined as "naturally recurring patterns of thought, feeling, or behavior that can be productively applied" (Clifton & Harter, 2003, p. 111), include ways of processing information, interacting with people, perceiving the world, or navigating the environment. Combined with authentic motivation and effort and the knowledge and skills acquired in the learning process, talents can be developed into strengths utilized to achieve academic as well as personal success. Peterson and Park (2004) note that "most individuals have 'signature strengths' and . . . use of these strengths at work, love, and play provides a route to the psychologically fulfilling life . . ." (p. 443).

The strengths-based approach represents a significant shift within higher education (Schreiner & Anderson, 2005). Currently, higher education, in practice if not in theory, focuses more on surviving than on thriving. It is more highly attuned to deficits than to strengths. A strengths-based approach to teaching fosters self-determination in students, impacting their engagement and thereby producing higher levels of learning, academic performance, and persistence in college (Cantwell, 2005). Instructors can utilize the following four strategies to foster students' authentic motivation and engaged learning:

1. *Develop a sense of community in the classroom by connecting to students in ways that enhance their learning and emphasize the strengths they contribute.* When students feel a sense of belonging and interdependence, they are more likely to become engaged in the campus community and in their own learning experiences (DeNeui, 2003). Experiencing a sense of community meets students' needs for relatedness and leads to higher levels of authentic motivation. With the proportion of commuter students increasing, the primary opportunity for developing a psychological sense of community on campus occurs through classroom experiences.

Strengths-based teaching builds this sense of community before, during, and after class, as instructors strive to learn about their students. In Kuh et al.'s (2005) study of 20 highly engaging colleges and universities, one common characteristic the institutions manifested was a campus-wide knowledge of their students—"where they came from, their preferred learning styles, their talents, and when and where they need help" (p. 301). Knowledge about the students an instructor encounters provides a foundation for connecting with those students' interests and prior learning. Relating to students authentically enables

professors to connect with them in the classroom, in an advising session, and outside the classroom.

The importance of such connections cannot be overestimated; in both Astin's (1993) and Pascarella and Terenzini's (2005) meta-analyses of decades of research on college outcomes, student–faculty interaction is consistently one of the strongest predictors of academic success and persistence to graduation. This interaction meets students' needs for relatedness by communicating care and support from faculty (Ryan & Deci, 2000), but it also creates a more secure attachment to a new community, the academic community created by the faculty. The modeling of community by the faculty then promotes competence beliefs and valuation within the students, leading to a greater likelihood that they will engage in the exemplary behaviors of the faculty (Ryan & Deci, 2000). As Pascarella and Terenzini (2005) documented, students who interact more frequently with faculty are not only more likely to graduate with higher grades, but are also more likely to pursue an advanced degree. Relatedness and competence, both of which are critically important for authentic motivation (Ryan & Deci, 2000), are supported by rewarding interactions between students and faculty.

A strengths-based approach to community building can begin on the first day of class. The instructor emphasizes that each student brings a unique constellation of strengths and experiences that, when combined with adequate preparation for class, can enhance the learning of all. This focus on "membership" fosters a sense of belongingness that contributes to a sense of community (McMillan & Chavis, 1986) and begins to build relatedness and competence among the students.

Asking students to complete an instrument outside of class that assesses their strengths and to reflect on specific ways they will apply their strengths to their learning experiences builds the sense of being a vital contributor to the community of learners. Two such instruments are of particular value; each offers a slightly different perspective on students' strengths. The Clifton StrengthsFinder™ (Gallup, 1999) measures 34 themes of greatest talent that can be productively applied in students' lives and provides their top five "signature themes." Psychometric studies specifically with college students have found the instrument to be reliable and valid for use in strengths development programs on college campuses (Schreiner, 2006), and there is a student textbook and Web site that outlines a strengths-based approach to the college experience

(Clifton, Anderson, & Schreiner, 2006). The VIA classification of strengths (Peterson & Seligman, 2002) is also a reliable and valid online measure that provides respondents with their top five "signature strengths" expressed as character virtues. The difference between the two instruments is primarily in their definition of strengths. The Clifton StrengthsFinder™ approaches strengths as developed talents that lead to excellence, while the VIA classification of strengths views strengths as elements of character that lead to the development of virtues valued across most cultures.

2. *Build positive emotions by designing active learning experiences that are connected to students' prior learning and current interests and that tap into the wide variety of students' strengths and learning styles.* Positive emotions are not only indicators of well-being, they also produce well-being and expand students' learning repertoire. According to Fredrickson's (2001; chap. 3) broaden-and-build theory, experiencing positive emotions builds personal resources and broadens the capacity for creativity, flexible thinking, and complex cognition. When positive emotions are experienced within the learning process, students' ability to solve problems and think critically and creatively is enhanced.

Positive emotions can be built from such active learning experiences as learning teams, debates, lively class discussions, simulations, case studies, role-playing, and jigsaw learning techniques (Silberman, 1996). Learning is about making connections, not only to other learners and their different perspectives, but also to what was previously known, to meaningful goals, and to one's own strengths and ways of seeing the world. Learning is an active process of making meaning (Tagg, 2003). Classroom learning experiences that actively engage students with the content and with each other lead to higher levels of enjoyment as well as to greater learning (Chickering & Gamson, 1987).

When such learning experiences also tap into students' strengths and learning styles, the beneficial impact multiplies. Giving assignments that enable students to reflect on their strengths and how they have helped them succeed academically can enable them to use those strengths more effectively to become better learners. Connecting to who students are, as well as to what they already know and how they learn, creates a powerful dynamic in the classroom that fosters all three needs identified by self-determination theory as crucial for authentic motivation: autonomy, competence, and relatedness (Ryan & Deci, 2000).

3. *Spark curiosity by creating meaningful assignments that provide clear expectations, choices, and an optimal level of challenge.* Curiosity contributes uniquely to the variation in student achievement, independent of the effects of positive emotions, hope, and well-being. Task curiosity leads to greater levels of attention and skill development in students, which then enhances positive emotions and feelings of mastery, leading students to be more likely to pursue similar experiences in the future (Kashdan & Fincham, 2004; chap. 34). Providing students with choices and opportunities for self-direction can spark curiosity and lead to greater levels of engaged learning. For authentic motivation to occur, students must see themselves as active agents engaged in a meaningful experience integrated with their own goals and values (Ryan & Deci, 2000). Instructors using a strengths-based approach to learning create meaningful assignments that connect to students' strengths, allowing them to capitalize on those strengths in demonstrating mastery of the course content (Anderson, Cantwell, & Schreiner, 2004). Inherently meaningful assignments tap into students' interests and require students to think about their talents and how to apply them in a learning situation. For classes where the structuring of assignments allows for limited choice, exams can be structured to allow students to select from different types of questions or among several questions to demonstrate their learning. To whatever extent students can see aspects of their academic tasks as chosen and relevant to their own goals, they are more likely to experience engaged learning.

Authentic motivation is also more likely to occur among students who perceive themselves as competent (Ryan & Deci, 2000). Competence can be supported by instructional environments that provide students with clear expectations and optimal challenges (Chickering & Gamson, 1987). Instructors can provide clear expectations through a syllabus that outlines how assignments will be assessed and provides helpful information on the structure of the tasks assigned. Emphasizing the meaningfulness of the activity and articulating the level of effort required to master it can also equip students with an increased sense of competence.

Optimal challenges occur when the assignment requires students to engage in tasks that realistically stretch their current capabilities (Csikszentmihalyi,

1990). Boredom and apathy occur when the challenge is too small; anxiety and withdrawal occur when the challenge is too great; curiosity and engagement occur when the challenge is optimal (Kashdan & Fincham, 2004).

4. *Increase students' academic self-efficacy by providing feedback that is timely, frequent, and constructive.* The relationship between academic self-efficacy and educational outcomes has been well researched. Students who perceive themselves as capable of accomplishing academic tasks are not only more likely to achieve, but also to persist and experience greater levels of personal adjustment (Chemers, Hu, & Garcia, 2001). Timely feedback from faculty fosters academic self-efficacy because it provides information that can be helpful in modifying future performance (Chickering & Gamson, 1987). Frequent feedback that provides information specific to the task enhances students' perceived competence as it targets specific actions the student can take to move to higher levels of excellence (Ryan & Deci, 2000). When feedback is constructive, rather than judgmental or critical, it also builds a sense of relatedness between the professor and student (Kuh et al., 2005). When students receive this type of feedback, their academic self-efficacy increases, as they perceive themselves to be capable of accomplishing the task.

Applying Positive Psychology to Academic Advising

Strengths-based advising explicitly attempts to promote excellence by building on students' natural talents to increase confidence and self-efficacy while motivating them to acquire the necessary knowledge and skills to succeed. Three phases of strengths-based advising have been outlined by Schreiner and Anderson (2005) as (a) identification and affirmation of students' talents; (b) teaching advisees ways of developing their talents into strengths by gaining skills and knowledge, then further developing the competencies that will help them meet their educational and life goals; and (c) helping students apply their strengths to new or challenging situations, such as the career planning process, course selection, and adjustment or academic difficulties. Two specific strategies of academic advisors can assist students in becoming engaged learners who persist to graduation.

1. *Build students' hope by teaching them to set goals that are connected to their values and strengths.* Assisting students in setting realistic and intrinsic goals, then teaching them how to apply their strengths to achieve those goals, engenders feelings of hope that can lead to greater success. A strengths-based approach to advising encourages students to identify life goals that are congruent with their values, then to determine which of their talents will contribute to reaching those goals. When students understand that strengths establish their pathways to goals (Lopez, 2004), and that the college experience provides the specific venues, knowledge, and skills they need to reach their destinations, they are more likely to internalize the behaviors necessary for full engagement in the college experience.

Students with high levels of hope are able to conceptualize their goals and then create specific strategies that they are motivated to use consistently in order to reach those goals (Lopez et al., 2004). In a 6-year study of college students that statistically controlled for their entrance exam scores, those students with higher levels of hope had higher grades and were more likely to graduate (Snyder, Wiklund, & Cheavens, 1999). The advising relationship engenders an ideal environment for accentuating hope, as advisors form a working alliance with students and assist them in setting realistic goals and brainstorming multiple pathways to reach their goals by capitalizing on their strengths. Advisors also can help students reframe potential obstacles to success as challenges that can be overcome with effort, providing the essential encouragement and support that can sustain the motivation necessary for reaching their goals. Students who feel both challenged and supported by persons who matter to them and believe they are capable of performing discover an environment that fosters the development of their intrinsic goals. The advisor who operates from a strengths perspective can provide this challenge and support.

2. *Bolster students' resilience by equipping them with a healthy explanatory style.* How students explain the setbacks and failures they experience in college affects their likelihood of recovering quickly from such setbacks and as well as their ability to approach future challenges. A healthy explanatory style is optimistic, attributing failures to controllable causes; such attributions build resilience by enabling a person to approach future events with greater confidence that success will be possible next time. As a result, students with a positive explanatory style are more likely to engage in the learning process, leading to higher levels of academic performance (Pintrich & Zusho, 2002).

As Weiner (1985) noted in his articulation of attribution theory, when students are able to attribute their poor performance to external or unstable causes rather than to internal or stable causes, this experience generates perceptions of greater control among students, fostering hope and leading to persistence (Perry et al., 2005). Students build resilience when they experience failure but are able to explain their performance in terms of insufficient effort. Equipping students with a healthy explanatory style is particularly important with first-year students, who are unfamiliar with the college environment and have yet to realize the amount of control they can have over their success (Perry et al., 2005).

A corollary to this healthy explanatory style is the ability to access thoughts about personal strengths. Dodgson and Wood (1998) noted that people with high self-esteem are significantly more likely to think about their personal strengths rather than their weaknesses after a failure. As a result, they rebound more quickly and reengage in achievement tasks. Their motivation and task persistence are, in fact, higher after a failure than after a success. Thus "focusing on strengths ... holds the potential for a relatively adaptive response to life's slings and arrows" (p. 198). Advisors who work with students to develop a healthy explanatory style and encourage them to access thoughts about their strengths and how they will apply them to the next challenge are able to foster resilience in students.

Applying Positive Psychology to Student Leadership Development

Programs designed to enable students to develop leadership potential during their college experience have increased dramatically in quantity, scope, and quality in the past 25 years (Troyer, 2004) as colleges and universities have designated the development of leaders as a primary objective. As authentic motivation provides a basis for engaged learning, authentic leadership forms a basis for organizational excellence and provides a viable theoretical framework for leadership programs on college campuses.

The authentic leader utilizes individual strengths, engenders positive emotions, stimulates hope, and reinforces consistent morals and values (Luthans & Avolio, 2003). The following suggestions for developing collegiate leadership programs are designed to translate positive psychological theories into relevant practices that will foster authentic leadership.

1. *Enable students to recognize and manage their emotions.* Current leadership theory views leadership as a relational process of mutual influence and emphasizes the role of emotion in effective leadership (Kezar, Carducci, & Contreras-McGavin, 2006). Yet the vital role of managing emotions has been an enduring theme in college student development theory since Chickering (1969) identified this task as central to the growth of 18–24-year-olds. Almost 40 years later, he describes emotional maturity as one of "the competencies needed to be an active citizen in a democracy" (Chickering & Stamm, 2002, p. 30), a view consistent with research on the role emotional intelligence plays in successful leadership (Caruso, Mayer, & Salovey, 2002).

To encourage the development of authentic leadership, college leadership development programs can teach students strategies that will build their emotional intelligence. Mayer, Salovey, and Caruso (2000) define emotional intelligence as the "ability to perceive emotions, to access and generate emotions so as to assist thought, to understand emotions and emotional knowledge, and to regulate emotions so as to promote emotional and intellectual growth" (p. 17). A student leadership development program based on emotional intelligence principles has four phases: (a) fostering students' self-awareness, including a recognition of their repertoire of emotional responses; (b) teaching strategies for managing emotional responses appropriately; (c) enhancing students' awareness of others' emotional responses; and (d) increasing their ability to manage complex human interactions. As students gain these skills, their sense of competence as future leaders increases; the relationships formed in the process will provide the support necessary for them to step into leadership roles.

2. *Design programs that encourage students to take a mindful approach to the leadership process.* Effective leaders develop the capacity to "think gray," that is, to simultaneously hold opposing points of view without rushing to make a judgment on the validity of either perspective (Sample, 2002). Thinking gray requires leaders to challenge habitual frames of reference through which they see the world and remain open to new perspectives.

Mindfulness has been conceptualized as a state of awareness characterized by actively noticing novelty and distinctions while remaining sensitive to context and to multiple perspectives (Langer, 1989; chap. 26). Mindlessness, in contrast, is produced by an overreliance on preexisting mental categories that can create rigid perspectives and lead to stereotyping, premature decision making, and diminished creativity. The value of mindfulness in leadership is beginning to be articulated by Boyatzis and McKee (2005), who assert that "great leaders are awake, aware, and attuned to themselves, to others, and to the world around them" (p. 3).

3. *Teach students to develop an incremental, growth mind-set approach to leadership challenges.* How students view themselves has a dramatic influence on their behavior. Dweck (2000) proposes that people possess one of two basic self-theories about personal qualities and abilities: an incremental theory or an entity theory. These self-theories lead to a mind-set that is either growth oriented or fixed. A person maintaining a growth mind-set adopts an incremental self-theory and believes that individual traits are malleable and can be altered with effort. Those with an entity self-theory maintain a fixed mind-set and view their personal characteristics as predetermined; thus, effort is seen as having little to do with their ultimate success. One's mind-set thus has a profound effect on how failure is interpreted.

For persons with a fixed mind-set, failure is a signal that they are lacking in personal ability; thus, failure is to be avoided at all costs. If failure does occur, entity theorists are more likely to attempt to cover up the failed attempt. Incrementalists, on the other hand, believe that failure affords an opportunity to learn and thus are quick to enter into challenges. Congruent with authentic leadership, persons who adopt a growth mind-set are more willing to confront the difficult facts facing an organization and assume responsibility for failures that naturally occur in moments of organizational change and growth. As Dweck (2006) asserts, "The lesson is: Create an organization that prizes the development of ability—and watch the leaders emerge" (p. 137). Communicating to students that intelligence and leadership qualities are malleable rather than fixed may better prepare them to successfully negotiate the challenges of leadership.

4. *Provide challenges that encourage students to capitalize on their strengths, recognize and develop the strengths of others, and promote the strengths of an entire organization.* A strengths-based approach to leadership requires that the leader (a) know his or her own strengths and leverage those strengths to attain excellence; (b) recognize, honor, and develop the strengths of others; and (c) capitalize on the strengths of the organization. Such an approach

leads to higher levels of organizational effectiveness (Clifton & Harter, 2003) and is an important component of student leadership development programs focused on authentic leadership.

Recognizing and learning to capitalize on one's own strengths in the leadership process provides a level of self-awareness and confidence that can contribute to a sense of self-efficacy about one's leadership potential. Identifying and affirming the strengths of others supports the collaborative models of leadership that have been found to be particularly effective. Utilizing appreciative inquiry methods, which investigate the strengths and successes of an organization, equips students with a powerful tool for organizational change (Whitney & Trosten-Bloom, 2003). As students are taught to focus on and develop the strengths of an organization, they will become immersed in the essence of authentic leadership.

Positive psychology has enormous potential to transform the existing theoretical foundations from which numerous college and university leadership development programs emerge. This transformation may inspire a future generation of leaders prepared to meet emerging challenges, as well as to lead individual lives of meaning and purpose.

Applying Positive Psychology to Promote Students' Psychological Well-Being

Engaging students in the learning process and encouraging their development as leaders aligns with typical goals of higher education, yet increasing numbers of students enter college with less than optimal levels of psychological well-being. Indicators of the increasing mental health crisis among college students abound in the professional literature. In an analysis of university counseling center client presenting problems over a 13-year period, Benton, Robertson, Tseng, Newton, and Benton (2003) reported an overall increase in 14 of 19 problem areas. More students are experiencing "difficulties in relationships and developmental issues, as well as the more severe problems such as anxiety, depression, suicidal ideation, sexual assault, and personality disorders" (p. 69). Despite mounting evidence of concern, university counseling center positions have faced increasing cuts over the past decade, along with a trend toward outsourcing clinical services to other agencies (Hodges, 2001).

The increased clinical demands and limited clinical resources pose significant challenges to the traditional service delivery models of university counseling centers. The three primary roles of such centers, as identified by the International Association for Counseling Services, include (a) counseling and psychotherapy for students experiencing adjustment, vocational, developmental, and/or psychological problems; (b) preventive outreach to help students identify and learn skills to help them meet educational and life goals; and (c) consultation and outreach to the broader campus community to support and enhance the healthy development of students. Positive psychology offers a unique framework for expanding these roles and thus holds promise for addressing the growing mental health needs of college students. Each of these areas is explored below for ways that positive psychology perspectives can be incorporated.

1. *Incorporate positive psychology perspectives within counseling and psychotherapy services.* Research has demonstrated that positive psychology principles can be effectively applied within clinical settings, either as specific therapeutic approaches or as adjuncts to more well-established treatments. Examples of positive therapeutic approaches include appreciative inquiry (Cooperrider & Whitney, 1999), well-being therapy (Ruini & Fava, 2004), hope interventions (Lopez et al., 2004), quality of life therapy (Frisch, 2006), and strengths-based therapy (Christine Perez, personal communication, June 23, 2008). Joseph and Linley (2004) suggest that positive therapeutic approaches do not require the abandonment of a preferred theoretical orientation or therapeutic modality, but rather emphasize positive aspects of human experience, value the therapeutic relationship as more important than the therapeutic technique, and attend to the social and political context of the therapeutic encounter. Indeed, Seligman and Peterson (2003) argue that most therapeutic approaches are, in part, effective because of the "deep strategies" (p. 312), including the instillation of hope and the building of strengths.

2. *Incorporate positive psychology perspectives within preventive outreach services.* One common trend is for university counseling centers to increase their efforts to reach students before they develop mental health problems that require counseling or psychotherapy. Typical outreach programs include psycho-educational workshops on suicide prevention, depression screening, and stress management. Although these workshops can be helpful for some students, positive psychology provides a framework for expanding the range of topics and approaches for preventive outreach. For example, Web-based positive psychology interventions, which have been demonstrated to reduce depressive symptomology and increase positive affect (Seligman, Steen, & Park, 2005), can be targeted toward particular student populations at higher risk for developing mental health problems. Hetzel, Matlock-Hetzel, and Marsh (2005) described an academic course designed to help provisionally admitted students increase their resiliency through building strengths and developing skills to persevere and adapt in the face of adversity. This course consisted of a standard study skills curriculum that was infused with eight class sessions in resiliency training. Based upon Reivich and Shatte's (2002) resiliency model, the resilience class sessions were developed and instructed by university counseling center staff. Preliminary data analysis indicated that students who received the resiliency training, compared with those students who participated in the standard study skills curriculum without resiliency training, reported higher levels of resilience, goal-directed determination (the agency component of hope), life satisfaction, and positive affect.

3. *Incorporate positive psychology perspectives within consultation and outreach to the broader campus community.* Lopez, Janowski, and Wells (2005) assert that positive psychology can be implemented within the curriculum and co-curriculum to promote positive personal and academic outcomes. With their training and knowledge in psychological theory, empirical research, and clinical services, counseling center staff are well suited to consult with the broader campus community about student development initiatives. Counseling center staff can support and enhance the healthy development of students by partnering with other departments and divisions (including, for example, academic and student life orientation, residence hall programming, career counseling, and academic departments that teach a large number of required general education courses) to expose students to strengths development in multiple contexts and settings.

Incorporating positive psychology perspectives within the roles and functions of counseling centers opens possibilities for addressing the burgeoning mental health needs on campus. The greatest benefit may well come through the outreach component of counseling services. Positive psychology offers a number of constructs that facilitate student growth and life satisfaction and can be offered to a broad audience through workshops or classroom settings. For many students who may never seek counseling, this type of service could be what they need to achieve well-being and be successful in the university setting.

Conclusion

The positive psychology approach to higher education should not be confused with fads (that are sometimes atheoretical and often are only loosely associated with an educational or psychological research base) that have swept through colleges and universities. It is neither a paradigm shift nor a revolution. It is actually a return to basic educational principles that emphasized positive aspects of student effort and achievement, as well as their strengths and well-being (Chickering & Reisser, 1993; Hurlock, 1925; Terman & Oden, 1947). And numerous educational philosophers (e.g., John Dewey, Benjamin Franklin, John Stuart Mill, Herbert Spencer) have reinforced educators' commitment to enhancing the best qualities of students. Here we attempt to connect positive psychological science with higher education practice to guide educators in their daily work with students.

Three Questions for the Future

1. How might we measure college students' ability to thrive during their college years? To what extent might such thriving predict their learning and persistence to graduation?

2. Strengths-based approaches to learning and leadership are believed to be significantly more effective than the current approaches utilized in higher education. How could this assumption be tested empirically?

3. What are the most effective ways of informing higher education practitioners about the potential applications of positive psychology to their work?

References

Anderson, E. C., Cantwell, L. D., & Schreiner, L. A. (2004). *Strengths-based teaching*. Azusa, CA: Noel Academy for Strengths-Based Leadership and Education. Retrieved August 25, 2006, from http://www.apu.edu/strengthsacademy

Astin, A. W. (1993). *What matters in college? Four critical years revisited*. San Francisco: Jossey-Bass.

Baxter Magolda, M. B. (1999). *Creating contexts for learning and self-authorship: Constructive-developmental pedagogy*. Nashville, TN: Vanderbilt University Press.

Benton, S. A., Robertson, J. M., Tseng, W. C., Newton, F. B., & Benton, S. L. (2003). Changes in counseling center client problems across 13 years. *Professional Psychology: Research and Practice, 34*, 66–72.

Boyatzis, R., & McKee, A. (2005). *Resonant leadership: Renewing yourself and connecting with others through mindfulness, hope, and compassion*. Boston: Harvard Business School Press.

Cantwell, L. D. (2005). A comparative analysis of strengths-based versus traditional teaching methods in a freshman public speaking course: Impacts on student learning and academic engagement. Unpublished dissertation, Azusa Pacific University, Azusa, CA.

Caruso, D., Mayer, J. D., & Salovey, P. (2002). Emotional intelligence and emotional leadership. In R. Riggio & S. Murphy (Eds.), *Multiple intelligences and leadership*. Mahwah, NJ: Lawrence Erlbaum.

Chemers, M. M., Hu, L., & Garcia, B. F. (2001). Academic self-efficacy and first-year college student performance and adjustment. *Journal of Educational Psychology, 93*(1), 55–64.

Chickering, A. W. (1969). *Education and identity*. San Francisco: Jossey-Bass.

Chickering, A. W., & Gamson, Z. F. (1987). Seven principles for good practice in undergraduate education. *AAHE Bulletin, 39*(7), 3–7.

Chickering, A. W., & Reisser, L. (1993). *Education and identity*. San Francisco: Jossey-Bass.

Chickering, A. W., & Stamm, L. (2002, May–June). Making our purposes clear. *About Campus, 7*(2), 30–32.

Clifton, D. O., Anderson, E. C., & Schreiner, L. A. (2006). *StrengthsQuest: Discover and develop your strengths in academics, career, and beyond* (2nd ed.). Washington, DC: Gallup.

Clifton, D. O., & Harter, J. K. (2003). Strengths investment. In K. S. Cameron, J .E. Dutton, & R. E. Quinn (Eds.), *Positive organizational scholarship* (pp. 111–121). San Francisco: Berrett-Koehler.

Connell, J. P., & Wellborn, J. G. (1991). Competence, autonomy and relatedness: A motivational analysis of self-system processes. In M. R. Gunnar & L. A. Stroufe (Eds.), *Minnesota symposium on child psychology* (Vol. 22, pp. 43–77). Hillsdale, NJ: Erlbaum.

Cooperrider, D. L., & Whitney, D. (1999). *Appreciative inquiry*. San Francisco: Berret-Koehler.

Csikszentmihalyi, M. (1990). *Flow: The psychology of optimal experience*. New York: HarperCollins.

DeNeui, D. L. C. (2003). An investigation of first-year college students' psychological sense of community on campus. *College Student Journal, 37*(2), 224–234.

Dodgson, P. G., & Wood, J. V. (1998). Self-esteem and the cognitive accessibility of strengths and weaknesses after failure. *Journal of Personality and Social Psychology, 75*(1), 178–197.

Dweck, C. S. (2000). *Self-theories: Their role in motivation, personality, and development*. Philadelphia: Taylor and Francis.

Dweck, C. S. (2006). *Mindset: The new psychology of success*. New York: Random House.

Fredrickson, B. L. (2001). The role of positive emotions in positive psychology: The broaden-and-build theory of positive emotions. *American Psychologist, 56*(3), 218–226.

Frisch, M. B. (2006). *Quality of life therapy: Applying a life satisfaction approach to positive psychology and cognitive therapy*. Hoboken, NJ: Wiley.

Gallup. (1999). *CliftonStrengthsFinder*. Washington, DC: Gallup.

Hetzel, R. D., Matlock-Hetzel, S., & Marsh, J. G. (2005). Positive psychology and university counseling centers: The

Baylor experience. *Section on Counseling and University Counseling Centers Newsletter, 1*(2), 8–9.

Hodges, S. (2001). University counseling centers at the twenty-for-ward, looking back. *Journal of College Counseling, 42,* 161–173.

Hurlock, E. B. (1925). An evaluation of certain incentives used in school work. *Journal of Educational Psychology, 16,* 145–159.

Joseph, S., & Linley, P. A. (2004). Positive therapy: A positive psychological theory of therapeutic practice. In P. A. Linley & S. Joseph (Eds.), *Positive psychology in practice* (pp. 354–370). Hoboken, NJ: Wiley.

Kashdan, T. B., & Fincham, F. D. (2004). Facilitating curiosity: A social and self-regulatory perspective for scientifically based interventions. In P. A. Linley & S. Joseph (Eds.), *Positive psychology in practice* (pp. 482–503). Hoboken, NJ: Wiley.

Kezar, A. J., Carducci, R., & Contreras-McGavin, M. (2006). Rethinking the "L" word in higher education: The revolution of research on leadership. *ASHE Higher Education Report, 31*(6). San Francisco: Wiley.

Kuh, G. D., Kinzie, J., Schuh, J. H., & Whitt, E. J. (2005). *Student success in college: Creating conditions that matter.* San Francisco: Jossey-Bass.

Langer, E. (1989). *Mindfulness.* Reading, MA: Addison-Wesley.

Lopez, S. J. (2004). *Naming, nurturing, and navigating: Capitalizing on strengths in daily life.* Paper presented at the Gallup Organization conference on Building a Strengths-Based Campus, Omaha, NE.

Lopez, S. J., Janowski, K. M., & Wells, K. J. (2005). *Developing strengths in college students: Exploring programs, contexts, theories, and research.* Unpublished manuscript, University of Kansas, Lawrence.

Lopez, S. J., Snyder, C. R., Magyar-Moe, J. L., Edwards, L. M., Pedrotti, J. M., Janowski, K., et al. (2004). *Strategies for accentuating hope.* In P. A. Linley & S. Joseph (Eds.), *Positive psychology in practice* (pp. 388–404). Hoboken, NJ: Wiley.

Luthans, F., & Avolio, B. C. (2003). Authentic leadership: A positive developmental approach. In K. S. Cameron, J. E. Dutton, & R. E. Quinn (Eds.), *Positive organizational scholarship* (pp. 241–261). San Francisco: Barrett-Koehler.

McMillan, D. W., & Chavis, D. M. (1986). Sense of community: A definition and theory. *Journal of Community Psychology, 14,* 6–23.

Mayer, J. D., Salovey, P. & Caruso, D. R. (2000). Models of emotional intelligence. In R. J. Sternberg (Ed.), *Handbook of intelligence* (pp. 396–420). Cambridge: Cambridge University Press.

Nakamura, J., & Csikszentmihalyi, M. (2003). The construction of meaning through vital engagement. In C. L. M. Keyes & J. Haidt (Eds.), *Flourishing: Positive psychology and the life well-lived.* Washington, DC: American Psychological Association.

Pascarella, E. T., & Terenzini, P. T. (2005). *How college affects students: A third decade of research* (Vol. 2). San Francisco: Jossey-Bass.

Perry, R. P., Hall, N. C., & Ruthig, J. C. (2005). Perceived (academic) control and scholastic attainment in higher educa-tion. In J. C. Smart (Ed.), *Higher education: Handbook of theory and research* (Vol. xx, pp. 363–436). Dordrecht, The Netherlands: Springer.

Peterson, C., & Park, N. (2004). Classification and measurement of character strengths: Implications for practice. In P. A.

Linley & S. Joseph (Eds.), *Positive psychology in practice* (pp. 433–446). Hoboken, NJ: Wiley.

Peterson, C., & Seligman, M. E. P. (Eds.). (2002). *The VIA classification of strengths and virtues.* Retrieved August 10, 2006, from http://www.viastrengths.org/index.aspx?ContentID=34

Pintrich, P. R., & Zusho, A. (2002). Student motivation and self-regulated learning in the college classroom. In J. C. Smart & W. G. Tierney (Eds.), *Higher education: Handbook of theory and research* (Vol. xvi, pp. 55–128). Dordrecht, The Netherlands: Springer.

Reivich, K., & Shatte, A. (2002). *The resilience factor: Seven keys to finding your inner strength and overcoming life's hurdles.* New York: Broadway.

Ruini, C., & Fava, G. A. (2004). Clinical applications of well-being therapy. In P. A. Linley & S. Joseph (Eds.), *Positive psychology in practice* (pp. 371–387). Hoboken, NJ: Wiley.

Ryan, R. M., & Deci, E. L. (2000). Self-determination theory and the facilitation of intrinsic motivation, social development, and well-being. *American Psychologist, 55*(1), 68–78.

Sample, S. (2002). *The contrarians' guide to leadership.* San Francisco: Jossey-Bass.

Schreiner, L. A. (2006). *A technical report on the Clifton StrengthsFinder with college students.* Princeton, NJ: The Gallup Organization. Retrieved October 20, 2006, from https://www.strengthsquest.com/Library/Documents/SQwebsiteversionofvaliditystudy.doc

Schreiner, L. A., & Anderson, E. C. (2005). Strengths-based advising: A new lens for higher education. *NACADA Journal, 25*(2), 20–29.

Seligman, M. E. P., & Csikszentmihalyi, M. (2000). Positive psychology: An introduction. *American Psychologist, 55,* 5–14.

Seligman, M. E. P., & Peterson, C. (2003). Positive clinical psychology. In L. G. Aspinwall & U. M. Staudinger (Eds.), *A psychology of human strengths: Fundamental questions and future directions for a positive psychology* (pp. 305–318). Washington, DC: APA.

Seligman, M. E. P., Steen, T. A., & Park, N. (2005). Positive psychology progress: Empirical validation of interventions. *American Psychologist, 60,* 410–421.

Shushok, F., & Hulme, E. (2006). What's right with you: Helping students find and use their personal strengths. *About Campus, 11*(4), 2–8.

Silberman, M. (1996). *Active learning: 101 strategies to teach any subject.* New York: Pearson, Allyn, & Bacon.

Snyder, C. R., Wiklund, C., & Cheavens, J. (1999, August). *Hope and success in college.* Paper presented at the annual meeting of the American Psychological Association, Boston.

Tagg, J. (2003). *The learning paradigm college.* Bolton, MA: Anker Publishing.

Terman, L. M., & Oden, M. H. (1947). *The gifted child grows up: Twenty-five years' follow-up of a superior group.* Stanford, CA: Stanford University Press.

Troyer, M. (2004). The challenges of leadership: A study of an emerging field. Unpublished doctoral dissertation, University of Kentucky, Lexington, KY.

Weiner, B. (1985). An attributional theory of achievement moti-vation and emotion. *Psychological Review, 92,* 548–573.

Whitney, D., & Trosten-Bloom, A. (2003). *The power of appre-ciative inquiry.* San Francisco: Berrett-Koehler.

Positive Workplaces

Fred Luthans *and* Carolyn M. Youssef

Abstract

Over the years, both management practitioners and academics have generally assumed that positive workplaces lead to desired outcomes. Unlike psychology, considerable attention has also been devoted to the study of positive topics such as job satisfaction and organizational commitment. However, to place a scientifically based focus on the role that positivity may play in the development and performance of human resources, and largely stimulated by the positive psychology initiative, positive organizational behavior (POB) and psychological capital (PsyCap) have recently been introduced into the management literature. This chapter first provides an overview of both the historical and contemporary positive approaches to the workplace. Then, more specific attention is given to the meaning and domain of POB and PsyCap. Our definition of POB includes positive psychological capacities or resources that can be validly measured, developed, and have performance impact. The constructs that have been determined so far to best meet these criteria are efficacy, hope, optimism, and resiliency. When combined, they have been demonstrated to form the core construct of what we term psychological capital (PsyCap). A measure of PsyCap is being validated and this chapter references the increasing number of studies indicating that PsyCap can be developed and have performance impact. The chapter concludes with important future research directions that can help better understand and build positive workplaces to meet current and looming challenges.

Keywords: human resource development, positive organizational behavior, positive organizational scholarship, psychological capital, workplace positive psychology

Given the highly turbulent but still but competitive nature of today's global economy, growth, excellence, and maximizing the return on both financial and human capital are receiving increasing attention. In line with the positive psychology initiative, management and organizational behavior researchers have begun taking a more balanced perspective by not only trying to fix what is wrong with dysfunctional organizations and employees, but also taking a positive, strengths-based approach to organizations and human resource management.

After briefly summarizing the roots and historical progression of a positive approach to the workplace, attention is devoted to specific positively oriented initiatives to the workplace at both the macro- (organizational) level (e.g., the University of Michigan's Center for Positive Organizational Scholarship or POS and Gallup University's strengths-based management) and micro- (individual) level (e.g., positive organizational behavior or POB, psychological capital or PsyCap, and authentic leadership development or ALD, primarily associated with the University of Nebraska's Leadership Institute). Although these are parallel developments in taking positive psychology to the workplace, they are very compatible and supportive of one another and we will touch on the points of convergence and divergence among them. Then, in the remainder of the chapter, the focus is on recent empirical findings, measures, and developmental interventions of positive organizational behavior and psychological capital.

Historical Progression of Positive Approaches to the Workplace

Similar to the field of psychology, management research in general, and specifically the areas that study the human side of enterprise, namely organizational psychology, organizational behavior, and human resource management, historically have constituted a wide spectrum of positively and negatively oriented constructs and approaches. For example, a half century ago, Frederick Herzberg (e.g., see Herzberg, Mausner, & Snyderman, 1959) offered the widely recognized two-factor theory of work motivation (i.e., motivators and hygiene factors). He highlighted the positive nature of job satisfaction being primarily related to job content factors (i.e., motivators) such as the specific work responsibilities and opportunities for growth and achievement that constitute the job. On the other hand, he proposed that the causes of job dissatisfaction (and the so-called hygiene factors for its prevention) were found in the context factors of the job (e.g., pay and working conditions).

Herzberg's empirical findings on the two-factor theory provided support for the beginning research in the field of organizational behavior from the famous Hawthorne studies in the 1920s (see Roethlisberger & Dickson, 1939). These original organizational behavior studies at the Hawthorne Works of the Western Electric Company had revealed that human productivity is influenced by more than simply improving physical working conditions such as light intensity or implementing rest pauses. Factors such as group dynamics, supervisory style, worker participation, and increased attention (commonly known as the "Hawthorne effect") serendipitously emerged as major contributors to workers' positive attitudes and higher performance.

This research (e.g., Herzberg et al., 1959, and at Hawthorne) suggested that just trying to eliminate the bad things in the workplace (e.g., low wages, poor working conditions, and autocratic supervision) did not automatically lead to positive outcomes such as job satisfaction and high levels of motivation and performance. In other words, these initial studies found that fixing what was wrong in the workplace may prevent dissatisfaction, but it did not lead to satisfaction and improved performance. Instead, a positive approach to managing human resources seemed necessary for attaining desired attitudes and performance impact.

These early workplace findings are in line with the position taken by positive psychology that seemingly opposite positive and negative constructs may not constitute extremes of a single continuum. Rather, positive and negative constructs are very divergent with different antecedents, dimensions, and outcomes (e.g., see Peterson & Chang, 2002). Taken to today's workplace, the study of popular issues such as work–life balance and diversity management viewed through a negatively oriented conflict lens (e.g., how to eliminate frustration and reduce stress) does not necessarily lead to or inform management research and practice on the positive effects of a balanced life or the potential advantages of a diverse workplace (Roberts, 2006). Similarly in psychological research, positive and negative emotions or affect have been found to vastly differ in their nature, variety, antecedents, and resultant action tendencies (Carver & Scheier, 1990; Fredrickson, 1998, 2001; Lazarus, 1991).

In addition to the pioneering workplace studies, positively oriented growth, development, and self-actualization are at the core of the historically important work motivation theories. For example, Maslow's (1943) hierarchy of needs and McGregor's (1960) Theory Y are very positive approaches associated with the effectiveness of the human side of enterprise. In fact, not only did Maslow directly call for the study of healthy rather than sick people, but a chapter in his classic book *Motivation and personality* was prophetically titled "Toward a positive psychology." Considerable contemporary management research also recognizes positive issues such as organizational justice (Colquitt, Conlon, Wesson, Porter, & Ng, 2001) and business ethics/ corporate social responsibility (Giacalone, Jurkiewicz, & Dunn, 2005).

Despite the considerable positivity associated with both historical and modern management research, the scarcity of resources, decreased employee loyalty and commitment, turnover, stress, burnout, discrimination in employment, dysfunctional leadership, and recurring business scandals of gigantic proportions certainly also contribute to negativity in the workplace with resulting research to better understand and fix the problems. However, especially in contrast to psychology, in both the academic and popular management literature, over the years there has probably been relatively more positivity than negativity. For example, in the field of organizational behavior, there have been frequent calls for shifting attention away from a narrow, short-term, management-by-exception orientation, with its predominant emphasis on mistakes, deficits, shortages, weaknesses, and dysfunctional behaviors, to proactive positive perspectives and approaches recognizing the value of human assets.

Multiple successes, with substantial increases in productivity performance and desirable employee attitudinal outcomes, have been accomplished through positively oriented initiatives in the organizational psychology and organizational behavior fields. This positive emphasis has been led by researchers and practicing managers toward a wider spectrum of new, untapped resources in actualizing the potential of human resources in organizations. For example, over two decades of behavioral performance management research support the importance of contingent positive rewards, positive feedback, and social recognition in the workplace (Stajkovic & Luthans, 1997, 2003). In the balance of the chapter, we present some recently emerging positive approaches to organizational behavior and human resource management that have been directly stimulated and drawn from positive psychology (see Luthans & Avolio, 2009; Luthans & Youssef, 2007, for comprehensive reviews of the literature and emerging issues surrounding positive organizational behavior).

Contemporary Positive Approaches to the Workplace

As mentioned, the positive approach primarily aimed at the organizational level is termed positive organizational scholarship (POS; see Cameron & Caza, 2004; Cameron, Dutton, & Quinn, 2003). The major emphasis of POS is the increased understanding and appreciation of optimal organizational states, outcomes, and dynamics that in turn can facilitate human flourishing at lower levels of analysis (e.g., dyads, groups, and individuals). Examples of topics studied by the POS group include organizational virtuousness, positive deviance, and courageous principled action (Cameron, Bright, & Caza, 2004; Cameron et al., 2003; Roberts, 2006; Spreitzer & Sonenshein, 2003).

In addition to POS, there are other noteworthy positive approaches applied to the workplace such as the Gallup Organization's strengths-based consulting practice (see Buckingham & Clifton, 2001; Buckingham & Coffman, 1999; Rath & Clifton, 2004). They provide evidence for the importance of objective assessment, placement, and development of talents and strengths that provide employees the opportunities to do what they do best every day in the workplace. They also provide basic research evidence on the relationship between engaged

employees and desired organizational outcomes such as productivity and customer satisfaction (Harter, Schmidt, & Hayes, 2002). This strengths-based approach represents a shift away from trying to fix weaknesses and what is wrong with employees and accompanying remedial training. Even promotion into positions based on technical expertise, which may result in transferring people out of their areas of highest potential, is cautioned against in this strengths-based approach.

Complementary to Gallup's strengths management are increasingly recommended high-performance work practices (HPWPs) such as multisource or 360-degree feedback, team-building, pay for performance, work-life balance programs, and others. As documented in Pfeffer's (1998) *Human equation* and the empirical assessment of work in America (O'Toole & Lawler, 2006), the recognition and consistent application of such positively oriented practices are used to explain the superior performance and sustainability of recognized world-class companies such as SAS, the large software development firm, and Southwest Airlines. Closing the "knowing–doing gap" in relation to such HPWPs is critical to realizing the full potential return on investment in human capital (Pfeffer & Sutton, 2000).

Despite these academically recognized positive approaches, there also have been a plethora of positively oriented management fads in the popular literature. Unfortunately, most of the best sellers lack any theory, measures, or research evidence of performance impact. This trend has culminated in the recent call for "evidence-based management" to help in narrowing the existing research–practice gap (Pfeffer & Sutton, 2006; Rousseau, 2006). With this brief historical and contemporary background serving as a point of departure, we now turn attention to the more micro-oriented theory, research and application of what is termed positive organizational behavior, or simply POB.

Positive Organizational Behavior

Drawing from positive psychology, several years ago Luthans (2002a, 2002b) called for a positive approach to organizational behavior (POB), which is defined as "the study and application of positively oriented human resource strengths and psychological capacities that can be measured, developed, and effectively managed for performance improvement in today's workplace" (Luthans, 2002b, p. 59; also see Nelson & Cooper, 2007; Wright, 2003). This definition provides several criteria that distinguish POB from the related initiatives discussed above. For example, psychological capacities that are included under this definition of POB must have a theoretical foundation and valid measurement. These two criteria align POB with other positive scientific domains of study such as positive psychology and POS, but differentiate it from the popular literature on positivity in the workplace. By the same token, the criteria of being state-like and open to development (as opposed to trait-like and relatively fixed) differentiate from much of positive psychology and POS. This open-to-development criterion also differentiates POB from Gallup's emphasis on talents and strengths as well as widely recognized streams of research in positively oriented mainstream organizational behavior such as the "Big Five" personality traits (Barrick & Mount, 1991) and core self-evaluation traits (Judge & Bono, 2001).

Most relevant to the positive workplace is the emphasis POB places on having performance impact. Whereas in positive psychology optimal human functioning may be of terminal value, applied to the workplace, value is largely determined by performance impact. Limited resources rarely can be secured or maintained in today's organizations without showing a quantifiable, sustainable impact on performance and, in business organizations, eventually bottom-line profitability.

Based on these criteria of being theory and research-based, measurable, state-like, and having performance impact, four positive psychological capacities have been initially identified for inclusion in POB theory building, research, and application: efficacy, hope, optimism, and resiliency (Luthans, 2002a; Luthans, Youssef, & Avolio, 2007a, 2007b).

- *Self-efficacy*, drawing from Bandura (1997), is defined for the workplace domain as "an individual's convictions (or confidence) about his or her abilities to mobilize the motivation, cognitive resources, and courses of action needed to successfully execute a specific task within a given context" (Stajkovic & Luthans, 1998b, p. 66). Self-efficacy has an established foundation in social cognitive theory (Bandura, 1986, 1997) and its positive relationship to work performance has extensive research support (Stajkovic & Luthans, 1998a). There are valid and reliable measures for self-efficacy applicable to the workplace (e.g., Maurer & Pierce, 1998; Parker, 1998) and widely recognized approaches for developing it. The sources for

developing efficacy include mastery experiences and success, vicarious learning and modeling, social persuasion and positive feedback, and physiological and psychological arousal (Bandura, 1997; chap. 31). In other words, self-efficacy meets the inclusion criteria for POB.

- *Hope* is defined as "a positive motivational state that is based on an interactively derived sense of successful (1) agency (goal-directed energy) and (2) pathways (planning to meet goals)" (Snyder, Irving, & Anderson, 1991, p. 287). State hope is measurable (Snyder et al., 1996) and related to performance in various domains, including the workplace (Adams et al., 2002; Luthans, Avolio, Avey, & Norman, 2007; Peterson Luthans, Avolio, Walumbwa, & Li, 2005; Peterson & Byron, 2007; Peterson & Luthans, 2003; Snyder, 1995; Youssef & Luthans, 2007). Recognized approaches for developing hope include setting challenging "stretch" goals, contingency planning, and when warranted, regoaling to avoid false hope (Lopez et al., 2004; Luthans & Jensen, 2002; Luthans & Youssef, 2004; Snyder, 2000). Thus, hope also meets the POB inclusion criteria.

- *Optimism* according to Seligman (1998) is "an explanatory style that uses personal, permanent, and pervasive causes to explain positive events and external, temporary, and situation-specific attributions for negative events." POB emphasizes the importance of realistic (Schneider, 2001) and flexible (Peterson, 2000) optimism. Recognized approaches for developing such optimism include leniency for the past, appreciation for the present, and opportunity seeking for the future (Schneider, 2001). Optimism has established measures (Reivich & Gillman, 2003; Scheier & Carver, 1985) and its performance impact in work settings has been demonstrated (Luthans, Avolio et al., 2007; Seligman, 1998; Youssef & Luthans, 2007). Thus, optimism meets the POB inclusion criteria as well.

- *Resiliency* is defined as "the developable capacity to rebound or bounce back from adversity, conflict, and failure or even positive events, progress, and increased responsibility" (Luthans, 2002a, p. 702; also see Masten, 2001; Youssef & Luthans, 2005). Resiliency is measurable (e.g., Block & Kremen, 1996; Wagnild & Young, 1993) and related to work performance (Coutu, 2002; Harland, Harrison, Jones, & Reiter-Palmon, 2005; Luthans, Avolio et al., 2007; Luthans et al., 2005). Drawing from the established theory building and empirical findings in clinical and developmental psychology, Masten's (2001; chap. 12) research supports that resiliency can be developed through asset-, risk-, and process-focused strategies (for specific applications of developing resiliency in the workplace see Luthans, Vogelgeslang, & Lester, 2006; Luthans & Youssef, 2004; Waite & Richardson, 2004). Thus, like efficacy, hope, and optimism, resiliency meets the POB criteria.

- *Other positive psychological capacities* also have been recently proposed as potentially meeting the POB criteria (see Luthans, Youssef, & Avolio, 2007b). Examples include wisdom, creativity, subjective well-being, flow, humor, gratitude, forgiveness, emotional intelligence, courage, authenticity, and spirituality. Although these positive constructs currently meet the POB criteria to varying degrees (e.g., see Luthans, Youssef, & Avolio, 2007b), their potential for the future seems especially promising. For example, authentic leaders have been defined as "those individuals who are deeply aware of how they think and behave and are perceived by others as being aware of their own and others' values/moral perspectives, knowledge, and strengths; aware of the context in which they operate; and who are confident, hopeful, optimistic, resilient, and high on moral character" (Avolio, Gardner, Walumbwa, Luthans, & May, 2004, pp. 803–804). Authentic leadership has been proposed as a predictor of positive performance and attitudinal outcomes in followers (Gardner, Avolio, Luthans, May, & Walumbwa, 2005) and recent empirical evidence supports the relationship between the positive psychological capacities of entrepreneurs and their authentic leadership (Jensen & Luthans, 2006).

Positive Psychological Capital

To transition POB more to the practice of human resource management and extend the recognized value that human and social capital may have for competitive advantage in today's workplace, we recently have proposed and empirically demonstrated a higher-order, core construct of psychological capital (Luthans, Avolio et al., 2007; Luthans & Youssef, 2004; Luthans, Youssef, & Avolio, 2007a, 2007b). We define this psychological capital, or simply PsyCap, as "an individual's positive psychological state of development that is characterized by: (1) having confidence (self-efficacy) to take on and put in the necessary effort to succeed at challenging tasks; (2) making a positive attribution (optimism) about succeeding now and in the future; (3) persevering toward goals and, when necessary, redirecting paths to goals (hope) in order to succeed; and (4) when beset by problems and adversity, sustaining and bouncing back and even beyond (resiliency) to attain success" (Luthans, Youssef, & Avolio, 2007b, p. 3).

Besides the foundation provided by POB briefly summarized previously, PsyCap as defined here is a higher-order, core construct based on the interactions of the positive states of efficacy, hope, optimism, and resilience. Similar to psychological resources theories (e.g., see Hobfoll, 2002, for a comprehensive review) and Fredrickson's (2001) broaden-and-build theory of positive emotions, we propose that PsyCap may have synergistic effects beyond the positive states that make it up. For example, in our research to date we have found support for PsyCap as being a higher-order, core factor and a better predictor of performance and satisfaction than any of the four capacities (i.e., efficacy, hope, optimism, and resilience) that make it up (Luthans, Avolio et al., 2007).

Although there are a number of established measures for each of the psychological states that constitute PsyCap (Lopez & Snyder, 2003), very few of these measures are specific to the context of the workplace, and none captures the additive and synergistic nature of these capacities. To fill this gap, a new measure has been recently developed and analyzed (Luthans, Avolio et al., 2007; Luthans, Youssef, & Avolio, 2007b). The Psychological Capital Questionnaire (PCQ) is a 24-item measure that draws from existing measures such as Parker's (1998) Role Breadth Self-Efficacy Scale, Snyder et al.'s (1996) State Hope Scale, Wagnild and Young's (1993) Resilience Scale, and Scheier and Carver's (1985) Optimism Scale. Our preliminary research indicates that the PCQ has evidence of construct validity and is significantly related to performance and satisfaction across diverse samples (Luthans, Avolio et al., 2007) and adds unique variance (Avey, Luthans, & Youssef, 2009).

In addition to a measure of PsyCap, we have also recently developed a micro-intervention strategy for developing PsyCap (Luthans, Avey, Avolio, Norman, & Combs, 2006). In a highly focused 1–3-hour training session, participants' hope is developed through coaching them on setting challenging, measurable, and personally valuable goals and "stepping" subgoals, as well as generating realistic pathways and "approach" (rather than avoidance) strategies to accomplish their goals and overcome potential obstacles. An optimistic explanatory style is also developed as participants anticipate and plan for potential adversities while engaging in positive self-talk and learning to exhibit internalized control. Success and mastery is experienced in a simulated but realistic setting, along with vicarious learning and social persuasion from the facilitator and other participants, in order to develop self-efficacy. In a similar manner, personal and social assets, risk management strategies, and adaptational processes are also inputs into the process of developing the participants' resiliency, which also take place in the context of participant-selected recent examples of personally challenging work-related situations.

In our preliminary research, this PsyCap microintervention has yielded positive results in terms of increasing participants' level of PsyCap (e.g., Luthans, Avey, & Patera, 2008) and their performance back on the job (Luthans, Avey, & Avolio, 2009). For example, in a very large high-tech manufacturing firm, engineering managers that went through the microintervention significantly increased their PsyCap and performance, while a matched control group showed no performance increase (Luthans et al., 2009). Based on the results of this study, using utility analysis from the human resource management literature (see Becker & Huselid, 1992; Boudreau, 1991; Cascio, 1991; Kravatz, 2004), a $73,919 1-year impact was calculated. Then, estimating the cost of the 2.5-hr intervention in terms of the participants' pay and benefits and conducting the session (i.e., a total cost of $20,000), the return on investment (or ROD, return on development of PsyCap) was calculated to be 270 percent (73,919–20,000/20,000; Luthans et al., 2006).

Creating Positive Workplaces

The evidence seems clear that work environments characterized by negativity, cynicism, incivility, and mistrust are not as productive nor satisfying as those characterized by positivity, confidence, hope, optimism, and resilience (see Luthans & Youssef, 2007; Luthans, Youssef, & Avolio, 2007b, for a summary of this literature). However, although there may be contagion effects from positive leadership (e.g., see Peterson & Luthans, 2003) and we are currently conducting such research, it also seems evident that merely hiring positive (e.g., optimistic) individuals is not sufficient for creating a positive

workplace (Youssef & Luthans, 2005). Organizational cultures are very fluid and complex. Creating a positive workplace requires human resource and leadership development. For example, Avolio and Luthans (2006, p. 2) in defining authentic leadership development (ALD) do include PsyCap, but also recognize other dimensions: "the process that draws upon a leader's life course, psychological capital, moral perspective, and a highly developed supporting organizational climate to produce greater self-awareness and self-regulated positive behaviors, which in turn foster continuous, positive self-development resulting in veritable, sustained performance."

Although the leader's personal background and PsyCap contribute to authentic leadership development, the organizational climate can facilitate, accelerate, hinder, or even reverse this process, as evident from the personal accounts in the news media of many top organizational leaders such as those found at Enron or WorldCom. On the other hand, a development process that is supported by one's psychological capital and a supporting inclusive, ethical, and caring organizational climate can be conducive to authentic leadership trickling down to followers with a positive impact on their performance and desirable attitudes (Avey, Wernsing, & Luthans, 2008; Avolio & Luthans, 2006; Gardner et al., 2005; Luthans, Norman, Avolio, & Avey, 2008). Even in the absence of a highly charismatic leadership style, this ALD process can be facilitated through the followers' increased trust in and identification with the authentic leader and the organization, as well as the leader's one-on-one modeling of positive values, attitudes, and emotions (Avolio et al., 2004; Gardner et al., 2005).

In addition to ALD, individual employees' efficacy can be enhanced or thwarted by the organizational context in which they work, or by their leaders or coworkers. In an organizational culture characterized by information sharing and cooperation, self-efficacy regarding one's areas of expertise can be integrated with that of others, creating collective efficacy, which Bandura (1997, p. 477) defines as "a group's shared belief in its conjoint capabilities to organize and execute the courses of action required to produce given levels of attainments." In such a positive organizational environment, interdependence is viewed as an opportunity to capitalize upon the work group's combined strengths and psychological capabilities, rather than a source of threat and vulnerability.

Besides the role that positive organizational contexts play in authentic leadership and collective efficacy, the same could be said for hope, optimism, and resilience at the organizational level. For example, organizational resiliency seems critical for individual employees' resiliency to develop and flourish (Youssef & Luthans, 2005). Organizations consistently make decisions to invest in or deplete their own or their participants' assets, expose themselves and their members to calculated risks, and build adaptive mechanisms and buffering processes that can help in best utilizing organizational and individual assets to manage relevant risk factors (Youssef & Luthans, 2005). Organizational values are also integral to employees' resilience because they provide stability, direction, and meaning in times of change and uncertainty (Coutu, 2002; Sutcliffe & Vogus, 2003; Weick, 1993; also see Youssef & Luthans, 2008).

The interactive, interdependent, and synergistic nature of positive workplaces and their leaders and employees is in line with social cognitive theory, in which individual-level biological, cognitive, and affective dimensions, as well as one's behavior, in addition to the external environment, including others' characteristics and behaviors, interact in triadic reciprocal causation (Bandura, 1986). This depiction of the positive organization is also consistent with the earlier-mentioned psychological resources theories (Hobfoll, 2002) and Fredrickson's (2001) broaden-and-build model, in which positive emotions exhibit upward spirals and contagion effects that expand the individual's and group's horizons and widens their scope for potential courses of action.

Future Directions

As indicated in this Handbook, the positive psychology initiative has stimulated and affected several related domains of research and practice, including, as shown in this chapter, at the workplace. In this concluding section, we highlight several potentially important directions for the further development of positive organizational behavior and psychological capital that may help positive workplaces "flourish" into the future:

- *Multilevel theoretical frameworks and empirical studies* are relatively scarce in organizational behavior research. They are difficult to accomplish in field settings. However, without studying cross-level linkages and discontinuities, the contributions of positivity in general and psychological capital in particular are likely to be limited. Both organizational- and individual-level positive constructs need to be operationalized and

measured in ways that can help establish and quantify various potential interactions and trickle-down, contagion effects. This is often difficult to accomplish in today's workplace environment, where sharing objective (especially performance-related) data is commonly perceived as added exposure to competitive and legal risks. This often leaves organizational behavior researchers with many perceptual variables, and results in incomplete testing of many complex but realistic multilevel conceptual frameworks.

- *A cross-disciplinary perspective* seems vital for better understanding of positive applications in the workplace, as well as for enriching positive psychology per se as an area of research and practice. It is becoming increasingly critical for organizational behavior researchers and practicing managers to gain additional depth in their understanding and application of not only positive psychology, but also related behavioral sciences such as sociology or cultural anthropology. This interdisciplinary bridge has been crossed in the past, which has resulted in many advances in the better understanding and management of human resources and organizations that could have never been accomplished had the field developed in isolation. Moreover, we believe that the workplace also provides positive psychologists with opportunities that should not be overlooked. After all, workplace productivity is a cornerstone of socioeconomic prosperity and flourishing. The workplace is where healthy, productive individuals tend to spend the majority of their time and energy. The workplace would seem to dominate the forgotten mission of facilitating "the good life" and nurturing people which was noted in the original charge for positive psychology (e.g., see Seligman & Csikszentmihalyi, 2000). In other words, leaders, employees, and the organizations they work at would seem to present positive psychologists with high-potential, largely uncharted, territories.

- *Cross-cultural applications* also represent a challenge to POB researchers and practitioners. For a positive approach to be important and effective, it has to take into notice the potential for cultural differences. For example, Fineman (2006) recently has criticized the indiscriminant assumption that always taking a positive approach is desirable and beneficial without recognizing that cross-cultural differences may render this assumption invalid. Our recent conceptual theory building and empirical research supports the relevance of PsyCap to several non-U.S. settings (Luthans, Avey, Clapp-Smith, & Li, 2008; Luthans et al., 2005; Luthans, Van Wyk, & Walumbwa, 2004; Luthans, Zhu, & Avolio, 2006; Youssef & Luthans, 2006). Cross-cultural research is necessary, both to establish the boundaries and external validity of PsyCap, and to better inform research within U.S. settings that are becoming increasingly diverse.

- *Virtual workplace settings* are becoming increasingly common. Being of a complex cognitive, affective, and social nature, developing and managing PsyCap in these settings is likely to yield meaningfully different challenges, dynamics, and outcomes. However, understanding the idiosyncrasies of virtual settings can present unprecedented opportunities for capitalizing on information technology to facilitate and leverage interpersonal, inter-unit, and interorganizational relationships that are meaningful and rewarding for a new workforce in spite of, but possibly because of, its lack of traditional face-to-face contact.

In conclusion, the positive lens for viewing the workplace has a long history, but only recently has an identifiable momentum in theoretical understanding, research, and application been building. The initial results of this effort seem to indicate that a positive approach may help meet the significant challenges facing workplaces now and in the future.

Future Questions

1. Does psychological capital extend to the group/team and organizational levels?

2. Can psychological capital development be sustained over time?

3. What other positive psychological resources besides efficacy, hope, optimism, and resiliency best meet the inclusion criteria of psychological capital?

References

Adams, V. H., Snyder, C. R., Rand, K. L., King, E. A., Sigmon, D. R., & Pulvers, K. M. (2002). Hope in the workplace. In R. Giacolone & C. Jurkiewicz (Eds.), *Handbook of workplace spirituality and organizational performance* (pp. 367–377). New York: Sharpe.

Avey, J. B., Luthans, F., & Youssef, C. M. (2009). The additive value of positive psychological capital in predicting work attitudes and behaviours. *Journal of Management, 35*, in press.

Avey, J. B., Wernsing, T. S., & Luthans, F. (2008). Can positive employees help positive organizational change? Impact of psychological capital and emotions on relevant attitudes and behaviors. *Journal of Applied Behavioral Science, 44*, 48–70.

Avolio, B. J., Gardner, W. L., Walumbwa, F. O., Luthans, F., & May, D. R. (2004). Unlocking the mask: A look at the process by which authentic leaders impact follower attitudes and behaviors. *The Leadership Quarterly, 15*, 801–823.

Avolio, B. J., & Luthans, F. (2006). *The high impact leader: Moments matter in accelerating authentic leadership development.* New York: McGraw-Hill.

Bandura, A. (1986). *Social foundations of thought and action.* Englewood Cliffs, NJ: Prentice-Hall.

Bandura, A. (1997). *Self-efficacy: The exercise of control.* New York: Freeman.

Barrick, M. R., & Mount, M. K. (1991). The Big Five personality dimensions and job performance: A meta-analysis. *Personnel Psychology, 44*, 1–26

Becker, B. E., & Huselid, M. A. (1992). Direct estimates of [SD.sub.y] and the implications for utility analysis. *Journal of Applied Psychology, 77*, 227–233.

Block, J., & Kremen, A. M. (1996). IQ and ego-resiliency: Conceptual and empirical connections and separateness. *Journal of Personality and Social Psychology, 70*, 349–361.

Boudreau, J. W. (1991). Utility analysis in human resource management decisions. In M. D. Dunnette & L. M. Hough (Eds.), *Handbook of industrial and organizational psychology* (Vol. 2, 2nd ed., pp. 621–745). Palo Alto, CA: Consulting Psychologists Press.

Buckingham, M., & Clifton, D. (2001). *Now, discover your strengths.* New York: Free Press.

Buckingham, M., & Coffman, C. (1999). *First, break all the rules.* New York: Simon & Schuster.

Cameron, K. S., Bright, D., & Caza, A. (2004). Exploring the relationships between virtuousness and performance. *American Behavioral Scientist, 47*, 766–790.

Cameron, K. S., & Caza, A. (2004). Contributions to the discipline of positive organizational scholarship. *American Behavioral Scientist, 47*, 731–739.

Cameron, K., Dutton, J., & Quinn, R. (Eds.). (2003). *Positive organizational scholarship.* San Francisco: Berrett-Koehler.

Carver, C. S., & Scheier, M. F. (1990). Origins and functions of positive and negative affect: A control-process view. *Psychological Review, 97*, 19–35.

Cascio, W. E. (1991). *Costing human resources: The financial impact of behavior in organizations* (3rd ed.). Boston: PWS-Kent.

Colquitt, J. A., Conlon, D. E., Wesson, M. J., Porter, C. O., & Ng, K. Y. (2001). Justice at the millennium: A meta-analytic review of 25 years of organizational justice research. *Journal of Applied Psychology, 86*, 425–445.

Coutu, D. L. (2002). How resilience works. *Harvard Business Review, 80*(3), 46–55.

Fineman, S. (2006). On being positive: Concerns and counter-points. *Academy of Management Review, 31*, 270–291.

Fredrickson, B. L. (1998). What good are positive emotions? *Review of General Psychology, 2*, 300–319.

Fredrickson, B. L. (2001). The role of positive emotions in positive psychology: The broaden-and-build theory of positive emotions. *American Psychologist, 56*, 218–226.

Gardner, W. L., Avolio, B. J., Luthans, F., May, D. R., & Walumbwa, F. O. (2005). "Can you see the real me?": A self-based model of authentic leader and follower development. *The Leadership Quarterly, 16*, 343–372.

Giacalone, R., Jurkiewicz, C., & Dunn, C. (Eds.). (2005). *Positive psychology in business ethics and corporate social responsibility.* Greenwich, CT: Information Age.

Harland, L., Harrison, W., Jones, J., & Reiter-Palmon, R. (2005). Leadership behaviors and subordinate resilience. *Journal of Leadership and Organizational Studies, 11*, 2–14.

Harter, J. K., Schmidt, F. L., & Hayes, T. L. (2002). Business-unit-level relationship between employee satisfaction, employee engagement, and business outcomes: A meta-analysis. *Journal of Applied Psychology, 87*, 268–279.

Herzberg, F., Mausner, B., & Snyderman, B. B. (1959). *The motivation to work.* New York: Wiley.

Hobfoll, S. (2002). Social and psychological resources and adaptation. *Review of General Psychology, 6*, 307–324.

Jensen, S., & Luthans, F. (2006). Relationship between entrepreneurs' psychological capital and their authentic leadership. *Journal of Managerial Issues, 18*, 254–273.

Judge, T. A., & Bono, J. E. (2001). Relationship of core self-evaluations traits—self-esteem, generalized self-efficacy, locus of control, and emotional stability—with job satisfaction and job performance: A meta-analysis. *Journal of Applied Psychology, 86*, 80–92.

Kravatz, D. (2004). *Measuring human capital.* Mesa, AZ: KAP.

Lazarus, R. S. (1991). *Emotion and adaptation.* New York: Oxford University Press.

Lopez, S. J., & Snyder, C. R. (Eds.). (2003). *Positive psychological assessment: A handbook of models and measures.* Washington, DC: American Psychological Association.

Lopez, S. J., Snyder, C. R., Magyar-Moe, J. L., Edwards, L. M., Teramoto Pedrotti, J., Janowski, K., et al. (2004). Strategies for accentuating hope. In P. A. Linley & S. Joseph (Eds.), *Positive psychology in practice* (pp. 388–405). New York: Wiley.

Luthans, F. (2002a). The need for and meaning of positive organizational behavior. *Journal of Organizational Behavior, 23*, 695–706.

Luthans, F. (2002b). Positive organizational behavior: Developing and managing psychological strengths. *Academy of Management Executive, 16*(1), 57–72.

Luthans, F., Avey, J. B., & Avolio, B. J. (2009). The development and performance impact of positive psychological capital: Micro-intervention studies. Manuscript under review.

Luthans, F., Avey, J. B., Avolio, B. J., Norman, S. M., & Combs, G. J. (2006). Psychological capital development: Toward a micro-intervention. *Journal of Organizational Behavior, 27*, 387–393.

Luthans, F., Avey, J. B., Clapp-Smith, R., & Li, W. (2009). More evidence on the value of Chinese workers' psychological capital: A potentially unlimited competitive resource? *The International Journal of Human Resource Management, 19*, 818–827.

Luthans, F., Avey, J. B., & Patera, J. L. (2008). Experimental analysis of a Web-based training intervention to develop positive psychological capital. *Academy of Management Learning and Education, 7*, 209–221.

Luthans, F., & Avolio, B. J. (2009). The "point" of positive organizational behavior. *Journal of Organizational Behavior, 30*, in press.

Luthans, F., Avolio, B. J., Avey, J., & Norman, S. (2007). Positive psychological capital: Measurement and relationship with performance and satisfaction. *Personnel Psychology, 60*, 541–572.

Luthans, F., Avolio, B. J., Walumbwa, F. O., & Li, W. (2005). The psychological capital of Chinese workers: Exploring the relationship with performance. *Management and Organization Review, 1*, 247–269.

Luthans, F., & Jensen, S. M. (2002). Hope: A new positive strength for human resource development. *Human Resource Development Review, 1*, 304–322.

Luthans, F., Norman, S. M., Avolio, B. M., & Avey, J. B. (2008). The mediating role of psychological capital in the supportive organizational climate–employee relationship. *Journal of Organizational Behavior, 29*, 219–238.

Luthans, F., Van Wyk, R., & Walumbwa, F. O. (2004). Recognition and development of hope for South African organizational leaders. *Leadership and Organization Development Journal, 25*, 512–527.

Luthans, F., Vogelgeslang, G. R., & Lester, P. B. (2006). Developing the psychological capital of resiliency. *Human Resource Development Review, 5*, 25–44.

Luthans, F., & Youssef, C. M. (2004). Human, social, and now positive psychological capital management: Investing in people for competitive advantage. *Organizational Dynamics, 33*, 143–160.

Luthans, F., & Youssef, C. M. (2007). Emerging positive organizational behavior. *Journal of Management, 33*, 321–349.

Luthans, F., Youssef, C. M., & Avolio, B. J., (2007a). Psychological capital: Investing and developing positive organizational behavior. In D. Nelson & C. L. Cooper (Eds.), *Positive organizational behavior* (pp. 9–24). Thousand Oaks, CA: Sage.

Luthans, F., Youssef, C. M., & Avolio, B. J. (2007b). *Psychological capital: Developing the human competitive edge.* Oxford: Oxford University Press.

Luthans, F., Zhu, W., & Avolio, B. J. (2006). The impact of efficacy on work attitudes across cultures. *Journal of World Business, 41*, 121–132.

Maslow, A. J. (1943). A theory of human motivation. *Psychological Review, 50*, 370–396.

Masten, A. S. (2001). Ordinary magic: Resilience process in development. *American Psychologist, 56*, 227–239.

Maurer, T. J., & Pierce, H. R. (1998). A comparison of Likert scale and traditional measures of self-efficacy. *Journal of Applied Psychology, 83*, 324–329.

McGregor, D. (1960). *The human side of enterprise.* New York: McGraw-Hill.

Nelson, D. L., & Cooper, C. L. (Eds.). (2007). *Positive organizational behavior.* Thousand Oaks, CA: Sage.

O'Toole, J., & Lawler, E. E. (2006). *The new American workplace.* New York: Palgrave Macmillan.

Parker, S. (1998). Enhancing role breadth self-efficacy: The roles of job enrichment and other organizational interventions. *Journal of Applied Psychology, 6*, 835–852.

Peterson, C. (2000). The future of optimism. *American Psychologist, 55*, 44–55.

Peterson, S. J., & Byron, K. (2007). Exploring the role of hope in job performance. *Journal of Applied Psychology, 28*, 785–803.

Peterson, C., & Chang, E. (2002). Optimism and flourishing. In C. L. M. Keyes & J. Haidt (Eds.), *Flourishing: Positive psychology and the life well-lived* (pp. 55–79). Washington, DC: American Psychological Association.

Peterson, S. J., & Luthans, F. (2003). The positive impact and development of hopeful leaders. *Leadership and Organization Development Journal, 24*, 26–31.

Pfeffer, J. (1998). *The human equation*. Boston: Harvard Business School Press.

Pfeffer, J., & Sutton R. I. (2006). Evidenced-based management. *Harvard Business Review, 84*(1), 63–74.

Pfeffer, J., & Sutton, R. I. (2000). *The knowing–doing gap*. Boston: Harvard Business School Press.

Rath, T., & Clifton, D. O. (2004). *How full is your bucket?* New York: Gallup Press.

Reivich, K., & Gillman, J. (2003). Learned optimism: The measurement of explanatory style. In S. L. Lopez & C. R. Snyder (Eds.), *Positive psychological assessment* (pp. 57–74). Washington, DC: American Psychological Association.

Roberts, L. M. (2006). Shifting the lens on organizational life: The added value of positive scholarship. *Academy of Management Review, 31*, 292–305.

Roethlisberger, F. J., & Dickson, W. J. (1939). *Management and the worker*. Cambridge, MA: Harvard University Press.

Rousseau, D. M. (2006). Is there such a thing as "evidence-based management"? *Academy of Management Review, 31*, 256–269.

Scheier, M., & Carver, C. (1985). Optimism, coping, and health: Assessment and implications of generalized outcome expectancies. *Health Psychology, 4*, 219–247.

Schneider, S. L. (2001). In search of realistic optimism. *American Psychologist, 56*, 250–263.

Seligman, M. (1998). *Learned optimism*. New York: Pocket Books.

Seligman, M., & Csikszentmihalyi, M. (2000). Positive psychology. *American Psychologist, 55*, 5–14.

Snyder, C. R. (1995). Managing for high hope. *R&D Innovator, 4*(6), 6–7.

Snyder, C. R. (2000). *Handbook of hope*. San Diego, CA: Academic Press.

Snyder, C. R., Sympson, S. C., Ybasco, F. C., Borders, T. F., Babyak, M. A., & Higgins, R. L. (1996). Development and validation of the State Hope Scale. *Journal of Personality and Social Psychology, 70*, 321–335.

Snyder, C. R., Irving, L., & Anderson, J. (1991). Hope and health: Measuring the will and the ways. In C. R. Snyder & D. R. Forsyth (Eds.), *Handbook of social and clinical psychology* (pp. 285–305). Elmsford, NY: Pergamon.

Spreitzer, G. M., & Sonenshein, S. (2003). Positive deviance and extraordinary organizing. In K. S. Cameron, J. E. Dutton, & R. E. Quinn (Eds.), *Positive organizational scholarship* (pp. 207–224). San Francisco: Berrett-Koehler.

Stajkovic, A. D., & Luthans, F. (1997). A meta-analysis of the effects of organizational behavior modification on task performance. *Academy of Management Journal, 40*, 1122–1149.

Stajkovic, A. D., & Luthans, F. (1998a). Self-efficacy and work-related performance: A meta-analysis. *Psychological Bulletin, 124*, 240–261.

Stajkovic, A. D., & Luthans, F. (1998b). Social cognitive theory and self-efficacy: Going beyond traditional motivational and behavioral approaches. *Organizational Dynamics, 26*, 62–74.

Stajkovic, A. D., & Luthans F. (2003). Behavioral management and task performance in organizations: Conceptual background, meta-analysis, and test of alternative models. *Personnel Psychology, 56*, 155–194.

Sutcliffe, K. M., & Vogus, T. (2003). Organizing for resilience. In K. S. Cameron, J. E. Dutton, & R. E. Quinn (Eds.), *Positive organizational scholarship* (pp. 94–110). San Francisco: Berrett-Koehler.

Wagnild, G., & Young, H. (1993). Development and psychometric evaluation of the resiliency scale. *Journal of Nursing Measurement, 1*, 165–178.

Waite, P., & Richardson, G. (2004). Determining the efficacy of resiliency training in the work site. *Journal of Allied Health, 33*, 178–183.

Weick, K. E. (1993). The collapse of sensemaking in organizations: The Mann Gulch disaster. *Administrative Science Quarterly, 38*, 628–652.

Wright, T. A. (2003). Positive organizational behavior: An idea whose time has truly come. *Journal of Organizational Behavior, 24*, 437–442.

Youssef, C. M., & Luthans, F. (2005). Resiliency development of organizations, leaders & employees: Multi-level theory building for sustained performance. In W. Gardner, B. J. Avolio, & F. Walumbwa (Eds.), *Authentic leadership theory and practice: Origins, effects and development, monographs in leadership and management* (Vol. 3, pp. 303–343). Oxford: Elsevier.

Youssef, C. M., & Luthans, F. (2006). Time for positivity in the Middle East: Developing hopeful Egyptian organizational leaders. In W. Mobley & E. Weldon (Eds.), *Advances in global leadership* (Vol. 4; pp. 283–297). Oxford: Elsevier Science/JAI.

Youssef, C. M., & Luthans, F. (2007). Positive organizational behavior in the workplace. The impact of hope, optimism, and resilience. *Journal of Management, 33*, 774–800.

Youssef, C. M., & Luthans, F. (2008). Leveraging psychological capital in virtuous organizations: Why and how? In C. C. Manz, K. S. Cameron, K. P. Manz, & R. D. Marx (Eds.), *The virtuous organization* (pp. 141–162). Hackensack, N.J.: World Scientific.

Positive Institutions, Law, and Policy

Peter H. Huang *and* Jeremy A. Blumenthal

Abstract

We analyze how positive institutions—democracy, strong families, free inquiry, free press, schools, businesses, communities, societies, work, and culture—can help foster human flourishing. We provide four examples of positive law and policy to illustrate the important role legal and social institutions can play in facilitating positive psychology. First, we explore positive psychology's potential interplay with law firm culture to reduce unhappiness of law firm associates. Second, we review the influence of civic participation in juries and democratic processes on citizens' well-being. Third, we identify the effects of policy changes on subjective perceptions of well-being in a wide range of contexts, and the complexities of evaluating such effects in light of individuals' cognitive and emotional tendencies. Finally, we speculate about the role of government or other third-party institutional intervention in enabling individuals and communities to flourish and thrive. Our overarching goal is to generate discussion about positive psychology's role in developing institutions that can help improve individuals' quality of life.

Keywords: democratic participation, Institutions, Paternalism, subjective well-being, workplace satisfaction

We analyze the third one of the three pillars of positive psychology: positive emotions, traits, and institutions (Seligman & Csikszentmihalyi, 2000). Positive institutions include democracy, strong families, free inquiry, and free press (Seligman, 2002); schools, businesses, communities, and societies (Peterson, 2006); and work and culture (Compton, 2005; Snyder & Lopez, 2007). We share the assumption that "positive institutions facilitate the development and display of positive traits, which in turn facilitate positive subjective experiences" (Peterson, 2006, p. 20) and therefore focus on how legal, public, and social policies and institutions can foster a good life.

We present four particular examples of positive institutions, law, and policy. First, we demonstrate how positive psychology suggests changes to make big law firm practice healthier by reforming institutional cultures (Huang & Swedloff, 2008). Second, we summarize how jury participation and direct participatory democracy improve life satisfaction.

Third, we analyze how various measures of subjective well-being assist policy evaluation in a number of diverse settings. Fourth, we speculate about what positive psychology implies for paternalistic government intervention. We choose these examples because they illustrate the important role legal and social institutions can play in facilitating positive psychology (Bohnet, 2006).

How to Make Big Law Firms Positive Institutions

Legal institutions, such as administrative agencies, courts, and legislatures, play ubiquitous roles in our lives. They also share two common features: they shape policy and involve lawyers. But, lawyers consistently rate poorly in surveys as to whom society trusts (e.g., Harris Poll, July 7–10, 2006). Lawyers have a negative image in popular culture: films increasingly portray lawyers negatively (Asimow, 2000; Post, 1987) and lawyer jokes abound (Galanter, 2005).

Some empirical studies find evidence that many lawyers have poor emotional, mental, and physical health, suffering from alcoholism, anxiety, depression, divorce, drug abuse, suicide, and unhappiness (Heinz, Nelson, Sandefur, & Laumann, 2005; Schlitz, 1999; Seligman, Verkuil, & Kang, 2001; but see Hull, 1999, for critical view of these studies). Lawyers at big law firms are among the unhappiest (Dinovitzer et al., 2004; Schlitz, 1999; but see Hull, 1999, for opposing perspective). Multiple causes explain unhappiness at big law firms, including long hours, organizational hierarchy, and competitive professional culture (Schlitz, 1999). Thus, a lawyer who wants to be happier and healthier should avoid firms that are or act like big law firms, including seeking alternatives to private practice (Schlitz, 1999). But, an important question remains: how to make lawyers at large law firms happier and healthier? Unhappy and unhealthy lawyers are unproductive lawyers.

Three fundamental psychological explanations for lawyer unhappiness are lawyer pessimism, junior associates' low decision latitude, and the zero-sum nature of adversarial systems (Seligman et al., 2001). Positive psychology offers coping strategies to reduce each of these sources of unhappiness (Seligman et al., 2001). First, flexible optimism (Seligman, Reivich, Jaycox, & Gillham, 1995) and learned optimism (Seligman, 1998) are well-documented antidotes for pessimism. Second, lawyers should have more personal control over their workday (Langer & Rodin, 1976; Seligman, 1992). Law firms can accomplish this by delegating more responsibilities, having partners mentor junior associates, offering more substantive training, permitting associates to have contact with clients earlier in associates' careers, and providing junior associates with voices in law firm management. Law firms can and should learn their associates' signature strengths to tailor work environments accordingly (Buckingham & Clifton, 2001; Peterson & Seligman, 2004). Third, law firms can strive to make litigation more cooperative and less adversarial (Croson & Mnookin, 1997; Gilson & Mnookin, 1994). In addition to law firms, law schools also can help to mitigate lawyer unhappiness by not fostering learned helplessness (Kurson, 2000; Seligman et al., 2001), by helping law students make better academic and career decisions based upon a realistic picture of the demands of a lawyer's professional life (Rodin, 1976), and by learning their signature strengths (Seligman et al., 2001). Lyubomirsky (2007) provides a number of happiness interventions that can help lawyers and others achieve sustainable increases of their happiness.

Subjective Well-Being and Civic Participation

Across a wide range of contexts, individuals derive substantial satisfaction from both participation in various activities and from the simple right to participate in the particular process. Research has long shown that with small-scale interactions, individuals' satisfaction with process can lead to their satisfaction with outcome—the notion of "procedural utility" (e.g., Frey, Benz, & Stutzer, 2004) or "procedural justice" (e.g., Lind & Tyler, 1988). But this is so at the larger institutional level as well: from trial juries to political institutions, individuals' subjective well-being from an institution in which they participate correlates with that institution's formal arrangement, and with those individuals' opportunity to participate in the institution.

Specifically, research findings demonstrate that people are happier with procedures or institutions when they are given a voice (Thibaut & Walker, 1975). When individuals participate in a process, express their opinions, or are given the opportunity to do so, they are generally more satisfied with that process. One of the classic opportunities for individuals to express their opinions in the legal system is in the trial jury. Jury trials, though increasingly rare, are an important part of today's justice system and are a constitutionally enshrined American institution. Despite substantial investigation of how juries function, however, surprisingly little evidence exists as to how jurors actually experience their time in service. Research shows that jurors who serve are generally satisfied with their experience and typically report willingness to serve again (Seamone, 2001–2002). The source of this satisfaction, however, is not always clear (see Cutler & Hughes, 2001, for review). We suggest that jurors' satisfaction with their experience may stem from their ability to participate, especially in the mini-democracy of jury deliberation. That is, jurors might be "motivated by a feeling of satisfaction with participation in the democratic process" (Prescott & Starr, 2006, p. 339, n. 190). For instance, for a small percentage of actual jurors surveyed, it was their "fellow jurors," rather than any other aspect of service, who "made the experience more positive" and changed their perception of the court system from "unfavorable" or "neutral" to "favorable" (Cutler & Hughes, 2001, p. 313, tbl. 4). In the same survey of over 4,600 jurors, 89% agreed that they "were satisfied with the jury deliberation process," the same percentage that agreed with the vaguer statement, "I was satisfied with the way the trial was conducted" (p. 315, fig. 2). Jury deliberation, in fact, generated the least dissatisfaction of all aspects of the experience about which jurors were asked (Cutler & Hughes, 2001). Further, civil juries operating under a unanimity decision rule deliberate longer and more thoroughly and seem to be more satisfied with their verdicts (see Diamond, Rose, & Murphy, 2006). Criminal juries too seem to "fee[l] better about themselves and their fellow citizens" under such a rule (Leib, 2006, p. 195).

Small group research supports these observations (e.g., Foels, Driskell, Mullen, & Salas, 2000; Peterson, 1999). Overall, individuals are more satisfied with democratic groups versus groups with autocratic leaders (e.g., Foels et al., 2000). This seems to derive directly from the increased opportunity to express one's voice, communicating that one is involved and participating in the group's decision and decision-making process (Peterson, 1999). Most fundamentally, such participation reinforces individuals' notions that their ideas, identities, and participation are of value: "the opportunity to express their thoughts . . . implies that [participants'] thoughts are worthy of being considered and that [they] are important individuals" (Peterson, 1999). This "group value" model of procedural justice (Tyler & Lind, 1992) emphasizes the importance of expressing oneself by participation in small groups, helping to affirm one's place in such groups and, thus, one's self-identity. Accordingly, jurors' satisfaction may stem from participating, from being active rather than passive participants (Dann, 1996).

Expressing one's opinions—or simply having the right to do so—is also of substantial importance at the level of political institutions. Participating in a democratic political culture, or having the chance to do so, can lead to increased subjective well-being (Frey & Stutzer, 2000, 2002). For instance, Frey and Stutzer (2000) interviewed thousands of residents in the various Swiss cantons about their overall life satisfaction. Controlling for a variety of demographic and economic factors, the opportunity to participate in direct democratic processes (e.g., referenda and other popular initiatives) was positively associated with individuals' self-reported subjective well-being concerning their life as a whole. Evidently, "citizens may gain procedural utility from such participation rights over and above the outcome generated in the political process, because they provide a feeling of being involved and having political influence, as well as a notion of inclusion, identity and self-determination" (Frey et al., 2004, p. 380).

Three lines of research might profitably develop these findings. First, both mock and actual jury research might ask jurors whether the participatory opportunities of deliberation lead to their generally high satisfaction with serving. Second, deliberation—deliberative democracy in particular—is an increasingly prominent topic for political researchers. Of particular interest is Fishkin and colleagues' Deliberative Polling (DP) project, in which small groups are informed, and then deliberate about, political and societal issues. Although some evidence suggests that such deliberation leads to increased support for the democratic process (Luskin & Fishkin, 2002), reported findings have focused on decision "outcomes." Further examination of DP participants' satisfaction with "process," "outcome," and "self" would be of interest. Third (and related), in light of recent arguments to increase direct democracy, profitable research might replicate Frey and Stutzer's (2000) study in the United States, examining whether increased availability and/or use of direct democratic processes such as referenda correlate with self-reports of subjective well-being across different states.

Subjective Well-Being Measures of Policy

Measures of subjective well-being are typically answers to questions asking survey respondents to self-report their subjective well-being on a numerical scale ranging from a low number such as 0 or 1 to a higher number such as 4, 7, or 10. Such measures are utilized in the Gallup World Poll (Gallup Organization, 2006), Eurobarometer (Inglehart & Klingemann, 2000), General Social Survey (Davis, Smith, & Marsden, 2001), World Values Survey (Inglehart, European Values Study Group, & World Values Survey Association, 2005), Experience Sampling Method (Andersson & Tour, 2005; Hektner, Schmidt, & Csikszentmihalyi, 2007; Stone & Shiffman, 1994), Daily Reconstruction Method (Kahneman, Krueger, Schkade, Schwarz, & Stone, 2004a), national well-being accounts (Diener, Kesebir, & Lucas, 2008; Kahneman, Krueger, Schkade, Schwarz, & Stone, 2004b) and brief indices (Diener, 2000, 2006; Diener & Seligman, 2004). Bhutan introduced a gross national happiness index to replace gross national product for measuring progress (Sherr, 2005). China recently announced plans to add a happiness index to its roster of key indicators

(Ford, 2006). Instead of designing public policy to achieve higher subjective well-being, there could be more emotional appeal to and political support for designing public policy to minimize subjective ill-being. An example of a subjective ill-being index is the U-index measuring the fraction of time that people spend in an unpleasant emotional state (Blanchflower, 2009; Kahneman & Krueger, 2006; Kreuger et al., 2009).

Subjective well-being measures offer nonmonetary metrics for evaluating policy in risk regulation (Huang, 2008a) or financial and securities regulation (Huang, 2008b). Such measures take into account investor confidence, financial euphoria, and market moods. Subjective well-being measures can lend insight into contexts as diverse as business ethics and social responsibility (Giacalone, Jurkiewicz, & Dunn, 2005), cigarette taxation (Gruber & Mullainathan, 2004), development economics (Graham, 2005; Graham & Pettinato, 2002), disadvantaged subpopulations (Delle Fave & Massimini, 2005), education (Martin, 2005; Noddings, 2003), employment discrimination litigation (Huang & Moss, 2006), environmental protection (Kahneman & Sugden, 2005), income inequality (Alesina, Di Tella, & MacCulloch, 2004); Graham & Felton, 2006), labor market regulation (Alesina, Glaeser, & Sacerdote, 2006), macroeconomics (Clark & Oswald, 1994; Di Tella, MacCulloch, & Oswald, 2003; Di Tella & MacCulloch, 2006; Eggers et al., 2006; Oswald, 1997; Stutzer & Lalive, 2004), marriage (Frey & Stutzer, 2005), obesity (Graham & Felton, 2005), organizational behavior (Baker, Greenberg, & Hemingway, 2006; Cameron, Dutton, and Quinn, 2003), political economy (Graham & Sukhtankar, 2004), poverty (Rojas, 2008), public housing (Kling, Liebman, & Katz, 2007), taxation (Bagaric & McConvill, 2005; Griffith, 2004; Kornhauser, 2004; Layard, 2005; Ring, 2004), terrorism (Frey, Luechinger, & Stutzer, 2007), and urban planning (Frey & Stutzer, 2004). In all these diverse settings, changes in policy are associated with changes in subjective well-being measures. Empirical findings that positive affect is positively correlated with physical health (Pressman & Cohen, 2005) and success (Lyubomirsky, King, & Diener, 2005) provide additional rationales for policies to foster positive affect.

Complicated issues about positive policy involve how people's own judgments of their subjective well-being vary over time (Sanna & Chang, 2006). People experience subjective well-being not only in the moment but also in savoring and memory (Elster & Loewenstein, 1992). Although future subjective well-being and past subjective well-being affect our current subjective well-being, they do so asymmetrically. Recent psychological studies find people feel more intense subjective well-being upon contemplating some future events than upon recalling past ones (Van Boven & Ashworth, 2006). Complexities multiply if our current subjective well-being depends upon not only our own anticipated subjective well-being and remembered subjective well-being, but also our anticipations and remembrances of others' subjective well-being. These varieties of subjective well-being can, in turn, depend on our current subjective well-being. Such dependencies are filtered through systematically inaccurate affective forecasting (Gilbert, 2006) and imperfect memory (Sutton, 1992). Incorrect predictions and recollections do help motivate us to pursue and strive for goals (Lench & Levine, 2006), and inaccuracies may also produce more financial economic activity than accuracies (Huang, 2005a, pp. 102–109). But irrational exuberance and unjustified anxiety raise normative questions about whether institutions and policies promoting accuracy about subjective well-being are socially desirable (Huang, 2005b). A final issue is whether to design policy to maximize aggregate subjective well-being or to assist people in advancing their individual and collective ideas of what is the good life (Frey & Stutzer, 2006a).

Positive Paternalism

One traditional concern about institutions is the possibility that they will engage in manipulation or improper influence against individuals. Indeed, a substantial body of economic and legal scholarship has recently developed about the propriety of "paternalism," that is, intervention by either the government or private parties into individual decision making and/or behavior in order to improve that person's welfare (e.g., Camerer, 2006; Jolls, Sunstein, & Thaler, 1998; Thaler & Sunstein, 2008).[1] This body of scholarship applies psychological findings documenting the prevalence of cognitive biases and heuristics to suggest that paternalism may sometimes be appropriate to protect people

[1] "Paternalism" has long had strongly negative connotations, in large part due to the perception that such intervention infringes on individual autonomy, on the right to make one's own choices (even if they are in error), and on individuals' preferences for the freedom to make such choices. Empirical research, however, may cast doubt on all of these rationales (Blumenthal, 2007).

from their own costly and self-injurious errors. Other analyses focus on emotional, rather than cognitive, influences on decision making (Blumenthal, 2005, 2007; Huang, 2006).

Little discussion of paternalism occurs, however, in the context of positive psychology. But to the extent that positive psychology is seen as prescriptive, not only descriptive (see, for example, Seligman & Pawelski, 2003), there may be a role in developing institutions that can intervene to enable individuals and communities to flourish and thrive. As we suggest above, a positive paternalism of institutions might supplement traditional paternalism, by helping to elevate individuals' and society's subjective well-being from some existing baseline.

We take no position here as to the normative propriety of such intervention. We do, however, suggest that both the positive and normative aspects of such possibilities be discussed and be investigated empirically. Public reluctance to accept paternalistic intervention is a formidable hurdle to overcome, and there are a variety of other social costs in developing paternalistic "interventions" (Blumenthal, 2007; Glaeser, 2006). However, private or governmental programming to promote "beneficial" outcomes might be more palatable to the public (as the loss aversion literature might suggest).

Consider, for instance, governmental response to the problem of poor physical health, including obesity or coronary heart disease. A remedial paternalistic intervention might prevent fatty and other unhealthy food from being sold in restaurants, cafeterias, or even supermarkets, to remove the option to purchase and consume such unhealthy food. In contrast, government mandating of an exercise program—perhaps even just for those at risk for heart disease—might be seen as less intrusive than the "remedial" approach. Avoiding juveniles' obesity and other health problems is of substantial current interest, and one approach has been the encouragement of requiring minimum levels of physical activity in schools, with potential accountability for schools that fail to provide appropriate physical education programs (e.g., Pate et al., 2006).

Similarly, consider the burgeoning research on "affective forecasting," the prediction of future emotional states (Wilson & Gilbert, 2003). Individuals are surprisingly poor at accurately predicting the intensity and duration of future emotions (Wilson & Gilbert, 2003). One application of this research has discussed its potential relevance to paternalism issues, but focused on remedial interventions (Blumenthal, 2007; see also Guthrie,

2003). Other examples of remedial interventions are to identify contexts where individuals are poor at recognizing what matters for their subjective well-being—and providing people better information about what will in fact matter for their subjective well-being (Frey & Stutzer, 2006b; Loewenstein & Ubel, 2006). A positive psychology approach would help individuals identify and develop their signature strengths so that people find their work more fulfilling and view it as a calling instead of a career or job (Huang, 2008c). If a metaphor for light paternalism is therapy designed to combat and correct for cognitive and emotional disturbances that detract from people's subjective well-being (Loewenstein & Haisley, 2008), then a metaphor for positive paternalism is positive therapy.

Finally, recent affective neuroscientific data provide evidence of a disjunction between two brain systems—wanting and liking (Nettle, 2005)—a gap that supplies a scientific language for normative and positive theories of paternalism (Camerer, 2006). Huang (2006) proposes that environments in which it is challenging to learn to want what you will like, such as those involving viscerally addictive experiences or substances, decisions having irreversible or very costly to reverse consequences, and infrequently repeated situations, justify some type of paternalism. Examples include possible choices about career, children, death, family, health, living wills, marriage, and retirement. For example, some people repeatedly fail to learn to distinguish between passionate love, which is "the love you fall into," and companionate love, which "grows slowly over the years" (see chap. 42). But the trajectories over time of these distinct kinds of love diverge in both the short and long run (Haidt, 2006). In particular, their short-term divergence creates "two danger points, two places where many people make grave mistakes." The first possible mistake is premature marriage during passionate love. The second is premature breaking up when passionate love fades, "because if the lovers had stuck it out, if they had given compassionate love a chance to grow, they might have found true love" (Haidt, 2006, pp. 126–127). Many states in the United States currently have laws that impose a waiting period before entering into or dissolving a marriage; but this research has implications for other contexts as well.

Clearly, the public's approbation of any such intervention by either government or private parties is a matter for further empirical research, as is, of course, such programs' effectiveness. Nevertheless, we hope to prompt both such research and further discussion about the normative aspects of such interventions.

Conclusion

Institutions maintain a variety of roles: creating incentives, coordinating behavior, guiding self-selection, providing information, facilitating causal explanations, and influencing preferences (Bohnet, 2006). Reviewing past and potential research on large law firms, civic participation, and policies designed to increase subjective well-being, we have sought to demonstrate one overarching goal: through these roles, institutions can help improve individuals' quality of life. We hope our review helps point to "recommendations for how to change institutions for the better of humankind" (Bohnet, 2006, p. 232).

Questions

1. How can empirical research identify optimal policies to relieve unhappiness, especially of employees at large law firms?

2. What are the costs and benefits of using measures of subjective well-being, rather than of economic well-being, as well-being criteria and standards for individuals, communities, and nations?

3. What is a government's role in intervening to enable individuals and communities to flourish and thrive that do not limit particular decisions and prohibit certain behavior?

References

Alesina, A., Di Tella, R., & MacCulloch, R. (2004). Inequality and happiness: Are Europeans and Americans different? *Journal of Public Economics, 88*, 2009–2042.

Alesina, A., Glaeser, E. L., & Sacerdote, B. (2006). Work and leisure in the U.S. and Europe: Why so different? In M. Gertler & K. Rogoff (Eds.), *NBER macroeconomics annual* (pp. 1–64). Cambridge, MA: The MIT Press.

Andersson, P., & Tour, R. (2005). How to sample behavior and emotions: A psychological approach and an empirical example. *Irish Journal of Management, 26*, 92–106.

Asimow, M. (2000). Bad lawyers in the movies. *Nova Law Review, 24*, 531–594.

Bagaric, M., & McConvill, J. (2005). Stop taxing happiness: A new perspective on progressive taxation. *Pittsburgh Tax Review, 2*, 65–91.

Baker, D., Greenberg, C., & Hemingway, C. (2006). *What happy companies know: How the science of happiness can change your company for the better.* Upper Saddle River, NJ: Prentice Hall.

Blanchflower, D. G. (2009). International evidence on well-being. In *National time accounting and subjective well-being.* Chicago: University of Chicago Press.

Blumenthal, J. A. (2005). Law and the emotions: The problems of affective forecasting. *Indiana Law Journal, 80*, 155–238.

Blumenthal, J. A. (2007). Emotional paternalism. *Florida State University Law Review, 35*, 1–72.

Bohnet, I. (2006). How institutions affect behavior: Insights from economics and psychology. In D. DeCremer, M. Zeelenberg, & J. K. Murnigham (Eds.), *Social psychology and economics* (pp. 213–237). Mahwah, NJ: Lawrence Erlbaum.

Buckingham, M., & Clifton, D. O. (2001). *Now, discover your strengths.* New York: Free Press.

Camerer, C. S. (2006). Wanting, liking, and learning: Speculations on neuroscience and paternalism. *University of Chicago Law Review, 73*, 87–110.

Cameron, K. S., Dutton, J. E., & Quinn, R. E. (2003). *Positive organizational scholarship: Foundations of a new discipline.* San Francisco: Berrett-Koehler.

Clark, A., & Oswald, A. J. (1994). Unhappiness and unemployment. *Economic Journal, 104*, 648–659.

Compton, W. C. (2005). *An introduction to positive psychology.* Belmont, CA: Wadsworth.

Croson, R., & Mnookin, R. H. (1997). Does disputing through agents enhance cooperation? Experimental evidence. *Journal of Legal Studies, 26*, 331–345.

Cutler, B. L., & Hughes, D. M. (2001). Judging jury service: Results of the North Carolina administrative office of the courts juror survey. *Behavioral Science and Law, 19*, 305–320.

Dann, B. M. (1996). From the bench: Free the jury. *Litigation, 23*, 5–6.

Davis, J. A., Smith, T. W., & Marsden, P. V. (2001). *General social survey, 1972–2000: Cumulative codebook.* Storrs, CT: The Roper Center for Public Opinion Research.

Delle Fave, A., & Massimini, F. (2005). The relevance of subjective well-being to social policies: Optimal experience and tailored intervention. In F. A. Huppert, N. Baylis, & B. Keverne (Eds.), *The science of well-being* (pp. 378–402). New York: Oxford University Press.

Diamond, S. S., Rose, M. R., & Murphy, B. (2006). Revisiting the unanimity requirement: The behavior of the non-unanimous civil jury. *Northwestern University Law Review, 100*, 201–230.

Diener, E. (2000). Subjective well-being: The science of happiness and a proposal for a national index. *American Psychologist, 55*, 34–43.

Diener, E. (2006). Guidelines for national indicators of subjective well-being and ill-being. *Journal of Happiness Studies, 7*, 397–404.

Diener, E., Kesebir, P., & Lucas, R. (2008). Benefits of accounts of well-being-for societies and for psychological science. *Applied Psychology: An International Review, 57*, 37–53.

Diener, E., & Seligman, M. E. P. (2004). Beyond money: Toward an economy of well-being. *Psychological Science in the Public Interest, 5*, 1–31.

Dinovitzer, R., Garth, B., Sander, R., Sterling, J., & Wilder, G. (2004). *After the JD: First results of a national study of legal careers.*

Di Tella, R., & MacCulloch, R. (2006). Some uses of happiness data in economics. *Journal of Economic Perspectives, 20*, 25–46.

Di Tella, R., MacCulloch, R., & Oswald, A. J. (2003). The macroeconomics of happiness. *Review of Economics and Statistics, 85*, 809–827.

Eggers, A., Gaddy, C., & Graham, C. (2006). Well-being and unemployment in Russia in the 1990s: Can society's suffering be individuals' solace? *Journal of Socio-Economics, 35*, 209–242.

Elster, J., & Loewenstein, G. (1992). Utility from memory and anticipation. In G. Loewenstein & J. Elster (Eds.), *Choice over time* (pp. 213–234). New York: Sage.

Foels, R., Driskell, J. E., Mullen, B., & Salas, E. (2000). The effects of democratic leadership on group member satisfaction: An integration. *Small Group Research, 31*, 676–701.

Ford, J. (2006, September 13). China to measure happiness (Radio broadcast). *Marketplace.* American Public Media, available at http://marketplace.publicradio.org/shows/2006/09/13/AM200609137.html

Frey, B. S., Benz, M., & Stutzer, A. (2004). Introducing procedural utility: Not only what, but also how matters. *Journal of Institutional and Theoretical Economics, 160,* 377–401.

Frey, B. S., Luechinger, S., & Stutzer, A. (2007). Calculating tragedy: Assessing the costs of terrorism. *Journal of Economic Surveys, 21*(1), 1–24.

Frey, B. S., & Stutzer, A. (2000). Happiness prospers in democracy. *Journal of Happiness Studies, 1,* 81–105.

Frey, B. S., & Stutzer, A. (2002). *Happiness and economics: How the economy and institutions affect human well-being.* Princeton, NJ: Princeton University Press.

Frey, B. S., & Stutzer, A. (2008). Stress that doesn't pay: The commuting paradox. *Scandinavian Journal of Economics, 110* 339–366.

Frey, B. S., & Stutzer, A. (2005). Testing theories of happiness. In L. Bruni & P. L. Porta (Eds.), *Economics and happiness* (pp. 116–146). New York: Oxford University Press.

Frey, B. S., & Stutzer, A. (2006a). *Should we maximize national happiness?* (Discussion Paper No. 306). Institute for Empirical Research in Economics, University of Zurich.

Frey, B. S., & Stutzer, A. (2006b). Mispredicting utility and the political process. In E. J. McCaffery & J. Slemrod (Eds.), *Behavioral public finance* (pp. 113–140). New York: Sage.

Galanter, M. (2005). *Lowering the bar: Lawyer jokes & legal culture.* Madison, WI: University of Wisconsin Press.

Gallup Organization (2006). Gallup World Poll. http://www.gallupworldpoll.com/

Giacalone, R. A., Jurkiewicz, C. L., & Dunn, C. (Eds.). (2005). *Positive psychology in business ethics and corporate responsibility.* Charlotte, NC: Information Age.

Gilbert, D. (2006). *Stumbling upon happiness.* New York: Knopf.

Gilson, R. J., & Mnookin, R. H. (1994). Disputing through agents: Cooperation and conflict between lawyers in litigation. *Columbia Law Review, 94,* 509–566.

Glaeser, E. L. (2006). Paternalism and psychology. *University of Chicago Law Review, 73,* 133–156.

Graham, C. (2005). Insights on development from the economics of happiness. *World Bank Research Observer, 20,* 201–231.

Graham, C., & Felton, A. (2005, September). *Variance in obesity across cohorts and countries: A norms based explanation using happiness surveys.* (The Center on Social and Economic Dynamics Working Paper No. 42). Washington, DC: The Brookings Institution.

Graham, C., & Felton, A. (2006). Inequality and happiness: Insights from Latin America. *Journal of Economic Inequality, 4,* 107–122.

Graham, C., & Pettinato, S. (2002). *Happiness & hardship: Opportunity and insecurity in new market economies.* Washington, DC: Brookings Institution Press.

Graham, C., & Sukhtankar, S. (2004). Does economic crisis reduce support for markets and democracy in Latin America? Some evidence from surveys of public opinion and well-being. *Journal of Latin American Studies, 36,* 349–377.

Griffith, T. D. (2004). Progressive taxation and happiness. *Boston College Law Review, 45,* 1363–1398.

Gruber, J., & Mullainathan, S. (2004). Do cigarette taxes make smokers happier? *Advances in Economic Analysis and Policy, 5*(1), article 4.

Guthrie, C. (2003). Risk realization, emotion, and policy making. *Missouri Law Review, 69,* 1039–1045.

Haidt, J. (2006). *The happiness hypothesis: Finding modern truths in ancient wisdom.* New York: Basic Books.

Harris Poll (2006). Values. http://www.pollingreport.com/values.htm

Heinz, J. P., Nelson, R. L., Sandefur, R. L., & Laumann, E. O. (2005). *The new social structure of the bar.* Chicago: University of Chicago Press.

Hektner, J. M., Schmidt, J. A., & Csikszentmihalyi, M. (2007). *Experience sampling method: Measuring the quality of everyday life.* Thousand Oaks, CA: Sage.

Huang, P. H. (2005a). Moody investing and the Supreme Court: Rethinking materiality of information and reasonableness of investors. *Supreme Court Economic Review, 13,* 99–131.

Huang, P. H. (2005b). Regulating irrational exuberance and anxiety in securities markets. In F. Paresi & V. L. Smith (Eds.), *The law and economics of irrational behavior* (pp. 501–541).

Huang, P. H. (2006, October). *Law and positive psychology: Happiness, affective neuroscience, and paternalism.* Paper presented at the Fifth International Positive Psychology Summit, Washington, DC.

Huang, P. H. (2008a). Diverse conceptions of emotions in risk regulation, *156 University of Pennsylvania Law Review PENNumbra 435,* http://www.pennumbra.com/responses/03-2008/Huang.pdf

Huang, P. H. (2008b). How do securities laws influence affect, happiness, & trust? *Journal of Business and Technology Law, 3,* 257–308.

Huang, P. H. (2008c). Authentic happiness, self-knowledge, and legal policy. *Minnesota Journal of Law, Science, & Technology, 9,* 755–783.

Huang, P. H., & Moss, S. A. (2006, October). *Implications of happiness research for employment law.* Paper presented at the First Annual Colloquium on Current Scholarship in Labor & Employment Law, Marquette, WI.

Huang, P. H., & Swedloff, R. (2008). Authentic happiness and meaning at law firms. *Syracuse Law Review, 58,* 335–350.

Hull, K. E. (1999). Cross-examining the myth of lawyers' misery. *Vanderbilt Law Review, 52,* 971–983.

Inglehart, R., European Values Study Group, & World Values Survey Association. (2005). *European and world values survey four-wave integrated data file, 1981–2004* [Data file]. Available from World Values Survey Web site, http://www.worldvaluessurvey.org/

Inglehart, R., & Klingemann, H. D. (2000). Genes, culture, democracy, and happiness. In E. Diener & E. M. Suh (Eds.), *Culture and subjective well-being* (pp. 165–183). Cambridge, MA: The MIT Press.

Jolls, C., Sunstein, C. R., & Thaler, R. H. (1998). A behavioral approach to law and economics. *Stanford Law Review, 50,* 1471–1550.

Kahneman, D., & Krueger, A. B. (2006). Developments in the measurement of subjective well-being. *Journal of Economic Perspectives, 20,* 3–24.

Kahneman, D., Krueger, A. B., Schkade, D., Schwarz, N., & Stone, A. (2004a). A survey method for characterizing daily life experience: The day reconstruction method. *Science, 306,* 1776–1780.

Kahneman, D., Krueger, A. B., Schkade, D., Schwarz, N., & Stone, A. (2004b). Toward national well-being accounts. *American Economic Review, 94,* 429–434.

Kahneman, D., & Sugden, R. (2005). Experienced utility as a standard of policy evaluation. *Environmental and Resource Economics, 32,* 161–181.

Kling, J. R., Liebman, J. B., & Katz, L. F. (2007). Experimental analysis of neighborhood effects. *Econometrica, 75,* 83–119.

Kornhauser, M. E. (2004). Educating ourselves towards a progressive (and happier) tax: A commentary on Griffith's progressive taxation and happiness. *Boston College Law Review, 45,* 1399–1411.

Krueger, A. B., Kahneman, D., Schkade, D., Schwarz N., & Stone, A. A. (2009). National time accounting: The currency of life. In *National time accounting and subjective well-being.* Chicago: University of Chicago Press.

Kurson, R. (2000, August). Who's killing the great lawyers of Harvard? *Esquire,* 82.

Langer, E. J., & Rodin, J. (1976). The effects of choice and enhanced personal responsibility for the aged: A field experiment in an institutional setting. *Journal of Personality and Social Psychology, 34,* 191–198.

Layard, R. (2005). *Happiness: Lessons from a new science.* New York: Penguin.

Leib, E. J. (2006). Supermajoritarianism and the American criminal jury. *Hastings Constitutional Law Quarterly, 33,* 141–196.

Lench, H. C., & Levine, L. J. (2006, August). *Emotion regulation across time: Relation of goals to anticipated and remembered emotions.* Paper presented at the International Society for Research on Emotions, Atlanta, GA.

Lind, E. A., & Tyler, T. (1998). *The social psychology of procedural justice.* Berlin: Springer.

Loewenstein, G., & Haisley, E. (2008). The economist as therapist: Methodological ramifications of "light" paternalism. In A. Caplin & A. Schotter (Eds.), *The foundations of positive and normative economics: A handbook* (pp. 210–248). New York: Oxford University Press.

Loewenstein, G., & Ubel, P. A. (2006, September). *Hedonic adaptation and the role of decision and experience utility in public policy.* Paper presented at the Conference on Happiness and Public Economics, London.

Luskin, R. C., & Fishkin, J. (2002, March). *Deliberation and "better citizens"* Paper presented at the annual Joint Sessions of Workshops of the European Consortium for Political Research, Turin, Italy. http://cdd.stanford.edu/research/papers/2002/bettercitizens.pdf

Lyubomirsky, S. (2007). *The how of happiness: A scientific approach to getting the life you want.* New York: Penguin.

Lyubomirsky, S., King, L., & Diener, E. (2005). The benefits of frequent positive affect: Does happiness lead to success? *Psychological Bulletin, 131,* 803–855.

Martin, P. (2005). *Making happy people: The nature of happiness and its origins in childhood.* London: Harper Perennial.

Nettle, D. (2005). *Happiness: The science behind your smile.* New York: Oxford University Press.

Noddings, N. (2003). *Happiness and education.* New York: Cambridge University Press.

Oswald, A. J. (1997). Happiness and economic performance. *Economic Journal, 107,* 1815–1831.

Pate, R. R., Davis, M. G., Robinson, T. N., Stone, E. J., McKenzie, T. L., & Young, J. C. (2006). Promoting physical activity in children and youth: A leadership role for schools: A scientific statement from the American Heart Association Council on nutrition, physical activity, and metabolism (physical activity committee) in collaboration with the councils on cardiovascular disease in the young and cardiovascular nursing. *Circulation, 114,* 1214–1224.

Peterson, R. S. (1999). Can you have too much of a good thing? The limits of voice for improving satisfaction with leaders. *Personality and Social Psychological Bulletin, 25,* 313–324.

Peterson, C. (2006). *A primer in positive psychology.* New York: Oxford University Press.

Peterson, C., & Seligman, M. E. P. (2004). *Character strengths and virtues: A handbook and classification.* New York: Oxford University Press.

Post, R. C. (1987). On the popular image of the lawyer: Reflections in a dark glass. *California Law Review, 75,* 379–389.

Prescott, J. J., & Starr, S. (2006). Improving criminal jury decision making after the Blakely revolution. *University of Illinois Law Review,* 301–356.

Pressman, S. D., & Cohen, S. (2005). Does positive affect influence health? *Psychological Bulletin, 131,* 925–971.

Ring, D. M. (2004). Why happiness? A commentary on Griffith's progressive taxation and happiness. *Boston College Law Review, 45,* 1413–1424.

Rodin, J. (1976). Density, perceived choice, and response to controllable and uncontrollable outcomes. *Journal of Experimental Social Psychology, 12,* 564–578.

Rojas, M. (2008). Experienced poverty and income poverty in Mexico: A Subjective well-being approach. *World Development, 36,* 1078–1093.

Sanna, L. J., & Chang, E. C. (Eds.). (2006). *Judgments over time: The interplay of thoughts, feelings, and behaviors.* New York: Oxford University Press.

Schlitz, P. J. (1999). On being a happy, healthy, and ethical member of an unhappy, unhealthy, and unethical profession. *Vanderbilt Law Review, 52,* 871–951.

Seamone, E. R. (2001–2002). A refreshing jury COLA: Fulfilling the duty to compensate jurors adequately. *New York University Journal of Legislation and Public Policy, 5,* 289–418.

Seligman, M. E. P. (1992). Power and powerlessness: Comments on "Cognates of personal control." *Applied & Preventive Psychology: Current Scientific Perspectives, 1,* 119–120.

Seligman, M. E. P. (1998). *Learned optimism.* New York: Free Press.

Seligman, M. E. P. (2002). *Authentic happiness: Using the new positive psychology to realize your potential for lasting fulfillment.* New York: Free Press.

Seligman, M. E. P., & Csikszentmihalyi, M. (2000). Positive psychology: An introduction. *American Psychologist, 55,* 5–14.

Seligman, M. E. P., & Pawelski, J. O. (2003). Positive psychology: FAQs. *Psychological Inquiry, 14,* 159–163.

Seligman, M. E. P., Reivich, K., Jaycox, L., & Gillham, J. (1995). *The optimistic child.* New York: Houghton Mifflin.

Seligman, M. E. P., Verkuil, P., & Kang, T. (2001). Why lawyers are unhappy. *Cardozo Law Review, 23,* 33–53.

Sherr, L. (2005, November). Gross national happiness? *ABC News 20/20 Original Report,* http://abcnews.go.com/2020/International/story?id=1296605

Snyder, C. R., & Lopez, S. J. (2007). *Positive psychology: The science and practical explorations of human strengths.* New York: Sage.

Stone, A., & Shiffman, S. (1994). Ecological Momentary Assessment (EMA) in behavioral medicine. *Annals of Behavioral Medicine, 16,* 199–202.

Stutzer, A., & Lalive, R. (2004). The role of social work norms in job searching and subjective well-being. *Journal of the European Economic Association, 2,* 696–719.

Sutton, R. I. (1992). Feelings about a Disneyland visit: Photography and the reconstruction of bygone emotions. *Journal of Management Inquiry, 1*, 278–287.

Thaler, R. H., & Sunstein, C. R. (2008). *Nudge: Improving decisions about health, wealth, and happiness.* New Haven, CT: Yale University Press.

Thibaut, J., & Walker, L. (1975). *Procedural justice: A psychological perspective.* Hillsdale, NJ: Lawrence Erlbaum.

Tyler, T. R., & Lind, E. A. (1992). A relational model of authority in groups. In M. P. Zanna (Ed.), *Advances in experimental social psychology* (Vol. 25, pp. 115–191). New York: Academic Press.

van Boven, L., & Ashworth, L. (2006, August). *Looking forward, looking back: Anticipation is more evocative than retrospection.* Paper presented at the International Society for Research on Emotions, Atlanta, GA.

Wilson, T. D., & Gilbert, D. T. (2003). Affective forecasting. In M. P. Zanna (Ed.), *Advances in experimental social psychology* (Vol. 35, pp. 345–411). New York: Academic Press.

PART 10

Specific Coping Approaches

Meditation and Positive Psychology

Shauna L. Shapiro

Abstract

Mental health, once defined in terms of absence of illness, has gradually become understood in a more holistic way, which also includes the positive qualities that help people flourish. This evolving definition of mental health has led to an exploration of other traditions and practices, including meditation, which for thousands of years have been devoted to developing an expanded vision of human potential. One result was the introduction of the practice of meditation into Western scientific study. However, the principal original intentions of meditation, to uncover the positive and to catalyze our internal potential for healing and development, have been largely ignored by the scientific community. Yet, a small number of researchers and theorists have explored and continue to explore the positive effects of meditation. The chapter focuses on this pioneering work.

Keywords: Buddhism, flourishing, intention, meditation, positive psychology

Mental health, once defined in terms of absence of illness (Ryff & Singer, 1998), has gradually become understood in a more holistic way, which also includes the positive qualities that help people flourish (e.g., Allport, 1961; Maslow, 1968; Seligman & Csikszentmihalyi, 2000). This evolving definition of mental health led to an exploration of other traditions, such as the Eastern, which for thousands of years have been devoted to developing an expanded vision of human potential (Shapiro, 1980).

One result was the introduction of the Eastern practice of meditation into Western scientific study. In the 1970s research on meditation began in earnest and has since increased exponentially (Murphy, Donnovan, & Taylor, 1997; Walsh & Shapiro, 2006). The transplantation of meditation occurred, however, within a traditional behavioral framework—emphasizing symptom reduction and alleviation—with little attention to development, enhancement, growth, and cultivation of positive psychological qualities and experiences (Shapiro & Walsh, 2003). As a result, one of the principal

original goals of meditation, to uncover the positive and to catalyze our internal potential for healing and development, has been largely ignored (Alexander, Druker, & Langer, 1990; Shapiro & Walsh, 1984; Walsh & Shapiro, 2006). Yet, a small number of researchers and theorists have explored and continue to explore the positive effects of meditation. This chapter focuses on such pioneering work.

Toward a Definition of Meditation

Meditation originally was conceived within the religious/philosophical context of Eastern spiritual disciplines but is an essential element in nearly all contemplative religious and spiritual traditions, including Judaism, Christianity, and Islam (Goleman, 1988). Various methods whose background and techniques are quite different from one another (e.g., transcendental meditation [TM], Zen meditation, and vipassana meditation) are placed collectively under the umbrella term of "meditation." To enhance clarity and avoid misunderstanding, in this chapter we will use the following definition: "Meditation refers to a family of techniques which have in common a conscious attempt to focus attention in a non-analytical way, and an attempt not to dwell on discursive, ruminating thought" (Shapiro, 1980, p. 14). The definition has three important components. First, the word "conscious" is used explicitly to introduce the importance of the "intention" to focus attention. Second, the definition is independent of religious framework or orientation (although not implying that meditation does not or cannot occur within a religious framework). Finally, the word "attempt" is used throughout, which places an emphasis on the "process," as opposed to the specific end goals or results (Shapiro, 1980).

The "family" of techniques traditionally has been divided into concentrative meditation and mindfulness meditation (Goleman, 1972). In all types of concentrative meditation, there is an attempt to restrict awareness by focusing attention on a single object. The practitioner attempts to ignore other stimuli in the environment and focus complete attention on the object of meditation. Attention is focused in a nonanalytical, unemotional way, in order to directly experience the object of meditation, which can be located in either the external or internal environment. Examples of the object include the breath, a mantra, a single word (e.g., "one"; see Benson & Proctor, 1984), or specific sounds (see Carrington, 1998).

In mindfulness meditation, an attempt is made to attend nonjudgmentally to all stimuli in the internal and external environment, but not to get caught up in (ruminate on) any particular stimulus. Mindfulness meditation is referred to as an opening up meditation practice. Some meditation techniques involve integrated elements of both concentrative and opening types. For example, a person may focus on breathing (Zen and vipassana meditation) or a mantra (e.g., TM), but be willing to allow attention to focus on other stimuli if they become predominant and then return to the breathing (or mantra).

Finally, in developing an understanding of meditation, it is crucial to note that meditation training differs both operationally and in its deep intentions from relaxation training (Kabat-Zinn, 2005). First, an emphasis of meditation is the development of greater understanding through the systematic cultivation of inquiry and insight, whereas the objective of relaxation training is to achieve a state of low autonomic arousal, with little or no emphasis on the cultivation of inquiry or insight. Relaxation is often a by-product of meditation, but it is not an objective of the process. Furthermore, relaxation is taught as a technique, to be used during stressful or anxiety provoking situations. Meditation, in contrast, is not a technique whose use is contingent upon stressful situations; rather, it is conceived as a "way of being" that is to be cultivated daily regardless of circumstances (Kabat-Zinn, 2005). The formal mediation practice seeps into daily life, bringing greater nonjudgmental consciousness to everything that one does, feels, and experiences.

Original Intentions of Meditation

Abraham Maslow (1968) stated, "what we call 'normal' in psychology is really a psychopathology of the average, so undramatic and so widely spread that we don't even notice it ordinarily" (Maslow, 1968, p. 16). Meditation disciplines have been suggesting this for over 2,500 years, teaching that our "normal" minds are untrained and often unconscious, which inhibits us from reaching our fullest potential. The intention behind meditation is to "wake up" from a suboptimal state of consciousness, wake up to our true nature.

Walsh (1983), a pioneer in the field of meditation research, identified the ultimate aims of meditation practice as "the development of deep insight into the nature of mental processes, consciousness, identity, and reality, and the development of optimal states of psychological well-being and consciousness" (p. 19). From a psychological growth perspective, it is essential to learn ways to free ourselves from the artificial and unnecessary limits we impose on our own minds, as well as to learn to expand our worldviews and consciousnesses. Meditation provides road maps to help recognize and let go of old structures and evolve toward new ways of seeing and being as we experience deep insights into the nature of mind and the path toward optimal health and freedom from suffering.

The intention behind meditation practice is to help develop and train the mind toward optimal states of empathy, joy, compassion, awareness, and insight, with the ultimate intention of total liberation. And yet, research exploring the effects of meditation to attain these goals has been scarce. With few exceptions, research has not measured the deeper levels of meditation's original intent, but instead has focused on traditional psychological variables (e.g., reducing anxiety, depression). Eleanor Rosch (1999) succinctly put it, "Yes, research on the meditation traditions can provide data to crunch with the old mind set. But they have much more to offer, a new way of looking" (p. 224).

Meditation Research

Over the past three decades, there has been considerable research examining the psychological and physiological effects of meditation (Murphy et al., 1997; Walsh & Shapiro, 2006). Moreover, meditative practices are being utilized in a variety of health-care settings (Baer, 2003). Research demonstrates that meditation is an effective intervention for cardiovascular disease (Schneider et al., 2005; Zamarra, Schneider, Besseghini, Robinson, & Salerno, 1996); chronic pain (Kabat-Zinn, 1982); anxiety and panic disorder (Edwards, 1991; Miller, Fletcher, & Kabat-Zinn, 1995); substance abuse (Gelderloos, Walton, Orme-Johnson, & Alexander, 1991); dermatological disorders (Kabat-Zinn et al., 1998); prevention of relapse of major depressive disorder (MDD); and reduction of anxiety and depressive symptoms in nonclinical populations (Shapiro, Schwartz, & Bonner, 1998).

As noted, few researchers have examined meditation's original purpose as a self-liberation strategy to enhance positive psychological qualities. Despite this, a small number of pioneering studies have addressed the effects of meditation on positive psychological health. The work described subsequently provides a valuable foundation upon which to build future research. Subsequently, we review specific studies, starting with the micro level (physiological) and moving to the macro level (transpersonal; for a review see Murphy et al., 1997).

Positive Physiological Findings

As Ryff and Singer (1998) aptly point out, "human wellness is at once about the mind and the body and their interconnections" (p. 2). Although the implications of the physiological correlates of meditation are as yet unclear, it seems likely that some of the changes represent "physiological substrates of flourishing" (Ryff & Singer, 1998, p. 2).

Improvements in immune system functioning or reversal of immune suppression may be an important marker of such physiological substrates of health and well-being. For example, a recent study (Davidson et al., 2003) found a greater increase in influenza antibodies among participants in an 8-week Mindfulness-Based Stress Reduction (MBSR) program than in waiting-list controls. Similarly, in cancer patients, MBSR had a number of effects on immune parameters that are consistent with a shift to a more normal profile (Carlson, Speca, Patel & Goodey 2004).

Another widely reported positive physiological effect of meditation is relaxation, as suggested by markers of physiological rest (e.g., reduced respiration rate and plasma lactate levels, and increased skin resistance). Statistical meta-analysis showed that changes in physiological states of relaxation are reliable across meditation studies (Dillbeck & Orme-Johnson, 1987). Also, consistent with increased calm are declines in blood cortisol and lactates (Jevning, Wilson, & Davidson, 1978), along with more stable phasic skin resistance (Alexander, Rainforth, & Gelderloos, 1991).

Although associated with physiological rest, there are several indicators that meditation simultaneously facilitates heightened alertness (Wallace, 1986). These changes are marked by increased cerebral blood flow; enhanced alpha and theta electroencephalogram (EEG) power and coherence in the frontal and central regions of the brain; marked increase in plasma arginine vasopressin; faster H-reflex recovery; and shorter latencies of auditory evoked potential (see O'Halloran, Jevning, Wilson, Skowsky, & Alexander, 1985; Orme-Johnson & Haynes, 1981; Wallace, 1986).

Research explicitly comparing meditation and relaxation confirms that they are physiologically distinct. For example, Dunn, Hartigan, and Mikulas (1999) compared concentration meditation versus mindfulness meditation versus a relaxation control condition. When collapsing mindfulness and concentration meditations into one group, results indicated that the EEGs of meditators were different from the EEGs of relaxed participants. These results suggest that meditations produce different cortical patterns relative to relaxation. Differences were also found between concentration and mindfulness states.

Another indication of physiological flourishing comes from recent research suggesting that meditation practice may enhance the left-to-right ratio of activation of the prefrontal cortex, which has been linked to positive emotions and mental health (Davidson et al., 2003). Participants in an 8-week MBSR program demonstrated increases in left frontal EEG activation as compared to a control group (Davidson et al., 2003). These findings lend physiological evidence of meditation's ability to actually change the structure of the brain and support preliminary research demonstrating that advanced meditators display unique degrees of lateralization of prefrontal cortical activity (a neural indicator of positive affect) and a unique high gamma EEG profile when cultivating compassion (Davidson et al., 2003; Lutz et al., 2004).

Further data providing structural evidence that meditation experience affects plasticity come from a recent study examining the effects of mindfulness meditation practice on changes in the brain's physical structure (Lazar et al., 2005). Magnetic resonance imaging was used to assess cortical thickness in 20 participants with extensive mindfulness practice. Brain regions associated with attention, interoception, and sensory processing were thicker in meditation participants than matched controls, including the prefrontal cortex and right anterior insula. These data provide preliminary evidence that meditation contributes to the development of the physiological structures that support intelligence.

Stress reactivity and recovery. Goleman and Schwartz (1976) compared 30 experienced meditators' and 30 control subjects' responses to laboratory stressors. Participants either meditated or relaxed with eyes closed or with eyes open, then watched a stressor film. Stress response was assessed by phasic skin conductance, heart rate, self-report, and personality scales. Meditators demonstrated heightened initial reactivity, but their heart rate and phasic skin conductance responses habituated more quickly to the stressor impacts and they experienced less subjective anxiety in comparison to the nonmeditators.

MacLean et al. (1997) extended the research in stress reactivity and recovery. They conducted a prospective random assignment study to examine the effects of TM on responses to laboratory stressors by four hormones: cortisol, growth hormone, thyroid-stimulating hormone (TSH), and testosterone. Healthy men were tested before and after 4 months of learning TM. The results indicated that basal cortisol level and average cortisol across the stress session decreased from pretest to posttest in the TM group but not in the control group. Cortisol responsiveness to stressors, however, increased in the TM group compared to controls. The baselines (stress responsiveness) for TSH and growth hormone as well as testosterone changed in opposite directions for the two groups. The results support previous data suggesting that "repeated practice of TM reverses effects of chronic stress" (p. 277).

Positive Psychological Findings

Memory and intelligence. Meditation appears to result in improvements in intelligence, school grades, learning ability, and short- and long-term recall (see Cranson et al., 1991; Dillbeck, Assimakis, & Raimondi, 1986; Lewis, 1978). For example, one study examined the effects of TM on performance on the Culture Fair Intelligence Test

(CFIT) and reaction time (RT) as compared to a control group (Cranson et al., 1991). Even when controlling for age, education level, level of interest in meditation, parents' education level, and annual income, the TM group improved significantly on both measures as compared to the control group. The results suggest that TM is a "promising educational tool for enhancing a learner's ability to learn" (Cranson et al., 1991, p. 1105).

Hall (1999) randomly assigned 56 undergraduates to two study groups: one group included meditation, the other did not. The meditation group was instructed in a simple meditation process that consisted of natural breathing techniques, attention focusing techniques, and relaxation exercises. The meditation process was practiced for a duration of 10 min at the start, and conclusion of a 1-hr study session. The intervention included a 1-hr session of meditation instruction twice a week for the academic semester. The meditation group was instructed to meditate before and after studying and before exams. The nonmeditation study group met for 1 hr a week to study and was not introduced to meditation. Significantly higher grades were found in the experimental group as compared to the control group.

There is also evidence that these improvements in memory and academic performance associated with meditation apply across the life span. Chang and Heibert (1989), in a review of relaxation procedures with children, reported that teaching meditation to children in public schools increased academic performance. In another study of elderly adults who were taught meditation, there were significant improvements in cognitive flexibility as compared to a control group (Alexander, Langer, Newman, Chandler, & Davies, 1989).

Creativity. Creativity is a complex construct consisting of various traits and capacities, including perceptual skill, ideational fluency, openness to experience, and emotional flexibility, all of which are theoretically fostered by meditation practice. Preliminary research confirms that meditation can cultivate creativity.

Cowger and Torrance (1982) studied 24 college undergraduates who were taught Zen meditation and 10 who were taught relaxation. The meditators attained statistically significant gains in creativity as defined by heightened consciousness of problems, perceived change, invention, sensory experience, expression of emotion/feeling, humor, and fantasy.

A series of studies by So and Orme-Johnson (2001) examined the effects of TM on cognition. One hundred fifty-four Chinese high school students were randomized into a TM group or a napping group (i.e., students were invited to lie down and rest or sleep). The TM technique and napping were practiced for approximately 20 min twice a day. At 6-month follow-up, the TM group demonstrated significantly increased practical intelligence, field independence, creativity, and speed of information processing, as well as significantly decreased anxiety compared to the control group. The results suggest that TM's effects extend beyond those of ordinary rest.

The findings of the above study were replicated in a sample of 118 junior high Chinese students who were randomly assigned to a TM group, a contemplative meditation group (involving reflection of specific insights and topics), or a no-treatment control group. All students practiced their respective meditation techniques for 20 min twice a day. At 6-month follow-up, the TM group showed improvement on creativity compared to the two other groups. Both TM and contemplation group improved on information processing time as compared to the control group.

Attention/concentration. To examine the effects of meditation on attention, Valentine and Sweet (1999) conducted an elegant study, which incorporated type of meditation (concentration vs. mindfulness), length of practice (long-term meditators > 24 months, short-term meditators < 24 months), and expectancy effects (expected vs. unexpected stimuli). Participants consisted of 24 controls, 5 short-term concentrative meditators, 4 short-term mindfulness meditators, 6 long-term concentrative meditators, and 4 long-term mindfulness meditators. A measure of sustained attention was employed with all participants. The meditation group was tested following their usual meditation practice. Results demonstrated that meditators' attention and accuracy were greater than the controls. Further, long-term meditators demonstrated greater attention processes than short-term meditators.

There were no differences in performance between concentrative and mindfulness meditators when the stimulus was expected. However, when the stimulus was unexpected, mindfulness meditators were superior to concentrative meditators. These differences may be due to the fact that, in concentration meditation, attention is focused on an expected stimulus. Therefore attention is impaired when the stimulus is unexpected. Conversely, in mindfulness meditation, attention is evenly distributed and therefore no stimulus or set of stimuli becomes more salient than others.

Interpersonal relationships. Practices for cultivation of love, compassion, empathetic joy, and equanimity have a long tradition in the meditative disciplines (Walsh, 1999). Most notable are the Brahma Vihara practices, which involve four distinct meditation practices focusing respectively on the cultivation of lovingkindness, compassion, empathetic joy, and equanimity (Salzberg, 2002). A recent study (Carson, Carson, Gil, & Baucom, 2004) incorporated the meditative practice of lovingkindness (*metta*), one of the Brahma Viharas, into a mindfulness-based intervention for couples. Forty-four couples that were in well-adjusted relationships and had been married an average of 11 years were randomly assigned to a waiting-list control or the meditation intervention. The program consisted of eight 2.5-hr sessions and a 6-hr retreat. In addition to components modeled on the MBSR program (Kabat-Zinn, 1990), a number of elements related to enhancing the relationship were added, including lovingkindness meditation, partner yoga exercises, focused application of mindfulness to relationship issues, and group discussions. Results demonstrated that the couples in the meditation intervention significantly improved relationship satisfaction as well as relatedness to and acceptance of the partner. In addition, individuals reported significant increases in optimism, engagement in exciting self-expanding activities, spirituality, and relaxation. Interestingly, increases in engagement in exciting self-expanding activities significantly mediated improvements in relationship quality (Carson, Carson, Gil, & Baucom, 2006).

The above study supports earlier research, which examined the effects of Zen breath meditation as compared to relaxation on college adjustment (Tloczynski & Tantriella, 1998). Seventy-five undergraduates, matched on initial anxiety, were randomized into meditation, relaxation, and control groups. The students received only 1 hr of instruction in either technique and were instructed to practice it once daily for at least 20 min. Anxiety and depression scores significantly decreased in both meditation and relaxation groups as compared to the control group; however, only the meditation group had a significant positive effect on interpersonal relationships.

Relapse prevention. In a multicenter randomized clinical trial, the effects of mindfulness-based cognitive therapy (MBCT) were evaluated for recovered recurrently depressed patients. The aim of this study was to determine if the meditation-based intervention could help prevent relapse of major depression.

One hundred forty-five patients who were currently in recovery/remission for major depressive disorder were randomized to continue with treatment as usual (TAU) which consisted of bimonthly assessment interviews, or in addition, to receive MBCT. The group intervention consisted of eight weekly 2-hr sessions and four monthly booster sessions.

Relapse/recurrence of major depression was assessed over a 60-week period. Findings indicated that for patients with recurrent major depression who had three or more episodes, MBCT approximately halved rates of relapse and recurrence during the follow-up period compared with patients who continued TAU. The absence of a comparison group limits the value of this study, since cognitive therapy by itself has been shown to reduce depression relapse rates. However, the study offers a promising avenue for future relapse prevention meditation research. These findings were recently replicated (Ma & Teasdale, 2004). Further study utilizing a comparison control group will yield greater answers.

Another innovative use of meditation for prevention is mindfulness-based relapse prevention (MBRP), a synthesis of relapse prevention and mindfulness meditation for addictive behaviors. The aim of MBRP is to help prevent relapse of substance abuse through developing awareness and acceptance of thoughts, feelings, and sensations and to utilize mindfulness in the face of high-risk situations.

Happiness and positive affect. Smith, Compton, and West (1995) investigated the impact of adding meditation to Fordyce's (1983) Personal Happiness Enhancement Program (PHEP). Thirty-six subjects were randomly assigned to an experimental group or a no-treatment control group. Experimental subjects were divided into two groups, both of which received instruction on the PHEP, but one experimental group was also taught meditation exercises that resembled Benson's Relaxation Response (Benson, 1975). Groups met for 12 sessions, 1.5 hr each, over a 6-week period. The meditation-plus-PHEP group significantly improved on measures of happiness, state-trait anxiety, and depression as compared to the PHEP-only group and the control group. Frequent meditators also report significantly higher level of positive affect, significantly fewer stressors and illness symptoms, and lower levels of anxiety, hostility, depression, and dysphoria (Beauchamp-Turner & Levinson, 1992).

Optimism. A recent study evaluated the effectiveness of a 10-day silent vipassana (mindfulness) meditation course on substance use and positive psychosocial outcomes in an incarcerated population (Bowen et al., 2006). Participants completed assessments 1 week before the start of the course, 1 week after the course, and 3 months following release from jail. Results indicated that participants in the meditation course, as compared to those in a TAU control condition, showed significant increases in optimism as measured by The Life Orientation Test (LOT; Scheier & Carver, 1985) 3 months after release. In addition, compared to the control condition, meditation participants demonstrated reductions in alcohol, marijuana, and crack cocaine use, as well as decreases in alcohol-related problems and psychiatric symptoms 3 months after release from jail.

Self-compassion. Self-compassion is defined as being kind and understanding toward oneself in instances of pain or failure rather than being harshly self-critical; perceiving one's experiences as part of the larger human experience rather than seeing them as isolating; and holding painful thoughts and feelings in balanced awareness rather than overidentifying with them (Neff, Kirkpatrick, & Rude, 2007). Two recent studies have found that mindfulness meditation–based intervention significantly increases self-compassion (Shapiro, Astin, Cordova, & Bishop, 2005; Shapiro, Brown, & Beigel, 2007). In the first study, health-care professionals were randomly assigned to an MBSR intervention or a waiting-list control group. Participants in the intervention group demonstrated significant increases in self-compassion as compared to the control group (Shapiro et al., 2005). The second study was a matched controlled design examining the effects of MBSR for counseling psychology students. Results support the findings of the health-care professional study, with participants in the MBSR intervention demonstrating higher levels of self-compassion compared to the control group (Shapiro et al., 2006).

Interestingly, a recent study found that self-compassion is significantly predictive of other positive psychological variables including wisdom, personal initiative, curiosity and exploration, happiness, optimism, and positive affect (Neff et al., 2007). Further, self-compassion remained a significant predictor of psychological health after controlling for shared variance with positive affect and personality. Therefore, self-compassion seems an important positive psychological variable that merits further research.

Empathy. All schools of meditation have emphasized concern for the condition of others and an intention to "promote an empathy with created things that leads toward oneness with them" (Murphy et al., 1997, p. 82). Recent research demonstrates that meditation practice does indeed lead to greater levels of empathy.

In a randomized controlled study, Shapiro et al. (1998) examined the effects of a mindfulness meditation–based program on 78 medical and premedical students. Results indicated increased levels of empathy and decreased levels of anxiety and depression in the meditation group as compared to the waiting-list control group. Furthermore, the results were found during the students' exam period, which is a stressful time, and thus reinforce the hypothesis that mindfulness training helps one cope with stress. The findings were replicated when participants in the waiting-list control group received the mindfulness intervention.

The findings of this study are supported by a recent study examining the effects of MBSR on counseling psychology students' empathy. Counseling students who participated in an 8-week MBSR course demonstrated significant pre–post increases in empathic concern for others as compared to a matched control group (Shapiro et al., 2006).

Self-actualization. Meditation has been described as a "technique to actualize and integrate the personality of human kind to those fulfilled states of personal integration" (Ferguson, 1981, p. 68). Important positive characteristics demonstrating self-actualization include "increased acceptance of self, of others and of nature . . . superior perception of reality" (Maslow, 1968, p. 26). These characteristics parallel some of the fundamental objectives of meditation. It is not surprising, therefore, that the most widely measured positive psychological outcome in the meditation literature is self-actualization (Alexander et al., 1991).

Alexander and colleagues (1991) performed a meta-analysis of studies examining the effects of TM and other meditation and relaxation interventions on self-actualization. The analysis included 42 independent treatment outcome studies (18 TM, 18 other meditation studies, 6 relaxation studies). The authors found significant improvements in self-actualization across all of the studies.

Moral maturity. Few questions in psychology are of greater social and global significance than how to foster moral maturity, but unfortunately traditional interventions, such as instruction in moral thinking, usually produce only modest gains. Meditative traditions emphasize the importance of moral development and regard moral maturity as both an essential foundation and product of practice. Meditation is said to enhance ethical motivation and behavior via several mechanisms. These include sensitizing awareness to the costs of unethical acts (such as guilt in oneself and pain produced in others), reducing problematic motives and emotions (such as greed and anger), strengthening morality supporting emotions (such as love and compassion), cultivating altruism, and identification with others via transpersonal experience (Walsh, 1999). Initial research support comes from reports of TM practitioners whose increased scores on scales of moral development correlate with duration of practice (Nidich, Ryncarz, Abrams, Orme-Johnson, & Wallace, 1983). Further research on this topic deserves high priority.

Spirituality. In the study by Carson and colleagues (2006) noted previously, the couples who received the mindfulness meditation relationship enhancement intervention reported significantly increases in spirituality compared to the control group. This supports earlier findings that MBSR intervention significantly increased spiritual experience in medical students as compared to waiting-list controls (Shapiro et al., 1998). These results were replicated when the control group received the same mindfulness intervention. Further, Astin (1997) demonstrated significant increases in spiritual experience in a randomized controlled study comparing a mindfulness meditation intervention to a control group of undergraduate students.

Summary and Critique

Meditation appears to enhance physiological, psychological, and transpersonal well-being. Specific enhancements observed include physiological rest, happiness, acceptance, sense of coherence, stress hardiness, empathy, and self-actualization. Thus, meditation may help human beings identify and actualize their potential strengths.

The results of past research are qualified by their limitations in methodology. We suggest the following criteria to insure rigorous design: (a) an adequate sample size of subjects should be randomized into experimental and control groups; (b) the type of meditation technique taught should be made explicit (e.g., mindfulness or concentrative); (c) frequency and duration of meditation practice should be recorded (e.g., meditation journals); (d) outcome variables should be included that are well established and consistent with the original intentions of meditation; (e) follow-up should include long-term as well as short-term assessment; and (f) researchers should include long-term meditators as well as beginning meditators. Also, when matching control subjects to long-term meditators in retrospective studies, in addition to age, gender, and education, it would be important to consider matching subjects on the dimension of an alternative attentional practice (e.g., playing a musical instrument). With such improvements, the inferences that we could make from results would be substantially strengthened.

Future Directions

There are multiple directions for future research. Rigorous and sensitive designs are needed that assess the multifaceted nature of health, including both the negative *and* the positive. We briefly outline five directions for future research in meditation and positive psychology.

First, in our research designs, we must examine dependent variables more closely parallel the original goals and objectives of meditation (e.g., self-actualization, cultivation of empathy, meaning, purpose). Second, we should explore the physiological states elicited during positive psychological experiences, including meditation practice, to further augment the emerging concept of the "physiological substrates of flourishing" (Ryff & Singer, 1998; for initial work in this area, see Davidson et al., 2003). Third, it is crucial to determine the most effective way to teach meditation in clinical, educational, and community settings by comparing differing lengths of meditation intervention, as well as different formats for the intervention (e.g., group vs. individual). Along these lines we must ask, "What works best for whom?" For example, are there specific types of meditation that fit better with specific individuals or specific goals? Different types "of meditation may have very different effects on the practitioner and thus may have different clinical applications" (Bogart, 1991, p. 385). It is crucial to consider what therapeutic goals (e.g., stress management, self-exploration, or transformative transpersonal experiences) are being sought when determining which type of meditation is most appropriate. Bogart (1991) suggests that concentration methods may allow the participant to feel inner balance, calm, and the ability to transcend the continuous flow of cognitions and emotions, whereas opening-up meditation may encourage insights into maladaptive cognitive, emotional, and behavioral patterns.

A fourth direction for future research involves operationalizing experience levels of participants. Researchers must assess both length of practice and have some index of depth of practice (e.g., teacher ratings). Fifth, we should ask, "What are the processes through which meditation brings about positive psychological changes?" The explanatory mechanisms of meditation are elusive and more attention needs to be given to them (for initial work in this area, see Baer, 2003; Shapiro, Carlson, Astin, & Freedman, 2006).

Conclusion

During the past four decades, research in meditation has developed a strong foundation, demonstrating significant psychological, physiological, and therapeutic effects. The field of positive psychology offers new opportunities and methodologies to examine the original intentions of meditation. In fact, meditation can be considered an applied positive psychology practice that has wide application for promoting positive health in medicine, business, and education.

The aim of positive psychology, according to Seligman and Csikszentmihalyi (2000), "is to begin to catalyze a change in the focus of psychology from preoccupation only with repairing the worst things in life to also building positive qualities" (p. 5). This aim of cultivating positive qualities, including wisdom, compassion, and generosity, is at the heart of the original intentions of meditation. Meditation offers paths to exceptional states of mental well-being and attentional control that have been systematically developed and practiced for 2,500 years. In this way, meditation may help positive psychology examine and reevaluate the current definition of "normal" and expand Western psychology's concept of mental health. Future research into the positive effects of meditation will help illuminate the richness and complexity of this age-old practice.

Acknowledgments

Acknowledgments to Gary Schwartz and Craig Santerre for their valuable contribution to the meditation chapter that appeared in the first edition of the *Handbook of Positive Psychology*, and to Willoughby Britton who contributed to portions of the physiological research review. Thanks also to Christin D. Izett for editorial assistance. Further thanks are due to the researchers in the field who are exploring an expanded vision of human health and healing.

Questions about the Topic

1. What are the physiological states elicited during positive psychological experiences, including meditation practice, and what are the physiological changes that result from meditation?

2. What is the most effective way to teach meditation in clinical, educational, and community settings?

3. What are the processes through which meditation brings about positive psychological changes?

References

Alexander, C. N., Druker, S. M., & Langer, E. J. (1990). Major issues in the exploration of adult growth. In C. N. Alexander & E. J. Langer (Eds.), *Higher stages of human development: Perspectives on adult growth* (pp. 3–32). New York: Oxford University Press.

Alexander, C. N., Langer, E. J., Newman, R. I., Chandler, H. M., & Davies, J. L. (1989). Transcendental meditation, mindfulness, and longevity: An experimental study with the elderly. *Journal of Personality and Social Psychology, 57*(6), 950–964.

Alexander, C. N., Rainforth, M. V., & Gelderloos, P. (1991). Transcendental meditation, self-actualization, and psychological health: A conceptual overview and statistical meta-analysis. *Journal of Social Behavior and Personality, 6*(5), 189–247.

Allport, G. W. (1961). *Pattern and growth in personality*. New York: Holt, Rinehart and Winston.

Astin, J. A. (1997). Stress reduction through mindfulness meditation: Effects on psychological symptomatology, sense of control, and spiritual experiences. *Psychotherapy and Psychosomatics, 66*, 97–106.

Baer, R. (2003). Mindfulness training as a clinical intervention: A conceptual and empirical review. *Clinical Psychology: Science and Practice, 10*, 125–143.

Beauchamp-Turner, D. L., & Levinson, D. M. (1992). Effects of meditation on stress, health, and affect. *Medical Psychotherapy: An International Journal, 5*, 123–131.

Benson, H. (1975). *The relaxation response*. New York: Morrow.

Benson, H., & Proctor, W. (1984). *Beyond the relaxation response*. New York: Putnam/Berkley.

Bogart, G. (1991). The use of meditation in psychotherapy: A review of the literature. *American Journal of Psychotherapy, XLV*(3), 383–412.

Bowen, S., Witkiewitz, K., Dillworth, T. M., Chawla, N., Simpson, T. L., Ostafin, B. D., et al. (2006). Mindfulness meditation and substance use in an incarcerated population. *Psychology of Addictive Behaviors, 20*(3), 343–347.

Carson, J. W., Carson, K. M., Gil, K. M., & Baucom, D. H. (2004). Mindfulness based relationship enhancement. *Behavior Therapy, 35*, 471–494.

Carson, J. W., Carson, K. M., Gill, K. M., & Baucom, D. H. (2006). Mindfulness-based relationship enhancement in couples. In R. A. Baer (Ed.), *Mindfulness-based treatment approaches: Clinician's guide to evidence base and applications* (pp. 309–331). Amsterdam: Elsevier.

Carlson, L. E., Speca, M., Patel, K. D., & Goodey, E. (2004). Mindfulness-based stress reduction in relation to quality of life, mood, symptoms of stress and levels of cortisol, dehydroepiandrostrone-sulfate (DHEAS) and melatonin in breast and prostate cancer outpatients. *Psychoneuroendocrinology, 29*, 448–474.

Carrington, P. (1998). *The book of meditation*. Boston: Element Books.

Chang, J., & Heibert, B. (1989). Relaxation procedures with children: A review. *Medical Psychotherapy, An International Journal, 2*, 163–176.

Cowger, E. L., & Torrance, E. P. (1982). Further examination of the quality changes in creative functioning resulting from meditation (zazen) training. *The Creative Child and Adult Quarterly, 7*(4), 211–217.

Cranson, R. W., Orme-Johnson, D. W., Gackenbach, J., Dillbeck, M. C., Jones, C. H., & Alexander, C. N. (1991). Transcendental meditation and improved performance on intelligence-related measures: A longitudinal study. *Personality and Individual Differences, 12*(10), 1105–1116.

Davidson, R. J., Kabat-Zinn, J., et al. (2003). Alterations in brain and immune function produced by mindfulness meditation. *Psychosomatic Medicine, 65*, 564–570.

Dillbeck, M. C., Assimakis, P. D., & Raimondi, D. (1986). Longitudinal effects of the transcendental meditation and TM-Sidhi program on cognitive ability and cognitive style. *Perceptual Motor Skills, 62*(3), 731–738.

Dillbeck, M. C., & Orme-Johnson, D. W. (1987). Physiological differences between transcendental meditation and rest. *American Psychologist, 42*(9), 879–881.

Dunn, B. R., Hartigan, J. A., & Mikulas, W. L. (1999). Concentration and mindfulness meditations: Unique forms of consciousness? *Applied psychophysiology and biofeedback, 24*, 147–165.

Edwards, D. L. (1991). A meta-analysis of the effects of meditation and hypnosis on measures of anxiety. *Dissertation Abstracts International, 52*(2-B), 1039–1040.

Ferguson, P. C. (1981). An integrative meta-analysis of psychological studies investigating the treatment outcomes of meditation studies (Doctoral dissertation, University of Colorado, 1981). *Dissertation Abstracts International, 42*(4-A), 1547.

Fordyce, M. W. (1983). A program to increase happiness: Further studies. *Journal of Counseling Psychology, 30*, 483–498.

Gelderloos, P., Walton, K., Orme-Johnson, D., & Alexander, C. (1991). Effectiveness of the transcendental meditation program in preventing and treating substance misuse: A review. *International Journal of the Addictions, 26*(3), 293–325.

Goleman, D. J. (1972). The Buddha on meditation and states of consciousness: Part I. The teaching. Part II. A typology of meditation techniques. *The Journal of Transpersonal Psychology, 4*(1–2), 1–44, 151–210.

Goleman, D. J. (1988). *The meditation mind*. Los Angeles: Tarcher.

Goleman, D. J., & Schwartz, G. E. (1976). Meditation as an intervention in stress reactivity. *Journal of Consulting and Clinical Psychology, 44*(3), 456–466.

Hall, P. D. (1999). The effect of meditation on the academic performance of African American college students. *Journal of Black Studies, 29*(3), 408–415.

Jevning, R., Wilson, A. F., & Davidson, J. M. (1978). Adrenocortical activity during meditation. *Hormones and Behavior, 10*(1), 54–60.

Kabat-Zinn, J. (1982). An outpatient program in behavioral medicine for chronic pain patients based on the practice of mindfulness meditation: Theoretical considerations and preliminary results. *General Hospital Psychiatry, 4*, 33–47.

Kabat-Zinn, J. (1990). *Full catastrophe living*. New York: Delacourte Press.

Kabat-Zinn, J. (2005). *Coming to our senses*. New York: Hyperion.

Kabat-Zinn, J., Wheeler, E., Light, T., Skillings, A., Scharf, M. J., Cropley, T. G., et al. (1998). Influence of a mindfulness meditation-based stress reduction intervention on rates of skin clearing in patients with moderate to severe psoriasis undergoing phototherapy (UVB) and photochemotherapy (PUVA). *Psychosomatic Medicine, 60,* 625–632.

Lazar, S. W., Kerr, C., Wasserman, R. H., Gray, J. R., Greve, D., Treadway, M. T., et al. (2005). Meditation experience is associated with increased cortical thickness. *NeuroReport, 16,* 1893–1897.

Lewis, J. (1978). The effects of a group meditation technique upon degree of test anxiety and level of digit-letter retention in high school students. *Dissertation Abstracts International, 38*(10-A), 6015–6016.

Lutz, A., Greischar, L. L., Rawlings, N. B., Ricard, M., & Davidson, R. J. (2004). Long-term meditators self-induce high-amplitude gamma synchrony during mental practice. *Proceedings of the National Academy of Sciences, 101,* 16369–16373.

Ma, S. H., & Teasdale, J. D. (2004). Mindfulness-based cognitive therapy for depression: Replication and exploration of differential relapse prevention effects. *Journal of Consulting and Clinical Psychology, 72*(1), 31–40.

MacLean, C., Walton, K. G., Wenneberg, S. R., Levitsky, D. K., Mandarino, J. P., Waziri, R., et al. (1997). Effects of the transcendental meditation program on adaptive mechanisms: Changes in hormone levels and responses to stress after 4 months of practice. *Psychoneuroendocrinology, 22*(4), 277–295.

Maslow, A. H. (1968). *Toward a psychology of being* (2nd ed.). New York: Van Nostrand Reinhold.

Miller, J., Fletcher, K., & Kabat-Zinn, J. (1995). Three-year follow-up and clinical implications of a mindfulness-based intervention in the treatment of anxiety disorders. *General Hospital Psychiatry, 17,* 192–200.

Murphy, M., Donovan, S., & Taylor, E. (1997). *The physical and psychological effects of meditation: A review of contemporary research with a comprehensive bibliography.* Sausalito, CA: Institute of Noetic Sciences.

Neff, K. D., Kirkpatrick, K. L., & Rude, S. (2007). Self-compassion and adaptive psychological functioning. *Journal of Research in Personality, 41* (1), 139–154.

Nidich, S. I., Ryncarz, R. A., Abrams, A. I., Orme-Johnson, D. W., & Wallace, R. K. (1983). Kohlbergian cosmic perspective responses, EEG coherence, and the TM and TM-Sidhi program. *Journal of Moral Education, 12,* 166–173.

O'Halloran, J. P., Jevning, R. A., Wilson, A. F., Skowsky, R., & Alexander, C. N. (1985). Hormonal control in a state of decreased activation: Potentiation of arginine vasopressin secretion. *Physiology and Behavior, 35,* 591–595.

Orme-Johnson, D. W., & Haynes, C. T. (1981). EEG phase coherence, pure consciousness, and TM-Sidhi experiences. *International Journal of Neuroscience, 13,* 211–217.

Rosch, E. (1999). Is wisdom in the brain? *Psychological Science, 10,* 222–224.

Ryff, C. D., & Singer, B. (1998). Human health: New directions for the next millennium. *Psychological Inquiry, 9*(1), 69–85.

Salzberg, S. (2002). *Lovingkindness: The revolutionary art of happiness.* Boston: Shambhala.

Scheier, M. F., & Carver, C. S. (1985). Optimism, coping, and health: Assessment and implications of generalized outcome expectancies. *Health Psychology, 4,* 219–247.

Schneider, R. H., Alexander, C. N., Staggers, F., Orme-Johnson, D. W., Rainforth, M., Salerno, W., et al. (2005). A randomized controlled trial of stress reduction in African Americans treated for hypertension for over one year. *American Journal of Hypertension, 18,* 88–98.

Seligman, M., & Csikszentmihalyi, M. (2000). Positive psychology: An introduction. *American Psychologist, 55,* 5–14.

Shapiro, D. H. (1980). *Meditation: Self-regulation strategy and altered state of consciousness.* New York: Aldine Publishing Company.

Shapiro, D. H., & Walsh, R. N. (Eds.) (1984). *Meditation: Classic and contemporary perspectives.* New York: Aldine.

Shapiro, S. L., Astin, J., Bishop, S., & Cordova, M. (2005). Mindfulness-based stress reduction and health care professionals. *International Journal of Stress Management, 12*(2), 164–176.

Shapiro, S. L., Brown, K. W., & Biegel, G. M. (2007). Teaching self-care to caregivers: Effects of mindfulness-based stress reduction on the mental health of therapists in training. *Training & Education in Professional Psychology, 1*(2), 105–115.

Shapiro, S. L., Carlson, L. E., Astin, J. A., & Freedman, B. (2006). Mechanisms of mindfulness. *Journal of Clinical Psychology, 62,* 373–386.

Shapiro, S. L., Schwartz, G. E. R., & Bonner, G. (1998). The effects of mindfulness-based stress reduction on medical and pre-medical students. *Journal of Behavioral Medicine, 21,* 581–599.

Shapiro, S. L., & Walsh, R. (2003). An analysis of recent meditation research and suggestions for future directions. *Journal of Humanistic Psychology, 31*(2–3), 86–114.

Smith, W. P., Compton, W. C., & West, W. B. (1995). Meditation as an adjunct to a happiness enhancement program. *Journal of Clinical Psychology, 51*(2), 269–273.

So, K., & Orme-Johnson, D. (2001). Three randomized experiments on the longitudinal effects of the transcendental meditation technique on cognition. *Intelligence, 29*(5), 419–440.

Tloczynski, J., & Tantriella, M. (1998). A comparison of the effects of Zen breath meditation or relaxation on college adjustment. *Psychologia: An International Journal of Psychology in the Orient, 41*(1), 32–43.

Valentine, E. R., & Sweet, P. L. G. (1999). Meditation and attention: A comparison of the effects of concentrative and mindfulness meditation on sustained attention. *Mental Health, Religion and Culture, 2,* 59–70.

Wallace, R. K. (1986). *The Maharishi technology of the unified field: The neurophysiology of enlightenment.* Fairfield, IA: MIU Neuroscience Press.

Walsh, R. (1999). *Essential spirituality: The seven central practices.* New York: Wiley.

Walsh, R. N. (1983). Meditation practice and research. *Journal of Humanistic Psychology, 23*(1), 18–50.

Walsh, R., & Shapiro, S. L. (2006). The meeting of meditative disciplines and western psychology: A mutually enriching dialogue. *American Psychologist, 61*(3), 227–239.

Zamarra, J. W., Schneider, R. H., Besseghini, I., Robinson, D. K., & Salerno, J. W. (1996). Usefulness of the transcendental meditation program in the treatment of patients with coronary artery disease. *American Journal of Cardiology, 77,* 867–870.

Spirituality: The Search for the Sacred

Kenneth I. Pargament *and* Annette Mahoney[1]

Abstract

To the founding fathers of psychology, spiritual phenomena represented critically important topics for psychological study. Since the early part of the twentieth century, however, psychologists have tended to (a) ignore spirituality; (b) view spirituality as pathological; or (c) treat spirituality as a process that can be reduced to more basic underlying psychological, social, and physiological functions. Fortunately, this situation has begun to change (Weaver, Pargament, Flannelly, & Oppenheimer, 2006), for several good reasons. First, spirituality is a "cultural fact" (cf. Shafranske & Malony, 1996): the vast majority of Americans believe in God (90%), engage in prayer (90%), and feel that religion is very important or fairly important to them (84%) (Gallup, 2004; Poloma & Gallup, 1991). Second, as we will see, empirical studies have linked spirituality to a number of aspects of human functioning. Finally, in a more practical vein, the American Psychological Association has defined religiousness as a "cultural diversity" variable. Although it has received relatively less attention than other diversity variables, psychologists are no less ethically obligated to attend to this dimension and reduce potential biases in their professional work with clients of diverse religious backgrounds (see Principle D, Ethical Principles of Psychologists and Code of Conduct of APA, 1992).

Keywords: coping, culture, religion, sacred, spirituality

In this chapter, we consider some of the intriguing findings that are emerging from the study of spirituality. Our review here will be selective rather than inclusive. We will discuss some of the ways that spirituality can be understood as another natural part of life. We will review some of the things we are beginning to learn from empirical studies of spirituality and its connections to well-being. Finally, we will illustrate some of the implications of spirituality for human functioning and positive psychology.[1]

Defining Spirituality

Psychological definitions of spirituality are diverse, ranging from the best of that which is human, to a quest for existential meaning, to the transcendent human dimension (Zinnbauer & Pargament, 2005). Even though any single definition of this rich, complex construct is unlikely to satisfy everyone, some characterization is needed to provide boundaries and order to this literature.

In moving toward a definition, it is particularly important to consider the relation between spirituality and religiousness. Traditionally, psychologists of religion did not distinguish between these constructs (Wulff, 1998). More recently, however, writers have begun to contrast the two, with some suggesting that religion is institutional, dogmatic, and restrictive, whereas spirituality is personal, subjective, and life enhancing (e.g., Elkins, 1995; Emblen, 1992). Elsewhere, we have argued against this polarization of the two constructs. Empirical studies indicate that most people appear to define themselves as both religious and spiritual (Zinnbauer et al., 1997). Moreover, both religion and spirituality can be expressed individually and socially, and both have the capacity to foster or impede well-being (Zinnbauer & Pargament, 2005). In short, we believe there are important points of overlap between the two constructs. We prefer to use the term "religion" in its classic sense as a broad individual and institutional domain that serves a variety of purposes, secular as well as sacred. "Spirituality" represents the key and unique function of religion. In this paper, spirituality is defined as "a search for the sacred" (Pargament, 1999, p. 12).

There are two key terms in this definition: "search" and the "sacred." The term "search" indicates that spirituality is a process, one that involves efforts to discover the sacred, hold onto the sacred once it has been found, and transform the sacred when necessary. People can take a virtually limitless number of pathways in their attempts to discover, conserve, and transform the sacred. What these diverse pathways share is a common end—the "sacred."

In our view, the sacred represents the substantively unique characteristic of spirituality. At its core, the sacred includes concepts of God, of the divine, and of transcendent reality; although such concepts cannot be proven as scientifically or ontologically "true," many people perceive one or more of these key elements as being real. As we have discussed at length elsewhere (Pargament & Mahoney, 2005), objects outside of this core can also be viewed as sacred by virtue of their association with, or representation of, this sacred core. We refer to imbuing objects with divine significance and character as "sanctification" and through this process many objects become sacred, including time and space (the Sabbath, churches); events and transitions (birth, death); materials (wine, crucifix); cultural products (music, literature); people (saints, cult leaders); psychological attributes (self, meaning); social attributes (compassion, community); and roles (marriage, parenting, work). We would describe persons as spiritual to the extent that they are trying to find, know, experience, or relate to whatever they perceive as sacred.

As Pargament (1999) has noted, this view of spirituality is broad enough to cover both traditional, theocentric, institutionally based spiritual expressions and nontheistic expressions that take place outside of traditional religious institutions, beliefs, and practices. The definition of spirituality, however, offers a basis for distinguishing between this construct and related phenomena. Unlike other psychological attributes, spirituality is centered around perceptions of the sacred. It overlaps with other human processes, many of which are described in this book (e.g., creativity, wisdom, forgiveness, meaning, hope, humility), only to the extent that they represent pathways to the sacred or become sacred in and of themselves. Of course, as we will see, many seemingly secular objects do, in fact, become sacred, and when they do, they become relevant topics for the study of spirituality. With this definition in mind, we now turn to the processes that are critical to spirituality.

Spiritual Processes
Discovery

The search for the sacred is dynamic, rather than static, evolving rather than fixed. As Figure 58.1 shows, it begins with the process of discovery, oftentimes in childhood. "How young we are when we start wondering about it all," Robert Coles (1990, p. 335) concluded from his study of the spiritual lives of children. Although some have questioned the child's capacity to grapple with religious abstractions (Goldman, 1964), social scientists have presented rich anecdotal accounts of children who appear to be engaged in a search for God. Consider the words of a 9-year-old boy:

> I'd like to find God! But He wouldn't just be there, waiting for some spaceship to land! He's not a person, you know! He's a spirit. He's like the fog and the mist. Maybe He's like something—something we've never seen here. So how can we know? You can't imagine Him, because He's so different—you've never seen anything like Him.... I should remember that God is God, and we're us. I guess I'm trying to get from me, from us, to Him with my ideas when I'm looking up at the sky!
> (Coles, 1990, pp. 141–142)

Social scientists have offered a variety of explanations for the propensity to seek the sacred. Some have suggested that there is a genetic basis for spirituality (e.g., Bouchard, Lykken, McGue, Segal, & Tellegen, 1990). Others have emphasized that conceptions of God are rooted in the child's intrapsychic capacity to symbolize, fantasize, and create superhuman beings (Rizzuto, 1979). Some have asserted that spirituality grows out of critical life events and challenges that expose human limitations and reveal a transcendent reality beyond the self (Johnson, 1959). Others have emphasized the importance of the social context (familial, institutional, cultural) in shaping the child's understanding of God (Kirkpatrick, 2005). And still others maintain that the spiritual capacity is basic to human character (Loewald, 1978).

Shaped by internal and external factors, perceptions of the sacred take many forms. In the United

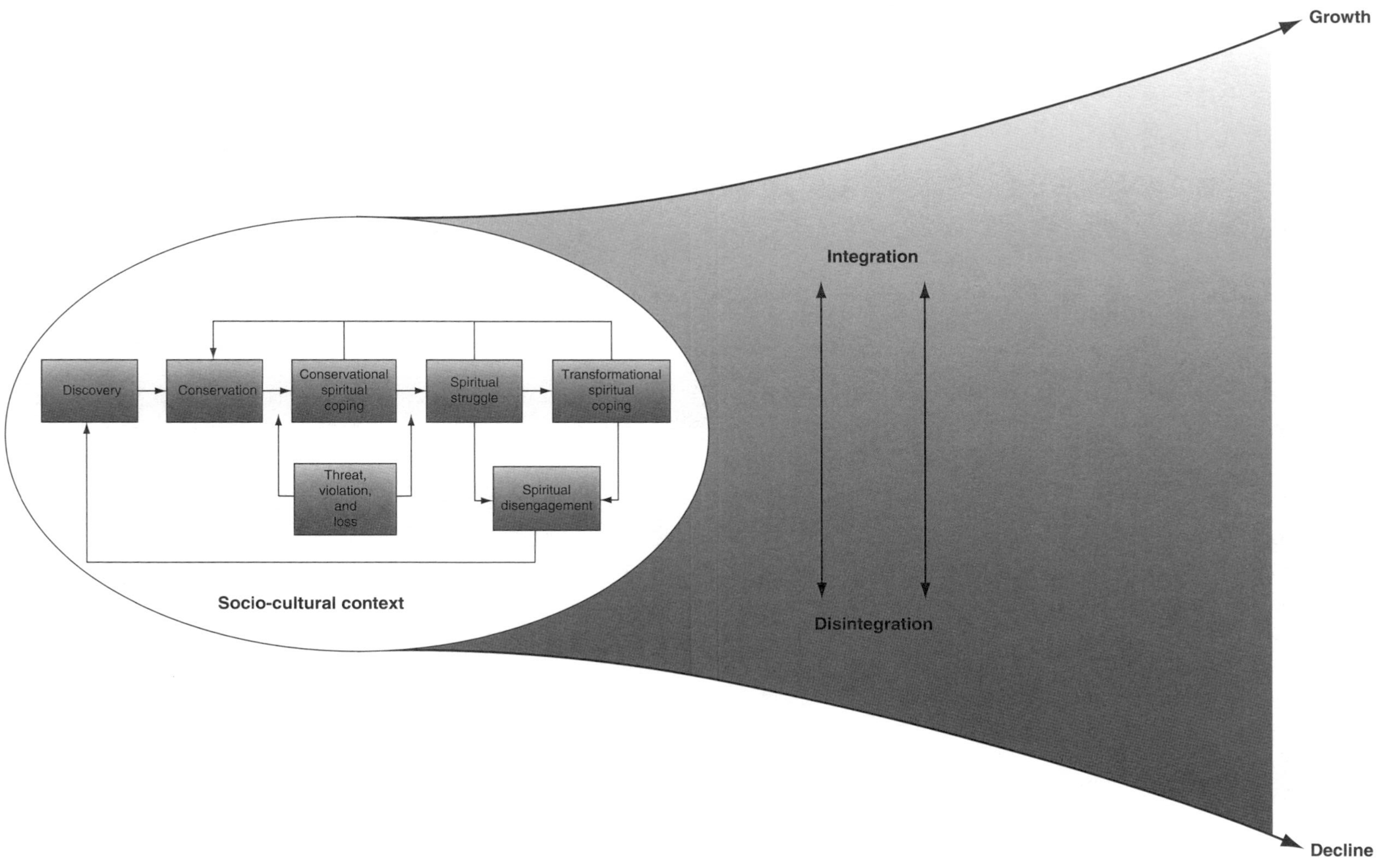

Fig. 58.1 The Search for the Sacred.

States, people hold diverse images of the divine, images that range from loving, kind, and forgiving to wrathful, strict, and controlling (Spilka, Armatas, & Nussbaum, 1964). As indicated previously, other aspects of life can also be sanctified, that is, perceived as manifestations of God or sacred in character (Pargament & Mahoney, 2005). For instance, many parents perceive their children as blessings (Murray-Swank, Mahoney, & Pargament, 2006), others view the body as something holy (Mahoney et al., 2005), and many describe love as eternal (see chap. 42). In short, people are able to discover the sacred in many parts of life, or life in its entirety.

Conservation

Figure 58.1 indicates that the search for the sacred does not end after it has been discovered. Once found, people strive to "hold on" to the sacred. Although social scientists generally have viewed religion and spirituality as mechanisms that help people maintain themselves physically, psychologically, and socially, the ultimate purpose of spiritual involvement for the religiously minded is not exclusively biological, psychological, or social (Pargament, 1997). Spiritual persons are, instead, concerned with developing, maintaining, and fostering their relationship with the sacred.

There is no shortage of examples of the human desire to hold on to the sacred, even at terrible costs. In a book aptly titled *With God in Hell*, Berkovits (1979) illustrates the great lengths to which many Jews went to preserve their faith during their imprisonment in the ghettos and concentration camps of World War II. One Jewish couple hurried to complete a ritual circumcision of their newborn son as the Gestapo were breaking into their homes to take them away, with the mother shouting "Hurry up! . . . They have come to kill us. At least let my child die as a Jew" (p. 45). Consistent with this example, researchers have found that levels of faith, and religious beliefs and practices are largely unchanged or even strengthened following traumatic events, such as accidents (Bahr & Harvey, 1979), war (Allport, Gillespie, & Young, 1948), and death of loved ones (Balk, 1983).

There are a number of spiritual pathways that conserve the individual's relationship with the sacred. Spiritual pathways include social involvements that range from traditional religious institutions to nontraditional spiritual groups, programs, and associations (e.g., twelve-step programs, meditation centers, Scientology). Pathways involve systems of belief that encompass those of traditional organized religions (e.g., Protestant, Roman Catholic, Jewish, Hindu, Buddhist, Muslim), newer spirituality movements (e.g., feminist, goddess, ecological spiritualities), and more individualized worldviews. Pathways are also made up of traditional religious practices that include prayer, Bible reading, watching religious television, and rites of passage, as well as other human expressions that have as their goal the sacred, including yoga, music, art, and social action (see Streng, 1976). In addition to these day-to-day forms of spiritual involvement, people can draw on a number of spiritual coping methods to help them conserve the sacred when it is threatened or violated, including spiritual support, purification rituals, and spiritual meaning making (see Pargament, 1997; Pargament & Ano, 2005, for reviews).

Transformation

Perhaps because of their involvement in these spiritual pathways, people demonstrate remarkable spiritual resilience. Nevertheless, Figure 58.1 shows that individuals experience internal or external events and transitions over the course of their lives that can be quite spiritually disorienting. As a result, they may struggle with whatever they hold sacred, with their system of spiritual beliefs, or with their religious communities. Spiritual struggles of these kinds have been linked to poorer mental and physical health, and even greater risk of dying (see Pargament, Murray-Swank, Magyar, & Ano, 2005). To resolve these struggles, transformation in the way the sacred is understood and experienced may be necessary.

Spiritual methods are available to facilitate this process of change (see Pargament, 1997, for a review). For example, religious rites of transition help people prepare for the deaths of those they hold most dear, acknowledge the loss, ease the deceased into the afterlife, incorporate the spiritual essence of the loved one into the inner experience of the survivors, and encourage the survivors to find new sources of sacred value in their lives once again. Spiritual conversion represents another transformational method in which those confronted by the limitations of their own self-contained worlds incorporate a sense of the sacred into themselves. The result is a fundamental change in the individual's self-definition, view of the world, and sense of purpose in life (see Paloutzian, 2005). Following transformation, the individual engages once again in efforts to conserve his or her new understanding of the sacred.

Not all attempts at transformation are necessarily successful, as Figure 58.1 indicates. The individual may be unable to find a new way to approach the sacred and disengage from the spiritual quest. Although some disengage permanently, others rediscover the sacred later in life and enter once again into the search for the sacred.

The process of discovering, conserving, and transforming the sacred is the essence of spirituality. It does not begin and end in childhood, nor does it conclude in early adulthood. It is a cycle that unfolds in different ways over the entire life span depending on a unique blend of biological, social, psychological, situational, and transcendent forces.

Spiritual Integration and Disintegration

Generally, involvement in the search for the sacred is associated with beneficial outcomes. People who pray and meditate more often, attend church more frequently, experience a greater sense of connectedness with the sacred, draw more on various spiritual methods of coping to deal with problems, and see the world through a sacred lens experience better health and well-being (see Koenig, McCullough, & Larson, 2001; Pargament, 1997; Pargament & Mahoney, 2005). But there are important exceptions to the rule: malignant spiritual expressions resulting in self-degradation, suffering, bigotry, and violence. Though spirituality speaks to the highest of human potentials, it also has been implicated in the lowest. Spirituality, in short, is not necessarily "good." People can take destructive as well as constructive spiritual pathways in the search for destructive or constructive representations of the sacred.

How do we determine whether spirituality is constructive or destructive? It would be overly simplistic to define the highest form of spirituality by a single belief, practice, emotion, or relationship. Instead, the most elevated form of spirituality is well integrated (see Pargament, 2002, 2007). At its best, spirituality is marked by pathways that are broad and deep, responsive to life's situations, nurtured by the larger social context, capable of flexibility and continuity, and oriented toward a sacred destination that is large enough to encompass the full range of human potential and luminous enough to provide the individual with a powerful guiding vision. At its worst, spirituality is disintegrated, defined by pathways that lack scope and depth, fail to meet the challenges and demands of life events, clash and collide with the surrounding social system, change and shift too easily or not at all,

and misdirect the individual in the pursuit of spiritual value. Thus, depending on the degree to which spirituality is well integrated or poorly integrated, an individual's spiritual trajectory may lead toward growth or decline (see Figure 58.1). Consider a few examples.

Problems of Spiritual Destinations

Problems arise when people pursue "small gods," that is, understandings of the sacred that leave people unable to come to terms with their own strengths and weaknesses and unequipped to face the full spectrum of life problems. On the one hand, exclusively harsh and punitive conceptions of God can interfere with the capacity to enjoy pleasures in life. These negative perceptions of the divine have been tied to higher levels of psychological distress (Exline & Rose, 2005). On the other hand, exclusively positive images of God as purely loving and protective may be difficult to reconcile with experiences of pain, suffering, and evil in the world. William James (1902) described this kind of "healthy-minded" religion as incomplete: "There is no doubt that healthy-mindedness is inadequate as a philosophical doctrine, because the evil facts which it refuses positively to account for are a genuine portion of reality; and they may after all be the best key to life's significance, and possibly the only openers of our eyes to the deepest levels of truth" (p. 160). Small gods who are seen by people as theirs and theirs alone can also pose problems for those who fall outside this sacred umbrella. For example, in a study of 11,000 people from 11 European countries, people who believed that "there is only one true religion" were significantly more prejudiced against ethnic minorities (Scheepers, Gijsberts, & Hello, 2002).

Problems also arise when people form attachments to inadequate substitutes for the sacred in their spiritual quest. Listen, for example, to the way one man described his descent into alcoholism: "As my alcoholism progressed, my thirst for God increasingly became transmuted into a thirst for the seemingly godlike experiences that alcohol induced. Alcohol gave me a sense of well-being and connectedness—and wasn't that an experience of God? Alcohol released me from the nagging sense that I was never good or competent enough—and wasn't that God's grace?" (Nelson, 2004, p. 31). False gods can take many forms—food, drugs, alcohol, self, others. Whatever its form, though, idolatry generally breaks down because the object of worship is unable to bear the full weight of the divine qualities that have been projected onto it.

Problems of Spiritual Pathways

In the search for the sacred, people encounter difficulties when their spiritual pathways lack breadth and depth. For example, people with a less extensive history of spiritual involvement are less likely to find spirituality helpful to them in difficult times. As Wink and Dillon (2001) put it: "Long-term investment in religious capital yields dividends that can compensate for subsequent declines in other human stock" (p. 102). Other studies have shown that a deeply internalized spirituality is tied to mental health benefits, unlike spiritualities motivated out of guilt or external pressures (Ryan, Rigby, & King, 1993). Finally, people who feel a more secure attachment to God report less psychological distress than those who describe a shakier attachment (Kirkpatrick, 2005).

Another set of problems occurs when the individuals' spiritual pathways do not fit with their destinations, their life situations, or larger social context. For example, by being overly scrupulous in the pursuit of spiritual goals, people can undermine the goals themselves, as in the case of a man who was so fearful of transgressing the injunction against praying when unclean that he spent too much time in the bathroom and missed his prayers entirely (Greenberg, Witztum, & Pisante, 1987). By failing to attend to the demands of situations, people can apply spiritual solutions inappropriately to life problems, as in the case of women who rejected medical help for lumps in their breasts and instead deferred the responsibility for the problem to God, with fatal consequences (Baider & De-Nour, 1987). And by virtue of their involvement in a larger unsupportive social context, people often experience considerable pain, as in the case of gay men and lesbians who report conflicts with the teachings of their traditions, prejudice from members and clergy in their congregations, and feelings of rejection, guilt, shame, and self-loathing (Schuck & Liddle, 2001).

Like other dimensions of life—physical, psychological, and social—spirituality is rich and complex. Over the course of their lives, people follow diverse spiritual trajectories, some leading toward growth and others toward decline. What determines the trajectory? Here we have suggested that there is no single key to distinguishing spirituality at its best from spirituality at its worst. Whether spirituality leads to growth or decline is instead determined by a configuration of factors and the degree to which they operate in harmony with each other.

Conclusions and Implications

The capacity to envision, seek, connect, and hold on to, and transform the sacred may be what makes us uniquely human. Spirituality cannot be reduced to purely biological, psychological, or social processes without distorting its essential character. Spirituality is an important human motive in and of itself (see also Emmons, 1999), one that deserves much greater study. Of course, we cannot speak to the actual existence of the sacred as social scientists. We have no instruments to measure God, the divine, or transcendent reality. We can learn, however, about the variety of ways that people try to discover, conserve, and transform what they perceive to be the sacred. We can also distinguish well-integrated from poorly integrated forms of spirituality. And we can examine how the search for the sacred impacts people's lives.

Psychologists and other social scientists are beginning to learn that spirituality holds a number of important implications for human functioning. But the study of spirituality is only beginning. Researchers have tended to study spirituality "from a distance," relying on surveys that contain global, distal measures, such as whether the individual believes in God, how often he or she goes to religious services, how often he or she prays, and his or her self-rated religiousness and spirituality. To develop a deeper understanding of this process, we will need to study it closer hand by getting to know spiritually oriented people; learning about their worldview, values, and relationships; participating in and observing their institutions and settings; and examining the specific resources and methods of spirituality in much greater detail. It will be important to consider the full variety of spiritual pathways and destinations, not only those associated with traditional religious institutions but also those tied to smaller, newer, culturally diverse, and nontraditional groups. Given the history of tension, antipathy, and misunderstanding between psychological and spiritual communities, research of this kind may be far from easy. Researchers need to gain some basic education in the psychology of religion and spirituality and to examine their own preconceptions and attitudes toward spirituality before they engage in this type of study. And yet, research in this area may be well worth its initial costs and challenges, for the study of spirituality holds promise not only for understanding a neglected dimension of life, but for practical efforts to help people enhance their well-being.

Spirituality offers, in some respects, a unique set of resources for living. As Pargament (1997) has noted elsewhere, much of psychology in the United States is control oriented. Making the unconscious conscious, increasing behavioral and cognitive control, and empowering the disempowered are hallmarks of an American psychology that tries to help people develop greater control over their lives. And yet, there are aspects of our lives that are beyond our control. Birth, developmental transitions, accidents, illnesses, and death are immutable elements of existence. Try as we might to affect these elements, a significant portion of our lives remains beyond our immediate control. In spirituality, however, we can find ways to understand and deal with our fundamental human insufficiency, the fact that there are limits to our control. Unfortunately, the language of spirituality—the sacred, letting go, forbearance, suffering, faith, mystery, finitude, sacrifice, grace, and transformation—is largely unfamiliar to psychologists. Even so, there may be much to be gained by bridging the worldviews, methods, and values of spirituality with those of psychology. Limitations and capacities are both a part of the human condition. After all, we grapple with both the possible and the impossible in any situation. Thus, a spirituality that helps us come to terms with our limits may complement rather than contradict a psychology that attempts to enhance our control.

Social scientists and health and mental health professionals are already starting to develop "psychospiritual interventions" that integrate spiritual resources into clinical practice. Spiritually oriented approaches have been interwoven with rational-emotive, cognitive-behavioral, psychoanalytic, marital-family, and existential therapies (see Nielsen, Johnson, & Ellis, 2001; Richards & Bergin, 2005; Shafranske, 1996). Although evaluations of the efficacy of these interventions are in short supply, initial results have been promising in several instances (e.g., Avants, Beitel, & Margolin, 2005; McCullough, 1999; Propst, Ostrom, Watkins, Dean, & Mashburn, 1992; Richards, Berrett, Hardman, & Eggett, 2006; Worthington, Kurusu, McCullough, & Sandage, 1996).

Researchers and practitioners have also begun to study a host of "virtues," constructs that have clear roots in religious traditions, and apply these spiritually related themes to preventive, educative, and therapeutic interventions (see Peterson & Seligman,

2004). For example, there is a burgeoning interest in the study of hope (Snyder, 1994; see also chap. 30), forgiveness (see McCullough, Pargament, & Thoresen, 2000; Worthington, 2005; see also chap. 40), love (Hazan, 2004; see chap. 42), acceptance (Sanderson & Linehan, 1999), and serenity (Connors, Toscova, & Tonigan, 1999). In the future, psychologists should also turn their attention to "vices," such as narcissism (Emmons, 1987) and evil (Baumeister, 1997; Peck, 1983). Helping people grapple with this darker side of spirituality represents another important direction for psychological practice. However, lest we slip back into a "negative psychology," this focus needs to be balanced with an appreciation for the resource that spirituality represents for many people.

In our efforts to help people, we have to be especially sensitive to the diverse ways they experience and express their spirituality. In the search for the sacred, people take many different pathways toward many different destinations. As psychologists we must respect the full range of worldviews, practices, and communities that people form in their spiritual journeys. Perhaps the best antidote to our professional arrogance will come from a willingness to develop closer, collaborative relationships with spiritual individuals and communities. We have much to learn from and about each other. With a relationship founded on mutual respect and trust, we may be able to pool our resources and extend our ability to enhance the well-being of people. And with a willingness to learn about, learn from, and work with each other, we may set the stage for a spiritually enriched, positive psychology.

References

Allport, G. W., Gillespie, J. M., & Young, J. (1948). The religion of the post-war college student. *Journal of Psychology, 25*, 3–33.

American Psychological Association. (1992). Ethical principles of psychologists and code of conduct. *American Psychologist, 47*, 1597–1611.

Avants, S. K., Beitel, M., & Margolin, A. (2005). Making the shift from "addict self" to "spiritual self": Results from a Stage I study of spiritual self-schema (3-S) therapy for the treatment of addiction and HIV risk behavior. *Mental Health, Religion, and Culture, 8*, 167–177.

Bahr, H. M., & Harvey, C. D. (1979). Widowhood and perceptions of change in quality of life: Evidence from the Sunshine Mine widows. *Journal of Comparative Family Studies, 10*, 411–428.

Baider, L., & De-Nour, A. K. (1987). The meaning of a disease: An exploratory study of Moslem Arab women after a mastectomy. *Journal of Psychosocial Oncology, 4*, 1–13.

Balk, D. (1983). Adolescents' grief reactions and self-concept perceptions following sibling death: A study of 33 teenagers. *Journal of Youth and Adolescence, 12*, 137–161.

[1] Portions of this chapter are adapted from Pargament, K. I. (2007). *Spiritually integrated psychotherapy: Understanding and addressing the sacred.* New York: Guilford.

Baumeister, R. F. (1997). *Evil: Inside human cruelty and violence.* New York: W. H. Freeman.

Berkovits, E. (1979). *With God in hell: Judaism in the ghettos and death camps.* New York: Sanhedrin Press.

Bouchard, R. J., Jr., Lykken, D. T., McGue, M., Segal, N. L., & Tellegen, A. (1990). Sources of human psychological differences: The Minnesota study of twins reared apart. *Science, 250,* 223–250.

Coles, R. (1990). *The spiritual life of children.* Boston: Houghton Mifflin.

Connors, G. J., Toscova, R. T., & Tonigan, J. S. (1999). Serenity. In W. R. Miller (Ed.), *Integrating spirituality into treatment: Resources for practitioners* (pp. 235–250). Washington, DC: APA Press.

Elkins, D. N. (1995). Psychotherapy and spirituality: Toward a theory of the soul. *Journal of Humanistic Psychology, 28,* 5–18.

Emblen, J. D. (1992). Religion and spirituality defined according to current use in nursing literature. *Journal of Professional Nursing, 8,* 41–47.

Emmons, R. A. (1987). Narcissism: Theory and measurement. *Journal of Personality and Social Psychology, 52,* 11–17.

Emmons, R. A. (1999). *The psychology of ultimate concerns.* New York: Guilford.

Exline, J. J., & Rose, E. (2005). Religious and spiritual struggles. In R. F. Paloutzian & C. L. Park (Eds.), *Handbook for the psychology of religion* (pp. 315–330). New York: Guilford.

Gallup Poll Organization. (2004). http://www.pollingreport.com/religion.htm

Goldman, R. (1964). *Religious thinking from childhood to adolescence.* New York: Seabury Press.

Greenberg, D., Witztum, E., & Pisante, J. (1987). Scrupulosity: Religious attitudes and clinical presentations. *British Journal of Medical Psychology, 60,* 29–37.

Hazan, C. (2004). Love. In C. Peterson & M. E. P. Seligman (Eds.), *Character strengths and virtues* (pp. 303–324). New York: Oxford University Press.

James, W. (1902). *The varieties of religious experience: A study in human nature.* New York: Modern Library.

Johnson, P. E. (1959). *Psychology of religion.* Nashville: Abingdon Press.

Kirkpatrick, L. A. (2005). *Attachment, evolution, and the psychology of religion.* New York: Guilford.

Koenig, H. G., McCullough, M. E., & Larson, D. B. (2001). *Handbook of religion and health.* Oxford: Oxford University Press.

Loewald, H. (1978). *Psychoanalysis and the history of the individual.* New Haven, CT: Yale University Press.

McCullough, M. E. (1999). Research on religion-accommodative counseling: Review and meta-analysis. *Journal of Counseling Psychology, 46,* 92–98.

McCullough, M. E., Pargament, K. I., & Thoresen, C. E. (Eds.). (2000). *Forgiveness: Theory, research, and practice.* New York: Guilford.

Mahoney, A., Carels, R., Pargament, K. I., Wachholtz, A., Edwards-Leeper, L., Kaplar, M., et al. (2005). The sanctification of the body and behavioral health patterns of college students. *The International Journal for the Psychology of Religion, 15,* 221–238.

Murray-Swank, A., Mahoney, A., & Pargament, K. I. (2006). Sanctification of parenting: Influences on corporal punishment and warmth by liberal and conservative Christian mothers. *The International Journal for the Psychology of Religion, 16,* 271–287.

Nelson, J. B. (2004). *Thirst: God and the alcoholic experience.* Louisville: Westminster John Knox Press.

Nielsen, S. L., Johnson, W. B., & Ellis, A. (2001). *Counseling and psychotherapy with religious persons: A rational emotive behavior therapy approach.* Mahwah, NJ: Lawrence Erlbaum.

Paloutzian, R. F. (2005). Religion, conversion, and spiritual transformation: A meaning-system analysis. In R. F. Paloutzian & C. L. Park (Eds.), *Handbook of the psychology of religion and spirituality* (pp. 331–347). New York: Guilford.

Pargament, K. I. (1997). *The psychology of religion and coping: Theory, research, practice.* New York: Guilford.

Pargament, K. I. (1999). The psychology of religion and spirituality? Yes and no. *The International Journal for the Psychology of Religion, 9,* 3–16.

Pargament, K. I. (2002). The bitter and the sweet: An evaluation of the costs and benefits of religiousness. *Psychological Inquiry, 13,* 168–181.

Pargament, K. I. (2007). *Spiritually integrated psychotherapy: Understanding and addressing the sacred.* New York: Guilford.

Pargament, K. I., & Ano, G. (2005). The religious dimension of coping: Advances in theory, research, and practice. In R. F. Paloutzian & C. L. Park (Eds.), *Handbook of the psychology of religion and spirituality* (pp. 479–495). New York: Guilford.

Pargament, K. I., Murray-Swank, N., Magyar, G., & Ano, G. (2005). Spiritual struggle: A phenomenon of interest to psychology and religion. In W. R. Miller & H. Delaney (Eds.), *Judeo-Christian perspectives on psychology: Human nature, motivation, and change* (pp. 245–268). Washington, DC: APA Press.

Pargament, K. I., & Mahoney, A. (2005). Sacred matters: Sanctification as a phenomenon of interest for the psychology of religion. *The International Journal for the Psychology of Religion, 15,* 179–199.

Peck, M. S. (1983). *People of the lie.* New York: Simon & Schuster.

Peterson, C., & Seligman, M. E. P. (Eds.). (2004). *Character strengths and virtues.* New York: Oxford University Press.

Poloma, M., & Gallup, G. H., Jr. (1991). *Varieties of prayer: A survey report.* Philadelphia: Trinity Press International.

Propst, L. R., Ostrom, R., Watkins, P., Dean, T., & Mashburn, D. (1992). Comparative efficacy of religious and nonreligious cognitive-behavioral therapy for the treatment of clinical depression in religious individuals. *Journal of Consulting and Clinical Psychology, 60,* 94–103.

Richards, P. S., & Bergin, A. E. (2005). *A spiritual strategy for counseling and psychotherapy.* Washington, DC: APA Books.

Richards, P. S., Berrett, M. E., Hardman, R. K., & Eggett, D. L. (2006). Comparative efficacy of spirituality, cognitive, and emotional support groups for treating eating disorder inpatients. *Eating Disorders: Journal of Treatment and Prevention, 41,* 401–415.

Rizzuto, A. M. (1979). *The birth of the living God: A psychoanalytic study.* Chicago: University of Chicago Press.

Ryan, R. M., Rigby, S., & King, K. (1993). Two types of religious internalization and their relations to religious orientation and mental health. *Journal of Personality and Social Psychology, 65,* 586–596.

Sanderson, C., & Linehan, M. M. (1999). Acceptance and forgiveness. In W. R. Miller (Ed.), *Integrating spirituality into treatment: Resources for practitioners* (pp. 199–216). Washington, DC: APA Press.

Scheepers, P., Gijsberts, M., & Hello, E. (2002). Religiosity and prejudice against ethnic minorities in Europe: Cross-national tests on a controversial relationship. *Review of Religious Research, 43*, 242–265.

Schuck, K. D., & Liddle, B. J. (2001). Religious conflicts experienced by lesbian, gay, and bisexual individuals. *Journal of Gay and Lesbian Psychotherapy, 5*, 63–82.

Shafranske, E. P. (Ed.). (1996). *Religion and the clinical practice of psychology*. Washington, DC: APA Press.

Shafranske, E. P., & Malony, H. N. (1996). Religion and the clinical practice of psychology: A case for inclusion. In E. P. Shafranske (Ed.), *Religion and the clinical practice of psychology* (pp. 561–586). Washington, DC: APA Press.

Snyder, C. R. (1994). *The psychology of hope: You can get there from here*. New York: Free Press.

Spilka, B., Armatas, P., & Nussbaum, J. (1964). The concept of God: A factor-analytic approach. *Review of Religious Research, 6*, 28–36.

Streng, F. J. (1976). *Understanding religious life*. Encino, CA: Dickenson.

Thoresen, C. E. (1998). Spirituality, health, and science: The coming revival? In S. Roth-Roemer, S. Kurpius Robinson, & C. Carmin (Eds.), *The emerging role of counseling psychology in health care* (pp. 409–431). New York: Norton.

Weaver, A. J., Pargament, K. I., Flannelly, K. J., & Oppenheimer, J. E. (2006). Trends in the scientific study of religion, spirituality, and health: 1965–2000. *Journal of Religion and Health, 45*, 208–214.

Wink, P., & Dillon, M. (2001). Religious involvement and health outcomes in late adulthood: Findings from a longitudinal study of men and women. In T. G. Plante & A. C. Sherman (Eds.), *Faith and health: Psychological perspectives* (pp. 75–106). New York: Guilford.

Worthington, E. L., Jr. (Ed.). (2005). *Handbook of forgiveness*. New York: Routledge.

Worthington, E. L., Jr., Kurusu, T. A., McCullough, M. E., & Sandage, S. J. (1996). Empirical research on religion and psychotherapeutic processes and outcomes: A 10-year review and research prospectus. *Psychological Bulletin, 119*, 448–487.

Wulff, D. (1998). *Psychology of religion: Classic and contemporary* (2nd ed.). New York: Wiley.

Zinnbauer, B. J., & Pargament, K. I. (1998). Spiritual conversion: A study of religious change among college students. *Journal for the Scientific Study of Religion, 37*, 161–180.

Zinnbauer, B. J., & Pargament, K. I. (2005). Religiousness and spirituality. In R. F. Paloutzian & C. L. Park (Eds.), *Handbook of the psychology of religion and spirituality* (pp. 21–42). New York: Guilford.

Zinnbauer, B. J., Pargament, K. I., Cole, B., Rye, M. S., Butter, E. M., Belavich, T. G., et al. (1997). Religion and spirituality: Unfuzzying the fuzzy. *Journal for the Scientific Study of Religion, 36*, 549–564.

CHAPTER 59

Sharing One's Story: On the Benefits of Writing or Talking About Emotional Experience

Kate G. Niederhoffer *and* James W. Pennebaker

Abstract

Over two decades of research devoted to the writing paradigm has resulted in substantial findings that translating emotional events into words leads to profound social, psychological, and neural changes. How and why would constructing stories about important personal events be so beneficial? The chapter describes the writing paradigm used in this research, offering an overview of the research findings and examination of its historical antecedents. While the precise mechanisms through which a narrative heals are still unrealized, we review three underlying processes that might explain its power: emotional inhibition, cognitive processes, and linguistic processes that echo changes in social orientation. Most recently, advances in computerized text analysis, in addition to the rapid development of the Internet, have afforded a new lens on the psychological transformations achieved through the writing paradigm. Linguistic Inquiry and Word Count (LIWC) is one such computerized text analysis program that captures style and content words. Originally created to better understand the language of emotional upheaval and recovery, with a focus on content and emotional valence, more recent research has focused on subtle stylistic differences in function words such as pronouns, articles, and prepositions. These "junk words" have proven to be reliable markers of demographics, biological activity, depression, life stressors, deception, and status. The chapter briefly reviews recent LIWC-based research regarding the often-overlooked stylistic components of sharing one's story.

Keywords: coping, emotional disclosure, Linguistic Inquiry and Word Count (LIWC), linguistic style, writing paradigm

One approach to positive psychology is to document the psychological factors that promote physical and mental health. Consistent with this approach, we have been exploring the psychological factors that operate when individuals cope with major emotional upheavals. We have been intrigued by the individual differences in response to a traumatic event. For example, some individuals are able to shrug it off and move on; others may talk about the event in detail for several days or weeks before getting on with their lives. Only a minority—perhaps about 20–30%—continue to suffer from the trauma for months or years afterward (cf. Wortman & Silver, 1989). What distinguishes those who quickly move past a trauma from those who become mired down

by it? More important, is there a way to use these naturally occurring processes to help individuals cope with a wide range of traumatic experiences?

Our interest in coping with emotional upheavals is rooted in people's apparent need to talk with others after a distressing event. It has long been argued that the self-disclosure of upsetting experiences serves as a basic human motive (Jourard, 1971). According to Rimé (1995), over 95% of emotional experiences are shared within the same day of occurrence, usually within a few hours. Although talking about traumatic events may be the norm, there are some experiences that people have great difficulty sharing—experiences such as rape, failure, or other secrets that many of us hold.

Is it possible that not talking about emotional upheavals can have adverse effects? If so, would people who are encouraged to talk or write about these secrets improve in mental and physical health?

For over two decades, researchers have been exploring the potential value of translating emotional experiences into words (cf. Pennebaker & Chung, 2007). One purpose of this chapter is to explore how and why constructing stories about important personal events is so beneficial. First, we will give a brief description of our paradigm and an overview of the research findings, followed by an examination of its historical antecedents. In the remainder of the chapter, we suggest some underlying processes that might explain the power of narrative. In this discussion, three recurring and overlapping processes are explored: those associated with emotional inhibition, cognitive processes, and linguistic processes that occur within the rubric of social dynamics. Specifically, not talking about important emotional events engages powerful, negative changes in each of these processes. However, by constructing stories through writing or talking, these dynamics can be reversed.

The Writing Paradigm: An Overview

The initial studies investigating the effect of putting emotional upheavals into words were founded on the hypothesis that giving people the opportunity to disinhibit or disclose their emotions would improve health. Students were brought into the laboratory and told they would be participating in an experiment to learn more about "writing and psychology." They were instructed to write about an assigned topic for 15 min daily, over 4 consecutive days. Participants were assured that their writing would be anonymous and that they would not receive any feedback. The only rule about the writing assignment was that once they began writing, they were to continue to do so without stopping, without regard to spelling, grammar, or sentence structure. Participants were then randomly assigned to either an experimental or a control group: One group was encouraged to delve into their emotions, and the other to describe objects and events dispassionately.

Those assigned to the experimental group were asked to spend each daily session writing about one or more traumatic experience in their lives. They were given the following instructions:

> For the next 4 days, I would like for you to write about your very deepest thoughts and feelings about the most traumatic experience of your life. In your writing, I'd

like you to really let go and explore your very deepest emotions and thoughts. You might tie your topic to your relationships with others, including parents, lovers, friends, or relatives. You may also want to link your experience to your past, your present, or your future, or to who you have been, who you would like to be, or who you are now. You may write about the same general issues or experiences on all days of writing, or on different traumas each day. All of your writing will be completely confidential.
> (Pennebaker, 1989, p. 215)

Those in the control group were asked to write about nonemotional topics. Examples of their assigned writing topics included describing the laboratory room in which they were seated or their own living room.

The most profound result of these writing studies was people's seemingly intuitive drive to disclose. Participants in the experimental condition enjoyed the writing process and found it to be extremely "valuable and meaningful." Similarly, 98% of participants reported that they would participate in the study again if given the choice (Pennebaker, 1997). Most surprising were the painful array of tragic and depressing stories about which these predominantly upper middle class college students wrote. Rape, family violence, suicide attempts, drug problems, and other horrors were common topics.

While the narratives themselves were compelling, our primary interest was the influence of the writing on physical health. The long-term effects (beginning at least 2 weeks after the studies) were overwhelmingly salutary. Participants in the experimental condition had significantly reduced numbers of physician visits in the next year (in comparison to those in the control condition). Contrary to the long-term effects, however, the immediate effects of the writing were not overtly positive; many students reported crying or being deeply upset by the experience. Understandably, in the hours after writing, participants in the experimental condition felt distressed and unhappy as they reexperienced the negative emotions that were elicited by the traumatic topics about which they wrote.

In further studies, we found similarly beneficial health outcomes for participants in the writing-about-trauma condition as measured by basic biological processes related to immune functioning (Pennebaker, Kiecolt-Glaser, & Glaser, 1988; Petrie, Booth, & Pennebaker, 1998) and positive influences on behavior—including increases in job offers received by a group of engineers after a massive layoff and increases in grades for incoming college students. Positive health and behavioral effects have also been found with maximum-security prisoners, medical students, community-based samples of distressed crime victims, arthritis and chronic pain sufferers, and women who recently gave birth to their first child. Furthermore, these findings are consistent across a variety of groups of individuals, including all social classes and major racial and ethnic groups in the United States, as well as samples in Mexico City, French-speaking Belgium, the Netherlands, Spain, and Japan (for a more complete review, see Smyth, 1998; Pennebaker & Chung, 2007).

Having demonstrated that the mere act of emotional disclosure through writing is a powerful therapeutic agent, we have since sought to more thoroughly investigate the possible mediators, moderators, and overall parameters of this relationship. We have explored the differential effects of writing versus talking about trauma, the topic of disclosure, time span of writing tasks, audience affects (via actual or implied feedback), individual differences in personality type and story-making abilities, and educational, linguistic, and cultural effects. Many of these variables will be considered in our discussion of individual differences.

History

Although the knowledge that disclosive writing can affect health and behavior has practical value, one of the more intriguing aspects of this research has been in trying to find the theories that best explain it. Because writing about emotional topics has been found to change biological processes, overt behaviors, and self-reports, we and others have adopted several theoretical approaches to try to capture these different levels of analysis. Our theoretical views, then, have evolved tremendously as the scope of the writing effects has broadened. As outlined here, the theoretical and research progression in this work began as a model of inhibition. Although the inhibition framework continues to provide valuable insights, a number of researchers began to emphasize the importance of cognitive processes. Most recently, we have begun to explore the role writing must have on the social dynamics of the people who write. Each of these theoretical positions is briefly discussed in the following sections.

The Role of Inhibition

Our original idea was that not talking about emotional upheavals was ultimately unhealthy.

This was based on the significant, salutary biological changes we witnessed among participants who expressed emotion while talking or writing about traumatic events. During confession in the laboratory or immediately after disclosure, for example, participants demonstrated reductions in blood pressure, muscle tension, and skin conductance (Pennebaker, 1989). More specifically, this verified that holding back or inhibiting one's thoughts, emotions, or behaviors was a form of physiological work that had the power to exacerbate stress-related problems.

The original theory motivating our writing studies was based on the assumption that not talking about important psychological events—constraining thoughts, feelings, and behaviors linked to emotional upheaval—is a form of inhibition. This active inhibition, in turn, is a form of physiological work, reflected in autonomic and central nervous system activity. Inhibition acts as a general stressor that can cause or exacerbate psychosomatic processes and thereby lead to long-term health problems (Traue & Deighton, 1999). Reducing inhibition as a strategy to improve health has been demonstrated by studies showing that both informal confiding and confiding in professionals through psychotherapy subsequently reduced illness (Mumford, Schlesinger, Glass, Patrick, & Cuerdon, 1998).

There are, of course, some striking similarities between our ideas about inhibition and Sigmund Freud and Joseph Breuer's talking cure. During their relatively brief collaboration, Freud and Breuer asserted that holding back pent-up feelings would result in the development of psychic tension, which in turn would result in neuroses. However, when people talked about the causes of their symptoms, they were cured of the symptoms. Freud went on to propose the "cathartic method" whereby talking about one's deepest feelings and thoughts, in a stream-of-consciousness manner, was thought to release pent-up emotions and cure people of their anxiety-related problems. Inhibition in Freud's world was ultimately linked to the deeper constructs of suppression and repression. The foundation of his theory was that the emotions associated with extreme stress must be deliberately and consciously "worked through," a concept we will return to in discussing the mechanisms by which writing brings about change (Freud, 1914/1958).

However, "letting go" of these thoughts as a way to reduce the stress of inhibition has not been sufficient in fully explaining the link of this process with better health outcomes. The method we now propose differs in its focus beyond the mere expression of pent-up emotions to an inclusion of the role of thought and insight. If merely expressing one's emotions was single-handedly effective, both verbal and nonverbal expression would bring about the same effects; however, recent studies have been unable to achieve similarly effective results using expressions such as art, music, and dance (Krantz & Pennebaker, 1997). We have come to realize that, in addition, there are two integral dimensions of disclosure beyond emotional disinhibition: cognitive and social.

The Role of Cognitive Processes

The cognitive roots of the paradigm are related to Gestalt psychologists' views on perception. When individuals experience trauma, they temporarily become disconnected from their core self or identity. This disconnection is exacerbated by the inhibition of the thoughts and feelings surrounding this emotional upheaval. Gestalt views explain our inherent need to integrate the many facets of a single event into a more coherent whole (Helson, 1925). An artifact of our ambiguous and unpredictable world is the anxiety of not attaining completion and not understanding a simple cause-and-effect explanation for traumatic disturbances. Alas, we naturally search for meaning and the completion of events; it gives us a sense of control and predictability over our lives.

In light of Bluma Zeigarnik's (1927/1938) finding that people have better memories for interrupted tasks than completed ones, it is easy to understand people's inherent need to obtain closure and resolve emotional upheaval. This, too, is related to Freud, who suggested that dreams were a symbolic way of completing unresolved tasks or wishes. Zeigarnik's, Freud's, and more recent research findings suggest that individuals tend to ruminate, talk, and dream about things that are not resolved in their minds, or about tasks that are not completed. Because we are motivated to complete our goal-related thoughts, these thoughts remain active when the task cannot be finished or resolved (Martin & Tesser, 1989). Furthermore, the more one tries to suppress these thoughts, paradoxically, the more frequently will they intrusively return to mind (cf. Wegner, 1994). The distressing nature of intrusive ruminations produces anxiety that can contribute to autonomic arousal.

Normally our drive to find meaning and obtain closure is helpful; once we understand why an event has occurred, we can put the thought out of mind

forever—or at least better prepare for future occurrences. However, in the face of a major upheaval or overwhelming trauma, which by definition disrupts life goals or tasks, we are driven to find meaning in a situation that might not lend itself to a plausible explanation. Nevertheless, our brains are constructed and/or our minds trained to move toward completion; this results in an endless obsession or preoccupation to figure out why the event happened and perhaps how we can cope with it.

Research in narrative psychology suggests that we make sense of our lives by putting them into story-like format (Neimeyer & Stewart, 2000). Similarly, modern psychotherapy is founded on the principle that clients must confront their anxieties and problems by creating a story to explain and understand past and current life concerns. Constructing a story facilitates a sense of resolution that gives individuals a sense of predictability and control over their lives—allowing them to be "in sync" with their core selves (a connection disrupted by emotional upheaval).

Through language, individuals can give structure to their experiences. An individual can create a coherent narrative, which, once formed, can be summarized, stored, and ultimately forgotten or, as narrative psychologists would say, "put away" more efficiently. Language serves as the scaffolding for individuals to organize their thoughts and feelings surrounding the traumatic event. Interestingly, recent research likens the process of narrative construction to an analog-to-digital conversion. That is, writing requires an individual to translate raw emotions into words, and therefore activates different areas of the brain (Pennebaker & Chung, 2007).

Innovative work in narrative psychology suggests that we use a "self-narrative" to account for the critical events in our lives (Gergen & Gergen, 1988; McAdams, 1996). Similar to a good story, these narratives include a guiding reason, or story goal with important events that are related in a sensible order to the goal. The beauty of the narrative is that it allows us to tie all the changes in our life together into a broad, comprehensive story. Indeed, we can create themes, plots, and subplots and arrange our multifaceted lives in an orderly, if not logical and hierarchical, fashion.

The Importance of Social Dynamics

The final component of not disclosing trauma involves the social repercussions. This phenomenon is described by Emile Durkheim (1951). An inherent benefit of forming a narrative involves being able to translate one's life story into a language that is both understandable and communicable. Not being able or willing to tell anyone about significant emotional upheaval disconnects people from their social worlds. Whether it is embarrassment, shame, or fear of incrimination that prevents an individual from disclosing, keeping a secret detaches one from society (see Kelly, 2001, for exceptions).

Research on secrecy suggests that having a secret will encourage obsessive preoccupation and rumination about the event (Wegner, Lane, & Dimitri, 1994). Suppressing thoughts on a daily basis is a large cognitive load, making it difficult to organize thoughts about the event and to make sense of what happened. Thus, the keeper of the secret will be more guarded, and the surrounding people who will be unaware of the individual's thoughts and feelings cannot offer sympathy or help. As a result, the individual becomes more isolated or, as Durkheim explained, less socially integrated.

Varied bodies of literature have established that social integration is one of the keys to both psychological and physical health. Durkheim (1951) argued that the less socially integrated people were, the more likely they were to commit suicide. Others have demonstrated that feelings of loneliness and isolation are associated with more health problems. Similarly, based on literature pertaining to the role of social support in health and illness, it appears that supportive interactions are key to maintaining mental health and that benefits arise not from the number of friends one has but from the quality of the friendships (Holahan, Moos, Holahan, & Brennan, 1996). However, social integration remains a somewhat ambiguous concept in psychology. We are yet unable to precisely label or measure its causes and constituents. Commonly, social integration is conceptualized as a sense of belonging, cohesion, confidence, and security with others. Our definition of social integration also incorporates the sense of coherence that one obtains in creating a synchrony in behaviors, beliefs, and language both within individuals and with their social group.

In the remainder of this chapter, our aim is to explain further the value of writing about emotional topics as a mechanism toward overall health and, more specifically, an important dimension of mental health, social integration. We will present a summary of our research findings, as well as hypothesized mechanisms by which these findings came about.

The Search for Process

As described previously, the writing research has evolved from three different theoretical perspectives. Because of this odd ancestry, research has been conducted that both extends the writing phenomenon and, at the same time, explores different explanations. Using the different historical backgrounds—inhibition, cognition, and social processes—we will trace the separate routes that have been taken by researchers to explain the beneficial effects of writing about emotional topics.

Research on Inhibition and Disclosure

There are many reasons that prevent people from disclosing trauma. Unfortunately, people who do not confide have greater risk for both major and minor health problems. In our early research we found that out of approximately 24,000 respondents to a survey in a popular magazine, 22% of females and 11% of males reported that they had had a traumatic sexual experience prior to age 17. These people also were more likely to have been hospitalized in the last year, to have been diagnosed with cancer, and to have high blood pressure, ulcers, and the flu (for a summary of this work, see Pennebaker, 1997). The significance of the relationship between these reported sexual traumas and such poor health outcomes is clearly not attributable to the nature of the trauma per se. Sexual trauma, however, is a prime example of an experience that is not readily discussed. Furthermore, subsequent studies have established that regardless of the type of trauma experienced, whether or not the trauma has been discussed strongly impacts health.

As our research progressed, we investigated the mechanism of disinhibition as the link between the disclosing of traumas and improved health. To do this, we used the previously discussed writing paradigm in which participants wrote consistently for 15 min daily over 4 consecutive days. Recall that in the experimental condition, participants were instructed to write about emotional topics: their "deepest thoughts and feelings about [their] most traumatic experience." In the control condition, participants simply wrote about nonemotional topics, such as the description of the room in which they were seated.

Whereas writing about traumas produced increased health benefits as compared with controls, in a variety of more recent studies, researchers have shown that simply writing about one's thoughts and feelings about coming to college, or about the experience of getting laid off (in the case of the unemployed engineers), produced comparable salubrious health outcomes. Similarly, when students were asked to write about imaginary traumas as though they had lived through them, they evidenced similar health benefits as compared with individuals who wrote about their own trauma (Greenberg, Stone, & Wortman, 1996).

The venting of emotions per se appears insufficient in the absence of cognitive processing. Although such venting may bring about subjective improvements and self-reports of improved mental health, health gains appear to require the translating of one's experiences into language. This was demonstrated in a study in which participants were asked either to express a traumatic experience using bodily movement, to express an experience using movement and then write about it, or to exercise in a prescribed manner for 3 days, 10 min per day. Only the "movement plus writing" group evinced significant improvements in physical health and grade point average (Krantz & Pennebaker, 1997). It is clear from all the studies that exploring emotions and thoughts—regardless of the content—is critical for the elicitation of health benefits.

Based on his meta-analysis, Smyth (1998) concludes that emotional disclosure is a necessary but not sufficient factor to beget the benefits from writing about trauma. Recent research findings support a two-step, multidimensional approach to explain the effects of disclosure. First, confiding traumas (a) reduces the physiological arousal associated with inhibition and (b) increases one's ability to understand and integrate the experience (Salovey, Rothman, & Rodin, 1998). Furthermore, as we will explain subsequently, it appears that one specific style of emotional confrontation is more effective than the others.

Cognitive Processes

In speaking to participants in the experimental conditions of the original writing studies, it was clear that they were gaining more through the writing than simply disclosing would suggest. In listening to the words that participants used to recount their experiences—such as "realize," "understand," "come to terms," and "getting past"—we gleaned that the writing was fostering a better understanding of both themselves and the situations about which they wrote. On an intuitive level, it seemed that an individual's cognitive reorganization was crucial for the positive outcomes we had been witnessing.

In two more systematic examinations, this point was substantiated: first in a topical analysis of the writings and, second, in a computer program that analyzed the linguistic components in more detail. In the first analysis, independent raters assessed the writing samples of participants whose health improved after writing, as compared with those whose health remained unchanged. Writing samples of participants who improved were judged to be more self-reflective, emotionally open, and thoughtful.

To investigate further the specific language that led to these assessments, we then developed a computerized text analysis program that could detect emotional and cognitive categories of words. The computer program, Linguistic Analysis and Word Count (LIWC), allowed us to reanalyze previous writing studies and link word usage among individuals in the experimental conditions with various health and behavioral outcomes. LIWC detects 70 word categories, 4 of which are of primary relevance (Pennebaker & Francis, 1999; Pennebaker, Booth, & Francis, 2007). The emotion categories include negative-emotion words (*sad, angry*) and positive-emotion words (*happy, laugh*), and the cognitive categories include causal (*because, reason*) and insight words (*understand, realize*). The two cognitive categories were designed to capture the degree to which participants were actively thinking in their writing, attempting to put together causes and reasons for the events and emotions they were describing. LIWC, in turn, produces a probabilistic rating for each linguistic category.

Thus, we reanalyzed six studies: two in which college students wrote about traumas where blood immune measures were collected; two in which first-year college students wrote about their deepest thoughts and feelings about coming to college; one study of maximum-security prisoners in a state penitentiary; and one using professionals who unexpectedly had been laid off from their jobs after over 20 years of employment (Pennebaker, Mayne, & Francis, 1997). In these efforts, we uncovered two important findings. The more that people used positive-emotion words, the more their health improved. Individuals who used a moderate number of negative-emotion words in their writing about upsetting topics evidenced the greatest drops in physician visits in the months after the study. Those people who used a very high rate of negative-emotion words and those who used very few were the most likely to have continuing health problems after participating in the study.

From a statistical perspective, the cognitive categories accounted for the most variance in predicting improvements in health. Specifically, people whose health improved the most used an increasing amount of causal and insight words over the 3–5-day course of the experiment. It was clear that participants demonstrating this pattern of language were constructing, over time, a story that was replete with causal implications. Stories were built on the foundation of causal links surrounding participants' experiences and feelings. Constructing this narrative appeared critical in reaching an understanding and achieving better health. Indeed, those participants who began the study with a coherent story that explained some past event did not benefit from writing; merely having a story is not sufficient to assure good health. The "process" of constructing a story is crucial.

Similarly, Clark (1993) asserts in her work on conversation and language that in order to convey a story, the speech act must be coherent. Linguistic coherence subsumes several characteristics, including structure, use of causal explanation, repetition of themes, and an appreciation of the listener's perspective. Constructing a coherent story resembles what many psychologists in the coping literature refer to as "working through" a problem. As a result of working through loss, an individual is thought to achieve resolution by accepting the loss intellectually. Indeed, the increased use of causal and insight words detected in our linguistic analyses provides good support for this process.

An inherent benefit of forming a narrative involves being able to translate one's life story into a language that is both understandable and communicable. Once constructed, this story not only helps the beholder to better understand himself and the causes of his trauma but also allows him to communicate it to others. Not being able to tell anyone or the unwillingness to be open and honest about significant emotional upheaval disconnects a person from his or her social world. The sharing of one's story leads us to the third proposed mechanism by which these benefits come about: social communication.

Social Processes

Traumatic events are socially isolating. Implicit in this statement is that by talking to others (or writing) about traumatic experiences, traumatized individuals can establish richer social connections to their social networks. The importance of human communication in mental health is of primary importance. Social support has been associated with mental and physical health, with speedier recovery from illness, and with the likelihood of remaining healthy when stressors occur (cf. Holahan et al., 1996). Indeed, social relationships especially protect individuals from ill health under periods of high stress.

It is important to maintain social connections because social groups offer a venue for growth, social experimentation, and change. Sharing our story alerts our friends to our emotional and psychological state. In contrast, keeping a secret engenders a social chasm between the secret keepers and their friends. Keeping a secret is a cognitively consuming load that prevents the secret keeper from being a good listener and thereby exacerbates the social disconnection.

In a study of mutual support, both online and face-to-face, we found that social support groups are a significant way by which people change their health behavior (Davison, Pennebaker, & Dickerson, 2000). With the onset of an illness or a traumatic experience come anxiety and uncertainty. The resulting intense emotions of an afflicted individual can be reduced through interpersonal exchange. Groups of others with similar concerns or conditions provide a standard of normalcy against which people can compare themselves, as well as to share their thoughts and feelings surrounding their conditions.

In our more recent studies, we have investigated the role of writing in facilitating social integration, specifically, whether one of the health benefits of writing enables individuals to better connect with their social group. Do people begin to interact differently with others, or perhaps see themselves in a new light, after writing about an emotional topic? In order to explore these ideas, we developed a method to capture how people naturally talk and interact with others using an electronically activated recorder (EAR)—a simple tape recorder with an attached computer chip that records for 30 sec every 12 min. The EAR is lightweight and nonintrusive like a Walkman, worn by participants for 2 consecutive days. A small external microphone allows us to hear pieces of conversations, as well as determine where participants are and what they are doing (Mehl, Pennebaker, Crow, Dabbs, & Price, 2001).

In the first study, participants wore the EAR for 2 consecutive days, 2 weeks prior to participating in a routine writing study and again 2 weeks afterward. Transcriptions of the conversations yielded promising results in terms of participants' physical behaviors, as well as their language as analyzed by LIWC. As compared with participants in the control condition, who were asked to write about time management, trauma writers began talking to their friends more, laughing more, and using significantly more positive emotions in their daily language. Trauma writers also demonstrated significant drops in their resting levels of both diastolic and systolic blood pressure. Similarly, writing about emotion encouraged participants to use more present-tense words and fewer past-tense words. Interestingly, these effects were far stronger for men, who are naturally less socially integrated than women.

One asset of the EAR is its ability to capture linguistic and acoustic data, thereby offering profound insight into social context, both physical and psychological. By chance, one project originally intended to capture the psychometric properties of the language of everyday life, using the EAR, began immediately prior to September 11, 2001 (Mehl & Pennebaker, 2003). The results were highly insightful with respect to linguistic changes and their concomitant social sequelae, during and after the intense psychological upheaval. Some of the more notable findings to emerge from this project include changes in first-person pronoun usage, decreasing immediately after the attack, alongside a preference or dyadic interactions above groups of a larger size. From the linguistic shift, we glean hints about how flexibly our perspective shifts in the face of trauma; from the change in group dynamics, we begin to understand that intimacy trumps information gathering in the face of trauma. In fact, participants who displayed this pattern of increased dyadic interactions were the ones to show the most improved health at follow-up.

Another line of research we have pursued originally intended to investigate the linguistic components of social integration that we refer to as "synchrony." Whereas other authors have conceptualized social integration from a self-report perspective, as a sense of belonging, cohesion, confidence, and security with others (Bille-Brahe, 1996), we defined social integration as a "synchrony" in behaviors, beliefs, and language within a social group. From a subjective perspective, synchrony among members of a dyad may be perceived as a "click" or feeling "in sync": having a conversation that is comfortable and fluid. Psychologists have demonstrated that synchrony (albeit among behaviors) communicates interest and approval (Kendon, 1970). Linguistically, we hypothesized that synchrony would be portrayed by similar patterns in the way people talk across LIWC word categories— for example, coordination in the number and types of words used within a dyad. Interestingly, linguistic style matching (LSM) emerged independent of all measures of subjective synchrony (Niederhoffer & Pennebaker, 2002). While it seems intuitive that a synchronized pattern of language would facilitate social integration, we found people are inclined to match conversation partners in linguistic style, regardless of their intentions and reactions. We interpret this as an inherent need and ability to coordinate our interactions, particularly when engaged in a conversation.

An important dimension to coping with stressors is the degree to which people discuss or confront traumas after their occurrence (Pennebaker, 1997). We propose that our paradigm facilitates confession by first enabling people to personally understand their trauma and ultimately allowing them to discuss it with others, thereby becoming socially integrated. In turn, social integration is an integral component of physical and psychological health. Although psychological health remains an ambiguous, sometimes illusory construct in psychology, our method of constructing and sharing one's story offers a way to reduce the physiological effects of a massive life stressor, as well as to gain control, find meaning, and facilitate social integration.

Individual Differences

Do some people benefit more from writing than others? In the first 15 years of the writing paradigm, no researcher was able to demonstrate consistently that one individual difference was linked to health. The problem may have been that health measures, such as physician visits, are notoriously variable. With such unstable dependent measures, it is exceptionally difficult to detect individual differences that are correlated with within-condition effects.

In recent years, some promising findings have begun to be reported. In Smyth's (1998) meta-analysis of 14 writing studies, men tended to benefit more from writing than did women. Christensen and Smith (1993) reported that individuals high in hostility evidenced greater immune response to writing than those persons who were low in hostility. Most recently, Paez, Velasco, and Gonzalez (1999) found that people who were high in the trait of alexithymia (a condition characterized by the inability to detect, interpret, or label emotions) benefited more from writing than did those low in the trait. The common thread of all these studies is that people who are *not* naturally emotionally open or likely to talk with others about feelings may be the very people who benefit most from writing about their internal states.

Recently individual differences in story making and narrative construction have been explored. Smyth, True, and Souto (2001) evaluated the role of narrative structuring by experimental manipulation and found that the self-reported health of people who wrote about a traumatic experience in a narrative fashion was better than for those who wrote about this topic in a disjointed, listlike way. Unfortunately, this may reflect the general task of writing more than a specific ability to write good stories. In a recent study, Graybeal, Sexton, and Pennebaker (2002) tried to evaluate if a person who was a good "story maker" in writing about traumas also was a good story maker in response to Thematic Apperception Test card or an inkblot test. There was virtually no relationship. Although the ability to construct a good narrative about one's own trauma apparently is beneficial, there does seem to be a group of very healthy story makers in the world who are accounting for all of our variance.

Linguistic Markers: Recent Research

Partially due to EAR technology and findings resulting from EAR studies, we have shifted the focus of our research from the writing paradigm to the writing, or language per se. That is, while researchers continue to investigate the precise boundary conditions for the writing paradigm, across various populations and conditions, the quest for the mechanism of change has concentrated on the analysis of linguistic changes over the course of emotional upheaval. Importantly, this necessitates an understanding of how the language of emotional upheaval and recovery compares to the language of everyday life and thus has created a growing body of research devoted to the psychometric properties of everyday language (cf. Mehl, 2003).

Pronouns, a category of common function words, which account for 50–55% of written and spoken words, are yielding the most prominent findings (Pennebaker, Mehl, & Niederhoffer, 2003). This is not surprising in the varied roles pronouns can play: subjects that act (e.g., I), objects of action (me), and possessors of things (my). Furthermore, unlike most other nouns and regular verbs, pronouns do not have stable referents. With every change of speaker in a conversation and every change of context in which a pronoun is uttered, pronouns shift referent (Ricard, Girouard, & Decarie, 1999). Developmentally, pronouns are inextricably bound to perspective-taking ability. Neuroscientific research also reveals that pronouns are processed differently in the brain than most other

nouns and regular verbs (Miller, 1995). What we are finding is that pronoun usage reflects the way people are thinking about themselves in relation to others, and referring to themselves and others (Pennebaker, 2002; Pennebaker & Chung, 2007).

From pronouns, one can glean information about self-awareness and integration with others, alleged ownership of statements, and social identity (Pennebaker, 2002). For example, the empirically driven profile of a frequent user of first-person singular pronouns (I, me, my) is a young (Pennebaker & Stone, 2003), honest (Newman, Pennebaker, Berry, & Richards, 2003) female (Mehl & Pennebaker, 2003; Newman Groom, Handelman, & Pennebaker, 2008), of lower social class (Pennebaker & King, 1999), low self-esteem, likely to be depressed, socially or emotionally isolated (Bucci & Freedman, 1981; Rude, Gortner, & Pennebaker, 2004; Weintraub, 1981;), and possibly prone to suicide (Stirman & Pennebaker, 2001).

A recent case study offers revealing fragments to the emerging picture of first-person pronoun usage and its relationship to emotional upheaval. Former New York Mayor Rudy Giuliani's speeches in 35 of his press conferences between 1993 and 2001 demonstrated significant changes in his pronoun usage in accordance with objective changes in his personal and professional lives (Pennebaker & Lay, 2002). During personal crisis, a 2-week period in which he was diagnosed with prostate cancer, withdrew from the Senate race, and separated from his wife, his usage of first-person singular pronouns (I, me, my) dramatically increased. In tandem, his usage of first-person plural ("we") dropped well below levels of his early mayoral days. This was indicative of his increasing introspection in order to express his thoughts and feelings. This humanized stance, linguistically, appeared in stark contrast to his original language.

In the beginning of his term, his more distant, objective language was marked by pomposity and aloofness, and an outward focus during times of public upheaval. His subsequent use of first-person plural (we) was a sign of power and privilege that he could speak for the masses. His highest levels of first-person plural were witnessed during the World Trade Center crisis; this was reflective of his attempts to build a strong sense of community by invoking connections with others. Interestingly, a comparison of King Lear's first and last speeches yield consistent usage of first-person singular and plural signifying this same shift from pomposity to humanization(Pennebaker, & Ireland, 2008).

Thus, flexibility in usage of pronouns (e.g., from "I" to "we") is deemed beneficial. Across multiple samples of participants in studies involving the writing paradigm, participants who alter their individual and social perspectives from day to day are the ones who benefit most from the exercise, as measured by a decrease in doctor visits (Campbell & Pennebaker, 2003). On another dimension, flexibility in pronouns can be both within (e.g., different meanings of "I") and across pronouns (e.g., from "I" to "we"). For example, Giuliani's flexibility manifested in fluid variation from an "I" of ownership to an "I" of openness, and likewise from a detached "we" to a personal "we." While the research around pronoun usage begins to paint a clear picture of their role in conveying intimacy, there are still many additional layers to explore.

Conclusions

Emotional upheavals can have a variety of adverse effects on people's mental and physical health. They make us think differently about life, our friends, and ourselves. They also have the potential to profoundly disrupt our ongoing relationships with others. As many researchers have begun to discover, disclosure— through writing or talking—has a remarkable potential in alleviating these effects. Putting upsetting experiences into words allows people to stop inhibiting their thoughts and feelings, to begin to organize their thoughts and perhaps find meaning in their traumas, and to reintegrate into their social networks.

Writing is not a panacea. Not everyone benefits from writing. We suspect that it has the potential to disrupt people's lives. As an example, a recent writing participant told us that, after writing, she reevaluated her life and her marriage. She then divorced her husband of 8 years and was forced to move with her children to a much smaller apartment. Although she reports being happier and healthier because of the writing, some might argue that writing had some very negative side effects.

It is somewhat ironic that the writing paradigm is discussed as a feature of positive psychology. Although we have demonstrated that writing about traumatic experiences can have significant health benefits, in a sense, our paradigm encourages participants to dwell on the misery in their lives. We are essentially bringing inhibited or secret negative emotions to the forefront. This can be an anxiety-provoking experience; recall that many participants in the experimental condition cry and report feeling greater sadness, depression, frustration, and guilt in the short run (Pennebaker, 1989). In fact, emotional state after writing depends on how participants are feeling prior to writing such that the better they feel before, the worse they feel afterward.

Is this distress necessary for the positive outcomes we witness in participants' health? If the achievement of insight is truly responsible for the benefits we have demonstrated, is emotional expression—when it appears to be the exact opposite of uplifting—a necessary component? Intuitively, participants' reports of distress seem antithetical to their reports of the value and meaningfulness they ascribe to participating in our experiments. Instead, it appears that they acknowledge the importance of distress as a prelude to overcoming trauma.

We have presented the writing paradigm as a "process" toward achieving mental health. We emphasize the importance of process in order to prevent the notion that one can automatically achieve health benefits. Clearly, one might have to endure some negativity to be healthy. Society has an obsessive focus on strategies aimed toward reducing the awareness of unpleasant emotions. Focus on negative emotions, however, may be necessary in order to genuinely overcome trauma and grow as a mentally healthy human being.

One cannot ascribe too much importance to positivity by neglecting what appears to be a necessary psychological cost. At the risk of sounding trite, we note that our research findings highlight the importance of being true to oneself—confronting negative thoughts and acknowledging negative emotions. The path to a satisfying and fulfilling life does not bypass difficulties and negative thoughts and feelings. Indeed, one of the goals in positive psychology is to increase our understanding and abilities to transverse those impediments more effectively. Thus, by openly facing our traumas, we no longer end up in such psychological ditches. Rather, we can begin to build bridges to the considerable strengths that we all possess. As such, the psychological road that heretofore has been less traveled may become a main thoroughfare of positive psychology.

Future-Oriented Questions

1. What are the boundary conditions of the writing paradigm: for whom is it most effective, when/how long after a trauma?

2. Is language a reflection of change or causal process? How prescriptive can a given style of writing be? Are there boundary conditions for

prescription, or is language best suited as a diagnostic marker?

3. Can we come to consensus on robust outcome measures to test the efficacy of the writing paradigm, balancing the speed and efficiency of self-report measures yet preserving the meaningfulness of real-world behaviors?

References

Bille-Brahe, U. (1996). Measuring social integration and social support. *Nordic Journal of Psychiatry, 50,* 41–46.

Bucci, W., & Freedman, N. (1981). The language of depression. *Bulletin of the Menninger Clinic, 45,* 334–358.

Campbell, R. S., & Pennebaker, J. W. (2003). The secret life of pronouns: Flexibility in writing style and physical health. *Psychological Science, 14,* 60–65.

Christensen, A. J., & Smith, T. W. (1993). Cynical hostility and cardiovascular reactivity during self-disclosure. *Psychosomatic Medicine, 55,* 193–202.

Clark, L. F. (1993). Stress and the cognitive-conversational benefits of social interaction. *Journal of Social and Clinical Psychology, 12,* 25–55.

Davison, K. P., Pennebaker, J. W., & Dickerson, S. S. (2000). Who talks? The social psychology of illness support groups. *American Psychologist, 55,* 205–217.

Durkheim, E. (1951). *Suicide.* New York: Free Press.

Freud, S. (1914/1958). Remembering, repeating and working through. In J. Strachey (Ed.), *The standard edition of the complete works of Sigmund Freud* (Vol. 12). London: Hogarth.

Gergen, K. J., & Gergen, M. M. (1988). Narrative and the self as relationship. In L. Berkowitz (Ed.), *Advances in experimental social psychology* (Vol. 21, pp. 17–56). New York: Academic Press.

Graybeal, A., Sexton, J. D., & Pennebaker, J. W. (2002). The role of story-making in disclosure writing: The psychometrics of narrative. *Psychology and Health, 17,* 571–581

Greenberg, M. A., Stone, A. A., & Wortman, C. B. (1996). Health and psychological effects of emotional disclosure: A test of the inhibition-confrontation approach. *Journal of Personality and Social Psychology, 71,* 588–602.

Helson, H. (1925). The psychology of Gestalt. *American Journal of Psychology, 36,* 494–526.

Holahan, C. J., Moos, R. H., Holahan, C. K., & Brennan, P. L. (1996). Social support, coping strategies, and psychosocial adjustment to cardiac illness: Implications for assessment and prevention. *Journal of Prevention and Intervention in the Community, 13,* 33–52.

Jourard, S. M. (1971). *Self-disclosure: An experimental analysis of the transparent self.* New York: Wiley-Interscience.

Kelly, A. E. (2001). Dealing with secrets. In C. R. Snyder (Ed.), *Coping with stress: Effective people and processes* (pp. 196–221). New York: Oxford University Press.

Kendon, A. (1970). Movement coordination in social interaction: Some examples described. *Acta Psychologica, Amsterdam, 32*(2), 101–125.

Krantz, A., & Pennebaker, J. W. (1997). Bodily versus written expression of traumatic experience. Unpublished manuscript.

McAdams, D. P. (1996). Personality, modernity, and the storied self: A contemporary framework for studying persons. *Psychological Inquiry, 7,* 295–321.

Martin, L. L., & Tesser, A. (1989). Toward a motivational and structural theory of ruminative thought. In J. S. Uleman, J. A. Bargh, et al. (Eds.), *Unintended thought* (pp. 306–326). New York: Guilford.

Mehl, M. R., & Pennebaker, J. W. (2003a). The social dynamics of a cultural upheaval: Social interactions surrounding September 11, 2001. *Psychological Science, 14,* 579–585.

Mehl, M. R., & Pennebaker, J. W. (2003b). The sounds of social life: A psychometric analysis of students' daily social environments and natural conversations. *Journal of Personality and Social Psychology, 84,* 857–870.

Mehl, M., Pennebaker, J. W., Crow, D. M., Dabbs, J., & Price, J. (2001). The electronically activated recorder (EAR): A device for sampling naturalistic daily activities and conversations. *Behavior Research Methods, Instruments, and Computers, 33,* 517–523.

Miller G. (1995). *The science of words.* New York: Scientific American Library.

Mumford, E., Schlesinger, H. J., Glass, G. V., Patrick, C., & Cuerdon, T. (1998). A new look at evidence about reduced cost of medical utilization following mental health treatment. *Journal of Psychotherapy Practice and Research, 7,* 68–86.

Neimeyer, R. A., & Stewart, A. E. (2000). Constructivist and narrative psychotherapies. In C. R. Snyder & R. E. Ingram (Eds.), *Handbook of psychological change: Psychotherapy processes and practices for the 21st century* (pp. 337–357). New York: Wiley.

Niederhoffer, K. G., & Pennebaker, J. W. (2002). Linguistic style matching in social interaction. *Journal of Language and Social Psychology, 21,* 337–360.

Newman, M. L., Groom, C. J., Handelman, L. D., & Pennebaker, J. W. (2008). Gender differences in language use: An analysis of 14,000 text samples. *Discourse Processes, 45,* 211–236.

Newman, M. L., Pennebaker, J. W., Berry, D. S., & Richards, J. M. (2003). Lying words: Predicting deception from linguistic style. *Personality and Social Psychology Bulletin, 29,* 665–675.

Paez, D., Velasco, C., & Gonzalez, J. L. (1999). Expressive writing and the role of alexithymia as a dispositional deficit in self-disclosure and psychological health. *Journal of Personality and Social Psychology, 77,* 630–641.

*Pennebaker, J. W. (1989). Confession, inhibition, and disease. In L. Berkowitz (Ed.), *Advances in experimental social psychology* (Vol. 22, pp. 211–244). New York: Academic Press.

*Pennebaker, J. W. (1997). *Opening up: The healing power of expressing emotions* (Rev. ed.). New York: Guilford.

Pennebaker, J. W. (2002). What our words can say about us: Toward a broader language psychology. *Psychological Science Agenda, 15,* 8–9.

Pennebaker, J. W., Booth, R. E., & Francis, M. E. (2007). *Linguistic Inquiry and Word Count: LIWC2007—Operator's manual.* Austin, TX: LIWC.net.

Pennebaker, J. W., & Chung, C. K. (2007). Expressive writing, emotional upheavals, and health. In H. Friedman and R. Silver (Eds.), *Handbook of health psychology* (pp. 263–284). New York: Oxford University Press.

Pennebaker, J. W., & Francis, M. E. (1999). *Linguistic Inquiry and Word Count (LIWC): A computer-based text analysis program.* Mahwah, NJ: Erlbaum.

Pennebaker, J. W., & Ireland, M. (2008). Analyzing words to understand literature. In J. Auracher & W. van Peer (Eds.), *New beginnings in literary studies* (pp. 24–48). Newcastle, UK: Cambridge Scholars Publishing.

Pennebaker, J. W., Kiecolt-Glaser, J., & Glaser, R. (1988). Disclosure of traumas and immune function: Health implications for psychotherapy. *Journal of Consulting and Clinical Psychology, 56,* 239–245.

Pennebaker, J. W., & King, L. A. (1999). Linguistic styles: Language use as an individual difference. *Journal of Personality and Social Psychology, 77,* 1296–1312.

Pennebaker, J. W., & Lay, T. C. (2002). Language use and personality during crises: Analyses of Mayor Rudolph Giuliani's press conferences. *Journal of Research in Personality, 36,* 271–282.

Pennebaker, J. W., Mayne, T. J., & Francis, M. E. (1997). Linguistic predictors of adaptive bereavement. *Journal of Personality and Social Psychology, 72,* 863–871.

Pennebaker, J. W., Mehl, M. R., & Niederhoffer, K. (2003). Psychological aspects of natural language use: Our words, our selves. *Annual Review of Psychology, 54,* 547–577.

Pennebaker, J. W. & Stone, L. D. (2003). Words of wisdom: Language use over the lifespan. *Journal of Personality and Social Psychology, 85,* 291–301.

Petrie, K. P., Booth, R. J., & Pennebaker, J. W. (1998). The immunological effects of thought suppression. *Journal of Personality and Social Psychology, 75,* 1264–1272.

Ricard, M., Girouard, P. C., & Decarie, T. G. (1999). Personal pronouns and perspective taking in toddlers. *Journal of Child Language, 26,* 681–697.

Rimé, B. (1995). Mental rumination, social sharing, and the recovery from emotional exposure. In J. W. Pennebaker (Ed.), *Emotion, disclosure, and health* (pp. 271–291). Washington, DC: American Psychological Association.

Rude, S. S., Gortner, E. M., & Pennebaker, J. W. (2004). Language use of depressed and depression-vulnerable college students. *Cognition and Emotion, 18,* 1121–1133.

Salovey, P., Rothman, A. J., & Rodin, J. (1998). Health behavior. In D. Gilbert, S. Fiske, & G. Lindzey (Eds.), *Handbook of social psychology* (Vol. 2, 4th ed., pp. 633–683). Boston: McGraw-Hill.

Smyth, J. M. (1998). Written emotional expression: Effect sizes, outcome types, and moderating variables. *Journal of Consulting and Clinical Psychology, 66,* 174–184.

*Smyth, J. M., True, N., & Souto, J. (2001). Effects of writing about traumatic experiences: The necessity for narrative structuring. *Journal of Social and Clinical Psychology, 20,* 161–172.

Stirman, S. W., & Pennebaker, J. W. (2001). Word use in the poetry of suicidal and non-suicidal poets. *Psychosomatic Medicine, 63,* 517–522.

Traue, H. C., & Deighton, R. (1999). Inhibition, disclosure, and health: Don't simply slash the Gordian knot. *Advances in Mind–Body Medicine, 15,* 184–193.

Weintraub, W. (1981). *Verbal behavior: Adaptation and psychopathology.* New York: Springer.

Wegner, D. M. (1994). Ironic processes of mental control. *Psychological Review, 101,* 34–52.

Wegner, D. M., Lane, J. D., & Dimitri, S. (1994). The allure of secret relationships. *Journal of Personality and Social Psychology, 66,* 287–300.

Wortman, C. B., & Silver, R. C. (1989). The myths of coping with loss. *Journal of Consulting and Clinical Psychology, 57,* 349–357.

Zeigarnik, B. (1927/1938). On finished and unfinished tasks. In W. D. Ellis (Ed.), *A source book of Gestalt psychology* (pp. 300–314). London: Routledge and Kegan Paul.

Benefit-Finding and Growth

Suzanne C. Lechner, Howard Tennen, *and* Glenn Affleck

Abstract

Following adverse life events, many people report positive outcomes, sometimes referred to as benefit finding and growth (or BFG). Some people experience a new appreciation of their own strength and resilience or an increased self-reliance. Others describe strengthened relationships and increased closeness with others, greater compassion or altruism, a heightened sense of the fragility of life, or changes in life philosophies and spirituality. This chapter addresses several unresolved issues in the study of BFG, including whether an individual's ability to find benefits in a stressful or traumatic life event is an important contributor to subsequent quality of life and adjustment; how BFG perceptions develop and are maintained over time; shortcomings of current indicators purporting to measure benefits in the context of adversity; future directions for research in this area; and clinical applications of research in BFG. In this chapter, we take a new look at the BFG literature, revisit concerns identified in the first edition of this Handbook, and raise new concerns regarding how BFG is currently assessed and translated into new treatments. We caution against the rush to create interventions to enhance BFG in light of the potential detrimental effects on victimized individuals created by our societal emphasis on the power of positive thinking.

Keywords: benefit finding, positive life change, posttraumatic growth, stress-related growth, thriving

Following adverse life events, many people report positive outcomes, sometimes referred to as benefit finding and growth (or BFG). For example, a man who had a heart attack now finds himself adopting a healthy lifestyle in terms of eating, exercise, and stress level, and spending more time with his family, all of which he attributes to his life-threatening wake-up call. An older woman diagnosed with breast cancer begins to notice the love and concern of her neighbors who take her to chemotherapy appointments and bring over dinner a few nights a week. She speaks to her daughter much more frequently now, and their conversations hold a depth that they had never shared before.

In its most basic sense, we are referring to an individual's perception that major changes have occurred as a result of a challenging life event. This is akin to the adage "When life hands you lemons, make lemonade." These changes may take the form

of transformations in an individual's perceptions of the self, the self in relation to others, and changes in life philosophy (Tedeschi, Park, & Calhoun, 1998). Thus, individuals may report a new appreciation of their own strength and resilience, an increased sense of self-reliance, and a keener awareness of their own vulnerability. Some people notice strengthened relationships and increased closeness with others, especially family and friends, whereas others report becoming more compassionate or altruistic. Following a traumatic event, some individuals describe a heightened sense of the preciousness and fragility of life. Life philosophies also may change. An enhanced appreciation of the little things in life and redirected priorities are commonly cited. Finally, some individuals note a new openness to spiritual or religious experiences. Although the particular benefits people find are idiosyncratic, most benefits reported following adversity can be categorized in the areas of relating to others, new life possibilities, personal strength, appreciation of life, and spiritual/religious change (Tedeschi & Calhoun, 1995). Finally, BFG is by no means rare, with estimates between 40% (Bower, Kemeny, Taylor, & Fahey, 1998) and 90% (McMillen, Smith, & Fisher, 1997) of individuals facing adversity reporting benefits.

Interest in the ways individuals grow or change following stressful life experiences has paralleled a broader interest in the positive aspects of human functioning. By focusing on well-being instead of pathology, study of BFG has articulated people's positive adaptation to stressful, traumatic, and negative life events. There are now reports of benefits resulting from various illnesses such as cancer, myocardial infarction and heart disease, HIV/AIDS, multiple sclerosis, fibromyalgia, severe acute respiratory syndrome (SARS), schizophrenia, chemical dependency, lower limb amputation, acquired brain injury, rheumatoid arthritis, psoriasis, and lupus. Adults, college students, adolescents, and children have reported benefits after negative life experiences. Individuals who were bereaved, victims of terror incidents, combat veterans, child survivors of the holocaust, survivors of childhood sexual abuse, victims of violence and trauma victims of natural disasters, former refugees and displaced people, political prisoners, parents who have lost a child to illness or violent death, caregivers of ill persons, therapists after disaster work or psychotherapy, and people who have experienced romantic relationship breakups have described to investigators a number of ways in which they feel they have grown or changed in positive ways as a result of their experience.

In fact, more than 300 articles related to BFG have been published, representing theoretical formulations and investigations across several disciplines. This chapter is not meant as a comprehensive literature review. Rather, we raise what we consider important issues and pose questions to guide future research. In this chapter, we take a new look at the BFG literature, revisit concerns identified in the first edition of this Handbook, and raise new concerns regarding how BFG is currently assessed.

Historical Roots

The study of positive changes following serious illness, trauma, and other life challenges has added a new dimension to our understanding of how people adapt to stressful encounters. Indeed, the stress and coping literature would otherwise be incomplete. In early interview studies (e.g., Affleck, Tennen, Croog, & Levine, 1987; Thompson, 1985), seriously ill individuals and trauma victims told investigators that positive changes co-occurred with negative changes in the aftermath of their stressful life encounters. Prior to these studies, most of the literature addressed the negative sequelae of trauma and illness. Although the seminal BFG studies pre-date positive psychology, this line of inquiry has been fueled by positive psychology's emphasis on thriving and human strengths and by cross-disciplinary investigations that have brought fresh ideas to our understanding of BFG. Investigators soon undertook the challenge of developing measures to assess posttraumatic growth (Tedeschi & Calhoun, 1995), stress-related growth (Park, Cohen, & Murch, 1996), adversarial growth (Joseph et al., 2005), and benefit finding (e.g., Antoni et al., 2001; Tomich & Helgeson, 2004), and there are now numerous BFG questionnaires.

Research in this area has been plagued by a lack of uniformity in terminology and measurement, resulting in a fragmented understanding of BFG. "Posttraumatic growth," "benefit finding," and "stress-related growth" are the most commonly used terms. However, the constructs of "adversarial growth," "found meaning," "experienced meaning," "meaning as outcome," "cognitive adaptation," "perceived benefits," "self-transcendence," "positive sequelae," and "thriving" show significant conceptual and measurement overlap with posttraumatic growth, benefit finding, and stress-related growth (Andrykowski, Brady, & Hunt, 1993; Carver, 1998; Collins, Taylor, & Skokan, 1990; Coward, 1991; Fife, 1994; Lewis, 1989; Linley & Joseph, 2005; Park et al., 1996; Park & Folkman, 1997; Taylor, 1983; Taylor, Lichtman, & Wood, 1984; Tedeschi & Calhoun, 1995; Thompson & Janigian, 1988). For clarity, we refer to BFG as the constellation of positive changes that are frequently reported following trauma, illness, or major stressful life events.

Investigators and theorists have recently offered distinctions among these terms that have not yet been reflected in the literature (Aldwin, 2005). Posttraumatic growth, for example, is increasingly considered by investigators to be wholly transformative and reflecting wisdom and a pervasive cognitive shift that is gained by relatively few of those who report positive changes following adversity. Benefit finding and stress-related growth, on the other hand, are constructs that capture lifestyle and behavior change and shifts in perception. Despite these emerging conceptual distinctions, extant measures of these constructs show significant overlap, each tapping posttraumatic growth, benefit finding, and stress-related growth. In one attempt to disentangle these related constructs, Sears, Stanton, and Danoff-Burg (2003) found that benefit finding, posttraumatic growth, and positive reappraisal coping had different predictors, which suggested that these were overlapping yet related concepts.

We also differentiate BFG from positive thinking and optimism. Although related to these constructs, BFG is purported to capture a different aspect of psychological functioning. In the same breath that a woman tells us that her rape showed her how strong and resilient she is, she also can describe her nightmares and sense of violation. BFG is not equivalent to dispositional optimism (Scheier & Carver, 1985). Whereas optimists view all aspects of their future through a lens of possibilities and positive expectations, individuals who find benefit in adversity tend to focus more narrowly on changes related to their adverse circumstances.

Despite people's conviction regarding the growth or benefits they have experienced from facing a threatening circumstance, and although we are confident that BFG is a phenomenon worthy of continued study, there is reason to be cautious in accepting these reports at face value, as some people may feel the need to present a socially desirable response and consequently report growth even when it has not occurred. Park and Lechner (2006) refer to this as "pseudogrowth." Ironically, many cases of pseudogrowth may occur in response to enthusiastic references to BFG in the lay literature and on professional Web sites, which subtly encourage victimized individuals to entertain the possibility of benefits, gains, or positive transformation.

Is BFG a Desirable Outcome or Associated with Known Desirable Outcomes?

Is an individual's ability to find benefits an important contributor to subsequent quality of life and adjustment (Park & Folkman, 1997)? Recent reviews have revealed significant inconsistencies across studies in the association between BFG and adjustment indicators. In their review of the literature examining BFG among individuals living with cancer, Stanton, Bower, and Low (2006) found that whereas some studies have shown that BFG is associated with lower levels of distress (Fife, 1995; Katz, Flasher, Cacciapaglia, & Nelson, 2001; Vickberg, Bovbjerg, DuHamel, Currie, & Redd, 2000;

Vickberg et al., 2001), higher self-esteem, less anxiety (Lewis, 1989), greater life satisfaction, and more optimistic estimates of future life satisfaction (Curbow, Somerfield, Baker, Wingard, & Legro, 1993) and other positive adjustment indices (Carver & Antoni, 2004; Coward, 1991; Petrie, Buick, Weinman, & Booth, 1999; Shapiro et al., 2001), other studies have found no relationship between BFG and adaptational outcomes (e.g., Antoni et al., 2001) or even a negative relationship (Tomich & Helgeson, 2004). Similarly, in their review of the literature on BFG, Zoellner and Maercker (2006) concluded that the literature "reveals a rather irritating and inconclusive picture" (p. 635) of the adaptive significance of BFG.

There are at least three explanations for these apparent inconsistencies in the association between BFG and indicators of positive adjustment. One explanation is that the relationship is neither linear nor unidirectional. Tedeschi and Calhoun (2004) have theorized that the relationship between BFG and well-being may be reciprocal and bidirectional. Some distress may be necessary to initiate the search for meaning, and finding benefits may serve to lower distress. Likewise, BFG and adjustment may be independent and unrelated during certain phases of a stressful encounter and more salient during other phases. Simple correlations, as have been used in numerous studies in the literature, cannot address such nuanced relationships. In fact, recent evidence indicates that the relationship may be quadratic for certain adjustment outcomes (an inverted U-shaped curve) in which persons with very low levels of distress and very high levels of distress show low levels of benefit finding (Lechner, Carver, Antoni, Weaver, & Phillips, 2006). These findings are consistent with BFG theory in that individuals who are not at all distressed may lack the motivation to search for meaning and thereby find benefits, and individuals experiencing very high distress levels may be precluded from finding meaning due to the extent of their suffering.

A second explanation for the somewhat inconsistent associations obtained between BFG and adjustment is that unmeasured moderators are at work. Future research will be challenged to identify and test conceptually relevant moderators of the BFG–adjustment relationship. A third explanation, proposed recently by Zoellner and Maercker (2006), offers a two-component model of BFG: a self-transcending or constructive side (as described by Tedeschi & Calhoun, 1995) and an illusory, self-deceptive, and potentially dysfunctional side.

According to Zoellner and Maercker's (2006) Janus-face model, the two components are coexisting and have different trajectories and different relationships with adjustment. They speculate that inconsistencies in the empirical literature linking BFG and adjustment are due, at least in part, to these two BFG components working simultaneously.

Benefit Finding and Growth: Still in Search of a Conceptual Home

In the first edition of this Handbook, Tennen and Affleck (2002) maintained that BFG needed first and foremost a conceptual home. This assertion is as true today as it was at that time. Theorists originally viewed victims' reports of benefits or gains as a positive illusory process (e.g., Taylor, 1983). Over the years this view has been supplanted by three other possibilities: (a) BFG is a selective appraisal; (b) BFG is a coping strategy; and (c) BFG reflects a genuine positive change that results from facing adversity.

After reviewing the literature, Tennen and Affleck (2002) concluded that there was little empirical support for the first two possibilities. Although finding benefits *may* for some individuals reflect a selective evaluation, there is still no evidence in the research literature that participants are making such evaluations when they report benefits in adversity. Similarly, while BFG *can* be a coping strategy, it has only rarely been measured in a way that would warrant such an inference.

After concluding that BFG as examined in the psychological literature is neither a selective evaluation nor a coping strategy, Tennen and Affleck (2002) entertained several alternative views. Their first alternative was that BFG represented a personality characteristic. McAdams (1993) has demonstrated that some individuals characteristically provide narratives in which misfortune or life tragedy contains a positive aspect or leads to a positive outcome. The second alternative explanation is that it represents a way in which people explain their characteristic hedonic level (Brickman, Coates, & Janoff-Bulman, 1978). Tennen and Affleck offer the example of the well-adjusted extrovert who feels relatively happy despite a recent life crisis. To make sense of her continued positive emotional state—which does not fit the stereotype of someone in the aftermath of crisis—she attributes it to what may seem like a newfound capacity to appreciate life's small pleasures or to feel grateful for past good fortune (McCrae, personal communication, May, 1996). Inherent in this interpretation of BFG is

that people hold personal theories regarding how they should be responding to adversity. A third explanation involves people's implicit theories of consistency and change. By its very nature, reporting benefits requires an individual to compare her current status on a particular dimension with her status on the same dimension prior to the event. Ross (1989) has argued convincingly that an exaggeration of positive change will occur when a person's theory of change leads him or her to anticipate such change when little or no change has actually occurred.

The fourth alternative interpretation of BFG offered by Tennen and Affleck (2002) is that BFG may represent a downward temporal comparison (Albert, 1977). Although individuals are inclined to evaluate the self as stable, when efforts to reduce negative discrepancies between the past and the present are unsuccessful, they will then construct positive changes, including subjective evidence of maturation, progress, and growth (Klauer, Ferring, & Filipp, 1998).

Finally, Tennen, and Affleck (2002) noted that the literature on posttraumatic growth (Tedeschi & Calhoun, 1995) and thriving (Epel, McEwen, & Ickovics, 1998) approaches BFG not as a cognitive construction designed to protect threatened assumptions nor as the product of implicit theories of change or a personality characteristic but rather as an indicator of genuine positive change.

In view of these compelling alternative conceptualizations of BFG, Tennen and Affleck (2002) urged positive psychology investigators to focus on formulating and evaluating various conceptualizations of BFG before rushing to improve its measurement. The conceptual challenges, they asserted, may be even more daunting than the methodological challenges facing this area of investigation. However, after reviewing the past 6 years of investigation, we conclude that the measurement of BFG is at least as challenging as its conceptualization. We now turn to what we consider serious flaws in the way we currently measure BFG.

The Measurement Quagmire: Do BFG Scales Measure Actual Benefits?

The upsurge in research on BFG has been hastened in large part by the availability of scales purporting to measure benefits in the context of adversity. Among the more widely used BFG scales are the Posttraumatic Growth Inventory (Tedeschi & Calhoun, 1996), the Stress-Related Growth Scale (Park et al., 1996), the Changes in Outlook Questionnaire (Joseph et al., 2005), and the

Benefit-Finding Scale (BFS; Tomich & Helgeson, 2004; see also Carver & Antoni, 2004). These questionnaires are easy to administer and demonstrate good internal consistency. They also have excellent face validity, and for this reason they are readily accepted by research participants, many of whom find that the scale items map well onto their personal experience. Similarly, BFG measured by interview has strong face validity. For example, Affleck, Tennen, Croog, and Levine (1987) and Affleck and Tennen (1991) asked their research participants, who had very recently experienced a first heart attack or had a newborn who required intensive care: "As difficult as it's been, have there been any benefits or gains that wouldn't have occurred if you hadn't experienced a heart attack/had a newborn in the NICU?" Armed with scales that have good psychometrics and interview questions that seemingly measure BFG in a straightforward manner, investigators have used these measures to examine BFG's nomological network (Cronbach & Meehl, 1955).

Although research participants readily complete BFG scales and respond easily to interview questions, an examination of scale items raises serious concerns as to whether people can accurately portray the benefits or growth they experienced. Table 60.1 presents sample items from the BFS (Mohr et al., 1999) and the Benefit-Finding Scale for Breast Cancer (BFSBC; Tomich & Helgeson, 2004) along with instructions to participants. Participants rate how much they have changed on each scale item as the result of the crisis they experienced. For

example, people are asked to share how much closer they feel to others as consequence of their crisis. Similarly, the BFSBC requires participants to evaluate how much they experienced each of the personal changes depicted in the scale as a result of their breast cancer. For example, someone completing this scale is asked to rate how much more patient she is with others as an upshot of her breast cancer.

Following Tennen and Affleck (2008) and Ford, Tennen, and Albert (2008), we find it instructive to consider the mental operations required to provide ratings for BFS and BFSBC items. A response to each scale item requires the respondent to engage in five assessments. She or he must (a) evaluate her or his current standing on the dimension described in the item, for example, a sense of closeness to others; (b) recall her or his previous standing on the same dimension; (c) compare the current and previous standings; (d) assess the degree of change; and (e) determine how much of that change can be attributed to the traumatic event or stressful encounter. By engaging in these five steps, the participant can respond to each scale item. It is tempting to argue that our research participants do not actually make such evaluations and calculations, but rather they offer global impressions of personal change. Yet this line of reasoning easily becomes a slippery slope. If people simply offer their global impressions of change, they are not reporting benefits of their threatening encounter, which is what these scales seek to measure. In other words, the best we can hope for is that individuals who complete scales measuring benefits and growth are actually engaging in the five appraisals, recollections, comparisons, and determinations we propose. We assert that people *cannot* accurately generate or manipulate the information required by currently available questionnaire measures to faithfully report benefits that result from threatening encounters (see Tennen & Affleck, 2008, for a detailed rationale). If we are correct, this represents a rather daunting measurement challenge to investigators studying BFG.

Directions for Future Research

In this chapter, we have addressed some key issues related to the study of BFG, each of which has implications for future research. We suggest that there are three main areas that need to be addressed in order to move the field forward.

First, there are plausible alternatives to the theory that people change in positive ways as a direct result of threatening encounters. Adequate tests of these

Table 60.1 Instructions and sample Benefit-Finding Scale (BFS; Mohr et al., 1999) and Benefit-Finding for Breast Cancer Scale (BFBCS; Tomich & Helgeson, 2004) items

BFS	BFBCS
As a result of experiencing...	Having had breast cancer has...
I have become more respectful of others	...made me more grateful for each day
I am more compassionate toward others	...led me to be more accepting of things
I am more motivated to succeed	...brought my family closer together
...has helped me to be closer to my family	...taught me to be patient
I keep in better touch with my family	...made me more productive

alternatives will not be found in cross-sectional study designs, still the mainstay of the BFG literature. Even longitudinal designs are limiting when they initiate measurement at an arbitrary time and then repeat measurements at arbitrary intervals. True prospective designs, while challenging to conduct, offer the best possibility of pitting alternative conceptualizations of BFG and its temporal trajectory. Researchers who identify a starting time frame during which BFG should begin to develop, and then conduct follow-up assessments within meaningful frames of time that are tailored to the type of trauma being studied, will be able to accurately measure and quantify changes in BFG. In so doing, we can then compare our current theories of BFG to other plausible alternative explanations.

Second, we have argued that existing questionnaire and interview BFG measures cannot assess BFG adequately. We urge investigators to develop measures that do not rely on retrospection, on comparing one's current and previous status on various dimensions, on subjective estimates of change, or on attributions to life events of any change one believes she or he has experienced. We suspect that measures fulfilling these criteria will look very different from the BFG measures that currently populate the literature.

Finally, although there is evidence from other cultures that BFG is not a purely Judeo-Christian phenomenon, cultural and ethnic differences in BFG need to be studied more fully. Although several studies conducted in China, Bosnia, and among various cultural groups that comprise Western society (African American, Hispanic) show similar rates and levels of BFG, we cannot assume that BFG in other cultures shares the same determinants or consequences as in Western cultures. To do so would obscure undoubtedly valuable information that could be generated by understanding the ways in which other cultures make sense of life's significant challenges and tragedies.

Interventions to Initiate or Enhance Benefit Finding and Growth?

Should clinicians develop and test interventions to initiate or augment BFG? Calhoun and Tedeschi (2001) dedicated an entire volume to this question. In brief, although there are interventions that may enhance BFG and lead to clinically meaningful outcomes among trauma survivors, these interventions have been applied in the context of a single client and single therapist. For several reasons, we caution against group-based and manualized interventions.

First, based on current knowledge, group-based interventions are premature. A cognitive-behavioral stress management intervention for women with early stage breast cancer increased BFG (Antoni et al., 2006), but the mechanisms of this intervention effect are unknown. More importantly, there are potential risks to clients. It was not long ago that Siegel's (1986) approach to the power of positive thinking was misapplied. During a time of heightened media attention on cancer, combined with societal beliefs that the mind could cause illness and the natural inclination of many people to try to better understand why bad events befall good people, some erroneously concluded that people cause their own cancer by "not being positive." This, in turn, signaled to cancer patients that they should feel responsible for their cancer and placed great pressure on individuals with cancer to feel positive even when they were feeling other than positive emotions. In a similar way, BFG interventions have the potential to contribute to a "tyranny of positive thinking" (Holland & Lewis, 2000), which could become an unintended legacy of positive psychology. Particularly in view of the clearly mixed findings linking BFG and positive adaptation, we urge clinicians to respect BFG when emerging spontaneously, while constraining their enthusiasm for inducing BFG among clients.

Concluding Thoughts

Theory and research on BFG has flourished in recent years. This theoretical and empirical attention has enhanced our understanding of BFG and provides new directions for future research. Yet progress has been slow, coming in fits and starts. There remain gaps in our theoretical formulations of BFG and equally troubling limitations in our current assessment strategies, which have confused realistic assessment with psychometric regalia. We hope that in the third edition of this Handbook we can report that theoretical formulations of BFG have gained great precision, that measurement no longer relies on retrospection, participants' personal theories of change, or on their subjective estimates of change, and that investigators have all but abandoned cross-sectional and arbitrary longitudinal study designs in favor of prospective inquiry.

Questions for Future Research

1. Is an individual's ability to find benefits in adversity an important contributor to subsequent quality of life and adjustment?

2. What are the determinants and consequences of the ways in which individuals in other cultures make sense of life's significant challenges and tragedies?

3. How can clinicians best integrate the BFG literature into practice?

Acknowledgment

The authors are grateful to Jessica Tocco for her assistance with editing and manuscript preparation.

References

Affleck, G., & Tennen, H. (1991). Appraisal and coping predictors of mother and child outcomes after newborn intensive care. *Journal of Social and Clinical Psychology, 10*, 424–447.

Affleck, G., Tennen, H., Croog, S., & Levine, S. (1987). Causal attribution, perceived benefits, and morbidity after a heart attack: An 8-year study. *Journal of Consulting and Clinical Psychology, 55*, 29–35.

Albert, S. (1977). Temporal comparison theory. *Psychological Review, 84*, 485–503.

Aldwin, C. M., Antoni, M. H., Bower, J. E., Carver, C. S., Helgeson, V. S., Lechner, S. C., et al. (2005). The state of the science in benefit finding research in health psychology. In S. C. Lechner (Chair), *Health psychology perspectives on positive life changes: Benefit finding and growth following illness.* Symposium conducted at the meeting of Health Psychology Perspectives, Storrs, CT.

Andrykowski, M. A., Brady, M. J., & Hunt, J. (1993). Positive psychosocial adjustment in potential bone marrow transplant recipients: Cancer as a psychosocial transition. *Psychooncology, 2*, 261–276.

Antoni, M. H., Lechner, S. C., Kazi, A., Wimberly, S. R., Sifre, T., Urcuyo, K. R., et al. (2006). How stress management improves quality of life after treatment for breast cancer. *Journal of Consulting and Clinical Psychology, 74*, 1143–1152.

Antoni, M. H., Lehman, J. M., Kilbourn, K. M., Boyers, A. E., Culver, J. L., Alferi, S. M., et al. (2001). Cognitive-behavioral stress management intervention decreases the prevalence of depression and enhances benefit finding among women under treatment for early-stage breast cancer. *Health Psychology, 20*, 20–32.

Bower, J. E., Kemeny, M. E., Taylor, S. E., & Fahey, J. L. (1998). Cognitive processing, discovery of meaning, CD 4 decline, and AIDS-related mortality among bereaved HIV-seropositive men. *Journal of Consulting and Clinical Psychology, 66*, 979–986.

Brickman, P., Coates, D., & Janoff-Bulman, R. (1978). Lottery winners and accident victims: Is happiness relative? *Journal of Personality and Social Psychology, 36*, 917–927.

Calhoun, L. G., & Tedeschi, R. G. (2001). Posttraumatic growth: The positive lessons of loss. In R. A. Neimeyer (Ed.), *Meaning reconstruction & the experience of loss* (pp. 157–172). Washington, DC: American Psychological Association.

Carver, C. S. (1998). Resilience and thriving: Issues, models, and linkages. *Journal of Social Issues, 54*, 245–266.

Carver, C. S., & Antoni, M. H. (2004). Finding benefit in breast cancer during the year after diagnosis predicts better adjustment 5 to 8 years after diagnosis. *Health Psychology, 23*, 595–598.

Collins, R. L., Taylor, S. E., & Skokan, L. A. (1990). A better world or a shattered vision? Changes in life perspectives following victimization. *Social Cognition, 8*, 263–285.

Coward, D. D. (1991). Self-transcendence and emotional well-being in women with advanced breast cancer. *Oncology Nursing Forum, 18*, 857–863.

Cronbach, L. J., & Meehl, P. E. (1955). Construct validity in psychological tests. *Psychological Bulletin, 52*, 281–302.

Curbow, B., Somerfield, M. R., Baker, F., Wingard, J. R., & Legro, M. W. (1993). Personal changes, dispositional optimism, and psychological adjustment to bone marrow transplantation. *Journal of Behavioral Medicine, 16*, 423–443.

Epel, E. S., McEwen, B. S., & Ickovics, J. R. (1998). Embodying psychological thriving: Physical thriving in response to stress. *Journal of Social Issues, 54*, 301–322.

Fife, B. L. (1994). The conceptualization of meaning in illness. *Social Science and Medicine, 38*, 309–316.

Fife, B. L. (1995). The measurement of meaning in illness. *Social Science and Medicine, 40*, 1021–1028.

Ford, J. D., Tennen, H., & Albert, D. (2008). A contrarian view of growth following adversity. In S. Joseph & P. A. Linley (Eds.), *Trauma, recovery and growth: Positive psychological perspectives on posttraumatic stress* (pp. 297–324). Hoboken, NJ: Wiley.

Holland, J. C., & Lewis, S. (2000). *The human side of cancer: Living with hope and coping with uncertainty.* New York: Harper Collins.

Joseph, S., Linley, P. A., Andrews, L., Harris, G., Howle, B., Woodward, C., et al. (2005). Assessing positive and negative changes in the aftermath of adversity: Psychometric evaluation of the Changes in Outlook Questionnaire. *Psychological Assessment, 17*, 70–80.

Katz, R. C., Flasher, L., Cacciapaglia, H., & Nelson, S. (2001). The psychosocial impact of cancer and lupus: A cross validation study that extends the generality of "benefit finding" in patients with chronic disease. *Journal of Behavioral Medicine, 24*, 561–571.

Klauer, T., Ferring, D., & Filipp, S. H. (1998). "Still stable after all this . . . ?": Temporal comparison in coping with severe and chronic disease. *International Journal of Behavioral Development, 22*, 339–355.

Lechner, S. C., Carver, C. S., Antoni, M. H., Weaver, K. E., & Phillips, K. M. (2006). Curvilinear associations between benefit finding and psychosocial adjustment to breast cancer. *Journal of Consulting and Clinical Psychology, 74*, 828–840.

Lewis, F. M. (1989). Attributions of control, experienced meaning, and psychosocial well-being in patients with advanced cancer. *Journal of Psychosocial Oncology, 7*, 105–119.

Linley, P. A., & Joseph, S. (2005). The human capacity for growth through adversity. *American Psychologist, 60*, 262–264.

McAdams, D. P. (1993). *The stories we live by: Personal myths and the making of the self.* New York: William Morrow.

McMillen, J. C., Smith, E. M., & Fisher, R. H. (1997). Perceived benefit and mental health after three types of disaster. *Journal of Consulting and Clinical Psychology, 65*, 733–739.

Mohr, D. C., Dick, L. P., Russo, D., Pinn, J., Boudewyn, A. C., Likosky, W., et al. (1999). The psychosocial impact of multiple sclerosis: Exploring the patient's perspective. *Health Psychology, 18*, 376–382.

Park, C. L., Cohen, L. H., & Murch, R. L. (1996). Assessment and prediction of stress-related growth. *Journal of Personality, 64*, 71–105.

Park, C. L., & Folkman, S. (1997). Meaning in the context of stress and coping. *Review of General Psychology, 1*, 115–144.

Park, C. L., & Lechner, S. C. (2006). Measurement issues in assessing growth following stressful life experiences. In L. G. Calhoun & R. G. Tedeschi (Eds.), *Handbook of posttraumatic growth: Research and practice* (pp. 47–67). Mahwah, NJ: Lawrence Erlbaum.

Petrie, K. J., Buick, D. L., Weinman, J., & Booth, R. J. (1999). Positive effects of illness reported by myocardial infarction and breast cancer patients. *Journal of Psychosomatic Research, 47*, 537–543.

Ross, M. (1989). Relation of implicit theories to the construction of personal histories. *Psychological Review, 96*, 341–357.

Scheier, M. F., & Carver, C. S. (1985). Optimism, coping, and health: Assessment and implications of generalized outcome expectancies. *Health Psychology, 4*, 219–247.

Sears, S. R., Stanton, A. L., & Danoff-Burg, S. (2003). The yellow brick road and the emerald city: Benefit finding, positive reappraisal coping and posttraumatic growth in women with early-stage breast cancer. *Health Psychology, 22*, 487–497.

Shapiro, S. L., Lopez, A. M., Schwartz, G. E., Bootzin, R., Figueredo, A. J., Braden, C. J., et al. (2001). Quality of life and breast cancer: Relationship to psychosocial variables. *Journal of Clinical Psychology, 57*, 501–519.

Siegel, B. S. (1986). *Love, medicine, and miracles.* New York: Harper & Row.

Stanton, A. L., Bower, J. E., & Low, C. A. (2006). Posttraumatic growth after cancer. In L. G. Calhoun & R. G. Tedeschi (Eds.), *Handbook of posttraumatic growth: Research and practice* (pp. 138–175). Mahwah, NJ: Lawrence Erlbaum.

Taylor, S. E. (1983). Adjustment to threatening events: A theory of cognitive adaptation. *American Psychologist, 38*, 1161–1173.

Taylor, S. E., Lichtman, R. R., & Wood, J. V. (1984). Attributions, beliefs about control, and adjustment to breast cancer. *Journal of personality and social psychology, 46*, 489–502.

Tedeschi, R. G., & Calhoun, L. G. (1995). *Trauma & transformation: Growing in the aftermath of suffering.* Thousand Oaks, CA: Sage.

Tedeschi, R. G., & Calhoun, L. G. (1996). The Posttraumatic Growth Inventory: Measuring the positive legacy of trauma. *Journal of Traumatic Stress, 9*, 455–472.

Tedeschi, R. G., & Calhoun, L. G. (2004). Posttraumatic growth: Conceptual foundations and empirical evidence. *Psychological Inquiry, 15*, 1–18.

Tedeschi, R. G., Park, C. L., & Calhoun, L. G. (Eds.). (1998). *Posttraumatic growth: Positive changes in the aftermath of crisis.* Mahwah, NJ: Lawrence Erlbaum.

Tennen, H., & Affleck, G. (2002). Benefit-finding and benefit-reminding. In S. J. Lopez & C. R. Snyder (Eds.), *Handbook of positive psychology* (pp. 584–597). New York: Oxford University Press.

Tennen, H., & Affleck, G. (2008). Assessing positive life change: In search of meticulous methods. In C. Park, S. Lechner, A. Stanton, & M. Antoni (Eds.), *Medical illness and positive life change: Can crisis lead to personal transformation?* (pp. 31– 49) Washington, DC: APA Press.

Thompson, S. C. (1985). Finding positive meaning in a stressful event and coping. *Basic and Applied Social Psychology, 6*, 279–295.

Thompson, S. C., & Janigian, A. S. (1988). Life schemes: A framework for understanding the search for meaning. *Journal of Social and Clinical Psychology, 7*, 260–280.

Tomich, P. L., & Helgeson, V. S. (2004). Is finding something good in the bad always good? Benefit finding among women with breast cancer. *Health Psychology, 23*, 16–23.

Vickberg, S. M., Bovbjerg, D. H., DuHamel, K. N., Currie, V., & Redd, W. H. (2000). Intrusive thoughts and psychological distress among breast cancer survivors: Global meaning as a possible protective factor. *Behavioral Medicine, 25*, 152–160.

Vickberg, S. M., DuHamel, K. N., Smith, M. Y., Manne, S. L., Winkel, G., Papadopoulos, E. B., et al. (2001). Global meaning and psychological adjustment among survivors of bone marrow transplant. *Psycho-Oncology, 10*, 29–39.

Zoellner, T. & Maercker, A. (2006). Posttraumatic growth in clinical psychology: A critical review and introduction of a two component model. *Clinical Psychology Review, 26*, 626–653.

Making Sense of Loss, Perceiving Benefits, and Posttraumatic Growth

Christopher G. Davis *and* Susan Nolen-Hoeksema

Abstract

Reports of personal growth following adversity are quite common, and a general model of the process has been proposed. However, very little research has been offered in support of the process model. We review studies that suggest that more than one process may be operating and propose that benefits should be distinguished from growth. Whereas benefits tend to be incidental and transient, personal growth emerges from a process of renegotiating goals and priorities and involves disengaging from or revising former core projects, activities, and strivings and initiating new ones that are intrinsically meaningful.

Keywords: benefits, loss, meaning, posttraumatic growth

> That which does not kill me makes me stronger.
> —*Nietzsche*

People often believe that adversity brings strength, understanding, and personal growth. But does it? In this chapter, we describe our program of research on people's attempts to see something positive in experiences of loss, tragedy, and other difficulties.

In our contribution to the first edition of the Handbook, we described our early research on meaning making and benefit finding in the context of loss (Nolen-Hoeksema & Davis, 2001). Drawing primarily from a longitudinal study on people coping with the loss of a terminally ill loved one (which we refer to as the "hospice study"), we observed that two meaning-making processes were evident: one centering on making sense of the loss and the second focusing on deriving benefit from the experience (Davis, Nolen-Hoeksema, & Larson, 1998; Nolen-Hoeksema & Davis, 2001). That research suggested that the two aspects of meaning seemed independent. They appeared to represent different issues to our bereaved participants, related to outcomes in different ways and at different times over the course of the longitudinal study, and were predicted by different pre-loss factors. Making sense of loss appeared to be more important early on in the process of coping (first

6 months) and was related to characteristics of the loss (e.g., age of the deceased) and whether the bereaved held religious or spiritual beliefs. In contrast, benefit finding appeared to be more strongly related to adjustment later in the coping process and was more strongly related to pre-loss optimism and a reflective coping style than to characteristics of the loss. It is important to note that although the relation of benefit finding to emotional adjustment increased in strength over the course of time, the proportion of the bereaved sample reporting benefits did not increase appreciably over time. People were as apt to report that they appreciated life more, were closer to their family, and so on at 6 months post loss as they were to report such things at 13 months post loss.

Finding Benefit versus Posttraumatic Growth

According to Tedeschi and Calhoun (2004), posttraumatic growth (PTG) is "positive psychological change experienced as a result of the struggle with highly challenging life circumstances" (p. 1; see also Joseph & Linley, 2005, for a similar definition). Tedeschi and Calhoun have described a model of the process, suggesting that PTG requires (a) a precipitating "seismic" disruption to one's assumptive world or sense of self; (b) the cognitive task of rebuilding a meaningful and coherent view of themselves and their world, referred to as a "schema reconstruction" process; (c) the recognition that one has changed for the better in some significant respect; and (d) an attribution of the positive change to the challenges one faced in the context of the precipitating event. That is, for growth to occur, the loss must be sufficiently disruptive to one's sense of identity, purpose, understanding of how the world "works"; one must process and reconcile the meaning of the loss for one's life, or more colloquially, "make sense of it"; recognize the changed self or worldview as an improvement over the former self or worldview; and finally, attribute the positive change to the event or one's working through of the experience. A burgeoning literature indicates that people who have experienced loss or other traumatic events often note that they come to see themselves (and others) in a different light, reevaluate their priorities, and come to appreciate life in a new way—and in this way are said to experience PTG (for reviews, see Helgeson, Reynolds, & Tomich, 2006, or Linley & Joseph, 2004).

Although the model suggested by Tedeschi and Calhoun (2004) is compelling, a number of authors have suggested that something akin to growth appears to occur by other means. McMillen (2004) has argued that positive changes sometimes have nothing to do with seismic disruption of worldviews, noting, for example, that positive changes in relationships can occur as one comes to share personal experiences with, and depend on, others; and that changes in goals can lead to the development of new skills and a new sense of personal mastery. Janoff-Bulman (2004), also responding to Tedeschi and Calhoun's model (2004), suggested three models of growth: one centering on changes in self-understanding that emerge from suffering; a second centering on changes in worldview, where one comes to realize that assumptions about control, the benevolence of others, and order are in need of revision; and a third centering on meaning making, reprioritizing, revaluing life, and spiritual change. Aldwin and Levenson (2004) have suggested that trauma is not required: people grow as they navigate their way through life stage transitions. Defining PTG broadly as any positive change has created a situation where almost anything could be considered "growth," and as a result, no single model of the process will be able to account for how growth might occur, what it means, and how it might be facilitated. By narrowing our definition of PTG, greater understanding of the process might ensue.

In our view, PTG should be distinguished from "benefits." Benefits are the common but relatively transient and incidental by-products of experiencing adversity and include such things as improved social relationships, minor or temporary adjustments to values and priorities, and the realization of new possibilities. We propose reserving the term PTG for significant sustained positive changes in major commitments and life goals.[1] One way of distinguishing significant changes from those less significant is that the former should be readily apparent in the behavior of the individual to the extent that the changes are evident to others in his or her social network. In this sense, PTG would include significant change in one's identity or life narrative (e.g., Neimeyer, 2005; Pals & McAdams, 2004) on the assumption that such changes are more than revisionist autobiography.

Unlike benefits, we suggest that PTG requires active processing of the meaning of a loss and time to set new goals and begin making significant progress toward those goals. It is not likely achieved overnight (but in rare instances might be, as described by Miller, 2004, in his account of quantum change) and not merely attributable to a reappraisal of the situation or one's past. In sum, we would argue that whereas the perception of benefits might be something that can occur relatively soon after trauma, and arise from a variety of processes, PTG—as we define it—follows the process outlined by Tedeschi and Calhoun, including a major shake-up of one's worldview or sense of self, significant cognitive processing of the meaning of the loss or trauma, and a new set of goals or commitments that change the meaning and direction of one's life. PTG is not simply adopting a revised set of priorities or a new philosophy of life but also engaging in and sustaining behavior directed toward achieving new goals.

---

[1] Elsewhere we have made a further distinction, noting a third category: insight or increased self-awareness. This category does not reflect change in what one does but rather a deeper understanding of self (Davis, 2008). It is also important to note that in our earlier work (Davis et al., 1998) we used the term "benefits" to refer generally to all perceived positive changes. Lacking evidence as to the degree to which these changes were significant, validated, and sustained, we opted to call such reported changes "benefits" rather than "growth."

Research on Processes of Growth and Benefit Finding

To assess whether statements of growth and benefits might reflect different processes, Davis, Wohl, and Verberg (2007) asked a group of people who had experienced the same traumatic loss to describe what they had lost, what they felt they had gained, whether their experience changed their philosophy of life, whether they felt anything positive had come of the experience, and other open-ended questions used to assess perceived growth and benefits. In an effort to determine whether schema reconstruction or sense making are critical components of the PTG process, participants also were asked whether they had searched to make sense of their loss, and whether they had been able to make some sense of it. We were interested in whether profiles of PTG would emerge consistent with the various models (Janoff-Bulman, 2004; Tedeschi & Calhoun, 2004; see also Joseph & Linley, 2005).

The participants in this study had experienced the traumatic loss of their husband, brother, son, or father in a mine explosion 8 years earlier. The explosion at the Westray mine in Plymouth, Nova Scotia, Canada, rocked the community in more ways than one. The event received overwhelming and sustained media attention, first as a calamity of national significance, and subsequently as a possible case of corporate crime, cover-up, and bureaucratic incompetence. The event became the subject of a public inquiry, a number of scholarly and popular books, a film documentary, and a dramatic play. Over 1,700 newspaper articles on the explosion and its aftermath were printed in the two daily papers of the province within the first 4 years (McMullan & Hinze, 1999). Criminal charges and civil lawsuits were launched against the company and its management, but for a variety of reasons none has been successful. For family members, the event was not merely a sudden, unexpected loss of their loved one, but also an ongoing saga of shattered beliefs, broken promises, deceit, and exploitation. As one family member noted,

> I might have been able to accept it if he had a car accident, or if he had cancer, or something, and dealt with it, but I'm not happy with it, no, and I probably never will be, because maybe there'll never be justice. I don't have any faith in it anymore.

Another said,

> If it was only the death of my husband, I could've been able to handle it, but it was the whole Westray story. It

was . . . just the circumstances, the public perception, . . .

Justice Peter Richard, commissioner of the public inquiry into the explosion, captured the essence of the situation when he described the explosion and its aftermath in the following terms:

> The tale that unfolds in the ensuing narrative is the Westray Story. It is a story of incompetence, of mismanagement, of bureaucratic bungling, of deceit, of ruthlessness, of cover-up, of apathy, of expediency, and of cynical indifference. . . . In all good common sense, [it] ought not to have occurred.
> (Richard, 1997)

Unlike many losses that have been the focus of research, this loss—in addition to being violent and untimely—struck many as senseless, unnecessary, and preventable, and therefore particularly likely to challenge assumptive worlds (Janoff-Bulman, 1992).

Davis et al. (2007) coded the responses of family members of the deceased miners for themes, and then assessed the degree to which each individual was similar to others in the study in terms of the themes he or she noted. The resulting similarity matrix was then subjected to a hierarchical clustering program. Of the three profiles (or clusters) derived, one clearly fit the PTG model suggested by Tedeschi and Calhoun (2004): People in this cluster tended to report losing a part of themselves, searching for and finding some meaning (typically noting that it was a source of personal growth), and describing positive changes (e.g., gained inner strength, learned about self).[2] As one person stated about her personal changes,

> I worked very hard to get it [something positive] . . . I think a lot of that was thinking of him and what he would want me to do . . . and I got a lot of strength from this . . . I don't think there is anything that I cannot handle, and I don't think that I had that before, and if I did, I don't think that I knew I had that inner strength.

A second cluster comprised people who were searching unsuccessfully to make sense of loss, and were perhaps as a consequence unable to perceive positive change or growth, reporting instead only negative changes and shattered assumptions. When asked how their loss experience affected their

---

[2] If one considers the three models suggested by Janoff-Bulman (2004), this group could be said to resemble the "suffering" model, yet central to the cluster is sense making, which is described as a feature of her third model.

philosophy of life, members of this cluster tended to report primarily negative changes. For example, one participant said, "I never thought that anybody could kill somebody and get away with it, so publicly... so my view on life has changed drastically."

The third cluster, however, was perhaps the most interesting. This cluster comprised individuals who reported that they did not search for meaning and reported modest "growth," primarily on dimensions of positive changes in philosophy of life (e.g., "It's made me value life more," "I try to live each day at a time and try to live it to its best"). It is debatable whether members of this group could be said to have experienced PTG. Although they described positive changes equivalent to items on common questionnaires designed to assess PTG, there was no sense that these participants had gone through a process of shattered self or worldview, searching for meaning, or rewriting one's life narrative. Moreover, the sense of growth that they did report was, for the most part, distinct from the sense of growth reported by those in the first cluster. They indicated that they "appreciate life more" and "live life in the present" but they did not report changes in how they see or understand themselves. Although we do not have any way of determining whether one set of changes is more substantial than the other, our sense is that the changes reported by the first cluster have more to do with a change in self, a "personal" growth. In contrast, the changes cited by the third cluster seemed more to reflect a refinement of a worldview, as suggested by the following statement by a member of this cluster in response to the question about whether he had searched for some meaning:

> I'm not a person who thinks there is a reason for everything that happens. I think it was just meant to be and I think maybe it would've been worse if it didn't happen.

These individuals seem to possess a worldview where it is accepted that bad things will happen, and thus one must focus one's life on living in the present.

In sum, the Westray study suggested some people fit a profile that features a "seismic" disruption of self, a search for purpose or meaning, and a sense that one has changed, matured, or developed significant personal qualities (such as strength, empathy, or coping abilities) that they attribute to having to cope with this experience. This profile is consistent with the model outlined by Tedeschi and Calhoun (2004). But others who report positive changes do not describe key features of the PTG model advocated by Tedeschi

and Calhoun. Not only do they indicate that they did not search for meaning, they also indicated somewhat different benefits or positive changes. Rather than describing changes in personal qualities, identity, or life purpose, they emphasized changes in attitude or values. Although these changes may be just as real as those reported by the first group, we suspect that they do not reflect a similar process and have different significance for the bereaved, themselves. We suggest that such changes not be considered instances of PTG.

The Meaning of Statements of Benefits and Growth

Both the mine explosion and the hospice studies suggest very clearly that sense making and benefit finding represented distinct, but conceptually related cognitive processes (see also Michael & Snyder, 2005). Whereas the sense that our hospice study participants drew from their loss primarily focused on the ways in which it could be understood within the assumptive worlds that they held (e.g., whether the death was perceived by the respondent to be predictable or just, or whether the patient accepted his or her imminent death), benefit finding in many cases seemed to us to involve a process of reflecting on one's own experience losing someone close.[3] The mine explosion study indicated that people attempt to make sense of their loss when the loss is perceived to be inconsistent with how or when these events are supposed to happen: either when the loss is off-time (e.g., the death of a young person), violent, or perceived to be unfair or unjust (see also Currier, Holland, & Neimeyer, 2006; Davis & Morgan, in press; Davis, Wortman, Lehman, & Silver, 2000). When such losses cannot be assimilated within existing knowledge structures or worldviews, people will either reject those aspects of the worldview in favor of one that can accommodate the meaning of the loss or downgrade the significance of the threat (e.g., "it could have been worse"). Successful meaning making under these conditions appears to involve developing a new worldview or understanding of self that guides or directs one toward new goals (e.g., a

---

[3] Although we maintain that the processes are distinct, this does not mean that efforts to make sense of loss may not be aided by perceiving benefits: For example, some participants in our studies have indicated that the sense they draw from their loss is that it has made them a better, more sensitive, or more focused person. What is suggested here is that perceiving benefits may result in less interest in making sense of loss.

commitment to help others, devote time to a cause, or take up new endeavors).

Perceiving benefit, however, appears to be largely unrelated to the nature of the loss, and consequently has little to do with making sense of the loss. In fact, a high proportion of people who experience any of a wide range of adversities report essentially the same set of benefits, and surprisingly soon after their adversity. Research suggests that the strongest peri-event predictors of perceived benefits are (a) retrospective ratings of the perceived stressfulness of the precipitating negative event (more stressful events are associated with greater perceived growth); and (b) personality traits (e.g., optimism; Davis et al., 1998; Helgeson et al., 2006; Park, Cohen, & Murch, 1996). The general lack of connection between statements of benefit and the precipitating event itself (aside from how stressful it was), and the finding that people who report various benefits often do not report higher scores on standard measures of conceptually similar constructs than those not reporting such benefits (e.g., Frazier & Kaler, 2006; Lehman et al., 1993), has led us to consider the possibility that some part of perceiving benefit might be better understood as a coping reaction to threat, and not necessarily to be taken at face value as bona fide growth.

In many cases, the perceived benefits that people report after adversity can be understood from the perspective of Taylor's (1983) cognitive adaptation theory (CAT). According to CAT, reports of personal growth may, to some extent, represent cognitive defenses or illusions which serve to maintain or shore up self-esteem and a sense of mastery over the event and over one's life more generally. Although Taylor (1983) does not deny that growth may result from trauma, the focus of CAT is on the self-protective function that these reports of personal growth serve. Thus, Taylor has noted that one can minimize the implications of a severe negative event by imagining worse situations, by construing benefit from the event, by selectively focusing on aspects that make one appear advantaged, or by comparing oneself to less fortunate others. Perhaps some of the perceived benefits (both changes in how one sees oneself and changes in values/attitudes) that our participants were describing were attributable to threats to self-esteem embedded within the loss experience. Implied within the characteristic statements that one is stronger now, has learned that one can cope, or has learned to appreciate the important things in life as a result of going through this experience, is the idea that at an earlier time one was weaker, that one suspected that one would be unable to cope, and that one formerly did not appreciate the important things in life—all of which might represent a threat to self-esteem.

A similar proposition derives from terror management theory (TMT; Greenberg, Solomon, & Pyszczynski, 1997). According to TMT, humans (unlike other species) are aware that they are mortal. Such knowledge would evoke debilitating anxiety (or terror) unless one is able to adopt a cultural worldview—a collection of beliefs that give meaning to one's everyday existence, such as a belief in a just world and a controllable world, where important outcomes are understood to be not random in their distribution but contingent on behavior under one's own control (e.g., Janoff-Bulman, 1989; Lerner, 1980)—and self-esteem, the belief that one is living up to the standards or expectations of one's culture. According to TMT, these beliefs give meaning to life, and thus buffer one from the terror associated with thinking of one's death.[4] Laboratory studies have demonstrated quite clearly that reminding people of their own mortality or threats to the legitimacy of one's worldview provokes a desire to increase self-esteem or to reassert the legitimacy of one's worldview (e.g., Florian & Mikulincer, 1997; Greenberg, Pyszczynski, Solomon, Simon, & Breus, 1994). When people for whom death has been made salient are able to affirm threatened worldviews, among other things, they report that life is more meaningful (Simon, Arndt, Greenberg, Pyszczynski, & Solomon, 1998).

When one considers that loss experiences are often poignant reminders of one's own mortality, and that these experiences may also represent a threat to one's worldview beliefs (e.g., of justice or control), then it follows that some part of the perceived benefits that people report following loss (or adversity more generally) might be understood as an attempt to reaffirm threatened worldviews and enhance self-esteem by perceiving oneself as better for the experience. One way to do this is to selectively interpret events so as to confirm that the world is still a good place (based, for example, on the observation that one's family and friends have

---

[4] Heine, Proulx, and Vohs (2006) recently have proposed a Meaning Maintenance Model, which posits that mortality concerns are but one aspect of a larger aspect of meaning. According to this model, people possess a need for meaning. When a core aspect of this meaning is threatened, people will attempt to affirm alternative representations of meaning. What we report below is consistent with this model as well as TMT. We present it in the context of TMT to be consistent with how the data were originally presented in Davis and McKearney (2003).

been extraordinarily supportive) or that one's life is still—or perhaps even more—meaningful (based, for example, on the realization that a meaningful life is one grounded in the quality of one's relationships rather than one's wealth, status, or achievements). Another way is to perceive that one has grown or developed in important ways as a result of the experience (e.g., developed spiritually, philosophically, or in terms of coping ability), again by selectively interpreting one's experience (McFarland & Alvaro, 2000; Taylor, 1983). What we are suggesting is that people participating in an interview or completing questionnaires about their loss (or trauma) experience are naturally reminded of mortality, and likely also reminded of how threatening the experience was to their worldviews and self-esteem. According to TMT (and CAT), one way of coping (consciously or not) with such threat is to take advantage of any opportunity presented in the interview or questionnaire to assert the meaningfulness and purposefulness of one's present life. Questions about positive changes, benefits, and perceived growth provide such an opportunity.

As a test of this proposition, we conducted an experiment in which we compared the effect of thinking briefly about trauma on the perception that one's life was meaningful and purposeful (study 1, Davis & McKearney, 2003). Participants in this experiment were undergraduate students who had indicated on a questionnaire administered at a mass testing session several months earlier that they had experienced the loss of a loved one or a situation where they themselves thought they might die (e.g., a serious accident), and might be willing to participate in research on their experience. In the context of the experiment, they were randomly assigned to think briefly either about death (i.e., a traditional mortality salience manipulation), a traumatic experience, or a control subject (i.e., what happens when one drinks a glass of water). After completing a number of filler tasks, they were asked to mark along a 100-mm line ranging from "not at all" to "extremely" the extent to which (among other filler items) they perceived that their life was currently meaningful, purposeful, and lacking in meaning (reverse scored).

Expecting that the trauma recall and mortality salience groups would report greater meaning in life than the control group, we were surprised by the extent to which trauma recall participants reported that their lives were meaningful. As shown in Figure 61.1, the trauma recall group showed a ceiling effect, with an average meaningfulness score (averaging over the three items) of 90 mm on the 100-mm response line. The data indicate, then, that the effect of recalling a traumatic episode was to increase the sense that life is "very" meaningful and purposeful. Research by McFarland and Alvaro (2000) suggests that this perception of increased meaningfulness comes from a tendency to perceive that they are better than they formerly were (or improved) for their experience. If nothing else, these data give reason to question the face validity of reports of benefits (or growth) by people participating in studies of trauma and loss. We are not suggesting that people are fabricating benefits, but rather that they may be motivated (again, consciously or not) to maintain or enhance self-esteem and to allay threats

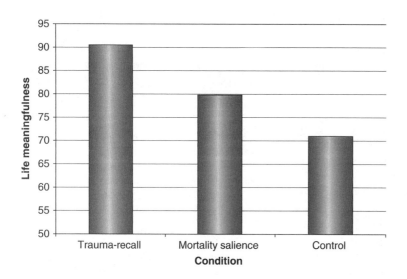

Fig. 61.1 Effects of trauma recall and mortality salience on life meaningfulness (from Davis & McKearney, 2003). Republished with permission.

to worldviews embedded in memories of loss or trauma, which leads them to capitalize on questions about life meaningfulness or about how much better off they are now as a result of their experience. Statements of benefits and PTG represent many things and should not be taken as unambiguous indications of growth.

Although perceiving benefit is likely not an indication of psychological well-being or adjustment, it is clear that people stuck in a loop of searching for meaning (Davis & Morgan, 2008; Davis et al., 2000; Michael & Snyder, 2005; Tait & Silver, 1989) or moodily pondering their emotions or their situation (which we refer to as "brooding"; Nolen-Hoeksema & Davis, 2004) are less likely to be coping well. These individuals may benefit from interventions that encourage people to reflect (rather than brood) on the beneficial aspects of their experience (Seligman, Rashid, & Parks, 2006; Stanton et al., 2002). Encouraging such positive reappraisals (or "benefit reminding"; see Affleck & Tennen, 1996) may lead people to focus less on the negative impact of the loss, including persistently asking "why me?" or what one might have done to prevent the death. Seligman et al. (2006), for instance, have reported significant declines in depressive symptoms in depressed persons (relative to baseline and vs. a depressed control group) from simply asking people to record daily three "blessings." Although such positive reappraisals may be biased and perhaps illusory, they may lead to the perception that the experience had positive value (Janoff-Bulman & Frantz, 1997).

Toward a More Refined Understanding of Posttraumatic Growth

Tennen and Affleck (2005) have argued that self-reports of PTG (or benefits) should not be accepted at face value. After all, for an individual to decide that he or she appreciates life more, is closer to one's family, has greater personal strength, or has a deeper faith in God, this person would have to assess his or her prior standing on each of these abstract, subjective dimensions (which in all likelihood were never previously considered, rated, or evaluated), assess his or her "current" standing on each dimension, and then, taking into account other factors (such as normal aging or maturation), attribute the difference to the event. Research indicates quite clearly that people are not very good at making such judgments (e.g., McFarland & Alvaro, 2000; Ross, 1989). In deciding whether and to what extent they have changed, people invoke a variety of change schemata and cultural assumptions that distort the extent of growth reported. Assessments are also influenced by motives for self-enhancement (McFarland & Alvaro, 2000; Wilson & Ross, 2001).

Given these problems in assessing PTG, we advocate an approach that focuses on changing goals. Rather than asking people directly about "growth," we suggest asking people to describe their goals pre loss (on the assumption that the loss was recent), and comparing these to post-loss goals, assessed over time. Specifically, we suggest that personal growth emerges from the process of renegotiating goals and priorities, which involves disengaging from or revising former core projects, activities, and strivings, and initiating new ones that are intrinsically meaningful. For example, in an ongoing study, we have observed some of the ways that people who have recently experienced a spinal cord injury (SCI) have adapted their pre-injury projects. Many of those formerly active in sports become very committed to wheelchair sports (basketball, rugby). One teacher who suffered an SCI has taken steps to reenter his profession as a specialist teacher for children with physical disabilities.

In summary, we advocate for a distinction between benefits and PTG, defining the latter as significant long-term (sustained) positive changes in major commitments and life goals. We propose that personal growth emerges from the process of renegotiating goals and priorities, which involves disengaging from or revising former goals, and initiating new goals that are intrinsically meaningful. Growth, from this perspective, is not just spending a bit more time with family, or learning a new skill, but rather is making sustained progress toward the commitment to family, or the goal that requires the new skill. Focusing on the movement toward goals over time helps distinguish tangible and lasting changes in one's life from the temporary provisions of support and the incidental gains following trauma and loss. Although this definition excludes many changes that others would consider indicative of PTG, the advantage of this approach is that it focuses attention on what people are doing, where they are heading, and where they derive their sense of meaning, purpose, and life satisfaction. This approach acknowledges that growth comes through action, from setting goals and working toward them and not merely reappraising a situation, or being the passive recipient of guidance, a helping hand, or financial compensation.

Seligman and Csikszentmihalyi (2000) and others (e.g., Joseph & Linley, 2005) have made a case for a psychology that focuses on positive outcomes following stress. PTG might be considered such an outcome. However, the current state of research on the topic of PTG tells us little about how PTG should be assessed, and this has impeded our ability to test complex models of the process of growth (e.g., Joseph & Linley, 2005; Tedeschi & Calhoun, 2004). We expect that future research that takes a more refined approach to the assessment of growth will uncover key mechanisms and processes that will, in turn, set the stage for interventions for promoting such positive outcomes following trauma and loss.

Questions for the Future

1. What is the process by which personal growth occurs? What promotes the acquisition of growth and what inhibits it?

2. In what way(s) does growth following adversity relate to psychological adjustment and well-being?

3. Does the perception of benefit following adversity promote acceptance and coping, and if so, why?

References

Affleck, G., & Tennen, H. (1996). Construing benefits from adversity: Adaptational significance and dispositional underpinnings. *Journal of Personality, 64*, 899–922.

Aldwin, C. M., & Levenson, M. R. (2004). Posttraumatic growth: A developmental perspective. *Psychological Inquiry, 15*, 19–22.

Currier, J. M., Holland, J. M., & Neimeyer, R. A. (2006). Sense-making, grief, and the experience of violent loss: Toward a mediational model. *Death Studies, 30*, 403–428.

Davis, C. G. (2008). Redefining goals and redefining self: A closer look at posttraumatic growth following loss. In M. S. Stroebe, R. O. Hansson, H. Schut, & W. Stroebe (Eds.), *Handbook of bereavement: 21st century perspectives* (pp. 309–325). Washington, DC: American Psychological Association.

Davis, C. G., & McKearney, J. M. (2003). How do people grow from their experience with trauma or loss? *Journal of Social and Clinical Psychology, 22*, 477–492.

Davis, C. G., & Morgan, M. S. (2008). Finding meaning, perceiving growth, and acceptance of tinnitus. *Rehabilitation Psychology, 53*, 128–138.

Davis, C. G., Nolen-Hoeksema, S., & Larson, J. (1998). Making sense of loss and benefiting from the experience: Two construals of meaning. *Journal of Personality and Social Psychology, 75*, 561–574.

Davis, C. G., Wohl, M. J. A., & Verberg, N. (2007). Profiles of posttraumatic growth following an unjust loss. *Death Studies, 31*, 693–712.

Davis, C. G., Wortman, C. B., Lehman, D. R., & Silver, R. C. (2000). Searching for meaning in loss: Are clinical assumptions correct? *Death Studies, 24*, 497–540.

Florian, V. & Mikulincer, M. (1997). A fear of death and the judgment of social transgressions: A multidimensional test of terror management theory. *Journal of Personality and Social Psychology, 73*, 369–380.

Frazier, P. A., & Kaler, M. E. (2006). Assessing the validity of self-reported stress-related growth. *Journal of Consulting and Clinical Psychology, 74*, 859–869.

Greenberg, J., Pyszczynski, T., Solomon, S., Simon, L., & Breus, M. (1994). The role of consciousness and accessibility of death-related thoughts in mortality salience effects. *Journal of Personality and Social Psychology, 67*, 627–637.

Greenberg, J., Solomon, S., & Pyszczynski, T. (1997). Terror management theory of self-esteem and cultural worldviews: Empirical assessments and conceptual refinements. In M. P. Zanna (Ed.), *Advances in experimental social psychology* (Vol. 29, pp. 61–139). New York: Academic Press.

Heine, S. J., Proulx, T., & Vohs, K. D. (2006). The Meaning Maintenance Model: On the coherence of social motivations. *Personality and Social Psychology Review, 10*, 88–110.

Helgeson, V. S., Reynolds, K. A., & Tomich, P. L. (2006). Meta-analytic review of benefit finding and growth. *Journal of Consulting and Clinical Psychology, 74*, 797–816.

Janoff-Bulman, R. (1989). Assumptive worlds and the stress of traumatic events: Applications of the schema construct. *Social Cognition, 7*, 113–136.

Janoff-Bulman, R. (1992). *Shattered assumptions: Towards a new psychology of trauma*. New York: Free Press.

Janoff-Bulman, R. (2004). Posttraumatic growth: Three explanatory models. *Psychological Inquiry, 15*, 30–34.

Janoff-Bulman, R., & Frantz, C. M. (1997). The impact of trauma on meaning: From meaningless world to meaningful life. In M. Power & C. R. Brewin (Eds.), *The transformation of meaning in psychological therapies* (pp. 91–106). New York: Wiley.

Joseph, S., & Linley, P. A. (2005). Positive adjustment to threatening events: An organismic valuing theory of growth through adversity. *Review of General Psychology, 9*, 262–280.

Lehman, D. R., Davis, C. G., DeLongis, A., Wortman, C. B., Bluck, S., Mandel, D. R., et al. (1993). Positive and negative life changes following bereavement and their relations to adjustment. *Journal of Social and Clinical Psychology, 12*, 90–112.

Lerner, M. J. (1980). *The belief in a just world: A fundamental delusion*. New York: Plenum.

Linley, P. A., & Joseph, S. (2004). Positive change following trauma and adversity: A review. *Journal of Traumatic Stress, 17*, 11–21.

McFarland, C. & Alvaro, C. (2000). The impact of motivation on temporal comparisons: Coping with traumatic events by perceiving personal growth. *Journal of Personality and Social Psychology, 79*, 327–343.

McMillen, J. C. (2004). Posttraumatic growth: What's it all about? *Psychological Inquiry, 15*, 48–52.

McMullan, J. L., & Hinze, S. (1999). The press, ideology, and corporate crime. In C. McCormick (Ed.), *The Westray chronicles: A case study in corporate crime* (pp. 183–217). Halifax, Nova Scotia: Fernwood.

Michael, S. T., & Snyder, C. R. (2005). Getting unstuck: The roles of hope, finding meaning, and rumination in adjustment to bereavement among college students. *Death Studies, 29*, 435–458.

Miller, W. R. (2004). The phenomenon of quantum change. *Journal of Clinical Psychology, 60*, 453–460.

Neimeyer, R. A. (2005). Re-storying loss: Fostering growth in the posttraumatic narrative. In L. Calhoun and R. Tedeschi (Eds.), *Handbook of posttraumatic growth: Research and practice* (pp. 68–80). Mahwah, NJ: Erlbaum.

Nolen-Hoeksema, S., & Davis, C. G. (2001). Positive responses to loss: Perceiving benefits and growth. In C. R. Snyder & S. J. Lopez (Eds.), *Handbook of positive psychology* (pp. 598–607). New York: Oxford University Press.

Nolen-Hoeksema, S., & Davis, C. G. (2004). Theoretical and methodological issues in the assessment and interpretation of posttraumatic growth. *Psychological Inquiry, 15*, 60–65.

Pals, J. L., & McAdams, D. P. (2004). The transformed self: A narrative understanding of posttraumatic growth. *Psychological Inquiry, 15*, 65–69.

Park, C. L., Cohen, L. H., & Murch, R. L. (1996). Assessment and prediction of stress-related growth. *Journal of Personality, 64*, 71–105.

Richard, K. P. (1997). *The Westray story: A predictable path to disaster. Report of the Westray Mine Public Inquiry* (Vol. 1: Executive Summary). Halifax, NS: Government Printer.

Ross, M. (1989). Relation of implicit theories to the construction of personal histories. *Psychological Review, 96*, 341–357.

Seligman, M. E. P., & Csikszentmihalyi, M. (2000). Positive psychology: An introduction. *American Psychologist, 55*, 5–14.

Seligman, M. E. P., Rashid, T., & Parks, A. C. (2006). Positive psychotherapy. *American Psychologist, 61*, 774–788.

Simon, L., Arndt, J., Greenberg, J., Pyszczynski, T., & Solomon, S. (1998). Terror management and meaning: Evidence that the opportunity to defend the worldview in response to mortality salience increases the meaningfulness of life in the mildly depressed. *Journal of Personality, 66*, 359–382.

Stanton, A. L., Danoff-Burg, S., Sworowski, L. A., Collins, C. A., Bransetter, A. D., Rodriguez-Hanley, A., et al. (2002). Randomized, controlled trial of written emotional expression and benefit finding in breast cancer patients. *Clinical Journal of Oncology, 20*, 4160–4168.

Tait, R., & Silver, R. C. (1989). Coming to terms with major negative life events. In J. S. Uleman and J. A. Bargh (Eds.), *Unintended thought* (pp. 351–382). New York: Guilford.

Taylor, S. E. (1983). Adjustment to threatening events: A theory of cognitive adaptation. *American Psychologist, 38*, 1161–1173.

Tedeschi, R. G., & Calhoun, L. G. (2004). Posttraumatic growth: Conceptual foundations and empirical evidence. *Psychological Inquiry, 15*, 1–18.

Tennen, H., & Affleck, G. (2005, May). *Positive change following adversity: In search of novel theories, meticulous methods, and precise analytic strategies.* Paper presented at Perspectives on Positive Life Changes, Benefit-Finding, and Growth Following Illness Conference, Storrs, CT.

Wilson, A. E., & Ross, M. (2001). From chump to champ: People's appraisals of their earlier and present selves. *Journal of Personality and Social Psychology, 80*, 572–584.

Happiness, Resilience, and Positive Growth Following Physical Disability: Issues for Understanding, Research, and Therapeutic Intervention

Dana S. Dunn, Gitendra Uswatte, *and* Timothy R. Elliott

Abstract

Do well-being and happiness change following acquired physical disability? The onset of physical disability occurs due to trauma or disease, either of which can mean a reduction in function (e.g., activities of daily living) or the literal loss of a body part (e.g., limb amputation). Restricted mobility, activity, or physical loss can have psychological consequences, so that some individuals report a variety of depressive symptoms and problem behaviors following disability onset. Yet many people with disabilities do not suffer from depression or behavioral difficulties; rather, they adjust to their circumstances reasonably well. Following the onset of disability and subsequent rehabilitation, then, many individuals report relatively favorable levels of subjective well-being (SWB) and happiness, and that they take pleasure in daily life, including work, play, and interactions with family and friends. The focus of this chapter is those individuals who exhibit positive reactions to living with disability. We hope that products and insights from their positive responses can develop new or revised existing therapies to promote the health and well-being of others, the goal of rehabilitation psychology. Our discussion is grounded in the theoretical and empirical perspectives of positive psychology; the constructive, person-situation focus of rehabilitation psychology; and the approaches emerging from the synergy of both research areas. Positive psychology emphasizes three complementary foci: subjective states, individual processes, and the creation and maintenance of positive social institutions. Against the backdrop of acquired physical disability, we consider the first two foci by examining happiness and then resiliency and positive growth. We then consider the implications of our review for future research and therapy.

Keywords: disability, happiness, positive growth, rehabilitation resilience

> Most observers have overlooked the potentially valuable experience of acquiring a physical disability. Writers have given only scant attention to positive growth and optimal living with chronic health problems, as well as the related searches for meaning, purpose, and fulfillment.
>
> —*Elliott, Kurylo, and Rivera* (2002, p. 687)

One of the most difficult facts for observers—a group often referred to as "outsiders" in the rehabilitation literature—to accept is that many people with disabilities (i.e., "insiders") adjust to their circumstances reasonably well (for discussion of the insider–outsider distinction, see Dunn, 2000; Wright, 1991). A second challenging fact for observers is that following the onset of disability and subsequent rehabilitation, many individuals report relatively favorable levels of subjective well-being

(SWB). Insiders often report being happy and taking pleasure in daily life, including work, play, and interactions with family and friends (e.g., de N Abrantes-Pais, Friedman, Lovallo, & Ross, 2007; Siosteen, Lundqvist, Blomstrand, Sullivan, & Sullivan, 1990; Wright, 1983). Insiders themselves are often surprised by their ability to cope with or adjust to physical disabilities and to learn that happiness and leading a relatively normal (if initially new and different) life is possible. Perceived quality of life, too, can be high in spite of physical limitations or a compromised physique (e.g., Albrecht, 1996; Delle Fave, 2006; Weinberg, 1988).

Although the appraisal processes of both insiders and outsiders are important to consider when studying disability, our focus in this chapter is largely on insiders' perspectives and assessments. We emphasize optimistic reactions to disability for two reasons. First, in line with positive psychology and exemplified by research summarized in this Handbook, the Zeitgeist in rehabilitation psychology is gradually becoming more salutary in focus. Second, some past efforts were overly negative in their portrayals of disability, highlighting distress and depression while creating the impression that people with disabilities were victims of cruel fate, objects of prejudice or pity, or simply health-preoccupied, passive recipients of medical care. We believe that a new focus on positive aspects of living with acquired physical disability will add needed balance to conceptualizations of well-being, and psychological and physical health.

Of course, the term "physical disability" is a broad one; some disabilities are due to trauma and therefore are sudden and unexpected. Other disabilities are disease related, which means those affected by them, as well as their families, often have time to anticipate or adjust to bodily as well as psychosocial changes. (Congenital disabilities constitute an important but separate category outside the scope of this review; see Dykens, 2006.) Physical loss, too, can mean a reduction in function (e.g., activities of daily living) or it can mean the literal loss of a body part (e.g., limb loss due to automobile accident), which, in turn, restricts mobility and activity. Physical loss can have psychological consequences and, naturally, some individuals report a variety of depressive symptoms and problem behaviors following the onset of disability (Elliott & Frank, 1996; Lawrence, Fauerbach, & Thombs, 2006; Turner, Lloyd, & Taylor, 2006). Treatment and rehabilitation options for such individuals are covered in great detail elsewhere (Frank & Elliott, 2000). Moreover, contemporary definitions of disability for understanding chronic conditions advanced by the World Health Organization (the International Classification of Functioning, Disability, and Health [ICF]; WHO, 2001; see also, Peterson & Elliott, 2008) deemphasize the explanatory utility of medical diagnosis, recognizing the role of socio-environmental factors in limiting ability and imposing limitations. This expanded view of disability complements alternative service models that promote independent living, improve access to institutions, and enhance role functioning and mobility to reduce disability across the WHO model's dimensions.

Our purpose is to discuss what is known about individuals who exhibit positive reactions to living with disability in order to learn from them. We hope that products and insights from their positive responses can develop new or revised existing therapies to promote the health and well-being of others, the goal of rehabilitation psychology. Our approach is grounded in the theoretical and empirical perspectives of positive psychology (e.g., Seligman, 2002; Seligman & Csikszentmihalyi, 2000), constructive, person-situation focus of rehabilitation psychology (e.g., Frank & Elliott, 2000; Frank, Caplan, & Rosenthal, in press; Wright, 1983), and approaches emerging from the synergy of both (e.g., Dunn & Dougherty, 2005; Elliott, Kurylo, & Rivera, 2002). To date, positive psychology emphasizes three complementary foci: subjective states, individual processes, and the creation and maintenance of positive social institutions. Against the backdrop of acquired physical disability, we will consider the first two foci by examining happiness and then resiliency and positive growth. We then consider the implications of our review for future research. We begin by examining the subjective state integral to positive psychology—happiness—and then consider how it may change following acquired disability.

Happiness After Disability

To be happy is to flourish in daily life. Happiness or SWB is frequently defined as having three interrelated qualities: regular positive affect, elevated life satisfaction, and sporadic negative affect (e.g., Diener, 1984; Diener, Suh, Lucas, & Smith, 1999). Happy people typically enjoy success in several life domains, including friendship, marriage, employment, work, income, mental health, and, not surprisingly, psychological well-being (for reviews, see Gilbert, 2006; Haidt, 2005; Lyubomirsky, King, & Diener, 2005; Myers & Diener, 1995; see also Ryff & Keyes, 1995). The main finding from happiness research is easily summarized: Most people report being happy. But what factors contribute to or maintain happiness? Recently, Lyubomirsky, Sheldon, and Schkade (2005) proposed that any individual's chronic level of happiness is governed by three factors: the person's set point of happiness, which is genetically determined, fixed, and stable; circumstantial factors, including personal qualities (e.g., age, gender, and life history), events (e.g., marriage, unemployment, and retirement), and situations (e.g., nation, location, and culture); and intentional actions, such as what people do and how they think in everyday life. These three factors constitute the "architecture of sustainable happiness" (Lyubomirsky, Sheldon, & Schkade, 2005).

We believe the pursuit of happiness following disability needs to be considered in light of this affective architecture. One set of reasons is that happy people engage in less negative self-reflection than unhappy individuals, dwell less on adversity and rebound more quickly from it, and react to distressing life events positively (Abbe, Tkach, & Lyubomirsky, 2003). Another reason is that some aspects of happiness following a disabling event may be relatively immune to rehabilitative or therapeutic intervention, whereas other aspects may offer clients opportunities to enhance their well-being. We begin by examining the extent to which an individual's range of happiness—the so-called "set point"—is affected by disability.

The Hedonic Treadmill, Set-Point Theory, and Disability

A milestone study in the study of happiness and disability found that individuals who acquired spinal cord injuries (SCIs) reported being almost as happy as people who could walk (Brickman, Coates, & Janoff-Bulman, 1978). This study also reported the ironic result that lottery winners generally end up being no happier than nonwinners. Brickman and colleagues argued that these findings implicated a "hedonic treadmill" where reactions to both positive and negative events are temporary—across time, people adjust to extreme good or bad fortune, returning to their individual set-point level of happiness. One implication of this model is that happiness is forever transitory because people adapt to whatever comes their way, whether good or ill. Yet, people potentially benefit from such adaptation when faced with negative events. Eventually, the impact of the distressing event is assimilated and individuals appear to return to their hedonically accustomed levels (e.g., Silver, 1982). Quite understandably, students of disability research were quick to interpret the hedonic adaptation of the individuals with acquired SCI as evidence that happiness returns even in cases of unexpected, traumatic loss.

A careful reanalysis of Brickman et al.'s (1978) findings, coupled with a revision of hedonic adaptation theory, suggests that happiness following some acquired disabilities is less robust than anticipated. Diener, Lucas, and Scollon (2006) note that the positive adaptation observed in Brickman et al.'s data was not quite so pronounced as claimed or later promulgated by sympathetic scholars. In fact, the participants with SCI actually reported being significantly less happy than the control group—the mean levels of happiness were approximately 0.75 standard deviations apart (Diener et al., 2006). One explanation could be depressive symptoms, which are a significant secondary complication of SCI (Elliott & Kennedy, 2004). Diener and colleagues also cite studies indicating that persons with SCI generally report lower levels of happiness compared to the general population (Dijkers, 1997, 2005; Hammell, 2004; Lucas, 2005, 2007). In other words, happiness set points can change in response to important life events, such as acquired disability, so that a return to previous levels may not occur. To quote Diener and colleagues (p. 307), "although people with paraplegia and other individuals with disabilities usually are not subjectively miserable, happiness levels do seem to be strongly affected by this important life circumstance." In some cases of SCI, then, one's set point of well-being can be substantially lowered even if depression or other psychological disorders do not occur.

Should researchers rule out the possibility of a resurgence of happiness following the onset of disability? Other research suggests that individuals with SCI sometimes report positive by-products (e.g., heightened compassion, closeness to family, and spirituality) as a result of acquired disability (McMillen & Cook, 2003). However, one problem is the mismatch between clients' self-reported benefits and those observed by family caregivers. To date, a reasonable approach for determining the validity of reported by-products, one combining methodological rigor with insider perspectives, remains to be devised. McMillen and Cook suggest that the validity of these particular reports remains uncertain. As will be discussed later, such skepticism is not new.

One also needs to consider individual differences in happiness among persons with disabilities. One intriguing individual difference is the relative financial standing of those who acquire a disability. Most cross-sectional studies find that once a certain level of material wealth is reached, additional income has little discernible impact on happiness (e.g., Myers, 2000). However, a recent study comprised of people at or near retirement age found that after the onset of disability, individuals whose finances placed their total net worth above the group's median showed smaller reductions in happiness than did those with assets below the median (Smith, Langa, Kabeto, & Ubel, 2005). In keeping with the set-point theory and the impact of circumstances (to be discussed shortly), the buffering effect of wealth was a short-term phenomenon. As time passed, the below-the-median group recovered some of their former happiness. Although suggestive, these results warrant further attention and replication.

The precise nature of the causal connections among happiness, disability, health, and income, as well as other between-group and individual difference variables, remains to be studied empirically using rigorous longitudinal designs like those employed by Lucas (2005). Moreover, set-point theory and the hedonic treadmill comprise only one factor affecting people's chronic happiness; circumstance and intentional actions also need to be considered.

Circumstances and Affective Forecasting Regarding Disability

Circumstances relevant to happiness are usually stable facts of life over which people have little control. Matters of personal history and life status variables (e.g., health and education) are exemplars of circumstance, as are major life events. A disabling experience, such as an industrial accident resulting in traumatic brain injury, is one such event. Lyubomirsky, Sheldon, & Schkade (2005) suggest that objective life circumstances have relatively little impact on happiness in the long run due to hedonic adaptation. Even things one can control to a degree, such as moving to a desirable part of the country, have little impact on well-being (Schkade & Kahneman, 1998). Where a severe disability is concerned, the affective impact would need to be considered in light of Diener et al.'s (2006) revised adaptation theory of well-being.

Lyubomirsky, Sheldon, & Schkade (2005) do suggest that some life status variables can potentially influence happiness but only within limits. In the short run, for example, happiness can be increased or decreased, respectively, as a result of positively (e.g., winning an award) or negatively (e.g., dissolution of a intimate relationship) valenced events. Changes in happiness levels due to many life status variables, then, are apt to be temporary.

We believe, however, that the effects of circumstances on happiness following disability should be examined for another reason: the potential for biased, especially unduly lowered, expectations regarding future well-being. Research on affective forecasting, the processes whereby people make predictions about their emotional reactions to future events, demonstrates that individuals routinely overestimate the strength and longevity of their affective reactions (Wilson & Gilbert, 2003, 2005). Many individuals do adapt physically and psychologically to health problems, including disability, while both they and the general public underestimate the ability to adjust (Frederick & Loewenstein, 1999; Loewenstein & Schkade, 1999). Wilson and Gilbert label this forecasting error the "impact bias" and suggest one source is undue focus on the event in question while simultaneously neglecting how other, competing events also shape thoughts and feelings. Different participant groups in different circumstances illustrate the bias, including people who anticipated undue sadness following a romantic breakup, women who overestimated their unhappiness following unwanted results from a pregnancy test, professors who overestimated their unhappiness several years after being denied tenure, and individuals who learned whether they were HIV positive, among others (Loewenstein, O'Donoghue, & Rabin, 2003; Mellers & McGraw, 2001; Sieff, Dawes, & Loewenstein, 1999; Wilson & Gilbert, 2003). Even the impact of wealth, including the desire to be richer, has an exaggerated and transient impact on happiness (Kahneman, Krueger, Schkade, Schwartz, & Stone, 2006).

Affective forecasting errors are relevant to acquired disability because of what Wilson and Gilbert (2003) refer to as people's "psychological immune system," which combats threats to emotional well-being via various social psychological processes (e.g., positive illusions, self-serving attributions). Most such processes are nonconscious, that is, people remain unaware that they possess or rely on such psychological defenses routinely. When projecting how he will feel later, say, a year following a traumatic accident, a person with a recently acquired disability will neglect the role of these subtle coping responses when he is predicting future feelings. Indeed, an important part of this process is the motivation to "make sense" of circumstances, especially unexpected ones. There is evidence, for instance, that people with acquired disabilities actively seek and find explanations for their experiences (e.g., Dunn, 1994).

What about the nature or severity of an event? Some research indicates that although major events have a larger emotional impact on people than minor ones, the motivation to make sense of the implications of the former is greater than that for the latter. Ironically, the affective anguish associated with minor events is apt to persist for a longer period of time (Gilbert, Lieberman, Morewedge, & Wilson, 2004). Indeed, people underestimate their capability to adjust and cope with life challenges (Gilbert, Pinel, Wilson, Blumberg, & Wheatley, 1998; Kahneman, 2000), just as they fail to notice how motivated they are to make sense of negative emotional events. What remains to be demonstrated empirically, of course, is whether these findings holds true for acquired disability. As with changes to happiness set points following disability, it may well be that different degrees of disability lead to shorter or longer periods of emotional adaptation.

Affective forecasts after disability are apt to be important for a variety of reasons. First, studying forecasting biases regarding disability adds depth to what is known about processes of subjective adaptation to and the potential identification of positive by-products following physical injury (Dunn & Dougherty, 2005). If so, then perhaps the knowledge gleaned from such research can be used to validate insiders' positive self-reports about disability, thereby convincing outsiders (including therapists) that adjustment claims represent normative, not maladaptive, responses (Dunn, in press).

Wilson and Gilbert (2005) note that affective forecasts play a significant role in people's lives because they sometimes guide decision making. Where everyday events are concerned, emotional mispredictions disrupt people's ability to accurately pursue or maximize happiness. In the case of sudden disability (e.g., stroke), an overestimate of the event's impact could lead to excessive upset and apprehension about one's future. As a result, some individuals (even families or health-care providers) might make less-than-optimal treatment choices by underestimating their abilities to adapt or overestimating the emotional toil a therapy regimen could create (Wilson & Gilbert, 2005). To date, however, attempts to improve the accuracy of people's forecasts have not succeeded (Ubel et al., 2001).

Construing Happiness Following Disability as an Intentional Act

While people's control over circumstances is limited, intentional activities are thoughts, behaviors, and volitional acts people choose to perform in daily life (Lyubomirsky, Sheldon, & Schkade, 2005; Sheldon & Lyubomirsky, 2006). These acts are novel or routine and generally involve some deliberate effort. In Lyubomirsky et al.'s model, happiness is linked with the three categories of effortful activities. "Cognitive activity" occurs in the form of hope for the future (e.g., Snyder, Ilardi, Michael, & Cheavens, 2000), for example, or finding side-benefits in an otherwise stressful situation (Affleck & Tennen, 1996). Treating others kindly or exercising ("behavioral activities") is also linked with enhanced levels of happiness (e.g., Keltner & Bonanno, 1997; Magen & Aharoni, 1991). Finally, performing acts of "volition," including pursuing or striving after personal goals (Ryan & Deci, 2000; Sheldon & Houser-Marko, 2001), being generative (e.g., de St. Aubin, McAdams, & Kim, 2004), or dedicating time to worthy causes, can lead to heightened well-being (Snyder & Omoto, 2001). In practice, all three categories work in concert with each other. However, selectively retaining distinctions among them are important for developing theory and creating interventions to increase chronic levels of happiness (Lyubomirsky, Sheldon, & Schkade, 2005; Sheldon & Lyubomirsky, 2006).

Electing to engage in positive, effortful, intentional acts following disability appears to be a constructive response, a means to stave off negative emotions, including depression. Behavioral responses to disability are probably the most common of the three types of intentional acts, and are often initiated by others during the course of rehabilitation. Although people respond differently, whether noted by insiders or outsiders, progress during rehabilitation can enhance well-being (Dettmers et al., 2005; Lai et al., 2006; Svendsen & Teasdale, 2006). According to Fredrickson's broaden-and-build model (Fredrickson, 1998, 2001), experiencing positive emotion helps to repair the deleterious effects of stress and broaden the repertoire of thoughts and behaviors available to individuals. Thus, the positive emotions resulting from progress in rehabilitation might help to repair the effects of stress and lead to other positive, intentional acts (e.g., maintaining health-related behaviors after rehabilitation).

Following disability, people's construal processes—how they appraise, explain, and draw meaning from their experiences—may well represent the sort of intentional act identified as a source of happiness by Lyubomirsky, Sheldon, and Schkade (2005). As Dunn (in press) argues, "Well-being should not be equated with absence of disability nor should chronic disability be misconstrued as 'permanent illness or loss'." Happiness is subjective and therefore subject to individual processes of construal. People both try to explain and search for meaning in disability once it occurs (Dunn, 1996), just as they try to understand and integrate threatening events into their lives (e.g., Taylor, 1983). Pursuing similar agendas, psychologists have been interested in how individual reactions to disability affect well-being in the context of rehabilitation (e.g., Elliott, Witty, Herrick, & Hoffman, 1991). Bulman and Wortman (1977), for example, examined construal following disability in the context of adjustment to SCI. The authors found that many individuals in their sample reevaluated their injuries as positive after asking "why me" questions, concluding that such defensive attributions were adaptive under the circumstances.

We suspect that intentional behavioral and cognitive acts can lead to volitional ones, especially when people with disabilities change their frame of reference from the negative to the positive. To understand disability experiences, we believe that an important quality of volitional acts is their future orientation. Volitional acts involve the choice to act in positive ways to work toward some desired state aligned with future happiness. For example, being encouraged to adopt a focus on one's strengths, real or potential, what one can do or can (re)learn to do, may lead to meaningful increases in happiness (e.g., Keany & Glueckauf, 1993). Several authors suggest that acquired disability encourages some individuals to adopt "reality negotiation strategies" or flexible self-beliefs that preserve a positive self-image while directing hopeful expectations toward positive outcomes despite dramatic life changes (e.g., illness and disability; Elliott et al., 1991; Snyder, 1989). Such strategies induce a variety of cognitive and behavioral acts linked with happiness, including planning and goal setting for the future (Elliott, Uswatte, Lewis, & Palmatier, 2000).

Happiness is clearly an important subjective response to acquired disability, albeit one selectively affected by positive interventions. We now turn to issues of resilience and positive growth, individual processes offering opportunities for psychosocial interventions following disability.

Resilience and Positive Growth Following Disability

"Resilience" describes a broad array of abilities for constructively and positively adapting to risk, adversity, or some monumental negative event. Resilient individuals not only cope with the event, they often learn from and are transformed by their experiences (Grotberg, 2003). Masten and Reed (2002), for example, argue that two criteria characterize an individual's response as resilient. First, the individual must be responding favorably on some set of agreed upon indicators of psychosocial well-being. Second, the stressful situation must be recognized as sufficiently threatening to reduce the likelihood of any good outcomes occurring. In spite of the "odds against them," resilient people bounce back from adversity (e.g., Carver, 1998) and do well regardless of the nature and impact of the traumas faced (e.g., Bonnano, 2004; Linley & Joseph, 2004).

Positive growth is one possible consequence of resilient reactions to negative events, including disability. Such growth has been examined in response to multiple sclerosis (Mohr et al., 1999), early-stage breast cancer (Sears, Stanton, & Danoff-Burg, 2003), living with HIV/AIDS (Milam, 2004; Siegel, Schrimshaw, & Pretter, 2005), cancer and lupus (Katz, Flasher, Cacciapaglia, & Nelson, 2001), and rheumatoid arthritis (Danoff-Burg & Revenson, 2005). People's perspectives on the nature and implications of such events can change in positive ways (Somerfield & McCrae, 2000). Changes include the construal processes noted earlier in this chapter (e.g., finding positive meaning and benefit finding), as well as favorably reinterpreting negative events (Scheier, Weintraub, & Carver, 1986), growth following trauma (e.g., Calhoun & Tedeschi, 2006), and positive illusions (Taylor & Brown, 1988), among other processes (for a review, see Tedeschi & Calhoun, 2004).

These responses are now largely accepted as both normative and adaptive among those facing traumatic events. In the past, where disability was concerned, such reactions were not viewed as real or true reflections of how people characterized their situations. Rather, under the circumstances (e.g., irrevocable change, physical loss), their accounts were viewed as perhaps understandable, if defensive, and in any case could not possibly be accurate portrayals of the experience of disability. Regrettably, this condescending outsider attitude toward insider views was even held by some rehabilitation professionals. In this section, we discuss some areas of resilience and growth that are linked with the experience of acquired physical disability, including known sources of resilience and growth, the benefit of narratives, the promise of positive emotion, and the cultivation of virtues. We also offer a caveat regarding promoting resilience and positive growth.

Possible Sources of Resilience and Growth Following Disability

Arguably, the most overlooked source for resilience and growth following disability is treating the individual with a disability *as* an individual. Disability is but one aspect of a person's life; it does not define a person or his or her self- or social worth. Wright (1983) claimed that a chief problem for people with disabilities was their frequent identification with their conditions rather than as individuals with a given condition. This "person-first" approach matters a great deal where eliminating the objectification of people with disabilities is concerned.

Wright (1983) also emphasized that the advent of any disability can be viewed as a surmountable challenge, something to be coped with, or as a disastrous undoing, something to succumb to. Individual differences can push people toward optimism or pessimism, that is, toward a coping or a succumbing frame of reference. We suggest that a client's family members and friends should be counseled to focus on his or her progress in rehabilitation while emphasizing a coping rather than succumbing orientation (Elliott, Shewchuk, & Richards, 2001; Olkin, 1999).

Sustained individuation and positive coping are also linked with the idea that no matter how severe or disruptive a disability may be, no physical condition eliminates people's other "assets" (Dunn & Dougherty, 2005). Assets represent a broad collection of existing or potential resources. These resources include a person's proficiencies, skills, or individual qualities connected to everyday life, such as self-concept, work, hobbies and interests, social networks, and social interactions. Assets are tangible (e.g., number of friends, income, and health insurance) as well as psychological (e.g., sense of humor, autonomy, and willingness to learn). Resilience and positive growth following disability can be promoted by reminding individuals of assets they possess or can acquire rather than unduly highlighting those they lost, lack, or may never gain back (Keany & Glueckauf, 1993). An important part of recognizing one's assets involves shifting from an old set of values regarding what matters in life to a new set based on living with disability.

A final way to promote resilience and positive growth is to involve clients in the rehabilitative process. The idea of clients as co-managers is a long-standing value of rehabilitation psychology that is gaining new currency in rehabilitative therapy (Balcazar, Keys, Kaplan, & Suarez-Balcazar, 1998; Wright, 1972). Involving clients, who are now often referred to as "consumers," emphasizes their role as stakeholders in what happens to them following the onset of disability. Clients can contribute insights about their conditions as well as express their desires where social, medical, psychological, and technological services are concerned.

What markers point to resilience and positive growth after a disabling injury? The relative absence of psychological problems (anxiety, depression, or social isolation), enhanced well-being, and general satisfaction with daily life point to both qualities. Wright (1983) and Taylor (1983) identify people's sense of personal worth (i.e., independent of altered appearance or physical limitation), gratitude for and enjoyment of family, and the development of spiritual, understanding, or thoughtful outlooks as compelling evidence. Elliott and colleagues (2000) suggest resilient reactions and positive growth can also be monitored by decreased risk for and infrequent incidence of secondary complications following disability onset (e.g., pressure sores; Elliott, Bush, & Chen, 2006). In addition, individuals displaying favorable responses would engage in successful problem-focused and emotion-focused coping activities aimed at maximizing their psychological and physical health (Lazarus & Folkman, 1984).

Narratives as Indicators of Resilience and Growth Regarding Disability

Life narratives are first-person accounts, the stories people tell about themselves to themselves and to others regarding their experiences following disability. Narratives represent a qualitative approach for studying resilience and growth, one that is case oriented and less focused on traditional issues of generalizability. The creation of coherent stories regarding major life events allows people to draw meaning from the event while shaping their identities in constructive ways (e.g., McAdams, 2001; McAdams, Josselson, & Lieblich, 2001; Rybarczyk & Bellg, 1997). In keeping with the themes discussed earlier in this review, life stories regarding disability tend to emphasize that living with a disability is not a defining quality but rather one among many (e.g., Cole, 2004; Elliott & Kurylo, 2000; Johnson, 2005; King, Brown, & Smith, 2003).

Narrative accounts foster outsiders' understanding about insiders' actual experience of disability (Dunn, 2005). Researchers should examine narratives not only for evidence of resilience or positive growth, but also to identify possible mechanisms driving favorable adjustment to disability. First-person accounts may be fruitful sources of hypotheses for more quantitatively focused studies. We suspect that many researchers ignore narrative data because they assume those are biased or merely representative of a typical American cultural script wherein negative experiences are necessarily perceived retrospectively as redemptive (McAdams, 1993, 2005). As other scholars suggest (Peterson, Park, & Seligman, 2006), such self-views on identity might not be inauthentic, but they should be regarded with healthy skepticism. We do not disagree; empirical validation is surely warranted. Yet, we believe narratives are an underutilized source of insider perspectives and insights on acquired disability.

Positive Emotion, Resilience, and Growth: Issues for Studying Disability

The cultivation of positive emotions is a promising avenue for promoting resilience with a growing body of evidence to support it (Fredrickson, 2006). There is substantial evidence that positive affect is an effective coping resource (Aspinwall, 2001). Resilient people are more likely than less resilient individuals to experience and benefit from experiencing positive emotions. Specifically, according to evidence from the broaden-and-build model of positive emotions, the latter affective states help undo any lingering effects of negative emotions (Tugade & Fredrickson, 2002). When linked with resilience, positive emotions cause a return toward baseline levels of psychological and physiological function (Tugade & Fredrickson, 2004). In a prospective field project involving data collection pre- and post-September 11, 2001, terrorist attacks, when compared to less resilient peers, resilient college students were less depressed and demonstrated post-event psychological growth (Fredrickson, Tugade, Waugh, & Larkin, 2003).

The research of Fredrickson and colleagues suggests that rehabilitation researchers should attend to the beneficial effects of positive emotion. In our judgment, researchers interested in coping with the consequences of disability should consider how rehabilitative progress coupled with social interaction can foster positive emotions. Recent work by Gable, Reis, Impett, & Asher (2004) implicates the intrapersonal and interpersonal consequences of sharing good things with others. When people "capitalize" on good events (e.g., successes) by telling the news to interested others (e.g., spouses) and then receive enthusiastic feedback in return, higher relationship well-being results. Such capitalization might be expected to serve two functions during rehabilitation: to mark treatment progress and to engender closer relationships with caregivers. As Gable and colleagues note, of course,

cultivating positive emotions through capitalization only operates when good news is responded to favorably. These capitalization findings imply that the quality of client–caregiver interactions play an important role in maintaining well-being following disability.

Cultivating Positive Strengths and Virtues

Can character strength and virtues be cultivated by people after a disabling experience? What impact do existing strengths or virtues have on adjustment to disability? Peterson and Seligman (2004) developed a framework for organizing and understanding 26 specific strengths or positive individual traits under six broad virtues: wisdom, courage, humanity, justice, temperance, and transcendence. Strengths are psychological processes or mental practices defining virtues, the core qualities of good character. Gratitude, hope, and humor, for example, are strengths that either singly or in combination implicate transcendence, a virtue connecting self to others and providing meaning to an individual's existence.

Space constraints preclude an extended discussion of strengths and virtues, but like Peterson and Seligman (2004), we believe that they can inoculate people by strengthening habits that engender flourishing, as well as providing sense and purpose in the face of adversity. In a large-sample, retrospective Web-based study, for example, individuals with a history of physical illness (e.g., diabetes, arthritis, cancer, cardiovascular problems) reported greater life satisfaction if they possessed the character strengths of kindness, bravery, and humor (Peterson, Park, & Seligman, 2006). Generally, life satisfaction is associated with love, zest, curiosity, gratitude, and hope (Park, Peterson, & Seligman, 2004). Peterson and colleagues suggest that, on occasion, physical recovery is linked with enhanced character strengths. However, these authors are not advocating adopting a "virtue in suffering" perspective on people's responses to physical problems. Rather, they believe that some people appreciate a return to physical health and well-being by developing certain strengths in the process.

Currently, no studies employing a longitudinal perspective tracking character pre- and post-physical or psychological crisis are available. Except for anecdotal accounts that many insiders and outsiders discount, there is no strong evidence that people with disabilities develop character strengths due to their conditions. Longitudinal studies would answer questions about how strengths may moderate the link between physical and psychological states, such as life satisfaction, happiness, and other measures of well-being. More to the point, however, we believe that researchers and practitioners who work with people with acquired disabilities should also look to develop interventions designed to increase strengths. There is evidence that some positive interventions do increase happiness and stave off depressive symptoms in nondisabled people (Seligman, Steen, Park, & Peterson, 2005).

A Caveat: Resiliency and Growth Should Be Encouraged, Not Required

We want to be clear about one important therapeutic issue: positive growth must not be mandated or forced upon clients. People with disabilities, like all individuals, have the right to self-determination and to participate in discussions and plans concerning care and treatment regimens. There is clearly a fine line between making clients aware of the possibility of improved quality of life and informing them that they must accept an enterprise designed to improve their well-being. To quote Wright (1983, p. 191), "Although there is good evidence that one *may* rise to great heights of emotional understanding from the depths of despair, this may not be the only or the best course" (italics in original). Indeed, not everyone may experience positive growth following a trauma (Wortman, 2004).

Not so long ago, well-intentioned researchers and therapists argued that people with acquired physical disabilities should be required to properly mourn their loss of function (e.g., Wright, 1980, 1983). Failing to grieve for lost capacities was portrayed as psychological denial or some other defensive reaction (e.g., Grzesiak & Hicock, 1994). The presumption was that postponing facing grim reality would undermine psychosocial well-being in the long run. Some individuals who become disabled did and do mourn the loss of function. Many, however, do not display grief reactions, at least not in any prescribed manner (similar variable responses are documented in the myths of coping with loss literature; Wortman & Boerner, 2007). Their reaction to their physical circumstances is normative, as research demonstrates there is no single way to respond to personal trauma. Rather, people display various reactions based on individual differences and particular situations. Indeed, whether a disabling event or other loss, some people portray the trauma as meaningless (Bulman & Wortman, 1977; Lehman, Wortman, & Williams, 1987). In short, there is no "right" way for individuals to respond to disability (Olkin, 1999; Trieschmann, 1988).

Finally, Henry (2006) cautions that some positive psychological strategies can promote or even achieve well-being and lasting change while others are ineffective. Individuals' differences may prevail; indeed, some personality factors may predispose some people to be more resilient than others after the onset of disability (Berry, Elliott, & Rivera, 2007). Some methods work for some people but not others. Henry reports that exhortations, such as urgent advice, admonishment ("Keep trying!"), and compassionate encouragement, are often seen as unhelpful. No doubt these observations do not apply universally, as many clients desire active, analytically focused guidance. The point is that any positive psychological intervention aimed at creating resilience must be carefully planned and empirically grounded rather than approached as a simplistic, cheerleading exercise.

Looking Forward

Advances in the psychology of positive subjective states and traits are a rich source of ideas for rehabilitation psychologists to plumb to enhance the well-being of people with disabilities. Possible approaches include helping consumers correct errors in affective forecasting when making decisions about rehabilitation, enhancing relationships with family caregivers by teaching both parties to reinforce each other's successes, and even employing well-known strategies, such as individuation, emphasizing assets, and setting treatment goals with the goal of fostering resilience. These approaches should be rigorously tested before adoption into clinical practice. Randomized controlled trials are necessary to find out which approaches are actually effective, followed by components' analyses to identify the therapeutic elements of the successful interventions.

At the same time, the study of adjustment to disability can be fertile ground for positive psychology. Rehabilitation psychologists study happiness under some of the more challenging circumstances encountered by men and women. The experience of people with disabling injuries also permits the study of character strengths that are not typically called upon frequently in the lives of able-bodied people. For example, bravery might be called upon in someone who is newly blind on a daily basis, whereas among able-bodied people this strength might be employed only in uncommon circumstances. The study of rehabilitation populations with focal damage to the brain, such as stroke survivors, might open the door to a neuropsychology of character strengths (e.g., Koenigs et al., 2007).

The Elliott et al. (2002) dynamic model of adjustment to disability reflects the Lewinian concept that behavior is a function of individual and environmental factors (Lewin, 1997). In their model, (a) enduring characteristics and individual differences and (b) social and environmental characteristics affect (c) phenomenological and appraisal process, which, in turn, influence (d) psychological well-being and (e) physical health. Psychological well-being and physical health influence each other. These five components are framed within a developmental continuum that permits changes in any of the five components as people age, technology advances, and public policy changes.

This framework offers guidance for the study of positive adjustment to disability. It directs the researcher to pay attention to both individual and environmental factors and to be open to dynamic interactions between all five components of the model. Importantly, the model also directs the researcher to examine the phenomenological and appraisal processes that connect enduring personal and environmental characteristics to psychological and physical outcomes. In general, rehabilitation psychology research to date, both in the positive psychology arena and otherwise, has examined the association between individual traits and psychological well-being and physical health. For the field to advance, it is important to examine what is "inside the black box," to delineate *how* particular traits are connected to desirable outcomes (Elliott, 2002). To accomplish this empirical goal, relevant behaviors, thoughts, and emotions, as well as relevant characteristics of the environment, need to be assessed at multiple time points during rehabilitation and in follow-up afterward. Multilevel modeling techniques, such as structural equation modeling and hierarchical linear modeling, can then be employed to help draw out relationships between the variables of interest across time (Elliott et al., 2002). This type of complex data and analysis will help ultimately to discover the psychological mechanisms that permit men and women to triumph over adversity and flourish.

Questions for the Future

1. When people's set-point of happiness decreases following disability onset, is the change a relatively permanent one? Can rehabilitation interventions reverse the change, thereby returning happiness to baseline levels?

2. Positive psychology tends to focus on the person, that is, psychological characteristics (e.g., strengths) that promote happiness and well-being, whereas rehabilitation psychology tries to link people's qualities with constraints and possibilities imposed by the environment. What methods and theories can positive psychology adopt and adapt from rehabilitation psychology (and vice versa)?

3. Rehabilitation research concerning happiness, resilience, and positive growth tends to be cross-sectional in nature. What sorts of longitudinal, multi-method research designs can be used to capture emotional, cognitive, and social change following the onset of disability?

References

Abbe, A., Tkach, C., & Lyubomirsky, S. (2003). The art of living by dispositionally happy people. *Journal of Happiness Studies, 4*, 385–404.

Affleck, G., & Tennen, H. (1996). Construing benefits from adversity: Adaptational significance and dispositional underpinnings. *Journal of Personality, 64*, 899–922.

Albrecht, G. L. (1996). Using subjective health assessments in practice and policy making. *Health Care Analysis, 4*, 284–292.

Aspinwall, L. G. (2001). Dealing with adversity: Self-regulation, coping, adaptation, and health. In A. Tesser & N. Schwartz (Eds.), *The Blackwell handbook of social psychology: Vol. 1. Intraindividual processes* (pp. 591–614). Malden, MA: Blackwell.

Balcazar, F. E., Keys, C. B., Kaplan, D. L., & Suarez-Balcazar, Y. (1998). Participatory action research and people with disabilities: Principles and challenges. *Canadian Journal of Rehabilitation, 12*, 105–112.

Berry, J., Elliott, T., & Rivera, P. (2007). Resilient, undercontrolled, and overcontrolled personality prototypes among persons with spinal cord injury. *Journal of Personality Assessment, 89*, 292–302.

Bonnano, G. A. (2004). Loss, trauma, and human resilience: Have we underestimated the human capacity to thrive after extremely aversive events? *American Psychologist, 59*, 20–28.

Brickman, P., Coates, D., & Janoff-Bulman, R. (1978). Lottery winners and accident victims: Is happiness relative? *Journal of Personality and Social Psychology, 37*, 917–927.

Bulman, R. J., & Wortman, C. B. (1977). Attributions of blame and coping in the "real world": Severe accident victims react to their lot. *Journal of Personality and Social Psychology, 35*, 351–363.

Calhoun, L. G., & Tedeschi, R. G. (Eds.). (2006). *Handbook of posttraumatic growth*. Mahwah, NJ: Erlbaum.

Carver, C. S. (1998). Resilience and thriving: Issues, models, and linkages. *Journal of Social Issues, 54*, 245–266.

Cole, J. (2004). *Still lives: Narratives of spinal cord injury*. Cambridge, MA: MIT Press.

Danoff-Burg, S., & Revenson, T. A. (2005). Benefit-finding among patients with rheumatoid arthritis: Positive effects on interpersonal relationships. *Journal of Behavioral Medicine, 28*, 91–103.

Delle Fave, A. (2006). The impact of subjective experience on the quality of life: A central issue for health professionals. In M. Csikszentmihalyi & I. S. Csikszentmihalyi (Eds.), *A life worth living: Contributions to positive psychology* (pp. 165–181). New York: Oxford University Press.

de N Abrantes-Pais, F., Friedman, J. K., Lovallo, W. R., & Ross, E. D. (2007). Psychological or physiological: Why are tetraplegic patients content? *Neurology, 49,* 261–267.

de St. Aubin, E., McAdams, D. P., & Kim, T.-C. (2004). *The generative society: Caring for future generations.* Washington, DC: American Psychological Association.

Dettmers, C., Teske, U., Hamzei, F., Uswatte, G., Taub, E., & Weiller, C. (2005). Distributed form of constraint-induced movement therapy improves functional outcome and quality of life after stroke. *Archives of Physical Medicine and Rehabilitation, 86,* 204–209.

Diener, E. (1984). Subjective well-being. *Psychological Bulletin, 95,* 542–575.

Diener, E., Lucas, R. E., & Scollon, C. N. (2006). Beyond the hedonic treadmill: Revising the adaptation theory of well-being. *American Psychologist, 61,* 305–314.

Diener, E., Suh, E. M., Lucas, R. E., & Smith, H. L. (1999). Subjective well-being: Three decades of progress. *Psychological Bulletin, 125,* 276–302.

Dijkers, M. (1997). Quality of life after spinal cord injury: A meta-analysis of the effects of disablement components. *Spinal Cord, 35,* 829–840.

Dijkers, M. P. J. M. (2005). Quality of life of individuals with spinal cord injury: A review of conceptualization, measurement, and research findings. *Journal of Rehabilitation Research and Development, 42,* 87–110.

Dunn, D. S. (1994). Positive meaning and illusions following disability: Reality negotiation, normative interpretation, and value change. *Journal of Social Behavior and Personality, 9,* 123–138.

Dunn, D. S. (1996). Well-being following amputation: Salutary effects of positive meaning, optimism, and control. *Rehabilitation Psychology, 41,* 285–302.

Dunn, D. S. (2000). Social psychological issues in disability. In R. Frank & T. R. Elliott (Eds.), *Handbook of rehabilitation psychology* (pp. 565–584). Washington, DC: American Psychological Association.

Dunn, D. S. (2005). Negotiating realities to understand others: Teaching about meaning and well-being. *Journal of Social and Clinical Psychology, 24,* 30–40.

Dunn, D. S. (in press). The social psychology of disability. In R. G. Frank, B. Caplan, & M. Rosenthal (Eds.), *Handbook of rehabilitation psychology* (2nd ed.). Washington, DC: American Psychological Association.

Dunn, D. S., & Dougherty, S. B. (2005). Prospects for a positive psychology of rehabilitation. *Rehabilitation Psychology, 50,* 305–311.

Dykens, E. M. (2006). Toward a positive psychology of mental retardation. *American Journal of Orthopsychiatry, 76,* 185–193.

Elliott, T. R. (2002). Defining our common ground to reach new horizons. *Rehabilitation Psychology, 47,* 131–143.

Elliott, T. R., Bush, B. A., & Chen, Y. (2006). Social problem-solving abilities predict pressure sore occurrence in the first 3 years of spinal cord injury. *Rehabilitation Psychology, 51,* 69–77.

Elliott, T. R., & Frank, R. G. (1996). Depression following spinal cord injury. *Archives of Physical and Medical Rehabilitation, 77,* 816–823.

Elliott, T. R., & Kennedy, P. (2004). Treatment of depression following spinal cord injury: An evidence-based review. *Rehabilitation Psychology, 49,* 134–139.

Elliott, T., & Kurylo, M. (2000). Hope over disability: Lessons from one young woman's triumph. In C. R. Snyder (Ed.), *The handbook of hope: Theory, measurement, and interventions* (pp. 373–386). New York: Academic Press.

Elliott, T. R., Kurylo, M., & Rivera, P. (2002). Positive growth following acquired physical disability. In C. R. Snyder & S. J. Lopez (Eds.), *Handbook of positive psychology* (pp. 687–699). New York: Oxford University Press.

Elliott, T. R., Shewchuk, R. M., & Richards, J. S. (2001). Family caregiver social problem-solving abilities and adjustment during the initial year of the caregiver role. *Journal of Counseling Psychology, 48,* 223–232.

Elliott, T. R., Uswatte, G., Lewis, L., & Palmatier, A. (2000). Goal instability and adjustment to physical disability. *Journal of Counseling Psychology, 47,* 251–265.

Elliott, T. R., Witty, T. E., Herrick, S. M., & Hoffman, J. T. (1991). Negotiating reality after physical loss: Hope, depression, and disability. *Journal of Personality and Social Psychology, 61,* 608–613.

Frank, R. G., & Elliott, T. R. (Eds.). (2000). *Handbook of rehabilitation psychology.* Washington, DC: American Psychological Association.

Frank, R. G., Caplan, B., & Rosenthal, M. (Eds.). (in press). *Handbook of rehabilitation psychology* (2nd ed.). Washington, DC: American Psychological Association.

Frederick, S., & Loewenstein, G. (1999). Hedonic adaptation. In D. Kahneman, E. Diener, & N. Schwartz (Eds.), *Well-being: The foundations of hedonic psychology* (pp. 302–329). New York: Russell Sage.

Fredrickson, B. L. (1998). What good are positive emotions? *Review of General Psychology, 2,* 300–319.

Fredrickson, B. L. (2001). The role of positive emotions in positive psychology: The broaden-and-build theory of positive emotions. *American Psychologist, 56,* 218–226.

Fredrickson, B. L. (2006). The broaden-and-build theory of positive emotions. In M. Czsikszentmihalyi & I. S. Czsikszentmihalyi (Eds.), *A life worth living: Contributions to positive psychology* (pp. 85–103). New York: Oxford University Press.

Fredrickson, B. L., Tugade, M. M., Waugh, C. E., & Larkin, G. (2003). What good are positive emotions in crises?: A prospective study of resilience and emotions following the terrorist attacks on the United States on September 11, 2001. *Journal of Personality and Social Psychology, 84,* 365–376.

Gable, S. L., Reis, H. T., Impett, E. A., & Asher, E. R. (2004). What do you do when things go right? The intrapersonal and interpersonal benefits of sharing positive events. *Journal of Personality and Social Psychology, 87,* 228–245.

Gilbert, D. T. (2006). *Stumbling on happiness.* New York: Knopf.

Gilbert, D. T., Lieberman, M. D., Morewedge, C., & Wilson, T. D. (2004). The peculiar longevity of things not so bad. *Psychological Science, 15,* 14–19.

Gilbert, D. T., Pinel, E. C., Wilson, T. D., Blumberg, S. J., & Wheatley, T. P. (1998). Immune neglect: A source of durability bias in affective forecasting. *Journal of Personality and Social Psychology, 75,* 617–638.

Grotberg, E. H. (2003). What is resilience? How do you promote it? How do you use it? In E. H. Grotberg (Ed.), *Resilience for today: Gaining strength from adversity* (pp. 1–29). Westport, CT: Praeger.

Grzesiak, R. C., & Hicock, D. A. (1994). A brief history of psychotherapy in physical disability. *American Journal of Psychotherapy, 48,* 240–250.

Haidt, J. (2005). *The happiness hypothesis: Finding modern truth in ancient wisdom.* New York: Basic Books.

Hammell, K. W. (2004). Exploring quality of life following high spinal cord injury: A review and critique. *Spinal Cord, 42,* 491–502.

Henry, J. (2006). Strategies for achieving well-being. In M. Csikszentmihalyi & I. S. Csikszentmihalyi (Eds.), *A life worth living: Contributions to positive psychology* (pp. 120–138). New York: Oxford University Press.

Johnson, H. M. (2005). *Too late to die young: Nearly true tales from a life.* New York: Henry Holt and Company.

Kahneman, D. (2000). Experienced utility and objective happiness: A moment-based approach. In D. Kahneman & A. Tversky (Eds.), *Choices, values, and frames* (pp. 673–692). New York: Russell Sage Foundation and Cambridge University Press.

Kahneman, D., Krueger, A. B., Schkade, D., Schwartz, N., & Stone, A. A. (2006). Would you be happier if you were richer? A focusing illusion. *Science, 312,* 1908–1910.

Katz, R. C., Flasher, L., Cacciapaglia, H., & Nelson, S. (2001). The psychosocial impact of cancer and lupus: A cross validation study that extends the generality of "benefit finding" in patients with chronic disease. *Journal of Behavioral Medicine, 24,* 561–571.

Keany, K. M. H., & Glueckauf, R. L. (1993). Disability and value change: An overview and reanalysis of acceptance of loss theory. *Rehabilitation Psychology, 38,* 199–210.

Keltner, D., & Bonanno, G. A. (1997). A study of laughter and dissociation: Distinct correlates of laughter and smiling during bereavement. *Journal of Personality and Social Psychology, 73,* 687–702.

King, G. A., Brown, E. G., & Smith, L. K. (2003). *Resilience: Learning from people with disabilities and the turning points in their lives.* Westport, CT: Praeger.

Koenigs, M., Young, L., Adolphs, R., Tranel, D., Cushman, F., Hauser, M., et al. (2007). Damage to the prefrontal cortex increases utilitarian moral judgments. *Nature, 446,* 908–911.

Lai, S. M., Studenski, S., Richards, L., Perera, S., Reker, D., & Duncan, P. W. (2006). Therapeutic exercise and depressive symptoms after stroke. *Journal of the American Geriatrics Society, 54,* 240–247.

Lawrence, J. W., Fauerbach, J. A., & Thombs, B. D. (2006). Frequency and correlates of depression symptoms among long-term adult burn survivors. *Rehabilitation Psychology, 51,* 306–313.

Lazarus, R. S., & Folkman, S. (1984). *Stress, appraisal, and coping.* New York: Springer.

Lehman, D. R., Wortman, C. B., & Williams, A. F. (1987). Long-term effects of losing a spouse or child in a motor vehicle crash. *Journal of Personality and Social Psychology, 52,* 218–231.

Lewin, K. (1997). *Resolving social conflicts & field theory in social science.* Washington, DC: American Psychological Association.

Linley, P. A., & Joseph, S. (2004). Positive change following trauma and adversity: A review. *Journal of Traumatic Stress, 17,* 11–21.

Loewenstein, G., O'Donoghue, T., & Rabin, M. (2003). Projection bias in predicting future utility. *Quarterly Journal of Economics, 118,* 1209–1248.

Loewenstein, G., & Schkade, D. (1999). Wouldn't it be nice? Predicting future feelings. In D. Kahneman, E. Diener, & N. Schwartz (Eds.), *Well-being: The foundations of hedonic psychology* (pp. 85–105). New York: Russell Sage.

Lucas, R. E. (2005). Happiness can change: A longitudinal study of adaptation to disability. Manuscript submitted for publication, Michigan State University, East Lansing.

Lucas, R. E. (2007). Adaptation and the set-point model of subjective well-being: Does happiness change after major life events? *Current Directions in Psychological Science, 16,* 75–79.

Lyubomirsky, S., King, L. A., & Diener, E. (2005). The benefits of frequent positive affect: Does happiness lead to success? *Psychological Bulletin, 131,* 803–855.

Lyubomirsky, S., Sheldon, K. M., & Schkade, D. (2005). Pursuing happiness: The architecture of sustainable change. *Review of General Psychology, 9,* 111–131.

McAdams, D. P. (1993). *The stories we live by: Personal myths and the making of the self.* New York: Guilford.

McAdams, D. P. (2001). The psychology of life stories. *Review of General Psychology, 5,* 100–122.

McAdams, D. P. (2005). *The redemptive self: Stories Americans live by.* New York: Oxford University Press.

McAdams, D. P., Josselson, R., & Lieblich, A. (Eds.). (2001). *Turns in the road: Narrative studies of lives in transition.* Washington, DC: American Psychological Association.

McMillen, J. C., & Cook, C. L. (2003). The positive by-products of spinal cord injury and their correlates. *Rehabilitation Psychology, 48,* 77–85.

Magen, Z., & Aharoni, R. (1991). Adolescents' contributing towards others: Relationships to positive experiences and transpersonal commitment. *Journal of Humanistic Psychology, 31,* 126–143.

Masten, A. S., & Reed, M. J. G. (2002). Resilience in development. In C. R. Snyder & S. J. Lopez (Eds.), *The handbook of positive psychology* (pp. 74–88). New York: Oxford University Press.

Mellers, B. A., & McGraw, A. P. (2001). Anticipated emotions as guides to choice. *Current Directions in Psychological Science, 10,* 210–214.

Milam, J. E. (2004). Posttraumatic growth among HIV/AIDS patients. *Journal of Applied Social Psychology, 34,* 2353–2376.

Mohr, D. C., Dick, L. P., Russo, D., Pinn, J., Boudewyn, A. C., Likosky, W., et al. (1999). The psychosocial impact of multiple sclerosis: Exploring the patient's perspective. *Health Psychology, 18,* 376–382.

Myers, D. G. (2000). The funds, friends, and faith of happy people. *American Psychologist, 55,* 56–67.

Myers, D. G., & Diener, E. (1995). Who is happy? *Psychological Science, 6,* 10–19.

Olkin, R. (1999). *What psychotherapists should know about disability.* New York: Guilford.

Park, N., Peterson, C., & Seligman, M. E. P. (2004). Strengths of character and well-being. *Journal of Social and Clinical Psychology, 23,* 603–619.

Peterson, D., & Elliott, T. (2008). Advances in conceptualizing and studying disability. In R. Lent & S. Brown (Eds.), *Handbook of counseling psychology* (4th ed., pp. 212–230). New York: Sage.

Peterson, C., Park, N., & Seligman, M. E. P. (2006). Greater strengths of character and recovery from illness. *The Journal of Positive Psychology, 1,* 17–26.

Peterson, C., & Seligman, M. E. P. (2004). *Character strengths and virtues: A handbook and classification.* New York: Oxford University Press/Washington, DC: American Psychological Association.

Ryan, R. M., & Deci, E. L. (2000). Intrinsic and extrinsic motivations: Classic definitions and new directions. *Contemporary Educational Psychology, 25,* 54–67.

Rybarczyk, B., & Bellg, A. (1997). *Listening to life stories: A new approach to stress intervention in health care.* New York: Springer.

Ryff, C. D., & Keyes, C. L. M. (1995). The structure of psychological well-being revisited. *Journal of Personality and Social Psychology, 69,* 719–727.

Scheier, M. F., Weintraub, J. K., & Carver, C. S. (1986). Coping with stress: Divergent strategies of optimists and pessimists. *Journal of Personality and Social Psychology, 51,* 1257–1264.

Schkade, D. A., & Kahneman, D. (1998). Does living in California make people happy? A focusing illusion in judgments of life satisfaction. *Psychological Science, 9,* 340–346.

Sears, S. R., Stanton, A. L., & Danoff-Burg, S. (2003). The Yellow Brick Road and the Emerald City: Benefit finding, positive reappraisal coping, and posttraumatic growth in women with early-stage breast cancer. *Health Psychology, 22,* 487–497.

Seligman, M. E. P. (2002). Positive psychology, positive prevention, and positive therapy. In C. R. Snyder & S. J. Lopez (Eds.), *Handbook of positive psychology* (pp. 3–9). New York: Oxford.

Seligman, M. E. P., & Csikszentmihalyi, M. (2000). Positive psychology: An introduction. *American Psychologist, 55,* 5–14.

Seligman, M. E. P., Steen, T. A., Park, N., & Peterson, C. (2005). Positive psychology progress: Empirical validation of interventions. *American Psychologist, 60,* 410–421.

Sheldon, K. M., & Houser-Marko, L. (2001). Self-concordance, goal-attainment, and the pursuit of happiness: Can there be an upward spiral? *Journal of Personality and Social Psychology, 80,* 152–165.

Sheldon, K. M., & Lyubomirsky, S. (2006). Achieving sustainable gains in happiness: Change your actions, not your circumstances. *Journal of Happiness Studies, 7,* 55–86.

Sieff, E. M., Dawes, R. M., & Loewenstein, G. (1999). Anticipated versus actual responses to HIV test results. *American Journal of Psychology, 112,* 297–311.

Siegel, K., Schrimshaw, E. W., & Pretter, S. (2005). Stress-related growth among women living with HIV/AIDS: Examination of an explanatory model. *Journal of Behavioral Medicine, 28,* 403–414.

Silver, R. L. (1982). Coping with an undesirable life event: A study of early reactions to physical disability. Unpublished doctoral dissertation, Northwestern University, Evanston, IL.

Siosteen, A., Lundqvist, C., Blomstrand, C., Sullivan, L., & Sullivan, M. (1990). The quality of life of three functional spinal cord injury subgroups in a Swedish community. *Paraplegia, 28,* 476–488.

Smith, D. M., Langa, K. M., Kabeto, M. U., & Ubel, P. A. (2005). Health, wealth, and happiness: Financial resources buffer subjective well-being after the onset of disability. *Psychological Science, 16,* 663–666.

Snyder, C. R. (1989). Reality negotiation: From excuses to hope and beyond. *Journal of Social and Clinical Psychology, 8,* 130–157.

Snyder, C. R., Ilardi, S., Michael, S. T., & Cheavens, J. (2000). Hope theory: Updating a common process for psychological change. In C. R. Snyder & R. E. Ingram (Eds.), *Handbook of psychological change: Psychotherapy processes and practices for the 21st century* (pp. 128–153). New York: Wiley.

Snyder, M., & Omoto, A. M. (2001). Basic research and practical problems: Volunteerism and the psychology of individual and collective action. In W. Wosinska, R. B. Cialdini, D. W. Barrett, & J. Reykowski (Eds.), *The practice of social influence in multiple cultures* (pp. 287–307). Mahwah, NJ: Erlbaum.

Somerfield, M. R., & McCrae, R. R. (2000). Stress and coping research: Methodological challenges, theoretical advances, and clinical applications. *American Psychologist, 55,* 620–625.

Svendsen, H. A., & Teasdale, T. W. (2006). The influence of neuropsychological rehabilitation on symptomatology and quality of life following brain injury: A controlled long-term follow-up. *Brain Injury, 20,* 1295–1306.

Taylor, S. E. (1983). Adjustment to threatening events: A theory of cognitive adaptation. *American Psychologist, 38,* 1161–1173.

Taylor, S. E., & Brown, J. D. (1988). Illusion and well-being: A social psychological perspective on mental health. *American Psychologist, 38,* 1161–1173.

Tedeschi, R. G., & Calhoun, L. G. (2004). Posttraumatic growth: Conceptual foundations and empirical evidence. *Psychological Inquiry, 15,* 1–18.

Trieschmann, R. B. (1988). *Spinal cord injuries: Psychological, social, and vocational rehabilitation.* New York: Demos.

Tugade, M. M., & Fredrickson, B. L. (2002). Positive emotions and emotional intelligence. In L. Feldman-Barrett & P. Salovey (Eds.), *The wisdom of feelings: Psychological processes in emotional intelligence* (pp. 319–240). New York: Guilford.

Tugade, M. M., & Fredrickson, B. L. (2004). Resilient individuals use positive emotions to bounce back from negative emotional arousal. *Journal of Personality and Social Psychology, 86,* 320–333.

Turner, R. J., Lloyd, D. A., & Taylor, J. (2006). Physical disability and mental health: An epidemiology of psychiatric and substance disorders. *Rehabilitation Psychology, 51,* 214–223.

Ubel, P. A., Loewenstein, G., Hershey, J., Baron, J., Mohr, T., Asch, D., et al. (2001). Do nonpatients underestimate the quality of life associated with chronic health conditions because of a focusing illusion? *Medical Decision Making, 21,* 190–199.

Weinberg, N. (1988). Another perspective: Attitudes of people with disabilities. In H. E. Yuker (Ed.), *Attitudes towards persons with disabilities* (pp. 141–153). New York: Springer.

Wilson, T. D., & Gilbert, D. T. (2003). Affective forecasting. In M. P. Zanna (Ed.), *Advances in experimental social psychology* (Vol. 35, pp. 345–511). San Diego, CA: Academic Press.

Wilson, T. D., & Gilbert, D. T. (2005). Affective forecasting: Knowing what to want. *Current Directions in Psychological Science, 14,* 131–134.

World Health Organization. (2001). *International classification of functioning, disability, and health.* Geneva, Switzerland: Author.

Wortman, C. B. (2004). Posttraumatic growth: Progress and problems. *Psychological Inquiry, 15,* 81–90.

Wortman, C. B., & Boerner, K. (2007). Beyond the myths of coping with loss: Assumptions versus scientific evidence. In H. S. Friedman & R. C. Silver (Eds.), *Foundations of health psychology* (pp. 285–324). New York: Oxford University Press.

Wright, B. A. (1972). Value-laden beliefs and principles for rehabilitation psychology. *Rehabilitation Psychology, 19*, 38–45.

Wright, B. A. (1980). Person and situation: Adjusting the rehabilitative focus. *Archives of Physical and Medical Rehabilitation, 61*, 59–64.

Wright, B. A. (1983). *Physical disability: A psychosocial approach* (2nd ed.). New York: Harper & Row.

Wright, B. A. (1991). Labeling: The need for greater person–environment individuation. In C. R. Snyder & D. R. Forsyth (Eds.), *Handbook of social and clinical psychology: The health perspective* (pp. 469–487). New York: Pergamon.

PART 11

Toward Better Lives

The Promise of Sustainable Happiness

Julia K. Boehm *and* Sonja Lyubomirsky

Abstract

From ancient history to recent times, philosophers, writers, self-help gurus, and now scientists have taken up the challenge of how to foster greater happiness. This chapter discusses why some people are happier than others, focusing on the distinctive ways that happy and unhappy individuals construe themselves and others, respond to social comparisons, make decisions, and self-reflect. We suggest that, despite several barriers to increased well-being, less happy people can strive successfully to be happier by learning a variety of effortful strategies and practicing them with determination and commitment. The sustainable happiness model (Lyubomirsky, Sheldon, & Schkade, 2005) provides a theoretical framework for experimental intervention research on how to increase and maintain happiness. According to this model, three factors contribute to an individual's chronic happiness level: (a) the set point, (b) life circumstances, and (c) intentional activities, or effortful acts that are naturally variable and episodic. Such activities, which include committing acts of kindness, expressing gratitude or optimism, and savoring joyful life events, represent the most promising route to sustaining enhanced happiness. We describe a half-dozen randomized controlled interventions testing the efficacy of each of these activities in raising and maintaining well-being, as well as the mediators and moderators underlying their effects. Future researchers must endeavor not only to learn *which* particular practices make people happier, but *how* and *why* they do so.

Keywords: construal, happiness, intervention, set point, well-being

> How to gain, how to keep, how to recover happiness is in
> fact for most men at all times the secret motive of all they
> do, and of all they are willing to endure.
> —*William James*

The quest for ever-greater happiness has existed since antiquity. Interest has not abated in today's society, whose preoccupation with becoming happier is evident in countless books and magazine articles promising the secret to a happy life. Indeed, the pursuit of happiness is not without reward, as empirical support is accumulating for the notion that happiness promotes multiple successful life outcomes (including superior health, higher income, and stronger relationships; see Lyubomirsky, King, & Diener, 2005, for a review). Nonetheless, conflicting evidence raises questions about whether it is even possible for people to realize and then sustain meaningful changes in well-being.

In this chapter, we examine several issues with respect to sustainable happiness. To begin, we describe what happy and unhappy people are like, paying particular attention to the strategies that chronically happy people appear to use to foster and preserve their well-being. Next, we address some of the scientific community's reservations and uncertainties with respect to the possibility of sustainably increasing happiness. Finally, we review evidence suggesting that people can indeed learn strategies to achieve durable increases in well-being.

What Are Happy and Unhappy People Like?

Why are some people happier than others? Is it due to their marital status or the salary they earn? Is it because of the experiences they have or the culture they grow up in? Hundreds of empirical articles to date have examined how these and other so-called "objective" circumstances relate to happiness. Surprising to many laypeople, such objective factors (including marriage, age, sex, culture, income, and life events) explain relatively little variation in people's levels of well-being (see Diener, Suh, Lucas, & Smith, 1999, for a review).

Given that circumstantial factors do not tell a satisfactory story to account for the differences between happy and unhappy people, one must look elsewhere to understand them. We propose that happy and unhappy individuals[1] differ considerably in their *subjective experience and construal* of the world (Lyubomirsky, 2001). In other words, happy people are inclined to perceive and interpret their environment differently from their less happy peers. This construal theory prompts us to explore how an individual's thoughts, behaviors, and motivations can explain her happiness over and above the mere objective circumstances of her life. A growing body of research suggests that happy people successfully enhance and maintain their happiness through the use of multiple adaptive strategies vis-à-vis construal of themselves and others, social comparison, decision making, and self-reflection (Liberman, Boehm, Lyubomirsky, & Ross, 2008; Lyubomirsky, Boehm, Kasri, & Zehm, 2008; Lyubomirsky & Ross, 1997, 1999; Lyubomirsky, Tkach, & DiMatteo, 2006; Lyubomirsky & Tucker, 1998; Lyubomirsky, Tucker, & Kasri, 2001; Schwartz et al., 2002).

Construal

Indeed, research suggests that happy individuals tend to view the world relatively more positively and in a happiness-promoting way. For example, when

[1] In the majority of the studies reported here, happy and unhappy people were identified using a median or quartile split on the widely used four-item Subjective Happiness Scale (Lyubomirsky & Lepper, 1999). In other words, those scoring in the top half (or quarter) of the happiness distribution were classified as chronically happy, whereas those in the bottom half (or quarter) were classified as chronically unhappy.

describing their previous life experiences, self-nominated happy people retrospectively evaluated the experiences as more pleasant at both the time of occurrence and when recalling them (study 1, Lyubomirsky & Tucker, 1998; cf. Seidlitz, Wyer, & Diener, 1997). Unhappy people, however, evaluated their past life events relatively unfavorably at both time points. Interestingly, objective judges did not rate the events described by happy people as inherently more positive than those described by unhappy people, suggesting that happy and unhappy people experience similar events but interpret them differently. Further supporting this finding, when participants were asked to evaluate hypothetical situations, dispositionally happy people rated the situations more positively compared with their less happy peers, even after current mood was controlled (study 2, Lyubomirsky & Tucker, 1998).

Self-nominated chronically happy people also have been found to use a positive perspective when evaluating themselves and others. For example, in one study, students interacted with a female stranger in the laboratory and were then asked to evaluate her personality. Happy students rated the stranger more positively, and expressed a stronger interest in becoming friends with her, compared with unhappy students (study 3, Lyubomirsky & Tucker, 1998; see also Berry & Hansen, 1996; Judge & Higgins, 1998). Furthermore, happy people tend to judge almost everything about themselves and their lives favorably, including their friendships, recreation, self-esteem, energy levels, and purpose in life (Lyubomirsky, Tkach, et al., 2006; see also Lucas, Diener, & Suh, 1996; Ryff, 1989).

Social Comparison

At its most basic level, the general finding from the social comparison domain is that happy people are less sensitive to feedback about other people's performances, even when that feedback is unfavorable. An illustrative study from our laboratory involved participants solving anagrams in the presence of a confederate who was performing the same task either much quicker or much slower (study 1, Lyubomirsky & Ross, 1997). When exposed to a slower confederate, all participants (regardless of how happy they were) reacted the same way to the experience—that is, performing the task bolstered confidence in their skills. In the presence of a faster confederate, however, happy students did not change their judgments of how good they were at the task, but unhappy participants derogated their own skills. This finding supports the argument that the self-perceptions of happy individuals are relatively invulnerable to social comparisons.

In another study, students were asked to "teach" a lesson about conflict resolution to a hypothetical audience of children while presumably being evaluated by experts (study 2, Lyubomirsky & Ross, 1997). After this teaching task, participants were supplied with an expert evaluation of their own—and a peer's—teaching performance. The results showed that happy people responded to the situation in a predictable and adaptive manner—they reported more positive emotions when told that their performance was excellent (even when a peer had done even better) than when told that their performance was poor (even when a peer had done even worse). Unhappy people's reactions, by contrast, were surprising and even dysfunctional. They reported more positive emotions after receiving a *negative* expert evaluation (accompanied by news that a peer had done even worse) than after receiving a positive expert evaluation (accompanied by news that a peer had done even better). Again, this suggests that happy people's emotions and self-regard are much less impacted by comparisons with others than those of their unhappy peers.

Happy individuals' inclinations to deemphasize social comparison feedback have been observed in a group context as well (Lyubomirsky et al., 2001). For example, in one study, students competed in four-person groups (or "teams") in a relay race involving word puzzles. The announcement of the winning team—or their individual rank on their team—did not influence happy participants' moods. In contrast, unhappy participants showed depressed moods after their team supposedly lost, and bolstered moods after learning that they had individually placed first on their losing team. The results of this study suggest that unhappy students are more responsive to both group and individual information, particularly in "failure" situations. Whereas unhappy people use individual ranking information (i.e., first place on their team) to buffer against unfavorable group comparisons (i.e., their team's underperformance), happy people do not appear to need such a buffer (see also Ahrens, 1991; Swallow & Kuiper, 1992; Wheeler & Miyake, 1992).

Decision Making

Besides using different strategies in the social comparison domain, happy and unhappy people also respond distinctively when making decisions. For example, empirical evidence suggests that happy and unhappy individuals show divergent responses to both inconsequential decisions (e.g., selecting a dessert) and momentous ones (e.g., selecting a college; Lyubomirsky & Ross, 1999). Happy people tend to be more satisfied with all of their available options (including the option they eventually choose) and only express dissatisfaction in situations when their sense of self is threatened. For example, when self-reported happy students were asked to rate the attractiveness of several desserts before and after learning which dessert they would get to keep, they increased their liking for the dessert they got and didn't change their liking for the dessert they couldn't get. This seems to be an adaptive strategy. In contrast, unhappy students found the option they were given to be minimally acceptable (derogating that dessert after learning they could keep it), and the forgone options to be even worse (study 2, Lyubomirsky & Ross, 1999; see also Steele, Spencer, & Lynch, 1993).

Similar patterns have been observed for happy and unhappy people facing a more significant decision-making situation—namely, the choice of a university (study 1, Lyubomirsky & Ross, 1999). After being accepted by individual colleges, self-described happy students boosted their liking and judgments of those colleges. To protect themselves, however, these happy students decreased their overall ratings of the colleges that had rejected them. This dissonance reduction presumably allowed the happy participants to maintain positive feelings and self-regard. By contrast, unhappy participants did not use the same strategy to maintain positivity; instead, they (maladaptively) maintained their liking for the colleges that had rejected them.

Happy and unhappy people also differ in how they make decisions in the face of many options. Research suggests that happy individuals are relatively more likely to "satisfice"—namely, to be satisfied with an option that is merely "good enough," without concern for alternative, potentially better options (Schwartz et al., 2002). Unhappy individuals, by contrast, are more likely to "maximize" their options—that is, they seek to make the absolute best choice. Although maximizers' decisions may ultimately produce objectively superior results (e.g., a more lucrative job), maximizers experience greater regret and diminished well-being relative to satisficers (Iyengar, Wells, & Schwartz, 2006). The maximizing tendencies of unhappy individuals may thus serve to reinforce their unhappiness.

Intrusive Dwelling

Happy people are much less likely than their unhappier peers to excessively self-reflect and dwell upon themselves. For example, in several studies, unhappy students led to believe that they had failed at a verbal task experienced negative affect and intrusive negative thoughts, which interfered with their concentration and impaired their performance on a subsequent intellectually demanding test (Lyubomirsky et al., 2008). These findings suggest that unhappy people engage in negative (and maladaptive) dwelling more so than do happy people, and their excessive dwelling not only makes them feel bad, but brings about significant detrimental outcomes (see also Lyubomirsky & Kasri, 2006). Notably, another study revealed that manipulating a person's focus of attention (i.e., reflecting vs. distracting) could eliminate the differences between the cognitive strategies and processes shown by happy and unhappy individuals (study 3, Lyubomirsky & Ross, 1999). This finding hints at a critical mechanism underlying differences between happy and unhappy people— namely, that one could "turn" a happy person into an unhappy one by instructing her to ruminate about herself. Conversely, one could make an unhappy person "look like" a happy person by directing his attention away from himself.

The way that people consider their past life events also may differentially impact happiness. A recent set of studies in the United States and Israel examined the relationship between well-being and two different thought perspectives that can be used to consider autobiographical experiences—namely, "endowing" (or reflecting on) life events versus "contrasting" them with the present (Liberman et al., 2008; cf. Tversky & Griffin, 1991). Happy people are relatively more likely to report endowing (or savoring) past positive life experiences and contrasting negative life experiences (i.e., considering how much better off they are today), whereas unhappy people are relatively more likely to report endowing (or ruminating about) negative experiences and contrasting positive experiences (i.e., considering how much worse off they are today). This evidence suggests that happy people's strategies of processing life events serve to prolong and preserve positive emotions, whereas the strategies of unhappy individuals serve to dampen the inherent positivity associated with positive events and to enhance the negative affect associated with negative events.

Can Less Happy People Learn Strategies to Achieve Sustainable Happiness?

Our current understanding of the differences between chronically happy and unhappy people suggests that happy people think and behave in ways

that reinforce their happiness. Given these findings, is it possible for unhappy people to learn deliberate strategies to achieve ever-greater well-being? Evidence suggests that in naturalistic settings people do try to become happier. For example, college students report a variety of strategies that they use to increase happiness, including social affiliation, pursuing goals, engaging in leisure activities, participating in religion, and "direct" attempts (e.g., act happy, smile; Tkach & Lyubomirsky, 2006). Although some of these techniques— especially social affiliation and direct attempts—are positively correlated with happiness, it is unclear whether such strategies *cause* increases in happiness or whether already happy people are simply more likely to practice them.

Sources of Pessimism Regarding Happiness Change

Doubts about the possibility of increasing and maintaining happiness have dominated the area of well-being and personality.

To begin with, twin and adoption studies suggest that genetics account for approximately 50% of the variation present in well-being (Lykken & Tellegen, 1996). For example, Tellegen and colleagues (1988) investigated the well-being of identical and fraternal twins who had been raised together or apart. The happiness levels of the identical twin pairs were strongly correlated, and this correlation was equally high regardless of whether such twins had grown up under the same roof ($r = .58$) or miles apart ($r = .48$). Pairs of fraternal twins, however, showed much smaller correlations between their levels of well-being, even when they shared the same upbringing and household ($r = .23$ vs. $r = .18$). Longitudinal studies of changes in well-being over time bolster these data even further. For example, although positive and negative life experiences have been shown to increase or decrease happiness in the short term, people apparently rapidly return to their happiness baselines (Headey & Wearing, 1989; Suh, Diener, & Fujita, 1996). These lines of evidence indicate that each person may have a unique set point for happiness that is genetically determined and immune to influence.

Another concern regarding sustainable changes in well-being is rooted in the concept of hedonic adaptation. Brickman and Campbell (1971) argued that after positive or negative life experiences, people quickly become accustomed to their new conditions and eventually return to their baseline happiness. This notion of a "hedonic treadmill" suggests that people adapt to circumstantial changes, especially positive ones. Many people still believe, however, that an incredibly exciting experience or major positive life change, such as winning a lottery, would make them considerably happier. In fact, a study comparing lottery winners and people who experienced no sudden windfall demonstrated that the lottery winners were no happier—and even appeared to obtain less pleasure from daily activities—than did nonwinners (Brickman, Coates, & Janoff-Bulman, 1978). This suggests that hedonic adaptation is another potent barrier to sustainably increasing well-being (cf. Diener, Lucas, & Scollon, 2006; Lucas, Clark, Georgellis, & Diener, 2003; see Lyubomirsky, in press, for a review).

A final source of pessimism about the possibility of real change in happiness is the strong association between happiness and personality (Diener & Lucas, 1999). Personality traits are characterized by their relatively fixed nature and lack of variation across time (McCrae & Costa, 1994). Thus, some researchers conceptualize happiness as part of a person's stable personality and, by extension, as a construct that is unlikely to undergo meaningful change (Costa, McCrae, & Zonderman, 1987).

The Sustainable Happiness Model

In their model of the primary determinants of happiness, Lyubomirsky, Sheldon, et al. (2005) challenge these reservations and offer an optimistic perspective regarding the possibility of creating sustainable increases in happiness. According to their model, chronic happiness, or the happiness one shows during a specific period in life, is influenced by three factors—one's set point, one's life circumstances, and the intentional activities in which one engages (see Figure 63.1). As mentioned, the set point is thought to account for

approximately 50% of the variance in individual differences in chronic happiness. Unfortunately, however, because the set point is "set" or fixed, it is resistant to change. Given its relative inflexibility, the set point is unlikely to be a fruitful direction to pursue increases in happiness.

Counter to many lay notions of well-being, a person's circumstances generally account for only about 10% of individual differences in chronic happiness (Diener et al., 1999). Life circumstances include such factors as a person's national or cultural region, demographics (e.g., gender and ethnicity), personal experiences (e.g., past traumas and triumphs), and life status variables (e.g., marital status, education level, health, and income). Given that such circumstances are relatively constant, they are more susceptible to adaptation and, hence, have comparatively little impact on happiness. Thus, circumstantial factors also do not appear to be a promising route through which to achieve sustainable well-being.

Interestingly, however, although the average person easily adapts to positive changes in her life, like getting married, winning the lottery, or acquiring sharper vision, individual differences have been found in degrees of adaptation. For example, in a study of reactions to marriage, some newlyweds reported substantial boosts in life satisfaction after the wedding and remained very satisfied even years later, while others rapidly returned to their baseline happiness and others still actually became less happy and stayed relatively unhappy (Lucas et al., 2003). These findings suggest that people vary in how they *intentionally behave* in response to changing circumstances—for example, the extent to which they might express gratitude to their marriage partner, put effort into cultivating their relationship, or savor positive experiences together.

The most promising factor for affecting change in chronic happiness, then, is the approximately 40% portion represented by intentional activity (see Figure 63.1; cf. Lyubomirsky, 2008). Characterized by committed and effortful acts in which people choose to engage, intentional activities can be behavioral (e.g., practicing random acts of kindness), cognitive (e.g., expressing gratitude), or motivational (e.g., pursuing intrinsic significant life goals). The benefits of intentional activities are that they are naturally variable and tend to have beginning and ending points (i.e., they are episodic). These two characteristics alone have the potential to work against adaptation. That is, it is much more difficult to adapt to something that is continuously changing (i.e., the

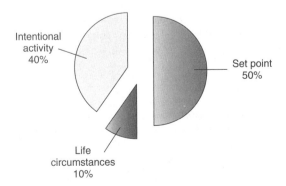

Fig. 63.1 The three factors that influence chronic happiness (adapted from Lyubomirsky, Sheldon, et al., 2005).

Intentional activity 40%

Set point 50%

Life circumstances 10%

activities that one pursues) than to something that is relatively constant (i.e., one's circumstances and situations).

Supporting this argument, when people were asked to rate various aspects of recent positive changes in their activities (e.g., starting a new fitness program) versus positive changes in their circumstances (e.g., moving to a nicer apartment), they described their activity-based changes as more "variable" and less prone to adaptation (Sheldon & Lyubomirsky, 2006a). Furthermore, activity-based changes predicted well-being both 6 and 12 weeks after the start of the study, whereas circumstance-based changes predicted well-being only at the 6th week. It appears that by the 12th week of the study, students had already adapted to their circumstantial changes, but not to their intentional activities.

Using Intentional Activities as the Basis of Happiness Interventions

Preliminary evidence suggests that happiness interventions involving intentional activities can be effective in increasing and sustaining happiness. One of the first researchers to teach volitional strategies to increase happiness was Fordyce (1977, 1983). Fordyce taught his "14 fundamentals" of happiness (e.g., socializing, practicing optimism, being present oriented, reducing negativity, and not worrying) to different classrooms of students. Across seven studies, students who were taught the happiness-increasing strategies demonstrated increases in happiness compared with students who received no training.

Fordyce's pioneering studies provide preliminary evidence that people have the potential to increase their short-term happiness through "training" programs. Extending this work, we have examined in depth several intentional happiness-enhancing activities in the laboratory and have sought to identify significant moderators and mediators of their effectiveness.

Committing Acts of Kindness

A randomized controlled intervention from our laboratory involved a behavioral intentional activity—in a 10-week experiment, participants were invited to regularly practice random acts of kindness (Boehm, Lyubomirsky, & Sheldon, 2008). Engaging in kind acts (e.g., holding the door open for a stranger or doing a roommate's dishes) was thought to impact happiness for a variety of reasons, including bolstered self-regard, positive social interactions, and charitable feelings toward others and the community at large. In this study, happiness was measured at baseline, mid-intervention, immediately post-intervention, and 1 month later. Additionally, two variables were manipulated: (a) the frequency with which participants practiced acts of kindness (either three or nine times each week) and (b) the variety with which participants practiced acts of kindness (either varying their kind acts or repeating the same acts weekly). Finally, a control group merely listed events from the past week.

Interestingly, the frequency with which kind acts were performed had no bearing on subsequent well-being. The variety of the kind acts, however, influenced the extent to which participants became happier. Those who were asked to perform a wide variety of kind acts revealed an upward trajectory for happiness, even through the 1-month follow-up. By contrast, the control group showed no changes in their happiness throughout the 14 weeks of the study, and those not given the opportunity to vary their kind acts actually became less happy midway through the intervention, before eventually rebounding to their baseline happiness level at the follow-up assessment.

In another kindness intervention from our laboratory, students were asked to perform five acts of kindness per week over the course of 6 weeks, and those five acts had to be done either within a single day (e.g., all on Monday), or across the week (Lyubomirsky, Sheldon et al., 2005). In this study, happiness levels increased for students performing acts of kindness, but only for those who performed all of their kind acts in a single day. Perhaps, when kind acts were spread throughout the week, the effect of each kind act was dispersed, such that participants did not differentiate between their normal (and presumably habitually kind) behavior and the kindnesses prompted by this intervention. Taken together, our two kindness interventions suggest not only that happiness can be boosted by behavioral intentional activities, but that both the timing and variety of performing such intentional activities significantly moderate their impact on well-being.

Expressing Gratitude

Another intervention from our laboratory—one examining the effect of expressing gratitude (or "counting one's blessings") on changes in well-being—conceptually replicated the kindness studies (Lyubomirsky, Sheldon et al., 2005). Being grateful was predicted to bolster happiness because it promotes the savoring of positive events and situations, and may counteract hedonic adaptation by allowing people to see the good in their life rather than taking it for granted. In this study, which was modeled after Emmons and McCullough (2003), participants were asked to keep gratitude journals once a week, three times a week, or not at all (a no-treatment control). In their journals, participants wrote down up to five things for which they were grateful in the past week. The "blessings" recounted included relatively significant things (e.g., health or parents), as well as more trivial ones (e.g., AOL instant messenger).

Well-being was measured both before and after the gratitude manipulation. Corroborating the results of our 6-week kindness study, the role of optimal timing again proved decisive. Accordingly, increases in well-being were observed only in participants who counted their blessings once a week rather than three times a week. This finding provides further evidence supporting the argument that not only an intentional activity can successfully increase happiness, but also the way that activity is implemented is critical.

Visualizing Best Possible Selves

Sheldon and Lyubomirsky (2006b) investigated yet another intentional activity that might be effective at elevating happiness—namely, the practice of visualizing and writing about one's best possible selves (BPSs; Markus & Nurius, 1986). This 4-week intervention also included a gratitude condition (in which participants counted their blessings) and a control condition (in which they recalled daily events). In the BPS condition, participants were encouraged to consider desired future images of themselves. King (2001) had previously demonstrated that writing about one's best future selves—a process that presumably enhances optimism and helps integrate one's priorities and life goals—is related to boosts in well-being. Results of our 4-week intervention indicated that participants in both experimental conditions reported increased positive feelings immediately after the intervention; however, these increases were statistically significant only among those who visualized BPSs.

Processing Happy Life Experiences

Another series of happiness intervention studies focused on the way that people consider positive life experiences (Lyubomirsky, Sousa, & Dickerhoof, 2006). We hypothesized that systematically analyzing and structuring one's thoughts and feelings

associated with the happiest moments in life would reduce some of the inherent joy associated with such experiences. In contrast, reexperiencing or savoring such moments (without attempting to find meaning or organization in them) was expected to preserve positive emotions and generally increase happiness. Two experiments tested these ideas using Pennebaker's (1997) expressive writing paradigm. In the first study, participants were asked to write about their life experiences (vs. talk into a tape recorder or think privately about them) for 15 min on each of 3 days. The findings revealed that those who thought about their happiest event reported higher life satisfaction relative to those who talked or wrote about it.

In the second study, participants wrote or thought about their happiest day by either systematically analyzing or repetitively replaying it. The combination of writing and analysis was expected to be the most detrimental to well-being, whereas thinking and replaying was expected to be the most beneficial to well-being. Indeed, those participants who repetitively replayed their happiest day while thinking about it showed increases in positive emotions 4 weeks after the study was over, when compared with the other groups. In sum, the evidence suggests that, when considering the happiest moments in one's life, strategies that involve systematic, planful integration and structuring (e.g., the processes naturally engendered by writing or talking) may diminish the accompanying positive emotions. A successful happiness-increasing strategy, by contrast, involves replaying or reliving positive life events as though rewinding a videotape.

Current and Future Directions

An important caveat to the happiness intervention research conducted to this date is that participants practicing a particular happiness-enhancing activity have not yet been followed in the long term. To be sure, a complete investigation of the sustainable impact of activity-based interventions on happiness must use a longitudinal perspective (i.e., assessing well-being many months and even years post intervention). Although some studies have measured happiness 6 months (Seligman, Steen, Park, & Peterson, 2005), 9 months (study 1, Lyubomirsky, Dickerhoof, Boehm, & Sheldon, 2008), and even 18 months later (Fordyce, 1983), it is unclear whether participants were still engaging in their assigned exercises for that period of time. Indeed, after the prescribed intervention period—when researchers are not encouraging, let alone enforcing, participants to practice their happiness-inducing activity—participants may or may not continue with the activity on their own accord. The committed effort shown by those who use happiness-enhancing strategies should be systematically measured and tested for the extent to which it moderates the effectiveness of strategy enactment.

Empirical evidence suggests, for example, that the participants likely to show long-term benefits of a happiness intervention are those who continue to implement and integrate the intervention activity into their lives, even after the active intervention period has ended (Seligman et al., 2005). For example, in our study that asked students to either express gratitude or visualize their best futures, positive affect was predicted 4 weeks later by continued performance of the intervention activity (Sheldon & Lyubomirsky, 2006b). Furthermore, those students who found the happiness-enhancing activity rewarding were the most likely to practice it. Similarly, a recent intervention study from our laboratory revealed that the well-being benefits of engaging in a happiness-inducing exercise (either gratitude or optimism) accrued only to those participants who were motivated to become happier (study 1, Lyubomirsky et al., 2008), and this effect was in evidence 6 months later. More to the point, after completing our intervention, participants who were still practicing their previously assigned exercise reported greater increases in well-being relative to others.

Future researchers also might find it valuable to investigate a variety of specific intentional activities that serve to enhance and sustain well-being. Fordyce (1977, 1983) proposed as many as 14 different strategies to increase happiness, and dozens of other candidates undoubtedly exist. Thus far, only a subset of strategies have been tested experimentally (e.g., expressing gratitude, imagining BPSs, practicing kind acts, and adjusting cognitive perspective). Although additional happiness exercises have been examined in Web-based interventions (e.g., applying personal strengths or thinking positively; Seligman et al., 2005), the investigation of specific intervention strategies in a controlled laboratory setting is critical, as it allows the testing of theory-based hypotheses about how and why a particular strategy "works."

The variety of questions that controlled laboratory studies can address include the role of variables that potentially moderate the effectiveness of any particular happiness-enhancing strategy. Exploring such moderators may be crucial to understanding the relationship between intentional activities and subsequent well-being. Several moderators, described briefly here, already have begun to be examined (e.g., timing, variety, and effort), but many others are untested or unknown. For example, one important moderator to consider in future studies is the "fit" between a person and an appropriate intentional activity—that is, the notion that not every activity is likely to benefit every person (Lyubomirsky, 2008; Lyubomirsky, Sheldon, et al., 2005). Supporting the critical role of fit, preliminary findings reveal that individuals who report a relatively high degree of fit with the activity they practice (i.e., performing it for self-determined reasons) report bigger gains in happiness (study 1, Lyubomirsky et al., 2008).

Happiness interventions also may be more effective when the participant has the support of close others. When training for a marathon, runners who are part of a "team" have others to provide encouragement and to share both the challenges and rewards of their endeavor. As a result, runners with emotional and tangible support are likely to be more successful than those training alone. Likewise, people practicing strategies to enhance well-being are also likely to benefit from social support.

Another important moderator to consider is culture. The individualist notion of personal happiness distinctive to North America and Europe actually may run counter to the values and prescriptives of collectivist nations. Indeed, the pursuit of happiness in general—or specific strategies in particular—may not be as accepted or well-supported in non-Western cultures (Lyubomirsky, 2001). Thus, cultural differences are critical to recognize when evaluating the effectiveness of well-being interventions (see also Suh, Diener, Oishi, & Triandis, 1998). Indeed, the results of a recent study support the intriguing idea that foreign-born Asian Americans may benefit less—and differently—from practicing grateful and optimistic thinking than their Anglo-American peers (study 2, Lyubomirsky et al., 2008).

Happiness in the Spotlight

This review of the sustainable well-being literature illustrates positive psychology's increasing focus on the causes, correlates, variations, and consequences of happiness. Why has happiness rapidly emerged into the scientific spotlight? Throughout the history of Western individualist societies, both laypeople and intellectuals alike have been preoccupied with attaining greater well-being. Indeed, people in a wide array of cultures report the pursuit of happiness as one of their most meaningful, desirable, and significant life goals (Diener & Oishi, 2000; Diener,

Suh, Smith, & Shao, 1995; Triandis, Bontempo, Leung, & Hui, 1990). It is not surprising then that happiness should become a topic of tremendous research interest. Furthermore, whereas earlier thinkers, lacking in the proper scientific tools, could only philosophize about the nature and roots of happiness, advances in assessment and methodology have enabled current researchers to investigate subjective well-being with greater confidence and increased precision (Diener, Lucas, & Oishi, 2002). Finally, as ever more people around the globe, and especially in the West, have their basic needs met, they have begun to enjoy the "luxury" of focusing on psychological fulfillment—that is, on psychological well-being rather than only on material well-being. And, for those with nonessential wealth, there may be a dawning recognition that material consumption—possessing the latest gadget or living in the grandest house—is not rewarding in and of itself (Diener et al., 2002).

Are there any costs to devoting energy and resources to the scientific study of well-being? We believe the costs are avoidable and few. Certainly, a single-minded obsession with the pursuit of happiness may obscure or preclude other important goals or activities for the individual—activities that may be "right," virtuous, or moral, but not happiness inducing. Furthermore, although many characteristics of happy individuals help them achieve success in many areas of life, some of their characteristics (e.g., reliance on heuristics or diminished attention to the self) may be detrimental in certain contexts (Lyubomirsky, King, et al., 2005). In sum, happiness may be a necessary condition of the good life—a healthy, well-lived life—but it is not a sufficient condition. Other concerns should motivate people too, like cultivating self-acceptance and nourishing strong social relationships (Ryff & Keyes, 1995). Then again, it is notable that many, if not most, important, worthy, and socially desirable life activities, which sometimes appear to be incongruent with the pursuit of happiness—like caring for a sick family member, cramming for the MCATs, or turning the other cheek—can all be used as strategies to ultimately enhance well-being (Lyubomirsky, 2008).

Concluding Remarks

Man is the artificer of his own happiness.
—*Henry David Thoreau*

We have reviewed a number of cognitive, judgmental, and behavioral strategies that happy people use to maintain their high levels of well-being and have suggested that less happy people can strive successfully to be happier by learning a variety of effortful, happiness-enhancing strategies and implementing them with determination and commitment. Lyubomirsky, Sheldon, et al.'s (2005) model of the determinants of happiness suggests that, despite historical sources of pessimism regarding change in well-being, people *can* become sustainably happier by practicing intentional activities—but only with concerted effort and under optimal conditions. We believe that hedonic adaptation to positive changes in people's lives is one of the most significant barriers to happiness. The intentional activities described here, and likely many others, can work to inhibit, counteract, or slow down the adaptation process.

Although empirical validation of our model is in the preliminary stage, increasing evidence suggests that engaging in purposeful activities leads to meaningful changes in well-being. Future researchers would do well to consider not only what strategies may successfully enhance happiness, but also under what conditions intentional activities are most effective.

Future Questions

1. Besides happiness, what other outcomes related to the "good life" might be affected by the practice of intentional activities?

2. Which additional intentional activities might serve to enhance happiness?

3. Would certain strategies to increase happiness be more effective in a collectivist versus an individualist culture?

4. Although the variable and episodic nature of intentional activities may serve to counteract adaptation, could people grow accustomed to a certain level of positivity in their lives and hence need more positive experiences just to maintain the same level of well-being?

5. Are activities to increase happiness more effective for happy people (who presumably already implement similar strategies in their daily lives) or for unhappy people (who presumably have more to gain in happiness)? Are some strategies a better fit for one group versus the other?

References

Ahrens, A. H. (1991). Dysphoria and social comparison: Combining information regarding others' performances. *Journal of Social and Clinical Psychology, 10*, 190–205.

Berry, D. S., & Hansen, J. S. (1996). Positive affect, negative affect, and social interaction. *Journal of Personality and Social Psychology, 71*, 796–809.

Boehm, J. K., Lyubomirsky, S., & Sheldon, K. M. (2008). Spicing up kindness: The role of variety in the effects of practicing kindness on improvements in mood, happiness, and self-evaluations. Manuscript in preparation.

Brickman, P., & Campbell, D. T. (1971). Hedonic relativism and planning the good society. In M. H. Appley (Ed.), *Adaptation-level theory* (pp. 287–302). New York: Academic Press.

Brickman, P., Coates, D., & Janoff-Bulman, R. (1978). Lottery winners and accident victims: Is happiness relative? *Journal of Personality and Social Psychology, 36,* 917–927.

Costa, P. T., McCrae, R. R., & Zonderman, A. B. (1987). Environmental and dispositional influences on well-being: Longitudinal follow-up of an American national sample. *British Journal of Psychology, 78,* 299–306.

Diener, E., & Lucas, R. E. (1999). Personality and subjective well-being. In D. Kahneman, E. Diener, & N. Schwarz (Eds.), *Well-being: The foundations of hedonic psychology* (pp. 213–229). Cambridge, MA: MIT Press.

Diener, E., Lucas, R. E., & Oishi, S. (2002). The science of happiness and life satisfaction. In S. R. Snyder & S. J. Lopez (Eds.), *Handbook of positive psychology* (pp. 463–473). New York: Oxford University Press.

Diener, E., Lucas, R. E., & Scollon, C. N. (2006). Beyond the hedonic treadmill: Revising the adaptation theory of well-being. *American Psychologist, 61,* 305–314.

Diener, E., & Oishi, S. (2000). Money and happiness: Income and subjective well-being across nations. In E. Diener & E. M. Suh (Eds.), *Culture and subjective well-being* (pp. 185–218). Cambridge, MA: The MIT Press.

Diener, E., Suh, E. M., Lucas, R. E., & Smith, H. L. (1999). Subjective well-being: Three decades of progress. *Psychological Bulletin, 125,* 276–302.

Diener, E., Suh, E. M., Smith, H., & Shao, L. (1995). National differences in reported well-being: Why do they occur? *Social Indicators Research, 34,* 7–32.

Emmons, R. A., & McCullough, M. E. (2003). Counting blessings versus burdens: An experimental investigation of gratitude and subjective well-being in daily life. *Journal of Personality and Social Psychology, 84,* 377–389.

Fordyce, M. W. (1977). Development of a program to increase personal happiness. *Journal of Counseling Psychology, 24,* 511–521.

Fordyce, M. W. (1983). A program to increase happiness: Further studies. *Journal of Counseling Psychology, 30,* 483–498.

Headey, B., & Wearing, A. (1989). Personality, life events, and subjective well-being: Toward a dynamic equilibrium model. *Journal of Personality and Social Psychology, 57,* 731–739.

Iyengar, S. S., Wells, R. E., & Schwartz, B. (2006). Doing better but feeling worse: Looking for the "best" job undermines satisfaction. *Psychological Science, 17,* 143–150.

Judge, T. A., & Higgins, C. A. (1998). Affective disposition and the letter of reference. *Organizational Behavior and Human Decisional Processes, 75,* 207–221.

King, L. A. (2001). The health benefits of writing about life goals. *Personality and Social Psychology Bulletin, 27,* 798–807.

Liberman, V., Boehm, J. K., Lyubomirsky, S., & Ross, L. (2008). Happiness and memory: Affective consequences of endowment and contrast. Manuscript under review.

Lucas, R. E., Clark, A. E., Georgellis, Y., & Diener, E. (2003). Reexamining adaptation and the set point model of happiness: Reactions to changes in marital status. *Journal of Personality and Social Psychology, 84,* 527–539.

Lucas, R. E., Diener, E., & Suh, E. (1996). Discriminant validity of well-being measures. *Journal of Personality and Social Psychology, 3,* 616–628.

Lykken, D., & Tellegen, A. (1996). Happiness is a stochastic phenomenon. *Psychological Science, 7,* 186–189.

Lyubomirsky, S. (in press). Surmounting a critical barrier to becoming happier: Hedonic adaptation to positive experience. In S. Folkman (Ed.), *Handbook on stress, coping, and health.* New York: Oxford University Press.

Lyubomirsky, S. (2001). Why are some people happier than others? The role of cognitive and motivational processes in well-being. *American Psychologist, 56,* 239–249.

Lyubomirsky, S. (2008). *The how of happiness: A scientific approach to getting the life you want.* New York: Penguin Press.

Lyubomirsky, S., Boehm, J. K., Kasri, F., & Zehm, K. (2008). The cognitive and hedonic costs of unwarranted dwelling. Manuscript under review.

Lyubomirsky, S., Dickerhoof, R., Boehm, J. K., & Sheldon, K. M. (2008). Becoming happier takes both a will and a proper way: Two experimental longitudinal interventions to boost well-being. Manuscript under review.

Lyubomirsky, S., & Kasri, F. (2006). [Levels of private self-consciousness and mood awareness among happy and unhappy individuals]. Unpublished raw data.

Lyubomirsky, S., King, L., & Diener, E. (2005). The benefits of frequent positive affect: Does happiness lead to success? *Psychological Bulletin, 131,* 803–855.

Lyubomirsky, S., & Lepper, H. S. (1999). A measure of subjective happiness: Preliminary reliability and construct validation. *Social Indicators Research, 46,* 137–155.

Lyubomirsky, S., & Ross, L. (1997). Hedonic consequences of social comparison: A contrast of happy and unhappy people. *Journal of Personality and Social Psychology, 73,* 1141–1157.

Lyubomirsky, S., & Ross, L. (1999). Changes in attractiveness of elected, rejected, and precluded alternatives: A comparison of happy and unhappy individuals. *Journal of Personality and Social Psychology, 76,* 988–1007.

Lyubomirsky, S., Sheldon, K. M., & Schkade, D. (2005). Pursuing happiness: The architecture of sustainable change. *Review of General Psychology, 9,* 111–131.

Lyubomirsky, S., Sousa, L., & Dickerhoof, R. (2006). The costs and benefits of writing, talking, and thinking about life's triumphs and defeats. *Journal of Personality and Social Psychology, 90,* 692–708.

Lyubomirsky, S., Tkach, C., & DiMatteo, M. R. (2006). What are the differences between happiness and self-esteem? *Social Indicators Research, 78,* 363–404.

Lyubomirsky, S., & Tucker, K. L. (1998). Implications of individual differences in subjective happiness for perceiving, interpreting, and thinking about life events. *Motivation and Emotion, 22,* 155–186.

Lyubomirsky, S., Tucker, K. L., & Kasri, F. (2001). Responses to hedonically conflicting social comparisons: Comparing happy and unhappy people. *European Journal of Social Psychology, 31,* 511–535.

Markus, H., & Nurius, P. (1986). Possible selves. *American Psychologist, 41,* 954–969.

McCrae, R. R., & Costa, P. T. (1994). The stability of personality: Observations and evaluations. *Current Directions in Psychological Science, 3,* 173–175.

Pennebaker, J. W. (1997). Writing about emotional experiences as a therapeutic process. *Psychological Science, 8,* 162–166.

Ryff, C. D. (1989). Happiness is everything, or is it? Explorations on the meaning of psychological well-being. *Journal of Personality and Social Psychology, 6*, 1069–1081.

Ryff, C. D., & Keyes, C. L. M. (1995). The structure of psychological well-being revisited. *Journal of Personality and Social Psychology, 69*, 719–727.

Schwartz, B., Ward, A., Monterosso, J., Lyubomirsky, S., White, K., & Lehman, D. R. (2002). Maximizing versus satisficing: Happiness is a matter of choice. *Journal of Personality and Social Psychology, 83*, 1178–1197.

Seidlitz, L., Jr., Wyer, R. S., & Diener, E. (1997). Cognitive correlates of subjective well-being: The processing of valenced life events by happy and unhappy persons. *Journal of Research in Personality, 31*, 240–256.

Seligman, M. E., Steen, T. A., Park, N., & Peterson, C. (2005). Positive psychology progress: Empirical validation of interventions. *American Psychologist, 60*, 410–421.

Sheldon, K. M., & Lyubomirsky, S. (2006a). Achieving sustainable gains in happiness: Change your actions, not your circumstances. *Journal of Happiness Studies, 7*, 55–86.

Sheldon, K. M., & Lyubomirsky, S. (2006b). How to increase and sustain positive emotion: The effects of expressing gratitude and visualizing best possible selves. *Journal of Positive Psychology, 1*, 73–82.

Steele, C. M., Spencer, S. J., & Lynch, M. (1993). Self-image resilience and dissonance: The role of affirmational resources. *Journal of Personality and Social Psychology, 64*, 885–896.

Suh, E., Diener, E., & Fujita, F. (1996). Events and subjective well-being: Only recent events matter. *Journal of Personality and Social Psychology, 70*, 1091–1102.

Suh, E., Diener, E., Oishi, S., & Triandis, H. C. (1998). The shifting basis of life satisfaction judgments across cultures: Emotions versus norms. *Journal of Personality and Social Psychology, 74*, 482–493.

Swallow, S. R., & Kuiper, N. A. (1992). Mild depression and frequency of social comparison behavior. *Journal of Social and Clinical Psychology, 11*, 167–180.

Tellegen, A., Lykken, D. T., Bouchard, T. J., Wilcox, K. J., Segal, N. L., & Rich, S. (1988). Personality similarity in twins reared apart and together. *Journal of Personality and Social Psychology, 54*, 1031–1039.

Tkach, C., & Lyubomirsky, S. (2006). How do people pursue happiness? Relating personality, happiness-increasing strategies, and well-being. *Journal of Happiness Studies, 7*, 183–225.

Triandis, H. C., Bontempo, R., Leung, K., & Hui, C. H. (1990). A method for determining cultural, demographic, and personal constructs. *Journal of Cross-cultural Psychology, 21*, 302–318.

Tversky, A., & Griffin, D. (1991). Endowment and contrast in judgments of well-being. In F. Strack, M. Argyle, & N. Schwarz (Eds.), *Subjective well-being: An interdisciplinary perspective* (pp. 101–118). Elmsford, NY: Pergamon.

Wheeler, L., & Miyake, K. (1992). Social comparison in everyday life. *Journal of Personality and Social Psychology, 62*, 760–773.

Meaning in Life

Michael F. Steger

Abstract

In this chapter, it is argued that meaning in life is an important variable for human well-being. Literature supporting this contention is reviewed, and complexities regarding defining meaning in life are discussed. Definitions of meaning have focused on several components, two of which appear central and unique to meaning in life, suggesting a conceptual framework of meaning in life comprised of two pillars: comprehension and purpose. Comprehension encompasses people's ability to find patterns, consistency, and significance in the many events and experiences in their lives, and their synthesis and distillation of the most salient, important, and motivating factors. People face the challenge of understanding their selves, the world around them, and their unique niche and interactions within the world, and the notion of comprehension unifies these domains of understanding. Purpose refers to highly motivating, long-term goals about which people are passionate and highly committed. In the framework presented in this chapter, it is suggested that people devote significant resources to the pursuit of their purposes and that the most effective and rewarding purposes arise from and are congruent with people's comprehension of their lives. Literature is reviewed regarding where meaning might come from, and other dimensions of meaning are considered (i.e., sources of meaning and search for meaning). Suggestions for future research are proposed.

Keywords: eudaemonia, existential, meaning in life, purpose in life, well-being

Life's central challenge is adaptively identifying, interpreting, and engaging with the most important features of one's environment. Among the many sights, sounds, aromas, and tactile stimuli one experiences, only some will be useful or important. Some of these stimuli may offer paths to valued goals, such as a "Help Wanted" sign. Some provide clues to one's status with other people, such as a warm smile. Others signify pernicious threats, and most amount to little more than random noise. The same stimulus can be viewed in completely opposite ways by two different people. One person might feel that a metropolitan smoking ban protects individual rights to be in public spaces without being subjected to cigarette smoke, whereas another person might feel the same ban transgresses individual rights to use a legal consumer product. The stimulus is the same, but the interpretation varies greatly because its *meaning* differs from person to person. In some ways, the ability to derive meaning from experience and environment is fundamental to the success of humanity. Our transactions are conducted through behaviors varying in content, intonation, rapidity, volume, and body language, each with enormous implications. Diplomatic endeavors grind to a halt over a few words among thousands. Burning paper stokes different reactions if it has been printed with a flag, or Thursday's tire sale advertisements. Oedipus did not pierce his eyes because he just found out Jocasta was his long-lost "*barber.*" Generating such examples could become a catchy new parlor game, and, in fact, we see children frequently playing with meaning ("Why does this person laugh and that person glower when I mention certain bodily functions?"), which is as it should be—meaning permeates our lives. Meaning matters.

As a species, we have developed profound abilities to harvest meaning from the world around us. Given human facility with and immersion in meaning, we should expect that just as people struggle to understand the meanings of natural disasters, medical diagnoses, works of art, or their marriages, they also strive to understand the meaning of their own lives. Meaning in this sense enables people to interpret and organize their experience, achieve a sense of their own worth and place, identify the things that matter to them, and effectively direct their energies. The term meaning in life has been used to describe the construct underlying all of these dimensions, and at its heart, meaning in life refers to people's beliefs that their lives are significant and that they transcend the ephemeral present.

Meaning in Life Research

The scientific study of meaning has largely concentrated on understanding the consequences of believing one's life is meaningful. Frankl (1963) famously argued that it is imperative for people to have a clear sense of what they are trying to do with their lives, in other words, what the purpose of their existence is. Since then, dozens of studies have been conducted which repeatedly demonstrate that people who believe their lives have meaning or purpose appear better off (for review, see Steger, in press). For example, they are happier (e.g., Debats, van der Lubbe, & Wezeman, 1993); profess greater overall well-being (e.g., Bonebright, Clay, & Ankenmann, 2000), life satisfaction (e.g., Chamberlain & Zika, 1988; Steger, Kashdan, Sullivan, & Lorentz, 2008), and control over their lives (e.g., Ryff, 1989); and feel more engaged in their work (Bonebright et al., 2000; Steger & Dik, in press). Those reporting high levels of meaning also report less negative affect (e.g., Chamberlain & Zika, 1988), depression and anxiety (e.g., Debats et al., 1993), workaholism (Bonebright et al., 2000), suicidal ideation and substance abuse (e.g., Harlow, Newcomb, & Bentler, 1986), and less need for therapy (Battista & Almond, 1973). Meaning also appears stable and independent from other forms of well-being over the course of a year (Steger & Kashdan, 2007).

Research has also illuminated the question of who has meaning, with results from several studies generally confirming what we might suspect. Those who have dedicated their lives to an important cause, or an ideal that transcends more mundane concerns, report higher levels of meaning than other people. For example, Anglican (Roberts, 1991) and Dominican nuns (Crumbaugh, Raphael, & Shrader, 1970), as well as Protestant ministers (Weinstein & Cleanthous, 1996) and recently converted Christians (Paloutzian, 1981) all report high levels of meaning in life. Likewise, those who are struggling with psychological distress, such as psychiatric patients (e.g., Crumbaugh & Maholick, 1964), members of substance abuse treatment groups (e.g., Nicholson et al., 1994), and disruptive presecondary school students (e.g., Rahman & Khaleque, 1996), report lower levels of meaning in life. Other researchers have reported that "normal" university students reported more meaning than both psychiatric patients and those who had availed mental health services more often (Debats et al., 1993). Finally, enhancements in meaning have been reported in psychiatric patients at posttreatment versus pretreatment (Crumbaugh, 1977; Wadsworth & Barker, 1976), and there is some evidence that treatment of psychological distress enables people to rebuild meaning in their lives (e.g., Wadsworth & Barker, 1976). Thus, research is consistent in affirming that meaning in life is part of the complex picture of human well-being and optimal functioning (see also King & Napa, 1998; Ryff & Singer, 1998).

Definitions

Despite consensus regarding the importance of meaning in life, definitions and operationalizations of meaning in life have varied across theoretical and empirical works, generally defining meaning in terms of purpose, significance, or as a multifaceted construct.

Purpose

Frankl's (1963, 1965) theory of meaning was heavily focused on the idea that each person has some unique purpose or overarching aim for their lives, comprehended in light of one's values, and enacted in reflection of one's community. Here, meaning is experienced as what people are trying to do to enact their values. Thus, meaning refers to people's pursuits of their most important strivings and aims in life. Others have defined meaning in terms of purpose and goals as well (Emmons, 2003; Klinger, 1977, 1998; Ryff & Singer, 1998).

Significance

Another approach to defining meaning is a semantic one, focusing on lives from an informational significance point of view (Baumeister, 1991; Crumbaugh & Maholick, 1964; Yalom, 1980). If one asks the question, "what does my life mean?" it is in some ways equivalent to asking, "what does this sentence mean?" Such an approach suggests that meaning in life consists of what a life signifies, and thus people experience meaning in life when their lives make sense or convey some comprehensible information or message. In other words, lives have meaning when they stand for something. A related extension of such a definition was suggested by Bering (2002), who argued that the same information processing abilities that enabled humans to discern what the behaviors of their social counterparts signified are those responsible for human efforts to understand what life signifies. Under this "existential theory of mind," meaning in life is created through people's efforts to interpret their experiences in terms of "life's" intentions and significance, whether "life" has inherent meaning or not.

Meaning-systems approaches yield a differently nuanced view of meaning as significance, describing people as meaning makers "insofar as they seem compelled to establish mental representations of expected relations that tie together elements of their external world, elements of the self, and most importantly, bind the self to the external world" (Heine, Proulx, & Vohs, 2006, p. 89). Baumeister and Vohs (2002), in their entry on the pursuit of meaningfulness in the previous edition of this Handbook, also argued that "the essence of meaning is connection," (p. 608), and that such connections are a primary way in which people attach a sense of stability to the fluctuating and dynamic conditions of their lives.

Multifaceted Definitions

Thus, the two major unidimensional approaches to defining meaning in life have been primarily motivational (purpose-centered definitions) or cognitive (significance-centered definitions). Multidimensional definitions of meaning in life often combine these two dimensions with an affective dimension referencing people's fulfillment in their lives. For example, Reker and Wong (1988) defined meaning in terms of the ability to perceive order and coherence in one's existence, along with the pursuit and achievement of goals, and feelings of affective fulfillment arising from such coherence and pursuits (see also Battista & Almond, 1973). From these perspectives, people who believe their lives are meaningful would think they have life figured out, have clear goals, and be filled with warm feelings about the grand scheme of things.

Issues in Defining Meaning in Life

There are theoretical and practical reasons to be cautious when incorporating affective fulfillment in definitions of meaning in life. From a theoretical point of view, the elements of meaning in life that make it most unique among many related psychological variables are the motivational and cognitive elements. Several motivational constructs exist that shed light on how people pursue their goals over short (current concerns, Klinger, 1977), intermediate (personal projects, e.g., McGregor & Little, 1998), and extended (e.g., life planning, Baltes & Kunzmann, 2004; life tasks, Cantor & Sanderson, 1999; personal strivings, Emmons, 1986) time frames. Motivational and goal constructs may be integral to understanding how people attempt to enact or attain meaning in their lives (see Emmons, 2003); however, they occupy more specific and time-constrained positions in a hierarchy topped by overarching missions, aspirations, and purposes at the most abstract and long-term level. Frankl's (1963) idea of purpose centered on understanding what people live their lives for, rather than what endeavors occupy people's attention and efforts for particular moments in time. Such a perspective is analogous to the desire to understand the intent behind the entirety of Hieronymus Bosch's triptych, "Garden of Earthly Delights," rather than any one of its figures, design elements, or panels.

Likewise, there are many cognitive constructs that focus attention on the importance of understanding one's self (e.g., identity) or one's world (e.g., worldviews), but the cognitive component of meaning in life provides a unifying framework for conceptualizing how people understand both themselves and their worlds, as well as how they view the interplay between themselves and the world (see Heine et al., 2006). Understanding one's life as a whole necessitates comprehension at the highest level of information organization. Such comprehension subsumes ideas about one's identity, one's world, and the many constituents of each and distills the most important, salient, and motivating features. It is difficult to imagine someone who could say they comprehend their existence but they do not understand who they are. Thus, the cognitive component of meaning in life theoretically organizes and prioritizes the most pertinent information about the myriad objects, facets, and domains of life into a coherent whole. By extension, this cognitive component also offers promise for understanding the particular niches, roles, and degree of fit people perceive for themselves in the world. In conjunction with the motivational component, the construct of meaning in life integrates personal ideas about self, world, interactions and fit between the self and world, as well as an understanding of what one is trying to accomplish and sustain in one's life (see also Steger & Frazier, 2005; Steger, Frazier, Oishi, & Kaler, 2006).

Recent research also challenges the place of affective fulfillment in the core of any understanding of meaning in life. Whereas multifaceted definitions of meaning suggest that fulfillment occurs *because* one has attained a sense of purpose of significance, experimental research suggests that inducing someone to experience positive emotion exerts a strong influence over meaning in life self-reports (King, Hicks, Krull, & Del Gaiso, 2006; Hicks & King, 2008). These findings, at the very least, suggest that the causal pathway between meaning and positive emotional states is bidirectional, leading both from meaning to positive emotions, as well as from positive emotions to meaning.

An additional implication of such findings is that efforts need to be made to identify the critical and unique components of meaning in life, in order to confirm its importance to human functioning and to distinguish it from other variables. There are numerous preexisting affective or fulfillment variables, and it is difficult to see how the type of fulfillment achieved through comprehending life and establishing overarching purposes would be distinguishable from the positive emotions that might arise from other sources. In fact, it is possible that truly meaningful moments might unfold in the absence of positive emotions (see Ryff & Singer, 1998). One such possibility is suggested by Frankl's (1963) emphasis on the attitude one takes toward suffering as a route to meaning. Other attempts have been made to identify uniquely existential experiences of fulfillment, and an analysis of the items used in such "existential happiness" measures reveals they rely heavily on the types of items already associated with existing constructs (e.g., "I am a happy person," "I often feel tense"; MacDonald, 2000). From a practical point of view, any degree of conflation of meaning in life assessment with affective items runs the risk of conjointly assessing mood-related constructs, such as affective disposition and personality (see Steger, 2006, 2007).

Definition of Meaning in Life

Purpose and significance appear central to psychological definitions of meaning in life, and they capture the idea that meaning is about understanding where we've been, where we are, and where we're going (see Steger, in press, for more discussion). In contrast, existential affective experience seems to be a by-product of purpose and significance and is hard to differentiate from several existing constructs. Because of these considerations, it seems prudent to define meaning in life as the extent to which people comprehend, make sense of, or see significance in their lives, accompanied by the degree to which they perceive themselves to have a purpose, mission, or overarching aim in life.

Where Does Meaning Come From?

It can be surmised that, depending on the definition, meaning in life should arise from comprehending one's existence, identifying and achieving valued goals, feeling fulfilled by life, or combinations of these three. Beyond this, several ideas have been forwarded regarding the elements essential to finding meaning in life. Frankl (1963) suggested that people find meaning by engaging in creative endeavors, through elevating experiences, or through their ability to reflect upon and grow from negative experiences and suffering. Baumeister (1991; Baumeister & Vohs, 2002) identified four domains that give rise to meaning: feeling a sense of purpose, having a basis for self-worth, clarifying the values system by which one judges what is right and wrong, and developing a sense of efficacy in the world. Perspectives that argue that people's sense of meaning is derived from the stories and narratives that explain their lives (e.g., McAdams, 1993; Niemeyer & Mahoney, 1995) are consistent with Baumeister's view (e.g., Baumeister & Newman, 1994) and are well suited for illuminating the creation of meaning. For example, it is thought that the process of writing about life events is beneficial because it facilitates the integration of events into a larger, overarching meaning system (see King & Pennebaker, 1996). Researchers have also found that people who tell a story in terms of their ability to overcome an adverse event and discover positive results of their efforts were better adjusted (e.g., higher generativity; McAdams, Diamond, de St. Aubin, & Mansfield, 1997).

Emmons (2003) identified a four-part "taxonomy" of meaning, consisting of work/achievement, intimacy/relationships, spirituality, and self-transcendence/generativity. In some ways, this taxonomy reflects investigations into the specific sources from which people draw meaning, rather than the broader theoretical underpinnings of the processes by which meaning is found. Research on specific sources of meaning will be more thoroughly addressed in a later section of this chapter. Seligman's (2002) proposal that meaning comes from the dedication of one's signature talents to some entity beyond one's self reflects the last item from Emmons' taxonomy, self-transcendence. Reker and Wong (1988) also argue for the importance of self-transcendence, predicting that people experience meaning in life more deeply as they achieve greater degrees of self-transcendence.

A related field of research has developed regarding event appraisals, or meaning making following adverse or traumatic life events, showing that those who find meaning in traumatic events report better outcomes than those who do not (e.g., Bower, Kemeny, Taylor, & Fahey, 1998; McIntosh, Silver, & Wortman, 1993). Although it is largely unknown how finding meaning in a particular event is related to finding meaning in one's life as a whole, as Frankl (1963) argued, people's experiences with suffering and overcoming adversity are likely linked to meaning in life (see Janoff-Bulman & Yopyk, 2004; Park & Folkman, 1997, for further consideration of the interplay between event appraisals and meaning in life).

Finally, some experimental work has been conducted to examine the causal mechanisms underlying meaning in life. Most directly related is the research by King et al. (2006), which used several experiments to demonstrate that inducing positive affect leads to higher assessments of meaning in life. A significant body of research has been conducted under the auspices of terror management theory (TMT; see e.g., Pyszczynski, Greenberg, & Solomon, 1999). TMT theorists postulate that existential motives are a primary influence over human social behavior, in that the human capacity to both value ourselves and also recognize our inevitable, unpredictable demise leads to efforts to quell our fear of death through championing our culture's worldviews and/or though bolstering our sense of self-esteem. Because it suggests we use our culture and self-esteem to force structure and meaning onto the chaos of life, TMT research has implications for the etiology of meaning in life. For example, following reminders of death, people feel their lives are more meaningful if they are given the opportunity to profess support for their culture's worldview and less meaningful if they are not given that opportunity (Simon, Arndt, Greenberg, Pyszczynski, & Solomon, 1998).

Thus, perspectives on the essential underpinnings of meaning are somewhat varied. Nonetheless, there is concordance around the idea that meaning is most fully achieved when people actively engage in pursuits that transcend their own immediate interests (e.g., religion or culture), possibly including transcending the short-term devastation of traumatic events. Meaning may be further enhanced when people engage in important pursuits while operating under a clear understanding of one's worth, capabilities, and attributes.

Dimensions of Meaning in Life Research

Meaning in life research has focused overwhelmingly on the presence or absence of beliefs that life is meaningful. However, the theoretical space of meaning in life also includes an emphasis on understanding the sources from which people say they draw meaning and the degree to which people are engaged in the search for meaning.

Sources of Meaning in Life

Research on sources of meaning in life has generally used one of two methods to understand the normative sources from which people draw meaning in life. The first method gathers responses to question such as "What gives your life meaning?" (e.g., Ebersole & DeVogler, 1981), which are analyzed and coded. This research has identified several common sources of meaning (e.g., relationships, religious beliefs, health, pleasure, personal growth). Across many studies, most people have indicated that relationships with others are the most important source of meaning in their lives. The second method presents people with a list of potential sources of meaning and asks them to rate each source's importance to them (e.g., Bar-Tur, Savaya, & Prager, 2001). Relationships are usually seen as most important using this method as well (see Emmons, 2003).

The Search for Meaning in Life

Another dimension of meaning in life concerns people's search for meaning. Empirical and theoretical work on meaning in life has argued for maintaining a distinction between having meaning and searching for meaning (e.g., Steger et al., 2006). The search for meaning in life refers to people's desire and efforts to establish and/or augment their understanding of the meaning, significance, and purpose of their lives. Some who are searching for meaning are struggling to establish some minimal level of meaning in their lives, whereas others might consider themselves to be engaged in a lifelong search for meaning, constantly striving to deepen their comprehension of the sense and significance of themselves and their lives (Steger, Kashdan, et al., 2008). Very little research has been conducted on the search for meaning in life. That which has been conducted has indicated that those searching reported having less meaning in life (Crumbaugh, 1977; Steger et al., 2006), although factor analysis has confirmed that the search for meaning is independent from its relative presence (Reker & Cousins, 1979; Steger et al., 2006). Research using a recently developed measure[1] has found that the search for meaning is associated with higher neuroticism, negative affect, anxiety, and depression (Steger et al., 2006) but also with openmindedness (Steger, Kashdan, et al., 2008). Finally, those searching for meaning seemed to prosper marginally more from meaning in life-focused therapeutic interventions than those not seeking meaning (Crumbaugh, 1977).

Both the sources of and search for meaning are deserving of vigorous empirical investigation. Numerous studies attest to the fact that the presence of meaning in life is associated with more positive human functioning. Although it is still interesting to continue to explore the nature of these relations, understanding the sources and search for meaning offers more dynamic ways to understand pressing, unresolved questions, such as how people find meaning, from where meaning comes, and why people benefit from having it. Gaining a clearer idea of the characteristics of those who are searching for meaning and the dynamics of their search, how people come to acquire sources of meaning, and whether such sources generate a general sense of meaning cannot be accomplished by focusing solely on the end product of the presence of meaning in life.

An Agenda for Future Research

Humans seem frequently stirred to ponder "the deep questions" about the ever-changing diversity, complexity, and inscrutability of the world around us. We might gaze at ancient ruins, the moon's face, or a cicada's discarded husk and wonder, "What does all this mean?" Such questions transcend psychology's bounds, but there is some consolation in knowing that psychology can help answer an equally important question—"What does 'my life' mean?" So far, psychologists can say that having an answer to

that question is important to a person's well-being. We can also say that our relationships will influence the answer and that we feel life is more meaningful when we feel good, whether because of positive affect, important religious commitments, or freedom from distressing psychopathology.

Future research should seek to examine these conclusions and, more importantly, expand our knowledge in several key directions. One important direction lies in understanding the development and change in meaning over the life span (e.g., Damon, Menon, & Bronk, 2003; Reker, Peacock, & Wong, 1987; Ryff, 1991; Steger, Oishi, & Kashdan, in press). For example, meaning in life predicted successful aging (i.e., greater well-being and physical health, less psychopathology) 14 months later, controlling for demographic variables and traditional predictors, such as social and intellectual resources (Reker, 2002). We should also endeavor to identify the neurological substrates (e.g., Urry et al., 2004) and biological markers (e.g., Ryff et al., 2006) of meaning in life. Future research should also prioritize assessing the role of meaning as a facilitator and an outcome of psychological treatment, clarifying how meaning contributes to optimal functioning, and investigating cultural expressions of, and influences on, meaning in life.

A combination of methods is necessary to advance these lines of research. Quasi-experiments comparing those with psychopathological symptoms and normal population samples would replicate some previous work, but meaning in life should receive scrutiny not only as a positive outcome of therapy but also as an active ingredient in the therapeutic process. Clinical research that tracks meaning across sessions could assess meaning as a mediator of improvement. Rigorously performed random clinical trials comparing meaning-centered interventions with validated treatments could help determine the viability of focusing on meaning as a therapeutic aid. Research suggests a potential interplay between event-specific meaning and broader meaning in life, and this possibility could be profitably investigated using multiwave longitudinal methods. Research also suggests a number of daily life activities that are associated with greater meaning in life (e.g., personal growth and relationship tending; Steger, Kashdan, & Oishi, 2008). Experimental methods gauging both the antecedents of meaning (e.g., positive affect) and the effects of temporary manipulations of meaning would help explicate the causal mechanisms of meaning in life. Cross-cultural research would expand our notions of

[1] The Meaning in Life Questionnaire (Steger et al., 2006) can be downloaded for free at http://michael.f.steger.googlepages.com/home or http://www.ppc.sas.upenn.edu/ppquestionnaires.htm

the constituents, expressions, and "meaning" of meaning in life. It appears that, like other well-being variables, those from cultures that emphasize individual happiness (i.e., United States) report higher meaning in life than those from cultures that stress collective harmony to a greater degree (e.g., Spain; Steger, Frazier, & Zacchanini, 2008; and Japan; Steger, Kawabata, Shimai, & Otake, 2008). Further comparisons should be considered, and efforts should be made to explore the specific mechanisms by which cultures encourage differences (see Matsumoto & Yoo, 2006).

Meaning and Life

Positive psychology emphasizes the necessity of understanding the factors that elevate human lives and exploring those features of life that make it not merely tolerable, but fulfilling, vital, and rich. Eliminating the meaning people perceive in their lives would also seem to dismantle the interconnecting filament on which are hung the most savory and desirable qualities of a full life. Life without meaning would be merely a string of events that fail to coalesce into a unified, coherent whole. A life without meaning is a life without a story, nothing to strive for, no sense of what might have been, or what has been. Perhaps, just as meaning links the moments of people's lives, meaning in life research holds some promise of uniting the many ways in which psychologists attempt to understand the events, states, traits, and institutions that define and determine human happiness.

Questions about the Future of Meaning in Life Research

1. The historical roots of psychological work on meaning in life lie in applied work. Given the similarities between the conceptual framework of meaning in life presented here and some of the core tenets of cognitive approaches to therapy (e.g., both emphasize people's interpretations of themselves and their interactions, and both emphasize the importance of goals), will future research show that focusing on meaning in life in the context of effective therapy helps consolidate gains or adds some other therapeutic benefit?

2. Emerging research suggests that positive affect serves a role in sustaining, and possibly stimulating or enhancing, people's judgments that their lives are meaningful. Will future research identify boundary conditions related to positive affect on the experience of meaning in life such that popular notions of "sadder but wiser" phenomena are invalidated to a degree?

3. There are few reliable methods of even temporarily enhancing people's experience of meaning in life. Yet, in order to fully understand the possible causes and benefits of meaning in life, the field needs interventions that are specific in increasing meaning in both the short term and long term in a general population. Will future research develop such interventions, or will it prove impossible to increase meaning in life without also increasing related constructs such as positive affect and life satisfaction?

References

Baltes, P. B., & Kunzmann, U. (2004). The two faces of wisdom: Wisdom as a general theory of knowledge and judgment about excellence in mind and virtue vs. wisdom as everyday realization in people and products. *Human Development, 47,* 290–299.

Bar-Tur, L., Savaya, R., & Prager, E. (2001). Sources of meaning in life for young and old Israeli Jews and Arabs. *Journal of Aging Studies, 15,* 253–269.

Battista, J., & Almond, R. (1973). The development of meaning in life. *Psychiatry, 36,* 409–427.

Baumeister, R. F. (1991). *Meanings of life.* New York: Guilford.

Baumeister, R. F., & Newman, L. S. (1994). How stories make sense of personal experiences: Motives that shape autobiographical narratives. *Personality and Social Psychology Bulletin, 20,* 676–690.

Baumeister, R. F., & Vohs, K. D. (2002). The pursuit of meaningfulness in life. In C. R. Snyder & S. J. Lopez (Eds.), *Handbook of positive psychology* (pp. 608–618). Oxford: Oxford University Press.

Bering, J. M. (2002). The existential theory of mind. *Review of General Psychology, 6,* 3–24.

Bonebright, C. A., Clay, D. L., & Ankenmann, R. D. (2000). The relationship of workaholism with work–life conflict, life satisfaction, and purpose in life. *Journal of Counseling Psychology, 47,* 469–477.

Bower, J. E., Kemeny, M. E., Taylor, S. E., & Fahey, J. L. (1998). Cognitive processing, discovery of meaning, CD4 decline, and AIDS-related mortality among bereaved HIV-seropositive men. *Journal of Consulting and Clinical Psychology, 66,* 979–986.

Cantor, N., & Sanderson, C. A. (1999). Life task participation and well-being: The importance of taking part in daily life. In D. Kahneman, E. Diener, & N. Schwartz (Eds.), *Well-being: The foundations of hedonic psychology* (pp. 230–243). New York: Russell Sage Foundation.

Chamberlain, K., & Zika, S. (1988). Religiosity, life meaning, and wellbeing: Some relationships in a sample of women. *Journal for the Scientific Study of Religion, 27,* 411–420.

Crumbaugh, J. C. (1977). The Seeking of Noetic Goals Test (SONG): A complementary scale to the Purpose in Life Test (PIL). *Journal of Clinical Psychology, 33,* 900–907.

Crumbaugh, J. C., & Maholick, L. T. (1964). An experimental study in existentialism: The psychometric approach to Frankl's concept of noogenic neurosis. *Journal of Clinical Psychology, 20,* 200–207.

Crumbaugh, J. C., Raphael, M., & Shrader, R. R. (1970). Frankl's will to meaning in a religious order. *Journal of Clinical Psychology, 26,* 206–207.

Damon, W., Menon, J., & Bronk, K. C. (2003). The development of purpose during adolescence. *Applied Developmental Science, 7,* 119–128.

Debats, D. L., van der Lubbe, P. M., & Wezeman, F. R. A. (1993). On the psychometric properties of the Life Regard Index (LRI): A measure of meaningful life. *Personality and Individual Differences, 14,* 337–345.

Ebersole, P., & DeVogler, K. L. (1981). Meaning in life: Category self-ratings. *The Journal of Psychology, 107,* 289–293.

Emmons, R. A. (1986). Personal strivings: An approach to personality and subjective well-being. *Journal of Personality and Social Psychology, 51,* 1058–1068.

Emmons, R. A. (2003). Personal goals, life meaning, and virtue: Wellsprings of a positive life. In C. Keyes & J. Haidt (Eds.), *Flourishing: Positive psychology and the well-lived life* (pp. 105–128). Washington, DC: American Psychological Association.

Frankl, V. E. (1963). *Man's search for meaning: an introduction to logotherapy.* New York: Washington Square Press.

Frankl, V. E. (1965). *The doctor and the soul: From psychotherapy to logotherapy.* New York: Vintage Books.

Harlow, L. L., Newcomb, M. D., & Bentler, P. M. (1986). Depression, self-derogation, substance use, and suicide ideation: Lack of purpose in life as a mediational factor. *Journal of Clinical Psychology, 42,* 5–21.

Heine, S. J., Proulx, T., & Vohs, K. D. (2006). The meaning maintenance model: On the coherence of social motivations. *Personality and Social Psychology Review, 10,* 88–110.

Hicks, J. A., & King, L. A. (2008). Religiosity and positive mood as information about meaning in life. *Journal of Research in Personality, 42,* 43–61.

Janoff-Bulman, R., & Yopyk, D. J. (2004). Random outcomes and valued commitments: Existential dilemmas and the paradox of meaning. In J. Greenberg, S. L. Koole, & T. Pyszczynski (Eds.), *Handbook of experimental existential psychology* (pp. 122–138). New York: Guilford.

King, L. A., Hicks, J. A., Krull, J. L., & Del Gaiso, A. K. (2006). Positive affect and the experience of meaning in life. *Journal of Personality and Social Psychology, 90,* 179–196.

King, L. A., & Napa, C. K. (1998). What makes a life good? *Journal of Personality and Social Psychology, 75,* 156–165.

King, L. A., & Pennebaker, J. W. (1996). Thinking about goals, glue, and the meaning of life. In R. S. Wyer (Ed.), *Advances in social cognition* (Vol. 9, pp. 97–106). Mahwah, NJ: Erlbaum.

Klinger, E. (1977). *Meaning and void.* Minneapolis, MN: University of Minnesota Press.

Klinger, E. (1998). The search for meaning in evolutionary perspective and its clinical implications. In P. T. P. Wong & P. S. Fry (Eds.), *The human quest for meaning: A handbook of psychological research and clinical application* (pp. 27–50). Mahwah, NJ: Lawrence Erlbaum.

McAdams, D. P. (1993). *The stories I live by: Personal myths and the making of the self.* New York: William Morrow.

McAdams, D. P., Diamond, A., de St. Aubin, E., & Mansfield, E. (1997). Stories of commitment: The psychosocial construction of generative lives. *Journal of Personality and Social Psychology, 72,* 678–694.

MacDonald, D. A. (2000). Spirituality: Description, measurement, and relation to the Five Factor Model of personality. *Journal of Personality, 68,* 153–197.

McGregor, I., & Little, B. R. (1998). Personal projects, happiness, and meaning: On doing well and being yourself. *Journal of Personality and Social Psychology, 74,* 494–512.

McIntosh, D. N., Silver, R. C., & Wortman, C. B. (1993). Religion's role in adjustment to a negative life event: Coping with the loss of a child. *Journal of Personality and Social Psychology, 65,* 812–821.

Matsumoto, D., & Yoo, S. H. (2006). Toward a new generation of cross-cultural research. *Perspectives on Psychological Science, 1,* 234–250.

Nicholson, T., Higgins, W., Turner, P., James, S., Stickle, F., & Pruitt, T. (1994). The relation between meaning in life and the occurrence of drug abuse: A retrospective study. *Psychology of Addictive Behaviors, 8,* 24–28.

Niemeyer, R. A., & Mahoney, J. J. (1995). *Constructivism in psychology.* Washington, DC: American Psychological Association.

Paloutzian, R. F. (1981). Purpose in life and value changes following conversion. *Journal of Personality and Social Psychology, 41,* 1153–1160.

Park, C. L., & Folkman, S. (1997). Meaning in the context of stress and coping. *Review of General Psychology, 30,* 115–144.

Pyszczynski, T., Greenberg, J., & Solomon, S. (1999). A dual-process model of defense against conscious and unconscious death-related thoughts: An extension of terror management theory. *Psychological Review, 106,* 835–845.

Rahman, T., & Khaleque, A. (1996). The purpose in life and academic behavior of problem students in Bangladesh. *Social Indicators Research, 39,* 59–64.

Reker, G. T. (2002). Prospective predictors of successful aging in community-residing and institutionalized Canadian elderly. *Ageing International, 27,* 42–64.

Reker, G. T., & Cousins, J. B. (1979). Factor structure, construct validity and reliability of the Seeking of Noetic Goals (SONG) and Purpose in Life (PIL) Tests. *Journal of Clinical Psychology, 35,* 85–91.

Reker, G. T., Peacock, E. J., & Wong, P. T. P. (1987). Meaning and purpose in life and well-being: A life-span perspective. *Journal of Gerontology, 42,* 44–49.

Reker, G. T., & Wong. P. T. P. (1988). Aging as an individual process: Toward a theory of personal meaning. In J. E. Birren & V. L. Bengston (Eds.), *Emergent theories of aging* (pp. 214–246). New York: Springer.

Roberts, G. (1991). Delusional belief systems and meaning in life: A preferred reality? *British Journal of Psychiatry, 159* (Suppl. 14), 19–28.

Ryff, C. D. (1989). Happiness is everything, or is it? Explorations of the meaning of psychological well-being. *Journal of Personality and Social Psychology, 57,* 1069–1081.

Ryff, C. D. (1991). Possible selves in adulthood and old age: A tale of shifting horizons. *Psychology and Aging, 6,* 286–295.

Ryff, C. D., Love, G. D., Urry, H. L., Muller, D., Rosenkranz, M. A., Friedman, E. M., et al. (2006). Psychological well-being and ill-being: Do they have distinct or mirrored biological correlates? *Psychotherapy and Psychosomatics, 75,* 85–95.

Ryff, C. D., & Singer, B. (1998). The contours of positive human health. *Psychological Inquiry, 9,* 1–28.

Seligman, M. E. P. (2002). *Authentic happiness.* New York: Free Press.

Simon, L., Arndt, J., Greenberg, J., Pyszczynski, T., & Solomon, S. (1998). Terror management and meaning: Evidence that the opportunity to defend the worldview in response to mortality salience increases the meaningfulness of life in the mildly depressed. *Journal of Personality, 66,* 359–382.

Steger, M. F. (in press). Experiencing meaning in life: Optimal functioning at the nexus of spirituality, psychopathology, and well-being. In P. T. P. Wong & P. S. Fry (Eds.), *The human quest for meaning* (2nd ed.). Mahwah, NJ: Lawrence Erlbaum.

Steger, M. F. (2006). An illustration of issues in factor extraction and identification of dimensionality in psychological assessment data. *Journal of Personality Assessment, 86,* 263–272.

Steger, M. F. (2007). Structural validity of the Life Regards Index. *Measurement and Evaluation in Counseling and Development, 40,* 97–109.

Steger, M. F., & Dik, B. J. (in press). Work as meaning. In P. A. Linley, S. Harrington, & N. Page (Eds.), *Oxford handbook of positive psychology and work.* Oxford: Oxford University Press.

Steger, M. F., & Frazier, P. (2005). Meaning in life: One link in the chain from religion to well-being. *Journal of Counseling Psychology, 52,* 574–582.

Steger, M. F., Frazier, P., Oishi, S., & Kaler, M. (2006). The Meaning in Life Questionnaire: Assessing the presence of and search for meaning in life. *Journal of Counseling Psychology, 53,* 80–93.

Steger, M. F., Frazier, P., & Zacchanini, J. L. (2008). Terrorism in two cultures: Traumatization and existential protective factors following the September 11th attacks and the Madrid train bombings. *Journal of Trauma and Loss, 13,* 511–527.

Steger, M. F., & Kashdan, T. B. (2007). Stability and specificity of meaning in life and life satisfaction over one year. *Journal of Happiness Studies, 8,* 161–179.

Steger, M. F., Kashdan, T. B., & Oishi, S. (2008). Being good by doing good: Eudaimonic activity and daily well-being correlates, mediators, and temporal relations. *Journal of Research in Personality, 42,* 22–42.

Steger, M. F., Kashdan, T. B., Sullivan, B. A., & Lorentz, D. (2008). Understanding the search for meaning in life: Personality, cognitive style, and the dynamic between seeking and experiencing meaning. *Journal of Personality, 76,* 199–228.

Steger, M. F., Kawabata, Y., Shimai, S., & Otake, K. (2008). The meaningful life in Japan and the United States: Levels and correlates of meaning in life. *Journal of Research in Personality, 42,* 660–678.

Steger, M. F., Oishi, S., & Kashdan, T. B. (in press). Meaning in life across the life span: Levels and correlates of meaning in life from emerging adulthood to older adulthood. *Journal of Positive Psychology.*

Urry, H. L., Nitschke, J. B., Dolski, I., Jackson, D. C., Dalton, K. M., Mueller, C. J., et al. (2004). Making a life worth living. *Psychological Science, 15,* 367–373.

Wadsworth, A. P., & Barker, H. R., Jr. (1976). A comparison of two treatments for depression: The antidepressive program vs. traditional therapy. *Journal of Clinical Psychology, 32,* 445–449.

Weinstein, L., & Cleanthous, C. C. (1996). A comparison of protestant ministers and parishioners on expressed purpose in life and intrinsic religious motivation. *Psychology: A Journal of Human Behavior, 33,* 26–29.

Yalom, I. D. (1980). *Existential psychotherapy.* New York: Basic Books.

The Future of Positive Psychology: Pursuing Three Big Goals

Shane J. Lopez

Abstract

Good positive psychological science is being disseminated to the general public. In turn, consumers are asking for solid, real-world applications of the science to make daily life better for individuals, families, and communities at large. Now, scientists, practitioners, and the consumers of our scholarly products potentially can collaborate to drive systemic changes in schools, families, and workplaces. In this chapter, I set three aspirational goals for positive psychology applications that could marshal the talent and resources of change agents throughout society.

Keywords: change, communities, education, families, positive psychology

"Positive Psychology, That's a Good Way to Spend Your Time"

The beginning of this final chapter picks up exactly where we left off in the "future of positive psychology" discussion in the first edition of this Handbook:

> As the other passengers were slowly boarding the plane, a white-haired woman sat down next to me (CRS [C. R. Snyder]). As we came to cruising altitude, we began a lively conversation that was to continue across the skies from Philadelphia to Kansas City. I learned that, because of a mandatory age retirement rule, this woman had to quit her teaching position over 15 years ago. She fondly recounted how she had spent those postretirement years with her grandchildren. In fact, on this occasion, she was going to visit her brand-new great-grandson. "What do you do for a living?" she asked. I recounted the short version of my life as a professor and mentioned my work in positive psychology. Upon hearing about this, she became very animated, asking question after question about positive psychology. The time passed quickly, and we soon were off the plane, walking up the ramp to the terminal building. She turned and opined, "Positive psychology,

that's a good way to spend your time." With that, she waved and disappeared into the outstretched arms of smiling family members. Positive psychology, that's a good way to spend your time.
> (Snyder & Lopez, 2002, p. 766)

Most scholars and practitioners of positive psychology would agree that the last 10 years have been well spent. New discoveries about strengths and positive emotions have augmented what we know about human functioning, talented professionals are committing themselves to studying and developing the best in people, promotion and intervention programs are being rigorously examined, and public policy makers are paying more attention to well-being. In short, we have moved from planning good bench science and survey research to attempting to improve people's lives through empirically examined treatments.

From Research to Practice to Big Goals

In 1999, a small group of social scientists gathered in Akumal, Mexico, to develop a scientific infrastructure and research agenda for examining the best in people. Their thoughts and some of their time quickly turned to developing the best in individuals and groups, as revealed in the proposed applications:

- Improving child education by making greater use of intrinsic motivation, positive affect, and creativity within schools
- Improving psychotherapy by developing approaches that emphasize hope, meaning, and self-healing
- Improving family life by better understanding the dynamics of love, generativity, and commitment
- Improving work satisfaction across the life span by helping people to find authentic involvement, experience states of flow, and make genuine contributions in their work
- Improving organizations and societies by discovering conditions that enhance trust, communication, and altruism between persons
- Improving the moral character of society by better understanding and promoting the spiritual impulse within humans

Clearly, these scientists and co-authors of the "Akumal Manifesto," which included Ken Sheldon, Kevin Rathune, Barbara Fredrickson, Mike Csikszentmihalyi, and Jon Haidt, were concerned with the implications and applications of their work. Their concern and the vision shared with other positive psychologists guided some of the twenty-first-century developments in field as reflected in new additions to the second edition of this Handbook: positive psychology applications (Linley et al.), family-centered positive psychology (Sheridan et al.), positive schools (Huebner et al.) and positive psychology on campus (Schreiner et al.), positive workplace (Luthans et al.), and positive institutions (Huang et al.). Now, with good science in place, practitioners and community change agents can put positive psychology to the test. In this chapter, I consider how we might spend our time over the next 10 years. Based on the assumption that positive psychology applications can promote growth and success in three domains of our lives—school, family, and work—I set one big goal for change in each of the areas.

Psychological Reform of Schools

School systems have been reformed and re-reformed. A positive psychology initiative for doing more reform may not be met with much support unless it is driven by research and new data and it goes well beyond traditional efforts for making schools perform better. Psychological reform of schools would also need to create conditions for students, teachers, and leaders to more easily do what they know works and what they do best. Finally, such an initiative would need to start with what is on the hearts and minds of students and involve the adults who make a difference in a children's lives.

Recently, I was asked to think about the future of positive psychology and education. This is what my Futuristic and Maximizer talents (see Rath, 2007, for a list of Clifton StrengthsFinder Themes) conjured up (Lopez, 2008):

What Would Happen If We Study What Is Right with People?

This year I attended a graduation ceremony at a small school in Omaha, Nebraska. The students marched proudly into the auditorium to the applause of their friends and family. After acknowledging the teachers and giving a quick speech, the school's head honcho, Dr. Reckmeyer, invited each student to join her on stage—one by one. She then shared a bit about what each student did best; she recognized their talents, their skills, and their hard work.

Dr. Reckmeyer described Eva as a creative visionary: "You have great artistic talent. You have an incredible ability to see things in a new and unique way. I hope you continue to enjoy and nourish your love of art throughout your life." Anna, an international student, was described as strong student with a warm personality. "You show great determination with each task you do. You work hard to complete each and every project to the best of your ability and love being praised for a job well done." In parting, Dr. Reckmeyer said, "[Anna] I will miss . . . your kindness . . . and your . . . smile. You have had an incredible journey and I feel blessed to have shared it with you." These students and the rest of their peers were truly known by those who taught them. And what was right with them was celebrated.

I learned from some of the parents that all of the kids in the graduating class were going to the Happiest Place on Earth. Now, you may be thinking, why would these students plan a group trip to Disneyland? Well, their destination was not Disney. They were going to a place where they could learn new things from smart people who cared about them, laugh with their friends, and dream about the future. These 17 preschoolers were headed to kindergarten, the Happiest Place on Earth.

Now, kindergarten has a big advantage over Disney. I know what you are thinking . . . much shorter lines. Yes, and, more importantly, good kindergarten programs and teachers encourage kids to do what they do best. Good teachers study what is right with each kid and propel each toward their future. Our students, clients, and the broader community we serve deserve nothing less ... and they need our help. We all know that the world is a scary place and modern society undermines our health, but I am more concerned about subtleties of the current educational system that can rob us of our hope as we transition from one grade or school to another, the small behaviors that make us less engaged and less energetic year by year—from fifth grade to senior year—and the shabby practices that take a thriving college freshmen, full of vim and vigor, and turn her into a struggling young adult. Nothing short of psychological reform of the educational system and intentional development of strengths, hope, engagement, and well-being will make schools, colleges, and universities what they all should be— some of the happiest places on earth.

Studying what is right with people, and more specifically the strengths of people young and old, was the bread and butter of one my professional heroes, the Nebraska educational psychologist Don Clifton, whose family bought Gallup in 1988. Don would ask me questions like, "Wouldn't it be great if every student could do what they do best every day?" Or, "Why not list a student's strengths on the report card, right alongside his grades?" The online tools are now available to reliably measure talents and strengths in all of our students, 10 years and older. So why don't we buck the status quo and train teachers and counselors to be strengths spotters and developers? Well, we are doing that right now. Through partnerships with school districts, colleges, and universities, including numerous Historically Black College and Universities, we are working toward a goal of training 500 strengths-based educators and identifying the strengths of 1 million students by the end of 2010. We are about one-fourth of the way to realizing our goal ... so we could use a little help.

As education becomes more strengths based, hope will rise. Ideas and energy for the future drive our academic success. Rick Snyder, my research mentor and close friend, found that hope trumped high school GPA, ACTs, and SATs when predicting college GPAs. Graduate student Matt Gallagher and I replicated these findings, and we have demonstrated that academic hope predicts academic retention (Gallagher & Lopez, 2008). So, then, why should we care about our old GPA and ACT/SAT scores when a score from an eight-item hope scale accounts for more variance in academic success? To some of us, these scores, along with our IQs and GREs, are like old friends that keep our self-esteem buoyant.

For others, the passage of time has endowed old test scores with a certain mystique and power. Hope also has a mystique ... and much more power. And, hope can be enhanced ... without the need for a 4.0 semester or a 6-month stint with Kaplan Prep.

Let's recap here. Capitalizing on strengths creates hope. Hope fuels academic success. And all of this happens within the emotional climates in schools and homes. These climates are determined by how much students feel safe, respected, and cared for. The quality of this climate also reflects the level of student engagement. In a nationwide study of 100,000 school children, Gallup researcher Gary Gordon and I found that about 40% are engaged, or tuned in; 32% are tuned out, or not engaged; and 28% of American students are actively disengaged or acting out and disrupting the teaching and learning process (Gordon & Lopez, 2008). These levels of engagement peak in the fifth grade and then slowly and steadily deteriorate year by year. The Happiest Place on Earth banners may provide truth in advertising for primary schools but not for middle or high schools. As the emotional climate changes, what also declines is a student's ability to be her best and be excited about shaping her future. The emotional climate in our schools can be improved, and some believe that it can be done in 30 days ... the first 30 days of the school year. Imagine faculty, staff, and administrators working together to welcome students and make them feel like they matter.

Now, while you have your imagination warmed up, imagine a ladder. The bottom rung—0—represents the worst possible version of your life. The top rung— 10—is your best life. Bottom rung, worst life, is 0. Top rung, best life, is 10. On which rung of the life ladder do you stand today? And, on which rung will you stand 5 years from now? Your responses to these two questions provide a snapshot of your well-being. 100,000 students, we have found that about 50% are thriving and 50% are struggling and, worse yet, suffering. Through the Gallup Student Poll, we will measure the well-being of students, from fifth grade through their senior year in college. We are hypothesizing that some of the big findings about kids and youth will parallel our findings from the polling of adults and related positive psychology research. Specifically, friends matter and positive affect drives success in school and work. And landing a good job in a newly flat world—a goal that connects our kids to kids around the globe—drives well-being in a way that we are barely beginning to understand.

What would happen if we study what is right with people? For starters, with the data we have today, we could bring psychological reform to our schools.

By capitalizing on strengths, making hope happen, fostering engagement, and transforming strugglers into thrivers, we could turn every school into a magic kingdom.

My hope is that we will lead, and that we can commit ourselves to a positive psychology mission—one that transforms education and the lives of our young people like my 3-year-old son, Parrish, who will be graduating from that little school in Omaha in 2010 and moving on to the Happiest Place on Earth. With a little help from us and lots of love from his mom, Alli, we can make sure that first grade through his first job will give him what he needs to reach the tenth rung of the life ladder.

Making schools strengths based, and tracking the hope, engagement, and well-being of kids, is a back-to-the-basics strategy that aligns with the thinking of educational philosophers such as John Dewey, Benjamin Franklin, John Stuart Mill, and Herbert Spencer. Turning this philosophy into practice in America would take commitment from the 17,000 school superintendents and 3 million plus teachers to approach the 50 million school children as individuals with the need to matter and the desire for daily feedback. One index of student well-being presented alongside state achievement scores, grades, and the dropout percentage could be the gauge of success for our work with kids. So, the big 10-year goal for positive psychology and education is to collaborate and create a national well-being or promise index for students and to develop empirically supported techniques for helping students move up the ladder of life.

Strong, Happy Families

Dysfunction dominates the family literature, but thanks to the work of Susan Sheridan and colleagues (chap. 52), this is changing. By studying family success, and specifically strong and happy families, we are learning more about the hallmarks of families that work. Barbara Kerr (personal communication, February 2008) got to know 30 families that function, families that thrive. Her findings, summarized subsequently, have greatly influenced the way I think about my family, and of the positive psychology of families.

What Are the Hallmarks of a Happy Family?

It's not money: No economic or social class has cornered the market on family happiness. Happy families have a religious affiliation or professed a strong "philosophy of life."

Storytelling and traditions: Storytelling is central in happy families, as are traditions and ceremonies. Making time to be together, often at mealtime, is a priority.

Rules: Happy families have only a few rules, stated broadly.

Kids and risks: Children are allowed to take some risks, especially in pursuits away from the family.

Individualization: The family's focus at times is directed toward one family member's goal, but that member knows the focus will shift.

Conflict resolution: Happy families have predictable ways to deal with conflict. Family members know that disputes will not threaten the family.

Private space: Family members have their own spaces, no matter how small, to be alone.

Gathering space: Some part of the house, often the kitchen, is the accepted gathering place. And, homes of happy families are gathering places for the neighborhood.

Modeling exemplar families and adopting a family-centered positive psychology approach to struggling families (chap. 52) will result in behavioral change that can lead a family in the right direction. Indeed, creating rituals, picking a few rules that work, rallying around individual family members' goals, and providing space for privacy and fun potentially can transform a family's functioning over time.

Despite the good work being done on positive psychology and family functioning, much more is needed. We know little about family strengths and how they come together to define a happy family. By discovering and developing the strengths of each family member and of the collective, children and adults can learn to do more of what they do best in the household, potentially through strengths family camps (Jerlene Mosely, Fursey Gotuaco, & Jennifer Gotuaco, personal communication, September, 2008). We can measure strengths of individuals but we have not created tools to measure and promote family strengths. So, the big 10-year goal for family-centered positive psychology is to create a robust measure of family strengths and to develop empirically supported techniques for helping families become stronger and happier.

Meaningful Work

Work has a bad rap in today's society. The capacity to work (and love and play) defines us as normal human creatures. Without work in our lives, we might feel a little less whole. Michael Steger (in chap. 64 he discusses the broader topic of meaning in life) argues that work brings meaning to our lives and meaningful work has many benefits, to individuals and organizations.

What Is Meaningful Work and Where Does It Come From?

People work for many reasons—some are obvious (I am paid to work), some are not as obvious (work is where my friends are). Many sources of evidence indicate that understanding how people approach work and what they get from it is vital to learning how to achieve the best possible outcomes for individuals and organizations. Few other avenues offer as much promise for accomplishing valued outcomes—both in terms of daily work and in terms of long-term, sustainable performance—as creating meaning in work.

Work is meaningful when people are able to understand who they are as workers, what their organization is about, and how they uniquely fit within—and contribute to—their organization. This sense of comprehension about themselves as workers helps people generate a purpose for their work. As they work toward a purpose in their work—whether self-generated or fostered by clear leadership from their organization—they will feel a sense of transcendence that encourages their identification with their organization and its mission.

Some people are endowed with an internally generated sense of meaning and purpose about their work. Research suggests that organizations should energetically seek to identify and recruit these individuals. They work better in groups, express more faith in management, and devote more discretionary effort to their organizations. There are also indications that they express less intent to turnover and more organizational commitment, thereby showing more promise of contributing to their organizations for a longer time.

Many people do not automatically approach their work with such a sense of meaning and purpose. Some research has identified specific organizational factors that hold promise for providing workers in organizations with meaningful work. My work focuses on two such factors: organizational mission and leadership. In order for the typical worker to feel like his or her work matters, a compelling organizational mission should be clearly communicated. Organizations that wish to attract or cultivate workers driven by a sense of meaning and purpose may consider developing a mission that is consistent with organizational identity and with the niche it serves.

Effective leadership is important not only to communicating the mission and identity of an organization, but also to creating an organizational environment that provides workers with a clear understanding of their role and fosters in them an identification with their organization's purpose. (retrieved from http://michael.f.steger. googlepages. com/thework-as-meaninginventory(wami)!!!)

If meaningful work is good for the bottom line and good for the employee, is it possible that meaningful work could be good for the family of an employee? We know little about how engagement or meaning at work affects life at home, but it seems to follow that leaving work with a sense of enthusiasm and purpose would translate into more positive interaction with one's partner and children (if a stressful commute doesn't moderate the potential benefits). So, the big 10-year goal for the positive psychology of work is to create research and measurement models that help us determine how engagement and meaning at work affect an employee's family's functioning and, in turn, how a family's functioning affects an employee's success at work.

Loftier Goals over the Long Term

Positive psychology has not and will not provide a magic bullet, elixir, and wand to solve the world's problems. The promise of positive psychology is in its success in rounding out the story of human nature. People suffer and people thrive. Weaknesses and strengths coexist. Joy and sorrow can be brought about in one interaction with a friend. We have always known this, and now psychology can better describe the good and bad in all of us and the roller-coaster ride of our days and lives. It is the greater understanding of human behavior that will allow us to tackle the loftier goals associated with school, family, and work: reducing the loss of talent through school dropout and disengaging work and workplaces and supporting and strengthening the families that shelter us all. Working on these goals is a good way for anyone to spend their time.

References

Gallagher, M. W., & Lopez, S. J. (2008). *Hope, self-efficacy, and academic success in college students*. Poster presented at the annual convention of the American Psychological Association, Boston.

Gordon, G., & Lopez, S. J. (2008). Gallup Student Engagement. [Unpublished raw data].

Lopez, S. J. (2008). *APA Division 17 Fellows Address: What would happen if we study what is right with people?* Presented at the annual convention of the American Psychological Association, Boston.

Rath, T. (2007). *StrengthsFinder 2.0.* Washington, DC: Gallup Press.

Snyder, C. R., & Lopez, S. J. (2002). The future of positive psychology: A declaration of independence. In C. R. Snyder & S. J. Lopez (Eds.), *Handbook of positive psychology* (pp. 751–767). New York: Oxford University Press.

INDEX

Stanford Time Perspective Inventory, 298, 300
Stanton, Annette L., 226–232, 306, 635
State Hope Scale, 135, 327, 583
Staub, E., 422, 431
Staudinger, U. M., 174, 175
Staw, B., 212
Steen, T. A., 20, 38–39, 441
Steger, M. F., 679–685, 692–693
Steinbeck, John, 465
Stein-Seroussi, A., 464
Stereotypes (beliefs), 71
Sternberg, R. J., 175, 238, 376, 449
Steward, J., 228
Strachman, A., 458
Stress-buffering hypothesis, 520
Stress-Related Growth Scale, 636–637
Stress-responsive systems, 520
Stroebe, M., 456
Stroebe, W., 456
Structured equation modeling (SEM), 157
Student's Life Satisfaction Scale (SLSS), 562
Stutzer, A., 590
Subjective well-being (SWB). *See also* Life satisfaction measures; Psychological well-being; Satisfaction With Life Scale (SWLS)
  civic participation and, 590–591
  convergent/discriminant validity of, 99
  cross-cultural investigations, 53
  culture and, 191
  curiosity and, 370–371
  defined, 651–652
  demographic correlates of, 190
  EI and, 242
  evidence of measurement variance, need for, 99–100
  forgiveness and, 430–431
  future research on, 191–192
  genetic influences, 189
  gratitude and, 441
  hedonic adaptation and, 190
  idiographic evidence, need for, 99
  love and, 452
  marital status and, 190
  measures of, 90, 98–99, 188–189
  mental aspects of, 190
  negative affect and, 561–562
  objective consequences of, 191
  optimism and, 304–305
  policy measures, 591–592
  positive affect and, 561
  research history and findings, 187–188, 191–192
  self-efficacy and, 338
  theoretical approach to, 189–190
  time perspective and, 299
Successful Aging (Rowe & Kahn), 168
Sue, D. W., 44
Sugimori, S., 494
Suh, E. M., 53, 188
Suicidal behavior, 348–349

Sullivan, Sarah J., 226–232
Surprise events, 326
Surveys, development of, 187–188
Sustainable happiness model, 671–672
Swann, W. B., Jr., 465, 466
Sweeny, P., 377
Sweet, P.L.G., 605
Syme, L. S., 135, 455
Sympathetic nervous system (SNS), 520, 522, 538, 540
Symptom Checklist-90, 347–348

T

Tafarodi, R. W., 494
Tajfel, H., 72
Talking about emotional experience, 621–631
Taoism, 381
Tarabulsy, G. M., 409
TAS-20. See Toronto Alexithymia Scale
Task focus, 79
Taylor, S. E., 533, 645, 657
Teasdale, J. D., 315
Tedeschi, R. G., 38, 635, 641–642
Tellegen, A., 189
Templeton, John, 26
Temporal balance (time concept), 297
Temporal continuity (time concept), 297
Temporal extension (time concept), 297
Temporal orientation (time concept), 297
Tendency to Forgive Scale, 428
Tennen, H., 229, 633–639, 647
Terenzini, P. T., 569
Terror management theory (TMT), 645–646, 683
Terry, D. J., 228
Thayer, R. E., 240, 457
Thematic Apperception Test, 629
Theokas, C., 158
Theory of Moral Sentiments (Smith), 398
Theory Y (McGregor), 580
Thinking flexibility, benefits from positive affect, 505–509
Thomas, C., 273
Thompson, R., 136
Thompson, Suzanne C., 271–276
Tiedens, L. Z., 20
Time, 295–301
  historical background, 295–296
  perspectives of, 296–301
Time Attitude Scale, 298
Time Competence Scale, 298
Time Reference Inventory, 298
Time Structure Questionnaire, 298
Tjeltveit, A., 107, 109, 110
Tobacco use (by adolescents) and EI, 242
Tocqueville, Alexis de, 398
Tomaka, J., 544
Tomkins, Silvan, 368
Tong, E.M.W., 20
Tonsager, M. E., 471
Topolski, T. D., 138
Toronto Alexithymia Scale (TAS-20), 252

Torrance, E. P., 604
Toughness/toughness theory, 537–546
  benefits from, 544–546
  definitions/physiological systems, 538
  evidence (when/where) of, 541–542
  extensions of toughness relationships, 543
  historical background, 540–541
  neuroendocrine mediators, 539–540
  nontoughening training, 542–543
  personality, performance, health, 540
  toughening manipulations, 539
Tov, W., 299
Trade-offs of character strengths, 31–32, 32*f*
Trait curiosity models, 369
Trait envy, 442
Trait gratitude, 439
Trait Hope Scale, 135, 326–327, 476
Transaction models (of resilience), 125–126
Transcendental Meditation (TM), 601, 604–605, 607
Transformational leadership, 40
Triandis, H. C., 50
Trivette, C. M., 554
True, N., 629
Trust and self-verification, 469–470
Tseng, W. C., 575
Turken, U., 20
Turner, R. A., 20, 40, 212
Twigger-Ross, C., 495
Twin studies, 189, 670
Two-continua model (of mental health), 90–92

U

Uchino, B. N., 455
Ulven, J. C., 83
Umberson, D., 455
Uncertainty, 40, 66, 181, 280–283
Uncontrollability, 272, 314, 315
Undo effect (of positive emotions), 19, 20
Unhappy people, 102, 190, 396, 668–672
Updegraff, J. A., 457
Upton, P., 138
Urada, M., 508
Uswatte, G., 651–660

V

Vaillant, George, 7, 533–534
Valentine, E. R., 605
Values and motives (of psychologists), 107
Values in Action (VIA) project
  campus application, 572
  classifications of, 27–28, 28*t*, 55
  correlates/consequences, 30
  courage and, 377, 379
  deliberate cultivation, 31
  distribution/demographics (findings), 29–30
  historical background, 26–27
  measures of, 28–29